NEW
INDIVIDUALIST
REVIEW

A Liberty Press Edition

NEW
INDIVIDUALIST
REVIEW

A Periodical Reprint of

Liberty Fund
Indianapolis

This is a Liberty Press Edition published by Liberty Fund, Inc., a foundation established to encourage study of the ideal of a society of free and responsible individuals.

The cuneiform inscription that serves as our logo and as the design motif for our endpapers is the earliest known written appearance of the word "freedom" *(ama-gi)*, or "liberty." It is taken from a clay document written about 2300 B.C. in the Sumerian city-state of Lagash.

Library of Congress Card #65–35281

ISSN #0028–5439 (320.51)
ISBN #0–913966-90-8
ISBN #0–86597-065-3 (pbk.)

10 9 8 7 6 5 4 3 2

CONTENTS

PUBLISHER'S NOTE

This volume contains all issues of the *New Individualist Review* in their entirety. A photo offset process was used to reproduce exactly the originals in all respects save color of covers.

The publisher has added only the general introduction by Milton Friedman and a cumulative index. The maroon numbers in the margin of each page provide the numbering for the cumulative index.

INTRODUCTION

By Milton Friedman

W hen the *New Individualist Review* was founded, belief in "free, private enterprise, and in the imposition of the strictest limits to the power of government" and in "a commitment to human liberty"—to quote from the editorial introducing volume 1, number 1 (April 1961)—was at a low ebb even in the countries of the so-called free world. Yet, at the same time, there were many signs of an intellectual reaction against collectivist views, of a resurgence of interest in the philosophy of classical liberalism.

Two organizations in particular served to channel and direct this resurgence: the Mont Pelerin Society, founded in 1947 primarily as a result of the initiative of Friedrich Hayek, whose book *The Road to Serfdom* did so much to spark the resurgence; and the Intercollegiate Society of Individualists, founded in 1953 by Frank Chodorov, a freelance writer and journalist and a dedicated opponent of collectivism.

The Mont Pelerin Society brought together relatively mature intellectuals—economists, historians, journalists, businessmen— who had kept the faith and had

Milton Friedman is Paul Snowden Russell Distinguished Service Professor of Economics at the University of Chicago, and Senior Research Fellow at the Hoover Institution on War, Revolution and Peace, Stanford, California. He is the author of numerous books, among them A Monetary History of the United States, 1867–1960 *(coauthored by Anna J. Schwartz) and* Capitalism and Freedom. *His most recent work is* Free to Choose *(coauthored by Rose Friedman). Dr. Friedman received the Nobel Prize for economic science in 1976.*

not succumbed to the temper of the times. Its members were representatives of a small minority, but one that had more than its share of independence, integrity, selflessness, and breadth of vision. The Intercollegiate Society of Individualists (ISI) operated at the other end of the age scale. It promoted the establishment of chapters among undergraduate and graduate students on college campuses throughout the country. The members of these chapters too were a minority, but also one that had more than its share of independence, integrity, selflessness, and breadth of vision.

As the *New Individualist Review*'s introductory editorial of 1961 put it,

> Two or three decades ago, individualism was held in contempt by American intellectuals, and a decade ago they regarded it as at least mildly eccentric. We certainly do not deny that the majority of today's intellectuals are still guided by the ideas which grew up in the 1930s. But the slogans which the New Deal shouted, and the stereotypes which it propagated, while perhaps fresh and exciting then, have lost their appeal to the generation which has emerged in recent years, one which sees no reason to consider our march toward the Total State to be as "inevitable as a law of nature."
> ... An increasing number of students in the past decades have recognized the inadequacies of the orthodox response to most of the present-day social and economic challenges. The party of liberty is steadily gaining adherents among students.

The University of Chicago played a key role in the preservation of liberalism and the resurgence of "the party of liberty." It was one of the few major universities in the world at which there persisted throughout the thirties and forties a strong liberal tradition, conveyed and maintained by eminent and respected members of the academic community like Frank H. Knight, Jacob Viner, Henry Simons, and others of their colleagues in the economics department, in other social science departments, in the Business School, and in the humanities. The university was by no means monolithic. Indeed, it had the general reputation of being a radical left-wing institution. Its student body and faculty had its share of Communist Party members, fellow travelers, and socialists. What distinguished it from most other institutions was that it also had a strong, cohesive, and intellectually respectable group of defenders of a free society.

After the war Hayek moved from the London School of Economics to the University of Chicago, where he became a professor in a newly formed Committee on Social Thought. Of the founding members of the Mont Pelerin Society, four were from the University of Chicago, more than from any other institution.

Both the time and the place were ripe for the emergence of the *New Individualist Review*. The time was ripe because the reaction against collectivism, and the resurgence of belief in individualism, had gone far enough to provide a sufficiently large and sophisticated audience—and pool of potential contributors—for a publication which aimed at a high intellectual level and proclaimed that "the viewpoints presented will generally be libertarian or conservative, but we will consider for publication any essay which indicates a reasoned concern for freedom, and a thoughtful valuation of its importance." The time was ripe also because the libertarian resurgence was still in an early enough stage that there were few periodical publications dealing with intellectual issues and offering a forum for their serious discussion. *National Review, Human Events,* and *The Freeman* were in existence but they were directed at an audience of concerned and interested citi-

zens of all professions and viewpoints, and served a different purpose, being devoted largely to reporting developments in the world of affairs or to commenting on and analyzing current issues primarily from a traditionally conservative—as opposed to libertarian—perspective.

The place was ripe because at the time the University of Chicago was almost surely the only academic institution at which there was a sufficient concentration of students not only committed to the values of a free society but also engaged in serious scholarly study of the intellectual and historical underpinnings of a free society. In particular, Hayek had attracted a group of able, dedicated, and like-minded students to the Committee on Social Thought. They formed the core group responsible for the *New Individualist Review*, reinforced by students in economics, business, and other areas who shared the value commitment although they were more technically and professionally oriented in their studies. Faculty support was also present and important. However, it cannot be too strongly emphasized that the *New Individualist Review* was throughout—in its conception, editing, and management—a student venture.

The ISI assisted at the birth of the *New Individualist Review*. The first three issues were described as being published by "the University of Chicago chapter of the Intercollegiate Society of Individualists"; thereafter as being published by the *New Individualist Review*. The first eleven issues carried full-page advertisements for the ISI—presumably the form that financial assistance took. In addition, Don Lipsett, the midwestern representative of the ISI, who was primarily responsible for founding the Chicago chapter, advised and assisted on business matters.

The initial editorial board consisted of editor-in-chief Ralph Raico; associate editors John McCarthy, Robert Schuettinger, John Weicher; and book review editor Ronald Hamowy. Each of these contributed an article to the first issue. Three were students in the Committee on Social Thought, one a student in the history department, one in the economics department. Raico served as editor-in-chief, alone or along with Schuettinger or Hamowy, for all but the final two issues. Joe M. Cobb served in that capacity for the final two issues and has been guardian of the tradition ever since.

The editorial advisory board initially consisted of myself from the economics department, F. A. Hayek from the Committee on Social Thought, and Richard M. Weaver from the English department. Aside from occasionally contributing articles, our role was strictly advisory and little advice was required. The students who undertook the project were not only dedicated; they were also extraordinarily able and talented, and that continued to be the case with the students who joined or replaced the founders. Most of them remain active and effective defenders of a free society, and have achieved careers that fulfill their initial promise. Few phenomena have so reinforced my own personal belief in the validity of the philosophy of freedom as the high quality, both intellectual and personal, of the young men and women who were attracted to the "party of liberty"—to use the *New Individualist Review*'s parlance— when it had all the appearance of being a lost cause.

The *Review* quickly established itself as the outstanding publication in the libertarian cause. Although every contributor to its first issue was from the University of Chicago (one faculty member, five students), by the second issue, two out of five were from outside the university, and in the third, five out of seven. As every reader of this volume will find for himself, the quality of the *Review* was consistently high. The contributions were directed at important and controversial issues; they were reasoned and thoughtful without being arid; they touched on both basic philosophical issues and important practical problems; they were, as the initial editorial promised, "generally . . . libertarian or conservative" but not narrowly parochial, and ranged over a wide variety of points of view.

The subsequent history of the *Review* and its ultimate termination were partly typical of student ventures—ups and downs as the student body changed and the number of persons interested in its subject matter and willing to devote the time to its publication fluctuated. But two other events played a role—one local, the other national.

The local event was Friedrich Hayek's retirement from the University of Chicago and his relocation to Freiburg, Germany. His students had formed the core of the initial founders and had remained an important component of the editorial staff throughout.

The national event was the Vietnam War. In the early 1960s there was, as the introductory editorial said, a rising tide of support among the young for the party of liberty, for the principles of free, private enterprise, and a strictly limited government. I believe that tide would have continued to rise if the passions of the young had not been diverted by the Vietnam War and above all by conscription. The antiwar, antidraft movement gained the support of young men and women of the left, the center, and the right; it absorbed their energies and their enthusiasm. The battle on the campuses deteriorated to an elemental level, as the very basic principles of civil discourse and reasoned, open-minded discussion came under attack. Little energy or possibility was left for more sophisticated examination of basic intellectual issues.

One of the final issues of the *Review* reflected one facet of this development: the spring 1967 issue devoted to a symposium on conscription. And even that was partly derivative from a conference on the draft held at the University of Chicago in December 1966.

Once the Vietnam War ended and the draft was replaced by an all-volunteer military, the former intellectual tide in favor of the party of liberty resumed, re-

xiii

inforced indeed by the antigovernment attitudes generated by the war and the draft. The result has been a veritable outpouring of publications, articles, and books devoted to examining and discussing the kinds of issues to which the *New Individualist Review* was devoted.

It is therefore highly appropriate that the progenitor of these publications be reprinted now. Most of the articles remain timely and relevant. More important, perhaps, this student venture, despite its narrow base and its limited resources, sets an intellectual standard that has not yet, I believe, been matched by any of the more recent publications in the same philosophical tradition.

NEW
INDIVIDUALIST
REVIEW

VOLUME 1
NUMBER 1
APRIL 1961

New INDIVIDUALIST Review

CAPITALISM AND FREEDOM

MILTON FRIEDMAN

POLITICS AND THE MORAL ORDER

JOHN P. McCARTHY

MODERN EDUCATION vs. DEMOCRACY

ROBERT SCHUETTINGER

HAYEK'S CONCEPT OF FREEDOM:
A CRITIQUE

RONALD HAMOWY

APRIL 1961   25 cents   Vol. 1 No. 1

NEW INDIVIDUALIST REVIEW

Volume 1 — Number 1

APRIL 1961

5

NEW INDIVIDUALIST REVIEW is published bimonthly (February, April, June, October, December) by the University of Chicago chapter of the Intercollegiate Society of Individualists, P.O. Box 4309, Chicago 80, Ill. Second Class mailing permit pending at the Chicago, Ill., post office.

Advertising and subscription correspondence should be sent to NEW INDIVIDUALIST REVIEW, P.O. Box 4309, Chicago 80, Ill. Editorial correspondence and manuscripts should be sent to NEW INDIVIDUALIST REVIEW, 7326 South Kingston Ave., Chicago 49, Ill. All manuscripts become the property of NEW INDIVIDUALIST REVIEW.

Subscription Rates: $2.00 per year (students, $1.00). Add $1.00 for foreign subscriptions.

An Editorial . . .

The **New Individualist Review** has been founded in a commitment to human liberty. We believe in free, private enterprise, and in the imposition of the strictest limits to the power of government. The philosophy which we advocate is that which was shared by some of the greatest and deepest political thinkers of modern times—by Adam Smith, Burke, Bentham, Herbert Spencer; it is responsible for most of the good that the modern world has accomplished in the way of material progress and increased freedom.

Two or three decades ago, individualism was held in contempt by American intellectuals, and a decade ago they regarded it as at least wildly eccentric. We certainly do not deny that the majority of today's intellectuals are still guided by the ideas which grew up in the 1930's. But the slogans which the New Deal shouted, and the sterotypes which it propagated, while perhaps fresh and exciting then, have lost their appeal to the generation which has emerged in recent years, one which sees no reason to consider our march towards the Total State to be as "inevitable as a law of nature."

College professors like to think of themselves as working far out on the frontiers of knowledge; the truth is, however, that in some respects, at least, they are not so very different from most people. They, too, think that old ideas, like old friends, are best. Accustomed to the premises of the collectivist ideology which they absorbed when they were students, they are understandingly comfortable with it, and are reluctant to change. But it is equally understandable that the best and most independent in each generation should want to test the premises of its predecessors, and seek out more veridical ones.

This is precisely what has been happening. An increasing number of students in the past decade have recognized the inadequacies of the orthodox response to most of the present-day social and economic challenges. The party of liberty is steadily gaining adherents among students: One of the purposes of this review will be to add to the growing number of libertarians in our colleges and universities.

In future issues we will publish articles and reviews by students and younger scholars, and occasionally by established authorities, in philosophy, economics, politics, history, and the humanities. The viewpoints presented will generally be libertarian or conservative, but we will consider for publication any essay which indicates a reasoned concern for freedom, and a thoughtful valuation of its importance.

Capitalism and Freedom

MILTON FRIEDMAN

IN DISCUSSING the principles of a free society it is desirable to have a convenient label and this has become extremely difficult. In the late 18th and early 19th centuries, an intellectual movement developed that went under the name of Liberalism. This development, which was a reaction against the authoritarian elements in the prior society, emphasized freedom as the ultimate goal and the individual as the ultimate entity in the society. It supported *laissez faire* at home as a means of reducing the role of the state in economic affairs and thereby avoiding interfering with the individual; it supported free trade abroad as a means of linking the nations of the world together peacefully and democratically. In political matters, it supported the development of representative government and of parliamentary institutions, reduction in the arbitrary power of the state, and protection of the civil freedoms of individuals.

Beginning in the late 19th century, the intellectual ideas associated with the term liberalism came to have a very different emphasis, particularly in the economic area. Whereas 19th century liberalism emphasized freedom, 20th century liberalism tended to emphasize welfare. I would say welfare instead of freedom though the 20th century liberal would no doubt say welfare in addition to freedom. The 20th century liberal puts his reliance primarily upon the state rather than on private voluntary arrangements.

Milton Friedman, Professor of Economics at the University of Chicago, is the author of *Essays in Positive Economics*, co-editor of the Cambridge Economic Handbook series, and a contributor of numerous articles to professional journals.

The difference between the two doctrines is most striking in the economic sphere, less extreme in the political sphere. The 20th century liberal, like the 19th century liberal, puts emphasis on parliamentary institutions, representative government, civil rights, and so on. And yet even here there is an important difference. Faced with the choice between having the state intervene or not, the 20th century liberal is likely to resolve any doubt in favor of intervention; the 19th century liberal, in the other direction. When the question arises at what level of government something should be done, the 20th century liberal is likely to resolve any doubt in favor of the more centralized level — the state instead of the city, the federal government instead of the state, a world organization instead of a federal government. The 19th century liberal is likely to resolve any doubt in the other direction and to emphasize a decentralization of power.

This use of the term liberalism in these two quite different senses renders it difficult to have a convenient label for the principles I shall be talking about. I shall resolve these difficulties by using the word liberalism in its original sense. Liberalism of what I have called the 20th century variety has by now become orthodox and indeed reactionary. Consequently, the views I shall present might equally be entitled, under current conditions, the "new liberalism," a more attractive designation than "nineteenth century liberalism."

It is widely believed that economic arrangements are one thing and political arrangements another, that any kind of economic arrangement can be associated with any kind of political arrangement. This is the idea that underlies such a term as "democratic socialism." The essential thesis, I believe, of a new liberal is that this idea is invalid, that "democratic socialism" is a contradiction in terms, that there is an intimate connection between economic arrangements and political arrangements, and that only certain combinations are possible.

It is important to emphasize that economic arrangements play a dual role in the promotion of a free society. On the one hand, "freedom" in economic arrangements is itself a component of freedom broadly understood, so "economic freedom" is an end in itself to a believer in freedom. In the second place, economic freedom is also an indispensable means toward the achievement of political freedom.

The first of these roles of economic freedom needs special emphasis. The citizen of Great Britain who after World War II was not permitted, by law, to spend his vacation in the United States because of exchange control was being deprived of an essential freedom no less than the citizen of the United States who was denied the opportunity to spend his vacation in Russia on the grounds of his political views. The one was ostensibly an economic limitation on freedom and the other a political limitation, yet there is no essential difference between the two.

The citizen of the United States who is compelled by law to devote something like 10% of his income to the purchase of a particular kind of retirement contract, administered by the government, is being deprived of a corresponding part of his own personal freedom. How strongly this particular deprivation may be felt, and its closeness to the deprivation of religious freedom, which all would regard as "civil" or "political" rather than "economic," was dramatized by the recent episode involving a group of Ohio or Pennsylvania farmers of a particular religious sect. On grounds of principle, this group regarded compulsory federal old age programs as an infringement on their own personal individual freedom and refused to pay taxes or accept benefits. As a result, some of

their livestock were sold at auction in order to satisfy claims for social security levies. A citizen of the United States who under the laws of various states is not free to follow the occupation of his own choosing unless he can get a license for it, is likewise being deprived of an essential part of his freedom. So economic freedom, in and of itself, is an extremely important part of total freedom.

The reason it is important to emphasize this point is because intellectuals in particular have a strong bias against regarding this aspect of freedom as important. They tend to express contempt for what they regard as material aspects of life and to regard their own pursuit of allegedly higher values as on a different plane of significance and as deserving special attention. But for the ordinary citizen of the country, for the great masses of the people, the direct importance of economic freedom is in many cases of at least comparable importance to the indirect importance of economic freedom as a means of political freedom.

VIEWED AS a means to the end of political freedom, economic arrangements are essential because of the effect which they have on the concentration or the deconcentration of power. A major thesis of the new liberal is that the kind of economic organization that provides economic freedom directly, namely, organization of economic activities through a largely free market and private enterprise, in short through competitive capitalism, is also a necessary though not a sufficient condition for political freedom. The central reason why this is true is because such a form of economic organization separates economic power from political power and in this way enables the one to be an offset to the other. Historical evidence speaks with a single voice on the relation between political and economic freedom. I cannot think of a single example at any time or any place where there was a large measure of political freedom without there also being something comparable to a private enterprise market form of economic organization for the bulk of economic activity.

Because we live in a largely free society, we tend to forget how limited is the span of time and the part of the globe for which there has ever been anything like political freedom. The 19th century and the early 20th century in the Western world stand out as striking exceptions from the general trend of historical development. It is clear that freedom in this instance came along with the free market and the development of capitalist institutions.

History suggests only that economic freedom is a necessary condition for political freedom. Clearly it is not a sufficient condition. Fascist Italy or Fascist Spain, Germany at various times in the last 70 years, Japan before World Wars I and II, Czarist Russia in the decades before World War I are all societies that cannot conceivably be described as politically free yet in which private enterprise was the dominant form of economic organization. So it is possible to have economic arrangements that are fundamentally capitalist and yet political arrangements that are not free.

Yet, even in those cases, the citizenry had a good deal more freedom than citizens of a modern totalitarian state like Russia or Nazi Germany in which economic totalitarianism is combined with political totalitarianism. Even in Russia under the Czars it was possible for some citizens under some circumstances to change their jobs without getting permission from political authority because the existence of private property and of capitalism provided some kind of offset to the centralized power of the state.

The relation between political and economic freedom is complex and by no means unilateral. In the early 19th century, Bentham and the Philosophical Radicals were inclined to regard political freedom as a means to economic freedom. Their view was that the masses were being hampered by the restrictions that were being imposed upon them, that if political reform gave the bulk of the people the vote, they would do what was good for them, which was to vote for *laissez faire*. In retrospect, it is hard to say that they were wrong. There was a large measure of political reform that was accompanied by economic reform in the direction of a great deal of *laissez faire*. And an enormous increase in the well-being of the masses followed this change in economic arrangements.

Later in the 19th century, when there began to be a movement away from freer economic arrangements and *laissez faire* toward a greater measure of collectivism and centralization, the view developed, as expressed for example by Lord Acton and in the 20th century by Henry Simons and Friedrich Hayek, that the relation was more nearly the opposite — that economic freedom was the means to political freedom.

In the period since World War II, I think we have seen still a different interconnection between political and economic freedom. In the post-war period, the fears that economic intervention would destroy political freedom seemed to be on the way to being realized. Various countries, and again Britain is perhaps the outstanding example because it has been so much a leader in the realm of ideas and social arrangements, did extend very greatly the area of state intervention into economic affairs and this did threaten political freedom. But the result was rather surprising. Instead of political freedom giving way, what happened in many cases was that economic intervention was discarded. The striking example in British post-war development was the Control-of-Engagements Order issued by the Labor Government. In trying to carry out their economic plans, the Labor Government found it necessary to do something which several years before it had said it would never do, namely, to exercise control over the jobs which people could take. Thanks to widespread popular objection, the legislation was never enforced at all extensively. After being on the books for one year, it was repealed. It seems clear that it was repealed precisely because it quite directly threatened a cherished political freedom. And from that day to this, there has been a trend toward a reduction in the extent of political intervention in economic affairs.

The dismantling of controls dates from the repeal of the Control-of-Engagements Order; it would have occurred even if

9

the Labor Government had stayed in power. This may, of course, turn out to be a purely temporary interlude, a minor halt in the march of affairs toward a greater degree of intervention into economic affairs. Perhaps only innate optimism leads me to believe that it is more than that. Whether this be so or not, it illustrates again in striking fashion the close connection between economic arrangements and political arrangements. Not only in Britain but in other countries of the world as well, the post-war period has seen the same tendency for economic arrangements to interfere with political freedom and for the economic intervention frequently to give way.

Historical evidence that the development of freedom and of capitalist and market institutions have coincided in time can never by itself be persuasive. Why should there be a connection? What are the logical links between economic and political freedom? In discussing these questions, I shall first consider the market as a direct component of freedom and then the indirect relation between market arrangements and political freedom. In the process, I shall in effect outline the ideal economic arrangements of the new liberal.

THE NEW LIBERAL takes freedom of the individual as his ultimate goal in judging social arrangements. Freedom as a value in this sense has to do with the interrelations among people; it has no meaning whatsoever to a Robinson Crusoe on an isolated island (without his man Friday). Robinson Crusoe on his island is subject to "constraint," he has limited "power," he has only a limited number of alternatives, but there is no problem of freedom in the sense that is relevant to the present discussion. Similarly, in a society, freedom has nothing to say about what an individual does with his freedom; it isn't an all-embracing ethic by any manner of means. Indeed, a major aim of the believer in freedom is to leave the ethical problem for the individual to wrestle with. The "really" important ethical problems are those that face an individual in a free society — what an individual should do

with his freedom. There are thus two sets of values that a liberal will emphasize — the values relevant to relations among people which is the context in which he assigns first priority to freedom; and the values that are relevant to the individual in the exercise of his freedom, which is the realm of individual ethics and philosophy.

Fundamentally there are only two ways in which the activities of a large number of people can be co-ordinated: by central direction, which is the technique of the army and of the totalitarian state and involves some people telling other people what to do; or by voluntary co-operation, whch is the technique of the market place and of arrangements involving voluntary exchange. The possibility of voluntary co-operation in its turn rests fundamentally on the proposition that both parties to an exchange can benefit from it. If it is voluntary and reasonably well informed, the exchange will not take place unless both parties do benefit from it.

The simplest way to see the principle at work is to go back to the economist's favorite abstraction of Robinson Crusoe, only to have a number of Robinson Crusoe households on different islands, each of which is initially self-sufficient. Let the households come into contact with one another. The possibility of trade now emerges. What is it that gives them an incentive to trade? The answer clearly is that if each household concentrates on a small range of activities, producing things for itself indirectly, by trade, rather than doing everything for itself, everybody can be better off. This possibility arises for two reasons: one is that an individual can achieve a higher degree of competence in an activity if he specializes in it rather than engaging in many activities; the other, closely associated but not identical, is that people are different and each can specialize in those activities for which he has special capacities. Even if everyone were identical in all his capacities and abilities, there would still be a gain from division of labor which would make a larger total return possible because each individual could concentrate on a particular activity. But in addition, diversity among people becomes a source of strength because each individual can concentrate on doing those things that he can do best. So the incentive for the households to engage in trade and to specialize is the possibility of a greater total output.

The protection to Household A is that it need not enter into an exchange with Household B unless both parties benefit. If exchange is voluntary, it will take place if, and only if, both parties do benefit. Each individual always has the alternative of going back to producing for himself what he did before so he can never be worse off; he can only be better off.

OF COURSE, specialization of function and division of labor would not go far if the ultimate productive unit were the household. In a modern society, we have gone much farther. We have introduced enterprises which are intermediaries between individuals in their capacities as suppliers of services and as purchasers of goods. And similarly, specialization of function and division of labor could not go very far if we had to continue to rely on the barter of product for product. In consequence, money has been introduced as a means of facilitating exchange and of enabling the act of purchase and of sale to be separated into two parts.

The introduction of enterprises and the introduction of money raise most of the really difficult problems for economics as a science. But from the point of view of the principles of social organization, they do not fundamentally alter the essential character of economic arrangements. In a modern complex society using enterprises and money it is no less true than in the simple idealized world that co-ordination through the markets is a system of voluntary co-operation in which all parties to the bargain gain.

So long as effective freedom of exchange is maintained, the essential feature of the market is that it enables people to co-operate voluntarily in complex tasks without any individual being in a position to interfere with any other. Many of the difficult technical problems that arise in applying our principles to actual economic arrangements are concerned with assuring effective freedom to enter or not to enter into exchanges. But so long as people are effectively free to enter into an exchange and are reasonably well informed the essential feature of the market remains that of our ideal example. It provides for co-operation without coercion; it prevents one person from interfering with another. The employer is protected from being interfered with or coerced by his employees by the existence of other employees whom he can hire. The employee is protected from being coerced by his employer by the existence of other employers for whom he can work; the customer by the existence of other sellers, and so on.

Of course, it is partly this feature of the market that leads many people to be opposed to it. What most people really object to when they object to a free market is that it is so hard for them to shape it to their own will. The market gives people what the people want instead of what other people think they ought to want. At the bottom of many criticisms of the market economy is really lack of belief in freedom itself.

The essence of political freedom is the absence of coercion of one man by his fellow men. The fundamental danger to political freedom is the concentration of power. The existence of a large measure of power in the hands of a relatively few individuals enables them to use it to coerce their fellow man. Preservation of freedom requires either the elimination of power where that is possible, or its dispersal where it cannot be eliminated. It essentially requires a system of checks and balances, like that explicitly incorporated in our Constitution. One way to think of a market system is as part of a broader system of checks and balances, as a system under which economic power can be a check to political power instead of an addition to it.

If I may speculate in an area in which I have little competence, there seems to be a really essential difference between political power and economic power that is at the heart of the use of a market mechanism to preserve freedom. With respect to political power, there is something like a law of conservation of energy or power. The notion that what one man gains another man loses has more applicability in the realm of politics than in the realm of economic arrangements. One can have many different small governments, but it is hard to think of having many different small centers of political power in any single government. It is hard for there to be more than one really outstanding leader, one person on whom the energies and enthusiasms and so on of his countrymen are centered. If the central government gains power, it is likely to do so at the expense of local governments. While I do not know how to formulate the statement precisely, there seems to be something like a fixed total of political power to be distributed.

There is no such fixed total, no law of conservation of power, with respect to economic power. You cannot very well have two presidents in a country, although you may have two separate countries, but it is perfectly possible to have a large number of additional millionaires. You can have an additional millionaire without there being any fewer millionaires anywhere else. If somebody discovers a way to make resources more productive than they were before, he will simply add to the grand total of economic wealth. Economic power can thus be more readily dispersed than political power. There can be a larger number of independent foci of power. Further, if economic power is kept in separate hands from political power, it can serve as a check and an offset to political power.

This is a very abstract argument and I think I can illustrate its force for our purpose best by turning to some examples. I would like to discuss first a hypothetical example that helps to bring out the principles involved and then an actual example from recent experience that also illustrates the way in which the market works to preserve political freedom.

I think that most of us will agree that an essential element of political freedom is the freedom to advocate and to try to promote radical changes in the organization of society. It is a manifestation of political freedom in our capitalist society that people are free to advocate, and to try to persuade others to favor socialism or communism. I want to contemplate for a moment the reverse problem. It would be a sign of political freedom in a socialist society that people in that society should be free to advocate, and try to persuade others to favor capitalism. I want to ask the hypothetical question: how could a socialist society preserve the freedom to advocate capitalism? I shall assume that the leading people and the public at large seriously wish to do so and ask how they could set up the institutional arrangements that would make this possible.

THE FIRST problem is that the advocates of capitalism must be able to earn a living. Since in a socialist society all persons get their incomes from the state as employees or dependents of employees of the state, this already creates quite a problem. It is one thing to permit private individuals to advocate radical change. It is another thing to permit governmental employees to do so. Our whole post-war experience with un-American activities committees and the McCarthy investigations and so on shows how difficult a problem it is to carry over this notion to governmental employees. The first thing that would be necessary would therefore be essentially a self-denying ordinance on the part of the government that would not discharge from public employment individuals who advocate subversive doctrines — since of course, in a socialist state the doctrine that capitalism should be restored would be a subversive doctrine. Let us suppose this hurdle, which is the least of the hurdles, is surmounted.

Next, in order to be able to advocate anything effectively it is necessary to be able to raise some money to finance meetings, propaganda, publications, writings and so on. In a socialist society, there might still be men of great wealth. There is no reason why a socialist society shouldn't have a wide and unequal distribution of income and of wealth. It is clear, however, that most, if not all of the people, of great wealth or income would be the leading figures in the government, directly or indirectly — high level civil servants or favored authors, actors, and the like. Perhaps it doesn't strain the bounds of credulity greatly to suppose that the government would countenance and tolerate the advocacy of capitalism by minor civil servants. It's almost incredible that it could tolerate the financing of subversive activity by leading civil servants. It is, therefore, hard to believe that these wealthy or high income individuals could be a source of finance. The only other recourse would be to try to get small sums from a large number of people. But this evades the issue. In order to get a lot of people to contribute you first have to persuade them. How do you get started persuading?

Note that in a capitalistic society radical movements have never been financed by small amounts from many people. They have been financed by a small number of wealthy people being willing to foot the bill. To take an example that is quite old but very striking, who financed Karl Marx? It was Engels, and where did Engels get his money? He was an independent business man of wealth. (In the modern day it's the Anita McCormick Blaines and Frederick Vanderbilt Fields, the Corliss Lamonts and so on who have been the source of finance of the radical movement.) This is the important source of the strength of freedom in a capitalist society. It means that anybody who has a "crazy" idea that he wants to propagate and promote has only to persuade a small number out of a very large number of potential backers in order to be able to get an opportunity to try out his crazy notions in the market place of ideas.

Moreover, the situation is even more extreme. Suppose somebody has an idea that he thinks will appeal to a large number of people. He doesn't even have to persuade somebody that he is right. He just has to persuade some capitalist in the society — in this particular case say a publisher or a magazine editor — that there's a chance that a lot of people will be willing to pay to read about his idea. A publisher, for example, will have an incentive to publish a book, with whose ideas he doesn't agree in the slightest, if there is a substantial chance

that the book will sell enough copies to make money.

By contrast, let's go back to the hypothetical socialist society. How does the proponent of capitalism in such a society raise money to propagate his ideas? He can't get it from the wealthy individuals in the society. It is hard to believe that it is feasible for him to raise the necessary amount by getting small sums from a large number of people. Perhaps one can conceive of the socialist society being sufficiently aware of this problem and sufficiently anxious to preserve freedom to set up a governmental fund for the financing of subversive activities. It is a little difficult to conceive of this being done, but even if it were done it would not meet the problem. How would it be decided who should be supported from the fund? If subversive activity is made a profitable enterprise, it is clear that there will be an ample supply of people willing to take money for this purpose. If money is to be got for the asking, there will be plenty of asking. There must be some way of rationing. How could it be rationed?

Even if this problem were solved, the socialist society would still have difficulties in preserving freedom. The advocate of capitalism must not only have money, he must also be able to buy paper, print his material, distribute it, hold meetings, and the like. And, in the socialist society, in each instance this would involve dealing with an instrumentality of the government. The seller of paper in a capitalist society doesn't care or indeed know whether the paper he's selling is going to be used to print the *Wall Street Journal* or the *Worker*.

In the circumstances envisaged in the socialist society, the man who wants to print the paper to promote capitalism has to persuade a government mill to sell him the paper, a government printing press to print it, a government post office to distribute it among the people, a government agency to rent him a hall in which to talk and so on. Maybe there is some way in which one could make arrangements under a socialist society to preserve freedom and to make this possible. I certainly cannot say that it is utterly impossible. What is clear is that there are very real difficulties in preserving dissent and that, so far as I know, none of the people who have been in favor of socialism and also in favor of freedom have really faced up to this issue or made even a respectable start at developing the institutional arrangements that would permit freedom under socialism. By contrast, it is clear how a free market capitalist society fosters freedom.

A striking example, which may be found in the January 26, 1959, issue of *Time,* has to do with the "Black List Fade-Out." Says the *Time* story, "The Oscar awarding ritual is Hollywood's biggest pitch for dignity but two years ago dignity suffered. When one Robert Rich was announced as top writer for *The Brave One,* he never stepped forward. Robert Rich was a pseudonym masking one of about 150 actors blacklisted by the industry since 1947 as suspected Communists or fellow travelers. The case was particularly embarrassing to the Motion Picture Academy because it had barred any Communist or 5th Amendment pleader from Oscar competition.

"Last week both the Communist rule and the mystery of Rich's identity were suddenly revealed. Rich turned out to be Dalton (*Johnny Got His Gun*) Trumbo, one of the original Hollywood Ten writers who refused to testify at the 1947 hearing on Communism in the movie industry. Said producer Frank King who had stoutly insisted that Robert Rich was a young guy in Spain with a beard, 'We have an obligation to our stockholders to buy the best script we can. Trumbo brought us *The Brave One* and we bought it . . .' In effect it was the formal end of the Hollywood black list. For barred writers, the informal end came long ago. At least fifteen per cent of current Hollywood films are reportedly written by black list members. Said producer King, 'There are more ghosts in Hollywood than in Forest Lawn. Every company in town has used the work of black listed people; we're just the first to confirm what everybody knows'."

One may believe, as I do, that Communism would destroy all of our freedoms, and one may be opposed to it as firmly and as strongly as possible and yet at the same time also believe that in a free society it is intolerable for a man to be prevented from earning his living because he believes in or is trying to promote Communism. His freedom includes his freedom to promote Communism. The Hollywood black-list is a thoroughly unfree act that destroys freedom. It didn't work, however, precisely because the market made it costly for people to preserve the black list. The commercial emphasis, the fact that people who are running enterprises have an incentive to make as much money as they can, protected the freedom of the individuals who were black listed by providing them with an alternative form of employment, and by giving people an incentive to employ them.

If Hollywood and the movie industry had been government enterprises or if in England it had been a question of employment by the BBC it is difficult to believe that the Hollywood Ten or their equivalent would have found employment.

The essential feature of the market which is brought out by these examples, and one could multiply them many fold, is essentially that it separates the economic activities of the individual from his political ideas or activities and in this way provides individuals with an effective support for personal freedom. The person who buys bread doesn't know whether the wheat from which it was made was grown by a pleader of the 5th Amendment or a McCarthyite, by a person whose skin is black or whose skin is white. The market is an impersonal mechanism that separates economic activities of individuals from their personal characteristics. It enables people to co-operate in the economic realm regardless of any differences of opinion or views or attitudes they may have in other areas. You and I may buy Mennen drug products even though we may think "Soapy" Williams was a terrible governor of the state of Michigan. This is the fundamental way in which a free-market capitalist organization of economic activity promotes personal freedom and political freedom.

Politics and the Moral Order

JOHN P. McCARTHY

THE EXISTENCE of our civilization is threatened today as the full implications of our prevailing philosophies are being actualized in the life of the common man. These philosophies have an inadequate conception of the nature of man and human liberty. Having been isolated in the academies up until now, they have had only a minimal effect on society as the bulk of the populace continued to be moved by its inherited traditions and beliefs, which provide a firm foundation for liberty, justice, and social harmony. Men accepted a moral order, and acted, or at least recognized their obligation to so act, with the purpose of attaining their own and society's moral perfection. However, the vast physical and social changes of the recent era have nullified the effectiveness of the traditional guides to wisdom and morality, thereby leaving man naked before the onslaught of the destructive philosophies.

Surprisingly enough, many of the political and economic institutions responsible for our great advances in liberty and progress have been inspired in part by the writings of the very same men who have postulated the destructive philosophies. The explanation for this paradox is that our pragmatic attitude towards theory and our traditional morality derived from ancient sources have shielded us from the full implications of these philosophies while we utilized their practical suggestions. Indeed, in their use of the practical suggestions of these

John P. McCarthy, a graduate of Fordham University, is at present a Woodrow Wilson Fellow in the Department of History, University of Chicago.

thinkers, the Americans were unconsciously motivated by a more ancient philosophical tradition quite at odds with the newer positions.

One alternative to the impending social chaos is a dehumanizing regimentation. Naturally rejecting this, we have no choice but to restore a philosophy of moral purpose and order as the foundation of our society. The age is past when we could rely solely on our pragmatic prudence and traditional morality as the safeguards of our liberty. This philosophy of liberty must be formulated in the academy by a thorough research into the works of its earlier exponents, as well as a new statement of its truths in an idiom and in a vein applicable to our age. Society must then positively commit itself to this view of man and the moral order. However, it is well to analyze the prevailing philosophies to see wherein lies their failure before attempting to state a positive position.

First, certain clarifications are in order. Since our crisis is primarily one of first principles, this discussion will not especially lend itself to the actual construction of our political institutions or to the effectiveness of their operations, even though such areas are of vital importance. Also by the way of clarification, the term "perfection" is used solely in the sense of the ideal to which free and responsible men are obliged to aspire. I am certainly aware of original sin and man's proclivity to evil, and admit the necessity of considering this in the actual structuring of society so as to fortify the cause of morality with institutional and traditional supports. Furthermore, I

Page Eleven

repudiate that notion of man's perfectability which would disregard his freedom, and interpret him in a deterministic light as raw material to be molded to a perfect image.

The notions which are at the root of our present crisis are the abandonment of a teleological view of man, the substitution of individual pleasure and life itself for justice and virtue as the ends of society, and the interpretation of natural law or rights as something pertaining to an earlier state in human history rather than as the code of man's perfection.

Thomas Hobbes, of course, introduced these concepts to the Anglo-Saxon world by depicting organized society as a contractual arrangement made by natural man. The state of nature was anarchistic savagery, where men followed but one impulse, namely, egoistic hedonism: to live and get pleasures. Natural man came to the conclusion that he stood a better chance to satisfy this impulse, or at least to preserve from the hedonistic impulses of his fellows that degree of satisfaction which he had already attained, by submitting himself to the authority of the state. There are no moral codes or limitations relevant to the state power; It exists solely because men think the gains of their own hedonism will be better preserved from the hedonistic ambitions of their fellows in an organized state.

John Locke also started with natural man. For Locke, however, the state of nature was not necessarily a state of savagery. Nonetheless, man surrendered certain of his powers which he used in defending himself and his possessions to the state for the purpose of obtaining more adequate protection. This is not a complete submission to the state because its authority is specifically limited to those powers which man delegates to it in the original social contract. These powers are for the sole purpose of protecting man's freedom of life and property. The natural law is a statement of the absence of restraint upon man, and is the standard to which man can appeal when the state transgresses the specific limitations of its power.

Locke does not concern himself with man's perfection or his obligations to his fellows or to society, but just insists on man's freedom from interference with his life and property. Consequently, his conception of man is basically hedonistic, with the nature of man being solely that of a property and pleasure-gathering agent, who of course, ought not to interfere with his fellows' similar pursuits. This ethic does not inspire one to seek his own moral perfection, or his brothers' or society's perfection as a good in itself. The only social impulse is to improve the instruments of protecting one's own freedom.

Granted that Locke's works are a magnificent contribution to the literature of constitutionalism, to the concept of restraining arbitrary power, they still fail to express a positive and noble statement of man's nature. He recognizes no good, no perfection to which we are in duty bound to aspire, but thinks only in terms of rights and unrestrained individuality.

Tom Paine pleads for the rights of man as liberties accruing to man by reason of his creation or existence. This would seem to suggest a notion that man has rights because he is by his nature a free agent. These rights include the pursuit of one's own happiness, but he also speaks of man's duty to God and to his neighbor. Paine was primarily a polemicist, rather than a philosopher, and one really cannot read too many profound meanings into his words. Yet, he seems to leave some room for an interpretation of man's nature as that of a free being responsible for pursuing a moral good, which is a nobler justification for human liberty than the blunt animal desire for self-preservation and pleasure.

However, Paine is anti-historical in his assertion that a government's legitimacy must be based on an original democratic grant of authority by the governed, and that each generation has the authority to change its government at will. His assertion that only those governments with delegated constitutions are legitimate could lead to anarchy. It is fine to plead for democratic reforms and constitutionalism, but the grounds for declaring a government to be illegitimate or for revolting are only present if the government is not a just one, or if it is not ruling for the benefit of all the nation.

William Godwin presented a new view of the nature of man. Man is by nature reasonable, and will always act for the utility of the whole of society. However, the institutions of organized society have corrupted man. The path back is to eliminate the corrupting institutions and restore human reasonableness by education. Then, once again, man will automatically follow the action dictated by reason, the action which serves the utility of society. There is no conception of human liberty or natural rights. Rather, man's behavior is determined either by institutions or by education. The latter promotes a behavior pattern serving the utility, not the moral perfection, of society. Nor is there any concern with the individual's own perfection and destiny.

This was the beginning of a reaction against selfish, dutiless individualism. Reaction denied not only virtue and justice, but liberty and natural rights as well. It demanded the forced subjection of the human being to the social end: the attainment of a maximum of utility in achieving the greatest amount of material pleasure for the greatest number of individuals. The utilitarian philosophers advocated unrestrained selfish individualism not out of a concern for liberty but because they believed in a natural harmony of selfish interests which would more efficiently advance the quantity and quality of human pleasures. A calculus of pleasure and pain was elaborated to induce men to a pattern of behavior which would avoid short-range pleasures, such as those which would interfere with the unrestrained activities of other pleasure-seekers, for the sake of achieving a greater quantity of pleasures in the long run. Education was also an instrument for showing individuals how to attain the greatest level of pleasure.

The utilitarian arguments for a rationalization of social institutions and for democracy were prompted solely by the exigencies of socal efficiency. A democratic society would prevent the short range selfishness of the few from interfering with the long range selfishness of the many.

The Lockean philosophy, despite its inadequate conception of the nature of man, had at least imposed distinct limitations on arbitrary governmental power. Utilitarianism, however, had abandoned any basis for human liberty. It denied natural rights, and did not even consider any notion of man's perfection or moral obligations. Rather, it simply sought to channel human liberties into the production of the maximum quantity of pleasure, and it just happened that unrestrained individualism was the most efficient method of doing so.

This heritage of man as a pleasure-seeker who, by nature has no special dignity which makes him free, and no essential grounds of appeal against arbitrary state power if such is exercised in the name of efficiency, has persisted to our day. But now it is maintained that the most efficient means of pleasure-production is direction of human enterprise by the state.

Modern politics no longer concerns itself with the nature of man, the ends of society, justice, virtue, or even the limits of governmental authority. Rather, it is the study of the techniques of administering the institutions of government, with the sole purpose of distributing pleasures and keeping the populace in a satisfied and contented status. However, it seems to be failing at even this, since it has forgotten the spontaneous efficiency of undirected human energies in the production of a greater material well-being.

The great aim of political science has become administrative efficiency and the adjustment of atomized individuals who are the members of the state. Men are adjusted and molded to an acceptance of society and to an efficient participation in its productive activities. Free and responsible individuals are no longer moved to exercise their liberty by dealing justly with their fellows and society according to an inner conviction of duty and morality.

Astonishingly, the only freedom to which our sensate culture adheres is freedom from any imposed intellectual and spiritual orthodoxy. Indeed, the multiplicity of concepts of man and his nature is considered a good in itself, thereby emphasizing the society's lack of concern with the nature of man. Yet, one of the essential ingredients of a just and liberal society is a commitment by the society — as reflected in the spirit of its institutions as well as in the personal convictions of the overwhelming majority of its citizenry — to the basic first principles of the nature of man and society.

The fundamental premises of the philosophy to which a society must be committed if it is to preserve its freedom is that a man is by his nature a free, social, and responsible being. Man is capable of knowing the truth which he must follow to attain his perfection. As a responsible being, he can only achieve this perfection by his own voluntary acts. To act as a responsible being, man must have control over his own person and must fulfill his duties by himself. This means he must have as much freedom in directing his personal affairs and in fulfilling his obligations to his fellow man and to justice as is possible. Governmental assumption of these duties would be a negation of personal responsibility.

Society is composed of individuals achieving their individual destinies and fulfilling their duties as required by justice towards one another. Man, by his nature, achieves his perfection as a member of society. Therefore, organized society is part of the natural order, and as such has a positive function to play in aiding man to achieve his perfection. Solitary man, without society, is helpless. Yet, society must not frustrate its own purpose of promoting human perfection by depriving man of the very means of achieving his perfection, his free and responsible direction of himself.

A recommitment by society to the principles of liberty and justice must be combined with an increasing awareness of society and the nation on the part of the individual. Men must renew their cognisance of their engagement in society, and must recognize their dependence on society, although, of course, not in the sense of being either a customer or a ward. A reverential attitude towards the traditions and heritage of our society and a commitment to its ideals of liberty and justice are essential for its preservation as a free society and for the prevention of its degeneration into a savage and irresponsible anarchy. This awareness of the nation and of its traditions will have a restorative effect and inspire free men to advance in the development of their civilization and moral order.

New Individualist Review welcomes contributions for publication from its readers. Essays should not exceed 3,000 words, and should be type-written. All manuscripts will receive careful consideration.

The Next Four Years: An Appraisal

JOHN WEICHER

THE PHILOSOPHY of individualism is on the offensive among scholars and students, but its practical counterpart, political conservatism, is still on the defensive, fighting a rear-guard holding action in day-to-day events. It is not entirely successful in doing even that; the conservatives have just lost one valuable short-run bulwark, as a result of the new Administration's success in packing the Rules Committee of the House of Representatives. This defeat, substantial as it is, has significance only in regard to domestic policy; there never was anything that Judge Smith and his fellow conservatives could do about the continuing unpoliced moratorium on nuclear tests or the disintegration of the Southeast Asia Treaty Organization in Laos or any of a large number of international problems where mistakes in policy could make the question of the minimum wage purely academic.

But for the time being, at least, the minimum wage and the welfare measures of President Kennedy's domestic program are very important, and despite his victory, about all the new President has accomplished is that his program will not be stillborn. Every Representative who voted against the packing scheme did so with the knowledge of what would happen to the President's legislative plans if the scheme failed. In effect, each took a stand on those legislative plans. Among that 212, the conservatives can expect to lose as many as 15 or 20 on specific issues, but it

Formerly a writer for *Human Events,* John Weicher is currently a graduate student in the Department of Economics at the University of Chicago. He received his B.A. from the University of Michigan.

should also be pointed out that about as many conservatives voted with the President; virtually all of these can be expected to vote against him on his specific proposals. Whatever impelled Thomas Curtis of Missouri, for example, to vote to give life to the Forand bill, he cannot be expected to support the measure itself, since he has been its best-informed and most effective opponent; nor can the Administration expect much further support from old Joe Martin, the former Speaker, or William Bates of Massachusetts, or Bill Ayres of Ohio. And the Louisianans and Texans and Arkansans who bowed to party pressure cannot bow further without committing political suicide, if they have not done so already.

The Rules Committee itself is by no means a tool of the President. Judge Smith is still Chairman and, like Adolph Sabath, his left-wing Democratic predecessor, even in the minority he will probably be able to stop a good deal of the legislation he opposes. The Judge's still formidable strength, added to the second line of conservative defense which is the House itself, will be likely to defeat most if not all of the President's proposals.

Therefore, since the general fate of the New Frontier has probably been settled by the conservative strength shown in the Rules Committee vote of January, the present offers a good opportunity to take a longer-range view of the political situation in the country. Here the prospects are much less encouraging than they are in the short-run Congressional skirmishing. In the longer view, the Rules Committee packing, important as it was, has simply ended a war which

Page Fifteen

19

the Republicans could never have won as long as they remain the minority party in the House. It is no accident that Judge Smith and Congressman Colmer are the first- and second-ranking Democrats on the Committee; both were first appointed to it in the 1930's, before the Southerners formed their alliance with the Republicans. Both are in their 70's. Should either retire or die, their replacements would be far to the left of them. The other two holdover Southern Democrats on the committee, Trimble of Arkansas and Thornberry of Texas, generally vote with the Northern wing except on civil rights or states' rights issues. The Democratic leadership has long since stopped appointing conservatives to Rules Committee vacancies.

The Republicans can sterilize the Administration's victory by regaining control of the House. In 1962 they will be aided by the natural advantages of the "outs"—the normal opposition that any administration creates will be working for them. But the 1962 election will be complicated by redistricting, particularly in the larger states, and the Republican failure to win the important state legislatures will probably cancel out their normal off-year gains. For instance, the Democrats are in full control in California, and have promised to gerrymander as many Republicans as possible out of their seats, especially in Los Angeles County. What they do could easily nullify all the Republican gains in the states west of the Mississippi River. Pennsylvania is also dominated by the Democrats, though there the gerrymandering danger is less. Of the large states which must redistrict, the Republicans hold only New York, and any conservative gains there are likely to be small. Elsewhere, the Republicans have at best a split with the Democrats. Moreover, many of the smaller states which lose Congressmen are conservative, such as Maine, Mississippi, Nebraska and North Carolina. It would not be too surprising if the Democrats were to show some small gains in 1962, barring a political rock by Kennedy.

Despite all the talk to the contrary, the Republicans did not do very well last year. Nixon ran well ahead of his

party in most of the nation, but the party itself, which he supposedly has been directing politically since 1954 and rebuilding since 1958, rebounded very slightly from the collapse of 1958. It failed to regain even one-half of the Congressional seats it lost that year, and the untimely death of Keith Thomson in Wyoming deprived it of one of the two Senate seats it was able to win (and also deprived the conservatives of their only Senate gain). It was a singularly inauspicious record for a party which has been claiming that it only gets its total vote out in Presidential election years; it raises the question of whether the Republican slide which began in 1954 has yet bottomed out.

On the more cheerful side, one of last November's significant results was the defeat of a disproportionately large number of Democrats who took extreme leftist positions on foreign policy or internal security matters. For example, Jimmy Roosevelt was forced to drop his campaign against the Un-American Activities Committee after the defeats of several of his supporters. Also, two of the three avowed advocates of recognizing Communist China were retired by their constituents. While William Meyer of Vermont would probably have been defeated regardless of his opinions on anything, his pacifism and stand on China undoubtedly contributed to the unusually large size of his defeat. Perhaps more important was the upset of Charles Porter while the other two Oregon Democrats were winning by their usual margins or more. Both Porter and his opponent, Edwin Durno, attributed Porter's loss to his views on foreign policy; he supported the Fair Play for Cuba committee, at least until recently, as well as advocating Red China recognition. This leaves only Thomas Ashley, from Toledo, who has voted against "sense of the House" resolutions opposing Communist China's admission to the United Nations, claiming the House doesn't need to pass such resolutions year in, year out. Thus the voters have rejected the open advocates of recognition while electing a President whose foreign policy advisors are at best wobbly on the issue. (Picture Adlai Steven-

20

son at the UN denouncing Communist China as an outlaw nation and the murderer of Tibet. It is inconceivable.)

It will be interesting to watch the fireworks in the House when and if Stevenson speaks on this issue, for the majority leader, John W. McCormack, is one of the nation's most outspoken opponents of Red China. If he does not bring up another "sense of the House" resolution before the next UN debate, it will be a sign that the administration is dropping the firm Truman-Eisenhower policy and is trying to prepare the public for the eventual recognition and UN admission of the Chinese Communists.

But these are just a few conservative gains, and while they may indicate a potential Republican issue for 1962, the Republicans will have redistricting and weak organizations going against them at the same time. In addition, 1962 offers little hope for Republican gains in the Senate; more Republicans than Democrats will be up for re-election. Senator Morse in Oregon and Senator Clark in Pennsylvania offer about the only chances for important Republican gains. Morse's likely opponent will be Governor Mark Hatfield, who has proclaimed himself a Modern Republican, so there is little comfort for conservatives there. A few smaller fry, such as Church in Idaho and Carroll in Colorado, will also be running, as well as some members of the Republican left, such at Javits, Kuchel and Wiley. But the over-all picture here is as gloomy as it is for the House. The Republicans have not yet begun to revive.

And the Republicans offer conservatives their only hope for recapturing political power. The conservative Democrats in the South and elsewhere are not a force in their party nationally, and there is simply not time to build a new individualist party; the exigencies of the international situation do not permit it. The Republicans are the only short-run possibility, and it is too dangerous for the individualists to put all their hopes in a long-run new party.

The picture is not entirely black, among the younger Republicans, individualism is becoming more and more popular, as it is on the college campuses.

But there is likely to be a gap while these younger men gradually move into positions of leadership in the party and while the rebirth of individualism is diffused through the voting population. During that gap the conservatives and the Republicans will be in their greatest danger. It is always possible, though not very likely, that Kennedy might make a major mistake that would bring down the wrath of the voters on his head and sweep the Republicans into power. Or the Republicans might rejuvenate themselves during the next two or four years, possibly under the leadership of Senator Goldwater, who seems to have an ability to excite people that might be the touchstone for a rapid Republican-conservative comeback.

There are, however, other forces that would like to rejuvenate the Republican party under their own leadership; during the next four years, while Kennedy battles Judge Smith, the more important battle will be fought between Senator Goldwater and Governor Rockefeller, both as persons and as representatives of different political philosophies. While the Republicans in Congress are creating a conservative record for the party, Governor Rockefeller's natural strategy will be to ally himself with the Republican governors. In many ways, their situations are similar to those of Senator Taft and General Eisenhower in 1952, but complicated by the presence of Nixon. Moreover, all three men are young enough to plan not only for 1964 but also for 1968. If any of the three runs for President four years from now and loses, he will automatically be out of contention later.

It is this circumstance that puts the individualists in such a ticklish situation. Goldwater may offer a great opportunity to them, should he win the Presidential nomination in 1964 and go on to win the election. At the same time, unfortunately, he would also present the last such opportunity, for the Republican left might be willing to concede him the nomination in 1964 on the certainty that he would lose. And if he should lose, no matter by what margin, political conservatism would take a very, very long time to recover from his defeat.

Page Seventeen

This is the first in a series of articles, by various authors, on past thinkers who have contributed to individualist philosophy. Future articles will deal with men such as Burke, Acton, Bastiat and Herbert Spencer.

Wilhelm von Humboldt

RALPH RAICO

22

WHEN Oswald Spengler in one of his minor books scornfully characterized German classical liberalism as, "a bit of the spirit of England on German soil," he was merely displaying the willful blindness of the school of militaristic-statist German historians, who refused to acknowledge as a true compatriot any thinker who did not form part of the "intellectual bodyguard of the House of Hohenzollern." Spengler had apparently forgotten that Germany had had its Enlightenment, and the ideals of freedom which were conceived and propagated in England, Scotland and France towards the end of the eighteenth century, had found an echo and a support in the works of writers such as Kant, Schiller and even the young Fichte. Although by 1899 William Graham Sumner could write that, "there is today scarcely an institution in Germany except the army," it is nevertheless true that there existed a native German tradition of distinguished, libertarian thought, which had, in the course of the nineteenth century, to some degree at least been translated into action. Of the thinkers who contributed to this tradition, Wilhelm von Humboldt was unquestionably one of the greatest.

Born in 1767, Humboldt was descended from a Junker family which had faithfully served the rulers of Prussia for generations — a fact which was later to cause surprise to some of those who heard young Humboldt in conversation passionately defend personal liberty. He was educated at Frankfurt-am-Oder, and later at Göttingen, at that time one of the centers of liberal ideas in Germany.

In the summer of 1789, Humboldt undertook a trip to Paris, in the company of his former tutor, Campe, who was a devotee of the *philosophes,* and now eager to see with his own eyes, "the funeral rites of French despotism." His pupil did not share his enthusiasm for the Revolution, however, for from what Humboldt had witnessed at Paris and from conversations with Friedrich Gentz (at that time a supporter of the French Revolution) there issued a brief article, "Ideas on the Constitutions of States, occasioned by the New French Constitution."[1]

This little essay, orginally intended as a letter to a friend, is noteworthy for a number of reasons. In the first place, Humboldt appears to have arrived at

Ralph Raico received his B.A. from City College of New York in 1959. He is presently studying under the Committee on Social Thought, University of Chicago.

[1] "Ideen über Staatsverfassung, durch die neue französische Constitution veranlasst," in Humboldt's *Gesammelte Schriften,* vol. i, (Berlin, 1903), pp. 77-85.

some of the major conclusions of **Burke**, without at that time being familiar with the latter's work. He states, for instance, that "reason is capable to be sure of giving form to material already present, but it has no power to create new material . . . Constitutions cannot be grafted upon men as sprigs upon trees." For a new political order to be successful, it is necessary for "time and nature" to have prepared the ground. Since this has not been the case in France, historical analogy compels us to answer no to the question whether this new constitution will succeed.

In addition, this essay is interesting because it anticipates an idea which was central to the thesis of Humboldt's most important work on political theory, and which was never far from his mind whenever he deliberated on the nature of man — the notion that, "whatever is to flourish in a man must spring from within him, and not be given him from without."

Nevertheless, Humboldt does not, in this essay, display the hostility towards the French people which was characteristic of Burke. He realizes that if the French had given themselves over to ill-considered schemes for remoulding their society according to a preconceived plan, it was a reaction which might have been expected, given the provocations of the Old Regime. "Mankind had suffered at the hands of one extreme; it understandably sought its salvation at the other."

On his return to Berlin, Humboldt had been given a minor post at the law court. But the relative freedom of thought which had been enjoyed in Prussia under Frederick the Great, was at this time being replaced by persecutions of the press and religious intolerance and Humboldt did not find the atmosphere of public life congenial. Added to this, was the disinclination which he felt to interfere in the lives of others (a nicety of feeling almost grotesquely out of place in a "public servant"). Most important of all, perhaps, was the new conception which he was beginning to formulate of the legitimate functions of government, a conception which virtually compelled him to look on the states of his time as engines of injustice. In the spring of

1791, Humboldt resigned his position.

The genesis of his major work on political theory, and the one of most interest to individualists, is also to be found in discussions with a friend — Karl von Dalberg, who was a proponent of the "enlightened" state paternalism then prevalent in Germany. He pressed Humboldt for a written exposition of his views on the subject, and Humboldt responded, in 1792, by composing his classic, *The Sphere and Duties of Government.*[2]

This little book was later to have a good deal of influence. It was of importance in shaping some of John Stuart Mill's ideas in this field, and may even have provided the immediate occasion for his *On Liberty.* In France, Laboulaye, the late nineteenth century individualist, owed much to this work of Humboldt's, and in Germany it exercised an influence even over such a basically unsympathetic mind as von Treitschke's. But it is also a book which has an inherent value, because in it are set forth — in some cases, I believe, for the first time — some of the major arguments for freedom.

Humboldt begins his work by remarking that previous writers on political philosophy have concerned themselves almost exclusively with investigating the divisions of governmental power and what part the nation, or certain sectors of it, ought to have in the exercise of this power. These writers have neglected the more fundamental question, "to what end ought the whole apparatus of the state to aim, and what limits ought to be set to its activity?" It is this question that Humboldt intends to answer.

"The true end of man — not that which capricious inclination prescribes for him, but that which is prescribed by eternally immutable reason — is the highest and most harmonious cultivation of his faculties into one whole. For this cultivation, freedom is the first and indispensible condition." Humboldt thus begins by placing his argument within the framework of a particular conception of man's nature, but it ought to be noted that the

---

[2] It was under this title that Humboldt's book appeared in English, in 1854. The German title is, *Ideen zu einem Versuch, die Grenzen der Wirksamkeit des Staats zu bestimmen;* in Humboldt op., cit. vol. i, pp. 97-254.

23

validity of his argument does not depend upon the correctness of his view of "the true end of man." Of primary importance are his ideas in regard to the mechanism of individual and social progress, and here even such a socially-minded utilitarian as John Stuart Mill could find instruction and inspiration.

For the full flourishing of the individual, Humboldt asserts, there is requisite, besides freedom, a "manifoldness of situations," which, while logically distinct from freedom, has always followed upon it. It is only when men are placed in a great variety of circumstances that those experiments in living can take place which expand the range of values with which the human race is familiar, and it is through expanding this range that increasingly better answers can be found to the question, "In exactly what ways are men to arrange their lives?"

A free nation would, according to Humboldt, be one in which "the continuing necessity of association with others would urgently impel each gradually to modify himself" in the light of his appreciation of the value of the life-patterns others have accepted. In such a society, "no power and no hand would be lost for the elevation and enjoyment of human existence." Each man, in applying his reason to his own life and circumstances, would contribute to the education of other men, and would, in turn, learn from their experience. This is Humboldt's view of the mechanism of human progress.

It should be clear, however, that this progressive refinement of the individual personality can only take place under a regime of freedom, since "what is not chosen by the individual himself, that in which he is only restricted and led, does not enter into his being. It remains foreign to him, and he does not really accomplish it with human energy, but with mechanical address." This is one of the central ideas of the book, and merits some discussion.

It is an idea which no one will dispute, when it is a question of scientific progress. No one expects worthwhile scientific thought to take place where the scientist is compelled or restricted in some important facet of his work. He must be free to develop his ideas, in accordance with the self-imposed standards of his profession, out of his own originality. But scientific knowledge is only one type of knowledge; there are other types, some at least as socially useful. There is the knowledge which consists in skills and techniques of production, and the type which, as we have seen, is embedded in values and ways of life: besides the sort of knowledge which is acquired through abstract thought, there is the sort acquired through practical thought and through action. The argument for freedom in the elaboration of scientific knowledge, therefore, is simply a special instance of the argument for freedom in general.

Professor Michael Polanyi has described the benefits of "individualism in the cultivation of science":

The pursuit of science can be organized . . . in no other manner than by granting complete independence to all mature scientists. They will then distribute themselves over the whole field of possible discoveries, each applying his own special ability to the task that appears most profitable to him. Thus as many trails as possible will be covered, and science will penetrate most rapidly in every direction towards that kind of hidden knowledge which is unsuspected by all but its discoverer, the kind of new knowledge on which the progress of science truly depends.[3]

Few will doubt that scientific progress would have been appallingly retarded if, for instance, Einstein had been compelled to obtain permission from a board in charge of "planning science" before he could undertake his researches (or if a government commission had been empowered to pass on Galileo's intended work!). But if men like Henry Ford had not been free to put their ideas into operation, industrial progress would have been no less stanched. We may freely concede that the abstract scientific thought of an Einstein is a loftier thing, representing a greater achievement of the human mind. But this has

_____
[3] Michael Polanyi, *The Logic of Liberty,* (London, 1951), p. 89.

no bearing on the argument.

We believe that individual scientists should be unhindered in the pursuit of their aims, because those who would be in charge of the central direction of scientific research, or those who had power to restrict scientists in essential ways, would not know as well as the scientists themselves — each of whom has an immediate knowledge of the relevant factors in his particular situation—which are the most promising lines to be explored. In addition, a self-chosen activity, or one which may be freely followed up in all of its ramifications, will summon forth energy which will not be available in cases where a task is imposed from without, or where the researcher meets up against countless frustrations in the pursuit of his goal — the free activity, in other words, will command greater incentive.

But both of these propositions are equally true of activities involving practical knowledge, or knowledge in action, of which techniques of production are an example. The socialist who believes in central direction of economic activity ought, consistently, to believe also in the central planning of science, and those who favor wide-spread government control of economic life, because the state "knows better," should, if they were consistent, favor a return to the system that shackled the scientific enterprise as well.

It was partly because force necessarily interferes with individual self-development and the proliferation of new ideas, by erecting a barrier between the individual's perception of a situation and the solution he thinks it best to attempt, that Humboldt wanted to limit the activities of the state as severely as possible. Another argument in favor of this conclusion is that a government wishing to supervise to even a modest degree such a complex phenomenon as society, simply cannot fit its regulations to the peculiarities of various concatenations of circumstances. But measures which ignore such peculiarities will tend to produce uniformity, and contract the "manifoldness of situations" which is the spur to all progress.

But what is the indispensible minimum of government activity? Humboldt finds that the one good which society cannot provide for itself is security against those who aggress against the person and property of others. His answer to the question which he posed at the beginning of his work, "what limits ought to be set to the activity of the state," is "that the provision of security, against both external enemies and internal dissensions must constitute the purpose of the state, and occupy the circle of its activity."

As for the services which it is commonly held must fall within the scope of government action, as, for instance, charity, Humboldt believes that they need not be provided by *political* institutions, but can safely be entrusted to *social* ones. "It is only requisite that freedom of association be given to individual parts of the nation or to the nation itself," in order for charitable ends to be satisfactorily fulfilled. In this, as, indeed, throughout his whole book, Humboldt shows himself to be a thoughtful but passionate believer in the efficacy of truly social forces, in the possibility of great social ends being achieved without any necessity for direction on the part of the state. Humboldt thus allies himself with the thinkers who rejected the state in order to affirm society.

Parts of Humboldt's book appeared in

25

two German periodicals in 1792, but difficulties with the Prussian censorship and a certain apparently innate lack of confidence in his own works, caused him to put off publication of the work until it could be revised. The day for revision never came, however, and it was only sixteen years after the author's death that *The Sphere and Duties of Government* was published in its entirety.

For ten years after the completion of this book, Humboldt devoted himself to traveling and private studies, principally in aesthetics and the classics, linguistics and comparative anthropology. From 1802 to 1808 he served as Prussian minister to Rome, a post which involved a minimum of official business, and which he accepted chiefly out of his love for the city. Humboldt's real "return to the state" occurs in 1809, when he became Director of the Section for Public Worship and Education, in the Ministry of Interior. In this capacity, he directed the reorganization of the Prussian public education system, and, in particular, founded the University of Berlin.

That so unquestionably sincere a man as Humboldt could have acted in such disharmony with the principles set forth in his only book on political philosophy (among them, that the state should have no connection with education), requires some explanation. The reason is to be sought in his patriotism, which had been aroused by the utter defeat suffered by Prussia at the hands of Napoleon. Humboldt wished to contribute to the regeneration of his country which was being undertaken by men such as Stein and Hardenberg, and the reform of the educational system fitted his abilities and inclinations.

This task completed, Humboldt served in various diplomatic posts for a number of years, including that of Prussian minister to the Congress of Vienna, and, after peace had been established, as a member of the Council of State. But the spirit which now predominated in Berlin, as well as throughout Europe, was the spirit of Metternich, who, always able accurately to identify the enemies of his system, had already in 1814 termed Humboldt a "Jacobin." Humboldt's opposition to the reactionary policies of his government gained for him as much ill-will at court as it did popularity among the people. He was hated and intrigued against by the reactionaries at court; they went so far as to open his mail, as if he had in actuality been a Jacobin. When, in 1819, Metternich induced Prussia to agree to the Karlsbad Decrees, which attempted to establish a rigid censorship for all of Germany, Humboldt termed the regulations "shameful, unnational and provoking to a great people," and demanded the impeachment of Bernstorff, the Prussian minister who had signed them.

It was clear that a man like Humboldt was an anomaly in a government which treacherously refused to fulfill its war-time promises of a constitution, and whose domestic policies were largely dictated by Metternich. In December, 1819, Humboldt was dismissed. He refused the pension offered him by the king.

The rest of his life he devoted to his studies, of which the researches into linguistics were the most important and gained for him the reputation of a pioneer in the field. He died in 1835.

If we ask what are the primary contributions of Humboldt to libertarian thought, we will find the answer in his ideas on the value of the free, self-sustaining activity of the individual, and of the importance of the unhindered collaboration — often unconscious — of the members of society. The first is a conception which is finding remarkable support and application in the work of the Client-centered, or Non-directive school of psychotherapists[4], while the second has been explored in the recent books of writers such as F. A. Hayek and Michael Polanyi[5]. That ideas which were set forth by Humboldt should be proving so relevant to contemporary research into man and society, is a sign of the clearly discernible trend towards individualism in present-day thought at the highest levels.

---

[4] On this very suggestive approach to psychotherapy, see Carl R. Rogers, et. al., *Client-Centered Therapy*, (New York, 1951).

[5] See, especially, F. A. Hayek, *The Counter-Revolution of Science*, (Glencoe, Ill., 1952), and *The Constitution of Liberty*, (Chicago, 1960), and Michael Polanyi, op. cit.

Modern Education vs. Democracy

ROBERT   SCHUETTINGER

"Observe that there is a certain flavor of totalitarianism about [progressive education]: it is just the form our totalitarianism would take — kindly, humane, fussy, bureaucratic, flat, insipid, like a minor civil servant's dream, without energy or power, hazard or enterprise, the standards set by people who cannot write English, who have no poetry or vision or daring, without the capacity to love or hate."—Professor A. L. Rowse, Oxford University.

IN THIS Year One of the New Frontier, there are few, if any, objective observers who will deny that whatever else the Deweyites did to America's schools, they did *not* turn them into centers of learning. It has, unfortunately become a commonplace that the sort of person who would commend the intellectual ability of the average education professor is precisely the sort who would have arisen, in another time, to praise the good intentions of Hitler or Stalin or, indeed, to defend the chastity of Messalina.

What the advocates of "modern" or "progressive" education **will** claim is that, while their students may not necessarily be able to read or write[1], they are all well-indoctrinated in certain "understandings and attitudes" which are far more vital to the educated man than mere literacy. That is, they have all been pumped full of the Standard Brand of "Democracy" . . . as approved by Teachers College, Columbia.

Robert Schuettinger, a graduate of Queens College, studied history at Columbia University before coming to the Committee on Social Thought, University of Chicago.

The fact of the matter is, however, that the educationists, as a profession, are doing more than any other organized group to destroy equality of opportunity in the United States today. Far from being apostles of democracy, they have, in reality, become its most effective enemies.

It is true, of course, that the educational bureaucrats who control most of our schools, talk and write a good deal about "our democratic way of life." Sometimes, it seems as though they talk about nothing else. They love to attend "workshops" where they can sit around in their shirtsleeves (what could be more democratic?) and devise "new and attractive" courses for the re-moulding of "our wonderful boys and girls"; courses with such grandiose titles as: "Eleventh and Twelfth Grade: Growth in Effective Living through Problem-Centered Experiences Directed Toward Achieving the Highest Possible Quality of Human Experience through Striving for Social, Political and Economic Democracy in Its Local, State and National Setting, and for Peace and Co-operation on the International Scene."[2]

[1] On the occasion of her appointment to the Educational Policies Commission of the NEA, Mrs. Rachel Royston Knutson, counselor at Sharples Junior High School, Seattle, made this contribution to educational thought: "Who's to say that everybody can read? Or write, or play the piano? Personally, I'm barely able to swim across a pool and I doubt if all the teaching in the world would make me a good swimmer." See *Council for Basic Education Bulletin*, September, 1959, p. 4. Mrs. Knutson's views are by no means unique among educationists.

[2] Douglas, Harl R., editor, *The High School Curriculum*, New York, 1956, p. 285.

On the surface, I suppose it is difficult to believe that these naive people, whatever short-comings they may have, are not sincere advocates of democracy. Yet I am convinced that, knowingly or unknowingly, they are doing great harm to the cause of democracy; in this essay I want to demonstrate precisely how and why this has come about.

If the word democracy has any meaning in relation to education (outside of its strict political use) it must stand for equality of opportunity for all students regardless of their racial, reigious or economic background. I believe that it can be demonstrated that most educationists (though they themselves are probably not fully aware of the implications of their own ideas) are working to deny equality of opportunity to many of their students — on the basis of their racial, religious or economic origins.

The largest lobby in Washington, the National Education Association, has been spending its members' dues on a lavish scale for many years in order to persuade Congress to pass a federal-aid-to-education bill. Apparently, the NEA leaders do not realize (or do not care) that such federal action would discriminate against students who prefer to attend religious or other non-public schools. The parents of private and parochial school students, in addition to paying their own tuitions, as well as their share of their community's school taxes, will be forced to pay higher federal taxes in order to provide more expensive facilities (not necessarily better education) for those children who choose to attend public schools. None of this money would go to any private or parochial school — which is as it should be. The point is, however, that many parents will be deprived of funds that they might have used to improve the non-public school attended by their own children. The result will be that private school students will be pressured into enrolling in the state system if they wish to share in the extra facilities which will be available to the public school student.

This withering away of the private schools is, of course, the eventual goal of such educators as Dr. Conant, who regards private schools as "divisive" and would like to see all children forced to attend the same school system so that they might all have the same opportunity to learn the officially-approved meaning of democracy.

It is true that the parents of many (though by no means all) private school students are wealthy and will be able to contribute sufficient funds to keep their schools in operation. This does not apply, however, in the case of church-related schools, whose students will suffer most, since few of their parents are well-to-do. In addition to many Catholics, Jews and Protestants, who may no longer be able to give their children an education of their own choosing, many Negroes in the South will also be set back several steps.

Since no federal education program is likely to be legislated over the opposition of Southern congressmen, a good part of the funds appropriated will be spent in strengthening the system of segregated schools in the South, many of which were becoming economically unfeasible even before the Supreme Court decision. I need hardly add that few, if any, of the State Education Departments in the South would be willing to divide federal money equally between white and Negro schools[3]. In the light of this, no one, unless he believed in the kind of totalitarian "democracy" preached by the Fascists and Communists, would call such government enforced discrimination democratic.

Perhaps the most widespread and most dangerous form of discrimination, however, is that directed against students from culturally deprived or lower-income families. Dr. George D. Spache, head of the Reading Laboratory and Professor of Education at the University of Florida, recently expressed[4] a point of view on this subject which is shared by many leading educationists.

"Reading," according to Dr. Spache, "is as much a sociological process as it is a

---

[3] The federal government is already a "silent partner" in the perpetuation of unequal schooling in the South. Federal funds now provide about 15 per cent of the revenues for state budgets for college education in the Deep South. State legislatures divert nearly all this money to white schools. See Edward P. Morgan's column in *The New York Post*, January 21, 1961.

[4] *Education Digest*, November, 1960.

psychological or personal one. Therefore, before we can expect to help the poor reader perform at what we consider a normal level, we must consider what is normal for his environmental setting. What part does reading play in the family's leisure time? What are the parental attitudes toward his reading? We should certainly attempt to improve the status symbols of breadth of reading, verbal fluency, reading tastes and interests. But we must recognize that these must be realistically related to the probable uses of reading for this child now and in the future in his environmental setting."

It would seem, then, that Dr. Spache is advocating a kind of educational and cultural determinism. He and others like him, who proclaim that they alone know what is best for the student, appear to be interested only in preserving the status quo. One report[5], which was received by most educationists as gospel truth, declared bluntly that 85% of our students are not capable of absorbing a genuine education and can only be given vocational training which will make them into "useful members of society." As Mortimer Smith remarked, those would-be "social-engineers" are saying in effect: "Bow, bow, ye lower middle casses, accept what is normal for your environmental setting — and continue to read comics and the tabloids."

It should not be supposed, moreover, that such anti-democratic attitudes are confined to a small minority of our educational philosophers. A widely used education text, *The High School Curriculum,* observes that "English teachers have suddenly discovered that many is the boy who says 'I ain't got no' because his parents say it, his friends say it and his community says it. Furthermore," say the educationists, *"these parents see no reason why they should change or why their sons should change."* (Italics mine)[6]. If I had not been informed to the contrary by so many experts, I would have thought (in my untutored simplicity) that it would be a rare parent indeed

who did not want his children to have a better education and a better start in life that he. Abraham Lincoln's illiterate father could never have known about the findings of such scholars as Dr. Spache; else he would never have permitted his son to read books which were clearly "not normal for his enviornmental setting."

It would be a serious mistake to write off such nincompoopery as the harmless prancing of would-be scholars who will never quite be recognized as such by the academic profession. Incredible as it may sometimes seem it is these people who are firmly in control of the great majority of the public schools in the United States today. If the present trend continues, only those students whose parents can afford to send them to a private school will know that the sentence "A great heap of books are on the table" is incorrect[7]. The very men who are talking most about democracy in education are also laying it down as dogma all over the country that no one has a right to speak like a cultivated person who was not born to parents who were themselves fortunate enough to have received a good education. It will not be too difficult to predict what will happen to the bright student who is poor but who is also presumptious enough to think that he might be able to raise his station in life. He will probably apply to a good college; however, in the entrance examinations and interviews he will be competing with boys who may be less gifted than he but who do know not to say "ain't" when talking to a Dean. Under these circumstances, there is no need to ask what chance he will have. If he is lucky he may still be admitted to an inferior college. There he may be trained to perform some second-rate task under the supervision of a gentleman's son who speaks English

[5] Conant, James, *The American High School Today,* New York, 1958.

[6] Douglas, *op. cit.,* p. 392.

[7] The Iowa Department of Public Instruction lists, in a handbook for English, a number of examples of poor usage (such as *these* kind of letters are scarce, a great heap of books *are* on the table, etc.) and then states: "Teaching corrections for these . . . is a waste of time and a source of confusion to the students. . . . Only in formal literary writing and in formal speech are finer distinctions made." See *CBE Bulletin,* September, 1958, p. 6.

instead of the vulgate and is, therefore, always called "Sir."

IT WOULD be interesting to know what motivates these educationists in their zeal for keeping their students on as low a level as possible. Laziness cannot be the answer since it surely requires far more effort to think up elaborate new reasons for **not** teaching reading and writing (to say nothing of history and science) than it would to simply respond to their students' natural desire to learn. If the prodigious energy which is diverted into making up gargantuan lists of the "aims and purposes of democratic education"[8] were devoted to teaching we would probably see a significant increase in the number of high school graduates who are able to fill out their driver's licenses without assistance.

I think that we may find a clue in Emile Faguet's perceptive book on the ills of democracy, *The Cult of Incompetence*. In his last chapter, M. Faguet asks himself why it was that the French public school teachers were so unanimous in taking a paternal attitude toward the lower economic classes. Despite their mediocre capacities, these teachers enjoyed considering themselves "Liberal intellectuals"; they eagerly aped the ideas of the latter-day *philosophes* and flitted from one fashionable brand of socialism to the next as they dutifully (and always self-righteously) espoused the "cause" of the workers. They affected a great contempt for the middle-class (from which most of them had sprung) and naturally held a bitter hatred for the upper classes, who possessed all the

advantages and power that they thought should have been given to themselves. After the Revolution, of course, genuine merit would receive its just due!

Eric Hoffer in his analysis of fanaticism, *The True Believer*, points out that the "non-creative man of words" (the would-be intellectual who will never produce the great work that he secretly believes himself capable of writing) very often finds an outlet for his frustrations in joining a cause which promises to shape the world into his own image of righteousness. M. Faguet's explanation for the monolithic Liberalism of the public school teachers is similar to Mr. Hoffer's and, I think, is, in the main, correct. These teachers, he notes, were clearly an inferior lot: not able enough to direct a business and not scholarly enough to become professors, they were denied the recognition that their egos so deeply carved.

They gained a deep satisfaction, therefore, in championing the aspirations of the lower classes but, at the same time, they never let the workers forget that they, their natural superiors, were performing an act of *noblesse oblige* by watching over their interests. A bright workingman's son would not fit into the picture; he must be kept at his own level and not be allowed to challenge the jealously guarded preeminence of the teacher in his own classroom. Most public school teachers in the United States now come from the lowest percentiles of university graduates, usually ranking below agriculture students. It should not be too surprising that such people fear, above all else, being "shown up" by a student of superior intelligence. To avoid this, therefore, bright students must be kept at the level of the slow learner, and all, so far as is possible, must be exposed to the bare minimum of education.

There is no shortage of evidence to substantiate the fact that most of our public school teachers denigrate competition and the pursuit of excellence in the classroom. Their own sense of mediocracy is so great, in fact, that the lengths to which they will go to avoid any comparison with their colleagues can only be described as desperate. A typical example of this passion for ano-

---

[8] In one education text the desirable "behavioral outcomes" of an ideal high school education are listed in a monumental classification extending for one hundred and twenty pages; the list is a prize example of what Stephen Leacock called "oceans of piffle." Outcome No. 1.122a is "writes and speaks with sufficient clarity and in good enough form to communicate with others." No. 1.241g is "helps when necessary to eliminate insects and vermin which carry germs." The ideal American student "wears (if a girl) with growing self-assurance, appropriate foundation garments and clothing properly styled for the maturing figure." (1.133i). See Will French and Associates, *Behavioral Goals of General Education in High School*, New York 1957.

30

nymity occurred recently in Racine, Wisconsin, where a group of 577 public school teachers rejected a proposed merit pay plan by a vote of 466 to 111. Instead, they adopted a plan whereby all teachers with the same length of service in a classification received the same pay regardless of individual ability.

Is it any wonder that such people are unlikely to encourage a bright but poor boy to improve himself and his family? Their watchword is "normality"; they heave a sigh of relief whenever they see it. The write "works and plays well with others" and reflect with satisfaction that one more American boy can be counted on never to do anything original.

I do not think it possible to exaggerate the dangers to our society emanating from our teachers' colleges and the NEA. I hope I have made it clear that if their policies are not checked the result will be the creation of what Disraeli called "two nations": one a nation of aristocrats forever set apart from the other, a nation of the poor, burdened by so many class distinctions, including language, that they will have little hope of ever changing their status for the better. No matter what their reasons may be, the inheritors of the mantle of Dewey are, in fact, building a static society which will end by enthroning the worst kind of reacton.

31

Hayek's Concept of Freedom: A Critique

RONALD HAMOWY

F. A. HAYEK, in his latest book, *The Constitution of Liberty* (University of Chicago Press, Chicago, 1960), attempts a thorough exposition of the theoretical and historical foundations of individual liberty. His main thesis is that freedom may be defined as the absence of coercion: it thus becomes clear that, in order fully to comprehend what he feels to be the basis of personal freedom in society, we must turn to his definition of coercion.

Professor Hayek states: "Coercion occurs when one man's actions are made to serve another man's will, not for his own but for the other's purpose." (p. 133.) But he goes on to make explicit that such coercion can occur only when the possibility of alternate actions is open to the coerced. "Coercion implies . . . that I still choose but that my mind is made someone else's tool, because the alternatives before me have been so manipulated that the conduct that the coercer wants me to choose becomes for me the least painful one." (p. 133.)

Let us examine this concept more thoroughly. Firstly, the absence of coercion, in terms of the above statement, would seem to be the following: Freedom (or the absence of coercion) obtains when the possible alternative actions before me are not such that, through the manipulation of such alternatives by another actor, the least painful choice for me is that which is the most bene-

ficial for him. Or, more simply, freedom obtains when no one else manipulates my environment in such a way that my action (or actions) benefits him. It shall be my purpose, throughout the remainder of this article, to indicate that such a concept of freedom is fundamentally incompatible with the one which forms the basis of a consistent libertarianism.

Now, the first difficulty arising out of such a definition is that of determining just what particular actions *are* coercive. Professor Hayek attempts to distinguish coercive acts from "the conditions or terms on which our fellow men are willing to render us specific services or benefits," in the following way: "So long as the services of a particular person are not crucial to my existence or the preservation of what I most value, the conditions he exacts for rendering these services cannot properly be called 'coercion'." But it would seem that this lends little if any clarity to the distinction between coercive and non-coercive acts, since we are still left to define and make precise Hayek's qualifications for characterizing an action as a coercive one; namely, being "crucial to . . . existence" and "preserving what one most values."

Let us take an example which Hayek himself uses. Suppose that the condition for my being invited to a certain party, which I had previously indicated I wanted very much to attend, were my wearing formal attire. Could it be said that my host, by demanding such an action on my part, was acting coercively towards me? It would appear, and so Hayek concludes, that the answer is

Ronald Hamowy did his undergraduate studies at City College of New York and Cornell University. He is at present a William Volker Fellow of the Committee on Social Thought, University of Chicago.

clearly "no." For, although it is true that my environment is being deliberately manipulated in such a way that my "least painful choice" is that which benefits the manipulator, this situation does not satisfy the terms of either of the above qualifications: i.e., neither "being crucial to my existence" nor "preserving what I most value." Yet, perhaps we are drawing our drawing our conclusion too hastily. It might be that I am a very social-conscious person, and not being invited to this party would greatly endanger my social standing. Further, my tuxedo is at the cleaners and will not be ready for several days. I do not have time to order a new one, and I am assured by my tailors that the fitting and altering involved will take at least a week and the party is this Saturday. Under these conditions, could it be said that my host's action in demanding my wearing formal attire as the price of access to his home is, in fact, a coercive one, since it clearly threatens the preservation of one of the things I most value, my social prestige?

The above situation might be altered slightly to present what might more clearly appear to be a coercive act, in terms of Hayek's definition. Suppose the price demanded by my host, in return for inviting me to his home, were a commitment from me that I wash all the silver and china used at the party. On the face of it this would seem to be nothing more than a contract relationship voluntarily entered into by the two parties to the agreement. But suppose all the other conditions concerning my attachment to social prestige still held. It then becomes the case, within the framework of Professor Hayek's terms, that such a contract is of a coercive nature.

On p. 136, he presents a case of "true coercion" of this same type. "A monopolist could exercise true coercion . . . if he were . . . the owner of a spring in an oasis. Let us say that other persons settled there on the presumption that water would always be available at a reasonable price and then found . . . that they had no choice but to do whatever the owner of the spring demanded of them if they were to survive: here would be a clear case of coercion." We assume that Hayek means that a contract entered into by the owner of the spring and the purchaser of water which allowed for renumeration to the spring-owner of any but a "reasonable price" would be of a coercive nature. But here we are faced with a difficult problem; namely, what constitutes "a reasonable price." By "reasonable," Professor Hayek might mean "competitive." But how is it possible to determine what the competitive price is in the absence of competition? Economics cannot attribute a cardinal magnitude to any price outside of the framework of the market. What, then, can we assume to be a "reasonable" price, or, more to the point, at what price does the contract alter its nature and become a coercive one? Is it at one dollar a gallon, ten dollars a gallon, one thousand dollars a gallon? What if the owner of the spring demands nothing more than the friendship of the settlers. Is such a price coercive? By what principle can we decide when the agreement is a simple contractual one, and when it is not?

But we must face yet a further difficulty. Is the owner acting coercively if he refuses to sell his water *at any price?* Let us suppose that he looks upon his spring as sacred to his gods and to offer up its holy water a gross sacrilege. Here is a situation which would not fall under Hayek's definition of coercion, since the owner of the spring forces *no* action on the settlers. Yet, it would appear that, within Hayek's own framework, this is a far worse situation, since the only "choice" left open to the settlers now is dying of thirst.

LET US NOW turn to Professor Hayek's use of the term "coercion" within the context of state activity. Here, just as many difficulties seem to arise. On p. 153, he states that "the conception of freedom under the law that is the chief concern of this book rests on the contention that when we obey laws, in the sense of general abstract rules laid down irrespective of their application to us, we are not subject to another man's will and are therefore free." The inference is, of course, that these abstract rules, when applied impartially without regard to person are non-coercive, despite any qualification as to their content. And Hayek himself says this: though "taxation and the various compulsory services, especially conscription . . . are not supposed to be avoidable, they are at least predictable and are enforced irrespective of how the individual would otherwise employ his energies: *this deprives them largely of the evil nature of coercion.*" (Italics mine).

Now, in a book dedicated to an investigation of the theoretical and historical groundwork of freedom, particularly within the context of a state structure, it is of the utmost importance that the boundary between coercion and non-coercion, as applied to the actions of the state, be clearly drawn. For how else are we to know when the state is exercising its legitimate functions or coercing its citizens? Hayek differentiates these two categories of actions by applying the concept of the Rule of Law. "Law," Professor Hayek asserts on p. 149, "in its ideal form might be described as a 'once-and-for-all' command that is directed to unknown people and that is abstracted from all particular circumstances of time and place and refers only to such conditions as may occur anywhere and at any time." We see, then, that the Rule of Law is the governance of society under a set of abstract rules which in no way discriminate among the citizenry and, hence, are equally applicable to all. An instance of such a law would be taxation (although *not* progressive taxation*) which applies equally to all those falling under the jurisdiction of the state. Having thus been robbed of either privilege or discrimination as regards "the classification of persons which the law must employ," such state action does not fall under the scope of coercion.

But we are forced to question the validity of this conclusion which rests on what is, in fact, a mistaken distinction between legitimate and illegitimate state actions. It would, for example, be perfectly consistent with the Rule of Law, as Professor Hayek presents it, to allow

*Cf. Hayek's discussion of progressive taxation on p. 314.

for the passage of legislation prescribing the enslavement of each male citizen for a period of two years, such enslavement to fall during the period of his prime (say, between the ages of 18 and 36). This is, in fact, the case with conscription, which Hayek explicitly states is consonant with a free society. Such a conclusion differs radically from that once made by Mr. William F. Buckley, Jr., that "conscription is the most naked form which tyranny assumes in our society today," and appears to be inconsistent with Hayek's own intention of laying down those principles which allow for a minimum of coercion in society.

Further, it would be just as consistent, within a free society governed by the Rule of Law, to interfere with many of our most basic freedoms — and such freedoms include economic ones as well**— provided such laws are applicable to all without distinction.

It is one of Hayek's purposes to build up a theoretical framework from which the necessity of private property can be deduced, a conclusion arrived at from an investigation of the nature of power and freedom in society. It would clearly seem to be subverting the very groundwork of such a principle if the theoretical system upon which it rests allows for the concentration and legitimate use of such powers in the hands of the state which can result in a system the nature of which aims at the overthrow of personal liberty. Hayek says: "the recognition of private property is . . . an essential condition for the prevention of coercion." Yet he succeeds in placing within the power of the state the very means of interfering with that right under the

** We are here dealing only with political, and not economic arguments. It could easily be shown that restrictions on trade and manufacture were highly detrimental to society in that they would necessarily lower the standard of living and the comfort and well-being of the citizens. But such arguments would be economic ones, and only economic ones, since we would have no recourse to political discussion except outside the terms of Professor Hayek's position. Once the Rule of Law is taken as a basis of legitimate state action, and all laws equally applicable to all fall under this rubric,. we can no longer bring to bear a discussion of the state's interference with personal freedom.

guise of acting consistently within the borders of its legitimate domain and consonant with the Rule of Law. Here, then, lies the main critique of Hayek's proposed framework: that it offers a rationale for what clearly are coercive acts of the state, e.g., conscription, interference in the economy (under the principle that it is attempting to minimize personal coercion) and alteration by fiat of the social structure of personal relationships which have developed spontaneously and undirected over the course of centuries.

Given that such situations as the voluntary contractualization of parties to a mutually beneficial agreement (e.g., the example cited above concerning the spring in the desert) can be classed under the heading of "coercion" within Hayek's system, and that what appear to be clear cases of coercive governmental action, such as conscription, are deemed legitimate and in accordance with the Rule of Law, it would seem that Hayek's position on the nature of coercion and freedom must, as it stands, be rejected.

NEW BOOKS AND ARTICLES

THE FOLLOWING IS A SELECT LIST OF BOOKS AND ARTICLES WHICH, IN THE OPINION OF THE EDITORS, MAY BE OF INTEREST TO OUR READERS.

F. A. Hayek, *The Constitution of Liberty*, (University of Chicago Press, Chicago, Illinois, 1960), 570 pp. $7.50.

Henry Hazlitt, editor, *The Critics of Keynesian Economics*, (Van Nostrand, Princeton, New Jersey, 1960), 427 pp. $7.00.

James D. Koerner, editor, *The Case for Basic Education*, (Atlantic-Little, Brown, Boston, Mass., 1960). $4.00.

Frank S. Meyer, *The Moulding of Communists*, (Harcourt, Brace, New York, 1961), 214 pp. $5.00.

Ludwig von Mises, *Epistemological Problems of Economics*, (Van Nostrand, Princeton, New Yersey, 1960), 239 pp. $5.50.

Felix Morley, *Freedom and Federalism*, (Henry Regnery, Chicago, Illinois, 1960). $5.00.

Albert Jay Nock, *Jefferson*, (Hill and Wang, New York, 1960), paper, $1.45.

Wilhelm Roepke, *A Humane Economy*, (Henry Regnery, Chicago, Illinois, 1960), 312 pp. $5.00.

Schoeck and Wiggins, editors, *Scientism and Values*, (Van Nostrand, Princeton, New Jersey, 1960), 270 pp. $6.50.

Louise Sommers, editor, *Essays in European Economic Thought*, (Van Nostrand, Princeton, New Jersey, 1960), 229 pp. $6.00.

P. T. Bauer, "Economic Development of Under-developed Countries," *Bulletin of the Atomic Scientists*, Vol. XVI, No. 8, (October, 1960).

Yale Brozen, "The New Competition—International Markets: How Should We Adapt?" *The Journal of Business*, Vol. XXXIII, No. 4, (October, 1960).

Hans F. Sennholz, "On Private Property and Economic Power," *The Freeman*, January, 1961. (Free copy available from the publisher, Foundation for Economic Education, Irvington-on-Hudson, New York.)

Richard Weaver, "Lord Acton: Historian as Thinker," *Modern Age*, (Winter, 1960-61).

In Future Issues....

NEW INDIVIDUALIST REVIEW will feature articles by young libertarian and conservative writers as well as by such scholars as **WILHELM ROEPKE, RICHARD WEAVER,** and **MURRAY N. ROTHBARD.**

To keep up with today's ferment of individualist ideas—subscribe to **NEW INDIVIDUALIST REVIEW** today.

ONE YEAR'S SUBSCRIPTION — $2.00, STUDENTS — $1.00

36

WE SHALL BE HAPPY TO SEND A FREE COPY OF THIS ISSUE TO ANY FIVE PERSONS WHOSE NAMES ARE ATTACHED TO YOUR SUBSCRIPTION.

VOLUME 1
NUMBER 2
SUMMER 1961

New
INDIVIDUALIST
Review

THE FALLACY OF THE "PUBLIC SECTOR"

MURRAY N. ROTHBARD

FEDERAL AID TO EDUCATION

JOHN WEICHER

TOCQUEVILLE AND THE
BLAND LEVIATHAN

ROBERT SCHUETTINGER

• • •

FREEDOM AND COERCION:
A REPLY TO MR. HAMOWY

F. A. HAYEK

Summer, 1961   25 cents   Vol. 1, No. 2

NEW INDIVIDUALIST REVIEW

Volume 1 — Number 2
SUMMER 1961

43

NEW INDIVIDUALIST REVIEW is published bimonthly (February, April, June, October, December) by the University of Chicago chapter of the Intercollegiate Society of Individualists, P.O. Box 4309, Chicago 80, Ill. Second Class mailing permit pending at the Chicago, Ill., post office.

Advertising and subscription correspondence should be sent to NEW INDIVIDUALIST REVIEW, P.O. Box 4309, Chicago 80, Ill. Editorial correspondence and manuscripts should be sent to NEW INDIVIDUALIST REVIEW, 7326 South Kingston Ave., Chicago 49, Ill. All manuscripts become the property of NEW INDIVIDUALIST REVIEW.

Subscription Rates: $2.00 per year (students, $1.00). Add $1.00 for foreign subscriptions.

In Future Issues....

NEW INDIVIDUALIST REVIEW will feature articles by young libertarians and conservative writers as well as by such scholars as WILHELM ROEPKE, RICHARD WEAVER, and RUSSELL KIRK.

To keep up with today's ferment of individualist ideas— subscribe to NEW INDIVIDUALIST REVIEW today.

ONE YEAR'S SUBSCRIPTION — $2.00, STUDENTS — $1.00

44

WE SHALL BE HAPPY TO SEND A FREE COPY OF THIS ISSUE TO ANY FIVE PERSONS WHOSE NAMES ARE ATTACHED TO YOUR SUBSCRIPTION.

The Fallacy of the "Public Sector"

MURRAY N. ROTHBARD

WE HAVE HEARD a great deal in recent years of the "public sector," and solemn discussions abound through the land on whether or not the public sector should be increased *vis-a-vis* the "private sector." The very terminology is redolent of pure science, and indeed it emerges from the supposedly scientific, if rather grubby, world of "national income statistics." But the concept is hardly *wertfrei;* in fact, it is fraught with grave, and questionable, implications.

In the first place, we may ask: "public sector" of *what?* Of something called the "national product." But note the hidden assumptions: that the national product is something like a pie, consisting of several "sectors," and that these sectors, public and private alike, are added to make the product of the economy as a whole. In this way, the assumption is smuggled into the analysis that the public and private sectors are equally productive, equally important, and on an equal footing altogether, and that "our" deciding on the proportions of public to private sector is about as innocuous as any individual's decision on whether to eat cake or ice cream. The State is considered to be an amiable service agency, somewhat akin to the corner grocer, or rather to the neighborhood lodge, in which "we" get together to decide how much "our government" should do for (or to) us. Even those neo-classical economists who tend to favor the free

market and free society, often regard the State as a generally inefficient, but still amiable, organ of social service, mechanically registering "our" values and decisions.

One would not think it difficult for scholars and laymen alike to grasp the fact that government is *not* like the Rotarians or the Elks; that it differs profoundly from all other organs and institutions in society; namely, that it lives and acquires its revenues by coercion and not by voluntary payment. The late Joseph Schumpeter was never more astute than when he wrote: "The theory which construes taxes on the analogy of club dues or of the purchase of the services of, say, a doctor only proves how far removed this part of the social sciences is from scientific habits of mind."[1]

Apart from the public sector, what constitutes the productivity of the "private sector" of the economy? The productivity of the private sector does not stem from the fact that people are rushing around doing *something,* anything, with their resources; it consists in the fact that they are using these resources to satisfy the needs and desires of the consumers. Businessmen and other producers direct their energies, on the free market, to producing those products which will be most rewarded by the con-

Murray N. Rothbard received his Ph.D. in economics from Columbia University and is presently a consulting economist in New York City. His forthcoming book, *Man, the Economy, and the State,* will be published this year.

[1] In the preceding sentences, Schumpeter wrote: "The friction or antagonism between the private and the public sphere was intensified from the first by the fact that . . . the state has been living on a revenue which was being produced in the private sphere for private purposes and had to be deflected from these purposes by political force." Precisely. Joseph A. Schumpeter, *Capitalism, Socialism, and Democracy* (New York: Harper and Bros., 1942), p. 198.

45

sumers, and the sale of these products may therefore roughly "measure" the importance which the consumers place upon them. If millions of people bend their energies to producing horses-and-buggies, they will, in this day and age, not be able to sell them, and hence the productivity of their output will be virtually zero. On the other hand, if a few million dollars are spent in a given year on Product X, then statisticians may well judge that these millions constitute the productive output of the X-part of the "private sector" of the economy.

ONE OF THE most important features of our economic resources is their scarcity: land, labor, and capital goods factors are all scarce, and may all be put to varied possible uses. The free market uses them "productively" because the producers are guided, on the market, to produce what the consumers most need: automobiles, for example, rather than buggies. Therefore, while the statistics of the total output of the private sector *seem* to be a mere adding of numbers, or counting units of output, the measures of output actually involve the important qualitative decision of considering as "product" what the consumers are willing to buy. A million automobiles, sold on the market, are productive because the consumers so considered them; a million b u g g i e s, remaining unsold, would *not* have been "product" because the consumers would have passed them by.

Suppose now, that into this idyll of free exchange enters the long arm of government. The government, for some reasons of its own, decides to ban automobiles altogether (perhaps because the many tailfins offend the aesthetic sensibilities of the rulers) and to compel the auto companies to produce the equivalent in buggies instead. Under such a strict regimen, the consumers would be, in a sense, compelled to purchase buggies because no cars would be permitted. However, in this case, the statistician would surely be purblind if he blithely and simply recorded the buggies as being just as "productive" as the previous automobiles. To call them equally productive would be a mockery; in fact, given plausible conditions, the "national

product" totals might not even show a statistical decline, when they had actually fallen drastically.

And yet the highly-touted "public sector" is in even worse straits than the buggies of our hypothetical example. For most of the resources consumed by the maw of government have not even been seen, much less used, by the consumers, who were at least allowed to ride their buggies. In the private sector, a firm's productivity is gauged by how much the consumers voluntarily spend on its product. But in the public sector, the government's "productivity" is measured — *mirabile dictu* — by how much *it spends!* Early in their construction of national product statistics, the statisticians were confronted with the fact that the government, unique among individuals and firms, could not have its activities gauged by the voluntary payments of the public — because there were little or none of such payments. Assuming, without any proof, that government *must* be as productive as anything else, they then settled upon its expenditures as a gauge of its productivity. In this way, not only are government expenditures just as useful as private, but all the government need to do in order to increase its "productivity" is to add a large chunk to its bureaucracy. Hire more bureaucrats, and see the productivity of the public sector rise! Here, indeed, is an easy and happy form of social magic for our bemused citizens.

The truth is exactly the reverse of the common assumptions. Far from adding cozily to the private sector, the public sector can only feed off the private sector; it necessarily lives parasitically upon the private economy. But this means that the productive resources of society — far from satisfying the wants of consumers — are now directed, by compulsion, *away from* these wants and needs. The consumers are deliberately thwarted, and the resources of the economy diverted from them to those activities desired by the parasitic bureaucracy and politicians. In many cases, the private consumers obtain nothing at all, except perhaps propaganda beamed to them at their own expense. In other cases, the consumers receive something far down on their list of priorities — like the buggies of our example. In either case, it becomes evident that the "public sector" is actually *anti*-productive: that it *subtracts from,* rather than adds to, the private sector of the economy. For the public sector lives by continuous attack on the very criterion that is used to gauge productivity: the voluntary purchases of consumers.

We may gauge the fiscal impact of government on the private sector by subtracting government expenditures from the national product. For government payments to its own bureaucracy are hardly additions to production; and government absorption of economic resources takes them out of the productive sphere. This gauge, of course, is only fiscal; it does not begin to measure the anti-productive impact of various government regulations, which cripple production and exchange in other ways than absorbing resources. It also does not dispose of numerous other fallacies of the national product statistics. But at least it removes such common myths as the idea that the productive output of the American economy increased during World War II. Subtract the government deficit instead of add it, and we see that the real productivity of the economy declined, as we would rationally expect during a war.

IN ANOTHER of his astute comments, Joseph Schumpeter wrote, concerning anti-capitalist intellectuals: ". . . capitalism stands its trial before judges who have the sentence of death in their pockets. They are going to pass it, whatever the defense they may hear; the only success victorious defense can possible produce is a change in the indictment."[2] The indictment has certainly been changing. In the 1930's, we heard that government must expand because capitalism had brought about mass poverty. Now, under the aegis of John Kenneth Galbraith, we hear that capitalism has sinned because the masses are too affluent. Where once poverty was suffered

by "one third of a nation," we must now bewail the "starvation" of the public sector.

By what standards does Dr. Galbraith conclude that the private sector is too bloated and the public sector too anemic, and therefore that government must exercise further coercion to rectify its own malnutrition? Certainly, his standard is not historical. In 1902, for example, net national product of the United States was $22.1 billion; government expenditure (Federal, state, and local) totalled $1.66 billion or 7.1% of the total product. In 1957, on the other hand, net national product was $402.6 billion, and government expenditures totalled $125.5 billion, or 31.2% of the total product. Government's fiscal depredation on the private product has therefore multiplied from four to five-fold over the present century. This is hardly "starvation" of the public sector. And yet, Galbraith contends that the public sector is being increasingly starved, relative to its status in the non-affluent nineteenth century!

What standards, then, does Galbraith offer us to discover when the public sector will finally be at its optimum? The answer is, nothing but personal whim:

> There will be question as to what is the test of balance — at what point may we conclude that balance has been achieved in the satisfaction of private and public needs. The answer is that no test can be applied, for none exists. . . . The present imbalance is clear. . . . This being so, the direction in which we move to correct matters is utterly plain.[3]

To Galbraith, the imbalance of today is "clear." Clear why? Because he looks around him and sees deplorable conditions wherever government operates. Schools are overcrowded, urban traffic is congested and the streets littered, rivers are polluted; he might have added that crime is increasingly rampant and the courts of justice clogged. All of these are areas of government operation and ownership. The one supposed solution for these glaring defects is to siphon more money into the government till.

[2] Schumpeter, *op. cit.*, p. 144.

[3] John Kenneth Galbraith, *The Affluent Society* (Boston: Houghton Mifflin, 1958), pp. 320-21.

47

But how is it that only *government* agencies clamor for more money and denounce the citizens for reluctance to supply more? Why do we never have the private-enterprise equivalents of traffic jams (which occur on government streets), mismanaged schools, water shortages, etc.? The reason is that private firms acquire the money that they deserve from two sources: voluntary payment for the services by consumers, and voluntary investment by investors in expectation of consumer demand. If there is an increased demand for a privately-owned good, consumers pay more for the product, and investors invest more in its supply, thus "clearing the market" to everyone's satisfaction. If there is an increased demand for a publicly-owned good (water, streets, subway, etc.), all we hear is annoyance at the consumer for wasting precious resources, coupled with annoyance at the taxpayer for balking at a higher tax load. Private enterprise makes it its business to court the consumer and to satisfy his most urgent demands; government agencies denounce the consumer as a troublesome user of their resources. Only a government, for example, would look fondly upon the prohibition of private cars as a "solution" for the problem of congested streets. Government's numerous "free" services, moreover, create permanent excess demand over supply and therefore permanent "shortages" of the product. Government, in short, acquiring its revenue by coerced confiscation rather than by voluntary investment and consumption, is not and *cannot* be run like a business. Its inherent gross inefficiencies, the impossibility for it to clear the market, will insure its being a mare's nest of trouble on the economic scene.[4]

In former times, the inherent mismanagement of government was generally considered a good argument for keeping as many things as possible out of government hands. After all, when one has invested in a losing proposition, one tries to refrain from pouring good

---

[4] For more on the inherent problems of government operations, see Murray N. Rothbard, "Government in Business," in *Essays on Liberty, Volume IV* (Irvington-on-Hudson: Foundation for Economic Education, 1958), pp. 183-87.

money after bad. And yet, Dr. Galbraith would have us redouble our determination to pour the taxpayer's hard-earned money down the rathole of the "public sector," and uses the very defects of government operation as his major argument!

Professor Galbraith has two supporting arrows in his bow. First, he states that, as people's living standards rise, the added goods are not worth as much to them as the earlier ones. This is standard knowledge; but Galbraith somehow deduces from this decline that people's private wants are now worth nothing to them. But if that is the case, then why should *government* "services," which have expanded at a much faster rate, still be worth so much as to require a further shift of resources to the public sector? His final argument is that private wants are all artificially induced by business advertising which automatically "creates" the wants that it supposedly serves. In short, people, according to Galbraith, would, if let alone, be content with non-affluent, presumably subsistence-level living; *advertising* is the villain that spoils this primitive idyll.

Aside from the philosophical problem of how A can "create" B's wants and desires without B's having to place his own stamp of approval upon them, we are faced here with a curious view of the economy. *Is* everything above subsistence "artificial"? By what standard? Moreover, why in the world should a business go through the extra bother and expense of inducing a change in consumer wants, when it can profit by serving the consumer's existing, un-"created" wants? The very "marketing revolution" that business is now undergoing, its increased and almost frantic concentration on "market research," demonstrates the reverse of Galbraith's view. For if, by advertising, business production automatically creates its own consumer demand, there would be no need whatever for market research—and no worry about bankruptcy either. In fact, far from the consumer in an affluent society being more of a "slave" to the business firm, the truth is precisely the opposite: for as living standards rise above subsistence, the consumer gets more particular and choosy about what he buys. The businessman must pay even greater court to the consumer than he did before: hence the furious attempts of market research to find out what the consumers want to buy.

There *is* an area of our society, however, where Galbraith's strictures on advertising may almost be said to apply — but it is in an area that he curiously never mentions. This is the enormous amount of advertising and propaganda *by government*. This is advertising that beams to the citizen the virtues of a product which, unlike business advertising, he never has a chance to test. If Cereal Company X prints a picture of a pretty girl declaiming that "Cereal X is yummy," the consumer, even if doltish enough to take this seriously, has a chance to test that proposition personally. Soon his *own* taste determines whether he will buy or not. But if a government agency advertises its own virtues over the mass media, the citizen has no direct test to permit him to accept or reject the claims. If any wants are artificial, they are those generated by government propaganda. Furthermore, business advertising is, at least, paid for by investors, and its success depends on the voluntary acceptance of the product by the consumers. Government advertising is paid for by means of taxes extracted from the citizens, and hence can go on, year after year, without check. The hapless citizen is cajoled into applauding the merits of the very people who, by coercion, are forcing him to pay for the propaganda. This is truly adding insult to injury.

IF PROFESSOR GALBRAITH and his followers are poor guides for dealing with the public sector, what standard does our analysis offer instead? The answer is the old Jeffersonian one: "that government is best which governs least." Any reduction of the public sector, any shift of activities from the public to the private sphere, is a net moral and economic gain.

Most economists have two basic arguments on behalf of the public sector, which we may only consider very briefly here. One is the problem of "external benefits." A and B often benefit, it is held, if they can force C into doing something. Much can be said in criticism of this doctrine; but suffice it to say here that any argument proclaiming the right and goodness of, say three neighbors, who yearn to form a string quartet, forcing a fourth neighbor at bayonet point to learn and play the viola, is hardly deserving of sober comment. The second argument is more substantial; stripped of technical jargon, it states that some essential services simply *cannot* be supplied by the private sphere, and that therefore government supply of these services is necessary. And yet, every single one of the services supplied by government has been, in the past, successfully furnished by private enterprise. The bland assertion that private citizens cannot possibly supply these goods is never bolstered, in the works of these economists, by any proof whatever. How is it, for example, that economists, so often given to pragmatic or utilitarian solutions, do not call for social "experiments" in this direction? Why must political experiments always be in the direction of more government? Why not give the free market a county or even a state or two, and see what it can accomplish?

49

The Question of
Federal Aid to Education

JOHN WEICHER

THE LARGEST LOBBY in Washington last year, according to the official statements of expenditure, was neither the AFL-CIO nor the National Association of Manufacturers, but the National Education Association. It spent its money largely to promote the most far-reaching of the proposals for Federal aid to elementary and secondary education, the Murray-Metcalf bill. Thus it fulfilled its promise of 1959 to wage an "all-out" fight for this measure, which provided over $1 billion each year for four years, to be divided among the states in accordance with their school-age populations, and available for school construction or teachers' salaries, as the states wished.

On behalf of this, the NEA out-spent the traditional lobbies; on behalf of this, or something close to it, the NEA and the Kennedy Administration are exerting every pressure they can bring to bear on the present Congress.

Few issues illuminate so sharply the contemporary left's faith in the Royal Touch of more money — preferably spent by government, by the largest possible unit of government. With the charm of several billion dollars, all the scrofulas of modern society will vanish. There may be a certain amount of truth in this in regard to sewage plants (ignoring the fact that local action is almost invariably cheaper), but it will not hold for education.

John Weicher is an Associate Editor of *New Individualist Review.*

The current agitation for Federal aid to education has resulted from the Soviet Union's being the first nation to launch a Sputnik and from its presumed lead in certain fields of space exploration and weapons development. But this lead has been achieved not through mere government aid to education, but through government *control* of education and, more immediately, of research. The Soviet Union has devoted its resources to fields which will yield results of direct value in its continued conflict with the free nations.

On our part, the United States has directed research into the military fields even before the National Defense Education Act. Its research contracts have long been a major item in the budgets of our leading universities. The Armed Forces have conducted their own language schools. Within the last two years, Congressmen A. Sydney Herlong and Walter Judd have sponsored legislation to create a Freedom Academy.

Admiral Hyman Rickover, perhaps the best-known critic of the nation's school deficiencies, has suggested that, if local and state agencies cannot educate children adequately, then Federal standards —Federal controls—should be set up. He has suggested these norms as a last resort, if other means of improving the schools fail. His chief emphasis has been on the scientific disciplines useful in defense, and he has based much of his argument on defense needs.

Federal control of education — particularly Federal control by Admiral Rickover and others devoted to excellence in schools — has some appeal as a short-run, *ad hoc* measure needed for national survival. But this is not really the central point at issue; the argument from defense needs is largely window-dressing and defense is not among the major aims of the NEA. It professes strongly its opposition to Federal control of education, and Federal control by Admiral Rickover is the *last* thing it wants.

Robert Schuettinger's article, "Modern Education vs. Democracy," in the April issue of *New Individualist Review,* set forth the prevailing educational philosophy of the NEA. It is not Admiral Rickover's, but it is that of most of the state departments of public instruction, and of the United States Office of Education in the Eisenhower Administration, under Commissioner Lawrence Derthick, who bitterly opposed the views of Admiral Rickover, the Council for Basic Education (CBE), and other groups seeking more rigorous standards. The CBE has expressed the hope that the new Commissioner, Dr. Sterling McMurrin, does favor solid intellectual achievement, but if he does, he will face a monumental housecleaning job in his department before those views can prevail.

The question of standards was carefully avoided by both President Kennedy's Task Force on Education, and by a panel of citizens reporting on the need to extend the National Defense Education Act. Professor Arthur Bestor of the University of Illinois, a member of the latter panel, evaluated its report in these terms:

"Committees, I discover, will always agree to spend more money, whether or not they agree on anything else. I cannot conscientiously subscribe to a report like the present that refuses to discriminate the conspicuously valuable program from the comparatively worthless one, and devoutly prays Congress to make its sun to rise on the evil and on the good alike.

"The National Defense Education Act of 1958 is a hodge-podge of different measures. Certain of these have contributed importantly to the improvement of American education. Others, it seems to me, have reinforced the very tendencies that produced American educational weaknesses in the first place . . . The various federal educational programs that point in this adverse direction should, I feel, be abandoned or curtailed . . .

"The resources of the federal government should be husbanded for the purpose of stimulating the full development of our *intellectual* resources. Local communities should pay the full cost of the frills to which they may be addicted."[1]

Apparently, Professor Bestor was alone in his views.

THE DECLINE of standards has been a major phenomenon in education over the last twenty or more years. While most colleges were talking of the increased competition among prospective freshmen in the wake of the Soviet Sputnik, a 1958 profile of Harvard in *Harper's* magazine commented that Harvard was taking a larger and larger share of its entering class from the private schools, and expected to continue to do so as long as public school standards continued to fall. This situation may be changing as some of the public school systems change their policies under public criticism, but if so it is changing not because of the NEA, which has gone so far as to advocate a boycott of the Luce publications when *Life* magazine attacked "life-adjustment" education a few years ago, but in spite of it.

A major point of controversy has been Federal aid to private and parochial schools. Enrollment at these schools has been growing more and more rapidly since 1940, in the face of a mounting tax burden which must deter many people who would like to send their children to parochial or private schools. This is discomfiting to those who regard private schools as divisive and would like to see them eliminated. If Federal aid to public education only is approved by Congress, the added burden will seriously curtail the freedom of choice of many people as to where to educate their children, and a major step toward the eventual uni-

---

1. *Council for Basic Education Bulletin,* February, 1961, p. 3.

51

formity of American education will be taken. But if Federal aid to private schools is approved also, then what has happened to the Constitutional separation of Church and State? Further, if Federal aid means Federal control, as it eventually must, we may then be on the way to a system similar to the French, where public and parochial schools offer identical curricula, both being administered by the state. Neither alternative is conducive to educational freedom.

In regard to whether Federal aid means Federal control, it should be noted that the state most in need of greater spending on education, according to the NEA statistics on per-capita spending and other indicators, is also the state whose opposition to Federal aid is likely to be most ferocious—Mississippi. The reasoning is quite simple: Federal aid is likely to mean integration, with or without the Powell amendment prohibiting funds to segregated schools.[2] If grants *are* made to the Southern states to build segregated schools, the interesting question arises of whether the Federal government is violating the law of the land as expressed in *Brown v. Board of Education.* But if integrated schools only are allowed, surely the Southern states will abstain from participating in the program; and since the Southern states are those most lagging in their educational programs, this would mean that the states for whom the program is designed are excluded, rendering the program largely useless, if not worse: for in that case the Southern states would be taxed to help support the educational programs of the richer, integrated Northern states, making it harder for the South to raise its educational standards and actually contributing to greater inequality of educational opportunity.

Even on the NEA's own quantitative basis, impressive evidence has been compiled to show that Federal aid is unnecessary. The classroom shortage, estimated at over 300,000 rooms five years ago, is now estimated at 132,400 by the Office of Education.[3] The accuracy of both these figures is open to question, however; each state department of public instruction is asked to estimate its own needs, based on its own definitions (which vary from year to year) of "substandard" and "over-crowded." Senator Strom Thurmond of South Carolina investigated his own state's reported shortage and discovered that a classroom was counted as "needed" for each classroom having more students than the desired ratio. If a classroom had 29 students and the desired ratio was 28, a "shortage" of one was counted.[4] Roger Freeman, in discussing the state estimates, wrote: "The so-called 10-year requirements . . . should not be treated as essential needs nor as attainable goals but as what most of them are: expressions of the desires of functional administrators who are conscientiously trying to promote what they believe to be in the best interest of the people but who cannot be expected to judge the relative priorities of the multitude of claims for public funds nor the over-all capacity of the economy to meet them."[5]

Everyone from President Kennedy to Freeman agrees that this country will need 60,000 new classrooms a year for the next ten years. But over the last five years, we have been building at a rate of approximately 70,000 classrooms per year—without Federal aid.[6] This means that if the state and local authorities continue to build at the current rate, the existing shortage (whatever it is), all new needs for the expanding population, and replacements for all classrooms which become unusable between now and 1970, will all be supplied.

---

2. In spite of the protestations of the advocates of the NDEA, it is clear that Federal aid means Federal control even in that act. Professor Claude J. Bartlett of George Peabody College for Teachers in Nashville, Tennessee, reported a startling example of Federal intervention in a Guidance and Counseling Institute set up under the NDEA at his college; eventually, the school dropped out of the program. See "Federal Control of Education: A Case History," in *Human Events,* March 10, 1961, p. 152.

---

3. Wilkinson, Ernest L., "A Report to Thruston Morton," *Human Events,* March 17, 1961, p. 165. Wilkinson quotes the United States Office of Education canvass for 1959.

4. *Congressional Record,* February 16, 1960.

5. Freeman, Roger A., *School Needs in the Decade Ahead* (Washington, 1958), p. 192.

6. *Ibid.,* p. 200, and Wilkinson, *loc. cit.,* p. 165.

The other chief "need" for Federal aid is to augment teachers' salaries. Freeman pointed out that teachers are now better off than they were in 1929, and that even according to the NEA's own figures, the supply of teachers is steadily catching up on the need for them. Moreover, in the fields where teachers are sought by outside employers—chiefly science—the teachers themselves refuse to permit higher salaries in these fields without across-the-board raises. At current rates of increase in salaries, teachers will be earning between $6,000 and $6,700 (in present dollars) by 1970. Freeman concludes: "The great majority of teachers do as well financially in teaching as they could anywhere else. Many do better."[7]

The real needs of the schools — which neither the NEA nor the Administration propose to remedy — are for higher standards and tighter discipline, which are inter-related. The former requires a change of philosophy among the departments of education and the NEA, the latter a change in philosophy among the children and their parents, and perhaps among teachers and administrators. When these problems are dealt with and we are near a reasonable working solution of them, we will find that Federal aid to education has ceased to be necessary to improve the schools. And these problems can best be handled on a local level. The NEA would be more useful if it stressed more rigorous training for its members in the subjects they teach, and if it sought to work with state and local officials to provide better discipline within the schools.[8]

7. Freeman, op. cit., Chapters III and IV, especially pp. 167-172.

8. The discipline problem, which is not discussed in the article, is widely recognized as extremely acute, particularly in the larger cities. Chicago has recently seen a 14-year-old fifth-grader confess the murder of his teacher during school hours; a number of teachers of my acquaintance have told me they will refuse to teach in the city at all rather than teach in certain schools. New York's problems are, of course, well known. It is questionable if any kind of Federal aid would be effective in these areas, short of sending in the National Guard.

53

Tocqueville and the Bland Leviathan

ROBERT SCHUETTINGER

[The power of government] covers the surface of society with a network of small complicated rules, minute and uniform, through which the most original minds and the most energetic characters cannot penetrate, to rise above the crowd. The will of man is not shattered, but softened, bent and guided; men are seldom forced by it to act, but they are constantly restrained from acting. Such a power . . . does not tyrannize, but it compresses, enervates, extinguishes and stupefies a people, until each nation is reduced to nothing better than a flock of timid and hard-working animals, of which the government is the shepherd.[1]

—*Alexis de Tocqueville*

ALEXIS DE TOCQUEVILLE was an aristocrat who was at the same time the most perceptive critic and the warmest friend that democracy ever had; he loved liberty, as he himself said, with "a holy passion," and his greatest fear was that in the new Age of the Common Man the ideal of equality would become the means by which freedom would be extinguished.

His two books, *Democracy in America* and *The Old Regime and the French Revolution,* earned for Tocqueville a lasting reputation primarily because he did not think that the historian's role should be confined to relating facts or that the sociologist should be merely a statistician; he was interested in something more than in *wie es gewesen.* What he wanted to do was to understand *why* institutions grew up and *why* events

Robert Schuettinger is an Associate Editor of *New Individualist Review.*

happened. Describing America he regarded as much less important than the task of analyzing democracy.

He read little and was indebted to few predecessors. Those few, however, included Plato, Aristotle and Burke, and these he mastered. It seems certain that his limited reading was not due to any lack of bookishness but rather to a conscious desire to think his own thoughts; because of this habit his works are packed with original ideas. In studying Tocqueville the reader is forced to proceed at a slow pace since he soon notices that almost every paragraph is the germ of another book.

He has been called "the prophet of the mass age," because he foresaw, in 1835, what were to become the two great movements of our time: the increasing centralization of government power and the irreversible trend toward equality. The first movement he condemned without hesitation; the second, he welcomed, with reservations. He knew that democracy, while inevitable, could come to any country in either one of two forms: a free variety or an unfree. By a free democracy, Tocqueville meant what we now call 19th century liberalism: a democratically-elected government in which the rights of the individual are supreme and are safeguarded by a constitution putting definite limits on the power of the state. Unfree democracy, according to Tocqueville, can again be divided into two types. The first of these is the totalitarian state which is based on the belief that one man (*Fuehrer-prinzip*) or group of men (dictatorship of the vanguard of the proletariat) effectively rep-

---

1. Alexis de Tocqueville, *Democracy in America* (New York, Vintage Books, 1954), vol. II, Bk. VI.

resents the will of the people and is mandated by them to eliminate all opposition. The second type is usually spoken of today as the welfare state; it is what I have called in the title of this essay "the Bland Leviathan," a despotism different from the first in that it is gentle and beneficient. This does not mean, however, that the second form of despotism is any more to be desired than the first; as Justice Brandeis has remarked, "Experience should teach us to be most on our guard to protect liberty when the Government's purposes are beneficient."[2]

TOCQUEVILLE SAW that the real threat to a democratic society in our age would not be what the Tories feared, anarchy, nor would it be the absolute dictatorship feared by the Old Liberals; rather it would be the mild tyranny of mediocrity, a standardization of mind and spirit, a gray uniformity enforced by a central government in the name of "humanity" and "social justice."

Tocqueville was able to make an analysis which has been confirmed by history because he divested himself of as many of his prejudices as he possibly could; he was determined to be interested in the *truth* and in nothing else. Politically, he was a critic of both parties and a member of none. "Intellectually," he once wrote, "I have an inclination for democratic institutions, but I am an aristocrat by instinct . . . I have a passionate love for liberty, law and respect for rights. . . . I am neither of the revolutionary party or of the conservative. Nevertheless, when all is said, I hold more by the latter than the former. For I differ from the latter more as to means than as to end, while I differ from the former both as to means and end."[3] Tocqueville could not be a revolutionary because, as he once noted, their "spirit combines very well with a love for absolute government"[4]; nor could he ever feel entirely comfortable with Tories since time and again their "insane fear of socialism" would "throw them into the arms of despotism."[5] Clearly, as he himself said, he was "a liberal of a new kind."[6]

Tocqueville was born in 1805 at a time when a people's emperor ruled France; his grandfather, the Comte de Tocqueville, had been imprisoned during the Revolution and his more distant ancestors were included in the rolls of the Norman conquerors. He never used his title, however, and determined to make a living for himself as a lawyer and writer. In 1831, with his friend Gustave de Beaumont, he toured the United States; upon his return he began to write *Democracy in America,* the book which placed him second only to Montesquieu among French political scientists. Shortly after its publication, he was elected to the presidency of the *Academie des Sciences Morales et Politiques.* In 1839, he was elected to the Chamber, serving as deputy from Valognes and, briefly, as foreign minister for the Second Republic. His political career was terminated abruptly by Louis Napoleon's *coup d'etat* in 1851; after spending two days in a make-shift jail, Tocqueville retired to his estate to write history instead of make it. He died at Cannes in 1859, his life cut short by a disease of the lungs.

TOCQUEVILLE APPLAUDED the men who had overthrown the Old Regime; in his own time, he ranked himself with those who were dedicated to destroying the power of privileged groups still hostile to liberty and equality. He saw, however, that as the old goals of equality before the law and equality of opportunity were reached, more and more men began to advocate the only possible means by which equality could be *further* extended: systematic

55

2. Justice Brandeis, in his dissenting opinion in *Olmstead v. United States* (XXX, 277, U. S. 479, 1927) went on to warn that, "The greatest dangers to liberty lurk in insidious encroachment by men of zeal, well meaning but without understanding." Quoted in F. A. Hayek's *The Constitution of Liberty,* (Chicago, 1960), p. 253.

3. Antoine Redier, *Comme disait M. de Tocqueville . . .* (Paris, 1925), p. 85.

4. Alexis de Tocqueville, *The European Revolution and Correspondence with Gobineau,* John Lukacs, editor, (New York, Anchor Books, 1959), p. 21.

5. *Ibid.,* p. 22.

6. Alexis de Tocqueville, *Oeuvres,* (Paris, 1866), vol. V, p. 431. I have used J. P. Mayer's translations in his *Alexis de Tocqueville* (New York, Harper, 1960).

regimentation directed by a centralized government. These men, who wanted economic equality even at the expense of liberty, were the socialists. As Tocqueville wrote, "They had sought to be free in order to make themselves equal; but in proportion as equality was more established by the aid of freedom, freedom itself was thereby rendered more difficult of attainment."[7]

By raising up the absolute sovereignty of the people to replace the old divine right of kings, men found that they had only exchanged one master for another, and erected a new despotism upon the ruins of the old. The idea that right is simply what the majority of the people want, Tocqueville dismissed as "the language of a slave."[8] In place of the notion that the supreme good is "the greatest happiness for the greatest number,"[9] Tocqueville believed in a natural law, an ideal of justice against which all men's actions must be measured.[10]

Tocqueville was not at all interested in the outward forms that state power assumed. As he once remarked, "When I see that the . . . means of absolute command are conferred on a people or a king, upon an aristocracy or a democracy, a monarchy or a republic, I recognize the germ of tyranny, and I journey onwards towards a land of more hopeful institutions."[11] What he *was* interested in was freedom.

But how did Tocqueville characterize the nature of freedom? If we are to distinguish between a genuinely free democracy and its perversion, this is the crucial question. In essence, he would have defined freedom as the right to do what you want to do, limited by natural obstacles but by no man-made restraints

except the law that no man has a right to interfere in another's rights. He looked upon the spiritual nature of freedom, however, as much more important than any of its material benefits. He believed that in the long run, freedom brings prosperity to those who know how to keep it, but he admitted that there are times when it interferes with material comfort; there are times, in fact, when despotism alone can insure

wealth or even subsistence. He knew that time and again the widespread craving for material well-being, for "security," had led men straight to servitude.

The chief value of liberty, he thought, was that it gave men the opportunity to be what human beings *ought to be.* This is why he wrote: "That which at all times has so strongly attached the affection of certain men is the attraction of freedom herself, her native charms independent of her gifts . . . apart from all 'practical considerations' . . . the pleasure of speaking, acting and breathing without restraint, under no master but God and the law. *The man who asks of freedom anything other than itself is born to be a slave.*"[12]

7. Alexis de Tocqueville, Oeuvres, vol. III, p. 514.

8. *Ibid.,* vol. II, p. 142.

9. In disagreeing with the utilitarianism of Bentham and J. S. Mill, Tocqueville avoided the intellectual trap in which the latter found himself. At one time in his career, Mill thought that if Communism did provide the most happiness for the most people it would be preferable to the risks of a free society. See J. S. Mill, *Principles of Political Economy,* (New York, 1883), vol. I, p. 269.

10. Alexis de Tocqueville, Oeuvres, Vol. II, p. 142.

11. *Ibid.*

12. Alexis de Tocqueville, *The Old Regime and the French Revolution,* (New York, Anchor Books, 1955), p. 169. (Italics mine.)

56

Tocqueville saw that no men, including confirmed tyrants, disputed the merits of freedom; in the case of despots, however, they wished to keep it for themselves, on the theory that lesser men were unworthy of it. He was aware that the value of freedom *per se* has never been at issue; what men are really quarreling about is their opinion of their fellow men. The more contempt men feel for those around them, the greater is their admiration for a strong central government which will show them how they ought to live.

In Tocqueville's own time, as in ours, there was never any shortage of what Wilhelm Roepke calls "the power-thirsty, cocksure and arrogant planners and organizers."[13] In a speech to the 1848 Constituent Assembly (published in this issue for the first time in English) Tocqueville pointed out the one characteristic which unites socialists of all schools: "a profound opposition to personal liberty." What the socialists wanted — a complete re-organization of society along "rational" lines — he saw could never be accomplished without instituting a new system of serfdom.[14]

UNLIKE HIS opponents on both the Left and the Right, Tocqueville had a strong faith in the democratic instincts of the majority of the people. Because he knew that nations accustomed to freedom would never voluntarily submit to totalitarian rule, Tocqueville was able to predict precisely what did come about: that "hot" socialism would be discarded in Western Europe and the United States and that democracies would instead be corrupted slowly and almost unnoticeably by "a servitude of a regular, quiet, and gentle kind."[15] He foresaw further that this "new despotism" would combine with some of the outward forms of

freedom[16] and that it would establish itself under the guise of the sovereignty of the people.

Three decades before the *Wohlfahrtstaat* of Bismarck and a full century before the Second New Deal, Tocqueville correctly perceived what many men of good minds and liberal education have difficulty in seeing even today. He understood that the time would come when "a new thing" which he could not name would have a power that is "absolute, minute, regular, provident and mild." Its authority would be like that of a parent, he wrote, except that a parent prepares his children for adulthood, while this power seeks, on the contrary, to keep its charges in perpetual childhood. This government willingly labors for the happiness of its subjects, "but it chooses to be the sole agent and the only arbiter of that happiness; it provides for their security, foresees and supplies their necessities, facilitates their pleasures, manages their principal concerns, directs their industry, regulates the descent of property, and subdivides their inheritances: what remains but to spare them all the care of thinking and all the trouble of living?"[17]

This then, as Tocqueville foresaw it, is the approximate condition of society in the United States today. We live in the shadow of a "Bland Leviathan," an overpowering influence predicated on the

57

---

13. Wilhelm Roepke, *A Humane Economy*, (Chicago, Regnery, 1960), p. 283.

14. In using the word "serfdom," Tocqueville was being precise. The British Labour Government, in 1947, passed an Act giving itself the power to assign any British worker to any job that it saw fit — for any length of time. See F. A. Hayek, *The Road to Serfdom*, (Chicago, Phoenix Books, 1957), p. xiii.

15. Alexis de Tocqueville, *Democracy in America*, vol. II, p. 337.

16. This point is of crucial importance for it is the distinctive characteristic of the welfare state; its proponents deny that they are socialists or authoritarians and, in most cases, they sincerely believe that their innovations would not seriously impair our freedoms. Prof. F. A. Hayek, in his *Constitution of Liberty*, (p. 259), explains, in one succinct paragraph, what Tocqueville's prophecy has come to mean:

"We shall see that some of the aims of the welfare state," he writes, "can be realized without detriment to individual liberty, though not necessarily by the methods which seem the most obvious and are therefore the most popular; that others can be similarly achieved to a certain extent, though only at a cost much greater than people imagine or would be willing to bear, or only slowly and gradually as wealth increases; and that, finally, there are others — and they are those particularly dear to the hearts of the socialists—that cannot be realized in a society that wants to preserve personal freedom."

17. Alexis de Tocqueville, *Democracy in America*, vol. II, p. 336.

root assumption that the needs of society, as determined by the planners, should take precedence over the liberties of individuals. He saw that this leviathan has three natural enemies: progress, excellence and freedom. Because it is bland, and because it lacks a definite purpose, it does not attempt to kill these enemies; instead, it imprisons, cripples or slowly suffocates them.

ANY LIMITATION on freedom, Tocqueville realized, must inevitably restrict progress. He feared, in fact, that the equalitarian oppression which was aimed at society's most original minds would result in a general deadening of civilization. "Man will waste his strength in bootless and solitary trifling," he wrote, "and swing backwards and forwards forever without getting fresh ideas."[18]

Ironically, it is many of our best and most creative minds who are bringing us to a point where our medical profession, most of our educational system, and the greater part of our scientists will be slowly absorbed under the all-protecting power of the federal government. Beguiled as they are by the humanitarian visions of the welfare state, these men have forgotten what, upon reflection, they must admit: that no man or group of men can hope to direct the creative energies of a nation without those energies being diverted into the safe and traditional patterns so congenial to administrators.

Progress has been defined as that which the rules and regulations do not foresee. Admiral Hyman Rickover,[19] among many others, has recently borne witness to the difficulties in any system where professional administrators are assigned to supervise intellectuals. The instincts of the two groups are almost completely opposed. The creative man wants plenty of room and time to follow his own hunches; he often harbors a disinterest in, or even a contempt for, the other "members of the team." The bureaucrat is trained to shun innovations; he is suspicious of reform; his life is dedicated to following precedents; in his world, there is no place for initiative.

Just as no society based on the principles of the welfare state can encourage progress, neither can it long endure the existence of excellence — except as a strictly private possession to be nurtured after-hours or in retirement. In all but a few parts of the "public sector" and in large areas of the private, everything above the average is being quietly smothered in the name of "equality" and "democracy"; examples are too many and too obvious to cite here. Since above-average talent in the right positions is a necessity for progress and productivity, however, it is not difficult to see where the road we are on will end. No one has ever been more uncompromisingly hostile to mediocrity than Tocqueville; he was certain that when the average, the norm, are consistently held up as standards to be identified with, individuality—and freedom itself—must soon perish.

After progress and excellence, freedom will be the last casualty of the welfare state—as it makes the transition to a totalitarian regime. The planners, someone has said, start by wanting to control things, but they end by controlling people. As government gets bigger and bigger, there is an increasing tendency for the democratically-elected legislature to delegate wider and wider powers to administrative agencies. These agencies are always supervised by non-elected officials who are practically independent of the President, the Congress or the courts.[20] Lord Ewart, in his important book, *The New Despotism*, cites as one

18. Quoted in Russell Kirk's *The Conservative Mind*, (Chicago, Regnery, 1960), p. 225. Tocqueville here almost exactly describes the modern bureaucrats' fondness for paperwork and for using words and phrases which convey the impression of activity while concealing their lack of accomplishments. Examples come readily to mind: "co-ordination," "stability," "continuing effort," "the situation is under analysis," etc.

19. Vice-Admiral Hyman Rickover, "Don't Hamstring the Talented," *Saturday Evening Post*, February 13, 1960.

20. Numerous examples of the harassment of private citizens by petty officials of the federal agencies (FTC, NLRB, FCC, etc.) are given in Lowell Mason's *The Language of Dissent*, (New York, 1959). The author enunciates "Mason's Law" which holds that bureaucracy, out of view of the public eye, will arrogate to itself all power available under a statute, despite constitutional limitations.

example of this trend the Rating and Valuation Act of 1925 in which it is provided that . . . "[the Minister] may modify the provisions of this Act so far as may appear to the Minister necessary or expedient for carrying [his orders] into effect."[21] Despite evidence which, by 1961, has become overwhelming, we are still solemnly assured by people who will insist that they are democrats, that we should not be afraid of state power because, after all, *we ourselves* are the government. Except for a few minor cases, this platitude was never true, and in this century, there is far less basis for the idea than there ever was.[22]

THE PROPER solution to the problems posed by democracy, according to Tocqueville, was not a reversion to aristocracy, but rather a renewed determination to harness the many virtues of the democratic process in order to insure that the rights of individuals would not be sacrificed to the demands of the state. He believed that free institutions could not be preserved except on a basis of equality. "Far from finding fault with equality because it inspires a spirit of independence," he wrote, "I praise it primarily for that very reason." By making all men conscious of their rights, he thought, "equality would prepare the remedy for the ills which it engenders."[23]

Tocqueville clearly showed the way in which modern society could, if it chooses, escape from "the new despotism." A proper concept of equality is the first necessity; everywhere we must strengthen the position of private individuals — at all levels of society — in their own rights and property. Almost as important, we must strengthen those *intermediate powers* which stand between the government and ourselves, that is, our

churches, labor unions, newspapers, political parties, business organizations, fraternal orders, etc. It is difficult, in a mass society, for one person to make himself heard but it can be done if he uses the amplifier provided by his like-minded associates. Following the same principle, we must maintain all the peculiar rights and duties of each of our independent governing bodies: the courts, Congress, the Presidency, the states, and the local administrations. At the same time we must be alert to promptly limit any or all of these bodies when they exceed their authorized powers.

We must also beware of slogans such as "national interest," or "national purpose." The words "national interest," especially in a time of war or emergency, often do mean something, but just as often they serve merely as a convenient device for justifying authoritarianism. The notion behind the idea of a national purpose, of course, is a dangerous one. It is based on the assumption that there is a collective interest which is separate and different from the interests of all the people which compose the society. In this country, until recently, we have always had individual hopes, ambitions, purposes; we have left the "national purposes" to the totalitarian states with their stadiums full of troops and flags.

Tocqueville, as usual, expressed what needed to be said when he wrote that:

> It would seem as if the rulers of our time sought only to use men to make things great; I wish that they would try a little more to make great men; that they would set less value on the work and more on the workman; that they would never forget that a nation cannot long remain strong when every man belonging to it is individually weak; and that no form or combination of social policy has yet been devised to make an energetic people out of a community of pusillanimous and enfeebled citizens.[24]

This is not an ideal to appeal to many politicians — who love power — but it should appeal to all those who love the ideals that Tocqueville worked so hard to preserve: progress, excellence, and liberty.

21. Lord Hewart, *The New Despotism*, (London, 1929), p. 10.

22. The possibility of a totalitarian state was not seriously considered until the 19th century and never put into practice until the 20th. Tocqueville writes: "No sovereign ever lived in former ages so absolute . . . as to undertake to administer . . . all the parts of a great empire; none ever attempted to subject all his subjects . . . to strict uniformity of regulation." See *Democracy in America*, Vol. II, Bk. IV, Ch. VI.

23. Alexis de Tocqueville, *Democracy in America*, vol. II, p. 305.

24. *Ibid.*, p. 347.

59

Tocqueville on Socialism

Translated by RONALD HAMOWY

Translator's Note:

In February, 1848, the July Monarchy of Louis Philippe was overthrown, and the Second French Republic established. The new republic believed that the unemployment problem which was plaguing Paris could be solved by setting up government work-projects, guaranteeing employment at a certain wage rate for all who desired it. On September 12th, the Constituent Assembly debated the continuance of this arrangement and Tocqueville rose to speak against it. In the course of his speech he entered onto the subject of socialism, which he considered the logical consequence of recognizing the "right to work," and devoted most of his time to a discussion of the socialist position.

This translation from the transcript of the proceedings, here appears for the first time in English.

NOTHING CAN be gained by not discussing issues which call into question the very roots of our society and which, sooner or later, must be faced. At the bottom of the amendment which is under consideration, perhaps unknown to its author but for me as clear as day, is the question of socialism. [*Prolonged Sensation — Murmurs from the Left.*]

Yes, gentlemen, sooner or later, the question of socialism, which everyone seems to fear and which no one, up to now, has dared treat of, must be brought into the open, and this Assembly must decide it. We are duty-bound to clear up this issue, which lies heavy upon the breast of France. I confess that it is principally because of this that I mount the podium today, that the question of socialism might finally be settled. I must

Ronald Hamowy is an Associate Editor of *New Individualist Review*.

know, the National Assembly must know, all of France must know — is the February Revolution a socialist revolution or is it not? [*"Excellent!"*]

It is not my intention to examine here the different systems which can all be categorized as socialist. I want only to attempt to uncover those characteristics which are common to all of them and to see if the February Revolution can be said to have exhibited those traits.

Now, the first characteristic of all socialist ideologies is, I believe, an incessant, vigorous and extreme appeal to the material passions of man. [*Signs of approval.*]

Thus, some have said: "Let us rehabilitate the body"; others, that "work, even of the hardest kind, must be not only useful, but agreeable"; still others, that "man must be paid, not according to his merit, but according to his need"; while, finally, they have told us here that the object of the February Revolution, of socialism, is to procure unlimited wealth for all.

A second trait, always present, is an attack, either direct or indirect, on the principle of private property. From the first socialist who said, fifty years ago, that "property is the origin of all the ills of the world," to the socialist who spoke from this podium and who, less charitable than the first, passing from property to the property-holder, exclaimed that "property is theft," all socialists, all, I insist, attack, either in a direct or indirect manner, private property. [*"True, true."*] I do not pretend to hold that all who do so, assault it in the frank and brutal manner which one of our colleagues has adopted. But I say that all socialists, by more or less roundabout means, if they do not destroy the principle upon which it is based, transform it, diminish it, obstruct it, limit it, and mold it into something completely foreign to what we know and have been familiar with since the beginning of time as private property. [*Excited signs of assent.*]

Now, a third and final trait, one which, in my eyes, best describes socialists of all schools and shades, is a profound opposition to personal liberty and scorn for individual reason, a complete contempt for the individual. They unceasingly attempt to mutilate, to curtail, to obstruct personal freedom in any and all ways. They hold that the State must not only act as the director of society, but must further be master of each man, and not only master, but keeper and trainer. [*"Excellent."*] For fear of allowing him to err, the State must place itself forever by his side, above him, around him, better to guide him, to maintain him, in a word, to confine him. They call, in fact, for the forfeiture, to a greater or less degree, of human liberty, [*Further signs of assent.*] to the point where, were I to attempt to sum up what socialism is, I would say that it was simply a new system of serfdom. [*Lively assent.*]

I have not entered into a discussion of the details of these systems. I have indicated what socialism is by pointing out its universal characteristics. They suffice to allow an understanding of it. Everywhere you might find them, you will be sure to find socialism, and wherever socialism is, these characteristics are met.

IS SOCIALISM, gentlemen, as so many have told us, the continuation, the legitimate completion, the perfecting of the French Revolution? Is it, as it has been pretended to be, the natural development of democracy? No, neither one or the other. Remember the Revolution! Reexamine the awesome and glorious origin of our modern history. Was it by appealing to the material needs of man, as a speaker of yesterday insisted, that the French Revolution accomplished those great deeds that the whole world marvelled at? Do you believe that it spoke of wages, of well-being, of unlimited wealth, of the satisfaction of physical needs?

Citizen Mathieu: I said nothing of the kind.

Citizen de Tocqueville: Do you believe that by speaking of such things it could have aroused a whole generation of men to fight for it at its borders, to risk the hazards of war, to face death? No, gentlemen, it was by speaking of greater things, of love of country, of the honor of France, of virtue, generosity, selflessness, glory, that it accomplished what it did. Be certain, gentlemen, that it is only by appealing to man's noblest sentiments that one can move them to attain such heights. [*"Excellent, excellent."*]

And as for property, gentlemen: it is true that the French Revolution resulted in a hard and cruel war against certain property-holders. But, concerning the very principle of private property, the Revolution always respected it. It placed it in its constitutions at the top of the list. No people treated this principle with greater respect. It was engraved on the very frontispiece of its laws.

The French Revolution did more. Not only did it consecrate private property, it universalized it. It saw that still a greater number of citizens participated in it. [*Varied exclamations. "Exactly what we want!"*]

It is thanks to this, gentlemen, that today we need not fear the deadly consequences of socialist ideas which are spread throughout the land. It is because the French Revolution peopled the land of France with ten million property-owners that we can, without danger, allow these doctrines to appear before us. They can, without doubt, destroy society, but thanks to the French Revolution, they will not prevail against it and will not harm us. [*"Excellent."*]

And finally, gentlemen, liberty. There is one thing which strikes me above all. It is that the Old Regime, which doubtless differed in many respects from that system of government which the socialists call for (and we must realize this) was, in its political philosophy, far less distant from socialism than we had believed. It is far closer to that system

61

than we. The Old Regime, in fact, held that wisdom lay only in the State and that the citizens were weak and feeble beings who must forever be guided by the hand, for fear they harm themselves. It held that it was necessary to obstruct, thwart, restrain individual freedom, that to secure an abundance of material goods it was imperative to regiment industry and impede free competition. The Old Regime believed, on this point, exactly as the socialists of today do. It was the French Revolution which denied this.

Gentlemen, what is it that has broken the fetters which, from all sides, had arrested the free movement of men, goods and ideas? What has restored to man his individuality, which is his real greatness? The French Revolution! [*Approval and clamor.*] It was the French Revolution which abolished all those impediments, which broke the chains which you would refashion under a different name. And it is not only the members of that immortal assembly—the Constituent Assembly, t h a t assembly which founded liberty not only in France but throughout the world — which rejected the ideas of the Old Regime. It is the eminent men of all the assemblies which followed it!

AND AFTER this great Revolution, is the result to be that society which the socialists offer us, a formal, regimented and closed society where the State has charge of all, where the individual counts for nothing, where the community masses to itself all power, all life, where the end assigned to man is solely his material welfare—this society where the very air is stifling and where light barely penetrates? Is it to be for this society of bees and beavers, for this society, more for skilled animals than for free and civilized men, that the French Revolution took place? Is it for this that so many great men died on the field of battle and on the gallows, that so much noble blood watered the earth? Is it for this that so many passions were inflamed, that so much genius, so much virtue walked the earth?

No! I swear it by those men who died for this great cause! It is not for this that they died. It is for something far

greater, far more sacred, far more deserving of them and of humanity. [*"Excellent."*] If it had been but to create such a system, the Revolution was a horrible waste. A perfected Old Regime would have served adequately. [*Prolonged clamor.*]

I mentioned a while ago that socialism pretended to be the legitimate continuation of democracy. I myself will not search, as some of my colleagues have done, for the real etymology of this word, democracy. I will not, as was done yesterday, rummage around in the garden of Greek roots to find from whence comes this word. [*Laughter.*] I look for democracy where I have seen it, alive, active, triumphant, in the only country on earth where it exists, where it could possibly have been established as something durable in the modern world — in America. [*Whispers.*]

There you will find a society where social conditions are even more equal than among us; where the social order, the customs, the laws are all democratic; where all varieties of people have entered, and where each individual still has complete independence, more freedom than has been known in any other time or place; a country essentially democratic, the only completely democratic republics the world has ever known. And in these republics you will search in vain for socialism. Not only have socialist theories not captured public opinion there, but they play such an insignificant role in the intellectual and political life of this great nation that they cannot even rightfully boast that people fear them.

America today is the one country in the world where democracy is totally sovereign. It is, besides, a country where socialist ideas, which you presume to be in accord with democracy, have held least sway, the country where those who support the socialist cause are certainly in the worst position to advance them. I personally would not find it inconvenient if they were to go there and propagate their philosophy, but in their own interests, I would advise them not to. [*Laughter.*]

A Member: Their goods are being sold right now.

Citizen de Tocqueville: No, gentlemen.

Democracy and socialism are not interdependent concepts. They are not only different, but opposing philosophies. Is it consistent with democracy to institute the most meddlesome, all-encompassing and restrictive government, provided that it be publicly chosen and that it act in the name of the people? Would the result not be tyranny, under the guise of legitimate government and, by appropriating this legitimacy assuring to itself the power and omnipotence which it would otherwise assuredly lack? Democracy extends the sphere of personal independence; socialism confines it. Democracy values each man at his highest; socialism makes of each man an agent, an instrument, a number. Democracy and socialism have but one thing in common — equality. But note well the difference. Democracy aims at equality in liberty. Socialism desires equality in constraint and in servitude. [*"Excellent, excellent."*]

THE FEBRUARY REVOLUTION, accordingly, must not be a "social" one, and if it must not be then we must have the courage to say so. If it must not be then we must have the energy to loudly proclaim that it should not be, as I am doing here. When one is opposed to the ends, he must be opposed to the means by which one arrives at those ends. When one has no desire for the goal he must not enter onto the path which necessarily leads him there. It has been proposed today that we enter down that very path.

We must not follow that political philosophy which Baboeuf so ardently embraced [*cries of approval*]—Baboeuf, the grand-father of all modern socialists. We must not fall into the trap he himself indicated, or, better, suggested by his friend, pupil and biographer, Buonarotti. Listen to Buonarotti's words. They merit attention, even after fifty years.

A Member: There are no Babovists here.

Citizen de Tocqueville: "The abolition of individual property and the establishment of the Great National Economy was the final goal of his (Baboeuf's) labors. But he well realized that such an order could not be established imme-

diately following victory. He thought it essential that [the State] conduct itself in such manner that the whole people would do away with private property through a realization of their own needs and interests." Here are the principal methods by which he thought to realize his dream. (Mind you, it is his own panegyrist I am quoting.) "To establish, by laws, a public order in which property-holders, provisionally allowed to keep their goods, would find that they possessed neither wealth, pleasure, or consideration, where, forced to spend the greater part of their income on investment or taxes, crushed under the weight of a progressive tax, removed from public affairs, deprived of all influence, forming, within the State, nothing but a class of suspect foreigners, they would be forced to leave the country, abandoning their goods, or reduced to accepting the establishment of the Universal Economy."

A Representative: We're there already!

Citizen de Tocqueville: There, gentlemen, is Baboeuf's program. I sincerely hope that it is not that of the February republic. No, the February republic must be democratic, but it must not be socialist —

A Voice from the Left: Yes! [*"No! No!"* (interruption)]

Citizen de Tocqueville: And if it is not to be socialist, what then will it be?

A Member from the Left: Royalist!

Citizen de Tocqueville (turning toward the left): It might, perhaps become so, if you allow it to happen, [*much approval*] but it will not.

If the February Revolution is not socialist, what, then, is it? Is it, as many people say and believe, a mere accident? Does it not necessarily entail a complete change of government and laws? I don't think so.

When, last January, I spoke in the Chamber of Deputies, in the presence of most of the delegates, who murmured at their desks, albeit because of different reasons, but in the same manner in which you murmured at yours a while ago— [*"Excellent, excellent."*]

(The speaker turns towards the left)

— I told them: Take care. Revolution is in the air. Can't you feel it? Revolution is approaching. Don't you see it? We are sitting on a volcano. The record will bear out that I said this. And why? —[*Interruption from the left.*]

Did I have the weakness of mind to suppose that revolution was coming because this or that man was in power, or because this or that incident excited the political anger of the nation? No, gentlemen. What made me believe that revolution was approaching, what actually produced the revolution, was this: I saw a basic denial of the most sacred principles which the French Revolution had spread throughout the world. Power, influence, honors, one might say, life itself, were being confined to the narrow limits of one class, such that no country in the world presented a like example.

That is what made me believe that revolution was at our door. I saw what would happen to this privileged class, that which always happens when there exists small, exclusive aristocracies. The role of the statesman no longer existed. Corruption increased every day. Intrigue took the place of public virtue, and all deteriorated.

Thus, the upper class.

And among the lower classes, what was happening? Increasingly detaching themselves both intellectually and emotionally from those whose function it was to lead them, the people at large found themselves naturally inclining towards those who were well-disposed towards them, among whom were dangerous demagogues and ineffectual utopians of the type we ourselves have been occupied with here.

Because I saw these two classes, one small, the other numerous, separating themselves little by little from each other, the one reckless, insensible and selfish, the other filled with jealousy, defiance and anger, because I saw these two classes isolated and proceeding in opposite directions, I said — and was justified in saying — that revolution was rearing its head and would soon be upon us. [*"Excellent."*]

Was it to establish something similar to this that the February Revolution took place? No, gentlemen, I refuse to believe it. As much as any of you, I believe the opposite. I want the opposite,

not only in the interests of liberty but also for the sake of public security.

I ADMIT that I did not work for the February Revolution, but, given it, I want it to be a dedicated and earnest revolution because I want it to be the last. I know that only dedicated revolutions endure. A revolution which stands for nothing, which is stricken with sterility from its birth, which destroys without building, does nothing but give birth to subsequent revolutions. [*Approval.*]

I wish, then, that the February revolution have a meaning, clear, precise and great enough for all to see.

And what is this meaning? In brief, the February Revolution must be the real continuation, the honest and sincere execution of that which the French Revolution stood for, it must be the actualization of that which our fathers dared but dream of. [*Much assent.*]

Citizen Ledru-Rollin: I demand the floor.

Citizen de Tocqueville: That is what the February Revolution must be, neither more nor less. The French Revolution stood for the idea that, in the social order, there might be no classes. It never sanctioned the categorizing of citizens into property-holders and proletarians. You will find these words, charged with hate and war, in none of the great documents of the French Revolution. On the contrary, it was grounded in the philosophy that, politically, no classes must exist; the Restoration, the July Monarchy, stood for the opposite. We must stand with our fathers.

The French Revolution, as I have already said, did not have the absurd pretension of creating a social order which placed into the hands of the State control over the fortunes, the well-being, the affluence of each citizen, which substituted the highly questionable "wisdom" of the State for the practical and interested wisdom of the governed. It believed that its task was big enough, to grant to each citizen enlightenment and liberty. [*"Excellent."*]

The Revolution had this firm, this noble, this proud belief which you seem to lack, that it sufficed for a courageous and honest man to have these two things, enlightenment and liberty, and to ask nothing more from those who govern him.

The Revolution was founded in this belief. It had neither the time nor the means to bring it about. It is our duty to stand with it and, this time, to see that it is accomplished.

Finally, the French Revolution wished —and it is this which made it not only beatified but sainted in the eyes of the people—to introduce charity into politics. It conceived the notion of duty towards the poor, towards the suffering, something more extended, more universal than had ever preceded it. It is this idea that must be recaptured, not, I repeat, by substituting the prudence of the State for individual wisdom, but by effectively coming to the aid of those in need, to those who, after having exhausted their resources, would be reduced to misery if not offered help, through those means which the State already has at its disposal.

That is essentially what the French Revolution aimed at, and that is what we ourselves must do.

I ask, is that socialism?

From the Left: Yes! Yes, exactly what socialism is.

Citizen de Tocqueville: Not at all!

No, that is not socialism but Christian charity applied to politics. There is nothing in it . . .

(*Interruption.*)

Citizen President: You cannot be heard. It is obvious that you do not hold the same opinion. You will get your chance to speak from the podium, but do not interrupt.

Citizen de Tocqueville: There is nothing there which gives to workers a claim on the State. There is nothing in the Revolution which forces the State to substitute itself in the place of the individual foresight and caution, in the place of the market, of individual integrity. There is nothing in it which authorizes the State to meddle in the affairs of industry or to impose its rules on it, to tyrannize over the individual in order to better govern him, or, as it is insolently claimed, to save him from himself. There is nothing in it but Christianity applied to politics.

Yes, the February Revolution must be Christian and democratic, but it must on no account be socialist. These words sum up all my thinking and I leave you with them.

65

Conservatives or Individualists: Which Are We?

EDWARD C. FACEY

Editor's Note: It is the policy of NIR to stimulate discussion of the fundamental principles of individualist philosophy. Accordingly, we are presenting here both a critique of a number of ideas current in conservative circles, and a comment on this critique, both articles written by individualists. Since there is not unanimity on the editorial board in regard to the issues discussed here, neither viewpoint should be taken to be the official position of this Review.

LAST YEAR, at Sharon, Connecticut, a group of right-wing college students and graduates passed a statement of first principles which they embraced as a sort of masthead for their new political action group, Young Americans for Freedom. The group was heavily conservative and I think an examination of its statement adds light to the debate in the May, 1960, issue of *The Individualist*.[1] But first, some preliminary remarks.

The individualist's position is that the individual man is the epistemological starting point in any social analysis. His nature and rights must be closely regarded before any consideration may be given to his place in society.

Unlike all the other animals in creation, man can continually make choices and direct his activity to the substitution of more suitable conditions for less suitable ones, i.e., he can act for ends. Since man is dependent here upon the material reality about him, the key right

significantly enabling these endeavors is the one that grants him the opportunity to convert or transform unused raw materials into desirable economic goods. Then, man must have the right to consume the goods or trade them with whomever he pleases. The latter activity is done within the free market, within the framework of society which encompasses the entire complex of all individuals and their multitudinous exchanges. Society is nothing more than a means by which the individual members may gain their sought-for ends more easily.

But there are some people who do not choose the economic means of producing and exchanging to gain ends. Instead, they would use force to acquire and enjoy the fruits of another man's labor. Franz Oppenheimer in *The State* calls this the "political means" of gaining wealth. It behooves the social members to divert a part of their production in order to establish institutions to expel looters so that man may continue existence secure in the right to produce and exchange property. This means that defense is another service that must be obtained in the market.

Conservatives, however, admire the historical solution to this problem: the establishment of an external non-social-market institution, government. They would install political officials and give them the power to seize wealth by taxation in order to repel the obstreperous persons mentioned previously. The individualist sees this as no solution but as merely the displacement of one set of

---

Edward C. Facey is a William Volker Fellow in economics at New York University.

1. "Individualist, Libertarian or Conservative—Which Are We?"

looters in favor of another "legalized" set. The individualist believes in each man's absolute rights and would move to cut off any group that insists on using the political means of gaining wealth rather than the economic means.

Still, individualists merge with the conservatives in urging a strict adherence to the Constitution in the United States. This is a tactical maneuver. It is the strategy of individualists to work a Fabianism in reverse until one by one the parts of the political structure, beginning with the most absurd, are upended and continuing until nothing is left. The Constitution, strictly interpreted, aids in this process.

THE CONSTITUTION in Article I, Section 8, in the enumeration of powers, says that Congress may call forth the Militia "to execute the Laws of the Union, suppress Insurrections and repel Invasions." This provision establishes a predisposition that the American government should concern itself with defending domestic society. If this is so, taxation can be kept light and social economic power may grow without serious let or hindrance.

Conservatives, however, are not restricting themselves to this interpretation of the extent of federal governmental power. Forgetting the individual, they are today engaged in a Messianic pledge to defend what they call Western civilization. In this caper they are urging bilateral alliances, collective alliances such as NATO, and actual combat, if necessary, in such far away places as Quemoy, Matsu, and Berlin. They urge that the enemy is Communism, and no sacrifice, seemingly, is too great to combat it. Witness the Sharon Conference statement:

"We, as young conservatives, believe...

"That the forces of international Communism are, at present, the greatest single threat to [liberty];

"That the United States should stress victory over, rather than coexistence with, this menace; and

"That all foreign policy must be judged by this criterion: does it serve the just interests of the United States?"

Individualists would disagree vigor-

ously on the first point, enough to say that statism or socialism is the threat and that Communism is merely one variant of this hydra-headed monster. The individualists would continue by saying that when the U. S. government is handed the vague, ambiguous power embodied in the "just interests" clause, subject to wide interpretation, we are on our way toward great diminution in liberty. What the conservatives, unwittingly perhaps, are getting at is that extensive statism must be adopted in order to defeat the international menace of Communism. In short, the conservatives would *use* the state rather than oppose it and in doing this induce a result likened to the foe they are supposed to be beating.

The growth of individual freedom is in the reduction of government harassment and intervention. Within the condition of the absence of interpersonal molestation a person should be allowed to do whatever he wants according to his wisdom and conscience. Yet, the Young Americans for Freedom are calling for the strengthening of the subpoena-empowered House *Un-American Activities* (whatever these two terms can or may mean) Committee. The individualist cannot countenance the coercing of peaceful individuals to appear before a tribunal unless there is evidence that these persons have injured others who are willing to press charges. Making people comply with a court order is a very serious matter.

THE CONSERVATIVES in Young Americans for Freedom acquit themselves similarly in other areas. Instead of committing battle against federal aid to education they ask that the aid be distributed to persons who have taken loyalty oaths. Instead of really contending with the Peace Corps they wish to make it "effective" with loyalty oaths for the members. They would even add a tax supported Freedom Academy. I wish these were minor activities of the Young Americans for Freedom but so far they seem to be the whole domestic program. All this while the Kennedy Welfare State grinds ceaselessly ahead.

In the international arena the program of the conservatives gives alarm. Make

67

no mistake, the attempt at world-wide defense of the West has taken the United States far from even Constitutional moorings. Not only is the U. S. not sticking to domestic defense but also it cannot stick to an international defense function if it would carry out the conservative mandate. America has had to engage in vast economic aid programs to keep the "Allies" from becoming "neutral" or selling out to Russia. Even then most, if not all, of the recipient countries are hanging onto a veto power over the use of American installations that may be placed within these foreign territories. Some may even kick the U. S. out of their countries after installations are built if no further U. S. aid is forthcoming or domestic political considerations warrant. Meanwhile, the U. S. gives them military money in hopes that they will add some troops of their own to defend the "West."

In the words of Garet Garrett, we have adopted the program of Empire. We are being forced to divert billions of dollars, some of which might better be spent on complex home defenses, into staking out a risky security via political internationalism. Even if the Federal Government did not engage in functions which conservatives and individualists agree are impermissible, such as federal aid to education, public power or social security, it is still possible for government to close in on our liberties through this American Empire idea. The U. S. government is spending $40 billion a year on "defense" and I rarely see this sum attacked in conservative journals as too high. Conscription is now an accepted institution in military operations because somehow many of us cannot get excited about fighting in foreign lands for some nebulous thing called the West or the Free World. Often the regime upheld may itself have little understanding of individual liberty.

Individualists will ever guard against the machinations of the state, any state. They view as *actually* present and more serious the inroads the domestic state has made on their absolute right to life and property. For the state is the real aggressor and it cannot be too often repeated that it is folly to extend and deepen the hegemony of one state in order to diminish that of another. Whatever the results of this attempt, collectivism or socialism is the winner; individualism and personal freedom, the loser. Let the conservatives beware.

Mr. Facey's Article: A Comment

MR. FACEY raises issues which have often divided those who consider themselves individualists. To some degree, I can sympathize with his fears in regard to the conservative position. There is no question that, historically, conservatives have tended to be paternalistic and nationalistic; nor have they shied away from power. While admitting this, we must take into consideration the objectives conservatives have had in view in seeking political power. If they have been interested in defending and extending the liberties of their fellow-citizens, they were right. It is clear that most American conservatives (including the members of Young Americans for Freedom) of the present day fall into this category, most certainly on the domestic issues where Mr. Facey attacks them.

Therefore, in the interests of a clearer terminology, I would suggest that Mr. Facey call himself an anarchist (as he is) or a Constitutional libertarian (a position he holds as a temporary expedient); I think it is unfair of him to try to pre-empt the word "individualist," because, as noted above, most American conservatives are primarily devoted to conserving personal liberty and limiting the power of the state. They thus consider themselves individualists, and rightly so. Conservatives and most libertarians agree that some government is necessary to maximize freedom; they believe that the police, the courts, and the armed services all restrict the freedom of various people at various times, but that the net effect is to increase freedom. The reasoning behind this position is well-known; John Locke is perhaps its most famous exponent.

Mr. Facey devotes most of his space to warning conservatives to beware of giving too much power to the federal government, on the excuse that a huge defense establishment is needed to fight the Communist menace. I think that most conservatives, including the military, would agree that the power of the military must always be restricted. But beyond the problem of growing military power, Mr. Facey is worried because many conservatives are interested in defending not only the United States but "what they call Western civilization."

This charge is true; conservatives are too well aware of the intensely difficult struggle through the last 2500 years to achieve and preserve our civilization to be willing to let it die undefended. One of its major traditions is individual liberty; in this, Western civilization is unique. It is within Western civilization that the liberty Mr. Facey wishes to extend has been developed. The only alternative that is currently available — Communism — will eliminate liberty, most particularly the economic liberty so important to both Mr. Facey and myself. The abolition or reduction of our military power now would be as disastrous to liberty as it would have been for the Athenians to abolish their own army and navy in the face of Darius and Xerxes.

ACCORDINGLY, the Conservatives prefer a strong military to Communist domination, even at an annual cost of $40 billion. They would indeed use the state to defeat Communism, but they would hardly term this "extensive statism," or "Empire." Many conservatives would join Mr. Facey in a vigorous attack on our present foreign aid program, while denying the practicality of the Fortress America concept he proposes instead — and wondering how he can suggest spending some of the foreign-aid billions on national defense and say that the defense budget is too high, in the same paragraph.

Mr. Facey and I both attended the Sharon conference; and while I must confess that I think he is manifestly unfair to Young Americans for Freedom, I, too, would like to see that organization devote more attention to domestic economic issues. But I would remind him first, that eight of the twelve principles of the Sharon Statement deal specifically with individual and economic liberty; and second, that Young Americans for Freedom is a political organization. While philosophically the hydra must be attacked *in toto,* politically it is necessary to cut off its heads, beginning with the most dangerous. To the conservative, the most dangerous is Communism.

To meet this threat, which has taken forms not previously seen in our history, the conservative supports the proposed Freedom Academy and the Un-American Activities Committee, though recognizing that the latter, like the courts, can restrict the freedom of some individuals. I do not suppose that Mr. Facey and I could agree on the value of laws proposed by this committee, or by anyone else, to prevent and punish sedition and subversion, but I believe he is radically misreading the hearings before that committee when he terms those it calls "peaceful." As to domestic politics, conservatives (including Young Americans for Freedom) do oppose federal aid to education, but they hold that if this aid is given as a defense measure — over their objections — it should at least be given to those who will defend the government which aids them. Moreover, on domestic issues conservatives and libertarians in Congress have some power to block the Administration's programs; they have much less in foreign policy and consequently much greater public pressure is necessary as a tactical matter to prevent the Administration from making mistakes which conservatives would consider disastrous to freedom.

In short, then, conservatives invite Mr. Facey to join them in fighting the great external threat to all our liberties, as they will join him in fighting the great internal threat.

JOHN WEICHER

Page Twenty-seven

69

Freedom and Coercion:

Some Comments and

Mr. Hamowy's Criticism

F. A. HAYEK

70

IN HIS REVIEW OF *The Constitution of Liberty*[1] Mr. Hamowy has raised points which are both important and difficult. In the space available I cannot attempt a complete answer but must concentrate on the chief problems. Before I turn to these I must, however, clear up a misunderstanding.

It was not the main thesis of my book that "freedom may be defined as the absence of coercion." Rather, as the first sentence of the first chapter explains, its primary concern is "the condition of men in which coercion of some by others is reduced as much as is possible in society." I believe I am etymologically correct in describing such a state as one of liberty or freedom. But this is a secondary issue. The reduction of coercion appears to me an objective of the first importance in its own right and it is to this task that the book addresses itself.

I sympathize with Mr. Hamowy's disappointment about my admission that I know of no way of preventing coercion altogether and that all we can hope to achieve is to minimize it or rather its harmful effects. The sad fact is that nobody has yet found a way in which the former can be achieved by deliberate

action. Such a happy state of perfect freedom (as I should call it) might conceivably be attained in a society whose members strictly observed a moral code prohibiting all coercion. Until we know how we can produce such a state all we can hope is to create conditions in which people are prevented from coercing each other. But to prevent people from coercing others is to coerce them. This means that coercion can only be reduced or made less harmful but not entirely eliminated. How far we can reduce it depends in part on circumstances which are not in the control of that organ of deliberate action which we call government. It is at least possible (to mention an extreme case which is the cause of one of Mr. Hamowy's chief complaints) that the use of so severe a form of coercion as conscription may be necessary to ward off the danger of worse coercion by an external enemy. I believe that the Swiss owe a long period of unusual freedom precisely to the fact that they recognized this and acted upon it; while some other countries protected by the sea were not under this unfortunate necessity. Where it exists the closest possible approach to perfect freedom may be much further from the ideal and yet the closest which can be achieved.

F. A. Hayek is Professor of Social and Moral Science at the University of Chicago and the author of numerous books, the most recent being *The Constitution of Liberty*.

[1] *New Individualist Review*, April, 1961, pp. 28-31.

THE TWO CRUCIAL issues which Mr. Hamowy raises concern, however, the definition of coercion and the practical means of limiting it. On the first his objections rest on a misunderstanding for which my exposition is perhaps partly responsible. I certainly did not intend to represent as coercion *every* change in a person's environment brought about by another with the intention of inducing the first to take some action beneficial to the second. Though both the possibility for the coercer to foresee the action of the coerced, and the former's desire to bring about this action, are necessary conditions for coercion, they are not sufficient. To constitute coercion it is also necessary that the action of the coercer should put the coerced in a position which he regards as worse than that in which he would have been without that action. (That was the meaning of the repeated emphasis in my book on the threatened harm.) Surely no change in the environment of a person which merely adds to his previously existing range of opportunities an additional one can without violence to language be called coercion. However certain I may be that somebody will be glad to buy from me a commodity if I offer it to him at a certain price, and however much I may gain from the sale, it would be ridiculous to suggest that I have coerced him by an offer which he regards as a clear advantage.

Normally, therefore, the terms on which somebody is prepared to render me services cannot be regarded as coercion: however important the service in question may be to me, so long as his action adds to the range of my choice something which I desire and which without his action would not be available to me, he places me in a better position than that in which I would be without his action — however high the price he makes me pay.

There seem to me, however, to exist cases which are superficially similar yet have to be judged differently, though the exact distinction may be difficult to state. The instance I discuss in my book is the situation in which somebody has acquired control of the whole water supply of an oasis and used this position to exact unusual performances from those whose life depends on access to that water. Other instances of the same kind would be the only doctor available to perform an urgent life-saving operation and similar cases of rescue in an emergency where special unforeseeable circumstances have placed into a single hand the power of rescue from grave danger. They are all instances where I should wish that those in whose hands the life of another is placed should be under a moral and legal obligation to render the help in their power even if they cannot expect any remuneration — though they should of course be entitled to normal remuneration if it is in the power of the rescued. It is because these services are regarded as rights to be counted upon that a refusal to render them except on unusual terms is justly regarded as a harmful alteration of the environment and therefore as coercion. That in such instances the unlimited control of the owner over his property has to give way is good old libertarian doctrine: see David Hume's discussion of the lapse of the rationale of property under the conditions of absolute scarcity in a state of siege.

THE SECOND CHIEF issue on which Mr. Hamowy dissents is the practical one of the manner in which the power of coercive action by government can be so limited as to be least harmful. Since government needs this power to prevent coercion (and fraud and violence) by individuals, it might at first seem as if the test should be whether it is in the particular instance necessary for that purpose. But to make necessity for the prevention of worse coercion the criterion would inevitably make the decision dependent on somebody's discretion and thereby open the doors to what has long been recognized as one of the most harmful and obnoxious forms of coercion, that dependent on some other man's opinion. While we want to allow coercion by government only in situations where it is necessary to prevent coercion (or violence, etc.) by others, we do not want to allow it in all instances where it could be pretended that it was necessary for that purpose. We need there-

71

fore another test to make the use of coercion independent of individual will. It is the distinguishing mark of the Western political tradition that for this purpose coercion has been confined to instances where it is required by general abstract rules, known beforehand and equally applicable to all. It is true that this by itself would not confine coercion to instances where it is necessary to prevent worse coercion; it leaves open possibilities of enforcement of highly oppressive rules on some dissenting group, especially in the field of religious observance and perhaps also in such restrictions on consumption as Prohibi-tion — though it is very questionable whether the latter kind of restriction would ever be imposed if they had to take the form of general rules from which no exceptions could be granted. Yet combined with the requirement that such general rules authorizing coercion could be justified only by the general purpose of preventing worse coercion, etc., this principle seems to be as effective a method of minimizing coercion as mankind has yet discovered. It certainly seems to me the best protection yet devised against that administrative despotism which is the greatest danger to individual liberty today.

72

BOOK REVIEW:

The Moulding of Communists, by Frank S. Meyer, (Harcourt, Brace, New York, 1961), 214 pp. $5.00.

Seldom does a book appear telling us what it is like to be a Communist. We have had a few biographies, most eloquently Whittaker Chambers' *Witness,* which, unfortunately, became a classic before most of the present student generation began to read; *Darkness at Noon;* the stories of some of the counterspies—Herbert Philbrick, Matt Cvetic — and some of the Soviet defectors, such as Victor Kravchenko. But the emphasis, especially in recent writing, has been on the ism, on the theory, the strategy or the conspiracy, and not on the man. Of the seven books in the Fund for the Republic's series on Communism in American Life, Frank S. Meyer's *The Moulding of Communists* is the first to treat specifically of the Communist as Communist, rather than as believer in Marxism or as worker in some specific subversive activity, for instance.

Unlike Chambers or Koestler, however, Meyer offers an *analysis* of how a Communist is made. Drawing upon his experience of 15 years in the Communist party, he abstracts the basic elements from the individual cases to present a systematic explanation of the process, in both its theory and practice. It is an infinitely painstaking process, from the recruitment of carefully-chosen specific individuals, through the development of the ideal Communist by intensive training, criticism and discipline. No other political, religious or military institution in Western experience has ever carried out such a continuous forced re-shaping of the personality and philosophy of the individual member. "The emphasis on development and training continues with greater rather than less emphasis in the higher levels of the movement . . . certainly I have found it as high as in National Secretaries of the Western Communist Parties — Browder, Pollitt, Thorez, Pieck . . ."

"The primary elements of the methodology of the Communist training process, then, are these: uncompromising insistence on the scientific character of reality, combined with continuing stress on responsibility, in a milieu where life is training and training is life. But a further element is necessary to fuse the others together." That element is pressure. Three chapters of the book specifically discuss the forms of pressure brought to bear upon the individual Party member. Training of the cadre, the inner core of elite "Communists in the full sense" of the book's title, differs from that of the rank-and-file member largely in that, at the cadre level, the pressure is self-imposed.

The pressure is applied in every conceivable situation; the Communist Party counts each small point as critical. "An 'error' in work is immediately assigned to 'theoretical weakness'; or a difference of opinion on even a comparatively minor organizational or technical question is debated with constant appeals to high theoretical principles." Meyer tells of the national Organizational Secretary of the French Young Communist League, whose "infuriatingly bureaucratic attitude" over a housing problem at an international anti-war conference led within six months to his expulsion from the French Party for "holding a semi-Trotskyist position on the allies of the proletariat." Incidents such as this, occurring continually on every level of party activity, and forcing all deviations from Marxism-Leninism into the open where they can be destroyed, mould the cadre. The description of the process forcefully brings home to the reader the nature of Communism as studies of theory or strategy cannot.

Meyer is admittedly less successful in explaining the role of theory in the day-to-day life of the Communist. He speaks

73

Page Thirty-one

of the concept of "unity of theory and practice" as central to Communism: "theory is not reducible to practice, but indissolubly united with it in a relationship where neither exists without the other, where each determines the other, permitting independent validity neither to abstract theory nor to empirical practice. It is a strange marriage of rationalism and empiricism, this unity of theory and practice which forms the intellectual mode of existence of the Communist." "But the unity of theory and practice enables the Communist to identify every act of the organization, even the most wanton exercise of authority over himself, as a necessity of History. His theoretical outlook enables him to 'recognize' that necessity. To recognize it is to be free. And this is not a matter of verbal gymnastics. It is simply the closest I can get to expressing in explicit terms the inner rationale which makes it possible for a feeling of independence and the actuality of subservience to exist side by side."

For a better description of this concept, which Meyer terms "mystical," we must turn to the imaginative writers. But for an unemotional explanation of the Communizing process and description of the Communist, with notes so full as to constitute a bibliography on the subject, *The Moulding of Communists* is unequalled. It is basic to any serious study of Communism.

JOHN WEICHER

74

NEW BOOKS AND ARTICLES

THE FOLLOWING IS A SELECT LIST OF BOOKS AND ARTICLES WHICH, IN THE OPINION OF THE EDITORS, MAY BE OF INTEREST TO OUR READERS.

Israel Kirzner, *The Economic Point of View,* (Van Nostrand, Princeton), 228 pp. $5.50.

Thomas Molnar (introduced by Russell Kirk), *The Future of Education,* (Fleet Press, New York).

Karl Brandt, "The Hard Core of the Farm Problem," *The Freeman,* April, 1961. (Free copy available from the publishers on request. Write: Foundation for Economic Education, Irvington-on-Hudson, New York.)

Ludwig von Mises, "On Equality and Inequality," *Modern Age,* Spring, 1961.

F. A. Hayek, "The *Non Sequitur* of the 'Dependence Effect'," *The Southern Economic Journal,* April, 1961.

George Reisman, "Galbraith's Modern Brand of Feudalism," *Human Events,* February 3, 1961.

Murray N. Rothbard, "Conservatism and Freedom: A Libertarian Comment," *Modern Age,* Spring, 1961.

John Weicher, "Inside Chicago Election Corruption," *Human Events,* February 24, 1961.

VOLUME 1
NUMBER 3
NOVEMBER 1961

New
INDIVIDUALIST
Review

"NATIONAL REVIEW":
 CRITICISM AND REPLY

RITUALISTIC LIBERALISM

AYN RAND'S
 "FOR THE NEW INTELLECTUAL"

JOHN COURTNEY MURRAY
 AND THE AMERICAN PROPOSITION

November 1961   35 cents   Vol. I, No. 3

NEW INDIVIDUALIST REVIEW

Volume 1 — Number 3
NOVEMBER 1961

81

NEW INDIVIDUALIST REVIEW is published bimonthly (January, March, May, Summer, November) by the University of Chicago chapter of the Intercollegiate Society of Individualists, Ida Noyes Hall, the University of Chicago, Chicago 37, Illinois. Second class mailing permit pending at the Chicago, Illinois post office.

Editorial, advertising and subscription correspondence and manuscripts should be sent to NEW INDIVIDUALIST REVIEW, Ida Noyes Hall, the University of Chicago, Chicago 37, Illinois. All manuscripts (which should not be longer than 3000 words) become the property of NEW INDIVIDUALIST REVIEW.

Subscription Rates: $2.00 per year (students, $1.00). Add $1.00 for foreign subscriptions.

The Readers of New Individualist Review . . .

include the usual "cross-section of American life." On our subscription list are lawyers, physicians, undergraduate students, bishops, explorers, graduate students, housewives, professors, statesmen and labor union members. Thinking that some of our readers might be interested in the reaction of other people to a new magazine, one of our editors blind-folded himself and drew a random sample of letters out of a well-mixed box. These are some of those comments.

"I am most grateful for . . . your excellent new magazine."

—William F. Buckley, Jr., Editor
"National Review"

"(NEW INDIVIDUALIST REVIEW) seems to me admirable both in coverage and the level of writing."

—Eugene Davidson, Editor
"Modern Age"

"This is a most impressive journal. I must rate it as one of the very best things coming out in the whole nation."

—Leonard Read, President
The Foundation For Economic Education

"I am sure you are acquainted with my belief that we must do everything we can to develop and direct the rising tide of conservatism on the college campuses and throughout the country. I think that your new publication will be a great help in this all-important endeavor. There is a great need for dissemination of well-thought-out conservative arguments and it is, I believe, a true sign of the times that the University of Chicago should become the source of such activity."

—Barry Goldwater
United States Senator

82

NEW INDIVIDUALIST REVIEW

IDA NOYES HALL
University of Chicago, Chicago 37, Illinois

Please enter my subscription for one year at $2.00 ☐   Students, $1.00 ☐

I also enclose a contribution of $..

NAME ....

ADDRESS ....

IF STUDENT: SCHOOL ....YEAR OF GRAD. ....

3

"National Review":

Criticism and Reply

RONALD HAMOWY

WILLIAM F. BUCKLEY, Jr.

83

SINCE ITS INCEPTION IN 1955, *National Review* has gradually assumed the leadership of the Right in America until today it stands practically unopposed as the intellectual spokesman of conservatism throughout the country. It boasts a staff of sophisticated and witty editors, the chief of whom is William F. Buckley, who has, in fact, achieved the status of national celebrity. Well-educated and self-assured, he has, in his countless appearances on television, at public lectures, and on dozens of college campuses including his own beloved Yale, impressed the general public with the fact that conservatives do not fall into the category of what H. L. Mencken used to call "yahoos."

So much is Mr. Buckley identified with everything intelligent on the Right that if in the common image of modern conservatism Senator Goldwater can justly be portrayed as the sword, Wil-

Ronald Hamowy is an Associate Editor of *New Individualist Review.*

William F. Buckley, Jr., the Editor-in-Chief of *National Review,* is widely known as a writer and lecturer. His published works include *God and Man at Yale* and *Up From Liberalism.*

liam Buckley is, without doubt, the pen. Given this phenomenon of Buckley as one of the directors of the Right, it becomes incumbent on all those who would attach themselves to this movement to carefully investigate the policies which he and his group espouse and to answer the crucial question of just where they are leading us. Nor should we be drawn away from this task by loud cries for "unity." It is the duty of all thinking men to reflect and examine before falling into step behind any leader. Indeed, it has always been an unfortunate disposition of most Right-wingers uncritically to follow the man and not the principle.

It is the contention of this article that William Buckley and *National Review* are, in fact, leading true believers in freedom and individual liberty down a disastrous path and that in so doing they are causing the Right increasingly to betray its own traditions and principles.

Better to see how far the Conservative movement has been straying under *National Review* guidance, let us briefly examine its genesis. The modern American "Right" was, in essence, a much-needed and healthy reaction against the New Deal, that revolution in domestic and foreign affairs wrought by Franklin D. Roosevelt which aimed at the radical transformation of the role of the State in American life and whose goal was the aggrandizement of government power at the expense of the individual. This modern Right represented the emerging opposition to such a shift and was, therefore, a movement stressing individual freedom. Domestically, the corollary of individual liberty was a call for free enterprise as against the socialist tendencies of the State; in foreign affairs, it stood for peace, neutrality, and isolationism as opposed to the Rooseveltian drive towards collective security, foreign entanglement, and war.

At a time when the Left had a virtual monopoly on all intellectual activity, during the early 40's, a small but evergrowing libertarian movement began to emerge. Its leaders were such eminent publicists and political thinkers as Isabel Paterson, Rose Wilder Lane, Garet Garrett, Albert Jay Nock, and Frank Chodorov. Philosophically, it was firmly dedicated to individual liberty, and consequently embraced free enterprise in economics, a strict adherence to the civil liberties of the individual, and peace. Historically, it ranked among its heroes Jefferson, Tom Paine, Thoreau, and Herbert Spencer.

Six years ago, however, a revolution took place "within the form," as Garet Garrett once wrote of the New Deal. The articulate publicists of *National Review,* founded at that time, have succeeded in remoulding the American Right until it travesties the intent of its original founders. Mr. Buckley and his staff have been able to achieve this transformation with such apparent ease simply because there has been no journal of opinion to oppose it, or even to call attention to the surgery that has been committed on the American Conservative movement.

How far this revolution within the form has gone may be gauged, for example, by the current conservative attitude towards Mr. Justice Frankfurter. Fifteen years ago, Justice Frankfurter was generally regarded by the Right as the personification of collectivist jurisprudence, as a destroyer of the Constitutional guarantees of liberty against the State. Today, he is considered to have become part of the Conservative movement and his name has actually been cheered by groups of conservative youth. To those who would take the trouble of investigating the judicial philosophy

of Mr. Frankfurter, however, it immediately becomes apparent that his position remains unchanged. He is guided solely by the principle that the courts must legitimize nearly every power the government decides to exercise. He is, and has always been, a thorough Statist. But now he is hailed by the Right because his most publicized decisions, especially in the Wilkinson and Uphaus cases, show him trampling upon the civil liberties of Leftists. His continued willingness to compromise with property rights is totally ignored by those who now reserve their zeal for the coercing of as many Communists and Communist sympathizers as they can lay their hands on. It is not Justice Frankfurter's position which has shifted, but that of the American Right.

And in this shift the lead has been taken by Mr. Buckley and his colleagues. *National Review* has time and again exerted its considerable intellectual influence *against* individual liberty. Through issue after issue of the journal we read of the "rights of the community," of five thousand years of conservative tradition, of authority and order, of the duty of the West to uplift the Negro with Bible and bullwhip, of the sacred obligation all free men have to coerce Communists at home and slaughter them abroad. Where once the Right was fervently devoted to the freedoms propounded in the Bill of Rights, it now believes that civil liberties are the work of Russian agents. Where once it stood for the strict separation of Church and State, it now speaks of the obligation of the community to preserve a Christian America through a variety of Blue Laws and other schemes for integrating government and religion. Where once the Right was, above all, dedicated to peace and opposed to foreign entanglements, it now is concerned with preparing for war and giving all-out aid to any dictator, Socialist or otherwise, who proclaims his unbending "anti-Communism." Where once the Right wanted America to exert its moral effect upon the world by being a beacon-light of freedom, it now wants to turn America into an armed camp to crush Communism wher-

84

ever it appears. Can it be less than fifteen years ago that the right-wing members of Congress voted against NATO and aid to Greece and Turkey? Can it be only a decade ago when Joseph Kennedy and Herbert Hoover were calling for withdrawal of our armies to our shores and when Howard Buffett, Taft's mid-west campaign manager, denounced this country's military bases abroad and the growing militarism in America?

It is not only on the Communist issue that the Right has abandoned its libertarian principles. All foreign policy questions are considered solely from the point of view of "historic traditions" or "American national interest." *National Review's* applause for the British-French-Israeli invasion of Suez is typical: for here was a situation where it could blend its fanatical opposition to anyone considered pro-Communist with its contempt for non-European and non-Christian peoples. The foreign policy position of the libertarian Right was essentially that held by Cobden and Bright in the nineteenth century: opposition to aggression, to imperialism, and to war. The foreign policy position of the new Right is that of Colonel Blimp and Rudyard Kipling, the pseudo-aristocratic outlook of "cane the bloody wogs" and "send the marines," coupled with the ever-present background mutterings of retired Generals and Admirals of "what they need is a whiff of grape."

These differences concerning foreign policy are of much greater importance than might first be realized, for they call into question the philosophic problem of moral principle. One of the outstanding features of *National Review* is its pretension of moral superiority, its insistence that it alone represents the conservator of two thousand years of Western Civilization and Christianity. But surely one who believes in natural law must hold that it be eternal and fixed, and that the natural rights of the individual apply at any time, for any place. Yet the position that *National Review* holds grants rights only, and then begrudgingly, to Anglo-Saxons. Spain must respect its heritage of the dictatorial *Caudillo;* Central Europe must revert to

the divinely-inspired Crown of St. Stephen; British colonies must be subjugated to the Mother Country; France's historical role is to be governed by a clique of fascist generals whose function it must be to hurl still more conscripts into the sacred task of crushing Moslems in Algeria. Surely there is no appreciable difference between this system of double morality and the contention often heard on the Left, when asked how they can reconcile a demand for civil liberties at home with support of such dictators as Nkrumah and Toure in modern Africa, that "the same standards cannot apply to the developing countries," and that "the African must be studied as a part of his cultural milieu."

The great moral principle of individual liberty has been superceded by the arrogance of the pseudo-aristocrat who preserves his civilized airs by exploiting the serf labor of "inferior" people; the libertarian principle of peace and non-intervention has been replaced by the heroics of a barroom drunk who proudly boasts that "he can lick anybody in the room." This posture is rendered tragic by the fact that the *National Review* group who proclaim "give me liberty or give me death" are willing to cremate countless millions of innocent persons whom they give no opportunity to make a choice.

Another touchstone of how far the Right has travelled is its position on conscription. Before and after World War II it fought the draft as unconstitutional, as slavery, and as the ultimate aggrandizement of the State. To the current conservative, anyone who dares to raise a principled voice against conscription is labeled a Communist or Communist dupe. The same libertarians who during the Second World War were accused by the Left of being "mouthpieces of the Goebbels line," are now accused, this time by the Right, of "doing the work of the Communists." One would expect libertarians to be reviled and slandered by the apologists of the State. It is, in fact, both noble and honorable to have such enemies. But that *National Review* should take the lead in this slander can mean only one thing: that the

Right, under the aegis of *National Review* has itself become a leading minion of the State. From an advocate of individual liberty against the State, the Conservative movement has now become a champion of the State against individual liberty. The entire concept of "right-winger," as it has been understood in America since the 1930's, has been taken by the Buckley group and, like the old word "liberal" at the hands of the Left, has been transformed into its very opposite.

We are left with one significant area: the economic. And even here, modern conservatism fares no better. It is true that there is still much talk about the free market, but a careful study of the literature of the Right today makes it quite clear that it is engaged in beating a steady, persistent retreat from libertarianism even in the economic sphere. One searches in vain, for example, in the concrete political programs of the Young Americans for Freedom, whose organizational meeting was held at Mr. Buckley's estate in Sharon, Conn., for any clear statement on the reduction of the economic intervention of the State. Nowhere, any longer, does a rollback or repeal of the New Deal seem to be seriously contemplated. The only real goal of the *National Review* Right is to keep the Federal government from advancing much further down the socialist road — a goal in itself contradicted by the war economy that it desires. And one is at a loss to find any genuine attempt on its part to examine the relationship between an ever-increasing military establishment and government interference in the economic affairs of the country. At no time has a disarmament agreement with Russia been given as serious consideration as it deserves nor has it been viewed as a welcome possibility. Rather, editors of *National Review* proceed to look on increased government spending not only as permissible but as desirable if it is earmarked for the production of bombs and other paraphernalia of death. On such questions the libertarian is almost forced to stand with the Leftists. If government spending is to be kept at such a high level, better

that it be used to build roads, schools, playgrounds, and other things which have some value, no matter how small, rather than be employed to manufacture a new and better type of H-bomb or rocket-launching satellite or used to finance some new inquisitorial government investigatory committee. A return to the free market is indeed hardly a burning issue on the Right today.

The new American Right would seem to reserve its real passion for such causes as giving Khrushchev bi-weekly ultimatums and suppressing civil liberties at home. Mr. Buckley himself has begun, of late, to show increasing asperity towards those misguided souls who still cling to individual liberty as their main political preoccupation by chiding us that social security is, after all, here to stay and really isn't so bad and by denouncing those libertarian "extremists" for cleaving to consistency and truth in speaking against government monopoly control of the roads and post-office. It seems that the desired unity behind our self-appointed leaders is being threatened by the tiny minority who have remained true to those very ideals of individual freedom which led them to become Right-wingers in the first place.

Just what *is* the direction in which *National Review* is leading the Right and would lead America? There is, of course, an inevitable diversity among the luminaries of that august journal. Willmoore Kendall believes that the Greek "community" had the duty, *a fortiori* the right, to murder Socrates. Frank S. Meyer finds the vision of a total nuclear holocaust not entirely unappealing. Garry Wills finds his pet peeve in capitalism. Frederick Wilhelmsen desires above all other earthly things that we venerate the Crown of St. Stephen. Hugh Kenner finds solace not only in the poetry but in the economics of Ezra Pound. But underneath this collection of attitudes there are manifested certain features that generally characterize them all. They may be summed up as: (1) a belligerent foreign policy likely to result in war; (2) a suppression of civil liberties at home; (3) a devotion to imperialism and to a polite form of white supremacy; (4) a tendency towards the union of Church and State; (5) the conviction that the community is superior to the individual and that historic tradition is a far better guide than reason; and (6) a rather lukewarm support of the free economy. They wish, in gist, to substitute one group of masters (themselves) for another. They do not desire so much to limit the State as to control it. One would tend to describe this devotion to a hierarchial, warlike statism and this fundamental opposition to human reason and individual liberty as a species of corporativism suggestive of Mussolini or Franco, but let us be content with calling it "old-time conservatism," the conservatism not of the heroic band of libertarians who founded the anti-New-Deal Right, but the traditional conservatism that has always been the enemy of true liberalism;* the conservatism of Pharonic Egypt, of Medieval Europe, of the Inquisition; the conservatism of Metternich and the Tsar, of James II and Louis XVI, of the rack, the thumbscrew, the whip, and the firing squad. I, for one, do not very much mind that a philosophy which has for centuries dedicated itself to trampling upon the rights of the individual and glorifying the State should have its old name back.

—Ronald Hamowy

————

* I use the term "liberalism" as it was employed in the 19th century in the hope that the dedicated libertarian might one day have *his* historic name again.

87

Three Drafts of an Answer to Mr. Hamowy

FIRST DRAFT

Dear me, thumbscrews, whips, firing squads, war, colonialism, repression, white supremacy, fascism — what a lot of things for *National Review* to have foisted upon the Right in a mere six years! There was a time when Associate Imperialist Henry Hazlitt, who appears on our masthead, was interested in personal liberty: now he wants war and white supremacy. Associate Torturer Erik von Kuehnelt-Leddihn, a founder of the neo-Liberal movement in Europe, and author of *Liberty or Equality,* has abandoned his views, to go authoritarian, along with *National Review.* "[What] a tremendous relief to read your periodical at a moment when we can only say, with Frederick the Great, 'Toute la boutique va au diable'." wrote Wilhelm Roepke, author of *Civitas Humana,* teacher of Ludwig Erhard, president of Mt. Pelerin Society, in a letter to *National Review* a week ago — how sad, to turn one's back on freedom, after so noble a lifetime spent in pursuit of it. (Contributing Torturer Kirk — what would you expect? — writes admiringly about Roepke in the current issue of *National Review*.) Senior Warmonger Frank Meyer argues that freedom is the meaning of life, that without freedom there is no life, that indeed that is why he would rather be dead than Red. He does not know that to be a true libertarian you must love freedom, but not *that* much — you must prefer to be Red than dead, or you cannot be in the libertarian tradition. Sad, is it not, to see Contributing Executioner John Chamberlain, who opposes the income tax, become a part of a statist movement; and Senior Suppressor James Burnham, who has written that the government has no business regulating the use of fireworks, end up trampling upon the rights of the individual and glorifying the State. And Associate Colonialist Frank Chodorov cracking the whip: "Call me Massa Frank," he growls at all black men, yellow men, and non-Christians, from the poop-deck of *National Review.* "Six of the best for the next man who says Uhuru," echoes Associate Racist Morrie Ryskind . . .

Pity the people whom
NR has led askew . . .

————

* October 21, 1961

SECOND DRAFT

1. The editorial section of the current issue of *National Review* includes: a) an analysis of the inflationary policies of the Federal Reserve, deploring the state's bureaucratic impositions on business; b) a joyful run-down on the accomplishments of the European Common Market, made possible by the dissipation of statist-enforced economic boundaries; c) a pat on the back for the government of Portugal for its phased increase of self-government in Angola and Mozambique, including extended programs for multiracial integration (a traditional Portuguese policy); d) an account of a poll by the Council for the Advancement of Small Colleges, yielding the happy news that two-thirds of the student leaders of the small colleges are unsympathetic to "the current trend of the federal government to increase its influence in all areas"; e) an analysis of the shifty legwork of the National Labor Relations Board which has the effect of circumventing the state right-to-work laws by the evasion of the agency shop, which requires a non-union member to contribute to the union's kitty; f) a report on the creeping sanity of Professor Paul Samuelson, who in the last five editions of his famous book on economics has reduced from 5 per cent to 1½ per cent the tolerable annual inflation; g) an appreciative obituary account for two men who had battled the overweening state for years; and h) renewed support for Editor William F. Rickenbacker's refusal to sign the Census Department's prurient questionnaire . . .

2. The Sharon (Charter) Statement of the Young Americans for Freedom includes the following asseverations: "political freedom cannot long exist without economic freedom . . . the purposes of government are to protect . . . freedoms through the preservation of internal order, the provision of national defense, and the administration of justice . . . when government ventures beyond these rightful functions, it accumulates power which tends to diminish order and liberty . . . the market economy, allocating resources by the free play of supply and demand, is the single economic system compatible w i t h the requirements of personal freedom . . . when government interferes with the work of the market economy, it tends to reduce the moral and physical strength of the nation; when it takes from one man to bestow on another, it diminishes the incentive of the first, the integrity of the second, and the moral autonomy of both . . ."

3. The last paragraph of the most recent address I have delivered is (in part): ". . . the direct problems that face the world are the making of governments in action; for only government can exercise the leverage necessary to transform individual vices into universal afflictions. It took government to translate *Mein Kampf* into concentration camps; it takes positive action by government to preserve many of the imbalances in our economic system; only government, with its monopoly of force, can perpetuate injustice that individuals, given the freedom to do so, might redress. It was long ago understood, in the evolution of political theory, that just about the only *in*tolerable answer to big government is *no* government. Government there must be, this side of paradise, so that the challenge is, and always will be, how to restrain and direct that government without which we cannot get on. The facile answer of the 19th century, when the body of the world's progressive social theorists seized intoxicatingly upon literacy and self-rule as the solvents of the enlightened and domesticated state, has proved naive. The insufficiency of democracy as a sole guarantor of enlightened public action is now perceptible. The only defense against the shortcomings and abuses of collective action by the state is concerted resistance by individuals. That resistance can only issue from an undamaged critical faculty and moral sense. If the entire thinking class indulges itself in the suppression of the intellect and the conscience, anything can happen: wars that should not be fought, are fought; and wars that should be fought are not fought; and human impulses that should be restrained are not restrained, and human impulses that should not be restrained, are restrained; and great nations are humbled."

THIRD DRAFT

Dear Mr. Hamowy:

Your article contains a number of factual errors (when on earth did *National Review* ever celebrate the existence of Felix Frankfurter? We have merely applauded his position on certain issues, as we applaud the position on certain issues of Sidney Hook or Paul Douglas or Lucifer); and, of course, your article seeks to make its points by caricature, which is okay by me, although by so doing, you impose upon me the responsibility of deciding where you are being merely playful, and where you mean to be taken seriously.

Putting aside the thumbscrews, I judge that your criticisms revolve around two central assumptions of *National Review*, which I herewith state, and attempt briefly to show why I judge that they come naturally to American conservatives. The first assumption is that freedom can only be defended in our time by the active use of one's strategic intelligence; and this calls for understanding the position of the Soviet Union in world affairs.

Among the corollaries of this assumption are: 1) it becomes necessary to forfeit a part of the freedom one might ideally exercise, in order to secure the greater part of our freedom; and corollary 2) our nation's role in world affairs, to the extent it is the state's responsibility to enact it, should turn on and be confined to the question of the national security.

The national security is a proper concern for the libertarian because without it he stands to lose — in this case — all his freedom. The conservative, who is a libertarian but other things, too, supports the large national effort that aims at neutralizing the Communist threat, because a conservative must be prepared to face reality. A conservative is not one of those pure and seraphic intellectualists Bishop Parker spoke about who, forsooth, despise all sensible knowledge as too gross and material for their nice and curious faculties. We conservatives are all for paradigmatic self-examinations

from time to time, that aim at drawing attention to all those freedoms we do not have: but we never lose sight of the value of what we do have, and the reason why we have it, namely, because we have a formidable military machine which keeps the Soviet Union from doing to us what it did to the Hungarians, and the Cubans. There is room in any society for those whose only concern is for tablet-keeping; but let them realize that it is only because of the conservatives' disposition to sacrifice in order to withstand the enemy, that they are able to enjoy their monasticism, and pursue their busy little seminars on whether or not to demunicipalize the garbage collectors.

* * * *

And the second assumption shared by the editors of *National Review* is that an approach to any human problem that calls for the ruthless imposition of any social schematic, whether Marxist or Benthamite, is self-defeating, for the reason that ideology can never replace philosophy. While it is true that freedom is good, it is not true that freedom can be promulgated in any given country simply by saying, Ready, Set, Be Free. The count-down is much longer. Sometimes it takes centuries. A conservative will argue for that system in a given country which will *maximize* freedom. But that system is not necessarily one that is based on one man, one vote; or even, necessarily, on the right of self-rule. We cannot, merely by renouncing colonialism instantly, write a script that will bring eudemonia to Upper Volta.

The American conservative needs to proceed within the knowledge of history and anthropology and psychology; we must live in our time. We must indeed continue to cherish our resentments against such institutionalized impositions upon our prerogatives (see my books) as social security. But we must not, if we are to pass for sane in this tormented world, equate as problems of equal urgency, the repeal of the social security law, and the containment of the Soviet threat. The problem of assigning priorities to the two objectives is not merely a problem of intellectual discrimination,

Page Nine

but of moral balance. Mr. Hamowy should examine the processes of thought even among his associates on the Committee for a Sane Nuclear Policy, which I am informed he has recently joined. I hope he will find there still is a differ-ence between him and the moral and intellectual emasculates among whom he mingles; I hope the difference is still discernible; I, and I am sure all conservatives, hope that.

— **William F. Buckley, Jr.**

A Rejoinder to Mr. Buckley in One Draft

It is always enjoyable to hear from Mr. Buckley; his style and wit make for relaxing reading. However, it is a fact of life which Mr. Buckley appears to ignore, that an abundance of charm coupled with good intentions is an inadequate substitute for cogency of thought. Had he dealt with my arguments, my task in defending them would have been simpler. As it stands, I can find few points worthy of serious reply. Therefore, I dismiss Mr. Buckley's First Draft with the admission that all those whose names appear on *National Review's* masthead are not, in any sense, consistent conservatives in the Buckley tradition and that, in particular, Henry Hazlitt and Frank Chodorov share few, if any, of the sentiments with which my article deals. Just one point more. Pray, of what neo-Liberal movement in Europe is Mr. Kuehnelt-Leddihn a founder? Does Mr. Buckley regard an intellectual attachment to enlightened despotism in Central Europe as in the tradition of Cobden and Bright?

Concerning the Second Draft. (1) The current issue of *National Review* also contains: (a) plaudits for the Supreme Court ruling on the registration of the Communist Party with the Justice Department. We are told that this is "a bright day for freedom." Someone or something (it is not indicated who or what) is "resourceful enough to bear down upon the unassimilable political minority for whom the normal rules cannot apply"; (b) an essay by James Burnham to the effect that one can either be for peace or against Communism but that to hold strongly to both positions is "a source of trouble"; (c) a defense of Franco Spain by Lev Ladnek. Mr. Ladnek feels that it is unrealistic to suppose that when idealists call for freedom they are not confining that freedom to just one group in Spanish society at the expense of another. He goes on to say that to champion freedom of expression and free elections is to invite civil war; (d) a report on the Mt. Pelerin Society by Russell Kirk in which he gleefully reports that Liberalism is slowly passing out of fashion as the new Conservatism sweeps all before it. We are informed that some old 19th-century individualists detracted from Kirk's enjoyment of the meeting but that on careful consideration "the moral and political doctrines of Bentham 'the great subversive' are fallen from favor nowadays, except in their *reductio ad absurdum,* Marxism."

(2) Despite the high-sounding phrases of the Sharon Statement, *no concrete political program* of the Young Americans for Freedom has concerned itself with a call for the reduction of the economic intervention of the State. Instead, they have devoted their time and energy to picketing in support of the House Committee on Un-American Activities and the American government's invasion of Cuba and against negotiations on Berlin. A charter member of this organization informs me that its Policy Committee has voted to decline to take a stand against the John Birch Society and State segregation laws. That they pay lip-service to freedom indicates nothing.

90

(3) Mr. Buckley's speech indeed expresses a noble sentiment. However, it bears no relevance to the arguments I present in my article.

The Third Draft presents 2 arguments, the first, that the external threat of Communism is of such magnitude that internal freedom becomes of minor importance. To this is added a sub-argument that it is ony thanks to people like Buckley sacrificing themselves "in order to withstand the enemy," that "tablet-keepers" like me might "enjoy their monasticism and pursue their busy little seminars on whether or not to demunicipalize the garbage collectors."

It might appear ungrateful of me, but I must decline to thank Mr. Buckley for saving my life. It is, further, my belief that if his view-point prevails and that if he persists in his unsolicited aid the result will almost certainly be either my death (and that of tens of millions of others) in nuclear war or my imminent imprisonment as an "un-American."

Mr. Buckley would seem to imply that my position rests on a personal fear of death, and if this is the case, it indicates a total misreading of the facts. I hold strongly to my personal liberty and it is precisely because of this that I insist that no one has the right to force his decisions on another. Mr. Buckley chooses to be dead rather than Red. So do I. But I insist that all men be allowed to make that decision for themselves. A nuclear holocaust will make it for them.

The second argument has as its underlying premise that "freedom cannot be promulgated . . . by saying, Ready, Set, Be Free," that it is something which is earned and often takes centuries to achieve. Promulgated by whom? Earned? Who is the paymaster? No one *gives* anyone else his freedom nor is anyone indebted to others for it. Mr. Buckley either rejects or is unfamiliar with the premises of political philosophy upon which our nation was founded. Namely, that freedom is, in fact, not earned, but the *right* of each human being. Mr. Buckley, I hold these truths to be self-evident, that all men are created equal, that they are endowed by their Creator with certain unalienable Rights, that among these are Life, Liberty, and the Pursuit of Happiness.

—**Ronald Hamowy**

91

Ritualistic Liberalism

RUSSELL KIRK

TO MR. CHESTER BOWLES, *ci-de-vant* advertising man, sometime ambassador to India, President Kennedy has issued letters of marque. Surveying, and perhaps helping to intensify, the problems of Ruanda-Urundi or Kashmir, Mr. Bowles is to scurry over the face of the world, scattering broadcast American optimism and good-will. Having been engaged in this scurrying for some years, between periods of lecturing and platform-writing in these United States, Ambassador Bowles may be counted upon to utter platitudes in fifty nations, and then write a new book repeating those platitudes for Americans. And his are illusory platitudes. They are the slogans and shallow understandings which have produced, for instance, the devastation and anarchy in the Congo today.

It was Professor Sidney Hook, I believe, who coined the term "ritualistic liberalism" to describe the condition into which much of American "liberal" opinion is fallen nowadays: an infatuation with old liberal slogans untempered by any prudential examination of the exigencies of our hour, an ideological fidelity to the liberal letter that forgets the liberal spirit. Mr. Hook was referring principally to the attitude that many American liberals take toward the Communist movement. A similar ritualism, I suggest — a like attitude that the mere repetition of liberal formulas and evoca-

tion of god-terms can suffice in dealing with our present discontents — may be discerned in the concept of American foreign policy entertained by many liberals.

Of such gentlemen, Mr. Bowles is an eminent representative; he is, indeed, the principal darling, more dear even than Mr. Adlai Stevenson, of the unreconstructed ritualistic liberals of Southern California. His popular and repetitious books — *Ambassador's Report, The New Dimensions of Peace, Ideas, People and Peace* — have exerted some influence, although not a power sufficient to get Mr. Bowles into the Senate, obtain him the presidential or vice-presidential nomination, or even to secure him a cabinet post. But these hasty works have secured him some national following and a good deal of attention in the press. The acerbic demolition of Mr. Bowles' notions about foreign policy by scholars such as Professor Hans Morgenthau may have caused responsible politicians to shy away from the Ambassador; but, curiously enough, these criticisms have not much affected Mr. Bowles' credit in certain quarters of the Academy.

Five years ago, Mr. Bowles seemed to be taken as a serious authority on foreign affairs in some of our leading universities. In 1956, he delivered both the Godkin Lectures at Harvard (named for E. L. Godkin of *The Nation*) and a somewhat similar series at the University of California; these soon were published under the respective titles of *American Politics in a Revolutionary World* and *Africa's Challenge to America*. That lectures so superficial should be heard re-

---

Russell Kirk, Research Professor of Political Science at C. W. Post College is the Editor of *The University Bookman* and is contributing Editor of *National Review*. He is the author of many books on conservative thought, including *The Conservative Mind, Academic Freedom* and *Prospects for Conservatives*.

spectfully by famous universities, and published by university presses, may suggest how far ritualistic liberalism still affects the higher learning in this country. For statecraft, professors of arts and sciences turn to an advertising-promoter.

Now that Mr. Bowles is lecturing to lesser breeds without the law on the way to peace and freedom, with the grand sanction of the American government, it may be worth while to glance again at these two slim books, presumably his most serious works, since they originated as university lectures. I do not find that they improve with time, or that Mr. Bowles was a true prophet. What a commonsensical liberal like old E. L. Godkin would have said to Bowles' band of liberalism, I think I know.

CHESTER BOWLES IS a thoroughgoing utilitarian and political universalist, convinced that all societies ought to be reconstituted in our American image, and that we ought to pay for the process. By an American-sponsored industrialization of "underdeveloped regions," under forced draft, he would have Americans out-materialize the Soviet materialists. (He sounds, indeed, oddly like Khrushchev, here and there — reminiscent, for instance, of Khrushchev's scowling admonition to the Javanese that they ought to abolish their handicrafts and turn to standardized industrial production.) The world is to become one immense copy of American society, repeating the campaign phrases of Jefferson and F.D.R., copying American technology, adopting our manners and institutions, and presumably inheriting all our problems and afflictions. Mr. Bowles' brand of One-Hundred-Per-Cent-Americanism — so the argument runs — may be imposed quite simply, with equal facility, upon the ancient civilizations of India and the primitive peoples of central Africa.

Such is Mr. Bowles' variety of liberalism, inherited (though possibly Mr. Bowles does not know it) from Bentham and James Mill. Whatever things are established — except, of course, the American liberal ideology — are anathema to

Ambassador Bowles. There comes to my mind Ambrose Bierce's definition of the word conservative, in *The Devil's Dictionary*. "Conservative, *n*. A statesman who is enamored of old evils, as contrasted with the liberal, who would replace them with new." Now Mr. Bowles is precisely that sort of liberal innovator; and nowhere does he reveal much awareness that we Americans possess the talent for distributing evils, as well as benefits.

I interject here a general proposition having some relation to American foreign policy. It seems to be a law governing all life, from the unicellular inanimate forms to Socrates and Gautama, that every living organism endeavors, above all else, to preserve its identity. Whatever lives, tries to make itself the center of the universe; and it resists with the whole of its power the endeavors of competing forms of life to assimilate it to their substance and mode. Every living thing prefers even death, as an individual, to extinction as a distinct species. Now if the lowliest alga struggles to the death against a threat to its peculiar identity, we ought not to be surprised that men and nations resist desperately and even unreasoningly any endeavor to assimilate their character to that of some other social body. This resistance is the first law of their being, extending deep below the level of consciousness. There is one sure way to make a deadly enemy, and that is to propose seriously to anyone, "Submit yourself to me, and I will improve your condition by relieving you from the burden of your own identity and reconstituting your personality in my image."

Yet this is just what Mr. Chester Bowles, with wondrous good will and innocence, proclaims as a rallying-cry for American policy makers in a revolutionary world. Mr. Bowles, to be sure, does not use precisely these phrases, and really seems to be unaware of the grand assumption behind his own humanitarian projects; but our author's naivete does not alter the nature of the first principles upon which his scheme is erected.

"The most powerful ideas and principles in the history of man are closely linked with the evolution of American democracy," Mr. Bowles writes in *American Politics*. "Today it is *our* revolution for self-determination, for human dignity, and for expanding economic opportunities which is alive and marching in Burma, India, and the Philippines, in Nigeria, the Sudan, and Tunisia, indeed throughout the non-communist world."

In both these books, as in his earlier writings, he implies repeatedly that modern revolutionary movements — Soviet movements excepted — have been directly inspired by knowledge of the American Revolution. *Africa's Challenge* concludes with "the fervent hope that we shall soon come to view the Soviet challenge not negatively as a mortal danger, but positively as an opportunity for which the continuing political, social, and industrial revolution of Jefferson, Lincoln, and Henry Ford has equipped us as no other people on earth." Revolutions are made, he informs us, out of devotion to the writings of "Locke, Rousseau, and Jefferson." A Revolution of Rising Expectations, in imitation of American theory and experience, "shapes the attitudes and aspirations of the one and a half billion people of India, Africa, and South America," and its objectives are "freedom from foreign domination, political or economic; a full measure of human dignity regardless of race, religion or color; and increased economic opportunities, broadly shared."

Liberal democracy is the passion of these rebels against things established: "The national revolutions in Europe and South America in the last century, the reform movements under the Tsar in Russia, Sun Yat-Sen's struggles in China, the Congress party effort in India, the beginnings of the independence movements in Africa, were all taken in the name of liberal democracy."

Well! Is this sort of breathless recitation of historical error and partisan cliche taken for political philosophy at Harvard and California nowadays? Mr. Bowles' phrases might have been written by one of the schoolboys in the first chapter of Aldous Huxley's *Antic Hay*, cribbed from a "liberal" ideologue's dull textbook. To pick his thesis to pieces is

to break a butterfly on the wheel, but if this manner of reasoning and proof is taken seriously at American universities, someone has to plumb the depths of Mr. Bowles' ignorance.

Even a hasty reading of a book such as Professor D. M. Brogan's *The Price of Revolution* ought to inform any undergraduate of Mr. Bowles' thorough incompetence as historian and political theorist. The revolutions of the twentieth century were made not in imitation of the American Revolution, but out of very different circumstances and materials; and so far as they were conscious imitations of any earlier revolution, it was the French Revolution. What lip-service these latter-day revolutionaries have paid to the American experience has come after the fact of their own revolutionary triumph. Mr. Bowles repeatedly confounds the concept of liberty with the concept of democracy, and the idea of nationalism with the idea of the dignity of man. Sun Yat-Sen took his principles from Marx, not from Jefferson and Adams; the Indian and African revolts against British dominion owed much more to the London School of Economics than they did to the Declaration of Independence; and we ascend into a Cloud Cuckoo Land of political fantasy if we pretend that American constitutionalism is the inspiration of the Westernized socialist regime in Burma, of the Sudanese tribes, and of the nationalists in Tunis.

THIS INDIFFERENCE to historical fact dominates the proofs for Mr. Bowles' thesis, as well as the general argument itself. The blunders are so numerous and obvious in both books that it is embarrassing to touch upon them. In *Africa's Challenge*, for instance, Mr. Bowles informs us that John Adams believed "the development of American democracy" to be "the 'opening of a grand scene and design of Providence for the emancipation of the slavish part of mankind all over the earth'." Then, in *American Politics*, he undoes himself by quoting Adams correctly. Adams did not write "American democracy," but "the settlement of America," which is a different thing. Of the Abyssinians, he writes in *Africa's Challenge*, "Their religion is Orthodox of the same strain as the Coptic Christian Church of Egypt." Neither Coptic nor Abyssinian churches are Orthodox, in plain fact; they are Monophysite. (This is one of the few instances in which Mr. Bowles touches at all upon religious opinion.) One may excuse a hasty traveller like Mr. Bowles, flying excitedly from celebrity to celebrity in Asia and Africa, for such slips; but when that hurried globe-trotter turns political pontiff. . . . He writes of "the Cambridge-Oxford liberal-arts system" with the presumption and the ignorance of a high-school debater. But we sink into bathos.

Thus the ideologue fits facts to his Procrustean bed. Charismatic phrases, godterms, are everything to a gentleman of Mr. Bowles' cast of mind; history and prudence are next to nothing. One of the phrases which especially fascinates Mr. Bowles is "self-determination." This is an end in itself, because Woodrow Wilson employed it, and Woodrow Wilson belonged to Mr. Bowles' party, and was Liberal a n d Progressive — Mr. Bowles thinks. Nothing must be allowed to stand in the way of immediate Self-Determination everywhere. Full speed ahead, a n d d a m n t h e consequences. "When harried American policy-makers suggest that under present-day conditions such principles as self-determination are valid in some years and not in others, or that they apply to white Poles but not to dark-skinned Africans, the disillusionment of the people in Asia, Africa, and indeed throughout most of the world, is profound."

Mr. Bowles displays not the slightest awareness of how destructive a force fanatical insistence upon "self-determination," down to the tiniest "cultural group," has been in our century; nor how this has been employed most advantageously by the tyrants of our age. In his scheme, there is no room at all for political prudence, nor for dull considerations of practical differences and limitations. The world must become one vast America — plus the Welfare State — be-

fore the decade is out. (The Welfare State, Mr. Bowles writes, also is of American origin!)

Although American society and the American economy, and a peculiar ideology of Americanism, are Mr. Bowles' pattern for a universal order, Mr. Bowles has singularly little appreciation of practical American political achievement and singularly small knowledge of American political thought. There is next to nothing about Order and Justice in Mr. Bowles' books; and by Freedom he usually means national Self-Determination, not private rights. What he seeks is not Order and Justice and Freedom, but conformity to an abstraction he calls Liberal Democracy, equalitarian and industrialized. And this Liberal Democracy does not seem to mean to Mr. Bowles the historical reality which we have known for the past century. His Liberal Democracy exists in a Utopian future. He feels some contempt for Britain and France, in their present difficulties with liberal democracy and the welfare state, and waxes impatient with America because of her stubborn attachment to prudence in politics. Where, then, are we to find our models for Liberal Democracy? This is what Mr. Bowles tells us on page 87 of *American Politics*: "In other democracies — Germany, India, Israel, Burma — where there is basic agreement upon a worthy national purpose *yet to be achieved,* there is no failure to mobilize the necessary energies and resources through the mechanisms of democracy."

So these are our models: Germany, with a pattern of government imposed by her conquerors and scarcely fifteen years old; India, dominated by a single party; Israel, the garrison-state complete; Burma, clawing at the brink of anarchy. It really would be entertaining to conjure Edwin Lawrence Godkin out of his grave and let him write a *Nation* editorial on Mr. Chester Bowles.

"Some insist that we can afford to put up with this political *sloganizing* in foreign policy," Mr. Bowles himself writes in *American Politics*. "After all, they say, the Republic has thus far survived similar sloganizing on domestic policy questions. . . . Foreigners, however, cannot reasonably be expected to play by American ground rules, and in foreign policy, we deal with foreigners. These calculated phrases, in my judgment, have cost us dear throughout the world — far more than we can easily afford." These are wise words — perhaps the only wise words in Mr. Bowles' two books. The Ambassador is referring, of course, to phrases employed by Mr. Dulles and other gentlemen who did not have the good sense to belong to Mr. Bowles' faction of Mr. Bowles' party.

True enough, there had been considerable sloganizing by members of Mr. Eisenhower's administration. To repeat political tags is so pleasant and easy — to murmur ideological cliches as if they were incantations; and it is so very painful to think seriously. And then Mr. Bowles, after this grave exhortation, proceeds to deluge his hearers and readers with as shallow and shopworn a set of slogans and god-terms as ever was em-ployed by anyone discussing American foreign policy — which is no mean feat.

If the United States should wish to make her influence detested throughout the world, her surest methods to attain this consummation would be to dispatch a naive liberal ideologue — a Wendell Willkie of the Democratic Party — globe-trotting, bestowing gratuitous counsel among the nations. Let this person tell every people to submit themselves to a recasting in the American image — that is, in F.D.R.'s concept of the American image; let him patronize and cajole revolutionary nationalists in every remote land where order is shaken; let him serve as a representative of American political authority. Let him be, in fine, Mr. Mennen Williams, or Mr. Chester Bowles. Let him talk vaguely but loudly about Liberal Democracy and Progress and Welfare States. "In this Nuclear Age," says Mr. Bowles, "without such a vision — the people perish." Without such a vision, Ambassador? Or because of it?

Ayn Rand's

"For the New Intellectual"

BRUCE   GOLDBERG

SURELY ONE OF the singularly most exciting intellectual occurrences of the last few years is that libertarianism has found a dynamic spokesman, a philosopher who seeks to discover the key to man's survival in the undeniable truth that A is A, an economist who seeks to demonstrate the superiority of capitalism by deducing it from that same truth, a moralist who defines the path to virtue as following from a single axiom — existence exists, and, in addition to all this, a novelist who makes the best-seller list of the *New York Times*. Her influence, especially on the college campus, cannot be denied, even by those who, whether on the left or the right, regard her as a knot on the tree of knowledge. Ayn Rand is unquestionably a figure to be reckoned with. Though her novels have contained philosophical passages, it has not been altogether easy to see how the various threads join. Now, her latest publication, *For the New Intellectual,* offers a selection of those passages, with an overtly philosophical introduction which places the rest of the system in perspective. At last the eager student can get some sort of overview of the intellectual edifice which is presented for his acceptance. I must say at the outset that I have not found the offering very palatable. Not, let me hasten to add, because I disagree with the conclusions —

Bruce Goldberg received his B.A. from the City College of New York and is currently doing graduate work in philosophy at Princeton University, where he holds the Proctor Fellowship.

free trade, a minimum of governmental interference in the economy, the immorality of altruism, are, I think, eminently justifiable intellectual positions. Rather it is the paucity of rational arguments, the frequency with which nonsense is offered as self-evident truth, the hysterical ranting against opponents who have had their views distorted beyond recognition, the amateurish psychologizing — in a word, the sloppiness of the whole thing, which forces me to regard it as a paradigm of philosophical incompetence. The temptation is to see it as a huge joke, a farce by means of which its creator can laugh at the gullible. But at the risk of being taken in I shall treat this book seriously, with perhaps only the popularity of the doctrine to justify the enterprise. My method shall be the following — I shall quote, sometimes at length, from the book, and then comment on the material presented.

The following passage contains, in an important sense, the core of Ayn Rand's "theory of man," i.e., a statement of the characteristics by virtue of which man is a moral agent. It is on the basis of this theory, together with certain other epistemological "truths" (which I shall consider later) that she hopes to construct a system of morality. For this reason, what Miss Rand says on this matter seems to me to deserve careful examination.

Man's consciousness shares with animals the first two stages of its development: sensations and perceptions; but it is the third stage, *conceptions*, that make him man. Sensations are integrated into perceptions automatically, by the brain of a man or of an animal. But to integrate perceptions into conceptions by a process of abstraction, is a feat that man alone has the power to perform — and he has to perform it *by choice*. The process of abstraction and of concept-formation is a process of reason, of *thought*; it is not automatic nor instinctive nor involuntary nor infallible. Man has to initiate it, to sustain it and to bear responsibility for its results. The pre-conceptual level of consciousness is non-volitional; volition begins with the first syllogism.[1]

In the first place, what are sensations and perceptions as the expressions are used here? On p. 153 the author says that "reason is the faculty that perceives, identifies and integrates the material provided by [man's] senses." But if perception is a function of reason then presumably if animals share with man the ability to perceive they too must be possessed of that faculty. Or does reason perform the perceptual function with regard to the material provided by an entity's senses if and only if that entity is a man? In this case it would seem that human and animal perception are significantly different since the former is rational while the latter is not. If this is so, then in what way are they similar? Is the similarity sufficient to call them a single stage which both animals and men go through? Briefly, either perception is a single stage which both men and animals go through or it is not. If it is then it is either rational or not. If it is a single stage which they go through and it is rational then animals are (to an extent which Ayn Rand would certainly be unwilling to admit) rational. On the other hand if it is a single stage and is not rational then the statement on p. 153 is false. Finally, if it is not a single stage (the only way out of the above dilemma) then it is not a stage which men and animals share, and the first sentence I have quoted from p. 9 is false.

---

[1] p. 9. In this, and all succeeding quotations, the italics are in the text.

Page Eighteen

A similar problem arises with the second sentence from p. 9. There it is held that sensations are integrated into perceptions automatically. But if reason is necessary for perception then reason is an automatic process (something the author repeatedly denies). However, if reason is not an automatic process and sensations are integrated into perceptions automatically then reason does not enter and again the statement on p. 153 which says it does is false.

Perhaps we can get Miss Rand out of this muddle by a terminological adjustment, using the paragraph on p. 9 to provide the clue. There it is said that reason (abstraction) enters when perceptions are integrated into conceptions. If we now identify the conceptions of p. 9 with the perceptions of p. 153 and regard "perception" on p. 9 as referring to something else entirely, the *internal* contradiction in Miss Rand's psychological theory (sic) is no more. With the hope that my house-cleaning has been of some help I let this matter rest.

Abstraction, we are told, is a process of thought which must be initiated by man. I take this to mean that an act of abstraction is volitionally produced. Since volition begins with the first syllogism it should be safe to assume that until one has gone through one's first syllogism one cannot abstract. This conclusion, I submit, is downright stupid. Often children are not able to see how the conclusion of a syllogism follows from its premises and, as anyone who has taught logic in college knows, some very mature students are not able to reason syllogistically at all. Are we to say that these latter are unable to abstract? Or even more absurdly, that they have no power of volition? As if this were not enough the author refers, on p. 152, to the first ray of light that one perceives (conceives) at the start of one's life as part of one's knowledge. Presumably what is meant is conceptual knowledge since the passage indicates that the first ray of light is regarded as on a continuum with the widest erudition one acquires in a lifetime. But how could it be conceptual knowledge? This is volitional and surely new-born infants cannot reason syllogistically. Apparently we must say either that babies *can* reason syllogistically or that the first ray of light one perceives at the start of one's life is not part of one's knowledge, in which case the statement on p. 152 is false. The choice between these two alternatives I leave as an exercise for the reader.

Miss Rand informs us that one has to *choose* to abstract. But on her own showing it should be impossible to do this. How can one choose to abstract if prior to abstracting one is not even able to form a single concept? In this pre-conceptual stage of development what reasons could there be either for abstracting or for abstaining from abstracting? Clearly there could be none. Reasons cannot be weighed by an entity which is not possessed of any concepts at all. What factors are involved in a person's choosing to abstract? Does he engage in a mental monologue like "Abstracting is really more rational than not abstracting, therefore I'll abstract"? But this is preposterous. Such a train of thought is inconceivable in an entity which does not already possess the power to abstract. The following should be patently obvious. One cannot choose to do anything until one has some notion of what it is that one is choosing to do. But such a notion could not be formed unless one could already form general concepts, i.e., until one has the ability to abstract. Apparently then, one must think (abstract) *before* one chooses to think and the prior act of thinking cannot (logically) be the product of a choice. From this dialectical mess I see no escape.

My detailed examination of this paragraph has not been without point. I hope to have illustrated, at least in part, the sloppy use of (undefined) technical terms, the lack of even a semblance of consistency, and above all, the shoddy reasoning that characterizes the writings of this lady. How ghastly must a philosophy be which is based in large measure on a paragraph such as this of which not a single sentence, not even a phrase, is true.

Miss Rand conceives herself to be warring against almost every philosophical system, past and present—and indeed she is. The enemy she regards as essentially two, designated with a dashing insight reminiscent of Harry Golden, as Attila and the Witch Doctor.[2] The former is

> the man who rules by brute force, acts on the range of the moment, is concerned with nothing but the physical reality immediately before him, respects nothing but man's muscles, and regards a fist, a club or a gun as the only answer to any problem.[3]

The latter is

> the man who dreads physical reality, dreads the necessity of practical action, and escapes into his emotions, into visions of some mystic realm where his wishes enjoy a supernatural power unlimited by the absolute of nature.[4]

Employing these "concepts" Miss Rand surveys a bit of history and the history of philosophy with an abandon and lack of concern for truth that is embarrassing. A few examples will serve to indicate what I mean.

> Plato's system was a monument to the Witch Doctor's metaphysics — with its two realities, with the physical world as a semi-illusory, imperfect, inferior realm, subordinated to a realm of *abstractions* (which means in fact, though not in Plato's statement: subordinated to man's consciousness) . . .[5]

Without condescending to discuss the relationship between Plato and Miss Rand's Witch Doctor, let us merely ask why, if the physical world is subordinated to the world of Forms (abstractions) does it follow that it is subordinated to man's consciousness. What is the justification for this statement which Miss Rand cavalierly tosses off with her characteristic disdain for logical argument? Suppose I say (and this is certainly part of what Plato meant) that the physical world is

99

---

[2] In all fairness I must bring to the attention of the reader the fact that Miss Rand is not to be held responsible for thinking of these titles, only for accepting them. She tells us in a footnote that their author is Nathaniel Branden.

[3] p. 8
[4] pp. 8-9
[5] pp. 19-20

inferior to the world of abstractions in the sense that in order to understand the nature of any physical entity one must subsume it under a universal concept. In order to understand what this object before me is I must subsume it under the general concept "table," a concept which applies not only to this object but to all other tables as well. (This, by the way, is an important part of the epistemology of Miss Rand's beloved Aristotle, whom she seems to understand no better than any of the other philosophers with whom she deals). In this sense then, the physical object, the table, is subordinated to the concept "table." Does it follow then that it is subordinated to human consciousness (an expression I take to mean dependent for its existence on some human beings perceiving it)? How does one get to the conclusion Miss Rand has drawn? I must confess that the connection remains a mystery to me. Perhaps it was an oversight, a slip, a free association . . . but I move on.

> Philosophy (in the Middle Ages) existed as a "handmaiden of theology," and the dominant influence was, appropriately, Plato's in the form of Plotinus and Augustine. Aristotle's works were lost to the scholars of Europe for centuries. The prelude to the Renaissance was the return of Aristotle via Thomas Aquinas.[6]

Miss Rand is either misinformed or else has allowed the demands of simplicity to take precedence over those of truth. The passage I have quoted gives the impression that Aristotle was unknown to or at least had no influence on medieval philosophers before St. Thomas. The slightest acquaintance with the writings of Boethius or Abelard or St. Thomas' teacher Albertus Magnus, would be sufficient to convince one of the falsity of Miss Rand's historical reporting. Again, she seems to attribute the doctrine that philosophy is the handmaiden of theology to the influence of Plato. But St. Thomas, in whom the influence of Aristotle was certainly greater than that of Plato, preached precisely this doctrine. As an historian I am admittedly a layman, but even my unpracticed eye can

---

[6] p. 21.

Page Twenty

detect that Miss Rand's historical writing is, not to be unkind, in need of improvement.

I pass over the offensive attack on Descartes with its irritating equivocations and groundless conclusions. Miss Rand's technique of vilification is most apparent when she turns to Hume, who is dismissed, without any rational argument at all, in two malicious paragraphs. A sample:

> When Hume declared that the apparent existence of an object did not guarantee that it would not vanish spontaneously next moment, and the sunrise of today did not prove that the sun would rise tomorrow . . . what men were hearing was the manifesto of a philosophical movement that can be designated only as Attila-ism.[7]

Does Miss Rand think that the *apparent* existence of an object guarantees that it will not vanish in the next moment? Does the fact that there is *apparently* a pink rat in the path of a drunkard guarantee that there will continue to be a pink rat in that path? Not only Hume but every sane person would answer this question negatively. And yet Miss Rand regards this as part of the manifesto of Attila-ism. And yet perhaps not. I do want to be fair to this lady. There seems to be, in the next phrase, a way out of the absurdity at which we have just arrived. Suppose we attribute the argument about apparent existence to sloppy formulation or something of the sort. The remark about the sunrise seems to be of sterner stuff so let us remain a moment with it. The problem toward which Miss Rand seems to be fumbling is the traditional philosophical problem of induction and it is Hume's view on this problem that she regards as evil. What is his view? Briefly, without introducing too much technical philosophical terminology, it is this. Hume distinguished between two sorts of propositions, those which express relations of ideas and those which express matters of fact. An example of the former is "A bachelor is an unmarried man." Such

---

[7] pp. 29-30. A few other doctrines are also held to be Hume's but their attribution to him is too silly to be worth comment.

a statement cannot possibly be false. As soon as one understands the meaning of the constituent expressions one understands that the statement is necessarily true. Its truth is absolutely certain. On the other hand, a statement expressing a matter of fact, such as "There is a table in the next room" can never be known with absolute certainty. (What I have just said is not a completely accurate rendering of Hume's view — of his distinction between philosophical and unphilosophical probability—but it will suffice here.) What Hume means by saying that propositions expressing matters of fact can never be known with absolute certainty is that their denial is not self-contradictory. There is no contradiction in either affirming or denying the statement "There is a table in the next room" while there is in affirming "A bachelor is a married man." Now he asks, is there a contradiction involved in saying "The sun rose today but it will not rise tomorrow." Since there is none, the fact that the sun rose today does not entail that it will rise tomorrow. Consider: A. The sun rose today; B. The sun will rise tomorrow. The first could be true while the second is false — therefore the truth of the first does not prove the truth of the second. Whatever one thinks of this argument, and I personally do not think it is correct, it is certainly not morally evil. But even further — and this is what irritates — what reasons does Miss Rand bring forth to persuade the reader that Hume is wrong? Not a one. Instead we are treated to still another of her nasty snears: "If it were possible for an animal to describe the content of his consciousness the result would be a transcript of Hume's philosophy."[8] This is indeed the very zenith of intellectual putrefaction. It might be worthwhile at this point to contrast Miss Rand's opinion of the great Scottish philosopher with that of a man who does occupy an important place in the libertarian tradition. Adam Smith, the philosopher's great friend, said this of him after his death: "Upon the whole, I have always considered him, both in his lifetime, and since his death, as approach-

ing as nearly to the idea of a perfectly wise and virtuous man, as perhaps the nature of human frailty will admit."[9]

Miss Rand's discussion of Kant is too puerile to be worthy of much discussion. The following is characteristic:

> His argument, in essence, ran as follows: man is *limited* to a consciousness of a specific nature, which perceives by specific means and no others, therefore, his consciousness is not valid; man is blind, because he has eyes — deaf, because he has ears — deluded, because he has a mind — and the things he perceives do not exist, *because* he perceives them.[10]

Where is the support for this sickening display of ill-concealed fabrication? Where did this hate blinded woman find Kant saying anything like what she attributes to him? One can only conclude that she either has never read Kant or else is deliberately misrepresenting him for her own ends. Again and again, in reading Ayn Rand, suffocating in her invective, one feels like crying out "Disagree if you want to, if you must, disagree even if you don't understand—but be honest!"

Again, in discussing Kant's morality Miss Rand is guilty of misinterpretation. She argues that, according to Kant, an action is moral only if one has no desire to perform it. This is simply false, though it must be admitted here that even some philosophers have made the same mistake Miss Rand makes (although none, I should add, have made it in quite so nasty a way).[11]

Hegel, Marx, Comte, Spencer, Nietzsche, and Bentham share similar fates at Miss Rand's hands. (If ever I felt sympathetic to Marx it was when I read her account

101

---

[9] Letter from Adam Smith to William Strahan. The entire text of the letter may be found in the Open Court Publishing Co. edition of Hume's *Enquiry Concerning Human Understanding* or on p. 604 of Ernest Campbell Mossner's *The Life of David Hume* (Thomas Nelson & Sons, 1954).

[10] p. 33.

[11] For those who are interested in what Kant really said, a scholarly and highly critical account is contained in H. J. Paton's *The Categorical Imperative* (Hutchinson's University Library, 1946). Paton discusses Miss Rand's error (though not, of course, with reference to the fact that she made it) on pp. 48-50.

[8] p. 30.

of his philosophy—no one, not even Marx, deserves this.) Finally we come to "the combined neo-mystic Witch-Doctory and Attila-ism of the Logical Positivists."[12] One turns the page expecting to find another victim in the tragical-comical-historical-pastoral existentialists but no such luck. The mood has changed and we are now instructed as eager aspirants to the club of New Intellectuals as to what to do to overcome the legacy of our wretched past, whose ills have been paraded before us.

I WANT TO TURN my attention now from the introduction to the last hundred pages of *For the New Intellectual* which, Miss Rand indicates, contain the essentials of her philosophy. Here, one hopes, will be a reasonably integrated set of arguments. But again the expectant reader is disappointed, for this section of the book, too, is filled with the same sort of fustian tirades against the enemy concerning which I have already commented. Here though, it must be admitted, it is decidedly more difficult to prove that the author is guilty of distortion, for while the introduction at least contained proper names which made Miss Rand's errors apparent, the enemy here remains anonymous. The mention of alien doctrines is generally prefaced by "you are told" or "they proclaim," the "they's" being "cheap little hypocrites" (p. 175), "college professors" (p. 196), "grotesque little atavists" (p. 208), "mystics" (two varieties—muscle and spirit *passim.*), "parasites" (p. 202), "sniveling neurotics" (p. 180), and "zero-worshippers" (p. 166). On occasion, though, there are clues as to who "they" really are and the interested reader might hazard a guess here and there.[13] If this exercise fails to make the arguments any more cogent it does provide a bit of much needed diversion.

---

12 p. 36.

13 I suggest as a start that the reader identify the mystics of muscle in this section with the Attila-people of the introduction and the mystics of the spirit with the Witch Doctors. If this results in no increase in clarity it might be tried the other way round.

For the present I want to ignore the assault on the enemy and examine very briefly selected doctrines which Miss Rand regards as essential ingredients in her own philosophy. An important word of qualification is necessary. The section of *For the New Intellectual* under consideration here is excerpted from Miss Rand's most recent novel *Atlas Shrugged*. With this in mind it is difficult for a reviewer to decide on the proper standards to employ in its criticism. On the one hand one may acknowledge that it is, after all, from a novel and regard it as a kind of literary exercise, a bit of *malslettres*. On the other hand, it is explicitly represented by its author as a presentation of her philosophy. Viewing it in this light would necessitate a critique employing the same standards which are proper to the examination of any other work of philosophy. I have chosen the latter alternative.

Man's life is the *standard* of morality, but your own life is its *purpose*.

. . . every man is an end in itself, he exists for his own sake, and the achievement of his own happiness is his highest moral purpose.

It is for the purpose of self-preservation that man needs a code of morality.

His own happiness is man's only moral purpose . . .[14]

What is one to conclude from these four statements? The first and third tell us that life (self-preservation) is the purpose of morality, while the second and fourth tell us that man's happiness is. Perhaps the contradiction has only an apparent existence and we can make it vanish semi-spontaneously by saying that life and happiness are the same thing. But this cannot be, for on p. 161 the author states that "happiness is the goal and the reward of life." Happiness and life then are different. Which is the purpose of morality? Are they both? This would be consistent with the statement from p. 150 which says only that happiness is the *highest* moral purpose. Certainly it could be the highest moral purpose with life playing the role of a

---

14 pp. 149, 150, 151, 161.

secondary, lower order purpose. But this won't do, since the statement on p. 161 expresses the "truth" that happiness is man's *only* moral purpose. One final attempt. Perhaps happiness is *man's* only moral purpose and life is *morality's* purpose. But this would be at best a sophistical solution. Surely to say that morality has a purpose is only an elliptical way of saying what *human* purposes morality serves. Morality is not the name of an entity which has purposes of its own. But if the purpose of morality is to keep people alive then presumably the purpose of a human being in being moral is life, which may lead to, but is certainly a different thing from, happiness. I cannot but regard Ayn Rand's pronouncements on the purpose of morality as hopelessly muddled. A parenthetical remark—generally when one says that a given thing is the highest of its type there are other things of that type which have a lower status. But if happiness is man's only moral purpose how can it also be man's highest moral purpose?

The root of Ayn Rand's moral code is to be found on p. 152. It is "the axiom that *existence exists*." How a moral code can rest on this "axiom" must surely be one of the sublimer truths of nature. This statement, unlike most of the others in the book, does not even have the merit of being false for, like "The Nothing noughts" of Heidegger fame, it is a patent piece of nonsense. Tables exist, people exist, but what sense does it make to say that existence exists? Is existence another thing, like tables and people which exists in its own right in addition to them? To say that existence exists is like saying that length is long or that circularity is round or that the truth is true.[15] The expression "existence exists" is a meaningless piece of verbiage which cannot be the root of anything. Yet this is what we are offered as the foundation of a moral code, this is what justified the spiteful insults hurled at Hume and Kant — but I must hold my tongue.

---

15 Indeed, on p. 216 Miss Rand assures us that the truth *is* true.

Even with all the irrationality contained in these pages it is, I think, most depressing of all when Miss Rand sets up a straw-man and then, by her ignorance of the most elementary logical principles, fails even to damage the caricature she has constructed.

If you search your code for guidance, for an answer to the question: "What *is* the good?"— the only answer you will find is *"The good of others."* . . . Your standard of virtue is not an object, not an act, not a principle, but an *intention.* You need no proof, no reasons, no success, you need not achieve in fact the good of others, —all you need to know is that your motive was the good of others, *not* your own. Your only definition of the good is a negation the good is the "non-good for me."[16]

Miss Rand has transformed the principle "The good of others" which is itself hardly an accurate rendering of the utilitarian principle, into the non-good for me. These two expressions are not at all synonymous nor are they logically equivalent. "X is good for non-me" does not mean the same as "X is non-good for me." The first doesn't even imply the second. Isn't it obvious that something can be both good for non-me *and* good for me — a free enterprise economy for example.

The rest of these hundred pages contains more of the same. I say in all honesty that I have never read a book (and I am not excluding *The Affluent Society*) which contained more contradictions and misstatements than this one. "Accept the fact that you are not omniscient . . . that your mind is fallible . . ." "Discard that unlimited license to evil which consists of claiming that man is imperfect."[17] Here I need only assure the doubters that Ayn Rand does indeed recommend both of these courses of action.

---

16 pp. 176-78. "Your code" here is utilitarianism, my evidence being the last sentence of the preceding paragraph in which the author speaks of a code whose major principle is the greatest good for the greatest number.

17 Both of these statements occur on page 224.

For the New Intellectual is an intolerably bad book. More than that it is a silly book; street corner rabble rousing can affect only the vulgar. That it should have come from the pen of the author of *The Fountainhead,* which is a genuinely fine novel, is not a little surprising. But as unfortunate as this book is, it would be even more unfortunate if it came to be regarded by anybody as a representative sample of libertarian thought. How easily the Left could shatter capitalism if this were its only defense! Fortuneately the superiority of free-enterprise *can* be demonstrated. But while von Mises, Hayek, and Friedman, to name only a few, make for more difficult reading and demand greater attentiveness than does Ayn Rand, the reward justifies the effort.

It is not difficult to understand the attraction Ayn Rand has for the uninstructed. She appears, I suppose, to be the spokesman for freedom, for self-esteem, and other equally noble ideals. However, patient examination reveals her pronouncements to be but a shroud beneath which lies the corpse of illogic. Those who are concerned with discovering the principles of a sound social philosophy can read and study libertarian thought at its best. The ludicrously mistitled *"philosophy* of Ayn Rand" is a sham. To those who are travelling her road I can only suggest its abandonment —for that way madness lies.

104

IN MEMORIAM

To those Hungarian students who gave their lives in the cause of liberty.

October — November
1956

Herbert Butterfield:

Christian Historian as

Creative Critic

LEONARD LIGGIO

HERBERT BUTTERFIELD, Professor of Modern History at the University of Cambridge, is generally recognized as the leading British historian whose writings reflect a Christian attitude. While Butterfield's application of such an attitude to the methodology of history and to the writing of British political history is familar, its application to international relations and to the history of diplomacy remains unknown to historians and to the educated public. Butterfield's views are scattered throughout his books on a variety of historical subjects, but, within his works certain topics and themes recur, allowing for the present investigation of his position on these questions.

Professor Butterfield has devoted much of his career to the study of historiography. This has led him to criticize what he refers to as "official history," the interpretation of foreign relations in a sense which would be favorable to a particular government and the interpretation of internal developments in a sense which would be favorable to the dominant world-view within one's society. Official history has its roots in "the arrogance of the modern pagan mythology of righteousness." The modern state and its historians have reverted to the legalism and Pharisaism which assumes "the primeval thesis: 'We are the righteous

ones and the enemy are wicked'." Official history imagines that

> masses of men on the one side have freely opted for wickedness, while on the other side there is a completely righteous party, whose virtue is superior to conditioning circumstances. The reasons for suspecting such a diagram of the situation are greatly multiplied if the ethical judgment is entangled with a political one — if, for example, the wickedness is charged against a rival political party, or imputed to another nation just at the moment when, for reasons of power politics, that nation is due to stand as the potential enemy in any case."

Lacking the urbanity and the charity of Christianity, official history plunges into the pseudo-moral judgments which the modern state, by its nature, passes upon other states and which the dominant intellectual position passes upon what lies outside the mainstream. "In any case, in the world of pseudo-moral judgments there is generally a tendency on the one hand to avoid the higher regions of moral reflection and on the other hand to make moral issues out of what are not really moral issues at all." Interacting with this myth-making has been what Butterfield refers to as an attitude of fear and suspicion. They are "not merely facts in the story, standing on a level with a lot of other factors. They give a certain quality to human life

Leonard Liggio is an historian living in New York City.

in general, condition the nature of politics, and imprint their character on diplomacy and foreign policy."

Butterfield indicates that the historian who is a Christian is obliged to assume a position in sharp contrast to the "pagan righteousness-myth" which is basic to official history. Not only may the Christian not judge others, but he must also make a special effort to appreciate and understand the positions of other peoples and other governments or of elements which stand outside the intellectually dominant framework. Thus, "the proper study of history requires a certain giving of ourselves — requires, in fact, that we shall do something with our personalities. What society needs is every possible variation and extension of the art of putting one's self — actually feeling one's self — in the other person's place." Further, the Christian, since he is obliged to be aware of his own personality, must be made conscious of the role of fear in human activity, which it is so natural to overlook, and must "recapture the fear, and the attendant high pressure, which so greatly affect the actions of men and the policy of governments." "Yet . . . the historian, surveying the past (like the statesman surveying rival powers in his own contemporary world), is apt to do less than justice to the part played by fear in politics, at any rate so far as concerns governments other than his own." In the face of the complete development in the twentieth century of the righteousness-myth and the domination of fear, the historian who is a Christian must make a creative response to "the real test of moral courage: namely, the exposure and the condemnation of our own sins as a nation and an empire."

The strength of official history lies in three sources: the increasing influence of governments, the uncritical acceptance of authorities, and the nature of historical writing itself. The official historians are not merely the historians who work directly for the government or for a political interest, or even "that new class of so-called 'independent historians' who have first to submit their scripts to the check or censorship," directly or indirectly, of some government

agent. There are also those historians who are connected with government or party through friendships and similar backgrounds. Butterfield believes "that nothing could be more subtle than the influence upon historians of admission to the charmed circle," within which a certain "auto-censorship" occurs. Even beyond that circle "a well-run State needs no heavy-handed censorship, for it binds the historian with soft charms and with subtle, comfortable chains." Since "the relations of a government with historical study are on a different footing from those which exist in the case of any of the other sciences, it is necessary for the outside student, therefore, always to be on his guard." Where freedom in the expression of thought exists, an independent science of history, an academic history, should develop standing over against the dominant political or intellectual position, but "such an independent science of history would always tend to find the dice loaded against it for the time being."

Butterfield feels that the purposes of official history are served by the tendency that "the reading of history has become less critical than it once was, the reviewing of books less scientific, and the faith in accepted 'authorities' more unthinking." Specialization has narrowed the range from which effective criticism can emerge and might result in the formation of a compact body of major historians who, from the nature of the situation, would become the official historians. Butterfield states:

> The tendency to look for an historian who will serve as an "authority" is one which seems to have increased during my lifetime, though history is a realm in which trust is the enemy of truth . . . I am not sure that the professionalizing of history has not resulted in the unconscious development of authoritarian prejudices among the professionals themselves; and it could happen that by 1984, if readers are not their own critics, a whole field of study might become the monopoly of a group or party, all reviewing one another and standing shoulder to shoulder in order to stifle the discrepant idea, the new intellectual system, or the warning voice of the skeptic.

107

Unlike mathematics which begins with the simplest things and proceeds in turn to the more complex, history starts with the studying of the most complex things, of broad generalizations, with the result that "the mere reading of history, the mere process of accumulating more information in this field, does not necessarily give training to a mind that was initially diffuse." Rather, it initiates "all kinds of generalizations, formulas, nicknames and analogies which answer to men's wishful thinking; and these come into currency without having to be submitted to any very methodical kind of test." These broad generalizations are the result of the abridgment of history which the necessities of teaching or of simple expression in conversation and in writing often seem to require. Butterfield does not think that it is a coincidence that this abridgment has worked to the advantage of official history, since "the total result of this method is to impose a certain form upon the whole historical story, and to produce a scheme of general history which is bound to converge beautifully upon the present — all demonstrating throughout the ages the working of an obvious principle of progress." Abridgment tends to make our present political system or our country an absolute and imparts an impression of the inevitability of the existing system or of a war, since it neglects the alternatives which exist at each point and which indicate the relativity of the existing political system or the foreign policy of our country.

BUTTERFIELD SUGGESTS that modern international relations represents the "tragic element in human conflict," in which the central fact "is a certain predicament, a certain situation that contains the elements of conflict irrespective of any special wickedness in any of the parties concerned." "What is required," he goes on, "is that we should stretch our imagination to the point of envisaging this particular international predicament in a purer form than either it or anything else ever exists in history." Such an abstraction of the irreducible

dilemma would postulate two groups of states each locked inside its system of righteousness, each moved by reasonable national self-interest, each desirous of avoiding a war, but each fearful, each desperately unsure about the intentions of the other party.

Suppose you have such a situation, and then one party to the predicament becomes over-exasperated and makes too willful a decision; suppose in particular that he does it because he thinks that somebody must take a strong line at last; and we will say that he even intends to bluff, but the bluff does not come off and so a greater war is brought about.

The origin lies in the predicament and not in the action of the man. Because the predicament is irreducible, the mind seeks an answer elsewhere, such as charges that the enemy is unrighteous. The diplomacy of righteousness says that this predicament does not exist, or, which is to them the same thing, that it should not exist. But the fundamental problem exists irrespective of the morality or ideology of each side.

In the midst of the predicament which Butterfield describes, it is difficult for people to conceive how two mutually hostile systems can achieve a relaxation of tension. It appears outside the range of possibility. But, Butterfield tells us, it would be wrong to rule out this possibility in advance because there have been similar irreducible conflicts in the past where it was possible to achieve a relaxation of absolute deadlocks. A function of the historian in such a period of crisis is to methodically analyze other periods of history which have achieved a relaxation of tension—a *detente*. Butterfield believes that the wars of religion "provide perhaps the closest analogy to the conflicts of the twentieth century," and that the Reformation period "presents the classical example of extreme tension followed by ultimate *detente*." He recalls that the conflict of that period seems strange to us because its underlying assumptions are not understood today, having lost their importance in the face of the tensions which the assumptions produced. The possibility of religious toleration was not realized, and

108

"above all, it was unthinkable that two forms of the Christian religion could co-exist within a given country." But, once the positions of stability which arose from the predicament were achieved, there was a tendency for people to actively desire its continuation. People began to work at those elements which would maintain that stability — acceptance of the principle of toleration which would transpose the conflict into the realm of persuasion, and the conduct of international relations in a way conducive to international order.

Butterfield is convinced that the historian who is a Christian is especially able to contribute to the analysis and understanding of international relations because he is "more interested in the processes and patterns of long-term history, in the principles that underlie foreign policy, in the ethical issues involved (particularly as they concern the Christian), and in the role of Christianity during an epoch of global revolution." In the first place, the role of the Christian in studying international affairs is enhanced by the fact that a certain amount of worldly wisdom has gathered around the Christian tradition and stands as a part of European civilization, especially of the tradition of European diplomacy. Since much of this wisdom has been secularized in its absorption into European civilization, there has been a tendency to lose sight of some of the Christian attitudes upon which they are based. As a result, the Christian can serve as a guardian of the elements of continuity in Western civilization and can prevent inflexible interpretations of them by the secular world which is unfamiliar with the underlying Christian attitudes. Since "Christianity in its essence is a risky religion, packed with the kind of ethical implications that are dangerous to *status quo's,* established regimes, and reigning systems," these Christian attitudes are capable of contributing to a breakthrough of the conventional framework of contemporary thinking on foreign affairs. The truths of Christianity are conducive to independence in thought and place the Christian in a position to achieve new perspectives and, by "not turning any mundane programme or temporal ideal into the absolute of absolutes — the Christian has it in his power to be more flexible in respect to all subordinate matters." The realization that Christ "calls men to constant self-criticism" and that Christians must confess themselves to be sinners requires Christians not to "assume too easily that their morality is identical with that of the political world in general." The Christian has principles — "the treatment of love, the insistence on humility, the attitude to human personality and the doctrine of sin . . . which can rescue him from the blindness of mere partisanship" and can give him a genuine understanding of the views of another person, group or country. Butterfield considers the Christian capable of contributing to international relations "those forms of intellectual explorations which are accessible only to men in a certain frame of mind, to human beings in love, human beings willing to make fools of themselves for love."

THE CHRISTIAN is alive to the failure of pacifism, militarism, the maintenance of the *status quo* or world government to solve the tragic predicament, and is able to move in directions which will be immediately more productive. While Butterfield agrees "that passive suffering and the willingness to be a martyr seem ultimately to move the world more than the resolution which meets force with force," and that eventually "the voluntary suffering of the pacifist might be the only lantern for the re-discovery of even the things which we call human values," he disagrees with those who withdraw their country from international affairs through complete unilateral disarmament. It would be wrong for pacifists to seek to impose such a disarmament on their fellow-citizens so long as those citizens do not impose on them contributions to armaments expenditures. In any case, whenever true pacifism emerges, Butterfield presumes "that Christians would protect it in vindication of conscience, and guard it as the kind of treasure which keeps its value when all prudential caluculations fail." Butterfield suggests that the best way in which a Christian can mitigate the effectiveness of power and limit its role in history is by that spiritual and intellectual influence which, "quietly penetrating free minds, acts as the leaven which leavens the whole lump."

Self-satisfied reliance upon a strong defense posture is not conducive to peace. Fear of our weapons by a prospective enemy will not maintain peace because "it is fear more than anything else which is the cause of war. Until very recently we ourselves had not lost the realization of the fact that mounting armaments, because they intensified fear and poisoned human relations, operated rather to provoke war than to prevent it." Much thought must be placed upon matters over and above the question of self-defense, which is something which may be pushed too far, as Butterfield indicates a supreme leader of Christianity has suggested. The paganism at the root of the "war for righteousness" has led to the psychology of total war. "The Christian doctrine of love, however, does have one important consequence which goes to the root of this type of superstition; for it carries the implication that war as a mere holocaust — war as a useless demonstration against sin — would be absolutely inexcusable."

In relation to those who would use the hydrogen bomb to secure justice, extend liberty or preserve Western civilization, Butterfield thinks that it should be clear that "the destructiveness which some people are now prepared to contemplate is not to be justified for the sake of any conceivable mundane object, any purported religious claim or supramundane purpose, or any virtue that one system of organization can possess against another." When faced with

a question of a war which would destroy mankind, or in which the effects of victory would be the same as the effects of defeat — then those people who argue that even such a war must be fought, that mankind must put itself on the altar, that we must destroy everything for a so-called righteousness of this particular sort, are not following either

Christian charity or the ordinances of Providence. What they are following is a pagan myth of righteousness; they are sacrificing mankind to the daemonic forces. In fact, there is an essential conflict, as there was in the Gospels, between Christian charity and another view of righteousness which survives from ancient dark mythologies.

The contemporary confusion of Christian with pagan elements has resulted in "a more high-powered mischief than either of the attitudes when taken separately; the corruption of the best becomes worse than anything else." Butterfield proposes that the countries who stand in direct descent from Christian civilization should take the initiative to resolve not to use or further manufacture such weapons, notwithstanding that this resolution will not be believed.

There is so great risk in having the hydrogen bomb that there can hardly be greater risk if we unplug the whole system, and if our governments refuse to have anything to do with the weapon. Even if there were, the radical difference in the quality of these risks would cancel it.

Since 1919, when the victorious Western powers systematized the international situation in such a way that any act to revise it or re-establish just relationships could be characterized as "aggression," the defense of the *status quo* has become the major means of increasing the role and scope of war. The flexibility which should be natural to the Christian in relation to mere temporal arrangements has special reference to the problems arising from the territorial and imperial *status quo*. Butterfield thinks that it is encumbent upon Christians that they realize that in international affairs, as in other aspects of life, one may share a partial responsibility for what may seem like the sins of others.

There are a number of ways in which we ourselves may provide aggression, or may so behave that we give occasion for sin. As defenders of the existing order of things, we may be committing a crime if we disdain protests and appeals from states which at the moment are not backed by power.

Dr. Butterfield indicates that in the nineteenth century statesmen recognized that responsibility for desperate resorts to violence must be attached to those who, allowing no real means of redress, strongly defend the *status quo,* and the great Western powers especially objected even to the use of international machinery to interfere with the revision of treaties or with revolutions. But, although the formation of international organizations since 1919 has given the appearance of the establishment of machinery to achieve equal justice, the real result has been "that we have devised no satisfactory machinery for the peaceful revision of the *status quo.* The new machinery tended to freeze this more definitely than the old had been able to do." The tendency of these international organizations has been the idealistic attempt to remove the unpleasant aspects of power politics, while the great powers continue to enjoy, unidealistically, the benefits acquired in the past centuries by power politics. These unjust benefits have been covered with the same cloak of international law which is supposed to bring harmony to international relations. Since the justice of revisionist demands can be screened by legalisms, "it is easier for some governments to be virtuous than for others, because the course of virtue happens to coincide with the requirements of self-interest."

AT THE BASIS of this recent situation has been the growth of legalism in international affairs and the increase of lawyers in international negotiations. This development is not without relation to the fact that recent international relations have been characterized by a legalistic mood of righteousness, and it is dangerous because "the legal mind is liable to be too rigid in the acts of judgment required." "Because there has been a tendency to take refuge in legalism, it would seem that those who desire revision can always be made to appear as aggressors." But, as Butterfield indicates, the so-called aggressor "may only be conscious of protesting against established injustices such as the other powers (and,

even in recent decades, the League of Nations itself) had often been prepared to leave untouched, out of regard for vested interests."

Under these circumstances, Butterfield thinks that it is necessary to recall the role which violence and the threat of violence played in traditional diplomacy: "to produce those marginal rectifications in the system which the system had been unable to achieve by its own automatic apparatus." In the twentieth century, the system has become even less automatic, much more frozen. "In the imperfect state of our international order, it is clear that it requires an act of violence to secure that a topic is in any effective sense put on the agenda at all." Even readiness to negotiate on the part of the possessing powers does not exclude the necessity of using those acts which we have associated with force and aggression, because once a topic is on the agenda there is no reason to concede anything in negotiations. Thus, "force is needed to jerk our attention (or the attention of the world) to the need for change in the *status quo.*"

> If, therefore, the Western powers have had to retreat after a violent demonstration or before the threat of violence, we ought not to regard this as necessarily a reverse or a cause of shame. It is rather a proof that, once we have been stung to attention, we are ready to listen to justice or make a concession to reasonableness.

Butterfield rejects the view that international organizations or a world government are the solution to the tragic predicament. Reference to an international conference does not solve the problem, it merely changes its position.

> Where the conflict is really a cutthroat one it seems to me that the conference method does not put an end to the predicament but merely changes the locality and the setting of it. The whole method is liable to break down if either the Communists or the non-Communists can be fairly sure in advance that on critical issues the other party is going to have the majority.

Even neglecting the fact that the long-run tendency of world government would

111

be to become frozen and to limit human freedom or that its misjudgment could universalize the disaster, such a system cannot make the world immune from total war. Butterfield recalls that the most terrible instance of such a war before 1914 was a conflict between one half of the United States and the other. Even should we have a world-state, civil wars would still be possibilities. Attempting to control and conceal conflicts, rather than to relax them, a world government is most likely to become an agency for aggrandizement of one set of interests against another.

In the realm of persuasion which can replace the predicament of conflict, the role of the Christian will increase in importance. In such a period, the missionary spirit of Christianity will be a vital counter-balance to the missionary spirit of Marxism. Under such conditions Butterfield suggests that it is important for Christians to realize what it is that they are confronting. Much of the ideological impact which Communism can make derives from elements which are essentially Western. Just as its anti-religious elements comes from the West so also do the more productive elements. The essentially Western character of Marxism means that it is performing a service of Westernizing large portions of the world "more radically in a few decades than Western Europe has managed to do in the course of centuries." Butterfield emphasizes the importance of knowing to what degree the evils which we face at the present time are due to heresies from an original liberalism which characterizes both the Marxist and the democratic systems. He wonders if Communism, due to its Western origins,

> does not possess colossal potentialities for future liberty—a liberty that we must not expect to be achieved before an international *detente* has made it more possible to have a relaxation at home. . . . all systems are going to move in the direction of liberty, if only somebody will open a window so that the world can breathe a more relaxed air and we can end the dominion of fear. If, however, we are unable to achieve this, the very measures which we are taking to preserve liberty in the world are bound to lead to the loss of liberty even in the regions that most prize it. They are bound — if we go on intensifying them — to make us become, in fact, more and more like the thing we are opposing.

> It may be a prejudice of mine, but I wonder whether Christians, if they could disentangle their minds from the conventional mundane systems that constrict them, might not within a decade contribute something creative to this deeper cause of human understanding.

One may conclude by wondering whether Butterfield has not gone far in fulfilling his own "prejudice."

The works of Herbert Butterfield which relate most directly to the topics dicussed in this article are: *Christianity and History*, (1949); *History and Human Relations*, (1951); *Christianity in European History*, (1952); *Christianity, Diplomacy and War*, (1953); *International Conflict in the Twentieth Century, a Christian View*, (1960).

An Approach for Conservatives

ROGER CLAUS

THE CONSERVATIVE magazine published at the University of Wisconsin, *Insight and Outlook,* carries a monthly feature, *The Nature of the Struggle,* of which I am in charge. Much of this feature is devoted to discussion as to how we may best conduct ourselves in the war of ideas. The result of my analysis of conservative methodology will constitute the subject of this brief essay; I want to discuss methods that can and will work, and I will discuss some which can never work. But first, the problem.

Our problem, both domestic and foreign, was thrust clearly into focus on that day nine months ago when Presidential Assistant Arthur Schlesinger, Jr., stated that *"the best defense against Communism is the Welfare State."* The problem was examined closely in the lead editorial of the March issue of *Insight and Outlook.*

Editor Gale Pfund wrote: "The Soviet Union is scoring victory after victory in the cold war, quite basically because of our own *moral indecision,* which prevents our taking a firm stand against the demands of Mr. Khrushchev. We, as a nation, have not firmly decided which system, capitalism or communism, ought to prevail. Ostensibly, we brandish our swords against an enemy whose avowed methods and purposes represent everything we abhor, but in reality we pursue policies more closely akin to *his* ideal than our own. We have overburd-

Roger Claus is a recent graduate of the University of Wisconsin where he was President of the Conservative Club and an Associate Editor of its publication, *Insight and Outlook.* The above article was adapted by him from a speech delivered to a conservative meeting in Chicago.

ened private property and private ownership of the means of production with government regulations and controls. We have convinced ourselves of the equitability of the progressive income tax (which in the U.S.S.R. isn't nearly as graduated as our own), the advisability of government handouts, the morality of federal social control, and the expediency of government intervention in the economy and federal manipulation of the money supply. *All of which* is closer to Karl Marx than Adam Smith.

"Although we do not necessarily hold the philosophical assumptions of historical and dialectical materialism, we nevertheless pattern our social and economic behavior directly upon the collectivist ideal. How can a nation, whose compromise with welfarism is more in sympathy with the communist ideal than the American, make a firm moral resolve that Western institutions ought to prevail and are ultimately worth fighting for? How can the United States stand up against a government whose strength and determination are unparalleled in the history of the world?

"In my time, it hasn't been able to do either. The moral irresolve of the West is pitted against the maniacal fanaticism of those in the Kremlin who labor day and night under the absolute conviction that communism is the *only* proper system of political, social, and economic organization.

"We are asking the Free World to join us in a cause, the merits of which we are still not firmly convinced. The Soviets, on the other hand, profess their beliefs with admirable solidarity and firmness,

113

and with an unwavering ideological consistency even more appealing to some nations than free American dollars."

This, then, is the problem; this is what Lenin foresaw 38 years ago when he wrote that they would never have to attack the U. S. . . . it would fall like an overripe fruit into their hands. He foresaw the day when our Republic would abound with active anti-communists who would, at the same time, fall for such subtle claptrap as the multitudinous government planning schemes for full employment, protectionism in the tariff field, minimum wage laws, support of small business, and "cradle-to-grave" social security.

What I want to do is to tell something about what a small group of students at the University of Wisconsin is doing about this dilemma. We have found a way, and I shall attempt to convince you that it is the *best* way.

Ever since *Time* and the AP mentioned our activities I have been deluged with letters asking the same question. "How do we escape being flunked for our political activity?" Although this is a bit strong, what they really mean is, "How do we, in a hotbed of 'liberalism,' escape adverse comment and reprisal for our activity?" To wit, how do we escape being called "neanderthals," "extremists," and "reactionary know-nothings?" My answer to them is this:

Ever since the Conservative Club was formed, we have bent every effort to keep it on the highest possible intellectual plane. Our magazine is scholarly and educational; it does not rant and bait. Our speakers are the best that intellectual conservatism can produce; we have not brought a single soapbox orator whose mission would be to pour fire and hell on the leftists. Our library contains the great works of conservative scholars; we keep the inflammatory pamphlets out.

What is the result of an approach of this sort? Well, when we were first organized, I knew what was running through the minds of many of the left-wing faculty. They thought that within a few years we would die out. Or, they expected that we would hop on every extreme movement that happened along,

whereupon they would be able to laugh us handily out of existence. Neither came true. Serious students of political science admired our studied approach to this new and unpopular conservatism. The more timorous came forward because we were eminently respectable. The professors were silenced because we demonstrated more regard for the true meaning of academic freedom than they did. In fact, many of them were badly shaken because they could see clearly the viability of our approach to the war of ideas.

Here is another result of this tack: the best way to win any argument is to know more about your opponent's subject than he himself does. From my own experience, I have found that it pays to know more about socialism than most socialists; it pays to know more about Communism than any left-winger I've met; it pays to have learned one's anti-communism, not from lurid depictions of internal conspiracies, but from long hours spent pouring over the works of Marx and Lenin. In short, we have done the impossible. *We have restored the conservative point-of-view to respectability.* And if any of you have any hopes of our cause catching on solidly across the nation, *you will have to demonstrate more regard for the intellectuals than many conservatives have been willing to do thus far.*

At this point you may be wondering: how can I be so positive that this method is best? Before I answer that, I will tender my thumbnail definition of a conservative, and point out its application here. The conservative holds each new innovation up against a yardstick composed of that which has proven worthwhile, viable and moral in the history and traditions of western civilization. In the adjacent sense, the conservative strives to keep what is good and workable and moral while striving to repeal and throw out what is proving to be harmful — by that same yardstick.

Now then, the *intellectual* approach to the promulgation of an ideology has given us a perfect example. As a matter of fact, it is more than a mere example; it, because of its success, is a conservative's roadmap — it is a mandate that we heed the oft-quoted aphorism that "History provides the lamp of experience for guidance in the present."

ON SEPTEMBER 12TH, 1905, ten men met at a Peck's restaurant in New York City. Upton Sinclair made a statement to that group the importance of which is incalculable. He declared, *"I decided that since the professors would not educate the students, it was up to the students to educate the professors."*

At that meeting, the Intercollegiate Society of Socialists was born. The I.S.S. started small. Jack London was the first president, and he was met with wisecracks and abuse. Feeling that education was too slow, and being dissatisfied with the conservatism of both major parties, the leftists of the time joked that "the aim of the society [was] to swat wage slavery with diplomas or smother it with degrees *or something.*" (That same year, 1905, a young man graduated *magna cum laude* from Princeton . . . his name was Norman Thomas.)

The tiny I.S.S. began to make headway in the next few years. In 1910, a petition of 300 students for a course in socialism was successful at Harvard. The president of the Harvard I.S.S., Walter Lippmann, declared: "Our object was to make reactionaries, standpatters; standpatters, conservatives; liberals, radicals; and radicals, socialists. In other words, we tried to move everyone up a peg." About this time, the publication *The Intercollegiate Socialist* was formed. Among the contributors was Paul H. Douglas, who in 1915 became president of the Columbia I.S.S. By 1912, the Society could fill Carnegie Hall. Then, with its first blush of glory abated, the Society settled down to twenty years of slow arduous work. Its purpose during these years is easily discernible. The organization stressed that it was educational in nature. Its aims were, "to acquaint collegians not only with socialist doctrines, writings and theories, but also to influence college-bred men and women [who were] rapidly assuming a growing part in the weightiest affairs of the nation."

In 1921, the Society changed its name to the *Student League for Industrial Democracy.* S.L.I.D. chapters were now spread over hundreds of campuses, and they continued in their avocations of leftism to the thousands of young intellectuals who were passing through the colleges. Whereas "socialism" had been a scare-word in 1905, the S.L.I.D. now claimed as national advisers such men as Clarence Darrow, Thorstein Veblen, Morris Ernst, and Paul Blanshard. On the whole, however, things remained quiet until 1932 when (as we all know) all-the-devil broke loose. Here I would stress a most significant point. How fitting it was that, upon election, Franklin Delano Roosevelt turned *not* to a team of political hacks, but to a "braintrust" of intellectuals. In addition, the early New Deal found S.L.I.D. graduates beginning to answer loudly the last charge that had been leveled against the effectiveness of the intellectual approach — *they began to reach the grass roots.* A Wayne University S.L.I.D. member, Walter Reuther, began to stir up labor; John Dewey, a League president of the 30's, sprouted as an "authority" on education; Reinhold Niebuhr, former president of the New York League, was to become a force in the field of religion. Think of the influence exerted upon the "grass roots" by the mass media; then look at these S.L.I.D. graduates: James Wechsler, editor of the *New York Post;* Columnist Murray Kempton; Columnist Walter Lippmann; Columnist Max Lerner; USIA Chief Ed Murrow — the list is endless. Leaf through the S.L.I.D. and you will see that it lists hundreds of these people in positions of influence — our whole society is riddled with them! And this is *not* the result of a multifarious conspiracy, but of *education.* Now who will venture to say that this movement couldn't reach the "grass roots"?

Nothing could be clearer than the fact that, in the last forty years, it has been the *intellectuals* who have steered America on a leftward bent. And I would emphasize again: the gospel of piecemeal socialism and appeasement of international communism which these men now preach from powerful positions was taught them when they were young,

115

when they were in college. The force generated by those ten men fifty years ago has prevailed; those ten men proved conclusively what Prof. Richard Weaver has told conservatives for years . . . *Ideas have consequences.* Actions can be defended, but it is *ideas* that shape the destinies of nations.

Now then, in view of what I have just said, the answer to the problem is clear. The hopes for a conservative revival depend on the rapid formation of a new corps of conservative scholars and writers — a new leadership for what Senator Goldwater calls "the Forgotten American," and, as you've seen in the newspapers, it is already on the march. For 5 years we have had an intellectual journal of conservative opinion, *National Review.* A nation-wide conservative group, Young Americans for Freedom, was born just last fall in the East; last month it filled Manhattan Center in New York. The rising tide of youthful conservatism is already beginning to *prove* that this is the best way. This is the counterthrust which, in time, will bail out the ship of state.

WE MUST NOW carefully define the direction we are to take in this war of ideas. We do not have the three decades that it took the left. There is little doubt in my mind but that another thirty years of the current economic nonsense will preclude any worry about Communism in the United States. The problem will then be theirs — how will they raise enough capital to make the remaining hulk of the U. S. into something they would even want as a satellite? Make no mistake about it. History abounds with evidence to prove this point. A monetary collapse, for instance, would do quite as well as a hail of I.C.B.M.'s to sink America. Therefore, we must make haste. A respectable, responsible conservatism must emerge to influence the economic policies of America. This is the rule against which we must measure the vagaries of contemporary rightist philosophy. If any short-range movement, no matter how well-intentioned, impedes the development and progress of this program by casting aspersion upon the respectability or responsibility of contemporary conservatism, it has a net effect of harm! And this applies to the anti-intellectual machinations of any elements which are ideologically obsessed w i t h domestically-rooted conspiracies and disreputable modes of combatting them.

Frank Chodorov has said, "You can't clean the Communists out of government — they grow there." If you root out one, he'll be replaced in a very short time; the *idea* is what we must fight—fight the "-ism" not the "-ist." William Buckley has said, "I'm sure that we can withstand the pressures emanating from the Kremlin; I am not so sure, however, that we can continue to resist the pressures emanating from Harvard University." This pressure is, of course, modern left-liberalism. In other words, the threat of communism could be checked and the tide of socialism rolled back if it were not for the ideological millstone that statist-liberalism has placed around our necks. We could deal with Socialism-Communism with master strokes if it were not for the flock of "liberals" that jump in to the benefit of the foe.

Fighting the *minions* of collectivism with activist methods, albeit questionable ones, can only frustrate us. Fighting the *idea* can marshal the lessons of history to our cause. A thought worth remembering — what good does it do to assail the latest left-wing front group with white-hot pokers when all the while universities are turning out the Lippmanns, the Murrows, the Reuthers, and the Wechslers of tomorrow? This is the nature of the struggle!

116

John Courtney Murray and
The American Proposition

JOHN P. McCARTHY

THE GROWING right-wing sentiment in American intellectual circles is caused almost certainly, by the awareness of the decline of liberty within the nation and of our inadequate strategy of defense against the external menace of communism. Too often, however, this awareness is simply a vague intuition rather than a precise understanding of our dilemma, and, as a result, many of the new rightists offer solutions that are unrealistic and self-defeating.

A man who appears to come to grips with the nature of the challenge to liberty, and from whom the American right can learn much, is the Jesuit theologian, John Courtney Murray. In his book *We Hold These Truths*, (New York: Sheed and Ward, 1960) he identifies as the substance of democracy the admission of "an order of rights antecedent to the state . . . (and) of another order . . . also antecedent to the state and regulative of its public action as a state . . . the order of justice." These are the self-evident truths, or, as he calls them, the proposition to which the founding fathers dedicated our nation, and the challenge to liberty is the result of the abandonment of this proposition as the basis of our public philosophy.

This might impress some as simply an attempt to impose Catholic "Natural Law" as the public philosophy of America. A careful reading, however, will show that it is more essentially an appeal for return to the philosophy or consensus of the founders of the nation; a

John P. McCarthy is an Associate Editor of *New Individualist Review*.

philosophy considerably closer to the Western tradition deriving from Medieval times than to much of what goes by the name of modern liberalism.

The essential Medieval contribution to the cause of liberty was the concept of the "freedom of the church," which asserted the right of the church to fulfill her spiritual duties of teaching, ruling, and sanctifying, as well as the freedom of the Christian people to live a Christian life. This meant that certain temporal things such as family life, various human relationships, and intellectual truths, were beyond the limits of political order and free "from profanation by the power of the state and other secular powers." "Freedom of the church," insofar as it was granted, served as a constitutional limitation on governmental sovereignty, as an instrument for judging the government according to a prior and higher standard, and as a means of insuring that the King would "fight for justice and the freedom of the people."

Modern politics would substitute the individual human conscience acting through free political institutions for the freedom of the church as a method for achieving the same ends. Philosophical rationalism asserted the autonomy of human reasons, which necessarily implied that all values are man-made. These rationalists conceived of the state simply as a construction of human reason designed to serve man's wants and interests. The notion of a higher and external standard from which to limit and judge the government's powers and actions was abandoned. The only standard for

117

political power was an internal one — adherence to the democratic procedure. Once this was complied with, there was no limit to the sovereignty of political power over all human activity. This monistic system resisted the claim of other authorities to speak on human affairs, for it admitted no standard outside of the democratic political process itself.

The libertarians in the Locke tradition sought at least to make the end of their activities the limitation of governmental interference with man's free direction of his own affairs. While this view did not consider the corporate nature of society, and the demands of justice arising from it, it did serve liberty. While the libertarian concerns himself with extending freedom, he cannot conceive of justice as demanding action by the state for ends other than the extension and protection of freedom. It is on this point that the Catholic and the libertarian necessarily differ, for the Catholic insists that justice can demand positive action by the state for attaining and distributing certain human needs. Both, however, are united in their opposition to the theories of our contemporary social engineers, which Murray labels "evolutionary scientific humanism."

This is the latest step in the monistic development of modern political thought. It is rationalist and insists on the complete independence of human reason, but differs from the old rationalism in that it is evolutionary. It does not conceive of a static law of nature waiting to be discovered. Rather, nature evolves, and the goal according to them then becomes the advancement of the evolutionary process by increasing the fullness of life. The necessary steps are determined by scientific examination. The total resources of government are devoted to the task of furthering the evolutionary process and forming the new citizen. Philosophies concerning a juridical order with limitations on government or standards to which the government must conform are simply dismissed as the aims or ideals of a particular society, lacking any necessary relationship to the real order.

We have come the full course from the Whig attempt to regard government

as man's instrument for protecting his freedom and property to an attitude towards the state as an end in itself from which man receives the interpretation of his own nature and guidance towards his destiny. "The state creates the ethos of society, embodies it, imparts it to its citizens, and sanctions its observance with rewards and punishments." Any source of authority which attempts to judge society other than the democratic process itself is viewed with distrust, for no standard is recognized other than that set by the democratic state itself. Such an attitude is the height of absolutism: the political process itself is deified.

This philosophy, or democratic religion, is most pronounced in the field of education, where the ideal is to mold a future citizen who will fit the pattern of social desirability as determined by the democratic process. This contrasts with the former ideal of educating a free citizen conscious of both his own liberty and the order of justice which the state must serve. This accounts for the violent objections of extremists of the scientific humanist camp to private religious education. They cannot help but regard as devisive a system of education which gives men an understanding of their own nature, as well as a higher standard on which to judge the actions of the state that conformity to the democratic process itself. The standard offered in the place of conformity is how well the state protects and advances liberty and justice.

Reflection on these matters suggests that American Catholicism, with its strong commitment to natural law may yet be one of the strongholds of the cause of liberty in America. The political philosophy of the founding fathers—the American consensus—finds one of its few and strongest modern sources of support in American Catholicism. This goes a long way towards explaining the basic compatibility, which history has demonstrated, between Catholicism and American democracy. Our public philosophy at its inception asserted the same principle as the medieval "freedom of the church" theory: that the government is limited and is subject to direction from standards outside of itself. The first amendment to the Constitution provides all that the church need demand from the state, namely, limitation of the state's powers and the exemption of certain realms of human life — especially those pertaining to moral and religious matters — from the political sphere. This guarantees the church just what the medieval notion guaranteed: freedom to fulfill its mission, and the freedom of Christian people to live as Christians.

This contrasts with the juridical omnipotence claimed for the state by the Jacobin liberals, who tolerate religion so long as it remains a purely individual matter and does not act as an authority for collective attitudes in opposition to the state's dictates. The American separation of church and state is a pragmatic arrangement devised to further the peace and common good of our pluralistic nation, not an institutional pronouncement of the irrelevance of religion as a guide for man and society.

For this reason the American system did not incur Papal condemnation as did continental liberalism, which asserted the thesis of the juridical omnipotence and omnicompetence of the state, and predicated freedom of religion and separation of church and state on this thesis.

* * *

In the light of these conclusions, Dr. Murray devotes a major segment of the book to an analysis of our struggle with Communism, and to a plea for the development of some sort of doctrine on the use of force. He examines the Soviet Union in its four unique aspects: first, as a state or power; secondly, as an imperium "organized and guided in accordance with a revolutionary doctrine"; thirdly, as an empire "mastering the older imperialistic techniques of military conquest, political puppetry, etc."; and lastly, as the "legate of a longer history . . . as the inheritor both of Tsarist imperialism and of mystical panslavist messianism." The Soviet Union can not be understood unless all these aspects are taken into consideration, and the Cold War is especially unintelligible unless the second aspect, the revolutionary doctrine, is considered. Without that doc-

trine the Soviet Union would not be a threat to the United States. Naturally the notion of a nation guided in its action by a strict doctrine is incomprehensible to the pragmatic American mind, and this accounts for much of our failure in the Cold War.

Professor Murray draws certain conclusions with regard to our cold war strategy from his understanding of the Soviet doctrine. These conclusions eliminate the need of relying solely on the resources of improvisation or practical wisdom in dealing with the Soviet moves, since they enable us to base our actions on certain expectations, for instance, that "communist leadership will yield only to calculations of power and success." Consequently, we should "put an end . . . to the Wilsonian era of diplomacy with its exaggerated trust in world assemblies," and rely on direct negotiations with the Soviets. Furthermore, we should negotiate to achieve certain policy objectives, rather than base our policies on negotiations. We should cease to enter negotiations with "sincerity" as the only guiding principle, and realize that the search for Soviet "sincerity" is a total waste of time.

This approach will rule out "disengagement," for, given the inherent aggressiveness of Soviet doctrine, the Soviet Union "continually probes for every vacuum of power and for every soft spot of purpose." Disengagement would "heighten the danger of war, most probably by permitting the creation of situations that we could not possible accept."

Soviet doctrine dictates a strategy of maximum security and minimum risk. Their first consideration is to take no action which will endanger the gains of Socialism. Since the Soviet Union acts under an internal dynamism, it will not be provoked into taking actions exceeding the minimum risk. We have also been following the same policy of maximum security and minimum risk, but this is disastrous for us since it inhibits us from blocking any aggressive thrust. It puts us in the position of taking decisive action only when the question is a matter of our survival, in contrast to the Soviets who use force for limited goals and seek to avoid being in the dilemma of having to use force as a matter of survival.

Realizing this situation, we should reverse our strategy and seek to create situations of risk for the Soviet Union, risks which they would wish to avoid. Only in this way can we seize the initiative in world affairs and reverse the pattern of Communist advances.

Murray goes on to examine the moral question of the use of force by the state. He criticizes the two common approaches in American thought, that of near-pacifism, which would seek to apply the beatitudes to the state, and that of moral ambiguism, which would have us avoid making moral decisions. The tradition of reason demonstrates that the nature of the state demands the exercise of force for the purpose of advancing and protecting liberty and justice. There are certain moral principles regulating the use of force, but the very exercise of force is not in itself immoral.

We Hold These Truths is a significant and insightful contribution to the appreciation of the present moral crisis, both in the philosophical realm and in the field of practical politics and diplomacy. It is a book to be recommended to all thoughtful readers anxious for a dispassionate analysis of the American philosophy.

NEW BOOKS AND ARTICLES

120

THE FOLLOWING IS A SELECT LIST OF BOOKS AND ARTICLES WHICH, IN THE OPINION OF THE EDITORS, MAY BE OF INTEREST TO OUR READERS.

Louis Baudin, *A Socialist Empire*: *The Incas of Peru,* (D. Van Nostrand, Princeton, New Jersey, 1961).

P. T. Bauer, *Indian Economic Policy and Development,* (Praeger, New York City, 1961).

Christopher Dawson, *The Crisis of Western Education,* (Sheed and Ward, New York City, 1961).

Harold M. Hyman, *To Try Men's Souls*: *Loyalty Tests in American History,* (University of California Press, 1961).

Bruno Leoni, *Freedom and the Law,* (D. Van Nostrand, Princeton, New Jersey, 1961).

John Lukacs, *A History of the Cold War,* (Doubleday and Co., New York City, 1961).

H. L. Mencken, *The Letters of H. L. Mencken,* (Alfred E. Knopf, New York City, 1961).

Charles Rist, *The Tyranny of Gold,* (Philosophical Library, New York City, 1961), paper.

R. J. Rushdoony, *Intellectual Schizophrenia,* (Presbyterian and Reformed Publishing Co., 1961).

Robert A. Rutland, *George Mason,* (Holt, Rhinhardt and Winston, 1961).

George B. Russell, *J. Bracken Lee: The Taxpayer's Champion,* (Robert Speller, 1961).

Helmut Schoeck and James W. Wiggins, *Relativism and the Study of Man,* (D. Van Nostrand, Princeton, New Jersey, 1961).

Robert Strausz-Hupe, *A Forward Strategy for Americans,* (Harpers, New York City, 1961).

A. J. P. Taylor, *Origins of the Second World War,* (Hamish Hamilton, London, 1961).

Klaus Epstein, "Shirer's History of Nazi Germany," *Review of Politics* (April, 1961).

Milton Friedman, "Economic Aid Reconsidered: A Reply," *Yale Review* (Summer, 1961).

Hans F. Sennholz, "Volunteers for the Peace Corps," *The Freeman,* September, 1961. (Free copy available from the publisher, Foundation for Economic Education, Irvington-on-Hudson, New York.)

Raghuveer Singh, "John Locke and the Theory of Natural Law," *Political Studies* (June, 1961).

George B. Sparks, "The Highway Dilemma," *The Freeman,* August, 1961.

VOLUME 1
NUMBER 4
WINTER 1962

New
INDIVIDUALIST
Review

Winter 1962   35 cents   Vol. 1, No. 4

NEW INDIVIDUALIST REVIEW

Volume 1 — Number 4   WINTER 1962

NEW
INDIVIDUALIST
REVIEW

EDITORIAL BOARD

Editors-in-Chief • Ronald Hamowy • Ralph Raico
Associate Editors • Robert M. Hurt • John P. McCarthy
Robert Schuettinger • John Weicher
Editorial Assistant • J. Edwin Malone

EDITORIAL ADVISORS

Milton Friedman • F. A. Hayek • Richard M. Weaver
University of Chicago

COLLEGE AND UNIVERSITY REPRESENTATIVES

128

NEW INDIVIDUALIST REVIEW is published quarterly (Spring, Summer, Autumn, Winter) by *New Individualist Review*, Ida Noyes Hall, University of Chicago, Chicago 37, Illinois. Second class mailing permit pending at the Chicago, Illinois post office.

Editorial, advertising and subscription correspondence and manuscripts should be sent to NEW INDIVIDUALIST REVIEW, Ida Noyes Hall, University of Chicago, Chicago 37, Ilinois. All manuscripts (which should not be longer than 3000 words) become the property of NEW INDIVIDUALIST REVIEW.

Subscription Rates: $2.00 per year (students, $1.00). Add $1.00 for foreign subscriptions.

Antitrust and Competition

ROBERT M. HURT

If [the businessmen] like freedom and don't want outright control, then they've got to stand up and be good citizens. They've got to quit their informal conforming and doing business the easy way. They're going to have to, we might say, expose themselves to the rigors of competition."

. . . .

"We must hold open opportunities for a man with an idea so that, with a little capital, he can go into business and have a fair chance, by his ingenuity, to grow and become big himself. This is very difficult if you subscribe to what is called "hard" competition. Competition of this kind is war in a jungle, where only the big man can survive."[1]

> Paul Rand Dixon, *Chrm. of the Federal Trade Commission*

GOVERNMENT AND PUBLIC alike are now exhibiting a case of schizophrenia in their attitude toward competition, complete with separate vocabularies. On the one hand, a group of business executives are given jail sentences for fixing prices in violation of the Sherman Antitrust Act and are paraded before the public as enemies of society. They are charged with obstructing the market and thereby injuring the public.

Robert M. Hurt received a B.A. from Wabash College and an L.L.B. from the Yale Law School. He is presently a Volker Fellow studying under Prof. F.A. Hayek on the Committee on Social Thought of the University of Chicago. He has recently joined the editorial board of *New Individualist Review* as an Associate Editor.

Even in those circles in which Adam Smith and his kin have been consigned to the innermost hell, his arguments against cartelization are accepted: independent pricing by each competitor in an effort to maximize his profit will result in lower prices and greater output than collusive pricing. Although collusion might bring greater security and greater profits to the participants, it is allegedly the philosophy of the antitrust laws that these are offset by disadvantages to the public. In the lexicon of our commentators, the goal is "competition" and the departure is marked by "conspiracy," "doing business the easy way," "oligopoly," and "directed prices."

On the other hand, in a continually expanding area, both federal and state governments embark on a calculated policy of encouraging the same results the price fixing prosecution was designed to prevent. In this area, the very type of competition which is likely to bring lower prices is prohibited. Here the vocabulary is given an Orwellian twist in its mimicry of the language used to describe a competitive market. The goal is "orderly competition" and "fair trade," the departure the "war of the jungle" and "unfair competition." The price cutter, in the words of President Roosevelt, is a "chiseler"; the competitor hurt by lower prices is deprived of his "fair chance" and "right to compete." It can be seriously argued that certain types of business conduct described as "unfair competition," especially in the area of fraud,

[1] *U. S. News and World Report*, July 17, 1961, p. 65.

129

can be proscribed with no adverse effect on price competition. This article deals with the sphere of government intervention which is clearly protectionist in character and acts to thwart the market at least as decisively as the conduct of the imprisoned executives.

The government's most grandiose attack on competition was the National Industrial Recovery Act of 1933, enforcing industry drafted codes, of which 85% contained provisions for fixing minimum prices. The President of the United States Chamber of Commerce stated the underlying philosophy of the Act:

> "The time has come when we should ease up on these laws and under proper government supervision, allow manufacturers and people in trade to agree among themselves on these basic conditions of a fair price for the commodity, a fair wage, and a fair dividend."[2]

After a period of horror, in which even an investigating committee appointed by Roosevelt denounced the whole undertaking as a "regimented organization for exploitation," the Supreme Court put the monster to death amidst sighs of relief even of some of its original supporters. This experiment with "corporativism" of the continental variety probably had the redeeming effect of leaving an understandable antipathy for such comprehensive legislation.[3]

The ghost of the NRA philosophy, however, lingers in a surprisingly large part of our economic life. Allocations of quotas to oil producers by state governments are enforced by the federal government. The producers argue that the purpose of the arrangement is conservation of dwindling reserves rather than higher profits, while they lobby for de-pletion allowances to allegedly encourage exploration and exploitation of oil fields. Over half the states have retail price maintenance laws (euphemistically dubbed "fair trade" laws) preventing price competition among retailers in a wide range of brand name products. These are exempt from the antitrust laws under the Miller-Tydings Act. While regulatory agencies are usually associated with the setting of maximum rates, there is an increased willingness on the part of the Interstate Commerce Commission and the Civil Aeronautics Board to set minimum rates to "protect competition." An increase in the minimum wage is openly advocated as a means of protecting Northern industry from the lower prices of low wage Southern industry. The avowed goal of our farm program is to keep prices high enough to enable all those wishing to remain farmers to achieve, as Kennedy promised during the election campaign, a return on investment equivalent to that obtained in business. And, of course, protective tariffs and other trade restrictions have from time immemorial sacrificed lower prices, greater output, and increased efficiency of specialization resulting from the free movement of goods for the greater security and profits of the protected industry.

While a complete list of clearly protectionist legislation, of which the above is a small sampling,[4] would be grim reading for persons of almost any political persuasion, I find the most distressing developments in that supposed citadel of free competition, the antitrust laws. The remainder of this article deals with these developments. In 1911, Justice White enumerated the evils which the Sherman Act was enacted to combat:

> "The power which the monopoly gave to one who enjoyed it, to fix the price and thereby injure the public; the power which it engendered of enabling a limitation on production, and the danger of deterioration in quality of the monopolized article."[5]

----

[2] Henry I. Harriman, quoted in Wilcox, *Public Policies Toward Business*, (Irwin, 1960), p. 351.

[3] The alleged purpose of the price control was to aid economic recovery. However, the expected result was born out by the Brookings Institute study which concluded that the Act, "on the whole, retarded recovery." Lyon, *et. al., The National Recovery Administration*, (Washington, D. C., Brookings Inst., 1935), p. 873.

----

[4] A complete list would include items not usually associated with price fixing, such as licensing of professional services.

Protection of the consumers from these evils—higher prices, lower output, and deterioration of quality — was accepted by the courts as the criterion of Sherman Act enforcement.[5] This standard roughly corresponds to the criteria developed by classical economists to demonstrate the superiority of competitive enterprise, although it is by necessity a cruder standard. It has frequently been argued that some, or even all, of the methods adopted by the antitrust laws have not or could not achieve these goals. But no student of the antitrust laws would deny that their enforcers have in the past at least sought to protect the public rather than to secure the position and profits of high cost competitors. The appearance of success has been sufficient to persuade the Common Market nations, long the ideological home of government aided cartels and the anti-competitive mentality, to include antitrust provisions strikingly like our own in the Rome Treaty.

Recently, however, the antitrust laws have been used to achieve those very results which they are allegedly designed to prevent — to thwart developments which will lead to lower prices and the other advantages which flow from competition. This trend is not irreversible, especially in view of the fact that many of the important cases are still to be reviewed by the higher courts. Three of the most important developments are: (1) the proposed consent decrees in the electrical equipment price fixing cases, (2) recent applications of the Celler-Kefauver Anti-Merger Act, (3) the attack on price discrimination and

the large buyer under the Robinson-Patman and Sherman Acts. Since this is a brief survey article, I cannot avoid some over-simplification; but the following discussion I believe captures the drift of the cases.

AFTER THE SEVEN executives were safely tucked away behind bars for conspiring to keep the price of electrical equipment "above the market price," the Justice Department proposed decrees which included a rule prohibiting the selling of equipment at an "unreasonably low price," to prevent competition which might drive smaller firms out of business.[7] Having prohibited agreements to thwart "competition," the Justice Department seems to desire that the big companies avoid actual competition. These companies would be left with the job of determining what is a "reasonable" price, with possible contempt proceedings, complete with jail sentences, threatening if they fail to calculate what the government and the courts consider an "unreasonably low price." Several customers of the convicted equipment suppliers, who are the very parties that the antitrust laws supposedly protect, have attempted to intervene in the case to protest this deprival "of the benefits of free price competition in the purchase of electrical equipment."

A ruling that big concerns should set their prices so as not to injure competitors would not only deprive customers of the benefits of lower prices; it would also place these larger companies in a preposterous situation. Should the price selected as consonant with safeguarding their small competitors be considered too high, the pubic is said to be the victim of "directed prices," and the authorities are exhorted to break up the "oligopoly." If the price is so low as to hurt some competitors, they are guilty of "monopolistic practices" and likewise subject to public outcry and prosecution. This would give a custodial role to large firms incompatible with any notion of

131

---

[5] Standard Oil of New Jersey v. United States, 221 *US* 1, 52, (1911).

[6] The courts have developed certain rules of thumb, declaring certain types of conduct illegal in all cases. (These are referred to as illegal per se). Into this category fall price fixing, market allocation, and joint boycotts. However, this was not considered a departure from the market standard, as the courts felt that these acts could have no other purpose than to injure the buying public. The market standard has been recently reaffirmed as the goal of antitrust enforcement in the important *Report of the Attorney General's National Committee to Study the Antitrust Laws*, (1955). p. 320.

[7] *U. S. News and World Report*, Dec. 4, 1961, p. 60.

a free market. The only completely safe course would be to obtain a clearance from the Justice Department before making a price change. The dilemma of the large firm is summed up by Leland Hazard, an antitrust lawyer:

"Antitrust doctrine forbids certain forms of hard competition. For example, GM would hesitate to price its cars as low as its efficiency might permit, for fear of driving Chrysler, American Motors, even Ford to the wall. As critics put it, businessmen must compete, but no one must win the competition. It is this aspect of antitrust which creates two standards, one for big business, another for small business. No matter how vicious the competition of the little fellow, the big fellow must not compete too hard."[8]

IN 1950 AS a result of fears that the merger movement was rapidly increasing monopoly power in American industry, the Celler-Kefauver amendment to the Clayton Antitrust Act was passed to prohibit mergers whose effect "may be to substantially lessen competition or tend to create a monopoly." While less of an immediate effect on competition was required when compared to the Sherman Act standard, the Congressional reports clearly indicate (1) that the goal was to protect competition rather than less efficient competitors and (2) that a "reasonable probability" rather than a mere possibility of injury to competition must be shown.[9] However, certain recent cases indicate that this act may be forged into one of the most sweeping anti-competitive devices in the hands of the Government.[10]

The Reynolds Metal Co., a producer of aluminum foil, was recently ordered by the Federal Trade Commission to divest itself of a recent acquisition, Arrow Brands, Inc., which converted aluminum foil into decorative foil for the florist

trade. Although Arrow was a customer of Reynolds before and after the acquisition, the main complaint of the Commission was that after the merger Arrow had priced so low that competitors were badly hurt. When Reynolds responded that they had not initiated the price cut but had lowered their prices to meet foreign competition, the Commission bluntly stated the new philosophy:

"Whether or not Arrow was actually the first to reduce prices was not too important. The significance in the situation is that Arrow could lower its prices and maintain them at low levels for an extended period which it could not have done before the merger. . . . In any event, we do not need to be particularly concerned with the justification Arrow may have had for reducing its prices below the cost of production. It is enough that the reductions show the exercise of a market power which Arrow achieved as a direct result of the acquisition."[11]

We leave to conjecture whether the Commission would recommend a protective tariff to fill the vacuum created by removing those firms which could meet foreign competition. Arrow's sin was what would, at one time, have been considered a virtue, its ability to compete more effectively. Though the Commission mentions pricing "below the cost of production," it hedges on whether Arrow did actually price below cost. Earlier the opinion admitted that "even if Arrow had not been selling below cost, it was selling at prices so near cost and so low that it virtually ran some of its competitors out of business."[12] In other words, even if after a merger the merged concern still makes a slight profit, should the lower prices "virtually run some of its competitors out of business," the merger injures "competition." This reasoning would apply whether the increased "power" results from greater efficiency or from greater financial "power."

---

[8] *Atlantic Monthly,* Nov. 1961, p. 57.

[9] Cf. Milton Handler, "A Decade of Administration of the Celler-Kefauver Act," 61 *Columbia Law Review,* 629, April, 1961.

[10] A more complete account of the anti-competitive enforcement of this act is given by Robert Bork in 39 *Texas Law Review,* 711, June, 1961.

[11] Reynolds Metal Co., 1960 *Trade Reg. Rep.* ¶28,533, p. 37,256.

[12] *Ibid.,* p. 37,255.

A recent decision by a hearing examiner, sent back for further findings of fact by the Commission, involves what is referred to as a conglomerate merger —a merger of two firms which neither are competitors nor do business with each other. Proctor & Gamble's acquisition of Clorox, a producer of liquid bleach, was found by the examiner to violate the Act.[13] Clorox's misdeed lay in being able to embark on a promotional campaign which allegedly succeeded at the expense of Clorox's competitors due to Proctor & Gamble's superior advertising and promotional experience and greater financial strength. Further, Proctor & Gamble, due to the large quantity of its advertising, received discounts unavailable to Clorox's competitors. This decision, if accepted by the Commission, would make explicit a completely new philosophy of antitrust. In previous cases, mergers were challenged because (1) by combining competitors they increased concentration in the market, (horizontal merger), or (2) by combining a buyer of a product with its seller, they "foreclose" competing sellers or buyers from a market (vertical merger). In the case of the conglomerate merger, the only grounds for objection must either be the increased financial ability to compete more effectively through advertising, price competition, or introduction of new techniques, or the economies of scale of management, mass advertising, etc. The former Chairman of the Commission has indicated that the Clorox case might lead the way to protection of small firms from the adverse effects of such mergers:

"The acquisition by a large and powerful diversified company of a small company in a discrete indus-

try historically shared by a number of small companies competing on equal terms followed by drastic competitive injury to the smaller competitors might be a demonstration of anti-competitive effect sufficient to satisfy the statutory requisites even if the acquisition was truly conglomerate."[14]

This philosophy, if accepted, could be used to freeze the structure of many American industries. When firms in a given industry are of a given size or structure, they would be kept that way if they could not generate the capital to introduce new cost saving techniques or the promotion necessary to expand the market. (This is especially likely at present, since a large percentage of equity capital is provided by large firms.) This can be compared to prohibiting a rich heir from buying a corner drugstore because by hard competition—advertising, new techniques—he could deprive competitors of a large part of their business, i.e., of a "fair opportunity to compete."

The Commission's endeavors have probably been surpassed by the recently replaced Robert Bicks of the Justice Department, who, you may recall, carried the torch of free competition in the price fixing case. An action has been brought against Von's Grocery Co. to disband its merger with Shopping Bag Food Stores. Together they comprise 8% of the grocery market in the Los Angeles area. At the time of the complaint there were twenty leading supermarket chains in the area; and experience indicates that competition, in the sense of lower prices, would be at least as great in such a market as in a market of small retailers, especially since entry is notably easy in the grocery business. But the complaint indicates that this is not what is meant by competition:

"Independent retailers of groceries and related products may be deprived of a fair opportunity to compete with the combined resources of Von and Shopping Bag."[15]

133

---

[13] Proctor & Gamble, (FTC Dkt 6901), remanded for further findings, *CCH Trade Regulation Reports* ¶15,245 (June 15, 1961). The Commission found that the Examiner's facts were not sufficient to support his conclusions. For instance the Nielson rating showed that Clorox was expanding its sales faster before the merger. However, the language of the opinion seems to indicate that the Commission supported the theory of the Examiner as to the "anti-competitive" effects of a conglomerate merger.

[14] Earl W. Kintner, quoted in Adelman, "The Anti-Merger Act," 51 *American Economic Review*, part 2, 1961. p. 243.

[15] United States v. Von's Grocery Co., *CCH Trade Regulation Reports*, 45,060, p. 66,427.

Mr. Bicks is more explicit as to what is undoubtedly the goal of the prosecution:

"This complaint reflects our continuing concern over the effects on small independent grocers resulting from combinations of large supermarket chains."[16]

It is not claimed that the merger will deprive the other twenty chains of the "opportunity to compete," as it undoubtedly would not. It cannot be seriously argued that price competition among the chains would be appreciably lessened, that there is a "reasonable probability" that prices are likely to be higher as a result of a merger. The objection is that the achievement of efficiencies from combined resources would deprive less efficient forms of business of a "fair opportunity to compete." Again, it is not the consumer but the competitor who is being protected.

Mr. Bick's *magnum opus,* however, is the Brown Shoe case,[17] now pending before the Supreme Court, in which Justice Weber ordered the merger of the Brown Shoe Company and the G. R. Kinney Company ended. The shoe industry is notably competitive; and, according to the Court's own figures, after the merger the combined firms had only 5.5% of the manufacturing market and 5.7% of the retail market.[18] Since these figures are singularly unimpressive even in present antitrust cases, Justice Weber made some almost ludicrous assertions, belied by his own figures, that there was a sufficient trend toward concentration to warrant fear for the future of competi-

tion. But the crux of the argument is that dangerous efficiencies are driving small and less efficient retailers to the wall:

"Company owned and company controlled retail stores have definite advantages in buying and credit; they have further advantages in advertising, insurance, inventory control and assists, and price control. These advantages result in lower prices or in higher quality for the same price, and the independent retailer can no longer compete in the low and medium price fields and has been driven to concentrate his business in the higher prices, higher quality type of shoes—and the higher the price, the smaller the market. He has been placed in this position, not by choice, but by necessity."[19]

"It is the Court's conclusion that the merger would establish a manufacturer-retailer relation which would deprive all but the top firms in the industry of a fair opportunity to compete."[20]

Justice Weber has made explicit what other protectionists are often loathe to admit. Economies which permit lower prices are a danger, not a benefit, when they hurt less efficient producers. This is what is meant by "fair opportunity to compete."

These cases cannot be dismissed as isolated instances, since they represent the attitudes of the agencies charged with enforcing the antitrust laws. Lee Loevinger, now heading the Justice Department's Antitrust Division, has indicated that we can expect increased activity in the merger area, and this policy is even more ominous when coupled with the "backward sweep" doctrine developed by the Supreme Court. In the DuPont-General Motors case, DuPont was ordered to give up stock of General Motors it acquired over thirty-five years ago, though there was no claim that the acquisition was "anti-competitive" at the time. If this doctrine is literally applied, when coupled with the "competitive opportunity" doctrine developed in the above

---

16 *Ibid.*

17 United States v. Brown Shoe Co., 179 *F. Supp.* 721 (ED Mo., 1959).

18 Justice Weber has to juggle statistics even to get the 5.7%. He takes Brown-Kinney's total retail sales as compared with the total sales of the 22,000 retail outlets classified by the Census Department as shoe stores. 70,000 stores sell shoes, but the Census Department included only those which do over 50% of their business in shoes, excluding department stores. However, shoes sold by Brown-Kinney in department stores are included in its total.

19 Brown Shoe Co., op. cit., p. 738.

20 *Ibid.,* p. 741.

cases, the government could function as a regulatory bureau over any firm which has had a merger since 1950 and attack it when things seem to get rough for competition due to the success of the merged operation.[21]

ALLEGEDLY TO prevent "monopolistic" price discrimination, the antitrust laws have been turned against one of the strongest vehicles for bringing lower prices to consumers—the large buyers, especially the chain stores. Large retailers have unquestionably reduced prices by passing on a great part of the benefits of large-scale economies in lower prices and improved services, by operating at a low unit profit (although the total profits may be high), and by procuring lower prices from suppliers. Due to the ease of entry into retailing and the intense competition between these large buyers, this is generally a most unlikely area for monopoly extractions from consumers. Supporters of competition in this field even have the dubious aid of Ambassador Galbraith, who has emphasized the benefits of large scale retailing to the public.[22]

But when prices are lowered, someone is likely to be hurt, in this case the small and high cost retailers as well as many suppliers of merchandise. Aided by one of the most vigorous lobbies in the nation, they have partially succeeded in thwarting low price competition through "fair trade" and compulsory mark-up laws. In addition, they have succeeded to a large measure in preventing price concessions from suppliers, even when justified by cost savings to the supplier due to large purchases and service performed, through the Robinson-Patman Act and, even, the Sherman Act.

The Robinson-Patman Act is a mire of legal draftsmanship and defies a short description. But, while clouded in the usual language of "competition" and ostensibly designed to prevent price discrimination, the Act seems to have but one unifying principle: "to enforce discrimination against the lower cost buyer or the lower cost method of distribution."[23] The Act, together with its administration, has been noted for its disregard for any economic analysis of the price discrimination problem. Certain types of price discrimination which economists would class as most likely to be "monopolistic" and lead to higher prices are ignored by the Act, since no competitors are immediately injured, while discrimination which injures someone's business is almost consistently condemned, though such discrimination may in some cases be highly conducive to competition and lower prices.[24]

Several of the provisions, taken almost directly from NRA codes, make discrimination against buyers in some cases compulsory. A firm which performs its own brokerage cannot receive a discount for the amount the seller thus saves, and the seller cannot give discounts for other services performed by a buyer (such as advertising) or make services available to a buyer unless an offer is made to smaller customers on "proportionally equal terms," which is in many cases impossible.

The Act's main provision effectively prevents price discounts given to buyers which prove particularly annoying to competitors of these buyers. It prohibits discounts which "injure competition" with any competing buyer. It has generally been sufficient to show that complaining competitors have suffered losses because of the differential to prove injury to this "competition." This is true when large buyers, by cutting into the profits of wholesale sellers, have been able to pass part of these savings on to the consumer, substituting vigorous competition among large retailers for the previous small firm, high price retail structure. Though some courts have

135

21 This danger is developed at length by Bork, op. cit., passim.

22 J. K. Galbraith, American Capitalism, (1956). pp. 119-120.

23 Adelman, "The Consistency of the Robinson-Patman Act," Stanford Law Review, Dec., 1953, p. 4

24 Cf. Ferrall, "Quantity Discounts and Competition," 3 Journal of Law and Economics 146, Oct., 1960.

used language to the contrary, the courts have generally substituted an "injury to competitors" for an "injury to competition" test.[25]

A price discount is exempt from the Act if it is equal to cost savings to the seller resulting from the size of the purchase or the method of delivery. However this has been so difficult to prove to the satisfaction of the Commission and the courts that the Act has effectively barred most discounts justified by cost savings. Discounts made in good faith to meet, but not undercut, the price of competitors, are also exempt. But the Commission recently held that this allows only "defensive" and not "aggressive" discounts, i.e., discounts cannot be made to meet the price of a competitor in order to win customers away from him.[26] As the dissenting Commissioner pointed out, this rule may effectively isolate suppliers in many markets from any price competition. The Commission has further held that a firm may not give a discount to meet the price of a competitor if consumer acceptance of its brand gives it an advantage.

In 1946 the biggest guns of antitrust were focused on a noted object of protectionist ire, the A&P, in a Sherman Act prosecution which is an epic in antitrust literature.[27] Even the judge convicting A&P proclaimed that "to buy, sell, and distribute to a substantial portion of 130 million people one and three-quarters billion dollars worth of food annually at a profit of 1¼ cents on each dollar is an achievement one may well be proud of." While selling less than 7% of the groceries in the nation, it had admittedly been a pioneer in introducing new techniques resulting in both lower prices and improved services to consumers. In the process, however, many had been hurt and were screaming loudly. There is legitimate disagreement as to just what the facts were and whether some action was warranted, but the government arguments and court decisions were landmarks in both economic confusion and protectionist sentiment. Only a few high points can be mentioned here.[28]

A&P was assailed for its policy of reducing prices so that volume of sales would eventually increase to a point where greater economies of scale would be realized and higher profits would be made. This practice would seem to lie at the very basis of competition, but to the government the notion of cutting prices to increase sales and realize economies seemed somehow un-American: "An honest retailer would attempt to price his merchandise in the traditional American way, that is, cost, plus expenses, plus a profit."[29] A&P's threat to manufacture its own products if its suppliers, often large ones, would not reduce their prices, was attacked as unfairly "coercive." A&P had performed its own brokerage, but it was forbidden by the Commission to receive discounts for the amount saved. It demanded allowances for its advertising and other services rendered its sellers, but these were attacked as giving A&P an "unfair advantage" without regard for the actual savings to suppliers in accepting these services. Though the action was

---

[25] The Supreme Court indicated that it identified injury to competitors with injury to competition in FTC v. Morton Salt Co., 334 *US* 37, (1948): "[The Commission] heard testimony from many witnesses in various parts of the country to show that they had suffered actual financial losses on account of respondent's discriminatory prices. Experts were offered to prove the tendency of injury from such prices. The evidence covers about two thousand pages, largely devoted to this single issue—injury to competition."

[26] Sunshine Biscuits, Inc., *CCH Trade Regulation Reporter*, ¶15,469 (Sept. 25, 1961).

[27] United States v. A&P, 67 *F. Supp.* 626, affirmed 173 *F2d* 79, (1949); and A&P v. FTC, 106 *F2d* 667. Representative Patman of Robinson-Patman fame unsuccessfully introduced a bill subjecting chain stores to a federal tax which would have imposed a $470,000,000 annual levy on A&P, creating a net loss of $390,000,000. Discriminatory taxes were placed on chains in 29 states, Wilcox, *op. cit., p.* 372.

[28] For a detailed analysis, see Adelman, "The A&P Case" 63 *Quarterly Journal of Economics* 238, (1949). For the opposing opinion, see Dirlam and Kahn, *Fair Competition: The Law and Economics*, (Ithaca, 1954), pp. 233-241.

[29] From the Main Brief of the Government, quoted in Adelman, "The A&P Case," p. 241.

brought under the Sherman Act with its market effect standard, the discounts received by A&P through hard bargaining were condemned without any attempt at showing that these policies were likely to injure rather than benefit buyers of groceries.

EVEN IF ONE agrees with the author that the antitrust laws have been perverted in recent years in certain areas, this, of course, does not demonstrate that they should be discarded. There is considerable honest dispute among economists as to what extent mergers resulting in increased concentration, price fixing and various other restrictive practices are likely to lead to higher prices and decreased output. Economists such as Stigler, J. M. Clark, and Machlup, to name a few, have advocated strong enforcement of the laws. Others, including Hayek, Mises, and Schumpeter, have been skeptical about the value of such action, especially as to the desirability of breaking up concentration. Machlup and others have suggested more may be accomplished by elimination or modification of patent law, tariffs, and other government policies which encourage concentration. But it is to be hoped that in the future the controversy over antitrust questions returns to this area and that the present anti-competitive tangent can be abandoned.

The present trend, however, might be destined to predominate in the years ahead, since it may well represent an attitude closer to the hearts of Americans than lip service paid to "free enterprise." (This is well illustrated by many "right wing" businessmen when their profits are threatened by competition.) The author suggests that the most likely statist trend in this country would not be toward "socialism," the present bogey of the right wing, but rather toward an indigenous hybrid of feudalism and economic fascism. In the extreme form of this type of social organization, each businessman would be guaranteed his margin of profit, just as each worker would be guaranteed his wage and each

farmer his income, sheltered against the forces which have made for a progressive, consumer oriented economy, with its painful adjustments for the marginal producer. The last few centuries have been viewed as dramatically displaying a movement away from such a society with its frozen relations toward a society characterized by mobility, freedom, and progress. This movement received Sir Henry Maine's famous characterization as the movement from "status" to "contract." Present popular attitudes as well as government policies may well indicate a reaction—from contract back to status.

While such a trend is to be noted not only in a wide area of governmental policy but also in private business and in labor relations, it can be seen in its purest form in the discussion of farm policy. Here the espousal of "just price" and the right of a farmer and his son (ad infinitum) to a "fair" return on their plot of land regardless of the greater efficiency of larger units and the conditions of demand, remarkably parallels the medieval attitude toward competition. We are asked to determine an intrinsic value of the farmer's performance separate from the market value of his production, and guarantee him a corresponding income.[30]

To those who accept this philosophy I can only suggest that they shed their hypocritical wrath directed at private price fixers. The philosophical arguments in support of such a position can certainly claim intellectual respectability. And I cannot deny the possibility that a government supervised static society, or one tending more in that direction, might, by more successfully satisfying urges for security and tranquility, provide greater "contentment" of a sort to the bulk of its members.

---

[30] "This nation owes to its farmers—not a fair income or a guaranteed income—but it owes to them conditions under which they have an opportunity to earn that kind of an income to which their industry and ability entitles them. This is the only answer that is consistent with our American ideals." Orville Freeman, *World,* Jan. 3, 1962, p. 17. If the reader can comprehend this distinction, please enlighten the author.

But to those who consider this sort of contentment repulsive and who prefer the values, material and otherwise, which are maximized in a free society, I urge that our present policies be carefully re-examined. It is a corollary to this position, although to some an uncomfortable one, that if the forces of competition are to have their desired effect, they will alter the structure of industries. And twenty similar sized firms in a market may be much more competitive than the two hundred previously existing in the market, notwithstanding the torturous demise of the firms not suited to remain. Once the distinction between preserving competition and protecting competitors is made clear, we can return to a fruitful debate on the policies most suited to maintain competition.

———

* Since this article was written the Justice Department has indicated that it will drop its demand for a rule against "unreasonably low prices" in the decree against GE. It is likely to do likewise with the other defendants.

138

With our last issue (November 1961) the single copy price of NEW INDIVIDUALIST REVIEW was raised from 25c to 35c. Our subscription rate, however, has remained the same. This increase was made necessary by our expanding from 32 to 40 pages.

With this issue, NEW INDIVIDUALIST REVIEW will become a quarterly; an issue of at least 40 pages will be published every three months. (We hope to be able to further increase the number of pages as soon as possible.)

Readers who enter their subscriptions prior to February 28, 1962 will receive five issues. Those who subscribe after that date will receive four issues a year at the original rate of $2.00 a year for non-students and $1.00 a year for students.

Reflections in Berlin

RALPH RAICO

THOSE AMERICANS WHO belong to the sophisticated academic circles which continue, in their hearts, to look on Communism as largely a myth invented by the John Birch Society ought to take a trip to Berlin. Here they will be able to ascertain for themselves that Communism does, indeed, exist. Hardly more perceptiveness will be required to see besides that, as a system having a claim on the sympathies of men who do not care to profit, economically or emotionally, from the servitude of others, Communism has ended in final, utter bankruptcy, a state of affairs symbolized by the wall which Ulbricht caused to be erected on August 13th of last year.

This is not to say that there was not every reason to condemn Communism before then. There were some men, stubbornly faithful to the reality-principle, who had not ceased to attack this form of totalitarianism from the very first year of the Bolshevik Revolution, when Lenin and Trotsky formed the Cheka and suppressed the Constituent Assembly, and the existence of such men is an unanswerable reproach to those others, less respectful of the facts which began emerging from Russia at a very early date, who were friendly to the Soviet regime in the 1920's, '30's, and '40's. The Berlin Uprising of 1953 and the Hungarian Revolution three years later should have made the issue quite clear in the minds of all men of good will; it is not mere partisanship which may lead one

to suspect the motives of a person who continues to support Soviet Communism after what happened in Budapest. But if anything *was* needed after Hungary, the events in Berlin last year have provided it. For here was realized what might have occurred to a mediocre author to put into an improbably sensationalistic novel on Communism: people were fleeing the Communist regime in such numbers that it was at last compelled *to build a wall* to keep them in!

We must, I think, agree with von Mises, who himself asserts, somewhere in his *Socialism*, that there is something grandiose about the socialist idea. This is especially true of the sub-species of socialism which is Communism. For the best and most enlightened spirits with full consciousness to, so to speak, lift their society out of history; to put an end, once and for all, to all the inherited superstitions and institutionalized abuses which "weigh like a nightmare on the brains of the living" and torture each generation anew — who can fail to be moved by the vision? And if one must employ means which even the old reactionaries—the Bourbons, the Romanoffs and the Hohenzollerns—would have found unacceptable? In that event—altogether probable, considering the scope of the changes aimed at—one can answer with the last words of Schiller's *Maid of Orleans*: "The pain lasts but a little while; the joy is eternal."[1]

Now, however, one can be excused for regarding the question as closed. A

Ralph Raico, an Editor-in-Chief of *New Individualist Review*, is currently a University of Chicago Exchange Fellow at the University of Paris. He recently returned from a trip to Berlin.

[1] "Kurz ist der Schmerz und ewig ist die Freude."

graphic comment on the above reasoning is provided by a photograph a reporter was clever enough to take, which may be seen at Amerika Haus, in West Berlin. It was snapped near the wall, and shows the office-building of a Communist newspaper, just over the boundary. The picture is taken at such an angle that the name of the newspaper, in big block letters on the side of the building, is framed by the barbed wire on top of the wall. The newspaper is—*Neue Zeit* ("New Age"). Those who, after the 13th of August, are looking for a more final condemnation of Communism can only justify their indecision by pointing to the fact that, after all, the Lord Himself has not yet come down from heaven to speak His judgment.

If you walk along Bernauer Strasse, which forms part of the boundary between the West and East Sectors, you will be able to see the nature of the threat to which the Communists responded by building their wall. Along this street there are four markers with wreaths, indicating the spots where people died, going to the extreme of jumping from the adjacent buildings in their attempt to escape to the West. One of the markers is for a German student who had been pursued across the rooftops by the Vopos (*Volkspolizisten* — "People's Police"). It sounds hackneyed, but only because the facts are so outrageously obvious: one can only think, *"This* badly do people want to leave a Communist country!" A sad little joke which is told in the East Sector asks, "What would you do if tomorrow the wall were dismantled?" The answer is, "I'd climb the nearest tree—I don't want to get trampled to death in the stampede to get out!"

What the people want to leave behind is not difficult to understand. To deal with the economic sphere first, Ulbricht's regime is in this regard a fiasco popularly and appropriately symbolized by the seven-year-old buildings on the fashionable Stalin Allee (now Karl Marx Allee) from the facades of which the tiles started a few years ago to fall off in clusters. There are continual shortages of some important food-items or others. Recently

it was potatoes (!) which were in short supply; currently, fruit is almost impossible to obtain. One can, it seems, buy all the *Wurst* one wants; any better meat is scarce and expensive. (A West Berliner told me how once tears came to the eyes of his relatives from the East Sector, as they looked on the abundance which can be found in any neighborhood grocery in the West Sector!) Clothing is expensive and decidedly inferior to any West European goods. Shoes are said simply not to be made to be walked in for a whole day. The Communist regime seems to be most negligent of all in regard to the little "luxuries" taken for granted everywhere in the West: cigarettes are expensive and tasteless; almonds and raisins for the traditional Christmas cakes were rarely to be had this year.

The Communist regime is well aware of its failure to provide its people with anything approximating the standard of living which has now become a matter of course in Western Europe, and it tries as best it can to cover up this failure. Sometimes it succeeds. I remember reading an account in the *Herald Tribune* by a reporter who visited the Leipzig Fair last year, and concluded that conditions in East Germany were not as bad as some maintain: he could see for himself that the people were living better than before. That this reporter could so unthinkingly accept at face value what he saw, testifies to an astounding naivete'. In Berlin I learned from a Saxon student who had fled to the West that the sudden manipulated annual rise in the living-standard of the Leipzigers at fair-time has become a standing source of humor in East Germany. According to one joke, the Leipzigers are the most pious people in Germany—they fast from *Messe* to *Messe*.[2]

The absence of political and intellectual freedom provides another important reason for the flight from the East Zone. The new "Socialist Legality" has either not been applied or not been of much use, if there is anything typical in the case (told me by a young lady in

_____
[2] *Messe* meaning both "mass" and "fast."

140

West Berlin and a relative of the man in question) of the Saxon who drank a bit too much at a Christmas celebration last year, began criticizing Ulbricht, and, as a consequence of the industry of an ever-alert Party member who was present, has been sentenced to five years in prison.

Most depressing of all, I found, was the climate of constant official *lying* under which people in the East must live.[3] They are, for instance, expected to believe, against their own personal knowledge, that those who fled to the West only went because they were kidnapped or bribed. In the East Sector, I saw, as another example, a sign with a statement by Ulbricht to the effect that the wall was built chiefly because an invasion by the Western powers was a real possibility. (As if, even if NATO *were* to invade East Germany, the invasion would come from isolated West Berlin!)

The almost eerie atmosphere of dishonesty is intensified by the existence, besides such explicit lies, of what might be termed "implicit," "institutionalized" lies. To this category belongs, for example, the continued maintenance of "other parties." On a walk in the East Sector, I was startled to see a neon sign across the top of a building: "Christlich-Demokratische Union" (Christian-Democratic Union)—Adenauer's party! Under this, however, was a placard the length of the building: "With the Peace Treaty for Peace and Unity of the Nation. With Socialism for the Happiness of the People." If the Communists really expect people to be impressed by such merely paper-organizations, with empty names standing for various political parties, they are reckless speculators indeed in the gullibility of man.

In the category of implicit lies must also be counted the re-naming of the old University of Berlin "Humboldt University." The use of the name of the greatest German theoretician of liberty by such a regime and for such an institu-

tion, seems to me to display almost as delicious a sense of irony as that which caused the Nazis to set above the gate at Auschwitz the motto, *Arbeit macht frei* ("Work makes one free").

A Communist-written history of "Humboldt University" states that, under the German Communist regime, the institution has "made a new start in the spirit of Humboldt." How much of this spirit exists in East Berlin may be gathered by a tour of the major book-stores, including those at the university. As observers have remarked before, they contain essentially only "Marx and technology." Of the large spirit of liberal education there is not a trace. We can take as an example the philosophy section of these shops. Besides being unusually small, they offered virtually only Marxist works. I noticed, for instance, that there were no works at all of Nietzsche or Schopenhauer. A sales-girl told me, "They are no longer published in Germany." Works of Kant were available, presumably because Engels somewhere mentions him and Fichte as "the great predecessors of Hegel and Marx." (If only Lenin had made a casual—uninformed but favorable—reference to Nietzsche in some letter!) Existentialism and modern positivism were represented only by Marxist critiques of these philosophers. The choice under the heading "Social Science" was even more limited: in the land of Max Weber and Wilhelm Dilthey, a sociology student must evidently be satisfied with the works of Walther Ulbricht and Ho Chi Minh. So much for the Communist method of realizing the spirit of Humboldt!

The suppression of intellectual freedom has, it would seem, become more, rather than less, pronounced in recent years. This, at least, is what is indicated by the statement published by Ernst Bloch, who, along with Peter Palitzsch (a well-known theater-director, said to have been Brecht's favorite pupil) was one of the East German intellectuals who broke with the regime after August 13th. The case of Bloch is an especially interesting one. One of the most prominent Marxist philosophers in Europe, Bloch had resided in

141

---

[3] This has, of course, frequently been noted and discussed by writers on Communism. For the case of Hungary, for instance, see George Mikas, *The Hungarian Revolution* (London, 1957).

the United States until 1949, when he went to the University of Leipzig to direct the *Institut fuer Philosophie*, having previously declined an offer by the (West German) University of Frankfurt-am-Main by remarking that he did not intend to become a servant of capitalism. In 1954, at the Second Congress of the National-Front, he asserted: "The peace speeches of Dulles and Adenauer only help along the war which they are planning." He was already living in the Bundesrepublik when the setting up of the wall led him to break with the East German Communists. In a letter to the (East) German Academy of Sciences, Bloch writes:

In the first years of my connection with the University, I enjoyed unhindered freedom of speech, of writing and of teaching. In recent years this s i t u a t i o n has increasingly changed. I was driven into isolation, was given no opportunity to teach, had my contact with students interrupted. My best students were persecuted and penalized, the possibility of published work was denied me, I was not able to publish in any periodical, and the *Aufbau* Press in Berlin did not fulfill its contractual obligations in regard to my work. . . . In contrast to this, universities, periodicals and my publisher in West Germany for a long time have given me an opportunity to publish and to continue unmolested the work I have done up until now. . . . At 76 years of age, I have decided not to return to Leipzig.[4]

In spite of all this, however, there are a number of important German intellectuals still loyal to Ulbricht's regime. To these, two West German publicists, W. Schnurre and G. Grass, addressed an

open letter on August 16th of last year, calling on them to denounce the erection of the wall. I do not think that much could really have been expected from these people. The novelist Anna Seghers, for instance, who is President of the (East) German Writers' League, and who was one of the persons addressed, had remarked at the time of the purge-trials under Stalin, when she was already a Communist, "I have succeeded in forbidding myself to reflect about that sort of thing."[5] As it turned out, the replies of the Communist writers who chose to respond[6] are in a way interesting. All of them passionately defended the action of "their government." They spoke of "West German militarism," "American imperialism," "the hangman-society" prevailing in the West (!), the necessity of changing the nature of man. The wall, according to the Communist composer Paul Dessau, represented a desire on the part of "the people of our republic to draw a thick line of demarcation between fascist degeneration and socialist construction." A person said to be a historian attached to the Central Committee of the SED (East German Communist Party) wrote, of West German agents in West Berlin, "They have blackmailed citizens of the German Democratic Republic into becoming secret agents, abducted children from their parents, driven young men to the Foreign Legion and young women to the white slave trade." (No proofs are offered, no sources cited.) The Presidium of the German Writers' League replied that, "The first space flights show us what man is capable of when he shakes off the burden of imperialism and its wars."[7] Not one of them in their defenses even once mentioned the fact that refugees had been streaming out of the East Zone in tens of thousands, or that this was the reason for the action of August 13th. Apparently, like Frau Seghers,

---

[4] Bloch's statement is reprinted in full in *Die Mauer, oder Der 13. August*, edited by Hans Werner Richter (Hamburg, 1961), pp. 140-141. Because of Bloch's change of camps, there has been a tendency among some writers to consider him a "hero," and to hint that now we in the West may begin to feel the discomfort of having such an "outspoken and fearless heretic" in our midst. It should be kept in mind that, as his letter makes quite clear, Bloch only left East Germany because he was personally beginning to have difficulties in freely expressing himself. In good left-Marxist form, he had never been much troubled by the Communist suppression of his philosophical opponents.

Page Sixteen

---

[5] Quoted by Walter Karsch, in *ibid.*, p. 106.

[6] As reprinted in *ibid.*, pp. 66-90.

[7] Do Newton and Einstein prove then "what man is capable of under capitalism"? Fortunately for these Communist intellectuals, they are assured that none of their colleagues will rise to point out the blunder.

these intellectuals had "successfully forbidden themselves to reflect about such things."

The position of the East German intellectuals is not an attractive one. After life-times spent in the service of a cause they at least at one time probably considered synomous with the freedom and well-being of the masses, they are now cruelly condemned to witness the results of their years of endeavoring.

Originally, as I have indicated before, it was thought that suppression of freedom of the press, abolition of academic freedom, and the dismantling of most of the rest of the legally-protected sphere of individual autonomy were justified, because, in spite of the pain caused to one or two generations, only in this way could a society at last be created where the great masses could live decently. But those who uncritically gave in to the hope that someday, somehow it would turn out this way must face the fact that the "Workers' and Peasants' State" of the Soviet Zone has proved itself utterly incapable of matching the achievements of free enterprise in the Bundesrepublik. What is left *now* as a rationale for dictatorship? That in one or two generations — or in one or two centuries — life will be better in the East than in the West? What reasonable grounds could anyone have for supposing this? And as the Communist intellectual searches for some reason, hidden in the recesses of the holy books of Marxism-Leninism, he is alone with the thought: an unarmed man was shot to death by the Vopos, as he attempted to swim across the Teltow Kanal into the West. As one French journalist wrote, addressing his Communist compatriots shortly after the erection of the wall: "Confess it: what weighs down on your minds, what makes you fear for the future, is that the Revolution and liberty have changed camps; is that you are for the jail-keepers and the hangmen, and that men everywhere are beginning to perceive it."[8]

Sad as is the personal case of these writers, however, we ought never to forget the great responsibility which, as intellectuals, they bore, and which they have acquitted quite poorly indeed. What I mean is this: the French worker who supports Communism in the vague belief that they will reduce the price of his daily bottle of wine, betrays nothing; he literally "knows not what he does." More rectitude was perhaps not to be expected from the Vopo who today murders an unarmed man fleeing to freedom: twenty-five years ago, this same Vopo would have marched with the SA and beaten old Jews in the street. That is the nature of the animal. But if the intellectuals themselves permit freedom to be destroyed—including the right to emigrate and the right to read Nietzsche—who will there be to defend it? Our French worker, or this Vopo? Freedom, especially intellectual freedom, is the immediate, urgent business of a very few people in the world. Although in the long-run freedom benefits all, almost everyone is prepared to jeer at concern with it as "ivory-tower," and to infringe it at the slightest supposed inconvenience to other interests. It is the duty of the intellectual, who should be more far-seeing than others and less liable to the shoddy emotions which are used to drown all regard for it, to guard freedom. This duty Communist intellectuals, particularly, have shamelessly betrayed.

It is, of course, difficult to defend uncompromisingly the abstract moral law against the pretexts employed by the existing powers in the world to justify their crimes; to be as uncompromising in this regard as, say, Acton was in the last century, or, to choose a contemporary American writer, as Dwight MacDonald has had the merit of being. Most intellectuals do not have the fortitude to bear the tensions such a position entails. How much easier to indulge the dream that someday "history will absolve us,"[9] to

143

---

[8] Henri A. Sabarthez, in *Rivarol*, August 24, 1961.

[9] *History Will Absolve Me* is the characteristic title of a collection of writings of Fidel Castro on sale at some American college book-stores a few months ago. Compare, from a Nazi "Folk-Book": "And even if they condemn us a thousand times over, the goddess of the eternal court of History will smile, tear up the accusation of the prosecution and the judgment of their court, for she acquits us . . ." Quoted in *Das Dritte Reich: Ansprung und Wirklichkeit*, by Hermann Glaser (Freiburg, 1961).

submit one's self to some Cause, especially one having something as grand as the Red Army, or the Awakening Nations (or the United States Air Force!) behind it, and, in a sort of moral Popular Front, to refrain from criticizing the wrongs committed in the name of this Cause. If one is fortunate enough to be able to summon the self-discipline which the Masters call for, then perhaps one can even "successfully forbid one's self to reflect" on such wrongs.

This has been the sad, sad treason of the intellectuals for decades now. It has contributed to the enslavement of the East Germans. As a look around in America today shows, it is still at work, leading intellectuals to applaud the enslavement of the Cubans, to excuse even that of the Chinese, to apologize for any immorality Power chooses to commit anywhere in the world in the name of "the masses."

For whose future enslavement, I wonder, is it even now preparing the way?

144

David Hume:

Whig or Tory?

EUGENE MILLER

DOES DAVID HUME, the leading English philosopher of the eighteenth century, deserve a place among those great political theorists of the past who valued individual liberty? This question has been debated since Hume's own century. Interpreters who deny such a place to Hume have viewed him as a Tory, rather than a Whig in the tradition of John Locke, and have insisted that he favored authority and monarchy, not liberty and free government. Russell Kirk echoes this view by describing him as an "ardent High Tory," who "stood for the Old Cause against Whiggery."[1] An opposing interpretation of Hume's political theory has come from such writers as F. A. Hayek, who emphasize Hume's influence on Adam Smith and classical liberalism. Hayek, who chooses Hume as a "constant companion and sage guide" throughout the pages of *The Constitution of Liberty*, places him in the "Old Whig" political tradition rather than in the Tory or conservative tradition.

The dominant interpretation of Hume's political philosophy places him in the Tory camp. The English Whigs writing during Hume's lifetime charged that his *History of England* and political essays favored absolute monarchy and the Tory

cause, and Thomas Jefferson branded him "the great apostle of Toryism" and claimed that his writings, along with Blackstone's, "have done more toward the suppression of the liberties of man, than all the millions of men in arms of Bonaparte."[2] In Jefferson's eyes, Hume was guilty of rejecting popular government, or government based on consent, and of defending the monarchy of the Stuarts. For this purpose, writes Jefferson, Hume

> suppressed truths, advanced falsehoods, forged authorities, and falsified records. . . . But so bewitching was his style and manner, that his readers were unwilling to doubt anything, swallowed everything, and all England became Tories by the magic of his art. His pen revolutionized the public sentiment of that country more completely than the standing armies could ever have done, which were so much dreaded and deprecated by the patriots of that day. . . . Hume, with Brodie, should be the last histories of England to be read. If first read, Hume makes an English Tory, from whence it is an easy step to American Toryism.[3]

[1] See Kirk's introduction to Hume's *Enquiry Concerning Human Understanding* (Chicago: Henry Regnery Co., 1956), p. vi.

[2] Quoted by Vernon L. Parrington, *Main Currents in American Thought* (New York: Harvest Paperbacks, 1954), I. p. 358.

[3] In *The Complete Jefferson*, ed., Saul K. Padover (New York: Duell, Sloan & Pearce, 1943), p. 1095.

Eugene Miller holds a B.A. degree from Emory University; he is currently a Danforth Fellow studying under Prof. F. A. Hayek on the Committee on Social Thought of the University of Chicago.

It is noteworthy that Jefferson believed Hume, rather than Burke, had been responsible for the growth of conservative sentiment in England during the late eighteenth century.

Recent findings concerning Hume's political theory, however, contradict the widely accepted notion that he was a Tory, and tend to support Hayek's belief that he was, in fact, an advocate of free government and individual liberty.

Ernest Campbell Mossner, Hume's biographer, has rejected the charge of Jefferson and others that Hume was a "Tory historian." According to Mossner, Hume was a sceptic who repudiated the dogmas of both the Whig and Tory *parties* of his time. Mossner does believe that Hume's political theory contains ideas in common with both the Whig and Tory *traditions*, which developed in the nineteenth century, and describes Hume as "a Liberal in the large, non-party (and, historically speaking, nineteenth-century) sense." Nevertheless he finds that Hume's political theory is "colored by a cautionary skepticism concerning the likelihood of continuous human progress that belongs to what may with equal justice be called the large, non-party, Conservative tradition."[4]

The belief that Hume opposed popular government has been undermined by the recent findings of Douglass Adair, who is recognized as an authority on *The Federalist*.[5] Adair seems to have been the first scholar to show that Hume's political essays served as a main source for James Madison's conception of republican government. In *The Constitution of Liberty*, Hayek places Hume and Madison in the same political tradition, but he does not suggest that the English philosopher might have directly influenced "the father of the Constitution." Adair shows that Hume's writings helped to transmit this political tradition to Madison.

While recent evidence discredits the opinion that Hume was simply a spokesman for the Tory cause, it does not justify the conclusion that he must therefore have been a Whig. The fact remains that Hume often ridiculed the Whig party and Whig beliefs. The practice of viewing Hume in terms of the Whig-Tory dichotomy rests on the dubious assumption that he can best be understood as a member of an eighteenth-century political party or a nineteenth-century political tradition. By the same token, it is not very helpful to ask whether Hume was a "conservative," a "liberal," or an 'individualist." These vague concepts came into use after Hume's time and have little meaning when applied to his thought.

How is Hume to be understood, if not as a Whig or a Tory? Hume provided an important clue to the proper interpretation of his political writings by referring to himself as a "philosopher." As he pointed out, a philosopher looks at political problems differently than a spokesman for a political party. The political philosopher poses such general questions as the nature of the best form of government or the proper goals of political life, and his thinking about specific issues is guided by general principles. Hume's interpreters have tended to focus on his specific statements about politics, which are often contradictory and obscure, without seeking the general principles which underly them.

The debate as to whether Hume was a Whig or a Tory must be settled in light of his over-all political philosophy. But no comprehensive account of that political philosophy has yet been offered. He has been virtually ignored by historians of political thought. His failure to write a systematic treatise on politics

---

[4] "Was Hume a Tory Historian?", *Journal of the History of Ideas*, II (April, 1941), pp. 235-36.

[5] Douglass Adair, "That Politics May Be Reduced to a Science. David Hume, James Madison, and the Tenth Federalist," *Huntington Library Quarterly*, XX (August, 1957), pp. 343-360. Gottfried Dietze, in *The Federalist* (Baltimore: The Johns Hopkins Press, 1960), cites Adair's findings in support of his own conclusion that "even before independence, there had existed complete accord between Hume and the colonists on the subject of liberty" (p. 316). Hume's influence on other founders such as Hamilton, and his sympathy for the American cause has long been recognized. The "neo-Burkeans" often refer to Burke's influence on American thought. Hume's influence has probably been far greater than Burke's, at least until the present generation of Americans.

has undoubtedly hindered the interpretation of his political theory. His brief political essays often appear contradictory, and it is difficult to formulate a unified view of political life from them.

While a full account of Hume's political philosophy is beyond the scope of a single article, some suggestions are possible as to its main features and their bearing on such issues as the Whig-Tory question, Hume's attitude toward individual liberty, and his place in the history of political theory. Mossner and Adair have provided suggestions for such an undertaking. Mossner has pointed out that Hume was sceptical of the dogmas of the Whig and Tory parties as well as of the notion of continuous human progress. Adair has called attention to Hume's emphasis on the dangers from political factions — an emphasis that is carried over into Madison's writings. These dangers may be said to have provided a starting-point for Hume's political philosophy. Adair goes on to show the importance of Hume's neglected essay on the "Idea of a Perfect Commonwealth" in shaping Madison's thought. This essay, which is crucial for a proper understanding of Hume's conception of the nature and tasks of political philosophy, indicates the purpose of his political writings.

THE DISPUTE as to whether Hume was a Whig or Tory must be settled in terms of his teachings about political factions. Hume regarded the Whigs and Tories as the leading English parties or factions of his time, and he traced their origin to the political struggles of the seventeenth century. For Madison, whose position in this area was greatly influenced by Hume's essays, factions arising from a common interest or passion are especially dangerous to the stability of popular government. He gave only passing notice, however, to a type of faction which Hume saw as particularly dangerous, i.e., "parties from principle."

Hume writes that "parties from principle, especially abstract speculative principle, are perhaps, the most extraordinary and unaccountable phenomenon that has yet appeared in human affairs."[6] As this passage shows, Hume anticipated the "age of ideology," in which bitter conflicts between opposing systems of ideas would predominate over moderate conflicts arising from opposed interests. Why had political and religious disputes become more bitter in modern times? Hume placed the blame on modern philosophers and theologians, who had allowed their speculative principles to become involved in factional disputes.

Hume viewed the Whigs and Tories as factions from principle. He observed that

as no party, in the present age, can well support itself without a philosophical or speculative system of principles annexed to its political or practical one, we accordingly find that each of the factions into which this nation is divided has reared up a fabric of the former kind in order to protect and cover that scheme of actions which it pursues.[7]

Underlying the Tory defense of monarchy is the principle that "the Deity is the ultimate author of all government." The Whigs trace government to an "original contract" and conclude that all just or legitimate government rests on the consent of the governed. Each faction insists on the absolute validity of its principle.

Hume's treatment of factions must be understood in terms of his frequent distinction between "philosophers" and "the vulgar." Factions arise among "the people" or "the vulgar," and "the people [are] commonly very rude builders, especially in this speculative way."[8] Just as the philosopher's knowledge transcends ordinary opinions, so is the philosopher above factions. Hume insists that to speak of "philosophers who have embraced a party" or faction is "a contradiction in terms."[9] To ask whether Hume was a Whig or a Tory, therefore, is to

---

[6] David Hume, *Essays Moral, Political, and Literary*, ed., T. H. Green and T. H. Grose (London: Longmans, Green, and Co., 1882), I, p. 130.

[7] *Ibid.*, p. 443.

[8] *Ibid.*

[9] *Ibid.*, p. 446.

147

miss the crucial point about his political philosophy. Whatever Hume says about the Whigs or the Tories is said not as a partisan but as a philosopher.

Hume did not conceive of the philosopher as merely a theorist, who lives apart from public affairs. While the philosopher is "above" factions, he is not indifferent to them. Hume believed that the philosopher is capable of performing certain political tasks for which ordinary citizens and even statesmen are unfitted. One of these tasks is to promote political stability by mediating between opposing factions to assuage the force of their disputes. The danger of factions provided a starting-point for Hume's political philosophy because he saw the philosopher as the citizen best fitted to mediate between competing factions, especially factions from principle. Hume's understanding of the task of the philosopher with respect to factions is stated concisely in his essay "Of the Protestant Succession":

> It belongs, therefore, to a philosopher alone, who is of neither party, to put all the circumstances in the scale, and assign to each of them its proper poise and influence. . . . If he indulges any passion, it is that of derision against the ignorant multitude, who are always clamorous and dogmatical, even in the nicest questions, of which, from want of temper, perhaps still more than of understanding, they are altogether unfit judges. . . . The following reflections will, I hope, show the temper, if not the understanding of a philosopher.[10]

Unless we understand this conception of the duty of the philosopher with respect to factions—and Hume does not allow us to forget that he is a philosopher—then we shall be unable to understand those writings in which he treats the English factions and their principles.

"Of the Original Contract" is probably the most important of the essays in which Hume discusses the principles of the two parties. He states the Tory doctrine of divine right in a brief passage at the beginning of this essay, but he does not explicitly criticize it. The remainder of this rather long essay is devoted to a vigorous and sarcastic attack on the

Whig notions of an "original contract" and government by consent. The style and emphasis of this essay might well give rise to the belief that he was sympathetic to the Tory and entirely opposed to the Whig principle. He ridicules the Whig "speculative system of politics" and claims that their "original contract" doctrine can make men "so much in love with a philosophical origin to government as to imagine all others monstrous and irregular."[11] He insists throughout this essay that the Whig principle is opposed to common sense and political stability: "Were you to preach, in most parts of the world, that political connections are founded altogether on voluntary consent or a mutual promise, the magistrate would soon imprison you as seditious for loosening the ties of obedience, if your friends did not before shut you up as delirious for advancing such absurdities."[12]

The passages in this essay that caution against violent innovations, a theoretical approach to politics, and a lack of respect for ancient ways are likely to remind the reader of some of Burke's statements.

It would be erroneous, however, to conclude from the most obtrusive statements in Hume's essays that he was simply a partisan of the Tories. As we shall see, his "perfect commonwealth," which provides for the annual election of all officials, is based on an extreme application of the doctrine of consent. The addition of a significant paragraph to the later editions of "Of the Original Contract" makes clear his intention:

> My intention here is not to exclude the consent of the people from being one just foundation of government. Where it has place, it is surely the best and most sacred of any. I only contend that it has very seldom had place in any degree, and never almost in its full extent, and that, therefore, some other foundation of government must also be admitted.[13]

Yet if Hume could agree with the Whigs that consent is the best and most

---

10 *Ibid.*, pp. 474-75.

11 *Ibid.*, pp. 448-49.
12 *Ibid.*, p. 447.
13 *Ibid.*, p. 450.

sacred basis of government, why would he ridicule and discredit the Whig principle, thereby provoking the suspicion that he was a Tory? The answer is to be found in Hume's conception of the practical tasks posed for the philosopher by factional disputes.

Hume states that one of his purposes in "Of the Original Contract" is "to encourage moderate opinions." It was to serve this purpose that Hume discredited in the minds of his readers those potentially dangerous political principles urged zealously by the Whig faction. In his attack on the Whigs and his silence concerning the Tories, Hume was guided primarily by practical rather than theoretical considerations. His intention was to say something beneficial, which is not necessarily something true. To consider principles with regard to their social effects is not the same as considering them with regard to their truth. Hume saw as clearly as Burke that a principle can be theoretically true and yet practically harmful.

At least part of the difficulty of interpreting Hume's writings can be explained by his recognition of the difference between true principles and beneficial opinions. The Whig principle of consent as the basis for just government was, from Hume's viewpoint, not so much philosophically false as practically dangerous. If Hume's purpose in writing his essays had been simply theoretical, then his sceptical philosophy would have provided him with far more reason to attack the Tory divine-right doctrine than the principle of consent.

Hume would have granted that in the past the divine-right doctrine had been used to justify political and religious oppression. By his time, however, there was no longer any likelihood that it would become a widely accepted and politically dangerous doctrine. Hume would appear to have foreseen an increasing acceptance and radicalization of Whig principles, and his attack was aimed more at the propaganda of intemperate Whig spokesmen than at the Lockean principle of consent.

It may seem strange to the modern mind that Hume would have thought it necessary to discredit noble principles or to teach opinions which are not simply true. Interpreters in the tradition of Jefferson would no doubt say that such actions reveal Hume's low opinion of human capacities, but Hume would undoubtedly reply that such critics show a lack of discrimination in failing to distinguish between philosophic men and ordinary citizens. Most citizens are guided by opinions, and what is philosophically true might be a very dangerous political opinion.

Thus Hume opposes the Enlightenment belief that all political problems can be solved by making true principles accessible to all men. In a letter to Turgot, Hume politely objects to the French economist's "agreeable and laudable, if not too sanguine hope, that human society is capable of perpetual progress towards perfection, that the increase of knowledge will still prove favorable to good government, and that since the discovery of printing we need no longer dread the usual returns of barbarism and ignorance. Pray, do not the late events in this country appear a little contrary to your system?"[14] Hume's own view is akin to the classical belief that political society must rest on "noble lies." Madison appears to agree to this when he refers in the forty-ninth *Federalist* to the proposition that "all governments rest on opinion."

In addition to attacking the opinions that he regarded as politically dangerous, Hume indicated which opinions are beneficial for citizens and should be protected. He holds that the political order stands or falls on the uncritical acceptance by most citizens of the belief that the existing laws and institutions are good simply because they are ancient and tested.

In the very essay in which Hume sets forth his "perfect commonwealth," he cautions that "the bulk of mankind [is] governed by authority, not reason, and never attribute[s] authority to anything that has not the recommendation of antiquity."[15] The Whig principle of

149

---

14 *The Letters of David Hume,* ed., J. Y. T. Greig (Oxford: The Clarendon Press, 1932), II, p. 180.

15 *Essays Moral, Political, and Literary,* op. cit., p. 480.

consent suggests that each generation and each individual is competent to judge which laws shall be obeyed. This principle undermines respect for traditional ways, which is a condition of the rule of law. As Jefferson made clear, the doctrine of consent implies that only popular government is just. Jefferson criticized Hume bitterly for suggesting that just power need not be based on majority consent, for Hume's suggestion implies that there are other legitimate forms of government in addition to the republican form. The reader may decide whether Hume or Jefferson had more foresight as to the ultimate practical consequences of the doctrine of consent.

PROFESSOR ADAIR has called attention to the influence of Hume's essay on the "Idea of a Perfect Commonwealth" in shaping Madison's view of republican government. This important essay shows that political philosophy, as Hume conceived it, involves broader practical tasks than the mediation of factional disputes.

Hume could assert that there are several legitimate forms of government besides the popular forms because he denied that consent is the *only* basis for legitimate government. Following tradition, he distinguished a variety of "pure" forms of government according to whether rule is by one person, a few men, or the many. In addition to the pure forms of government — monarchy, aristocracy, and democracy — Hume spoke of constitutions which are mixtures of two or more pure forms. He suggested that under certain conditions, any of these forms, including absolute monarchy, might be legitimate. Hume also divided governments according to whether rule is by law or by discretion.

In writing about the several forms of government, Hume did not deny, as would later relativism, that one form could be proved better than another. He agreed with the classical tradition in his belief that the forms of government must be ranked according to their merit. He avoided both the ordinary citizen's error of identifying his own form of government with the best form and the parti-

san's error of asserting that there is but one form of government that is best for all situations.

Hume's essay on the "Idea of a Perfect Commonwealth" indicated that he regarded a properly constructed republic as the best of these forms. In contrast to the Whig spokesmen, however, he set an example for the true friends of republican government by advancing his proposals with the utmost caution. His opening paragraphs are devoted to a warning against trying "experiments merely upon the credit of supposed argument and philosophy." The wise magistrate "will bear a reverence to what carries the marks of age; and though he may attempt some improvements for the public good, yet will he adjust his innovations as much as possible to the ancient fabric and preserve entire the chief pillars and supports of the constitution."

Plato and Aristotle had held that the best regime is rarely if ever possible. By the same token, Hume suggests the possibility but not the likelihood that the best regime might be established:

And who knows, if this controversy were fixed by the universal consent of the wise and learned, but, in some future age, an opportunity might be afforded of reducing the theory to practice, either by a dissolution of some old government or the combination of men to form a new one in some distant part of the world?

Speculation about the best regime need not depend for its justification, however, on the assumption that the best regime can be instituted:

In all cases it must be advantageous to know what is the most perfect in the kind, that we may be able to bring any real constitution or form of government as near it as possible by such gentle alterations and innovations as may not give too great disturbance to society.[16]

Hume's purpose in depicting the "best commonwealth" is to help statesmen and founders to formulate new constitutions or to improve old ones. Significantly, Madison refers to Hume as a "lawgiver."

---

16 *Ibid.,* pp. 480-81.

There is no need to enter here into the details of Hume's ideal commonwealth. He provided, in Madison's words, "a republican remedy for the diseases most incident to republican government." Hume believed that the main affliction of popular government in ancient times had been its turbulence, which transformed it into either anarchy or tyranny. Hume's republic, by contrast to the small republics of former times, is quite large in both territory and population. He held that factional disputes would be less violent and dangerous in a large republic. The large republic is made possible by a system of representation; checks and balances are devised by Hume to insure that the elected representatives will act in the public interest: "A republican and free government would be an obvious absurdity if the particular checks and controls provided by the constitution had really no influence and made it not the interest, even of bad men, to act for the public good."[17]

Hume's reputation as a political economist points to another mainstay of his "perfect commonwealth." He believed that the large republic could be made stable and prosperous by basing it on a commercial economy. Adam Smith, Hume's close friend, adopted the view that commerce is favorable to republican liberty and developed it at length in *The Wealth of Nations*. In that work, Smith describes Hume as the first writer to take notice of the fact that "commerce and manufactures gradually introduced order and good government, and with them, the liberty and security of individuals." [18]

Hume's conception of the tasks of political philosophy closely resembles that of Aristotle and the classical political philosophers. However, he chose a different standard to judge the forms of government. The ancients had taken their bearings by human excellence. They had insisted that in the best regime, wise statesmen would promote moral virtue in the citizens through wise laws, education, and honors. Hume took his bearings by liberty rather than virtue, and he insisted that the best regime is one that promotes the liberty of its subjects.

The ancients had believed that good government requires virtuous citizens and virtuous rulers. If liberty rather than excellence is taken as the political standard, the right of political authorities to produce moral virtue through coercive means—a right granted by the ancients—becomes questionable. Hume's "science of politics" finds a substitute for virtue through the skillful arrangement of political institutions. Thus, he was able to combine good government with minimal coercion. Human excellence was not essentially a political problem for Hume. In Hume's view, the political problem *par excellence* is to reconcile liberty which is not licence with authority which is not oppression: "Liberty is the perfection of civil society, but still authority must be acknowledged essential to its very existence."[19]

Hume's contemporary, Rousseau, also insisted that liberty should be the political standard. Rousseau did not, however, agree with Hume, that a large republic was possible. His perfect republic, which was modeled after Sparta, is harsh and austere. It is sustained by courage and other virtues, which require the restraint of the passions and the banishment of luxury. Hume shared Rousseau's belief that the ancient republics had necessarily been harsh and austere because their existence had depended on virtuous citizens. The modern commercial republic, however, would make possible the enjoyment of republican liberty without the sacrifices necessary in ancient times to sustain it. Indeed, the functioning of a commercial economy depends on the release of the passions rather than their restraint. Hume showed how liberty and luxury could be made compatible.

THE PROBLEMS surrounding the interpretation of Hume's political writings

151

---

[17] *Ibid.*, p. 99.

[18] (New York: The Modern Library, 1937), p. 385.

[19] *Essays Moral, Political, and Literary, op. cit.,* pp. 116-17.

must be seen in the light of the practical purpose of those writings, which is to carry out a broad conception of the tasks of the political philosopher. One of these tasks is to moderate factional disputes. Another task is to depict the best form of government as a guide for legislators and founders of governments. Still another is to give advice on the improvement of existing governments. These tasks are partly in conflict with each other. This conflict, which is reflected in Hume's writings, is partly responsible for his having been charged with Toryism and inconsistency.

Hume's seemingly contradictory statements about monarchies and republics can be explained by these conflicting tasks. Hume believed firmly that the establishment of the best form of government is seldom possible. The most pressing tasks for the legislator and the political philosopher, therefore, are to improve existing regimes and to decide which forms of government are suitable for existing circumstances.

Hume was certain that republican government could not be instituted successfully in England. He believed that limited monarchy, which admittedly is an imperfect form of government, was best for his contemporary England. In his writings, he was confronted with the delicate task of depicting the best form of government without weakening support in England for the existing form. In the "Idea of a Perfect Commonwealth," therefore, Hume discusses "the chief alterations that could be made on the British government, in order to bring it to the most perfect model of limited monarchy."[20] He does not mention the possibility of bringing England to the most perfect model, i.e., the republican form.

While this practical purpose helps to explain Hume's apparent vacillation between a preference for republican government and a preference for limited monarchy, it does not explain his explicit approval of absolute monarchy, which Locke had called "no form of civil government at all."

As Mossner points out, Hume was sceptical of the notion of continuous human progress. Hume shared the classical position that political systems inevitably decline. He rejected Harrington's view that the best commonwealth can be so constructed as to escape decay. Thus, he was forced to take into account the possibility that conditions in England might someday be unsuited for even a limited monarchy. He had to prescribe for such an eventuality and to prepare public opinion for it and entered upon these tasks in the essay "Whether the British Government Inclines More to Absolute Monarchy or to a Republic." In this essay, Hume predicts that the time will come when England will have to choose between absolute monarchy and republican government. Convinced that republican government would be disastrous for England, Hume writes: "I would frankly declare that, though liberty is preferable to slavery in almost every case, yet I should rather wish an absolute monarch than a republic in this Island."[21] In other essays, Hume develops the possibility that even absolute monarchy can be tempered by the rule of law.

THE CONFUSION as to whether Hume was a Whig or a Tory as well as other problems in his political writings can be resolved largely in terms of his conception of the practical problems of political philosophy. Hume was faced with the delicate task of setting forth what is best in theory without weakening public acceptance of what was best under particular circumstances. He had to write for the present and the future, for England and other nations, for philosophic men and the vulgar, about topics which are essentially controversial. In order to reconcile Whigs and Tories and to encourage moderate opinions, he was forced to emphasize not what is theoretically true, but what was beneficial under existing conditions. Hume cannot be identified with either

---

[20] *Ibid.*, p. 491.

[21] *Ibid.*, p. 126.

faction, for he wrote always as a philosopher and not as a partisan.

In order to understand Hume's writings properly, it is necessary to grasp his conception of the tasks of political philosophy. One reason for the failure of recent interpreters to understand the intention of Hume's political writings is the change just after his time in the meaning of political philosophy. Adair calls attention to this change when he writes that after the French Revolution, " 'philosopher' would be a smear-word, connoting a fuzzy-minded and dangerous social theorist—one of those impractical Utopians whose foolish attempts to reform society according to a rational plan created the anarchy and social disaster of the Terror."[22]

Many of the differences between Hume and Burke can be traced to their differing attitudes toward philosophy. Hume recognized as fully as Burke that imprudent philosophers could be highly dangerous. Yet unlike Burke, Hume saw that practical political activity is ultimately dependent on theoretical guidance. Hume believed that one task of the philosopher is to advise legislators on proper forms of government. It was in this respect that Madison, who calls Hume a "lawgiver," was influenced by Hume's writings. Burke's hostility to theory as such, and not merely misused theory, blinded him to the sense in which constitutions are created rationally. Hume's praise for the founders of governments contrasts sharply with Burke's statement that "the very idea of the fabrication of a new government is enough to fill us with disgust and horror."[23] Burke tended to hold that whatever survives historically is best. Philosophy furnished Hume with a trans-historical standard. The practical consequence of this difference is to be seen in the fact that while Burke tended to accept the British Constitution as the model, Hume, by virtue of his theoretical understanding of the nature of the best regime, fully recognized its imperfections.

153

---

[22] Adair, *op. cit.,* p. 344.

[23] *Reflections on the Revolution in France* (Chicago: Henry Regnery Co., 1955), p. 50.

New Individualist Review welcomes contributions for publication from its readers. Essays should not exceed 3,000 words, and should be type-written. All manuscripts will receive careful consideration.

The Judicial Philosophy of
Felix Frankfurter

MARTIN GLASSER

IN HIS DISCUSSION of the causes of the dissolution of the United States in 1861, Lord Acton stated that "democracy . . . must stand or fall according to its choice, whether to give the supremacy to the law or to the will of the people."[1] Since the end of the Civil War we have been more or less continuously choosing in favor of the supremacy of the will of the people. During this period only the branch of government not responsible to the populace, the Supreme Court, resisted the popular will and stood as a bulwark in defense of the law and the concept of limited government proclaimed by the Constitution. In doing its traditional task of defending liberty against the encroachment of the State, it earned the scorn of the many "progressive" social thinkers who looked with anger at the Court for striking down their legislation.

As the tradition of liberty gradually eroded under the pounding of its critics, the Court slowly renounced its duty to enforce the Constitution and eventually capitulated. Foremost among the present members of the Court who have led in this renunciation is Associate Justice Felix Frankfurter. Appointed to the Court in 1939, he personifies the Court's efforts to prostrate itself at the feet of the popular branches of government.

With the New Deal came a series of laws which violated the spirit of the Constitution. Twelve of these laws were struck down by the Supreme Court as unconstitutional. But even while the Court was dealing setback after setback to the New Deal, the minority of the justices who supported the interventionist legislation were erecting the judicial philosophy of "self-limitation" or "self-restraint" which was later to dominate the Court. Justice Stone's statement that "the only check upon our own exercise of power is our own sense of self-restraint,"[2] set the pace for this group.

The Justices who opposed the interventionist measures of the legislature were following the classical doctrine of judicial review, first applied by Chief Justice Marshall in the famous case of *Marbury vs. Madison.*[3] Marshall stated that it is the duty of the Judiciary to decide which among conflicting rules governs a case. If the conflicting rules are the Constitution and ordinary law, the Constitution as the paramount law of the land must prevail. If the legislature is free to pass laws without regard for the Constitution, the Constitution must be rendered ineffectual. To the Judiciary evolves the duty of seeing that constitutional limits are observed, since it cannot be expected that the legislature will enforce the Constitution against itself. The conservative Justices rather than the "judicial restraint" wing

Martin Glasser is a senior majoring in political science at the City University of New York.

---

[1] "Political Causes of the American Revolution," *Essays on Freedom And Power,* ed. Gertrude Himmelfarb (New York, 1955), p. 171.

[2] *United States v. Butler,* 297 U.S. 1, p. 79 (1936).

[3] 1 Cranch 137 (1803).

of the Court were in the classic stream of constitutional interpretation when they struck down the interventionist economic legislation, although these same conservative justices were often as unwilling to apply judicial review in defense of civil rights as the present court is to apply it in defense of property rights.

Those who upheld the Marshallian view were soon crushed. In 1937 the Court capitulated and the New Deal went on a rampage. Eventually, with the death and retirement of the alleged reactionaries, the Court became entirely dedicated to the ideal of judicial self-restraint. However, there arose a faction which put limits on the idea of judicial self-restraint. This faction did not derive from those judges who followed Marshall. but found its roots in the decisions of Justice Brandeis. Brandeis was one of the earliest American advocates of government intervention, but was also one of the staunchest defenders of civil liberties. It was he who said that "experience should teach us to be most on our guard to protect liberty when the government's purposes are beneficent."[4] This school of thought is known as "activism" or "dynamism" because of its advocacy of judicial review in cases concerning civil rights. It stands for an absolute view of the First Amendment. Its opponents sneeringly refer to its position as the defense of "preferred liberties."

In opposition to the activists, those who followed judicial self-restraint all the way put up the old arguments which were founded on the decisions of Justice Holmes and which were used against the conservatives who defeated Roosevelt's pre-1937 legislation. They represented an extreme reaction to the conservative view. Whereas the conservatives vetoed freely those laws they thought to be unconstitutional, the self-restraint school insisted on abstention from almost all interference with the "representatives of the people." They claimed that the conservatives abused judicial review. Of course, judicial re-

view was not abused, the legislature merely abused the Constitution. This confusion is not rare. The conservative Justices were accused of asserting property rights to the detriment of human rights, whereas they only maintained that property rights are an inseparable part of human rights.

With this extreme fear of judicial review, the self-restrainers saw no reason to make exceptions in civil liberties cases. Needless to say, the controversy over whether civil liberties are to follow property rights out of the fold of judicial protection has totally obfuscated any thought of property rights. The main issue today is that between Justices Douglas and Black on the activist side, and Justice Frankfurter on the self-restraint side, in the battle over whether civil rights shall remain exempt from the popular will in the form of Congress, the President, and the state governments.

From a liberal point of view, neither side is attractive.[5] However, the Douglas-Black activist position does have two things in its favor:

(1) It is in favor of protecting civil rights which should be dear to all true classical liberals.

(2) It keeps alive the spark of a judiciary which is alert to its duty of enforcing the Constitution against the government and gives us hope that this spark may someday burst into a flame that will topple the interventionists and their laws.

As mentioned previously, the Frankfurter position was loosely derived from Holmes. Holmes once said to Justice Stone: "About seventy-five years ago I learned that I was not God. And so, when the people . . . want to do something I can't find anything in the Constitution expressly forbidding them to do, I say, whether I like it or not, 'Goddammit, let 'em do it!' "[6] Frankfurter's judicial philosophy builds on this brief and informal statement.

155

[4] *Olmstead v. United States*, 277 U.S. 438, p. 479 (1928).

[5] I use the term liberal according to its 19th century meaning. The 19th century liberal attempted to limit state power and activity and to foster the liberty of the individual.

[6] As quoted in Bernard Schwartz, *The Supreme Court* (New York, 1957), p. 23.

An admirer of Frankfurter has said of him that:

> He would resolve all reasonable doubt in favor of the integrity of sister organs of government and the people to whom they must answer. He would adhere, that is, to the deepest of all our constitutional traditions, the dispersion of power — though, as in the "flag salute" cases, the immediate result offends his own generous heart's desire. He is wary of judicial attempts to impose justice on the community; to deprive it of the wisdom that comes from self-inflicted wounds and the strength that grows with the burden of responsibility. It is his deepest conviction that no five men, or nine, are wise enough or good enough to wield such power over the lives of millions. In his view, humanitarian ends are served best in that allocation of function through which the people by a balance of power seek their own destiny. True to the faith upon which democracy ultimately rests, the Justice would leave to the political processes the onus of building legal standards in the vacuum of doubt. For in his view only that people is free who chooses for itself when choice must be made.[7]

Readers of Orwell's *Nineteen Eighty-Four* will recall the insidiously illiberal effects of altering the definitions of words. The above panegyric illustrates Orwell's contentions. One may easily assume that the person described is a liberal and not suspect that he defends the government's aspiration to omnipotence.

Professor Wallace Mendelson, the author of this plethora of praise, establishes Frankfurter as the champion of the people. It is indeed a noble task to defend the free choice of the people! However, one must be forgiven for closer investigation of precisely what comprises the "people" as defined by Professor Mendelson and Oliver Wendell Holmes, Jr. They were, it appears, under the impression that the people and the legislature are coextensive. But no less a thinker than John Stuart Mill was of the opinion that "the 'people' who exercise the power, are not always the same people with those over whom it is exercised, and the 'self-government' spoken of, is not the government of each by himself, but of each by all the rest."[8] In a manner similar to Rousseau's wonderful transposition of the people into the General Will, the apologists for unlimited legislative power have transposed the people into the legislature.

PRACTITIONERS OF Hitler's "big lie" technique would be unsurprised at the effectiveness of this method. Expedience is the only criterion for a self-aggrandizing politician. Why is the politician aided in his task by those who should be disinterested in these matters? Yet they do aid him by confusing free individual action with the decisions of the legislature. So liberally-oriented minds become confused in their efforts to distinguish between demagoguery and the liberal point of view. America's tradition could absorb the New Deal only through semantic tricks which identified it with its arch-enemy, liberalism. In this spirit Frankfurter and company scream about the "essential democracy," free choice, and seeking one's own destiny, while opting for elective despotism.

Of course the villains of these Statist theatrics are the Supreme Court Justices, for whether they exercise it or not, they hold the constitutional power to veto the alleged free choice of the people. And "even the narrow judicial authority to nullify legislation . . . serves to prevent the full play of the democratic process."[9] Further, by refusal to exercise their veto, they inevitably place the stamp of constitutional authorization on interventionist legislation in the eyes of the public.

According to Frankfurter, "to fight out the wise use of legislative authority in the forum of public opinion and before legislative assemblies . . . serves to vindicate the self-confidence of a free people."[10] That is, the democratic process justifies the confidence of the people and aids in their growing political

---

[7] Wallace Mendelson, *Justices Black and Frankfurter: Conflict in the Court* (Chicago, 1961), p. 131.

[8] *On Liberty* (New York, 1873), p. 14.

[9] *West Virginia v. Barnette*, 319 U.S. 624, p. 650 (1943).

[10] *Minersville v. Gobitis*, 310 U.S. 586, p. 600 (1940).

156

maturity. The legislature must assume responsibility for public policy and not the Supreme Court.

The only thing that grows with the burden of legislative responsibility is power, and as power mounts, freedom recedes. The legislature assumes responsibility which rightfully belongs to the people, and I use the term "people" in its simple, ungarnished definition. The only thing that can teach the legislature responsibility—and by this I mean, the knowledge of its proper *limits*—is to have the Court remind them of the exact extent of its power, whenever this power is exceeded.

Thus the idea that each man should decide for himself has been twisted to mean that the legislature should decide for itself without being called to account by the Court. In fact, the Statists have assigned to the Court the position that the liberals have assigned to the legislature; and, further, they have assigned to the legislature the position that the liberals have assigned to the people. The result is that freedom has become power.

Even the venerable concept of judicial impartiality has been violated by such reasoning. Frankfurter contends that "it can never be emphasized too much that one's own opinion about the wisdom or evil of a law should be excluded altogether when one is doing one's duty on the bench."[11] A judge should not write his "private notions of policy into the constitution."[12] What does Frankfurter suppose *he* is doing when he abstains from invalidating laws? Inaction, as well as action, is a manifestation of "private notions."

This is only an aspect of Frankfurter's type of judicial impartiality. The crux of his injustice to this concept is his complete misuse of it. The idea of judicial impartiality implies that the judge should unbiasedly apply the law in all cases. Frankfurter wants the Court to generally refrain from invalidating any legislation as being unconstitutional. He has dressed the policy of judicial self-restraint in the robes of an impartial re-fusal to impress one's personal ideas on the adjudication of a case. An independent judge, not to be influenced by any considerations but constitutionality, is seen to be biased, whereas a judge who slavishly follows the legislature is hailed as one who refrains from imposing his own feelings on a case.

Translated into action Frankfurter's ideals turn out such decisions as those in the flag salute cases.[13] In these cases Frankfurter talks about the problems of national security and individual freedom in a most grandiloquent manner, concluding that if we are to cater to each individual conscience we must weaken our national security.

It seems that the threat to our national security came from certain young school children who refused to salute the flag on the basis of sincere religious belief. More confusion: this time highfaluting principles were related to irrelevant facts. Will the United States crumble if a group of children refuse to salute the flag? God save America if this be so, because the compulsory flag salute won't. Nobody can deny the primacy of national security; anybody can deny that the few school children in this case threatened it.

But Frankfurter states that it isn't his duty to decide on the wisdom of an act of a legislature (i.e., in at least one of these cases, the Board of Education which was constituted by the legislature). Although those Justices who decided in favor of the school children probably thought that they had acted wisely on the basis of some extraconstitutional moral standard, they voted for the school children strictly on the basis of their constitutional position — that the fourteenth amendment guarantees religious liberty through its incorporation of the first amendment. The ones who acted emotionally in these cases were Frankfurter and his followers, and they voted according to their emotional attachment to unrestricted majority rule.

The only thing that Frankfurter can offer to the Jehovah's Witnesses is the glory of the democratic process. What does this mean? A hopeless minority

---

[11] *West Virginia v. Barnette*, p. 647.
[12] *Ibid.*

[13] *Minersville v. Gobitis* and *West Virginia v. Barnette.*

must campaign to change the prejudicial laws of a hostile majority. But it was precisely the purpose of the Constitution to guard against the majority's incursions into minority rights, so that the minority would not have to rely on the capricious tolerance of the majority. It is essential to democracy that the polls be open to all; it is essential to liberty that individual rights are not determined at the polls.

In these cases, Justice Brandeis' warning against governmental interference with liberties in the name of some beneficent purpose has been ignored. National security has been set up as a basis for trampling on religious liberty just as political freedom was trampled on in cases where allegedly subversive activity was subject to restrictive legislative activity.

In voting against the Communists' political freedom, Frankfurter tells us that the government must be strong enough to survive. The German Communists, along with the Jews, were the first inmates of Hitler's concentration camps. Both of these groups represented a threat to the safety of the Reich. By legislative inquisition and prior arrest (i.e., arrest for yet to be committed crimes, or such committed crimes as advocacy or conspiracy), we follow the same path. Just as flag salutes will not save us, deprivation of the Communists' political liberties will not save us. However, it cannot be denied that the latter method will most definitely preserve a land that bears a striking geographical resemblance to the United States, but with none of its political characteristics.

In the Dennis case, Frankfurter asserts that the decision as to whether freedom or national security shall prevail entails the utilization of a balancing process. Needless to say this process is the function of the Congress for the "Courts are not representative bodies. They are not designed to be a good reflex of a democratic society."[14]

After listing the usual facts against the Communists, Frankfurter poses these questions to the Court: "Can we then say that the judgment Congress exercised was denied it by the Constitution? Can we establish a constitutional doctrine which forbids the elected representatives of the people to make this choice? Can we hold that the First Amendment deprives Congress of what it deemed necessary for the Government's protection?"[15] The answer is clear. The first amendment deprives the federal government of the power to abridge freedom of speech.

The defendants in *Dennis* were convicted of such nebulous crimes that one is reminded of the prosecutions common to Czarist or Communist Russia. The Constitution provides for treason. No one would oppose the conviction of seditioners. *These men are accused of conspiring to teach conspiracy!*

THE PROBLEM IS that we have simply ignored the form the internal Communist threat is taking. And Frankfurter seems to realize this when he quotes George Kennan's plea for an end to the use of Communist technique in the struggle against them.[16] However, Frankfurter insists policy decisions are within the sphere of the Congress and not the Court. He may acknowledge that a policy is unwise, but he may not strike it down on this basis. The formula of leaving it to Congress is nothing more than a declaration that the only restraint on Congress is its own self-restraint. It is merely deceptive to talk about a balancing process between national security and freedom of speech when the only spokesman for the latter side has disqualified itself. In a word, the whole thing adds up to the end of freedom for anyone who does not have the votes to protect himself.

The most horrible thing about all this is Frankfurter's usually persistent advocacy, especially in the flag salute cases, of keeping open the "remedial channels" of the "democratic process." This should be sacrosanct and beyond legislative interference. Everyone must be entitled to campaign for seeing his own point of view prevail in the legislature. Everyone? Obviously the American Communist

---

14 *Dennis v. United States*, 341 U.S. 494, p. 525 (1950).

15 *Ibid.*, p. 551.
16 *Ibid.*, pp. 554-555.

is of a certain gender which finds no place in the expression "everyone."

It is true that Frankfurter maintains in *Dennis* that "the democratic process at all events is not impaired or restricted."[17] But the Communist Party was outlawed and prevented by law from partaking in the democratic process. It is true that non-Party members could restore its liberty, but it cannot be denied that the remedial channels had been all but completely blocked through the illiberal rules of the Smith Act.

Individual liberty has found no friend in Frankfurter in a variety of other cases. In *Beauharnais v. Illinois*[18] his opinion upheld a criminal libel statute as applied to an area of discussion proscribed by the state: publications which expose "the citizens of any race, color, creed or religion to contempt, derision or obloquy." The defendant had distributed leaflets expressing opinions against the Negro race which, however reprehensible, were probably shared by a large percentage of Americans. He was not permitted to defend himself by showing either the truth of the statements or the fact that they were not likely to produce a clear and present danger of public disturbance.

In *Korematsu v. United States,*[19] it was determined that the Constitution allows the nation to conduct war. Frankfurter maintains that "to talk about a military order that expresses an allowable judgment of war needs by those entrusted with the duty of conducting war as an unconstitutional order is to suffuse a part of the Constitution with an atmosphere of unconstitutionality."[20] In other words, constitutional guarantees are to be overruled by the generals (with the aid of Congress) whenever they feel that it is good tactics, because they have the power to wage war. American citizens who committed no other crimes, but to be of a minority racial origin, must be placed in concentration camps, because the generals think that it is good tactics. It becomes quite obvious that in wartime we are subject to the generals, and we may

enjoy what liberty they care to bestow, if this rule is to be followed. The amazing thing in this case is that the uncontradicted evidence points to Korematsu's unswerving loyalty to the United States.

In his pre-Supreme Court writing and activity, Frankfurter had demonstrated a high regard for aspects of freedom. I think particularly of his part in the Sacco-Vanzetti case and the post-World War I red-baiting activity. However, his judicial thinking has been so dominated by the idea of majority supremacy as manifested by the legislature, that it is impossible to think of him as being in any way a friend of freedom. His attacks on the preferred freedoms of Justice Black and Douglas indicate that he prefers no freedom other than what the representatives of the people care to bestow. And as Lord Acton suggests, freedom has no basis in arbitrary will—even the will of the majority.

IN HIS CLASSIC essay, *On Liberty*, John Stuart Mill states that the aim "of patriots, was to set limits to the power which the ruler should be suffered to exercise over the community; and this limitation was what they meant by liberty."[21]

Frankfurter's patriot would not acknowledge any limit to the power of the state (which he would spell with a capital "S"). Alexis de Tocqueville described this mentality: "The French, under the old monarchy, held it for a maxim . . . that the King could do no wrong . . . . The Americans entertain the same opinion with respect to the majority."[22] So the Divine Right of kings becomes the Divine Right of majorities.

Liberals have always fought authority, and the most perceptive did not give up the fight when the *anciens regimes* of Europe disintegrated. Instead they noted and took issue with a new source of authority. Lord Acton, Mill, and Tocqueville all warned against the tyranny of the majority.

Acton stated: "By liberty I mean the assurance that every man shall be protected in doing what he believes his duty

[17] *Ibid.*, p. 552.
[18] 343 U. S. 250 (1951).
[19] 323 U.S. 214 (1944).
[20] *Ibid.*, pp. 224-225.

[21] Pp. 10-11.
[22] *Democracy in America* (New York, 1900), I, pp. 259-260.

against the influence of authority and majorities, custom and opinion."[23]

Mill held that "the majority, or those who succeed in making themselves accepted as the majority: the people, consequently, *may* desire to oppress a part of their number; and precautions are as much needed against this, as against any other abuse of power."[24]

Tocqueville forecast: "If ever the free institutions of America are destroyed, that event may be attributed to the unlimited authority of the majority."[25]

But the lessons of these men have not been heeded and today Frankfurter rests his case for democracy on the right of the citizen to cast a vote for the demagogue who promises the most. His "democratic process" is the only thing that distinguishes our system as it is now from self-admittedly reactionary systems. No longer is the individual sovereign in his own sphere—the majority is. All limits have been thrown to the wind. There is no convincing the alleged progressive that a living Constitution is not a dead Constitution. They firmly believe that "true" democracy can only be manifested by unhindered majority rule and individual or minority conscience is irrelevant to the definition of democracy.

The framers of the Constitution were not so cavalier about minority rights. They viewed their product as being analogous to a corporation charter. The charter allows the corporation to undertake certain activities and forbids them others. When the corporation acts *ultra vires*, it acts illegally. The Constitution is the charter of the federal government and it defines the limits of the government's powers. When the government exceeds these limits, it acts illegally. The sovereign majority is supreme within the public sphere, but acts illegally when it acts beyond that constitutionally-defined sphere.

John Locke favored the right to revolt when the government acted beyond its limits. In the United States the judicial safeguard to the Constitution was invented as a peaceful substitute. That is, the courts are to look after our liberty, and for this purpose they must be totally independent of the ebb and flow of political events.

It is Frankfurter's contention that "to the legislature no less than to the courts is committed the guardianship of deeply-cherished liberties."[26] In reply to this it may be worthwhile to quote James A. Bayard:

> How vain is a paper restriction if it confers neither power nor right. Of what importance is it to say, Congress is prohibited from doing certain acts, if no legitimate authority exists in the country to decide whether an act done *is* a prohibited act? Do gentlemen perceive the consequences which would follow from establishing the principle that Congress have the exclusive right to decide on their own powers? This principle admitted, does any Constitution remain? Does not the power of the Legislature become absolute and omnipotent? Can you talk to them of transgressing their powers, when no one has a right to judge of those powers but themselves?[27]

Of course liberty cannot long endure if the spirit of the nation is hostile to it, regardless of even a determined Court. The Court can only check occasional lapses from constitutionality; in the long run, the Congress will approve only those judges who will abide by its policy. The people must be shown that the policy of liberty is still valid.

Conservatives today speak much of a renaissance of their ideals. Unfortunately, liberalism cannot make the same claim. There is no popular opposition to the principles of Statism today. Liberalism is hardly known, let alone followed. Intellectuals either regard it as outdated or as having organically developed into what is called liberalism today. Many think of John Stuart Mill's development from a liberal to an admirer of moderate socialism as symbolic of the development of liberalism.

Although the future looks bleak, the liberal acknowledges no laws of history and therefore knows liberty will remain within reach as long as he strives for it.

---

[23] "The History of Freedom in Antiquity," *Essays On Freedom And Power*, op. cit., p. 55.
[24] On Liberty, p. 14.
[25] Democracy In America, I, p. 273.

[26] *Minersville v. Gobitis*, op. cit., p. 600.
[27] As quoted in Schwartz, op. cit., p. 7.

The Intellectual Collapse of European Socialism

WILHELM ROEPKE

THERE HAS BEEN occurring recently in Europe something which can hardly be surpassed in significance. For more than a century the idea of socialism and the socialist movement have so shaken the foundations of our civilization that one could well write the history of these hundred years—let us say, from the *Communist Manifesto*, in 1847, to the challenge directed against the world by the Communist Empire—from the perspective of the intellectual, social and political struggle over socialism.

The intellectual origin of modern socialism lies in the French Revolution of 1789 and its painful consequences. But no country has been more important for the further advance of socialism in Europe, and in the rest of the world, than Germany. It was three German intellectuals — Marx, Engels, and Lassalle — who cast the socialist idea into the form in which it captured the masses, and among these three, Marx quickly became the real leader. It is, then, the socialist party of German, which, in the name and spirit of Karl Marx, but also making use of Prussian discipline and talent for organization, has made this country into a model of the socialist movement. No socialist party was more respected than this one, none had greater power and authority.

From the German Social Democrats — this was the new name which the German socialists soon took for themselves— the socialist leaders of other countries derived the spirit and the technique of the modern mass-party, and its program became a model to the others. It is obvious that, without Marx, there would have been no Lenin, and ultimately, no Khrushchev. But it is even questionable whether the triumph of Communism in Russia would have been at all possible without the preliminary work of German Social Democracy and its great leaders from Liebknecht to Bebel.

And, now what is the great event of which I spoke at the beginning? Nothing less than the fact that this German Socialist Party, on November 15, 1959, at Bad Godesberg, adopted a new program which leaves scarcely anything over from its socialist tradition but the name. This tradition meant that the socialists demanded "socialization," i.e., the expropriation of banks, mines or industrial firms by the state. This demand has now been buried. The tradition further demanded the ordering of economic life through a planned economy, which would replace the market, competition, the free play of supply and demand, and the unhampered initiative of free entrepreneurs by the decree of the state and the administration of the economy by the state's bureaucracy. This demand, too, has disappeared from the program of German Social Democracy. The party now explicitly confesses to the tried and proven merits of com-

Wilhelm Roepke is a professor in the graduate school of the University of Geneva and an economic advisor to the German Federal Republic. His most recent book is *A Humane Economy*.

This essay is translated from the German by Ralph Raico.

petition, of free prices and of entrepreneurial initiative, thereby appropriating to itself the liberal economic policy of the hitherto so bitterly attacked and derided Economic Minister Erhard. Just a few years ago the socialists — the Germans and those of other countries—were prophesying an ignominous end for this "social market economy": now they acknowledge it to be incomparably superior to the socialist concept of the planned economy, and the German socialists have taken it up themselves. The name "Marx" appears nowhere in the whole program. Moreover, there is virtually not a trace left of his spirit. Adam Smith, the founder of liberal economic theory, has triumphed over Marx.

The socialist party of Germany, in a word, no longer wishes to bring about that economic order which has hitherto been its principal aim, and which is realized in its purest form throughout the Communist world empire. The socialists confess that they set greater store by free competition, free prices and free entrepreneurial initiative than by a planned economy, state-run enterprises and central direction of production and consumption. This is indeed astounding but will surprise no one who has attentively followed the development of socialism in Germany, as well as in other countries. In Germany, as in Switzerland and Great Britain, it has become especially evident that the old socialists' program of socialization and the planned economy has not only lost its previous overpowering force, but actually repels the great masses of voters. For these voters fear that the realization of this program might imperil the extraordinary prosperity which t h e masses in these countries are enjoying. They have been furnished with an object lesson in political economy, such as no previous generation ever experienced. The fiasco that socialist parties have suffered in every case in which they were offered the opportunity to carry out their program of socialization and the planned economy is as gross and palpable as the success of the opposite, liberal course of the market economy and economic freedom. The last great nations in Europe

which have once more demonstrated this have been Great Britain and France.

If the socialist parties do not take this development into consideration, they will be in danger of losing more and more political ground. They run the risk of "perishing as sects," as the Chairman of the German Social Democrat Party, Herr Ollenhauer, exclaimed at Bad Godesberg, in his effort to have the new program adopted.

It is certainly doubtful whether this complete capitulation of the German socialists to the principles of economic liberalism is the expression of an honest conviction. That would be more than one could expect. The fight over the new program was not settled without the supporters of the socialist tradition and the modernists finally coming to terms, and a great deal of compromise between socialism and liberalism was necessary. One can even be of the opinion that these compromises would allow a socialist government much of the "old" socialism, without the government having openly to disavow its program. In short, the capitulation of socialism to liberalism is neither absolute nor free from the suspicion of being, to a certain degree, a political maneuver. But, in the first place, it is that to a certain degree only: in the case of many German socialists, the conversion is genuine and honest. And, in the second place, the new program demonstrates, at any rate, the compelling power that the liberal economy, i.e., the economic system based on the market, competition, free prices, private property and entreprenurial initiative—has gained over the voting masses through its own success and through the failure of the socialist economy. It is important to recognize that this turnabout of German Social Democracy would scarcely have been possible if the Communist Party had not been outlawed as incompatible with the Constitution. It has been only through this that Social Democracy won the freedom of maneuver necessary for the change in program: otherwise, it would have had to fear the defection of its radicals leftwards, to the Communists.

On Freedom and the Law[1]

MURRAY N. ROTHBARD

WHILE AT LEAST a corporal's guard of libertarian economists exists in America today, the situation in the other disciplines of human action is indeed bleak. Most political scientists, for example, are either engaged in spinning fallacious scientistic "models" or in solemnly recording the empirical *minutiae* of the workings of government bureaucracy. The small minority of political philosophers (those who still grapple with such basic questions as the nature and proper function of the State) trumpet the alleged glories of Order, Tradition, Community, the "Leap in Being," and Good Manners, but somehow remain silent about the liberty of the individual. This pervading miasma makes all the more welcome the publication of a notable series of lectures by Professor Bruno Leoni, eminent jurist and political scientist of the University of Pavia, Italy. For here at last is a political scientist with strong libertarian inclinations.

Professor Leoni's major thesis is that even the staunchest free-market economists have unwisely admitted that laws must be created by governmental legislation; this concession, Leoni shows, provides an inevitable gateway for State tyranny over the individual. The other side of the coin to increasing intervention by government in the free market has been the burgeoning of legislation, with its inherent coercion by a majority —or, more often, by an oligarchy of pseudo-"representatives" of a majority— over the rest of the population. In this connection, Leoni presents a brilliant critique of F. A. Hayek's recent writings

on the "rule of the law." In contrast to Hayek, who calls for general legislative rules as opposed to the vagaries of arbitrary bureaucracy or of "administrative law," Leoni points out that the real and underlying menace to individual freedom is not the administrator but the legislative statute that makes the administrative ruling possible.[2] It is not enough, demonstrates Leoni, to have general rules applicable to everyone and written down in advance; for these rules themselves may—and generally do—invade freedom.

Leoni's great contribution is to point out to even our staunchest *laissez-faire* theorists an alternative to the tyranny of legislation. Rather than accept either administrative law *or* legislation, Leoni calls for a return to the ancient traditions and principles of "judge-made law" as a method of limiting the State and insuring liberty. In the Roman private law, in the Continental Civil Codes, in the Anglo-Saxon common law, "law" did not mean what we think today: endless enactments by a legislature or executive. "Law" was not *enacted* but *found* or discovered; it was a body of customary rules that had, like languages or fashions, grown up spontaneously and purely voluntarily among the people. These spontaneous rules constituted "the law";

163

Murray N. Rothbard received his Ph.D. in economics from Columbia University. He is the author of *Man, Economy and State*, recently published by Van Nostrand.

---

[1] A review of Bruno Leoni, *Freedom and the Law* (Princeton: D. Van Nostrand, 1961).

[2] Leoni also presents an effective critique of Hayek's defense of special "administrative courts." If there is to be one law for bureaucrats and yet another for ordinary citizens, then there is no equality under the law for everyone, and therefore there is no genuine "rule of law." Here, as elsewhere, Leoni rehabilitates the stringent rule of law championed by the great nineteenth century English jurist, A. V. Dicey, as contrasted to the weaker modern versions of Hayek and C. K. Allen.

and it was the works of experts in the law — old men of the tribe, judges, or lawyers — to determine what the law was and how the law would apply to the numerous cases in dispute that perpetually arise.

If legislation is replaced by such judge-made law, says Leoni, fixity and *certainty* (one of the basic requirements of the "rule of law") will replace the capriciously changing edicts of statutory legislation. The body of judge-made law changes very slowly; furthermore, since judicial decisions can only be made when parties bring cases before the courts, and since decisions properly apply only to the particular case, judge-made law — in contrast to legislation — permits a vast body of voluntary, freely-adopted rules, bargains, and arbitrations to proliferate as needed in society. Leoni brilliantly shows the analogy between these free rules and bargains, which truly express the "common will" of *all* participants, and the voluntary bargains and exchanges of the free market.[3] The twin of the free market economy, then, is *not* a democratic legislature ever grinding out new *diktats* for society, but a proliferation of voluntary rules interpreted and applied by experts in the law.

While Leoni is vague and wavering on the structure that his courts would take, he at least indicates the possibility of privately competing judges and courts. To the question: who would appoint the judges. Leoni answers with the question: who now "appoints" the leading doctors or scientists in society? They are not appointed, but gain general and voluntary acceptance on their merits. Similarly, while in some passages Leoni accepts the idea of a governmental supreme court which he admits becomes itself a quasi-legislature,[4] he does call for the restoration of the ancient practice of *separation* of government from the judicial function. If for no other reason,

Professor Leoni's work is extremely valuable for raising, in our State-bemused age, the possibility of a workable separation of the judicial function from the State apparatus.

A GREAT DEFECT in Leoni's thesis is the absence of any criterion for the *content* of the judge-made law. It is a happy accident of history that a great deal of private law and common law is libertarian, that they elaborate the means of preserving one's person and property against "invasion." But a good deal of the old law was anti-libertarian, and certainly custom can not always be relied on to be consistent with liberty. Ancient custom, after all, can be a frail bulwark indeed; if customs are oppressive of liberty, must they still serve as the legal framework permanently, or at least for centuries? Suppose ancient custom decrees that virgins be sacrificed to the gods by the light of the full moon, or that red-heads be slaughtered as demons? What then? May not custom be subject to a higher test—reason? The common law contains such anti-libertarian elements as the law of "conspiracy," and the law of "seditious libel" (which outlawed criticism of the government), largely injected into the law by kings and their minions. And perhaps the weakest aspect of the volume is Leoni's veneration for the Roman law; if the Roman law provided a paradise of liberty, how account for the crushing taxation, the periodic inflation and currency debasement, the repressive network of controls and "welfare" measures, the unlimited imperial authority, of the Roman Empire?

Leoni offers several different criteria for the content of the law, but none are very successful. One is *unanimity*. But while superficially plausible, even explicit unanimity is not necessarily libertarian; for, suppose that there are no Moslems in a country, and everyone unanimously decides—and it passes into custom—that

---

[3] This contrasts to the mocking claim of "democratic" legislatures which coercively impose their rules upon dissenters, to be expressions of the "common will." To be "common," Leoni points out, the common will must be a *unanimous* one.

[4] At one point, Leoni seems to believe that the requirement of unanimity on the Supreme Court bench for any change over previous rulings

would approximately establish the "Leoni model" on the American scene. But here all depends on the "zero point" at which a unanimity requirement is introduced. In the present heavily State-ridden world, a unanimity requirement for change would tend to fasten our Statist regulations permanently upon society.

all Moslems should be put to death. And what if, later, a few Moslems should appear in the land? Further, as Leoni recognizes, there is the problem of the *criminal;* certainly *he* does not join in favoring his own punishment. Here Leoni falls back on a tortured construction of implicit unanimity, i.e., that, in such a case as murder or theft, the criminal *would* agree to the punishment if *anyone else* were the criminal, so that he *really* agrees to the justice of the law. But suppose that this criminal, or others in the community, have the philosophical belief that certain groups of people (be they red-heads, Moslems, landlords, capitalists, generals, or whatnot) *deserve* to be murdered. If the victim is a member of one of these abhorred groups, then neither the criminal nor others holding this belief would agree to the justice of either the general law against murder or to the punishment of this particular murderer. On this ground alone, the implicit unanimity theory must fall.

A second proffered criterion for the content of the law is the negative Golden Rule: "Do not unto others what you would not wish them to do unto you." But this too is unsatisfactory. For one thing, some acts generally considered criminal would still pass the negative Golden Rule test: thus, a sado-masochist can torture another person, but since *he* would be delighted to be tortured, his act, under the negative Golden Rule, could not be considered criminal. On the other hand, the Golden Rule is much too wide a criterion; many acts would be condemned as criminal which should certainly not be. Thus, the Rule decrees that men shouldn't lie to each other (a man would not want to be lied to) and yet few would urge that all lies be outlawed. Also, the Golden Rule would decree that no man should turn his back on a beggar, because the former would not want the beggar to turn his back on him were they to change places—and yet, it is hardly libertarian to outlaw the refusing of alms to a beggar.[5]

Leoni hints at a much more promising criterion: that freedom be defined as the absence of constraint or coercion—except against constrainers. In this case, the *initiation* of coercion is outlawed, and the "governmental" function becomes strictly limited to coercing the coercers. But, most unfortunately, Leoni falls into the very same trap that snared Hayek in his *Constitution of Liberty*: "coercion" or "constraint" is not defined in a proper or cogent manner.[6] At first, Leoni gives promise of a correct understanding of coercion when he says that a man cannot be said to "constrain" another when he refuses to buy the latter's goods or services, or when he refuses to save a drowning man. But then, in his unfortunate Chapter 8, Leoni concedes that constraint may occur when a religiously devout person *feels* "constrained" because another man does not observe the former's religious practices. And this feeling of constraint may appear to justify such invasions of liberty as Sunday blue laws. Here again, Leoni errs in placing his test of constraint or coercion, not on the objective acts of the defendant, but on the subjective feelings of the plaintiff. Surely this is an extremely wide highroad for tyranny!

Furthermore, Leoni apparently does not see that taxation is a prime example of coercion, and is hardly compatible with his own picture of the free society. For if coercion is to be confined to the coercers, then surely taxation is the unjust coercive extraction of property from a vast body of *non*-coercing citizens. How, then, is it to be justified? Leoni, again in chapter 8, also concedes the existence of some legislation in his ideal society, including, *mirabile dictu*, some nationalized industries![7] One specific nationalization favored by Leoni is the lighthouse industry. His argument is that

165

---

[5] A critical error—in this and other places—is Leoni's tendency to make the test of criminality the *subjective feelings* of participants, rather than their objective actions.

[6] For an excellent critique of Hayek's conception of coercion, see Ronald Hamowy, "Hayek's Concept of Freedom: A Critique," *New Individualist Review*, (April, 1961), pp. 28-31.

[7] Thus, Leoni asserts that, in those fuzzy cases where criminality or constraint cannot be objectively determined, there exists room for coercive legislation on the subject. But surely the proper —and libertarian—rule is that fuzzy cases be decided in favor of *"laissez-faire"*—of letting the activity go on.

a lighthouse could not charge individual consumers for its service, and that therefore it should be supplied by government. The basic answers to this argument are threefold: (1) the taxation for lighthouses imposes coercion and is therefore an invasion of freedom; (2) even if the lighthouse could not charge individuals, what prevents shipping lines from constructing or subsidizing their own lighthouses? The usual reply is that then various "free riders" would benefit from the service without paying. But this is universally true in *any* society. If I make myself a better person, or if I tend my garden better, I am adding to the benefits enjoyed by other people. Am I then entitled to levy tribute upon them because of this happy fact? (3) In fact, lighthouses *could* easily charge ships for their services, *if* they were permitted to *own* those surfaces of the sea which they transform by their illumination. A man who takes unowned *land* and transforms it for productive use is readily granted ownership of that land, which can henceforth be used economically; why should not the same rule apply to that other natural resource, the sea? If the lighthouse-owner were granted ownership of the sea-surface that he illuminates, he could then charge each ship as it passes through. The deficiency here is a failure, not of the free market, but of the government and the society in not granting a property right to the rightful owner of a resource.

On the necessity of taxing for government lighthouses and other services, Leoni adds the astonishing comment that "in these cases the principle of free choice in economic activities is not abandoned or even put in doubt." (p. 171) Why? Because "it is admitted" that people would be willing to pay for these services anyway, if available on the market. But *who* admits it, and to what extent? And which people would pay?

Our problem can be solved, however; a cogent criterion *does* exist for the content of libertarian law. That criterion defines coercion or constraint, simply, as: the initiation of violence, or the threat thereof, against another person. It *then* becomes clear that the use of coercion (violence) must be confined to coercing the initiators of violence against their fellow-men. One reason for confining our attention to violence is that the unique weapon employed by government (or by any other enforcing agency against crime) is precisely the threat of violence. To "outlaw" any action is precisely to threaten violence against anyone who commits it. Why not then use violence *only* to inhibit those who are initiating violence, and not against any other action or non-action that somebody might choose to define as "coercion" or "constraint"? And yet, the tragic puzzle is that so many quasi-libertarian thinkers have, over the years, failed to adopt this definition of constraint or have failed to limit violence to counteracting violence, and have, instead, opened the door to statism by using such vague, jumbled concepts as "harm", "interference", "feelings of constraint", etc. Decree that no violence may be initiated against another man, and all the loopholes for tyranny which even such men as Leoni concede: blue laws, government lighthouses, taxation, etc., would be swept away.

In short, there exists *another* alternative for law in society, an alternative not only to administrative decree or statutory legislation, but even to judge-made law. That alternative is the libertarian law, based on the criterion that violence may only be used against those who initiate violence, and based therefore on the inviolability of the person and property of every individual from "invasion" by violence. In practice, this means taking the largely libertarian common law, and correcting it by the use of man's reason, before enshrining it as a permanently fixed libertarian code or constitution. And it means the continual interpretation and application of this libertarian law code by experts and judges in privately competitive courts. Professor Leoni concludes his highly stimulating and important book by saying that "lawmaking is much more a theoretical process than an act of will." (p. 189) But certainly a "theoretical process" implies the use of man's reason, to establish a code of law that will be an unbreachable and unflawed fortress for human liberty.

Fertig's

"Prosperity Through Freedom"[1]

J. EDWIN MALONE

FOR SOME TIME the average reader in this country has been inundated with the semi-mystical economics of the New Liberals, the authors ranging from such men as Galbraith and Schlesinger to the small-town *literati* writing in the Sunday supplements. They defend, and the next minute attack, individual freedom with all the aplomb of consistent thinkers. While there are several scholarly books which present detailed analyses of the Statists' programs, works of the quality and simplicity of, for example, Hazlitt's *Economics in One Lesson* are rare. Lawrence Fertig, nationally syndicated columnist, has made a worthwhile contribution to this field with his recently published *Prosperity Through Freedom*, a work one could honestly recommend, although it leaves something to be desired as an argument for conservatism. The book ignores what may be an important motivation of our predominantly welfare-oriented public, and a few of the arguments are not as convincing as they might have been had the author risked being more sophisticated in his argumentative style. Mr. Fertig has, perhaps, underestimated both the strength of the public's fear of capitalism's so-called "plague"—depressions —and the public's requirement that unpopular opinions be presented in a more systematic manner.

Private enterprise must be preserved,

Mr. Fertig begins, because it achieves those goals which are generally accepted as the ends of a political society; it guarantees human freedom, it provides the most efficient economic system, and it responds to the self-expression of every individual. In view of the brevity and level of analysis of this work, the author is surprisingly successful in showing that welfare statism and socialism consistently fail to accomplish any one of these goals.

There is an outstanding number of widely-accepted illusions in this country about the success of European and Asian experiments with socialist economics, and the author carefully examines the most important of these.

Although *Prosperity through Freedom* is presented in the form of a series of essays covering a great multitude of topics, it is essentially an elaboration of four important contentions introduced in the first chapter. The first of these is that, ". . . today socialism stands repudiated by leading Socialists of the Western world . . . [i.e., the] doctrines formulated by Karl Marx which were at the apex of [their] popularity only a decade ago, are now dead."

Mr. Fertig clearly shows that there is an increasing awareness on the Left of the dangers of concentrating economic power in the hands of government and of the impossibility of reconciling government domination of large industries and the maintainance of a

J. Edwin Malone is an undergraduate majoring in the history of ideas at the University of Chicago. He has recently joined *New Individualist Review* as an Editorial Assistant.

[1] A review of Lawrence Fertig, *Prosperity Through Freedom* (Chicago: Regnery, 1961).

167

free market. Here he compares the development of West Germany and Great Britain at the end of World War II. It is well known that the British Labor Party, then in control, renounced the doctrine of nationalization of major industries subsequent to their abortive experiment. But in Germany things turned out differently. The United States sent an advisory commission with instructions to help the Germans revamp their economy. According to Mr. Fertig, a U. S. government document, not declassified until 1961, states, in brief, that the committee prescribed inflation. The Economics Minister of Germany, Ludwig Erhard, threatened to resign if this policy were adopted. The German government supported Erhard and the commission left, probably shaking their heads in anticipation of the ruin to come. Interestingly enough, one member of the committee was Walter W. Heller who now heads President Kennedy's Council of Economic Advisers.

Most revealing is Mr. Fertig's contention that we are being urged to embark on a dangerous course of radically altering our economic system to meet the Soviet surge of growth. This, of course, becomes one more reason for increased government interference in the market. But, the author points out, no one has yet been able to prove either that our present growth rate would not be insufficient if the government would cease its interventionist policies, or that Soviet claims concerning their own growth rate are true. He shows, in fact, that present government policy is the real villain in hindering America's economic growth, that several Soviet economic projects have admittedly been rather ludicrous flops, and, by the admission of a leading Soviet economist, the widely accepted growth-rate figures in the Soviet Union are a myth.

The liberals seem to have a special aptitude for piling false premise upon false premise, thereby deriving a maze of unrealistic conclusions. We are told that the Soviet system is the more dynamic, although this is clearly not the case. Next, the liberals say that underdeveloped countries are more interested in food

than freedom, and are, therefore, naturally inclined to ally themselves with the more dynamic economic system. In conclusion, they claim, the only way we can compete with the Soviets for popularity is to buy neutrals off. After examining instances in which the "spend-to-defeat communism" program has been attempted, the author contends that even if such a program could be maintained, it could not succeed. He concludes, "You do not kill communism by raising standards and you need not necessarily get it where the standard of living is very low. Communism flourishes where there is no strong opposing ideal to offset it."

Finally, the author examines the argument that the welfare of the people can only be achieved and maintained by increased government spending. He finds that this is a conception not only based on false premises, but, moreover, a very dangerous one for the economic and political future of the nation:

Who provides the countless improved conveniences of life — from automobiles and wonder drugs to electric dishwashers and frozen foods? Who provides the means by which people get more education, more medical care, more opportunity for expressing themselves and making progress in life according to their own lights? Plainly, it is business and professional organizations and the people who work in them who advance everybody's welfare and give us the remarkable kind of life which exists in this country. The government has had little to do with this throughout our national history.

Government, states Mr. Fertig, already spends a third of the gross national product and is apparently planning to spend more. It is precisely this that stifles investment in industry and thereby prevents an increase in productivity. Sharing with the government the responsibility for depreciation of the dollar is union labor. But even here, the responsibility is easily traceable to government. It is the legal immunity of labor unions that has allowed them to cut their own throats by totally unrealistic wage demands. Such demands seriously endanger their members' real wages, not to speak of the incomes of the majority of workers who have chosen not to join a union, and retired persons who perhaps bear the brunt of inflationary union demands. Of course, the fact that these retired people have savings in what is now an inflated currency becomes merely another reason for increased government welfare spending.

Prosperity Through Freedom does not present sophisticated and detailed analyses of these problems. It is directed primarily to the reader who has little more than an introductory knowledge of economics. Mr. Fertig's arguments are presented in quite readable style, often citing actual examples to contradict the beliefs of the New Liberals. The drawback to this method of argumentation lies in the fact that it will take only a perceptive reader, not necessarily a sophisticated economist, to notice that the author's heavy reliance on example isn't really conclusive. Only detailed and logical analysis of these problems can successfully refute the New Deal philosophy. Well chosen examples, by themselves, can be, and often are, explained away by claiming that they are merely exceptions to the rule.

Only once does the author make what appears to be a mistake common to conservative critics. He is perfectly justified in his criticism of the strong Keynesian bias in college economics courses. But he extends his argument by saying that teachers should be "subjective" in pointing out the advantages of the free enterprise system—i.e., college courses should be biased in favor of the conservative position. Why conservatives who are convinced that the facts clearly justify capitalism still hesitate to approve an objective presentation of those facts in the classroom is something of a mystery to the reviewer.

More important, Lawrence Fertig fails to come to grips with what may well be the central issue. It is probably the case that most people are content to allow the government to play a dominant role in the economy because of their belief that the free-market system is inherently plagued with periodic depressions. Although realizing the importance of this view, he offers no argument against it. In failing to do so, I believe that he has done a serious disservice to the purpose of the book.

In short, while *Prosperity Through Freedom* will win few converts to *laissez faire*, it will at least demonstrate to our unaware public the practical dangers to individual liberty and well-being of an increasingly large and dominant government.

169

NEW BOOKS AND ARTICLES

THE FOLLOWING IS A SELECT LIST OF BOOKS AND ARTICLES WHICH, IN THE OPINION OF THE EDITORS, MAY BE OF INTEREST TO OUR READERS.

Campaigne, Jameson G., *Check-Off: Labor Bosses and Working Men*, (Regnery, Chicago, 1961).

Conant, James, *Slums and Suburbs*, (Harper, New York, 1961).

Evans, M. Stanton, *Revolt on the Campus*, (Regnery, Chicago, 1961).

Hazlitt, Henry, *Economics in One Lesson*, (new paperback edition published by the Foundation for Economic Education, Irvington-on-Hudson, New York: 50¢).

Jacobs, Jane, *The Death and Life of Great American Cities*, (Harpers, New York, 1961).

Meyer, Frank S., *Freedom, Tradition, Conservatism*, and Evans, M. Stanton, *A Conservative Case For Freedom*, (The Intercollegiate Society of Individualists, Philadelphia, 1961. Free copy available from ISI, 1014 Lemcke Building, Indianapolis 4, Indiana).

St. John-Stevas, Norman, *Life, Death and the Law*, (University of Indiana Press, 1961).

Talmon, J. L., *Political Messianism: The Romantic Phase*, (Praeger, New York, 1960).

Walcutt, Charles C., (ed.) *Tomorrow's Illiterates*, (Little, Brown and Co., New York ,1961)

Weaver, Richard M., "The Importance of Cultural Freedom," *Modern Age* (Winter 1961-1962).

THE EDITORS OF NEW INDIVIDUALIST REVIEW . . .

have been much encouraged by the enthusiastic response which the appearance of a new periodical has elicited from people all over the United States. One of our editors blind-folded himself and drew a random sample of these letters out of a well-mixed box. These are some of those comments.

"Although your magazine purports to be Right-wing, it is obvious to any informed person that most of your articles are designed to subtly brain-wash uncritical readers. Your advocacy of freedom of speech for Godless Communistic conspirators is but one obvious example. We know that the enemies of our Republic are very adept at the techniques of infiltration so I am not too surprised that their handiwork is visible in the New Individualistic Review."

Elizabeth Carpin, Houston, Texas

"In tone, style and content, this piece reminds one of a Sunday tabloid expose . . . [Bruce Goldberg's review of Ayn Rand's "For the New Intellectual"] is less accurately described as an attempt at philosophical analysis than an act of juvenile delinquency . . . Mr. Goldberg has not . . . learned the elementary rules of civilized discourse . . . What I primarily object to is his manner of expressing his views—the personal abuse, the hooligan style, and Mr. Goldberg's barbarian hysteria."

Nathaniel Branden, New York City

". . . bright young fascists like yourselves are well-qualified to join the intellectual Swiss Guard of the economic royalists. I envy the futures you have ahead of you; in return for your talents as propagandists the leaders of the military-industrial complex will see to it that you are well-supplied with fat expense accounts, call girls, champagne and with any other indulgences your hearts may desire . . . "

Richard MacDonnell, New York City

"Please cancel my subscription to your Red magazine."

Joseph Kelly, Indianapolis, Ind.

170

NEW INDIVIDUALIST REVIEW   4
IDA NOYES HALL
University of Chicago, Chicago 37, Illinois

Please enter my subscription for one year at $2.00 ☐   Students,$1.00 ☐

I also enclose a contribution of $..

NAME ....

ADDRESS ....

IF STUDENT: SCHOOL...........................YEAR OF GRAD.................

"SOCIALISM is only an idea, not an historical necessity, and ideas are acquired by the human mind. We are not born with ideas, we learn them. If socialism has come to America because it was implanted in the minds of past generations, there is no reason for assuming that the contrary idea cannot be taught to a new generation. What the socialists have done can be undone, if there is a will for it. But, the undoing will not be accomplished by trying to destroy established socialistic institutions. It can be accomplished only by attacking minds, and not the minds of those already hardened by socialistic fixations. Individualism can be revived by implanting the idea in the minds of the coming generations. So then, if those who put a value on the dignity of the individual are up to the task, they have a most challenging opportunity in education before them. It is not an easy job. It requires the kind of industry, intelligence and patience that comes with devotion to an ideal."

—*Frank Chodorov*, Founder and President, Intercollegiate Society of Individualists, Inc.

INTERCOLLEGIATE SOCIETY OF INDIVIDUALISTS
For the Advancement of Conservative Thought on the Campus

410 LAFAYETTE BUILDING ~ PHILADELPHIA 6, PENN. • WAlnut 5-5682
Midwest Office: 1014 LEMCKE BUILDING • INDIANAPOLIS 6, INDIANA • MElrose 9-5551
Western Office: 1436 EL CAMINO REAL • MENLO PARK, CALIFORNIA • 325-4553

VOLUME 2
NUMBER 1
SPRING 1962

New INDIVIDUALIST Review

Spring 1962   35 cents   Vol. 2, No. 1

NEW INDIVIDUALIST REVIEW

Volume 2 – Number 1   **SPRING 1962**

NEW INDIVIDUALIST REVIEW is published quarterly (Spring, Summer, Autumn, Winter) by *New Individualist Review, Inc.*, at Ida Noyes Hall, University of Chicago, Chicago 37, Illinois.

Opinions expressed in signed articles do not necessarily represent the views of the editors. Editorial, advertising, and subscription correspondence and manuscripts should be sent to NEW INDIVIDUALIST REVIEW, Ida Noyes Hall, University of Chicago, Chicago 37, Illinois. All manuscripts become the property of NEW INDIVIDUALIST REVIEW.

Subscription rates: $2.00 per year (students $1.00). Add $1.00 for foreign subscriptions.

A. J. P. Taylor and
the Causes of World War II

HARRY   ELMER   BARNES

IT IS A privilege and pleasure to be invited to appraise the epoch-making book of Professor A. J. P. Taylor on *The Origins of the Second World War*[1] for the readers of a magazine made up mainly of earnest members of the younger generation who are seeking to understand the novel and complicated world into which maturity has cast their lot. No field of study could be more useful in promoting such aspirations for rational orientation than that of history. Unless we know how we got here, we are bound to be confused as to how to deal with the present or to plan for the future.

Those who are now coming to maturity are greatly handicapped in regard to historical information and realism as compared to my own generation. The 1920's and early 1930's were an era of iconoclasm and debunking, well symbolized by Mencken and Nathan and the *American Mercury*, the writings of Theodore Dreiser, Sinclair Lewis, Scott Fitzgerald, and the like. It was difficult in those days to maintain an intellectual blackout anywhere, even in the realm of historical writing. My first ardent attack on any form of his-

torical blackout appeared in the first number of the *Mercury* at Mencken's suggestion, even insistence.

The iconoclastic trend in history took the form of what has come to be known as "Revisionism," which was devoted to wiping out the vestiges of the wartime propaganda of the previous decade. It got its name because it was hoped that the facts this movement revealed relative to the causes of the first World War would lead to the revision of the notorious Treaty of Versailles. Had this been done, there would have been no second World War, although there might have been a militant lineup of Western Europe against Soviet Russia.

The generation which was born or has been educated since 1936 or thereabouts is, historically speaking, a lost generation—a group of youthful Rip van Winkles. By 1937, the majority of American liberal intellectuals were adopting the internationalist ideology of the Popular Front and "collective security," which Litvinov had so successfully propagated at Geneva. Nearly all liberals, and a surprising number of conservatives, jumped on the interventionist and anti-German bandwagon then being chartered and steered by President Roosevelt and Harry Hopkins. The great majority of American historians belonged to the liberal camp and became ardent interventionists.

Harry Elmer Barnes is the author of numerous books and articles on twentieth century history, among which is the *Genesis of the World War* which deals with the responsibility for the outbreak of World War I. He is co-author of *Perpetual War for Perpetual Peace*, (1953), characterized by Raymond Moley as "the most solid of recent books published on foreign policy."

[1] New York: Atheneum Publishers, 1962, 296 pp. $4.50.

From this time onward, most history teaching and writing in this country, in dealing with recent world events, increasingly took on the form of a fanciful, and in part unconsciously malicious fairy-tale. It presented the pattern of the late 1930's and the 1940's as a planetary crusading arena in which a triumvirate of St. Georges—Franklin D. Roosevelt, Winston Churchill and Joseph Stalin—were bravely united in a holy war to slay the Nazi dragon. Even before the latter had shot himself in a Berlin bunker, Roosevelt and Churchill had begun to suspect that their erstwhile Soviet fellow crusader for freedom, justice and peace was more of a menace to utopia than the Nazi "madman." In due time, even his successor was revealed to be a threat to the Free World, although he had snatched Stalin from the Kremlin display window and buried him like any ordinary mortal.

In the 1920's, the evidence of the mistakes which the United States had made in its first crusade in Europe under the leadership of Woodrow Wilson were frankly brought forth and displayed before the American educational world and reading public. Not so with the far greater blunders of our second global crusade. The disagreeable facts were consigned to the Orwellian "memory hole," and the few books which sought to present the salutary truth were either ignored or viciously derided. The generation which grew up during this ill-fated crusading era has been thoroughly brainwashed in regard to the historical basis of world affairs and the role of the United States therein. It has passed little if any beyond the intellectual and informational confines of President Roosevelt's colorful but misleading "Day of Infamy" rhetoric.

It has long since been observed that historical truth is the first casualty of a war. American historiography was sadly ailing before September, 1939, and was mortally ill by Pearl Harbor, in December, 1941. The great majority of historians ardently supported intervention in the European maelstrom. A surprisingly large group accepted posts involved in the war effort and propa-

ganda, a number of them of much prominence and responsibility. Hence, they had a powerful vested interest in preserving and defending the dragon-killing legend.

Most historians were ardently inflamed by the emotions engendered by the wartime propaganda. Many of them, no doubt, were honestly convinced of the soundness of this interventionist and crusading propagandism. Those few who had kept their heads and really knew the score were wise enough to keep their counsel to themselves in order to hold their posts and have some assurance of promotion. Whatever the reasons for the debacle, it is certain that historical standards and products at all affected by recent world events declined to a lower level, so far as integrity and objectivity are concerned, than at any period since the close of the Counter-Reformation. For anything comparable in this country one would have to look back to the political tracts of the period of the Civil War and Reconstruction.

In the 1920's there was a strong reaction against the military obsession for intervention in foreign quarrels. For more than a decade a trend towards peace, isolation and anti-militarism ensued. Historical writing and teaching rather generally adjusted to this climate of intellectual opinion. Revisionism sprang up and, by and large, had won the battle against the bitter-enders of the previous decade before the end of the 1920's. Leading revisionist historians, such as Sidney Bradshaw Fay and Charles Callan Tansill, were lavishly praised by members of their craft. The journalistic culmination of revisionist spirit and lore, Walter Millis' *Road to War,* became one of the outstanding best sellers of the 1930's.

THERE WAS NO such cooling-off period or escape from militant emotions after V-J Day in 1945. Along with the perpetuation of propaganda in the guise of history came a powerful effort to prevent those who had some real regard for historical truth from getting their facts and thoughts before the American public. This project has come to be known as the "Historical Blackout." It involved a comprehensive effort since the outbreak of the second World War to suppress the truth relative to the causes and merits of the great conflict that began in 1939 and the manner in which the United States entered it. This has consisted in ignoring or suppressing facts that ran counter to the wartime propaganda when writing books on these subjects, and in suppressing, ignoring or seeking to discredit those books which have taken account of such facts.

It has often been asserted that this historical blackout is today a sinister and deliberate plot to obstruct the truth and degrade history. This is undoubtedly the truth with respect to the program and activities of some minority groups and ideological organizations which have a special vested interest in perpetuating the wartime mythology. But, for the most part, it is more the unconscious product of nearly three decades of indoctrination that grew out of interventionist and wartime propaganda. Even most professional historians who began their teaching career after 1937 have automatically come to accept as truth the distortions of pre-war and wartime interventionism. The current blackout is more an automatic reaction to brainwashing than a perverse conspiracy. But this does not make it any less difficult to resist or overcome.

This situation following the second World War is, thus, a complete reversal of what happened after the first World War when Revisionism carried the day in the historical forum in less than a decade after the Armistice of November 11, 1918. Even some of the outstanding leaders of Revisionism after the first World War, such as Sidney B. Fay and William L. Langer, recanted their Revisionism, succumbed to the historical blackout, and gave warm support to the dragon-slaying fantasy. In only about a year and a half after the Armistice of 1918 Fay had blasted for all time the myth of the unique guilt of a Hohenzollern gorilla, as the Kaiser had been portrayed during the conflict. Within a decade after the close of the War a veritable library of revisionist books had been produced on responsibility for the calamity of 1914.

Despite the fact that the documentary material to support Revisionism after the second World War is more profuse, cogent and convincing than after 1918, as of 1962 not a single volume by an American scholar devoted exclusively to the causes of the second World War has been published in the United States— some twenty-three years after the outbreak of the War and seventeen years after its close.

To be sure one book related to the field was published, *Back Door to War*, by Charles Callan Tansill, now dean of diplomatic historians. It has about as much material on responsibility for 1939 as Professor Taylor's book, is more thoroughly documented, and arrives at much the same conclusions as Taylor. But the Tansill book was designed primarily to indicate by impressive documentation how, as Clare Boothe Luce had expressed it, President Roosevelt had lied the United States into war from 1937 to 1941. Hence, there was much more interest in the antecedents of Pearl Harbor than in the responsibility for the European War in 1939, and Tansill's extensive and valuable material on the latter was generally ignored. There have been a number of important and distinguished books by American writers which have supplemented Tansill's account of American entry into the second World War but for the most part they have been ignored or smeared, and the dragon-slaying fiction still remains almost immaculate and impregnable.

Professor Tansill's book, *America Goes to War*, which was published in 1938, and is far and away the best account of American entry into war in 1917, was declared by Dr. Henry Steele Commager to be "the most valuable contribution to the history of the pre-war years in our literature and one of the most notable achievements of historical scholarship of this generation." His *Back Door to War* is an equally learned, scholarly and erudite account of our entry into the second World War, but ortho-

181

dox historians have been inclined to dismiss it as merely superficial counter-propaganda. Even Charles Austin Beard, dean of American historians and political scientists, was ruthlessly smeared for presuming to protect Clio's chastity.

Although several impressive books by informed experts, including Tansill, have detailed the facts about the Pearl Harbor disaster and scandal, Professor Foster Rhea Dulles, writing in the most formidable historical series recently launched in the United States and co-edited by Professor Commager, declared that "there is no evidence to support such charges."

Publishers who might wish to make available the truth about the second World War are intimidated by the more powerful Book Clubs, which are without exception dominated by those supporting the historical blackout. The most influential advisory service, which has great weight in recommending book purchases by public libraries and book stores, makes a specialty of deriding and discouraging the purchase of revisionist books. The fable of the dragon-killers remains almost inviolate, so far as the general public is concerned.

William Henry Chamberlin's *America's Second Crusade,* the only substantial but popular account of our entry into the second World War, was highly comparable to Millis' *Road to War* on 1917. But, whereas Millis' book sold a quarter of a million copies, a year after the Chamberlin book was published there was still not one copy listed in the New York Public Library or in any of its many branches. It need not be alleged that all those who operate book clubs and book services deliberately aim to pervert or frustrate historical truth relative to world affairs. They are presumably supporters of truth in theory. They just do not know what it is. They are emotionally congenial to the wartime legends and most historians they know seem to agree with them. Both have been brainwashed for a generation.

The essence of what has preceded is that the generation which has gained its historical knowledge and perspectives since the late 1930's has been deprived,

cheated and handicapped by the distortion and suppression of historical facts relative to world affairs. This is especially unfortunate because of the transcendent role of world relations and policies in the everyday life, interests, decisions and destiny of the American citizen of today. This handicap is true even if a person has been a history major in college. Indeed, it is likely that he will have been more victimized by historical errors as a result of more copious and intensive indoctrination with historical fiction than one who has specialized in literature, art or music.

The importance of Professor Taylor's highly controversial volume lies in the prospect that it will prove unusually potent in blasting through the historical blackout. Through a fortunate combination of circumstances, the book has shaken up Britain more than any other historical work in the field of world affairs since the writings of E. D. Morel just about forty years ago. It may be hoped that the American edition can do as well in producing a flash of light which will penetrate the historical blackout of nearly a generation's duration.

For the generation represented by most of the readers of this article, the great value of the Taylor book is that it can be the logical starting-point for them in recovering the all-important lost pages of history, out of which they have been cheated by brainwashing and the historical blackout. Those who are stimulated to continue the process will find most useful J. J. Martin's *Liberal Opinion and World Politics,* 1931-1941 (Devin-Adair); C. C. Tansill's *Back Door to War* (Regnery); G. N. Crocker's *Roosevelt's Road to Russia* (Regnery); W. H. Chamberlin's *Beyond Containment* (Regnery); and John Lukacs' *A History of the Cold War* (Doubleday). These carry the story consecutively from the Hoover Administration to that of Kennedy.

HAVING THUS presented at some length the background and setting of Professor Taylor's book, we may now consider the nature and significance of the book itself. First and foremost, it is the first book to be published in any language which is exclusively devoted to the task of debunking the dragon-slaying travesty which has colored and distorted historical perspective for nearly a quarter of a century.

It is probable that no living historian could be more appropriate as an effective and convincing author of such a book. In the first place, he is an English scholar. Due to Rhodes scholarships and other allied items which promote Anglophilism in the United States, there is a special aura attaching to English historians, their scholarship and their implied words of wisdom. This gives Taylor and his book special prestige in this country. Then, he is easily the best known and most popular of contemporary British historians. Further, he is the author of a number of substantial historical works dealing with contemporary history and diplomatic relations, most of them devoted in part at least to recent German history. In other words, he is a specialist in the field covered by his book under review here, which is not the case with such bitter critics as A. L. Rowse and Hugh R. Trevor-Roper, the former a specialist in Tudor history and poetry and the latter in Stuart ecclesiastical history and, also, poetry.

In all of his previous books, Taylor has invariably shown a rather strong antipathy to German politics and leaders. Hence, he could not logically be suspected of any pro-German sympathies or any desire to clear Hitler or any other German politician of political errors or public crimes which could be supported by reliable documentation. Finally, he has been closely associated with British left-wing activities, the Labor Party, disarmament, and other attitudes and policies which make it quite impossible for him to be imagined as having any sympathy with totalitarianism of any sort, least of all with that of National Socialist Germany in the 1930's. Clement Attlee and the Laborites were, if anything, more vehement in their hatred of Hitler and so-called appeasement than the Tories who were in power in Britain in 1938-1939.

Hence, it would be difficult to conceive of any historian who could give greater assurance that his criticisms of the dragon-slaying hypothesis are no more than those which historical accuracy and reliable documentation makes necessary. They are a product of historical integrity and professional courage, probably more of the latter than has been displayed by any other historian of our generation. It is interesting to note that since his book on the causes of the second World War has appeared, a number of critical reviewers have accused Taylor of being a publicity-seeking vendor of sensationalism who must not be taken seriously as a historian. But these same critics were actually the very ones who had previously lauded his profound scholarship when his books reflected a strong hostility to Germany and its policies.

While indicating Professor Taylor's attitude towards Germany, and especially the Germany of the 1930's and Hitler, it may be well to make clear my own approach to such matters. As a lifelong exponent of freedom of thought and political action, and a veteran critic of any racial theory of history, it will be a little difficult to hang any pro-Hitler label on me. Further, I probably lost more in the way of prestige, influence and contacts in Germany than any other American intellectual as a result of the rise of Hitler and National Socialism, surely far more than any other historian. William L. Shirer and Dorothy Thompson were catapulted into fame and fortune by the ascendency of the Nazis and should have been exceedingly grateful for the emergence of Hitler.

My contention is that there are enough valid reasons for repudiating the social system represented by National Socialism without resorting to the most extensive, lurid and indefensible body of lies and distortions which have ever degraded so-called historical science and have caused Clio to bed down with the Gadarenes for a quarter of a century. My extensive revisionist labors in the 1920's and early 1930's were designed to encourage the revision of the Treaty of Versailles and prevent the rise and ascendency of Hitler or anybody like him.

183

AFTER THESE preliminary observations, which are indispensable for judging the importance and validity of Professor Taylor's work, we can now get down to the outstanding facts and conclusions which are expressed in the book.

The vital core of the volume is the contention that Hitler did not wish a war, either local, European, or world, from March, 1933, right down into September, 1939. His only fundamental aim in foreign policy was to revise the unfair and unjust Treaty of Versailles, and to do this by peaceful methods.

This is a most remarkable and unusual contention, however well defended in the book. Hitherto, even those who have sympathized heartily with the justice and need of revising the Versailles Treaty have, nevertheless, usually maintained that, even if Hitler's revisionist program was justified in its general objectives, he carried it out in a reprehensibly brusque, provocative and challenging manner, gladly or casually risking war in each and every move he made to achieve the revision of the Versailles system. In other words, even if his goal were justifiable, his methods of seeking to obtain it were unpardonably violent, deceitful and inciting.

Professor Taylor repudiates and refutes this interpretation as thoroughly as he does the charge that Hitler wished to provoke war at any time. He holds that Hitler was unusually cautious and unprovocative in every outstanding step he took to undermine Versailles. He let others create situations favorable to achieving his ends and then exploited them in a non-bellicose manner.

One thing is certain, even if one takes a most hostile attitude towards Hitler and Professor Taylor's thesis. This is that the Allies had some thirteen years in which to revise the Treaty of Versailles in a voluntary and peaceful manner. But they did nothing about it, although one of the main ostensible functions of the League of Nations was stated to be carrying forward a peaceable revision of Versailles. Professor Sidney B. Fay had proved by 1920 that the war-guilt clause of the Treaty of Versailles, proclaiming that Germany and her allies were solely responsible for the first World War, had no valid historical foundation whatever.

Professor Fay and the rest of us revisionists of the 1920's hoped that the facts we brought forth had completely undermined the war-guilt clause, and would lead to the revision of the Treaty in political fact. But they did not, and the failure to do so accounts for the rise of Hitler and all the many results for good or evil which ensued.

After he came into power, Hitler waited patiently for some years for the Allies to make some practical move to revise the Versailles system before he occupied the Rhineland on March 7, 1936. Even on the heels of this action he publicly proposed on March 31, 1936, what Francis Neilson has called "the most comprehensive non-aggression pact ever to be drawn up." But the Allies made no cooperative response whatever; they totally ignored it.

In the meantime, Hitler had barely attained power when, on May 17, 1933, he proposed the most sweeping disarmament plan set forth by any country between the two World Wars, but neither Britain nor France took any formal notice whatever of it. Even after he had introduced conscription in March, 1935, in response to the expansion of military conscription in France, Hitler declared that "the German Government is ready to take an active part in all efforts which may lead to a practical limitation of armaments." This proposal received no more response from Britain, France or the United States than that of May, 1933. Hence, if Hitler was to revise Versailles at all, it had become completely evident by March, 1936, that it must be by unilateral action.

We may now consider what Professor Taylor concludes about the moves whereby Hitler accomplished all of his revisionist program except for the settlement with Poland, the failure of which, due to British support of Polish intransigence, brought on the European war in September, 1939. In doing so, we should always keep in mind Taylor's fundamental assumption about Hitler, to the effect that he was not a fanatical and bellicose psychopath—a veritable madman intent upon war—but a shrewd and rational statesman, notably in his handling of foreign affairs.

It will hardly be necessary for any sane person to emphasize the fact that Professor Taylor does not seek to present Hitler as any combination of Little Lord Fauntleroy, George Washington at the cherry tree, Clara Barton and Jane Addams. He could be devious, shrewd, inconsistent, self-contradictory, cruel and brutal, although he did balk at saturation bombing of civilians until he was compeled to do so in retaliation. The main point here is that, unlike Churchill, Roosevelt and Stalin, he did not wish to have a war break out in 1939.

Professor Taylor takes up in order the main items and acts which have been exploited for decades by Hitler's critics and orthodox historians to demonstrate Hitler's combined depravity and bellicosity.

The occupation of the Rhineland in March, 1936, was long overdue. It should have been returned to Germany years before Hitler took over power. His forceful occupation was pure bluff. Even a strong protest from France and Britain would probably have restrained him, and an order of mobilization by France would have produced an ignominious retreat. Moreover, the act had no serious results and at least a few advantages for Britain and France.

Historians bent on maintaining Hitler's responsibility for the second World War and his grandiose plans for world conquest have based their indictment mainly on the Hossbach Memorandum, a record made of a meeting at the German Chancellery on November 5, 1937, by a German general staff liason officer by the name of Hossbach. It was attended by Hitler, Goering, the chief army and navy officers, and the Foreign Minister.

What took place was a general consideration of the European situation, past, present, and future, and of possible German policies in relation to existing and potential developments—the type of discussion that was common, even routine, in the higher counsels of any great state. Those who were present gave little serious attention to what was said after the conference broke up, and a majority of

them were out of office or command before the summer of 1939. The memorandum had been lost sight of until the Allies dug it up about a decade later and sprang it maliciously as a surprise on Goering at the Nuremberg Trial.

Taylor dismisses the Hossbach Memorandum with deserved contempt: "Hitler, it is claimed, decided on war and planned it in detail on 5 November, 1937. Yet the Hossbach Memorandum contains no plans of the kind . . . Hitler did not make plans for world conquest or for anything else . . . [His speculations] bear hardly any relation to the actual outbreak of war in 1939."

Although the public at large knew little about the Hossbach Memorandum, world opinion was well aware of the occupation of Austria on March 12, 1938, the so-called *Anschluss* or union of Germany and Austria. The circumstances were quite different from what Hitler had planned and wished, and were forced on him by the stupidity and duplicity of Schuschnigg. Hitler had planned to take over control gradually by infiltration and political operations from within Austria. He was annoyed by being compelled to make a show of force and was humiliated by the spectacle that his ill-prepared army made in marching into Vienna.

The *Anschluss* itself had been recommended by most fair-minded and realistic observers of the post-war situation, and it was greeted with enthusiasm by the majority of the people of Austria. But for the short-sighted opposition of Britain and France it would have been accomplished during the era of the Weimar Republic and might have helped to bolster the fortunes of both the Weimar regime and Austria, even to the point of saving both from National Socialism.

FEW EPISODES or events in the history of civilized mankind have been more vehemently attacked and viciously pilloried than the Munich Conference of September 29-30, 1938. It has been depicted and denounced as a veritable incarnation of the cowardly betrayal of all principle and public ethics in international dealings. It gave rise to the most widely used political smear term of the present generation—"appeasement"—which is actually the procedure whereby most normal diplomacy had been carried on for centuries, namely, by rational and peaceful negotiations. Munich has also been especially portrayed as the most ignominious and irresponsible defeat Britain ever met in her entire diplomatic experience and the main cause of the second World War. Professor Taylor, on the contrary, finds that Munich "was a triumph for all that was best and most enlightened in British life."

That Munich did not work out as had been hoped at the time was due more to British action and policy on the heels of Munich than to any deeds of Hitler. Chamberlain did not, and perhaps could not, stand up effectively against the myopic and bitter criticisms of Munich by both the British Conservatives and Laborites. Halifax was already in the process of betraying the peace efforts at Munich and taking over the leadership of the war party in the cabinet. Churchill proclaimed that Germany was getting too strong to be tolerated and must be smashed, if necessary by force of arms. Duff Cooper contended that the balance of power on the Continent of Europe must be preserved at all costs. Taylor fails to mention the fact that Clement Attlee also attacked Munich with as great vehemence and bitterness as any Conservative.

Instead of defending his Munich policy on the high level of statecraft and public morality to which Taylor has ascribed his motives, Chamberlain, in the face of criticism by the British war party, fell back on the lame and dishonest excuse that Britain surrendered at Munich because it had been too weak to fight rather than negotiate; hence, it now had to rearm speedily and thoroughly. "In this way, Chamberlain did more than anybody else to destroy the case for his own policy."

The usual explanation that Munich failed to preserve peace because Hitler violated his pledge not to make further territorial demands in Europe after the Sudetenland transfer cannot be main-

tained on a factual basis. He actually made this pledge at a *Sportpalast* speech in Berlin on September 26, 1938, three days before Munich. Hitler made no demand for Czechoslovakian territory after the Munich Conference and the cession of the Sudetenland, and his demands for the return of the German city of Danzig, on which Poland had no valid claims, and for the railroad and motor road across the Corridor, could hardly be regarded as any literal, or even moral, violation of this pledge. Czechoslovakia inevitably fell apart in the natural course of the political disintegration which had been set in motion by the return of the Sudeten territory to Germany. Taylor emphasizes this fact at length.

Of all the silly and preposterous allegations made against Hitler, surely the outstanding was that his occupation of Prague proved his determination on world conquest. Although Chamberlain, Halifax, and the British war party made this charge to beguile the British public, they knew better than to base their case in diplomatic channels on this travesty. Rather, in collusion with the Rumanian minister in London, they concocted a transparent fraud, immediately repudiated by the Rumanian Foreign Minister, charging that Hitler had just made demands on Rumania which threatened her sovereignty and forecast an attempt at wholesale penetration of the Balkans.

Aside from inadequate emphasis on the extent and manner in which Lord Halifax and Sir Howard Kennard, the British ambassador at Warsaw, encouraged Poland not to negotiate a peaceful settlement with Hitler in August, 1939, Professor Taylor's account of the German-Polish crisis of October, 1938, to September, 1939, accords with his general thesis that Hitler did not want war. He makes it clear that Hitler wished a permanent and peaceful settlement with Poland rather than war.

THE TERMS Hitler suggested to Poland, beginning on October 24, 1938, were extremely reasonable—indeed, the most moderate of any in his whole revisionist procedure from 1933 to 1939 and were far less drastic than many British leaders had suggested between the two World Wars. Even Churchill, at about the very time Hitler came to power, had declared in the House of Commons on April 13, 1933, that the question of the Polish Corridor was a leading issue that had to be adjusted if European peace were to be preserved.

Hitler only asked for the return of Danzig and a railroad and motor road across the Corridor. Indeed, he proposed much more in return than he requested; he offered to guarantee the Polish boundaries as settled at Versailles after the first World War, something the Weimar Republic would never even remotely consider. Britain has been invariably presented in the traditional story of 1939 as the moral custodian of Europe, even willing to risk war to protect the integrity of Poland, which Hitler was seeking to gobble up. The facts are precisely the reverse.

There is conclusive evidence that the Polish leaders believed that Hitler's terms of 1938-1939 were sincere, and were not merely the first step in a sinister program to absorb Poland later on by military force or political intrigue. But Josef Beck, the Polish Foreign Minister, refused to accept Hitler's generous terms, and on March 26, 1939, broke off negotiations with Germany. They were never again resumed down to the time war broke out on September 1, 1939.

The stubborn refusal of Poland even to negotiate with Germany during the crisis of August, 1939, is fully revealed by Taylor, although he does not bring out the extent to which Beck was encouraged in this intransigeance by Halifax and Kennard, especially the latter. Taylor does, however, make it crystal clear that the Poles were far more willing to envisage war than was Hitler. Right down to the final crisis Hitler had hoped for peaceful revision. Even during the last hours of peace he only increased his demands to include a plebiscite in the northern tip of the Corridor. It would have taken a year of peaceful negotiations to complete the arrangements under this plan, and the important Polish port of

Gdynia was explicitly excluded from the proposed plebiscite area.

Those who refuse to be convinced by Taylor's demonstration that Hitler's operations in revising the Treaty of Versailles prove that he did not desire to provoke war, fall back on the allegation that his whole economic policy had been to gear German industry to warlike plans, that he had spent enormous sums of money to create a great military machine, sufficient for and ready to start a war of world conquest, and that he had converted Germany into a great military camp.

Taylor refutes all this very effectively. Hitler had not spent more money for armament, relatively, than either France or Britain, and he was in no way prepared for even a Europeon war, to say nothing of a war of world conquest. He was only ready for a short *Blitzkrieg* of a couple of months, such as he waged in Poland. Out of a hundred divisions he put into war in Poland, only three were mechanized and not one completely motorized. The combined military forces of Britain and France were far more than equal to those of Germany in 1939.

The final line of defense of those who reject the facts of both diplomatic history and economic history from 1933 to 1939 is that the real proof of Hitler's plan to conquer the world is to be found in his *Mein Kampf*, written in 1924, and his alleged "Second Book," putatively composed in 1928, not in what he actually did from 1933 to 1939. This implies that Hitler was the only prominent public figure in 1939 who had never changed his mind over the years despite revolutionary alterations in surrounding circumstances. Yet, these same critics of both Hitler and sound history have been the very ones who have contended for three decades that if there was one invariable characteristic of Hitler it was his explosive nature, his undependability, his instability, vacillation and fickleness, and his general irresponsibility. They cannot very well have it both ways.

Mein Kampf furnishes little or no clue as to what was going on in Hitler's mind in 1939, any more than Churchill's violent attacks on Russia in 1918-1920 provide a

187

true reflection of his attitude towards Russia at the Teheran or Yalta Conferences, or his assurance to the House of Commons after his return from Yalta that he knew of no country which honored its public promises with greater fidelity than Soviet Russia. The *Mein Kampf* subterfuge is like seeking the motives and policies of President Roosevelt on the eve of Pearl Harbor in his isolationist and pacifist speeches during the campaign of 1936 —only five years earlier.

In his final conclusion as to the coming of war in September, 1939, Professor Taylor rejects the verdict which has been accepted for more than two decades, namely, that it was the inevitable product of a long premeditated and wicked plot on the part of a maniacal Nazi dictator.

He contends, to the contrary, that it was a calamitous mistake, not premeditated by either side, and was primarily the product of diplomatic and political blunders on both sides: "This is a story without heroes; and perhaps even without any villains . . . The war of 1939, far from being welcome, was less wanted by nearly everybody than almost any war in history . . . The war of 1939, far from being premeditated, was a mistake, the result on both sides of diplomatic blunders . . . Such were the origins of the second World War, or rather the war between the three Western Powers over the settlement of Versailles; a war which had been implicit since the moment the first war ended."

PROFESSOR TAYLOR is quite correct in stating that, in so far as the general publics were concerned, the second World War was one of the most unwanted wars in history, but it was not unwanted by Halifax, Kennard, and the British war party in the summer of 1939. Chamberlain was rather wavering and schizoid on the matter, but in the end he joined with Halifax and Kennard and stood out against Sir Nevile Henderson, the British ambassador at Berlin, who resolutely opposed the war to the last moment.

As Foreign Secretary, Halifax was the responsible leader of the war group. He had taken over control of British foreign policy within a week after the Munich Conference. He carried through the war program in a ruthless and undeviating manner and with consummate skill, craftiness, duplicity, and determination, from mid-October, 1938, to the sending of the final ultimatum to Germany on September 3, 1939. If there was any "villain" in 1939 it was Lord Halifax, far more so than Churchill. The latter had little to do with British diplomacy at the time, and actually did not know much about what was going on at the end of August when Halifax was craftily, skillfully, and relentlessly piloting England and Europe into war.

While affecting a personal piety almost akin to that of Thomas a Kempis, Halifax planned, engineered and gratuitously let loose on the world the most cruel and devastating war in history, the ultimate result of which may be the extermination of the human race, with no more justification than the perpetuation of an obsolete British political tradition—the balance of power on the European continent—which had been fashioned in the sixteenth century by Cardinal Wolsey.

As to the motives of the group which backed up Halifax, they were both varied and numerous. Some were chronic German haters. Others were alarmed by Germany's economic recovery and the methods whereby this had been accomplished. Some may have honestly feared that Hitler did have a program of extensive military conquest, although surely none of them believed that this would be directed against Britain. Some, like Churchill, believed that they could improve their political status in the event of war. Laborites and other Leftwing groups hated conservative totalitarianism.

Certainly, the British blank check to Poland, either when made in March or when confirmed on August 25th, was a hypocritical fraud which did not offer any honest guarantee or comprehensive protection to Poland, and was not intended to do so. It was purely a provocative war stratagem. It merely encouraged Poland to stand firm against reasonable German demands and thus make inevitable a war against Germany. It was Hitler who offered the genuine guarantee to Poland.

When, in the autumn of 1939, Russia brazenly occupied eastern Poland, the question was raised in the House of Commons as to whether the British guarantee of Poland covered aggression against her by Russia. Richard A. (Rab) Butler, who answered for the government, had to admit that it did not. It was only a guarantee against Germany, which at the outset did not contemplate annexing any Polish territory. Rather, Germany offered to guarantee the Versailles boundaries of Poland.

It is well established that no responsible leaders in Germany, France, or Italy wished war in 1939. President Roosevelt apparently desired to have the European war break out as soon as possible, pressed Chamberlain to go ahead, and encouraged Polish arrogance and stubbornness. But Roosevelt was in no position to exert any directly decisive influence on European decisions in 1939, and Halifax did not need any encouragement from Roosevelt.

It is unlikely, however, that Britain would have dared to adopt the policy she did in 1939 in regard to Poland and Germany if Roosevelt had not already promised British leaders, notably through Anthony Eden and George VI, all possible American aid in the event of war and had agreed to make every conceivable effort to bring the United States into war on the side of Britain if one broke out. This is well brought out in the so-called "Kent Documents," the nearly two thousand secret messages that were exchanged between Roosevelt and Churchill in American code and embodied, as Churchill had admitted, most of the vital Anglo-American diplomatic commitments and arrangements, beginning even before Churchill became Prime Minister.

To summarize realistically the matter of war responsibility in 1939, one may quite safely say that Professor Taylor is entirely correct in holding that the broad general responsibility, running over two decades, was divided among all the parties and was the outcome of blunders by all of them.

In regard to the direct and immediate responsibility for the outbreak of hostilities in September, 1939, the blame for the German-Polish War was divided between Poland, Britain and Germany, with the so-called guilt ranking in this order.

The primary and direct responsibility for the European War, which grew into the second World War, was almost solely that of Great Britain and the British war group, made up of both Conservatives and Laborites. If Britain had not gratuitously given Poland a blank check, which was not needed in the slightest to assure British security, Poland might have risked a war with Germany. Nevertheless, even in this case there would still have been no justification for British intervention in such a war or for the provocation of a European war.

This sole immediate British responsibility for the outbreak of the European War in September, 1939, stands out in contrast to the direct responsibility for starting a European war in August, 1914, which was divided between Russia, France and Serbia, in the order given. If Alexander Izvolski, the Russian ambassador to France in 1914, was more responsible than any other individual for war in 1914, so was Lord Halifax more to be blamed than any other person for the coming of war in 1939.

ALREADY THERE has arisen a line of criticism designed to discredit the significance of Professor Taylor's book, even granting its accuracy as to the general responsibility for war in 1939. It is held that, although Hitler and the Nazis may not have started the war in 1939, or even wished to start it, the brutal outrages of which they were guilty after the war got started proved them such degenerate gangsters that Halifax and his associates were justified in resorting to any degree of plotting and duplicity required to produce a war to smash and annihilate them, and that President Roosevelt performed a great moral service in "lying the United States into the war" to make it certain that this salutary and needed act of extermination would be accomplished.

Any such argument is even more fallacious and deplorable than the *ex post facto* jurisprudence on which the Nuremberg Trials were founded. Further, there is no reason whatever to believe that the brutal wartime actions which have been alleged against Germany would have taken place if peace had been preserved. Finally, as Milton Mayer, Victor Gollancz, and others, have already suggested, it seems likely that the whole question of the wartime crimes of Germany will ultimately be submitted to as drastic a type of revisionism as the conventional views about the responsibility for the second World War have been subjected to by Taylor. Many thousands were executed after war-crime trials in Germany and Iron Curtain countries—trials which are still going on today—and far over 100,000 were executed or massacred in France and Italy during the "Liberation."

Two great wrongs do not make a right but even a casual survey of Allied atrocities, which does not even include those in the Asiatic area, aside from the atom bombings, makes it amply clear that there is no validity to the argument that the second World War simply had to be waged to rid the world of a totally unique gang of German scoundrels—unique both as to moral depravity and deeds of brutal violence.

Hitler's evil deeds have been told and retold, beginning long before 1939. After the Cold War started, the Western World began to learn something about the monstrous and nefarious doings of Stalin—that "man of massive outstanding personality, and deep and cool wisdom," as Churchill described him—which far exceeded those of Hitler. But we have heard little of the horrors which were due to the acts and policies of Churchill and Roosevelt, as, for example, the saturation bombing of civilians, the incendiary bombings of German cities such as Hamburg and of Tokyo, the bombing and destruction of the beautiful city of Dresden which had no military significance whatever and in which more lives were lost than in the bombings of Hiroshima and Nagasaki, the atom bombings of the Japanese cities (planned by Roosevelt), the expulsion of about fifteen million Germans from their former homes and the death of four to six millions in the process as a result of massacre, starvation and

190

exposure, the brutalities practised on German SS prisoners of war, the cruel and barbarous treatment of Germany from 1945 to 1948, and the return of around five million Russian refugees in Germany to Stalin to be butchered or enslaved. The greatest horror that could be fairly traced to their doings is still held in reserve for us—the nuclear extermination of mankind.

In short, there is no unique or special case against Nazi barbarism and horrors unless one assumes that it is far more wicked to exterminate Jews than to massacre Gentiles. While this latter value judgment appears to have become rather generally accepted in the Western world since 1945, I am personally still quaint enough to hold it to be reprehensible to massacre either Jews or Gentiles.

Professor Taylor, logically and wisely, deals only slightly and incidentally with the domestic policy of Nazi Germany, although he does hint correctly several times that this probably did more to produce the war than Hitler's foreign policy. Of all of Hitler's domestic policies, the one which brought upon him the greatest opprobrium and hatred and the one which played the most important public role in encouraging war on Germany, was his treatment of the German Jews, a piece of folly which I have condemned for nearly thirty years in numerous articles, books and lectures. Indeed, the famous American Rabbi, Stephen S. Wise, reprinted a series of articles I wrote for the Scripps-Howard newspapers criticizing Hitler's anti-Semitism and distributed tens of thousands of copies.

There could, however, be no greater paradox in history than a war in behalf of Poland on the basis of the Jewish issue. There were in Poland, in 1933, six times as many Jews as in Germany, and they were surely treated as badly as were the German Jews under Hitler. Moreover, by 1939, Hitler's anti-Jewish program had moderated and more than half the German Jews had left Germany, usually with many of their possessions, whereas the Polish Jewish population had declined relatively slightly and their treatment had not improved to any notable extent.

In the 1930's, when I was actively engaged in journalism, I received much praise from Jewish readers for my columns and editorials criticizing Hitler's treatment of the Jews, but this was interspersed with frequent and insistent suggestions that I should not overlook the far more extensive plight of the Jews in Poland. Several of my more responsible correspondents charged that the Polish government was laying plans to exterminate the Polish Jews as communist revolutionaries. This was several years before it is alleged that Hitler even planned any extermination project. Nor should Russia be overlooked. Writing in October, 1938, Walter Duranty observed that "Stalin has shot more Jews in two years of purges than were ever killed in Germany."

IT IS WORTHWHILE here to indicate briefly the significance of the book by Professor Taylor for citizens of the United States. So far as revisionist scholarship is concerned, this is greatly strengthened and its basic contentions are confirmed. It will now be easier to treat the causes of the second World War realistically and honestly without being accused of mental defect or moral depravity.

The awe and reverence with which English historians are customarily regarded by the American historical guild will make it the more difficult and embarrassing for the latter to laugh off Professor Taylor's confirmation of the basic tenets of American revisionist historical scholarship. The frenetic reviews of the American edition have already revealed their schizoid reaction—a sort of intellectual "twist" dance.

The Taylor book underlines the accuracy of American anti-interventionism which had been supported by revisionist historical writings in this country. The interventionists based their policy on the fantastic assumption, actually voiced by such able historians as Samuel Flagg Bemis, top commentators like Walter Lippmann, and superb journalists of the type of Walter Millis, that the United States was in mortal danger of infiltration and attack by Nazi Germany. Professor Taylor's book further emphasizes the grotesque fallacy of this contention. Hitler did not even wish to attack England or France, to say nothing of proceeding westward across the Atlantic. Nor was it necessary for the United States to enter the war to protect Britain or France. Hitler sought peace after the Polish War and again after the fall of France, and Dunkirk.

In the light of the facts brought forward by Professor Taylor, which are not at all new to American revisionist historians and had previously been well stated by Tansill, Beard, and others, President Roosevelt's allegation that Hitler planned to invade the United States by way of Dakar, Rio de Janeiro and Panama —his notorious timetable for the Nazi occupation of Iowa—is shown to be as fantastic and untenable as his statement that he was "surprised" by the Japanese attack in December, 1941.

191

Professor Taylor's book should serve as a warning that a third world war will not be prevented by an avalanche of stale Germanophobia, or by merely mouthing arrogant platitudes and benign homilies about the virtues and superiorities of democracy and the "Free World." These semantic gestures must be supplemented and implemented by all the wisdom, precaution, foresight and statecraft that can be drawn from the disastrous experience with two world wars and their ominous aftermaths. Failing this, we shall not have another opportunity.

We are not likely to succeed so long as we resolutely reject searching self-examination but continue to seek a scapegoat on whom we may lay the blame for all international tragedies. The effort to make a scapegoat out of the Kaiser and Germany after the first World War produced the Versailles Treaty and, in time, the second World War. The same process was continued on a more fantastic scale after the second World War, and it has already led us to the brink of nuclear war several times. Professor Taylor has made clear the folly in seeking to make Hitler's foreign policy the cause of all the miseries and anguish of the world since 1939—or even 1933.

Page Fifteen

We can get no valid comfort from the illusion that nuclear warfare will be withheld in the third World War, as poison gas was in the second. As F. J. P. Veale pointed out so well in his *Advance to Barbarism,* the Nuremberg Trials took care of that. These showed that the rule in the future will be that defeated leaders, military and civilian, will be executed. Hence, no leader in wartime will spare any available and effective horrors which may avert defeat. Field Marshal Bernard Law Montgomery got this point when he stated in Paris in June, 1948: "The Nuremberg Trials have made the waging of unsuccessful war a crime: the generals on the defeated side are tried and then hanged." He should have added chiefs of state, prime ministers, foreign ministers, and even secretaries of welfare.

While it is easy to demonstrate that the second World War and American entry into it constituted the outstanding public calamity in human history, and perhaps the last—surely, the next to the last—of such magnitude, the question is always asked as to what *should* have been done.

There is no space here to write a treatise on world history or to combine prophesy with hindsight. But a reasonable answer can be suggested.

Britain should not have started the second World War. The British leaders knew that Hitler was no threat to them. Next to assuring German strength, he was mainly interested in bolstering the British Empire. Even after Dunkirk he offered to put the German *Wehrmacht* and *Luftwaffe* at the service of Britain if she would make peace.

Germany and Russia had made a pact in August, 1939, and both were interested in turning east and south. If they remained friendly they could have developed and civilized these great untamed areas. If they quarrelled and fought, they would thereby have reduced the two great totalitarian systems to impotence through military attrition. Once the war started and Germany had invaded Russia, the United States should have remained aloof and allowed these totalitarian rivals to bleed themselves white and thereby end their menace to the Western World.

The wisdom of such procedure was recognized by public leaders in both major political parties, such as ex-President Herbert Hoover, Senator Robert A. Taft, and Senator Harry S. Truman. Communism would not now dominate a vast portion of the planet or have over a billion adherents. Nor would we be faced with a war of nuclear extermination.

But the combined power of Roosevelt's lust for the glamor of a war presidency, the communist line about "collective security," so successfully propounded by Litvinov at Geneva and adopted by American liberals as the ideological basis of their interventionism, and Churchill's gargantuan vanity and vast enjoyment of his prestige as wartime leader, was far too great to be overcome by either factual information or political logic. The dolorous results of the folly of American intervention and Roosevelt's concessions to Stalinite Communism dominate the material in every daily newspaper and every political journal of our time.

192

The New Conservativism

JAMES M. O'CONNELL

AS SOME recent articles in the *New Individualist Review* and other magazines have indicated, the intellectual Right in the United States is divided into at least two large factions. Each of the factions has its own firmly-held ideology, its own history, its own roster of heroes and demons. And some members, at least, of each faction are not at all sure that large numbers of their fellow-Rightists are not more profoundly in error and more dangerous to the Republic than are even the infernal legions of the Left.

In the interests of harmony and good-fellowship, many conservatives have lately suggested that such discussions be played down and that the Right return to its principle business: exposing the foibles and inanities of the American Left. Were the differences minor ones, then the airing of them in public would do little or no good for the advancement of the principles held by those commonly referred to as "conservatives." However, when such differences are radical, when the only area of agreement is anti-communism, then to call for harmony in the interest of a united "anti-communist" and "anti-socialist" front is as reprehensible now as the actions of those who called for a Popular Front in the closing years of the Thirties "to oppose Fascism."

These articles, especially those by Mr. Hamowy and Mr. Facey in this magazine,[1] indicate that the differences are radical, and that the older philosophies of libertarianism, *laissez-faire* economics, and constitutionalism have little in common with what has been called the "new conservatism." It is the attempt of this article to point out these differences and to show why they are incompatible with the older philosophy, which might be called, as it had been before the name was pirated by the statists and interventionist of the Left, "liberalism." The task is complicated, for, as Professor F. A. Hayek points out: "Since it [conservatism] distrusts both abstract theories and general principles, it neither understands those spontaneous forces on which a policy of freedom relies nor possesses a basis for formulating principles of policy."[2] An analysis of this new conservatism must begin, then, with an investigation of the ideas put forth by its proponents in their writings.

Those who read the works of the new conservatives are struck first of all by the contempt in which reason is held. Russell Kirk, so it seems, cannot write a book without sneering at "defecated rationality" or the "puny private stocks of reason" possessed by individuals. Mr.

193

James M. O'Connell is a Ph. D. candidate in mathematics at the University of Wisconsin. He is a contributing editor of *Insight and Outlook* and writes a column for the University of Wisconsin *Daily Cardinal*.

[1] Ronald Hamowy, "*National Review*; Criticism and Reply," in *New Individualist Review*, November, 1961, pp. 3-11; Edward C. Facey, "Conservatives or Individualists: Which Are We?," *New Individualist Review*, Summer, 1961, pp. 24-26.

[2] F. A. Hayek, *The Constitution of Liberty* (University of Chicago Press, Chicago, 1960), p. 401.

194

Kirk prefers to remain an "intellectual dwarf perched on the shoulders of a g i a n t — Christian, Western tradition." But the errors of reasoning made by those Professor Hayek calls the "rationalist liberals" in no way invalidate the tool used: reason. As a method for combatting the errors of the planners and interventionists, reason is far superior to appeals to tradition. Indeed, Professor Ludwig von Mises asks, in *Human Action,* if the traditional doctrines so constructed are in agreement with the actual beliefs held by the ancestors so venerated. Tradition and custom possess no validity *per se*; their rightness or wrongness depends solely on their agreement with those principles, discoverable by reason, which regulate human action.

To the new conservative, such ideas are "the murkiest Bentham." These traditionalists make much of the fact that many libertarian authors use a utilitarian cause-and-effect approach in their writings on economics. Utilitarianism is "materialistic," they claim, ignoring the fact that it studies, especially the modern agathistic utilitarianism, not only material pleasures, but all human desires, for one purpose: to discover the correct method of fulfilling such desires. Others would condemn it for ignoring the irrational, the unusual in life. Such a censure is foolish, for it ignores the fact that economics limits itself to the study of the analyzable; it does not attempt to comment on the goals and desires of an acting individual. As Prof. Mises puts it:

> The teachings of economics and praxeology are valid for every human action without regard to its underlying motives, causes and goals. The ultimate judgments of value and the ultimate ends of human action are given (that is, undefined in the logical sense) for any kind of scientific inquiry; they are not open to any further analysis.[3]

More often than not, the new conservative will content himself with simply sneering at utilitarian ideas. They are "immoral," they are "relativistic" or, to use a phrase common to conservative polemicists, "the ideas of Bentham, 'the great subversive,' find their *reductio ad absurdum* in Marxism." Such criticism is meaningless, for modern utilitarianism is neutral with respect to final choices; charges of "immorality" or "relativism" when applied to it are absurd. As for its alleged connection with Marxism, one could, with more justice, establish an ideological relationship between conservatism and fascism. It is but a few steps from Burke's veneration of the "oaks of the English aristocracy" to Maistre's veneration of "throne and altar," Metternich's censorship, t h e racism of a Carlyle or a Gobineau, the nationalism of a Barres, until we reach our *reductio* — the fascism of a Maurras. Even those supposedly in the Burkean tradition were eager, at times, for a man on horseback — Irving Babbitt, founder of the New Humanism and intellectual mentor of new conservative Russell Kirk, declared, in his passion for order, that there would be a time when "we may esteem ourselves fortunate if we get the American equivalent of a Mussolini; he may be needed to save us from the equivalent of a Lenin."[4] That Millian socialism and its bastard brother Marxism are, in fact, perversions of Benthamite utilitarianism seems to escape the new conservatives; the fault lies not in utilitarianism itself, but in the minds of those misinterpreting it.

It is this rejection of reason for tradition and custom that has brought out what Mr. Hamowy called "the whips, thumbscrews and firing squads" in his article;[5] it is obvious that, if the only defense of the new conservatism is tradition, then that tradition must be maintained, no matter what the cost to liberty. It is the love of custom that brings forth the shibboleths of the new conservatives commonly applied against libertarian-liberalism — the system considers men as an individual; it is "rational" and "atomistic." To the new conservative, "community" is all. Indeed,

---

[3] Ludwig von Mises, *Human Action,* (Yale University Press, New Haven, 1949), p. 21.

Page Eighteen

[4] Irving Babbit, *Democracy and Leadership,* (Houghton Mifflin, Boston, 1924), p. 312.

[5] Hamowy, *op. cit.,* p. 7.

Mr. Kirk makes merry over a group of people who wished to found a society of individualists; in considering their choice of intellectual mentors, he declares:

These same gentlemen (who profess to be individualists, but are really conservatives in their impulses) cried up a pantheon of philosophers after their taste: Lao-Tse, Zeno, Milton, Locke, Adam Smith, Tom Paine, Jefferson, Thoreau, John Stuart Mill, and Spencer. No thinking conservative would be much inclined to pull these chestnuts out of the fire for the sake of the commonwealth. I suggested that if they were to substitute Moses or St. Paul for Lao-Tse, Aristotle or Cicero for Zeno, Dante for Milton, Falkland for Locke, Samuel Johnson for Adam Smith [!], Burke for Paine, Orestes Brownson for Ralph Waldo Emerson, Hawthorne for Thoreau, Disraeli for Mill, and Ruskin [—yes, Ruskin!] or Newman for Spencer, then indeed they might make the dry bones speak, and kindle the imagination of the rising generation.[6]

This alone would be enough to validate the thesis of this article: new conservatism has nothing to do with the individualism of American libertarian-liberalism; the inclusion of a socialist and a few rabid monarchists in the renovated pantheon indicates that it is as hostile as it ever was to individualism. And why not? The individual, especially the innovator and the dissenter, is hostile to the ideas of "order" and "tradition"; he prefers to cut his own way. In so doing, he may increase the good of all, but this idea never occurs to our tradition-minded gentlemen.

NOR ARE conservatives content only to celebrate the existence of such anti-individualists; they are ready and willing to go to further impositions on individual liberty. Willmoore Kendall is unalterably opposed to the open society; Revilo Oliver sees in an established church — preferably high-church Episcopal or Roman Catholic — the salvation of America; all join in supporting the

House Committee on Un-American Activities, despite its questionable status in a nation dedicated to a Rule of Law. Yet, such people assure us that they stand for "liberty" over equality. In contrast to these opinions, the ideas of H. L. Mencken, who was not only an anti-communist but an anti-democrat, bear repeating:

"I believe in only one thing and that thing is human liberty. If ever a man is to achieve anything like dignity, it can happen only if superior men are given absolute freedom to think what they want to think and say what they want to say. I am against any man and any organization which seeks to limit or deny that freedom." Mr. Mencken was speaking to Hamilton Owens at the time, and when Owens asked if Mencken would limit freedom to superior men, Mencken replied that "the superior man can be sure of freedom only if it is given to all men."[7]

Together with his strong dislike of individualism, the new conservative is contemptuous of the system it produced: the *laissez-faire* economy. Indeed, one can find almost any other kind of system outside of socialist collectivism praised in their writings — despite the fact that such systems are unworkable. Some, like Mr. Kirk, would restore "community" to economics. What is needed is a higher morality, a "humanity," among businessmen and workers. The new system will not be socialism, for private property will be preserved, not interventionism, for there will be no need for government intervention in a "moral economy," nor capitalism, for the profit motive will be supplanted by conscience. While such a system is, apparently, non-coercive, it makes an assumption which is almost as unjustifiable as that which suggests that all men can be made reasonable: that all men can be made moral. If it seeks to bring such a moral millenium about by force, it will fail. We need only consider Prohibition to understand the futility of attempts to enforce a morality above and beyond the normal laws needed for co-operation in society.

195

---

[6] Russell Kirk, *A Program for Conservatives*, (Regnery, Chicago, 1955), p. 49.

---

[7] Quoted in the *Freeman*, March, 1962, p. 64.

Plans to restore "community and morality" overlook one fact: such things can only come about, if they ever existed, spontaneously; they cannot be forced.

AN ECONOMIC system more pleasing to new conservatism is corporatism. Rejecting even the idea of a "moralized" capitalism, our new conservatives seek the solution of the "problem of community" in the guild system of the Middle Ages. Whether the system advocated is "guild socialism" or corporatism, the idea is easy enough to grasp. Each branch of business forms a monopoly which is fully autonomous; the only purpose of the state is to settle quarrels between different bodies. Unfortunately, such a system ignores the fact that the market cannot be divided in such a manner. It serves to protect inefficiency and prevent the diversion of capital to other sources where it would be more productive. Under such a system, the worker *qua* worker might enjoy a feeling of security and community; as a consumer, however, he would suffer.

In the times it has been tried, either it has failed miserably, as in the case of the American NRA experiment, or has resulted in continued bureaucratic control, as in the case of Italian Fascism. We are offered a new collectivism, a collectivism of the Right, to save us from both the "inhumanity" of capitalism, with its "rootless individualism," and the collectivism of the Left. In offering this as a substitute for the market economy, the new conservatives, for all their wrath against rationalist planners, become planners themselves and triflers with individuals.

It will be objected that my notion of freedom is dangerous in that it ignores values. Such an objection indicates a basic misunderstanding of the concept of freedom. It does not posit the right of every man to act as he pleases; such is a definition of license rather than freedom. Freedom is the right of an individual to think and act as he pleases, so long as he bears full responsibility for his actions, and refrains from using coercive or aggressive force against the life, liberty or property of any other. Such a definition implies the recognition of a set of absolute values binding on all men which govern interpersonal relations; it implies the existence of personal values in each individual and it implies that these values serve as a standard of right and wrong, which serves to fix responsibility for actions. It is the new conservative who is more of a relativist, for he, in his search for order, would destroy such standards. Why else the desire for an "American Mussolini?" Why the hatred of capitalism and the support for socialistic measures which has, at times, marked conservatism. It is a desire for freedom for an elite, rather than a desire for freedom for the individual, that provides conservatism with a relativistic outlook.

This, then, is the new conservatism: a doctrine which is not only anti-rationalistic, in that it opposes the wild dreams of the planners, but anti-rational, in opposition to all reason; it holds to a creed of anti-individualism and anti-capitalism; in its search for "order," it embraces a relativism of its own. It has its sources in neither the libertarianism of an Albert Jay Nock nor in the constitutionalism of a Liberty League; if we seek its sources, we find them in the ludicrous union of the New Humanists, Eliot, More and Babbitt, on the one hand, and southern agrarians, men such as Robert Penn Warren, on the other, well salted with mediaevalists, Distributists and followers of the socio-ethical theories of Carlyle and Ruskin. In its extremes, it either drifts over to a fascism or, in its attempts to reject capitalism, to a mild socialism. Indeed, so foreign are its principles to those of libertarianism that it can be hailed by the Left as a good. Mr. Kirk quotes, with some pride, the words of one interventionist on the new conservatism.

. . . Mr. Arthur Schlesinger, Jr., writing in the quarterly journal *Confluence*, remarks that "the aim of the New Conservatives is to transform conservatism from a negative philosophy of niggling and self-seeking into an affirmative movement of healing and revival, based on a liv-

196

ing sense of human relatedness and on a dedication to public as against class interests, all to be comprehended in a serious and permanent philosophy of social and national responsibility.[8]

In short, the new conservatism is not what most people would call "conservative" at all; it favors, not freedom, but an exchange of power, from the present bureaucrats to an "aristocratic elite." In calling the attention of individualists to its beliefs and dogmas, I am not trying to attack the Right, or cause a "schism"; I am trying to point out that the doctrines of individualism are being misrepresented and that those who are misrepresenting these ideas are doing more harm than good, and should be repudiated.

---

[8] Kirk, op. cit., p. 35.

Individual Freedom and
Economic Security

G. C. WIEGAND

THE POPULAR slogan "freedom from want," which links freedom and economic security, is either an anachronism or a semantic illusion which helps to becloud the socio-economic problems which face the free world.

There was a time when individual freedom and economic security went hand-in-hand. In a world of general insecurity —out at the fringe of the Frontier—the freedom of the individual to make the fullest possible use of his physical and mental resources was the only assurance he possessed that he would survive in a hostile world. Similarly, at the time of John Locke, the late 17th century English defender of the rising middle class, freedom from government oppression and repression enabled the individual to use his faculties in order to acquire property and thus gain economic security and social status. The economic well-being of the middle class was dependent upon freedom of enterprise, freedom of trade and protection of private property, all three of which had been previously hampered by absolutism and mercantilism. It was for that reason that Locke argued that "life, liberty and property," are inherent rights of the individual which no government could, or should take from him.

G. C. Wiegand is Professor of Economics at Southern Illinois University and is the author of numerous articles on monetary theory and the history of economic thought.

This, however, is not the type of personal freedom and economic security which the advocates of the modern "freedom from want" slogan have in mind but, rather, a policy under which the individual surrenders much of his personal freedom as a producer and consumer in return for economic security provided by a more or less powerful and benevolent state.

This is obviously not a new idea. The same trend of thought regarding freedom and security prevailed during the troubled decades of the declining Roman Empire. The entrepreneurial middle class was increasingly subjected to rigid government controls; the acquisition of personal wealth was pictured by writers of the time, both Christian and pagan, as a useless, if not immoral occupation; and slaves and free peasants alike came under the "protection" of the large landowners. By the 5th century, the economic liberalism which had prevailed in Rome during its centuries of power, had given way to an economic system, characterized by those features which in the following centuries blossomed into feudalism and serfdom. No doubt the slaves and serfs of this period, if theirs was a good master, enjoyed a fairly high degree of economic security, considering the general low standard of living of the time. But good masters have a tendency of turning into tyrants, and who assures the people of today who rely on the benevolence of the welfare state, that it will remain benevolent?

More than any other industry, American agriculture has been the beneficiary of government aid for many years. But instead of solving the problems of agriculture, government aid has deepened and prolonged them. Here is what the President of the American Farm Bureau Association, one of the two large farm organizations in America, has to say about the effects of government interference: "America has been known as the land of opportunity, but opportunity depends upon freedom, and freedom means individual responsibility—not the rule of force by government. The government interventionist abandons freedom of choice because he is contemptuous of the ability of individuals to know what is best for them." And Mahatma Gandhi, the great Indian philosopher and humanitarian warned: "While apparently doing good by minimizing exploitation, the state does the greatest harm to mankind by destroying individuality which is the root of all progress. . . . The state is a soulless machine; it can never be weaned from violence to which it owes its very existence."

The rapid economic growth during the 19th century, the rising standard of living and the unprecedented expansion of personal freedom coincided with, and to a large extent were due to, the rise of the entrepreneurial middle class which followed the overthrow of 17th and 18th century collectivism through the Glorious Revolution of 1688 in England, the American Revolution of 1776, and the French Revolution of 1789. Only after political and economic power had passed from the aristocracy and its proliferating bureaucracy to the middle class, whose vitality and strength sprang from personal freedom and private initiative, did the western world achieve its greatest economic, social and political advance.

Yet today we are turning away from the ideals of 19th century liberalism, which during the past 150 years have turned the western world from "underdeveloped countries" plagued by poverty and hunger into the "affluent societies" of today. What is causing the declining faith in personal initiative and freedom and the widespread demand by the people for "freedom from want" on the one hand, and on the other, the promise of the government to provide the country with a "great living program of human renewal?" Technological, institutional, social, political and cultural conditions have changed rapidly during the past 50 years; and rapid changes make for insecurity, which is undoubtedly one of the reasons for the craving of the millions for security provided by the state.

IN A WORLD of handicraft and small shops, of small towns and small farms, man was able to make a living without too much dependence upon the rest of society. He produced—or at least could produce—the food he needed. Most of his clothing was homemade, his house was not filled with gadgets which only an expert could keep in repair, home remedies were used in times of illness, and the aged found a spare room in their children's home. Life was, of course, neither idyllic nor comfortable, if measured by modern standards. There was little variety in food, houses were hot in summer and cold in winter, sanitary facilities were primitive, the infant birth rate was twice as high as it is today, and the chances of surviving a major illness were poor. But these material short-comings of the "good old days" were offset by two great advantages: man could and to a large extent did preserve his economic independence, at least in the United States, and whatever man created by his hand or his mind was an expression of his own spirit and his own personality— and his personal property.

Science and technology have wrought a radical change. They have taken from man's shoulders many of the burdens he carried for thousands of years. They have flooded the western world with consumer goods, have raised the quality and quantity of our food and raiments, have put dozens of intricate gadgets into our homes which replace human labor, have produced sanitation and medical knowledge which have doubled man's lifespan; but

199

they have also deprived man of his economic independence and his individuality as producer and consumer.

URBANIZATION, like mass production, produces interdependence. A subsistence farmer can survive a depression; an unemployed industrial worker, living in a metropolis far removed from the soil, cannot survive by his own resources. A strike of elevator operators or tugboat crews can paralyze New York. By destroying a power line, a windstorm can deprive hundreds of people many miles away of heat, water, light and their ability to cook a meal. Having thus lost the economic basis of his independence, his ability to survive without the coordinated effort of society, modern man naturally seeks security, and only a strong and well organized state seemingly can assure the necessary order to prevent economic chaos and give the individual the security which he lost when he traded his handtools for a place at the assembly line, and his subsistence farm for an apartment in the big city. As the dependence of the individual upon nature in an agrarian society gradually shifted to increasing reliance of the people on government in an industrial society, man's attitude toward government intervention changed.

But the changes in modern man's mode of living do not tell the full story. Man's outlook on life is no doubt influenced by his physical make-up, his environment, and his religious beliefs; but neither the flow of glandular secretions, nor subconscious influences of a Freudian nature, nor theological doctrines, and—contrary to Karl Marx—most certainly not man's physical surrounding can deprive man from choosing one course or another. Being free to make decisions distinguishes man as a moral being from an electronic computer. The same holds true of nations. At the end of the war, England was partly destroyed and generally impoverished; devastation and poverty were infinitely worse in Germany. Nations were free to choose between welfare state socialism and free enterprise. England adopted the former, and under the rule of the Labor Government her economy skidded from one near-crisis to the next. Western Germany on the other hand, having learned from fifteen years of bitter experience the consequences of statism and economic interventionism, turned to free enterprise, and within less than a decade the world began to talk of the "German miracle." Just as the British and the Germans were not forced by circumstances to adopt the policies which they chose, industrialization and mass production do not compel the American people to turn to welfare state socialism.

THERE ARE other and deeper reasons, however, which help to explain the politico-economic shifts of the recent decades. During the past 50 years western civilization has experienced a radical change in its concept of the individual and of the nature of society. For two hundred years, since the days of the Enlightenment, man had been regarded essentially as a rational being, able to judge what was best for him. Modern psychology no longer subscribes to this assumption. Freudian man is impelled by subconscious drives; his actions are supposedly often irrational; and with the population growing at an extremely rapid rate during the past 100 years and with the spread of mass-education, the masses have swamped the intellectual and cultural elite. One writer speaks of the "vertical barbarian invasion" of western civilization by the masses resulting in an overemphasis of material goods and a disregard of basic cultural values; the desire for security on the part of the *Massemench* which has overwhelmed the demands for personal freedom of the superior individual.

"Our people in a body are wise," wrote Thomas Jefferson to Joseph Priestley, "because they are under the unrestrained and unperverted operation of their own understanding." "I believe, as I believe in nothing else, in the average integrity and the average intelligence of the American people," wrote President Wilson more than a hundred years later.[1] This

---

[1] Woodrow Wilson, *The New Freedom*, (New York: Doubleday, 1913), pp. 64, 89.

200

was not campaign oratory; Jefferson and Wilson believed in the rationality and goodness of man.

The spirit has changed in the past 30 years. "Without results we know that democracy means nothing and ceases to be alive in the minds and hearts of men," warned the President's Committee on Administrative Management in 1937.[2] Government had come to look upon the people as being not primarily interested in abstract ideals—"freedom buys no milk for the baby" was a popular phrase during the depression years—but in material results, in security. As Lord Keynes put it: "In the long run we are all dead." Instead of assuming that man is able to judge the nature and long-range effects of a government policy, which is the basic assumption upon which democracy rests, we have come to "tax and tax, and spend and spend, and elect and elect," because, in the words of Harry Hopkins, one of the best-known exponents of New Deal philosophy, "the people are too damned dumb."

Just as the concept of man has changed during the past few decades, so has our social philosophy.

THERE ARE two basic concepts of society, the atomistic and the organic. We can postulate that society consists of a large number of small independent atoms, namely human beings, who represent ultimate reality, while, the state is merely an agglomeration of individuals. This was the premise of 19th century economic and political liberalism. The state, having no independent existence of its own, was not expected to provide either welfare or economic security. In vetoing an appropriation of $25,000 to buy seed corn for drought-stricken farmers, President Cleveland wrote: "There is no warrant in the Constitution of the United States for taking the funds which are raised from taxes and giving them from one man to another . . . while the people support the government, the government does not support the people."

[2] *Report with Special Studies,* (Washington, 1937).

On the other hand, we can picture society as an organism, somewhat like the human body. Human beings then become cells of the social organism, unable to exist by themselves. Society alone can provide the necessary security. The emphasis thus shifts from the individual to the group. The latter becomes ultimate reality and the individual and his wants are subordinated to the needs and wants of "society." This was the philosophy which prevailed throughout the Middle Ages and down to the 18th century, and which was gradually replaced by the atomistic view. In our own days we seem to have returned to a large extent to the organic concept of society.

The growing dependence of the individual upon society, the declining faith in the rationality of man, and the growing emphasis upon society rather than the individual have resulted in the development of a new branch of economics, macro-economics, which today accounts for almost two-thirds of the typical college curriculum.

While nineteenth-century economics concerned itself primarily with the economic problems which confronted the individual and the firm, such as price and value and the distribution of income, twentieth-century economists are primarily interested in the problems which affect the nation as a whole: growth and stagnation, monetary and fiscal policies, welfare economics, and economic planning.

In the construction of their analytical models, nineteenth-century economists made two basic assumptions: (1) The mainsprings of economic activity were thought to be rational individuals who were intent on maximizing their income while minimizing their efforts; and (2) the economy was assumed to be governed by so called "economic laws," conceived as somewhat similar to the causal laws of Newtonian physics, which, if not interfered with by man, would produce an economic equilibrium which most economists assumed would provide the greatest good for the greatest number. Twentieth-century economics has largely dropped both assumptions. The rationality of man and the profit motive are regarded as premises which are neither helpful nor realistic; and the notion that automatic forces, if not interfered with, would automatically promote the greatest general welfare has been replaced by the modern postulate that the economy is constantly in need of state intervention. The "perfect machine," our social organism, which the Enlightenment thought had been created for the benefit of man by an all-wise and all-kind God, appears to the twentieth-century badly in need of repairs by economic planners.

While the term macro-economics is the creation of our time, and while the approach is new as far as the twentieth-century is concerned, modern macro-economics offers many parallels to the mercantilism of the absolutist age. There is, however, one striking difference. While economic planning in the totalitarian countries is directed almost exclusively toward the strengthening of the state, at the expense of the freedom and well-being of the people, just as it was under mercantilism 300 years ago, economic planning in the western world is directed primarily toward the improvement of the economic status of those members of society who seem unable to achieve by their own efforts the standard of living which the government regards as appropriate.

THE MOST significant move in this direction has been the Employment Act of 1946. Its basic philosophy was outlined by President Roosevelt in a message to Congress in 1944 and restated in the Democratic Platform of the same year. It calls for the federal government to provide "full employment for the unemployed and guarantee . . . a job for every man released from the armed forces and the war industries at fair pay and working conditions." A year later, Secretary of Commerce Henry Wallace restated the principle that "the essential idea is that the federal government is ultimately responsible for full employment," and the Employment Act itself provided that "it is the policy and the responsibility of the Federal Government to use all practical means . . . to promote maximum employment."

The Employment Act of 1946 did not immediately impair the personal freedom of the American people and, since cause-and-effect relationships are often not clear to the untrained observer, the eventual loss of personal and economic freedom, which may well be the result of the job security created by the Employment Act, has not yet dawned upon the great mass of the American people.

Employment depends upon demand, demand upon prices, and prices, in turn upon the cost of production. As wages rise the cost of production increases, and as prices rise the demand declines, which results in a drop in employment. Under the Employment Act, however, the Federal Government is required to prevent unemployment and it can do so by creating additional demand through the expansion of credit and the creation of more money, which means inflation. While the labor unions need not worry any longer that an increase in wages might lead, via higher prices and declining demand, to unemployment, the price which the American people as a whole, including the workers, have paid for this type of job security has been high. The cost of living has increased steadily since the end of the war. The retail price index stood at less than 77 in 1945 and had almost reached 129 by the end of 1961. Since 1950, moreover, the United States has steadily suffered a deficit in her balance of payments. Since the "gold crisis" in the fall of 1960, the dollar has been dependent upon international support in order to prevent a run on the sharply reduced gold reserves of the nation. The weakening of America's international monetary position has affected her political stature as well. While the totalitarian countries directed their economic planning toward the strengthening of the state, economic planning in the western nations has been aimed thus far primarily toward a higher standard of living for the people, even though, as we have come to realize today, this has resulted in a relative weakening of the American position in world affairs.

Obviously, this trend cannot continue indefinitely if we are to survive as a nation. The American people are confronted with a far-reaching choice. Will there be a turning away from the welfare state policies of the past decade and a return to greater reliance on private initiative, or shall we increase further the power of the state, as Rome did in its time of trouble?

When Diocletian came to power toward the end of the third century, after decades of civil wars, the weaknesses of the Roman Empire were far more pronounced than are the difficulties which face the United States today. Inflation had progressed much further and the Roman economy was stagnating, while the American economy of today is booming. But Rome had one advantage: while it had many border conflicts—the Koreas, Laos's and Congos of those days—it was not challenged by a major power comparable to modern Russia.

Diocletian's efforts to restore the strength of the Roman Empire followed methods which are quite similar to those which economic and political leaders suggest today. In order to stop inflation, he "fixed" prices and wages by law, with the death penalty for those who violated the ceilings; made local trade associations responsible for price maintenance and in some instances for production quotas; and froze workers, especially farm laborers, in their jobs. His "emergency" measures designed to restore economic stability at the beginning of the 4th century affected the freedom of the people of Europe for 1500 years. The trade associations, which Diocletian entrusted with price maintenance, set the pattern for the medieval guilds which regulated prices, production, working conditions, and entry into the trade. While these guilds could well have developed without Diocletian's reforms, the latter helped to set the pattern. Farm workers, whom Diocletian froze in their jobs to assure the necessary food supplies, eventually became the medieval serfs.

Lord Beveridge, the father of the full employment philosophy, recognized at the outset that a full employment policy can easily produce chronic inflation and suggested that the government, if necessary, freeze wages and prices and regulate production and employment, i.e., tell the entrepreneur what and how much to produce, and the worker where he can work and at what wages. The attempt of the 1940's to provide job security may thus very well lead, in the 1960's, to federal wage and price regulations, and, when these fail, to more rigid regulations of production and employment.

TWO OTHER Congressional efforts to assure economic security—and one can, of course, list many more—illustrate the danger that man can easily lose in freedom as he gains in security. The National Labor Relations Act of 1936 was intended to protect the worker against oppression and exploitation by the employer, but an integral part of the same legislation was the creation of powerful unions and of the union shop provision—or its various equivalents—under which a worker has to pay union dues in order to retain his job. The courts have even held, that if a worker, during a national election, advocates a view opposed by his union, he can be expelled from the union even though this may automatically result in his discharge from his job and may prevent him from getting another job in the occupation for which he is trained.

The farm aid program is designed to provide the farmer with "parity" income by placing a floor under farm prices. Aside from the fact that the program has failed to provide a minimum of income security for the small farmer—the average subsidy for about 3.5 million small farmers amounts to less than $125 a year—the American farmer had to surrender a substantial portion of his personal and economic freedom in exchange for the security which the program was intended to provide.

In Wickard vs. Filburn[3] and in a number of other decisions, the Supreme Court has ruled that Congress can not only regulate the flow of farm products in interstate commerce, but that it can also prescribe how much a farmer may raise on his own farm for his own consumption. Acreage allotments, production and marketing quotas—all of them restrictions on the freedom of the farmer to use

3 317 *U.S.* 111 (1942).

203

Page Twenty seven

his land and his ability to produce—are the logical concomitant of the attempt of the federal government to place a floor under farm prices, and thus provide "security" for the farmer.

IN THEIR search for "economic security" the American people are in danger of chasing a phantom. We live in a world of rapid technological and economic change which results in insecurity for the investor, the entrepreneur and the worker. Growth means change, and change means insecurity. Yet the same people who advocate maximum economic growth very often also clamor for maximum economic security.

Economic security is relative. Simpler societies of the past enjoyed a feeling of abundance and security, while we, despite our riches, are plagued by the frustrating sense of want and insecurity, because we have replaced the more or less stable requirements of necessities with spiraling desires for more goods and services. Nobody questions the need for "minimum security." As St. Thomas wrote 700 years ago, "A minimum of comfort is necessary in life for the efficient practice of virtue." The danger lies in the fact that the American people, and for that matter, western civilization as a whole, may succumb to the temptation of trading their individual freedom for the promise of economic security and an ever rising standard of living.

Mass production and urbanization, which impose upon us interdependence, make us security-minded, and the intellectual climate of our time seems to favor the same trend. We have gone a long way during the past 50 years toward trading away our personal freedom, and the 1960's are not likely to bring a reversal of the trend. In fact, men like Professors Hansen and Galbraith assure us that henceforth the well-being of the American people as a whole will be advanced more by "social" rather than by "individual" consumption. Instead of permitting the individual to "fritter away" his income on tail-finned cars, martinis and hula-hoops, the government should channel, via increased taxation, an ever greater share of the national income into social consumption: schools and hospitals, recreational facilities and roads. After all, we are told, America spends almost three times as much on liquor, tobacco and cosmetics as on education; five times as much on dog food as on college textbooks. Perhaps our standard of values, as reflected in the buying pattern of the consumer, is basically unsound. But will it be changed for the better, if we transfer the responsibility for the allocation of the nation's resources—together with the people's freedom as producers and consumers—to government officials, politicians and "experts?" This is the fundamental question which faces the American people during the 1960's.

New Individualist Review welcomes contributions for publication from its readers. Essays should not exceed 3,000 words, and should be type-written. All manuscripts will receive careful consideration.

Sin and the Criminal Law

ROBERT M. HURT

The freedom we enjoy extends also to ordinary life; we are not suspicious of one another, and do not nag our neighbor if he chooses to go his own way.[1]

Pericles

He who imagines that he can give laws for the public conduct of states, while he leaves the private lives of citizens wholly to take care of itself; who thinks that individuals may pass the day as they please, and that there is no necessity of order in all things; he, I say, who gives up the control of their private lives, and supposes that they will conform to law in their common and public life, is making a great mistake.[2]

Plato

WHILE ONE would expect the criminal arm of the New York City bureaucracy to be fully occupied with more momentous problems, it was able in February of this year to find time to hail a group of girls before the bar of justice for "glue sniffing," allegedly for the narcotic effect. Though we think of the criminal law as designed to protect individuals against the acts of other individuals, these girls were charged with "impairing their own health and morals." In a nation which allows persons to be punished on such grounds, those of us who are interested in the maximization of personal liberty should consider whether John Stuart Mill's maxim that the state should not interfere in the private acts of individuals is a minimum condition for a free society.

The maxims are, first, that the individual is not accountable to society for his actions, in so far as these concern the interests of no person but himself. Advice, instruction, persuasion, and avoidance by other people if thought necessary by them for their own good, are the only measures by which society can justifiably express its dislike or disapprobation of his conduct.[3]

Most conservatives will be quick to agree with Mill's refusal to let the law interfere in the private sphere when some new economic regulation is under consideration. Ambassador Galbraith's vendetta against tailfins and his desire to protect the consumer against his imprudent free choice, Ambassador Stevenson's indignation at the "myth of privacy," and Social Security taxes designed to provide workers to provide for themselves in their old age, are all greeted by the "right" as attempts to subvert our liberty. Yet, conservative "defenders of freedom" are often found shouting the loudest for coercion to enforce their particular moral concepts or standards of decency in situations directly affecting only those who are voluntary parties to an act. (And, to compound the paradox, it is often the interventionist liberal who most vigorously upholds personal freedom in these areas.)

At the risk of offending those who not only support these prohibitions but also feel they are too delicate to be discussed in a scholarly journal, I invite the reader to examine an area of law which is all

Robert M. Hurt is an Associate Editor of *New Individualist Review*.

---

[1] Thucydides, *The Peloponnesian War*, (New York: Random House, 1951) p. 104.
[2] *Laws*, vi., 780.
[3] *On Liberty*, (Chicago: Gateway, 1952) p. 119.

too often ignored in analyses of the role of the state. If adherents to the libertarian-conservative philosophy of limited government are to deserve the intellectual respectability which they claim, they have a duty to develop a more consistent practical application of that philosophy.

LIKE MOST important intellectual controversies, the proper role of state intervention in the private affairs of citizens was a point of vigorous dispute among the early Greeks. Little is known of that Greek libertarian tradition which received one of its most eloquent formulations in the funeral oration of Pericles and seems to have been advocated by Democritus, Protagoras, and Lycophron.[4] Lycophron is quoted by Aristotle as demanding that the state should be merely a "covenant by which men assure one another of justice" and a "co-operative association for the prevention of crime." In reaction to this first known advocacy of an "open society" came the totalitarianism of Plato, who urged the complete regulation of every important aspect of the citizen's moral life as a necessity for a "virtuous society." Though seeing more value in freedom of action than Plato, Aristotle still saw "virtue" as the end of the *polis*, an end to which the secondary value of freedom of action readily gave way. While this Platonic-Aristotelian tradition triumphed over its libertarian alternative and was not successfully attacked until recent centuries, the early Christian and medieval period gave far more deference to individual freedom than is commonly supposed. St. Augustine viewed the state as completely unable to improve the moral constitution of its already corrupted citizens and consequently advocated severe limitations on state intervention. While St. Thomas, like Aristotle, saw virtue as the principal end of the state, he emphasized the

importance of "individual autonomy" and the necessity of allowing free choice between right and wrong. The last few centuries have seen an erosion of this Platonic-Aristotelian tradition and a return in the Protestant countries to the social contract and policeman state concepts of Lycophron. Ironically, most Catholic countries do not proscribe many of those acts which are penalized in some supposedly more liberal Protestant nations: gambling, use of alcoholic beverages, homosexuality, adultery, and fornication.[5]

The early nineteenth century saw England, under Benthamite influence, gradually move toward the position that the state should not interfere in the private lives of its citizens. It was, however, in the United States that lovers of freedom placed their greatest hopes. Lord Acton was prompted to write:

> Europe seemed incapable of becoming the home of free states. It was from America that the plain idea that men ought to mind their own business, and that the nation is responsible to Heaven for the acts of State, burst forth like a conqueror upon the world they were destined to transform, under the title of the Rights of Man.[6]

Unfortunately, the "home of free states" has had to endure periods of legal moralizing on such a hysterical scale that even Plato might have blanched to see it. Characteristic of the "yahooism" so vividly described by H. L. Mencken was the career of Anthony Comstock, who in the 1870's led a nationwide campaign for legal proscription of conduct which he considered sinful. He succeeded, as leader of the New York So-

---

[4] Cf. Popper, *The Open Society and Its Enemies*, (Princeton: Princeton University, 1950), pp. 112-14, 165 ff., and Hayek, *The Constitution of Liberty* (Chicago: University of Chicago, 1960), pp. 164-66.

[5] Catholic intolerance in areas such as birth control and censorship has tended to obscure the facts that Catholic scholars are by no means agreed on many areas of state intervention and that the most restrictive moral legislation is often due to pressure from Protestant groups. An excellent book which represents the more liberal Catholic tradition is St. John-Stevas, *Life, Death and the Law*, (Bloomington, Ind.: Ind. Univ. Press, 1961). He concludes that birth control should not be outlawed in countries with large non-Catholic populations.

[6] Acton, *History of Freedom*, p. 55, as cited in Hayek, *op. cit.*, p. 176.

ciety for the Suppression of Vice and later as special agent for the Post Office, in preventing the circulation through the U. S. mails of birth control information and other literature considered by persons of his turn of mind to be obscene or immoral. This *jehad* against sin which characterized the Populism and Bryanism of the turn of the century had not even the mitigating value of being directed by a Platonic elite; rather it was a grassroots movement based largely on religious moralizing and a dislike of the "strange ways" and religious trends in the urban centers of the East.

The crowning glory of this radical democracy was the Prohibition Amendment, which stands as one of the most striking examples in the history of a **free nation of an** attempt by one group to impose its personal mores on others. Since the beginning of the New Deal and the repeal of Prohibition in all but a few states, government action against private immorality has tended to decline. The grassroots citizenry has since turned to the more lucrative pastime of regulating the economic lives rather than **the moral** lives of others. Though state regulation of private conduct is at present far less pervasive than economic intervention, it is still extensive enough to constitute a serious limitation on freedom.

A long **and** comprehensive list of the areas of personal morality regulated by law, from federal statute down to minute municipal ordinance, could easily be composed, but some of the more far-reaching are: (1) prohibitions against the sale of birth control devices or the dissemination of birth control information, (2) statutes forbidding the intermarriage or cohabitation of persons of different racial groups, (3) statutes classifying suicide or attempted suicide as a crime and classifying voluntary euthanasia (the killing of a suffering and hopelessly incurable person at his own request) or otherwise aiding a person in committing suicide as murder, (4) prohibition of fornication, prostitution, and homosexual and other unnatural sex acts between consenting adults, (5) prohibitions against the sale of narcotics

and alcoholic beverages, (6) statutes prohibiting gambling, (7) censorship of allegedly "obscene" or "immoral" books or movies.[7]

Even should we accept the classical liberal maxim that a person should not be punished for his own "sins" as long as no non-consenting party is injured, other problems are raised by the laws mentioned above. If we hold that the law should not protect adults from themselves, we still must deal with the thorny problem of special protection for juveniles, the insane, and possibly the feeble-minded. Should the sale of certain narcotics or alcoholic beverages be likely to lead to crime, it has been argued that legal prohibition is needed to protect innocent parties. Moreover, are persons to be born entitled to any protection? Should measures be taken to protect their genetic stock from deterioration? In examining the extent of government coercion in these areas of private conduct, I will attempt to show that almost none of this legislation can be justified as preventing harm to juveniles or innocent third parties. I conclude with a theoretical proposal concerning the proper delineation of the private sphere from the sphere of allowable government intervention.

NOT ONLY IS the Comstock Act, which prohibits distribution of contraceptives or birth control information for other than medical purposes through the mail, still federal law but, also, twenty-two states prohibit or limit the sale of contraceptives. In five states, Connecticut, Kansas, Massachusetts, Mississippi, and Nebraska, the statute makes no exceptions; even if pregnancy would result

---

[7] I have not included certain laws which raise complicated issues involving possible injury to third parties which cannot be easily answered by any general principle as to the right of government to regulate private lives. For instance, abortion raises the issue as to whether an unborn child is an innocent party that should be protected against murder, and polygamy and artificial insemination raise the question as to whether a future child should be protected agains the social stigma of "illegitimacy."

207

in death or serious injury to the wife, the sale of contraceptives or dissemination of information still can technically land the party in jail. In Connecticut the use of contraceptives is also a criminal offense. While the status of these laws is unclear in Mississippi, Kansas, and Nebraska, high courts in Connecticut and Massachusetts have held that the health or life of the wife does not prevail against legislative fiat.[8] To any future widowers as a result of this statute, the highest Connecticut court offers this brutal condolence: the legislature left them free to practice the alternative of "abstention." The United States Supreme Court has thus far avoided testing the constitutionality of these statutes, but it will soon be forced to reach a decision. On November 1st of last year a Planned Parenthood Center was opened in New Haven, Connecticut, to disseminate birth control information. Ten days later officers of the center were arrested. There seems to be no gimmick by which the Supreme Court can avoid deciding this case, now on appeal, on the constitutional issues involved.

These anti-birth control laws, though reduced in importance because of the reluctance of officials to enforce them, (except when their hand is forced, as in New Haven, by deliberate publicity) make a travesty of that "plain idea that men ought to mind their own business." No injury is claimed to third parties, unless one is willing to argue that a potential person deprived of existence is somehow entitled to legal protection. Protection of juveniles seems to raise no special problem, as it might in the case of narcotics and alcoholic beverages. These laws seem to be a clearcut example of a partially successful attempt to impose a personal religious and moral code on dissenters.

THE SUPREME COURT has also avoided passing on the constitutionality of state laws which touch on one of the

most personal decisions in an individual's life: the choice of a spouse. Twenty-two states, six of them outside the South, still prohibit interracial marriages. While one-eighth Negro blood is enough to constitute a person a Negro in most of these states, in Georgia and Virginia an "ascertainable trace" is sufficient.[9] The record of such prohibitions is sanctified with age; a Jamestown ordinance proclaimed that a white man should be publicly whipped "for abusing himself to the dishonour of God and the shame of Christians by defiling his body in lying with a Negro." After passage of the Fourteenth Amendment, state courts generally upheld the constitutionality of these statutes. The Alabama Supreme Court summed up the usual rationale for these laws in an 1877 case:

> The natural law, which forbids their intermarriage and that amalgamation which leads to a corruption of races, is as clearly divine as that which imparts to them different natures.[10]

The California Supreme Court is the only high court which has thus far struck down such a statute as violating the federal constitution.

Unlike some "moral legislation," which is allowed to lie dormant on the statute books, these statutes are still often vigorously enforced, especially in the South. The depravity to which "protectors of the white race" will resort in enforcing these statutes is illustrated by the fate of Davis Knight, who at the age of twenty-three was sentenced to five years imprisonment in Mississippi for marrying a white girl. He was classified as a Negro because his great-grandmother was a Negro, a fact which neither he nor his

---

[8] Tileston v. Ullman, 129 *Conn* 84 (1942), and Cw. v. Allison, 227 *Mass* 57 (1917).

[9] These ratios make a mockery of the notion that the statutes are designed to protect equally the integrity of the white and Negro races. A consistent application would require a person with less than one-half Negro blood to marry only a person of the white race.

[10] Green v. State, 58 *Ala* 190 (1877).

parents knew at the time of his marriage.[11]

These fantastic laws fail to arouse the attention they deserve both because they affect only a small group of people and because they have for so long been a part of the judicial landscape. In a nation where social security or the banning of a Communist speaker bring forth cries of tyranny, one might expect more indignation at prohibitions in this area of private choice. If we require injury to innocent parties as the basis for criminal liability, these laws clearly cannot be justified on the grounds by which they are usually defended: that intermarriage is inherently sinful, contrary to the Bible, or opposed to natural law. Likewise, the notion that the "white race has a right to protect itself" is necessarily a collectivist and mystical sentiment which can hardly give justification for criminal sanctions if freedom is a serious goal. These laws are defended by the more sophisticated on a eugenic basis: intermarriage will allegedly lower the genetic quality of unborn generations; hence anti-miscegenation laws prevent injury to unborn persons. But even if this argument is admitted to have a sound scientific basis, few if any of the proponents of this legislation would admit the general principle that the state may regulate marriage whenever justified by "scientifically proven" eugenic principles. As a general principle, the choice of a spouse is one decision almost all of us want left to the individual, regardless of the genetic consequences; it is only when the additional prejudices and fears surrounding intermarriage are involved that we allow such restrictions.

PERHAPS THE ACID test of one's belief in freedom of choice arises when we are asked: does a person have the legal right to terminate his own life? Further, may a person, without incurring criminal liability, assist another in terminating his own life? Though our Christian tradition has regarded suicide as a heinous crime, authorities have been understandably vexed in applying sanctions. By canon of King Edgar in 967, English suicides were denied burial rites; this tradition was later embellished by burial on a highway with a stake through the heart, coupled with forfeiture of the suicide's possessions to the Crown. In a famous early case the court outlined the reasons for treating suicide as a crime:[12] (1) it is against nature "because it is contrary to the rules of self-preservation, which is the principle of nature, for everything living does by instinct of nature defend itself from destruction, and then to destroy one's self is contrary to nature and a thing most horrible," (2) to kill one's self is a breach of God's command "thou shalt not kill," (3) the king loses a subject, "he being the head has lost one of his mystical members."

Classification of suicide as a felony is not an academic matter when applied to attempted suicides and accomplices to a suicide. Attempted suicide is a crime in England; from 1946 to 1955, 5,794 cases were tried by courts and 308 persons actually went to prison. In the United States neither suicide nor attempted suicide is a crime in most states, and in those states that do make attempted suicide a criminal offense, prosecutions are rare. However, assisting a person in committing suicide at his own request is generally punished as murder in both England and the United States.[13]

209

---

[11] *Time*, Dec. 27, 1948, p. 18. The police were informed by a relative who as a result of an old family feud, dug up Knight's genealogy. Mississippi's zealousness also extends to nipping the threat to racial integrity in the bud. Section 2339 (1959) of the Mississippi Code reads: "Any person, firm, or corporation who shall be guilty of printing, publishing, or circulating printed, typewritten, or written matter urging or presenting for public acceptance or general information, arguments or suggestions in favor of social equality or intermarriage between whites and negroes shall be guilty of a misdemeanor and subject to a fine not exceeding five hundred dollars or imprisonment not exceeding six months, or both . . ."

[12] Hales v. Petit, 1 *Plow* 253 (C.B. 1563).

[13] Assisting a suicide is only manslaughter in New York, and in Texas no crime is committed if the accused merely encourages or assists without actually killing the suicide. Many European writers accept the position of the Italian positivist, Enrico Ferri, who argued that, since a man has the right to dispose of his own life as he chooses, he has the right to consent to his own destruction by another. But Ferri's suggestion

The legality of voluntary euthanasia, or "mercy killing," provides a particularly controversial variation to this general question. Courts are frequently called upon to decide whether a doctor commits murder when he kills a patient who is in serious pain from an incurable disease, and requests that the doctor end his misery. Polls have indicated that about half of Americans and an even larger portion of Britons favor mercy killings;[14] this is reflected in the frequent refusals of juries to find that a killing was committed, even when the defendant had admitted the killing.[15] Though euthanasia societies in both Britain and the United States have pressed for a change in legislation,[16] only Uruguay has enacted a law legalizing voluntary euthanasia. Since many of the objections to mercy killing may be overcome by proper legal draftsmanship — the danger of a hasty decision due to a temporary whim induced by suffering, and the danger that the doctor could get away with actual murder for selfish reasons — the argument against it rests largely on theological and ethical strictures concerning *felo de se*, a crime against one's self.[17] We are told that suicide, of which voluntary euthanasia is a form, is a sin which must be discouraged by the law. According to St. Thomas and the mainstream of Catholic thought, "suicide is the most fatal of sins, because it cannot be repented of."[18] Further, God reserved the right to take away life at the appointed time, an argument which would seem to prohibit the use of any medicine to prolong life beyond the time when the patient would otherwise die. Finally, the Biblical commandment against killing, as well as the nobility and desirability of suffering as part of a "divine plan," is invoked. Advocates of personal liberty may or may not agree that suicide to prevent a slow and agonizing death is sinful. Undoubtedly, they would unanimously admire the person who would voluntarily stick it out to the bitter end on moral or religious grounds. And certainly they would not argue that such a person should be killed against his will; the compulsory euthanasia centers for the feeble-minded and the deformed set up by the Nazis have left a bad taste in the mouth of humanity. But even to those who accept this view of the sinfulness of suicide and who would live by this principle themselves and fervently urge it on others, it should appear as an act of barbarity to urge state coercion against those who choose relief from pain over the moral principle involved. Imposition of religious views here smacks not only of cruelty but of hypocrisy, when those who would let the "absolute value of human life" prevail against the voluntary choice of the subject refuse to take an unqualified stand against the involuntary taking of human life through capital punishment or war.

210

---

has been adopted only in the Swiss Criminal Code, which provides that whoever assists the suicide of another commits no crime unless he is actuated by "selfish motives."

[14] Fifty-four percent of Americans favored mercy killings in an Institute of Public Opinion Poll in the *New York Herald Tribune*, Jan. 17, 1937, but 46 percent of Americans and 68 percent of Britons favored it in a Gallup Poll recorded in the *New York Times* Index (1939), p. 1414.

[15] A New Hampshire case, State v. Sander, received nation-wide publicity in 1950.

[16] The proposed legislation would allow a patient to petition a court for euthanasia, provided he is over twenty-one, of sound mind, and suffering from an incurable disease accompanied by severe pain. After an investigation to determine whether the patient fully understands what he is doing and whether his malady is incurable, euthanasia would be administered before court appointed witnesses. While these proposals would avoid some objections to euthanasia—it could not be used as a result of a temporary whim, and a court would not have to rely on the doctor's word that the patient desired death—this legal ritual might be viewed as governmental encouragement of euthanasia. Glanville Williams' suggestion, that murder would be presumed and the physician would be required to show that the patient requested death upon mature reflection and was incurably ill, seems preferable.

[17] Additional objections are that killing violates the Hippocratic Oath, although the oath also requires a physician to relieve suffering, and that, as Chesterton has asserted, this might be extended to involuntary euthanasia in the future. The non-religious arguments against euthanasia are summed up in Kamisar, *Minnesota Law Review*, 42: 16 (May, 1958).

[18] *Summa Theologica*, ii-ii q. 64, art. 5.

Joseph Fletcher, a noted physician and writer, has commented on this strange double standard:

> We are, by some strange habit of mind and heart, willing to impose death but unwilling to permit it: we will justify humanly contrived death when it violates the human integrity of its victims, but we condemn it when it is an intelligent voluntary decision. If death is not inevitable anyway, not desired by the subject, and not merciful, it is righteous! If it is happening anyway and is freely embraced and merciful, then it is wrong.[19]

Probably the most common ground for attacking voluntary euthanasia is the fallibility of doctors. Either the malady might be erroneously diagnosed as incurable or a cure might be discovered in time to save the patient. Since it is certainly possible that, even with the checks provided by legislation, some would choose euthanasia who might have been cured, we are driven back to the original question: should it be a criminal offense to aid a person in taking his own life, regardless of whether he is doomed to a painful death in the near future. If we hold strictly to the principle that the criminal law should protect only innocent parties and should not recognize "crimes against one's self," we could not sanction the use of law to prevent a person from seeking aid in his own destruction. (As a corollary we could not punish the person who gave the aid.) Unlike some of the other issues raised in this article, this would appear to be an unambiguous and clearcut application of this principle. However, this conclusion runs so directly counter to certain threads in our political and moral thought that it would be a bitter pill even for many strong advocates of freedom to swallow. The notion of the "absolute sanctity of human life" has been a vital part not only of our religious tradition but also of the classical liberal tradition from which our attachment to freedom largely derives. (Another related and possibly more difficult question is whether dueling should be permitted when both parties agree to the duel.) While sanctions against voluntary euthanasia might be liberalized or even abandoned in the future, emotions and countervailing philosophical attitudes are probably too strong to make a change in the law in regard to aiding a suicide likely in the near future.

WHILE CRIMINAL sanctions against voluntary euthanasia raise serious issues for a philosophy of freedom, our attempts to regulate the private sexual conduct of adults through state coercion have been more in the nature of a very bad joke. At present, the fantastic hodgepodge of statutes and ordinances of the various states prohibiting fornication, adultery,[20] and those acts amorphously grouped as "unmentionable crimes against nature," even when in private between consenting adults, cover such a wide range of sexual conduct that, according to Kinsey's sampling, ninety-five percent of all males have committed a criminal sexual offense sometime in their lives.[21] These statutes, if literally applied, would in most states not only result in criminal sanctions against all those engaged in sexual relations of any sort outside the marriage bond, but would, under the fantastic statutory definitions of "crimes against nature," etc., result in criminal penalties against a large percentage, probably a majority, of married couples for their private relations. State interference in private sexual affairs was not extensive in the western world until rather recently; at present, statutory meddling in the Anglo-Saxon countries is probably more comprehensive and detailed than it has ever been.

Most of the advanced nations of the world attach no criminal penalty to fornication, though they probably do this

---

[19] Fletcher, *Morals and Medicine*, (Princeton: Princeton Univ. Press, 1954) p. 181.

[20] Adultery presents a special problem because it is justified as protecting the spouse from injury. In almost every European nation, however, the civil remedy is considered adequate.

[21] Kinsey, Pomeroy, and Martin, *Sexual Behavior in the Human Male*, (Philadelphia: Saunders, 1948).

211

out of recognition of the fact that the practice is well-nigh universal and literal enforcement would lead to a call to arms by the citizenry rather then out of a feeling that this is none of the state's business. Further, even adultery is normally not a statutory offense, though the injured spouse usually has civil redress. The *Code Napoleon* abolished such offenses between consenting adults, and France's example has been followed throughout Western Europe. American crusaders against sin, however, have been able to hold the line in most state legislatures in an unsuccessful attempt to enforce their moral code on a population that generally rejects it. All but eleven states make fornication a criminal offense, penalties ranging from a three-year jail sentence in Arizona to fines alone in seven states. The federal government has plunged into the battle with the Mann White Slave Act, which prohibits the transporting of a woman across a state line for "immoral purposes." The courts have held that a federal crime is committed should one have relations with one's girl friend on an interstate drive.[22] But the interventionists have had their reverses; the California courts recently struck down all municipal legislation prohibiting fornication and adultery (because state legislation, which contained no bar, had preempted the field), in the face of the warning of the Los Angeles Police Chief that this was a "Bill of Rights for prostitutes" and that "a hedonistic philosophy is filling the void created by the destruction of the Victorian culture."[23]

Until rather recently, criminal law codes in western countries had paid little attention to homosexual acts between consenting adults, and the civil and ecclesiastical sanctions which did exist were justified in large part by the notion that God would visit the fate of Sodom and Gomorrah on those nations where such conduct was tolerated. Since we optimistically assume that this belief has lost wide acceptance, we might expect the laws to likewise disappear. All

the nations of Western Europe except West Germany and Austria have repealed laws penalizing these "crimes against nature" except when juveniles are involved or when the crime occurs in a public place. But in Britain and the United States the statutes have been extended rather than repealed and now in most states cover such a wide variety of allegedly "unnatural acts" that husband and wife are no longer safe from legislative meddling. Practices widely recommended by most modern marriage manuals and in no conceivable way the legitimate concern of "organized society" are technically criminal even though probably practiced by a majority of married couples.[24] While there is fantastic variety and confusion in the laws of the various states (partly due to the embarrassment of legislators who wanted to prohibit the act without mentioning its name or describing it), every state except Illinois makes some form of private homosexual conduct between consenting adults a prison offense. In England the maximum penalty for sodomy is life imprisonment. Many states impose a high minimum sentence; for example, Rhode Island sets seven years. Maximum sentence varies from life in Nevada and sixty years in North Carolina to three years in several states. Some states, such as Colorado, underline the social danger by depriving those convicted of the right to vote, serve on a jury, or hold public office.

Perusing the statutes and ordinances alone, we might assume that minute government regulation of almost every form of sexual activity has reached a level of intensity which would gratify Orwell's Anti-Sex League. But the citizenry has been given a reprieve: Big Brother seldom enforces these laws. Only in Massachusetts is the adultery statute widely enforced, and prohibitions against fornication and the various "unnatural acts" between male and female in private are only sporadically enforced by exceptionally vigorous upholders of community mores. (Witness the zeal of the

---

[22] Neff v. U. S., 105 *F. 2nd* 688 (1939).

[23] *Newsweek*, Jan. 8, 1962, p. 18.

[24] Ploscowe, *Sex and the Law*, (New York: Prentice Hall, 1951) p. 202.

Atlanta ordinance which required that shades should be pulled when mannequins were being undressed.) Even homosexuals, though subject much more to public indignation, are rarely imprisoned for voluntary private acts between adults. In both Britain and the United States, most arrests involve either juveniles or "public indecency" of some sort. However, sporadic round-ups by the police, even when resulting in probation rather than a jail sentence, have been so blatantly unjustifiable as a necessary police measure, that respected jurists in both Britain and this country have argued vigorously for abolition of this offense. The authoritative American Law Institute, upon the recommendation of such noted jurists as Learned Hand, has urged that such laws be repealed. Thus far, their recommendation has been adopted only in Illinois, where the legislature this year removed all criminal penalties for private relations between consenting adults. In Britain, the Wolfenden report recommending that all such prohibitions be removed is still the subject of heated debate.

Jeremy Bentham classified prohibited sex acts in which there is neither violence, fraud, nor interference with the rights of others, as "imaginary offenses" in which no penalty is justified. Fornication (including prostitution) and homosexuality, when juveniles are not involved and when not occurring in a public place, obviously qualify under this criterion as "imaginary offenses": no question of violence or fraud is involved (these are covered by separate statutes) and no third parties are directly injured except insofar as they are somehow offended or indignant that such things occur in their vicinity. The most important exception would be that fornication could be viewed as injuring resulting children due to social opprobrium placed upon illegitimacy. The usual motivation for such legislation, however, is to either protect the offender from himself or to give vent to community indignation and to enforce its notion of sin. This fact seems to be generally recognized by informed persons who have a high regard for individual freedom, as is indicated by the widespread support for the Wolfenden Report in Britain and by the attempts to liberalize the law in this country. In an otherwise statist era, this is probably one field in which the trend will be toward more individual freedom rather than less.

WHILE ALCOHOLIC beverages are barred in only a few states, a pervasive net of state and federal laws and international treaties provide almost universal prohibition or regulation of addicting narcotics. In addition to the desire to save the potential addict from his own misconduct, to prevent him from metaphorically "selling himself into slavery," these prohibitions are motivated by two other important considerations. Addiction allegedly leads to crime either through its direct effect on the mind or due to the need for money to buy more of the drug; hence, innocent parties are protected by these laws. Further, it is argued that if drugs are sold freely, there is no practical way to prevent them from falling into the hands of juveniles, who it is felt should be protected from addiction. As to the first consideration, a recent joint American Bar Association-American Medical Association report has accepted the position of most modern authorities that drugs themselves reduce the propensity to commit crimes of violence. Addicts are forced to commit crimes mainly to pay the exorbitant prices of illegal narcotics which can be supplied only by the underworld.[25] Narcotics, if traded on a free market, would be among the cheapest of commodities.

213

———
25 *Drug Addiction: Crime or Disease,* Final Report of the Joint Committee of the American Bar Association and American Medical Association on Narcotic Drugs (Bloomington, Ind.: Ind. Univ. Press, 1961) p. 165: "In terms of numbers afflicted, and in ill effects on others in the community, drug addiction is a problem of far less magnitude than alcoholism. Crimes of violence are rarely, and sexual crimes are almost never, committed by addicts. In most instances the addicts' sins are those of omission rather than commission, they are ineffective people, individuals whose great desire is to withdraw from the world and its troubles into a land of dreams."

Anti-gambling statutes, as well as the traditional unwillingness of courts to enforce gambling contracts, are, like narcotics laws, attempts to protect individuals from their own sinfulness and imprudence. Like alcohol, gambling is regarded by many religious groups not only as a "vice of Babylon" but as one justifying state interference. Just as Galbraith would prevent the consumer from imprudently wasting his money on "unnecessary" car appliances, many anti-gambling zealots would mark off this area as one where consumer choice should not be allowed. The money could, in their estimation, be put to better use. While anti-gambling and anti-narcotics laws are both to an extent honestly motivated by a desire to prevent crimes of violence, these very laws have provided a new haven for organized crime, evicted from its most lucrative business by repeal of Prohibition, since it is now the only institution that can carry on the trade.

Censorship statutes and ordinances are too complex and present too many issues to be covered adequately here. Book-banning to prevent "immoral" and "obscene" literature from passing into the hands of the citizenry by local and state officials as well as by the Post Office has been one of the most comprehensive devices for imposition of the tastes and values of a majority or of a vocal group upon the rest of the community. The Supreme Court itself applies a majoritarian test in determining whether a book may be constitutionally banned:

> Whether to the average person, applying contemporary community standards, the dominant theme of the material taken as a whole appeals to prurient interest.[26]

[26] Roth v. United States, 354 U. S. 476 (1957). A letter by a Commander of the Catholic War Veterans illustrates the majoritarian and "low boiling point" attitude toward censorship: "The Illinois Department of Catholic War Veterans would like to go on record as opposing distribution of a book that shocks a judge the first time he reads it. Further, the Department would like to state for its members . . . that their standards of decency still do not accept the use of dirty words or the description of lewd and vulgar incidents into their homes. They have a right, therefore, to resent a book which brings these things into their community."

However, many advocates of censorship are undoubtedly motivated not by a desire merely to impose their tastes and sentiments by force but by a genuine concern for the effect pornography will have on juveniles and on juvenile crime. While the effect of pornography on juveniles is still an open question, a comprehensive recent study concludes that there is no evidence that pornography has harmful effects on juveniles and promotes crime, and that there is some indication that attempts to keep pornography from juveniles may be harmful.[27]

The problems discussed above are only some of the more spectacular and controversial examples of moral legislation. A complete survey would deal with laws regulating or prohibiting commercial activity on the Lord's day, artificial insemination, voluntary sterilization, polygamy, incest, and physical injury to a consenting subject. We have dealt exclusively with criminal laws; civil laws making various "immoral" contracts unenforceable or otherwise interjecting community moral values into the process of civil recovery raise similar issues. Instead of extending this survey of state intervention into the sphere of private morality, I propose to devote the remainder of this article to the more fundamental question: *why* should the state be prevented from legislating morality?

WHILE ALL GENUINE friends of freedom will be distressed at this panorama of official meddling, it is admittedly more difficult to translate this sentiment into a practical and consistent principle delineating a sphere of private moral conduct with which the state may not interfere. Mill would bar the state from interfering with a person's acts which "concern the interests of no person but himself." Unfortunately, this maxim can be stretched to sanction almost any conceivable state intervention, since it is difficult to conceive of any act which could not adversely affect others. Exces-

[27] Cf. Kronhausen, *Pornography and the Law,* (New York: Ballantine, 1959).

214

sive drinking, excessive TV watching, or refusal to go to college may make a person less productive, thereby lessening his ability to support a family, to produce goods desired by others, and to pay taxes. One who regularly reads the *Congressional Record* might conceivably be driven insane and commit homicide. An improper diet could make one less attractive or pleasant. Birth control might lower the population growth, which could arguably hinder the defense effort. Even when practiced in an outpost isolated from public view, poker games, nudist colonies, rock 'n' roll dancing, even theatre going may be offensive through their mere presence to some citizens.

While the primary purpose of this article is to present the problem rather than to propose an airtight theoretical answer, a few suggestions may be ventured. Juveniles and other persons given a similar status because of insanity or judicially declared incompetence will undoubtedly be given a special protective status under the criminal law; the limits of such protection present too complex a problem to be subsumed under a general principle. After side-stepping this problem, the following general maxim can be offered: the criminal law may punish no category of acts which are not directly injurious to persons who do not consent to the act.[28]

"Directly" in this context is an admittedly ambiguous term. I employ it in a sense analogous to the legal term "proximate cause."[29] Under this criterion I would exclude the following acts from the area of legitimate concern of criminal legislation: (1) Injury to a consent-ing party would not be grounds for punishing another party. (2) Mere outrage or indignation that such acts are going on would not constitute direct injury. (3) Acts which injure others only insofar as they make the actor a less able, virtuous, or pleasant person (by affecting his money-making capacity, etc.) or which deprive others of his contributions altogether (*e.g.*, suicide) will not be sufficient grounds for government interference. (4) Acts which, when taken in the aggregate, might injure others in a remote and secondary way, as by tending to decrease the birth rate or to debase the genetic stock of the community, or by tending to lower the "moral tone" of the community by causing changes in attitudes, will not be grounds for punishment, especially when the alleged tendency is hypothetical and supported only by popular attitudes rather than by conclusive scientific evidence.

This position, held implicitly or explicitly by classical liberals for the last two centuries, has been the subject of intense criticism, some eloquent and penetrating, in recent years. The most frequent criticisms might be mentioned.

First is the "civil libertine" charge: *those who would not punish vice by jail sentences thereby spend their nights practicing it.* While classical liberals might incur their proportionate share of sin, this argument needs no reply. The personal habits of advocates of an idea can hardly affect the validity of the idea.

Second, *those who would not penalize immorality either do not believe in absolute values or do not have any system of values at all.* This assessment may be valid to the extent that one who rejects a system of fixed, absolute values is more likely to object to state enforcement of such alleged values. One is more likely to reject state enforcement of morals if he agrees with F. A. Hayek that:

> . . . even what we regard as good or beautiful is changeable — if not in any recognizable manner that would entitle us to take a relativistic position, then in the sense that in many respects we do not know what will appear as good or beautiful to another generation.[30]

[28] This, of course, does not imply that all acts which do directly injure innocent persons should be criminal. Vigorous commercial competition is desirable even though competitors are "injured" in one sense; many acts which result in injuries, such as hurting a person's feelings, would not be made the subject of law by all but the most ardent statists. And most injuries will be redressed by civil damages rather than criminal sanctions.

[29] Black's Law Dictionary gives this definition of proximate cause: "That which in a natural and continuous sequence, unbroken by any efficient intervening cause, produces the injury, and without which the result would not have occurred."

[30] Hayek, *op. cit.*, p. 35.

215

and rejects W. F. Buckley's claim that, as to moral values

> . . . all that is finally important in human experience is behind us; that the crucial explorations have been undertaken, and that it is given to man to know what are the great truths that emerged from them.[31]

However, libertarians number among their ranks those who base their position on absolute moral values and who find freedom a necessity because it is a condition precedent to moral choice and because the state, by its intervention, will inevitably thwart morality.[32] At any rate, to condemn a political position merely by linking it with a philosophical position completely begs the issue of its validity.

Third, *by repealing laws prohibiting immoral acts, "society" somehow appears to condone and encourage them.* This argument, like its twin brothers in the economic realm — if you vote against Kennedy's farm program, you are against the farmer; if you are against forced desegregation of private dwellings, you are against the Negro — is based on a pernicious premise: the state condones and encourages those things which it does not condemn or act to prevent. Holding to such a doctrine presupposes a rejection of the concept of limited government, whereby most decisions in vital matters, both moral and economic, are left to individual choice. This area of unrestricted freedom is narrowed in principle as much when the state acts as moral conscience as when it acts as policeman. Such is true even when the law is not enforced, though the policy will be less effective.

It has been urged with more plausibility that it would be better to leave such statutes on the books and not enforce them or only enforce them sporadically, since repeal would be taken as a posi-

tive encouragement to engage in the prohibited act. If it were true that such statutes would actually remain dead and would not be gleefully "rediscovered" by some zealot, there would be little advantage in repeal other than the possibility that by not enforcing certain laws we breed disrespect for the remaining laws. However, playing Russian roulette through sporadic enforcement wreaks havoc with the rule of law. The selection of persons to be prosecuted becomes arbitrary and rests solely on the whims of the bureaucrat who happens to be charged with its enforcement. In any case, no evidence has been offered that persons will engage in acts simply because they think repeal of a criminal law showed that "society" or the government thereby encouraged and condoned it.

Fourth, *one cannot separate law and morals, as those who would not punish private immorality allegedly would do.* This criticism is at least in part due to the tendency of liberal legal philosophers, such as H. L. A. Hart,[33] to emphasize the "separation of law and morals" and to couple this with a plea that the law not enforce morality. Actually, neither criminal nor civil law can be divorced from community moral concepts (a close reading of Hart shows he does not deny this), and this in no way undermines the position advocated generally by classical liberals. Generally speaking, an act must be considered in some way "immoral" or "evil" before a criminal sanction can be applied to it. If the criminal law is radically out of step with what Eugen Ehrlich dubbed the "living law," *i.e.*, if acts are punished which are not considered meriting punishment by most members of society, the statutory law will probably be changed to parallel this living law. Prohibition is the usual example given. Further, the severity of punishment will be determined in large measure by the degree of turpitude attached to the crime. However, this "moral turpitude" is clearly at most a necessary, not a sufficient, condition for criminal sanction. No one would argue that

---

[31] Buckley, *Up from Liberalism,* (New York: Hillman, 1959) p. 172.

[32] The articles by M. Stanton Evans and Frank S. Meyer in the Fall, 1960, *Modern Age* and by Murray N. Rothbard in the Spring, 1961, *Modern Age* illustrate how libertarian political philosophies can be based on a belief in absolute moral values.

[33] "Positivism and the Separation of Law and Morals," *Harvard Law Review,* 71:593 (Feb., 1958).

all acts considered immoral—lying, indolence, not going to church — should be punished. The position taken here is that *not only* must the penalized act be condemned morally by members of society, but that *also* some non-consenting party must be directly injured by this category of act.

Fifth, *coercive enforcement of a moral code is necessary to prevent society from "disintegrating."* Sir Patrick Devlin has eloquently argued, in an attack on the Wolfenden Report's contention that there must be a realm of private morality which is "not the law's business," that the threat of such disintegration gives a justification to moral legislation which has no theoretical limit.[34] "Society means a community of shared ideas," of which moral and ethical ideas are a part. Without fundamental agreement on good and evil, "society will fail." Since a recognized morality is necessary to society's existence, *"prima facie,* society has the right to legislate against immorality as such,"* just as it has a right to legislate against subversion. As "society" is used here in a vague sense and has, at first glance, a suggestion of mysticism, we need to pin down just what is meant by "disintegration of society."

Two possibilities suggest themselves. The way people live and interact becomes changed in a manner short of the breakdown of law and order — *i.e.*, violence is still controlled by law and commerce continues. Let us say that "society" consisted of shared ideas A, B, C, D. Then A disappears and is replaced by E. Since the original society, that is, shared ideas A, B, C, D, no longer "exists," in this definitional sense, society has disintegrated. This is what Devlin seems to have had in mind when he asserts that since monogamy is part of the structure of our society, it "could not be removed without bringing it down." No assertion is made that polygamy is not workable where practiced or that its adaption or partial acceptance would lead to any breakdown in law and order. Merely, the society in question would cease to exist because

monogamy is claimed to be an essential ingredient of this society. In this sense the statement that "society has a right to protect itself" is a mystical guise for the assertion that certain persons have a right to prevent, by use of the policeman, the adoption by others of a practice which *they* do not like. Devlin's "society," "a community of shared ideas" is an abstraction which, as such, is incapable of any action whatsoever.

Devlin may be interpreted to mean, however, that if an established morality is not enforced, anarchy and a breakdown of law and order will result, as allegedly occurred in Rome. This would be a more concrete and persuasive argument. One could object to this thesis that there seems to be no evidence that private immorality has been the cause rather than a symptom of any descent into chaos; and if an immoral trend was actually threatening chaos, laws would be ineffectual to stem it, due to enforcement difficulties. Actually, this "trend" would certainly be impossible to properly diagnose, and such an alleged danger could be used to justify almost any moral legislation. Devlin, however, gives little indication that he is concerned with this problem. He makes no offer of criteria to determine when immorality threatens chaos. Instead, he contends that the state may intervene in private affairs whenever an act is considered "a vice so abominable that its mere presence is an offense." This is a mere thermometer of intolerance, and is unrelated to any analysis of the danger to law and order. I would conclude that Devlin and others who argue about "society's right to defend itself" are, in company with those who propound "the white race's right to defend itself," are merely urging that changes in voluntary relations between individuals which they strongly dislike be stopped. It is undoubtedly true that a certain consensus as to morality may be an absolute necessity to prevent chaos. If the majority of persons believed in the goodness of indiscriminate theft or murder, the strongest law enforcement would probably not be sufficient to uphold minimum order. But as to conduct not directly injuring third

217

---

[34] *The Enforcement of Morals*, (London: Oxford Univ., 1959).

parties, there seems to be no indication that a divergence of practice will do any more than prove vexatious to an indignant majority.

Even if the usual attacks on our maxim are rejected, the basic query remains. Why should "society" permit individuals to act according to their own dictates, even if the course chosen is one considered markedly evil or immoral? The reasons are identical with those which lead us to urge that economic decisions be left to private individuals rather than government, even when, in our estimation, not enough books and education and too many large cars and cigarettes are being purchased. While we may regret the result of freedom in particular cases, we hold that on balance the good will outweigh the bad.

Virtually all readers of a conservative-libertarian journal accept, to some degree, that aspect of Western political theory which has made it unique — the emphasis on what is broadly described as the "innate dignity of the individual." This notion can only be given content if these individuals are free to make their own mistakes as well as to make "correct" decisions. Freedom of choice becomes either an intrinsic good or a necessary prerequisite for truly moral decisions. The Platonic tradition of paternalism, in which obedience and uniformity replace freedom as ultimate goals, leaves no place for an autonomous individual to whom is accorded the dignity and responsibility of making by his own decisions a success or failure of his life. If we agree that the "innate dignity" of an individual implies his right to make his own mistakes, this principle would nowhere be more applicable than in those areas of allegedly sinful acts which injure no one but the consenting actors.

A more subtle but probably more forceful argument is that developed by those writers in the Anglo-Saxon Whig tradition, which has received its most recent formulation in F. A. Hayek's *Constitution of Liberty*. Writers in this tradition, who include David Hume and Lord Acton, argue that civilization will advance more rapidly and more satisfactorily if decisions are left to the spon-

taneous interaction of individuals acting voluntarily rather than to the edict of a governmental body with a monopoly of coercion. Even the great conservative Edmund Burke, who derived most of his political philosophy from this tradition, argued that, contrary to the latent totalitarianism of the French Revolution (which he successfully predicted would burst forth into actual totalitarianism), the inalienable rights of Englishmen provide that, "whatever each man can separately do, without trespassing on others, he has a right to do for himself."[35]

This view is based on a pessimistic view of man's nature and his knowledge, rather than an optimistic one, as is sometimes charged. Man's ignorance of the factors of his environment and his inability to take into account more than a few facts at a time make it difficult enough for him to plan out his own life, even with his knowledge of his own desires and of those factors of his immediate environment which most directly affect his existence. To place such decisions in the hands of a central legislature or executive merely compounds a thousandfold this ignorance. The Authority not only has no way of effectively collecting and assimilating data on the desires of all those it controls, but it cannot assimilate the fantastic amount of other relevant data that individuals would use in making their decisions.

There was also no assumption that men were by nature good. On the contrary, defects in human nature would be magnified when persons were given extensive power of political coercion over others; this was pithily summed up in Acton's warning about absolute power corrupting absolutely. They concluded that balanced progress could best be obtained by allowing human institutions to adjust to changed conditions and changed desires through a gradual process of free, voluntary interaction of individuals. Through trial and error this evolutionary process would reject what was found to be unsuited. This theory is, consequently, not built on an optimistic but on a pessimistic view of man's

---

[35] *Reflections on the Revolution in France,* (New York: Liberal Arts, 1955) p. 67.

218

nature and knowledge. It is only more optimistic than its "conservative" counterparts in that it holds that when men are given as much freedom as is possible while still providing for protection of innocent persons from violence, civilization will descend into neither chaos nor a grand Saturnalian debauchery.

While this position is most commonly associated with freedom in the economic sphere, it applies to all aspects of our lives which might come under central regulation, including our very value structure. As Hayek has noted:

> It would be an error to believe that, to achieve a higher civilization, we have merely to put into effect the ideas now guiding us. If we are to advance, we must leave room for a continuous revision of our present conceptions and ideals which will be necessitated by further experience. We are as little able to conceive what civilization will be, or can be, five hundred or even fifty years hence as our medieval forefathers or even our grandfathers were able to forsee our manner of life today.[36]

Consequently, even our patterns of accepted morality should be open to some experimentation and change. It, too, in large part has been adapted through a continuous process of experimentation and evolution to suit the more basic problems of the times. Social pressure and the odium attached to conduct considered "immoral" are sufficient to insure a considerable degree of uniformity in moral conduct. However, if "immoral" conduct is not punished by the government, a few individuals will risk social odium if the incentive is great enough; as a result, there is room for some experimentation a n d gradual change.

It will be argued that, granted the general argument for freedom, certain immoral acts have no redeeming features whatsoever, and punishment of these acts can in no conceivable way impede progress. However, even if we can only see advantages in an *ad hoc* piece of legisla-tion, we are much better off sticking to a general principle which bars all prohibitions of private immorality:

> The argument for liberty, in the last resort, is indeed an argument for principles and against expediency in collective action . . . Not only is liberty a system under which all government action is guided by principles, but it is an ideal that will not be preserved unless it is itself accepted as an overriding principle governing all particular acts of legislation. Where no such fundamental rule is stubbornly adhered to as an ultimate ideal about which there must be no compromise for the sake of material advantages — as an ideal which, even though it may have to be temporarily infringed during a passing emergency, must form the basis of all permanent arrangements —freedom is almost certain to be destroyed by piecemeal encroachments. For in each particular instance it will be possible to promise concrete and tangible advantages as the result of a curtailment of freedom, while the benefits sacrificed will in their nature always be unknown and uncertain.[37]

We cannot tell in advance whether freedom in a given area will bring results which we or a later generation will consider desirable. If we could tell exactly in which areas beneficial results would flow from freedom, the general case for freedom would disappear, since it is the unforeseeable results of free interaction of individuals on which the case for liberty largely rests. Consequently, we may expect to be forced to put up with immediate results which we do not like if we are to consistently apply our doctrine. It is in the belief that on balance men will be better able to solve their problems if they are left as free as the necessary protection of others will permit, as well as out of the conviction that only maximum freedom of choice is consistent with our belief in man as a creature of inherent dignity and with moral responsibility, that we conclude that the sphere of private morality and immorality is none of the law's business.

219

---

[36] Hayek, *op. cit.*, p. 23.

[37] *Ibid.*, p. 68.

The Shortcomings of
Right-Wing Foreign Policy

JOHN P. McCARTHY

IN A RECENT article commenting on "American Conservatives," a perceptive European champion of liberty suggested as a problem for the consideration of American intellectuals the capacity of a democracy to have a sensible foreign policy.[1] This is a problem which will have to be answered and analyzed by the American Right before it can assert its claim for power or effectively exercise national office. This is because the Right has not been immune to certain long-standing inadequacies which have characterized American thinking on foreign policy. These shortcomings appeared in the foreign policy of Robert A. Taft, and appear also in the drastically different foreign policy position of Barry Goldwater. But before discussing these two men in particular, let us look at the historical background of these weaknesses in our traditional posture toward the rest of the world.

American foreign policy has long been crippled by two ideas which have persisted throughout our history: moralism and belief in American invincibility. By moralism I mean the tendency to apply ethics and canons of perfection governing individual action to collective action by society or the state. Such naivete, in the name of righteousness, would call for the state to follow the dictates of the beatitudes and the counsels of individual spiritual perfection and would decry the

use of power in influencing diplomacy or foreign affairs. This false moralism fails to appreciate that political action should be governed by moral imperatives derived from the nature and purposes of the state, which is to exercise its authority and force, if need be, to promote justice, freedom, security, the general welfare, and civil unity or peace.[2] The other attitude, overconfidence in American invincibility, is the paradoxical belief that the "innocent, moral United States" will be strong enough by itself to defeat and punish any potential aggressor. In short, these attitudes unite so as, first, to prevent American involvement in any balance of power politics which would hinder the development of aggressive nations and, second, to cause us to rely exclusively on our own capacity to repel and defeat those aggressors whose development we refused to prevent.

These attitudes probably derive from the twofold uniqueness of the American experience: our isolation behind the Atlantic Ocean and our orthodoxy of constitutional liberalism. Lacking the continental strife between an old and a new order (in our case the old order was the new order; there had been no old order

---

John P. McCarthy is an Associate Editor of *New Individualist Review*.

[1] E. v. Kuehnelt-Leddihn, "American Conservatives: An Appraisal." *National Review*, (March 13, 1962), p. 167.

[2] *Vide* John Courtney Murray, *We Hold These Truths*, (New York: Sheed and Ward, 1960), p. 286.

or establishment to be overthrown), and secure in our isolation, we lacked all empathy with the objectives of nineteenth century European statesmen. We refused to understand their attempts to preserve a balanced concert of nations which could meet and absorb the various nationalist and revolutionary movements and thereby insure the organic and peaceful development of political liberty. Our national policy was to keep our hands clean of the "immoral" power-balancing machinations of the European nations.

At the time, isolationism was probably the policy best suited for the national interest. But the unfortunate attitudes engendered by it were to result in disastrous consequences when the force of events and technological progress would involve the United States in world affairs. The American leaders would have to invoke the slogans of a moralistic crusade to gain popular support for our intervention. During the first world war, for example, the popular attitude was rapidly changed from moralistic isolation and detachment from the "corrupt, fratricidal strife" of the European "war lords" only by an appeal to a mixture of anti-German racism and a crusading zeal in behalf of the secular religion of democracy.

The Wilson Administration did not base its case for our entry into the war on the legitimate grounds that the impending German domination of the seas would be incompatible with our national interest. Rather, we remained aloof from these balance of power considerations and stressed American idealism and our determination to fight "to end all wars" by making the world "safe for democracy."

The duty of the statesman should be to determine the policies required by the national interest, and then to educate and lead the nation in the acceptance and implementation of those policies. He should lead public opinion and not follow it. It is dangerous for statesmen to start to follow public opinion, or to cater to public misunderstanding of foreign policy by justifying measures with crusading slogans. By doing so they run the risk of unleashing the engines of mass enthusiasm on a course of action which will be difficult to control or restrain. These engines may well follow through the logic of the crusade's slogans to ends quite opposed to the designs of those who issued the call for a crusade.[3]

This danger was borne out by our post-World War I experiences. A public which had been called upon to fight a war to end all wars could scarcely be expected to bear the burdens of keeping the peace and international order when these tasks required the very same instruments which European statesmen had used for a century and against which America had allegedly fought in the war for "democracy." The American flight from international responsibility was all the more tragic, since the temporizing influence of American power could perhaps have dampened the nationalistic passion for "final solutions" which developed out of the disillusionment of the democratic masses who had sacrificed so much in the war. These final solutions ranged all the way from "hang the Kaiser," through demands for security, Bolshevism, to the madness of Nazism.

The debate preceding American entry into the Second World War was based on the same mistaken premises of American invincibility and moralism. Isolationists insisted that America could remain secure behind the Atlantic ocean no matter what happened abroad, and the interventionists called for us to enter the fray, arm in arm with British Toryism, Bolshevism, and the Kuomintang, carrying forth the banners of "anti-fascism," the United Nations, and a world-wide New Deal.[4] Our confusion of purpose in entering the war is easily appreciated by observing the present world situation and recalling some of the objectives for which the West then fought: Polish In-

221

---

[3] Vide Walter Lippman, *The Public Philosophy*, (New York: Mentor Books, 1955), pp. 15-24.

[4] There were spokesmen for both positions who reasoned from practical foreign policy considerations. For instance, Herbert Hoover hesitated about intervening wholeheartedly in a war in which the major outcome would be the strengthening of the position of international Communism.

dependence, the security of the Western position in the Far East, and Chinese National Independence. The former two are probably less near realization today than in 1939, and the latter has been secured, but with rather dire consequences for the West. In view of the debilitating attitudes which have continually marred American foreign policy, let us proceed to examine the role of the American Right-wing spokesmen as critics of our post-war foreign policy.

THE AMERICAN Right, out of office since 1932, was untiring in its criticism of the utopianism which had dictated our wartime collaboration with the Soviet Union, and no doubt much political capital was gained by such. But the Democratic Administration had, to all intents and purposes, admitted these mistakes by changing its attitude towards international Communism and by shaking itself loose from the lingering proponents of the wartime policy, such as Henry Wallace. Hence, the post-World War II Right has to be judged by its criticism of the new policy which had been adopted by the Truman Administration in its attempt to check further Communist expansion: the containment policy.

Under it, aid was furnished to the anti-Communist forces in Greece and Turkey, European economic recovery was sought by such means as the Marshall Plan, an attempt was made to strengthen the economies and societies of the free world by Point Four aid, and NATO was formed. The primary shortcomings of this policy were its purely defensive nature and its tendency to regard the Soviet danger solely as a military threat. It relied primarily on military defenses and economic well-being to meet the expansion of Communism. This was a refusal to wage the Cold War in the ways which the Communists had initiated. No practical proposals were put forth for making inroads on the Communist empire, nor for meeting and countering the multi-faceted Communist challenge, particularly in the realm of political, diplomatic, and psychological warfare.

As a result, by refusing to exploit our atomic and military superiority we permitted the consolidation of the Communist gains of the Second World War, we failed to halt the expansion of Communism in the Far East, and, worst of all, we permitted ourselves to become embroiled in a drawn-out struggle on the enemy's terms over territory we had originally written off. We had to settle for an unsatisfactory truce as exaggerated fears of provoking a general war inhibited us from utilizing our military and technical advantages in that action.

In Congress and out, the Right-wing opposition successfully exploited the public discontent with the Korean War and the concern over domestic Communism. However, the heritage of isolationism and the strong persistence of the traditional attitudes of moralism and American invincibility kept the Right from advancing any serious alternative proposals to the containment policy. At best, these limitations were overcome by a belated acceptance of some of the containment policies, but a continuing distrust of alliances and a basic lack of feeling for foreign affairs prevented the nationalist and anti-Communist enthusiasm of the American people from being channeled into a serious foreign policy alternative to containment. Thus, should they have assumed office, the actions of the American Right would probably have been just a poor imitation of the old containment thesis pursued with reservations and with less competence than it could be by the original authors of that policy.

This probability is borne out by the record of the Eisenhower Administration. Eisenhower was a conservative who simply expanded his isolationism and pacific moralism so as to include a broader area than the Western Hemisphere. His foreign policy was, to a large extent, an imitation of Truman's. The major difference was that Eisenhower tended to withdraw himself from considerations of power politics in his apparent belief that the simple expression of his good intentions would be enough to secure international peace.

Naturally, today's articulate Right-wingers disown Eisenhower, but let us examine the foreign policy ideas of the man who would have been their choice in 1952, Senator Robert A. Taft.

THE TAFT foreign policy, as outlined in his book, *A Foreign Policy for Americans,* was in general a critical and hesitant acceptance of the goals and measures of the containment policy. His criticism of specific ventures of the containment plan was based on the old Whiggish grounds of their formidable expense, their tendency to undermine American diplomatic independence, and their disregard for the authority of the Congress in declaring war. He feared the possible over-extension of the U. S. in an attempt to defend the whole free world. Furthermore, since he only hesitatingly abandoned his faith in the United Nations as an instrument of international law and peace, he was reluctant to enter defense or military alliances which would arrogate to themselves the functions of the UN and which did not have a foundation in international law.

Taft's attitude toward the Atlantic Pact revealed his basic premises on international affairs. He approved the policy of notifying Russia that an attack on Western Europe would involve her in a war with the United States, for such was to him simply "the extension of the Monroe Doctrine to Europe."[5] Despite this, he voted against the ratification of the Atlantic Pact, because he considered it to be "contrary to the whole theory of the United Nations Charter, which had not then been shown to be ineffective; . . . because . . ., at least by implication, it committed the United States to the policy of a land war in Europe."[6] He had considered the pact to be a violation of the spirit of the United Nations since N.A.T.O. would not harmonize its actions with, nor seek authorization from, the Security Council.

Taft, however, gradually became convinced of the UN's inadequacies, as he realized that in practice it was not based on a system of international law nor justice to which all the signatories would be bound. The use of the veto especially prevented this. As a result, deception and expediency became the rule for all sides in the organization. Taft criticized as expediency the Truman Administration's attempts to cloak its independent anti-Communist activities in Europe and Korea under the mantle of the world organization. The disharmony between these legitimate anti-Communist measures and the United Nations, which was called upon to approve them, would eventually paralyze the implementation of the former.

Taft criticized Truman's intervention in the Korean War under the UN mandate as an expedient use of the UN, because, in contrast to the organization's rules, the mandate was not based on the consent of all the permanent members of the Security Council. He insisted that this expediency put us in a trap which would prevent us from getting a mandate to continue the war effectively once Russia returned from her "walkout."

The Ohio Senator prophetically opposed our attempt to bypass the Security Council and the Russian veto by appealing to the General Assembly on certain issues. He pointed out that no nation had contracted to abide by any decision of the General Assembly. "Furthermore," he remarked, "we would have only one vote among sixty, which sometime in the future, even in the very near future, may subject us to very arbitrary treatment."[7]

Taft's classic opposition to Truman's use of American troops in the Korean War without Congressional consent reveals a determining factor in his foreign policy. As a strict constitutionalist he opposed any undermining of the authority of Congress in declaring war. Consequently, he opposed the committing of American troops without Congressional authorization to any spot where they were liable to come under attack or be-

---

[5] *A Foreign Policy for Americans,* (Doubleday, 1952), p. 88.

[6] *Ibid.,* p. 89.

[7] *Ibid.,* p. 43.

come involved in a war. Under this reasoning, the sending of troops to Europe, where they would serve as part of the N.A.T.O. defenses, was prohibited unless it received previous authorization from Congress. He likewise challenged the validity of committing troops simply under a UN mandate without Congressional approbation, for "on the same theory, he [the President] could send troops to Tibet to resist Communist aggression or to Indo-China or anywhere else in the world without the slightest voice of Congress in the matter."[8]

Taft was, no doubt, an excellent theorist of the principles of international organization and law, and a perceptive critic of the expedient disharmony between our independent containment policy and our United Nations policy. Yet he lacked the creative imagination in foreign affairs for constructing serious alternatives to the administration's containment policy or for appreciating the full nature of the Communist challenge. His tendency to rely almost exclusively on American air power for deterring Soviet expansion demonstrated an inflexibility in molding the necessary means for meeting the various facets of the Communist challenge. Furthermore, he devoted only three paragraphs in his book to a suggestion that we seek to promote anti-Communist movements behind the Iron Curtain, and his suggestions on political warfare are limited to proposals for the creation of a propaganda agency. He expressed no notion of exploiting diplomatically the internal situation of the Communist world, not even as a counter to their various threats and demands. In short, his criticism of the Truman Administration's foreign policy was an attempt to modify its policy by the application of his strict Whiggish principles, as well as to note the imprudence of certain of its steps, rather than to postulate an alternative. Perhaps such was in accord with his ideas that the duty of the opposition party is to oppose rather than to present alternative policies.

THE AMERICAN Right never felt at home in the Eisenhower Administration, although large segments of the old Taft bloc played significant roles in that administration. Then in the twilight of the failing Eisenhower Administration, a charismatic new leader, Barry Goldwater, arose on the national scene and was assigned the mantle of Taft as the leader of American political conservatism.

In his foreign policy views Goldwater took a position quite unlike that of Taft, whose primary criticism of Truman had been of the arbitrary executive commitment of American forces abroad and who had stressed the defensive task against Communism. Goldwater, however, insisted that the national goal of "peace in which freedom and justice will prevail . . . is a peace in which Soviet power will no longer be in a position to threaten us and the rest of the world. A tolerable peace . . . must follow victory over Communism."[9]

Where Taft had worried about overextending and over-committing ourselves in the Cold War, Goldwater notes that even our "alliance system is not coextensive with the line that must be held if enemy expansion is to be prevented."[10] Sharing with Taft a realization of the inadequacy of American conventional ground forces to meet the Communist challenge in all corners of the globe, Goldwater called for the West to develop a nuclear capacity for limited war and "to learn to meet the enemy on his own grounds" of political warfare. Goldwater's major criticism of the Western alliance system is of its completely defensive nature and outlook *vis-a-vis* the area of world Communism.

In subsequent foreign policy statements, Goldwater has insisted that the continuing expansion of Communist domination and political influence has resulted from the Western failure to deal with "the key problem of international relations," namely, the uses a nation makes of power. He claims that for the

---

[8] *Ibid.*, p. 33.

---

[9] Barry Goldwater, *The Conscience of a Conservative*, (New York: Hillman Books, 1960), p. 92.

[10] *Ibid.*, pp. 94-5.

policy makers of the United States the "effort to please world opinion . . . has become a matter of grand strategy, . . . the guiding principle of American policy."[11] He urges us to abandon this preoccupation, and to fully commit ourselves to the Cold War and to the use of Western power to "defeat" international Communism. Specifically he would repudiate disarmament discussions, eliminate Castro, declare Africa a Western protectorate, and encourage, and prepare to assist, uprisings within Eastern Europe.[12] More recently he has denounced "coalition governments" as a "tactic of the enemy," and has asserted that all Communist regimes must be opposed whether in Yugoslavia, Moscow, or North Vietnam.[13]

The Goldwater foreign policy is immensely different from that of Taft. Goldwater basically advocates what might be called American Imperialism, or the extension of American power to more and more areas of the globe, whereas Taft postulated the traditional Whig principles of limited foreign involvement and legislative control over the commitment of the military power. Taft's policy was basically defensive with a premium placed on limiting our commitments, our expenses, and the executive power. Few have called attention to this remarkable difference of views, a divergence as vast as the difference between Gladstone and Disraeli.

This disagreement is all the more startling when one considers that the bulk of the Goldwater support comes from the old Taft circles. This fact should evoke some reflection from those who may see Goldwater as a potential answer to their hopes for a policy for the West which would assume the diplomatic initiative against Communism, which would not hesitate to exercise Western power, and which would develop the capacity for meeting the Communists on all levels and indeed carrying

the struggle to the other side of the Iron Curtain. Can a man be an effective proponent of such a policy who is, in reality, beholden to or dependent for support on the vast bulk of the old Taft forces? Aside from his own possible inadequacies in the sphere of intellectual power or of leadership skill, would Goldwater really be an effective fighter in the "protracted conflict" with Communism, or would he revert to the older traditions of his party and of the principal part of his supporters: isolationism, withdrawal, and pre-occupation with strict internal constitutionalism?

The hard core of intellectual conservatism in the United States sees Goldwater through the eyes of the *National Review*. And Goldwater, in his writings for, and communications with, *National Review*, echoes to a large extent the *National Review* line on the waging of the Cold War, the use of American power, and the carrying of the battle to the enemy's territory. But the *National Review*, after all, despite its pre-eminent position in conservative intellectual circles and its close contact with the greater Western conservative tradition and the hard-line strategists and theoreticians of the world-wide anti-Communist movement, is a relatively minor force in the broader Goldwater movement.

Indeed, Goldwater's mass appeal does rest partly on the heightening anti-Communist enthusiasm of the electorate and in a revival of basic American nationalist and patriotic sentiments. But these elementary emotions need guidance, and, I fear, a large part of the political leaders of the Goldwater movement who are benefitting from these emotions are pre-occupied with different concerns than those of the cold war strategists of the *National Review*, or, more emphatically, of the Foreign Policy Research Institute.[14] These leaders can deliver much more important votes to Goldwater than can the *National Review*, with its subscribers occupying their minority posi-

225

[11] Barry Goldwater, "A Foreign Policy for America," *National Review*, (March 25, 1961), p. 179.

[12] *Ibid.*, pp. 180-81.

[13] Barry Goldwater, "To Win the Cold War," *New Guard*, (March, 1962), p. 37.

[14] The research institute at the University of Pennsylvania which sponsored the studies, *Protracted Conflict* and *A Forward Strategy for America*, by Robert Strausz-Hupé, Stefan Possony, et. al.

tions in the electorate of the Eastern States.

The primary concerns of these local political leaders, who will be contributing so much to the Goldwater movement, are the traditional concerns of midwestern Republicanism: federal fiscal responsibility, states' rights, and a friendly environment for their business activities. In foreign affairs they have a general determination to resist Communism, but it is doubtful if they have really adapted themselves to the exigencies of modern international relations. Basically, they believe in the traditional notion of American invincibility, and, as a result, pay little heed to the task of strengthening the non-Communist areas of the world, so as to enhance the use of Western power and halt Communism. For example, they have their doubts about our associating with the European Common Market, and enter alliances hesitantly and only after someone else has demonstrated their necessity. They show no inclination to participate in any ventures for strengthening and modernizing the underdeveloped nations both economically and politically. Their response to direct Soviet challenges is always a determined resolve to use force if necessary, and to not give in, but they are slow in developing the means for resisting the various short-of-general-war techniques of Soviet aggrandizement. They profess their sympathies with the captive nations of Eastern Europe, yet limit their suggestions for assuming a diplomatic offensive against the Communist world to a few useless condemnatory resolutions.

The basic failure of these elements of the Republican Party, as with Taft, is their lack of that imaginative understanding of foreign affairs which is essential for securing the free world and waging the intricate and difficult diplomatic maneuvers essential to making inroads on the Communist Empire, so as to make it no longer a threat to peace and freedom. An administration based on such forces might be startlingly like the Eisenhower Administration, which also relied heavily on "heartland" Republican support: an administration that would half-heartedly accept the frustrating containment policy and thereby not even achieve its own primary goals of fiscal responsibility and governmental decentralization.

226

J. B. Conant's

"Slums and Suburbs"

ROBERT M. SCHUCHMAN

IF THERE IS one observation about Dr. James Bryant Conant which the esteemed scholar has, himself, made painfully apparent, it is that he is a firm supporter of the notion that the public school should assume a vast societal role which would virtually supplant the traditional functions of the home, the church, and private education. In *Slums and Suburbs,*[1] Dr. Conant offers a provocative potpourri of self-assured assertions of opinion, as well as some extremely perceptive insights concerning the ills of contemporary urban education. The book is a hurried summation of several of the findings of the Carnegie Foundation's "Study of the American High School," an inquest which is yet to be completed.

The initial premise of this study is "that to a considerable degree what a school should do and can do is determined by the status and ambitions of the families being served." Thus, there is no ideal or single purpose or curriculum which should dominate secondary education: the function of the school is to be determined by the "socio-economic composition" of its students. Proceeding from this thought, Dr. Conant explores the relative needs of secondary schools in the well-to-do suburbs of our large central cities, where Johnny's parents

are determined that their son shall be enrolled in an Ivy League college, and in the cultural vacuums of America's urban slums, neighborhoods which the New York State Department of Education would have us call "older, more overcrowded areas."

Dr. Conant refuses to cloak his recommendations in the silly euphemisms of the social-worker set. He recognizes, forthrightly, that the American slum problem is largely a Negro problem, and that it cannot be remedied without this fact in mind. As a result of decades of patent discrimination, the Negro in our cities rarely expects job opportunities commensurate with his abilities: hence, there is little desire in the Negro slum to progress academically, since the white establishment will not recognize any such progress.

One observation of Dr. Conant should provide a lesson for those who build new slums at public expense in the name of "urban development." He emphasizes that there is a far greater correlation between desirable social attitudes and job opportunities than there is between such attitudes and housing conditions. Unfortunately, the Conant solution to the lack of slum opportunity is to use the school as the vocational training ground for future employment, a solution which would tend to freeze the urban Negro permanently in his present

Robert M. Schuchman received a B.A. in history from Queens College and an LL.B. from the Yale Law School where he was an Earhart Fellow in economics. He is National Chairman of Young Americans for Freedom.

---

[1] *Slums and Suburbs*, by James Bryant Conant, (McGraw-Hill: New York, 1961), 147 pp.

status as unskilled or semi-skilled worker. One would think it preferable to improve Negro education for the sake of instilling academic excellence among Negro youth, but Dr. Conant has concluded that "in a heavily urbanized and industrialized free society the educational experiences of youth should fit their subsequent employment." Such "experiences" almost invariably turn out to be a vocationalized edition of life-adjustment education. The best that Dr. Conant can say about the fine "Higher Horizons" project of New York City (which is an eminent example of the use of the school to raise the cultural level and interests of slum youth) is that the project is "encouraging." Vocational training, on the other hand, is "necessary," and not just encouraging.

Not all of Dr. Conant's recommendations are restatements of the vocational heresy, however. He notes that slum parents must be encouraged to support education, perhaps with an adult education program sponsored by the community high school: this would help to create a home environment more conducive to academic success. Dr. Conant also recognizes the futility of arbitrarily shifting Negro and white students to far-away schools as a method of improving the education of Negro slum children. The slum schools should be improved where they are, he concludes; inter-neighborhood integration only lowers the standards of the white schools without appreciably improving Negro education.

Perhaps the most significant finding made by Dr. Conant is the presence of what he calls "social dynamite" building up in our urban slum areas among unemployed, out-of-school youth. The unemployment problem here is directly traceable to the hiring policies of labor unions and management. Dr. Conant believes that the frustration engendered by this incapacity to secure employment may erupt into actual physical violence in slum neighborhoods if the situation is not soon corrected. He would entrust such social treatment to the high school, an institution which, it would seem, is not intended to perform this type of surgery.

Slums and Suburbs serves a valuable function in isolating several significant maladies afflicting urban high schools and their students. But the book suffers from Dr. Conant's faith in the schoolroom as the central correction agency of American society. He would expand the functions of the public school in the slums to the point where its academic purposes would become at best peripheral. There may well be a need for social action to remedy the problems elucidated by this study, but, we submit, Dr. Conant has offered the wrong blueprint.

F. J. Johnson's

"No Substitute for Victory"

IN *No Substitute for Victory*[1] Frank J. Johnson, a former naval intelligence specialist on Soviet affairs, proposes what he believes to be the only strategy by which the United States can be certain of maintaining both peace and freedom. He asks us to deliberately adopt a policy of victory over Communism; *only* such a policy, he holds, can prevent an atomic holocaust.

By using the phrase "victory over Communism," Mr. Johnson is *not* suggesting that we conquer the Soviet Union and make it a United States satellite; what he does propose is that we should pursue "creative initiatives" (to borrow a pet Liberal term). These initiatives will be aggressive in character and will be designed to convince the Soviet rulers that it is in their own interest to terminate the Cold War and to dismantle the world-wide Communist conspiracy. Mr. Johnson believes this can be accomplished if we recognize the fact that "peaceful co-existence," as propounded by Khrushchev, is a fraud, that the Soviets are willing to negotiate and to trade territory back and forth in the "war zone" (the non-Communist world) but not in the "peace zone" (the Communist world). By using paramilitary warfare, subversion, terror, sabotage, strikes, guerilla techniques and other means short of nuclear war, the United States could carry the Cold War to the Soviet Union by invading the "peace zone" and endangering the security of the Communist rule in the mother country. Our object should be to encourage rebellion in the satellites and thus make Eastern Europe a liability and not an asset to the Russian government. The price for ending these pressures on the Communist bloc will be iron-clad guarantees from the Politburo that they. in turn, will abandon their adventurous foreign policy. Our hope will be that the peoples under Communist rule will eventually achieve their own freedom, either through peaceful means or by force.

The alternative to this policy — appeasement— must ultimately lead to a nuclear war since the Soviet Union will not attack the United States until the greater part of the world has been brought under Communist control by paramilitary means. An appeasement policy by the West will allow this timetable to be carried out; a firm counter-offensive, however, will prevent the Soviets from reaching the take-off stage of their plan for world conquest. Readers of this book will understand that we are not left with only two choices ("Red or dead"). There is a third course, one that will enable us to avoid both war and submission, and Mr. Johnson has outlined that course with clarity. It only remains for Mr. Kennedy to follow it.

229

Robert Schuettinger is an Associate Editor of *New Individualist Review*.

[1] *No Substitute for Victory*, by Frank J. Johnson, with introduction by Admiral Arleigh Burke, (Regnery: Chicago, 1962), 230 pp.

Page Fifty-three

No Substitute for Victory is aimed directly at the person who must ultimately be convinced in a democracy: the average voter. This is both a strength and a weakness. It is of necessity plainly written and so contains a number of over-simplifications. The emphasis on the essential un-Americanism of Communism — its European origins — could, for instance, have been easily omitted. Although it must be classed as an introduction to its subject[2] it is a solid and generally reliable work; it contains almost none of the unfortunate vulgarizations perpetrated by so many of the "authorities" on Communism currently cropping up all over the lecture circuit. These half-educated, unthinking popularizers may be well-meaning, but their wild outcries have the effect of obscuring and even discrediting the serious proposals of reputable spokesmen for an anti-Communist strategy. For this and other reasons, they are doing far more harm than good. It is even more unfortunate, however, that most of the West's intellectuals (who lack the excuse of ignorance) still believe that "peaceful co-existence," as defined by Khrushchev, is possible with the present governments of the U.S.S.R. and Communist China.

Although the West is weakened in its struggle by the (let us hope) temporary neutrality of so many of its finest minds, we should probably not be too surprised by this phenomenon. After all, the greatest part of Europe's intellectuals believed, at one time, in the flatness of the earth, just as they once fervently upheld chattle slavery, blood-letting and leeches, witchcraft and the theory that the sun revolves around the earth. History demonstrates, however, that even intellectuals can learn, so we can hope that hard experience will eventually triumph over wishful thinking and that the myth of "co-existence" will someday go the way of the Ptolemaic theory. Mr. Johnson's book will do much to hasten this process.

---

[2] Most readers of this review will be familiar with a more complete work, *A Forward Strategy for America*, by Strauz-Hupe, Kintner and Possony (Harper, New York, 1961).

NEW BOOKS AND ARTICLES

THE FOLLOWING IS A SELECT LIST OF BOOKS AND ARTICLES WHICH, IN THE OPINION OF THE EDITORS, MAY BE OF INTEREST TO OUR READERS.

John Davenport, Herrell DeGraff, F. A. Hayek, Felix Morley, *The Spiritual and Moral Significance of Free Enterprise, A Symposium,* pamphlet, available from the National Association of Manufacturers, 2 E. 48th St., New York 17, N. Y.

Milton Friedman, "Tariffs and the Common Market," *National Review,* (May 22, 1962).

Albert Hunold, ed., *Freedom and Serfdom,* (Reidel, Dordrecht, Holland, 1961).

Simon Kuznets, *Capital in the American Economy,* (Princeton University, Princeton, 1961).

Thomas Molnar, *The Decline of the Intellectual,* (Meridian Books, New York, 1961).

John U. Nef, *A Search for Civilization,* (Regnery, Chicago, 1962).

Sylvester Petro, "Trade Unionism and the Public Sector," *Modern Age,* (Spring, 1962).

Leonard E. Read, *Elements of Libertarian Leadership,* (Foundation for Economic Education, Irvington-on-Hudson, New York, 1962).

Murray N. Rothbard, *Man, Economy and State,* (Van Nostrand, Princeton, 1962), two volumes.

Murray N. Rothbard, *The Panic of 1819,* (Columbia University Press, New York, 1962).

Ernest van den Haag, *The War in Katanga,* available from the American Committee for Aid to Katanga Freedom Fighters, 79 Madison Avenue, New York 16, New York, $1.50.

Eliseo Vivas, "Art and the Artist's Citizenship," *Modern Age,* (Spring, 1962).

230

NEW INDIVIDUALIST REVIEW . . .

as the mail-clerk in Ida Noyes Hall can testify, is the beneficiary of a world-wide correspondence. Most NIR readers are more articulate than the average citizen; most of them are the kind of people which are known in the trade as "opinion-molders." Here is what a few of these "influentials" (who care enough about NIR to pay the extra dollar required of foreign subscribers) have written to us lately.

"I was delighted with your last issue. I can testify from bitter experience that your Dr. Rothbard is entirely correct when he demonstrates that public ownership of lighthouses is the first step on the road to communism. Please prepare a Chinese edition of 600,000,000 copies; I would like to mail them (bulk rate, of course) to selected opinion-molders in the occupied provinces of my country."

President Chiang Kai-shek

232

"I congratulate you for having published, and I congratulate myself for having read, the Winter issue of NIR. Although nothing in this universe is of real importance (excepting, of course, the life to come and the Honour of France) your magazine is rather relaxing. Your discussion of whether or not David Hume was a whig or a tory was charming but quite needlessly prolonged. He was a tory."

President Charles de Gaulle

"What are your rates for original poetry?"

Chairman Mao Tze-tung

"Please send 20 copies air mail of your stimulating magazine. I am trying to convince the members of the Politburo that economic progress will come much faster if we adopt a freer trade policy. None of my colleagues is yet in favor of private ownership of the streets but I am working on them."

Deputy Premier Anastas Mikoyan

NEW INDIVIDUALIST REVIEW   5

IDA NOYES HALL
University of Chicago, Chicago 37, Illinois

    Please enter my subscription for one year at $2.00 ☐   Students,$1.00 ☐

    I also enclose a contribution of $................................

    NAME ....

    ADDRESS ....

    IF STUDENT: SCHOOL........................YEAR OF GRAD...............

"SOCIALISM is only an idea, not an historical necessity, and ideas are acquired by the human mind. We are not born with ideas, we learn them. If socialism has come to America because it was implanted in the minds of past generations, there is no reason for assuming that the contrary idea cannot be taught to a new generation. What the socialists have done can be undone, if there is a will for it. But, the undoing will not be accomplished by trying to destroy established socialistic institutions. It can be accomplished only by attacking minds, and not the minds of those already hardened by socialistic fixations. Individualism can be revived by implanting the idea in the minds of the coming generations. So then, if those who put a value on the dignity of the individual are up to the task, they have a most challenging opportunity in education before them. It is not an easy job. It requires the kind of industry, intelligence and patience that comes with devotion to an ideal."

—*Frank Chodorov*, Founder and President, Intercollegiate Society of Individualists, Inc.

INTERCOLLEGIATE SOCIETY OF INDIVIDUALISTS
For the Advancement of Conservative Thought on the Campus

410 LAFAYETTE BUILDING ∗ PHILADELPHIA 6, PENN. • WAlnut 5-5682
Midwest Office: 1014 LEMCKE BUILDING • INDIANAPOLIS 6, INDIANA • MElrose 9-5551
Western Office: 1436 EL CAMINO REAL • MENLO PARK, CALIFORNIA • 325-4553

VOLUME 2
NUMBER 2
SUMMER 1962

New

INDIVIDUALIST

Review

Summer 1962   35 cents   Vol. 2, No. 2

NEW INDIVIDUALIST REVIEW

Volume 2 – Number 2   SUMMER 1962

239

NEW INDIVIDUALIST REVIEW is published quarterly (Spring, Summer, Autumn, Winter) by
New Individualist Review, Inc., at Ida Noyes Hall, University of Chicago, Chicago 37, Illinois.

Opinions expressed in signed articles do not necessarily represent the views of the editors.
Editorial, advertising, and subscription correspondence and manuscripts should be sent to NEW
INDIVIDUALIST REVIEW, Ida Noyes Hall, University of Chicago, Chicago 37, Illinois. All manu-
scripts become the property of NEW INDIVIDUALIST REVIEW.

Subscription rates: $2.00 per year (students $1.00). Add $1.00 for foreign subscriptions.

Is a Free Society Stable?

MILTON FRIEDMAN

THERE IS A STRONG TENDENCY for all of us to regard what is as if it were the "natural" or "normal" state of affairs, to lack perspective because of the tyranny of the status quo. It is, therefore, well, from time to time, to make a deliberate effort to look at things in a broader context. In such a context anything approaching a free society is an exceedingly rare event. Only during short intervals in man's recorded history has there been anything approaching what we would call a free society in existence over any appreciable part of the globe. And even during such intervals, as at the moment, the greater part of mankind has lived under regimes that could by no stretch of the imagination be called free.

This casual empirical observation raises the question whether a free society may not be a system in unstable equilibrium. If one were to take a purely historical point of view, one would have to say that the "normal," in the sense of average, state of mankind is a state of tyranny and despotism. Perhaps this is the equilibrium state of society that tends to arise in the relation of man to his fellows. Perhaps highly special circumstances must exist to render a free society possible. And perhaps these special circumstances, the existence of which account for the rare episodes of freedom, are themselves by their nature

Milton Friedman, Professor of Economics at the University of Chicago, is an Editorial Advisor to *New Individualist Review*. His most recent book is *Price Theory*.

transitory, so that the kind of society we all of us believe in is highly unlikely to be maintained, even if once attained.

This problem has, of course, been extensively discussed in the literature. In his great book, *Lectures on Law and Public Opinion in the Nineteenth Century*, written at the end of the nineteenth century, A. V. Dicey discusses a very similar question. How was it, he asks, that toward the end of the nineteenth century there seemed to be a shift in English public opinion away from the doctrine of liberalism and toward collectivism, even though just prior to the shift, individualism and *laisser-faire* were at something like their high tide, seemed to have captured English public opinion, and seemed to be producing the results that their proponents had promised in the form of an expansion of economic activity, a rise in the standard of life, and the like?

As you may recall, Dicey dates the change in public opinion in Britain away from individualism and toward collectivism at about 1870-90. Dicey answers his question by essentially reversing it, saying that in its original form, it may be a foolish question. Perhaps the relevant question is not why people turned away from individualism toward collectivism, but how they were induced to accept the queer notion of individualism in the first place. The argument for a free society, he goes on to say, is a very subtle and sophisticated argument. At every point, it depends on the indirect rather than the direct effect of the policy followed.

241

Page Three

If one is concerned to remedy clear evils in a society, as everyone is, the natural reaction is to say, "let's do something about it," and the "us" in this statement will in a large number of cases be translated into the "government," so the natural reaction is to pass a law. The argument that maybe the attempt to correct this particular evil by extending the hand of the government will have indirect effects whose aggregate consequences may be far worse than any direct benefits that flow from the action taken is, after all, a rather sophisticated argument. And yet, this is the kind of argument that underlies a belief in a free or *laisser-faire* society.

If you look at each evil as it arises, in and of itself, there will almost always tend to be strong pressures to do something about it. This will be so because the direct effects are clear and obvious while the indirect effects are remote and devious and because there tends to be a concentrated group of people who have strong interests in favor of a particular measure whereas the opponents, like the indirect effects of the measure, are diffused. One can cite example after example along this line. Indeed, I think it is true that most crude fallacies about economic policies derive from neglecting the indirect effects of the policies followed.

The tariff is one example. The benefits that are alleged to flow from a tariff are clear and obvious. If a tariff is imposed, a specified group of people, whose names can almost be listed, seem to be benefited in the first instance. The harm that is wrought by the tariff is borne by people whose names one does not know and who are unlikely themselves to know that they are or will be harmed. The tariff does most harm to people who have special capacities for producing the exports that would pay for the goods that would be imported in the absence of a tariff. With a tariff in effect, the potential export industry may never exist and no one will ever know that he might have been employed in it or who would have been. The indirect harm to consumers via a more inefficient allocation of resources and higher prices for the resulting products are

spread even more thinly through the society. Thus the case for a tariff seems quite clear on first glance. And this is true in case after case.

This natural tendency to engage in state action in specific instances can, it would seem, and this is Dicey's argument, be offset only by a widespread general acceptance of a philosophy of non-interference, by a general presumption against undertaking any one of a large class of actions. And, says Dicey, what is really amazing and surprising is that for so long a period as a few decades, sufficiently widespread public opinion developed in Britian in favor of the general principle of non-intervention and *laisser-faire* as to overcome the natural tendency to pass a law for the particular cases. As soon as this general presumption weakened, it meant the emergence of a climate of opinion in favor of specific government intervention.

Dicey's argument is enormously strengthened by an asymmetry between a shift toward individualism and a shift away from it. In the first place, there is what I have called the tyranny of the status quo. Anyone who wants to see how strong that tyranny is can do no better, I believe, than to read Dicey's book now. On reading it, he will discover how extreme and extensive a collectivist he is, as judged by the kinds of standards for governmental action that seemed obvious and appropriate to Dicey when he wrote his lectures. In discussing issues of this kind, the tendency always is to take *what is* for granted, to assume that it is perfectly all right and reasonable, and that the problem to argue about is the next step. This tends to mean that movements in any one direction are difficult to reverse. A second source of asymmetry is the general dilemma that faces the liberal — tolerance of the intolerant. The belief in individualism includes the belief in tolerating the intolerant. It includes the belief that the society is only worth defending if it is one in which we resort to persuasion rather than to force and in which we defend freedom of discussion on the part of those who would undermine the system itself. If one departs

242

from a free society, the people in power in a collectivist society will not hesitate to use force to keep it from being changed. Under such circumstances, it is more difficult to achieve a revolution that would convert a totalitarian or collectivist society into an individualist society than it is to do the reverse. From the point of view of the forces that may work in the direction of rendering a free society an unstable system, this is certainly one of the most important that strengthens Dicey's general argument.

PERHAPS THE MOST FAMOUS argument alleging the instability of a free enterprise or capitalist society is the Marxian. Marx argued that there were inherent historical tendencies within a capitalist society that would tend to lead to its destruction. As you know, he predicted that as it developed, capitalism would produce a division of society into sharp classes, the impoverishment of the masses, the despoilment of the middle classes, and a declining rate of profit. He predicted that the combined result would be a class struggle in which the class of the "expropriated" or the proletarian class would assume power.

Marx's analysis is at least in part to be regarded as a scientific analysis attempting to derive hypotheses that could be used to predict consequences that were likely to occur. His predictions have uniformly been wrong; none of the major consequences that he predicted has in fact occurred. Instead of a widening split among classes, there has tended to be a reduction of class barriers. Instead of a despoilment of the middle class, there has tended to be, if anything, an increase in the middle class relative to the extremes. Instead of the impoverishment of the masses, there has been the largest rise in the standard of life of the masses that history has ever seen. We must therefore reject his theory as having been disproved.

The lack of validity of Marx's theory does not mean that it has been unimportant. It had the enormous importance of leading many, if not a majority, of the intellectual and ruling classes to regard tendencies of the kind he predicted as inevitable, thereby leading them to interpret what did go on in different terms than they otherwise would. Perhaps the most striking example has been the extent to which intellectuals, and people in general, have taken it for granted that the development of a capitalist society has meant an increased concentration of industrial power and an increase in the degree of monopoly. Though this view has largely reflected a confusion between changes in absolute size and changes in relative size, in part also, I think, it was produced by the fact that this was something they were told by Marx to look for. I don't mean to attribute this view solely to the Marxian influence. But I think that in this and other instances, the Marxian argument has indirectly affected the patterns of thinking of a great many people including many who would regard themselves as strongly anti-Marxian. Indeed, in many ways, the ideas have been most potent when they have lost their labels. In this way, Marx's ideas had an enormous intellectual importance, even though his scientific analysis and predictions have all been contradicted by experience.

In more recent times, Joseph Schumpeter has offered a more subtle and intellectually more satisfactory defense of essentially t h e Marxian conclusion. Schumpeter's attitude toward Marx is rather interesting. He demonstrates that Marx was wrong in every separate particular, yet proceeds both to accept the major import of his conclusions and to argue that Marx was a very great man. Whereas Marx's view was that capitalism would destroy itself by its failure, Schumpeter's view was that capitalism would destroy itself by its success. Schumpeter believed that large scale enterprises and monopoly have real advantages in promoting technological progress and growth and that these advantages would give them a competitive edge in the economic struggle. The success of capitalism would therefore, he argued, be associated with a growth of very large enterprises, and with the spread of something like semi-monopoly

243

over the industrial scene. In its turn, he thought that this development would tend to convert businessmen into bureaucrats. Large organizations have much in common whether they are governmental or private. They inevitably, he believed, produced an increasing separation between the ultimate owners of the enterprises and the individuals who were in positions of importance in managing the enterprises. Such individuals are induced to place high values upon technical performance and to become adaptable to a kind of civil-service socialist organization of society. In addition, this process would create the kind of skills in the managerial elite that would be necessary in order to have a collectivist or governmentally controlled society. The development of this bureaucratic elite with its tendency to place greater and greater emphasis on security and stability and to accept centralized control would tend, he believed, to have the effect of establishing a climate of opinion highly favorable to a shift to an explicitly socialized and centralized state.

The view that Schumpeter expressed has much in common with what Burnham labelled a managerial revolution although the two are not by any means the same. There is also much in common between Schumpeter's analysis and the distinction that Veblen drew in his analysis of the price system between the roles of entrepreneurs and engineers, between "business" and "industry." There are also large differences. Veblen saw the engineer as the productive force in the society, the entrepreneur as the destructive force. Schumpeter, if anything, saw matters the other way. He saw the entrepreneur as the creative force in society, and the engineer as simply his handmaiden. But I think there is much in common between the two analyses with respect to the belief that power would tend to shift from the one to the other.

For myself, I must confess that while I find Schumpeter's analysis intriguing and intellectually fascinating, I cannot accept his thesis. It seems to me to reflect in large part a widespread bias that emphasizes the large and few as opposed to the small and numerous, a

tendency to see the merits of scale and not to recognize the merits of large numbers of separate people working in diverse activities. In any event, so far as one can judge, there has been no striking tendency in experience toward an increasing concentration of economic activity in large bureaucratic private enterprises. Some enormous enterprises have of course arisen. But there has also been a very rapid growth in small enterprises. What has happened in this country at least is that the large enterprises have tended to be concentrated in communication and manufacturing. These industries have tended to account for a roughly constant proportion of total economic activity. Small enterprises have tended to be concentrated in agriculture and services. Agriculture has declined in importance and in the number of enterprises, while the service industries have grown in both. If one leaves government aside, as Schumpeter's thesis requires one to do, so far as one can judge from the evidence, there seems to have been no particularly consistent tendency for the fraction of economic activity which is carried on in any given percentage of the enterprises to have grown. What has happened is that small enterprises and big enterprises have both grown in scale so what we now call a small enterprise may be large by some earlier standard. However, the thesis that Schumpeter developed is certainly sophisticated and subtle and deserves serious attention.

THERE IS ANOTHER DIRECTION, it seems to me, in which there is a different kind of a tendency for capitalism to undermine itself by its own success. The tendency I have in mind can probably best be brought out by the experience of Great Britain — Great Britain tends to provide the best laboratory for many of these forces. It has to do with the attitude of the public at large toward law and toward law obedience. Britain has a wide and deserved reputation for the extraordinary obedience of its people to the law. It has not always been so. At the turn of the nineteenth century, and earlier, the British had a very different reputation as a nation of people who would obey no law, or almost no law, a nation of smugglers, a nation in which corruption and inefficiency was rife, and in which one could not get very much done through governmental channels.

Indeed, one of the factors that led Bentham and the Utilitarians toward *laisser-faire,* and this is a view that is also expressed by Dicey, was the self-evident truth that if you wanted to get evils corrected, you could not expect to do so through the government of the time. The government was corrupt and inefficient. It was clearly oppressive. It was something that had to be gotten out of the way as a first step to reform. The fundamental philosophy of the Utilitarians, or any philosophy that puts its emphasis on some kind of a sum of utilities, however loose may be the expression, does not lead to *laisser-faire* in principle. It leads to whatever kind of organization of economic activity is thought to produce results which are regarded as good in the sense of adding to the sum total of utilities. I think the major reason why the Utilitarians tended to be in favor of *laisser-faire* was the obvious fact that government was incompetent to perform any of the tasks they wanted to see performed.

Whatever the reason for its appeal, the adoption of *laisser-faire* had some important consequences. Once *laisser-faire* was adopted, the economic incentive for corruption was largely removed. After all, if governmental officials had no favors to grant, there was no need to bribe them. And if there was nothing to be gained from government, it could hardly be a source of corruption. Moreover, the laws that were left were for the most part, and again I am over-simplifying and exaggerating, laws that were widely accepted as proper and desirable; laws against theft, robbery, murder, etc. This is in sharp contrast to a situation in which the legislative structure designates as crimes what people individually do not regard as crimes or makes it illegal for people to do what seems to them the sensible thing. The latter situation tends to reduce respect

for the law. One of the unintended and indirect effects of *laisser-faire* was thus to establish a climate in Britain of a much greater degree of obedience and respect for the law than had existed earlier. Probably there were other forces at work in this development but I believe that the establishment of *laisser-faire* laid the groundwork for a reform in the civil service in the latter part of the century — the establishment of a civil service chosen on the basis of examinations and merit and of professional competence. You could get that kind of development because the incentives to seek such places for purposes of exerting "improper" influence were greatly reduced when government had few favors to confer.

In these ways, the development of *laisser-faire* laid the groundwork for a widespread respect for the law, on the one hand, and a relatively incorrupt, honest, and efficient civil service on the other, both of which are essential preconditions for the operation of a collectivist society. In order for a collectivist society to operate, the people must obey the laws and there must be a civil service that can and will carry out the laws. The success of capitalism established these preconditions for a movement in the direction of much greater state intervention.

The process I have described obviously runs both ways. A movement in the direction of a collectivist society involves increased governmental intervention into the daily lives of people and the conversion into crimes of actions that are regarded by the ordinary person as entirely proper. These tend in turn to undermine respect for the law and to give incentives to corrupt state officials. There can, I think, be little doubt that this process has begun in Britain and has gone a substantial distance. Although respect for the law may still be greater than it is here, most observers would agree that respect for the law in Britain has gone down decidedly in the course of the last twenty or thirty years, certainly since the war, as a result of the kind of laws people have been asked to obey. On the occasions I have been in England, I have

245

had access to two sources of information that generally yield quite different answers. One is people associated with academic institutions, all of whom are quite shocked at the idea that any British citizen might evade the law — except perhaps for transactions involving exchanging pounds for dollars when exchange control was in effect. It also happens that I had contact with people engaged in small businesses. They tell a rather different story, and one that I suspect comes closer to being valid, about the extent to which regulations were honored in the breach, and taxes and customs regulations evaded — the one thing that is uniform among people or almost uniform is that nobody or almost nobody has any moral repugnance to smuggling, and certainly not when he is smuggling something into some country other than his own.

The erosion of the capital stock of willingness to obey the law reduces the capacity of a society to run a centralized state, to move away from freedom. This effect on law obedience is thus one that is reversible and runs in both directions. It is another major factor that needs to be taken into account in judging the likely stability of a free system in the long run.

I HAVE BEEN EMPHASIZING forces and approaches that are mostly pessimistic in terms of our values in the sense that most of them are reasons why a free society is likely to be unstable and to change into a collectivist system. I should like therefore to turn to some of the tendencies that may operate in the other direction.

What are the sources of strength for a free society that may help to maintain it? One of the major sources of strength is the tendency for extension of economic intervention in a wide range of areas to interfere directly and clearly with political liberty and thus to make people aware of the conflict between the two. This has been the course of events in Great Britain after the war and in many other countries. I need not repeat or dwell on this point.

A second source of strength is one that has already been suggested by my comments on law obedience. In many ways, perhaps the major hope for a free society is precisely that feature in a free society which makes it so efficient and productive in its economic activity; namely, the ingenuity of millions of people, each of whom is trying to further his own interest, in part by finding ways to get around state regulation. If I may refer to my own casual observation of Britain and France a few years after the war, the impression that I formed on the the basis of very little evidence but that seemed to me to be supported by further examination was that Britain at the time was being economically strangled by the law obedience of her citizens while France was being saved by the existence of the black market. The price system is a most effective and efficient system for organizing resources. So long as people try to make it operate, it can surmount a lot of problems. There is the famous story about the man who wrote a letter to Adam Smith, saying that some policy or other was going to be the ruin of England. And Adam Smith, as I understand the story, wrote back and said, "Young man, there is a lot of ruin in a nation."

This seems to me an important point. Once government embarks on intervention into and regulation of private activities, this establishes an incentive for large numbers of individuals to use their ingenuity to find ways to get around the government regulations. One result is that there appears to be a lot more regulation than there really is. Another is that the time and energy of government officials is increasingly taken up with the need to plug the holes in the regulations that the citizens are finding, creating, and exploiting. From this point of view, Parkinson's law about the growth of bureaucracy without a corresponding growth of output may be a favorable feature for the maintenance of a free society. An efficient governmental organization and not an inefficient one is almost surely the greater threat to a free society. One of the virtues of a free society is precisely that the market tends to be a more efficient organizing principle than centralized direction. Centralized direction in this way is always having to fight something of a losing battle.

Very closely related to this point and perhaps only another aspect of it is the difference between the "visibility" of monopolistic action whether governmental or private and of actions through the market. When people are acting through the market, millions of people are engaging in activities in a variety of ways that are highly impersonal, not very well recognized, and almost none of which attracts attention. On the other hand, governmental actions, and this is equally true of actions by private monopolies, whether of labor or industry, tend to be conducted by persons who get into the headlines, to attract notice. I have often conducted the experiment of asking people to list the major industries in the United States. In many ways, the question is a foolish one because there is no clear definition of industry. Yet people have some concept of industry and the interesting thing is that the result is always very similar. People always list those industries in which there is a high degree of concentration. They list the automobile industry, never the garment industry, although the garment industry is far larger by any economic measure than the automobile industry. I have never had anybody list the industry of providing domestic service although it employs many more people than the steel industry. Estimates of importance are always biased in the direction of those industries that are monopolized or concentrated and so are in the hands of few firms. Everybody knows the names of the leading producers of automobiles. Few could list the leading producers of men's and women's clothing, or of furniture, although these are both very large industries. So competition, working through the market, precisely because it is impersonal, anonymous, and works its way in devious channels, tends to be underestimated in importance, and the kinds of personal activities that are associated with government, with monopoly, with trade unions, tend to be exaggerated in importance.

Because this kind of direct personal activity by large organizations, whether it be governmental or private, is visible, it tends to call attention to itself out of all proportion to its economic importance. The result is that the community tends to be awakened to the dangers arising from such activities and such concentration of power before they become so important that it is too late to do anything about them. This phenomenon is very clear for trade unions. Everybody has been reading in the newspapers about the negotiations in steel and knows that there is a labor problem in the steel industry. The negotiations usually terminate in some kind of wage increase that is regarded as attributable to the union's activities. In the post war period, domestic servants have gotten larger wage increases without anyone engaging in large scale negotiations, without anyone's knowing that negotiations were going on and without a single newspaper headline except perhaps to record complaints about the problem of finding domestic servants. I think that trade unions have much monopoly power. But I think the importance of trade unions is widely exaggerated, that they are nothing like so important in the allocation of labor or the determination of wage rates as they are supposed to be. They are not unimportant — perhaps 10 or 15% of the working force have wages now some 10 or 15% higher than they otherwise would be because of trade unions, and the remaining 85% of the working class have wages something like 4% lower than they would otherwise be. This is appreciable and important, but it does not give unions the kind of power over the economy that would make it impossible to check their further rise.

The three major sources of strength I have suggested so far are the corroding effect of the extension of state activities and state intervention on attitudes toward the enforcement of the law and on the character of the civil service; the ingenuity of individuals in avoiding regulation; and the visibility of government action and of monopoly. Implicit in these is a fourth, namely the general inefficiency in the operation of government.

These comments have been rather discursive. I have been attempting simply to list some of the forces at work tending to destroy a free society once established, and tending to resist its destruction. I have left out of consideration the force that in some ways is our most important concern; namely, the force of ideas, of people's attitudes about values and about the kind of social organization that they want. I have omitted this force because I have nothing to say about it that is not self-evident.

No very clear conclusion can be drawn from this examination of the forces adverse and favorable to a free society. The historical record suggests pessimism, but the analysis gives no strong basis for either great optimism or confirmed pessimism about the stablity of a free society, if it is given an opportunity to exist. One of the most important tasks for liberal scholars to undertake is to examine this issue more fully in the light of historical evidence in order that we may have a much better idea of what factors tend to promote and what factors to destroy a free society.

248

An Opportunity

for the Republican Party

THE ARENA WAS filled to overflowing. At the microphone the carefully-coached candidate was rolling out pleasant-sounding generalities. At each pause for breath, the crowd would respond with roof-raising cheers and stamping of feet.

At the back of the hall, two Yankees—visitors from the country-side—watched quietly. Finally one, puzzled by the performance, turned to his companion and demanded:

"What's he talking about?"

"He don't say," the friend replied, starting for an exit.

The humbug portrayed in the foregoing anecdote is standard performance today for both the New Frontier and the modern GOP. The result is that millions of voters are as puzzled and disgusted as the two Yankees who walked out.

At this moment in national affairs this conclusion may sound unwarranted. Recent months have recorded several striking conservative victories in Washington. Nevertheless, the bitter truth is this: that for 30 years we have been marched towards collectivism despite occasional repulses by conservative forces.

The Hon. Howard Buffett is a former Republican Congressman from Nebraska. In 1952 he served as campaign manager for Senator Robert A. Taft.

Why has this happened? For freedom-loving Americans the answer to this question transcends all other issues. The answer is not hard to discover once we recognize two political realities:

(1) Despite a sizable dissenting element, the Democratic Party has a definite political faith. That faith is collectivism — the Welfare State. Every measure that Party promotes is designed to give the government more power and contrary-wise to shrink the area of individual freedom.

(2) Since the 'thirties the Republican Party has had no coherent or recognizable political faith. When out of power it has occasionally brilliantly resisted the collectivist drive. But mostly it has collaborated with the Democrats in diminishing individual freedom, calling such action bi-partisan. Foreign Aid and Military Conscription are examples.

During the recent eight-year GOP administration the New Deal remained intact. While elements in the GOP stood for the principles of free individualism, the Party followed a me-too policy. This political perversion started many years ago. It first became evident when Wendell Willkie, a Democrat switch-over, was made GOP presidential nominee in 1940. In that campaign, both candidates, Franklin Delano Roosevelt and Wendell Willkie, promised to keep us out of for-

Page Eleven

eign wars. Yet both supported actions that would get us into the European war already raging. Me-tooism became the pattern of the Republican Party. Control of the GOP had been quietly seized by Eastern Internationalists who hold it to this day. In the two decades that followed 1940, political sterility characterized the Republican Party. Many factors contributed. The most obvious causes were global intervention and the gigantic expansion of government expenditures. This strategy enabled the Democrats to pose as world-saviors and at the same time scatter political or financial rewards to all who would become their lackeys — Repubican or Democrat.

By 1952 the Republican Party had been out of power twenty years. Desperate, it was determined to win at any price. What happened?

The GOP discarded their great leader of the difficult war and post-war years — Senator Robert A. Taft. Instead, they nominated General Dwight D. Eisenhower, candidate of the powerful Internationalists. He was elected President like war hero candidates before him — Zachary Taylor and Ulysses S. Grant. Freedom-loving Americans were assured collectivism would be halted — that swollen governmental power would be whittled down.

The 1952 GOP platform declared: "We charge that they (the Democrats) have arrogantly deprived our citizens of precious liberties by seizing powers never granted."

What happened? As Al Smith used to say, "Let's look at the record." In its first months the Eisenhower administration did achieve one commendable change. The sickening and senseless slaughter of American boys in Korea was halted. But in domestic affairs no serious effort was made to repeal a single New Deal measure.

By 1957, Norman Thomas, frequent Socialist candidate for President, was boasting:

> The United States is making greater strides toward Socialism under Eisenhower than even under Roosevelt, particularly in the fields of federal spending and welfare legislation.

This program can be credited to President Eisenhower and is particularly significant because it is being done by a Republican administration.

In the 1958 elections, despite a GOP administration in the White House, Republican Congressional strength was thinned down to its minority status of the 1930's.

The 1960 election is probably fresh in your mind. Both platforms were full of bromides and pious platitudes. Both candidates had the okay of the Eastern Internationalists. Their debates showed their views were close together. The election of either was to advance collectivism, but the GOP would not collectivize the country as fast as the Democrats. Conservative Americans generally voted for Nixon. That was about the only way to protest the continuing socialist drive of the Democrats.

The foregoing is history. The question now is: Where do we go from here?

Three possibilities exist. (1) The GOP will be rebuilt into a genuine and respected party; (2) a new party will be formed and become effective; and (3) the forces favoring a totalitarian state will have only intra-party opposition.

Those are the alternatives.

The difficulties are sobering. But the American people can solve them if competent leadership is found. The primary requirement is an aroused people — determined to be true both to their heritage and to their children. They can make either alternative (1) or (2) come into reality. The preferable solution would seem to be a massive reformation by the GOP.

Both parties still give lip service to freedom. Consider these recent utterances:

> "I am here to promote the freedom doctrine," declared President Kennedy in one of his first messages to Congress.
> "THE GREAT ISSUE OF 1962— [is] . . . which party acts more effectively to preserve and enlarge human freedom?" declared a statement of Republican principles issued in June 1962.

The fact is that the lamps of American liberty have been going out, one by one. A recent tabulation shows nine important American freedoms have been wholly or partially lost in the thirty years between 1931 and 1961.

Not one of these freedoms was abridged by consent of the people. These freedoms were destroyed in Washington without resistance from either major party. Me-tooism reigned.

Yet the Republican Party was born and nourished to greatness on action for freedom. Organized in 1854, the GOP nominated their first presidential candidate in 1856, John C. Fremont. He lost. But something important happened in 1856. Consider these stirring words:

> The battle of freedom is to be fought out on principle. Slavery is a violation of the eternal right. We have temporized with it from the necessities of our condition, but as sure as God reigns and school children read, that black foul lie can never be consecrated into God's hallowed truth.[1]

This stand for freedom marked Abraham Lincoln's speech as he joined the Republican Party in 1856 — and broke with the Whig Party that had elected him to Congress and other offices.

The Republican Party stood firm against the spread of slavery. Was that highly controversial action politically unwise and impractical? "Yes," declared the experienced Whigs. A few years later, the Whig Party was only an unmourned memory.

The new-born Republican Party, with Lincoln at the helm, won the next presidential election — 1860. That victory was repeated in 10 out of 12 presidential elections in the half-century that followed — a record never equaled in American history. Taking a stand for freedom was not simply a righteous move — it was dynamic political action.

AMAZINGLY, AN ISSUE of actual physical freedom, as vital and fundamental as the infamous Negro slavery, exists in America today. Its abolition

awaits a political party courageous enough to champion liberty as the Republicans did a century ago. I refer, of course, to the Old World evil of conscription, carried out here under the soothing label of Selective Service.

Today, all American boys, at eighteen, are registered into military conscription and become subject to physical bondage by the government. This occurs even before these boys are of age.

The grim aspects of this law have been obscured. But their awesome meaning has been spelled out by a long-revered scholar of the Constitution, the late Professor John W. Burgess of Columbia University:

> The power in the government to raise and employ conscript armies for, and in, foreign war . . . is the most despotic power which government can exercise. It can be so exercised, at any moment and on occasion created by government itself, as to sweep every vestige of individual liberty and put the last drop of blood of every man, woman and child in the country at the arbitrary disposal of the government.[2]

Sobering details of the Conscription Law are reported by Lewis B. Hershey, Director of Selective Service:

> Every young man must register with a local board of the Selective Service System on his eighteenth birthday or within five days thereafter. . . . A registrant who fails to comply with all his selective service obligations because he leaves the United States after his registration . . . becomes a violator of the Act and is subject to severe penalties prescribed in the Act.

The meaning of Hershey's statement is that every American boy, as he reaches the age of eighteen, goes into bondage. He must not leave the jurisdiction of U. S. military authorities except by their permission. In some respects, he may seem like a free person. He may be permitted to go to school, work, or loaf, but he is actually a captive in that his person and services are

251

[1] Spoken at Bloomington, Illinois, May 29, 1856.

[2] John W. Burgess, *Recent Changes in American Constitutional Theory* (New York: Columbia University Press, 1923).

subject to military control for a period of years.

If his parents should emigrate to Canada, England or some other land, no law stops them. But their eighteen-year-old son cannot get out. He cannot leave America until the U. S. military is through with him. Then, if he is still alive, he becomes free.

Many objections can be advanced against the GOP facing up to this situation. Similar arguments were raised against Lincoln and the Republican Party when they talked against Negro slavery.

In its abolition of freedom, peacetime conscription overshadows all other collectivism and regimentation. When the American government conscripts a boy to go 10,000 miles to the jungles of Asia without a declaration of war by Congress (as required by the Constitution) what freedom is safe at home? Surely, profits of U. S. Steel or your private property are not more sacred than a young man's right to life.

By a stand against the peacetime conscription of American youth, the Republican Party could again become the party of freedom. Without this action, pledges in other areas of American life have little significance.

Will the Republican Party seize this opportunity? Who knows? It would seem to be the GOP's best, if not only, hope for the future. The Democratic Party has preempted and permanently occupied the socialistic and collectivist position in American politics.

If America is again to have government "by consent of the governed," one party must offer the alternative position. That alternative is, of course, individual freedom and private enterprise. Lacking that choice, America will end up in socialism without a single, genuine, ballot-box opportunity to reject it. Remembering the glorious history of our political system and its fruits, a greater tragedy to the world is hard to envision.

All this is not to say that otherwise the GOP will be counted out immediately. Suppose it continues to dodge action for freedom? The stock market crash and the economic effects it portends may bring GOP gains this fall. But that respite would only postpone its last rites if the me-too pattern of the last 30 years continues.

A return to faith in freedom by the GOP would not solve all its problems. But that action is the decisive step to assure its future. Then, as it was for Lincoln and the GOP in 1856, victory and a rebirth of freedom would come into sight.

For political action that sets men free has proven the most dynamic force in all history.

In turn, the rededication of America to freedom could reverse the totalitarian tide now sweeping over the world.

252

H. L. Mencken:

The Joyous Libertarian

MURRAY N. ROTHBARD

The extortions and oppressions of government will go on so long as such bare fraudulence deceives and disarms the victims — so long as they are ready to swallow the immemorial official theory that protesting against the stealings of the archbishop's secretary's nephew's mistress' illegitimate son is a sin against the Holy Ghost.

— H. L. Mencken

IT IS TYPICAL of American *Kultur* that it was incapable of understanding H. L. Mencken. And it was typical of H. L. Mencken that this didn't bother him a bit; in fact, quite the contrary, for it confirmed his estimate of his fellow-countrymen. It is difficult for Americans to understand a *merger* of high-spirited wit and devotion to principle; one is either a humorist, gently or acidly spoofing the foibles of one's age, or else one is a serious and solemn thinker. That a man of ebullient wit can be, in a sense, all the more devoted to positive ideas and principles is understood by very few; almost always, he is set down as a pure cynic and nihilist. This was and still is the common fate of H. L. Mencken; but it is no more than he would have cheerfully expected.

Murray N. Rothbard is the author of *Man, Economy, and State,* a systematic treatment of economics. He received his Ph.D. in economics from Columbia University and is presently a consulting economist in New York City.

Any man who is an individualist and a libertarian in this day and age has a difficult row to hoe. He finds himself in a world marked, if not dominated, by folly, fraud, and tyranny. He has, if he is a reflecting man, three possible courses of action open to him: (1) he may retire from the social and political world into his private occupation: in the case of Mencken's early partner, George Jean Nathan, he can retire into a world of purely esthetic contemplation; (2) he can set about to try to change the world for the better, or at least to formulate and propagate his views with such an ultimate hope in mind; or, (3) he can stay in the world, enjoying himself immensely at this spectacle of folly. To take this third route requires a special type of personality with a special type of judgment about the world. He must, on the one hand, be an individualist with a serene and unquenchable sense of self-confidence; he must be supremely "inner-directed" with no inner shame

Page Fifteen

or quaking at going against the judgment of the herd. He must, secondly, have a supreme zest for enjoying life and the spectacle it affords; he must be an individualist who cares deeply about liberty and individual excellence, but who can — from that same dedication to truth and liberty — enjoy and lampoon a society that has turned its back on the best that it can achieve. And he must, thirdly, be deeply pessimistic about any possibility of changing and reforming the ideas and actions of the vast majority of his fellow-men. He must believe that *boobus Americanus* is doomed to be *boobus Americanus* forevermore. Put these qualities together, and we are a long way toward explaining the route taken by Henry Louis Mencken.

Of course, Mencken had other qualities, too: enormous gusto, a sparkling wit, a keen and erudite appreciation of many fields of knowledge, a zest for the dramatic events of the everyday world that made him a born journalist. Despite his omnivorous passion for intellectual fields and disciplines, he had no temperament for fashioning rigorous systems of thought — but then, how many people have? All these qualities reinforced his bent for what he became.

A serene and confident individualist, dedicated to competence and excellence and deeply devoted to liberty, but convinced that the bulk of his fellows were beyond repair, Mencken carved out a role unique in American history: he sailed joyously into the fray, slashing and cutting happily into the buncombe and folly he saw all around him, puncturing the balloons of pomposity, gaily cleansing the Augean stables of cant, hypocrisy, absurdity, and cliche, "heaving," as he once put it, "the dead cat into the temple" to show bemused worshippers of the inane that he would not be struck dead on the spot. And in the course of this task, rarely undertaken in any age, a task performed purely for his own enjoyment, he exercised an enormous liberating force upon the best minds of a whole generation.

It is characteristic of Mencken that one of the things he enjoyed the most was a Presidential convention, which he almost never failed to attend. Here he plunged into the midst of the teeming, raucous and absurd throng: into all the hilarity and inanity and excitement of the great American political process itself, his jacket off, swigging beer, partaking of all the fun while missing none of the folly. And then he would write up what he saw, slashing at the cant, hypocrisy, and concentrated nonsense of our governors in action. No one truly immersed in Mencken could emerge quite the same again; no one could retain the same faith in our "statesmen" or in the democratic political process itself, no one could ever be quite the same sucker for all manner of ideological, social, and political quackery, the same worshipper of solemn nonsense.

Mencken's liberating force, of course, was exerted not on the mass of men, but on the scattered but intelligent few who could appreciate and be influenced by what he had to say; in short, like his old friend and fellow-libertarian, Albert Jay Nock, Mencken wrote for (and liberated) The Remnant who would understand.

The style is truly the man, and not the least of Mencken's deeds of liberation was the shattering impact of his style. A scholar in the English — or the *American* — language, Mencken had a love for the language, for precision and clarity of the word, a deep respect for his craft, that few writers have possessed. It was not hyperbole when the eminent critic and essayist Joseph Wood Krutch referred to Mencken as "the greatest prose stylist of the twentieth century;" this, too, has gone unrecognized because Americans are generally incapable of taking a witty writer seriously.

The tragedy — for us, not for Mencken himself — is that most of The Remnant didn't understand either; the bulk of his supposed followers made the same mistake as everyone else in presuming wit and serious purpose cannot be joined; blinded by the wit, they did not realize the positive values which should have been evident in his work. And so those who happily joined Mencken in scoffing at Babbittry, at Prohibition and the Anti-Saloon League, at the wowsers and the Uplift of the 1920's, abandoned Mencken to enlist in the ranks of the intensified Uplift and the more extravagant wowsers of the 1930's. The very scorners of the politicians and political nostrums of the 'twenties, promptly and fiercely subscribed to the far more pernicious nostrums of the political quacks of the New Deal. The same Menckenians who clear-sightedly saw the folly of America's immersion into World War I, beat the drums loudly and with no trace of humor or hesitation for the equal or greater folly of our entry into World War II. The failure of Mencken's would-be followers to understand his "message" (a concept he would have abhorred) certainly did not depress Mencken; it only confirmed him in his judgment of the pervasiveness of the "booboisie." But it was a calamity for the country.

If Mencken was not a nihilist, what positive values did he hold? His values included a devoted dedication to his craft — to his work as editor, journalist, linguist. This in turn reflected his thorough-going and pervasive individualism, with its corollary devotion to individual excellence and to individual liberty. They included a life-long passion for music. They included a perhaps excessive zeal for science, the scientific method, and medical orthodoxy; along with the zeal for science came a mechanistic type of determinism which undoubtedly helped to shape his pessimistic view of the possibility of changing the ideas and actions of men.

Mencken's pervasive individualist *Weltanschauung* gave an unappreciated consistency to his views on many different subjects. It gave a system to his superficially piecemeal forays into innumerable fields. Let us take, for example, such a supposedly "non-political" field as folk-music. It is not accidental that both the Socialist Left and the Nationalist Right — those twin enemies of individualism — in our century have made a virtual fetish of the "people's" folk-song. Mencken cut to the heart of the matter in his inimitable review of Dr. Louise Pound's *Poetic Origins and the Ballad*:

Dr. Pound's book completely disposes of the theory upon which nine-tenths of all the pedagogical discussions of the ballad and its origins are based. This is the theory that the ballads familiar to all of us ... are the product, not of individual authors, but of whole herds of minnesingers working together . . . in brief, that the primitive balladists first joined in a communal hoofing, then began to moan and hum a tune, and finally fitted words to it. It is difficult to imagine anything more idiotic, and yet this doctrine is cherished as something almost sacred by whole droves of professors and rammed annually into the skulls of innumerable candidates for the Ph.D. Dr. Pound proves . . . that the ballads really did not originate that way at all — that they were written, on the contrary, by individual poets with talents . . . and that most of them first saw the light, not at vulgar shindigs on the village green, but at fashionable and even intellectual ale-parties in castle halls.

The notion that *any* respectable work of art can have a communal origin is wholly nonsensical. The plain people, taking them together, are quite as incapable of a coherent esthetic impulse as they are of courage, honesty, or honor. The cathedrals of the Middle Ages were not planned and built by whole communities, but by individual men; and all the communities had to do with the business was to do the hard work, reluctantly and often badly. So with folk-song, folk-myth, folk-balladry. . . . German folk-song . . . used to be credited to a mysterious native talent in the German yokelry, but scientific investigation reveals that some of the songs regarded as especially characteristic of the folk-soul were actually written by the director of music at the University of Tubingen, Prof. Dr. Friedrich Silcher. . . .

The English ballads are to be accounted for in the same way. Dr. Pound shows that some of the most famous of them, in their earliest forms, are full of concepts and phrases that would have been as incomprehensible to the English peasantry of Elizabeth's time as the Ehrlich hypothesis of immunity—that it is a sheer impossibility to imagine them being composed by a gang of oafs whooping and galloping around a May pole, or even assembled solemnly in an *Eisteddfod* or *Allgemeinesangerfest*. More, she shows the process of ballad making in our own time — how a song by a Paul Dresser or a Stephen Foster is borrowed

255

by the folk, and then gradually debased.[1]

The myth of Mencken as a mocking nihilist has pervaded literary criticism; it was with surprise and much admiration, then, that the eminent critic Samuel Putnam read Mencken's great collection of short pieces — selected and edited by himself—the *Mencken Chrestomathy*. In a perceptive review, Putnam wrote that it was now evident that Mencken was a "Tory anarchist." "Tory anarchist" is indeed an excellent summation of Mencken's life-long worldview.

Mencken's guiding passion was individual liberty. To his good friend Hamilton Owens, he once solemnly declared: "I believe in only one thing and that thing is human liberty. If ever a man is to achieve anything like dignity, it can happen only if superior men are given absolute freedom to think what they want to think and say what they want to say. I am against any man and any organization which seeks to limit or deny that freedom . . . [and] the superior man can be sure of freedom only if it is given to all men."[2] At another time he wrote that he believed in absolute individual liberty "up to the limit of the unbearable, and even beyond." In a privately written "Addendum on Aims," Mencken wrote that "I am an extreme libertarian, and believe in absolute free speech. . . . I am against jailing men for their opinions, or, for that matter, for anything else."[3] And in a letter to one of his biographers, Ernest Boyd, Mencken wrote: "So far as I can make out, I believe in only one thing: liberty. But I do not believe in even liberty enough to want to force it upon anyone. That is, I am nothing of the reformer, however much I may rant against this or that great curse or malaise. In that ranting there is usually far more delight than indignation."[4]

The *Chrestomathy* contains some brilliant writing on what Mencken captioned as the "inner nature" of government:

All government, in its essence, is a conspiracy against the superior man; its one permanent object is to oppress him and cripple him. If it be aristocratic in organization, then it seeks to protect the man who is superior only in law against the man who is superior in fact; if it be democratic, then it seeks to protect the man who is inferior in every way against both. One of its primary functions is to regiment men by force, to make them as much alike as possible and as dependent upon one another as possible, to search out and combat originality among them. All it can see in an original idea is potential change, and hence an invasion of its prerogatives. The most dangerous man, to any government, is the man who is able to think things out for himself, without regard to the prevailing superstitions and taboos. Almost inevitably he comes to the conclusion that the government he lives under is dishonest, insane and intolerable, and so, if he is romantic, he tries to change it. And even if he is not romantic personally he is very apt to spread discontent among those who are. . . .

The average man, whatever his errors otherwise, at least sees clearly that government is something lying outside him and outside the generality of his fellow-men — that it is a separate, independent and often hostile power, only partly under his control, and capable of doing him great harm. In his romantic moments, he may think of it as a benevolent father or even as a sort of *jinn* or god, but he never thinks of it as part of himself. In time of trouble he looks to it to perform miracles for his benefit; at other times he sees it as an enemy with which he must do constant battle. Is it a fact of no significance that robbing the government is everywhere regarded as a crime of less magnitude than robbing an individual? . . .

What lies behind all this, I believe, is a deep sense of the fundamental antagonism between the government and the people it governs. It is apprehended, not as a committee of citizens chosen to carry on the communal business of the whole population, but as a separate and autonomous corporation, mainly devoted to exploiting the population for the benefit of its own members. Robbing

---

[1] H. L. Mencken, *A Mencken Chrestomathy* (New York: Knopf, 1949), pp. 471-72.

[2] Guy J. Forgue, ed., *Letters of H. L. Mencken* (New York: Knopf, 1961), p. xiii.

[3] *Ibid.*, p. 189.

[4] *Ibid.*, p. 281.

it is thus an act almost devoid of infamy. . . . When a private citizen is robbed a worthy man is deprived of the fruits of his industry and thrift; when the government is robbed the worst that happens is that certain rogues and loafers have less money to play with than they had before. The notion that they have earned that money is never entertained; to most sensible men it would seem ludicrous. They are simply rascals who, by accidents of law, have a somewhat dubious right to a share in the earnings of their fellow men. When that share is diminished by private enterprise the business is, on the whole, far more laudable than not.

This gang is well-nigh immune to punishment. Its worst extortions, even when they are baldly for private profit, carry no certain penalties under our laws. Since the first days of the Republic, less than a dozen of its members have been impeached, and only a few obscure understrappers have ever been put into prison. The number of men sitting at Atlanta and Leavenworth for revolting against the extortions of government is always ten times as great as the number of government officials condemned for oppressing the taxpayers to their own gain. . . . There are no longer any citizens in the world; there are only subjects. They work day in and day out for their masters; they are bound to die for their masters at call. . . . On some bright tomorrow, a geological epoch or two hence, they will come to the end of their endurance. . . .[5]

Mencken had little faith in the ability of revolutions to effect an overthrow on behalf of liberty: "Political revolutions do not often accomplish anything of genuine value; their one undoubted effect is simply to throw out one gang of thieves and put in another. After a revolution, of course, the successful revolutionists always try to convince doubters that they have achieved great things, and usually they hang any man who denies it. But that surely doesn't prove their case." This blend of libertarian doctrine and pessimism on achieving it was summed up by Mencken: "The ideal government of all reflective men . . . is one which lets the individual alone—one which barely escapes being no govern-

ment at all. This ideal, I believe, will be realized in the world twenty or thirty centuries after I have passed from these scenes and taken up my public duties in Hell."[6]

Mencken saw clearly the fallacy of treating government officials as uniquely motivated by the public weal:

These men, in point of fact, are seldom if ever moved by anything rationally describable as public spirit; there is actually no more public spirit among them than among so many burglars or street-walkers. Their purpose, first, last and all the time, is to promote their private advantage, and to that end, and that end alone, they exercise all the vast powers that are in their hands. . . . Whatever it is they seek, whether security, greater ease, more money or more power, it has to come out of the common stock, and so it diminishes the shares of all other men. Putting a new job-holder to work decreases the wages of every wage-earner in the land. . . . Giving a job-holder more power takes something away from the liberty of all of us. . . .

Mencken goes on to add, on the nature of government and attempts to stem its incursions:

It is, perhaps, a fact provocative of sour mirth that the Bill of Rights was designed trustfully to prohibit forever two of the favorite crimes of all known governments: the seizure of private property without adequate compensation and the invasion of the citizen's liberty without justifiable cause. . . . It is a fact provocative of mirth yet more sour that the execution of these prohibitions was put into the hands of courts, which is to say, into the hands of lawyers, which is to say, into the hands of men specifically educated to discover legal excuses for dishonest, dishonorable and anti-social acts.[7]

One of the major forces keeping governmental tyranny unchecked, Mencken pointed out, was the credulity of the masses of men: "The State is not force

257

[5] *Mencken Chrestomathy,* pp. 145-48.

[6] *Ibid.,* p. 146.

[7] H. L. Mencken, *Prejudices: A Selection,* ed. by James T. Farrell (New York: Vintage Books, 1958), pp. 180-82.

alone. It depends upon the credulity of man quite as much as upon his docility. Its aim is not merely to make him obey, but also to make him want to obey."[8]

Is government sometimes useful? Answered Mencken:

> So is a doctor. But suppose the dear fellow claimed the right, every time he was called in to prescribe for a bellyache or a ringing in the ears, to raid the family silver, use the family tooth-brushes, and execute the *droit de seigneur* upon the housemaid?[9]

Neither did Mencken have any greater affection for the military caste than for the civilian bureaucracy:

> The military caste did not originate as a party of patriots, but as a party of bandits. The primeval bandit chiefs eventually became kings. Something of the bandit character still attaches to the military professional. He may fight bravely and unselfishly, but so do gamecocks. He may seek no material rewards, but neither do hunting dogs. His general attitude of mind is stupid and antisocial. It was a sound instinct in the Founding Fathers that made them subordinate the military establishment to the civil power. To be sure, the civil power consists largely of political scoundrels, but they at least differ in outlook and purpose from the military. . . .[10]

NO ONE EXCELLED MENCKEN in what he called "Utopian flights"—hilarious and magnificent projects for libertarian reform of government, or of society in general. Thus, in a piece written in 1924, before, as he put it, "the New Deal afflicted the country with a great mass of new administrative law and extra-tyrannical jobholders," Mencken proposed a searching reform in our system of administrative law. He begins by saying that "in the immoral monarchies of the continent of Europe, now happily abolished by God's will, there was, in the old days of sin, an intelligent

<hr/>

[8] H. L. Mencken, *Minority Report: H. L. Mencken's Notebooks* (New York: Knopf, 1956), p. 217.

[9] Mencken, *Prejudices*, p. 187.

[10] Mencken, *Minority Report*, p. 217.

and effective way of dealing with delinquent officials." Not only, he adds, were they subjects to ordinary criminal law, but *also* to special courts for "offenses . . . peculiar to their offices." Prussia maintained a court where any citizen was free to lodge a complaint against an official, and a guilty official could be punished in many ways — forced to pay damages against a victimized citizen, removed from office, and/or sent to jail. "Had a Prussian judge in those far-off days of despotism, overcome by a brainstorm of *kaiserliche* passion, done any of the high-handed and irrational things that our own judges, Federal and State, do almost every day, an aggrieved citizen might have hailed him before the administrative court and recovered heavy damages from him. . . ." Furthermore, the law "specifically provided that responsible officials should be punished, not more leniently than subordinate or ordinary offenders, but more severely. If a corrupt policeman got six months a corrupt chief of police got two years. More, these statutes were enforced with Prussian barbarity; and the jails were constantly full of errant officials."

Mencken adds that he does not precisely propose, "of course," the Prussian system for the United States:

> As a matter of fact, the Prussian scheme would probably prove ineffective in the Republic, if only because it involved setting up one gang of jobholders to judge and punish another gang. It worked very well in Prussia before the country was civilized by force of arms because, as everyone knows, a Prussian official was trained in ferocity from infancy, and regarded every man arraigned before him, whether a fellow official or not, as guilty *ipso facto*; in fact, any thought of a prisoner's possible innocence was abhorrent to him as a reflection upon the *Polizei*, and by inference, upon the Throne, the whole monarchical idea, and God. But in America . . . judge and prisoner would often be fellow Democrats or fellow Republicans, and hence jointly interested in protecting their party against scandal and its members against the loss of their jobs.

"What is needed," concluded Mencken, "is a system (a) that does not depend for its execution upon the good-will of fellow jobholders, and (b) that provides swift, certain and unpedantic punishments, each fitted neatly to its crime." Mencken's proposed remedy

provides that any [citizen] . . . having looked into the acts of a jobholder and found him delinquent, may punish him instantly and on the spot, and in any manner that seems appropriate a n d convenient — and that, in case this punishment involves physical damage to the jobholder, the ensuing inquiry by the grand jury or coroner shall confine itself strictly to the question whether the jobholder deserved what he got. In other words, I propose that it shall no longer be *malum in se* for a citizen to pummel, cowhide, kick, gouge, cut, wound, bruise, maim, burn, club, bastinado, flay or even lynch a jobholder, and that it shall be *malum prohibitum* only to the extent that the punishment exceeds the jobholder's desserts. The amount of this excess, if any, may be determined very conveniently by a petit jury, as other questions of guilt are now determined. . . . If it decides that the jobholder deserves the punishment inflicted upon him, the citizen who inflicted it is acquitted with honor. If, on the contrary, it decides that the punishment was excessive, then the citizen is adjudged guilty of assault, mayhem, murder, or whatever it is, in a degree apportioned to the difference between what the jobholder deserved and what he got, and punishment for that excess follows in the usual course. . . .

The advantages of this plan, I believe, are too patent to need argument. At one stroke it removes all the legal impediments which now make the punishment of a recreant jobholder so hopeless a process. . . . Say a citizen today becomes convinced that a certain judge is a jackass — that his legal learning is defective, his sense of justice atrophied and his conduct of cases before him tyrannical and against decency. As things stand, it is impossible to do anything about it. . . . Nor is anything to be gained by denouncing him publicly and urging all good citizens to vote against him when he comes up for re-election, for his term may run for ten or fifteen years, and even if it expires tomorrow and he is defeated the chances are good that his successor will be quite as bad, and maybe even worse.

But now imagine any citizen free to approach him in open court and pull his nose. Or even, in aggravated cases, to cut off his ears, throw him out of the window, or knock him in the head with an ax. How vastly more attentive he would be to his duties! How diligently he would apply himself to the study of the law! How careful he would be about the rights of litigants before him![11]

Mencken's concern for the parlous state of liberty in America, and with the virtual immunity granted to its oppressors, was never expressed with more hilarity or bitter irony than in his article on "The Nature of Liberty"—written in the early 1920's but in no sense out of date. His theme is the police vs. the individual citizen. He begins in irony: "Every time an officer of the constabulary, in the execution of his just and awful powers under American law, produces a compound fracture of the occiput of some citizen in his custody, with hemorrhage, shock, coma and death, there comes a feeble, falsetto protest from specialists in human liberty." "Is it a fact without significance," Mencken continues, "that this protest is never supported by the great body of American freemen, setting aside the actual heirs and creditors of the victim? I think not." For the plain people understand that policemen are given night-sticks "for the purpose of cracking the skulls of the recalcitrant plain people, Democrats and Republicans alike."

It is clear, therefore, Mencken continued to spoof, that this minority of intellectuals concerned with civil liberty and individual rights as against the police are subversive and un-American:

The specialists aforesaid are the same fanatics who shake the air with sobs every time the Postmaster-General of the United States bars a periodical from the mails because its ideas do not please him, and every time some poor Russian is deported for reading Karl Marx, and every time a Prohibition enforcement officer murders a bootlegger who resists his levies, and every time agents of the Department of Justice throw an Italian out of the window, and every

259

---

[11] Mencken *Chrestomathy,* pp. 384-387.

time the Ku Klux Klan or the American Legion tars and feathers a Socialist evangelist. In brief, they are Radicals, and to scratch one with a pitchfork is to expose a Bolshevik. They are men standing in contempt of American institutions and in enmity to American idealism. . . .

What ails them primarily is . . . that . . . having mastered . . . the theoretical principles set forth in the Bill of Rights, they work themselves into a passionate conviction that those principles are identical with the rules of law and justice, and ought to be enforced literally, and without the slightest regard for circumstance and expediency.

They did not realize, added Mencken, that the Bill of Rights as originally

adopted by the Fathers of the Republic . . . was gross, crude, idealistic, a bit fanciful and transcendental. It specified the rights of a citizen, but it said nothing whatever about his duties. Since then, by the orderly processes of legislative science and by the even more subtle and beautiful devices of juridic art, it has been kneaded and mellowed into a far greater pliability and reasonableness. On the one hand, the citizen still retains the great privilege of membership in the most superb free nation ever witnessed on this earth. On the other hand, as a result of countless shrewd enactments and sagacious decisions, his natural lusts and appetites are held in laudable check, and he is thus kept in order and decorum. . . . Once a policeman, he is protected by the legislative and judicial arms in the peculiar rights and prerogatives that go with his high office, including especially the right to jug the laity at his will, to sweat and mug them, to subject them to the third degree, and to subdue their resistance by beating out their brains. Those who are unaware of this are simply ignorant of the basic principles of American jurisprudence, as they have been exposed times without number by the courts of first instance and ratified in lofty terms by the Supreme Court of the United States.[12]

Mencken's devoted services to civil liberty, his opposition to censorship as editor of the *American Mercury*, are too

well-known to need repeating here. But less known is Mencken's searching dissection of the myth of Mr. Justice Holmes as, in his dissenting opinions, a great civil libertarian. Mencken keenly pointed out that "it is impossible to see how . . . [Holmes' opinions] can conceivably promote liberty." It was misleading to consider Holmes an advocate of the rights of man; rather,

he was actually no more than an advocate of the rights of law-makers. There, indeed, is the clue to his whole jurisprudence. He believed that the law-making bodies should be free to experiment almost *ad libitum*, that the courts should not call a halt upon them until they clearly passed the uttermost bounds of reason, that everything should be sacrificed to their autonomy, including, apparently, even the Bill of Rights. If this is Liberalism, then all I can say is that Liberalism is not what it was when I was young.[13]

Mencken had no particular interest in economic matters, but he saw clearly that capitalism, the consequent of individual liberty in the economic sphere, was the most productive and rational economic system. He bitterly opposed the New Deal for being anti-capitalist as well as anti-libertarian. Of capitalism, Mencken wrote:

We owe to it almost everything that passes under the general name of civilization today. The extraordinary progress of the world since the Middle Ages has not been due to the mere expenditure of human energy, nor even to the flights of human genius, for men have worked hard since the remotest times, and some of them had been of surpassing intellect. No, it has been due to the accumulation of capital. That accumulation . . . provided the machinery that gradually diminished human drudgery, and liberated the spirit of the worker, who had formerly been almost indistinguishable from a mule.[14]

His old friend, Hamilton Owens, writes of Mencken's vehement anger at Roosevelt's taking America off the gold standard. "With all the vehemence of which

___
[12] Mencken, *Prejudices*, pp. 138-43.

[13] *Mencken Chrestomathy*, p. 259.
[14] *Ibid.*, p. 294.

260

he was capable he insisted it was down-right robbery. He talked about taking court action in person."[15] In correspondence with the famous socialist, Upton Sinclair, who had evidently plied him with the old well-tested bromide on the supposed efficiency of government post offices, fire departments, public health services, etc., Mencken, instead of hastily retreating and compromising, as most conservatives do when faced with similar challenges, riposted:

Your questions are easy. The government brings my magazine to you only unwillingly. It tried to ruin my business, [*The American Mercury*] and failed only by an inch. It charges too much for postal orders, and loses too many of them. A corporation of idiot Chinamen could do the thing better. Its machine for putting out fires is intolerably expensive and inefficient. It seldom, in fact, actually puts out a fire; they burn out. . . . The Army had nothing to do with the discovery of the cause of yellow fever. Its bureaucrats persecuted the men who did the work. They could have done it much more quickly if they had been outside the Army. It took years of effort to induce the government to fight mosquitoes, and it does the work very badly today.[16]

And, in a significant but forgotten review of the individualist Sir Ernest Benn's *The Confessions of A Capitalist*, Mencken wrote that Benn

devotes most of his book to proving what the majority of Americans regard as axiomatic: that the capitalistic system, whatever its defects, yet works better than any other system so far devised by man. The rest of his space he gives over to proofs that government is inevitably extravagant and wasteful — that nothing it does is ever done as cheaply and efficiently as the same thing might be done by private enterprise. I see nothing to object to here.

And Mencken immediately adds:

Even the most precious functions of government—say, collecting taxes or hanging men—would be better

---

15 Mencken, *Letters*, p. xii.

16 *Ibid.*, p. 295.

done if the doing of them were farmed out to Ford.[17]

The great individualist Albert Jay Nock has written that, while in the 1920's he was generally considered a flaming "radical," and in the 1930's as a bitter "reactionary," his political philosophy remained, in these decades, exactly the same. The same might be said of his friend Mencken, who also remained, throughout, an individualist and a libertarian. In the 1920's, Mencken directed his fire against the tariff and other special privileges to favored business groups, against laws and edicts against free speech and other personal liberties, and especially against the monstrous tyranny of Prohibition. In the 1930's, Mencken directed his major attacks against the major threat to liberty of that era: the New Deal. The former Menckenites of the 1920's and his new-found conservative champions of the 1930's, each, in believing that Mencken had now shifted from Left to Right, showed that they understood neither Mencken nor the principles of liberty. Often, what was mistaken for anti-capitalism was simply a cultural and esthetic distaste that Mencken had for the bulk of businessmen ("Babbitts") as persons — a distaste which they shared with the common run — the "mass-men"— of other occupations. But Mencken's antipathy to the cultural tastes of individual capital*ists* must not be confused — as he never did — with opposition to capital*ism* as such.

Looking back on the two eras as early as 1934, Mencken wrote to a friend:

If I really believed that I had Left a Mark upon my Time I think I'd leap into the nearest ocean. This is no mere fancy talk. It is based on the fact that I believe the American people are more insane today than they were when I began to write. Certainly the Rotarians at their worst never concocted anything as preposterous as some of the inventions of the Brain Trust. They were

---

17 [H. L. Mencken], "Babbitt as Philosopher," *The American Mercury* (September, 1926), pp. 126-27. For a definitive bibliography of Mencken's writings, see Betty Adler, comp., *H. L. M.: The Mencken Bibliography* (Baltimore: Johns Hopkins Press, 1961).

harmless fools, seeking to formulate a substitute for the Christianity that was slipping from them. But the Brain Trusters, at least in large part, are maniacal fanatics, and will lead us down to ruin if they are not soon suppressed.[18]

One of the delightful aspects of Mencken, indeed, is the constancy of his views. As he once, at the age of sixty, playfully wrote to a friend: "On all known subjects, ranging from aviation to xylophone-playing, I have fixed and invariable ideas. They have not changed since I was four or five years old."[19]

In his charming, mellow, affectionate, and witty autobiography on his life as a child, *Happy Days*, Mencken recalls imbibing his "reactionary" views at his father's knee:

> His moral system, as I try to piece it together after so many years, seems to have been predominantly Chinese. All mankind, in his sight, was divided into two great races: those who paid their bills, and those who didn't. The former were virtuous, despite any evidence that could be adduced to the contrary; the latter were unanimously and incurably scoundrels.
>
> He had a very tolerant view of all other torts and malfeasances. He believed that political corruption was inevitable under democracy, and even argued, out of his own experience, that it had its uses. One of his favorite anecdotes was about a huge swinging sign that used to hang outside his place of business in Paca street. When the building was built, in 1885, he simply hung out the sign, sent for the city councilman of the district, and gave him $20. This was in full settlement forevermore of all permit and privilege fees, easement taxes, and other such costs and imposts. The city councilman pocketed the money, and in return was supposed to stave off any cops, building inspectors or other functionaries who had any lawful interest in the matter, or tried to horn in for private profit. Being an honorable man according to his lights, he kept his bargain, and the sign flapped and squeaked in the breeze for ten years. But then, in 1895, Baltimore had a reform wave, the councilman was voted out of office, and the idealists

in the City Hall sent word that a license to maintain the sign would cost $62.75 *a year*. It came down the next day.

> This was proof to my father that reform was mainly only a conspiracy of prehensile charlatans to mulct tax-payers. I picked up this idea from him, and entertain it to the present day. I also picked up his doctrine that private conduct had better not be inquired into too closely — with the exception, of course, of any kind involving beating a creditor.[20]

The firmness of Mencken's libertarianism may also be gauged by the numerous quotations from libertarian and even unknown anarchist authors in his *New Dictionary of Quotations*.[21] Thus, in his section on the "State," the great bulk of the quotations are anti-State, and the remainder are so extremely pro-State that the effect on the reader is emphatically ironic. An example of the latter is "The National Socialist party is the state — Adolf Hitler." And the anti-State quotations are taken largely from highly individualist or anarchist sources: Emerson, Max Stirner, Thoreau, Bakunin, William Graham Sumner, Kropotkin, Tolstoy, and Benjamin R. Tucker. It is doubtful if someone not highly sympathetic with these authors would (1) know their writings with such familiarity, and (2) "pack" such sections with their quotations. The section on "Speech, Free" is, again, almost exclusively filled with pro-free speech quotations, including not only Macaulay, Jefferson, James Mill, and various judges, but also the quasi-anarchistic English individualist, Auberon Herbert.

H. L. MENCKEN's contempt for democracy is well-known. It stemmed largely from his primary devotion to individual liberty, and his insight that the bulk of men — the democratic majority — is generally inclined to suppress rather than defend the liberty of the in-

---

18 Mencken, *Letters*, pp. 374-75.
19 *Ibid.*, p. 444.

20 H. L. Mencken, *The Days of H. L. Mencken* (New York: Knopf, 1947), pp. 251-52.
21 H. L. Mencken, *A New Dictionary of Quotations: On Historical Principles from Ancient and Modern Sources* (New York: Knopf, 1942).

262

dividual. Mencken once summed up his view of the nature of democracy, the common man, and the State in this eight-word definition of "democracy": "Democracy is the worship of jackals by jackasses." Other Menckenian definitions: "Democracy is the theory that the common people know what they want, and deserve to get it good and hard." "If x is the population of the United States and y is the degree of imbecility of the average American, then democracy is the theory that x times y is less than y." All of democracy's axioms "resolve themselves into thundering paradoxes, many amounting to downright contradictions in terms. The mob is competent to rule the rest of us — but it must be rigorously policed itself. There is a government, not of men, but laws — but men are set upon benches to decide finally what the law is and may be."[22] On democracy's inherent tendency to suppress liberty, Mencken wrote in a private letter:

All appeals to any intrinsic love of free speech are futile. There is no such passion in the people. It is only an aristocracy that is ever tolerant. The masses are invariably cocksure, suspicious, furious and tyrannical. This, in fact, is the central objection to democracy: that it hinders progress by penalizing innovation and non-conformity.[23]

Mencken's atheism is, again, well-known, but for him passionate hostility was reserved for those religious groups which persisted in imposing their moral codes by coercion upon the rest of the population. In Mencken's day, the prime example was Prohibition: and therefore Mencken's hostility was directed chiefly toward the Methodists and Baptists. In contrast, Mencken had no particular animus against the Roman Catholics (especially the non-Irish sections): "Catholics are not Prohibitionists, they have more humor than the Methodists," he is supposed to have said once, and he was apparently friendly with quite a few members of the Catholic clergy.

The linkage in Mencken's thought between religious coercion of morals, de-mocracy, the common man, and tyranny over the individual, may be seen in one of his most uproarious articles — his blistering attack upon the American farmer:

The same mountebanks who get to Washington by promising to augment his [the farmer's] gains and make good his losses devote whatever time is left over from that enterprise to saddling the rest of us with oppressive and idiotic laws, all hatched on the farm. There, where the cows low through the still night, and the jug of Peruna stands behind the stove, and bathing begins, as at Biarritz, with the vernal equinox — there is the reservoir of all the nonsensical legislation which makes the United States a buffoon among the great nations. It was among country Methodists, practitioners of a theology degraded almost to the level of voodooism, that Prohibition was invented, and it was by country Methodists . . . that it was fastened upon the rest of us, to the damage of our bank accounts, our dignity and our viscera. What lay under it, and under all the other crazy enactments of its category, was no more and no less than the yokel's congenital and incurable hatred of the city man — his simian rage against everyone who, as he sees it, is having a better time than he is.[24]

Mencken's view of the hostility of the common man toward liberty was also expressed in his insight into the truly puzzling question: How did the overwhelming majority of conscripts manage to adjust so readily to the enslavement of Army life?

All save a small minority of them came from environments a great deal less comfortable than an Army camp. . . . At one stroke they were relieved of that haunting uncertainty about subsistence which is the curse of all poor and ignorant young men, and also of all need to experiment and decide for themselves. They were fed and clothed at the public expense . . . and could engage freely in sports and other divertissements forbidden in their native places. Their lives, in brief, were not unlike those of the inmates of a well-run prison, but with . . . the constant expectation of release on some near tomorrow — not as

263

[22] *Mencken Chrestomathy*, pp. 167-68.
[23] Mencken, *Letters*, p. 109.
[24] *Mencken Chrestomathy*, pp. 363-64.

wards of nosey cops and parole officers, but as heroes. . . . Not only did someone else decide what they should wear, where they should sleep, when they should get up and when they should go to bed, and what they should eat and when: all these accommodations were provided for them plentifully, and at no expense to themselves. In brief, the burden of responsibility was lifted from them altogether. . . .

The average soldier . . . found in the Army a vastly more spacious life, with many of the privileges of a chartered libertine. . . . If he did a little stealing it was one of his privileges as a savior of humanity. If he was rough and brutal it was a sign of his fighting spirit. Moreover, he could look forward to distinction and respect for the rest of his life, with a long list of special privileges. In every community in America, however small, there are local notables whose notability rests wholly on the fact that they were once drafted into some war or other. . . . Their general intelligence is shown by the kind of ideas they advocate. They are, in the main, bitter enemies of the liberty of the individual, and are responsible for some of the worst corruptions of politics. The most grasping of all politicians is the war veteran.[25]

Mencken, in fact, was an arch "isolationist" who bitterly opposed American entry into both World Wars I and II. He often remarked that he was opposed to intervention in both wars, but that if America *had to* intervene, it should have intervened on the other side. In April, 1942, he wrote jocularly to a friend: "The coming summer promises to provide Christian men with the best show seen on earth since the Crusades. I am looking forward to it with the most eager anticipations. I only hope that if the Japs actually take California they are polite to you."[26] And to his old friend Harry Elmer Barnes, Mencken wrote, in September, 1943, that "I am so constituted that I have to either Tell It All or stay silent altogether. In this war, as in the last, it seems to me to be most rational to save up what I have to say until it can be said freely."[27]

Mencken's reaction to the dropping of the atom bomb was understandably bitter. Two years after the event, he wrote to Julian Boyd that

The atom bomb, I have long preached, is the greatest invention that Yahweh has made since leprosy. Certainly it has given great glory to the Christian physicists of this country. Try to imagine a decent cannibal throwing it on a town full of women and children.[28]

Mencken was particularly concerned with the well-nigh absolute suppression of civil liberties that seems inevitably to stem from participation in war, and in the conduct of World War I he saw the exemplar of his jaundiced view of democracy, the State, foreign intervention, and the common man. One of Mencken's funniest "buffooneries" was his proposal to decorate lavishly the "home front" heroes of World War I:

What I propose is a variety of the Distinguished Service Medal for civilians . . . to mark off varying services to democracy. . . . for the university president who prohibited the teaching of the enemy language in his learned grove, heaved the works of Goethe out of the university library, cashiered every professor unwilling to support Woodrow for the first vacancy in the Trinity, took to the stump for the National Security League, and made two hundred speeches in moving picture theaters —for this giant of loyal endeavor let no 100 per cent American speak of anything less than the grand cross of the order, with a gold badge in stained glass, a baldric of the national colors, a violet plug hat with a sunburst on the side, the privilege of the floor of Congress, and a pension of $10,000 a year. . . .

Palmer and Burleson I leave for special legislation. If mere university presidents, such as Nicholas Murray Butler, are to have the grand cross, then Palmer deserves to be rolled in malleable gold from head to foot, and polished until he blinds the cosmos. . . .[29]

There is no space here to discuss Mencken's other notable contributions — his dissections of Veblen, Wilson, and Theo-

[25] *Ibid.,* pp. 93-95.
[26] Mencken, *Letters,* p. 463.
[27] *Ibid.,* p. 476.

[28] *Ibid.,* p. 501.
[29] *Mencken Chrestomathy,* pp. 601-05.

264

dore Roosevelt, his being the first person to write books on Nietzsche or George Bernard Shaw, his. . . . But let it suffice to say that America desperately needs another Mencken, and that the reader should consider the above a tantalizing sample of Menckeniana to spur him toward more of the rich and copious product available. There is no better way of concluding than to turn to Mencken's noble and moving Credo, written for a "What I Believe" series in a leading magazine:

> I believe that no discovery of fact, however trivial, can be wholly useless to the race, and that no trumpeting of falsehood, however virtuous in intent, can be anything but vicious.
> I believe that all government is evil, in that all government must necessarily make war upon liberty, and that the democratic form is as bad as any of the other forms. . . .
> I believe in complete freedom of thought and speech — alike for the humblest man and the mightiest, and in the utmost freedom of conduct that is consistent with living in organized society.
> I believe in the capacity of man to conquer his world, and to find out what it is made of, and how it is run.
> I believe in the reality of progress.
> I ——
> But the whole thing, after all, may be put very simply. I believe that it is better to tell the truth than to lie. I believe that it is better to be free than to be a slave. And I believe that it is better to know than to be ignorant.[30]

---

[30] H. L. Mencken, "What I Believe," *The Forum* (September, 1930), p. 139.

265

Individualism and Corporations

RICHARD   W. DUESENBERG

A GREAT PARADOX OF AMERICA in the decades at midcentury has been the dual assumption that the inevitable corporateness of a growing and more complex society is evil, and that this evil can only be corrected by actions of the government. Acting as though the government were something other than collective coercion, politicians and public alike have ignored its invasion of our private lives as they have given it the power to clip the wings of some and to nourish the power grabs of others.

The whipping boy of the New Deal was big business. And it still is. A steady stream of "bright young men" from the colleges has been entering government service with the express purpose of doing as much damage as possible to an industrial complex that has provided the American people with the highest standard of living in the history of mankind.

In addition, much popular literature of recent years has devoted itself to deploring the conformity allegedly demanded by modern corporateness. This has been the theme of many best-selling novels and professors, clerics and journalists have taken up the cry—bemoaning the loss of individuality and the depersonalization of modern man. There may indeed be such a trend, but it is not necessarily because corporate activ-

Richard W. Duesenberg is Associate Professor of Law at the New York University School of Law and editor of the *Annual Survey of American Law* and *Survey of New York Law*.

ity is not individualistic. In this essay, I propose to analyze the ideas of individualism and corporateness and to make plain what I believe to be the sole preservative of true individualism.

Before denouncing or criticizing the corporate society, a fair-minded person ought to first analyze the nature of concerted action. We hear much these days about John Doe's being a mere number among many thousands in the Gary Steel mills. Yet, can one argue that the endless lines of flaming stacks and giant furnaces are in themselves an evil? They are inanimate objects, capable of performing only upon human direction; and they are a means of production which a heavily-populated world needs for survival. Insofar as they serve that purpose they are of positive value. Criticism of the corporate society must be more than a nostalgic brief for the pleasures of a former time. However, many and varied were the virtues of the agrarian past, and the task we have before us is that of carrying into the new age the best of the old.

To do this we must first be clear about what it is that we are trying to preserve; that is, we must define "individualism." This is not easy to do since the idea includes all of human personality. And yet, the very vastness and complexity of individuality is the strongest support for individualism as a political and economic creed. No single mind can know all of history, all of biology, all of the myriads of desires of a single person in any one of a multitude of circumstances, let alone all of these and more combined. Yet, it is the assumption that this is possible, or nearly possible, which underlies much collectivistic thought.

I regret that this vogue of planners and bureaucratic demagogues includes many college and university professors who seem either to miscomprehend freedom's heritage or to be obsessed with visions of themselves as administrative princes.

The best definition of the term that I know of is to be found in the writing of F. A. Hayek. Individualism, he says quite correctly, is a theory of society, "an attempt to understand the forces which determine the social life of man. . . . Its basic contention . . . is that there is no other way toward an understanding of social phenomena but through our understanding of individual actions directed toward other people and guided by their expected behavior." It contends further that the "institutions on which human achievements rest have arisen and are functioning without a designing and directing mind." In substance, Hayek's definition is that "individualism is freedom lived."

The primary point of this definition is, of course, the insistence on the genius of undesigned progress. A society of men, free to choose individually, and therefore free to make as many successes or failures as there are choices freely made, is definitely greater than the controlled society, limited to the powers and finite qualities of its collective controlling mind.

This does not mean that individualists are only concerned with the economic wastefulness of error on the part of the planners; they are even more concerned with the tragedies that occur when a brilliant man or a useful idea is left undiscovered by society because the "powers-that-be" were short-sighted or petty men. The defenders of freedom, of course, hold no brief for crackpots, but they permit crackpots to try out their ideas since they know that this is the only way we can insure that viable inventions will be introduced to society.

The amalgamation of the individual into a collective unit manifests itself in many ways and consequences. Organization is, however, a phenomenon consistent with the best traditions of freedom and individualism. It is patently obvious that most of what is considered materially beneficial would be unavailable without concerted effort and concentrated capital. It is important not to confuse organization *per se* with the depersonalization of the individual, for the individual choice to unite with others for a common achievement is as much a manifestation of individualism as is one's decision to go anything alone. This is so, at least as long as the joining is freely entered, free, that is, of a conscious coercion by a planning entity's commands. If the right not to join, or having joined, to withdraw, is reserved and implemented by legal sanctions, the propensity toward depersonalization is minimized. I do not believe it necessary to view a corporate society as necessarily destructive of or conducive to the breakdown of individualism. What is essential is a construction of a legal order which permits the manifestations of free choice, and which denies to any legal personality the absolute power to compel collectivism.

A *sine qua non* for maximization of individual choice is the formulation of principles upon which a society is to be constructed and the application of them to all units therein. The pragmatism of deciding each issue or case "on its merits" as an *ad hoc* proposition fails for want of a necessary ingredient of any good law, predictability. The alleged judiciousness of a society which does not feel itself bound to fixed principles is, in fact, not judiciousness, but simply a lack of principle, a drifting toward the point of not more, but less free will.

If we were to ask which characteristics of the Anglo-American legal system were most indispensable to individual freedom, we would have to head our list with the right to freedom of contract and the right to private property.

Many seem to be of the notion that private property and individuality are not necessarily related. Such a notion is preposterous, since neither can endure without the other. Some element of private property has existed in every known society, free and unfree, and the degree of freedom varies in direct proportion to the scope of private property rights. In view of this, it is startling that some theologians and parts of the organized church are among the antagonists, until, it should be noted, the deprivation comes too close to home (urban planning and the zoning off of religious institutions, for instance).

In his *Essays in Individualism*, Felix Morley has written that: "It would seem that those American theologians whose collectivism induces them to pick from anthropology what they think supports their view on the unrelatedness of private property to human nature, have not only falsified anthropological data but also by implication attack the universality of the family. It is significant that the only truly equalitarian communities in our present world, certain villages in Israel, operate under a system that keeps children from the day of birth until age eighteen in communal nursing homes with the express purpose of extirpating the notion of private property."

Most of what can be said for private property as a necessary prop of individualism can also be said of freedom of contract. Private property permits one to acquire, to keep, and to dispose. Freedom to contract permits contracting, acquiring the right to insist on the benefit contracted for or claim damages, or not to contract. Each enlarges the security of the individual to do as he will and is able, to acquire and keep what is legally his, a point worth bearing in mind when listening to the current suggestion that the choice of modern man is between freedom and security. Freedom is the best means to security. Sociologists often talk of the absolute security of a prisoner, when attempting a contrast of freedom and security. It is like saying a slave is secure. Secure he is, secured to the whim, caprice, love, hatred, fits and passions of his master, secured to his property, to the unappealable decision of his master to extinguish his life. The same is true of a prisoner, be he behind bars, or a member in a society

where the dictatorship of the General Will prevails. To recall a perceptive quote of John Locke's: "For I have reason to conclude that he who would get me into his power without my consent, would use me as he pleased when he had got me there, and destroy me, too, when he had a fancy to it; for nobody can desire to have me in his absolute power unless it be to compel me by force to that which is against the right of my freedom, i.e., make me a slave."

The concept of a society, of course, does not rule out limitations on property and contract. The maximization of one's enjoyment from his property implies a restraint from injury to another's. Likewise, the right to contract means to contract voluntarily, free from coercion and fraud. An involuntarily entered contract is not, properly speaking, a contract at all. Contracts against public policy, such as not to marry, not to have children, in restraint of trade, to murder or to plot the destruction of another's rights, have never been recognized or enforced. A contract not to join a union while in a given employment might well be argued to be unenforceable, because it invades the choice of the individual employees. In the converse, a closed shop, the now illegal requirement to be unionized before employed, might be held to be unenforceable under concepts of free contract and property rights. Indeed, the compulsion to join a union after taking employment (the union shop as distinguished from the closed shop) might be illegal for the same reason. The authority given by the state to unions to monopolize the labor market is demonstrably responsible for the exaggerated corruption n o w infesting American organized labor, and it is as hideous an example of the degeneration of individuality as is conceivable. And why is it not recognized that the poorest excuse for the existence of anything, including a union, is the fact that it can perpetuate itself by the power given it through legislation, rather than the acceptance won by it in the operation of the marketplace? Because it is demonstrable that a religious rearing contributes substantially to the prospects of maturing into a well-disciplined adult, it is just as logical to argue that churches should be given the power to compel membership in them as a condition to receiving a public education.

The greatest threats to individuality, without a doubt, come from the government, either itself acting as agent to extract co-operation from individuals, or acting indirectly by giving to another the power to compel submission. If interventionist policies are looked at from a moral perspective, they are considerably inferior to the free and voluntary actions of society. There is no moral merit to support of social welfare if non-support lands the recalcitrant in jail. Morally, state intervention in social security, federal aid to education, subsidies, etc., however ornamented by glossy phrases of humanitarianism, are reactionary and retrogressive. And the growing galaxy of governmental paternalism poses a real threat to the multitude of privately sponsored organs of our society which have depended in the past on the voluntary charitable support of individuals choosing to further their objectives. It may well be that private education, like other private actions, and consequently the scope of available choices, will in time be starved out of existence because of the tax extortions which paralyze the source of support for concerted private action.

There are some areas of American law where individuality may still prosper almost without restraint. Free speech is staunchly protected by a whole line of Supreme Court cases. One of the paradoxes of the Court in the past several decades has been its singling out of some civil rights for shielding from state intervention, while ignoring or actually permitting others to be eroded away. Actually, such action can be explained by the almost Bohemian-like concept some people, usually collectivists, have of individuality. One such writer recently declared that:

A final ambiguity in the problem of individualism remains to be faced. "Individualism" is used in American discourse, particularly in political argument, to refer to economic endeavor and enterprise. It connotes striving in some self-reliant and rela-

tively unfettered (particularly by government) way for achievement and success, in short, the acquisitive urge. This notion is not identical with what we call "individuality"— the right to "be one's self," to develop one's own individual personality as far as possible according to one's own values and tastes, to be different, to be a non-conformist, to dissent from orthodoxy if one thinks it necessary, in short, the right to diversity.

Such a definition is blatantly short-sighted, indeed dishonest, if it does not include first and foremost the right to pursue the satisfaction of what the writer called the acquisitive urge. America has been the most individualistic country in history because of this right, and because the practical result of this right has been the widest conceivable assortment of goods with which each could satisfy to the best of his ability the pleasures he craved. I wonder seriously if the author learned his individualism by observing ONLY the incarcerated, the denizens of Greenwich Village, or the inhabitants of a Chinese commune.

Though organization may be inevitable, and may substantially alter the shape of things present from the past, it is not at all incompatible with individual expression. The task of modern man, if he is genuinely concerned with individuality, is to elevate to the status of an immutable moral principle the concept of individual freedom, by which is meant not equality, not happiness, not poverty, not unlimited choice, not security, not necessarily any or all of these, but the opportunity for each man to achieve his own ends, each in his own way.

When libertarians say that individualism should be made a matter of moral principle, they emphatically do not mean that this shall be the objective of society. The value of individualism lies in the fact that it encourages pluralism, thrives on dissent and permits the pursuit of all legitimate objectives while it resolves disputes as collisions of interests arise. It permits the pursuit of particular objectives by everyone, individually or collectively, without the coercion of state intervention.

269

Page Thirty-one

Conservatives, Cities,
and Mrs. Jacobs[1]

JOHN WEICHER

FOR MANY YEARS, conservative political theorists and practical politicians, attempting to demonstrate the relevance of their beliefs to the twentieth century, have regularly run into the rebuttal, "But you don't have any solutions to city problems. What you say about states' rights or self-reliance, or individualism, used to be valid, but it isn't now when most Americans are living in cities and super-cities. What are you going to do about *them?*"

Conservatives and libertarians have seldom had an answer. Many of them tend to regard cities as things to be avoided; advocates of this view range from philosophers in solitary retreats to small-town politicians denouncing Big City Democratic Machines. Others have said the only problem is that conservatives just haven't tried to organize and sell their message in cities. This is true enough. But one reason they have not tried is that nobody has told the organization what to say; nobody has worked out implications of conservatism or libertarianism for cities. About the only talking point conservatives have had is that property taxes are too high. If they have opposed urban renewal, it has been because they don't like Federal inter-

vention in local affairs, and they have offered no substitute plan for dealing with the obvious problems confronting our cities.

Although it was not her intention, Jane Jacobs has gone far toward providing conservatives with an urban program. Mrs. Jacobs says little about politics, and what she does say is not particularly conservative; she favors government subsidies for low-income housing, for example. But her politics are not important, and her book is. *The Death and Life of Great American Cities* is permeated with conservative and free-market attitudes. As she castigates the planners of housing-project Utopias that leave no room for their inhabitants to make any plans of their own, one is reminded of Edmund Burke: "The nature of man is intricate; the objects of society are of the greatest possible complexity; and therefore no simple disposition or direction of power can be suitable either to man's nature, or to the quality of his affairs. When I hear the simplicity of contrivance aimed at and boasted of in any new political constitutions, I am at no loss to decide that the artificers are grossly ignorant of their trade, or

---

John Weicher is an Associate Editor of *New Individualist Review.*

1. A review of Jane Jacobs, *The Death and Life of Great American Cities* (New York: Random House, 1961).

totally ignorant of their duty." Mrs. Jacobs says much the same thing. "City processes in real life are too complex to be routine, too particularized for application as abstractions. They are changes made up of interaction among unique combinations of particulars." Her whole book is an elaboration upon two themes: "Rome wasn't built in a day," and Burke's statement, "I must see the things, I must see the men." Mrs. Jacobs shows us the things and the men.

Diversity, she insists, makes a city or city neighborhood successful. The various components of this diversity support each other in creating liveliness. After an illuminating discussion of how city neighborhoods f u n c t i o n socially, in which she establishes her case for diversity as a good thing, Mrs. Jacobs gets to "the most important part of this book," the four ingredients which generate it:

(1) A neighborhood must have two or more primary functions, in order that people are outdoors at different times for different purposes.

(2) It must have short blocks, so that streets are not isolated and the neighborhood can be knit together.

(3) It must have old as well as new buildings, in varying conditions.

(4) It must have a high density of population, both working and residential.

Each prerequisite — and almost every other statement in the book — is illustrated with examples from existing American cities, generally New York or others on the East Coast. I am inclined to wonder if Mrs. Jacobs' apparent greater familiarity with Eastern cities may not have led her into a few mistakes. For instance, she sets the minimum density for her fourth prerequisite at 100 dwelling units to the net residential acre, a figure which is higher than now exists in most of Chicago. Mrs. Jacobs herself points out that the very successful Back-of-the-Yards neighborhood in Chicago has a density of "well under" 100, which she explains by pointing out that it covers a larger geographical area than the usual mile and a half square of most neighborhoods, and that it is politically powerful and skillful. As on

most other subjects, Mrs. Jacobs has interesting things to say about city politics, including examples of how to fight City Hall and how to get money for gradual redevelopment of a neighborhood (instead of being blacklisted by banks or subjected to huge projects financed by "cataclysmic money"). But she does not suggest any special reasons why other neighborhoods could not be as politically potent as the Back-of-the-Yards, even if they were also below 100 dwelling units per acre.

However, with the way population is growing in this country, this question may become academic quickly; cities may have to be as dense as Mrs. Jacobs desires simply in order to absorb people. In the Chicago area, huge apartment houses are being proposed for the North Shore suburbs, which now contain only single-family homes.

The one important factor Mrs. Jacobs leaves out is race and ethnic background. She is quite right in pointing out that successful and unsuccessful neighborhoods are not those which keep Negroes out and let them in, respectively. When whites with freedom of choice leave a neighborhood, something is wrong with it, and the lower-income Negroes (or whites) who move in are an effect and not a cause of failure. But this is not the whole story.

Mrs. Jacobs credits the unionization of the packinghouse workers living in Back-of-the-Yards with helping to overcome the old nationality antagonisms and creating an effective district. My own impression is that anti-Negro feeling also played an important part. In 1956, I worked in a packing plant during the summer, when the Democratic National Convention was held in the International Amphitheatre two blocks away. A few days before the convention, the United Packinghouse Workers of America held a rally during the lunch break, at which officials of the UPWA and NAACP spoke. I asked another worker after the rally what it was all about, and he said, "They told us to support Harriman because Stevenson was against the Negroes." He added, "If Stevenson is, he gets my vote." This man represented the general attitude in

271

the neighborhood, I think; certainly he was representative of the plant. Of course, people want to preserve a neighborhood because they like it, and not just to "keep the Negroes out," but the latter motive can be a powerful catalyst in the process of preserving and upgrading a neighborhood. On the positive side, as Mrs. Jacobs admits, "strong city neighborhoods are frequently ethnic communities," because one factor which can promote a sense of community is a common ethnic background. A series of articles in the *Cleveland Plain Dealer* in 1959, "Why Neighborhoods Stay Good," noted that several of the successful neighborhoods were composed almost entirely of one or another nationality group. Probably in time this factor will become less and less important, but it does not seem accurate to ignore it now.

272

CITY PLANNERS get a thorough going-over in *The Death and Life of Great American Cities*. Mrs. Jacobs attacks the concept of public housing projects, which destroy neighborhoods and call attention to the poverty of their residents. She offers a proposal that, for those who support the idea of subsidized housing, is far more rational than 15-story prison towers and "grass, grass, grass." She also has some trenchant criticism of the accounting practices used in evaluating costs and benefits of public housing and urban renewal; a full accounting would include the losses of businessmen who are forced to leave the project area, being wiped out in the process and receiving next to nothing for their property. "They are subsidizing these schemes, not with a fraction of their tax money, but with their livelihoods, with their children's college money, with years of their past put into hopes for the future—with nearly everything they have. . . . The community as a whole has not seen fit to bear that whole expense, and it is never going to. Redevelopment officials and housing experts blanch when it is suggested. . . . Were the involuntary subsidies which make these schemes possible included as public costs, the enlarged public costs

would bear no conceivable relationship to anticipated tax returns [i.e., increased taxes from the improved area].

This is a familiar story in public finance. The Army Engineers have been notorious for their fantastically inflated estimates of benefits for public works projects, but cost-benefit studies of individual projects by competent academic economists have started to push the Engineers toward more realistic accounting. Similar results might be expected from studies of urban renewal projects which included the losses of businesses wiped out by the project and other costs now overlooked, particularly real estate taxes, which are now not charged on public housing. If, as Mrs. Jacobs believes, the additional costs make urban renewal projects totally uneconomic, then those who advocate them should either base their arguments on non-economic criteria, or else drop the projects altogether; justification by false accounting is the least defensible alternative.

MRS. JACOBS also has written the finest short discussion of Metropolitan Government that I know of. She points out that city governments currently are unable to solve the problems of interdepartment communication, and that there is no point in creating still larger governmental units when the largest ones we now have are unfathomable bureaucratic labyrinths. What is needed is a system of geographic administrative districts within cities. In each district, locally, municipal services would be planned and coordinated, since it is on a local scale that most city planning is really carried out. The administrators of the police and other services would know their districts intimately; also, each district would be helped to function as a unit, politically and socially. Not all services could be so decentralized, of course, but many could be. I would be inclined to add one more to those Mrs. Jacobs mentions: schools, with locally-elected school boards. Mrs. Jacobs is critical of efforts to plan city neighborhoods on a basis of elementary school districts, but in Chicago, at least, the average public high school district contains about 80,000 to 90,000 people, which is just under her estimate of minimum effective district size. Schools can be effective means of unifying districts, particularly if local control is established.

I have mentioned just two of the areas in which Mrs. Jacobs clarifies a problem for us. In discussing automobiles, neighborhood parks, already-existing public housing, *The Death and Life of Great American Cities* offers new ideas. Moreover, from the number of quotations taken from urban specialists, one gets the impression that the ideas have been gradually occurring to the professional students of cities, so that we may see a revamping of current city planning within a reasonably short period of time; Mrs. Jacobs is a pioneer, but not a solitary one. In parts she is synthesizing the work of other people who have mentioned some of the points she makes. And this is all to the good, because we ourselves, the city dwellers, have made the mess we live in. "It is so easy to blame the decay of cities on traffic . . . or immigrants . . . or the whimsies of the middle class. The decay of cities goes deeper and is more complicated. It goes right down to what we think we want, and to our ignorance about how cities work." "We have, therefore, no one to blame for this but ourselves." Mrs. Jacobs has given us new visions and new techniques for achieving them. It may yet be that conservatives can show they have something relevant to say about cities, and all of us will find that cities are not inherently unmanageable, and can be made fit to live in.

273

Housing in Latin America,

Public and Private[1]

SAM PELTZMAN

274

ALAN CARNOY DEVELOPED a successful home building business in the suburbs of New York City in the post World War II building boom. Since much of his building experience was concentrated in low priced homes, why not, he reasoned, apply this experience to the construction of homes for the rising middle class in Latin America; American building techniques had theretofore been almost non-existent in that part of the world. Thus it was that Carnoy American Building Corp. became Carnoy de Mexico, S. A. However, Carnoy soon found that there was more to duplicating American building techniques in Latin America than mere change of venue. In the U. S. he had had the benefit of a highly developed mortgage market and a relatively tractable legal system, both essential to large scale home development. In Mexico the situation was drastically altered. There he found extensive government interference, red tape, and an overly complex and ambiguous legal system, all of which encouraged an almost universal government corruption. Needless to say, such an environment had hardly been con-

ducive to the development of a smoothly functioning mortgage market either. This same pattern, Carnoy found, was general in all of Latin America. Thus, to this day his plan for bringing the advantages of low cost privately owned homes to Latin America has hardly been a rousing success, in spite of the fact that a potential market for such homes does exist in all of the larger cities of Latin America.

This rather r u d e awakening has greatly affected Carnoy's policy proposals. He is deeply convinced that widespread home ownership in Latin America is both economically feasible and a potential a n t i d o t e to the spread of communism there. Therefore, he argues, it is in our own cold war interest to encourage the spread of home ownership. The basic hurdles to be overcome are, as just mentioned, excessive government regulation with its attendant red tape, archaic laws and corruption, and the lack of a highly developed market for mortgages without which widespread home ownership is impossible. We can do very little to change the former, but, Carnoy claims, we can do something to change the latter. If only

Sam Peltzman, a graduate of City College of New York, is now a Ford Foundation Fellow in the Department of Economics, University of Chicago. He has recently become business manager of *New Individualist Review.*

1. A review of *Democracia — Si! A Way to Win the Cold War* by Alan Carnoy (New York: Vantage Press, 1962).

our foreign aid authorities undertook a small program to provide loans to private home builders in Latin America at going interest rates and guaranteed against default of principal, we will have gotten the ball rolling. Once one sizeable project has been so financed and its success demonstrated, the Latin American governments will be encouraged to modify their laws and so encourage the growth of local capital markets for home construction; widespread home ownership there will become a reality, and Latin America will be safe for democracy.

One might, with much justification I would think, dismiss this out of hand as mere special interest pleading for a subsidy. However, I would prefer to deal with the proposal on its own merits and argue that it is not likely to accomplish Carnoy's objective. Certainly Carnoy knows better than I whether low cost private homes in Latin America are economically feasible or not, and neither will I quarrel with his premise, overly simple as it is, that widespread home ownership can be of assistance in the fight against communism. However, I am sure that Carnoy would agree that his objective can ultimately be realized only if the Latin American governments themselves remove the interferences, red tape and corruption which have heretofore retarded the growth of capitalist enterprise in home building as well as other industries. Indeed, Carnoy spends a good portion of his book chronicling the enormous potential and actual achievements of private enterprise in home construction (about which more below) and decrying the obstacles he found to private enterprise in Latin America. Yet, what would be an important result if his proposal became law? It would, even if initially successful, remove any incentive the Latin governments might have had to engage in needed reforms. The home builders, who might before have brought some pressure to bear on the local govern-

2. One recalls in this context that our domestic farm price support program was initiated merely to tide the farmers over the depression of the 1930's.

ments to relax restrictions on the free flow of capital, would now have that capital provided them on attractive terms from Washington. Why should they worry about the chaotic state of the local mortgage market? Indeed, given that this credit made home building easier and less costly, would not the government bureaucrats have an incentive to actually increase the red tape and so siphon off some of the *norteamericano* largesse in increased bribes? Of course, Carnoy sees this as only a small once-for-all project to "show the way." However, who can really believe that, with both builders and local politicians benefiting, it will remain so?[2] Also, it must be considered that the proposal would make land expropriation on the part of the Latin governments much more attractive than at present. With Washington guaranteeing the principal of the loan, the builder would lose nothing and the government gain the monthly mortgage payments by expropriating the developments. The ultimate result of Carnoy's proposal, it seems to me, can only be to encourage even more interference with the free flow of capital than now exists, and impose the costs thereof on the U. S. taxpayer.

IN CONTRAST TO the weaknesses of his major policy proposals, Carnoy is on far more substantial ground when he deals with the home building industry as he has known it. In fact, his chapter entitled, "Government Building vs. Private Building" is one of the best discussions of the subject I have ever seen. Here Carnoy employs his considerable knowledge of the economics of home building, public and private, North American and Latin American, and comes to one simple conclusion: "I do not see how [public housing] can ever be to the advantage of the majority of the people in any country." He backs this conclusion up with numerous references to his own experience with the monumental inefficiency of public housing. Consider, for example, Carnoy's experience with a public housing project in Westchester County, New York:

275

The (budgeted) cost of a 750 square foot (five room) apartment in this [public housing] project is $14,250. [I] can build an 800 square foot (5½ room) private home on a 50 x 100 foot lot for $9,000 (*including the land . . . and I did.*)[3]

Much the same story is outlined for Latin America. Yet, even given this fairly incredible waste of resources, what manner of product is it that the taxpayer is subsidizing? From the White Plains, New York project where a tenant confided to the author: "We all dream of getting out of here," to the French housing project which won a prize for design but was full of tenants complaining of the shoddy construction, to the Middle Eastern project devoid of any tenants, complaining or otherwise, because it had been built in the middle of the desert far away from the necessary utilities, the answer is the same — too little for too much. The reasons for the superiority of private over public building are stated so simply and succinctly by Carnoy that they deserve repetition here:

1. Private enterprise does not cost the country anything. An independent builder invests his own money, and when he borrows from the bank, he has to pay his loan back. When people buy his houses or rent his apartments, *they* will pay for them . . .

2. Private enterprise has a powerful master — the public. If the prospective clients don't like the location, they will not rent or buy. The prices are subject to public acceptance and competition, and this is the monumental factor in favor of the purchaser or the tenant.[4]

What then is the reason for the growth of public housing, inferior as it is? On

this, Carnoy is quite blunt:

I think that the political power which a government gets through housing is probably its primary reason for going into the building business.[5]

Carnoy details how, for example, in Latin America, favored labor unions get government credit while these same governments restrict the availability of credit to private builders, how space in projects is distributed on the basis of favoritism and bribery, etc. Using public housing as a means to political power has also had some interesting side results. Carnoy tells of the Venezuelan government's attempt to curry favor with the labor unions by building a public housing complex for them. This had the incidental effect of herding thousands of workers together in a central location where they could be effectively harangued *en masse* by left-wing agitators. The result was the Caracas riots of 1960.

In summary, the reader will find *Democracia—Si!* a curious mixture of noble sentiments far more difficult of attainment than the author realizes and well informed commentary on the realities of his own industry today, all embellished by a steady stream of anecdotes derived from a life far more varied than has even been indicated here. The book permits of no easy judgment, except that it recalls some of Adam Smith's remarks on the advantages of specialization.

---

3. Italics mine.
4. Italics mine

5. To be sure, the desire for political power is not the only motive behind public housing. Another factor which Carnoy feels important is the collectivist mystique which is operative in the most well intentioned government planners: "Somehow, to a government official this word [housing] implies thousands of attached units rather than .. .. .. detached homes with gardens."

276

NEW BOOKS AND ARTICLES

THE FOLLOWING IS A SELECT LIST OF BOOKS AND ARTICLES WHICH, IN THE OPINION OF THE EDITORS, MAY BE OF INTEREST TO OUR READERS.

Martin Bailey, *National Income and the Price Level*. (New York: McGraw-Hill, 1962).

Paul Bakewell, Jr., 13 *Curious Errors About Money*. (Caldwell, Idaho: Caxton Press, 1962).

George C. S. Benson, *et al.*, *Essays on Federalism*. (Claremont, California: Claremont College, 1962).

H. N. Brailsford, *The Levellers and the English Revolution*. (Stanford, California: Stanford University Press, 1962).

Jeremy Bentham, *Handbook of Political Fallacies*. (New York: Harper Torchbooks, 1962). Paper.

Paul V. Birdsall, *Versailles* 20 *Years After*. (Hamden, Connecticut: Shoestring Press, 1962).

Frank Chodorov, *Out of Step*. (New York: Devin-Adair, 1962).

Smith Hempstone, *Rebels, Mercenaries and Dividends*: *the Katanga Story*. (New York: Praeger, 1962).

Gertrude Himmelfarb, *Lord Acton*. (Chicago: University of Chicago Press, 1962). Paper.

William R. Kintner and Joseph Z. Kornfeder, *The New Frontier of War*. (Chicago: Henry Regnery, 1962).

John McCormick and Mairi MacInnes, *Versions of Censorship*. (Chicago: Aldine Press, 1962).

Francis J. Nock, ed., *Selected Letters of Albert Jay Nock*. (Caldwell, Idaho: Caxton Press, 1962).

G. Warren Nutter, *The Growth of Industrial Production in the Soviet Union*. (Princeton: Princeton University Press, 1962).

Claude Robinson, *Understanding Profits*. (Princeton: Van Nostrand, 1962).

Christian Rochefort, *Children of Heaven*. (New York: McKay, 1962).

George Rude, *Wilkes and Liberty*. (Oxford: Oxford University Press, 1962).

Francis Russell, *Tragedy in Dedham*. (New York: McGraw-Hill, 1962).

M. K. Singleton, *H. L. Mencken and the* American Mercury *Adventure*. (Durham, North Carolina: Duke University Press, 1962).

Lewis L. Strauss, *Men and Decisions*. (New York: Doubleday, 1962).

Philippa Schuyler, *Who Killed the Congo?* (New York: Devin-Adair, 1962).

Edward Bennett Williams, *One Man's Freedom*. (New York: Atheneum, 1962).

Dover Woodcock, *Anarchism*. (New York: Meridian, 1962). Paper.

W. F. Rickenbacker, "A Proposal for the Airlines," *National Review*, July 17, 1962.

George V. Taylor, "The Paris Bourse on the Eve of the Revolution, 1781-1789," *American Historical Review*, July, 1962.

Richard Weaver, "A Great Individualist," (Review of *The Letters of H. L. Mencken*), *Modern Age*, Spring, 1962.

Richard S. Wheeler, "Deliver Us from Evil," *Insight & Outlook*, Summer, 1962.

277

New Individualist Review welcomes contributions for publication from its readers. Essays should not exceed 3,000 words, and should be type-written. All manuscripts will receive careful consideration.

In Future Issues . . .

NEW INDIVIDUALIST REVIEW will feature articles by young libertarian and conservative writers as well as by such scholars as WILHELM ROEPKE, RICHARD WEAVER, and MURRAY N. ROTHBARD.

To keep up with today's ferment of individualist ideas — subscribe to NEW INDIVIDUALIST REVIEW today.

* * * *

NEW INDIVIDUALIST REVIEW has come a long way since we made the above promise to readers of our first issue, over a year ago. Our circulation has grown steadily with each succeeding issue. Students at campuses across the country have volunteered their time to make NIR available to their colleagues. We have readers in nearly every state and more than a dozen foreign countries. Our original staff of five editors has more than doubled; most of the new members are undergraduates who will ensure that NIR continues after the founders have left school. We are well on the road to permanence.

Perhaps as important, NIR has brought libertarian and conservative ideas to a wider readership than its circulation. Articles have been reprinted in the "Wall Street Journal," the "Freeman," "Under Thirty," and other newspapers and magazines. We have been praised by other publications and individuals — the "Chicago Tribune," the "Portland Oregonian," "America," "National Review," the "New Republic," William F. Buckley, Jr., Russell Kirk, and Leonard Read, among them.

Articles have been translated into Spanish and published in Mexico and Venezuela. Professors at several colleges have requested permission to use articles for reading assignments in their courses.

In our first issue, we also said: "The NEW INDIVIDUALIST REVIEW has been founded in a commitment to human liberty. We believe in free, private enterprise, and in the imposition of the strictest limits to the power of government." If you share that belief, we invite you to subscribe to NIR, in order "to keep up with today's ferment of individualist ideas," and to help those ideas reach still more people. If you do not share it, we think you will find NIR stimulating and challenging, and perhaps persuasive.

278

"SOCIALISM is only an idea, not an historical necessity, and ideas are acquired by the human mind. We are not born with ideas, we learn them. If socialism has come to America because it was implanted in the minds of past generations, there is no reason for assuming that the contrary idea cannot be taught to a new generation. What the socialists have done can be undone, if there is a will for it. But, the undoing will not be accomplished by trying to destroy established socialistic institutions. It can be accomplished only by attacking minds, and not the minds of those already hardened by socialistic fixations. Individualism can be revived by implanting the idea in the minds of the coming generations. So then, if those who put a value on the dignity of the individual are up to the task, they have a most challenging opportunity in education before them. It is not an easy job. It requires the kind of industry, intelligence and patience that comes with devotion to an ideal."

—*Frank Chodorov*, Founder and President, Intercollegiate Society of Individualists, Inc.

INTERCOLLEGIATE SOCIETY OF INDIVIDUALISTS
For the Advancement of Conservative Thought on the Campus

629 PUBLIC LEDGER BLDG., PHILADELPHIA 6, PA., WAlnut 5-5632
Midwest Office: 505 Lemcke Bldg., Indianapolis 6. Ind., MElrose 9-5551
Western Office: 1436 El Camino Real, Menlo Park, California, 325-4553

VOLUME 2
NUMBER 3
AUTUMN 1962

New
INDIVIDUALIST
Review

Vol. 2, No. 3   35 cents   Autumn 1962

NEW INDIVIDUALIST REVIEW

Volume 2 — Number 3   **AUTUMN 1962**

285

NEW INDIVIDUALIST REVIEW is published quarterly (Spring, Summer, Autumn, Winter) by *New Individualist Review, Inc.,* at Ida Noyes Hall, University of Chicago, Chicago 37, Illinois.

Opinions expressed in signed articles do not necessarily represent the views of the editors. Editorial, advertising, and subscription correspondence and manuscripts should be sent to NEW INDIVIDUALIST REVIEW, Ida Noyes Hall, University of Chicago, Chicago 37, Illinois. All manuscripts become the property of NEW INDIVIDUALIST REVIEW.

Subscription rates: $2.00 per year (students $1.00).

NEW

INDIVIDUALIST

REVIEW

EDITORIAL BOARD

Editors-in-Chief • Ronald Hamowy • Ralph Raico
Associate Editors • Robert M. Hurt • John P. McCarthy
Robert Schuettinger • John Weicher
Business Manager • Sam Peltzman
Editorial Assistants • Jameson Campaigne, Jr. • Joe Cobb
Burton Gray • Thomas Heagy • Jerome Heater
R. P. Johnson • Robert Michaels • James Powell
James Rosenholtz

EDITORIAL ADVISORS

Milton Friedman • Richard Weaver
University of Chicago
F. A. Hayek
University of Freiburg

286

The Intellectual
and the Market Place

GEORGE J. STIGLER

THE INTELLECTUAL has never felt kindly toward the market place; to him it has always been a place of vulgar men and of base motives. Whether this intellectual was an ancient Greek philosopher, who viewed economic life as an unpleasant necessity which should never be allowed to become obtrusive or dominant, or whether this intellectual is a modern man, who focuses his scorn on gadgets and Madison Avenue, the basic similarity of view has been pronounced.

Now you and I are intellectuals, as this word is used. I am one automatically because I am a professor, and buy more books than golf clubs. You are intellectuals because you are drawn from the most intelligent tenth of the population, most of you will go on to graduate school, and you would rather be a United States Senator or a Nobel Laureate than the head of the Great Atlantic and Pacific Tea Company. The question I wish to pose to us is not whether we should love the market place — even a professor of economics of outrageously conservative tendencies cannot bring himself to say that the chants of five auctioneers rival a Mozart quintet. The questions are rather: what don't we like

---

George J. Stigler, Walgreen Professor of American Institutions at the University of Chicago, is President-elect of the American Economic Association. He is the author of numerous books on economic theory, including the well known text, *Theory of Price*, and is a contributor of numerous articles to professional journals. The above article is adapted from a speech given before a college audience.

about the market place; and, are we sure that our attitudes are socially useful?

Let us begin by noticing that from certain important viewpoints one would have expected the intellectuals to be very kindly disposed toward that system of private enterprise which I call the market place.

First, if I may introduce a practical consideration, intellectuals by and large have elevated tastes — they like to eat, dress, and live well, and especially to travel. Walton Hamilton once said that our customary salutation, "Good Day," was a vestige of an agricultural society where people were asking for good weather, and he expected city dwellers eventually to greet each other with the phrase, "Low Prices." If Hamilton's theory is correct, the intellectuals will come to the salutation, "Fair Fulbright."

Since intellectuals are not inexpensive, until the rise of the modern enterprise system no society could afford many intellectuals. As a wild guess, the full-time intellectuals numbered 200 in Athens in the extraordinary age of Pericles, or about one for every 1500 of population, and at most times in later history the intellectuals fell far, far short of this proportion. Today there are at least 1,000,000 in the United States, taking only a fraction of those who live by pen and tongue into account, or one for each 200 of population. At least four out of every five of us owe our pleasant lives to the great achievements of the market place. We professors are much more beholden to Henry Ford than to the foun-

287

Page Three

dation which bears his name and spreads his assets.

Not only have the productive achievements of the market place supported a much enlarged intellectual class, but also the leaders of the market place have personally been strong supporters of the intellectuals, and in particular those in the academic world. If one asks where, in the western university world, the freedom of inquiry of professors has been most staunchly defended and energetically promoted, my answer is this: Not in the politically controlled universities, whether in the United States or Germany — legislatures are not over-populated with tolerant men indifferent to popularity. Not in the self-perpetuating faculties, such as Oxford and Cambridge from 1700 to 1850—even intellectuals can become convinced that they have acquired ultimate truth, and that it can be preserved indefinitely by airing it before students once a year. No, inquiry has been most free in the college whose trustees are a group of top quality leaders of the market place — men who, our experience shows, are remarkably tolerant of almost everything except a mediocre and complacent faculty. Economics provides many examples: if a professor wishes to denounce aspects of big business, as I have, he will be wise to locate in a school whose trustees are big businessmen, and I have.

But debts are seldom the basis for friendship, and there is a much more powerful reason the intellectual might be sympathetic to the market place: the organizing principles of both areas are the same.

An enterprise system is a system of voluntary contract. Neither fraud nor coercion is within the ethics of the market system. Indeed there is no possibility of coercion in a pure enterprise system because the competition of rivals provides alternatives to every buyer or seller. All real economic systems contain some monopoly, and hence some coercive power for particular individuals, but the amount and the extent of such monopoly power are usually much exaggerated, and in any case monopoly

is not an integral part of the logic of the system.

The intellectual world, and I speak chiefly but not exclusively of scholarship, is also a voluntary system. Its central credo is that opinions are to be formed through free discussion on the basis of full disclosure of evidence. Fraud and coercion are equally repugnant to the scholar. The freedom of thought is preserved by the open competition of scholars and ideas. Authority, the equivalent of monopoly power, is the great enemy of freedom of inquiry. Competition in scholarship is in some ways more violent than in business: the law sets limits on the disparagement of a rival's product, unless it is done in a book review in a learned journal.

Just as real markets have some fraud and monopoly which impair the claims for the market place, so the intellectual world has its instances of coercion and deception, with the coercion exercised by claques and fashion. But again these deviants are outside the logic of the system.

Both areas, moreover, are democratic. The intellectual believes that every able and willing young person should get a good education whatever his race or financial background. The market believes every able and willing person should be permitted to enter any industry or occupation, whatever his race or educational background. There is food for thought in the fact that racial discrimination has diminished earlier, faster, and more quietly in the market place than in political life.

The analogies could be pursued much farther, although not without danger of alienating all professors and most businessmen. I shall therefore merely mention, in passing, that both fields pay a fair amount of attention to packaging and advertising, and both fields place an absurdly high value on originality. There are also many minor differences, such as that the intellectual has no desire to know the market place, whereas the businessman wishes, or at least believes he wishes, to know the world of the intellectual. The basic fact is that the intellectual believes in the free market in ideas and, what is not quite the same thing, in words.

Yet **whatever** the latent sympathies of the intellectual for the market place, the hostilities are overt. The contempt for the "profit motive" which directs economic activity is widespread, and the suspicion of the behavior to which it leads is deep-seated. The charge that American society is materialistic has been recited more often than the Declaration of Independence, and has been translated into more foreign languages.

In one basic respect I believe that the criticism by the intellectuals is misplaced, and at times even hypocritical. The American economy produces many goods that are vulgar, silly, or meretricious, as judged by standards which I share with many intellectuals. It seems only proper to cite a few examples, if only to show how selective these standards are. I shall not propose the currently most popular item, the large and powerful automobile, because I have observed that mostly intellectuals of short stature criticize our cars. But other examples are at hand. I am dissatisfied with the tastes of the nine-tenths of the population which believes that nonfictional books are to be read only by young people working for their B.A. I am dissatisfied with a population whose love for interesting music is so narrow that every symphony orchestra requires subsidies. I consider it shocking that more Americans have read *The Affluent Society* than *The Wealth of Nations*.

At the risk of appearing reasonable, I wish to qualify this complaint by observing that the tastes of the American public are more elevated than those of any other large society in history. Most societies have been judged by their cultural aristocracies — indeed in earlier periods the vast majority of the population was not even considered to be a part of the culture of the society, for this vast majority was illiterate, tradition-bound, with most people living brutishly in peasant huts. Our society's tastes are judged by those of the vast majority of the population, and this majority is generous, uncomplacent, and hard-working w i t h unprecedentedly large numbers engaged in further self-education, or eagerly patronizing the arts. Our market-supported legitimate theatre, which is surely the best in the world, is a suggestive measure of popular tastes.

These qualifications are not intended to withdraw the charge that the public's tastes should be better, and for that matter, that the intellectual's tastes should be better. It is, in fact, a basic function of the intellectual to define the standards of good taste more clearly, and to persuade people to approach them more closely. It is proper to denounce vulgarity of taste, and to denounce it more strongly the more popular it is. It is permissible to reject certain desires completely — as we do when by compulsory education laws we reject the desire for illiteracy — although there is a strong presumption against the use of force in the area of tastes.

When I say that the complaints of deficiencies in tastes are misplaced when they are directed to the market place, I mean just that. The market place responds to the tastes of consumers with the goods and services that are salable, whether the tastes are elevated or depraved. It is unfair to criticize the market place for fulfilling these desires, when clearly the defects lie in the popular tastes themselves. I consider it a cowardly concession to a false extension of the idea of democracy to make *sub rosa* attacks on public tastes by denouncing the people who serve them. It is like blaming the waiters in restaurants for obesity.

To escape this response, the more sophisticated intellectuals have argued that people are told what to want by the market place—that advertising skillfully depraves and distorts popular desires. There is no doubt an element of truth in this response, but it is an element of trifling size. The advertising industry has no sovereign power to bend men's wills — we are not children who blindly follow the last announcer's instructions to rush to the store for soap. Moreover, advertising itself is a completely neutral instrument, and lends itself to the dissemination of highly contradictory de-

289

sires. While the automobile industry tells us not to drink while driving, the bourbon industry tells us not to drive while drinking. The symphony orchestra advertises, and gets much free publicity, in its rivalry with the dance band. Our colleges use every form of advertising, and indeed the typical university catalogue would never stop Diogenes in his search for an honest man.

So I believe the intellectuals would gain in candor and in grace if they preached directly to the public instead of using advertising as a whipping boy. I believe they would gain also in virtue if they would examine their own tastes more critically: when a good comedian and a production of Hamlet are on rival channels, I wish I could be confident that less than half the professors were laughing.

The main indictment by the intellectual, however, is that the market place operates on the principle of self-interest, and in fact through competition compels even the philanthropic businessman to become self-serving. Self-interest, often described with such neutral words as egotism, greed, and dog-eat-dog, is viewed as a crass, antisocial element of man's character, and an economic system that rests upon, and inculcates, this motive achieves little admiration. In fact, a dislike for profit-seeking is one of the few specific attitudes shared by the major religions.

I also find naked selfishness an unendearing trait, but I have trouble in separating it from the more admirable motives related to it. A prudent regard for one's own survival is generally applauded even if the individual does not say, "I got out of the way of the oncoming train only to spare my Sunday School class pain." The violent endeavors of an athlete to defeat his rivals are much admired, providing the contest is more or less fair, even though the winner is expected not to say, "I am glad I won chiefly because I'm vain, but secondarily for the honor of Sheboygan High School."

Even in fields somewhat removed from the athletic arena, the roles of self-interest and what for lack of a better name I shall call benevolence are perplexingly interwoven. I have spent my life among college teachers, although admittedly in the most competitive branch of research and publication. In one sense the disinterest of my colleagues is beyond doubt: I have seen silly people — public officials as well as private, by the way — try to buy opinions, but I have not seen or even suspected any cases in which any important economist sold his professional convictions. It is also true that many of the best professors, and many of the worst, could earn more in other callings.

But on the other hand, the motives that drive them and me are not completely clear, either. When we strive to solve a scientific problem, is ambition for our own professional status completely overshadowed by our love of knowledge? I wonder. When we write an article to demonstrate the fallacies of someone else's work, is our hatred for error never mixed with a tiny bit of glee at the display of our own cleverness? I wonder.

To shift elsewhere, I have never encountered a political candidate who said, "I am running for office because I, with my dear wife and future administrative assistant, can earn more in politics than elsewhere." Nor do I expect to. But the language of public interest surely covers a good many acres of self-interest.

A major source of the view that the market place places special values on self-interest, beyond those more or less evident in all human behavior, is the belief that one man's gain is another's loss — that business, like the so-called friendly poker session, is a zero-sum game. Not so.

On the one hand, it must be recognized that the great source of market gains is the productivity of the participants. Unlike the poker game, the wealth of our society has been doubling even on a per capita basis every 25 years, and the doubling has been due to the labors and ingenuity of the men in the market place. Of course there are also incomes achieved by monopoly rather than by efficiency, by fraud rather than by output, but it would be a wholly extravagant estimate that they amount to 10 per cent of the income of the market place. There is room for improvement here, but there is vastly more room to admire the prodigious production achievements of the market place.

On the other hand, I would emphasize that most of the gains from innovation in the market place are passed on to the community at large. A new idea may yield handsome profits for a time, but the rapid rush of competition soon drives the price of the product down to a modest level. Ball-point pens were first marketed at $12.50 to those penmen eager to write under water (and, judging by my experience, only under water); they rapidly fell in price and as you know are now so cheap that you have no economic excuse if you do not write the Great American Novel. Sears, Roebuck and C o m p a n y and Montgomery Ward made a good deal of money in the process of improving our rural marketing structure, but I am convinced that they did more for the poor farmers of America than the sum total of the federal agricultural support programs of the last 28 years.

It is an interesting illustration of the great influence of the intellectual that the market place itself has become apologetic of its pursuit of profit. The captains of industry now list, in a world in which public relations are becoming as important as efficiency, among their major achievements the great number of bowling alleys or college fellowships they have given to their employees. To boast that large profits demonstrate great efficiency in producing existing products and introducing new ones is considered even by them to be too archaic a form of thought for public consumption. The patron saint of economics, Adam Smith, once wrote:

> I have never known much good done by those who affected to trade for the public good. It is an affectation, indeed, not very common among merchants, and very few words need be employed in dissuading them from it.

I wonder what those very few words were.

To return to the intellectuals, their dislike for the profit motive of the market place no doubt rests in part on a failure to understand its logic and workings. It is a fact painful to record that the level of economic literacy has not risen noticeably in the twentieth century. Indeed as professional economics becomes more complicated and its practitioners use an increasingly more formidable apparatus, there seems to have been retrogression in our ability to communicate with other intellectuals. Less than a century ago a treatise on economics began with a sentence such as, "Economics is a study of mankind in the ordinary business of life." Today it will often begin, "This unavoidably lengthy treatise is devoted to an examination of an economy in which the second derivatives of the utility function possess a finite number of discontinuities. To keep the problem manageable, I assume that each individual consumes only two goods, and dies after one Robertsonian week. Only elementary mathematical tools such as topology will be employed, incessantly."

But misunderstanding is not the whole explanation: I cannot believe that any amount of economic training would wholly eliminate the instinctive dislike for a system of organizing economic life through the search for profits. It will still appear to many intellectuals that a system in which men were driven by a reasonably selfless devotion to the welfare of other men would be superior to one in which they sought their own preferment. This ethic is deeply imbedded in the major religions.

I personally also believe that the good society will be populated by people who place a great value on other people's welfare. This is, however, not the only attribute of the good society, and in particular in the good society a man should be free within the widest possible limits of other men's limitations on his beliefs and actions. This great ethic of individual freedom clashes with that of benevolence, for I can seldom do positive good to another person without limiting him. I can, it is true, simply give him money, but even in this extreme case where I

291

seem to place no bonds on him, he inevitably faces the question of what conduct on his part will lead me to give money to him again. Usually I will find it hard to be content to do so little good—giving money to improve a man's food or housing or health will seem as inefficient as giving him gasoline so he will drive more often to museums. Hence when I give money I shall also insist that it be spent on housing, or on medical care for his children, or on growing wheat in the way that I think is socially desirable, or on the collected works of Burke and de Tocqueville, or of Marx and Lenin. A patron tends to be paternalistic, in a nice way, of course. I am not saying that benevolence is bad, but that like everything else it can be carried to excess.

One final question on motives — why are they so important? Am I to admire a man who injures me in an awkward and mistaken attempt to protect me, and to despise a man who to earn a good income performs for me some great and lasting service? Oddly enough, I suspect our answer is that motive makes a difference — that it is less objectionable to be injured by an incompetent benefactor than by a competent villain. But I leave with you the question: are motives as important as effects?

Several charges related to the dominance of self-interest have rounded out the intellectual's indictment of the market place:

First, the system makes no provision for men whose talents and interests are not oriented to profit-seeking economic activity.

Second, there are cumulative tendencies toward increasing inequality of wealth, which—if unchecked—will polarize the society into a great number of poor and a few very rich.

Third, the game in the market place is unfair in that inheritance of property plays an immensely larger role in success than the efforts of the individuals themselves.

I shall comment briefly on each of these assertions.

The first charge is true — the market place will not supply income to a man who will not supply something which people want. People have enormously varied desires, but not enough of them wish to hire men to engage in research on ancient languages nor, sixty years ago, did they hire men to study quantum mechanics. The market place does not provide an air force or alms for the poor. It does not even supply babies. I conclude that a society needs more than a market place.

The second charge, that there are cumulative tendencies to ever-increasing inequality of wealth, is untrue. I would indeed ignore the charge for fear of reprimand from the Society for the Prevention of Cruelty to Straw Men, were it not that this strawman is so popular. In plain historical fact, the inequality in the distribution of income has been diminishing, and the diminution has been due to market forces even more than to governmental efforts. It is also worth noting that a modern market economy has a less unequal income distribution than either centrally directed or unindustrialized economies.

The third charge, that inheritance of property plays a dominant role in the distribution of income in the market place, is an overstatement. Inheritance of property is important, but it will give some perspective to the charge to notice that property income is only one-fifth of national income, and inherited property is less than half of all property, so less than 10 per cent of all income is governed by inheritance of property.

No useful purpose would be served by trying to appraise the proper role of inheritance of property in a few passing remarks. We should have to look carefully at the effects of inheritance on incentives; we should have to look at gifts during life, which are almost equivalent to bequests; and we should have to decide whether privately endowed colleges do enough good to offset the inevitable high-living heirs—whether we can have Carleton without having Tommy Manville.

But our greatest problem would be that inheritance extends far beyond a safe-deposit box full of bonds and stocks. I have told you that you are intelligent; I now add that the chief reason you are intelligent is that your parents are intelligent. Some of you, especially the younger of you, may find this unbelievable. Mark Twain said he was astonished by how much his father had learned during the short time it took Mark to grow from 18 to 21. But inheritance of ability is important, probably more important in its effects on the distribution of income than is the inheritance of property. So a full account of the proper role of inheritance would have to extend to ability, and perhaps even to name and reputation, as the junior senator from Massachusetts might agree. The social and legal institutions governing inheritance in our society are surely open to improvement, but we are unlikely to improve them if we are guided by nothing more than naive egalitarianism.

And now to my final point. We are great believers in the human mind, we intellectuals, and in its ability to conquer an ever larger part of the immense domain of ignorance. But we have not made much use of the mind in reaching our views on the economic organization appropriate to the good society so far as its basic cultural values go. It is clear that the kinds of traits that are fostered in man are influenced by (but of course not only by) the way economic life is organized — after all, throughout history men have spent half their waking hours in economic activity.

Important as the moral influences of the market place are, they have not been subjected to any real study. The immense proliferation of general education, of scientific progress, and of democracy are all coincidental in time and place with the emergence of the free enterprise system of organizing the market place. I believe this coincidence was not accidental: the economic progress of the past three centuries was both cause and effect of this general growth of freedom. The dominant era of the free market place was in the Nineteenth Century. I believe, but with less confidence, that the absence of major wars in that century — the only peaceable century in history — was related to this reign of liberty. I believe, again with less confidence, that the contemporary transformation of the British public from a violent and unruly people into a population of almost painful Victorian rectitude was related to this reign of liberty.

These beliefs may be right or wrong, but they are not matters of taste. They are hypotheses concerning the relationship between economic and social organization, and are subject to analytical development and empirical testing. It is time that we did so, high time. Our ruling attitude toward the market place has not changed since the time of Plato. Is it not possible that it is time to rethink the question?

293

Observations on the
Soviet "Lost Generation"

ROBERT M. HURT

THE AMERICAN PUBLIC tends to think of the youth of Communist nations in terms of certain newsreel images—hundreds of youths marching in step to martial music, with identical uniforms and presumably with identical thoughts. Visitors to Russia have been amazed to find that the young people they meet are out of step not only with this stereotype but, what is much more important, with the announced goals of communist society itself. I would like to pass on some observations I made on this subject while in the Soviet Union this past summer.

During my first stop off in a major Russian city I learned that, contrary to my misgivings about the language barrier and the willingness of Russians to talk to Americans, it is often easier to get to know Russian students than even the students of Western Europe. To give an example, I found myself the main attraction at an informal discussion in the center of a small park during my first evening in the town. One student asked if most American families have cars. Another informed us that all American workers lived in constant dread of unemployment and consequent starvation. A boy of high school age stated that Benny Goodman's appearance was a great event in his life and asked when Louis Armstrong was coming to Russia.

An older girl asked quietly about Pasternak's prestige in the West and later warned me privately about the omnipresent security police. One student hoped that we would not invade Cuba; another whispered to me as I left, "Yankee si, Cuba no!"

This diversity of opinion illustrates a phenomenon noted frequently by commentators on the Russian scene. In spite of what is undoubtedly history's most determined and scientific attempt at total indoctrination for any prolonged period, the Kremlin has failed to produce a generation of "socialist men" who would swallow *in toto* the Gospel according to Nikita. Some writers have gone so far as to assert that Russia's youth constitutes one of the greatest long range threats to the regime. Edward Crankshaw, in a book which generally praises Khrushchev, sees the present generation as Khrushchev's greatest problem. He noted in 1959 that "the communist idea has long ceased to be an active faith," and that rejection of this idea was most pronounced in the generation under thirty.[1]

The communist leadership displays its uneasiness by its defensiveness in regard to the youth problem. *World Student News*, mouthpiece of the International Union of Students, the Prague-based puppet international communist student

Robert M. Hurt is an Associate Editor of *New Individualist Review*.

[1] *Khrushchev's Russia* (Baltimore: Penguin, 1959) p. 139.

organization, felt called upon to refute the image painted in a *Time* feature article of a "lost generation" in Russia. Their portrait of Russian youth marching arm-in-arm to a Brave New World represents the wishful thinking of the leadership and would have been a bad joke to most of the Russians with whom I talked:

> The whole of Soviet youth is preparing to engage in building the nation's economy, in getting ready to change the mentality of more and more human beings, so as to raise them to the level which the new society they desire demands of each and everyone of them . . . the struggle to strengthen their country, to build, has become a revolutionary factor which stirs their minds and hearts. Just as revolutionary ideals mobilized former Soviet generations, so the revolutionary ideal of today is work, work, and work.[2]

Communist propagandists themselves give the lie to this ecstatic vision with their omnipresent posters in every town square exhorting the population against "teddy boys" and "hooligans" and their articles castigating those young people who seek to emulate "decadent capitalist ways."

THE STUDENTS WITH whom I talked can be roughly divided into three groups. The first would be those who seemingly are unquestioningly accepting everything they have been taught and will defend every article of the communist dogma with a religious fervor. While most of the Russians I had met at the Helsinki Youth Festival and at the International Union of Students Congress in Prague, as well as Russian exchange students I have talked to, would fall in this category, only two students I met in Russia itself were of this type. (One was our Intourist guide, who was dubbed Little Izvestia by our group.) I suspect that these young militants, while predominant at

2 "Soviet Youth: A Lost Generation?" *World Student News,* vol. 16, no. 6, 1962, p. 10.

events where official selection is necessary, are only a small proportion of Russian youth.

In the second category I would place those Russian youth who are in open and contemptuous rebellion against communist ideals and Soviet society. These are grouped together as "teddy boys" by the Soviet press. American tourists inevitably run into the most daring of these young men almost as soon as they step off the train or plane in Moscow. Operating near the most popular tourist establishments, especially Gorki Park and the GUM Department Store, they offer to buy American suits, ties, synthetic shirts, and especially shoes. (I received eight tempting offers for my suit during my first two days in Moscow.) Sometimes they offer to pay in American dollars, even though it is a serious crime for Russians even to possess American dollars. (Some of the most important black market operations in dollars are conducted by students who purchase dollars from Russian sailors.) They are equally willing to sell phony seventeenth century icons to gullible American tourists.

These rebellious young men are found throughout the social spectrum. The "hooligans" are the children of workers, the *stilyagi* are of the middle class, and the "jet-set" are the parasitic and completely shiftless children of the very rich.

At best they do absolutely nothing; at worst they are juvenile delinquents of the most violent sort.

Those with whom I talked seem to have consciously and emphatically rejected their indoctrination. They are most eager, often without fear of being overheard, to tell just how horrible they think life in Russia is. (The black marketeers might think that this would increase the chance of commercial transactions with Americans.) Their ideal seems to be the United States, but unfortunately a parody of the United States which would horrify us. They worship at the altar of American rock 'n' roll. (I was asked several times to my chagrin to demonstrate the "twist.") Elvis Presley is a hero. Moscow streets are popularly named after American counter-

295

Page Eleven

parts; for instance, Gorki Street is dubbed Broadway. They dress in what they presume to be American styles, though they are closer to the zoot suits of the early forties. I was shocked to learn that an anti-American film had to be closed out because a showing of automobile "chicken races" had backfired in its propaganda effect. One Muscovite asked me with awe, "Do you really do that in America?"

Needless to say, when listing their grievances against communism, they failed to indicate any appreciation of the values which we prize in the West. Their main grievance seems to be that they do not now receive the material benefits and opportunities for sensual thrills that they think they would receive in the United States. Though the *stilyagi* and "hooligans" have received considerable attention in the Western press, they clearly do not comprise a majority of Russian youth, and their importance should not be overemphasized.

INTO MY THIRD CATEGORY I would put most of the students I met during my brief Russian stay. These are the young people who on the one hand are honest and somewhat intellectually bent, and desire to lead useful, productive lives, and on the other hand are disillusioned and skeptical in varying degrees about the goals and actualities of Soviet society. I was frankly surprised that so many Russians were of this opinion, and I might well have had different results if I had been able to talk to more people. The fact that I could only converse with persons who spoke English might have given me an inaccurate cross-section. But the discovery that many born and reared under communism develop such attitudes is a cause for amazement. And both the Americans and Russians I talked to in Moscow agreed that a significant proportion of the present generation is skeptical and disillusioned without resorting to the extremes of the "teddy boy" set.

For obvious reasons I cannot be too specific in describing these young people.

In contrast to some of the bolder *stilyagi*, they usually fear reprisals for over-familiarity with Americans. Almost as soon as we crossed the Russian-Polish frontier we noticed the manifest uneasiness of our acquaintances when a stranger walked by or seemed to be staring. Whenever we would approach within a few blocks of a major hotel, an area with a notoriously high concentration of plainclothesmen, the Russians usually would politely excuse themselves or bluntly announce that they were afraid to go further. (This attitude is not universal. Two loquacious and critical college students showed no fear whatsoever.) Fantastic rumors abound concerning new electronic listening devices and an apparatus which reads letters without opening them. While commenting on the common belief that there are hidden microphones in most public buildings, one student remarked that Russians give a quite literal meaning to the epigram, "The walls have ears." Twice to my knowledge students were warned by plainclothesmen not to talk to me; once one of these ever-present gentlemen even interrupted our conversation and warned the Russian with whom I was talking to discontinue our acquaintance.

The fears of these students are offset, however, by a passionate desire to talk to Americans and learn of the United States and the West. There is the inevitable interest in the material benefits of American life: Does your family have a car? A house? What will a worker's or doctor's wage buy? How much are shoes? Have you been to Disneyland? And even the serious students are obsessed with jazz and Louis Armstrong, although not with rock 'n' roll.

But the most gratifying revelation to me was their strong concern with questions of individual freedom. No conversation passes without questions about Pasternak, who is a heroic symbol to a large segment of the young Russian intelligentsia. I found a hunger for information about Western writers and artists, especially American and French. I spent two hours one evening describing contemporary controversies in philos-

296

ophy to two brilliant university students who were particularly bothered by the narrow limits of philosophic inquiry in the Soviet Union. The ideas of Ayer and Wittgenstein, of Maritain and Sartre, represented a forbidden frontier to them. They noted with special irony that the philosophic works of such heroes of Soviet propaganda as Russell and Sartre (as well as the paintings of Picasso) are forbidden, with the exception of carefully selected extracts. One student remarked disgustedly, "While you explore the whole world of philosophy, we stop at Lenin's *Materialism and Empiro-Criticism.*"

Almost everyone felt that conditions had improved in some ways since the pre-1956 period. However, Khrushchev's brutal crackdown on "liberal" writers after the literary thaw period of 1956-57 came in for especially bitter criticism. Several students commented angrily on Khrushchev's speech at a party for writers in 1957 at his own villa. Though it was omitted from the published report, they claim he asserted that the Hungarian trouble could have been avoided if the Hungarian government had shot a few writers. He warned that if similar trouble arose in Russia, "My hand would not tremble." This remark seemed especially brutal since it was coupled with an attack on the "incorrect" opinions expressed by Margaret Aliger, one of the most daring of the "thaw" writers.[3] Khrushchev has curtly summed up his attitude toward cultural freedom: "For anyone who faithfully serves his people in a socialist society, the question of whether or not he is free in his creative work simply does not exist. . . ."[4] Fortunately, for many in the new genera-

tion of creative minds in Russia it is a question that does exist.

These young Russians were even more bitter in their criticism of restrictions on travel to the West in particular and of their isolation from the West in general. Everyone was amazed that I could travel to Russia without special State Department permission. One Russian who had been unable to obtain permission to travel to communist Poland switched from an attitude of mild cynicism to anger at his lot in the world when he heard of the ease with which I travelled through almost every country in Europe. He pointed out that it was considered a great improvement when Russians were allowed to travel more than twenty kilometers from their residence without special permission. University students were especially interested in the ease and cheapness of travel between Western nations. When I suggested that this might gradually lead to valuable cultural cross-fertilization and eventually to a cultural synthesis as well as a political federation of Western nations, one student summed up a typical attitude: "And we will be left out!"

This official stifling of the creative spirit, and officially imposed isolation from the rest of the world, when coupled with a realization that a monstrous and cumbersome bureaucracy attempts to manipulate every aspect of personal life, has produced a feeling that, figuratively speaking, the individual lives in an atmosphere so stifling that one can scarcely breathe. This not only was a metaphor that cropped up several times in personal conversation, but it is a recurring theme among the best young Soviet writers.[5] Incessant loud speakers in the centers of large cities, with their stream of martial music and purring feminine voices, symbolized to two of these students the stifling atmosphere of

---

[3] While Miss Aliger reportedly fainted upon hearing Khrushchev's thinly veiled threat, her later "recantation" may have been written satirically: "I think that I will be able fully to explain the profound conclusions which I have drawn for my future only by working wholeheartedly, by remembering always that the main task of a Soviet writer is political work, and that it can only be performed honorably by following unwaveringly the Party line and Party discipline."

[4] Quoted in *The Current Digest of the Soviet Press* (New York), October 9, 1957.

[5] This tendency is illustrated by the works of Russian and satellite authors collected in *Bitter Harvest,* ed. Edmund Stillman, (New York: Praeger, 1959). Francis Bondy's introduction points out that some of these authors have more in common with Kafka than with the authors of socialist realism. On one occasion a young Russian writer informed me he felt more kinship with Kafka than with any Russian writer.

Page Thirteen

their society. Even as a brief visitor to the Soviet Union I found these an annoying intrusion into my privacy. The effect of a dictatorial bureaucracy in stifling life was well summer up in an article by one of the Party's most renowned writers, Ilya Ehrenburg, who, surprisingly, was allowed to subtly voice this opinion even after Krushchev's threats:

> A tyrant can be intelligent or stupid, good or evil, but all the same he is all-powerful and powerless; he is frightened by conspiracies, he is flattered and deceived; the jails fill up; cowardly hypocrites whisper, and a silence settles in that is enough to stop the heart . . . .
>
> . . . the guilt rests with a society that demands hypocrisy, condemns the truth, and tramples large feelings for the sake of its many conventions.[6]

In reaction to this feeling of suffocation large segments of Russian society have in one way or another tried to attain a little privacy. The official press has bitterly assailed the "antisocial" tendency among the members of the new wealthy class to isolate themselves in small *dachas* hidden in the woods. Writters react by turning from the "social" themes required by socialist realism and either remaining silent or turning to an introspective, even egocentric theme. The very silence of writers after the end of the thaw was recognized by the officialdom as a danger. Soviet writers were told by a high party official in 1957:

> It is known that in music a pause sometimes expresses more feeling and thought than the melody. Your silence is dangerous. It causes disorientation among the readers. What does it mean? What does it conceal? An arrogant contempt for the opinon of others? A contemptuous belief in one's own infallibility? An insulting "How could you possibly understand us?" The pathos of readiness for sacrifice? What does this silence signify? We do not understand it. Neither do the people.[7]

The brilliant young poet Evgeni Evtushenko, who now sticks close to permissible themes, was assailed as a representative of the new tendency to turn from social themes and engage in introspection:

> When Evtushenko was roaming the countryside around Zima, it never occurred to him to take hold of the controls of a combine-harvester or the wheel of a lorry, or a rake or a scythe or a fork . . . Evtushenko has not portrayed the heroism of labor. . . .[8] .

Pasternak's *Dr. Zhivago* was correctly recognized by the literary officialdom as an extreme representative of this new attitude. The famous *Novy Mir* letter rejecting *Dr. Zhivago* for publication, the only official comment with any vestige of integrity, ignores the most obvious political remarks, which were really no worse than many which had already been published in some recent works, and concentrates on the underlying attitude toward life. Pasternak is attacked for making a hero of Doctor Zhivago, a man who is egocentric and concerned mainly with his own personal salvation, as well as indecisive and unheroic in the physical sense, the literary antithesis of the new socialist man just as the book is the antithesis of socialist realism.

Khrushchev's revelations of Stalin's crimes, which are continuing in lurid detail, have contributed more than anything else to destroying the faith of these young intellectuals in their government and system. An announcement that Beria, once one of the triumvirate that ruled Russia, had personally murdered prisoners in his office was a crowning blow. In Orwell's *1984*, no one noticed when Big Brother rewrote history. In Russia this rewriting has created the gravest doubts. If what we believed then was a lie, why should we believe what we are told today? How could one

6 "The Lessons of Stendhal," *Bitter Harvest,* pp. 230-31.

7 Leonid Sobolev in a 1957 speech to the Soviet Writers' Union, as quoted in *Soviet Survey,* (London), September, 1957.

8 V. Solukhin, *Literaturnaya Gazeta* (Moscow), as quoted in *Soviet Survey* (London), July-September, 1958.

Page Fourteen

of history's worst tyrants take power under a system which we are told is the world's best? How do we know it will not happen again? Is it still happening? Some Russians believe almost nothing emanating from government sources. One did not believe there was segregation in the United States until he heard it admitted on the Voice of America.

Others are confused and skeptical. I recall one instance which illustrates the depth of this doubt. A student was arguing with two others that Khrushchev was completely different from Stalin and actually desired a transition to more freedom. I threw out a query which I thought would have only slight rhetorical value: "What will you say after the de-Khrushchevization period? Will you contend that the next leader is different from Stalin and Khrushchev?" While the other students nodded in agreement, she gave a look of terror, and tears actually came to her eyes. She later admitted that her attitude had been one of desperate hope rather than conviction.

All this does not in any sense mean any significant number of the young generation have embraced capitalism as their ideal or are looking to American military liberation of Russia. Their political goals are usually nebulous and uncertain. Sometimes I encountered a belief in a highly decentralized "syndicalism" in which workers owned their factories and people were free in their personal lives. The ideas of Gorky seemed to have had more of an impact among them than those of Lenin. There is pride in Russia's rapid technological development, although not as much as I had anticipated. Many Russians are clearly not impressed with their space achievements, and several felt it was a tragic waste of money with so much misery to be alleviated.

Their attitudes toward the United States and the Cold War vary considerably, but I never found them either completely uncritical or particularly hostile. No one doubts that the average worker is much better off materially in the United States, although there is much misunderstanding and exaggera-tion as to the unemployment problem. They usually express criticism of the condition of the Negro, though not with the vehemence of the average Englishman. They sometimes express concern over the John Birch Society, often demonstrating such misinformation that they might have been readers of the *New York Post*. Their views on the Cold War, though usually blaming the United States for creating "war tensions," were often surprisingly sophisticated, considering difficulties in obtaining information, and rarely completely echoed official propaganda. Most tend to attribute guilt for present tensions to both sides; the Russian military and American arms producers are singled out as the culprits. American bases around Russia, the U-2 flight, and our policy towards Cuba are singled out for criticism, although I found them open-minded and willing to re-examine their opinions when I explained the reasons for American policy. Their willingness to reject a previously held opinion probably was another indication of the extreme skepticism with which they often receive official information. All but two were well informed about the Hungarian repression and were horrified at their government's action; several had guessed at the real reason for the Berlin Wall. And many fear and are repelled by the Communist regime in China.

299

BECAUSE OF OUR language barrier, I could enter into only a few detailed conversations on deeper issues, the attitudes of these people toward the purpose of their existence and the hopes they had for the future of Russian and mankind. I cannot say how typical the attitudes expressed in these conversations were, but I pass them on as some of the most interesting observations of my trip. I found a surface optimism concealing a pessimisim which ran deeper than mere cynicism. Goals, though vague and uncrystallized, are phrased in terms of absolutes. This vividly contrasts with the more pragmatic and cynical attitude of the Czechs, for instance, to look to a little more than survival and a general improvement in their present condtion. Philosophies such as pragmatism and neo-positivism in my opinion would be utterly unacceptable to this Russian mentality, because the attitude of mind which has engendered them in the West, the skeptical mind which is willing to suspend judgment and to be content with partial answers, is alien to this Russian intellectual temperament. Likewise, in the political field these young Russians seem to be looking for absolute commitment to a system which provides answers to all questions rather than for a set of provisional solutions to vexing problems. Just as the Russian has always been either theist or atheist, never agnostic, there is a strong tendency for the Russian, unlike the American, Englishman, or Czech to be a political extremist and uncompromising idealist. Dostoevski meticulously probed this desire for total commitment, and Berdyaev has shown how the intellectual success of Marxism is bound up with his mentality.

All the disillusionments of recent years, the Stalin revelations, Hungary, the fanatic turn taken by China (and I am sure their government's vociferous denial, then admission of missile bases in Cuba can now be added to the list), and Khrushchev's crude crackdown on the 1957 literary thaw, have had a traumatic psychological effect on these young Russians, who emotionally are intensely patriotic to "Mother Russia" and desire so strongly to "believe" in her. Several times I detected what might have been a feeling of personal guilt, a slight tinge of masochism. Descriptions of the worst aspects of life in Russia are all too often accompanied by remarks such as "This is our shame," and "We are so embarrassed to admit this to an American." Also, when they undertook to defend their government on some point, I felt they were all too willing to give in to my arguments. They found them much more convincing than I did on several occasions, and stated that they were "humiliated" to admit I must be right.

If I am warranted in drawing any conclusions from these observations of the Russian attitude, I would say that this helps to explain why Marxism as a closed theory and ideal had such an attraction to the Russian intellect and why the theoretical justification for a capitalist and pluralist system, admittedly offered as merely the best of imperfect systems, might have little intrinsic appeal. However, when a system falls so blatantly short of any set of ideals justifying commitment, such a mentality is likely to engender more hostility than a more moderate and pragmatic one.

NOW I COME TO the task of drawing practical conclusions from my disjointed mass of observations. First I would note that Russia is in a perverted way a more open society than we might expect. Rigid government control of the nation's economic life is circumvented to a fantastic degree by various illegal operations: black market, bribery, and theft of state property. Recent administration of the death penalty for various economic crimes (murder and rape are not punishable by death) seems to be a feeble attempt to deal with a way of life that in many areas is the rule rather than the exception. Likewise, the official monopoly of informational media is circumvented by an all pervasive grapevine. In Moscow we received slightly confused reports of the riots and subsequent repression near Rostov, when the government was stopping tours bound for Rostov because of an "epidemic." A slight Soviet relaxation of controls has also contributed to alleviating the situation in regard to information. English language Voice of America broadcasts can be easily picked up, although Russian language broadcasts are usually jammed. The United States government publication *America,* which is sold in very limited amounts under our cultural exchange program, had been read by almost everyone to whom I talked. And, of course, the mass inflow of Western tourists offers an important respite from isolation to these people, at least in the large tourist centers.

300

Second, almost every American visitor is surprised by the special friendship and respect accorded Americans. Not only do Americans find themselves well-received; we found almost no hostility toward the United States and its government. As I have already pointed out, among a significant portion of the young, American culture, or at least what we regard as the worst aspects of it, is set up as an ideal. And among the more serious I found a respect for America and its institutions greater in many cases than is usually found in Western Europe. To the young generation, events such as Benny Goodman's tour are magnified in importance. Not only is this music they want to hear, it is contact with America. On several occasions I was touched by the special attention I received when a Russian learned I was an American. Once a boy of about twenty, after telling me how to get to my destination on the other side of Moscow, asked me if I was an Englishman. When I informed him I was an American, he spent the next hour accompanying me to my destination. When no one was looking he proudly displayed the contents of his gym bag—a copy of *America.*

But of what significance is all this? Does the attitude of the Russian young generation make one iota of difference as to Russian policy when all decisions rest in the hands of the top men? Senator Goldwater, in his *Conscience of a Conservative,* has no trouble finding an answer. In one sentence he asserts that contacts with the Russian people are useless because they have no say with the government. Although I do not plan to go into the reasons here, I would contend, but with some reservation, that broadening contacts and attempting to explain our position may in the future be of considerable importance.

But one sentiment that is difficult to rid oneself of after associating with these people is a fervent hope that some day they will see an end to the oppression under which they live, coupled with a hope that in some way we may help them to do so. I was especially moved by an event which occurred when I was being questioned on Pasternak by a very small group of adult Russians late at night in a public square. The eldest, a worker who was interpreting for the group, asked if I remembered any of Pasternak's poems. I stumbled through the first two stanzas of "Beast in an Enclosure" while it was translated to the entranced group:

> I am lost like a beast in an enclosure
> Somewhere are people, freedom, and light
> Behind me is the noise of pursuit
> And there is no way out
>
> Dark forest by the shore of the lake
> Stump of fallen fir tree,
> Here I am cut off from everything
> Whatever shall be is the same to me.

301

I could remember no more, but one of the Russians picked up the remaining two stanzas, as tears formed in the eyes of every Russian in the group:

> But what wicked thing have I done
> I the murderer and villain?
> I who force the whole world to cry
> Over the beauty of my land.
> But in my case, I am near my grave
> And I believe the time will come
> When the spirit of good will conquer
> Wickedness and infamy.

Seconds after these stanzas were completed, several passersby seemed to be moving too close for the comfort of the Russians. We shook hands and departed.

Economic Growth
vs. "Growth" Economics

JOHN VAN SICKLE

AS WORLD WAR II drew to a close, the prevention of massive unemployment was generally regarded in the West as *the* major continuing postwar problem. In the underdeveloped countries, however, it soon appeared that *the* number-one problem was growth, and not just any kind of growth, but industrial growth. At that time Russia's forced growth convinced many in the West that some minimum rate was required for national survival, and that governments must see to it that this minimum rate is attained.

To old-fashioned liberals[1] this concern for growth seems excessive. To them growth is a form of change and the only kind of change worthy of the name is one resulting from spontaneous changes in consumer tastes and preferences. If people want and can secure more leisure or more children rather than more material things, then that is growth. In brief, to the liberal, growth is only meaningful within the context of freedom.[2]

The liberal does not deny, of course, that in the world of today national survival does depend on growth in output per capita of goods people really want. But he believes that spontaneous forces can and will provide both freedom *and* adequate growth, in this more

restricted sense, if government will but provide the proper framework. To him the best way to produce more of what people want is to work harder, save and invest more, and devise better tools and better methods of organizing production. Assuming as he does that human wants are virtually unlimited, he lays his bets on the enormous potentialities inherent in individual initiatives. He relies on free prices and competition to direct resources to all sectors of the economy in such proportions as to keep the returns to capital and to labor approximately equal at all margins. Out of the resulting abundance he would, of course, have the governments of the free world take whatever is needed for defense, urging only that the burden be so distributed as to maintain as fully as possible the incentives which free people must rely on to meet the Communist challenge.

The liberal is rationally as well as emotionally an internationalist. It is obvious to him that no national market is broad enough to yield the full potentialities that specialization offers. He is further convinced that only through free and private trading can national markets be peacefully and effectively integrated.

John Van Sickle is Professor Emeritus of Economics at Wabash College and co-author of the college textbook *Introduction to Economics*. This article is taken from his forthcoming book, *A Framework for Freedom.*

[1] The term "liberal" is used here and throughout this article in its original and proper sense.

[2] For an effective statement of this view of growth, see P. T. Bauer, *Economic Analysis and Policy in Underdeveloped Countries,* (Durham, North Carolina: Duke University Press, 1957), pp. 113-114.

Page Eighteen

302

Properly speaking there is no single "new theory" of growth, but rather a family of theories, differing from one another in detail, but alike in their denial of the liberal concept and explanation of growth, and in their distrust of the spontaneous forces of the market. Common to all variants of the "new theory" is the conviction that growth must be in accordance with the overriding directives of a comprehensive plan. Just as the 1949 United Nations *Report on Full Employment*[3] represents the "new look" at the employment problem, so its 1951 Report [4] on ways of promoting the rapid development of poor countries represents the "new look" at the growth problem.[5]

A CHARACTERISTIC OF the new theories is the modest role assigned to agriculture. For a variety of reasons, some perfectly valid [6] and some wholly fallacious,[7] it is held that an appreciable proportion of the farm population in the underdeveloped countries could be withdrawn from that sector without any adverse effect on total output. Anything these workers could do elsewhere would represent a net gain. But they cannot be put to work without tools. Conse-

---

[3] *National and International Measures for Full Employment*, United Nations, (New York, 1949).

[4] *Measures for the Economic Development of Underdeveloped Countries*, United Nations, (New York, 1951).

[5] There is little in the subsequent flood of interventionist literature that runs counter to the analysis and policy recommendations to be found in this 1951 report.

[6] For a clear statement of this sophisticated theory, see *Economic Development in Latin America and Its Principal Problems*. An analysis of this theory by B. A. Rogge appeared in the Spring, 1956, issue of *Inter-American Affairs*, (vol. 9, no. 4), pp. 24-49.

[7] For a perceptive discussion of this whole issue of the place of agriculture in a growing economy, see P. T. Bauer and B. S. Yamey, *The Economics of Under-developed Countries* (London and Chicago, 1957), Chapter XV. For actual evidence against this thesis, see H. T. Oshima, "Under-employment in Backward Countries," *Journal of Political Economy*, June, 1958, and T. W. Schultz, "Latin-American Economic Policy Lessons," *American Economic Review*, May, 1956.

quently investment in the non-farm sector of the economy is the key to growth, with industrial development given top priority.

It is further held that the needed rate of industrial development cannot be had by adherence to measures consistent with orthodox theory. Investment would be spread too thin. What is needed is such a massive concentration of capital on a relatively limited non-farm target as to enable the whole economy to "take off" and to "break through" the vicious circle of proverty and stagnation. Where a single factory might not pay, fifty plants properly brought together might prove highly profitable because they would provide each other with external economies and further justify the provision of the roads, power, ports, education, health services—the much-talked-of infra-structure—which would otherwise represent a waste of scarce resources.[8]

This variant of the "new theory" explicitly rejects the marginal-productivity principle. "Economic analysis," we are told, "provides two general principles for the use of resources. One is the marginal principle." Another, and a better one, to which no name is attached, "arises from the fact that large movements of resources within the economy will have effects which are disproportionately different. In consequence the planner must satisfy himself not only that further marginal movements would serve no useful purpose but also that there is nothing to be gained by larger movements of resources, amounting to a considerable alteration in the structure of the economy." The new principle must be grasped intuitively. The planners "must soak themselves thoroughly in the facts of each particular case and must then use their best judgment." [9] Furthermore they must rely primarily on "direction" rather than on "inducement" despite the fact that direction requires a costly bureaucracy which is "liable to corruption," "gives rise to black markets," causes "great irritation

---

[8] *Measures for the Economic Development of Under-developed Countries*, op. cit., parag. 185.

[9] ibid., parags. 148-151.

303

Page Nineteen

and frustration" and "cannot be applied to new foreign resources to be attracted from abroad."[10]

The immensity of the task assigned to the governments of the underdeveloped countries is revealed in the following list of public functions which the United Nations experts cite as representative rather than complete: market research; prospecting; establishment of new industries; creation of financial institutions "to mobilize savings and to channel them into desirable private enterprise"; operation of public utilities, of agencies for marketing agricultural produce, of factories for processing the output of small farmers; confiscation of "unearned increments" that arise in economic developments; land reform; "creating credit institutions and insurance schemes which satisfy the farmers' legitimate needs for credit"; some compulsory standardization of products in particular industries; planning and organization of "industrial centers"; compulsory consolidation of land holdings; "influencing the movement of resources in directions which it considers to be more appropriate," including the location of industry; control of new building by restrictive licensing; acting as guarantor for particular investments; licensing of new in-

vestment; and perhaps controlling the consumption of the rich.[11]

Governments of underdeveloped countries obviously cannot mobilize the talents needed to discharge this range of tasks. The Pakistani people were recently told just this by two distinguished German bankers who were invited to visit the country in the hope, of course, that they could help the Pakistani government find foreign capital. The visitors stated that "because of lack of experience, efficiency and discipline," the administration was "incapable of running a system of physical controls."[12] Similarly a Mission sent by the International Bank to study economic conditions in India and Pakistan suggested very discreetly that "selective controls over industrial development present certain hazards in a country where administrative talent is spread so thin."[13]

This is in brief the new theory. It denies that economic freedom alone will produce growth; it insists that government's role in this area is critical, central and substantial. It is now in competition with orthodox theory for acceptance by policy-making bodies in all countries. Is it an improvement on the old?

THERE IS TRUTH in the new theory, but most of what is true is not new and most of what is new is of dubious validity. Indeed, the valid part of the theory is largely a restatement of two exceptions to the principles of "natural liberty" which have been recognized by economists from the days of Adam Smith on.

First, there is the infant-industry argument. Economists have always recognized the possibility of speeding up by temporary protection the development of industries for which an industrially young country possesses a potential com-

[10] ibid., parags. 216, 217. An item about Indonesia in Newsweek (February 14, 1960) strikingly confirms the reality of these dangers which the U.N. Report identifies and then dismisses: "Meanwhile, the art of government seems to elude Indonesia. Its vast mushrooming bureaucracy (more than 1 million Indonesians are on the public payroll) is riddled with twin ills: incompetence and corruption. More than anything else, these evils have got the nation's economy into such a shambles that U. S. observers in Indonesia simply throw up their hands when the subject is brought up.

"Bribes and Bad Fish: Corruption is the normal way of business. One man recently paid a 50,000 rupiah bribe in order to be allowed to pay a 200 rupiah tax he'd forgotten; another was asked to pay 50,000 rupiahs for a residence permit to be allowed to live in his own house. (The rupiah itself, on the black market, has gone up as high as 750 to $1, though the legal rate is 45.) As for bureaucratic incompetence, government purchasing agents consistently buy bad rice and rotting fish; one importer recently bought 100,000 tons of Swedish cement and had to throw 30,000 tons into the ocean after it got wet because there was no place to store it."

[11] The above list of duties and the ensuing comment borrows heavily from Ben A. Rogge, "The Role of Government in Latin-American Economic Development," Inter-American Economic Affairs, (vol. 9, no. 3, Winter, 1959), p. 43.

[12] International Monetary Fund, International Financial News Survey, March 27, 1959, p. 298.

[13] ibid., April 28, 1960, p. 333.

parative advantage. In so far as economic theorists reject the conclusion, it is on practical and political grounds.

Then there are what have come to be called "neighborhood effects." Adam Smith's third "duty of the sovereign" covers some of these; Professor Pigou has made us familiar with others. Whenever uncompensated benefits and uncompensated damages result from private actions, traditional theory recognizes the propriety, in principle at least, of public interventions of an encouraging or restraining sort, if returns to resources at all margins are to be kept equal. Here again the liberal's scepticism is due to his doubts regarding the ability of governments to resist the pressures to carry investment far beyond the point indicated by marginal-productivity theory, and to handle satisfactorily the resulting administrative and fiscal problems.

Both these arguments slight the political and fiscal aspects of the problem. When a poor country invokes tariffs and subsidies in a large way, there is apt to be such a misuse of scarce resources as to seriously retard growth. Until a government can discharge tolerably well the first of Adam Smith's "duties of the sovereign" — national defense and the maintenance of domestic tranquility — the undertaking of these optional and more difficult tasks is likely to create a situation in which growth with freedom becomes impossible.

Ambitious public programs call for large public expenditures. It is difficult to raise the required revenues entirely through indirect taxes. Consequently, governments are under pressure to impose heavy and sharply progressive direct taxes modeled on Western standards, or else to resort quite frankly to inflation. Both methods impede growth.

Inflation distorts investment decisions, creates balance-of-payments problems, works hardships on fixed-income groups, provokes flights of domestic capital and discourages the entry of foreign capital. Consequently investment via this route frequently explodes into galloping inflation with complete destruction of confidence in the nation's money, or degenerates into "suppressed" inflation with its accompanying arsenal of detailed and paralyzing price and production controls, its black markets and the widespread "irritation and frustration" to which the United Nations' experts referred.[14]

Progressive taxation is likely to be equally harmful to growth. In so far as the law is enforced, it slows down the rate of increase in precisely that resource which is most scarce and most needed for growth. In fact, of course, underdeveloped countries simply cannot enforce highly progressive taxes, but this does not mean that the attempt does not have unfavorable consequences. Administration is apt to be arbitrary, capricious, and corrupt, and the yield is sure to fall short of expectations. Hence, poor countries which attempt to finance grandiose development schemes through a modern progressive income tax are forced to fall back finally on either inflation or on indirect taxes. Neither is adequate to the task, but of the two, inflation is by far the more damaging.

The development plans called for by the new theory invariably require a greater investment than can be had from voluntary savings. Consequently, internal compulsions are recommended, though they are frequently spoken of as "inducements." But it is also recognized that the "revolution of rising expectations" cannot be satisfied by any combination of voluntarism and compulsion. Foreign capital is essential and it is generally taken for granted that the underdeveloped countries neither can nor should be expected to pay the price needed to attract this capital from the private-capital markets of the West. The governments of the West are said to have a moral obligation to force the savings of their people into the service of the

305

----

14 See Professor Karl Brandt's *The Threat of Inflation in the Under-developed World,* at the Stanford Business Conference on Economic Growth and Inflation, held at Stanford University, Stanford, California, July 20, 1959 (mimeograph copy). A convincing statement of the case against inflation as a means of promoting growth will be found in an article by Gottfried Haberler, Galen L. Stone Professor of International Trade at Harvard University, *Inflation: Its Causes and Cures* (revised and enlarged edition, American Enterprise Association, Washington, D.C., June, 1961).

peoples of the underdeveloped countries roughly on the basis of need.

Is it wise to encourage this belief? Leaving aside the moral aspects of the problem, it is well to ask whether in fact the underdeveloped countries are likely to get more or less foreign capital by relying on compulsion rather than on voluntarism.

Unless the compulsions applied within the poor countries are extremely severe they defeat themselves by driving capital out of the country or into hiding. Success, therefore, will depend upon the willingness of the people of wealthy countries to tax themselves and to see their funds used year after year to keep in power regimes whose actions are in many respects at variance with the ideals which the aid is supposed to promote. Will the people of the West be willing to give enough and give long enough to enable *all* underdeveloped countries to grow in numbers and in wealth at rates corresponding to their several "expectations"? The amounts required are so gigantic that no responsible government in the West should give the impression that they will be forthcoming,[15] and no responsible government among the underdeveloped countries should build its plans on the expectation that they will be forthcoming. Almost any underdeveloped country, on the other hand, can expect to see a very substantial inflow of foreign capital and foreign managerial skills, if it puts at the very center of its development plans the necessity for creating those social psychological, economic and institutional arrangements which represent the veritable infrastructure for voluntary growth.

NOTHING SAID SO FAR should be interpreted as a denial of the deep concern of all true liberals in the growth of freedom and well-being everywhere. What they object to is the method favored by the new theory. If the people of the West are really sincere in their protestations of concern with poverty in less-favored parts of the world, they must be prepared (a) to open on durable and reasonable terms their own markets to the products of the underdeveloped countries; and (b) to refrain both directly and through such agencies as the International Labor Organization from urging the governments of the underdeveloped countries to impose wage and welfare standards they cannot yet afford. And if the peoples of the underdeveloped countries really want growth with freedom, they must be prepared (a) to accept the disciplines of free markets; (b) to see to it that their governments discharge efficiently, adequately and honestly the "primary functions" that all governments must perform; and (c) to resist the natural and generous impulse to convert the high productivity which capital and modern know-how make possible too quickly into increased consumption. Development, whether planned or unplanned, is uneven in its timing and in its impact. It lifts productivity in narrow sectors of the economy far above that prevailing in the sectors where, for the time being, traditional methods persist.

When governments of poor countries call upon these narrow sectors to provide incomes to public officials and to the workers directly involved which are a multiple of those enjoyed by the vast majority of the people, a "domestic gap" is created which is probably more conducive to envy and more detrimental to growth than the international gap about which we hear so much. The high wages, whether imposed by minimum-wage laws or collective bargaining or industry commissions, create a "contrived scarcity" of labor where there is no real scarcity,

---

[15] Professor J. Spengler's warning is very pertinent: "Unless population growth is reduced, the stork will gobble up capital faster than it can be introduced . . . in consequence per capita income will not be able to rise rapidly and America will be damned for having supplied a drop of water, when allegedly a bucket was needed, even though in the absence of a salutary change in the people's habits, not even a barrel could have helped much in the long run." This is from an address Professor Spengler gave at the Third Duke American Assembly, May 18-21, 1961. The whole address ("National Goals, Growth and the Principle of Economy") deserves careful reading. It is an exceptionally convincing statement of the pitfalls involved in setting up national goals.

and thus make it necessary for the private firms which are subject to these imposed costs to use more capital-intensive methods than would otherwise be the case. As a result the work force in the less-developed sectors of the economy is deprived of the simple tools which would contribute more to national output than the highly modern plant and equipment which planners in the underdeveloped countries delight in as evidence of progress.

To conclude, we can find no reason either in theory or in the historical record why governments of poor countries must play a larger role in economic affairs than the governments of wealthy countries. Development is an unending process. It is needed by poor and rich countries alike. The public policies which promote growth with freedom are much the same everywhere.

WHAT YOU CAN DO TO HELP NIR . . .

During the past year, the circulation and staff of NEW INDIVIDUALIST REVIEW has been expanding rapidly. This journal is now being sold at many local newsstands and at over 40 colleges and universities. Despite a few dissenting notes, the general reaction of libertarian and conservative leaders has been favorable. The author of "The Conservative Mind," Prof. Russell Kirk, for instance, has said that NEW INDIVIDUALIST REVIEW is a work of "genuine intellectual power" and the editor of "National Review," William F. Buckley, Jr. has called it "by far the best student magazine on our side of the fence." If you agree that this is a useful magazine which ought to be read by more people, there are four things that you can do to further the growth of libertarian-conservative ideas.

(1) You can urge your college library or your local public library to subscribe. A library subscription makes an excellent donation since it may introduce the magazine to dozens of people.

(2) You can urge your friends to subscribe or to donate subscriptions to students.

(3) If you are a college student, you can volunteer to act as our representative on your campus.

(4) Our student subscription price ($1.00 a year) does not cover the cost involved; this price is purposely kept low to encourage as wide a readership as possible among undergraduates. Our deficit is made up by voluntary contributions from individuals. Any donation which you might be able to afford at this time would be gratefully received. None of our staff, by the way, receives any remuneration of any kind.

Civil Liberties in the Welfare State

ROBERT   SCHUCHMAN

IT IS GENERALLY conceded that the concept of limited government is a keystone of the political structure preferred by consistent adherents of the libertarian or conservative philosophy. The notion of limited government rests upon the conviction that the primary fount of sovereignty, the well-spring of civilized existence, resides in the individual. The rights and liberties of the individual in a democracy thus assume a rank of such importance that they may not be nullified by the wishes of any class, any race, any combination of powers, or even by the majority of the electorate itself.

The philosophy of limited government was epitomized by the great Enlightenment penologist, Marquis Beccaria-Bonesana, when he argued that "every act of authority of one man over another, for which there is not an absolute necessity, is tyrannical."[1] To protect ourselves from such a tyranny, we agree consensually to what are essentially self-denying ordinances: to constrain some individuals from using the power of government to interfere with the free exercise of the rights of speech, press, property, and movement, by other individuals, we enjoin the government from exercising any prior restraint in these areas of human activity. In their ideal existence, these self-denying ordinances restrict the enactment of positive law by majorities as well as by minorities: collectively, they form the constitutional framework of what we generally call civil liberties. It may be observed that the extension of civil liberty has always gone hand in hand with the limitation of government by the governed.

With these basic ideas in mind, we may proceed to the central thesis of this paper: that the adoption and extension of what is called "the welfare state," together with current Liberal responses to national economic and diplomatic inadequacies, constitute a serious threat to the maintenance of civil liberties in America today. I do not speak of the economic manifestations of welfarism, a subject which has been commented upon at length by conservative and libertarian scholars. Furthermore, I shall make little or no attempt here to offer alternatives to the shortcomings I enumerate. My sole purpose is to suggest that lawful policies born of political necessity have been so extended as to infringe upon the civil freedoms guaranteed by our Constitution. For the purposes of this argument, I shall throughout even assume the validity of the underlying governmental functions cited and single out for objection only their anti-libertarian effects.

Robert M. Schuchman, who received a B.A. from Queens College and an L.L.B. from Yale Law School, is former National Chairman of Young Americans for Freedom.

---

[1] Caesar Bonesana, Marquis Beccaria, *An Essay on Crimes and Punishments*, (London: Nicklin, 1819), p. 16.

The programmes of Liberalism are apparently motivated by a desire to correct certain inequalities in the human condition. Rather than advocate a general redistribution of wealth, the modern Liberal redistributes on an *ad hoc* basis, attempting to correct what he considers social inequities as he finds them. Unfortunately, the most obvious force for such *ad hoc* exercises of government power is the ballot box. As a number of voters become assured that they constitute a group in their collective capacity, they increasingly tend to utilize the coercive powers of the state to reap benefits from the public till. With the encouragement of political candidates seeking their votes, other groups respond in like measure, until, as H. L. Mencken put it, "there are now only two classes of men in the United States: those who work for their livings, and those who vote for them."[2]

The welfare state, insofar as it exists in this country, is a patch-work of interferences in the private life of the citizen: yet all of these interferences are justified in the name of equality and humanitarianism. It is this fact which makes welfarism so grave a threat to our liberties. No less an observer of the status of American freedom than Mr. Justice Brandeis emphasized that "Experience should teach us to be most on our guard to protect liberty when the Government's purposes are beneficent. Men born to freedom are naturally alert to repel invasion of their liberty by evil-minded rulers. The greatest dangers to liberty lurk in insidious encroachment by men of zeal, well meaning but without understanding."[3]

I submit that this "insidious encroachment" on our civil freedoms is already a reality. As temporary majorities form in our state and national legislatures to enact a statute benefiting still another special interest group, the "oppression of one part of society by the injustice of the other part" becomes further en-trenched in our law.[4] Because of the generality of these assertions, it would be well to cite several instances of the anti-libertarian effects of welfarism and the extensions of government activity enacted by a Liberal-minded government.

The sphere of human endeavor which is most peculiarly sensitive to government interference is the quest of the individual for knowledge upon which to base his political and social judgments. Intelligent action may be impossible without access to information leading to an understanding of the alternatives open to the actor. In a free society, such action should be the resultant of autonomously derived preferences. As Professor F. A. Hayek has said, "The conception that government should be guided by majority opinion makes sense only if that opinion is independent of government. The ideal of democracy rests on the belief that the view which will direct government emerges from an independent and spontaneous process. It requires, therefore, the existence of a large sphere independent of majority control in which the opinions of the individuals are formed."[5]

A similar conclusion may be reached concerning private decision-making: we are less free to the extent that we must depend upon government as a source of knowledge, or are limited in our access to knowledge by the regulatory actions of government. The entry of the Federal Government into the field of scientific, medical, and sociological research, almost to the exclusion of private philanthropy, poses a unique danger insofar as the relevant bureaus of government may now determine which subjects are to be investigated and which allowed to atrophy. Political control of research is rapidly becoming the technological counterpart of the President's power over political information. It has been said of the President's use of his periodic

309

---

[2] H. L. Mencken, *A Mencken Chrestomathy*, (New York: Knopf, 1949), p. 622.

[3] Dissenting opinion, *Olmstead v. United States*, 277 U. S. 479 (1927).

[4] James Madison, *The Federalist*, No. 51, (New York: Modern Library, 1936), p. 339. See also Bruno Leoni, *Freedom and the Law*, (Princeton: Van Nostrand, 1961).

[5] F. A. Hayek, *The Constitution of Liberty*, (Chicago: University of Chicago Press, 1960), p. 109.

press conference that, "He uses it as a tool. He makes the news, chooses the emphasis and decides where to put it."[6] In much the same way, the financial monopoly over technical research increasingly being enjoyed by the government allows this power to choose the emphasis and decide where to put it in a host of non-political areas.

At the same time as the Federal Government is increasing its sphere of activity, we see a trend in Washington encouraging official censorship of bureaucratic proceedings, again enlarging the area where access to knowledge is limited by the political power. Much of this silencing is excused in terms of cold war requirements. The celebrated "muzzling of the military" controversy is novel not because of the fact of censorship but because of the apparent extent of it. It would be tragic if the trend towards official censorship was a reflection of the extraordinary conclusion by Senator J. William Fulbright, in his now famous "Memorandum," that, "Fundamentally, it is believed that the American people have little, if any, need to be alerted to the menace of the cold war." Yet, if this conviction that the electorate must be kept in ignorance of complex international problems does not influence the Administration, why has the President granted the power of censorship to at least six Federal agencies since he assumed office?[7]

Closely related to the need for independent sources of information is the requirement that methods of *communicating* knowledge be allowed freedom from government compulsion or persuasion. If the state exercises restraint upon the mechanical communicators of ideas and opinions, liberty of expression may become a luxury of personal correspondence. Those who advocate an expansion of the powers of the Federal Communications Commission to include

compulsory national programming for radio and television justify their beliefs by reference to the public welfare: even if the masses prefer the twist, we must elevate them with Beethoven. Although I personally prefer Bach and Handel to Rock and Roll, I can see no excuse for foisting my views on others, with the assistance of government power. The possibilities of coercing the common citizen through central control of the popular news media are appalling. It is, perhaps, not too far-fetched to suggest that the well-intentioned Newton Minow of today may find himself establishing administrative machinery usable by a Joseph Goebbels in the future.

We have already seen the government postal monopoly used to deny the use of the mails for literature deemed "subversive" or "obscene" by the authorities. If bureaucratic yahoos are ever allowed to ban the novels of D. H. Lawrence again, I suspect that there will be no limit to postal censorship. Another extension of the postal power to limit dissent is illustrated by the recent successful attempt to deny postal meter privileges to a company which printed Mr. Robert Welch's slogan "This is a Republic, not a Democracy" on its metered envelopes. Regardless of what we may think of this epigram of the Birch Society, it would be salutary if the postmen would stick to delivering the mail and cease reading it.

The power of the Federal Government over passports and visas has also been used to limit speech and access to information for political reasons. When the Young Americans for Freedom invited President Moise Tshombe of Katanga Province to address their rally in New York City last March, the State Department refused to grant a visa to the Congolese leader because to do so would not be in the "best interests" of American policy in central Africa. Under our laws, the denial of a visa may not be appealed to the courts. Presumably, Mr. Tshombe has a point of view on the late United Nations invasion of his province. It is unlikely that one can make a seriously intelligent decision on so complex a problem as the Congo crisis unless he is allowed to hear all relevant points of

---

[6] Statement by Benjamin McKelway, editor, *The Washington Star*.

[7] These agencies are the Peace Corps, Office of Emergency Planning, Agency for International Development, President's Foreign Intelligence Advisory Board, United States Arms Control and Disarmament Agency, and the Federal Maritime Commission.

310

view. The denial of the visa to Tshombe implies that assent to official policy is the only acceptable position — truly a negation of the civil liberties view of the desirability of independently derived opinion.

The use of government power, in the name of welfare, to limit effective opinion and dissent is further illustrated by our labor laws. Under this legislation, a worker may be compelled to join a union in order to keep his job, once a union contract has been signed. Not only must the dissenting employee join this supposedly voluntary organization, thereby denying him the basic liberty of association, but he must contribute monies to the union which are spent in support of candidates for public office which he may not approve. Thus the dissenter is put in the anomalous position of enhancing the very opinions with which he does not agree: as in old England, even the atheist must pay for the Church.

IN ADDITION TO direct government interferences with dissent and access to information, there has been a tendency to use the taxing and spending powers to influence thought and speech. The vast increase in government contracts, for example, has created a demand that such contracts be conditioned upon the institution of "acceptable" hiring policies by the private contractor. The problems of racial discrimination are more fully discussed below; however, I suspect that public statements by the contractor might also become an important factor governing eligibility for Federal funds.

The government's power to give leads to its power to take away. Tax exemptions, which are pretty much left to the discretion of Congress, may become extremely valuable tools for subverting civil liberties. Already, one company has felt the censorial powers of the Internal Revenue Service, which has denied a tax deduction to the Timken Roller Bearing Company for certain advertisements it ran in the years 1951 to 1954. These were "institutional" ads which published various messages that

Timken thought were in the public interest and likely to engage the good will of the public. Needless to say, they espoused the conservative position. If the taxing authorities can pick and choose the policy-oriented advertisements for which they will allow a deduction, a most valuable method of free communication may be selectively denied. The same argument applies to tax-exempt foundations: to the extent that we give the Commissioner the discretion to grant or deny such exemptions, we allow the government to enhance "acceptable" ideology at public expense.

A highly important area where the Liberals would like to extend Federal power is in the field of education. The question of Federal aid to education has been debated at great length over the past few years and little can be added to this controversy. The conservatives warned that Federal control would follow Federal aid: the Liberals disputed this contention. Then the National Defense Education Act was passed, along with over a dozen Federal controls, including the famous loyalty oath and disclaimer affidavit provisions. It should not be surprising that political strings were attached to the financial grants under the Act; if the advocates of "progressive" education or Admiral Rickover have their way, we will soon see a national curriculum established as well. What could be a more perfect weapon for thought control than a centrally determined curriculum for our schools?

Government assistance to the arts is a final instance I will cite of the danger that welfare enactments can infringe upon our access to knowledge and dissenting opinion. An excellent presentation of "The Case Against Government Aid to the Arts" appeared in the March 25, 1962 edition of the *New York Times Magazine*, by Russell Lynes, managing editor of *Harper's*. Mr. Lynes emphasizes the danger that mediocrity may prevail and the controversial or experimental arts may suffer if we permit a "marriage between the fine arts and the Government." After citing the objections of several Congressmen to the art exhibits sponsored by our State Department, Mr. Lynes notes that

311

There is no way for the arts to get Federal subsidies without accountability to the people for how the money is spent. This means, of course, that those who administer the subsidies first must decide what is art and what is not art, and they will have to draw the line between the "popular" arts and the "serious" arts, a distinction that is increasingly difficult to define. . . . Having decided what is serious, it will follow that those who dispense the funds will also decide what is safe . . . [and] able to be defended with reasonable equanimity before a Congressional committee.

Enough has been recited of Mr. Lynes' article to convince us that Robert Benchley was almost clairvoyant when he predicted that political assistance to the arts might lead to such campaign slogans as "Vote for John A. Ossip! He kept us out of post-impressionism!" and "Down with the nude in art! Vote for Horace W. Pickerell and the sanctity of the home!"[8]

Beyond the limitations and coercions by which welfarism and the extension of government activity adversely affects our liberties of access to information and communication of dissenting ideas, there exists in the welfare state "a network of small and complicated rules, minute and uniform,"[9] which tend to stifle freedom of association and limit the privacy of the individual. What once had been deemed matters for private decision have become public questions: the once-voluntary relations of men are now subjected to state regulation. Just as the President may now compel an eighty day postponement of a strike by a labor union, there have been suggestions, following the proposed rise in steel prices, that the Chief Executive be granted the power to set the price for important goods when it is deemed in the public interest to do so.

We learned a lot about government power during President Kennedy's crusade against the steel industry. The Chief Executive summoned an enormous host of coercive weapons against Messrs. Blough and company: he harangued the steel executives on all the mass communications media in the country; he threatened to withhold defense contracts from the recalcitrant companies; his brother had the F.B.I. wake up newspapermen at three o'clock in the morning; and, to top it off, the President publicly accused Mr. Blough of *treason*. The crime of the steel companies was, of course, their desire to set their own prices on their own products.

Private decision making would be further limited under a recommendation by former Secretary of Labor Goldberg, that the Federal Government should participate in collective bargaining disputes and "provide guidelines to the parties" that would "insure 'right settlements' that take into account the public interest [as "asserted and defined" by the government] as well as the interests of the parties."[10]

IN A SIMILAR VEIN as these interferences are the host of recent statutes which attempt to enforce a public policy on *private* race relations. Originally, Southern states enacted legislation which prohibited inter-racial private housing, private schools, and private accommodations. There is little doubt that such interferences restrict the liberty of the citizen to buy, sell, and associate with whom he pleases. Now, under Liberal sponsorship, many Northern states have passed laws prohibiting racially restrictive private housing, private employment, and private accommodations and restaurants. It is difficult to see any essential difference between these statutes and the Southern ones: both speak in the name of a "public policy"; both are justified in terms of the welfare of the community; and both equally restrict the liberties of the citizen.

In an attempt to eradicate the blight of racial prejudice, created in part by laws which required such prejudice in private relations, the Liberals have

---

[8] Quoted from "Art in Politics," by Robert Benchley, *Vanity Fair*, March, 1919.

[9] Alexis de Tocqueville, *Democracy in America*, (New York: Vintage, 1956), vol. II, p. 337.

[10] *The New York Times*, February 28, 1962, pp. 1, 10.

merely substituted a new form of invasion of private rights. In the past, the Federal Housing Administration *required* racially restrictive covenants in all FHA-insured mortgages; today, an individual may not enforce such a covenant even if he has voluntarily agreed to it. The problem of racial discrimination in our private relations is indeed a serious one in this country, and there are many private and voluntary movements currently attempting to correct the situation. But, serious as the race problem may be, I submit that the personal liberty of the individual to associate or not to associate with whomever he chooses, for whatever reasons, rational or irrational, is too great a freedom to be sacrificed even in the name of "civil rights." "The chief danger today is that, once an aim of government is accepted as legitimate, it is then assumed that even means contrary to the principles of freedom may be legitimately employed."[11]

The classic instance of Tocqueville's "network of small complicated rules" in the United States today is in the field of agriculture. No American may grow cotton, sugar beets, tobacco or wheat without an acreage allotment from the Government. This is true even if the farmer wishes to consume the crops himself.[12] Fines are levied on farmers who grow more than their Federal quota. Moreover, the program enunciated by Secretary of Agriculture Freeman would add jail sentences to these fines, and would also provide for prison sentences for dairy farmers who keep inadequate records. It is restrictions like these which persuaded Michigan farmer Stanley Yankus to remove his family to Australia, after the Government had told him how much wheat he could grow on his own land to feed to his own chickens.[13]

The tragedy of extending government power, in the name of social welfare, is not only what it does to the liberty of the citizen, but also the way in which

it makes the bureaucrat indifferent or even callous to the deprivations and hardships inflicted on individuals. Two examples of this will suffice. The first concerns the administration of Social Security, surely the sacred cow of the welfare state. Under the law, F. I. C. A. payments are compulsory taxes, not voluntary insurance premiums. This fact was not evident to an Amish farmer in Pennsylvania named Byler, whose religion prohibits him from accepting government old-age assistance. Byler was not aware of the paternal nature of welfare legislation: since he did not intend to accept the benefits therefrom, he never paid any social security premiums. The beneficent Internal Revenue Service finally caught up with him last year, demanded all back payments with interest, and finally levied on his workhorse (he has no tractor) and sold it to make up the deficiency. As a result of a program aimed at easing the financial woes of retirement, farmer Byler has been deprived of his only means of sustenance. Since he will not accept government hand-outs, he has been made a charge on his family and denied his source of livelihood.

Even more blase in his callousness than the Tax Commissioner is our ubiquitous Interior Secretary, Stewart Udall. Secretary Udall was searching for land to condemn in Kansas last November, when he spied the ranch of one Carl Bellinger from his helicopter. The Secretary simply alighted on Bellinger's land and began to explore it, at which point Bellinger informed him that he was trespassing and would he please get off the land. Secretary Udall later commented: "It's too bad that when a member of the President's Cabinet tries to take a walk on a hill he is told to get off, but the National Park will remedy that!"[14]

It is always possible to "remedy" the exercise of individual liberty through the use of government and its coercive powers. The dangers to freedom which I have tried to illustrate were all established by what Mr. Justice Brandeis

[11] F. A. Hayek, *op. cit.*, p. 260.
[12] See *Wickard v. Filburn*, 317 U. S. 111 (1942).
[13] *The Freeman*, April, 1962, p. 34.

[14] Quoted in *National Review*, December 16, 1961, p. 401.

called "men of zeal, well meaning but without understanding." An understanding of the threat to liberty resulting from the abandonment of the idea of limited government is absolutely necessary if we are to maintain the existence of the autonomous individual as more than a mere legal fiction. I can think of no more eloquent description of the depressing effects of welfarism on liberty than the comments of Alexis de Tocqueville in a chapter appropriately titled, "What Sort of Despotism Democratic Nations Have to Fear," from his *Democracy in America*:

Above this race of men stands an immense and tutelary power, which takes upon itself alone to secure their gratifications and to watch over their fate. That power is absolute, minute, regular, provident, and mild. It would be like the authority of a parent if, like that authority, its object was to prepare men for manhood; but it seeks, on the contrary, to keep them in perpetual childhood . . . it provides for their security, foresees and supplies their necessities, facilitates their pleasures, manages their principal concerns, directs their industry, regulates the descent of property, and subdivides their inheritances: what remains, but to spare them all the care of thinking and all the trouble of living?

Thus it every day renders the exercise of the free agency of man less useful and less frequent; it circumscribes the will within a narrower range and gradually robs a man of all the uses of himself. The principle of equality has prepared men for these things; it has predisposed men to endure them and often to look on them as benefits.

After having thus successively taken each member of the community in its powerful grasp and fashioned him at will, the supreme power then extends its arm over the whole community. It covers the surface of society with a network of small complicated rules, minute and uniform, through which the most original minds and the most energetic characters cannot penetrate, to rise above the crowd. The will of man is not shattered, but softened, bent, and guided; men are seldom forced by it to act, but they are constantly restrained from acting. Such a power does not destroy, but it prevents existence; it does not tyrannize, but it compresses, enervates, extinguishes, and stupefies a people, till each nation is reduced to nothing better than a flock of timid and industrious animals, of which the government is the shepherd.[15]

Although written in the 1830's, de Tocqueville's prognostication of the American dilemma becomes more and more accurate with the years. The extension of government and the idea of welfarism often compel a choice between liberty and equality. We must recognize that these goals are not synonymous, that we may lose our liberties in the search for a chimera of equality.

---

[15] Alexis de Tocqueville, *op. cit.*, vol. II, pp. 336, 337.

New Conservatives and Old Liberals

BENJAMIN A. ROGGE

AS MANY OF my readers may know, a college dean is not paid to think — or, at least, to think about matters extraneous to the operation of his college. For him even to continue an interest in his old pre-deaning discipline is thought by many to be evidence of a frivolous approach to administration. In line with this tradition, I have limited myself in recent years to one non-dean-type thought at a time, and I can never predict what that thought will be at a given moment. When I came to jotting down some notes for this essay, I found myself bemused by the new conservatism; thus, I had no choice but to take it as my topic.

This choice makes some sense in that I am considered to be a conservative by that embarrassingly small number of people who have thought me worth classifying. Also, there is much talk and writing these days about the new conservatism or the "revival of conservatism," or, as some would put it, the "recrudescence of conservatism."

So as to remove any element of suspense from this presentation, let me say immediately that, from the vantage point of *my* particular brand of conservatism, much of the new conservatism is a hindrance rather than an aid to the cause.

Benjamin A. Rogge, Dean of Wabash College, is co-author of the college textbook *Introduction to Economics* and is a contributor to professional journals.

Or, to put it differently, with some of these people as my friends, I don't need any enemies.

It should be obvious to you now that we are about to play a game of semantics. What is a "conservative"? What is a "liberal"? There is the story of three famous umpires discussing the calling of balls and strikes. The first one says, "I calls them as I sees 'em." The second one says, "I calls them as they *are*." The third one, and my hero, says, "They ain't nothin' 'til I calls 'em!"

I'm going to play the role of the third umpire and begin by saying that, of course, I am not properly identified when I am called a conservative. Rather, I am a classical (or, if you prefer, a primitive) liberal. The distinguishing characteristics of a classical liberal are: (1) a deep and abiding distrust of government, and (2) a belief that each individual should be free to do and believe and say anything he wishes so long as he is not using force or fraud against some other individual. The political philosophy that follows from these beliefs is one that limits the government to the night-watchman's role, to preventing one individual from using force or fraud against another. The economic philosophy is basically that of *laissez-faire*. My intellectual mentors would be such men as Adam Smith, David Ricardo, the early John Stuart Mill, Frederick Bastiat, de Tocqueville, Lord Acton and, among the moderns, Frank Knight and F. A. Hayek.

IF THIS BE TRUE LIBERALISM, what then is true conservatism? The distinguishing characteristics of true conservatism are: (1) a deep mistrust of human reason, and (2) a belief that order and continuity are of paramount importance in nurturing and preserving the humane and civilized virtues of human beings in society. The true conservative sees society as always threatened by a return to barbarism, with the only effective restraints on brute man being those of religion, custom, recognition of an aristocracy of birth, etc. Thus an Edmund Burke sees in a French Revolution, not the coming of the new and enlightened Jerusalem, but a break in the pattern of society so violent that only barbarism or tyranny can result from it. Personally, I think it clear that Burke was right, and, in fact, I find much with which I can sympathize in this, the true, conservatism. Modern representatives of this point of view are such men as Peter Viereck and Russell Kirk.

However, it is not this kind of sophisticated and philosophical conservatism that is being revived. Nor can I ever forget that over the centuries, in actual operation this true conservative philosophy has brought man, not freedom, but bondage. The prototype of the unfree man has been the one living in a tyranny, supported by religion, administered by an hereditary monarch, and made impotent by the dead-weight of custom. The ancient kingdom of Sparta, a truly conservative state, finally defeated Athens, but it is not a society I would care to see reborn. I realize that that the true conservative would say that Sparta was conservatism exaggerated and made rigid, but this seems often to be the end of true conservatism in practice.

However, as I said before, the new conservatism is not the true conservatism. What then is it? It is, in fact, an odd mixture of many conflicting elements. It is, for example, a Robert Welch and a John Birch Society. A Robert Welch would give man his freedom in economic life, as I would. But he would not give man freedom to preach the end of freedom, e.g., to preach Communism, and I

would. I do not know Mr. Welch but I do know a number of the members of his society. They are serious, sincere people, who see this nation facing a crafty and terrible enemy, in fact, so crafty that he is able to enlist the conscious or unwitting support of many of our own people. National survival then depends on exposing and defeating this enemy wherever he might be found. I say these people are serious and sincere, but so were the Athenians who sentenced Socrates to death for subverting the youth of the city. So were the men who devised the Spanish Inquisition; so was Martin Luther when he advised the ruler of a German province to shoot down like dogs the German peasants who threatened the stability of the society; so was John Knox, the father of the Presbyterian Church, when he urged that all Catholics in Scotland be put to death; so were the people who gave trouble to my German-born grandfather in World War I, in spite of the fact that he had a son fighting in the AEF; so were the Americans who ordered imprisonment for thousands of Japanese-Americans in World War II. So are they always who, in fright, hope to solve their problems by hunting out the "bad" guys, and eliminating them.

Let us remember now the spirit of David Ricardo, the great classical economist of the early 19th century, who, born a Jew, turned Quaker, yet spent part of his personal fortune to end legal discrimination against Catholics in Great Britain, and in Parliament defended a book-seller who had been imprisoned for selling the free thought works of Tom Paine. Freedom of belief and advocacy means exactly that — and for Communist and John Bircher alike.

A second much-talked-about element in the new conservatism is campus conservatism, or the phenomenal growth of conservative clubs on college and university campuses. There is much in this that I can find interesting and attractive, but much that I find disturbing as well. Many of the young men and women seem to be concerned with the central issues of the individual vs. the state. But many others seem to be only self-importantly and noisily anti-communist. They seem to see their tasks as those of identifying and exposing the left-wingers on the faculty and protecting the House Committee on Un-American Activities. The super-patriot is never a true friend of individual liberty, nor is he who would advance the cause of liberty by restricting the freedoms of all those who disagree with him.

I MUST CONFESS that I can never be very optimistic about the contribution to the cause of freedom of college-age youth. Classical liberalism is essentially an end-of-innocence philosophy. It requires accepting the imperfect nature of man and hence the imperfect nature of all human constructs. It sadly, but firmly, insists that the New Jerusalem is never to be realized. It denies that man can consciously and deliberately plan himself into the good life and the good world. It places its restricted faith in the unpredictable and unplanned consequences of the individual decisions of free men and women.

This is a philosophy of the mature human being. It has little real appeal to the confident, hyper-critical mind of the young person. It is the young who believe in the possibility of a heaven on earth brought into being by the conscious exercise of their mighty power of reason — and who are prepared to sweep aside those whose feeble minds or weak wills make them an obstacle to the cause. It is later in life, if ever, that a man reconciles himself to living in an imperfect world in which imperfect people make imperfect decisions — and is willing to let them do so, so long as they do not infringe on his freedom and the freedom of others. In sum, while I am encouraged by the increasing interest of college students in the cause of individual freedom, I must confess that I think much of this interest is about as well-grounded in philosophic commitment as their interest in panty raids and school spirit. If freedom survives in the decades ahead, it will be because age and not youth has had its way.

A third element in the new conservatism is reflected in a group of senators, but particularly Representatives in Congress, who belligerently identify themselves as conservatives. Some of these men I find very attractive and indeed some of them seem to be consistent classical liberals. But most of them prove their conservatism by (1) urging the United States to use its military might to crush Communism, (2) supporting all restrictive measures against domestic Communism and fellow-travelers, (3) vigorously upholding the rights of the individual states to deny Negroes equality before the law, and (4) always supporting the "business" interest, whether it be by tariffs, right-to-work laws, fair trade acts, special tax treatment or what have you. In none of this do I find any evidence of a true commitment to the principle of freedom and its corollary, the rule of law.

I am no more attracted by government intervention in economic life to give special treatment to business groups than I am to the anti-business interventions supported by the modern liberal. This brings me at last to the other side, the belligerent non-conservatives, the authors of the New Frontier, the Fair Deal, the New Deal — and Modern Republicanism. If I don't like my fellow conservatives, why don't I ally myself with those who are called liberals today?

THE ANSWER IS that these people are no more truly liberal than my conservative friends. Admittedly, they usually come down on the right (or freedom) side of the fence when the issue relates to freedom of speech or of press or of belief — although some of them are inconsistent even here. But they have absolutely no commitment to economic freedom—nor any recognition of its relationship to all other freedoms. They are the would-be philosopher-kings who are going to protect, guide, manipulate, subsidize and control those who are less blessed with wisdom than they. They are the legal Robin Hoods, who in never-ending gallantry, are going to use the coercive power of the state to take from one man and give to another. They are the planners of great plans, whereby this country is going to achieve an annual growth rate of 6.12 per cent, and all the underdeveloped countries of the world are to be brought quickly into the modern world. Their point of view is magnificently represented by Mr. Minow of the Federal Communications Commission, whose complaint against the television industry is that it is giving the viewers what they (the viewers) want. Under this philosophy, workers and farmers are forced by law to do that for which businessmen are sent to jail. Under this philosophy, the blindfolded Goddess of Justice has been permitted — nay encouraged — to peek, and she now says with the jurists of the ancient regime, "First tell me *who* you are and then I'll tell you what your rights are."

No, there is no commitment to freedom in this philosophy, nor is there any of that fear of the state, of government, upon which any philosophy of freedom must be grounded.

What then is left for a classical liberal? With which side is he to ally himself — the conservative or the modern liberal? In answer and in closing I would like to describe one of my favorite cartoons from *The New Yorker*. In the picture, a mother is feeding a vegetable to a little girl in a high chair and the little girl is obviously having none of it. In the caption, the mother says, "But dear, it's broccoli"; to which the little girl replies, "I say it's spinach and I say the hell with it."

Whether on the one hand it is called patriotism or true Americanism, or anti-communist, or pro-business, or anti-labor; whether on the other hand it is called humanitarianism, liberalism, the wave of the future, economic democracy, the welfare state, the New Frontier or the New Deal, I say it's spinach and I say the hell with it.

(The following is reprinted from the front page of the Book Review Supplement of a prominent American metropolitan newspaper, with the kind permission of the original publishers. Due to technical inadequacies, we are not able to reprint the illustration accompanying the review. It was a reproduction of the Picasso mural, "Guernica," set in the middle of the first page, with the caption: "That it might not happen here . . .")

When America Spoke

With One Voice

Fascism in Retreat, by Harold Forstman (New York, 1966). 278 pp. $4.95.

Reviewed by Wesley Mouchner

THROUGH THE AGES, commentators on the human scene have sadly observed that men find it difficult, if not impossible, to learn from experience. (Santayana added that those who refuse to learn from history are condemned to repeat its errors.) A glorious exception to this rule, however, occurred two years ago, appropriately enough in the United States (a nation whose whole history demonstrates that its only deeply-rooted tradition has been the tendency to break with all tradition). At that time, society, recalling the way in which the Nazi Party had gained control of a powerful nation and used it to further its own diabolical schemes, decided that it would simply not be permitted to happen here. It is this episode which Mr. Forstman has set himself to chronicle, with the meticulous scholarship and engaging prose style which are his trademark.

Fascism in Retreat concerns, of course,

the Great Sedition Trial of the three young would-be Hitlers, arrested, tried and executed in New York, in 1964. But primarily it deals with the public reaction to this seditious conspiracy, and, in this way, it serves as a vindication of the proud claim of democracy: a pluralistic society, in time of crisis, *is* ready and willing to learn from the evident successes of closed societies—it *can* and *will* summon forth the unanimity which alone insures national survival in the modern world.

Since it is a commonplace that the newspaper headlines of today are virtually obliterated from memory, once they give way to the headlines of tomorrow, it might be well to recapitulate the chief events of the Great Sedition Trial. The facts, briefly, are these:

It was on December 31, 1964, that death came to John Williams, 22, Hugh Marlowe, 21, and Richard Phillips, 17, in the electric chair at Sing Sing Prison. (Polls indicated that the execution, the first to be shown on television, had an audience of 79 million, a record for the industry.) The executions climaxed a series of trials and appeals which had been the focus of world attention. The youths, you may remember, were indicted on January 16, 1964, for plotting a war against society and the United States Government, and conspiring to violate the United Nations Declaration of Human Rights. During the lengthy

319

Mr. Mouchner, a Professor of Thought and Civilization at Brandeis University, is an authority on the history of ideas, and a frequent contributor to this Book Review Supplement. His most recent book, *Radicalism from Francis of Assisi to Karl Marx,* was reviewed here last week by Harold Forstman.

trial the prosecution established a well-developed conspiracy of sixteen youths between the ages of 12 and 25, with the long-range purpose of exterminating Catholics, Jews and Masons throughout the country. To implement the conspiracy, they had procured Nazi arm-bands, blank membership cards and records of Hitler speeches. Annotated copies of *Mein Kampf, The Merchant of Venice,* and *Oliver Twist* were found in Williams' room, where the meetings were held.

One of the most encouraging aspects of this whole story is the part played by the American judiciary, which renounced a sterile, and, in any case, impossible, "impartiality," in favor of a forthright and courageous defense of democratic society. By a six-three decision, the Supreme Court refused to grant the appeal of the Fascist leaders. (A motion for the impeachment of the dissenting Justices was introduced in the House by the senior member of the Brooklyn delegation.)

An especially interesting sidelight in connection with the Court's decision was that Justice Clerk, writing for the majority, for the first time in judicial history employed a quantifiable formula, utilizing higher mathematics in order to arrive at a verdict. Thus, he has shown that American law will not permit itself to fall behind in the grand movement aimed at converting jurisprudence into a branch of bio-physics. His formula was an improvement of the rule devised by the Second Circuit in the Dennis case:

$$C_L{}^* = i_p \bullet \log_e d^m \over \det [D_{fp}]$$

___

[1] Where: i_D = intensity of the danger.

$\log_e d^m$ = naperian logarithm of the danger raised to the power of its immediacy.

$\det [D_{fp}]$ = determinant of the matrix of all possible dangers to freedom from prohibition of the act.

$C_L{}^*$ = constitutionality of the lower court decision.

If the first order partial derivative of $C_L{}^*$ with respect to i_p exceeds zero, the decision is constitutional; if zero or less, it is unconstitutional, provided of course that $\det [D_{fp}]$ is positive definite.

Page Thirty-six

Since with the aid of a team of mathematicians and cyberneticists from the Massachusetts Institute of Technology and a BUM 70707070 computer, Justice Clerk found the relevant partial derivative to be well in excess of zero, he concluded that there was obviously no constitutional problem.

Justice Hamburger, in a concurring seventy-nine page opinion, which represented an expression of true judicial statesmanship, pointed out that English law had permitted similar proceedings in the past, notably in the reign of Charles I. He demonstrated, by citing his own concurring opinions in previous cases, that the ordered liberty prescribed by the Constitution allowed interference with government action only when o u r civilized conscience was shocked, and he further pointed out that he wasn't shocked at all.

Justices Hugo Blank and William O'Doodle both wrote dissenting opinions. Justice O'Doodle noted that, "While this power is now being exercised by a beneficent executive in the best interest of society, it might in the future be used against communists and radicals." One cannot help but sympathize with the Justice's concern. When one remembers the McCarthy era, when irresponsible accusations were hurled even at such liberal organizations as Americans for Demogogic Action, the Conspiracy of Industrial Organizations, OGPU and SMERSH, one realizes that the safeguards of freedom for progressive groups cannot be too firmly maintained. Nevertheless, when such liberty is extended to ultra-rightist groups, it seems difficult to avoid the conclusion that it has become a thin veil for license.

THE ACLU EXTENDED help to the defendants. In the aftermath of this action, however, approximately one-third of its membership, including a preponderance in the New York area, switched to a rival civil liberties group, which had, in a unanimous resolution, upheld the decision of the Supreme Court for what it was, "a great landmark in the glorious struggle to protect the legitimate rights of minorities." The Special Committee to Protect the Feelings of Minorities (SCPFM), composed of New York and Washington civil liberties lawyers, proclaimed that, "Any rational definition of freedom must include the freedom of the members of society to not be subjected to the views of anti-social and racist elements. Racist views are clearly in a different category from views against a class (which are, of course, deserving of protection), for the latter views can be supported by rational arguments." Meanwhile, liberal students at Berkeley and the University of Chicago postponed protest demonstrations against the flight of refugees from Cuba and East Germany, in order to express their approval of the Court's action.

The larger perspective of history was opened up on the Conspiracy by William L. Shyster, the noted journalist and historian. After much research, he uncovered and published the fact that three of the sixteen young men involved in the case were of German descent, demonstrating the absolute incorrigibility and congenital degeneration of this race. "The totalitarian mentality of the Germans is an old story," he declared in an article published in a prominent popular magazine, and later beamed to West Germany by the Voice of America. "It began with Luther and Bach, was carried on by Hegel, Nietzsche, and the mad monster, Franz Schubert, and culminated in the perfect expression of the 'German soul': Hitler and Himmler." When it was pointed out to Mr. Shyster that, of the three youths, two were descended from ancestors who had left Germany after having participated in the unsuccessful Revolutions of 1848, he remarked that this "merely shows the hypocrisy of those people." To the further observation that there were also in the group two Swedes, four Scotch-Irish and three Armenians, he retorted with his customary humor and verve: "Try to sell *that* to the Book-of-the-Month Club!"

One of the most surprising outcomes of the Trial was the manner in which certain groups, especially those on the Responsible Right, sided with the majority consensus, and thereby, for the first time, entered the Dialogue. (Certain isolated individuals, like extreme civil libertarian lawyers, left the Dialogue in the course of this episode. Others, such as nihilistic libertarians of the Manchester variety, the Austrian-type economists etc., were, naturally, never within the Dialogue.) The organizational manifestation of this new turn of events was the liaison meeting between the Anti-Fascist Committee of the Americans for Demogogic Action, and the newly formed League to Protect Virtue, headed by Helbent Moselle and Wantmore Kindling (the famed authority on subversion and the disposal of heretics). The joint statements that were issued by these groups indicate that, although there were still certain differences in regard to substantive matters, surprisingly little disagreement existed as to form. Both groups agreed that while freedom in the abstract might be desirable,[2] any doctrinaire absolutism on this issue would lead to the breakdown of the consensual framework without which social life is impossible. Abridgments of freedom in the abstract are indispensible, in order to protect freedom in the concrete. One of the practical consequences of this agreement was rather interesting, as an example of the spirit of give-and-take which must govern the actions even of ideological antagonists in a democratic society. In return for a brilliant editorial in the nation's leading conservative journal, which castigated the supporters of acquittal for the Fascists for being guilty of no less than eleven Christian heresies, the liberal organization agreed that, in the media of mass communication which it controlled, the term "responsible right" would be used three times for every one reference to the "ultra-right."

As the distinguished columnist, Marx Larner, pointed out at the time, however, the rightest intellectuals still appeared wedded to certain of their former incon-

321

---

[2] Mr. Moselle had waged an unsuccessful fight to have the statement read, "might or *might not* be . . ."

sistencies. In particular, they were guilty of the time-worn fallacy that persecution of Communists is as justified as persecution of fascists! While applauding the new amalgamation, Larner went on to warn that, "Such reactionaries are, unfortunately, still unable to recognize the essential difference between fascism and communism, just as they cannot see the difference *in kind* between, on the one hand, the mad-dog mass murders of the Nazis, and, on the other hand, the —admittedly *regrettable* and *inexcusable* —elimination of millions of *kulaks* under the pressure of economic necessity."

WHILE THE CONSENSUS in favor of the convictions was well-nigh unanimous as concerns each and every respectable group in the nation, there were, of course, certain scattered lunatic fringe elements which were shrill in their frenzied opposition. The tiny Society of Christian Soldiers, for instance, announced that the executions (which they claimed had been engineered by the Council on Foreign Relations) were symbolic re-enactments of the Crucifixion, designed to return us to the era before Christ. The chief journalist among the unreconstructed Roosevelt-haters proclaimed in his column that the conviction "marks the complete triumph of Warren, Myrdal, Stalin and Freud. They are now able to destroy physically, as well as economically, the best of the native patriotic forces which offer hope of salvation from alien cosmopolitan enslavement." On a self-consciously more "sophisticated" plane, the handful of allies which these hate-peddlers have at various universities worked the tired old cliche' about "rule of law" into the ground. And so on, *ad nauseam*. It should be obvious that there was nothing either new or correct in the reactions of these few persons. They are the same ones who have opposed TVA, Social Security and the dismantling of American industry for shipment to India. In perusing their polemical outbursts, one cannot help agreeing with modern psychology, sociology and astrology, which have all conclusively proven that mental imbalance and latent social status tensions are at the base of such extreme right-wing positions.

This then is the story Mr. Forstman tells in his new book. He tells it with compassion, humor and philosophical detachment, e.g.: "No one will ever convince the American people that such Fascist scum have a right to life." It remains only to sum up the more long-range significance of the episode of which Mr. Forstman has shown himself the able historian.

I would say that its greatest significance is this: another victory was won in a great age-old battle. The contenders have changed in each generation: Galileo against t h e Inquisition; Milton against a government which claimed the right to license presses; Voltaire, Zola and the American Establishment in their defenses of Jean Callas, Alfred Dreyfus and Alger Hiss, respectively. And I insist that the Great Sedition Trial represented a victory *in this very struggle*. It might appear superficially that what was at stake in these contests were some metaphysical dogmas, "freedom" of speech and belief, or protection of certain individuals and minorities against the arbitrary power of the rest of Society (as if any individual or group could exist *outside* of Society!). But in fact the real issue has always been *reform* or *reaction*, or, as it used to be put in my student days, in the Thirties (before the present-day intellectual sterility and political apathy set in), "the Revolution *vs.* the Counter-Revolution." The Sedition Trial, and the magnificent way in which the American people responded to its challenge, prove again that the great American promise, as exemplified in Jefferson, Lincoln, the Knights of Labor, and Chester Bowles, can survive and flourish in the modern world.

A New Treatise

on Economics[1]

LUDWIG VON MISES

MOST OF WHAT goes today under the label of the social sciences is poorly disguised apologetics for the policies of governments. What Santayana once said about a teacher of philosophy of the—then Royal Prussian—University of Berlin, that it seemed to this man "that a professor's business was to trudge along a governmental towpath with a legal cargo," is today everywhere true for the majority of those appointed to teach economics. As these doctors see it, all the evils that plague mankind are caused by the acquisitiveness of greedy exploiters, speculators and monopolists, who are supreme in the conduct of affairs in the market economy. It is the foremost task of good government to curb these scoundrels by suppressing their "economic freedom" and subjecting all affairs to the decisions of the central authority. Full government control of everybody's activities—whether called planning, socialism, communism, or any other name — is praised as the panacea.

To make these ideas plausible one had to proscribe as orthodox, classical, neoclassical and reactionary all that economics had brought forward before the emergence of the New Deal, the Fair Deal and the New Frontier. Any acquaintance with pre-Keynesian economics is considered as rather unsuitable and unseemly for an up-to-date economist. It could easily raise in his mind some critical thoughts. It could encourage him to reflect instead of meekly endorsing the empty slogans of governments and powerful pressure groups. There is, in fact, in the writings and teaching of those who nowadays call themselves economists no longer any comprehension of the operation of the economic system as such. These books and articles do not describe, analyze or explain the economic phenomena. They do not pay attention to the interdependence and mutuality of the various individuals' and groups' activities. In their view, there exist different economic spheres that have to be treated as by and large isolated domains. They dissolve economics in a number of special fields, such as economics of labor, of agriculture, of insurance, of foreign trade, of domestic trade and so on. They deal, e.g., with the height of wage rates as if it were possible to treat this subject independently of the problems of commodity prices, interest, profit and loss, and all the other issues of economics. They assemble, without any idea for what purpose they are doing it, a vast array of statistical and

Ludwig von Mises is currently a Professor at the Graduate School of Business at New York University. His many books include *Human Action, Socialism, The Anti-Capitalistic Mentality,* and most recently, *The Free and Prosperous Commonwealth.*

[1] A review of *Man, Economy and State,* Murray N. Rothbard (Princeton, New Jersey: Van Nostrand, 1962), 2 vols., 987 pp. $20.

other historical data about the recent past which they choose to style the "present." They entirely fail to comprehend the interconnectedness and mutual determination of the actions of the various individuals whose behavior results in the emergence of the market economy.

The economic writings of the last decades provide a pitiful story of progressing deterioration and degradation. Even a comparison of the recent publications of many older authors with their previous writings shows an advancing decline. The few, very few, good contributions that came out in our age were smeared as old-fashioned and reactionary by the government economists, boycotted by the universities, the academic magazines and the newspapers and ignored by the public.

324

LET US HOPE that the fate of Murray N. Rothbard's book *Man, Economy and State* will be different. Dr. Rothbard is already well known as the author of several excellent monographs. Now he joins the ranks of the eminent economists by publishing, as the result of many years of sagacious and discerning meditation, a voluminous work, a systematic treatise on economics.

The main virtue of this book is that it is a comprehensive and methodical analysis of all activities commonly called economic. It looks upon these activities as human action, i.e., as conscious striving after chosen ends by resorting to appropriate means. This cognition exposes the fateful errors of the mathematical treatment of economic problems. The mathematical economist attempts to ignore the difference between the physical phenomena in the emergence and consummation of which man is unable to see the operation of any final causes, and which can be studied scientifically only because in their concatenation and succession there prevails a perceptible regularity on the one hand, and, on the other, the praxeological phenomena that lack such a regularity but are conceivable to the human mind as purposeful aiming at definite ends chosen. Mathe-matical equations, says Rothbard, are appropriate and useful where there are constant quantitative relations among *unmotivated* variables, they are inappropriate in the field of conscious behavior. In a few brilliant lines he demolishes the main device of mathematical economists, viz., the fallacious idea of substituting the concepts of mutual determination and equilibrium for the allegedly outdated concept of cause and effect. And he shows that the concepts of equilibrium and the evenly rotating economy do not refer to reality, but are, although indispensable for any economic inquiry, merely auxiliary mental tools to aid us in the analysis of real action. The equations of physics describe a process through time, while those of economics do not describe at all a process, but merely the final equilibrium point, a hypothetical situation that is outside of time and will never be reached in reality. Furthermore, they cannot say anything about the path by which the economy moves in the direction of the final equilibrium position. As there are no constant relations between any of the elements which the science of action studies, there is no measurement possible and all numerical data available have merely a historical character; they belong to economic history and not to economics as such. The positivist slogan, "science is measurement," in no way refers to the sciences of human action; the claims of "econometrics" are vain.

In every chapter of his treatise, Dr. Rothbard, adopting the best of the teachings of his predecessors, and adding to them highly important observations, not only develops the correct theory but is no less anxious to refute all objections ever raised against these doctrines. He exposes the fallacies and contradictions of the popular interpretation of economic affairs. Thus, for instance, in dealing with the problem of unemployment he points out: in the whole modern and Keynesian discussion of this subject the missing link is precisely the wage rate. It is meaningless to talk of unemployment or employment without reference to a wage rate. Whatever supply of labor service is brought to market can be sold, but only if wages are set at whatever rate will clear the market. If a man wishes to be employed, he will be, provided the wage rate is adjusted according to what Rothbard calls his discounted marginal value product, i.e., the present height of the value which the consumers—at the time of the final sale of the product—will ascribe to his contribution to its production. Whenever the job-seeker insists on a higher wage, he will remain unemployed. If people refuse to be employed except at places, in occupations, or at wage rates they would like, then they are likely to be choosing unemployment for substantial periods. The full import of this state of affairs becomes manifest if one gives attention to the fact that, under present conditions, those offering their services on the labor market themselves represent the immense majority of the consumers whose buying or abstention from buying ultimately determines the height of wage rates.

Less successful than his investigations in the fields of general praxeology and of economics are the author's occasional observations concerning the philosophy of law and some problems of the penal code. But disagreement with his opinions concerning these matters cannot prevent me from qualifying Rothbard's work as an epochal contribution to the general science of human action, praxeology, and its practically most important and up-to-now best elaborated part, economics. Henceforth all essential studies in these branches of knowledge will have to take full account of the theories and criticisms expounded by Dr. Rothbard.

THE PUBLICATION of a standard book on economics raises again an important question, viz., for whom are essays of this consequence written, only for specialists, the students of economics, or for all of the people?

To answer this question we have to keep in mind that the citizens in their capacity as voters are called upon to determine ultimately all issues of economic policies. The fact that the masses are ignorant of physics and do not know anything substantial about electricity does not obstruct the endeavors of experts who utilize the teachings of science for the satisfaction of the wants of the consumers. From various points of view one may deplore the intellectual insufficiency and indolence of the multitude. But their ignorance regarding the achievements of the natural sciences does not endanger our spiritual and material welfare.

It is quite different in the field of economics. The fact that the majority of our contemporaries, the masses of semi-barbarians led by the self-styled intellectuals, entirely ignore everything that economics has brought forward, is the main political problem of our age. There is no use in deceiving ourselves. American public opinion rejects the market economy, the capitalistic free enterprise system that provided the nation with the highest standard of living ever attained. Full government control of all activities of the individual is virtually the goal of both national parties. The individual is to be deprived of his moral, political and economic responsibility and autonomy and to be converted into a pawn in the schemes of a supreme authority aiming at a "national" purpose. His "affluence" is to be cut down for the benefit of what is called the "public sector," i.e., the machine operated by the party in power. Hosts of authors, writers and professors are busy denouncing alleged shortcomings of capitalism and exalting the virtues of "planning." Full of a quasi-religious ardor, the immense majority is advocating measures that step by step lead to the methods of administration practiced in Moscow and in Peking.

If we want to avoid the destruction of Western civilization and the relapse into primitive wretchedness, we must change the mentality of our fellow citizens. We must make them realize what they owe to the much vilified "economic freedom," to the system of free enterprise and capitalism. Those who call themselves educated and the intellectuals must use their superior cognitive faculties and power of reasoning for the refutation of erroneous ideas about social, political and economic problems and for the dissemination of a correct grasp of the operation of the market economy. They must start by familiarizing themselves with all the issues involved in order to teach those who are blinded by ignorance and emotions. They must learn in order to acquire the ability to enlighten the misguided many.

It is a fateful error on the part of our most valuable contemporaries to believe that economics can be left to specialists in the same way in which various fields of technology can be safely left to those who have chosen to make any one of them their vocation. The issues of society's economic organization are every citizen's business. To master them to the best of one's ability is the duty of everyone.

Now such a book as that of Rothbard offers to every intelligent man an opportunity to obtain reliable information concerning the great controversies and conflicts of our age. It is certainly not easy reading and asks for the uttermost exertion of one's attention. But there are no short cuts to wisdom.

326

A "Fusionist" Approach
to Freedom[1]

JOHN WEICHER

FOR A LONG TIME Frank S. Meyer has been seeking a synthesis between the two main streams of contemporary conservative thought: streams which have their sources in the conservatism and liberalism, respectively, of the last century. *In Defense of Freedom* is his most ambitious effort to achieve that synthesis, which is a "combination of freedom and moral authority," or a "simultaneous belief in objectively existing moral value and in the freedom of the individual person." Meyer is not satisfied with asserting that this "combination" is the generally-held view of most American conservatives today; his book attempts to prove that such a combination is theoretically sound. Since a good many books and articles recently — by those both within and without the conservative "movement"— have maintained that such a synthesis is *not* sound, it is good to have someone willing to argue at some length that it *is*.[2]

Meyer's synthesis is that freedom and objectively existing moral value are

> . . . axioms of different though interconnected realms of existence. How can true ends be established elsewhere than in the intellectual, the moral, the spiritual order? Where can the conditions for freedom be established but in . . . the political order? A good society is possible only when both these conditions are met: when the social and political order guarantees a state of affairs in which men can freely choose; and when the intellectual

John Weicher is an Associate Editor of *New Individualist Review.*

and moral leaders, the "creative minority," have the understanding and imagination to maintain the prestige of tradition and reason, and thus to sustain the intellectual and moral order throughout society.

Of these two conditions, however, only one is to be fulfilled by political means: the establishment of freedom. Deciding which ends are true, is left, by implication, to the creative minority; Meyer says no more about this problem, except that the creative minority cannot impose its decisions by force upon the rest of the population.[3]

This seems to me to be a perfectly acceptable position. Whether it is a synthesis is another question. Most libertarians will probably say that this has been their position all along. As long as no one is compelled by the creative minority to accept the "true ends" as determined by that minority—or is compelled to believe that "true ends" exist at all—where does this good society differ from that of the libertarians? Libertarians are not going to object to anyone

---

[1] A review of *In Defense of Freedom*, by Frank S. Meyer. (Chicago: Henry Regnery Co., 1962.)

[2] Two recent publications on the other side are *The Conservative Illusion*, by M. Morton Auerbach, and "Freedom or Virtue?" by L. Brent Bozell, in the September 11, 1962, issue of *National Review.* Bozell's article, though published earlier, often seems to be a reply to Meyer's book.

[3] "Given the most elevated intellectual, moral, and spiritual understanding, the subordination of the political order to the enforcement of that understanding, the denial to men of the freedom to accept it or reject it, would make virtue meaningless and truth rote."

else's belief that there are objectively determinable moral values, whether or not the libertarians share that belief, in the absence of any effort to compel agreement.

Before we welcome or condemn Meyer to the ranks of the libertarians, however, there are several points in his book which need clarification. For instance, the only specific discussion of religious freedom occurs in a footnote to a chapter on "The Locus of Virtue," in which Meyer maintains that virtue exists only in individuals and can only be inculcated by individuals, and not by organizations or institutions. That footnote says in part:

> That no civilization can come into being or develop without being informed by one kind or another of relationship between the men who make it up and God, I am certain; that Christianity, which informs Western civilization, is the highest and deepest relationship to the Divine that men can attain, I am also certain; but I am not able to say that any single institutional church is the bearer of God's spirit on earth. And this makes it impossible for me to discuss the church in the terms of this book. At the very least, it is of the category of those institutions which fulfill a function that is necessary, but which can be fulfilled in a number of different ways. If, however, it should be true that a single church is the direct expression of God's love for men, then that church would be, like the state and the family, necessary in its essential form to human existence.

The basic problem in that paragraph is the meaning of "necessary in its essential form to human existence." If a particular church is "necessary," does Meyer's good society permit freedom of religion? He does not say. Or, going back to the beginning of the paragraph, does the good society exclude atheists? After all, no civilization can exist "without being informed by one kind or another of relationship between the men who make it up and God." This question too is unanswered.

Much earlier, it is true, Meyer has said, "freedom can exist at no lesser price than the danger of damnation; and

if freedom is indeed the essence of man's being, that which distinguishes him from the beasts, he must be free to choose his worst as well as his best end." This and similar statements appear to imply that the freedom to choose the wrong religion, or none, is included in the good society, and perhaps Meyer means the earlier statements to be applicable to the question of religious freedom. Perhaps he thinks further repetition of the need for freedom would be superfluous in that footnote. However, at the point at which he says, "freedom can exist at no lesser price than the danger of damnation," Meyer has not mentioned religion at all; nor has he discussed the state and the family, the other two institutions which are necessary in their essential form to human existence.

We do not get any help when we turn to his discussions of these other two institutions. In regard to the state, "Some form of order is a human necessity. *Without it, freedom itself is impossible.* The state . . . is therefore an institution called into being by the very nature of men's existence."[4] Meyer has said at the outset of the book that "innate freedom is of the essence of [man's] being." But now freedom is impossible without the state.[5] It is not at all clear where this puts the anarchists. Do they have the right to advocate the abolition of the state? Or does the fact that man cannot realize the essence of his being without a state, mean that those who would prevent him from realizing this essence, are themselves to be prevented? Man must be allowed to choose to be damned, but a state is necessary for him to have the opportunity to make that choice. There are some people—anarchists—who do not believe that a state is necessary. Thus, apparently, they would prevent men from choosing. Can man choose not to have the opportunity to choose salvation or damnation? Once again, the question is not answered.[6] But without some kind of answer to all

---

[4] Italics mine.

[5] It should be stressed that Meyer's state has the sole functions of supplying justice and national defense.

these questions, Meyer's synthesis is incomplete.

THERE IS A MORE fundamental problem in Meyer's exposition. The statement quoted above, that "innate freedom is of the essence of [man's] being," is an assumption. In fact, it is more than an assumption; it is the "central axiom on which this critique of political thought is founded." The argument rests on the validity of this axiom. But all Meyer says in support of it is: "No objective methodology, however strict, can disprove the existence of the autonomous self and validate determinism." This statement "rests upon data derived from apprehension of the external world." The only description of these data seems to be that the study of human beings is "a study where we are richly provided with direct knowledge of consciousness."

Much more needs to be said about this axiom. Meyer cites Marx, Freud, and one or two contemporary social scientists who disagree with it, but he does not attempt to refute them; he simply asserts that they are wrong. This axiom, however, is what the argument is really all about. Meyer's critiques of collectivist liberalism and New Conservatism both depend heavily upon it.

Meyer's criticism of New Conservatism is largely a criticism of Russell Kirk. He specifically states that he is *not* criticizing a number of other writers — Leo Strauss, Eric Voegelin, Willmoore Kendall, Richard Weaver, Frederick Wilhelmsen, and a number of European writers — on the ground that they differ from New Conservatism by "the high value they place upon the faculty of reason for the establishing of conservative principles," while the New Conservatives "insist upon the undifferentiated virtue of tradition, not merely as guide and governor of reason, but over against reason." (In addition to the "central axiom," Meyer further "assumes that the primary mode of achieving understanding in the study of man . . . is the use of reason operating within and upon tradition, reason deriving extended conclusions from simple apprehensions of the nature of man.") But Meyer's book is a defense of *freedom*, not reason, and one can cite quotations from several of these writers which would indicate that they do not share his view of the essence of man's being.[7] Meyer seems to have no argument with, e.g., Kendall and Wilhelmsen, as opposed to Kirk, because much of his argument against Kirk is a defense of the second axiom, which he shares with Kendall and Wilhelmsen. But when he argues for a free society against Kirk's stress on "community" or "society," as independent entities separate from the individuals within them, he is arguing on the basis of the "central axiom." Because he says so little about it, we cannot be sure whether Kendall and Wilhelmsen and the others do share it with him. Clarification here would be useful.

329

I HAVE GIVEN disproportionate emphasis in this review to those parts of Meyer's book with which I disagree, and I do not want to end on a critical note. In large part the book *is* an eloquent defense of freedom, and one which deserves to be widely read. Meyer's critiques of liberalism and New Conservatism are both cogent, and should lead to an interesting and instructive discussion, at least with Kirk and other New Conservatives. As far as his synthesis has been spelled out, I think most American conservatives can support it as the kind of society that they are trying to establish, while they wait for the further development and clarification of Meyer's views, which will be well worth waiting for.

---

6 Similarly with the family, into which children are born involuntarily. It is a voluntary contract between individuals. But there is no discussion of whether a man may form such a voluntary contract with two women simultaneously, or whether a member of the creative minority may advocate polygamy, wife-switching on alternate nights, etc. Is the family "necessary" only to the child who is an involuntary member?

---

7 See, for instance, "Baloney and Free Speech," by Willmoore Kendall, and " 'My Doxy is Orthodoxy,' " by Frederick Wilhelmsen, both in the May 22, 1962, issue of *National Review*.

NEW BOOKS AND ARTICLES

THE FOLLOWING IS A SELECT LIST OF BOOKS AND ARTICLES WHICH, IN THE OPINION OF THE EDITORS, MAY BE OF INTEREST TO OUR READERS.

Allen Drury, *A Shade of Difference.* (New York: Doubleday).

M. Stanton Evans, Allan H. Ryskind, William Schutz, *The Fringe on Top.* (New York: American Features, Inc.).

Foundation for Economic Education, *Essays on Liberty, Vol. IX.* (Irvington-on-Hudson: Foundation for Economic Education.

Milton Friedman, *Capitalism and Freedom.* (Chicago: University of Chicago Press).

Elgin Groseclose, *Money and Man.* (New York: Frederich Ungar).

Erik von Kuehnelt-Leddihn, *Democracy Revisited.* (Intercollegiate Society of Individualists pamphlet, 629 Public Ledger Bldg., Philadelphia).

John Lively, *The Social and Political Thought of Alexis de Tocqueville.* (Oxford: Oxford University Press).

John Stuart Mill, *Essays on Politics and Culture*, ed. by Gertrude Himmelfarb. (New York: Doubleday).

Ludwig von Mises, *The Free and Prosperous Commonwealth.* (Princeton: Van Nostrand).

Heinrich Rickert, *Science and History.* (Princeton: Van Nostrand).

Earl E. T. Smith, *The Fourth Floor.* (New York: Random House).

David McCord Wright, *The Keynesian System.* (New York: Fordham University Press).

James Burnham, "Emancipation Proclamation", *National Review,* November 8, 1962.

W. Allen Wallis, "Neo-Mercantilism and the Unmet Social Need-ers", *Modern Age,* Summer, 1962.

George Winder, "The British Nationalized Health Service," *The Freeman,* August, 1962.

New Individualist Review welcomes contributions for publication from its readers. Essays should not exceed 3,000 words, and should be type-written. All manuscripts will receive careful consideration.

"SOCIALISM is only an idea, not an historical necessity, and ideas are acquired by the human mind. We are not born with ideas, we learn them. If socialism has come to America because it was implanted in the minds of past generations, there is no reason for assuming that the contrary idea cannot be taught to a new generation. What the socialists have done can be undone, if there is a will for it. But, the undoing will not be accomplished by trying to destroy established socialistic institutions. It can be accomplished only by attacking minds, and not the minds of those already hardened by socialistic fixations. Individualism can be revived by implanting the idea in the minds of the coming generations. So then, if those who put a value on the dignity of the individual are up to the task, they have a most challenging opportunity in education before them. It is not an easy job. It requires the kind of industry, intelligence and patience that comes with devotion to an ideal."

—*Frank Chodorov*, Founder and President, Intercollegiate Society of Individualists, Inc.

331

INTERCOLLEGIATE SOCIETY OF INDIVIDUALISTS

For the Advancement of Conservative Thought on the Campus

629 PUBLIC LEDGER BLDG., PHILADELPHIA 6, PA., WAlnut 5-5632
Midwest Office: 505 Lemcke Bldg., Indianapolis 6. Ind., MElrose 9-5551
Western Office: 1436 El Camino Real, Menlo Park, California, 325-4553

In Future Issues . . .

NEW INDIVIDUALIST REVIEW will feature articles by young libertarian and conservative writers as well as by such scholars as WILHELM ROEPKE, RICHARD WEAVER, and MURRAY N. ROTHBARD.

To keep up with today's ferment of individualist ideas — subscribe to NEW INDIVIDUALIST REVIEW today.

* * * *

NEW INDIVIDUALIST REVIEW has come a long way since we made the above promise to readers of our first issue, over a year ago. Our circulation has grown steadily with each succeeding issue. Students at campuses across the country have volunteered their time to make NIR available to their colleagues. We have readers in nearly every state and more than a dozen foreign countries. Our original staff of five editors has more than doubled; most of the new members are undergraduates who will ensure that NIR continues after the founders have left school. We are well on the road to permanence.

Perhaps as important, NIR has brought libertarian and conservative ideas to a wider readership than its circulation. Articles have been reprinted in the "Wall Street Journal," the "Freeman," "Under Thirty," and other newspapers and magazines. We have been praised by other publications and individuals — the "Chicago Tribune," the "Portland Oregonian," "America," "National Review," the "New Republic," William F. Buckley, Jr., Russell Kirk, and Leonard Read, among them.

Articles have been translated into Spanish and published in Mexico and Venezuela. Professors at several colleges have requested permission to use articles for reading assignments in their courses.

In our first issue, we also said: "The NEW INDIVIDUALIST REVIEW has been founded in a commitment to human liberty. We believe in free, private enterprise, and in the imposition of the strictest limits to the power of government." If you share that belief, we invite you to subscribe to NIR, in order "to keep up with today's ferment of individualist ideas," and to help those ideas reach still more people. If you do not share it, we think you will find NIR stimulating and challenging, and perhaps persuasive.

332

VOLUME 2
NUMBER 4
SPRING 1963

New
INDIVIDUALIST
Review

Vol. 2, No. 4   35 cents   Spring 1963

NEW

INDIVIDUALIST

REVIEW

EDITORIAL STAFF

Editors-in-Chief ● Ronald Hamowy ● Ralph Raico
Associate Editors ● Robert M. Hurt ● John P. McCarthy
Robert Schuettinger ● John Weicher
Business Manager ● Sam Peltzman
Editorial Assistants ● Jameson Campaigne, Jr. ● Joe Cobb
Burton Gray ● Thomas Heagy ● Jerome Heater
R. P. Johnson ● Robert Michaels ● James Powell
James Rosenholtz

EDITORIAL ADVISORS

Milton Friedman ● George J. Stigler ● Richard Weaver
University of Chicago

F. A. Hayek ● Benjamin Rogge
University of Freiburg *Wabash College*

COLLEGE AND UNIVERSITY REPRESENTATIVES

NEW INDIVIDUALIST REVIEW

Volume 2 – Number 4 **SPRING 1963**

339

Due to unavoidable technical difficulties, we have been forced to omit the Winter, 1962 issue of *New Individualist Review*. The present Spring, 1963 issue follows the Autumn, 1962 issue as Volume 2, Number 4. Subscriptions will not be affected by this omission; each subscriber will receive four issues for a one-year subscription.

NEW INDIVIDUALIST REVIEW is published quarterly (Spring, Summer, Autumn, Winter) by *New Individualist Review, Inc.*, at Ida Noyes Hall, University of Chicago, Chicago 37, Illinois.

Opinions expressed in signed articles do not necessarily represent the views of the editors. Editorial, advertising, and subscription correspondence and manuscripts should be sent to NEW INDIVIDUALIST REVIEW, Ida Noyes Hall, University of Chicago, Chicago 37, Illinois. All manuscripts become the property of NEW INDIVIDUALIST REVIEW.

Subscription rates: $2.00 per year (students $1.00).

IN MEMORIAM

Richard M. Weaver

Few men have been as important in the intellectual renaissance of American conservatism as Richard M. Weaver. His first book, Ideas Have Consequences, has been regarded as one of the starting-points of that renaissance, and its influence has continued to grow in the fifteen years since it was published. He wrote the lead article in the first issue of Modern Age, and he was an associate editor of that magazine. He taught English for twenty years at the University of Chicago, where his teaching ability and his stress on the importance of language, his "respect for words as things," earned him in turn the respect of his students and his colleagues.

He was also one of our editorial advisors, and we shall miss him very much. He was always willing to help us in any way that he could, and he was ready to advise us when asked, but he believed firmly in editorial freedom, and he never sought to press his views upon us. His patience and good humor were invaluable in sustaining this magazine and reassuring us when difficulties arose.

A few weeks before his death, Professor Weaver spent an evening with our staff and several other students. He talked about the book he was writing and the three or four more that he planned to write, but he was more interested in the future of conservatism, particularly its intellectual future. He looked forward to that future, and he was confident that it would be exciting, and that eventually conservatism would again prevail. If it does so, much of the credit will belong to him.

ICC: Some Reminiscences on the Future of American Transportation

CHRISTOPHER D. STONE

The Commission . . . can be made of great use to the railroads. It satisfies the popular clamor for a government supervision of the railroads, at the same time that the supervision is almost entirely nominal. Further, the older such a commission gets to be, the more it will be found to take the business and railroad view of things. It thus becomes a sort of barrier between the railroad corporations and the people and a sort of protection against crude legislation hostile to railroad interests. . . . The part of wisdom is not to destroy the Commission, but to utilize it.

341

> —Letter of Attorney General of the United States Richard Olney to Charles E. Perkins, President of the Chicago, Burlington and Quincy Railroad, Dec. 28, 1892. [1]

DISSATISFACTION WITH the Interstate Commerce Act and its administrator, the Interstate Commerce Commission, has inspired a great number of proposals, currently before the Congress, to revise the transportation regulatory scheme. An understanding of problems which presently beset the transportation industry may be somewhat advanced (they will certainly not be solved) by a few observations on the state of affairs which brought Congress to the juncture of federal regulation, and upon the evolution of the Interstate Commerce Commission as an agency to do the job which Congress wanted done.

By the time the Second Session of the Forty-ninth Congress convened, on December 6, 1886, it had become fairly certain that some sort of railroad regulatory body was going to emerge. Only six weeks before, the Supreme Court's decision in *Wabash, St. Louis and Pacific Ry. Co. v. Illinois*[2] had voided practically all state regulation in this field upon the grounds that the Constitution vested in the federal government alone the power to legislate upon interstate railroad transportation. The unexpected Wabash decision had thus left the nation without so much as a shell of governmental regulation to point to as an excuse for continued debate.[3] In Washington and with-

Christopher D. Stone received an A.B. from Harvard College and an L.L.B. from the Yale Law School. He has been the author of several articles appearing in law reviews and is at present the Law and Economics Fellow at the University of Chicago Law School.

[1] Quoted in Josephson, *The Politicos* (New York: Harcourt, Brace, 1938), p. 526.

[2] 118 *U.S.* 557 (1886).

[3] In deed, if not in word, the Wabash decision was a reversal of a series of 1876 decisions popularly known as the Granger cases. See Munn v. Illinois, 94 *U.S.* 113.

out, for, some years previous, both railroad and anti-railroad interests had been lobbying intimately with Congress; and the imminence now of the first of the federal government's modern regulatory agencies, so long in gestation, brought both sides to an uneasy bed-watch—for even at this late date, it was uncertain whose child it would prove to be.

Although the coming federal regulatory board, whatever powers might shortly be conferred upon it, symbolized a cross-roads in the relations of government to industry, it would be wrong to suppose that prior to 1886 the federal government had steadfastly refused to intercede in the conduct of the nation's business affairs. The transportation industry, perhaps more than any other, had been fostered from the start by a series of measures which lay beyond the pale of *laissez-faire*. The very first tariff act (1789) set a precedent for lower duties to be charged on goods entering the United States in American bottoms. The Embargo Act of 1808 had presented the American shipping industry with a ban on foreign ships in the U.S. coastal trade; and by 1830, Congress had instituted the practice of doling out public funds to ship owners—in the form of handsome mail subsidies—thereby paving the way for the sensational investigations of Senators Gerald Nye and Hugo Black, one century later. State finance of early turnpikes made the business of transportation by wagon feasible on a theretofore unrealizable scale. Public reaction was satisfactory enough "to inaugurate a strong movement in favor of a national system of roads constructed with the aid of the federal government,"[4] although the only upshot, to this time, had been partial construction of the Cumberland Road — the "National Pike" — projected from Washington to the Mississippi. The success of the State of New York's Erie Canal (1808-1825) set off a flurry of publicly financed canal construction, thus drawing the expenses from society in general, rather than from the waterway operators and industrialists who stood most directly in the line of benefit.

But of all the bountiful intrusions upon the sanctity of free enterprise, that which had been accorded the railroads loomed the largest.

Initially (1830-50) the government's policy toward the railroads had been moderately *laissez-faire*. It may be assumed that early railroad development roughly paralleled, through time, the probable returns on railroading investment relative to returns elsewhere in the young economy—and thus relative to the economies of, and demand for, transportation by competing modes of carriage.

But at least by the year 1850, agitation for a less modest expansion of the rails had reached a high pitch in the Congress, and it was proposed that the federal government cede to the states vast tracts of public domain to be applied as land grants for otherwise reticent railroad entrepreneurs. Senator Davis of Georgia commented sourly that "the Government seems to me to be becoming a great eleemosynary institution,"[5] while in the House, North Carolina's Representative Venable warned of "Wall Street speculators," and predicted that, "The House were [sic] asked today to tie together ... the various sections in a system of log rolling and corruption which would absorb the entire public domain."[6]

The government proceeded to offer up an estimated 242,000 square miles of public domain—an area greater by one-fifth than the territory of France—as a lure to further the construction of rails. Seven Western states were to give up from a fifth to a quarter of their birthrights. Gifts and loans by the federal, state, and local governments totalled an additional 700,000,000 nineteenth century dollars. According to one commentator, "The Lone Star state discovered in 1882 that in her youthful ardour she had given away some 8,000,000 acres more than she possessed."[7]

The campaign of construction had immediate and dramatic effects. In the decade from 1850 through 1859 over 20,000

---

[4] S. Rep. 46, Part 1, 49th Cong. 1st Sess. (1886) p. 5.

[5] *Congressional Globe*, 31st Cong. 2nd Sess. (1851) p. 322.

[6] *Congressional Globe*, 31st Cong. 1st Sess. (1850) p. 1887.

[7] Sharfman, *The American Railroad Problem* (New York: Century, 1921), pp. 34-5.

342

miles of rail were built, nearly three times that which had been built in the twenty years preceding. The Civil War slowed construction markedly; but the peace was followed by unprecedented railroading vigor. 1869 saw completion of the Union Pacific-Central Pacific link from the Missouri River (Omaha) to the Pacific (Sacramento). In 1871, a cobweb of rails having been spun in and between the East and Midwest, and a second, third, and fourth transcontinental line having threaded their ways to the Pacific, the land grant program was brought to an end. The country was by this time on the verge of a financial panic and depression sponsored by the "construction mania" itself (1873-78).

Neither the conclusion of the land grant program, however, nor the panic of the seventies, halted economically questionable ventures and the trend towards overcapacity. For though the *operation* of railroads had proven profitable enough as a legitimate pastime, the truly memorable fortunes were being lavished upon those who promoted new construction with absurdly watered stock, or speculated in any number of the ingenious ways by which railroads were born for purposes of swindle, and not soberly predicated upon the expectation of a sustaining demand. But whatever the sum of the causes, by 1886 the nation looked back to see that with the planting of the roots of a great industrial power, the previous three decades had witnessed a helter-skelter dedication to the establishment of railroad capacity far out of proportion to the foreseeable demands of traffic. In 1886, the country found itself saddled with 7¼ billion dollars invested in railroads and railroad equipment, representing more than one half that year's gross national product,[8] one-fifth the entire wealth of the nation.[9] Track was still being laid so fast that by 1890 perhaps

80% of today's road mileage would be accounted for.[10]

Once virtual monopolists wherever they chose to build, the railroads were feeling the press of competition. Marginal roads had begun to fail. Even though it was in the interests of the railroads as a group to keep rates high, each individual competitor found himself with significant excesses of rail and rolling stock on hand, which made it tempting to succumb to any rate offer which would utilize capacity, cover direct costs, and make some contribution to overhead. To "stabilize" rates, railroads operating along competing routes made arrangements to divide earnings equally among themselves; such collusive "pooling" (not then illegal) partly obviated the mutually disadvantageous incentive to compete for shippers' favors. But even where pools existed, they were fraught with suspicions, and railroad managers who wanted to retain prize accounts took to effecting rate reductions through secret rebates— secret from other shippers, who would, if they knew of them, insist upon equal treatment, and secret from other railroads, who would, when they found out, set off a new round of price cutting. The elaborate network of rebates, preferences and suspicions which evolved was, of course, not only inimical to the railroads, but to the majority of the business community as well. Small and average sized businesses saw the hand of their most powerful competitors strengthened, while rational marketing decisions were frustrated by the impossibility of ascertaining the transportation costs which faced one's rivals.

Pooling, which forestalled but never halted competition's whittling away at the level of rates, and personal preferences, were but two of the plaints which were agitating the nation towards an inevitable rail reform. Because of the manner in which the duplicated and un-

343

---

[8] U.S. Bureau of the Census, *Historical Statistics of the United States* (Washington, D.C., 1960), pp. 428, 139. *Transport Statistics in the United States for Year Ended December 31, 1961* (Washington, D.C.: ICC, 1962) Part 1 lists "investment in railroad property used in transportation services" today at $35,132,559,881. p. 114, l. 91.

[9] S. Rep. 46, Part 1, 49th Con. 1st Sess. (1886) p. 49.

[10] *Transport Statistics in the United States, supra* n. 8, lists "miles of road owned" as of December 31, 1961, at 187,782 (p. 120, l. 207). *Historical Statistics of the United States, supra,* n. 8, lists road owned in 1890 at 163,359 miles (p. 427). The respective figures for all track (including second main track, yard switching tracks, etc.) are 300,551 at present, 208,152 for 1890.

derutilized rail facilities had spread themselves across the country, certain locations afforded shippers who located there a number of competitive alternatives for the transportation of their wares; whereas other communities were, as a practical matter, wholly dependent upon a single carrier. In cities which were becoming the great hub-like rail centers (as in cities along the waterways and upon the seas), businessmen could play off one railroad manager against another, or against barge and ship owner. Rates not only fell in such centers, but the effect was self-perpetuating. The lower rates in the favored locales held out to new industry the promise of cheap access to raw materials and strategic flexibility in seeking out markets; and the influx of new industry brought still more carriers to their doorsteps. As a result, the industrial map of the nation was being etched in such manner that the fortunes of some centers of commerce were guaranteed—while vast areas were foredoomed to the less rewarding and more menial tasks which running a country call for.[11] Inhabitants of the less favored areas viewed this trend with especial indignation since they imagined the high rates they had to pay as in some sense defraying or offsetting those of the favored regions.

THE IMPOTENCE of state legislation to quell discontent had been tempting federal intercession at least as early as

---

[11] In the 1870's, a Rochester manufacturer shipped his goods destined for Cincinnati first *eastward* to New York, and from there back *westward* to Cincinnati via Rochester again, because by such a roundabout passage he was able to save himself 14¢ a hundred pounds; but the effect more than forfeited the natural advantage he might have enjoyed in competing with the easternmost manufacturers for the Ohio market. Complaints of this nature were widespread. And if some discriminatory rates might be ascribed to alternative means of carriage, and the dictates of competition, in the background of still other inequities there seemed to lurk merely an unarticulated scheme to perpetuate certain centers of commerce at the expense of others. Thus, the rate on gloves from San Francisco to Denver was $2.00 per hundred pounds, but if someone were imprudent enough to establish a glove factory in Denver, the rate for him to San Francisco would be $3.00. Jones, *Principles of Railway Transportation* (New York: Macmillan, 1924), p. 106.

1872, but no concrete legislation had resulted. In March, 1885, the Senate authorized a five man Select Committee on Interstate Commerce (the Collum Committee) "to investigate and report upon the subject of the regulation of transportation."[12]

The Collum Committee enjoyed a full presentation of the basic issues which to this day divide the bulk of the public from the bulk of the transportation industry. The "public" rallied around the standard saw of the economics primers, that the evil effects of monopoly (of which collusion is a struggling imitator) are high prices, low output, and, more broadly, a misallocation of resources. From the same fundamental observation on competition and monopoly derives the early railroad executive's probably unwitting epigram: "the evil effects of competition upon net earnings."[13] Each side wished to resist the onslaught of its own particular evil.

One of the public's grievances with pooling was, of course, that truly competitive bidding would have given it the benefit of lower rates. On the other hand, the implications of collusion for the transportation dilemma, then and now, go beyond the price of carriage and can only be understood in relation to the misallocation of resources which it was destined to effect. From this point of view, to the extent that collusion succeeded in holding prices up, it prohibited the transportation of certain marginal commodities which might otherwise have been able to enter into commerce; and so restricted the growth of all firms which produced, distributed or utilized them. Further, by interfering with the free market mechanism, price "stabilizing" abetted the overinvestment in railroad capacity which land grants, fiscal subsidies, and speculation by promoters had begun. For to the extent that collusion successfully "stabilized" prices, investment returns from railroading were reduced not by a decline in the level of prices which the public had to bear, but

---

[12] The "Collum Report" is S. Rep. 46, Parts 1 (report proper) and 2 (testimony), 49th Cong. 1st Sess. (1886).

[13] Haines, *Restrictive Railway Legislation* (New York: Macmillan, 1906), p. 233.

344

solely by a further division of traffic among the "in" roads and each successive newcomer, whose very reason to enter the industry was the attractiveness of uncompetitively high rates. The result was to decrease the utilization of capacity between given points; where three roads could economically have carried the freight, five sprang up, each lamely operating at 3/5 capacity or less. There was that much less steel for the rest of the economy, that much less land, entrepreneurial skill and mobile capital.

The railroads' answer to the problem of overcapacity was federal intervention, too—but not the outlawing of pooling. The existing railroads were perfectly willing, as Colonel Fink, their commissar of pooling proposed, to submit to legislation barring the threat of new competitors.[14] As for collusive rate making, moreover, here, too, federal power could be brought to the railroads' own advantage: to prevent the debilitation of pooling they asked that "Congress should legalize pooling, and impose a heavy penalty for any violations of the pooling agreement."[15]

This was, no less than the request for the government imposed strictures upon entry, tantamount to a hope that, as the railroads' own efforts at cartelization were faltering, the sanctions of federal power should come to the rescue of Colonel Fink. In addition, only the federal government (if anyone) could effectively cope with the Achilles heel of collusion: secret rebates, with their ineluctable tendency to reduce rates to a competitive level. Chairman Collum asked the eminent Charles Francis Adams (then president of the mighty Union Pacific), "Suppose Congress were to pass a law, not interfering with pooling, but prohibiting the payment of drawbacks and rebates . . .?" Adams' answer is instructive.

It would be the greatest boon you could confer, because that would do away with the lack of confidence of which I just now spoke. If you could provide any way by which all passenger and freight agents could be absolutely debarred from making reductions from published rates, and from deceiving each other while doing it, *you would be very much more successful than I have been in my limited sphere.*[16]

Indeed, even if price changes were freely allowed, there was good reason to believe that price competition could be discouraged if only the federal government would enforce a requirement that *intentions* of rate changes be prepublished.[17]

These requests for government assistance to stabilize the railroads' faltering cartel sought a common justification: the glut of rail capacity, which all were prepared to concede. But was there such overcapacity that, but for the right to collude, something called "destructive competition" would have "destroyed" the railroads? The railroads tried to create this impression before the Collum Committee, but whatever the proposition may mean precisely, it seems unconvincing as a basis for legislative action. The literal *survival* of existing facilities (as opposed to their rusting away) would depend upon the railroads' abilities to cover fixed

---

[14] S. Rep. 46, Part 2, 49th Cong. 1st Sess. (1886) pp. 117-18.

[15] S. Rep. 46, Part 2, 49th Cong. 1st Sess. (1886) p. 1205 (testimony of Charles Francis Adams) and p. 117 (testimony of Albert Fink). Up to this date pooling had not been made *illegal* (as the anti-rail elements were now proposing) in the sense that parties to a pooling agreement could not be criminally prosecuted. On the other hand, under the common law, pooling arrangements were *unenforceable* as contractual obligations. Thus, if the parties to such an agreement were "wronged" by one of their number, they could have no redress in the courts. The result must have been to encourage independent price setting when it seemed more promising than commitment to the pool.

[16] *Ibid.,* p. 1210.

[17] For one thing, the rationale for an oligopolist to cut prices to select shippers is the short run profits he can make from added volume *until the others find out;* then they will have to lower their prices, too, and when the rates have resettled, the temporary advantage of the maverick has been lost and road rates are lower all around. A government enforced thirty day public notice of rate reduction would stand competitor roads on guard, so that not even short run profits could be anticipated by the price cutter. Besides, he would, in effect, be standing up and confessing a sin which might bring reprisals. And thirdly, the reduction would have to apply to a general class of goods: well calculated selective price cuts would be hampered. cf. P. W. MacAvoy, "Trunk Line Railroad Cartels and the Interstate Commerce Commission (1870-1900)," p. 28 (unpublished, Univ. of Chicago).

Page Seven

and variable costs from year to year and this was no widespread problem. Certainly, if demand did not pick up in the coming years faster than competition reduced earnings, some roads would not be able to replenish obsolescent stock and a few roads, undoubtedly, would sell out to other roads at a price reflecting their nuisance value, or go bankrupt and be operated by creditors. But if such were the mandate of the free market, was there any reason to resist it? Is this not the sense in which all competition is by its very nature "destructive"?

IN 1963, IT IS to a large extent true that all the various pleas the railroads made in 1885-87, for Congress to cartelize the transportation industry, have since wended their way into law. But the same shoe, today, must also fit truckers, waterway operators, intercoastal shippers, freight forwarders, and pipeline companies, as a result of which the railroads are feeling the pinch.

Government cartelization did not spring into being with the Interstate Commerce Act of 1887. This first legislation emerged on sort of a middle ground and, partly through judicial evisceration, was not terribly significant in any direction, except to establish the principle of federal surveillance. The original Act applied to carriage wholly by railroad, and partly by railroad, partly by water, where both were under joint control. Pooling was prohibited (rate bureaus, mergers, and joint banking control took its place). The Act declared that all rates must be "just and reasonable" (but the Supreme Court soon pointed out that there was no actual power to amend "unjust, unreasonable" rates). Personal and geographic preferences were prohibited in word (but the Commission turned out to have no power to prescribe non-discriminatory rates). Carriers could not charge more for a short haul than a long haul (the New York, Rochester, Cincinnati problem, n. 11 *supra*) but the provision contained a loophole which made it little more than a sentiment. Within ten years of its establishment, it might have appeared that the federal

commission was destined to be as powerless as its state predecessors.

"The part of wisdom is not to destroy the Commission, but to utilize it."[18]

Utilize it the railroads did, and soon. In 1903, the Elkins Act amended the Interstate Commerce Act to close up the loopholes in the anti-rebate provision they had sought. Any deviation from published tariffs (except the most ingeniously contrived) were unlawful. The rail lobby soon organized "the most reckless publicity campaign . . . ever known in the history of railroad control"[19] to combat Teddy Roosevelt's attempts to bring them under effective control. The Hepburn Act of 1906 (which significantly extended the breadth of activities over which the Commission had jurisdiction) gave the rails the provision they had been seeking for thirty days notice in advance of rate changes. Departures from published tariffs now could be punished by imprisonment—for both those giving and those receiving rebates—a move which was another step toward the "stabilization" of rates. The railroads were no longer "allowed" to give free passes, a freedom they had always preferred to be without.

Nonetheless, the most far reaching innovation of the Hepburn Act, vesting the Commission with the power to review maximum rates, might have been detrimental to the railroads, should they have been unable to secure the appointment of commissioners sympathetic to the problems of owning railroad stock. As it turned out, the early attitude of the Commission (certainly until 1918) was such that it granted only a minor fraction of railroad demands. But by the time the railroads had struck back with passage of the Transportation Act of 1920, directing the ICC to maintain rates which would yield a "fair return" (a provision since repealed as unworkable) the sentiment on the Commission had turned congenial enough to grant boosts of 25% to 40%, in some cases more than the railroads them-

---

[18] *Supra,* n. 1.
[19] Dixon, *Railroads and Government* (New York: C. Scribner's Sons. 1922), p. 3.

selves had deigned to ask.[20] In fact, the Commission had proved itself so over-indulgent that rates had to beat a partial (10%) retreat within two years when traffic balked.

Still, the Commission's attitude towards maximum rate "control" was such that from 1924 through 1929, freight rates were stabilized at about 165% of the 1913 level, whereas wholesale prices had fallen back to 140% of that same standard. During the depression, with the wholesale price index down 30% from the 1929 level, the Commission's contribution to the emergency was to continue to grant price increases anyway. In fact, the Commission has not denied *in toto* a railroad request for a general price increase since 1926.[21] Today, authorized carload rates may be as much as 25% *more*, on the average, than the railroads are finding it profitable, in their discretion, to levy.[22] Indeed, the railroads' major pricing concern today has shifted to seeking *lower* rates, and the Commission's power over maximum rates is becoming more and more superfluous.

The year 1920 saw enactment of Colonel Fink's request that strictures be placed in the path of prospective competitors who seek to enter the business of railroading. The device was the Certificate of Public Convenience and Necessity which, henceforth, would have to be issued before further railroad line capacity could be constructed. Another proviso gave the Commission power to legitimize pooling agreements once more, if the Commission, in its enlightened omniscience, found such collusion "in the interest of better service to the public." In a similar about-face of policy, the Congress relieved from the operation of the antitrust laws ICC approved mergers and acquisitions of control over a competing road through lease or stock ownership.

The Transportation Act of 1920 had not only resulted in a sudden upswing of rail rates, but the 1920 Act broke ground for a cartelization device even the indus-

try spokesmen of the 1880's had not deigned to suggest: the Esch-Cummins Bill gave the Commission *power to set federally enforceable minimum rates.* Perhaps to this, as well as to the extravagantly high maximum rates which the Commission decreed in the same year, can be ascribed the fact that between 1920 and 1924, truck registration in the United States nearly doubled.[23] Thus, the artificially high rate structure had a backlash to it, much as it had had in the nineteenth century; but now, with the entry-stalling certificates of public convenience and necessity having closed the doors on rail expansion as an equalizer of investment possibilities, trucks were driving through the windows.

The railroad industry first tried to meet truck competition by advising friends in state legislatures as to the evils of trucks on highways, suggesting a variety of enactments such as would prescribe maximum truck speeds, maximum gross tonnage, and upper limits to truck drivers' working hours, all of which inured to the respective "safeties" of public and railroad.

But when these and other devices failed, and trucks had asserted themselves as here-to-stay, the railroads took the more enlightened path. The truck industry was so fragmented that truckers couldn't hold their rates up to non-competitive levels *inter se,* much less as against the railroads. As a result, both were threatened with competitive pricing. For that reason, the railroads felt that if only the trucks were cartelized, too, the both of them could fight it out with a little more imagination for the interests they shared mutually against the shipping public. By securing passage of the Motor Carrier Act of 1935, the railroads gave the trucks (and indirectly themselves) some of the benefits they had been enjoying: the ICC was to limit entry through certificates of public convenience and necessity, and rates were to be published and adhered to. The Director of the Commission's new Bureau of Motor Carriers even went on the road to give the truckers fatherly lectures on the elementary economics of collusion.

[20] Jones, *op. cit.,* p. 568.

[21] Huntington, "The Marasmus of the I.C.C.," 61 *Yale L. J.* 467, 482 (1952).

[22] Hearings before the Committee on Commerce, United States Senate, on S. 3242 and S. 3243, 87th Cong. 2nd Sess. (1962) p. 345 and chart, p. 359.

[23] *Historical Statistics of the United States,* p. 462.

The Commission wants to work with the industry and wants to work with you operators . . . but we can't work with the industry if there are 57 varieties of rates in the industry. The result of that is going to be that if you folks don't get together yourselves in the interest of uniformity of rates, you may get by with it initially but a little later the Commission is going to have to prescribe them for you.[24]

The Commission not only encouraged unlawful "rate conferences" as between the truckers themselves, but as between truckers and railroaders jointly.[25] Nonadherents to the "rate bureau's" determination might find their low rates cancelled on the grounds that "competitive rate making . . . has resulted in unduly low, depressed, and non-compensatory rates and charges, and instability and unsound economic conditions. . . ."[26]

Because of the large number of truckers (even despite the certificate requirement) the ICC's attempts at giving the transportation industry "stability" were less than perfect, and railroad attempts to help out went so far as undertaking (through the medium of Kuhn, Loeb & Co., the railroad bankers) two efforts to consolidate the truckers into a more happily manageable whole.[27] Though these efforts were blocked, the Association of American Railroads had been able to announce that the American Trucking Assn., Inc. ". . . has shown a disposition to work constructively with the railroads. . . . In many instances the trucking association has insisted on getting low rates that were bothersome to the rail carriers brought to the rail level."[28]

One problem with cartelization is, though those within the cartel can work to mutual advantage, anyone outside the cartel gets a "free ride" in the sense of having a rate umbrella: he can charge as high as the cartel does if it suits his purposes, but if cutting into the cartelists' volume with lower prices is more profitable, he can do that, too. This threatens injury to the cartel. After 1935, the railroads and truckers (and the pipelines, brought under the ICC in 1906) turned about to see the water carriers in just such a position. In 1940, though there was no public clamor for regulation of the water carriers (and a lot against it) the "industry" brought the watermen "in" to the federal regulatory scheme with a righteous and Orwellian doublethought on the old saw about competition and survival: "If one or more forms of transportation cannot survive under *equality of regulation* [!], they are not entitled to survive."[29] Thus: rate "stability" for existent barge and ship owners; limits on competition between them, the rails, and truckers; and certificates of public convenience and necessity for prospective competitors. Predictably, freight forwarders were tapped for ICC membership two years later.

HAVING SO MANY modes of transportation entrusted to its protection was destined to put a strain upon the ingenuity of the ICC, even granted a staff which, by 1962, had passed 2000 employees, and a budget which, for the same year, was pre-estimated at $22,-000,000.[30] Not the least perplexing problem was, of course, how to allocate rates (and, hence, traffic) between the various modes. The dedication to competition which appears elsewhere in the economy —even to the point of banishing electrical industry executives to prison—has never commended itself to the commissars of transport. But what better way to proceed?

---

[24] *Transport Topics,* Dec. 2, 1935, quoted in Wiprud, *Justice in Transportation* (Chicago: Ziff-Davis, 1945), p. 97.

[25] Rates between Arizona, California, New Mexico and Texas, 3 M.C.C. 505, 511 (1937), quoted in Wiprud, *op. cit.,* pp. 97-98. The unlawfulness is *ex post facto* implied, if it was not always obvious, by Georgia v. Pennsylvania R.R., 324 *U.S.* 439 (1945) and the subsequent Reed-Bulwinkle Act, exempting railroad rate bureaus from the anti-trust laws. (Public Law 662, 80th Cong.)

[26] Ex Parte No. MC-21, Central Territory Motor Carrier Rates, 8 M.C.C. 233, 257 (1938).

[27] Wiprud, *op. cit.,* pp. 33-34.

[28] Hearings before Senate Interstate Commerce Committee on S. 942, Regulation of Rate Bureaus, 78th Cong. 1st Sess. (1943) p. 747.

[29] S. Rep. 433, Part 1, 76th Cong. 1st Sess. (1939) pp. 2-3.

[30] *Interstate Commerce Commission Activities, 1937-62* (Washington, D.C.: I.C.C., 1962), pp. 18-19.

348

In regards to adjusting rates between railroads, motor carriers, water carriers and freight forwarders, Congress' mandate to the ICC, via the Interstate Commerce Act, was cliche ridden and inscrutable.[31] The Commission decided that what it was supposed to do was to keep all of its brood in business. In a typical case, the railroads' traffic of bulk petroleum had been nearly cut in half by truck competition, and in an effort to regain it, the railroads reduced their rates below those of the truckers. The trucks said that *their* costs prohibited any further reduction in highway rates. As a result, the Commission cancelled the railroad reduction on the theory that rates must be "so related that they will not be unreasonable, unfair, or destructive . . . and [must] preserve the *inherent advantages* of both."[32] How was the "inherent advantage" to be proven, other than in the ability and willingness of the railroads to carry the petroleum for less? In other cases, the Commission saw its task to be the exercise of minimum rate power whenever it became necessary "to prevent destructive competition and to stabilize the rates at a level which will permit each mode of transportation to participate in the traffic in a just and reasonable manner."[33] It is tempting to imagine what would have happened had the ICC been created at the time of the nation's birth, and exercised continuing jurisdiction over the stage coach: would the government have interceded to keep every competitor's rates above those of Wells, Fargo & Co., to enable that mode to continue participation in the traffic in what the ICC divined to be "a just and reasonable manner"?

Railroad discontent with the Commission's minimum price policy led to a 1958 amendment which directed that "rates of a carrier shall not be held up to a particular level to protect the traffic of any other mode of transportation. . . ." But there was enough resistance on the part of less confident modes of carriage to continue the amendment to read ". . . giving due consideration to the objectives of the national transportation policy. . . ." The irony is that the National Transportation Policy (1940) is a mandate that the courts and the Commission *"preserve a national transportation system by water, highway and rail, as well as other means. . . ."* Thus, the second proviso of the enactment is open to construction as cancelling out the first, which is just what the Commission appears to have been doing, as a rule, post 1958. A proposed railroad rate reduction on newsprint was disallowed recently, because "a differential of approximately 10% under the rail rates is necessary to enable the water carriers to be in a position fairly to compete."[34] When the bankrupt New York, New Haven & Hartford Railroad tried to raise a little revenue by meeting the rates of competing cargo ships, the Commission forbade them to maintain a differential of less than 6%.[35] This from the agency which, in the eyes of much of the public 75 years ago, was going to emancipate them from excessive and burdensome charges.

Not all transportation has been dragged within the embraces of the ICC scheme. The hauling of bulk commodities by water carrier is exempt from regulation, as is motor carrier transportation of agricultural and fishery products. Similarly, producers who own their own transportation media (private carriage) may operate outside the pale of rate control. In past years, there has been a marked trend towards carriage by unregulated carriers; it has been estimated that since 1946, the ICC regulated fleets have been losing 1% each year of the total intercity freight volume to non-ICC regulated carriers.[36]

349

---

[31] The Commission had been told to consider, e.g., "The facts and circumstances attending the movement of traffic by the carrier or carriers to which the rates are applicable." See 49 U.S.C. §§15a (2), 316 (i), 907 (f), 1006 (d).

[32] Petroleum Products from Los Angeles to Arizona and New Mexico, 280 I.C.C. 509, 516 (1951).

[33] Canned Goods in Official Territory, 294 I.C.C. 371, 390 (1955).

[34] Newsprint Paper from Tenn. & Ala. to Houston, Tex.; I&S No. 7144; CCH Federal Carrier Cases ¶35,134 (1961).

[35] The I.C.C.'s decision was reversed by a three-judge federal court in New Haven on November 15, 1961. New York, New Haven and Hartford Railroad v. U.S., 199 F. Supp. 635. The government currently has an appeal pending before the Supreme Court, Dkt. No. 108.

[36] I.C.C. Staff Report, *Gray Areas of Transportation Operations* (1960), p. 13.

If the present trend continues, private and exempt carriage can be expected to account for 39% of intercity freight not later than 1975.[37]

The implications of these findings would appear to be, first, the ICC is administering rates so high, that an increasing number of producers are finding it more economical either to buy their own carriers (those producers with sufficient traffic demands) or, where possible under the law, to apply for the services of exempt for-hire carriers. And, second, the striking growth of exempt carriers is powerful testimony that trucks, barges, etc., *can* be operated profitably at rate levels less than those now being administered by the ICC.[38]

In fact, one of the most telling commentaries upon the effects of ICC regulation centers about the "agricultural commodities" exemption clause. In 1953, by an interpretation of the statute, a United States District Court in Iowa ruled that eviscerated poultry was such an exempt commodity, and that therefore the ICC could not regulate the rates for the carriage of fresh slaughtered poultry by truck.

The ICC fought the ruling all the way up to the Supreme Court, but without success. A similar ruling with respect to frozen poultry was affirmed by the Supreme Court in 1956. Subsequently, the United States Department of Agriculture undertook a study to compare the transportation rates on unfrozen and frozen poultry, both before and after the respective decisions which freed them from ICC stewardship. The results showed that in 1956-57, poultry firms were paying 33% less for the transport of unfrozen poultry than they had had to pay in 1952, the last full year of ICC control. In the same 1956-57 period, frozen poultry rates had settled 36% below the prices the Commission had been supporting in 1955.[39]

WHAT MAKES THE ICC's protectionism especially serious is that today, as in 1887, the transportation industry is marked by overcapacity, which appears to be increasing at an accelerating rate. The so-called "Doyle Panel," commissioned by the Senate Committee on Commerce to undertake a study of the field, claims that *The social investment (public and private costs) of transportation per unit of transportation performed is growing at a fantastic rate.* By 1975, *"transportation social investment will outrun the gross national product."*[40]

The result of expansion of carrier investment and capacity at a rate that so far exceeds the growth of gross national product has resulted in an

---

[37] Report No. 445, 87th Cong. 1st Sess. (1961) pp. 81-82. (Hereinafter referred to as the "Doyle Report.") The author does not vouch for the accuracy of any of the Doyle Report's "findings." Note that on page 49 the Report seems to contradict itself in claiming that "private and exempt carriage can be expected to account for half of intercity freight not later than 1975." The Panel asserts on page 7 that since 1916 "the cumulative total of federal expenditures in highways, airways and waterways has come to approximately $23 billion. . . . "On page 166, the Panel sets the "monetary magnitude" of Federal aids to "highway transportation, to navigation, to aviation, and to the merchant marine" at "no less than $33.6 billion" since 1917. The Panel's chairman, John P. Doyle, is a retired air force general, and as such may not have been trained to trifle over $10 billion here or there.

[38] Although it ought to be noted that, to a certain extent, the duties the law imposes upon a regulated common carrier place certain "costs" (broadly defined) upon them which an unregulated carrier escapes. This need not, however, be an argument against unregulated carriage more than an argument against the imposed "costs."

[39] "Interstate Trucking of Fresh and Frozen Poultry under Agricultural Exemption," *Marketing Research Report No. 224* (Washington, D.C.: Dept. of Agriculture, 1958), p. 1. Certain objections to this study ought to be noted. First, it is not immediately apparent why the surveys chose 1952 and 1955, respectively, as the last years of regulation; in one case the District Court's opinion was selected as the terminal point (rather than the denial of certiorari by the Supreme Court in 1954) and in the other case the date was the Supreme Court's affirmance (rather than the District Court's opinion). The reasons should have been explained. Also, there was no "control" experience relating to the rate movements of regulated commodities by truck, during the same period, nor was there an attempt to correlate transport rates with, say, the wholesale price value of these commodities over the periods studied. The sampling of firms was conscientiously broad (those sampled in the 1956-57 period shipped 1.4 billion pounds), but the number of years analyzed deprived the study of some force.

[40] Doyle Report. p. 10. Italics in the original.

350

excess of transportation capacity that is unequalled in this century except during the major economic depressions of the thirties. Already decreased utilization of transportation plant has reached unusual proportions, and competition between carriers consequently has increased.[41]

Confronted with such a problem, and armed with experiences which were unavailable to the Collum Committee, some analysts might advocate freer competition to prune out the inefficient and to bring rates to a level which would discourage further superfluous capacity. But like the railroads of the 1880's, the Doyle Report's concern goes off along the opposite line of thought, advocating that there be "restraint of cutthroat competition from shipper pressures which is made possible by oversupply of transportation capacity. . . ."[42] Though the conclusion may seem paradoxical, it is the reasoning which is truly an affront. "Cutthroat competition" must be prevented, we are told, in order that the industry can meet the capital requirements necessary "to maintain and develop these facilities,"[43] i.e., the facilities which, so it is said, are already overdeveloped and too rapidly growing. In other words, read as a whole: we must have non-competitive prices, because under the current and lamented *excess of capacity*, if competitive pricing were allowed, the lower rates which would surely ensue would make the field less attractive to investors, and so frustrate *the maintenance and increasing of capacity*.

It is in line with this illogic—and from their inherent senses of "fair play" —that the Commissioners wish to continue to exercise their minimum rate power. And as for unregulated carriage, the fact that many an American businessman is rebelling against the ICC's family has provoked the Commission to spread its protective wings, rather than to surrender power: "The public interest in stable, reasonable and properly regulated rates cannot find expression in the complete absence of control of such a large segment of the bulk carrying trade." The

ICC's alternative legislative "solution" would be simply to abolish unregulated water carriage and to limit severely the agricultural commodities loophole.[44]

These views are just symptomatic of a broad range of Commission attitudes which portend a continuing uneconomical investment in transportation capacity— along roads which promise the public no end to uncompetitively high rates.

WRITING IN THE *Yale Law Journal* a decade ago, Harvard Professor Samuel Huntington suggested that "the ICC should be abolished as an independent agency" for the failure of its outlook to be "as comprehensive as the interests of the whole country."[45] Some years later, his colleague, Louis Jaffe, responded in the same forum that the critics' "real quarrel" with the administrative agencies, "if they would but recognize and admit it, is with Congress." Using the Interstate Commerce Commission as an example, he observed:

> . . . can anyone find in the legislation of 1935 and 1940 an intention to establish competition as the presumptive norm of transportation regulation? . . . Everyone seems to be agreed that the railroads and the large truckers were the dominant forces in procuring that legislation. Was this in the name of competition? When somewhat later the Supreme Court came close to holding that railroad rate conferences were a violation of the antitrust laws, Congress, immediately immunized them. Was this another indication of a congressional mandate for competition?[46]

Though Jaffe conceded that "The ICC . . . is, at times, more tender of the railroad interests than even a fair reading of its mandate would require, and it may be less adventurous in permitting new competition than it might be,"[47] upon

---

[41] *Ibid.*, p. 8.
[42] *Ibid.*, p. 56.
[43] *Ibid.*, p. 50.

[44] *Ibid.*, p. 134.
[45] Huntington, "The Marasmus of the ICC," 61 *Yale L.J.* 467, 508 (1952), criticized in Jaffe, Book Review, 65 *Yale L.J.* 1068 (1956) and Jaffe, "The Effective Limits of the Administrative Process: A Re-evaluation," 67 *Harvard L. R.* 1105 (1954).
[46] Jaffe, Book Review, 65 *Yale L. J.* 1068, 1072, (1956).
[47] *Ibid.*, p. 1073.

351

his view, it ought to be recognized that the Commission is generally doing the job which Congress wanted done.

These two views need not be inconsistent. One could agree both with Jaffe —that the ICC staff is not to be blamed for doing the job that "Congress" wanted done—and with Huntington—that the ICC ought to be abolished rather than permitted to continue a job so often irreconcilable with the public interest.

Huntington's "s o l u t i o n," however (rather astonishing in the context of his documented cynicism about federal regulation), was to replace the abolished ICC with *three new* commissions: one, it may be presumed, to be dominated by water interests, one by truckers, and one by the railroads.[48] Perhaps a more worthwhile future for transportation regulation would be to divest the ICC at least of the powers discussed in this article, and to explore the withdrawal of federal financial patronage to an already over-invested segment of the economy.

No doubt the problems which deregulation would raise are extraordinarily complex. To take one specific problem (outside the immediate concern of the ICC), permanent federal subsidization of the inland waterways is a fine example of indefensible governmental intrusion. Why should those who do not directly benefit from the waterways pay for those who do? Many have suggested as an alternative that a "user charge" be imposed to make the users of the waterways bear the full expenses of their maintenance. On the other hand, even granted that the present transportation network is the child of economically irrational forces, one must recognize, too, that as the system has developed, patterns of commerce have adjusted themselves to it. The Ohio Valley (with the important Pittsburgh-Youngstown iron and steel district) has in no small way been built upon cheap water transportation. Much of Southern industry, too, has been driven to the banks of the Mississippi by improvidently high rail charges. Until we know more about the repercussions a user charge would have upon such fundamental industrial networks, more

about the ability of railroads and trucks to "fill in" with service at comparable cost to users, and more about the competitive implications in the product market of increasing the raw material costs of waterway industry, changes ought to be instituted with some respect for the awesome magnitude of the task.

Nonetheless, the future direction of governmental control is indicated. The transportation industry can and ought to be sheared of its supports, whether they be the meting out of direct subsidies or ICC regulation of prices. Artificial props can be removed gradually, one by one, so that the impact may be gauged without taking an eye off any imagined danger spots. No doubt many persons in the transportation industry will agree with the Doyle Report's advice that "Experience in the United States . . . with unrestricted competition in ratemaking by carriers has not been happy."[49] But assuming that General Doyle means "not been happy" for the public (rather than for the transportation industry, with which the report appears more tenderly concerned), it ought to be remarked that unrestricted competition has not been widely *tried* in 75 years. And where it has been tried, as with agricultural exempt commodities, the experience has indeed been "happy"—for the farmers and for the consuming public.

Moreover, since the foundation of the ICC, two other developments have greatly altered the need for regulation. First, the relative railroad power of the 1880's has considerably diminished. As of a few years ago, an ICC study on percentage distribution of intercity freight traffic revealed that the railroads accounted for 45% of revenue ton-miles; motor vehicles, 22%; the inland waterways (including the Great Lakes), 15%; and oil pipelines, 18%.[50] Second, a large body of antitrust law has developed in the interim. It is true that a well oiled transportation lobby has managed to produce some special exemptive legislation (and the Doyle Panel would extend present exemptions

---

[48] Huntington, *op. cit.,* p. 508.

[49] Doyle Report, p. 419.

[50] *Intercity Ton Miles* (Washington, D.C.: ICC, Bureau of Transport Economics and Statistics, 1961).

352

to legitimize rate-rigging by every mode of carriage). On the other hand, if only the antitrust umbrella would be repealed, the existence of the antitrust laws would actually make the withdrawal of institutionalized regulation more feasible today than ever before. Antitrust, thoughtfully applied to transportation, could allay many of the past fears about abusive practices and huge amalgamations of power.

Indeed, one can not help but wonder how much substance there is to some of the fears voiced against deregulation. The supposed need for minimum rate regulation is a case in point. Advocates of maintaining the Commission's power have maintained (1) that if the railroads are allowed to put lower rates in force along waterways and major highway trunk routes, the rates will "have to be" raised in the less competitive areas; (2) that if control is relaxed, the railroads will lower their rates and destroy competing modes of carriage; (3) that, having destroyed competing modes, the rails will raise their rates to a higher level than that which had obtained previously, to the detriment of the public.

The first of these arguments sounds like a restatement of the "recoupment fallacy" so ably and decisively repudiated by Professor Morris A. Adelman of MIT in another context.[51] The railroads, generally, are maintaining rates well below the maxima the Commission has allowed them (much less the maxima the Commission probably would allow them on request). If the railroads could make more net revenue in the less competitive areas by raising their rates higher than those which presently obtain, they would have done so already; it is hard to see how rate changes in the competitive areas alter either the feasibility or the profitability of rate advances in non-competitive regions. Thus, it is not credible that "because" the railroads lower their rates to meet water and truck competition, they "will have" to raise them else-

where. The argument is based on some rather primitive theories about pricing.

The second supposed justification for rate minima is no more compelling: that the railroads will use their potential for better service and lower rates to destroy competing modes. If the underlying assumptions of the argument are correct, the issue so stated is as simple as whether we want to sustain and encourage investment in inefficient transport media by recourse to artificial price supports.

The third argument is the one which demands the most attention although it, too, may well prove dubious. Even if the railroads could lower their prices enough to drive truck competition from select major routes, it is not immediately apparent how the rails could thereafter "simply" recoup their short-term losses with new, higher-than-ever rates. Their ability to do so would be a function of the costs to truckers of reestablishing themselves in the affected area. And trucks, once driven off (the image of "destroyed" is unfortunately misleading), could probably swarm back like flies; higher-than-ever rates would be frustrated by attracting a more-than-ever number of trucks.

Water transportation, however—especially by intercoastal carrier—is subject to certain economies of scale which make the long-run effects of railroad price depressing less amenable to *a priori* analysis. What is needed is a follow-up study of the actual effects of cases in which lowered rates have driven away intercoastal competitors, to determine whether the railroads have, in fact, been able to enlarge their power over the public. The entire area is, indeed, riddled with a number of intangibles. But even if there proves to be some risk of objectionable price cutting, one may wonder whether the mere possibility justifies the imposition of an objectionable rate umbrella. If there are bona fide victims of *"predatory* prices" (as opposed to victims of *lower* prices and their own inefficiency), it would seem as though the established procedures for private antitrust suits would be a solution preferable to the perpetuation of the ICC.

353

---

[51] Adelman, "Effective Competition and the Antitrust Laws," 61 *Harvard L. R.* 1290 (1948).

THE REGULATORY BUREAUS:

CAB: Freedom from Competition

SAM PELTZMAN

BACK IN THE days when air travel was still considered something of a stunt, the early pioneers of the civil aviation industry begged to be taken seriously. They wanted their industry to be treated just like any other form of transportation, and that meant being regulated and subsidized by a full-fledged federal authority. The federal government had, after all, granted its protection to the railroads, ships, trucks, and busses, and civil aviation remained much the neglected child of the transportation industry. The federal government's insouciance ended when, in the summer of 1938, Congress passed the Civil Aeronautics Act in which the Civil Aeronautics Authority (now Civil Aeronautics Board) was formed. The industry exulted:

> Tension relaxed. The battle had been won. At last civil aviation had come into its own with its own agency....[1]

> The Civil Aeronautics Act is the Magna Charta of aviation. With some defects and some uncertainties, it is nevertheless the finest thing that has happened to aviation since the World War conclusively proved its practicality.[2]

This "Magna Charta" gives the Civil Aeronautics Board extremely broad powers to regulate the economic aspects of civil aviation,[3] the most important of which concern the routes flown by air lines and the fares they charge.

Sam Peltzman is Business Manager of *New Individualist Review*.

All passenger, cargo, and mail rates, while they are initially set by the airlines, require approval by the CAB. In addition, the CAB may, when it deems these rates not "just and reasonable," fix maximum or minimum rates or both. Operation of an airline in interstate commerce requires a certificate of "public convenience and necessity" from the CAB, except that the so-called "grandfather carriers" (those airlines in operation at the time the Act was passed) received such certificates automatically. The CAB determines which airline may serve which cities, and it may regulate the number of flights to a city. Additionally, the CAB is empowered to grant subsidies to the airlines and to rule on mergers. These regulatory powers remain essentially the same today as those granted in the 1938 Act. It was thought at that time that, as an "infant industry," civil aviation required subsidies and pro-

---

[1] 3 *American Aviation* No. 23, May 1, 1940, p. 1, cited in Lindsey, John M., *The Legislative Development of Civil Aviation, 1938-1958* (Washington: Civil Aeronautics Board, 1962), p. 3n.

[2] Logan, "Aeronautical Law Developments, 1939," 11 *Journal of Air Law and Commerce* 1 (1940), 16, cited in Lindsey, *op. cit.*, p. 1n.

[3] The Civil Aeronautics Board has two major functions in addition to economic regulation; it assists the State Department in negotiating the rights of U. S. international airlines with foreign governments, and it investigates air accidents and makes recommendations on air safety rules to the Federal Aviation Agency. The Federal Aviation Agency, created in the Federal Aviation Act of 1958, administers air safety laws and the air traffic control system. This article will deal only with economic regulation by the CAB of domestic airlines.

tection from competition if it were to develop properly. However, as is the case with many such infants, they never seem to grow old enough for the subsidies and regulation to be discontinued. In fact, while consideration of the "public interest" is supposed to provide the *raison d'etre* for economic regulation of the airlines, there is much to indicate that the CAB acts in great measure to protect the airlines at the expense of the public interest.

The case of the non-scheduled airlines (today known as "supplemental" airlines) provides perhaps the clearest illustration of this. These are small carriers which do not operate on published schedules or fixed routes, but rather seek to utilize their aircraft as fully as possible by adjusting quickly to changes in air traffic patterns. This results in a considerable cost reduction over the type of service provided by regularly scheduled airlines. After World War II, these airlines, which were exempted from CAB regulation in 1938, began using this cost advantage to undercut the rates of the regularly scheduled airlines.[4] They grew in number and some began providing fairly regular service. The regularly scheduled airlines, facing real competition for the first time, retaliated by inaugurating low cost air-coach service. This was nothing more than the normal results of increased competition such as would obtain in any other growing industry—lower prices, more variety of service, etc. However, the regularly scheduled airlines, unlike other industries, had available the full force of federal law, incarnate in the CAB, with which to escape the rigors of competition. In 1947 non-scheduled airlines were required to register with the CAB; in 1949 the blanket exemption from regulation was dropped, and each of the nonskeds (as these airlines were popularly known) was required to file for exemption individually; in 1951 the CAB began limiting nonsked operations. With the aid of an important Supreme Court decision affirming CAB control over the nonskeds,[5] this limita-

tion has proceeded more or less systematically. The number of nonskeds dropped from 150 in 1947 to 50 by 1957.[6] In 1959 the CAB ordered 12 of those remaining to cease operations; the lines allowed to continue flying received temporary operating certificates for from two to five years. Several of the two-year certificates have recently lapsed without being renewed. Thus, for example, on the New York-Chicago route, most heavily traveled in the country, the number of supplemental flights is now only ten per month as against thirty in 1961. The day may not be far off when the supplemental airlines will be eliminated altogether. This systematic reduction of competition cannot be justified on grounds of public interest. It might possibly be justified on grounds of safety if, as has been charged, the supplemental carriers do not maintain as safe operations as the scheduled airlines. However, the CAB itself dismisses this as a cause for forcing the supplementals out of business:

> There is no factual showing that the applicants [for operating certificates] have failed to adhere to required safety standards. . . . Moreover regulatory control for safety purposes is maintained over supplemental carriers as it is over holders of route certificates.[7]

Rather, the CAB pointed to lack of "going concern status" and lack of "ability to operate" as the major reasons for denying applications.[8] At best, these vague criteria are merely lame excuses for restricting competition; at worst, they constitute a blatant interference on the part of a regulatory body with the right of management to take financial risks.[9]

355

---

[4] Cf. Wilcox, Clair, *Public Policies Toward Business* (Homewood, Ill.: Irwin, 1960), p. 680.

[5] North American Airlines v. C.A.B., 353 *U.S.* 941.

[6] Wilcox, *op. cit.*, p. 676.

[7] 28 *C.A.B.* 224 (1959), 238.

[8] *Loc. cit.*

[9] Unfortunately criteria such as these are employed constantly at CAB hearings. Thus, to take a recent example, Continental Airlines is denied a certificate for operation between Los Angeles and San Francisco because, among other things: "*Continental* would be required to install new terminal facilities at San Francisco and Oakland and incur substantial promotional and advertising expenses in establishing itself in the market," while TWA is favored because it "has the advantage of a long standing identity in this market." *Pacific Southwest Local Service Case*, Order E-17950, January 25, 1962 (Washington, D. C.: Civil Aeronautics Board), p. 27 (italics supplied).

The CAB's attitude toward the supplementals was neatly summarized by its chairman at the time of a Congressional inquiry into the supplemental air carrier industry. He told that inquiry:

> . . . we have felt it to be our duty under the Civil Aeronautics Act to see to it that the irregular [supplemental] air carriers should do the job which we authorized them to do and . . . not to compete with the certificated air-transport structure of the nation.[10]

Putting the supplementals out of business has not been the only way in which the CAB has protected the certificated air-transport structure of the nation from the scourge of competition. In an industry which has grown as rapidly as has civil aviation, it is inevitable that many new firms will seek to enter the field. The CAB has in fact received over 150 applications for the establishment of new scheduled airline companies since it was formed. *In all the years of its existence, it has not approved a single one of these applications.*[11] While the CAB insists that it is trying to promote competition in the air transport industry,[12] all that it has done in this regard is to shuffle routes among the favored "grandfather carriers." Further, it is now trying to make the club even more exclusive. The current CAB chairman has issued a call for mergers to reduce "excess competition."[13]

EVEN IF THE CAB has stifled competition by limiting and even reducing the number of firms engaging in air transport, the situation might still be mitigated if it encouraged competition among already existing airlines in the fares they charge for their services. However, the CAB's record does not show that it has acted this way, nor is it clear that the CAB could, given the legal framework under which it operates, have done much to encourage competition. The very fact that all fares must by law be filed with the CAB and receive its approval after a hearing creates a natural tendency away from price competition. When an airline is required to publicize a rate cut before the fact and when it knows that its rivals will likely retaliate before the first CAB hearing, the temporary gains of price cutting, which so often stimulate it in other industries, disappear. There is thus a strong incentive for individual airlines not to initiate rate cuts, and this is endemic to the legal structure. In general, however, the CAB has not been anxious to promote price competition even where it might have been able to do so. The prevailing CAB attitude here is perhaps best seen in its decision in the *General Passenger Fare Investigation.* This four-year investigation into the fare structure sought to determine what a "fair and reasonable" return on investment would be for the trunk (inter-regional) airlines and to set rate making standards to achieve that return. It found 10.5% to be such a "fair and reasonable" return for the airline industry.[14] It is hardly surprising, in view of the CAB's solicitude for the airlines as shown in its policy toward the nonskeds, that this was a rate considerably in excess of that being earned by the airlines at the time of the investigation.[15] The CAB then set forth the rate-making standard which would be applied in attaining this goal:

> Where the bulk of the carriers fall within a reasonable range of the rates of return found herein to be proper . . . fare adjustments should normally be based upon the results for the *industry as a group.*
>
> In effect, the entire domestic trunk-line industry would be regulated so as to produce an over-all rate of return to the industry equal to [10.5] percent.[16]

This standard, which is to govern future rate making decisions by the CAB, dis-

---

[10] *Future of Irregular Airlines in United States Air Transportation Industry. Hearings before a sub-committee of the Select Committee on Small Business, U. S. Senate* (Washington, D. C., 1953), p. 8.

[11] Wilcox, *op. cit.,* p. 677.

[12] For just one example of this insistence, see discussion at 27 *C.A.B.* 829.

[13] *New York Times,* Nov. 4, 1961.

[14] *General Passenger Fare Investigation,* Order E-16068, Nov. 25, 1960 (Washington, D. C.: Civil Aeronautics Board), p. 13.

[15] *Ibid.,* Appendix A, p. A-1.

[16] *Ibid.,* p. 75 (italics supplied); p. 72.

356

tinctly reduces the possibility of significant price competition. For, suppose an airline were to come up with some method to cut its costs. One way it could capitalize on this would be to cut its fares and win business from its competitors. However, it is possible that, if it did so, the losses of its competitors might exceed the gains to the rate cutting airline, and the rate of return to the industry would fall below the "fair and reasonable" rate. The Board, if it felt this was likely to be the result of the fare cut, would be required, under the standard it has set up, to reject any proposed fare reduction. What seems likely to evolve is something like rate setting by majority vote of the airlines or by that faction which can convince the CAB that its particular rate proposal will bring the 10.5% return to the industry. Clearly, if the industry is to be treated as a group, independent and diverse rate setting policies could not be tolerated. This is hinted at when the Board states:

> It is thus clear that the proper fare level must be found at some point between the needs of the most profitable and least profitable carriers. . . .[17]

If this means anything, it surely means that an efficient airline could not be permitted to institute fare reductions which threatened the existence of inefficient carriers, as this would surely be contrary to the "needs" of the latter. In treating the industry as a corporate entity, the benefits of price competition to the consumer are thus to be made subservient to the "needs" of the carriers. The CAB did not wait long before implementing its announced policy. Even before the *General Passenger Fare Investigation* report was issued, it made permanent a temporary fare increase and authorized a new increase, the total of the two being 6½% plus $2 per ticket.[18] This applied to all trunk airlines, and all of them adopted the new fares immediately. This uniformity, in the face of the great variety of market conditions in an area as large as the United States, is hardly the mark of a vigorously competitive industry.

This absence of reliance on price competition apparently stems from the CAB's view of the airline industry as a public utility,[19] about which the CAB examiner in the fare investigation had this to say:

> Unbridled competition tends to be destructive in the case of utilities resulting in widely fluctuating prices, equally fluctuating profits, and bankruptcy for most of the competitors. Thus, bankruptcy eliminates the competition and tends toward monopoly, which without the check of competition has no economic regulator on prices or profits. Consequently, regulation was developed to do the job competition could not do with respect to public utilities.

How this can possibly be taken to apply to the airline industry where it was not "unbridled competition" but deliberate, pertinacious CAB policy which reduced the number of competitors is something beyond the ken of this author. The examiner goes on to say:

> . . . the restriction on entry of new carriers into the business and of existing carriers into areas not covered by their certificates renders it impossible to conclude . . . that free-market forces can be depended upon to prevent either too low or too high returns on capital.[20]

However, if it then follows that free-market forces will be efficient regulators of prices and profits under conditions of free entry, the CAB must explain why it has not permitted first free entry and then free competition.

That the collective pricing judgment of a dominant group will not always be wiser than that of a single aggressive innovator can be seen in a recent case in which the CAB temporarily relented in applying its rate making standards. In 1961, Continental Airlines, eleventh largest of the twelve domestic trunk airlines, attempted to reduce coach fares 20% on its Chicago-Los Angeles route. Its three competitors, United, American, and TWA (first, second, and third, respec-

357

---

[17] *Ibid.*, p. 74.
[18] CAB Press Release, June 17, 1960.

[19] Cf. *General Passenger Fare Investigation*, Appendix A, p. 2 ff.
[20] *Ibid.*, Appendix A, pp. 3-4.

tively), filed protests with the CAB.[21] Consistent with its rate making policy, the CAB ruled against Continental and the fare reduction.[22] Recently, however, the CAB has permitted the reduction for a trial period, and Continental's three competitors have been forced to meet its fares. The results to date: non-stop traffic between Chicago and Los Angeles rose about 30% in the last four months of 1962 (the time in which the new fares were effective), revenues rose 15%. This contrasts with reductions of 7% and 9% in traffic and revenues respectively in the previous months of 1962. Continental's expenses were cut by $360,000 on an annual basis by eliminating free meals on the coach flights.[23] It is still an open question as to how far the CAB will allow this attempt at price competition on an important route to go, but the Continental case illustrates what a gross mistake it is to treat the airline industry as a single public utiilty. In the airline industry, no less than in any other, it is the experimentation and innovation of independent firms and individuals which can, if it is given free reign, bring about the greatest progress.

While the Continental Chicago-Los Angeles fare reduction is still classed as an "experiment" by the CAB, and its permanence is in doubt, one of the few important routes in the country which has seen extensive and permanent price competition is the San Diego-Los Angeles-San Francisco route. This occurred when Pacific Southwest Airlines purchased new equipment and proceeded to undercut the fares of its bigger competitors. This has been a highly successful policy for Pacific Southwest (and, we may assume, for its customers).[24] The "catch" here is that Pacific Southwest operates wholly within the state of California, and, since the CAB's jurisdiction on fares extends only to firms engaged in interstate commerce, it is free of CAB rate-making policy.

ON THE BASIS of its record over the past 24 years, it is obvious that the CAB has acted as a focal point for the organization of a compulsory cartel in domestic civil aviation. The CAB itself has actively restricted entry into civil aviation by new firms and eliminated old ones, and it has reduced the scope of price competition between airlines. While it may be true that it could do little, given the law, about the lack of price competition, it is interesting to ask why it should have restricted entry to the extent it has. The simplest answer is that it is a deliberately perverse organization beholden to the regularly scheduled airlines. This is not necessarily the correct answer, however. Quite often regulatory agencies, set up in the "public interest," sincerely identify that interest with the interests of the industry they are supposed to regulate. Looked at from the viewpoint of the regulators, this does not seem unreasonable. To them the "public interest" presents itself as a highly diffuse quantity, in the case of the CAB a traveling public of millions of individuals, with a viewpoint seldom articulated at hearings. The interest of the airlines (always set forth by them as the same as the public interest) is seen in concrete, specific terms and is always pressed insistently before the CAB. The airlines have, after all, a far greater incentive to win the CAB over to their mode of thinking than does any individual purchaser of their services. It is thus natural to expect the airlines to expend more money and effort to convince the CAB that their interest is identical to the general interest. These efforts have not been without success. As one commentator put it:

> The present regulatory system for civil aviation with its primary emphasis on protection of the regulatees from competition, was "sold" partly on the basis of the . . . vague identification of the financial welfare of particular carriers with the satisfaction of national need. . . .[25]

The way in which the CAB confused special interest with the general interest can

[21] Cf. *New York Times*, Oct. 31, 1961; Nov. 16, 1961.
[22] *New York Times*, Nov. 23, 1961.
[23] Cf. *Wall Street Journal*, Jan. 22, 1963.
[24] *Wall Street Journal*, Nov. 9, 1959.

[25] Keyes, Lucile S., "National Policy Toward Commercial Aviation—Some Basic Problems," 16 *Journal of Air Law and Commerce* 280 (1949), 294.

be seen in the Congressional hearings on the non-scheduled airlines. The regularly scheduled carriers took the position that the nonskeds were "skimming the cream" off their business on major routes, leaving them unremunerative business in small towns. If the regularly scheduled carriers were to continue to provide service to small towns at unremunerative rates, they needed the profits on major routes; hence, the nonskeds had to be restricted, since the "public interest" clearly required extensive air routes all over the country.[26] Superficially, it might seem reasonable that the "public interest" indeed required the provision of scheduled air service to small towns at unremunerative rates, and, in fact, the CAB chairman took that stand at the hearings. Yet, even if we accept what is doubtful—that rates to small towns were in fact "unremunerative" in any meaningful sense, the uneconomic utilization of transport facilities this entails (diversion of planes from routes òn which their services are more valuable, underutilization of existing rail and highway facilities, etc.) is not in the public interest. At best, it serves the interests of the particular group of people who use scheduled air service to small towns at the expense of those who travel on major routes. Were the subsidies and protection withdrawn, this inefficient rate structure would disappear. So it is with the two other reasons most frequently cited in defense of limiting entry into the airline industry, namely that it is essential to the maintenance of proper safety standards and that it is necessary to the maintenance of regularly scheduled service.[27] As to the first of these, we have already seen that the CAB doesn't really believe it itself; safety regulation and economic regulation are essentially separate matters. As to the second, one authority has concluded that the competitive pressures in the airline industry are such as to work toward greater rather than less regu-

larity of service.[28] More to the point, we need ask why regularly scheduled service is in the public interest if it is true that the public doesn't want it. Undoubtedly, the CAB's defense, that limiting competition is in the public interest, is completely sincere, though, in this writer's opinion, it is without a convincing argument in its favor. This is a situation, however, which typically arises when the uncoerced decisions of the market-place are replaced by the arbitrary decisions of an agency of the State.

IT IS INTERESTING to examine the economic situation of the airline industry after 24 years of regulation by the CAB. In addition to limiting entry and discouraging price competition, the CAB has provided outright subsidies to the major airlines; it now provides them indirectly by subsidizing local service carriers which provide much "feeder" traffic to the trunk lines. The industry is further subsidized by federal aid to airport construction under the Federal Airport Act of 1946. Moreover, along with all this assistance to the airlines, the public's acceptance of air travel has made it one of the fastest growing industries in the United States. From 1947 to 1961, for example, the number of passenger-miles (number of passengers times miles flown per passenger) flown by the airlines has increased from 6.0 billion to 29.5 billion, or about 400%.[29] This is a combination of circumstances which, one would have thought, would have been highly profitable for the airlines. However, this has not been the case. In the face of a slowdown in the *rate* of increase in revenue (revenues still grew absolutely), domestic trunk lines lost 34.6 million dollars in 1961.[30] One major trunk line (Capital) averted bankruptcy by merger, another (Northeast) has been temporarily saved from bankruptcy by financial assistance

---

[26] See testimony of any certified airline executive in Select Committee on Small Business, op. cit.

[27] Kaysen, Carl, and Donald Turner, *Antitrust Policy: An Economic and Legal Analysis* (Cambridge, Mass.: Harvard University Press, 1959), p. 205.

[28] Keyes, Lucile S., "A Reconsideration of Federal Control of Entry into Air Transportation," 22 *Journal of Air Law and Commerce* (1955) cited in Kaysen, loc. cit.

[29] *Moody's Transportation Manual* (1962 edition), p. a69.

[30] *Ibid.*, p. a71.

from the Hughes Tool Co. Trans World Airlines, third largest in the nation, suffered a loss of 38.7 million dollars in 1961.[31] The largest domestic trunk line, United, had a return on stockholders' investment of about 2% in the same year as opposed to the roughly 10% which is average in other industries.[32] While it would be wrong to say that the domestic airline industry faces a financial crisis, it is apparent that, in spite of all the help it has received, important segments of it are not in the most robust health. Though it may seem paradoxical, this state of ill-health has been induced, to some degree, by an overdose in its adult life of what was the airlines' sustenance as an infant—CAB regulation and subsidies.

Regulation contributes to the current financial difficulties of the airlines by introducing inflexibility into their operations. Abandonment of a route, to cite one example, requires often lengthy CAB hearings and CAB permission. Thus, except in periods of rapid overall growth in which every route shares to some degree, an airline is liable to find itself flying virtually empty planes on routes experiencing falling traffic for some time, before (and if) it is permitted to abandon them. Similarly, these empty planes cannot readily be shifted to new, more rapidly growing routes before the necessary hearings and certificates of convenience and necessity are obtained. The inefficiencies inherent in such a situation will, if anything, become more troublesome now that the period of most rapid growth for the airlines is apparently ending. Another type of inflexibility induced by regulation finds its source in the rate-making policies fostered by the Civil Aeronautics Act and CAB policy. Airlines, finding it difficult to engage in price competition with each other, compete primarily in the services they offer—e.g., free meals, lavish terminals, faster schedules. Thus, when the jet transport was introduced, each airline felt compelled to introduce them as rapidly as possible to meet its competitors with little regard to the slow-

down in traffic growth occurring at the same time. No real attempt was made to create new classes of service (such as those offered by the supplementals) which would have, by lowering the fares on piston planes, utilized them more fully and caused the jets to be introduced at a rate more in keeping with the growth of traffic. Certainly, no new airlines were chartered which might have utilized the piston planes being sold by the airlines converting to jets. All that happened was that piston fares were kept constant while a jet surcharge was introduced. On many routes, the passenger is not even afforded the chance to take advantage of the lower relative cost of piston flights because these routes are currently being served only by jet flights. The net result of an inflexible rate structure in a period of rapid expansion of the jet fleet has been a sharp increase in the number of empty seats on scheduled flights. At $5,000,000 per jet plane, this can be and has been, quite costly. Given a continuation of the present regulatory set-up, however, we will likely witness much the same thing when the supersonic passenger plane is introduced in the 1970's.

We can conclude that the heavy protection and subsidization of the airlines has been only a mixed blessing even to them. It has, by choking off new sources of competition and discouraging competition among existing airlines, worked against the "public interest" it was created to serve. Quite clearly, it is legitimate to ask what the alternatives to the present regulatory policy are.

In the opinion of this writer, one simple alternative presents itself as the most preferable—abolition of the CAB in all its economic functions. (While I am also in favor of having both the CAB and FAA withdraw from safety regulation, discussion of this is beyond the scope of this article.) If what we mean by "public interest" here is the satisfaction of market demands, in all their variety, at lowest social cost and, as part of this, the quick adaptability to changing market conditions, then our history indicates that this interest is best served by competition free of arbitrary interference by State power. It is not served by reserving

---

[31] *Ibid.*, p. 1298.

[32] *The Fortune Directory* (New York: Time, Inc., 1962), p. 31.

civil aviation as the exclusive domain of "grandfather carriers;" it is not served by government supervision of minimum rates; it is not served by compelling the community to pay, in the form of government subsidies, for services provided by and to favored groups. It is true the end of government interference and protection of the airlines will cause some painful readjustments in the air transport industry. Allowing new firms to enter the industry freely and permitting all firms to serve whatever routes they choose to will, judging by the success of the supplementals before their ranks were decimated by the CAB, and the success of Pacific Southwest on the west coast, likely lead to a reduction in the fare level. It will cause a reduction in service on subsidized and poorly patronized routes, increases in service on other routes. With the pressures of competition substituted for bureaucratic controls, airlines would be compelled to adjust services and fares as quickly as possible to changing market conditions. Failure to do so, given the relative ease with which the airline business could be entered into and the great mobility of the basic capital equipment, would result in quick loss of business to new competitors. All of this is surely in the public interest, but it just as surely will force inefficient airlines out of business. However, unless inefficiency is constantly penalized, the airline industry itself will not be healthy for long. We have already seen what has happened to certain parts of the industry in the face of a mere slowdown in the rate of traffic growth. Further protection of inefficiency will only lead to further financial difficulties, more controls and possible ultimate nationalization of the industry. There is no compelling reason for allowing this to happen. Neither is there any reason to believe that the benefits of free competition cannot serve the general interest as well in the air transport industry as it has in other industries. So far, however, we have not given free competition a chance in this industry. We might do worse than to try it.

361

THE REGULATORY BUREAUS:

FCC: Free Speech,
"Public Needs," and Mr. Minow

362

THE PANORAMA confronting television viewers may recently have passed the cost of living as a universal cause for complaint. It is no wonder that FCC Chairman Newton Minow's crusade to induce broadcasters to cater to our nation's more refined tastes (meaning of course your tastes and mine!) has been greeted with considerable enthusiasm. In this case most of the iceberg is well below the surface; the popularity of Minow's cause has obscured the challenge to a free society implicit in his approach. In this article I hope to point out some of the dangers inherent in both past Commission policy and in Minow's present course. While the Commission performs such diverse functions as regulation of private telephone and telegraph rates,[1] research in communication technology, and supervision of future communications satellites, I deal here with the Commission's most controversial function: allocation of available radio and television frequencies among applicants and subsequent supervision of their use. I conclude with some brief suggestions as to how the problems discussed might be solved.[2]

My position can be summed up as follows: When some form of legal regulation of the air waves became inevitable, Congress chose a method that would lead to problems of excessive government con-

trol no matter how well intentioned those appointed to supervise the air waves would prove to be. As a result, during the next three decades a philosophy of public ownership and control of the airwaves became crystallized, although the Commission was generally restrained in its application of this philosophy. Finally, when public sentiment against broadcasters became strong enough, we were so accustomed to according a special "public" status to the broadcasting industry that the appearance of Minow as a tribune of the public interest seemed natural. The seemingly benevolent and non-despotic nature of his crusade obscures the fact that his program requires markedly increased bureaucratic supervision of what "the public interest requires" in the way of programming. Nowhere in the vast structure of govern-

---

[1] Problems raised by rate regulation are covered in the preceding two articles. FCC rate regulation is often as exotic as that of the ICC and CAB, as is indicated by a recent report in the *Wall Street Journal:* "The FCC found that both companies were earning about 3% on their private telegraph services and ordered [!] them to boost rates so that AT&T would earn about 7¼% and Western Union about 9%." January 30, 1963.

[2] My suggested solutions, as well as much of my background material, are taken largely from an article by R. H. Coase which this writer considers a classic of applied economic theory: "The Federal Communications Commission," *Journal of Law and Economics,* October, 1959, pp. 1-40. I recommend this article for those who wish a more sophisticated development of the issues presented here.

Robert M. Hurt is an Associate Editor of *New Individualist Review.*

mental regulation of our way of life can one better apply Tocqueville's warning against that

> . . . immense and tutelary power which takes upon itself alone to secure [men's] gratifications and to watch over their fate. This power is absolute, minute, regular, provident, and mild.

WHILE RADIO WAS first used commercially at the turn of the century, there was no urgent need for legal regulation of broadcasting until 1922, when the number of broadcasting stations increased from 60 to 564. Secretary of Commerce Herbert Hoover, who was authorized to grant broadcasting licenses under a 1912 Act of Congress, attempted to prevent new stations from interfering with one another and with existing stations by writing into new licenses the wave lengths the licensee could use and the hours he could broadcast. However, in 1926 a federal court held that the Secretary could not attach such conditions to a license under the 1912 Act. The result of this decision was chaos and confusion. Over two hundred stations were built during the next nine months, and existing stations no longer limited themselves to frequencies allocated in their licenses. Interference was rampant and radio reception was described as a "Babel of tongues."

Obviously some form of legal intervention was necessary here. Available radio and television frequencies are like any scarce resource in that they are not open to universal and unrestricted use without their value being destroyed or seriously impaired. There is room on the frequency spectrum for only 106 AM radio channels, 50 FM radio channels, 12 very high frequency television channels, and 70 ultra high frequency television channels, if interference is to be avoided. Since stations far enough apart can operate on the same frequencies without interference, there would be room in the entire nation for 3,000 AM stations, 2,000 FM stations, 619 VHF stations, and 1,432 UHF stations.[3] Invariably there have been many more potential users than available airspace.

Consequently, broadcasting frequencies, like land, would have to be rationed in some way among potential users. Just as the same frequencies cannot be used in a community by two broadcasters without interference which would drown out or seriously hinder one or both, a tract of fertile land would lose most of its value if everyone were free to attempt to sow or reap it. To give an analogy closer to the problem of radio interference, land would lose its value for cultivation if anyone could graze his domestic animals on it. The same is true of any scarce factor of production, whether a natural resource such as iron ore or a finished product such as a machine. In these cases the rationing problem has been met by rules of property laid down by courts and legislatures, by which property rights are defined and protection is given against interference.

363

Several alternative forms of legal regulation were available at this point, and we will explore some of them later. But a 1925 Senate resolution set the pattern to be followed by declaring that the "ether" was an "inalienable possession of the people of the United States . . ." and the first Congressional response to the 1926 court decision was to require all licensees to execute "a waiver of any right or of any claim to any right, as against the United States, to any wave length or to the use of the ether in radio transmission." This was due partly to a reaction against the scandalous giveaway of public lands before the turn of the century to railroads and other private interests. But while it may not have been universally recognized at the time, the first corollary to "public ownership of the ether" would be the doctrine that broadcasters were in some sense trustees bound to act in the interest of the public,

---

[3] Wilcox, *Public Policies Toward Business* (Homewood, Ill.: Irwin, 1959), pp. 697-701. These figures are based, first, on the rather arbitrary Commission allocation of available airspace among broadcasters and other domestic and governmental users, and, second, on the Commission's fixed rules determining how many frequencies each station may use. As Coase suggests, op. cit., different methods of allocation might result in a substantially different number of stations. These figures merely demonstrate that there will be a substantial limitation on the number of stations.

Page Twenty-five

since they were using the property of the public. The inevitable second corollary is that government is the tribune of the people that must enforce this duty.[4]

In 1927 an Act of Congress created the Federal Radio Commission, which was authorized to issue licenses for use of airwaves only when "the public interest, necessity, or convenience would be served" by so doing. Licenses were issued for only three years, subject to renewal by the Commission, and could be transferred to another party only with its consent. In 1934 the powers and functions of the Federal Radio Commission were transferred to the seven man Federal Communications Commission, but the regulatory system of the 1927 Act was retained.

Congress had specified in the Acts of 1927 and 1934 that the Commission was not to act as a censor and was not to infringe freedom of speech. The drafters of this legislation may have legitimately hoped that this provision would eliminate the spectre of bureaucrats determining or influencing the content of radio communication. The stated purpose of the Act was "to make available so far as possible . . . a rapid, efficient nationwide and worldwide wire and radio communication service. . . ." It has been argued that the act relegated the Commission to the role of a "traffic officer policing the wave lengths to prevent stations from interfering with each other." And as late as 1940 the Supreme Court declared that the broadcasting field was open to anyone showing "competency, the adequacy of his equipment, and financial ability to make good use of assigned channels."

However, no matter how anxious the Commissioners might have been to obey these strictures against censorship, they were faced with a dilemma. In most cru-

cial cases they are confronted with several applicants for a given frequency range, each possessing the necessary technological and financial qualifications. They were forced to make choices on some other basis, and their only legislative guide was the empty "public interest, necessity, or convenience" standard. Inevitably the Commissioners turned to the only other really important criterion, and decisions were made, either directly or indirectly, on the basis of prospective program content (or past program content when passing on renewal applications). This was approved by the Supreme Court in 1943, when Justice Frankfurter correctly pointed out that the rationing function delegated by Congress necessarily involved passing on the *quality* of programming.[5]

THE COMMISSION IS not immune to the most spectacular method used from time immemorial by bureaucrats when called on to award exclusive rights, as was demonstrated by the Commissioner Mack bribery scandal. And it is notoriously guilty of the sin of arbitrariness, which we find associated with almost any allocation process where political replaces market allocation. According to Professor Louis Jaffe of the Harvard Law School, the Commission's announced criteria for awarding licenses were "spurious criteria used to justify results otherwise arrived at." They were "announced only to be ignored, ingeniously explained away, or so occasionally applied that their very application seems a mockery of justice."[6] The process of awarding

---

4 Both these corollaries are echoed today by Chairman Minow in his famous Wasteland Speech before the National Association of Broadcasters: "Your license lets you use the public's airwaves as Trustees for 180,000,000 Americans. The public is your beneficiary. If you want to stay on as Trustees, you must deliver a decent return to the public—not only to your stockholders." "For every hour that the people give you—you owe them something. I intend to see that your debt is paid with service." *Vital Speeches,* June 15, 1961, p. 533, 535.

5 "The Commission's licensing function cannot be discharged, therefore, merely by finding that there are no technological objections to the granting of a license. If the criterion of 'public interest' were limited to such matters, how could the Commission choose between two applicants for the same facilities, each of whom is financially and technically qualified to operate a station? Since the very inception of federal regulation of radio, comparative considerations as to services to be rendered have governed the application of the standard of 'public interest, necessity or convenience.' " National Broadcasting Co. v. U.S., 319 U.S. 190, 217 (1943).

6 "The Scandal in TV Licensing," *Harper's Magazine,* September, 1957, p. 79, 84.

licenses is characterized by inconsistency, uncertainty, fantastic delay, and favoritism, placing a serious barrier in the way of managers attempting to make rational business calculations. But these are problems which we can expect to crop up with any regulatory bureau. The FCC presents a special problem because its present procedure brings it into direct conflict with the constitutional guarantee of free speech and free press, and it is to this issue that I address the bulk of this article.

The original Act of 1927 prohibited programs containing "obscene, indecent, and profane" language as well as radio lotteries. Enforcement of these provisions has been relatively restrained, although the Commission has sometimes stretched the meaning of these terms. For instance station KVEP of Portland, Oregon, was dropped from the air and a character known as the "Oregon Wildcat" was criminally convicted for broadcasting profane statements, because of his use of the expressions "damn scoundrel," "by God," and "I'll put on the mantle of the Lord and call down the curse of God on you."[7] Such stringent censorship would probably be a violation of the First Amendment if applied to newspapers. The Commission also placed a ban on the popular giveaway shows of the 1940's, arguing that this constituted a lottery. This ban was struck down by the Supreme Court as not within the Commission's legislative mandate.

However the Commission has challenged freedom of speech more directly by determining what is proper or improper editorializing. In its earliest days the Commission closed down stations for personal vendettas and broadcasts which constituted a "disruptive influence." In the first case of this sort, the Federal Radio Commission in 1928 refused to renew the license of WCOT in Providence, Rhode Island, because the owner made "false and defamatory" statements about personal enemies. (This characterization was based on a Commission decision and not on a jury trial for defamation.)

An amazing case, more for the language of the decision than for the actual holding, was the refusal to renew the license of KTNT, Muscatine, Iowa, where the licensee had pushed his quack cancer cures and attacked the state medical association and other enemies:

[The medical association's] alleged sins may be at times of public importance, to be called to the attention of the public over the air in *the right minded way*. But this record discloses that Mr. Baker does not do so in any *high minded way*. It shows that he continually and erratically over the air rides a personal hobby [sic], his cancer cure ideas and his likes and dislikes of certain persons and things. Surely his infliction of all this on the listeners is not the proper use of a broadcasting license. Many of his utterances are vulgar, if not indeed indecent. Assuredly they are *not uplifting or entertaining*.

* * *

Though we may not censor [!] it is our duty to see that broadcasting licenses do not afford mere personal organs, and also see that a standard of refinement fitting our day and generation is maintained.[8] [italics added]

In 1932 the Commission refused to renew the license of KGEF, operated by the Trinity Methodist Church of Los Angeles, because its minister, Robert Shuler, had engaged in personal vendettas, made guardedly anti-Catholic and anti-Jewish statements and accused judges of personal immorality. The Commission was upheld by the Circuit Court:

If it be considered that one in possession of a permit to broadcast in interstate commerce may, without let or hindrance from any source, use these facilities reaching out as they do, from one corner of the country to the other, to obstruct the administration of justice, offend the religious susceptibilities of thousands, inspire political distrust and civic discord, or offend youth and innocence by the free use of words suggestive of sexual immorality, and be answerable for slander only at the instance of the one offended, then this great science, instead of a boon, will become a scourge, and the nation a theatre for the display of individual passions and the collision of personal interests.[9]

365

---

[7] Duncan v. U.S., 48 Fed 2nd 128, 132, 133 (1931).

[8] FCC Docket #967, June 5, 1931, quoted from Coase, *op. cit.*, p. 9.

[9] Trinity Methodist Church, South v. F.R.C., 62 Fed 2nd 850, 852 (1932).

The Commission and courts demonstrated at this early date that the federal government would supervise the content and standards of radio broadcasters to a degree that would have been immediately rejected as a violation of freedom of press if applied to newspapers. They were willing to pass on what was and was not "the high minded way" and "uplifting and entertaining." The statement that "we may not censor" was obvious double-talk; the Commission and courts spoke in the language of blatant censorship if the word is to have any meaning.

Cases such as the above, however, were rare; and the holdings themselves were not as extreme as the language used to rationalize them. The most spectacular infringement of free speech was the Mayflower Doctrine of 1940, which prohibited all editorializing by radio stations.

> A truly free radio cannot be used to advocate the cause of the licensee. It cannot be used to support the candidacies of his friends. It cannot be devoted to the support of principles he happens to regard most favorably. In brief, the broadcaster cannot be an advocate.[10]

Although this rule was almost unquestionably unconstitutional, it was obeyed without challenge for nine years. In 1949 the rule was implicitly repudiated by the Commission, and the "fairness doctrine" was substituted in its place. When a station allows a given controversial viewpoint to be presented, it must allow an opportunity for the contrary viewpoint to be presented:

> Only when the licensee's discretion in the choice of the particular programs to be broadcast over his facilities is exercised so as to afford a reasonable opportunity for the presentation of all *responsible* positions on matters of *sufficient importance* to be afforded radio time can radio be maintained as a medium of *freedom of speech for the people as a whole*.[11]
> [italics added]

---

[10] Mayflower Broadcasting Co., 8 F.C.C. 330, 340 (1940).

[11] Editorializing by Broadcast Licensees, 13 F.C.C. 1246, 1250 (1949). The fairness doctrine was devised by the FCC and should not be confused with the "equal time rule," which was written into the 1927 Act and requires stations to give equal time to all political candidates. This rule raises separate problems not dealt with here.

The Commission switched from a position of banning editorials on radio to actively encouraging them. At present an applicant for a license is expected to include time for discussion of public issues on his proposed schedule, and Chairman Minow has castigated broadcasters for neglecting this area. But two aspects of this doctrine need to be examined, for it is potentially more dangerous tnan the absolute ban of the Mayflower Doctrine. This issue is by no means academic, since more than 400 fairness complaints were received by the Commission in 1961, more than double the 1960 number.

First, the expression "freedom of speech" has undergone a transformation as complete as that of the word "liberal." The First Amendment proclaims that "Congress shall make no law abridging freedom of speech or of the press." Freedom of speech has been viewed quite naturally as a negative freedom—the right not to be restrained from expressing oneself. And the Constitution barred only the government from restraining individuals. But the Commission, while admitting that radio came under the First Amendment, proceeded to give the concept an opposite meaning:

> But this does not mean that the *freedom of the people as a whole* to enjoy the maximum possible utilization of this medium of mass communication may be subordinated to the freedom of any single person to exploit the medium for his own private interest. . . . The most significant meaning of freedom of the radio is the right of the American people to listen to this great medium of communcation free from any governmental dictation as to what they can or cannot hear and *free alike from similar restraints of private licensees.*
> [italics added]

Freedom of speech has become the "right" of "the people as a whole" to receive broadcasts free from "restraints" of those who make the broadcasts; the violators of this freedom are those who decide what they will broadcast according to their "own private interest," and the government is the interpreter and enforcer of this "freedom." This seems an unconscious parody of a recent explanation by Mikoyan as to why the

366

Russian press is free and the Western press is not.

A more concrete problem is raised by the assumption that there is an objective standard of fairness. Undoubtedly opinions which would fit into what we might irreverently dub the "Establishment Consensus" will be held entitled to a reply— attacks on the flag, the New Frontier, religion, racial equality, labor unions will almost certainly fall within the fairness doctrine. But what of the hard cases, the less "respectable" opinions, which always constitute the crucial arena when freedom of speech is involved. Would Ross Barnett be entitled to reply to an attack on his position? Harry Bridges? Jimmy Hoffa? The Commission inserted "weasel words" to provide a way out. Only "responsible positions" "on matters of sufficient importance" are entitled to replies. And the government must of course decide what is responsible and of sufficient importance. Hence the Commission must make crucial value judgments to apply its standard.

The record indicates that, in spite of self-righteous denials, the Commission has done just this. Labor unions and cooperatives have received Commission help when stations were charged with anti-labor or anti-cooperative bias,[12] as have various other groups representing what we view as responsible opinions. But an atheist named Robert Scott did not fare so well in an attempt to reply to direct attacks on the atheist position. An initial decision in 1946 denied Scott's request for revocation of the licenses of stations that refused to give him time, but the Commission indicated that atheistic views were controversial and might be entitled to a hearing.[13] This dictum provoked the expected furor on Capitol Hill, complete with a committee investigation. Here was one of those great issues of righteousness which so obsess the souls of Congressmen and allow them to sound off to the constituency without

antagonizing any sizeable group.[14] As a result the Commission backed off, and in a later challenge by Scott refused him even a hearing. More recently the NBC documentary, "Battle of Newburgh," which this writer and many conservative commentators felt was a grossly biased report of a domestic controversy, was given a clean bill of health by the Commission. In response to a fairness complaint by City Manager Mitchell, the Commissioners hailed it as a "conscientious and responsible effort to report a controversial issue."[15] While we may be as opinionated as the Commission here, the tragedy is that the Commissioners are able and willing to base their decisions on such opinion in a matter where reasonable men can obviously disagree.

It seems obvious that a "fairness doctrine" is not likely to be applied fairly, not only because there can be no objective criteria for applying it, but also because a politically sensitive agency will almost certainly be unwilling or unable to apply it symmetrically. (A symmetrical application would mean that if advocates of opinion B could be challenged by advocates of opinion A, then advocates of opinion B could challenge advocates of opinion A.) And in the hands of Commissioners who are not well intentioned, this would become a potent weapon for control of our nation's thought. The possibilities are indicated by recent urgings that the Commission should investigate southern stations that did not give a fair hearing to President Kennedy's position in the Mississippi integration crisis.

A related problem is raised by the "good character" requirement for licensees. An applicant is required by the Commission to show that he is "of good character and possesses other qualifications sufficient to provide a satisfactory public service." Under this regulation the Commission has denied licenses to appli-

367

---

[12] Smead, *Freedom of Speech by Radio and Television* (Washington, D.C.: Public Affairs Press, 1959), p. 50 *et. seq.,* and Wilcox, *op. cit.,* p. 713.

[13] In re Petition of Robert Scott (FCC release 96050) July 19, 1946, quoted in Smead, *ibid,* p. 61.

[14] Representative Charles J. Kersten demonstrated typical Congressional tolerance: "Atheists have no more standing to ask equal time with religious programs over the air than violators of the moral law would have the right to expound immoral ideas on an equal basis with time granted to those who defended the moral law." Quoted from Smead, *op. cit.,* p. 62.

[15] *New York Times,* August 12, 1962.

cants who make false statements on their application forms and who have been convicted of crimes.[16]

The Commission is on much weaker ground when it attempts to ascertain the character of applicants by examining their opinions and associations.[17] When the New York *Daily News* applied in 1942 for an FM station, the American Jewish Congress intervened, arguing that the newspaper's alleged editorial bias against Jews and Negroes had disqualified it as a radio operator. The Commission allowed this evidence to be admitted to help it determine "whether [the applicant] is likely to give a fair break to those who do not share [these beliefs]."[18] According to the Commission this evidence was relevant to the "character" of the applicant and was not used to determine his beliefs. (If the Commission were sincere and not really interested in specific beliefs, consistency would require it to admit evidence of an anti-racist bias as relevant to the question of the applicant's willingness to give racists a fair break. This hardly seems likely.) The evidence submitted was dismissed by the Commission as being unscientifically prepared and thus having no probative value. The license was denied, allegedly on other grounds, and it is impossible to determine what actual effect the evidence had.

In a later case a clergyman was denied a license because he was found to be "intemperate in his writings, sermons and broadcasts . . . an expert in vituperation and vilification." However the Commission recognizes some limits. When a rival applicant attacked the application of WHDH because Al Capp was a minority shareholder and his comic strip "Li'l Abner" had allegedly been condemned by a New York legislative committee, the Commission dismissed the argument, stating with a straight face that Capp was obviously not in control of WHDH.

Inevitably the alleged Communist or pro-Communist connections of applicants have become involved in license controversies. Applicants have been rejected for refusal to disclose whether they were members of the Communist party. The case of Edward Lamb, a founder of the far left National Lawyers' Guild, raised one of the greatest rows in Commission history. In 1954, when Lamb applied for license renewal for his station WICU, a pioneer television station, the Commission charged that he had lied during hearings for his license in 1948. He had not told of alleged Communist affiliations and associations and had not mentioned a pro-Russian book he had written in 1935 (the book would seem to have been a matter of public record). During lengthy and well-publicized hearings two Commission witnesses recanted and accused Commission representatives of urging them to lie under oath. (One of these witnesses, however, was later convicted of libeling a Commission staff member with these charges.) The hearing examiner found no evidence that Lamb had engaged in Communist activity, and the license was eventually renewed.

This is an incomplete catalog of some of the more dramatic absurdities of Commission activity up through the last two years. It should be noted that these cases were exceptions rather than the rule, and the language of the decisions and rulings was usually much worse than the actual holdings. The Commissioners usually exhibited a healthy desire not to force their tastes, prejudices and views on broadcasters and the public. Its most potent weapon of coercion, the threat not to renew a license, was used so sparingly that the Commission earned from certain leftist quarters the *ne plus ultra* of insulting epithets: *laissez-faire*. However, during this period a philosophy of special responsibilities on the part of broadcasters and of a duty to supervise and control on the part of the Commission had become

---

16 The Commission recently held up a renewal for a General Electric station because of the antitrust suit against G.E. *Wall Street Journal*, June 16, 1961. After heated hearings, J. S. Love was granted a license in Mississippi even though he openly ignored the state's prohibition law as a hotel keeper, a law which was such a dead letter that the state also taxed the sale of liquor. Brown, *infra*, n. 17, p. 647.

17 The cases mentioned here are discussed at greater length in an article by Prof. Ralph S. Brown, "Character and Candor Requirements for FCC Licensees," *Law and Contemporary Problems*, Autumn, 1957, p. 644 *et. seq.*

18 WBNX Broadcasting Co., 12 F.C.C. 805 (1948).

so well established that the stage was set for a Caesar who would not view his role with such self restraint.

THIS POTENTIALITY for abuse inherent in our public philosophy of radio and television regulation has unfortunately taken on a magnified importance since the arrival of the New Frontier and Newton Minow in Washington. Since his famous "Wasteland" speech in May of 1961, Minow has embarked upon the imposing task of forcing stations and networks to fulfill their alleged trust obligation to the American public. Broadcasters are constantly exhorted to act in the "public interest," which he treats as an entity as ascertainable as the specific gravity of lead. Much of his crusade thus far consists of verbiage which can be dismissed with a condescending smile usually reserved for overly enthusiastic cheerleaders: "Never have so few [the broadcasters] owed so much to so many [the public]." "Gentlemen, your trust accounting with your beneficiaries is overdue." And of course: "Ask not what broadcasting can do for you. Ask what you can do for broadcasting."[19]

But other remarks and actions cannot be dismissed so easily. He has coupled his warnings that programming standards must be improved with explicit threats not to renew licenses if this is not done. He assures us that no censorship is planned:

I am unalterably opposed to governmental censorship. There will be no suppression of programming which does not meet with bureaucratic tastes. Censorship strikes at the tap root of our free society.

It might seem that a decision as to what is or is not improved programming involves a value judgment on the part of the Commission, involves what we would call censorship and the application of bureaucratic tastes. But we misunderstand the meaning of censorship, and Minow sets us straight on this. The Commission does not censor, since the courts

have upheld its authority to concern itself with a licensee's programming. Rather it is the *broadcasters* who censor. This censorship takes two insidious forms, "rating censorship" and "dollar censorship." Rating censorship

. . . is a result of the almost desperate compulsion of some licensees to live by the numbers, always striving to reach the largest possible audience in order to attract and hold the mass advertising dollars.[20]

In other words censorship occurs when broadcasters give the listeners what they want! Dollar censorship occurs when a broadcaster lets his advertiser—the party footing the bill—determine what will be shown.

But even if we are overawed by Minow's rhetoric and concede that only broadcasters indulge in "censorship" under the New Frontier redefinition, certain dilemmas remain which cannot be avoided by facile cliches about "public interest" and "the people's airwaves."[21] Clearly the broadcasters and networks are not presenting the type of programs Minow and his cohorts expect (in this they are supported by the most vocal segments of national opinion), and he intends to bring about a change. His objection is not that the broadcasters are failing to give the public what it wants but precisely that they are giving the public what it wants but not what it "needs." "Some say the public interest is what interests the public. I disagree. . . . It is not enough to cater to the public whims —you must also serve the nation's needs." To implement this program there is no alternative to substitution of "bureaucratic tastes," so strongly eschewed by Minow, for the tastes of the marketplace as indicated by the ratings. This raises a more fundamental conflict for a free, pluralistic, and ostensibly consumer-

369

---

[19] The Wasteland Speech again. *Vital Speeches,* June 15, 1961, p. 533, 534, 537.

[20] *Wall Street Journal,* August 4, 1962.

[21] A typical example of Minow doubletalk: "[We do not] contemplate any invasion by the Commission of the programming function of the broadcasters. However, we are equally determined that every broadcaster to whom we issue a license shall make an honest, sincere effort to serve the public interest." *Wall Street Journal,* January 24, 1962.

oriented society than even control of editorials under the "fairness" doctrine. The logical extension of this elitist desire to use government to subordinate popular tastes in favor of more "edifying" ones can be seen in England, where the government's Pilkington Report advocates placing commercial television under government control (even though now it is run by government-appointed trustees) precisely because it is drawing viewers away from the more uplifting BBC programs and forcing the BBC to lower its standards to compete.[22]

I would not claim that the present mediocrity in television does not present a problem, and it is possible that Minow's non-coercive attempts at moral suasion may in some cases have a desirable effect. I will deal with this problem more thoroughly below. But first we need to examine some of his specific responses to the problem.

First, he holds that there is no problem of censorship or invasion of the broadcaster's programming function if the Commission cracks down on overall program balance rather than on individual programs. "I told the Senate committee that if someone puts on a lousy Western it's none of the Government's business—but if someone puts on nothing else for three weeks, then it is." (He will of course find no station which shows nothing but Westerns; he obviously refers to "too many Westerns"— in somebody's judgment.) Before his appointment the Commission had established a policy of viewing overall program balance as a major criterion for granting and renewing licenses,[23] al-

though few renewals were denied for not complying with promises. He has announced that he will vigorously enforce this policy, especially by denying renewals. Of course any judgment as to what constitutes a balanced schedule— or which of two competing schedules is more balanced—must involve some standard of taste or value just as much as passing on the worth of an individual program.

Second, Minow continually refers to another pseudo-objective standard which he would have us believe would not involve bureaucratic value judgments. Broadcasters must meet "local needs," and these needs are to be ascertained by calling in local groups before Commission hearings.

> Renewal hearings should be held in the local community. Let anybody come and say what kind of programs the local stations have been showing. League of Women Voters, P.T.A., Church groups, everybody. I think that pretty quickly you'd have better television programming. I don't think people realize they own the air, and the broadcaster is using it with their permission.[24]

Recently a license was denied Suburban Broadcasters in Elizabeth, New Jersey, specifically because the applicant "made no attempt to determine the program needs of Elizabeth."

While this policy might appear to some to express an admirable "democratic" sentiment, he never specifies precisely what is meant by local needs. But we can get a good idea of the emphasis it is likely to take by looking at the recent Commission hearings in Chicago which were held to determine such local needs. The Radio and TV director of the Catholic Archdiocese complained that the shows *given free of charge* to the

---

[22] *New York Times,* June 28, 1962. Fortunately several Tory government spokesmen have indicated their disapproval of the report.

[23] In a pre-Minow statement, "Network Programming Inquiry Report and Statement of Policy," 25 Federal Regulations 7291 (1961), the Commission, Commissioner Hyde dissenting, laid down the following categories as essential to a balanced schedule: (1) Opportunity for local self expression, (2) Development and use of local talents, (3) Programs for children, (4) *Religious programs* (possible constitutional question?), (5) Educational programs, (6) Public affairs programs, (7) *Editorialization by licensees* (remember the fairness rule), (8) Political broadcasts, (9) Agricultural programs, (10) News programs, (11) Weather and

market reports, (12) Sports programs, (13) Service to minority groups, (14) Entertainment programming. (p. 7295) There is a strong indication that all these must be included in a successful application prospectus; cf. *Nebraska Law Review,* June, 1962, p. 826. And failure to carry out the program set forth in the prospectus is sufficient grounds for refusal to renew a license.

[24] "The Big Squeeze," *Saturday Evening Post,* November 11, 1961, p. 62.

Archdiocese were produced in "the smallest and most inadequate studio in Chicago" and charged the stations with a "lack of concern" for religious programming. The head of the Broadcasting Commission of the Chicago Board of Rabbis complained that religious programs are scheduled for Sunday morning, when TV sets are allegedly not in use. The publisher of the Chicago *Daily Defender* complained that "generally the Negro as a normal human being doesn't exist in the programming eye of the local TV stations." He reported that there had been some improvement, but the stations still "haven't come around to our satisfaction." The President of the Joint Civic Committee of Italian-Americans found a number of programs, such as "The Untouchables," portraying "persons of Italian extraction as gangsters." And the Chairman of the Japanese-American Citizens League complained of anti-Japanese World War II movies on late shows.[25]

One important reason for television's mediocrity has been the fear of offending minority and special interest groups. Making a politically sensitive government bureau a champion of "local interests" certainly would not work in the other direction. The "public" which makes itself heard at government hearings is invariably composed of the best organized interest groups. This is a variety of democracy that is all too prevalent today.

Third, Minow sees TV's programming "wasteland" as largely due to sordid attempts by advertisers and broadcasters to maximize profits. He notes with indignation that far too many broadcasters operate "not in the public interest but rather to get the greatest financial return possible out of their investment." He somehow hopes to improve radio and

---

[25] *Wall Street Journal*, March 20, 1962, and March 22, 1962. Minow places great store by such complaints: "We received substantial complaints from the three major religious faiths and other citizens requesting a chance to comment on local service [in Chicago]. I say to you frankly and positively; we will not ignore such complaints and neither should you." *New York Times*, April 4, 1962.

television fare with various restrictions on advertisers which will inevitably make sponsorship less attractive to them, including proposals to prevent any control by advertisers of the programs they sponsor and to place severe limits on the length and content of commercials. While a more "uplifting" television program is not necessarily a more costly one, a policy which is designed to make sponsorship less attractive to advertisers would seem to be the worst way to entice them into improving their programs. A more plausible effect would be to cause advertisers to shift their advertising dollars out of radio and television and into media where the return is higher. His policy becomes all the more incomprehensible when we consider that he wishes to apply the more stringent advertising controls to radio, where he asserts that earnings are "too low," and where he is looking for methods of raising earnings. Following the regulatory tradition of the CAB and ICC, he has suggested that radio is "too competitive," and that earnings might be increased by making it less competitive—i.e., by encouraging concentration.

Thus far Minow has met with opposition to his policies on the Commission itself; he has seldom been able to obtain a majority to support his promises to use revocation and refusals to renew licenses to enforce his ideas of proper programming. Commissioners Rosel Hyde and John Cross have publicly criticized his regulation mania, and Hyde has warned that, "The unattractive office of censor can be made to appear as guardian of integrity." But in December of 1962 President Kennedy, an avid supporter of Minow's policies, appointed Kenneth Cox, a Minow partisan, to replace the retiring Cross. And in 1965, assuming the New Frontier goes rolling on, we can count on an absolute majority of Minow men.

Thus the near future may bring the full fruits of our nation's acquiescence in broadcasting control. The likelihood that many renewal applications will be denied takes on special significance. As was mentioned earlier, during its entire

371

history the Commission had acted with restraint in this matter. But in 1961, the first year of the Minow dispensation, 588 applications for renewal were deferred for investigation, many times more than the total for any previous year. And the Commission's refusal to renew the license of WDKD in Kingstree, South Carolina, for "coarse, vulgar, suggestive, indecent, double meaning statements" of a disc jockey as well as for alleged "overcommercialization," has been interpreted as marking a reversal of previous leniency on renewals.[26]

The Commission's past restraint in the matter of renewals has been a most effective check on bureaucratic control of our radio and television fare. The administrative bureau offers a tremendous opportunity for coercion to satisfy the whims and prejudices of the bureaucrats in control, since a bogus basis can be found for almost any decision (and decisions are essentially non-reviewable on the facts by higher courts). But the greatest danger will not be in the actual use of this power, but rather in the fear that it might be used. When we consider Professor Jaffe's observation that announced criteria are largely ignored by the Commission and that the licensing process is characterized by marked arbitrariness and uncertainty, we can be certain that similar uncertainty about the likelihood of obtaining a renewal every three years could wreak havoc with attempts by managers to make rational business calculations about the future.

And what of the effects on freedom of expression? Witness the Mayflower Decision, which, though obviously unconstitutional, was obeyed for nine years without challenge. If significant numbers of licenses are revoked or not renewed, no one can be certain of the real reasons. Even if objective and high sounding criteria are offered, who will risk offending the New Frontier editorially before re-

newal time? Who will risk defying the opinions and prejudices which Commissioners express off the record? Broadcasters devote exhaustive effort to determining "public whims;" it would seem even more urgent to them to guess at and satisfy the whims of the Commissioners, who hold the power of life or death over their business every three years.

WITH THESE DISTURBING problems raised by government regulation, why do we single out radio and television for a comprehensive and in some ways unique form of regulation, one that we would not allow for a moment with newspapers or public speeches? There is of course the fear of monopoly concentration because of scarcity of airspace and consequent difficulty of entry into the industry. Such a danger might well exist; but we have an elaborate structure of antitrust laws, and these have been frequently applied to the broadcasting field. From a strictly economic perspective imperfect competition in radio and television presents the same problems which in other industries we have been content to leave to the antitrust laws.

But there are other more important difficulties which allegedly distinguish radio and television from newspapers and movies. Radio and especially television are more accessible to children than printed matter; hence it is argued that immorality, violence, and other subject matter which might have a bad effect on children should be more strictly controlled. This argument is in the writer's opinion the only one which might support greater program control of airwaves than of newspapers. The difference, however, is one of degree and not of kind; objectionable printed matter, as well as television pictures, can find its way into the home. And in a free society the duty of censorship of material likely to influence children should rest primarily with the parent.

It is also persuasively argued that anyone can start a newspaper, but only a limited and privileged number can oper-

---

[26] "An End to Laissez Faire?" *Saturday Review*, March 24, 1962, p. 35, and *New York Times*, July 26, 1962. The hearing examiner in the case stated that a Commission decision to uphold him would "help signalize abandonment by the Commission of a laissez faire policy of regulation in the field of programming."

ate a television station. Hence, aside from the danger of monopoly profits, this most important channel for the dissemination of ideas is not really open to the "marketplace of ideas," as is the newspaper business. Any point of view can allegedly find expression in the newspaper world, but radio and especially television are controlled by those who were fortunate enough to get a special privilege. This argument has only a grain of truth. In the first place radio and television stations must compete with newspapers in the marketplace as well as with other stations, and there is no persuasive evidence that stations have generally been more effective proponents than newspapers. Even more important, our fifty largest cities have an average of from three to four television stations but only two newspapers.[27] Just as there are technological limitations on the number of radio and television stations in a geographic area, a community will only be capable of supporting financially a small number of newspapers. A few persons will control each medium in any community. The argument is valid only insofar as anyone with sufficient capital can attempt to found a newspaper but cannot found a broadcasting station without a government grant.

Two factors do seem to differentiate broadcasting from other communications media and need to be dealt with at greater length. In both cases I suggest that we should consider possible market solutions utilizing the price mechanism.

The first problem (which I must deal with in a somewhat oversimplified fashion) arises from the fact that broadcasting is financed by advertising rather than by direct payments from its audience. Consequently, voting by viewers cannot be "weighted" as it is in other areas. By this I mean that, if a given minority wants a better magazine or a better car enough to pay more for it, it will be produced if the higher price they are willing to pay will make production profitable. But there is no analogous way for television viewers to weight their vote. Though John Doe might be willing to pay $5.00 to see one show and little or nothing to see another show that he watches, this cannot be recorded by the market. Consequently, it can be said with only minor qualifications that the sponsor is interested only in paying for a show that, for a given cost, will reach the largest possible audience.[28] Hence our radio and television fare tends to be pitched to the lowest common denominator, and minority tastes will often be unsatisfied.

This has been a major reason for Minow's acclaim among vocal segments of American opinion for his demands that our television wasteland be renovated. One can debate whether it is necessarily undesirable to have a low-brow communications medium. But if we fell that at least a portion of our television fare should be devoted to what we consider higher quality material, pay television offers one solution to this problem. A minority, no matter how small, could make it advantageous to produce a given type of show merely by being willing to pay enough to make it profitable. The Commission has moved hesitatingly in the right direction by allowing tests of pay television in Hartford and Denver, after much delay due largely to Congressional pressure. The amazing aspect is that this can be done only under close Commission supervision and that the Commission's *power to grant permission* could be seriously challenged in the courts by associations of theatre owners and broadcasters with the argument that they would be deprived of business. Another possibility is the increased use of closed circuit pay television, which is not under FCC jurisdiction and does not

373

[27] *Nebraska Law Review*, June, 1962, p. 824.

[28] Even when attempting to attract the largest audience, an advertiser will often cater to minority tastes: an historical documentary might receive a higher numerical rating than a western because there are so many westerns competing for those who prefer westerns to historical documentaries. And an advertiser may prefer a select audience even if smaller; farm appliance dealers would cater to farmers and soap manufacturers to housewives. In a few cases advertisers are concerned with the "stamp of quality" for their product which they hope will be derived from a high quality show. The "Hallmark Hall of Fame" is a good example.

interfere with open circuit stations on the same frequencies, although there are serious technological problems in establishing a profitable system of this sort.

Pay television raises certain problems that space does not permit me to deal with here. But if we feel that television standards must be improved, the alternative to pay TV seems to be a bureaucratic determination as to what is necessary to elevate and educate the American citizenry.

The second and more crucial problem was alluded to above: how can available frequencies be allocated so as to avoid the pitfalls outlined above? A startling but plausible suggestion (and one that I have not too subtly hinted at throughout the article) is that we view the available frequencies as another scarce resource and examine alternative methods by which the impersonal market might ration this resource.

The homesteading principle was one method of allocating land, and this principle was actually applied by some courts to radio before the Act of 1927.[29] In these cases the station first to put equipment into use which used certain frequencies received a property right in these frequencies, that is, a right to use these frequencies without interference from other operators. The courts used the analogy of the homesteader who obtained ownership of the land that he put to use first. Many problems, such as the limits of the geographic area covered by this property right and the control of interference, would be left to the courts to decide. But the courts have successfully faced analogous problems in property law before and they were developing such a body of law when Congress intervened in 1927.

Professor R. H. Coase of the University of Virginia presents a more radical but probably more acceptable plan: *he suggests that property rights in available frequencies be auctioned by the govern-*

ment to the highest bidder.[30] He presents a lengthy and convincing case for a market allocation of available frequencies, and I can only give a brief outline of his position here. The successful bidder would be free to sell, lease, or otherwise contract for the use of these frequencies and would be entitled to government protection against interference in his allocated frequency range, just as a property owner is entitled to government protection against interference with the use of his property.

By this device the price system rather than the bureaucratic process would allocate the airwaves just as it allocates other fixed factors of production such as land and labor: available airspace would go to those who would use it most profitably. And the argument for allocation of land, labor, and minerals, to those who could use them most profitably would apply here. To state it a bit crudely, the most profitable use is the one, among all competing uses, which is valued most highly by consumers.[31]

Broadcasting would consequently be placed on a basis similar to newspapers. Both would purchase all their factors of production on the market, and each community would support only a few of each, selection being made by the largely impersonal market mechanism. The strongest arguments for the "trustee" role of broadcasters would disappear. Not only would the people no longer "own" the airwaves, but the licensee would no longer receive from the state a free grant, often worth large sums of money, from which special duties to the public could be reasonably inferred. Elimination of huge windfalls which accrue to successful licensees would be one advantage to this plan. At present stations sell for as much as $20 million, and a sizeable portion of this is for the mere license.

This plan has been naively dismissed by some on the grounds that it would

[29] Cf. Tribune Co. v. Oak Leaves Broadcasting Station (Cir. Ct., Cook County, Ill., 1926), cited in Coase, *op. cit.*, p. 31. The operator of a station was held to have established a sufficient property right, acquired by priority, to bar a later established station from causing any interference.

[30] *Op. cit.*, n. 2.

[31] In the case of non-pay TV and radio, the direct consumers are advertisers rather than the audience, and the problems brought about by the inability of listeners to weight their votes would still exist if airspace was auctioned.

award stations to those with the most money. Actually, the price mechanism allocates resources to those who can put them to the most profitable use; and, assuming a fluid capital market, this will only coincidentally be the party possessing the most money. On the other hand, the Commission has in fact tended to favor large, financially prosperous and experienced firms; it is certainly not implausible that newer and smaller firms would obtain more stations under an auctioning system.

In addition to eliminating the need for regulation of program content with its dangers for freedom of speech and press, use of the market mechanism would eliminate other problems inherent in centralized decision-making. Program broadcasting occupies a relatively small portion of available frequencies, the rest being allocated to various private users—oil companies, taxis, telephone companies, etc.—and to governmental users—military, forest services, etc. The Commission, which is overworked and operating on a tiny budget, has been forced to arbitrarily assign ranges of frequencies to various categories of use. Consequently the Commission often rations available broadcasting frequencies among eager applicants while equally serviceable frequencies go unused. An auctioning system would ration out all available frequencies among all possible uses according to the relative monetary returns to various uses, as reflected in the bids.

These seem like strange and radical proposals largely because we have grown to look at broadcasting in a way which is not warranted by the facts. As Professor Coase states it: "It is difficult to avoid the conclusion that the widespread opposition to the use of the pricing system for the allocation of frequencies can be explained only by the fact that the possibility of using it has never been seriously faced."

There would of course be serious problems in implementing such a system to-day; since expectations have been built around the present system, it would be more difficult to convert to a pricing system today than to implement it in the 1920's. Alternative measures might be explored which would invoke some of the benefits of the market and reduce the role of government. If sale of frequencies for all time to the highest bidder were unacceptable, the government might lease the frequencies to the highest bidder for a period of years, with the lessee having the right to freely sublease or otherwise use the frequencies as he saw fit. If we feel that it would be unfair to require existing stations, who have invested large amounts in the expectation of continued free use of their frequencies, to either bid high or lose their frequencies, we might restrict bidding to presently unused frequencies. The price mechanism would prevail to a large extent even under the present system if licensees were free to sell or otherwise dispose of their frequencies to anyone without Commission approval and if renewals were made automatic.[32]

The suggestions advanced above are offered with some trepidation; there are many difficulties which space does not permit me to deal with here. But we should at least explore them more thoroughly, for the alternative is abdication to the present system, which not only has operated unsatisfactorily in the past but is showing portents for the future that a free society cannot accept.

---

[32] Full utilization of ultra high frequencies, which can be expected in the future, will more than double the number of television stations and will consequently lessen the need for rigorous rationing. It is possible that there will be airspace available in many areas for more stations than the area will support economically. At present UHF is not fully utilized, largely because most television sets are not equipped to receive it (although in other ways UHF is inferior to VHF). FM broadcasting was slow in becoming established for the same reason, and market pressures will undoubtedly increase the use of UHF just as it did FM. This process will be accelerated by the recent law which requires television manufacturers to adapt all sets to UHF.

375

Czecho-Slovakia and the USSR

IT IS CUSTOMARY in the Free World to consider the so-called satellite countries as having more or less identical standing within the Warsaw Pact system. This is a fallacy. In fact, there are basic differences from Moscow's point of view.

The history of the last fourteen years proves that Eastern Europe is not the monolithic bloc that Khrushchev pretends it is. In two states, the population has shown, not only its overwhelming hostility against Communism and foreign rule, but also its readiness to make the supreme sacrifice in a desperate attempt to overthrow the tyranny. In Hungary, at least nine-tenths of the nation rose against colonial oppression in October, 1956. Khrushchev needed 21 armored divisions and protracted heavy artillery fire on the centers of resistance, especially Budapest, to impose the puppet regime of Janos Kadar on the vanquished country. The strength of continued opposition despite military defeat is shown by Kadar's repeated purges and obvious efforts to placate the nation.

In the Soviet-occupied zone of Germany, the so-called "German Democratic Republic," the oppressed population and especially the factory-workers of East Berlin and of the industrial areas of Halle and Leipzig, rose on June 17, 1953, and

for several days fought valiantly against dictator Ulbricht's police. Here, too, the Russian army had to step in, in order to keep the Communists in power.

In Poland we have had strikes and other acts of resistance in 1956, even before the Hungarian uprising. After Budapest fell to the Russians, the situation remained extremely critical for two months. Finally, a *de facto* compromise was reached: the Polish people represented primarily by the Catholic bishops, led by Archbishop Cardinal Wyszinsky, renounced — in the light of what had happened in Hungary — the use of violence, in exchange for an easing of the Soviet pressure and the elimination of the so-called Natolin-Stalinist group. The Soviets, on the other hand, recognized that a war in Poland would entail more dangers for them than the one in Hungary, since Poland has a mighty army and direct access to the sea, where it could receive arms and equipment from the West via the ports of Stettin and Danzig. Poland has thus obtained up to this day a special position in the Eastern Bloc. True, Gomulka is not a democrat, as certain Western observers would like to believe. Still, there are areas of freedom in Poland which Moscow tacitly accepts in both cultural and economic life, especially agriculture.

Compared to these developments, it is surprising that since 1948 only Czecho-Slovakia among the central European satellites has accepted without serious resistance both Soviet hegemony and the integrally Communist policies of its gov-

---

Otto von Habsburg is the present head of the House of Habsburg. He is a member of the Mt. Pelerin Society and a keen student of current international affairs, and has contributed numerous articles on historical and political topics to scholarly journals.

ernments. In all that period only the liquidation of the Slansky group might be regarded as an attempt at liberalization, since the eleven Communist leaders hanged had been the most important liaison men between the Czech government and the Soviet Union. Even after the 20th Party Congress all remained quiet in this model Communist Republic. Never did Stalin or Khrushchev feel the need to intervene in Prague.

Slovakia is the only area in Czecho-Slovakia where major security measures have been called for. This shows an essential difference within the nation, which has deep historic roots.

The overwhelming majority in Slovakia has always opposed the fiction of the Czecho-Slovak nation. During the First World War, the leader of the Czech emigration and later head of the Czecho-Slovak Provisional Government, Thomas G. Masaryk, pledged to the American Slovaks in the Treaty of Pittsburgh that, in exchange for their political support, full autonomy would be given to their country, including an independent Parliament and administration. This agreement was never honored by the Czechs, despite strong Slovak protests. Masaryk later stated that he had only meant to make a non-committal declaration. To prove that this was not true, a delegation of American Slovaks brought the original document from Pittsburgh to Europe in 1938. The Slovaks, led by Mr. Hletko, entered their country through Poland and, at great popular gatherings, exhibited the signature of Masaryk. The energetic demands of the Slovaks for the fulfillment of the treaty contributed decisively to the collapse of President Benes' regime in the summer of 1938.

The Slovaks considered themselves a separate nationality not "Czecho-Slovaks." The same can be said of the Czechs, who never call themselves "Czecho-Slovaks." The Slovak, Hodza, who was Prime Minister at the hour of the great crisis in 1938, went one step further and spoke of "Czechs, Moravians and Slovaks," thus showing that he considered even the Slavs of Moravia as a nation. There is a Slovak language. Even the casual traveler will see it

while reading public inscriptions. In the trains, compartments where smoking is forbidden are marked in Czech territories *Nekuraci,* while in Slovakia it is *Nefajfarov.* The difference between Czech and Slovak is approximately the same as between Slovene and Croat, Danish and Norwegian, or Dutch and German. Furthermore, the predominantly rural population of Slovakia is deeply religious and consequently resented the laicistic cultural policy pursued by the Czechs from 1918-1919 on.

The Slovak question turned out to be the fatal handicap of the Second Czecho-Slovak Republic from October, 1938, to March, 1939. The hyphen between the two parts of the State's name was obtained by the Slovaks immediately after the Munich agreement. They also received a far-reaching autonomy with independent Diet and ministries. But new conflicts soon arose. When the central authority violated the constitution by removing the autonomous Slovak government, German diplomacy had no great trouble encouraging the Slovaks in their demand for a complete break with Prague. On March 13, 1939, the independent Slovak Republic was proclaimed in Bratislava. This was the cause of President Hacha's ill-fated trip to Berlin.

The Slovaks, in whose make-up we find many Magyar and Polish elements, are much more temperamental than the Czechs. During the Second World War they rose in the autumn of 1944 against the Nazi occupier, while the Czech territories, the Protectorate, remained cooperative and quiet. The so-called Prague uprising of May 5, 1945, took place only because a false rumor had spread that American combat units had already entered the town. On the morning of May 9, the Red Army entered Prague and thus secured the victory of the Communists.

In Slovakia, resistance against Communism was much stronger than in the Czech areas despite the fact that the Communists at first recognized Slovak autonomy and abandoned the fiction of "Czechoslovak" by including the hyphenated version of the word in the constitution. It is practically unknown in the

Free World that in the 1946 elections, the last which were relatively free, only the Slovaks gave a clear and sizeable majority against the Communists; this was not the case for the historically Czech provinces of Bohemia, Moravia and Silesia. In May, 1946, 61.4% of the Slovak voters supported the strongly anti-Communist Slovak Democratic Party. While Communist votes amounted to 38% in the whole nation, Communist returns in the Czech territories exceeded 40%. The Socialist Party, led by Zedenek Fierlinger, closely allied with the Communists, received 12.8% of the total, almost exclusively from Czech areas. Thus the Communists and their satellites had, from 1946 on, a 50.8% majority in the State. Without the massive anti-Communist votes of the Slovaks this majority would have been much greater.

Had the Czechs voted in 1946 as did the Slovaks it might have been possible to form in Prague a government without Communists, or at least a cabinet in which the Communists would not have held the top positions such as the Presidency of the Council, the Ministry of Interior (with its control over the police), or the Ministries of Propaganda, Agriculture, Education and Culture. An "Austrian solution" would have been possible.

A realistic appraisal leads thus to the conclusion that, contrary to the Poles, the Hungarians and the East Germans, a majority of the Czechs gave in to the left wing totalitarians and dragged the unwilling Slovaks along with them into the catastrophe. Only 15.8% of the Czech voters gave their ballots in May, 1946, to the only party which presented a true alternative to the Communists, namely the Christian Lidova Strana, whose press had the courage in the years 1945-46 to expose the crimes of the Communists and to warn of their gradual take-over of the State. Especially the columnist Helena Kozeluhova, who later was able to escape to the West, spoke out with great courage and raised the hopes that her party might become a strong rallying point.

The Social Democrats were, as we mentioned, satellites of the Communists. It

is true that in the year 1947, when the Social Democratic youth became restless, Fierlinger was removed as head of the party and replaced by Bohumil Lausman. Nevertheless, in 1948 Lausman was the first to recognize the new order demanded by the Communists and sanctioned by President Benes. Later on Lausman escaped to the West but very soon returned to Czecho-Slovakia and made his peace with the Gottwald-Fierlinger regime. There are good reasons to believe that he did not come to the West as a bona fide emigrant but as an agent sent to carry out propaganda actions in favor of the Communists.

Concerning the present-day situation in the country, one has to be most skeptical regarding alleged secret information coming f r o m emigre political groups. There is no tangible evidence of an effective underground movement. Escapees and prisoners who were used as forced labor in the coal pits, stone quarries and uranium mines, and thus had the opportunity to speak with Czech co-workers or prisoners, report unanimously that there unquestionably is dissatisfaction in the country, but that real resistance can only be found in Slovakia.

This surprising attitude of the Czechs has its roots in three reasons which the West scarcely knows:

(1) the expulsion of the German population from the Czecho-Slovak Republic prepared systematically by Dr. Benes since 1939;

(2) Benes' consistent policy of close alignment of his country with the Soviet Union; and

(3) the bloody so-called revolution organized by Dr. Benes after the liberation which did more than anything else to deliver the nation to the Communists.

The Germans were already in the First Czecho-Slovak Republic, from 1918 to 1938, a bulwark against Communism. Thus in the parliamentary elections of 1925, 42 of 182 Czecho-Slovakian seats went to Communists; of the 66 German seats only 6 were held by followers of Moscow. When the Social Democratic Party split in 1920 the majority of Czech Social Democrats joined the Communists, while only one-fifth of the Germans did the same thing. Thus the expulsion of the Germans was bound to be beneficial to the Communists. To this must be added the fact that the Communists very ably used the expropriation of the Sudeten Germans to strengthen their position in the nation's economy by gaining the lion's share of the spoils. On July 25, 1947, Godfrey Lias, one of President Benes' most active apologists, wrote in the London *Times*: "Through their control of the Ministry of Interior and Agriculture the Communists were able to create in the frontier regions a party-state within the state." This was the first time that in the pages of the *Times,* which to that moment had fully supported the Benes regime, the Communist danger in Czecho-Slovakia was being mentioned. The *Times'* readers suddenly learned that through the banning of the Agrarian Party, many farmers had been pushed into the arms of the Communist Party: "Probably the strongest group of Communist supporters among the peasants were those who had received German land in the frontier regions."

Farmers enriched by the expropriation of Germans were not the only followers which the Communists were able to gain with the help of Dr. Benes. The decisive role in the battle between the Communist and the non-Communist parties — in 1946 the Christian People's Party, the Slovak Democratic Party and, to a lesser degree, the Czech National Socialist Party — was played by the decree which gave complete amnesty for all acts of violence carried out during the so-called revolution. The presidential decrees were issued in violation of the constitution. Benes had resigned from the Presidency in October, 1938, not because of strong foreign pressure, but because he was compelled to give in to adverse public opinion. He had sent his congratulations to the newly elected President Hacha from America. At first the Allies had refused to recognize the government which he formed in 1940 in London. The only genuine supporter he had was Anthony Eden. Thus in order to bolster his power and to destroy his opposition, Benes made a complete alliance with the Soviet Union. He rode into Czecho-Slo-

vakia on the coat-tails of the Red Army coming from the East; he thus passed through the Podkarpatska Rus which, in a secret treaty, he had already offered to the Soviets in exchange for financial and diplomatic aid. This completely illegal decision was to give Russia the essential military bridgehead on the southern slopes of the Carpathian mountains. In April, 1945, Benes formed a government in Kosice in which the Communists already held the decisive positions. His "program of Kosice" was inspired by the Communists. In order to prevent the expression of public opinion, the President decided to rule by decree in a period of transition, although it would have been easy to elect a Constituent Assembly immediately following liberation, as Austria did in November, 1945. Benes thus established a personal dictatorship. He permitted elections only in May, 1946, when he and the Communists had successfully weakened the social fabric of his nation and changed the legal order.

On May 16, 1945, Benes had entered Prague. In his first speech he declared that "the country must be completely purged of Germans." On May 25 the Communist Minister of Propaganda stated that the Army was in readiness "to clean out the border areas of Germans and Hungarians and to give back all these old Slav territories to the Czechs." These German "colonists" had settled in the area in the 12th and 13th century. The Germans had developed these virgin lands at the invitation of the Bohemian dukes and kings, 400 years before the Pilgrim Fathers landed in America.

On June 19, 1945, Benes issued a decree which ordered the confiscation and division of all land owned by Germans and Magyars, as well as by all "enemies and traitors" to the Czech and Slovak people. The confiscation extended not only to land, houses, factories and machinery, but also to all the private property of German-speaking citizens, such as clothes, furniture and household goods. During the deportation (*Odsun*) every German-speaking citizen was only permitted to take with him 70 kilograms, including no valuables. In most instances the Germans had already been robbed

379

in the concentration camps to the point that they had nothing but the clothes they were wearing.

IN THE MONTHS following May, 1945, Czecho-Slovakia was the scene of innumerable crimes. According to the official statistics of the German Federal Republic,[1] 225,000 of 3,000,000 Sudeten Germans were killed — every 13th German-speaking citizen of Czecho-Slovakia was slaughtered during the orgy of terrorism. The first official Czecho-Slovak statistic[2] stated that the number of Czechs killed during the Nazi regime amounted to 60,000 — that is, one Czech out of 150. Later, the Prague Communists increased this number to 335,000, an obviously fantastic exaggeration. But even if it were true, the losses of the Czechs and the Slovaks would be much smaller than those of the Germans: one dead out of 27 inhabitants.

With indignation, a true Czech resistance fighter wrote in the Socialist weekly *Cil*:[3] "We witnessed how human rats who had shown nothing but cowardice sallied from their holes against the vanquished enemy in order to avenge themselves in shameful manner for their own dishonor. We also saw uniformed and non-uniformed mobs who had insolently put on the Red armband of the revolutionary guards, attack dwelling places and plunder them. . . . This wave of crimes finally influenced even some among the true freedom fighters. It was the tragic consequence of the general demoralization brought by these hyenas."

This state of affairs laid the ground for what happened in the 1946 and 1948 elections. Dr. Benes personally was largely responsible for the disregard of human rights in his country. On May 8, 1946, he proclaimed spontaneously the so-called amnesty-law, whose first paragraph stated: "Any action carried out in the period between Sept. 3, 1938, and Oct. 28, 1945, with the intention to help the fight for the reestablishment of Czech

and Slovak freedom or which was a just vengeance for the crimes of the occupants and their associates is not illegal even if it is punishable by law." Of course this paragraph in fact exclusively covers what happened between May 8 and Oct. 28, 1945. In most cases, as the long period of 5½ months after Germany's surrender shows, acts covered by the amnesty were not emotional vengeance, as might have occurred in the first days of the liberation; indeed the great majority of these were crimes organized in cold blood.

In Prague alone, according to Czech newspapers published in June, 1945, there were 27,000 "suicides" of Germans within the three weeks following May 8. On that day there lived roughly 60,000 Germans in Prague, to which must be added a large number of wounded soldiers in hospitals who were killed almost without exception. In other words, according to the Czech press itself, we are asked to believe that almost 50% of all Germans committed suicide. It is quite obvious that, in reality, the word is simply a euphemism for murder and execution. No nation can stand such a wholesale outbreak of bloodlust without deep-seated moral and psychological consequences. This may well be an important cause of the Czech flight into Communism, which alone would give them protection from their bad conscience and a possible future vengeance. One must add that literally hundreds of thousands of Czechs were also imprisoned, robbed and even killed for alleged collaboration. There is good reason to believe that in the statistic of Czech victims of the war published by the Communists, these dead were also included and simply put to the German account.

Dr. Benes' Secretary, Edvard Toborsky, admitted that his chief had already thought of the expulsion of the Germans in 1939,[4] that is to say, at a time when there was as yet no cause for such cruel vengeance. In 1943 the Czech President-in-exile received Moscow's consent for his plan. In exchange he offered to the Russians the transformation of his state into a Communist province. In the so-

[1] *Vertreibungsverluste* (Wiesbaden, 1958), p. 325 ff.; p. 355.
[2] *Encyclopedia Americana*, vol. VIII, p. 383.
[3] No. 19 (May, 1947), p. 23.

[4] *Pravda Zvitezila* (Prague, 1947), p. 207.

called "Narodni Fronta" which ruled the country after the manifesto of Kosice of April, 1945, and which gave Benes his dictatorial powers, only those parties were represented which in the emigration had supported Benes' close alliance with Moscow: Communists, Social Democrats, National Socialists and Populists. On the other hand, the Republican Party (or Agrarians)—which had between 1925 and 1939 the strongest party in the Czech parliament and which from 1920 to 1939 had given the country all its Prime Ministers, a party which had produced first rate personalities l i k e Antonin Svehla and Milan Hodza — was banned by presidential order. A similar fate befell the National Democratic Party, which was headed until 1937 by the great Czech patriot Karel Kramar, who had been condemned to death during the First World War, been released by Emperor Charles and had become Czecho-Slovakia's first Prime Minister. If, in the case of the Agrarians, one could argue that one of their members had been for a time Prime Minister in the Hitlerite Protectorate, not a single act of collaboration could be charged against the strongly nationalistic National Democrats. Their only crime was that they had opposed Benes' policy of alignment with the Soviet Union.

IT WAS OBVIOUS that these measures were aimed at the extermination of those national Czech forces which had prevailed during the critical days of May, 1945, and had tried to establish ties with the West. Thus the path was open for the Communists. Gen. Ingr, who had been Minister of War in Benes' London exile government and had escaped to England after the events of February, 1948, declared immediately upon his arrival, in an interview with the London *Catholic Herald,* that the Army, which was in majority anti-Communist, was completely ready to prevent the Communist take-over and to guarantee a liberal order. But, as in 1938, Benes had been too cowardly to give the order. He had betrayed his people and liberty. This statement, coming from one of the most prominent collaborators of Dr. Benes,

seems to show that the latter was driven by lust for personal power, had tried desperately to retain his position, and had hoped, even in 1948, to stay on as head of the State by carrying out the will of the Communists unquestioningly. That is why he remained in office despite the murder of two of his faithful friends, Jan Masaryk and Drtina, and the transformation of the People's Democracy into open Communist Party dictatorship. Maybe his attitude was logical from his point of view. He had made his alliance with the Soviet Union in 1935 and had been elected President with the help of the Communist votes. In 1941 and 1943 he had delivered himself into the hands of the Communists and in 1945 had covered with the mantle of his name and authority all the crimes committed by left wing totalitarians. He had thus destroyed the moral foundations of a democratic community and delivered to the totalitarians the most important positions in the State. Such premises made final surrender to Gottwald just a matter of time. A few months after this last step, Benes was to die, alone, dishonored, and dismissed from the office to which he had clung so desperately and for which he had sacrificed all higher principles.

The Sudeten German leader, Wenzel Jaksch, who during the war was an emigre in London and at present is a Socialist member of the German *Bundestag,* has shown in his remarkable book, *Europe's Road to Potsdam,*[5] that Benes not only betrayed his own people and the Slovaks to Moscow, but also contributed decisively to the loss of Poland by giving President Roosevelt false information on Stalin's plans, and selling the American public on the pipedream of a democratic Russia.

Thus the moral fiber of the Czech people was destroyed. This is felt even today. Khrushchev's strongest support in the Eastern bloc comes from Czecho-Slovakia. It is only when Communism will have been defeated in Warsaw, Budapest and East Berlin that we can expect an end of totalitarian rule in Prague.

[5] Stuttgart, 1958, p. 378 ff.

381

The Case Against Coercion

ROBERT CUNNINGHAM

IT IS A RATHER easy sport to show how particular collectivist measures have gone awry. But we conservatives cannot neglect the task of attempting to articulate a theoretical justification for our position. And this is especially important for a journal such as *New Individualist Review*. In this article I have attempted to outline some of the more general and abstract arguments for limiting governmental coercion to the narrowest possible sphere. While one cannot in so brief a space show conclusively where the line between governmental and non-governmental action should be drawn, I hope to provide support for the premise that is fundamental to the conservative position: that a *prima facie* case exists against governmental coercion when extended beyond its role of preventing violence by private individuals, and that consequently the burden of proof is always on its proponent.

To avoid the usual arguments over the "true meaning" of coercion, I will stipulate the following definition. Coercion is violence or threatened violence designed to cause a person either to perform an act or to refrain from performing one. Most would agree that governmental coercion in this sense ought to be used against the private coercive action of one citizen directed against another, and

Robert Cunningham is an Associate Professor of Philosophy at the University of San Francisco. He received his Ph.D. from Laval University and is the author of articles in *Mind* and other philosophic journals.

against those agents of foreign governments who initiate coercion against us. Are there good reasons for wanting to minimize the overall coercion of one man by another, whether by an agent of government or by anyone else? Are there reasons for wanting to maximize "freedom" (which I stipulate to mean the absence of coercion initiated by one man against another)?[1]

When coercion is exercised upon a man, he does not act according to his own plans and for his own ends, but out of fear, acts as a tool in the hands of him who coerces. Not only are certain choices closed to him, but the opportunities freedom offers for self discipline are closed to him. Whenever the sphere of fully voluntary acts is thus narrowed, the number of choices open to the agent is reduced and he will consequently find it impossible to act in accord with the best judgment of his own conscience; and so not only the egoist, the man who lives for himself, but even the altruist prefers to be left free to make his own choices.

---

[1] Freedom is a word with many meanings: Isaiah Berlin tells us that over 200 have been recorded by historians of ideas. I have given one of them, and when I use the word without qualification, "absence of initiated coercion" is substitutable for it. I do not in so defining "freedom" wish to deny that there are other goods which ordinary usage in some contexts may justify calling "freedom," "freedoms," "liberty," etc.; if one wishes to say that other "freedoms" are more valuable than the absence of initiated coercion, I shall be willing to hear him out—for in giving a definition I have proved nothing.

Coercion may be justified insofar as it removes obstacles to virtuous acts, and it is on this ground that coercion of children by parents may be justified: the bulldozer of coercion cannot build the house of virtue, but can push away the obstructions of unrestrained passion. Coercion of adults cannot be justified for this reason because nothing similar to the loving interest and detailed knowledge that parents can be presumed to have of their own children—and how many are the blunders of parents!—can be found on the part of governors of adults. Such interest and knowledge *may* exist, but there is no institutionalized way of picking out those who possess it. The appropriate means for one adult to lead another to a good end is persuasion, example, moral suasion, etc.—all of which attempt to affect only the choice and not the physical environment or body of the actor.

Unless an adult is permitted to guide himself to his own ends, he will fail to concern himself with matters which he knows best and cares for most. And unless there were some assurance that the governor's circumstantial knowledge of and concern for what is good for each individual exceeds that of the individual, it could not be justifiably claimed that the governor is right to coerce individuals for their own good. As Thoreau said, "If I knew for a certainty that a man was coming to my house with the conscious design of doing me good, I should run for my life."

There is a question one might raise about this analysis: "How distinguish coercion from other forms of non-rational influence?" One cannot of course deny that people differ in ability to withstand pressures of various sorts, and that there are circumstances in which some individuals will fear certain moral sanctions as strongly as they would fear threatened violence. But though at the margin non-coercive forms of pressure may be as strongly felt as the threat of physical violence, one must not blur the difference between the two: Not only is it far easier for a man of conviction to resist jeers than it is to resist a club, but it is also true that while one can usually accomplish his ends though he feels the force of social disapproval, one cannot usually accomplish his ends when in jail.

Thus far we have said, in sum, that governmental coercion is desirable as a means of reducing overall coercion, and that there is an initial prejudice against using coercive measures for other reasons, because an act done under coercion fails to be a fully voluntary and thus a fully valuable human act. On this analysis, governors are the guardians of the peace, not spiritual directors. The conservative position is that governors hold a warrant only to promote that outward peace without which social life is impossible. As Jefferson said in his first inaugural address, government is to confine itself to restraining men from injuring one another: "this is the sum of good government, and this is necessary to close the circle of our felicities." There is no way to guarantee the possession by agents of government of the special wisdom and other virtues demanded to know and carry out progress which uses coercion to make people *good*, or *better*. To put this point another way: I may believe I know what is good for you, but I do not trust you to know what is good for me. And if I might lose my power to coerce you for your own good, and if you might gain power to coerce me for my own good—then I want to deny myself the power to coerce you, and want to try to persuade you to deny yourself the power to coerce me. Surely it is true that individuals often act against their own best interests. Surely it is true that there are some who could use coercion to make people really better. But the problem is, how can we find these paragons of wisdom and virtue?

It should be clear that on this view of government, the most important question is not the classic *"Who* should rule?" but *"How* can we stop rulers from ruling too much?" For only if political sovereignty is thought to be essentially unlimited would the question "Who is to be sovereign?" be the only important question left.[2] The problem of getting rulers

390 383

[2] Cf. Karl Popper, *The Open Society and Its Enemies* (Princeton, N.J.: Princeton University Press, 1960), p. 120 *et seq.*

who will always, or even more often than not, know and act for what is really in the best interests of all, beyond the minimizing of coercion, is practically insoluble; though of course every ruler and candidate professes love of and devotion to the "common good"—equivalent only to a denial that he is motivated by purely sectional concerns—and certainly no one could fault even Hitler in this respect. I am not maintaining the theory of the "outlaw conscience," *conscientia ex lex*, the theory that the individual's conscience is unrestrained and unrestrainable by anything other than its own subjective imperatives. Rather I approve a form of natural-law theory according to which certain moral truths (the Ten Commandments, let us say) are known with very little discourse. But I deny that any civil governor or governors, or even the majority of people in a democracy, will always or even usually act wisely when it is a matter not of minimizing overall coercion, but of coercing people to be better. This is not to say that one should not sometimes use every means short of coercion to lead others to what he considers to be virtuous activity or intelligent thinking about some matter. But he will either convince all or only some: if all are convinced, coercion will be unnecessary; if only some are convinced, coercion is, in my opinion, undesirable.

One must be willing to distinguish accurately between what is valuable in itself and what is a desirable goal of men acting through the instrumentality of the coercive state. To illustrate: one may believe that some men are "natural slaves" (in the Aristotelian sense); and yet, because of the difficulties of identifying these slaves and the dangers of giving to some men the power so to identify others, one may deny the desirability of a political order in which men are distinguished as "naturally" free or "naturally" slave.

Now even though the principle that state coercion is justified to minimize overall coercion be accepted, it must be in somebody's discretion to answer the question: is such-and-such a coercive measure necessary to prevent worse coercion? The formula "better prevention than cure" would tend to stifle spontaneity and to presume more knowledge on the part of governors than can reasonably be expected. So there is no easy answer to this question and at the margin there will be room for dispute. But some administrative arbitrariness may be avoided if the *onus probandi* be placed on those who propose new legislation and if such coercive measures as are adopted be general abstract rules, known beforehand, and equally applicable to all.[3]

A number of other reasons have been offered by political theorists for justifying the reduction of coercion to a minimum. Among them we find the alleged fact that there exists a sphere of private, non-social activity in which no one but the individual concerned is interested, a sphere which does not involve the well-being of others; and so in this sphere no government coercion is justified. But no such purely private sphere exists; all behavior affects others at least indirectly and remotely, and those effects of my actions, though relatively unpredictable, may be quite as important to others as the obvious and immediate effects. One cannot, furthermore, assume the relativist position that no one knows what is morally or otherwise good for the individual better than he himself does; to my mind, at least, relativism is an indefensible position. Nor can one assume that most men are morally good and can well be left alone to pursue their own interests; the contrary I believe more likely: most men are morally bad in that most men seek the good of sense in opposition to the good of reason. The only telling argument for minimizing governmental and other coercion is this: there is no way of getting rulers who will know and do what is best for all concerned. If there were a way of getting rulers who would use force when necessary to teach us to use our liberty rightly, to become strong in resisting the determination of our own instincts, to stand firm against non-coercive sanctions—the curled lip, the raised eyebrow, the cancelled invitation, the economic depriva-

---

[3] Cf. F. A. Hayek, "Freedom and Coercion: A Reply to Mr. Hamowy," *New Individualist Review* (Vol. I, No. 2).

tion, the scorn and ridicule, or the applause, the bonus and the medal—then one might not unreasonably be willing to give up a measure of freedom; to stop insisting on as large a protected "private" sphere of activity as possible. This is not to say that each of us is a little god, almighty and allgood, who asks only to be left alone to enjoy himself and his works; it is only to say that the state is not in Hegel's words "a Big god almighty and allgood," whose will is carried out by angelic agents.

To sum up in a sentence: We need governmental coercion, but we want no more than is "necessary." But how much is necessary beyond what is called for by internal and external aggression? The conservative answer is: none. The hypothesis the conservative defends might be stated: if no more coercion be admitted than is necessary to reduce coercion to an overall minimum, then the conditions of the "good life" will be preserved. How could we verify this hypothesis? By attempting to falsify it, and failing. If we could find some interventionist measure (one by which government interferes with the voluntary actions of individuals to force them to do or refrain from doing certain non-coercive acts) whose consequences would be on the whole beneficial, then we should have falsified the hypothesis. Now the conservative does not hold that should one, or even a number of interventionist measures be introduced, the sky will crack and the world tumble about our ears. Some governmental interventions have worse consequences than others; one should take the middle path when the best path is closed; etc. But the conservative does hold that the fact that coercive measures are introduced "democratically" does not make them less undesirable. And he does believe that the better arguments can be found on the side of those who oppose interventionist measures—measures such as minimum wage laws; price and rent control; Social Security; FEPC legislation; Communist Party registration; the establishment of "free" and public schools; tariffs and quotas; regulatory commissions such as the ICC, the FCC, and the like; government monopoly of the post office; state licensing provisions; and the TVA. Now every such interventionist proposal would require a careful critique if one expected to convince a reasonable person of the rightness beyond question of the conservative position. It seems to me, however, that at a minimum the considerations we have just educed on the undesirability of coercion unmistakably throw the burden of proof on those who announce plans to increase the scope of governmental activity.

385

Ireland,

Victim of Its Own Politicians

JOHN P. McCARTHY

IRISH - AMERICANS a r e earnestly proud of their Irish heritage. At the annual St. Patrick's Day festivities they vigorously assert their determination to further Ireland's freedom and national unification, and indulge in a few Anglophobic outbursts. But as soon as the ceremonies are over, they return these Fenian enthusiasms to the attic storerooms and once again become preoccupied with the problems and concerns of those institutions to which they owe their primary loyalties: the United States and the Catholic Church. This is fortunate, not only for American politics which has one less overseas political loyalty to have to appease, but also for Ireland herself. Irish-American involvement in Irish problems would scarcely benefit Ireland. Because of their lack of understanding about Ireland's real needs, Irish-American circles would probably only aid the nationalist politicians in Ireland who are primarily responsible for Ireland's present difficulties. These Irish politicians would use Irish-American sympathy for Ireland solely to cover up their own inadequacies by reassuring the Irish electorate that there is overwhelming support in America for their policies. For instance, Ted Kennedy's two-day visit to Ireland last spring is used by Irish politicians to assure their constituents that all will go well because Ireland has an ardent champion in the American Senate.

John P. McCarthy is an Associate Editor of *New Individualist Review*.

Ireland's present difficulties are attributable not to British tyranny nor to partition, but to the ineptitude of many of the people who have been governing Ireland since national independence was won, especially since Eamon de Valera's assumption of power in 1932. A further tragedy is that the natural Irish rebelliousness and political ingenuity has been lulled to sleep because of self-satisfaction with the very fact of having independence. Probably because of a political inferiority complex, Irishmen will scarcely criticize their own government in front of foreigners lest their listeners think the Irish are unfit to govern themselves.

Simply because an activity or policy is followed by an independent Irish government, Irishmen tend to think that it has to be supported regardless of its merits. As a result, Ireland has let herself be dominated in the past thirty years or so by a band of fattened revolutionaries, who are profiting from the memory of their exploits during the revolution of 1916-1921, but who are scarcely concerned or competent to deal with Ireland's most pressing needs. This incompetence especially injures the greatest section of the Irish population, the people living on farms. The greatest gains made by the Irish farmers — the ability to own their own land and the initiation of the co-operative creameries — began in the last few years of British rule. They have had no comparable gains since then. But before discussing these politicians and their policies, let us examine the history and development of Irish independence.

PRIMARILY BECAUSE of the political genius of Irish leaders, such as O'Connell and Parnell, most of the frightful injustices under which the Irish suffered had been removed. Catholics had been admitted to Parliament in 1829, the Episcopal Church in Ireland was disestablished in 1867, and in the 1890's and early 1900's landlordism disappeared as the British Government assisted the Irish peasants in becoming the proprietors of their own land. In earlier history, especially during the penal days in the eighteenth century, British power in Ireland was used solely to benefit the land-grabbing Protestant "Establishment." But in the thirty years before World War One, the British ministry and Parliament had begun to govern for the benefit and well-being of all the Irish population. Railroads were extended to the neglected Irish western seaboard, a Department of Agriculture was set up to help the new peasant proprietors modernize their farming methods, and educational opportunities were extended, including the establishment of a non-denominational National University.

The major remaining objective of the Irish Nationalist representatives in Parliament was to gain Home Rule for Ireland, that is, an independent legislature for Ireland with responsibility for Irish domestic affairs. By 1911, the British ministry itself was committed to the passage of a Home Rule Act. Since the veto power of the Tory House of Lords had been removed, a Home Rule Act seemed certain of success.

The only obstacle was the refusal, even to the point of arms, of the Protestant section in Northern Ireland, Ulster, to accept being ruled by a Home Rule Parliament. An attempt at compromise was made as the Unionist leader, Edward Carson, modified his total opposition to any Home Rule to simply an insistence on the exclusion of six of the Ulster counties from a Home-Ruled Ireland. John Redmond, the Nationalist

leader, was willing to accept the exclusion of part of Ulster, but insisted that two of the six counties, Tyrone and Fermanagh, which had Catholic and Nationalist majorities, should be included under Home Rule. The Unionists would not agree to this, and when the World War began the ministry postponed any action on Home Rule. The prospects for it at the end of the war were bright, though, for, as King George V told Redmond in a private conversation, everyone, himself included, regarded Home Rule as inevitable.[1]

But then, on the virtual eve of the attainment of Home Rule, a futile uprising occurred in Dublin in Easter Week, 1916. The rebels, led and inspired by a group of Gaelic language revivalists, labor leaders, and intellectuals, rejected the Irish Nationalist Party's policy of working within the British Parliament to achieve Ireland's objectives. To them, Ireland's political independence was not something to be requested from the British Parliament. Wanting not just legislative independence or Home Rule, they proclaimed "the Irish Republic as a Sovereign Independent State."

Irish popular sentiment was still behind the parliamentary Nationalists. However, the heavy-handed treatment of the rebels by the British military authorities and Lloyd George's decision in April, 1918, to request an extension of the draft to Ireland caused a shift in public feeling to the Sinn Fein, the political party of the rebels. Irish sensitivity had been offended by Lloyd George's move because there were already many Irish volunteers in the British forces, and Redmond's offer to have Irish Volunteer Militia units called to active service had been rejected by the War Office.

The Sinn Fein won 73 of the Irish seats to Parliament in the 1918 general election, against 6 for the Nationalists, and 26 for the Unionists. Yet, the Sinn Fein M.P.'s refused to sit in the British Parliament (where they would have been able to take part in the probable passage of Home Rule legislation). Instead, they

[1] Edgar Holt, *Protest in Arms, the Irish Troubles, 1919-23* (New York: Coward-McCann, 1961), p. 47.

387

declared a *de facto* Parliament of Ireland (Dail Eireann), and demanded the removal of the British forces from Ireland as well as the dissolution of the Royal Irish Constabulary, the police force in Ireland. Then, following a series of attacks on the British military by the Irish Republican Army, the military arm of the insurgent Irish government, fierce guerrilla warfare was initiated and covered Ireland for the next two years.

A compromise between the different sections in Ireland became even more improbable now that southern sentiment had shifted from the Parliamentary Nationalists to the Sinn Fein. The Sinn Fein refused any compromise solution, but insisted that the north must be governed by and accept, not a Home Rule Parliament granted by the British Government, but the *de facto* republican government which the Sinn Feiners claimed to be the government of all Ireland. The Redmond party, at least, would have accepted the exclusion of some northern counties from the Home Rule section of Ireland. Home Rule Ireland would also have maintained some connection with Britain. This and the control of the independent Irish Parliament by experienced parliamentary leaders might have made the Unionists amenable to an eventual re-unification.[2]

LLOYD GEORGE PASSED a Government of Ireland Act, which set up two separate Home Rule Parliaments, one for the twenty-six southern counties and one for six Ulster counties, including the predominantly Catholic and Nationalist Tyrone and Fermanagh. King George V opened the northern Parliament on June 22, 1921, expressing his wish for eventual re-unification. The Sinn Feiners had been elected to the southern Parliament, but they refused to operate it since it was not the republican Parliament of all of Ireland.

---

[2] Michael Sheehy in *Divided We Stand* (London: Faber and Faber, 1955) argues that southern extreme nationalism following the decline of the Parliamentary Nationalist Party did more than anything else to insure the permanence of partition.

Then, the British Government entered into direct negotiations with representatives of the rebel government. A treaty was drafted and was accepted by the rebel Parliament in January, 1922, whereby Ireland was given more independence than had been sought for by the pre-Sinn Fein Irish leaders. The twenty-six counties received not just legislative independence, but a complete government as well as the evacuation of the British military. The only restriction on the independence of this Irish Free State was that it was to be a member of the British Commonwealth, with a representative of the Crown present in Ireland and an oath to the King required of members of the Irish Parliament. Also, the Irish Free State was to allow several Irish harbor facilities and defenses to be maintained by the British forces.

Many republicans, such as Eamon de Valera, regarded the treaty's acceptance of membership in the Commonwealth, the oath to the King, and the continuing partition as a betrayal of the Sinn Fein principles of an independent Irish Republic. The pro-treaty forces had won the Parliamentary election of the Irish Free State's provisional government. However, civil war broke out between the die-hard rebel army, the IRA, and the new professional Irish Free State Army being recruited in accord with the treaty.

The republicans were defeated (although the Chairman of the provisional government, Michael Collins, had been killed in an ambush), and ended fighting in April, 1923. The political arm of the republicans, the Sinn Fein, continued its opposition to the treaty as its members refused to sit in or recognize the Free State Parliament to which many of them had been elected. Then de Valera organized a new republican party, the Fianna Fail, whose members would accept their seats in the Parliament. In the 1927 elections, the pro-treaty party, now called Cumann na nGaedheal, maintained its majority with W. T. Cosgrave remaining as President.

In 1925, a Boundary Commission (with representatives f r o m Northern and

Southern Ireland and Britain), called for by the 1922 treaty, suggested, over the dissent of the southern Irish member, that the *status quo* boundary between Northern and Southern Ireland be maintained, despite the fact that there were nationalist majorities in many northern areas. This was rationalized on the grounds that the economic survival of Northern Ireland as a separate entity necessitated the inclusion of these predominantly nationalist areas in Northern Ireland.

The southern government's dissatisfaction with this report was resolved by a new agreement in December, 1925, which replaced the 1922 treaty. The Boundary Commission and the contemplated "Council of Ireland," where both sections could have met together on common problems, were dissolved, but the *status quo* partition was accepted. At the same time the British Government and the Free State cancelled their respective liabilities towards each other. Then, by an agreement reached in March, 1926, the Free State agreed to transmit to the British Government the annual payments on land annuities collected from the former tenants who had purchased their estates under the 1903 Land Act.

Under this Act many Irish tenants were enabled to buy the land on which they lived solely by promising to pay the annuities over a period of 68 years to the British Government which had compensated the landlords. The landlords had been compensated by being issued stock on which interest was paid out of the monies collected as annuities. As a result of this 1926 agreement the Irish Government agreed to collect and to transmit to the British Government the annuities which amounted to about £5 million annually.

IN THE 1932 GENERAL elections de Valera's Fianna Fail Party won control of the Free State Government which they, as republicans, had originally refused to recognize. With the two short exceptions of 1948-51 and 1954-57, the Fianna Fail has since been in power.

Therefore, the record of Irish development in the past thirty years must to all intents and purposes be considered as the Fianna Fail record.

Intent on achieving the old republican goal of breaking all ties with Great Britain, the Fianna Fail Government removed the oath to the King from the Free State constitution, and continually slighted the King's representative in Dublin, the Governor-General, whose legal powers were removed. The right of appeal from the Irish courts to the British Privy Council was abolished.

These gestures naturally made the Unionist Government of Northern Ireland permanently opposed to any re-unification, for it realized that re-unification with the Fianna Fail Government would involve dissolution of the British connection to which the Unionists were so committed. Those who suffered most from de Valera's strict republicanism were, of course, his nationalist allies in the north, for the possibility of a compromise whereby they would find themselves in a united Ireland was now removed. The only alternative course for the northern nationalists (who in County Tyrone and County Fermanagh were the majorities, justly entitled to incorporation with the Southern Government) was some sort of rebellion. To prevent this, the Unionist Government placed stringent restrictions on the nationalist and Catholic minorities in the north.

De Valera then refused to abide by the 1926 agreement to transmit the land annuities to the English Government. This refusal would have been justified if de Valera had based it on the grounds that the former landlords really had no right to have owned the land in the first place, since they had gained it by confiscating it from the original owners in the 16th and 17th centuries. The tenant-purchasers were the true successors of the rightful owners whose land had been taken in those centuries, and therefore they should have no obligation to compensate the illegitimate "landlords" nor to pay annuities for their own land.

But de Valera contradicted this reasoning, for he did not end the obligation

389

of the tenant-purchasers to pay annuities. The only thing he did was to insist that the annuities be collected for his government rather than for the old "landlords."

The British Government naturally retaliated against de Valera's action by raising special duties on imports from the Irish Free State. De Valera replied by imposing higher duties on imports to Ireland from Great Britain, and an economic war between both nations began. Naturally, Ireland, the agrarian and exporting country which had always relied on British markets to sell its products in and which was dependent on British manufactured goods, was bound to be the loser.

As a result of the economic war, Irish agriculture became so disorganized that its export capacity fell by 50%. But this did not trouble the Fianna Fail theorists, who saw the war as an opportunity to further their ideals of separation from Britain and of economic nationalism. It should be remembered that the social forces behind the Irish Revolution had not been the impoverished farming community, which had supported the nineteenth century struggles, especially those against landlordism. Rather, it came from the many children of the farmers who had been forced to seek work in the towns and cities. "Surplus children squeezed into the towns and cities, and found there that all the power and most of the wealth was in the hands of people of a different religion, racial origin, or political loyalty." It was this ambitious urban class which had come to power in Ireland.

This class was not a laboring class. Rather, "the more able among them were petit bourgeois, middle-men, importers, small manufacturers . . . a new twentieth-century middle-class to fill the vacuum created by the departure or depression of the earlier alien middle-class . . . they were rising to sudden wealth behind protective tariff-walls . . . [and] had a vested interest in nationalism and even in isolationism."[3]

---

[3] Sean O'Faolain, "Fifty Years of Irish Writing," *Studies*, Vol. LI, no. 201 (Spring, 1962), p. 97.

During the economic war and ever since then, there has been considerable industrial expansion in Ireland, part of it, no doubt, having been encouraged by protective tariffs as well as by government credits. Furthermore, a sizeable part of industrial progress in Ireland has been due to government investment, as state-sponsored boards and companies cover an extremely wide field in production, communications, marketing, research, development, finance, and sports. No doubt much employment has resulted from this industrial development, but its long range effect on Ireland's welfare is still to be determined. This is especially so if government protection and subsidization of certain industries penalizes other activities such as agriculture, which have much more basic importance to Ireland.

In 1938 the economic war ceased, following an argument between de Valera and Neville Chamberlain. The land annuities dispute was resolved by English acceptance of a final Irish payment of only £10 million, and both nations removed the special duties imposed during the economic war. Chamberlain would not heed the Irish request that he put pressure on the Northern Government towards unification, but he did agree to revoke the 1922 agreement by withdrawing the British forces from the Southern Irish ports of Cobh, Berehaven, and Lough Swilly.

A new Irish constitution was drawn up whereby the name "Ireland" was substituted for "Irish Free State," and the only remaining connection with Britain was by membership in the Commonwealth. The King was regarded as the head of that association, but not someone entitled to an oath of allegiance. De Valera assumed the new office of Prime Minister or "Taoiseach," and Douglas Hyde, a leader of the old Gaelic League, was elected to the honorific Presidency. Then in 1949 Ireland broke the last ties with Britain, as it withdrew from the Commonwealth and Ireland was proclaimed a Republic. Paradoxically this was done not by the Fianna Fail Party, but by a coalition government headed by J. A. Costello of the Fine Gael Party, the successors of the Cosgrave Free State Party. Costello had agreed to leave the Commonwealth as a bargain to gain the parliamentary votes of an extremist republican party.

IN CONTRAST TO the industrial expansion, Irish agriculture has hardly developed as one might have expected since the achievement of national independence. This agrarian failure is partly attributable to the economic war of the 1930's. This was a loss which could not be compensated by the numerous welfare schemes offered to the farmers by the de Valera government. In Ireland there are many pensions for the elderly people, widows, and orphans; new houses are provided, and there is an extensive government sponsored hospitalization scheme. Despite these welfare advantages, however, the number of agrarian workers in Ireland has declined since the 1920's. The growing industrial capacity of Ireland has scarcely been able to absorb those leaving the farms. Instead, most have emigrated to the industrial areas of England and the United States. Emigration from Ireland is so great that Ireland shares with only East Germany and North Vietnam the dubious distinction of being a nation with a declining population.

The standard of living, measured by the increased amounts spent on food, tobacco, drink, clothes, fuel, light, entertainment, and on motor cars, has improved — but this is only because there was so much emigration which prevented mass unemployment and limited to a low level the total number dependent on the national income.

The emigration from rural areas to industrial urban areas is a common feature in the modern world. But accompanying the decline of agricultural laborers in many nations has been a substantial modernization of agricultural methods and a sizeable increase in agricultural productivity. In comparison with many of these nations, though, Ireland is failing to modernize significantly its agricultural methods or improve its productivity.

Irish leadership should be aware that Ireland's natural resources are too limited to create a serious manufacturing economy in Ireland. Fortunately, the new ministry of Sean Lemass, who succeeded de Valera as the Fianna Fail leader when the latter assumed the nonpolitical office of President in 1959, is receding from the old ideals of economic nationalism. Instead of protecting and subsidizing industries which would be incapable of meeting foreign competition and would penalize the domestic Irish consumer, the Government is now encouraging private investment in Ireland by foreign capital. Tax concessions are granted to the imported industries with hopes that these industries will be successful in foreign markets.

However, it is not enough simply to encourage manufacturing. Ireland's economy can only prosper by emphasizing and developing the most naturally advantageous industries: agriculture and fishing. This is especially so if Ireland is to join the Common Market, where Ireland will scarcely be able to compete in manufactured goods with the other Common Market members. As an agrarian country, Ireland will have to reconcile herself to a certain amount of emigration. But, by improving her agricultural methods and expanding productivity, the amount of emigration can be lessened and greater prosperity and well-being can be obtained for the bulk of the population.

The government should not expect to encourage agricultural improvement by the present system of welfare assistance, pensions, and housing grants. These forms of assistance to the farmer are scarcely large enough to serve as capital with which to improve his methods. Indeed, by providing a certain amount of minimum comforts they probably engender a spirit of self-satisfaction and disdain to change or improve himself.

Government facilitation of more liberal credit terms in acquiring new machinery is, of course, more useful to the farmer than would be unproductive doles. At the same time, the farmer has to be encouraged to abandon the traditional Irish small 30-acre farm, which is incapable of competing in a modern economy, in favor of larger scale co-operatives. The dairy products co-operatives encouraged by the Agricultural Department set up under British rule probably did more than anything else to improve the lot of Irish farmers.

Irish fishing needs more encouragement. In view of the frequent presence of so many Danish trawlers within a few miles of the Irish coast, it should be expected that a modernized and well-equipped Irish fishing fleet could successfully compete in the European market and provide thousands of job opportunities in Ireland. At present, however, the Irish fishing industry is in a relatively primitive state, with much fishing being done by independent fishermen with unmotorized craft.

Until the leaders realize the full potentials of Irish agriculture and fishing, and recognize the marginal value of so much of the manufacturing and tourism which the government encourages, the Irish economy will scarcely be able to hold its own, never mind prosper, in the Common Market.

A curious policy of the Irish Government has been its efforts to encourage the revival of the Gaelic language. Irish enthusiasm for the old language is understandable. In other centuries, the Anglo-Irish Establishment had deposed the Gaelic-speaking Catholics from their own land and insulted the natives by making English the official language of Ireland. The Irish people were successfully induced to speak English in national schools, and an attitude was nurtured to regard the inability to speak English as a sign of ignorance.

But the Gaelic enthusiasts should reconcile themselves to the fact that the overwhelming majority of Irishmen are English speaking, and are unlikely to be won over to a Gaelic revival. This, despite the compulsory studying of Gaelic in the national schools as well as the requirement to speak Gaelic in most civil service positions. There are many areas in western Ireland, known as Gaeltacht, where a high percentage of the people can speak Gaelic. But even in these areas most of the people, especially the younger ones, speak English despite their eligibility for government grants for the ability to speak Gaelic. Significantly, it is the Gaeltacht areas that have the highest rate of emigration, emigration to such non-Gaelic speaking areas as London and New York.

Another feature of the Irish Government's policy has been its "neutralism" in foreign affairs. It justified its non-involvement in World War Two and its refusal to join NATO on the grounds that part of Ireland had been "imprisoned" by one of the Allies, Great Britain. Most of the Irish people are firmly anti-Communist and very sympathetic to the policies of the United States (especially since the election of John F. Kennedy). However, it is becoming fashionable in many Irish intellectual and political circles, especially since Ireland's entry into the UN, to consider their nation as one of the peaceful nations uninvolved in the Cold War and allied only with the anti-imperialist struggles in Asia and Africa. All of this would have been very innocent except for Ireland's commitment to the UN assault on Katanga, where quite a few Irish soldiers lost their lives as a result of the policies of the historian-turned-diplomatic-adventurer, Conor Cruise O'Brien.

IT IS NECESSARY that new leadership arise in Ireland to replace the romantic and opportunistic governing circles who have refused to acknowledge the twentieth century. Ireland must shake itself loose from its Gaelic romanticism and accept the rightful burdens, concerns, and *Weltanschauung* of a modern Western European nation. Unless it does so, Ireland will be neither a modern nation nor a romantic Gaelic "other world." Instead it will be simply a tourist resort, with most of its native population having departed through emigration.

392

NEW BOOKS AND ARTICLES

THE FOLLOWING IS A SELECT LIST OF BOOKS AND ARTICLES WHICH, IN THE OPINION OF THE EDITORS, MAY BE OF INTEREST TO OUR READERS.

James M. Buchanan and Gordon Tullock, *The Calculus of Consent.* Ann Arbor, Mich.: University of Michigan Press, 1962. $6.95. An attempt to apply a rigorously scientific approach, based primarily on game theory and marginal utility analysis, to the problems of democratic government.

Milton Friedman, *Capitalism and Freedom.* Chicago: University of Chicago Press. $1.50, paper. Happily, a paperback reprint of Prof. Friedman's book, published last year, has already been issued. Tightly-reasoned and bold in its conclusions, this volume is an excellent example of the approach of the "Chicago school" of neo-liberal economists.

George B. de Huszar, editor, *Fundamentals of Voluntary Health Care.* Caldwell, Idaho: Caxton Press. $6. An intelligent selection of pertinent and cogent essays on voluntary as against socialized medicine, by a number of experts in the field.

Michael Oakeshott, *Rationalism in Politics.* New York: Basic Books. $6.50. A collection of essays on politics, ethics and related subjects, permeated with Burkeanism and written by one of the leading contemporary British conservative writers.

393

Edmund A. Opitz and Robert LeFevre, *Must We Depend upon Political Protection?* Colorado Springs, Colo.: The Freedom School. 75¢. A debate on "limited" vs. "no" government.

Hans Rothfels, *The German Opposition to Hitler.* Chicago: Regnery, 1962. $4.00. A new edition of the classic introduction to the internal opposition to Nazism, which culminated in the attempted *coup d'etat* of July 20, 1944. A stimulating review of Rothfels' book appears in the Winter, 1962-63, *Modern Age.* Prof. Klaus Epstein here argues that Roosevelt's foreign policy in regard to Germany and Russia was so perverse that, within its framework, we must be grateful that the *coup* did *not* succeed!

Eliseo Vivas, *Relativism: Its Paradoxes and Pitfalls.* Pamphlet; free copy available from Intercollegiate Society of Individualists, 629 Public Ledger Building, Philadelphia 6, Pa. An interesting, if oblique, handling of the thesis of the relativism of moral values, by a distinguished professional philosopher.

J. K. Zawodny, *Death in the Forest.* South Bend, Ind.: Notre Dame University Press. $6.50. A detailed and comprehensive examination of the facts concerning the massacre of 10,000 Polish officers and intellectuals at Katyn Forest in 1940 by the Russian Army.

Robert E. Gaskins, Jr., "The Voluntary Society," *The Standard,* December, 1962. Free copy available from The Standard Publishing Co., Lawrence, Kans. A young libertarian presents a proposal for extending the principle of private ownership to the court system and the police force.

William McCord, "Long Night in Ghana," *New Leader,* Nov. 26, 1962. A professor of sociology reports on the totalitarian state being erected by the *Osagyefo* ("In Accra today one sees phlanxes of 'Young Pioneers,' aged 12, chanting their oath: 'Nkrumah is always right! Nkrumah will never die!'"), and replies point by point to the Establishment's apologia for the African dictator.

Know Your Enemy !!

The editors of NEW INDIVIDUALIST REVIEW have recently, through their highly placed contacts in the Communist Empire, come into possession of a fantastic and hitherto secret Communist blue-print for world domination. Entitled BLUE-PRINT FOR WORLD DOMINATION, it was composed in the depths of the Kremlin in 1920, by a noted Bolshevik writer, and has been ratified and re-ratified by numerous Communist Congresses and countless Communist deeds. Every patriotic American must familiarize himself with this shocking and sobering document! Here are the Conclusions, as set forth by its author, the well-known Bolshevik leader, V. I. LENIN.

"In order to conquer the world for our Godless Creed we must employ infinite craftiness and patience. The most difficult nation to vanquish will be the United States, for there the people are basically prosperous, moral, and un-revolutionary, because of the inspiring achievements of free enterprise. After the United States has been initially softened up by the abolition of the gold standard and the introduction of welfare legislation, we will begin this Three-Point Program for victory over America:

"(1) First we will trick them into banning prayer in the public schools. Just as fluoridation of water destroys the body, so the elimination of public-school prayer destroys the spirit.

"(2) Then, in keeping with our almost Oriental immoralism, we will begin the steady introduction of pornographic materials—both those which are rankly so, and those which we will camouflage as "avant-gardism"—into American society. Pornography will be the chief weapon in our campaign to rot out the moral fibre of America, but abstract art and 12-tone music are not to be neglected in this connection.

"(3) Our final take-over will be preceded by an unparalleled crusade to destroy the magazine, NEW INDIVIDUALIST REVIEW. This quarterly journal, because it is so highly informative, entertaining and intellectual, is perhaps our single most serious problem in the United States, rivalled only by the Strategic Air Command. To destroy NEW INDIVIDUALIST REVIEW is to make America a plum ripe for the picking!"

Block Communist Plans for World Domination Today! Subscribe to NEW INDIVIDUALIST REVIEW!

WHAT YOU CAN DO TO HELP NIR . . .

During the past year, the circulation and staff of NEW INDIVIDUALIST REVIEW has been expanding rapidly. This journal is now being sold at many local newsstands and at over 40 colleges and universities. Despite a few dissenting notes, the general reaction of libertarian and conservative leaders has been favorable. The author of "The Conservative Mind," Prof. Russell Kirk, for instance, has said that NEW INDIVIDUALIST REVIEW is a work of "genuine intellectual power" and the editor of "National Review," William F. Buckley, Jr. has called it "by far the best student magazine on our side of the fence." If you agree that this is a useful magazine which ought to be read by more people, there are four things that you can do to further the growth of libertarian-conservative ideas.

(1) You can urge your college library or your local library to subscribe. A library subscription makes an excelent donation since it may introduce the magazine to dozens of people.

(2) You can urge your friends to subscribe or to donate subscriptions to students.

(3) If you are a college student, you can volunteer to act as our representative on your campus.

(4) Our student subscription price ($1.00 a year) does not cover the cost involved; this price is purposely kept low to encourage as wide a readership as possible among undergraduates. Our deficit is made up by voluntary contributions from individuals. Any donation which you might be able to afford at this time would be gratefully received. None of our staff receives any remuneration of any kind.

Society lives and acts only in individuals
. . . Everyone carries a part of society on
his shoulders; no one is relieved of his share
of responsibility by others. And no one can
find a safe way for himself if society is
sweeping toward destruction. Therefore
everyone, in his own interests, must thrust
himself vigorously into the intellectual battle. None can stand aside with unconcern;
the interests of everyone hang on the result. Whether he chooses or not, every man
is drawn into the great historical struggle,
the decisive battle (between freedom and
slavery) into which our epoch has plunged
us.

—Ludwig Von Mises

The Intercollegiate Society of Individualists, a non-partisan, non-profit educational organization, deals with ideas. ISI places primary emphasis on the distribution of literature encompassing such academic disciplines as economics, sociology, history, moral philosophy, and political science. If you are a student or teacher, you are invited to add your name to the ISI mailing list. There is no charge, and you may remove your name at any time. For additional information, or to add your name to the list, write the nearest ISI office.

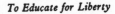
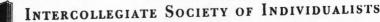

VOLUME 3
NUMBER 1
SUMMER 1963

New
INDIVIDUALIST
Review

EDUCATION: FREE AND PUBLIC?

"CONSUMER SOVEREIGNTY"
AND THE LAW

ON THE PREMISES
OF GROWTH ECONOMICS

THE NEGRO REVOLUTION

Vol. 3, No. 1   35 cents   Summer 1963

NEW INDIVIDUALIST REVIEW

Volume 3 — Number 1   SUMMER 1963

401

NEW INDIVIDUALIST REVIEW is published quarterly by *New Individualist Review, Inc.,* at Ida Noyes Hall, University of Chicago, Chicago 37, Illinois.

Opinions expressed in signed articles do not necessarily represent the views of the editors. Editorial, advertising, and subscription correspondence and manuscripts should be sent to NEW INDIVIDUALIST REVIEW, Ida Noyes Hall, University of Chicago, Chicago 37, Illinois.   All manuscripts become the property of NEW INDIVIDUALIST REVIEW.

Subscription rates: $2.00 per year (students $1.00).

NEW

INDIVIDUALIST

REVIEW

EDITORIAL STAFF

Editors-in-Chief ● Ronald Hamowy ● Ralph Raico
Associate Editors ● Robert M. Hurt ● John P. McCarthy
Robert Schuettinger ● John Weicher
Business Manager ● Sam Peltzman
Editorial Assistants ● Jameson Campaigne, Jr. ● Joe Cobb
Burton Gray ● Thomas Heagy ● Jerome Heater
R. P. Johnson ● Robert Michaels ● James Powell

EDITORIAL ADVISORS

Yale Brozen ● Milton Friedman ● George J. Stigler
University of Chicago
F. A. Hayek ● Benjamin Rogge
University of Freiburg *Wabash College*

402

COLLEGE AND UNIVERSITY REPRESENTATIVES

UNIVERSITY OF ALABAMA
Dianne Hastings

UNIVERSITY OF ARIZONA
Stephen Sala

BALL STATE COLLEGE
Geoffrey Scott

BELOIT COLLEGE
Alfred Regnery

BROOKLYN COLLEGE
Howard Seigel

BRYN MAWR COLLEGE
Sheila Bunker

CITY COLLEGE OF NEW YORK
Kathie Fiesel

COLUMBIA UNIVERSITY
John P. McCarthy

UNIVERSITY OF DELAWARE
John M. Tobin

DE PAUW UNIVERSITY
David Prosser

UNIVERSITY OF DETROIT
George McDonnell

DUKE UNIVERSITY
Robert B. Fisher

EARLHAM COLLEGE
David Lindsey

GROVE CITY COLLEGE
A. Bruce Gillander

HARVARD UNIVERSITY
David Friedman

UNIVERSITY OF IDAHO
Robert D. Brown

UNIVERSITY OF ILLINOIS
Bill Jacklin

INDIANA UNIVERSITY
Karl K. Pingle

UNIVERSITY OF KANSAS
Larry F. Glaser

UNIVERSITY OF KENTUCKY
James G. Otto

KNOX COLLEGE
Kip Pencheff

LOUISIANA STATE UNIVERSITY
William Thomas Tete

LOYOLA UNIVERSITY
(Chicago)
William Ford

MANHATTAN COLLEGE
Stephen J. Kerins

MIAMI UNIVERSITY
(Ohio)
Thomas R. Ireland

NEW YORK UNIVERSITY
Jeffrey Jay Weiser

NORTHWESTERN UNIVERSITY
S. Kent Steffke

OCCIDENTAL COLLEGE
Goetz Wolff

OREGON STATE UNIVERSITY
John Charles Neeley

PACIFIC COAST UNIVERSITY
Ernest Talaganis

PROVIDENCE COLLEGE
Raymond LaJeunesse

PURDUE UNIVERSITY
Ted Sigward

QUEENS COLLEGE
Robert J. Malito

QUINCY COLLEGE
Michael J. Hill

REGIS COLLEGE
Edwin J. Feulner, Jr.

SOUTHERN ILL. UNIVERSITY
John Lulves, Jr.

STANFORD UNIVERSITY
Richard Noble

SYRACUSE UNIVERSITY
Irwin H. Rosenthal

TUFTS UNIVERSITY
William G. Nowlin, Jr.

VANDERBILT UNIVERSITY
Peter Chamberlain

UNIVERSITY OF VIRGINIA
Robert Stuart Redfield

WABASH COLLEGE
Ronald Rettig

UNIVERSITY OF WISCONSIN
Theodore Cormaney

UNIVERSITY OF WISCONSIN
(Milwaukee)
Wells H. Perkins

●

UNIVERSITY OF FRANKFURT
Werner Krebs

UNIVERSITY OF PARIS
Ronald Hamowy

OXFORD UNIVERSITY
Robert Schuettinger

Education: Free and Public?

ROBERT L. CUNNINGHAM

ONE IS RIGHTLY suspicious when he comes across what purports to be an easy solution to a complex of difficult problems. Knowing that a **preference** for shortcuts springs from deep-seated intellectual laziness, he is suspicious when told that all would change if only people would become pacifists, or abandon Aristotelian logic, or adopt the social credit system. Yet sometimes it is the simple solution which is the best solution. This may well be the case with regard to the major educational problems we face in the United States today: the religious-school problem, the problem of raising educational standards, and the segregation problem.

I propose in this paper to ask, and offer an answer to, two questions: Why do we need schools that are "free"? and, Suppose our schools were "free" but not "public," what would be the consequences? To the first question I shall answer: We do not need schools that are "free," but will find it impossible in the short run to persuade people that we do not. To the second I shall answer: The consequences of a system where most schools are "free" but "non-public" are such that our major problems will be solved, and no new problems of consequence will be raised.

Robert L. Cunningham is an Associate Professor of Philosophy at the University of San Francisco, and the author of numerous philosophical articles in scholarly journals.

WHY THEN DO WE need a free school system? Suppose we examine the hypothesis that, given parental rights and duties, there is no need for a free school system, and that government has only two roles in the field of schooling: the first that of a truant officer, of making a minimum standard of education compulsory; the second, the paternalistic role of paying the costs of educating those children whose parents are demonstrably unable to pay.

The first, truant-officer role of government, can be perhaps justified on the grounds that unless some schooling were compulsory, a significant number of parents would give their children little or no schooling—which would put the child at a disadvantage with respect to his peers, and cause external diseconomies, such as a lower level of political understanding and of productive power. Knowledge is the sort of good or value whose goodness is obvious only to those who have some, and if there are illiterate parents who do not appreciate the value of literacy, it is generally thought that government interference is justified in the name of the child and the "common good"; the grounds are that the whole social cost of sub-standard education is borne not by the uneducated individual and his family alone, but by society as a whole, for the fact is that the educated child confers political, material, and cultural benefits upon others.[1] We must recognize, however, that by making schooling compulsory, we fly in the face of the principle stated by Thomas Jefferson, "It is better to *tolerate* that rare instance of a parent's refusing to let his child be educated, than to shock the common feelings by a forcible transportation and education of the infant against the will of his father."[2] Whether one agrees with Jefferson or not, it is worth noting how far we have come from Jefferson's notion of parental liberty and control — few of us feel any "shock of the common feelings"!

If one could make the assumption that the great bulk of families were capable of paying the costs of schooling for their own children, the only other role of government, if private charity proved insufficient, would be the paternalistic one of paying the costs of educating those children whose parents are demonstrably unable to pay; just as it now gives subsistence aid to those children whose parents are demonstrably unable to furnish food, clothing, and shelter.

Can one make the assumption that the great bulk of families are capable of paying directly the costs of educating their own children? One could, of course, point out that state and local taxes would be cut by 45% (which amount now goes to the public school system), thus leaving that much more money in the hands of individuals to pay the costs of schooling for their own children. One might point to the example of the Catholics who, though a lower-middle income class, built and paid for a system of parochial schools, costing them three-quarters of a billion dollars a year, that compares favorably with the public schools — even while a substantial proportion of their state and local taxes was spent to make education "free" for oth-er people's children. Again, one might point to the rise in the number of those who send their children to private schools, which indicates an increasing demand and ability to pay for private schooling; for in 1950, one in seven attended private schools, in 1960, one in 5.7, and if extrapolation is legitimate, one in four will attend private schools in 1970.

We have, I think, answered the first question: Why do we need schools that are free? The answer is: we do not. Yet, practically, there is no real likelihood that people can be persuaded that it is desirable to leave to private initiative the demand for schooling. The reasons are easy to see: conservative resistance to any kind of change, insufficient attraction to exercise of individual choice, the educationist lobby, egalitarianism, and the failure to see that even though public education is "free," it must be paid for.

But even more important than all this is the fear that the great bulk of parents would not see the advantages of paying for at least as much schooling as their children receive now, and we should have a relatively uneducated American populace, with all the disadvantages this entails. But, one might answer, although parents now take schooling as a matter of course and give it little attention, under the proposal referred to, parental attitudes, interest, and sense of responsibility, would be greatly strengthened and developed. Consider an analogy: suppose that 50 years ago children's clothing had been made a "free" commodity, given regularly to children out of government warehouses. Suppose that this had become institutionalized and a part of our American way of life. Now consider the difficulty one would have today in seeing that parents could be led to take an interest in clothing their children; the difficulty of convincing people that the principle of equal opportunity would not be irreparably damaged if rich parents purchased better clothing for their children than the poor could afford for *their* children; the difficulty of conservative inertia; the difficulty of arousing parents to

---

[1] Cf. J. C. DeHaven, *Some Economic Features of Public Education,* p. 3ff. H. R. Bowen points out that price exclusion (unwillingness to pay for some benefit leads to exclusion from its use) is as impractical for the social benefits of education as for the benefits of national defense. *Toward Social Economy* (New York: Rinehart, 1948), pp. 172-3.

[2] Saul Padover, *Jefferson* (New York: Harcourt, Brace, 1952), p. 196.

404

overcome their distaste for assuming greater responsibility than before; the difficulty of making people see that "free" clothing must be paid for; etc.[3]

TO SUM UP: a system of schools that are non-free (and non-public) is impractical. But now our second question: Suppose our schools were "free" but not "public," what would be the consequences? At present the great majority of our schools are free and public. Let us consider the nature and consequences of a system in which the majority of our schools were free but not public, a system in which *government subsidizes the demand for but not the supply of education,* a system in which government pays the costs of but does not supply or run schools. Such a system is not really a new sort of thing; in most of the countries of Western Europe, schooling is at least partly free and at most only partly administered publicly. And in the United States we have witnessed an application of free but non-public schooling in the G.I. Bill, under which a veteran attends, if he wishes, the private school of his choice, the costs of schooling being met out of public tax funds.

One might justify such a proposal by arguing this way: parents are compelled by law to send their children to school. If the capacities of parents to obey this law are unequal, provision should be made to equalize these capacities. But parents are relevantly unequal in respect of their ability to pay for schooling. So, because some of the benefits of educating children accrue to society as a "neighborhood effect," in the form of more cultured, more productive citizens, society may find it to its interests to raise money to pay for the education of children through taxation.[4]

Now, the crucial considerations in arranging for the distribution of the edu-

---

[3] Adapted from O. B. Johannsen, *Private Schools for All* (1959), p. 7.

[4] Cf. W. Gorman, "A Case of Distributive Justice," in Robert Gordis, *et al., Religion and the Schools* (New York: The Fund for the Republic, 1959).

cational funds are these two: first, when the government distributes goods, the distribution should be made impartially and equally to all in such a way that no irrelevant differentiating criteria such as those of race, color, or creed be made excluding conditions; second, the distribution should be made in accordance with the principle of subsidiarity, the principle that the individual should be permitted to do for himself whatever he alone or in conjunction with like-minded people can do as well or nearly as well as some agency of government can. This is to say that acceptance of government control over the use of these funds should not be made an enabling condition for the very reception of the funds. Thus, those parents who give evidence of ability to reach the ends for which the compulsory law was instituted, either by educating their own children or delegating this function to a qualified schoolmaster in a non-government school, should not be excluded from sharing in the tax funds raised to guarantee an educated population. (Is there any reason to believe that a government-appointed schoolmaster is a better educator than a schoolmaster who has won the support of the parents whose children he offers to educate?)

One way of institutionalizing the distribution of an educational fund is by means of a "voucher" system. Suppose individual parents, in California let us say, were given a "voucher," a certificate, for a certain amount (say $400, which is somewhat less than the normal per-pupil cost in California per year) which could be "spent" only by offering it as full or partial payment for schooling to a schoolmaster, who could then receive cash for it out of local and state tax funds. (Of course, in small, relatively isolated communities, the small size of the educational-consumer public might offer little scope for competition— and so *the* one school would likely remain "public.") Suppose, too, that the majority of parents exercise their option of sending their children to a private school of their choice. What would be the consequences of a sort of "G.I. Bill"

405

for all children down at the elementary and secondary levels?[5]

The first and perhaps most important consequence is that really effective control over the education of the child would be in the hands of his parents. Most parents who have $400 school vouchers to spend would give at least as much attention to choosing a school for their child (supplementing the voucher with money directly out of pocket, perhaps[6]) as they do to choosing a family automobile. And just as parents are now responsible for choosing food, clothing, and shelter for their children, so then they would be responsible for choosing the food, clothing, shelter, and *education* of their children. Of course, not all parents are now expert dieticians but they can and do come to know, and choose, perhaps with the expert advice and instruction of Dr. Spock and others, appropriate food for their children; so, too, parents could and would come to know, and choose, perhaps with expert advice and instruction, appropriate education for their children. Few are expert in medicine, but a man wants to choose his own doctor, even though he does not expect to tell the doctor what to do.

First, then, there is the advantage of extending, in an important way, the scope of parental free choice; the other side of the coin is the elimination of the possibility of dangerous public control, of the power of the state to dominate the formation of the minds of the young.[7] *Only* if there were: first, truly scientific answers to educational problems; and second, no danger that the authority to whom education is entrusted would fail to apply these answers; and third, no possibility of disagreement about what kind of human being is desirable — *only* if all these conditions were met might we not fear to entrust this power over the young to the state. But scientfic answers to educational problems, tested objectively, are not available;[8] past and recent history does not encourage us to trust the state without reservation; and there is a good deal of disagreement at all levels about what sort of human being is ideal. The recent development and growth of psychological and psycho-pharmacological techniques which increase our power to mould men's minds deliberately, should —at least when we're in a 1984 mood— lead us to be concerned about the temptation to make use of these newly found powers. Consider too the possibilities of television—the possibility of an expanding uniformity, the spectre of a single All-Informing Eye teaching all the children of the land. Consider the possibilities of psychic "conditioning," already feasible through "counseling and guidance." In a unified public school system the temptation to use these new powers might conceivably sooner or later prove irresistible; and there is reason to want a disinterested institution to act as an impartial protector of men's minds against the use of such powers—a function government at its various levels could perform were it not committed, through an often powerful educational bureaucracy, to the application of the then currently most fashionable educa-

406

[5] Cf. esp. Milton Friedman, "The Role of Government in Education," in Robert A. Solo, ed., *Economics and the Public Interest* (New Brunswick: Rutgers University Press, 1955), and Milton Friedman, *Capitalism and Freedom* (Chicago: University of Chicago Press, 1962), ch. 7; and V. Blum, *Freedom of Choice in Education* (New York: Macmillan, 1958).

[6] C. S. Benson, *The Economics of Public Education* (Boston: Houghton Mifflin, 1961), p. 324: "There is evidence to show that high expenditures on education offer real, not fictitious, improvements in quality, and that there is no tendency for quality to level off as the support level goes up." See also Lorne H. Woollatt, *The Cost-Quality Relationship on the Growing Edge* (New York: Bureau of Publications, Teachers College, Columbia University, 1949).

[7] Cf. Arnold J. Toynbee, *Study of History* (London: Oxford University Press, 1934), Vol. IV, pp. 196-97. The degree of seriousness of the danger is no doubt a function of the degree of unified federal control. The federal government in the United States, according to Clayton D. Hutchins of the U. S. Office of Education, is currently spending $2.5 billion annually to support educational programs of various sorts.

[8] It is perhaps worth noting that we should be grateful that the firing of the Russian Sputnik shook the confidence of educators and their clients alike that educational problems were, in the main, licked.

tional curriculum, methods, and techniques.[9] Most obviously, in a system in which almost all schools are private there would be less danger of domination by the "scientific" theories of some one group of educators.

Another consequence of the introduction of the voucher-system would be the relegation of the religious-school problem from the area of political decision to the area of private decision. The problem of paying for their religious-schools is giving Catholics, and others, increasingly great concern. They pay the whole cost of their own schools and a share of the far more expensive schooling of their neighbors' children; and costs are rising on the local, state, and federal levels. This leads Catholics to ask for public funds of one kind or another to help ease the burden they have voluntarily adopted. Unless we can arrive at some substantially unanimous agreement on how to resolve this conflict, we shall likely enter a period of religious-versus-secular school conflict like that indigenous to France for generations.

It is difficult to see, given the mainly-public school system, a way out of this political and social predicament. People might sooner or later be brought to find it desirable to assist the parochial schools in a substantial way on grounds of self-interest, on the grounds that anyone who does a fairly decent job of educating the young serves the interests of the rest of the citizenry as a whole. But if more state aid were given, would not a degree of government control follow, such that, for example, an atheist or a Zen Buddhist would be effectively able to demand admission for his child at a tax-supported parochial school and be effectively able to demand that no religious doctrine be taught his child?

Some Catholics claim that they are being (and have been for over 100 years) treated unjustly according to the canons of "distributive justice." They are being "penalized financially for the exercise of their constitutional rights," so that they are not "free" to send their chil-

dren to parochial schools, since "freedom at a price is not freedom." It appears to me that there is some basis for this sort of claim, though perhaps the language of "penalized" and "freedom" is somewhat queer. Let us use an analogy. Suppose "the government" felt it necessary to raise the level of consumption of sweets by the population. And suppose that instead of handing out vouchers for the purchase of sweets, it decided to hand out chocolate bars to all who applied. And suppose also that some people preferred jelly beans to chocolate bars, but, since the government does not offer "free" jelly beans, those who prefer jelly beans must purchase them privately. This would presumably constitute a case of government's "penalizing" those who prefer jelly beans, since the jelly bean eaters would be, in their own chosen way, seeing to it that their own consumption of sweets was raised. But if the charges of the jelly bean eaters and the Catholics be allowed, many other similar charges must be allowed. For socialized medicine, socialized housing, and the like, are as objectionable as are socialized schooling and socialized candy distribution: all entail practical limitations on the exercise of choice among alternative means to the same goal. This is to say that if I object to living in a particular housing project — but would qualify if I wished to live there — then I have a right in distributive justice to government support for the sort of housing I prefer (or "need"). And if I have a right to publicly supported recreation facilities, but happen to prefer Disneyland to Yosemite, I have a right in distributive justice to spend "my share" in Disneyland. Thus any government "welfare" measure, unless it meets with absolutely unanimous agreement in every detail, may be said to limit freedom, to "penalize" those who would choose otherwise.

But if the school-system were mainly private, it is quite likely that the reality of effective parental control in this area would be quite as important to most Protestants, and others, as to Catholics. Though both Catholics and Protestants

9 Cf. F. A. Hayek, *The Constitution of Liberty* (Chicago: University of Chicago Press, 1960), pp. 380-81.

realize that, given our government public school system, the application of the least-possible-common-denominator principle is imperative in the field of religion and morality, many Protestants and others would exercise their option in a mainly-private system by choosing a school that teaches a preferred religion and morality. For, of course, schools catering to the demand for religious, or irreligious, training would be developed in numbers approximating effective market desire for them — a development which displeases no one but those who are convinced that parents should be permitted no alternative to that offered by the wisdom of majority decision.

Another development to be anticipated would make Catholics stand out in the crowd less than they do at present. The parochial school system would be weakened and, at least in the long run, would tend to break down. For the parochial school, which is tied to a parish church in respect of location, size, and administration would prove to be less efficient in meeting the demands of Catholic parents than would the more adaptable private school. Catholic religious teachers would of course make the most efficient use of their limited numbers by concentrating on the teaching of religion and related subjects, since if the voucher system were introduced, only one of three schools serving Catholics could be wholly staffed by religious teachers.

And now, as one analyst of this proposal has put it, to go from the Gordian Knot of the church-related school problem to the Augean Stables of the school segregation issue. What would be the effects of the introduction of the voucher plan on the segregation issue?[10]

At the moment, the segregation issue is being decided on the basis of majority wishes: the majority of people in the United States have opted for compulsory integration; the majority of people in some Southern states have opted for compulsory segregation. It is characteristic of activities that depend on political decisions that if even the smallest change is to be made peacefully, it is necessary to convince a political majority to favor making the desired political decision. Now those who are interested in the fullest possible measure of human freedom find themselves in a dilemma when asked to choose between compulsory segregation and compulsory integration. But is such a choice necessary? Not under the voucher system, which would obviate such a choice. Under this system there would be white schools, and Negro schools, and mixed schools, in numbers approximating the desires of various elements of the local population. There would be no coercion; and for those who are willing to permit free speech and other civil rights even to those with whom they disagree, this is an important value.

There are no integrated grade or high schools in Alabama. It is therefore difficult to show the majority of Alabamans that discrimination solely on the basis of color is quite unreasonable. But under the voucher system those parents in Alabama, and of course there are some, who believe that the presence of an intelligent Negro child in class with their children will not only fail to lower but will likely improve the class standard, have no effective way of demonstrating their preference. Under the voucher system it would be a matter of convincing one's next door neighbors. It would not be unreasonable to expect that if the voucher system were introduced, there would be, overnight as it were, substantially more integration in the South than can be anticipated *by the use of coercion,* which clearly tends to strengthen opposition and prejudice.[11]

10 For an excellent analysis, cf. Friedman, *op. cit.;* and for an interesting sketch of the philosophy behind, and the working of, the "Virginia Plan," see Leon Dure, "The New Southern Response: Anatomy of Two Freedoms," *Georgia Review,* Vol. XV, No. 4, 1961, and his "Individual Freedom v. 'State Action,'" *Virginia Quarterly Review,* Summer, 1962; for criticism of the plan see H. C. Dillard, "Freedom of Choice and Democratic Values," in the same issue of *VQR.* For data on the working of the plan, see "The Freedom of Education Plan," in *The Reporter,* Oct. 11, 1962.

11 "Resegregation," according to the estimates of some Southern educators, has brought about a state of affairs in which there are more all-Negro schools in the South now than there were

The appropriate method of eradicating prejudice is not for the majority to coerce the minority, but for one person to use rational persuasion and moral suasion to convince another that the latter's position is wrong-headed and the fruit of prejudice. I deplore segregation and racial prejudice, but it is not, in my view, the function of government to force the individual to act in accordance with my or anyone else's views—whether about racial prejudice or whom to vote for—so long as he does not employ violence and physical coercion on others.

Further, the *de facto* segregation of Negroes and others in public schools by reason of the stratification of residential areas would tend to diminish when like-minded people, whether white or black, offered their vouchers to a schoolmaster who had demonstrated his ability to provide just the sort of education *these* parents want for their children.

With regard to the prospective consequences of the proposed competitive school-master system in improving school standards, one can be brief: "monopolies do not, whether in manufacturing, services, *or education,* provide incentives for increasing productivity or quality;"[12] under the voucher system

the forces of competition between school-masters would increase educational quality, variety, and innovation. Even if the prediction that the number of government schools would in time diminish drastically is wrong, the competition of private schools would offer the individual parent quite an effective way of expressing disapproval of what was done in some public school, namely by withdrawing his voucher from one schoolmaster and giving it to another.[13] At present, an individual parent can express disapproval only as one of perhaps 50,000 or 100,000 or 1,000,000 voters for a school board, and has ordinarily little power to change educational policy which offers but one standard model for a community.[14] The forces of competition would give parents the sort of schooling they want for their children: there would be schools which offer traditional academic training and schools which emphasize science, or the core curriculum, or modern languages, etc., in numbers approximating the proportions of those who want such education for their children; and if a parent wanted to send his child to a school for pickpockets, a law enforcing minimum standards, as we have today for private schools, would eliminate such an obviously unwise choice.

But, one might ask, if parents are faced with so wide a range of schools to choose from, how will they know which is best for their child? How will they make an intelligent, responsible choice? The answer is, of course, that they will not always know with certitude, as they do not now know precisely what quan-

409

---

before the U. S. Supreme Court's desegregation decision of 1954 — the desegregation order has led to less mixing of races than before. Cf. *U. S. News and World Report,* December 4, 1961, pp. 86-7.

[12] DeHaven, *op. cit.;* in Benson's opinion: "there is a lack of genuine diversity in educational programs and practices." But ". . . without diversity it is extremely difficult to test whether some innovation in method or staffing pattern is efficient. . . . Lack of diversity would seem to prevail on two counts. First . . . the public schools are local monopolies and hence cannot in fairness make any kind of radical change which would be repellent to some group of parents. Second, invention and innovation normally cost money. They are processes involving risk, in the sense that the 'payoff' is uncertain, with respect to whether any good thing will occur, and, if so, *when* it will occur. It follows that expenditures on development, broadly considered, are hard to defend against the attacks of the zealous skeptic. But school authorities, as we have said, must continually be ready to defend expenditures against the opposition (a) of non-parents and (b) of parents who are quite satisfied with the existing program." Benson, *op. cit.,* pp. 326-27.

[13] One may now go to the principal or to the superintendent with complaints, but as school districts become larger, access to the administrator becomes more and more difficult. And as Benson says, ". . . physical access to the office of the administrator is not equivalent to access to the man." *Ibid.,* p. 228.

[14] "He can work through cumbrous political channels to promote change. As anyone who is familiar with schools knows, change will be slow. There is reason to suspect that change in public schools is necessarily slow by the fact of public operation. In short, measurable change will occur only after the parent's child has passed beyond that part of the program with which the parent was dissatisfied." *Ibid.,* p. 325.

tity of what food, or which toy, or which musical instrument, is best for their child; but, of course, in all these latter cases, expert advice and the experience of others is available, and so also would it be with respect to schooling. If a man wanted a new car, it would take less of his time and attention if there were only one model in one make offered, but he would probably not find that car satisfying his desires or serving his purposes so well as one he chooses after examining a number of models in a number of makes. The myth that parents do not know anything about their own children, and would not act on this knowledge if they did, is an educationist's myth, as fanciful and unreal as any ever dreamed of; but few myths are held and defended with greater vigor.

Further, educational economists tell us that the size and location of most public schools, based as they are on political considerations, are uneconomic and inefficient.[15] Others go on to tell us that desirable innovations find their way into the school, if they ever do, only after an unconscionably long time.[16] A mainly-private school system, based at least in part on profit, would tend to correct such manifestations of head-in-the-sand conservatism. It is characteristic of a monopoly, most particularly of a government-administered monopoly such as the public-school system, that stagnation sets in. (At the elementary and secondary levels, private schools, because of their higher costs and fear of being out of step, offer no effective competition.)

What would be the effect of such a program on the teacher? Better teachers would, under such a system, receive higher pay not based entirely on seniority and post-graduate "education" credits; there would, furthermore, be differential pay scales for different subjects, so as to make it possible to hire and retain those teachers, especially in the pure sciences, who are well qualified to teach.

A final advantage of the voucher sys-

tem is described by C. S. Benson, the Harvard educational economist:

> Further, it would be possible for a family to adjust its expenditures somewhat in accordance with the needs of its different children, e.g., unusually bright or slow children might be provided with special programs in schools that offered such work. It would be possible, furthermore, for a family voluntarily to increase its expenditures on elementary and secondary education at the time when it enjoyed an increase in income. For instance, suppose a head of a household receives a $500 increment in annual earnings, after taxes. If the family had already attained a reasonably comfortable standard of living, it might wish to spend as much as $250 of this gain on education. A child might be shifted, say, from a lower-cost to a higher-cost private school. Under our present system, however, there is no good way for this $250 to be spent on elementary and secondary education. Even the total increase in income would not pay for tuition in a good private school, and it would certainly not represent the cost of changing residence to a better school district. Instead of spending it on elementary or secondary education, the prudent family might put the sum aside for college education. Of course, school taxes might go up, but they would be unlikely to increase by $250 in a year. In short, certain families might want to use part of their gains in income for the purpose of education in amounts substantially in excess of an annual rise in tax rates, provided they thought that they were getting what they wanted in education. The present system does not have a place for this gradual, voluntary rise in educational expenditures.[17]

WE HAVE SEEN now the desirable consequences. But are there undesirable consequences? Let us see. The main objection now made against private schools is that they are divisive. This charge has certainly never been documented, but it is a common theme of educationists, who speak of private schools as "inherently undemocratic" by contrast with the "democratic public school system." Dr. James B. Conant

---

15 Cf. Procter Thomson, "Free Public Education," *School Review*, 1955.

16 Cf. Paul R. Mort and Francis G. Cornell, *Adaptability of Public School Systems* (New York: Teachers College, Columbia University, 1938).

---

17 Benson, *op. cit.*, pp. 327-28.

410

has said, "To my mind our schools should serve all creeds." (Conant's statement can mean either: (1) all people should go to the public schools, whether they are satisfied with them or not; or (2) all people should be satisfied with the public schools.) He goes on, "the greater the proportion of our youth who attend independent schools, the greater the threat to our **democratic unity.**"

The nature of a desirable democratic unity is certainly difficult to assess, being of not-too-much, not-too-little variety: we want "unity," but not "conformity;" we want "differentiation," but not "divisiveness." And how much of a "threat to democratic unity" should we permit? Should these "threats" be absolutely prohibited? After all, free speech is divisive; freedom of the press is divisive; political democracy itself, with candidates who actually compete against each other, is divisive.

It is generally accepted that in any stable society there must be a set of common ideas and assumptions without which even rational discussion and persuasion is impossible; and that without commonly held moral beliefs, maintenance of order will require extreme coercion. On the other hand, *it seems reasonable to expect that the majority opinion which in a limited area guides democratic government should, in order to avoid circularity and stagnation, be independent of the control of government in its formation.* Otherwise, there will be a tendency to prevent a minority from trying to alter majority opinion—and to do this is to cut the roots of progress, to destroy the principle of minority opposition by which civilization has grown and spread. ". . .the conception that government should be guided by majority opinion makes sense only if that opinion is independent of government. The idea of democracy rests on the belief that the view which will direct government emerges from an *independent* and spontaneous process. It requires therefore the existence of a large sphere independent of majority control in which the opinions of individuals are formed."[18] Consider an ex-

ample: the judgment of the desirability of the United States' maintaining its membership in the United Nations or in NATO or in SEATO is a judgment that should be made, no doubt, on majority grounds. But suppose a measure of government control such that the great majority of children are *indoctrinated* to hold that membership in the UN, NATO, SEATO, etc., is in the best interests of the U. S. The majority at some one moment could use a unified public school system to impose its position on the minds of the young; there would be no real possibility of change, even if conditions change.[19]

Applying these principles to the controversy over the private schools as a threat to democratic unity, and assuming that it is generally true that schools are a mirror of society, it follows that, unless substantial evidence is forthcoming, unless it could somehow be shown that private schools will not reflect parents' wishes or that parents will wish to train their children in un-American ways, there may be grounds for wondering, but no grounds for acting as though private schools are a threat to desirable democratic unity. Since there are far more historical precedents for being careful to avoid a school system that is nationally controlled, one should want to make very sure that a minority having doubts about the wisdom of a majority decision is not to be denied an opportunity to use rational discussion and persuasion to alter the conviction of the majority. This may appear to be an exaggeration, but consider an editorial in the *New Republic* (March 20, 1960) which informs us that "to accept the principle of equal support of public and private schools out of public funds is to abandon *the mission of the state* . . . the State is committed to exerting a *secular, unifying egalitarian* force."

411

[18] Hayek, *op. cit.,* p. 109.

[19] Cf. F. Lilge, "The Politicizing of Educational Theory," *Ethics,* April, 1962; and C. Bay says: "It is the ability to resist manipulation I wish to see increased, and this ability can best be developed in institutions in which not impartiality but controversy is fostered. . . . On this score I swear to the wisdom of Socrates." *The Structure of Freedom* (Stanford: Stanford University Press, 1958), p. 98.

This appears to me very like the analysis by John Stuart Mill of "state education," which, however, he deplores:

That the whole or any large part of the education of the people should be in State hands, I go as far as anyone in deprecating. All that has been said of the importance of individuality of character, and diversity of opinions and modes of conduct, involves, as of the same unspeakable importance, diversity of education. A general State education is a mere contrivance for moulding people to be exactly like one another; and as the mould in which it casts them is that which pleases the predominant power of the government, whether this be a monarch, a priesthood, an aristocrat, or the majority of the existing generation; in proportion as it is efficient and successful, it establishes a despotism over the mind, leading by natural tendency to one over the body. An education established and controlled by the state should only exist, if it exists at all, as one among many competing experiments, carried on for the purpose of example and stimulus, to keep the others up to a certain standard of excellence.[20]

In sum, a mainly-private school system seems to destroy the balance between democratic unity and democratic diversity as judged by the rule-of-thumb: avoid what tends to make rational discussion more difficult. Thomas Gilby, O. P., has said, "Civilization is formed by men locked together in argument. From this dialogue the community becomes a political community." There is no evidence that a school system where parents have a choice between alternative types of schooling, will fail to mirror our society as it is, or make rational discussion more difficult. "It is unlikely that private demand will purchase, or that private supply will offer, kinds of education which threaten or even marginally undermine the beliefs we hold and the knowledge and skills we deem essential. . . . An enterprise which emphasized instruction in the Koran or the Communist Manifesto would be unlikely to be established or, if established, to endure."[21]

Another objection is raised by Benson:

The compelling argument for maintaining the present pattern of public operation is, we believe, found in the imperative of social mobility. In this country (in Dr. Conant's words) there is a "devotion to the ideals of equality of opportunity and equality of status." The *ideal that every child have an equal start in life* is impossible of close attainment, but the public schools have been the major instrumentality for moving as far as we have toward that goal. It seems clear, moreover, that quality of education is becoming a more important determinant than before of an individual's income and status. The justification for public *operation* of the schools rests, then, on the control of the public school system in preserving social mobility.[22]

This objection is quite obviously based on the egalitarian assumption that everyone should have an equal start, and takes the dog-in-the-manger attitude that if everyone cannot have the better, then no one shall. It is not said that some would receive a worse education than any do now, but rather that not all would benefit to the same degree. (Under the voucher system, the exchange value of vouchers would differ from community to community, but there is no reason to believe that there would be a wider range of expenditure than exists now: in 1959-60, the per-pupil cost in Arkansas was $191, but was almost three times that amount, $559, in New York.) Some parents would supplement the voucher directly out of their own pockets, and thus give their children a better start in life.[23] Egalitarians, however, look at matters this way: if a child is born having great *natural* talents, well and good—this is *natural*—and he can eventually develop and use these talents for the common welfare. Yet the useful qualities which are welcomed when a

---

20 John Stuart Mill, *On Liberty* (New York: Appleton-Century-Crofts, 1947), p. 108.

21 Thomson, *op. cit.*

22 Benson, "Rebuttal," *op. cit.*, pp. 328-29. First italics mine.

23 The educational tax level would tend to rise to the level at which those parents who constituted a majority of the whole population voting on educational funds would pay no additional subsidy to the schoolmaster.

412

result of a person's natural endowment are suspect when they are the result of circumstances such as a good home and intelligent parents. Of course, we believe that the family is so valuable because we believe that as a rule parents can prepare their children better for a satisfactory life than can anyone else. (If we did not believe this, we would likely follow the example of the Russians, who take children out of the family at a very early age and put them into State nurseries for the preferred moral and intellectual training to be got there.) But we seem not to be aware that "there is, indeed, good reason to think that there are some socially valuable qualities which will be rarely acquired in a single generation but which will generally be formed only by the continuous efforts of two or three." We are simply not willing to admit that "belonging to a particular family is part of the individual personality, that society is *made up* as much of *families* as of individuals, and that the transmission of the heritage of civilization within the family is as important a tool in man's striving towards better things as is the heredity of beneficial physical attributes."[24] It is as unreasonable to take away from parents a good chance of providing their children with a head-start in cultural and educational qualities as it would be to take away from parents the chance of providing their children with a head-start because they were given a finer moral training.

One might now reasonably ask: why is it that people so devoted to freedom as were our Founding Fathers did not develop a mainly-private school system? The answer is that of course no large-scale educational system was developed until the second third of the 19th century—and a *public*-school system was then developed for a number of reasons which have little or no application today: first, the scope of mass-immigration made defensible the concept of the public-school as a "melting-pot;" second, the very technical administrative difficulties of a publicly-supported private school system, of handing out vouchers to indi-

viduals, and checking their use, made such a system impractical (today, of course, an I.B.M. engineer could outline a rational approach to this problem on his day off); third, Catholics under the leadership of some bishops made the fatal mistake of fighting the school question as a Roman Catholic question rather than as a question of a desirable exercise of parental rights;[25] fourth, there was a measure of belief among the most influential Protestant bodies that public schools could be Christian though nonsectarian — a belief that proved unfounded, especially once the courts began, around the turn of the century, to defend minority rights in this sphere; fifth, the "natural monopoly" argument was much stronger in earlier days: a given locality can support only one school, and that had best be publicly administered and finally, the intellectuals of the day looked upon the Prussian public-school system as an ideal model.

UNDER THE SYSTEM proposed, whereby the financing of education is a government function but the educational institution itself is privately administered, what happens to higher education? According to Friedman and Hayek, we must first of all distinguish between three sorts of education beyond the high-school: *first*, education for leisure and leadership, or liberal education; *second*, vocational education offered in professional schools — those which train dentists, veterinarians, beauticians, etc.; *third*, advanced research at the "frontiers" of knowledge. Different things must be said of each, though it is often admittedly difficult to distinguish between them in practice.

What about college-level liberal arts education? Limited by the wealth of the community, a case for subsidizing the demand for this sort of education can be made along the same lines as the case for subsidizing the demand for elementary and secondary education —

413

---

[24] Hayek, *op. cit.*, p. 90.

[25] Cf. Zachariah Montgomery, *"The School Question"* (Washington: Gibson Bros., Printers, 1886), esp. p. 45 ff.

Page Thirteen

though, of course, the case for financing education for all at some lower level is stronger than it is at a more advanced level. Here the student's family would be given a voucher for a limited sum, which could be supplemented by the family's own resources, scholarships, etc.—a sort of G.I. Bill extended to all. There would tend to be fewer if any State administered liberal arts schools remaining. And the limitations of this program would be imposed by the limitations of the material and human resources of the community.

What should be the functions of the State with respect to vocational education? Let us look a little more closely at, say, the training of a dentist. A young man is attracted by the material (and, conceivably, non-material) rewards of dentistry. He must invest a certain number of years, and a certain amount of money, but when he gets his certification, he gains the rewards of his investment. As things now are, it is usually a great deal easier for the wealthy young man to invest the requisite time and money; it would appear desirable that loans (analogous to equity capital) be made available, in the absence of private investors, by some federal institution which could offset this advantage the wealthy have; this would tend to increase competition and promote the full development of human resources. Note that it is *loans,* not gifts, which are in issue — for since the major part of the advantages of such professional education (those which increase the individual's economic productivity) accrue directly to the individual in greater earning power, it is undesirable that government make this sort of education free, for that would tend to promote over-investment in human beings.

What, finally, should be the functions of the State with respect to advanced research in all the fields of knowledge? It is clear that major contributions to knowledge are made at advanced-research institutions — universities which provide education as a by-product of research. Unlike the benefits which training in dentistry confers, the benefits which the research-scholar's work produces do not accrue to him personally. "The benefits that a community receives from its scientists and scholars cannot be measured by the price at which these men *sell* their particular services, since much of their contribution becomes freely available to all."[26] Financing such research may be a desirable function for government when private resources are not wholly adequate. And here it is a matter of a gift to an institution or to an individual, since success in this field does not usually bring proportional financial returns to the institutions or individual researchers.

TO TURN TO the immediately practical order, what chance does the voucher plan have of achieving recognition and approval? There are some formidable obstacles, most notably the roadblock the educationists are likely to erect in the way of a plan which would do so much to weaken their power and prestige. As Albert Lynd wrote a few years ago, "The educationists have copper-riveted one of the neatest bureaucratic machines ever invented by any professional group in any country since the priesthood of ancient Egypt." Then consider the difficulty of rousing the interest of the 20th-century-liberal intellectuals, who concern themselves with some sorts of infringements of individual liberty but favor over and over again increasing the role of government *vis-a-vis* individual initiative — though if this group ever came down on the side of effective parental choice, the battle would be over. And conservatives may be of two minds: opposition to innovation and change will struggle with the desire to roll back the influence of government in an important area of national life. Of course, both Catholics and Protestants could be expected to approve on the grounds that an extension of parental initiative is desirable; but some Protestants would dislike the idea that Catholics would no longer be at a financial disadvantage. Negroes would have good reason to favor the plan if they

26 Hayek, *op. cit.,* p. 283.

414

were shown that their status would gradually improve, but the fact that the plan was first introduced in the South is a strike against it; and they might prefer seeing coercion used on their side for a change.

There are, however, two quite hopeful straws in the wind: first, the current interest in Gov. Nelson Rockefeller's "scholar incentive program" to strengthen the private colleges and universities in New York, and second, the interest in strengthening private schools evidenced by the number of congressional bills (163 from 1953 to 1960) for reducing taxes by an amount proportionate to tuition costs. Further, since the voucher plan is quite open to being introduced gradually on the local level, and since costs are rising, economy — attainable by giving as an alternative to public schooling a voucher for an amount less than estimated public school costs—may offer an additional motive for its introduction, at least in those areas where Catholics are not numerous.

To conclude, it may be that the current debates over our various educational problems in the United States will lead increasing numbers to consider seriously proposals like the voucher-system, systems which remove most educational choice from the sphere of yes-or-no political decision. The test of the desirability of considering such systems is not speedy enactment but the contribution they make to orderly thinking about basic issues of educational policy. And perhaps what David Riesman has said in another context may prove to be the case here: "Radical and what were previously regarded as 'impossible' changes come about almost instantaneously once people discover that views they had previously regarded as unacceptable or idiosyncratic are in fact widely shared."[27]

---

[27] *Atlantic Monthly*, April, 1961, p. 43.

415

"Consumer Sovereignty" and the Law

BRUNO LEONI

CONTEMPORARY TECHNOLOGY has accustomed us to the manufacturing of the most varied things, and not only of things never previously produced or conceived, but also of those which in the not too distant past were produced but not *manufactured*, as, for instance, pre-fabricated houses, and the famous Liberty Ships which contributed so much to the victory of the Allies in the last war. With the help of technology, long and costly processes of production have been eliminated, costs reduced, and delivery dates accelerated, with increased satisfaction for the consumer, and, naturally, for the producer as well. These technological processes have, as has already been emphasized by many, posed a series of problems in other fields, by bringing about often radical changes in the social environment and even in our ways of thinking.

A widespread commonplace concerning contemporary culture is the position affirmed by — among others — the distinguished American jurist, W. Friedman, in his recent book, *Law in a Changing Society*:[1] namely, that technical progress has necessarily and directly entailed a profound revolution of legal institutions. In this age of space satellites and astronauts, we often hear it asked, how can we possibly limit ourselves to, say, the concepts inherited from the Romans on the subject of property or contractual obligations, and so on? In reality, however, the modifications of legal institutions through the agency of technical innovation are not so numerous nor so important as they seem; in any case, it is very doubtful, and surely at least debatable, that such innovations of themselves entail radical modifications of the institutions and relations which have ruled our societies for thousands of years. While, for example, the private ownership of property admittedly no longer reaches *usque ad sidera* in any country of the world, nevertheless, it still persists and fulfills its necessary role. In the same way, the word or signature given by telephoto, or any other ultra-modern method, serves the same necessary function that it has had for some millenia. The modern man who communicates by television and travels in jets is of the same flesh and blood as, is psychologically and physically similar to, his distant ancestors who communicated by voice and travelled in chariots and sailing ships.

But notwithstanding the relative stability of legal institutions, at least in the countries of the West, a noteworthy change has arisen during the last 150 years precisely *in the way in which people had for centuries, and even millenia, conceived the nature, origin and functions of the law.*

Bruno Leoni is a Professor of Jurisprudence at the University of Pavia. He is the author of *Freedom and the Law,* and the editor of the scholarly journal *Il Politico.* This essay was translated from the Italian by William Campbell, an American student studying under Professor Leoni at Pavia.

[1] W. Friedman, *Law in a Changing Society* (London: Stevens, 1959).

The decline of the idea that the law is on the whole independent of the will of the rulers, and that it cannot be identified immediately and completely with the laws and decrees emanating from time to time from the holders of political power, is a most striking development, for its implications no less than for its diffusion in almost all societies in the contemporary period.[2] Strangely enough, this development — p e r h a p s through the continuity and gradualness with which it has taken place since the beginning of the last century — has seemed so natural, especially in Europe, that very few scholars up to now have addressed themselves to the task of considering it in its whole import or have dedicated to it the attention, and, I would wish to add, the *apprehensiveness*, that it deserves.

If only one word had to be used to define this widespread change in the idea of the law, I would say that according to the man on the street the law today is something which must be *manufactured*, or even *pre-fabricated*. That is, it is something produced with the minimum of time and effort judged necessary, according to plans prepared in advance, by the "suitable" people in the "suitable" places (the national legislatures), and presented to those who must obey the laws. The latter people (we might say the "consumers," if the word were not misleading for reasons which we shall shortly see) do not have — or are thought not to have — any other role than that of using the product ready made for them, just as they use the automobile or the washing machine.

The production of the law today by other procedures would seem to many people slow, inadequate and imprecise. Habits, customs, judicial precedents and the opinions of experts in this matter were the classical instruments of the production of the law in classical Rome, in medieval and modern England, in the United States, and, notwithstanding some contrary appearances, in the majority of the countries of Europe until the compilation of the current legal codes, that is, generally speaking, until the beginning of the last century. But these instruments appear today, at least to the superficial glance of many, as outmoded tools of an "artisan" society, inadequate for the needs of a "rapid" civilization on the vast scale that we are familiar with today.

THE ANALOGY BETWEEN juridical "products" and the products of our technical and industrial civilization is not, however, so suitable as it appears at first glance. In fact, considered more attentively, it turns out to be wholly deceptive and false. A fundamental difference exists in the relationship, on the one hand, between the producers and consumers of the goods manufactured with the resources of industrial technique, and, on the other hand, between the "producers" and "consumers" of legal rules manufactured, even mass-produced, by the wielders of political power with the resources of legislative techniques.

In spite of every contrary appearance, the industrial productive process in the countries of the West is still originated and sustained by the initiative of private individuals — that is to say, by individuals who do not have at their disposal the police or the army to constrain the consumers to buy the products which these private individuals put on the market. "One dollar, one vote," describes very well the nature of that continuous process with which the consumer directs and dominates the conduct of the producers in the free market. While the latter study how to entice the consumer (and sometimes even how to deceive him), they know that in the final analysis they must serve the consumer, satisfy his will, and cater to his whim

417

---

[2] The phenomenon concerns not only the countries of continental Europe (where, as is well-known, the "will of the prince" has been repeatedly regarded as the fount of the law), but also the Anglo-Saxon countries, where it used to be maintained, at least up to the beginning of this century, and still is in part, that the "prince" (today we should say "parliament," and through it the government, when the parliament delegates to it the necessary powers) *is not so much the creator of the law as the guardian of justice*, which the judges administer in the prince's name, but in full independence of his personal will.

under penalty of going into the red, and thus having to cease their productive activity.

There is a radically different relation between the "producers" and "consumers" of the legal rules manufactured through the use of legislative technique. The vote of the "consumers" in this case is discontinuous, a circumstance arising from the fact that it can be given only at certain times and under certain conditions, with a meaning almost always empty or equivocal, and with effects not predicted, often unpredictable and frequently unwanted. We may also add that not all "consumers" can vote, whereas on the market even a five year old boy who has ten cents to buy himself an ice cream cone casts his "ballot." Further, there are always some voters who will find themselves in the minority of any political vote and despite every contrary electoral invention and device are destined purely and simply to *waste* their votes. To control the production of legislation, in this case, is for the "consumers," the people for whom the rules themselves are intended, an evidently hopeless job.

It is said that these differences between economic processes and legislative techniques are inevitable, and that it is therefore necessary to know how to resign oneself to them. Our civilization does not allow us to take into consideration the desires of all the electorate on the political level, the argument goes, and consequently political representation is the best substitute that can be offered us for that real "representation" which would otherwise be unfeasible. This position would make sense if the people for whom the laws are intended could control the production of these laws in no other way than through the institution of "representation." But it is exactly this claim—that there is no other way to produce law than through the institution of representation—which has to be demonstrated, since this technique of production of the law (legislation) reveals its grave inefficiency. It is the problem of defining "law" that must be entirely reconsidered and, in particular, the problem of whether the

law, and, especially the above-mentioned private law, can be "manufactured," as today a washing machine or automobile is manufactured. Might it not be, instead, that the law is something that evades the rules of industrial production and consumption, something not susceptible of being manufactured by a limited number of "entrepreneurs" for the use of everyone else?

One can cite the contemporary experience: the law of today which denies that of yesterday evening, and which will be superseded by that of tomorrow morning; the two thousand laws manufactured every year by 500 men in our own, as in other countries, without the majority of the citizens even knowing of the existence of these laws; the obviously ephemeral character of much legislative activity, owing to the transitory triumph of no less ephemeral majorities in parliaments; the consequent impossibility of the citizens making long-range plans which could take for granted the constancy of juridical rules; the equally serious consequence that the law of today can be the result (as frequently happens) of the oppressive design of a slender majority, or even of an effective *minority* (the "pressure groups," as they are called today), who tomorrow will see themselves oppressed in their turn by a new minority in the seats of power. All these are reasons for profound perplexity on the nature and the function of the law "manufactured" by the legislators who produce laws on a vast scale. This process of "production'" may seem to be equivalent to the techniques evolved for manufacturing industrial items, but, unlike the industrial sector, in the case of law there are actually very few reasons for preferring those techniques to the ancient methods of the "artisans" for the ascertainment and the "production" of the customary and judicial law.

Perhaps one day the common man will understand a truth with which he appeared to be instinctively acquainted in times not far distant from us, although they seem to fade more and more into the past. In reality, the law is something which is not pre-fabricated in some specially-designated place, by some specially-designated producer and with some pre-established technique. In much the same way, no followers of the artificial languages such as Esperanto and Volapuk have yet succeeded in finding a substitute for the language that we speak every day, which also is *not* prefabricated. The law is in the last analysis something which everyone makes every day with his behavior, his spontaneous acceptance and observance of the rules that everyone helps to establish, and finally, even if it seems paradoxical, with the disagreements themselves which eventually arise among the various individuals on the observance of these rules.

The consequences of this old but always valid conception of the law will not necessarily consist in the total abandonment of the "manufacturing" of the law. But certainly our law-factories will have to limit very much their "production," and renounce sooner or later (if the West is not destined to fall into servitude) many of their "products." Finally, "law-consumers" will take back their true function of being producers of their own laws or at least of those laws—and they are not few—whose production they would otherwise control but today cannot.

On the Premises
of Growth Economics

ISRAEL M. KIRZNER

THERE ARE FEW topics concerning which economists are currently more able to secure respectful public attention, than that of economic growth. "To foster a more rapid growth rate" has become an almost unquestioned goal of governments throughout the world. A very considerable fraction of the research efforts of economists is, and has been now for several years, directed to the problem of how this goal is to be achieved. The course of political and economic history in recent decades has focused both professional and lay attention upon the problem of growth and development, pushing out of the limelight even such long-time favorites as the problem of economic stability. Elections have revolved around economic growth, commencement day orators, columnists and editorial writers consider the topic suitable grist for their mills, and books on this supposedly esoteric subject have become popularly accepted as fare for the masses.

There are a number of points of view from which this preoccupation with growth and development appears to be based on misconception and misunderstanding. This article is concerned with the dangers which this preoccupation must seem to imply for all who are concerned with the maintenance of

Israel M. Kirzner is an Associate Professor of Economics in the School of Commerce at New York University. His published books are *The Economic Point of View* and *Market-Theory and the Price System*, just published by Van Nostrand.

individual liberties. We will analyze the growth problem in order to expose those fallacies in popular thinking on the subject that are responsible for the potential dangers to a free society arising out of this preoccupation. Many of these fallacies will be seen to have their counterparts in the writings of economists themselves; this is not entirely a matter for surprise, but in any event makes our task no less pressing.

That the popular growth preoccupation carries with it implications that must seem menacing to the individualist, hardly needs elaborate demonstration. A growth policy invariably means a government policy. A growth or development policy may call, at worst, for a completely socialized economy; at best it implies a degree of regimentation forced upon an otherwise free enterprise system. Those preoccupied with growth generally believe, first, that growth is *per se* desirable; second, that the spontaneous growth of a market economy is likely to fall short of its full potential; and third, that this full potential may be achieved by appropriate governmental policies. Many even of those who have some understanding of the allocative functions of the price system, and who appreciate the market as an engine of social efficiency, are convinced that for growth purposes it is necessary to resort to governmental direction of economic activity. Like Keynes, they see no reason to suppose that the market seriously misemploys the factors of production which are in use;[1] perhaps, unlike Keynes, they see no reason even to believe that the market fails seriously in providing employment for all factors that can be efficiently employed, but they do nonetheless believe that the unhampered market fails to direct economic activity along the channels required for growth.[2] It is this belief that leads to the advocacy of programs of government activity that must necessarily impinge more or less heavily upon the range of opportunities open to individuals.

This article will focus critical attention on the analytical underpinnings of these beliefs, and will specifically deal with the following four aspects of the problem:

1) We will examine the view that distinguishes sharply between the current allocation of resources on the one hand, and the task of making provision for future growth on the other. It is this postulated distinction that is responsible for the possibility of a posture of simultaneous acceptance of the short-run allocational capabilities of the market, and distrust of its long-run propensities. At the same time it is to this alleged distinction that must be attributed the uncritical acceptance of growth as a goal appropriate to all situations.

2) We will examine the claim that long-run market-achieved results may be expected to be rendered inadequate because of what the economist calls "externalities" operating over time. We will examine both the claim itself, as well as the corollary drawn from it to the effect that, in consequence, government interference with the market may be desirable.

3) We will examine the uncritical use, in the growth literature, of national income (or related) figures as a means of judging and measuring the extent of achieved desirable growth.

4) We will subject to critical examination the welfare theory that is implicit in much of the current literature and discussion of growth. This theory will be scrutinized and held up for comparison with the more limited welfare propositions that are acceptable to economics seen as a science of human action, and to individualist-minded critics.

As we shall discover, these different aspects are intimately bound up with one another. Fallacies which we will expose in connection with one of these aspects, will be found to have great relevance to others. Nonetheless, for the sake of clarity, it appears expedient to deal with one matter at a time.

421

WE TURN TO the first aspect: that of the postulated distinction between the goals of short-run allocation, and long-run growth. This distinction is one that is made repeatedly in the economic literature. (It is not met with quite as frequently in lay writings, probably because the allocation problem itself is poorly understood in these writings.) Many textbooks of economics inform students that allocation and the provision of growth are *separate* functions of economic systems.[3] An outstanding British economist has declared that the study of growth, rather than of allocation of scarce resources among competing ends, should be seen as the core of economic science.[4] Certain economists suggest that the Soviet economy may not be successful in allocating its resources, but is successful in achieving

[1] See J. M. Keynes, *The General Theory of Employment, Interest, and Money* (New York: Harcourt, Brace, 1936), p. 379.

[2] For some recent examples of this widespread belief, see Karl de Schweinitz, "Free Enterprise in a Growth World," *Southern Economic Journal*, October, 1962; Stephen A. Marglin, "The Social Rate of Discount and the Optimal Rate of Investment," *Quarterly Journal of Economics*, February, 1963; review by Joan Robinson, *Economic Journal*, March, 1963, p. 125.

[3] For examples see Paul T. Homan, Albert Gailord Hart, and Arnold W. Sametz, *The Economic Order* (New York: Harcourt, Brace, 1958), p. 10.; George J. Stigler, *The Theory of Price* (New York: Macmillan, 1952), p. 4; Richard H. Leftwich, *The Price System and Resource Allocation* (New York: Holt, Rinehart & Winston, 1960), p. 20; see also Frank H. Knight, *The Economic Organization* (New York: Kelley, 1951), pp. 12-13.

[4] Peter J. D. Wiles, *Price, Cost and Output* (Oxford: Blackwell, 1956).

rapid growth.[5] And the list could easily be prolonged.

The rationale of the distinction is a simple one. At any one time an economy finds itself with given resources that set the ceiling on current productive potential. Over time the volume and composition of these resources may change, bringing about corresponding changes in the productive possibilities of the economy. Two separate problems are then distinguished. First, there is the problem of squeezing the greatest possible volume of current output, in value terms, from the currently available body of resources. This is the allocation problem. Second, there is the problem of ensuring that the change over time in the volume of available resources be so arranged as to permit rapid growth.

422

But the superficiality of the distinction can be shown with equal simplicity. Insofar as the change over time in the volume of resources can be consciously manipulated, this second problem reduces itself immediately to an aspect of the first one. A policy today for tomorrow's resource availability must mean, if it means anything at all, a choice with respect to current production with today's resources that will have an impact on the availability of resources tomorrow. Such a choice clearly involves a particular aspect of the general problem of the allocation of today's resources.

So the writers who profess to have confidence in the ability of the market to allocate resources, but not in the ability of the market to achieve a desirable growth rate, are open to the charge of inconsistency. For the very same price mechanism through which the market system allocates current resources as between the production of shoes and the production of sausages, is available for the allocation of resources as between the production of shoes for today and the production of shoe factories for the future. In fact, the market has developed a wide range of institutions through which intertemporal exchanges can be made between individuals, in this way achieving an allocation of resources over time. There seems no obvious reason to assume the market to be any less efficient in this allocative task than in its others. Writers who wish to express doubts on this score can do so more easily by diverting attention altogether from the intertemporal allocation of resources involved in a growth policy. Their pursuance of this course must appear distinctly dangerous to individualists, if only because this procedure masks the extent to which a governmental growth policy interferes with the pattern of allocation that would emerge from the actions of free individuals acting through the market.[6]

In particular, the spurious distinction between "allocation" and "growth" must be held largely responsible for the uncritical adoption of growth as a desirable goal in all situations. And here, as elsewhere, it is the duty of the economist to point out the *costs* associated with an otherwise desirable outcome — costs which may be of such a magnitude as to render the outcome no longer desirable at all. By implying that a growth policy is not at the same time a policy with respect to the allocation of current resources, growth writers are able to create the illusion that growth involves no cost — and is hence unquestionably desirable. By ignoring the costs required for growth, such writers are led to point accusing fingers at the performance of the market, charging that it does not achieve a sufficiently rapid growth rate. As soon as the growth problem is placed in proper perspective as an allocation problem, however, it is no longer at all obvious that growth *per se* is necessarily desirable. One no longer has the right, then, to condemn the market for not achieving a given rate of growth, when it is by no means clear *a priori* whether such a rate justifies the costs involved. In fact, the costs may be such that the most desirable goal turns out to be not

---

[5] J. M. Montias, "Planning with Material Balances in Soviet-Type Economies," *American Economic Review*, December, 1959, p. 982.

[6] See, e.g., the paper by de Schweinitz cited above, n. 2, for statements concerning the necessity to abrogate freedom for growth purposes.

to grow at all, or even to decline. The propensity to ignore the costs of achieving growth, therefore, can only facilitate government interference with the intertemporal choices of individuals through the market, by concealing this kind of cost of a growth policy altogether.

A MORE SOPHISTICATED rationalization for not relying on the market for growth purposes, is provided by economists concerned with external economies and diseconomies. Externalities have roughly to do: (a) with cases in which an individual is held back from undertaking a project the costs of which would be more than offset by the benefits accruing to the economy, because the project requires that while he shoulder all the costs himself, he share the benefits with many others; (b) with cases in which an individual is induced to undertake a project the costs of which fail to be offset by the accruing benefits, because he is able to escape some of these costs while reaping the full benefit for himself. Such possibilities would constitute instances in which private costs or benefits fail to coincide with "social" costs or benefits. Critics of the market economy have pointed to such cases as instances calling for government intervention to prevent an otherwise faulty allocation of "social resources."

A special example of the externalities argument occurs where a large project (or series of complementary projects), in which many people would participate jointly in both costs and benefits, would be of net benefit to each of them — but which no single individual wishes to embark upon by himself for fear that he might be left to bear all the costs while sharing the benefits with others. It is this kind of possibility that is frequently implied when the necessity for central direction of a developing economy is advocated. It is argued, that is, that the profitability of investment projects frequently hinges on the simultaneous undertaking by others of complementary investment projects. A railroad will extend a commuter line to the outskirts of a city only if a series of housing projects is expected to be built there; but the housing projects may in turn be contingent on the prospect of the commuter line extension.[7] In the words of one recent writer, "an atomistic market provides no means of breaking the deadlock: none of us is willing to invest unilaterally, each of us is prepared to if we all do."[8]

Nonetheless it is not clear that externalities and interdependence provide sufficient justification for persuading a society of free men to surrender significant degrees of their liberties. This position is based on two grounds. First, it can be shown that externalities do not render the market as impotent an engine of efficiency as might appear at first blush. Second, it can be argued that even where externalities cannot be overcome by the market process, the situation does not obviously justify coercion as a solution. We take up these two points in order.

Externalities may not seriously impair the efficiency of the market, because the market itself is able to exert forces capable of overcoming many of the obstacles raised by these externalities. The existence of interdependence sets up market forces making for conglomeration. External economies tend to become internalized by mergers of firms into larger units, or by voluntary cooperative activity.[9] This can be as true for long range projects as for immediate ones. So long as the size of the proposed projects remains relatively small as compared with the size of the economy as a whole, this process can be carried on without seriously affecting the competitiveness of the system, and provides, in effect, a market alternative to central planning of interrelated projects.

With special regard to intertemporal allocation, too, the market is capable of considerable flexibility in developing in-

---

[7] See J. de V. Graaff, *Theoretical Welfare Economics* (Cambridge: Cambridge University Press, 1957), p. 104.

[8] Marglin, *op. cit.*, p. 103.

[9] See Otto A. Davis and Andrew Whinston, "Externalities, Welfare, and the Theory of Games," *Journal of Political Economy*, June, 1962.

stitutions to cope with problems of interdependence. The relatively long-range plans of market participants can interact very powerfully through intertemporal markets of all types. Forward markets, bond markets, and securities exchanges are all market institutions through which the diverse expectations of prospective investors can become mutually adjusted.

Fully as important, however, as the recognition of the capabilities of the market in overcoming problems of interdependence is the recognition of the significance of problems of this kind that still remain unresolved. Such a recognition will show that it is far from obvious that discovery of unresolved problems of interdependence constitutes an automatic case for central direction. The fact is that consideration of the hypothetical case of interdependence frequently leads one to appreciate the obvious benefits that would accrue from concerted action, without a full understanding of the associated costs. It is easy to compare one situation in which the possibilities of concerted action are not exploited, with the situation in which they are exploited, and become convinced of the resulting gains. But it is also easy to do so without taking into account the fact that the organization of concerted action involves an unavoidable cost in terms of communication of knowledge, persuasion of individuals to participate, ensuring conformity with the agreement, and so forth. These costs must, in the nature of the problem, be borne if concerted action is to take place. If these costs can be covered by the gains, there is a market basis for expecting that the task of securing concerted action will be undertaken. If the market does *not* achieve such concerted action, either through merger or co-operative agreement, this is then *prima facie* evidence that these costs are excessive and render concerted action no longer desirable on a net basis.

Under such conditions, central direction in order to achieve concerted interdependent actions by a group, becomes visible in its true light. Central direction

is not a short-cut method of pushing aside the senseless obstacles to progress erected by stubborn externalities. Central direction is seen rather as involving costs of a particular kind, *alternative* to those other direct costs of achieving concerted action — costs that the market has pronounced to be so high as to make such group action not worthwhile. These particular costs involved in central direction include, of course, the liberties that must be sacrificed in the process. The argument that interdependence problems call for solution by central direction, like other such arguments, rests heavily on forgotten costs. *All* group action requires some degree of surrender of individual decision-making authority. The members of a golf club have given the club's governing body the power to make a range of decisions affecting the members. Where the market finds it unprofitable to form such clubs, this means that the costs of persuading potential members to make such a surrender are excessive and not justified by the anticipated result. Central direction does not avoid these costs; it merely substitutes its own. (After all, forcing people to join a club is not necessarily a desirable way of getting recalcitrant potential members to do what is good for them.)

A PIVOTAL POSITION is occupied in the literature on growth, especially that relating to proposals for a centrally-directed growth program, by the *measurement* of national product, or income, or similar quantities, through such aggregative measures as national income figures. These figures, perhaps adjusted to a per capita basis, are employed to show how slow our "growth rate" has been, and thus how unsuccessful our market economy has been in this respect. It is to be stressed that only because such tools of measurement are available for use, and are widely known (by, among others, journalists), is it that the concept of a "growth rate" has gained popularity. But for the ready availability of these aggregative measures, the growth concept itself might not have been able to have been crystallized sufficiently so as to capture public attention. These aggregative figures are used in growth discussions as reflecting the level of economic well-being of a nation. It will be pointed out in this section that the indiscriminate use of such figures in the growth literature has had harmful results for two distinct reasons: (a) such aggregative measures suffer from serious (and well-recognized) limitations in respect to their ability to serve as measurements of economic well-being; (b) the use of these measures, by ignoring the serious conceptual problems which they involve, helps to create the image of a "national" rate of growth, that corresponds to no rigorous theoretical concept whatsoever.

Gross National Product figures[10] measure the annual physical output of an economy valued at market prices. Placed on a per capita basis, historical figures are frequently used to measure achieved growth, which may then be held up for comparison with similar figures for other countries. It will be pointed out here that because national product figures can necessarily measure output defined only in a particular way, their use in this manner in the growth literature — usually as indices of rising standards of economic well-being — may be highly misleading. These limitations[11] do not preclude the figures from having great usefulness, properly used. The growth problem, however, is precisely one where these limitations (or at least some of them) become crucial. These figures measure the physical output in value terms, but it is well-known that the resulting figure cannot take into consideration many important items of output that do not flow through the market; and, in addition, the output figure makes no attempt to measure the enjoyment of leisure by the members of the econo-

my. This latter omission is, of course, not open to criticism, in a measure of output as such; but it does render the resulting figure quite misleading as a measure of economic growth, especially for comparative purposes. We are entitled to assume that the concept of economic growth, for the layman certainly, refers broadly to increases in economic well-being, rather than to increases in purely physical output. After all, as one writer has pointed out, an economy specializing in breeding rabbits could reach a very high growth rate, in physical terms.[12] But if this is granted, then a figure that reflects nothing of the leisure-dimension of well-being must seem highly distorted. Two economies growing at the same rate, according to these measurements, but which differ in the rate of addition to their leisure time, can surely in no wise be described as keeping pace with one another.[13]

The fact is that aggregate measures such as Gross National Product must necessarily fail to express sensitively many of the variations and refinements that must be taken into consideration in assessing the increase in over-all economic well-being. The current fashion of measuring growth in Gross National Product terms, and of proceeding to use the resulting calculations in policy contexts, cannot fail to exert powerful constraints on the direction of subsequent individual activities. Insofar as policy is deliberately directed to accelerating growth in terms of GNP, it must necessarily nudge the expansion of economic activity away from those dimensions of progress which find no expression in these aggregates, towards those which do. This may well, for example, encourage rabbit breeding at the expense of leisure, free individual preferences possibly being to the contrary notwithstanding.

Perhaps even more important, however, than the omissions that unavoid-

425

<hr>

[10] We use Gross National Product (GNP) figures for our purposes here, but other similar figures are open to similar criticism. Of course nothing in these remarks refers to the use of such figures with due awareness of their limitations.

[11] See P. T. Bauer and B. S. Yamey, *The Economics of Underdeveloped Countries* (Chicago: University of Chicago Press, 1957), Chapter II, for an excellent survey.

[12] See E. Malinvaud, "An Analogy Between Atemporal and Intertemporal Theories of Resource Allocation," *Review of Economic Studies,* June, 1961, pp. 148-150, for a sophisticated critique of the "rate of growth" concept.

[13] This, of course, vitiates growth comparisons between the U. S. and the U.S.S.R.

ably cloud aggregates such as GNP, is the fact that the widespread use of these figures draws attention completely away from the numerous well-nigh insoluble problems involved in measuring at all the almost incredibly elusive "quantity" which GNP purports to represent, and in distilling "its" rate of growth. The truth is that the "level of economic well-being" and similar entities, during any one period, are vexingly but inescapably multi-dimensional—they involve innumerable heterogeneous goods, valued by innumerable different people. To collapse this concept into a single figure raises theoretical and statistical problems so serious that almost any use of the resulting figure in popular media can hardly fail to mislead. When this use is glibly extended to hatch out a rate-of-growth concept, it is to be feared that economists are permitting this apparently simple measure—their own creature—to foster habits of thought in their own minds and in those of the public, which would perhaps never have emerged had the intrinsic conceptual and measurement problems been borne in mind. There can be few more obtrusive examples of the tissue of fallacies that can emerge from ill-considered aggregation than this GNP-inspired notion of a "national" rate of economic growth — a notion whose appeal to the lay intellect is so suspiciously complete as to propagate an entirely new set of attitudes towards economic affairs.[14]

WE TURN TO appraise the welfare theory that is implicit in much of the growth literature. Of all the habits of thought embedded in the growth litera-

ture, it is this that offers the most serious threat to the free society. There is, in fact, a profound difficulty (from a welfare theory point of view) that seriously affects all discussions of growth "policies," and especially those relevant to long-range policies for the future. This difficulty arises from the fact that in formulating any such policy, one is necessarily involving the welfare of unborn generations; so that, before even attempting the task of policy formulation, it is necessary to clear up the problem of precisely how the welfare of as yet non-existent people is to be taken into consideration. This problem is crucially relevant to the maintenance of a free society; it is moreover relevant to the "scientific" quality of growth propositions underlying government policy in this context.

The truth of the matter is that economists are incapable of asserting *any* propositions concerning welfare that do not depend in some way on necessarily arbitrary individual judgments of value. To the extent that economists make welfare propositions, they are either acting in a non-scientific capacity, or they are *applying* scientific propositions in the context of given dominant arbitrary value judgments.[15] All this is true of welfare propositions in general; it is *a fortiori* true of propositions involving unborn generations (and thus of growth literature) in particular.

To put the matter in a different way, economists are unable to state as a scientific proposition that any given change yields a net benefit to "society." The reason for this is that ultimately no scientific meaning can be attached to the phrase "the net benefit to society."[16] The economist may be able to assert that acts freely performed by individuals have made *them* better off; but this does not preclude *others* from having been made worse off by these acts. And even if a change benefits every single indi-

---

[14] Among the more serious theoretical problems raised by the use of GNP figures as indices of growth are: (a) the aggregation of market values which individually reflect only marginal decisions and valuations; (b) the extent to which production for investment should be reflected in these measures. See J. Bonner and D. S. Lees, "Consumption and Investment," *Journal of Political Economy*, February, 1963; see also P. A. Samuelson, "The Evaluation of 'Social Income,' Capital Formation and Wealth," in F. A. Lutz and D. C. Hague, eds., *The Theory of Capital* (New York: St. Martin's Press, 1961), p. 56.

[15] See the large welfare literature on these points, especially Murray N. Rothbard, "Toward a Reconstruction of Utility and Welfare Economics," in Mary Sennholz, ed., *On Freedom and Free Enterprise* (Princeton: Van Nostrand, 1956).

[16] In the more important realm of metaphysics, things are of course quite different.

vidual (or benefits some without harming others), we have no scientific meaning to attach to the concept of "society's being better off," other than the fact that some *individuals* in society are better off.

"Group decision-making" can in no sense help us escape this impasse. Unless we *define* the social "good" as that emerging from some specified machinery for group decision-making, like majority rule (thereby making what seems to be a dangerous misuse of language), we cannot hope that any such group decision should "represent" the composite values of its members in a consistent fashion. To demonstrate this was the outstanding contribution of Arrow.[17]

But if all this is the case, what basis in consistent thought exists for long-range growth policies on the part of the state? We have shown in this essay that such policies can claim to be plans only if the benefits anticipated for the future are weighed against the associated current costs. But even if such a comparison is attempted, one is left facing the problem of how to *evaluate* the planned future gains. Ordinarily a plan involves a balance of yield against costs. In the growth case, not only are those who will enjoy the benefits *different people* from those who must bear the cost — these beneficiaries do not yet *exist*: their value scales are as yet non-existent. How then can cost and benefit be meaningfully compared?

The problem can be restated in terms less skeptical of the possibility of scientific welfare propositions. Let us for the sake of argument concede that due attention to appropriate welfare criteria makes it possible to enunciate such propositions. These propositions are built out of changes in the welfare of *individuals*. Such changes can be defined only in terms of the value scales of the individuals themselves (so long as we eschew references to an absolute, metaphysical welfare). A person is made better off by a change if he prefers the new situation to the old. But such a preference can be described only against

a background of *given* tastes. Should the change in situation be accompanied by a change in tastes, there may possibly exist no unambiguous meaning to the term "the preferred situation." Comparisons of benefit and cost are thus ruled out in this scheme of things, even between persons existing simultaneously; between persons not existing simultaneously, it seems hardly possible even to define what such a comparison should mean.[18]

IT SHOULD BE noticed that the sweeping implications of these considerations for growth "policies" have reference only to those of the state. As far as individuals are concerned, nothing need prevent them from exercising their own arbitrary judgments as to their current choices that might affect future generations. They may wish to consume all their capital and exhaust all the natural resources which they possess, leaving nothing left for posterity. Or they may conserve resources, accumulate capital, to prepare a wealthier environment for the future. It is perfectly in order that these choices be made on a non-scientific basis.

The devastating implications of the above considerations for state growth policies arise precisely from the fact that the state can hope to formulate such policies *only* as an individual does — that is, on the basis of arbitrary judgments of value. And it is here that the crucial issue for a free society is encountered. The arbitrary choices of the state can hardly fail to conflict with the arbitrary judgment of some of the citizens.

In effect, state growth policies, consciously or otherwise, require that the state set itself apart from the current wishes of its citizens, scan the future

427

---

[17] Kenneth Arrow, *Social Choice and Individual Values* (New York: John Wiley, 1951).

[18] All this is well recognized in the literature. See I. M. D. Little, *A Critique of Welfare Economics* (Oxford: Clarendon Press, 1957, 2nd edition), p. 85; see also Jerome Rothenberg, *The Measurement of Social Welfare* (Englewood Cliffs: Prentice-Hall, 1961), pp. 52-58; Richard S. Weckstein, "Welfare Criteria and Changing Tastes," *American Economic Review*, March, 1962; Malinvaud, *op. cit.*, pp. 146-147.

history of society, and pass judgment as to the most "desirable" inter-generation allocation of the "nation's" resources. The state becomes the guardian of the interests of its future citizens, it conserves resources for them, it deprives present citizens in order to accumulate capital for them — all this in a manner that *must* be arbitrarily different from the allocation pattern desired by at least some of the affected present citizens. Sometimes, indeed, this is explicitly recognized. Pigou deemed it the responsibility of the state to protect the long-run interests of society from the short-sighted selfishness of the current property-holders.[19]

At issue are some very fundamental questions concerning private property rights, and the proper functions, powers, and responsibilities of government. This is not the place to clarify these questions. Here it is merely desired to point out that government growth programs cannot avoid rigidly circumscribing the concept of property rights. Such programs involve the deliberate acceptance of a stewardship notion of property rights; they involve moreover the notion of a government elected by *today's* citizens, that should represent the interests also of *future* citizens (possibly in directions undesired by many of today's citizens). The implications of these matters require no elaboration.

A FEW FINAL remarks concerning one further aspect of the fashionable emphasis on governmental growth policies may not be completely out of place. We have referred to the pattern of development that would emerge from freely-made multi-period choices of individual citizens acting through the intertemporal market. Whether growth or decline, this development may at least express the choices of today's citizens. (It may clearly be desirable in some contexts to allocate a larger portion of resources to earlier than to later periods). Whatever the pattern of development, it depends for the success with which it reflects the wishes of the people, on the accuracy of the intertemporal market in registering the multi-period value rankings of individuals. And it is here that governmental growth (and other) policies may inhibit the desirable expression of these multi-period value rankings. An atmosphere in which individuals fear such things as chronic inflation, possible eventual abrogation of property rights, confiscatory taxation, and the like, cannot but distort the multi-period plans that individuals would otherwise make. Intervention in the intertemporal markets must, moreover, inevitably prevent them from registering individual multi-period value rankings as sensitively as possible. All this may lead conceivably to a pattern of historical development substantially different from what might have emerged from the free choices of the people working through the free intertemporal market.

---

[19] See citations (and references to other writers) in de Graaff, *op. cit.,* p. 101.

New Individualist Review welcomes contributions for publication from its readers. Essays should not exceed 3,000 words, and should be type-written. All manuscripts will receive careful consideration.

The Negro Revolution

MURRAY N. ROTHBARD

DESPITE INCREASING USE of the term, it is doubtful that most Americans have come to recognize the Negro crisis as a revolution, possessed of all the typical characteristics and stigmata of a revolutionary movement and a revolutionary situation. Undoubtedly, Americans, when they think of "revolution," only visualize some single dramatic act, as if they would wake up one day to find an armed mob storming the Capitol. Yet this is rarely the way revolutions occur. Revolution does not mean that some sinister little group sit around plotting "overthrow of the government by force and violence," and then one day take up their machine guns and make the attempt. This kind of romantic adventurism has little to do with genuine revolution.

Revolution, in the first place, is not a single, isolated event, to be looked at as a static phenomenon. It is a dynamic, open-ended process. One of its chief characteristics, indeed, is the rapidity and acceleration of social change. Ordinarily, the tempo of social and political change is slow, meandering, inconsequential: in short, the typical orderly America of the political science textbooks. But, in a revolution, the tempo of change suddenly speeds up enormously; and this means change in all relevant

---

Murray N. Rothbard, a consulting economist in New York City, is the author of several books on economic subjects: *Man, Economy and State* (2 vols.), *The Panic of 1819*, and, most recently, *The Great Depression.*

variables: in the ideas governing the revolutionary movement, in its growth and in the character of its leadership, and in its impact on the rest of society. Another crucial aspect of Revolution is its sudden stress on *mass* action. In America, social and political action has taken place for a long while in smoke-filled rooms of political parties, in quiet behind-the-scenes talks of lobbyists, Congressmen, and executive officials, and in the sober, drawn-out processes of the courts. Outside of football games, the very concept of mass action has been virtually unknown in the United States. But all this has been changed with the onset, this year, of the Negro Revolution.

As in the case of most revolutions, the Negro Revolution began with a change in the ruling values and ideas of American intellectuals. At the turn of the century, and through the 1920's, most American intellectuals were fundamentally "racist," i.e., they upheld two guiding postulates: (1) that the white race in general, and the Anglo-Saxon wing of that race in particular, are inherently superior, intellectually and morally, to other races and ethnic groups, and particularly the brown and black races; and (2) that *therefore* the superior races had the right and perhaps even the duty to exercise political power over the inferior. Although (2) does not at all follow from (1), few people, whether pro- or anti-racist, have seen that this political conclusion is a *non sequitur.*

In the 1930's and 1940's, an enormous

change occurred among American intellectuals on the race question. Influenced partly by the racist excesses of Hitler and the atmosphere of World War II, American intellectuals, during the 1930's and '40's, swung around to almost the opposite position. In their anxiety to preclude a racist brand of statism, the intellectuals adopted the opposite brand of egalitarianism. Their two new guiding postulates became: (1) all races and ethnic groups are intellectually and morally equal or identical, and (2) that *therefore* no one should be allowed to treat anyone else as if they were not equal, i.e., that the State should be used to compel absolute equality of treatment among the races. Here again, few people noticed that another *non sequitur* was being employed.

It should be noted that this shift is by no means identical to the well-known shift (sometimes attributed by conservatives to a Fabian "conspiracy") of intellectuals from *laissez-faire* liberalism to interventionism a n d socialism. *That* shift occurred decades earlier, and the racist postulates were as common among American socialists and progressives as among conservatives. This shift by intellectuals from racism to egalitarianism then began to filter down, inevitably, to the rest of the population. And this had two crucial effects: it inspired the Negroes to begin to struggle, at long last, for their rights as they saw them; and it disarmed the whites from offering any effective opposition to such a change.

NOW THE PATTERN of racism in America, of course, has been *political* and therefore enforced by police power in the South; voluntary and therefore much looser in the North. The focus of the Negro movement thus had to be the South. And even though the Negroes are a submerged minority in the South, the growth of education and therefore receptivity to intellectual influences, has led the white majority to agree that the Negroes are *right,* that morality, at least, is on the side of the Negro people. Here we have the indispensable condition for success of a *minority* revolution; for even though

Negroes are a minority in this country, general white agreement on the righteousness of the Negro cause has provided the framework for majority support.

The first step, then, was an ideological conversion of the intellectuals and then the bulk of the people; the second was the stirring of the Negroes themselves against segregation and for egalitarian goals. Since the outstanding racist center is the South, the drive began there, and proceeded in the most "moderate," non-revolutionary way possible: through the orderly, staid processes of the government and its courts. This was the way of the oldest and by far the most conservative of the leading Negro organizations, the NAACP. Financed largely by wealthy whites, the NAACP's technique was to employ the power of the Federal Government—its courts and hopefully its legislature, to change conditions in the South. That the NAACP is moderate and non-revolutionary, incidentally, does not mean that it is less statist than more radical Negro groups. On the contrary, the hallmark of the NAACP technique has been to use the "courts instead of the streets," i.e., to confine the Negro movement to State processes, instead of direct action by the masses. It is precisely action *outside* and against the State apparatus that forms the hallmark of a social revolution.

The NAACP went ahead, slowly and gradually, and its use of the Federal arm bore fruit; but the processes of gradualism and legalism, typified by the snail's pace of school desegregation years after the Supreme Court's decision in *Brown v. Board of Education,* began to make the Negroes restive, and understandably so. If they were indeed *right,* as almost everyone up to the Supreme Court was proclaiming, why shouldn't right prevail quickly, even immediately? How long were the Negroes to wait for what nearly everyone, since the previous "revolution" in values, now conceded was their right and due?

There then began among the Negroes a series of sporadic, isolated, uncoordinated actions: beginning with the Montgomery bus boycott in 1955, and continuing with sit-ins, Freedom Rides, etc.

The significant points about this third phase of the Negro movement are: (1) that they were direct *mass* actions, actions "in the streets," voluntary actions by Negroes themselves, casting off dependence on the quiet and seemingly peaceful operations of the State; and (2) as such, they quickly went beyond the established NAACP framework. Because the NAACP was not geared for this type of revolutionary action, new, far more radical organizations began to replace the NAACP in the leadership of the demonstrations. As in the French Revolution, each succeeding wave of organizations able to capture the leadership of this dynamic movement is more radical than the one before: has to be, in order to gain and keep that leadership. And, as the process accelerates, each succeeding organization takes the risk of being tagged with that chilling label "Uncle Tom," apologist for white domination. And, therefore, the older organizations, in this fierce inter-group competition for the loyalty and leadership of the increasingly radicalized Negro masses, themselves become more radical or claim to; thus the NAACP, until recently an opponent of mass demonstrations, now must take a stand in favor of them — or lose all standing in the Negro community.

The Reverend Martin Luther King brought to the Negro movement the truly revolutionary concept of non-violent mass action. The Gandhian concept of non-violent action had several advantages for the Negro movement, especially in that relatively early stage. For one thing, it imbued the movement with the prestige of a "philosophy," however shaky much of the philosophy was; it was able to make use of the common Christianity of the country to appeal to the great Christian tradition of non-violence; it placed a great moral advantage in the hands of the non-violent demonstrators as against their armed opponents; and, finally, it was the most practical course for an oppressed, unarmed minority facing the armed brutality of the Southern police. Probably, the most important of these advantages is the moral: for, nothing could be more potent in mobilizing support throughout the country, among Negroes and whites, than the news or pictures of unarmed and helpless Negroes beaten or clubbed by armed whites. And this despite the philosophical fuzziness of the King concept of "non-violence;" for mass invasion of private restaurants, or mass blocking of street entrances is, in the deepest sense, *also* violence. But, in the generally statist atmosphere of our age, violence against property is not considered "violence;" this label goes only to the more obvious violence against *persons*.

AS MORE AND MORE Negroes participated in mass action, the ideology and especially the tactics of the Negroes became increasingly radical and militant. But in the main the King type of strategy prevailed. As this process grew, however, and as the non-violent strategy met defeats as in Albany, Georgia, a new and far different voice began to emerge — with a far different strategy. This newest and most revolutionary movement, as yet still waiting in the wings, is typified, in their different ways, by Robert F. Williams and by the Black Muslims. Essentially, men like Williams and the Muslims asked of the Kings a very intelligent question: why must only the *Negroes* exercise non-violence? Why may the white oppressors, whether in the form of Ku Klux Klan-type mobs or as armed police, be armed and violent, while only the Negroes must remain meek and disarmed? Why not preach non-violence to the whites for a change? In short, these radicals asserted the perfectly incontrovertible thesis: everyone has the right to defend himself against violence *with* violence; and therefore the Negroes have the right to defend themselves with violence agains armed attacks. The views of Williams and the Muslims have generally been distorted in the press as advocating *aggressive* violence against whites; but they have been quite clear that they would only use violence defensively (although they, too, of course, would not consider such acts as sit-ins to be "violence").

The leading white advocate of this extreme left, Truman Nelson, cites as reflecting his views the following quote

431

from William Lloyd Garrison's review of *Uncle Tom's Cabin*:

That all slaves of the South ought to repudiate all carnal weapons, shed no blood, be obedient to their masters, wait for peaceful deliverance and abstain for all insurrectionary movements is everywhere taken for granted, because the *victims are black!* . . . . *They* are required by the Bible to put away all wrath, to submit to every conceivable outrage without resistance. None of *their* advocates may seek to inspire them to imitate the example of the Greeks, the Poles, the Hungarians, our revolutionary sires, for such teaching would evince a most un-Christian and blood-thirsty disposition. But for those whose skin is of a different complexion, the case is materially altered. Talk not to the whites of peacefully submitting, of overcoming evil with good when they are spit upon and buffeted, outraged and oppressed. . . . Oh no, for them it is, let the blood of the tyrants flow! Is there one law of submission for the black man and another law of rebellion and conflict for the white man?[1]

Against *whom* would this militant revolutionary wing direct its defensive violence? Not, to be sure, against such private citizens as store-keepers or owners of golf courses; *their* rights are already invaded, in a "non-violent" manner, by the established Negro "Center." The proposed revolutionary violence would be directed against two groups: (a) white armed mobs, of the Ku Klux Klan variety, and (b) the armed forces of (white) governments, specifically the Southern police.

By the spring of 1963, the "Negro liberation movement" had grown steadily, in numbers and intensity, with the dominant *motif* one of disciplined non-violence, but with advocates of defensive violence gaining in strength around the fringes. But the movement, though developing, was not yet a revolutionary one in the truest sense; its mass demonstrations were still sporadic, limited, and largely confined to a majority of students and other dedicated groups.

---

[1] Quoted in Robert F. Williams, *Negroes with Guns* (New York: Marzani and Munsell, 1962), p. 22.

IT IS POSSIBLE to pinpoint the time and place when the Negro movement became a revolution: the time, May, 1963, the place, Birmingham, Alabama. In the Birmingham struggle, the stories and pictures of masses of women and small children non-violently refusing "to be moved," and being set upon by fire hoses and police dogs, galvanized the Negro cause throughout the country. This spectacle provided the spark for an amazingly rapid and thorough-going radicalization of the Negro masses. Since that date, the Negro masses throughout the country have become revolutionized, are willing and even eager to demonstrate, sit-down, even fill the jails, and, in some cases, to fight back violently. Not only are the Negro masses eager to join in the fight, but they have since Birmingham exhibited a remarkable alienation and thoroughgoing disgust that is essential to the flourishing of any revolutionary movement. James Baldwin's words which so shocked Robert Kennedy, that the Negroes will not fight for "their" country against, e.g. Cuba, as long as they do not receive their full rights, typifies this growing, radical alienation.

But the Birmingham crisis-point needs to be analyzed in more detail. For the Birmingham struggle took place in two phases: the first phase, of the non-violent children, was on behalf of desegregation, and also compulsory integration of restaurants and forced hiring of Negroes in various jobs. This phase ended with the negotiated agreement of May 10. In retaliation for the Negroes' success, white gangs resorted to violence: to the bombing of a leading Negro motel and the house of the Rev. King's brother. It was this act that provoked an entirely different set of Negroes to action: to committing retaliatory violence on the night of May 11-12. These were not the sober, church-going, lower middle-class Negroes committed to the Rev. King and non-violence. These were the poorest strata of the Negro workers, the economically submerged who help to form that group which suffers from unemployment at a depression-rate, a rate twice the average for American workers as a whole. Interestingly and significantly enough, their aim was not compulsory integration, nor was their particular target the white employer or restaurant-owner. No, it was the police.

A reporter for the *New York Post* described these militants:

> They were not the fresh-faced youngsters who paraded so solemnly for justice last week.
>
> They were not those parents who stood proudly by as they saw their children off to jail.
>
> No, instead they are Birmingham's dispossessed, and the truth is that they will remain non-privileged even when the new day dawns. . . . They will not benefit from Birmingham's new deal because they will never be qualified, or acceptable, for jobs as clerks or salesmen.
>
> They have known only two kinds of white men—the boss and the cop. The boss is none too good. . . . But the cop is much worse. The cop accosts them at any hour and arrests them on any pretext.
>
> In every town there's gossip of what cops do in the back room. There was no need for a backroom in Birmingham. The cops often beat Negroes senseless in full public view on the street. . . .
>
> They had always cowered before the cops and held back their hatred—to protect their skulls. But suddenly, without forewarning, for they had been in no church rallies and ridden in no freedom rides, they saw Negroes defying the hated cop.
>
> So, the non-privileged decided to make it a fight of their own. . . .[2]

Demonstrating Negroes have taken to a favorite chant: "What do we want? Freedom! When do we want it? Now!" An admirable sentiment, but "freedom," at best a word of fuzzy meaning in recent decades, is a vague portmanteau, and hopelessly ambiguous word as used by the Negro movement. To some groups it means desegregation, to others compulsory integration, to yet others a racial quota system in all jobs, to still others, as we have seen, the ousting of the Southern police and the Southern sheriff from arbitrary rule over Negro citizens (and whites as well). And to still more radical groups, as we shall see, it means a "Negro nation" in the Black Belt of the South. But the very vagueness of the term adds fuel to the dynamics of

[2] *New York Post,* May 13, 1963.

the revolution. For it makes the goals of the Negroes open-ended, distant, ever-receding into the future. In short, the very fuzziness of the goal permits the Negroes to accelerate and increase their own demands without limit regardless of how many demands are met. No movement with strictly limited goals can ever become revolutionary; it is the very sweep and vagueness of the demands that make the movement insatiable, and hence ever-open to rapid growth.

ONCE THE REVOLUTIONARY crisis-point is passed, the revolution becomes almost unbeatable, because: (1) if the white governments yield to the stated demands, this adds fuel to the revolutionary movement and induces them to increase their demands; but (2) if savagely repressive measures are taken, as at Birmingham, this will make martyrs out of the Negro victims, multiply their revolutionary fervor, and greatly intensify support of the revolution throughout the country, among white and Negro alike. Indeed, it was this treatment, as we have seen, that made the Negro cause a revolution. In short, the governments are now damned if they do and damned if they don't. With the Negro movement now in a revolutionary situation, it seems therefore *impossible* for the governments to stop or defeat it.

This does not mean, however, that the Negro Revolution will inevitably be victorious. There are two ways by which it might be crippled and defeated. First, the retaliatory creation of a white counter-revolutionary mass movement, equally determined and militant. In short, by the re-creation of the kind of Ku Klux Klan that smashed Reconstruction and the Negro movement in the late 19th century. Since whites are in the majority, they have the capacity to do this *if* they have the will. But the will, in my opinion, is gone; this is not the 19th century, nor even the 1920's. White opinion, as we have seen, has drastically shifted from racism to egalitarianism; even the Southern whites, particularly the educated leadership, concede the broad merit of the Negro cause; and, finally, mob action no longer

433

has respectability in our society. There *have* been attempts, to be sure, at mass counter-revolutionary white action: the Ku Klux leader in Georgia told a rally that "we must fight poison with poison," armed conflict between white and Negro mobs has broken out in Cambridge, Maryland, and white hoodlums have repeatedly assaulted Negro pickets in the Bronx. But all this is a feeble replica of the kind of white action that would be necessary to defeat the revolution; and it seems almost impossible for action to be generated on the required scale.

There is a second, and far more subtle, method by which the Negro Revolution might be tamed and eventually crippled: through a "sellout" by the Negro leadership itself. It has happened time and again in the history of unsuccessful revolts that the masses, after having been indoctrinated and radicalized by their leadership, are then betrayed by the leadership itself, and left floundering and inchoate, finally to collapse from lack of direction or guidance. Betrayals occur for a variety of reasons, but usually from a combination of venality and timorousness; and because it is much easier for counter-revolutionaries to put pressure on the leadership, the few who stand out from the crowd, than on the broad base of the masses themselves.

There are very strong indications that this betrayal-process has already begun; for so radicalized were the Negro masses by the events of May that they have now outstripped almost all of the Negro leadership, even those considered the "crackpot" fringe only a year ago. In particular, we are seeing more and more the openly expressed fear on the part of *all* the established Negro organizations that the Negro masses will get out of hand, will pass beyond the safe-and-sane limits desired by the leadership, and begin to "resort to violence" against the government. Desperately fearful of violence and hence of genuine militancy, all these established organizations, from NAACP to CORE to SNCC, have banded together in the Council for United Civil Rights Leadership, heavily financed by equally fearful white Liberals, to keep the Negro masses "under control."

Of course, the Negro Establishment will not be able to dump their own revolution quickly and abruptly, else they would be totally repudiated by their followers. The strategy, on the contrary, appears to be as follows: to pressure for the "safe-and-sane" course of Federal intervention and civil rights bills, and, with the plum of this concession to the Negro masses, to keep the damper down on mass demonstrations.

The following quotes indicate the dimensions of this attempt to cripple the revolution and channel it into "safe," orderly statist directions:

> Administration and Negro leaders view the passage this year of the Kennedy civil rights bill, with the "public accommodations" section relatively intact, as absolutely essential to keep the fire under control.
> "If we don't get the public accommodations section, the Negroes won't talk to us any more," said one important Administration figure. "If we can't talk to them, advise them, there's no telling what might happen."[3]

> Why are white religious, business and civic leaders so anxious to deal with men like [the leaders of the Council for United Civil Rights Leadership]. . . . "You should see what's waiting in the wings to take over, if these non-violent people fail," said one influential white private citizen. . . .[4]

It seems clear, furthermore, that President Kennedy's sudden decision for all-out action on civil rights legislation and his intervention in general were caused precisely by the new revolutionary mood of the Negro people. It was immediately after the Negro violence of the night of May 11-12, that the President decided to send Federal troops to Alabama — causing Malcolm X, articulate young spokesman for the radical Black Muslims, to comment acidly that Kennedy only intervened after the onset of *Negro* violence. Nothing had been done by the Federal government, he added, when white (government) violence had been rampant in Birmingham.

---

[3] *New York Daily News,* July 26, 1963.
[4] *New York Daily News,* July 25, 1963.

OUR PROGNOSIS FOR the Negro problem in this country depends on whether or not the Establishment strategy for curbing and containing the Negro Revolution will succeed. Success for this strategy depends upon two factors: (a) whether Congress will pass a "tough" civil rights bill this year, and (b) whether the Negro masses will find a leadership willing at least to keep up with the radical temper of the masses or even to go beyond it. *If* Congress does pass the civil rights bill, *and* no popular radical leaders emerge among the Negroes, then it is fairly certain that the Negro Revolution will be curbed, will be satisfied with limited concessions, and will finally simmer down or perhaps fizzle out. But *if*, on the other hand, the civil rights bill is stopped by a filibuster, *and* a popular radical leadership comes to the fore, then a full-scale Negro Revolution seems inevitable. Should one of the conditions hold and not the other, then the outcome becomes doubtful.

As to the second condition for the continuation of the Revolution, it is rare that a revolution has succeeded without truly radical leaders to constitute a vanguard. But as yet, the Negro Revolution has not found its Lenin, its Castro, or its Hitler. Who are the "extremist" groups "waiting in the wings"? So far, they consist largely of the followers of Robert F. Williams and the Black Muslims, with smaller groupings around the Trotskyites and the Maoist "Hammer and Steel." There are also new and so far small groups of militants such as the *Uhuru* and GOAL movements in Detroit.

The Black Muslims have a substantial following, but largely limited to the poorer working class in the Northern cities. The Muslims are a highly interesting movement, which received favorable publicity years ago in the ultra-right-wing *Right* magazine. The Muslims have a far more libertarian program than the other Negro organizations, opposed to compulsory integration. Indeed, as a Negro nationalist movement, they favor voluntary segregation of the races, preferably in a Negro nation in the "Black Belt" of the South, or in a Negro return to Africa. The Muslims have also been able, paradoxically, to do a remarkable job in instilling the "Protestant ethic" into the most criminal groups of the Negro population. The Muslims, however, have not been able to attract any Negro support in the South; and, at the most, its Muslim religion would limit its mass base. Malcolm X will never be the "Lenin" of the Negro Revolution; at the most, the Muslims could be a co-operating but subsidiary organization in such a struggle.

Robert F. Williams had a substantial following in the South, but he fled to Cuba after being charged with kidnapping, and it is doubtful if he commands any organizational support at present. William Worthy is emphatically on the left of the Negro movement, but again, he is an independent journalist without an organizational base.

The fact that no over-riding leaders are in sight, however, does not mean that they will not emerge. For one of the main characteristics of a revolutionary situation is that change is unprecedentedly swift. As long as the situation continues to be revolutionary, a prominent radical leader and organization could emerge out of the blue in a matter of months.

Suppose that the Establishment strategy fails, and the Negro Revolution succeeds, what form might we expect it to take? Here again, prognosis is risky, but we might expect several developments. In the first place, there seems no doubt that a revolutionary leadership would be generally "leftist," i.e., for some form of socialism at home, and opposed to the Cold War foreign policies of the United States. We can infer this from the fact that the current radical leadership, each in its separate way, has a strong tendency to identify "white oppression" at home with "white American imperialism" abroad, especially against the "colored countries" of Asia and Africa.

As an example of this trend of thought, we may take the Negro journalist William Worthy. In a speech in Harlem on June 1, Worthy called for a Negro "third party" in America (toward which the Muslims and others are also sympathetic) to "co-ordinate . . . unsung local heroes into one gigantic effective national movement." A Negro party, added Worthy, would wield the political balance of power, and upset the entire "white power structure" of the country. It would also "change the nuclear-racist-colonialist course of American history, and thereby the destiny of the entire world."

A revolutionary N e g r o leadership would concentrate, as we have indicated, far more on direct opposition to all levels of *government,* especially the local police. That this would be true North as well as South is seen by the recent prominence of new, militant groups in protesting police brutality in Detroit. Protesting the killing of an alleged Negro prostitute by a white ' policeman, were none of the established organizations; only radical groups participated, including the Black Muslims, *Uhuru* and GOAL.

Another factor has already served to radicalize all sectors of the Negro movement. More and more reference appears, in the Negro literature, to the "white power structure;" Negroes were highly impressed with the fact that negotiations in Birmingham were conducted, not so much with the elected public officials, as with the leading businessmen of the community. This has caused many Negroes, of varying political stripe, to adopt the radical view that the "real rulers" of government are not the elected officials, but the big businessmen of the community or, in the final analysis, of the country. We can expect that many of them will draw Marxist conclusions from this premise; and the Marxists near and among the radical Negro groups will do their best to see to it that these conclusions are drawn.

Many conservatives are irretrievably convinced that the Communists are somehow "behind" the whole Negro Revolution. Paradoxically, however, in the spectrum of Negro organizations that we have outlined, the Communist Party can best be described as "moderately left of center." Their main idol is the Rev. Martin Luther King, and they wax almost as hysterical over the possibility of Negro violence as do the most determined racists. Anyone considering this far-fetched is invited to turn to a

lengthy article by the Negro editor of *The Worker,* James E. Jackson, on the Negro question. Jackson devotes a large part of his article to a savagely vituperative attack on the Black Muslims, calling them "ultra-reactionary forces . . . with the strategic assignment to sow ideological confusion . . . a leach on the Negro freedom movement — sucking its blood. . . ." Jackson is particularly bitter that Malcolm X dared to attack the Rev. King as an "Uncle Tom." Jackson even goes on to denounce militant, revolutionary Negroes in general as self-glorifiers and ignorant egotists. The radical *Liberator* magazine is denounced for daring to criticize the Rev. King, and even Robert F. Williams is bitterly attacked for his "utterly irresponsible attacks upon . . . Negro leaders and their allies. . . ."[5]

In denouncing the Muslim proposal for a Black nation in the South, James Jackson carefully refrained from pointing out that this was the Communist Party line several decades ago. Still holding to this program, however, is perhaps the "furthest out" and most radical of all the revolutionary organizations in and around the Negro Left: Hammer and Steel. A Maoist splinter group of men formerly in the Communist Party, Hammer and Steel considers the Negro movement to be a "national liberation movement," which "must be prepared to answer violence with greater violence directed at Wall Street and their agents." Non-violence might have worked against relatively civilized Britain, says Hammer and Steel, but could not work against "brutal and genocidal" American imperialism. To have true civil rights, the "Negro nation" must have its "freedom" and self-determination in the South, and "special rights" must be granted the Negro minority in the North and West. "A Free Negro nation will determine whether its best interest lie [sic] in separation or as an autonomous part of the U. S." As for the best means of attaining this goal, Hammer and Steel envisages a "national liberation front" in the South similar to the fronts in Viet Nam

---

[5] James E. Jackson, "A Fighting People Forging New Unity," *The Worker,* July 7, 1963.

and Algeria. Hammer and Steel ends its discussion with a series of slogans for our time: "Disarm the White Oppressors in the South!", "Arms for the Negro People!", and "Self-Determination, State Power for the Negro Nation!"[6]

TO PASS BRIEFLY from the analytical to the evaluative, what should be the libertarian position on the Negro movement? Perhaps the most important point to make here is that the issue is a complex one; the Negro Revolution has some elements that a libertarian must favor, others that he must oppose. Thus, the libertarian opposes compulsory segregation and police brutality, but also opposes compulsory integration and such absurdities as ethnic quota systems in jobs. The ethnic quota is no less objectionable than Hitler's *numerus clausus;* if 25% of bricklayers must be Negro, must not the proportion of Jewish doctors be forcibly reduced to 3%? Must every occupation in the land have its precise quota of Armenians, Greeks, Montenegrans, etc. *ad infinitum?*

For his over-all estimate of the Negro movement, the libertarian must weigh and formulate his conclusions according to what he believes to be the most important priorities. In doing so, incidentally, he should not overlook a generally neglected point: some Negroes are beginning to see that the heavy incidence of unemployment among Negro workers is partially caused by union restrictionism keeping Negroes (as well as numerous whites) out of many fields of employment. If the Negro Revolution shall have as one of its consequences the destruction of the restrictive union movement in this country, this, at least, will be a welcome boon.

[6] *Hammer and Steel Newsletter,* June, 1963.

437

Foreign Aid in Latin America

ROBERT   SCHUETTINGER

THE PROBLEM OF how best to bring about economic, educational and political progress in the underdeveloped nations is certainly one of the major challenges of our time. For this reason, it is particularly discouraging that the great body of our college graduates (who mould the public opinion of this country) have been content to follow the lead of publications such as the *New York Times* and adopt a simplistic and essentially thoughtless attitude toward what will perhaps be remembered as the Gordian Knot of the Twentieth Century.

If you ask the average modern Liberal intellectual what sort of economic system he considers best suited to the "emerging"[1] nations, nine times out of ten you will receive almost exactly the same cliche in reply: "For the advanced nations, I am all in favor of free enterprise (under adequate safeguards, of course) but I think that some form of socialism is necessary for the developing countries — at least until they develop sufficient thrust to pass the 'take-off stage'."[2] The results of such little polls would not be especially noteworthy were it not for the fact that most of the available economic data point in precisely the opposite direction.[3]

It is a rather alarming commentary on the state of public discussion in America

(and on our intellectual community in general) that almost all of the talking and writing done on the subject of foreign aid each year is uninformed and emotional. This, of course, is an indictment not of one party only, but of both sides of the case. The Liberals as a rule dismiss all critics of foreign aid as reactionary, anti-humanitarian and isolationist; the Conservatives, on the other hand, too often attack foreign aid as a general principle without pausing to ask what are the actual effects upon the

---

[1] It would be tiresome to list all of the various euphemisms tossed up in order to avoid using the Anglo-Saxon word "backward." I have come across twelve such circumlocutions in my reading, and I invite the reader to try to top my score.

[2] The most widely-discussed exposition of this view is W. W. Rostow, *The Stages of Economic Growth* (Cambridge: Cambridge University Press, 1960). In *Man, Economy and State* (Princeton, N. J.: Van Nostrand, 1962), Murray N. Rothbard remarks, "Perhaps some of the popularity of this work may be due to the term 'take-off,' which is certainly in tune with our . . . space-minded age."

[3] F. A. Hayek, in *The Constitution of Liberty* (Chicago: University of Chicago Press, 1960), notes (p. 367) that, "However strong a case there may exist in such countries for the government's taking the initiative in providing examples and spending freely on spreading knowledge and education, it seems to me that the case against over-all planning and direction of all economic activity is even stronger there than in more advanced countries. I say this on both economic and cultural grounds. Only free growth is likely to enable such countries to develop a viable civilization on their own capable of making a distinct contribution to the needs of mankind."

Robert Schuettinger is an Associate Editor of *New Individualist Review*. He is currently doing graduate work at Oxford University as an Earhart Fellow.

United States and the receiving country of a particular program. In the light of this background then, I would like to discuss the operation of the Peace Corps and some other aspects of our foreign economic aid program in Latin America.

This past winter, I spent a month of my vacation touring three Latin American countries, stopping on the way to visit friends who are currently serving in the Peace Corps.[4] My impression of this much-publicized organization, based on the Volunteers I have met in the United States as well as in Latin America, is that it does not attract into its ranks the very highest level of college graduates; with a few exceptions it attracts the solid, competent, intelligent, second-level type. There are good and obvious reasons why this should be so. Most really first-rate students simply can not spare two years for this kind of work; they are committed to long stretches of graduate study interrupted, in most cases, by the Armed Services. There are, however, notable exceptions. Some of the Volunteers I met will certainly be leaders in their fields; but, as in most government agencies, these are few and far between. Tocqueville's comment that the most able Americans, as a rule, avoid public service is as true in 1963 as it was in 1830.

Most of the Volunteers I met had no strong political convictions; the great majority fitted in unobtrusively with the American consensus. The beatnik types are clearly a small minority in the Corps. The hardships of the two-month training period, I was told, weeded out the few of them who did apply. At one Peace Corps "boot camp" I visited, the training was indeed rigorous in the physical and busy-work sense; anyone who completed it had more than his share of conscientiousness and endurance. These are the two qualities the Corps is most interested in and it is for this reason

that only a few Volunteers have returned to this country prematurely. On the other hand, the training program can not be said to be *intellectually* demanding and it is primarily for this reason that Harvard University has declined to have anything more to do with it. What *is* demanded is staying-power, including the capacity to sit through twelve hours a day of classes which, in many cases, are boring and trivial.

The Peace Corps now consists of over 5,000 persons and it is still growing rapidly. It is not at all surprising, therefore, that such an organization should have faults. but it is surprising that it has managed to do so effective a job with so little money under such adverse conditions and in so short a time. That it has been able to do so is largely due to the quality of the Volunteers themselves, almost all of whom do more than their jobs require. Despite a generally favorable press, however, and the support of most politicians, strong criticism of the Corps is still to be heard, most of it centering around two main points.

Some conservatives have taken pains to point out that the Peace Corps Volunteers are inadequately trained in methods of combatting Communism. Since it is highly unlikely, however, that a recent college graduate could be trained to be an effective anti-Communist agent in less than a year, it would seem that the return would not be worth the investment. Under existing circumstances all that can be reasonably expected of the Volunteers is that they be able to explain with some clarity,[5] whenever it seems appropriate, why they prefer democracy[6] to totalitarianism.

A complaint frequently heard from classical Liberals is that the Peace Corps, for all its good intentions, teaches young people to rely unduly upon government as a panacea. This would be a damning

439

---

[4] This article, then, is inspired by some personal observations, but I would not want to say that it is based on them. It seems to me that man-hour for man-hour invested, more important and reliable information is to be derived from printed sources (assuming they are well-chosen, of course) than is to be derived from so-called "first-hand experience."

[5] If this seems like too modest a goal, it might be helpful to recall that a man who was to serve twice as President of the United States (Dwight Eisenhower) confessed that he could not explain to Marshal Zhukov why democracy was better than Communism. It is really not as easy as it may sound at first.

[6] Or republicanism, if any reader has a marked preference for that word.

charge if it were true, but I don't believe that it is. It certainly cannot be denied that all Peace Corps Volunteers are employees of the United States government; the important point, however, is that in almost all countries they have been assigned jobs which have traditionally been under government direction. Unlike other parts of the foreign aid program, the Peace Corps has caused almost no displacement of private enterprise. For instance, well over half of all Peace Corpsmen are teachers, who are, in underdeveloped countries as in the United States, largely government employees.

Nor can it fairly be said that the Peace Corps has ignored private organizations working in the same fields. Since its policy is to stimulate and advise and not to preempt it has usually sought (and usually received) the co-operation of local businesses, newspapers, labor unions, church groups and independent relief agencies as well as individuals interested in contributing something to a particular project.

In some parts of Latin America, Peace Corpsmen work alongside members of a private "peace corps" called *Accion*. This "rival firm" was launched by a California student who had read William James' essay, "A Moral Equivalent for War." In 1958, he decided to put into action the psychologist's exhortation to the youth of the advanced nations to abandon militarism and to channel their restless energies instead into a great effort to spread civilization to the remotest parts of the earth. Two years after this idea was first revived in California, the then Senator Kennedy began talking about a "Point Four Youth Program." A year before the campaign of 1960, however, a group of students aided by several businessmen had already put the first "peace corps" into operation.

THE PRIOR EXISTENCE of *Accion*, of course, was enough to raise the question of what justification there could be for a government Peace Corps if the same work could be done well by private enterprise. I would answer that the Peace Corps is probably the single most effective part of our entire economic aid network, and, since it is one of the few cases where our foreign aid funds are being spent in the right way, it serves as a valuable example. This assumes, of course, that the principle of foreign aid can itself be defended insofar as: (1) it actually improves the economic well-being of the people in the receiving country, and (2) it furthers the foreign policy aims and thereby the security of the United States. A good deal of our present foreign aid does not even fulfill the second criterion and almost none of it fulfills the first. The Peace Corps, to its credit, fulfills both.

Our foreign policy objectives have clearly been furthered by the Peace Corps primarily because every Peace Corps Volunteer is a visible demonstration of the friendship of the American people for the people of the host country. Since most people are more interested in other people than they are in machines, the propaganda value of a $75-a-month (plus expenses) Peace Corpsman is a far better investment for the United States than the equivalent value in, say, fertilizer. Also, as one Volunteer told me, a Peace Corpsman is probably the only variety of foreign aid which cannot be stolen by a politician somewhere along the line. He can, of course, be wasted, and a certain number of Volunteers are sitting around right now waiting for their assignments to emerge from some Kafka-esque local bureaucracy. But these are the exceptions and not the rule.

Economically, the Peace Corps has concentrated on spreading knowledge and education. Most economists would agree that this is the best way for governments to lay the groundwork for advance and thereby encourage economic progress.[7]

An additional benefit of the Peace Corps and one not foreseen by the planners in Washington is the effect upon thousands of Volunteers of seeing exactly how governments go about their announced goals of raising living standards

---

[7] See footnote 3 for F. A. Hayek's comment on the proper role of governments in furthering education as the foundation for economic growth.

Most Peace Corpsmen left the United States with a prejudice in favor of foreign aid and government economic planning; as a result of their experiences many are certain to revise their opinions. Indeed, the most idealistic and naive observer[8] can not help but notice that corruption, inefficiency and wastefulness are the hallmarks of almost all Latin American governments; in these nations a political career is regarded simply as a means to self-enrichment (as it is still looked upon today in some parts of the United States).

EVEN IF WE set corruption and political instability aside, however, at least three major impediments to economic progress in Latin America remain: (1) the threat of nationalization of industry, (2) economic nationalism, and (3), perhaps most fundamental of all, the resistance to change which is firmly rooted in the Latin American way of life. None of these obstacles to a rising standard of living is likely to be reduced by our foreign aid program as it is presently designed. The plain truth is that Latin America (and the underdeveloped countries generally) can not expect to make real economic progress without first effecting drastic internal reforms. And these changes can only be brought about by the governments themselves; any hint of United States interference will bring outraged cries of "Yankee imperialism." By the rules of the game we are forbidden to insist that money be allocated first for such basics as education, sanitation, vocational training, roads and water and sewage systems.[9] Nor may we insist upon the necessary controls to minimize graft and guarantee competent management.

The single most important reason why capital, which is needed so badly to create new industries and jobs, has been fleeing Latin America at such an increasing rate is the threat of nationalization. In a Senate speech recently, Jacob Javits pointed out that, "Additional North American investments are losing the battle against the flow of Latin Americtn local capital, whose flight is calculated between nine and fifteen billion dollars, a great part of which is deposited in Swiss banks. I ask you to imagine the tonic effect that would result," he went on, "if only these depositors, who have in Swiss banks the 'fugitive' capital of Latin America, would invest but one half of the balance of their accounts in their own countries. The same political instability and economic doubts that caused the emigration of Latin American capital, is [sic] responsible for the decline of North American direct investments in Latin America. . . . These negative tendencies are reciprocally reinforced by a vicious circle which causes greater doubts and instability — and finally violent nationalistic acts and unjust expropriations. It is evident that a great responsibility lies upon the Latin American nations for the improvement of their climate for investments."

The extent of this hostility to private enterprise may be gauged by the fact that the Chamber of Commerce of America, meeting recently in Florida, passed a resolution specifically requesting President Kennedy and the Latin American governments concerned to allow the participation of private industry in the United States foreign aid program.[10]

Economists have estimated that the investments planned over a ten year period by the United States government could be brought about in only a few months if only Latin American governments would abandon their hostile attitude toward private capital, domestic and foreign. It is not too hard to imagine what a great difference this speed-up

441

---

[8] As a matter of fact, Chester Bowles has recently returned from one of his journeys and has presented a report urging that foreign aid be decreased or denied to those countries which fail to meet minimum standards of co-operation and self-help.

[9] These, of course, are the areas where the Peace Corps has been concentrating its efforts. Would that the rest of our foreign aid program would profit by this example.

[10] This despite the fact that many Liberal writers on economics, including the last Ambassador to India, John Kenneth Galbraith, have recently said that what the underdeveloped countries need is more private enterprise, not less. See Galbraith's new book, *Economic Development in Persepective* (Oxford: Oxford University Press, 1962).

could make to millions of people now living in utter poverty; but as things stand today, these people will just have to wait.

The truth is that Latin America's dictators[11] do not care how long their people wait so long as *they* get full credit for any new jobs created or new industries founded. This, of course, is a major source of the economic nationalism which is one of the biggest millstones around Latin America's neck. The ruling groups, supported by Washington, are interested primarily in creating "show-case industries"— which require large capital investments and small numbers of employees. Such industries include automobiles, petrochemicals, machine tools and other mass production items which use highly automated processes. There are several reasons why spending money on such projects actually hurts rather than helps the welfare of the people in the countries concerned. First, "show-case industries," while satisfying the pride of the planners, divert needed capital from economically sound to economically unsound uses. Unemployment is aggravated, not helped, by this concentration on highly automated industries. By insisting on manufacturing their own automobiles at a high cost, when they could buy them at a much lower cost from the United States, the planners are making certain that their citizens will have less to spend for other products. As consumers have less money to spend, fewer imports can be bought and fewer new jobs created both at home and abroad. Our own economy is hurt by these policies just as it would be helped if our foreign aid programs could achieve their announced objectives. All this nonsense-on-stilts is simply mercantilism, the inward-looking and backward-glancing system that Adam Smith exploded in 1776.[12]

The planners thus refuse to acknowledge the importance of the free flow of private capital, and the ordinary citizen is denied the advantages of geographic specialization and the international division of labor. Rather than come down to earth and help their citizens concentrate on what they can do well, the dictators prefer to weave grandiose schemes which they are being encouraged to charge off to the United States taxpayer. Everyone would laugh if the United Fruit Company poured vast sums of money into growing bananas near its Boston headquarters; otherwise intelligent people, however, greet such follies as a new Diesel-engine plant in Nicaragua as "an important step forward."[13]

BUT ALL OF Latin America's economic ills cannot be blamed on Washington and her own governments; the people themselves must shoulder a good part of the responsibility. Like many North Americans, most Latin Americans distrust change. As long as they have barely enough to eat and some kind of a roof over their heads they are content

---

[11] Most objective political scientists would estimate that, at the very most, three or four Latin American nations are *not* governed by dictators.

[12] Milton Friedman, in his "Foreign Aid: Means and Objectives," *(Yale Review*, Summer, 1958, p. 505) cites a classic example of this sort of "planning": "The Pharaohs raised enormous sums of capital to build the Pyramids; this was capital formation on a grand scale; it certainly did not promote economic development in the

fundamental sense of contributing to a self-sustaining growth in the standard of life of the Egyptian masses. Modern Egypt has under government auspices built a steel mill; this involves capital formation; but it is a drain on the economic resources of Egypt . . . since the cost of making steel in Egypt is very much greater than the cost of buying it elsewhere; it is simply a modern equivalent of the Pyramids, except that maintenance expenses are higher."

[13] As F. A. Hayek (op. cit., p. 366) points out: "Much of this endeavor . . . seems to be based on a rather naive fallacy of the *post hoc ergo propter hoc* variety: because historically the growth of wealth has regularly been accompanied by rapid industrialization, it is assumed that industrialization will bring about a more rapid growth of wealth. This involves a clear confusion of an intermediary effect with a cause. It is true that, as productivity per head increases as a result of more capital in tools, and even more as a result of investment in knowledge and skill, more and more of the additional output will be wanted in the form of industrial products. It is also true that a substantial increase in the production of food in those countries will require an increased supply of tools. But neither of these considerations alters the fact that if large-scale industrialization is to be the most rapid way of increasing average income, there must be an agricultural surplus available so that an industrial population can be fed."

to let come what may. The people for whose benefit our optimistic foreign aid plans were supposedly launched are just not much interested in progress. If anyone doubts this, he has only to look at what has happened in those countries where free land in the interior has been offered to anyone who would go out and settle it. Wherever such offers have been made there has been almost no response; the supposedly land-hungry *campesinos* have been too lazy and too conservative to move their families 200 miles in order to get a farm of their own. Of course, these same people will accept a piece of the neighboring *hacienda* if it is handed to them on a silver platter by a benevolent (and vote-conscious) government. I know of at least two instances where formerly landless peasants took over a large farm and duly harvested the crops planted by the previous owners. The next year, however, there was no crop at all; the new owners claimed that they "didn't know what to do." This is what "land reform," as it is usually practiced in Latin America, means — not opening up new land to productivity but destroying formerly productive land by incompetent management. No doubt it is unfair to expect a largely uneducated population to change its way of living in a short period of time. And yet if Latin America is even to maintain its present standard of living, in the face of a rapidly rising birth rate and a declining death rate, it is essential that change *does* come, and soon.

Our economic aid program as now constituted, however, will not promote this change. Despite all the rhetoric about "the winds of change sweeping across a continent," the planners in Washington are doing their best to assist the reactionaries' struggle against change. Far from being a "liberating force," the program is actually a support for sagging dictatorships, a buttress for a decaying feudalism, and the keystone of a revived mercantilism.

443

"*Economics of the Free Society*"[1]

444

AS ONE OF the chief architects of West Germany's post-war "economic miracle," Wilhelm Roepke has exerted a powerful influence on contemporary practical affairs. However, it is in his role as an academic economist that Professor Roepke comes to us in this book. *Economics of the Free Society* is the English translation of what has become a popular textbook on the Continent. In a very few pages, it is able to cover just about every aspect of the workings of the free market system, always with a view to demonstrating the superiority of this system over its collectivist rivals. The book is aimed at the reader with no formal training in economics — the "intelligent layman"— and many in this audience will find it a good, easily-read introduction to the problems a modern economy must solve and the means by which a system of free markets solves them. Beginner or not, however, the reader will be satisfied only in inverse proportion to the degree of logical rigor he demands.

Roepke sets forth his arguments almost exclusively by analogy and example. While this can be helpful and certainly contributes to the readability of the book, it is no substitute for lucid logical argument. At those points in the exposition where some central theoretical concept is being elucidated, a geometric presentation could usefully be inserted into the text. This would do much more for the book than simply clothe it in the trappings of elegance. The Cartesian plane remains the basic tool of the economist, and, even for the beginner, it is an invaluable device for tying together diverse concepts into a logical whole. By his almost exclusive reliance on analogy and anecdote, Roepke seriously dilutes the content of economics, sometimes to the point of permitting himself to make glib assertions he might not care to defend under a more rigorous analysis.[2] While it might be claimed that glibness and superficial analysis are tolerable in a book for beginners, it is precisely this audience which can most benefit from a good grounding in the logical re-

---

[1] A review of *Economics of the Free Society* by Wilhelm Roepke (Chicago: Regnery, 1963), 273 pp.

[2] An example of this may be found on page 149 where Roepke claims: "It is quite possible . . . that a fall in agricultural prices may provoke an increase rather than a reduction in cultivation as a consequence of each farmer seeking to compensate for price declines by raising his output." A farmer can compensate for a price decline by an increase in output only if the costs of the additional output are at least covered by the receipts from the additional output at the new, lower price. However, if such a situation in fact obtains, the farmer would surely have been able to cover the costs of the added output by the receipts from its sale at the original, higher price. He would thus have expanded his output previous to any fall in price. Unless Roepke is willing to claim that farmers are less interested than others in making money, the quoted assertion is sheer nonsense.

Sam Peltzman is Business Manager and Associate Editor of *New Individualist Review*.

quirements of economic analysis. To the extent that a knowledge of the methods of economic analysis equips one to refute the numerous collectivist fallacies, Roepke is doing a disservice to the cause he champions.

The cause he is championing, it must be noted, is *not* the *laissez-faire* capitalism of the last century (a period Roepke identifies as the era of "paleo-liberalism"). Roepke recognizes the inherent social efficiency of a competitive market system, and for the attainment of such a system Roepke is willing to use the power of the state to destroy or regulate private monopoly. Though he is unspecific as to methods, Roepke also advocates use of state power in some form to gain a more equitable distribution of income (p. 197 ff.). Yet, in this respect, Roepke differs hardly at all from certain other supporters of the free market system, e.g., Henry Simons. It is when he charges that the logic of capitalist development, entailing as it does a rapid extension of the specialization of economic functions, has contributed to the "inhumane," depersonalized condition of modern industrial society, that Roepke differs from most of his intellectual bedfellows. This is a charge, of course, often made by the collectivist critics of capitalism, particularly those of the fascist stripe; it is one seldom made by a defender of capitalism like Roepke. At the same time, however, Roepke takes great pains to point out the futility of hoping for, much less seriously advocating, a return to some pre-Raphaelite utopia. The rapid extension of specialization has been the motive force behind a great increase in the productivity of modern industry, but this very development has made possible an equally great increase in population, which population is consequently dependent for its very existence on the productivity of the specialized industrial system. Thus, every contemporary social system, collectivist or otherwise, is constrained to preserve the present degree of specialization, for "to turn back the clock would be tantamount to ordering the destruction of millions of lives." While one may agree or disagree

with Roepke's pessimistic view of the social effects of specialization (and I do think he tends to greatly underemphasize some of the contributions to a "good society"—the unprecedented extension of general education to all strata of society has been made possible only because the specialized economy has been productive enough to release the necessary human and material resources), his analysis should serve as a strong antidote to policy recommendations based on "the fond reveries of economic romanticists and autarkists."

HELPFUL AS ROEPKE'S analysis of particular economic and social problems may be, one can hardly fail to be disappointed by the inattention to rigorous analysis which pervades his book. Nowhere is this more evident than in his section on "The Impact of Keynesianism" (p. 221 ff.). Roepke totally eschews a frontal attack on the logic or the empirical relevance of Keynes' analysis. In fact, he concedes that "the services which Keynes rendered to the advancement of theory . . . . are considerable," and further "we will readily concede that the use of Keynesianism as a logical apparatus . . . in the struggle against inflation is (and was) thoroughly legitimate . . . ." If the reader wonders why Roepke is ready to concede so much to the Keynesian analytic system, he need only turn back a few pages to Roepke's presentation of his own theory of business cycles. It bears a close family reresemblance to the Keynesian theory. Roepke: "Expansion and contraction of investments, which go hand in hand with expansion and contraction of the supply of credit, constitute the real core of the cyclical movement" (p. 212). Keynes: "The Trade Cycle is best regarded, I think, as being occasioned by a cyclical change in the marginal efficiency of capital [the demand curve for investment] . . . ."[3] Given such close agreement between Roepke and Keynes on the analytical level, there would seem

445

---
[3] Keynes, John Maynard, *The General Theory of Employment, Interest and Money* (New York: Harcourt, Brace, 1936), p. 313.

to be little room for Roepke to take issue with Keynes as an economist. What Roepke proceeds to do, then, is to attack Keynes on several irrelevant fronts: in contrast to the "deistic moralist," Adam Smith, who left us, "in addition to his magnum opus on the *Wealth of Nations* (1776) a book on the *Theory of Moral Sentiments* (1759)," Keynes was a (presumably amoral) "**exponent of positivistic scientism**," who can claim only "a monograph on the theory of probability" in addition to his ecomonic works. With absolutely no analysis of the substantive content of Keynes' works, Roepke permits himself to label them "the end product of a process of disintegration in which the crisis of an exclusively rationalistic society finds its **ultimate expression**." Not only is Keynes' *economics* to be discredited because he failed to write books on morality, but he must be saddled with the immorality of his followers as well:

> . . . the real tragedy of the Keynesian legacy is that what Keynes regarded as intellectual "working capital," i.e., ideas easily shifted from the service of one ideal to that of another, became for his less flexible disciples intellectual "fixed capital," the profits of which were protected by every means available, including that of monopolistic exclusion. *Keynes cannot be spared the reproach of having failed to take this fateful result of his writings and teachings into account.* (p. 225, italics supplied.)

We are thus asked to blame the doctor for the death of his patient when the latter takes a prescription for moderate exercise as license for an attempt at the four-minute mile. Such procedure, I would submit, is simply inadmissable in any rational evaluation of economic theories. If Roepke were concerned to give us a critical biography of Keynes, he should have made his intention clear.

To pass off a few derogatory remarks on Keynes and the Keynesians as a sufficient critique of the substance of Keynes' economics is, however, a form of intellectual laxity which contributes little either to biography or economics. The fact is that Adam Smith's economics *qua* economics stands solely on its ability to give us a useful, i.e., empirically relevant, framework within which to analyze economic problems, not on the fact that Smith happened to be a deist or that his followers were prudent men. It is on this same basis that Keynes' economics should and will ultimately be judged. Personal and social values may well find themselves confirmed in economic writing, and conversely we may reject recommendations which conflict with our values though they are founded on good economic reasoning. It is important, however, especially in a book about economics, to make a distinction between economics and ethics. Roepke, especially in his discussion of Keynes, has failed to do this, and it detracts greatly from his book.

AT A TIME when various collectivist programs gain ever greater acceptance among the most influential groups in our society, there can be no doubt of the need for a good introductory economics textbook which explicitly emphasizes the method by which the free market solves economic problems. *Economics of the Free Society* is an attempt to fill this need, but it does so only partially. There are areas in which its analysis can be quite effective, but these are too lightly interspersed in a book which avoids logical analysis at almost every point. Since most collectivist programs suffer precisely from a deficiency in their underlying logic, it is to be regretted that Roepke chose not to exploit this weakness.

446

NEW BOOKS AND ARTICLES

THE FOLLOWING IS A SELECT LIST OF BOOKS AND ARTICLES WHICH, IN THE OPINION OF THE EDITORS, MAY BE OF INTEREST TO OUR READERS.

Yale Brozen, *Automation: The Impact of Technological Change* (Washington, D.C.: American Enterprise Institute, 1963), $1.00. A professional economist analyzes the arguments on automation, pro and con, and cites some remarkable statistics in its behalf. A noteworthy study.

James Dugan, *American Viking* (New York: Harper, 1963). The saga of the shipping magnate Hans Isbrandtsen, the rugged individualist who successfully challenged the international shipping cartel and took on the meddling bureaucrats of many nations with less success.

F. A. Hayek, ed., *Capitalism and the Historians* (Chicago: University of Chicago Press, 1963), $1.50, paper. A reprint of six essays, examining the "supreme myth which more than any other has served to discredit the economic system to which we owe our present-day civilization . . . the legend of the deterioration of the position of the working class in consequence of the rise of 'capitalism' . . ." Contributors to this valuable symposium are T. S. Ashton, Louis Hacker, W. H. Hutt, Bertrand de Jouvenal and the editor.

Helmut Schoeck and James W. Wiggins, eds., *The New Argument in Economics: The Public vs. the Private Sector* (Princeton, N. J.: Van Nostrand, 1963), $5.95. The latest in the stimulating and high-level symposia on various philosophical and political subjects edited by the two Emory University sociologists. This volume contains papers by George Stigler, W. Allen Wallis, Ernest van den Haag, and others, dissecting the "public squalor argument."

Neil McInnes, "Half a Century of Rent Control," *Barron's*, July 8, 1963. A review of French rent control policies, which have "turned France into a nation of slum-dwellers."

Benjamin A. Rogge, "Is Economic Freedom Possible?" *The Freeman*, April, 1963 (free copy on request from Foundation for Economic Education, Irvington-on-Hudson, New York). An examination of the charge that private monopoly will inevitably make free enterprise impossible.

Richard M. Weaver, "Two Types of American Individualism," *Modern Age*, Spring, 1963. In his last published article, Prof. Weaver contrasts the aristocratic individualism of John Randolph with the "high but irresponsible thinking of Thoreau," and argues for reinstitution of the former in our society, which has too curtly dismissed both. The same issue of *Modern Age* contains an article by A. A. Shenfield, "Economic Planning in Great Britain: Pretense and Reality." Here the author, a noted English economist, reviews the elusive goals and chaotic results of Labor Party policies, and lauds the re-emergence of liberal principles up until 1955 under the Conservative Party. Regrettably, he observes, it has since relapsed into a fascination with centralized planning, which often seems to have "the power of magic over men's minds—and the inability of magic to master men's problems."

The fourth volume of *The Journal of Law and Economics* (dated Autumn, 1961) has been issued, and includes articles by George Stigler, Milton Friedman, and others. Of all American scholarly journals, this annual publication is undoubtedly the one most solidly in the classical liberal tradition. A complete set (four numbers) may be obtained for $10 (students, $4) by writing: Prof. Aaron Director, The Journal of Law and Economics, University of Chicago Law School, Chicago 37, Illinois.

447

In the Coming Year . . .

NEW INDIVIDUALIST REVIEW will NOT publish articles by James Baldwin, Ralph McGill, Walter Lippmann, J. William Fulbright, Arthur Schlesinger, Jr., Gore Vidal, Jean-Paul Sartre, Nehru, or Howard N'Bongo-Bongo, Prime Minister of Anthropophagia;

NIR will not tell you how affluent you are, or urge you to write your Congressman to triple your income-tax, so that the country can eliminate squalor in the public sector;

NIR will not attempt to distinguish between in-itself and for-itself in the Theatre of the Absurd, or compare Bertholt Brecht favorably with Shakespeare;

NIR will not claim that Portuguese rule in Angola is the single greatest threat to world peace today;

448

NIR will not try to convert you to Zen Buddhism;

NIR will not assert that American businessmen are morally inferior to the Mau Mau.

This alone would be worth the price of a subscription, even if we sent you 60 pages of blank paper every three months. (After all, how many other magazines can make this guarantee: DOUBLE YOUR MONEY BACK if we break any of these promises.) But we do more—we send you a magazine full of thoughtful and thought-provoking discussions of individualist ideas and proposals, by some of the leading conservative and libertarian writers of today and tomorrow—articles like those in the issue you've just read.

HOW CAN YOU POSSIBLY LIVE WITHOUT NIR? SUBSCRIBE TODAY!

Society lives and acts only in individuals
. . . Everyone carries a part of society on
his shoulders; no one is relieved of his share
of responsibility by others. And no one can
find a safe way for himself if society is
sweeping toward destruction. Therefore
everyone, in his own interests, must thrust
himself vigorously into the intellectual battle. None can stand aside with unconcern;
the interests of everyone hang on the result. Whether he chooses or not, every man
is drawn into the great historical struggle,
the decisive battle (between freedom and
slavery) into which our epoch has plunged
us.

—Ludwig Von Mises

*The Intercollegiate Society of Individualists, a non-partisan, non-profit
educational organization, deals with ideas. ISI places primary emphasis on
the distribution of literature encompassing such academic disciplines as
economics, sociology, history, moral philosophy, and political science. If
you are a student or teacher, you are invited to add your name to the ISI
mailing list. There is no charge, and you may remove your name at any
time. For additional information, or to add your name to the list, write the
nearest ISI office.*

To Educate for Liberty

INTERCOLLEGIATE SOCIETY OF INDIVIDUALISTS

629 PUBLIC LEDGER BUILDING • PHILADELPHIA 6, PENN. • WAlnut 5-5632
Midwestern Office: 505 LEMCKE BUILDING • INDIANAPOLIS 4, INDIANA • MElrose 9-5551
Western Office: 1436 EL CAMINO REAL • MENLO PARK, CALIFORNIA • 323-0047

VOLUME 3
NUMBER 2
WINTER 1964

New
INDIVIDUALIST
Review

KINDS OF ORDER IN SOCIETY

Vol. 3, No. 2   35 cents

NEW INDIVIDUALIST REVIEW

Volume 3 — Number 2

455

NEW INDIVIDUALIST REVIEW is published quarterly by *New Individualist Review, Inc.,* at Ida Noyes Hall, University of Chicago, Chicago 37, Illinois.

Opinions expressed in signed articles do not necessarily represent the views of the editors. Editorial, advertising, and subscription correspondence and manuscripts should be sent to NEW INDIVIDUALIST REVIEW, Ida Noyes Hall, University of Chicago, Chicago 37, Illinois. All manuscripts become the property of NEW INDIVIDUALIST REVIEW.

Subscription rates: $2.00 per year (students $1.00).

NEW

INDIVIDUALIST

REVIEW

EDITORIAL STAFF

Editors-in-Chief ● Ronald Hamowy ● Ralph Raico
Associate Editors ● Robert M. Hurt ● John P. McCarthy
Robert Schuettinger ● John Weicher
Business Manager ● Sam Peltzman
Editorial Assistants ● J. Michael Cobb ● James Powell
Jameson Campaigne, Jr. ● Burton Gray ● Thomas Heagy ●
Robert Michaels ● James Rock

EDITORIAL ADVISORS

Yale Brozen ● Milton Friedman ● George J. Stigler
University of Chicago
F. A. Hayek ● Benjamin Rogge
University of Freiburg *Wabash College*

456

Kinds of Order in Society

F. A. HAYEK

WE CALL A MULTITUDE of men a society when their activities are mutually adjusted to one another. Men in society can successfully pursue their ends because they know what to expect from their fellows. Their relations, in other words, show a certain order. How such an order of the multifarious activities of millions of men is produced or can be achieved is the central problem of social theory and social policy.[1]

Sometimes the very existence of such an order is denied when it is asserted that society—or, more particularly, its economic activities—are "chaotic." A complete absence of an order, however, cannot be seriously maintained. What presumably is meant by that complaint is that society is not as orderly as it should be. The orderliness of existing society may indeed be capable of great improvement; but the criticism is due mainly to the circumstance that both the order which exists and the manner in which it is formed are not readily perceived. The plain man will be aware of an order of social affairs only to the extent that such an order has been deliberately arranged; and he is inclined to blame the apparent absence of an order

in much of what he sees on the fact that nobody has deliberately ordered those activities. Order, to the ordinary person, is the result of the ordering activity of an ordering mind. Much of the order of society of which we speak is, however, not of this kind; and the very recognition that there exists such an order requires a certain amount of reflection.

The chief difficulty is that the order of social events can generally not be perceived by our senses but can only be traced by our intellect. It is, as we shall say, an abstract and not a concrete order. It is also a very complex order. And it is an order which, though it is the result of human action, has not been created by men deliberately arranging the elements in a preconceived pattern. These peculiarities of the social order are closely connected, and it will be the task of this essay to make their interrelation clear. We shall see that, although there

---

F. A. Hayek, an editorial advisor of NEW INDIVIDUALIST REVIEW, is Professor of Political Economy at the University of Freiburg and Honorary President of the Mt. Pelerin Society. He is the author of several books, including *The Road to Serfdom, The Counter-Revolution of Science,* and, most recently, *The Constitution of Liberty.*

[1] The concept of order has recently achieved a central position in the social sciences largely through the work of Walter Eucken and his friends and pupils, known as the Ordo-circle from the yearbook *Ordo* issued by them. For other instances of its use, see: J. J. Spengler, "The Problem of Order in Economic Affairs," *Southern Economic Journal,* July, 1948, reprinted in J. J. Spengler and W. R. Allen, eds., *Essays on Economic Thought* (Chicago: Rand McNally, 1960); H. Barth, *Die Idee der Ordnung* (Zurich: E. Rentsch, 1958); R. Meimberg, *Alternativen der Ordnung* (Berlin: Duncker & Humblot, 1956); and, more remotely relevant as a treatment of some of the philosophical problems involved, W. D. Oliver, *Theory of Order* (Yellow Springs, Ohio: Antioch Press, 1951).

is no absolute necessity that a complex order must always be spontaneous and abstract, the more complex the order is at which we aim, the more we shall have to rely on spontaneous forces to bring it about, and the more our power of control will be confined in consequence to the abstract features and not extend to the concrete manifestations of that order.[2]

(The terms "concrete" and "abstract," which we shall have to use frequently, are often used in a variety of meanings. It may be useful, therefore, to state here in which sense they will be used. As "concrete" we shall describe particular real objects given to observation by our senses, and regard as the distinguishing characteristic of such concrete objects that there are always still more properties of them to be discovered than we already know or have perceived. In comparison with any such determinate object, and the intuitive knowledge we can acquire of it, all images and concepts of it are abstract and possess a limited number of attributes. *All* thought is in this sense necessarily abstract, although there are degrees of abstractness and it is customary to describe the relatively less abstract in contrast to the more abstract as (relatively) concrete. Strictly speaking, however, the contrast between the concrete and the abstract, as we shall use it, is the same as that between a fact of which we always know only abstract attributes but can always discover still more such attributes, and all those images, conceptions, and concepts which we retain when we no longer contemplate the particular object.[3]

The distinction between an abstract and a (relatively) concrete order is, of course, the same as that between a concept with a small connotation (intention) and a consequently wide denotation on the one hand, and a concept with a rich connotation and a correspondingly narrow denotation on the other. An abstract order of a certain kind may comprise many different manifestations of that order. The distinction becomes particularly important in the case of complex orders based on a hierarchy of ordering relations where several such orders may agree with respect to their more general ordering principles but differ in others. What is significant in the present context is that it may be important that an order possesses certain abstract features irrespective of its concrete manifestations, and that we may have it in our power to bring it about that an order which spontaneously forms itself will have those desirable characteristics, but not to determine the concrete manifestations or the position of the individual elements.)

THE SIMPLE CONCEPTION of an order of the kind which results when somebody puts the parts of an intended whole in their appropriate places applies in many parts of society. Such an order which is achieved by *arranging* the relations between the parts according to a preconceived plan we call in the social field an ,*organization*. The extent to which the power of many men can be increased by such deliberate co-ordination of their efforts is well-known and many of the achievements of man rest on the use of this technique. It is an order which we all understand because we know how it is made. But it is not the only nor even the chief kind of order on which the working of society rests; nor can the whole of the order of society be produced in this manner.

The *discovery* that there exist in society orders of another kind which have not been designed by men but have resulted from the action of individuals without their intending to create such an order, is the achievement of social theory—or, rather, it was this discovery

---

[2] For a more extensive treatment of the problem of the scientific treatment of complex phenomena, see my essay, "The Theory of Complex Phenomena," in Mario A. Bunge, ed.: *The Critical Approach: Essays in Honor of Karl Popper* (New York: The Free Press of Glencoe, Inc., 1963).

[3] For a helpful survey of the abstract/concrete relation and especially its significance in jurisprudence, see K. Englisch, *Die Idee der Konkretisierung in Rechtswissenschaft unserer Zeit* (Heidelberg: *Abhandlungen der Heidelberger Akademie der Wissenschaften*, Phil.-Hist. Klasse, I, 1953).

458

which has shown that there was an object for social theory. It shook the deeply-ingrained belief of men that where there was an order there must also have been a personal orderer. It had consequences far beyond the field of social theory since it provided the conceptions which made possible a theoretical explanation of the structures of biological phenomena.[4] And in the social field it provided the foundation for a systematic argument for individual liberty.

This kind of order which is characteristic not only of biological organisms (to which the originally much wider meaning of the term organism is now usually confined), is an order which is not made by anybody but which forms itself.

It is for this reason usually called a "spontaneous" or sometimes (for reasons we shall yet explain) a "polycentric" order. If we understand the forces which determine such an order, we can use them by creating the conditions under which such an order will form itself.

This indirect method of bringing about an order has the advantage that it can be used to produce orders which are far more complex than any order we can produce by putting the individual pieces in their appropriate places. But it has the drawback that it enables us to determine only the general character of the resulting order and not its detail. Its use in one sense thus extends our powers: it places us in a position to produce very complex orders which we could never produce by putting the individual elements in their places. Our power over the particular arrangement of the elements in such an order is however much more limited than it is over an order which we produce by individually arranging the parts. All we can control are certain abstract features of such an order, but not its concrete detail.

All this is familiar in the physical and biological field. We could never produce a crystal by directly placing the individual molecules from which it is built up. But we can create the conditions under which such a crystal will form itself. If for that purpose we make use of known forces, we can, however, not determine the position an individual molecule will occupy within a crystal, or even the size or position of the several crystals. Similarly, we can create the conditions under which a biological organism will grow and develop. But all we can do is create conditions favorable to that growth, and we are able to determine the resulting shape and structure only within narrow limits. The same applies to spontaneous social orders.

IN THE CASE OF certain social phenomena, such as language, the fact that they possess an order which nobody has deliberately designed and which we have to discover, is now generally recognized. In these fields we have at last outgrown the naive belief that every orderly arrangement of parts which assist man in the pursuit of his ends must be due to a personal maker. There was a time when it was believed that all those useful institutions which serve the intercourse of men, such as language, morals, law, writing, or money, must be due to an individual inventor or legislator, or to an explicit agreement of wise men who consented to certain useful practices.[5] We understand now the process by which such institutions have gradually taken shape through men learning to act according to certain rules — rules which they long knew how to follow before there was any need to state them in words.

But if in those simpler instances we have overcome the belief that, wherever we find an order or a regular structure which serves a human purpose, there must also have been a mind which deliberately created it, the reluctance to recognize the existence of such spontaneous orders is still with us in many other fields. We still cling to a division, deeply embedded in Western thought since the

459

---

[4] All three independent discoverers of biological evolution, Darwin, Wallace, and Spencer, admittedly derived their ideas from the current concepts of social evolution.

[5] Cf., e.g., the examples given by Denys Hay, *Polydore Vergil* (Oxford: Clarendon Press, 1952), ch. 3.

classical antiquity, between things which owe their order to "nature" and those which owe it to "convention."[6] It still seems strange and unbelievable to many people that an order may arise neither wholly independent of human action, nor as the intended result of such action, but as the unforeseen effect of conduct which men have adopted with no such end in mind. Yet much of what we call culture is just such a spontaneously grown order which arose neither altogether independently of human action nor by design, but by a process which stands somewhere between these two possibilities which were long considered as exclusive alternatives.

Such spontaneous orders we find not only in the working of institutions like language or law (or, more conspicuously, the biological organisms) which show a recognizable permanent structure that is the result of slow evolution, but also in the relations of the market which must continuously form and reform themselves and where only the conditions conducive to their constant reconstitution have been shaped by evolution. The genetic and the functional aspects can never be fully separated.[7]

That division of labor on which our economic system rests is the best example of such a daily renewed order. In the order created by the market, the participants are constantly induced to respond to events of which they do not directly know, in a way which secures a continuous flow of production, a co-ordination of the quantities of the different things so that the even flow is not interrupted and everything is produced at least as cheaply as anybody can still provide the last quantities for which others are prepared to pay the costs. That it is an order which consists of

the adaptation to the multitudinous circumstances which no single person can know completely is one reason why its existence is not perceived by simple inspection. It is embodied in such relations as those between prices and costs of commodities and the corresponding distribution of resources; and we can confirm that such an order in fact exists only after we have reconstructed its principles in our minds.

THE "ORDERING FORCES" of which we can make use in such instances are the rules governing the behavior of the elements of which the orders are formed. They determine that each element will respond to the particular circumstances which act on it in a manner which will result in an overall pattern. Each of the iron filings, for instance, which are magnetized by a magnet under the sheet of paper on which we have poured them, will so act on and react to all the others that they will arrange themselves in a characteristic figure of which we can predict the general shape but not the detail. In this simple instance the elements are all of the same kind and the known uniform rules which determine their behavior would enable us to predict the behavior of each in great detail if we only knew all the facts and were able to deal with them in all their complexity.

Some order of a determinate general character may form itself also from various kinds of different elements, i.e., of elements whose response to given circumstances will be alike only in some but not in all respects. The formation of the molecules of highly complex organic compounds provides an example from the physical sciences. But the fact is especially significant for many of the spontaneous orders which form themselves in the biological and social sphere. They are composed of many different elements which will respond to the same circumstances alike in some respects but not in others. But they will form orderly wholes, because each element responds to its particular environment in accord-

---

[6] Cf. F. Heinimann, *Nomos und Physis* (Basel: F. Reinhardt, 1945).

[7] On the inseparability of the genetic and the functional aspects of these phenomena as well as the general relation between organisms and organizations, see Carl Menger, *Untersuchungen uber die Methode der Sozialwissenschaften und der politischen Oekonomie insbesondere* (Leipzig: Duncker & Humblot, 1883), which is still the classical treatment of these topics.

ance with definite rules. The order results thus from the separate responses of the different elements to the particular circumstances which act on them and for this reason we describe it as a "polycentric order."[8]

The physical examples of spontaneous orders we have considered are instructive because they show that the rules which the elements follow need of course not be "known" to them. The same is true more often than not where living beings and particularly men are the elements of such an order. Man does not know most of the rules on which he acts;[9] and even what we call his intelligence is largely a system of rules which operate on him but which he does not know. In animal societies and in a great measure in primitive human society, the structure of social life is determined by rules of action which manifest themselves only in their being obeyed. It is only when individual intellects begin to differ sufficiently (or individual minds become more complex) that it becomes necessary to express the rules in communicable form so that they can be taught by example and deviant behavior can be corrected and differences of view expressed about what is to be decided.[10] Though man never existed without laws which he obeyed, he did exist for millennia without laws which he knew in the sense that he was able to articulate them.

Where the elements of the social order are individual men, the particular circumstances to which each of them reacts are those which are known to him. But it is only when the responses of the individuals show a certain similarity, or obey some common rules that this will result in an overall order. Even a limited similarity of their responses—common rules which determine only some aspects of their behavior—suffice, however, for the formation of an order of a general kind. The important fact is that this order will be an adaptation to a multitude of circumstances which are known only to the individual members but not as a totality to any one of them; and that such an order will result only because, and in so far as, the different individuals follow similar rules in these responses to the particular circumstances known to them. This does not mean, nor is it necessary for the production of an order, that in similar circumstances different persons will do precisely the same thing. All that is meant and required is that in some respect they follow the same rule, that their responses are similar in some degree, or that they are limited to a certain range of actions which all have some attributes in common. This is true even of the iron filings in our former illustration which may not all move with the same speed because they will be different in shape, smoothness, or weight. Such differences will determine the particular manifestation of the resulting pattern which, in consequence of our ignorance of these particulars, will be unpredictable; but the general character of the pattern will be unaffected by them and will therefore be predictable.

Similarly, the responses of the human individuals to events in their environment need be similar only in certain abstract aspects in order that a definite overall pattern should result. There must be some regularity but not complete regularity in their actions: they must follow some common rules, but these common rules need not be sufficient to determine their action fully; and what action a particular individual will take will depend on further characteristics peculiar to him.

461

---

[8] Cf. Michael Polanyi, *The Logic of Liberty* (London: Routledge and Kegan Paul, 1951), p. 159.

[9] On the whole issue of the relation of unconscious rules to human action, on which I can touch here only briefly, see my essay, "Rules, Perception, and Intelligibility," *Proceedings of the British Academy*, v. 48 (1962-63).

[10] There thus seems to be some truth in the alleged original state of goodness in which everybody spontaneously did right and could not do otherwise, and to the idea that only with increased knowledge came wrongdoing. It is only with the knowledge of other possibilities that the individual becomes able to deviate from the established rules; without such knowledge, no sin.

The question which is of central importance both for social theory and social policy is what rules the individuals must follow so that an order will result. Some such common rules the individuals will follow merely because of the similarity of their environment, or, rather, because of the similar manner in which this environment reflects itself in their minds. Others they will all follow spontaneously because they are part of the common cultural tradition of their society. But there are still others which it is necessary that they be made to obey, since it would be in the interest of each individual to disregard them, though the overall order will be formed only if the rule is generally obeyed.

The chief regularity in the conduct of individuals in a society based on division of labor and exchange follows from their common situation: they all work to earn an income. This means that they will normally prefer a larger income for a given effort—and possibly increase their effort if its productivity increases. This is a rule which is sufficiently generally followed in fact for those who follow it to impress upon society an order of a certain kind. But the fact that most people follow this rule in their actions leaves the character of the resulting order yet very indeterminate, and it certainly does not by itself insure that this order will be of a beneficent character. For this it is necessary that people also obey certain conventional rules, i.e., rules which do not follow simply from the nature of their knowledge and aims but which have become habitual in their society. The common rules of morals and of law are the chief instance of this.

It is not our task here to analyze the relation between the different kinds of rules which people in fact follow and the order which results from this. We are interested only in one particular class of rules which contribute to the nature of the order and which, because we can deliberately shape them, are the chief tool through which we can influence the general character of the order which will form itself: the rules of law. These rules differ from the others

which individuals follow chiefly by the circumstances that people are made to obey them by their fellows. They are necessary because only if the individuals know what means are at their respective disposals, and are made to bear the consequences of their use of these means, will the resulting order possess certain desirable attributes. The appropriate delimitation of these individual spheres is the main function of the rules of law, and their desirable content one of the chief problems of social policy. This is not altered by the fact that their desirable form has been found largely by the accumulated experience of ages and that their further improvement is also to be expected more from slow experimental piecemeal evolution than from redesign of the whole.

THOUGH THE CONDUCT of the individuals which produces the social order is guided in part by deliberately enforced rules, the order is still a spontaneous order, corresponding to an organism rather than to an organization. It does not rest on the activities being fitted together according to a preconceived plan, but on their being adjusted to each other through the confinement of the action of each by certain general rules. And the enforcement of these general rules insures only the general character of the order and not its concrete realization. It also provides only general facilities which unknown individuals may use for their own ends, but does not insure the achievement of any particular results.

In order to enforce the rules required for the formation of this spontaneous order, an order of the other kind, an organization, is also required. Even if the rules themselves were given once and for all, their enforcement would demand the coordinated effort of many men. The task of changing and improving the rules may also, though it need not, be the object of organized effort. And in so far as the state, in addition to upholding the law, renders other services to the citizens, this also requires an organized apparatus.

The organization of the apparatus of government is also effected in some measure by means of rules. But these rules which serve the creation and direction of an organization are of a different character from those which make possible the formation of a spontaneous order. They are rules which apply only to particular people selected by government; and they have to be followed by them in most instances (i.e., except in the case of judges) in the pursuit of particular ends also determined by government.

Even where the type of order chosen is that of organization and not a spontaneous order, the organizer must largely rely on rules rather than specific commands to the members of the organization. This is due to the fundamental problem which all complex order encounters: the organizer wants the individuals who are to cooperate to make use of knowledge which he himself does not possess. In none but the most simple kinds of social order it is conceivable that all activities are governed by a single mind. And certainly nobody has yet succeeded in deliberately arranging all the activities of a complex society; there is no such thing as a fully planned society of any degree of complexity. If anyone did succeed in organizing such a society, it would not make use of many minds but would instead be altogether dependent on one mind; it would certainly not be complex but very primitive —and so would soon be the mind whose knowledge and will determined everything. The facts which enter into the design of such an order could be only those which could be perceived and digested by this mind; and as only he could decide on action and thus gain experience, there could not be that interplay of many minds in which a lone mind can grow.

The kind of rules which govern an organization are rules for the performance of assigned tasks. They presuppose that the place of each individual in a fixed skeleton order is decided by deliberate appointment, and that the rules which apply to him depend on the place he has been given in that order. The rules thus regulate only the detail of the action of appointed functionaries or agencies of government—or the functioning of an organization created by arrangement.

Rules which are to enable individuals to find their own places in a spontaneous order of the whole society must be general; they must not assign to particular individuals a status, but rather leave the individual to create his own position. The rules which assist in the running of an organization, on the other hand, operate only within a framework of specific commands which designate the particular ends which the organization aims at and the particular functions which the several members are to perform. Though applicable only to particular, individually designated people, these rules of an organization look very much like the general rules underlying a spontaneous order, but they must not be confused with the latter. They enable those who have to carry out commands to fill in detail according to circumstances which they, but not the author of the command, know.

In the terms we have used, this means that the general rules of law aim at an abstract order whose concrete or particular manifestation is unpredictable; while both the commands and the rules which enable those who obey commands to fill in the detail left open by the command, serve a concrete order or an organization. The more complex the order aimed at, the greater will be the part of the circumstances determining its concrete manifestation which cannot be known to those whose concern it is to secure the formation of the order, and the more they will be able to control it only through rules and not through commands. In the most complex type of organizations little more than the assignment of particular functions to particular people will be determined by specific decisions, while the performance of these functions will be regulated only by rules. It is when we pass from the biggest organization, serving particular tasks, to the order of the whole of society

463

which comprises the relations between those organizations as well as the relations between them and the individuals and among the individuals, that this overall order relies entirely on rules, i.e., is entirely of a spontaneous character, with not even its skeleton determined by commands. The situation is, of course, that, because it was not dependent on organization but grew as a spontaneous order, the structure of modern society has attained a degree of complexity which far exceeds that which it is possible to achieve by deliberate organization. Even the rules which made the growth of this complex order possible were not designed in anticipation of that result; but those peoples who happened to adopt suitable rules developed a complex civilization which prevailed over others. It is thus a paradox, based on a complete misunderstanding of these connections, when it is sometimes contended that we must deliberately plan modern society because it has grown so complex. The fact is rather that we can preserve an order of such complexity only if we control it not by the method of "planning," i.e., by direct orders, but on the contrary aim at the formation of a spontaneous order based on general rules.

We shall presently have to consider how in such a complex system the different principles of order must be combined. At this stage it is necessary, however, at once to forestall a misunderstanding and to stress that there is one way in which it can never be sensible to mix the two principles. While in an organization it makes sense, and indeed will be the rule, to determine the skeleton by specific command and regulate the detail of the action of the different members only by rules, the reverse could never serve a rational purpose; if the overall character of an order is of the spontaneous kind, we cannot improve upon it by issuing to the elements of that order direct commands: because only these individuals and no central authority will know the circumstances which make them do what they do.

EVERY SOCIETY of any degree of complexity must make use of both ordering principles which we have discussed. But while they must be combined by being applied to different tasks and to the sectors of society corresponding to them, they cannot successfully be mixed in any manner we like. Lack of understanding of the difference between the two principles constantly leads to such confusion. It is the manner in which the two principles are combined which determines the character of the different social and economic systems. (The fact that these different "systems" which result from different combinations of the two ordering principles, are sometimes also referred to as different "orders" has added to the terminological confusion.)

We shall consider further only a free system which relies on spontaneous ordering forces not merely (as every system must) to fill in the interstices left by the commands determining its aim and structure, but also for its overall order. Such systems not only have many organizations (in particular, firms) as their elements but also require an organization to enforce obedience to (and modify and develop) the body of abstract rules which are required to secure the formation of the spontaneous overall order. The fact that government is itself an organization and employs rules as an instrument of its organization, and that beyond its task of enforcing the law this organization renders a multitude of other services, has led to a complete confusion between the nature of the different kinds of rules and the orders which they serve.

The abstract and general rules of law in the narrow sense (in which "the law" comprises the rules of civil and criminal law) aim not at the creation of an order by arrangement but at creating the conditions in which an order will form itself. But the conception of law as a means of order-creation (a term which, as a translation of the equally ambiguous German *Ordnungsgestaltung*, is now invading Anglo-American jurisprudence[11]) in the hands of public lawyers and civil

464

servants who are primarily concerned with tasks of organization rather than with the conditions of the formation of a spontaneous order, is increasingly interpreted as meaning an instrument of arrangement. This conception of law, which is the conception prevailing in totalitarian states, has characteristically been given its clearest expression by the legal theorist who became Hitler's chief legal apologist, as "concrete order formation" (*konkretes Ordnungsdenken*).[12] This kind of law aims at creating a concrete preconceived order by putting each individual on a task assigned by authority.

But though this technique of creating an order is indispensable for organizing the institutions of government and all the enterprises and households which form the elements of the order of society as a whole, it is wholly inadequate for bringing about the infinitely more complex overall order.

We have it in our power to assure that such an overall order will form itself and will possess certain desirable general characteristics, but only if we do not attempt to control the detail of that order. But we jettison that power and deprive ourselves of the possibility of achieving that abstract order of the whole, if we insist on placing particular pieces into the place we wish them to occupy. It is the condition of the formation of this abstract order that we leave the concrete and particular details to the separate individuals and bind them only by general and abstract rules. If we do not provide this condition but restrict the capacity of the individuals to adjust themselves to the particular circumstances known only to them, we destroy the forces making for a spontaneous overall order and are forced to replace them by deliberate arrangement which, though it gives us greater con-

trol over detail, restricts the range over which we can hope to achieve a coherent order.

IT IS NOT IRRELEVANT to our chief purpose if in conclusion we consider briefly the role which abstract rules play in the coordination not only of the actions of many different persons but also in the mutual adjustment of the successive decisions of a single individual or organization. Here, too, it is often not possible to make detailed plans for action in the more distant future (although what we should do now depends on what **we shall want** to do in the future), simply because we do not yet know the particular facts which we shall face. The method through which we nevertheless succeed in giving some coherence to our actions is that we adopt a framework of rules for guidance which makes the general pattern though not the detail of our life predictable. It is these rules of which we are often not consciously aware—in many instances rules of a very abstract character—which make the course of our lives orderly. Many of these rules will be "customs" of the social group in which we have grown up and only some will be individual "habits" which we have accidentally or deliberately acquired. But they all serve to abbreviate the list of circumstances which we need to take into account in the particular instances, singling out certain classes of facts as alone determining the general kind of action which we should take. At the same time, this means that we systematically disregard certain facts which we know and which would be relevant to our decisions if we knew all such facts, but which it is rational to neglect because they are accidental partial information which does not alter the probability that, if we could know and digest all the facts, the balance of advantage would be in favor of following the rule.

It is, in other words, our restricted horizon of knowledge of the concrete facts which makes it necessary to coordinate our actions by submitting to

465

[11] Cf., e.g., E. Bodenheimer, *Jurisprudence, the Philosophy and Method of Law* (Cambridge: Harvard University Press, 1962), p. 211.

[12] See Carl Schmitt, *Die drei Arten des rechtswissenschaftlichen Denkens* (Hamburg: Schriften fur Akademie fur deutsches Recht, 1934).

Page Eleven

abstract rules rather than to attempt to decide each particular case solely in view of the limited set of relevant particular facts which we happen to know. It may sound paradoxical that rationality should thus require that we deliberately disregard knowledge which we possess; but this is part of the necessity of coming to terms with our unalterable ignorance of much that would be relevant if we knew it. Where we know that the probability is that the unfavorable effects of a kind of action will overbalance the favorable ones, the decision should not be affected by the circumstance that in the particular case a few consequences which we happen to be able to foresee should all be favorable. The fact is that in an apparent striving after rationality in the sense of fuller taking into account all the foreseeable consequences, we may achieve greater irrationality, less effective taking into account of remote effects and an altogether less coherent result. It is the great lesson which science has taught us that we must resort to the abstract where we cannot master the concrete. The preference for the concrete is to renounce the power which thought gives us. It is therefore also not really surprising that the consequence of modern democratic legislation which disdains submitting to general rules and attempts to solve each problem as it comes on its specific merits, is probably the most irrational and disorderly arrangement of affairs ever produced by the deliberate decisions of men.

466

New Individualist Review welcomes contributions for publication from its readers. Essays should not exceed 3,000 words, and should be type-written. All manuscripts will receive careful consideration.

The Results of Planning in India

B. R. SHENOY

PLANNING IS NOT, like Communism. a way of life, though planning and Communism necessarily go together. In democracies, planning may be defended only as a means to an end. The aim of planning in India is fourfold: abolition of poverty, liquidation of unemployment, reduction of income inequalities, and industrialization. By emphasizing the third objective — reduction of income inequalities — it is sought to establish, simultaneously with economic progress, a socialist pattern of society, the principal characteristics of which will be absence of concentrations of wealth, income and economic power, and prevention of the stifling of talent for want of opportunities.

Indian planners believe that these objectives cannot be achieved with the speed necessary to prevent a social explosion, if the economy and society are left free to trudge along on their own. In common with their counterparts in other countries, they have a deep-seated distrust of the ability of the free-market mechanism to realize striking overall progress; they believe that the profit motive animating it is apt to divert productive resources into fields where they may yield the highest private gains rather than the highest social good. They

B. R. Shenoy is Director of the School of Social Sciences at Gujarat University, in Ahmedabad, India. He is a contributor of numerous articles to scholarly journals, and a member of the Mt. Pelerin Society.

maintain that a planning commission, on the other hand, would be actuated by considerations of the advance of the community as a whole, not by any private or sectional interests. Though this assertion is unsupported by any rigorous reasoning or empirical evidence, it represents the conviction of the policy makers and of the people that count in India.

It is now possible to put to the test this claim of Indian planners by assessing our achievements during the past decade of planning. We shall attempt this in terms of each of the four objectives of Indian economic planning.

ORDINARILY, PROGRESS in the abolition of poverty may be broadly gauged by the expansion of production. From 1950-51, the last pre-Plan year, to 1961-62, Indian national income (at constant prices) rose by 47 per cent, or at an annual rate of 3.6 per cent. This figure, however, is highly misleading as evidence of our progress in overcoming poverty. For such evidence, the increase in national income must be modified by four deflators.

First, it must be adjusted for the rise in population, as per capita income is more meaningful as an indicator of well-being than the income of the community as a whole. According to the 1961 Census, Indian population rose by 22 per cent during the past decade. On this basis,

467

per capita income rose by but 18.5 per cent, from $51.98 in 1950-51 to $61.61 in 1961-62, or by less than one-half of the increase in overall national income.

Secondly, since the ultimate test of economic welfare is the marketed output of consumer goods, due allowances must be made from national income statistics (a) for the unduly large output of non-consumer goods as reflected by excess production capacities, and (b) for excessive additions to inventories. Excess capacities exist both in the capital goods and consumer goods industries and in the public as well as the private sector. They are estimated at 35 per cent in the major and minor irrigation works, of a lesser order in the power projects and at an average of 40 to 50 per cent in 40 industries.

Additions to inventories are common under inflation, though it is not always possible to assess their precise magnitude. Circumstantial evidence confirms the build-up of inventories of foodgrains during the three years ending 1958-59 when foodgrains prices rose by 18 per cent. Total foodgrains supplies — domestic production plus imports — went up from 65.81 million tons in 1955-56 to 77.70 million tons in 1958-59. This was a much faster rate of increase (over 5 per cent per year) than the increase in money incomes (3.9 per cent per year). Since, in spite of this increased production, prices rose, it seems safe to infer that part of the increase in supplies was hoarded; if the whole of the enhanced supplies had flowed into the market, prices should have fallen. Since then, on the same reasoning, some decumulation of foodgrains stocks has probably taken place. This is evidenced by the fact that, though money incomes were 20.6 per cent higher in 1962 than in 1958-59, and foodgrains supplies rose by but 5 per cent, foodgrains prices remained steady, the index of foodgrains prices being 100.1 in 1959-60 and 100.0 in 1961-62 (1952-53=100). Apparently, the supplies placed on the market were larger than the domestic output plus imports, inventories being drawn upon for the difference.

Thirdly, as the well-being of a people must be assessed by the economic condition of the masses, not by the overall magnitude of the national income, due allowances must be made for the considerable sums of unmerited and illicit shifts of income which have taken place during the past decade in favor of the upper-income groups. Such income shifts have taken place (a) as a result of inflation, which has corroded the incomes of the fixed and "sticky" money income groups—the masses of the people—and has correspondingly added to the incomes of a fraction of the community— the traders, businessmen and industrialists; (b) because of controls which, in addition to corruption, have created sheltered markets and semi-monopolistic positions, bringing windfall gains to the beneficiaries of controls; and (c) from the great expansion of the public sector, which has added phenomenally to the illicit gains of contractors and other participants in this expansion.

In recent years, the magnitude of these income shifts may be of an annual order of $1.6 billion, or more than the rate of increase in the national income, which has averaged $1.5 billion per year during the past seven years. Large as this income shift might seem at first sight, it is, possibly, an underestimate, as is suggested by a review of the components of the income shifts.

The inflationary expansion of money —if this may be defined to be expansion of the money supply in excess of the needs of expanded production at constant prices—during the seven years ending 1961-62 amounted to $1.3 billion, or about $180 million per year. This may be taken as a rough measure of the "anti-social" income shifts resulting from inflation.

By law, private importers must buy a license from the government. Such licenses have been issued in an amount averaging $1.3 billion per year over the past seven years. However, the resale value of an import license is anywhere from 30 to 500 per cent or more above its face value, depending on the commodity concerned. Assuming an average mark-up of 75 per cent, total net gains from these licenses may be on the order of $1.0 billion per year. The bulk of the gains from these licenses accrues to well-to-do, or comparatively well-to-do, people, such as corrupt functionaries of the state, touts and "contact" men, and the recipients of the licenses.

Public sector investment outlays have shot up from $4.1 billion in the First Plan to $9.7 billion in the Second. However, when $100 is accounted as "invested" in a public sector project, all of this does not, in fact, go into the project concerned. A part, varying with circumstances, gets siphoned off into private incomes in the form of illicit payments made for obtaining business by the contractors and successful bidders. Assuming that such illicit payments, which again accrue to the well-to-do, average 20 per cent of "investment," they have amounted to about $400 million per year in the Second Plan period.

If to the above is added monopoly revenues accruing from controls, the total anti-social income shifts, even excluding illicit earnings from price controls, distribution controls, and other restrictions, may come to $1.6 to $1.7 billion per year.

Fourthly, national income at constant prices is arrived at mainly by deflating national income at current prices by index numbers of prices. However, the latter understate the actual level of prices, since, where price controls apply, they are based on controlled prices, which are generally lower than free-market prices. This is evidenced by the disparate movements of the price index and the money supply. From 1960-61 to 1962-63, while the money supply rose by 15.3 per cent, prices rose by but 2.4 per cent. Allowance being made for the larger money requirements of the expanded national product, prices should still have risen by at least 11 per cent. The use of these defective index numbers has led to the national income at current prices being insufficiently deflated, the statistics of national income at constant prices being correspondingly exaggerated. This exaggeration may be of an order of 8 per

cent during the three years ending 1962-63, so that the actual rate of growth of income during the period may be less than the rate of growth of population.

The net result of these adjustments may well be that the well-being of the masses of the people has stagnated during the past decade of planning. Eloquent evidence of this is in the consumption of food and cloth. In the context of Indian poverty, even apart from other data, the level of food and cloth consumption alone should be a sufficient indicator of plan achievements. Data on food consumption are in the *Economic Survey,* issued with the Union budget. Per capita "availability" of foodgrains per day fluctuated downward with the progress of planning, from 15.7 ozs. in 1954 to 14.0 ozs. in 1958, recovered to 16.2 ozs. in 1961, and was at 15.8 ozs. in 1962. These figures are not adjusted for additions to stocks by traders and farmers. With such adjustments, per capita consumption would be less than the "availabilities." Jail rations are 16 ozs., army rations 19 ozs. and the nutritional norm 18-19 ozs. During the five years ending 1960, annual per capita consumption of cloth, statistics of which are published in the *Indian Textile Bulletin,* issued by the Textile Commissioner, Ministry of Commerce and Industry, declined from 14.66 metres in 1956 to 13.98 metres in 1960.

THE NET GAIN FROM PLANNING in the field of employment seems to be negative. The additional employment produced by the First Plan was 4.7 million and from the Second 6.5 million—an improvement of 35 per cent—despite the steep rise of 110 per cent in investment outlays from $7.9 billion in the First Plan to $16.6 billion in the Second. Moreover, since the increase in employment has been less than the natural increase in the labor force, the Second Plan will bequeath to the Third Plan vastly more unemployed—conjectured at 9 million — than it inherited from the First—conjectured at 5.3 million. These computations are based on a population increase of 5 million per year—the rate indicated by the 1951 Census—of which 40 per cent is treated as additions to the labor force. The 1961 Census, however, revealed that the population has actually been rising at a rate of 7.9 million per year. If we take the latter figure, plan achievements in the field of employment appear even poorer. These employment statistics, however, cannot be taken at face value. Though issued officially, they are guesses, and the margin of error they embody may be large. But perhaps it may be broadly correct to say that the expansion of employment has probably lagged behind the expansion of the labor force.

REFERENCE HAS BEEN MADE to the anti-social income shifts resulting from inflation and statist economic measures. The experience of West Germany appears to have been similar; we are told that, while planning lasted in West Germany, there emerged "a thin upper crust able to afford anything" on top of a "broad lower stratum with insufficient purchasing power." Statism in India has concentrated power in the hands of the Administration—the politician and the civil servant. It has done this through public sector investment outlays, which amounted to $9.7 billion under the Second Plan and would be $16.9 billion under the Third—or a rise from 58 per cent to 66 per cent of total investment outlays, including foreign aid; and it has done this through permits, licenses, concessions and other instruments of statist direction and control of the economy, which enable their recipients to siphon from the community colossal gains to which they have neither economic nor moral claims. Unmerited and anti-social income shifts seem to be inevitable under statism.

Under economic freedom, on the other hand, control over investment resources would be acquired by tens of millions of entrepreneurs competing in the open market, and economic power would be correspondingly diffused over the community as a whole. Financial success

would be governed by efficiency, quality and price of the output, i.e., in proportion to what the individual adds to the national product. Under statism, however, financial success often rests overwhelmingly on contacts and "pull" in obtaining patronage, and not wholly on the use of talent to contribute to the stream of the national product. Statism is apt to bring into being a body of parasitical functionaries.

IN CONTRAST TO the disappointing record in regard to the three objectives of planning reviewed above, production statistics exhibit striking progress in industrialization, the fourth objective of the planners, the General Index of industrial production going up at an annual rate of 6.7 per cent, from 100 in 1951 to 191.8 in 1961. This has not lifted up the overall national product at a comparable rate, because industries account for but a minor part, 16 to 19 per cent, of total economic activity. Though progress was recorded in all categories of production, the expansion in the output of capital goods—machinery, electrical motors, machine tools and automobiles—and intermediate goods—coal, iron and steel, other metals, cement, heavy chemicals, paints, tanned hides, rubber goods and electricity—was outstanding. In 1960, the output of capital goods ranged from 2.9 times (automobiles) to 8.9 times (diesel engines) their output in 1950; the corresponding rise in intermediate goods was from 1.6 times (coal) to 21 times (rayon yarn).

Among consumer goods, the output of cotton textiles showed the least progress, the index of cotton textiles production rising from 100 in 1951 to 117 in 1961 (1951=100). The production indices for consumer goods used by the relatively well-to-do classes of the Indian people—sewing machines, electric lamps, electric fans, radio receivers, sugar, vegetable oil products and cigarettes—went up much faster, their increases varying from 1.9 times (vegetable oil products) to 9.6 times (sewing machines) their output in 1950. Most of these goods are still little more than curiosities to the masses of the people.

This pattern of industrial production corresponds to the foregoing analysis. It reflects the unduly large diversion of resources into heavy industries to the neglect of agriculture. The pattern of consumer goods production reflects the anti-social income shifts and the vastly larger improvement in the well-being of the upper income groups as compared with the masses of the people, the well-being of the latter remaining stagnant at best.

Most of the industrial expansion has taken place in defiance of the doctrine of comparative costs; it is forced by official policy, rigorous import restrictions and exchange controls. The unsalability abroad of Indian sugar surpluses because of the heavy price differential—the price of Indian sugar is about $242 per ton as against the world price of $66 per ton—is an example of the unconscionably heavy costs of industrialization in a closed market. Fertilizer, penicillin and refrigerators provide other examples. The landed cost of imported penicillin is 2¢ per million units, while the estimated cost of production in India is 26¢ per million units. The import of refrigerators is banned. The cost of a refrigerator in India is about $473. The cost of a comparable refrigerator in England is about $190. These are but a few instances of what applies extensively to the whole range of industrial production in India, though there may be striking exceptions here and there.

The wastages of forced industrialization are examples of what we may term "Walt Disney economics." Manifestations of waste may be seen in abundance in those under-developed countries which have embarked on the "exciting national pilgrimage" of "development" through "planned" industrialization, on which their economic salvation is believed to rest. Productive resources, which are extremely scarce, are devoted to fabricating commodities at home which may be imported—in unlimited amounts, in superior quality and at prices vastly lower than those charged for the poor quality home products. Were free competition permitted, the domestic manufactures would have little or no chance against the imported products. But the domestic manufactures are protected against this competition by autarchic policies reinforced by exchange restrictions.

A unique phenomenon of interest to this discussion is the vast gap between the landed costs and the market prices of virtually the whole range of import goods; these gaps have emerged as a consequence of inflation, an unrealistic exchange rate and exchange controls. The gaps vary from 30 per cent to 500 per cent or more of the landed costs, depending upon commodities. These price gaps are a rough measure of the unmerited windfall gains which accrue to the recipients of the import licenses; of the near-ransom prices paid by domestic consumers for imported goods and for their domestic substitutes; and of the waste of resources in producing goods at home which may be had much more cheaply through imports. If the resources thus wasted were employed in export industries with comparative cost advantages, the national product would rise commensurately. Such a policy would also put a stop to the prevailing anti-social income shifts from the general body of consumers to the holders of import licenses, dealers in imported goods and industrialists fabricating domestic substitutes for imported goods.

It is bad enough to produce goods at home which may be acquired at much lower costs from abroad. However, when the domestic output exceeds the demands of the home market, the surplus is sold abroad at knock-down prices subsidized by the government. The manufacturer-exporters have their losses made good by cash payments and other benefits which the government grants to certain categories of exporters as part of its "export promotion" schemes. Apparently, the under-developed countries are prepared to pay any price, however fantastic, to foster the growth of industry and "a technologically mature society." It is interesting to note that a part of this

471

price is paid by the industrially advanced countries in the form of massive "developmental" aid to the under-developed countries.

The phenomenal pace of progress in the industrialization of India is thus not a matter to be enthused over. It is a species of Pyrrhic victory. Obviously, the consumer does not stand to benefit from it. To continue the example of the refrigerator, what good can accrue to him to get mulcted of $473 and receive but a refrigerator in exchange, when, if imports were unrestricted—as in the pre-Plan days—he could not only have had a much better refrigerator, with fewer breakdowns and a longer life-span, but would still have had about $280 to furnish the kitchen with other goods.

Forced industrialization has been detrimental to the national product and to the expansion of employment, through the callous and wasteful disposal of resources which it has produced. Resources have been diverted from sectors where they produce greater output into sectors where real costs are higher and returns lower. It has been estimated that an additional investment of $2.1 million would yield a gross yearly output of $1.2 million to $1.4 million in agriculture and a gross output of $0.3 million to $0.9 million in five manufacturing industries —cement, paper, iron and steel, cotton textiles and sugar, the output in iron and steel being $0.4 million. The same amount of investment would provide employment for 500 persons in large-scale investment goods industries, 1,150 persons in large-scale consumer goods industries and 4,000 persons in agriculture and small-scale and household industries. To press the development of heavy industry in such a context is uneconomic and seems inhuman.

Historically, advances in agriculture appear to have almost always preceded industrial expansion, and progress in lighter industries to have preceded the development of heavy industry. Growth of agriculture provided a broad-based demand for the output of industry, and the growth of light industry provided an assured demand for the out-

put of heavy industry. This pattern of economic development, one sector sustaining and aiding the progress of the other, would eliminate the present wastages and so contribute to a more rapid growth of the Indian economy.

Planning in India, however, has amounted to a reversal of this natural process. We are developing heavy industry ahead of light industry—among the latter, throttling the growth of cotton textiles, the most important consumer goods industry, accounting for about 36 per cent of industrial output—and developing both at the expense of agriculture. This topsy-turvy progress is inherently unstable. Persistence in such a policy might render the Indian economy more vulnerable to setbacks. The edifice that is being built might run into a storm, and it could even come crashing to the ground, if its principal support, foreign aid, should be drastically curtailed or withdrawn. If, on the other hand, production and international trade had been allowed to be directed by the basic economic forces of comparative costs and efficiency, India might have had both progress and stability. Indian national income might then have increased at a much faster rate than it actually has, perhaps at 8 to 10 per cent per year. This possibility is well supported by the striking economic and social progress made by countries—like West Germany, France, Italy, the Netherlands and Japan —which have pursued liberal economic policies.

STATIST TAMPERING with the market mechanism in the name of "planning" has brought on us the worst of both worlds—the evils of planning and the evils which the market mechanism produces when tampered with. The consequences of statist tampering have been the opposite of its intentions; we have had, if anything, an *increase* of poverty, unemployment and income inequalities. Statist policies might have been abandoned before now but for the intervention of three factors.

First, generous foreign aid—$479 mil-

472

lion or 6 per cent of the outlay of the First Plan and $3.1 billion or 19 per cent of the outlay in the Second Plan—seems to have more than compensated for the prodigalities of "planning." The actual significance of foreign aid is much greater than these percentages might indicate. The dollar amount of Plan outlays is given here as converted from Indian money at the highly over-valued official exchange rate of the rupee. To measure the real significance of foreign aid to the Indian economy, it must be assessed in terms of the market prices of the goods imported by its means. On this basis, foreign aid may represent 11 per cent of total investments in the First Plan and 33 per cent of total investments in the Second Plan. Currently, this percentage may be very much higher. Despite reductions in domestic saving, foreign aid has raised investment from 7 per cent of national income at the end of the First Plan to 11 per cent at the end of the Second. That per capita income has, nevertheless, remained semi-stagnant, is testimony to investment extravagance, wastages and corruption. To put it bluntly, our socialist policies in India are being supported by the savings of free societies overseas.

Secondly, the thinking behind statist policies, though much of it is fallacious, and empirical evidence against it is growing, has received considerable moral support from visiting economists. Their chits carry great weight with the Indian public.

The Indian public has been assured by others that inflation, born of a big Plan, could be contained if an abundant flow of foodgrains was provided under U. S. Public Law 480. This assurance is given on the ground that foodgrains constitute the major part of the budget of the average Indian laborer. The Government of India seems to have accepted this assurance. India has also been told by Professor J. K. Galbraith that there was no "alternative to extensive public enterprise;" this has been interpreted as expert blessing on the Indian policy of unrestrained expansion of the public sector. The latest appreciative pat is from Dr. T. Balogh, which comes after a two-month sojourn with kindred souls in a monastery at Calcutta. Dr. Balogh has commended "Soviet planning" for India, and he was confident that we might undertake this without damage to democracy "thanks to the great authority which the Prime Minister wielded." He has also certified that Indian "economic thinking" was ahead of that of the rest of the world, though it is not clear whether this applied as well to the unrepentant adherents of a free society.

Somehow, visiting economists to this country, being hand-picked, have a habit of belonging to a certain economic persuasion. Professors Milton Friedman and P. T. Bauer were the exceptions which prove the rule. It is time that the Indian public had the advantage of hearing the views of those opposed to statism.

This is not to argue against foreign aid or against a voluntary Point Four program. The need for accelerated capital formation is obvious. However, if the burden of debt-service is not to break our back, aid must be channeled into the best among alternative investments. The best investment, the one which contributes most to national income, it must be noted, is not always the most spectacular. However, there seems to be no easy device to guarantee that aid will be so channeled in the absence of fiscal and monetary stability.

There is little hope of a reversal of the socialist policies of the Indian Government unless foreign aid is scaled down or abandoned—which might happen only in the event of the aid-giving countries' running into serious trouble —or, unless the aid-giving countries adopt a positive foreign aid policy, linking aid to domestic economic, fiscal, monetary and social reforms. Though the linking of foreign aid to domestic policies may present many challenges to diplomacy, there is a precedent to such a linkage; the International Monetary Fund requires assurances of appropriate domestic policies before borrowings from a country's third and fourth allotments are agreed to.

Page Nineteen

473

We seem to be living in peculiar times. Freedom-loving people, in the name of preserving and spreading freedom, are unwittingly financing and otherwise sustaining socialist policies which thus far —sensational projects and schemes apart —have yielded little else than social injustice, unemployment, poverty and conflict. Though the Indian planners and their overseas supporters are full of promises and hope, these policies can hold out prospects of nothing better for the future.

WE MAY NOW summarize the principal conclusions emerging from this discussion:

1. Judging from its four principal objectives and taking an overall view, statist economic policies have not been a success in India.

2. During the 11 years ending 1961-62, Indian national income rose by 47 per cent, or 3.6 per cent per year. However, this figure is misleading as evidence of Indian progress in overcoming poverty. For a more reliable measure, it must be deflated by the rise in population, the unduly large output of non-consumer goods, the creation of excess production capacities, the unduly large accumulation of inventories, the unmerited and illicit income shifts from the masses of the people to the upper-income groups, and the use of the general price index, which understates the actual price level, in computing national income at constant prices.

3. Progress in the welfare of the people in recent years is best reflected in the statistics of food and cloth consumption. Since 1952-53, the per capita consumption of food has fluctuated downward, being below the jail ration of 16 ounces per day most of the time; the nutritional norm is 18-19 ounces. The per capita consumption of cloth, which improved until 1956, has since declined, from 14.66 metres in 1956 to 13.98 metres in 1960.

4. The gain in employment from planning has been negative. The expansion of employment has fallen short of the natural growth of the labor force. The volume of unemployment has thus grown despite a more than doubling of Plan investments, from $7.9 billion in the First Plan to $16.6 billion in the Second.

5. Since planning began, the pattern of income distribution has probably become more unequal than ever. Statism in India has involved concentration of power in the Administration—in the politician and civil servant—on a Himalayan scale. It has centralized in the state control of over two-thirds of national investment resources, including foreign aid, and colossal powers of control of economic activity through licenses, permits, quotas and concessions. Antisocial income shifts are inevitable under statism. The magnitude of these antisocial income shifts may be of an order of $1.6 billion per year.

6. Alone among the four objectives of planning in India, industrial production has shown remarkable progress, the index of industrial production rising by 92 per cent in 10 years. However, much of this progress is in defiance of the doctrine of comparative costs. By diverting resources from other sectors of the economy, principally agriculture, where returns are vastly higher, it has detracted from a maximization of the national product, and, therefore, from the pace of progress in overcoming poverty and unemployment. In the context of a semistagnant agriculture, this development has rendered the Indian economy highly vulnerable to setbacks. The unstable structure that is being erected might topple over if its principal support, foreign aid, should be drastically cut or withdrawn.

7. Statist policies in India might have been abandoned long ago, but for the intervention of foreign aid, which kept the coffers of the prodigal replenished as they got depleted, the moral support lent to statist policies by visiting "experts" from overseas, and the colossal gains in money and power which these policies yield to the politician and civil servant.

474

Red China's Great Leap Backward

MICHAEL F. ZAREMSKI

TILLMAN DURDIN, in his introduction to *Report from Red China,* relates that when sixteen-year-old Mao Tse-tung was on his way to enroll in a school some distance from his home, he met a small boy walking with an old man. Liking their companionship, but irked by their inability to keep up with his steady pace, he derided them and provoked the youngster to tears with his incessant, scornful cries of "Faster! Faster! Faster!"

In a broad sense, this episode characterizes the whole attitude of the Chinese dictator with regard to the 700 million people he rules. With unrelenting, brutal determination, he led his unwilling followers into a complete program of rapid collectivization a n d industrialization, which, leaving no sector of Chinese life untouched, brought the country "even one step beyond the Soviet Union" on the road to the pure Communist state. But despite the heady optimism with which the project was launched, it proved a dismal failure, and now, after the disastrous flirtation with Communism-in-practice, the Chinese economy is again languishing in chaos.

The country Mao Tse-tung took control of when the Communists conquered the Chinese mainland in 1949 was one which manifestly showed the results of thirty years of civil war and almost a decade of Japanese incursions. Cities were in rubble; the countryside, ravaged by the unpredictable floodings of the Yellow River, the Yangtze, and the Huai, lay in waste; and the few industries, concentrated in Manchuria, were decimated when the departing Soviet occupation troops dismantled most of the machinery and brought it back with them into Russia. Compounding these difficulties was China's perennial problem, agriculture.

The basic cause of the country's farm troubles can be traced to the lack of arable land. While mainland China encompasses 9.6 million square kilometers of territory, only an estimated 250 million acres are cultivable. Per capita land distribution in pre-war China was only 0.45 acres, as compared with 2.01 in Russia and 8.04 in the United States.[1] Since almost 90 per cent of the population earned their living from the soil and the Chinese rules of inheritance dictated that land be distributed among all a person's heirs, farm units were kept small. In 1933, the average land holding was 4.23 acres, while at the same time it was 39.74 in Denmark, 77.30 in England and 156.85 in the United States.[2]

The Communist remedy for the situation was not long in coming. The first few years after their seizure of power witnessed the first stage of the "great agricultural experiment," the liquidation

475

Michael F. Zaremski, who holds a B.A. from Iona College, is a graduate student in the Department of Public Law and Government at Columbia University.

[1] A. K. Chiu, "Agriculture," in *China,* edited by H. F. MacNair (Berkeley: University of California Press, 1946), p. 468.

[2] J. L. Buck, *Land Utilization in China* (Chicago: University of Chicago Press, 1937), pp. 267-69.

of the large land holdings and the execution of the landlords and other "Counter-revolutionaries." Estimates of the total number of landlords killed range from a conservative figure of 3 million — based on official estimates — to upwards of seven times that sum.[3] That done, the

[3] Sripati Chandra-sekhar, *Red China: An Asian View* (New York: Praeger, 1961), p. 24.

A former Chinese government and party official estimates that "conservatively speaking, in each of the more than two hundred thousand villages *(hsiang)* in China, an average of five landlords were killed and another five were terrorized into committing suicide. This totals more than two million people." Chow Ching-wen, *Ten Years of Storm* (New York: Holt, Rinehart & Winston, 1960), p. 105.

Another observer states: "The Communists issued many sets of figures when it came to summing up the results of their Campaign against Counter-revolutionaries in October 1951. In some areas they gave precise numbers while in others their figures were vague and suggested inadequate statistical work. . . . It is worth while to cite a few of the figures given by the Communists in order to point up the intensity of violence involved in this campaign.

"In his report on the situation in the Central-South Region on 21 November 1951, Teng Tzu-hui stated that from the winter of 1949-50 until November 1951 more than 1,150,000 'native bandits' had been inactivated and that 28 percent of these or 322,000 had been executed. These were figures for only one of the six major administrative areas in China. The *Southern Daily* in Canton reported that in the ten months between 10 October 1950 and 10 August 1951, 28,332 'criminals' had been executed in Kwangtung province. The figures published for October 1949 to October 1950, before the drive to eliminate counter-revolutionaries got under way in earnest, are illuminating: a total of 1,176,000 were liquidated in four of the six administrative regions, according to the chairmen of the regions involved. Yet according to statements of Communist officials themselves the campaign did not assume major proportions until 1951. By 1952 Peking no longer reported in such detail on the number of people liquidated; the figures were being used against the Communists on the world propaganda front.

"It is on the basis of these incomplete figures and others provided by the Communists that the Free Trade Union Committee of the American Federation of Labor estimated in October, 1952 that the Mao regime had been responsible for the deaths of more than 14,000,000 people over the previous five years. This total included more than 5,000,000 executed in the rural areas and more than 2,600,000 executed as 'bandit agents' or counter-revolutionaries. It is difficult to keep in mind that these are human beings rather than mere statistics. . . ." Richard L. Walker, *China Under Communism* (New Haven: Yale University Press, 1955), pp. 218-19.

Agrarian Reform Law of 1950 was adopted, establishing the complex machinery whereby the confiscated land — 117 million acres—would be redistributed among 300 million farm laborers and poor peasants.

But China's Red rulers have never left much doubt about the real purpose of agrarian reform — as a necessary preliminary stage in their program for China's industrial development. Immediately before the adoption of the Agrarian Reform Law, on June 14, 1950, Liu Shao-chi, then the chief theoretician of the Party, commented:

The basic reasons for and the aim of agrarian reform are different from the view that it is only designed to relieve the poor people. . . . The results of agrarian reform are beneficial to the impoverished laboring peasants, helping them partly to solve their problem of poverty. But the basic aim of agrarian reform is not purely one of relieving the impoverished peasants. It is designed to set free the rural productive forces from the shackles of the feudal ownership system of the landlord class in order to develop agricultural production and thus pave the way for New China's industrialization.[4]

No sooner had the land been divided and subdivided into small, individual plots than the Communists initiated a new program designed to help the Chinese to discover the inefficiency of small-scale farming. The peasants were now subjected to a new propaganda line exhorting them to join "mutual aid teams." By thus pooling their resources, so they were instructed, they could benefit from the increased knowledge of modern farming methods and could have access to costly mechanical implements otherwise beyond their means.

The Chinese Communist Party then adopted a resolution establishing the Agricultural Producers' Co-operatives. Under this system the peasants pooled their labor, tools and livestock, worked the land jointly, and were paid a part of the crop-yield in proportion to the value of the material they originally "invested" in the co-operative.

[4] Chandra-sekhar, *op. cit.*, p. 25.

476

The program, which began inauspiciously with 300 experimental co-operatives in 1952, soon burgeoned. By 1953, 14,000 units had been established, and the next year the number rose to over half a million. In 1956 there were 1,300,000 such organizations in operation, encompassing, as the Communists boasted, over 90 per cent of the peasant households. Thus the peasant was suddenly and unceremoniously deprived of the very land which a few years before he had been given with so much fanfare and at a cost of so many lives.

This step taken, the next was viewed by the Communists as inevitable; it was "the logical result of the march of events." In August, 1958, the Chinese Communist leadership approved a measure calling for "The Establishment of the People's Communes in the Rural Areas." The land was totally communized, private property nearly completely eliminated, and the workers fully regimented. What was to be the final stage in the "great agricultural experiment" was reached.

THE DRIVE TO modernize China's economy through industrialization was carried forward with no less brutal determination. The first aim of the Party's leadership was the re-establishment of the factories in southern Manchuria, a goal achieved through a provision of the treaty of alliance signed between the Soviet Union and the Chinese People's Republic in early 1950, by which Moscow agreed to lend Peking $300 million in five yearly instalments. Then, in January, 1953, Chou En-lai announced China's first Five-Year Plan, an ambitious program of forced industrialization to be carried out with Russian administrative and technical assistance.

Under the Plan the Communist leadership called for all available capital and labor to be directed into the development of heavy industry, machines, fuel and electrical power, with little channeled into those sectors of the economy producing consumer goods. Over the five year period, according to official statistics, 58.2 per cent of the total capital investment of $18 billion went into in-

dustrial projects, with only 7.6 per cent going to agriculture, forestry and water conservation. Moreover, of the total industrial investment, 88.8 per cent went into heavy industry, leaving 11.2 per cent for light industrial projects. As a result of this order of priority, China, at the end of the first economic plan, could boast of factories making automobiles, electrical equipment, machine tools and military goods, while such staple commodities as wearing apparel were in short supply and of poor quality.

Nonetheless, if the low priority given to consumer commodities produced an unfortunate situation, the results of the concentration on capital good industries were impressive. The total value of industrial output at the end of the five year period exceeded the original goal by 21 per cent — 141 per cent higher than in 1952. The average annual rate of growth was planned to be 14.7 per cent; it actually surpassed 19 per cent.[5] Steel production, for example, which was 1.35 million metric tons in 1952, reached 4.45 million tons in 1956, thereby passing, a year ahead of schedule, the original target of 4.12 million tons.

Yet despite the rapid and in some cases startling gains made under the first Five-Year Plan, the program manifested numerous signs of inefficiency and waste. In August, 1954, the *People's Daily* (Peking) published an article which revealed that "the products of a number of machine-producing factories have a rate of wastage as high as 40 per cent, with only a very low passing grade in quality.[6]

A more graphic account of inefficiency was carried in that same publication in February, 1955. In a story describing a government inspection of a machine shop in Shenyang, the following was noted:

The safety devices were not functioning properly. . . . Some of the drills stopped working within 20 seconds after being started — electrical switches did not function well; some

[5] Cheng Chu-yuan, *Communist China's Economy, 1949-1962* (South Orange: Seton Hall University Press, 1963), pp. 132-33.
[6] Paul S. H. Tang, *Communist China Today* (New York: Praeger, 1957), p. 301.

477

sliding surfaces could not be lubricated properly; the gears made a great noise; and the shaft cases leaked oil. Closer examination revealed that many of the parts did not comply with the specifications. Iron filings, dirt, and sand were found in the moving parts. A further check showed that all of the drills and drill presses of these two models on hand in the stock room were defective.[7]

Accounts of similar situations appeared too frequently in the official press to discount the above as isolated cases.

UNDER THE SECOND Five-Year Plan, announced in 1957, priority continued to be given to heavy industry, though the growth rate for this sector of the economy was now revised downward. The growth rate for agricultural output, on the other hand, was set at 10 per cent above the corresponding rate for the 1953-1957 period.

This increased agricultural quota underlines one of China's more pressing problems: In order to finance her industrialization projects, marketable grains and raw materials must be exported from the mainland. But population increases continually absorb any gains in agricultural production; how then is additional revenue to be accumulated? The answer, as the Communists worked it out, was to order output raised, give a lower percentage of income back to the local authorities, and divert more and more money into reserve funds to be distributed by the central government for top-priority industrial projects. After the communes were established, the point was reached where only 20 per cent of the total income reverted to the commune, with the remainder invested in the industrial program. The still further decline of the living standard of the peasant and the stifling of local initiative were defects in the system which Peking either could not or would not recognize.

But these difficulties, compounded by waste and inefficiency in the administration of the program, soon assumed alarming proportions, and in an apparent about-face, China's rulers reversed the system, allowing the local bureaucracy to utilize a large percentage of the commune's income. Counting on a great burst of enthusiasm on the local level, Peking announced, in 1959, the beginning of the "Great Leap Forward." Under this program, the peasant laborers, in addition to working at their regular communal jobs, were expected to devote their "free" time to such occupations as making cement in backyard kilns, operating neighborhood steel furnaces, mining coal in small, otherwise unproductive seams, or working with teams on public works projects.

While oppression was still the order of the day, opposition could not be stifled among the peasants. Reports conspicuously appeared in the Chinese press relating such anti-regime activities as work slow-downs, deliberate damage to property, attacks on local cadres and the slaughter of livestock.

In an obvious attempt to put down the government's increasingly vociferous "rightist" critics, Chou En-lai was forced, in late 1959, to declare that the commune system "was in fact very good and not at all a terrible mess . . . , that its rise was not premature."[8]

The actual agricultural and industrial production figures, however, failed to support his case. The second Five-Year Plan called for a 12 per cent increase in the value of agricultural output during 1960, but the crop-yield failed by far to match this goal. Three successive years of bad harvests, in 1959, 1960, and 1961, depleted whatever supply of food China had, forcing her to import a great quantity of grain from abroad to feed her soldiers and other security personnel. In addition to these difficulties, by mid-1961 the livestock population had fallen by 40 per cent. In October, 1961, the *People's Daily* (Peking) was forced to admit that "three consecutive years of grave natural disasters have resulted in the reduction of agricultural production" and this has "affected light industry production and also heavy industry and consequently commodity supplies and the people's livelihood."

---

[7] *Ibid.*

[8] *Wall Street Journal*, March 10, 1960.

Industrial output during the 1959-1962 period *decreased* by more than 30 per cent. Steel production, estimated at 15 million metric tons in 1960, dropped to about 12 million tons in 1961, and below 10 million tons in 1962. Coal output in 1962 was about half as much as in 1960.

Consumer industries fared no better. As late as October, 1962, an official government statement declared that "the goods we produce are still insufficient to meet the needs of the rural people." Industry must "increase the variety and raise the quality of products," it advised.

There can be no doubt that the institution of the commune system was the major factor in the deterioration of China's whole economy. In their major policy statements, the Red leaders declared that the nation's economy would thrive because of the benefits to be gained from the "rational" use of land and labor and unified planning and management. Yet, as it happened, it was precisely for these reasons — and others — that China's economic structure collapsed.

For the Chinese leadership, with their advocacy of rapid and large-scale industrialization, "rational" use of labor meant pulling every possible man off farming projects and putting him to work building up heavy industry. While this sector of the economy may have benefitted from the move, the effect on agricultural production was disastrous. The shortage of farm workers, confessed the *People's Daily* (Peking) in 1960, was the main cause of the devastation of grain fields that year. Further, as the correspondent of the *London Times* reported,

> Some of the measures taken to stimulate grain production imply that it has not been drought and flood alone that are to be blamed, but the misuse of manpower in the communes. The excesses of backyard steel were corrected when the steel was found to be useless . . . . the small-scale factory production of the communes was one of the great claims made for the new system of human organization and it is these factories that seem to have drawn off too much able-bodied manpower so that grain production has suffered.[9]

Similarly, centralized planning also proved to be extremely damaging. In an effort to achieve uniformity in farming techniques and management throughout the country, Peking issued sets of regulations which totally ignored the differences necessarily existing between one locality and another. Peculiar needs were sacrificed to an impossible goal; the results of the indiscriminate advocacy of such techniques as "close-planting" and "deep-plowing" were evident in the final production figures.

Another aspect of communal life contributing to the agricultural crisis was the fact that in the commune there was no incentive to make the peasant want to work harder to fulfill the promises of the "Great Leap." To be sure, the workers were driven hard to meet production goals; but when every worker gets the same payment for his work, when all live under the same conditions and eat the same amount of food, there are few who will do more than the bare minimum necessary to gain admission to the communal dining hall. Those who had had high production levels lost all incentive; those who were slothful or unskilled remained so or become worse.

Even more damaging to the economy as a whole was the anti-specialist attitude manifested by the Party bureaucracy. The expert was held in reproach, and book learning was described as "a heap of garbage;" scientific achievements born in the West were similarly condemned as worthless.[10] Party officials were given the managerial jobs on the farms and in the factories; it did not seem to matter if they knew what they were doing so long as they followed the Party line in doing it.

The absence of trained technical personnel in positions of authority wrought devastating results, especially in industry. Gross mismanagement was in evidence everywhere; doctrine-bound party cadres, more interested in meeting goals on target dates than in building securely, embarked on impractical schemes and fostered poor production standards. Mechanical equipment in factories was badly made and improperly operated. When

479

---

[9] *London Times*, September 27, 1960.

[10] *Wall Street Journal*, February 2, 1962.

machines broke down, they remained inoperable because there were no spare parts available for repairing them.

THESE LESSONS were not entirely lost on the Chinese Communist leadership. The first signs of a change in Peking's policy line were manifested in October, 1959, when the basic unit of agricultural production was shifted from the commune to the production brigade, similar in size to the former agricultural co-operative. Ownership of land, tools and draft animals was given to the smaller unit, which divided its income among the members of the group without any consideration of the other brigades. Thus, in an effort to gain more production through increased incentive, the much vaunted egalitarian feature of income distribution was repudiated.

A step farther was taken in the spring of 1961 when the brigades were subdivided into production teams. Incentive wages tied to productivity were given laborers, and small plots allowed them for individual cultivation. Moreover, the village "free-markets," where the peasant could sell certain commodities for personal profit, were re-established.

Early in the year, evidence of a drastic reform of China's whole economic program came out of the ninth plenary session of the Communist Party's Central Committee. Ordering a reduction of capital outlays for heavy industry, it initiated a policy of "consolidation, adjustment and filling out" for the country's economy; henceforth, agricultural production would be emphasized. The plan, calling for "diligence, thrift and hard work," was reiterated at the meeting of the People's National Assembly in April, 1962.

The degree to which China's rulers have repudiated the "Great Leap" was underlined in an article which appeared in an issue of *Hung Chi,* the official organ of the Party's Central Committee. The gist of the piece was that industry would have to make do with the labor resources and machinery now at its disposal; no sizable new capital investments would be forthcoming.

Factories were called upon to "unfold technical innovation in existing enterprises and bring out fully the potentials of existing equipment. . . . By this method labor productivity can be raised rapidly and effectively with little investment."

Significantly, the article went on to say that "the process of realizing socialist industrialization can only be a gradual process, and the process of improving working equipment, too, can only be a gradual process." "Real results," it added, "can be obtained only if we consider the problem of mechanization and automation on the basis of the present level of industrialization."

Reluctantly following capitalist example, the author of the article advised the institution of a system of rewards and penalties tied to production: "Special material incentives should be given to individuals and units for special accomplishments in production. . . . Necessary economic penalties should be imposed on individuals and units for poor production because of insufficient subjective effort."[11]

Indicative of the seriousness of Red China's continuing agricultural crisis is the fact that the country's rulers have had to forsake their political dogmatism in an effort to avoid widespread famine and disease by importing grain from the West. While the government has insisted that economic necessity would never force it to compromise its position, the Chinese pattern of trade in recent years would seem to indicate otherwise.

Since 1959 general trade with the nations of the Soviet bloc has been halved, mainly because neither Russia nor her European satellites, plagued by farming difficulties of their own, have been able to supply China with the massive aid she requires. The only recourse left the Chinese Communists was to turn westward, which they have been doing with increasing frequency.

In 1961, for example, Red China signed a three-year, $362 million trade agreement with Canada, and negotiated other contracts with Australia, France, Argentina and a number of other Western

---

11 *New York Times,* September 20, 1962.

nations. To pay for this grain a high percentage of China's exports has gone to Western Europe, Canada, Hong Kong, Southeast Asia, and even Japan, with whom the Chinese had broken off trade relations for political reasons in 1958.

But an even more radical policy change — and one which is certain to have widespread effects — may be in the making. For the grain reserves of the nations with which China is now trading are rapidly shrinking. If the agricultural output on the mainland cannot be considerably increased in the very near future, the only country which has food supplies large enough to be able to give sizable assistance to China is the United States.

CERTAINLY, THE MAJOR problem now facing China is her population, presently expanding at a rate of from 2 to 3 per cent annually, and calculated to exceed 800 million before the end of the decade. At present, however, the problem is one which the dogmatic Communists cannot even acknowledge: unemployment.

When the emphasis in the economic program was shifted from industry to agriculture, the hordes of peasants forced into the cities were no longer needed. With the withdrawal of Soviet assistance,[12] a multitude of various projects were cancelled and factories closed down. In addition, those factories which remained in operation were ordered to cut personnel to the barest minimum.

The Chinese leadership pursued the only course left open: to effect the mass transfer of these workless peasants back to the country. The already over-populated and impoverished rural areas, however, had neither need nor room for more people, and even with the current emphasis on farming no work could be found. Many of these people thereafter resorted to begging and stealing, becom-

ing a source of constant discontent among the rural populace.

While the Chinese Communists rode into power on their pledge to remedy the agricultural situation, an examination of pre-war conditions as compared to those of today reveals that in actuality their program of compulsory collectivism has radically aggravated rather than alleviated the problem; the peasant could never boast of his condition, but it was even worse now.

In 1956, for example, the Communist leadership initiated a large-scale program of water conservation. But:

> As most of the canals and reservoirs were dug and constructed without proper geological investigation or technical design, the new projects not only destroyed the natural irrigation system and hindered the regular function of the main rivers, . . . but also made roughly a million acres of arable land alkaline.[13]

Whereas before the canal construction the area of flood and drought had never exceeded 30 million acres, it now increased to 38 million acres in 1957, 78 million in 1958, 108 million in 1959, and 150 million acres in 1960.[14]

These errors in economic planning had their effect on the Chinese peasant, whose living standard was reduced to the lowest recorded level. Official statistics for 1956, the peak year of the first Five-Year Plan, reveal that per

481

---

[12] An editorial on the subject of Russia's withdrawal of assistance appeared in the *People's Daily* (Peking) on July 19, 1963. It revealed that the ordering home of all the Soviet experts and the cancellation of numerous Russian contracts was totally "unexpected" and inflicted "incalculable difficulties" on China's economy.

[13] Cheng Chu-yuan, *op. cit.*, p. 142.

[14] *Ibid.*
"By 1959 the *People's Daily* sensed something was wrong: 'During the past one or two years, the alkalization of much soil in many irrigated areas in the North is spreading.' But the canal digging went on. In 1960, the same paper again reported that saltpetre, which normally appears only in serious drought, had affected millions of acres of farmland. In April 1961, the *Kuang Ming Daily* said: 'Arable land is continuously shrinking and alkali soil spreading.' In August 1962, the Party's authoritative mouthpiece *Red Flag* reported that nearly 20 million acres of farmland in Manchuria and in the North, Northwest and Central China had turned alkaline, and that the peasants were unwilling to till the swiftly alkalizing farms which soon became barren land, thus reducing the already limited arable land of the country." Valentin Chu, *Ta Ta, Tan Tan (Fight Fight, Talk Talk): The Inside Story of Communist China* (New York: Norton, 1963), pp. 66-67.

capita annual consumption amounted to only $35. Personal consumption in 1957 was estimated to have been 18 per cent below the figure for 1933.[15]

Caloric intake has also shown a marked decrease. In 1957, the per capita intake was set at 1,830 units daily, as compared to 1,940 for 1933. While the 1933 figure indicates bare sustinence level, the food ration allowed in 1957 was 110 calories lower, and thereafter steadily decreased until in late 1961 a diet of 600 calories was average.[16]

Above the appreciable reduction in their already pitiable standard of living, the Chinese have suffered more acutely from something else, something more intangible though no less important — the dehumanizing character of the Communist system.

A dispassionate picture of this aspect of life under the "Great Leap" is drawn by Robert Loh, one of three sons of a successful Chinese businessman, who, while enjoying a secure position as a university instructor, underwent the familiar infatuation-disillusion-despair process that marks the life of many living under totalitarian tyranny. "Any worker who lived through the Great Leap," he writes,

> knows that the campaign had the effect of suppression. The people were made to work constantly to the

very limit of human endurance — and in many cases beyond. . . . It was as though the authorities, in a vicious fury at the antagonism shown them by the people during the blossom period, had sentenced the whole population to the slave gangs of labor reform. Proof of the punitive nature of the campaign was in the fact that people from the other classes and strata who incurred the Party's disfavor were sent as *punishment* to 'learn from the masses' by giving their labor along with the workers and peasants.[17] (Author's emphasis.)

THE CHINESE EXPERIENCE demonstrates a number of economic facts of life which especially the under-developed countries would do well to take into careful consideration. Coercion of the populace, bureaucratic mismanagement, shoddy work, economically unsound experiments, public apathy or outright opposition — all diminished where the free market is allowed to operate — are commonplace in China.

Any government worthy of the name seeks economic progress primarily as a means of raising the standard of living of its citizens; China has sought it as a springboard to recognition as a world power. To their detriment, the Communists have ignored the individual, the key to economic progress. While the Chinese leadership has often been forced to reverse their policies, they have in no sense repudiated the communes of the "Great Leap." It is almost certain that similar projects will be launched in the future; it is likewise certain that they, too, will meet an ignominious fate. George Santayana wrote, "He who does not learn from history is condemned to repeat it;" those nations seeking economic progress should be mindful of the experience of post-war China.

---

[15] Cheng Chu-yuan, *op. cit.*, pp. 159-60.

[16] *Ibid.*
Newsweek reported on March 27, 1961, that the average rice ration in the commune, originally 12 ounces daily, had then been cut to 4 or 5 ounces, about one bowlful. It added that visitors reported that the people blamed the government, not nature, for this situation.
Writing of more recent conditions, Valentin Chu commented: "A normal man in Asia requires a minimum of 2,300 calories of food daily. In food-short India, according to a United Nations survey, the daily average food intake is 2,000 calories. In pre-war China it was 2,234 calories. In Taiwan it is 2,310 calories. Most of the peasants in Communist China, who must work long hours at hard labor, have been getting about 1,000 calories." Chu, *op. cit.*, pp. 72-73.

[17] Robert Loh, as told to Humphrey Evans, *Escape from Red China* (New York: Coward-McCann, 1962), pp. 369-70.

482

Skinner's Behaviorist Utopia

BRUCE GOLDBERG

483

THAT A STATEMENT or a theory is true or false is a matter which is, presumably, to be decided by the employment of the various canons of scientific (in the widest sense of that term) observation and inference. A theory, for example, is tested by its ability to explain the facts on the basis of which it was introduced, and also by its ability to explain new facts which were not explicitly taken into account in its construction. And there are considerations irrelevant in determining the acceptability of putative truths. One obviously irrelevant factor is the aesthetic satisfaction anyone might get from contemplating a given theory. Whatever the poet may have thought, beauty is not the same as truth. Less obvious, and perhaps worth mentioning for that reason, is that the moral consequences of a statement are not relevant determinants of its truth or falsity. It may be that the general acceptance of some statement would lead to universal misery. Conceivably this could be a reason for keeping the statement secret. It could *not* be a reason for concluding that it was false. All men *are* mortal, whatever *Angst* might be occasioned by recognition of the fact.

That these considerations are not truth determinants would seem to be hardly susceptible of dispute. And yet,

Bruce Goldberg did graduate work in philosophy at Princeton and Oxford Universities, and is presently an instructor in philosophy at the University of Illinois. He is a contributor to *Analysis* and *The Journal of Philosophy*.

without explicit avowal, antagonists of scientific theories have all too often allowed aesthetic or moral upset to count against those theories. The Einsteinian conception of time as a relativistic magnitude did indeed shatter a well-established *Weltanschauung*. The relatively simple picture of Newtonian mechanistic interactions embedded in an absolute temporal framework died hard. That death, however, should have been an easy one. The major test of a scientific theory is its ability to explain the phenomena, and the new theory was better at this than the old. And for most (although not absolutely all) physicists, this was enough. But for others—theologians, philosophers, aestheticians, even laymen (though certainly not for all the members of any of these groups)—this was not enough. The aprioristic defenses of the old order began. "It's perfectly self-evident," ran one defense, "that time is absolute throughout the universe. One simply can't conceive of it being any other way." "It's in the nature of time," ran another, "to be the same everywhere." And in the background was the—unexpressed—objection that the adjustment was too difficult to make, that the new picture was not anything so much as repulsive.

Nowhere does this anti-scientific resistance to new theorizing assume more vigor than with respect to explanations in psychology. While physicists may displease, they are in possession of a mathematical apparatus which frightens. The critics, for all their resistance, remain more or less quiet and, at times, even a little ashamed. However, the language of, say, Freudian theory is ordinary English (or German). The technical terms are no more awe-inspiring than those of a competent aesthetician: "drive cathexis" is no more intimidating than "aesthetic distance." This releases inhibitions, and the defenders of received opinion feel that they have a free hand.

But there is a feature of psychological theory more important in this connection than that its propositions are unmathematized.[1] Psychological theory concerns people. It attempts, among other things, to explain why they act the way they do. And often the answers are such that the actor would not unreflectively acknowledge their correctness. Further, the critic may have a stake in the answers' being incorrect. How often has Freudian theory been attacked because of its "repulsive" doctrines of infantile sexuality? Or on the ground that our traditional views of human responsibility would have to be discarded? But such objections are absolutely worthless. The repulsiveness of Freudian theory is no more relevant to its truth or falsity than its country of origin. But it is one thing to point up the utter irrationality of an objection, and quite another to dispel the fears which prompt it.

As objectionable as Freudian theory was, however, it was sufficiently anthropomorphic to pose less of a threat to "man's dignity" than the mechanistic view associated with a certain other psychological theory. While Freud, the standard version goes, moved the springs of action from the conscious mind to the unconscious, later twentieth century psychology removd it from the psyche altogether. This new dehumanization of man is called behaviorism. Behaviorism not only eliminated the mental as a factor—it combined this with a thoroughgoing determinism which left no room for free action at all. The moral conscience revolted. Behaviorism was castigated as evil, and therefore, presumably, false.

But the argument is no more legitimate here than it was in the preceding cases. Behaviorism simply cannot be shown to be incorrect by showing that its alleged consequences are undesirable, morally repugnant, or even evil. Those who adopt this approach deserve our ears no more than the critics of another theory, who insisted that man's dignity required that his planet be at the center of the universe.

THESE OBSERVATIONS ON what is relevant and what is irrelevant in the evaluation of a scientific theory such as behaviorism are necessary, for in this essay I shall be concerned with the behaviorist-based recommendations for social organizations of Professor B. F. Skinner, the eminent Harvard University psychologist, as set forth in his utopian novel, *Walden Two*.[2] If his proposal for a society rigidly controlled by behaviorist psychologists is to be rejected (as I think, in reason, it must be), it will have to be on the basis of logical analysis, and not of foolish sloganizing.

The blurb on the book informs us that *Walden Two* "provocatively pictures a society in which human problems are solved by a scientific technology of human conduct—and in which many of our contemporary values are obsolete." That anyone has presented us with a solution for human problems should make us listen, especially when the donor is a psychologist of unquestionable achievement. If in the end we will be skeptical, no part of the cause should be lack of gratitude for the attempt.

Walden Two is an attempt, in fictional form, to outline a system of social organization based on behaviorist psychological theory. "The methods of science have been enormously successful wherever they have been tried," Skinner says in another place;[3] "let us then apply them to human affairs." The scene of most of the book is a utopian community (Walden Two). Frazier, the creator

---

[1] I am, of course, ignoring those areas of psychology where mathematics is becoming increasingly important, e.g., learning theory.

[2] Originally published in 1948. I have used the paperback edition published by Macmillan in 1962.

[3] *Science and Human Behavior* (New York: Macmillan, 1953), p. 5.

of the experiment, defends his theories of social organization against Professor Burris, a slightly skeptical but generally sympathetic antagonist, and Professor Castle, a tender-minded philosopher and a bumptious, nasty, and unreasonable caviller, who interrupts the discussion from time to time with generally straw-mannish objections.

A good deal is said in this novel, and I shall not try to examine every point that is made. What I shall do is consider certain of the central ideas of *Walden Two,* on the falsity of which the claims of the book would founder. Occasionally I shall bring to bear illustrative evidence from one of Skinner's non-fiction works, *Science and Human Behavior.*

The initial picture of the inhabitants of Walden Two with which we are presented is an attractive one. "These were delightful people," Professor Burris muses; "their conversation had a measure and a cadence more often found in well-wrought fiction than in fact. They were pleasant and well-mannered, yet perfectly candid; they were lively, but not boisterous; affectionate, but not effusive" (page 28). And in the course of the book, we come to learn that the inhabitants of Walden Two possess most of the desirable character traits one can think of and almost none of the bad ones. Indeed, with the exception of Frazier himself (who did not have the benefit of a Walden Two upbringing) everyone seems to be supremely happy and well-adjusted. This is not to be scoffed at. Only those with no social concern at all (and they don't count) could be indifferent to the possibility of establishing a form of social organization which has such results.

How does one go about producing such desirable characters? Well, babies at Walden Two are reared in community nurseries. At the age of one year, they graduate to community playgrounds, being subjected during these formative years to an intensive and highly scientific program of conditioning. All this provokes much resistance from the antagonistic Castle. But the questions of the techniques of Walden Two seem to me less interesting than the question of whether Skinner has even provided a coherent account of what can be accomplished by those techniques. If that account is itself internally inconsistent, the details are unimportant.

What I mean is this. Skinner's general program is the behavioral conditioning of certain kinds of emotions and behavioral responses. This conditioning is to have the result that only certain kinds of emotions appear in the members of Walden Two, while others, the undesirable ones, disappear through lack of positive reinforcement. The result is lots of people with good emotions, and very few or none with bad ones. It might immediately be objected that this could never come about, that human nature cannot be changed, or something of the sort. But this Castle-type move is a bad one. Talk about human nature is far too vague to permit a reasonable decision to be made as to whether or not it could be changed.

"As to emotions—we aren't free of them all, nor should we like to be. But the meaner and more annoying—the emotions which breed unhappiness—are almost unknown here, like unhappiness itself. We don't need them any longer in our struggle for existence, and it's easier on our circulatory system, and certainly pleasanter, to dispense with them" (page 101). To the objection that emotions are fun, Frazier replies, "Some of them, yes. The productive and strengthening emotions—joy and love. But sorrow and hate—and the high-voltage excitements of anger, fear and rage—are out of proportion with the needs of modern life, and they're wasteful and dangerous. Mr. Castle has mentioned jealousy—a minor form of anger, I think we may call it. Naturally we avoid it" (page 102). And so it is conditioned out, along with the other unpleasant emotions, presumably simply by never receiving any positive reinforcement on any occasion of its occurrence. This is the account one must examine, not, I should add, to determine whether or not it would be *advisable* to condition out the emotions referred to but to determine whether such a conditioning out would be even a theoretical *possibility.*

485

The behaviorist picture (at least as Skinner presents it) is in some ways an excessively simplistic one. There seems to be the idea that, with respect to any given person and the various emotions he is capable of experiencing, one could, given a proper technology, pluck out some while leaving the others intact. Occurrences of emotions are, on this account, something like pains. Just as one can eliminate a given pain (by administering a drug, say), so one can eliminate a given emotion (by a proper administration of behavioral engineering). In this sense, the account of the emotions is an atomistic one. Each emotion can be considered separately, and the relevant conditioning techniques can be applied to it. The good ones stay and the bad ones go.

486

THIS PICTURE IS A radically misconceived one, and it requires no experimentation at all to show this. Is it even possible to become clear about what the picture suggests? Skinner wants to retain joy (because it is productive) and eliminate sorrow (because it isn't). Under what circumstances might one experience joy? Well, suppose one has not seen one's mother for twenty years. One goes to meet the plane on which she is expected to arrive. The door opens, she descends the stairs and comes running to meet one, arms outstretched, tears in her eyes. Presumably, on this occasion one is happy, joyful, and the inspiration provided enables one that very evening to make some important new contribution to knowledge.[4] But

---

[4] For joy, Skinner tells us, is a productive emotion (page 102). This seems hardly to be a "scientific" remark. What is it for an emotion to be "productive"? Is the view something like that joyful people do more productive work than sad ones? Is there any empirical evidence for this? Skinner provides no experimental evidence; and even if one were to make a historical survey which showed that joyful people are, in fact, more productive than sad people, that wouldn't establish the claim. Their greater productivity might be attributable to all sorts of other factors. But Skinner probably doesn't mean anything as precise as this. More likely, all he means by calling joy a productive emotion is that he has a favorable attitude towards joy and not towards sorrow. In any case, nowhere are any criteria presented for what is to count as a productive emotion.

suppose that just as one is about to embrace one's mother, an unknown assailant shoots her in the back. Doesn't one then feel at least sorrow, or even grief? Is one neutral? Indifferent? Isn't it obvious that joy and sorrow are not atomistic states with no stronger connection than that they are both emotions? If the death of one's mother (in the situation described above) did leave one indifferent, how *could* the embrace produce joy? In order for one to experience joy in the situation described, it must (logically must) be true that whether or not one's mother lives or dies makes *some* difference to one. But if that's true, then one could not remain indifferent if she does die.

Perhaps another example will make the point clearer. Skinner is pro-happiness. The people in Walden Two are a happy group. They are often engaged in creative enterprises, and they are happy in their work. But unhappiness is unproductive. Presumably it's also to be conditioned out. Again, the question arises about the theoretical possibility of such a state of affairs, i.e., a state of affairs in which people are only happy. Suppose I have been working on a project for ten years, have constructed an elaborate theory which has only to receive its final experimental confirmation. The laboratory technicians bring in the results of a series of experiments which they have been running for the past two weeks. Now what is Skinner's claim? Am I indifferent to the results of my experiments? Suppose I am. In that case, it's odd to say that I'm very happy, even overjoyed, when I learn that my theory has been confirmed. Suppose that I'm not. Then it's equally odd to say that I'm not even a little bit unhappy when I learn that the experiments have falsified the theory. Given that people sometimes fail to achieve what they want very much (and not even *Walden Two* promises to fulfill all desires), it follows that they are sometimes unhappy. Isn't it patently obvious that happiness and unhappiness are not independent atomic states? But if that's true, then it doesn't even make sense to suppose that one could condition people never to experience the one and always (or almost always) to experience the other.

The principle illustrated by these examples is that many emotions have what might be called quasi-logical counterparts. Pairs such as love-hate, joy-sorrow, happiness-unhappiness are familiar. To suppose that (whatever technique one might employ) one could condition out one member and leave the other intact is to believe a fiction. And this has nothing to do with the nature of man or the limitations of scientific technique. It is, rather, a matter of the logic of emotional predication. "Whenever a particular emotion is no longer a useful part of a behavioral repertoire, we proceed to eliminate it," Frazier tells us (page 103). Presumably, on this account we could, if we wanted, "engineer" a person to feel only grief or only love or only nostalgia. We decide which emotions we want, and then instill them. But this is something we shall never be able to do (at least not in the way implied in *Walden Two*). And the reason is that to say that we can do it doesn't even make sense.

The above is not mere philosophic pedantry. One of the attractions of *Walden Two* is that it seems to offer us an escape from the unpleasant, and this through the application of an allegedly scientific theory. But that theory, whatever its other merits, cannot at least succeed in this. If the inhabitants of Walden Two can experience joy, then they can experience sorrow. And it is a logical mistake to suppose that things could be otherwise.

WE HAVE, THEN, eliminated one major piece of the theoretical groundwork of *Walden Two*, at least as Skinner views his system. There is another view advanced by Skinner, of even greater importance than the view that one can selectively condition emotions. This is the idea that free will is an illusion. Skinner regards a behavioral technology as being incompatible with free will. Since he regards the former as possible, he denies the latter. Now, the problem of free will is an enormously compli-

cated one. What I shall try to do here is merely to show that Skinner's view of what it would mean to have free will is a confused one, and that nothing he says even tends to show that free will is an illusion.

Skinner regards adherence to the idea that man has free will as essentially a relic of pre-scientific ways of thinking. And this is a fairly widespread notion. Without discussing the merits of this claim—my own opinion is that it is much too vague for argumentation on either side—it might be worthwhile to see just how Skinner proposes to demonstrate the falsity of the free will doctrine. In a way, this is a difficult thing to do, for Skinner seems not altogether clear about what view he is attacking. Sometimes it is the view that human actions are spontaneous, at other times it is that their actions are the actions of responsible agents, at still other times it is the view that human actions are uncaused. This last is probably the most substantial, so let us deal with that one. Skinner argues that it is a mistake to regard actions as uncaused. The most we are justified in saying is that for various actions we do not know what the causes are. However, the advancing march of science gives us every reason to believe that in time the causes of human behavior will present no greater problem than the causes of heat transfer in gases. The issue of free will is often discussed in these terms. That is, those who assert that we have free will generally regard this as committing them to the view that human action is uncaused. Those who opt for a general determinism regard this as implying that human action is unfree.[5] One of the unfortunate aspects of this controversy is that both sides seem to have thought that they had pretty clear ideas about the meaning of the key expression, i.e., determinism. The allegedly unproblematic explication of this notion has most often been: "the theory that every event has a cause." But a number of

---

[5] There have been exceptions in the history of philosophy. Hume and John Stuart Mill accepted both determinism and free will. But this is no place for a historical account of the question.

487

contemporary philosophers have seen that this explication is by no means as clear as has been thought. Some have gone so far as to assert that they do not know what the thesis of determinism is.[6] And there is good reason for this. For example, if one sees how Skinner fills out his account of what determinism with respect to behavior is, one cannot but find it surprising that he does regard the truth of determinism as incompatible with human freedom.

In Chapter Three, "Why Organisms Behave," of *Science and Human Behavior,* Skinner says that "we are concerned . . . with the causes of human behavior. We want to know why men behave as they do. Any condition or event which can be shown to have an effect upon behavior must be taken into account. By discovering and analyzing these causes we can predict behavior; to the extent that we can manipulate them, we can control behavior" (page 23).

Initially such a picture of a general determinism of behavior seems to many people to be a frightening one. The suggestion is that we are mere ciphers in a causal stream over which we have no control. And this is a picture to which Skinner frequently alludes in a favorable way in the course of his writings. We can manipulate causes and control people. A Brave New World (if one is frightened) or a Walden Two (if one is pleased) looms up before us.

But is there reason, given Skinner's view (which is a widely held one), for either fear or pleasure? Is there, indeed, anything excitingly new being said?

What are the causes of behavior on Skinner's showing? "Any condition or event which can be shown to have an effect upon behavior. . . ." Suppose I am a devotee of Shakespeare and a friend tells me that a new production of *King Lear* has just come to the Lido. Excited, I rush down to reserve tickets for the next performance. Now it is unquestionably true that my friend's informing me that the play was being performed is

an event which had an effect on my behavior. If he hadn't told me I wouldn't have done what in fact I did do, *viz.,* go to the theater to reserve the tickets. Of course I might later have learned on my own that the play was being performed and would have then bought the tickets, but I wouldn't have done that when, as a matter of fact, I did. Suppose that I go to the play, and, after having thoroughly enjoyed it, applaud wildly when the performers take their curtain calls. Again, the appearance of the performers on the stage is an event which had an influence on my behavior. If they hadn't come out I would have returned home without applauding, wondering what went wrong, and perhaps feeling a bit sad because I didn't have the opportunity to show my appreciation. We have here, then, two examples of events which had an influence on my behavior. Were they causes of it?

It is not altogether easy to answer this question. For Skinner, of course, the answer is clear. They *are* causes. According to the quoted passage *any* condition or event which has an influence on behavior is a cause. But there are difficulties. Consider another kind of case. I tell someone, "I was just in the psychology laboratory with John and I caused his leg to rise." When asked how, I reply that I hit his knee in the familiar spot with a small hammer. But suppose that, when asked how I caused John's leg to rise I reply, not that I hit his knee with a small hammer, but that I asked him if he would raise his leg. Ordinarily, we would say that if *this* is how I got John's leg to rise (by asking him to raise his leg), then I didn't *cause* his leg to rise, although what I said was certainly relevant to bringing it about that John's leg did rise. It would at least be misleading, under these circumstances, to say that I did cause his leg to rise. In a context like this one, it would in general be assumed that if I *caused* John's leg to rise, I did something which in some way put it out of John's control that his leg did rise. When this assumption turns out to be wrong, i.e., when it turns out that I simply asked John to raise his leg and he did so, then it sounds very odd indeed

6 Cf. P. F. Strawson, *Freedom and Resentment* (London: Oxford University Press, 1962), p. 187.

to say that I caused his leg to rise. This is not always true. If John were hypnotized and raised his leg at my command, then it would be perfectly in order for me to say that I caused what occurred. One can easily think of other cases in which it wouldn't sound odd to say that I caused John's leg to rise. But in the case where I simply ask John to raise his leg (and he's fully conscious—not hypnotized, etc.), it does. But why should this be true if, as Skinner says, a cause is *any* condition or event which can be shown to have an effect upon behavior? Why does it sound at all odd to say that the performers' appearing on the stage *caused* me to applaud?

Above I hinted at what seems to me to be at least a partial explanation. It seems to be a legitimate inference that if someone is caused to do something, then that thing is in some way out of his control, that he is in some way not at liberty not to do it. And Skinner appears to be aware of the legitimacy of this inference. Notice that he says that to the extent to which we can manipulate behavior we can *control* it. If I am controlling someone's behavior, then he certainly isn't. This is surely the source of the doctrine that if someone's behavior is determined, then he isn't free. If the behavior is determined, then it's caused; if it's caused, then it is out of his control; and if it is out of his control, then he's not free. Assuming this argument to be legitimate, then one cannot at the same time grant that a bit of behavior was determined and that it was free. From the fact that the behavior was determined, it would follow that it was not free. But does it follow from the fact that there were events which *influenced* the behavior that the behavior was unfree? Put in another way, from the fact that the agent was influenced by certain circumstances to act in a certain way, does it follow that the action was out of his control? As we ordinarily speak about behavior, this certainly does not follow. Let us take still another example.

One of the factors influencing a general's decision to attack may be the intelligence information that the enemy is shortly going to concentrate its forces against his weak flank. Is his subsequent behavior (giving instructions to his subordinates to attack, preparing certain false reports which he is going to allow to fall into enemy hands, etc.) something which is out of his control? Surely not. Such a situation is just the sort of situation in which we say someone's behavior *is* under his control. Under what circumstances would we say that his behavior was out of his control? Well, suppose that he received the intelligence information and instead of calmly preparing plans for the coming attack, went berserk. Suppose he ran out of the Command Headquarters raving about the imminent destruction of his forces, and ordered each individual soldier (with or without a weapon) to attack the enemy at once. Suppose, too, that he himself starts running in the direction of the enemy camp, knife in hand, screaming that he is going to kill the mad beasts. Here, most probably, we would say that his behavior was not under his control. Surely our estimate of the situation must be different when he calmly sits down to prepare the attack, and gives his subordinates intelligent instructions, involving what, in the opinion of all, is a master military move. And yet there are events which influenced this behavior, just as there are events which influenced the berserk behavior. But if we allow that, in the case of the intelligent action, simply from the fact that there were indeed events which influenced his behavior it does not follow that the behavior was out of his control, then we must either reject the argument that causality implies non-freedom or reject Skinner's assumption that any event which influences behavior is a cause of that behavior.

And indeed how would one go about trying to show that any event which influences behavior *is* a cause of that behavior? Skinner, in the passage I quoted, seems to want to do this by definition. But this can show absolutely nothing. Presumably Skinner must regard the assertion that all behavior is, because determined, unfree, as an interesting assertion about behavior, i.e., about actions which people perform.

489

Page Thirty-five

That is, presumably he doesn't regard the contention that behavior is unfree as a simple definition. For if it were a mere definition, then while we might agree (accepting his definition for a moment) that "behavior" will imply unfreedom, we could not say about any of the events which we normally call cases of human action that they were in fact cases of "behavior."

Let us assume, then, that the statement at issue is not a simple definition. Now, to say that behavior is determined, is to say that it is caused. Therefore, by the original argument, caused behavior is unfree. And if any event or condition which influences behavior is a cause, then behavior which is to any extent influenced by events or conditions is unfree. What is it to say that a bit of behavior was influenced by an event or condition? Presumably, that the event or condition would be relevant in explaining why the behavior occurred, why the man acted as he did. From all of the above, it follows logically that the only behavior which *could* be free is that behavior for which there is no explanation at all. The only behavior which could be free is that behavior which is completely irrelevant to the circumstances in which it occurred, in the sense that nothing could be brought to bear to explain why the agent acted as he did. And from this it follows that every case of goal-directed behavior (that is, behavior in which the agent acts to achieve some end) is, to the extent to which the end was relevant to his behavior, *unfree*. And finally, it follows that all behavior, in so far as it is rational, is unfree. This, I submit, is absurd, for if behavior is unfree, then it is impossible that it be rational. Any argument which has as its conclusion the assertion that all rational behavior is unfree (in the last analysis, *because* it is rational) must be rejected. Skinner's argument about free will thus results in a palpable contradiction. His reasons for thinking that free will is an illusion are no reasons at all.

I have spent a good deal of time on what might be called the philosophical underpinning of *Walden Two*, the two theses, namely, that it is possible selec-

tively to condition emotions and behavior, and that all behavior is unfree. If the truth of these theses were granted, much (though not all) of what Skinner recommends would be extremely difficult to deny. Mere charges that it is all diabolical would, in this case (and actually, in any case), be pointless. Now that we have seen that they are false, we can go on to see how they lead to the advocacy of Walden Two.

IN WALDEN TWO, things are controlled from the top. There are various managers (of play, of social activity, of work, etc.) who decide what sorts of enterprises are conducive to the psychological welfare of the members of the community, and are therefore to be permitted. The society is thus a rigidly controlled one, and the reason is that "when a science of behavior has once been achieved, there's no alternative to a planned society. We can't leave mankind to an accidental or biased control" (page 264). Why, one might ask, is the only alternative to planning (controlling) the lives of people by Skinnerian managers that of leaving them to the (accidental and/or biased) control of others? The historical tradition of liberalism would seem clearly to have shown us another alternative, that of letting people shape their own lives as they see fit. But, it should by now be clear, this is not an alternative which Skinner, in terms of the framework he has constructed, could even suggest. Since all behavior, whether we like it or not, is, in fact, controlled, we might as well let it be controlled by the good guys. Why is all behavior controlled? In the last analysis, because there are events and conditions which influence that behavior. Because of his mistaken idea that no behavior can be free, Skinner is rendered incapable of seeing the distinction between planning someone's life and letting him plan it himself.

This is a most important point. *Prima facie* there would seem to be two alternatives (with lots of gradations in between)—either people are controlled, or they are not. But for Skinner, this last is not even a possibility. The argument about free will makes it impossible that anyone is uncontrolled. The only real alternatives are good control and bad control (page 263). But this is simply the product of a bit of sham reasoning. What, one wants to ask, do you say about the possibility of establishing a society in which people are not subject to a rigid conditioning process in the hands of "behavioral engineers," but in which they are able to encounter many and diverse influences and make up their own minds about which they regard as the more important and which the less? Skinner's answer is clear. This, he would presumably say, is just the situation I am trying to avoid; it is the one I was talking about when I described a situation in which there was accidental and biased control.

It seems to me that therein lies, for the superficial reader, the main attraction of *Walden Two*. Only the unreasonable would prefer a system of biased and accidental control to one of intelligent control. Walden Two is, after all, better than Russia. It is to expose the view that these are our only choices that I spent as much time as I did examining Skinner's argument about free will.

In actuality, there are a number of alternatives open to us who would recommend a form of social order. There are at least the three just alluded to: a Russian system controlled from the top by foolish and arbitrary men, a Walden Two in which this control is exercised by intelligent men of good will, and an uncontrolled society.[7] These are, of course, not the only alternatives, but if we recognize the fallaciousness of Skinner's free will argument, we see that there are at least these three.

And, granting that Walden Two is

preferable to Soviet society, we must raise the question concerning whether it is better than an uncontrolled one. Frazier, in effect, raises this very question, ". . . what do you say to the design of personalities? Would that interest you? The control of temperament? Give me the specifications, and I'll give you the man! . . . Let us control the lives of our children and see what we can make of them" (page 292). Notice that Skinner relies, in characterizing his own alternative, on the view which we discovered earlier was not even coherent. It is not true, irrespective of the techniques one employs, that one can generate people according to any arbitrary list of specifications: one could not (logically) make people who were only happy. But leaving this aside, the question is whether we should allow a central committee in control of society consciously to design personalities. *Prima facie* the answer to the question would seem to depend on which values the central committee is concerned to instill. It might seem that if these values are good ones, then we can accept Skinner's recommendation, and that if they are bad ones, we should reject it. What are the character traits and social values which Skinner accepts? In general, they are the very best. Happiness, productivity, lovingness, etc. This is another reason, I suspect, for the attraction which *Walden Two* exerts. If the answer to the question *did* depend on whether or not Skinner's choices were good ones, then there would be little more to say.[8] But it does not. What must be decided is the question of the desirability of a controlled society.

An initial question, preparatory to deciding the matter, might be the following: given that we can produce artists, scientists, musicians, at will, how could anybody reasonably decide about the desirable proportions? This seems to be the sort of value question which the behavioral scientist is in no better position to answer than any of the rest of us. Suppose that the behaviorist were to reply

491

---

[7] It should be clear that by uncontrolled society I don't mean one in which there is *no* control over behavior. Obviously, a society which prohibits certain acts *(e.g.,* murder) is to that extent controlling behavior. By an uncontrolled society, I don't mean an anarchic one. This is not the place to enter upon an extended discussion of the semantics of "control." For my purposes it is enough to say that by an uncontrolled society I mean one in which the sorts of control that are characteristic of both Walden Two and Soviet society are absent—thought control, thoroughly propagandized education, etc.

[8] Of course, in this discussion I am accepting something which I spent much time earlier in denying, *viz.,* the possibility of creating people to order.

that this isn't a value question at all. It's purely an economic matter, i.e., the question is one of the allocation of resources: we want to provide the people in our behaviorist utopia with the maximum possible satisfaction of their various desires, and our decision about what sort of people to produce (artists, musicians, scientists, etc.) will depend not on our values, but on the values of the community.

Now there would be difficulties in proceeding in this way. I mean that the behaviorist in his controlled socialist society would have the same problems in the effective allocation of resources as any other socialist planner. But this sort of objection is, at this point, not the relevant one. Can we really allow that, as far as we have presented it, the behaviorist's problem is one of resource-allocation? I think not. Remember that the important idea about Walden Two is that we are conditioning values, i.e., likes and dislikes. We are not simply taking an arbitrary society and discussing the question about how best to satisfy the needs of that society given its (and not our) set of values. What this means in the present case is that the problem about how many musicians to produce is not an economic question. We are deciding not merely how to satisfy desires—we are deciding what those desires shall be, i.e., we must decide how many people are going to want to hear music, how many people enjoy art, etc.

Thus the behavioral scientist is faced with a question of value, a question of the order in which various goods are to be placed on a preference scale, and the behavioral scientist is in no better position to resolve this problem than we are. Indeed what criteria *could* be employed to decide such a question? This is surely not a scientific question, in the sense that there are generally accepted ways of finding out the answer. *finding out* the answer. The very best one could do is suggest an answer, and that answer will be an expression of the particular value scheme embraced by the suggester. There is no reason at all to suppose that the behaviorist is possessed of any expertise in this matter which is denied to the rest of us.[9]

Page Thirty-eight

IT BEGINS TO LOOK as though distinctly unscientific elements of arbitrariness (which arbitrariness, remember, Skinner was concerned to avoid) are being introduced into the design of the behaviorist utopia. But there are further difficulties. Skinner argues that a free society (in the ordinary sense) is an extremely undesirable thing. The reason is that all sorts of elements of arbitrariness and haphazardness are introduced by people pursuing incompatible (and often unpraiseworthy) goals. The various efforts which these people make in the attempt to persuade their fellows that the goals are desirable ones are causal factors which can change, in the last analysis, the value orientation of that society. This arbitrariness, the possibly of bad values being substituted for good ones as a result of the free (again in the ordinary sense) interplay of competing goals, is perhaps the chief evil against which *Walden Two* is directed. This is *the* reason Skinner advocates a controlled society.

We must then investigate whether or not it is *possible*, even on Skinner's terms, to eliminate arbitrariness in this sense. Let us suppose that we have a scientific procedure for determining not only how to condition various abilities, character traits, and values, but

---

[9] While Skinner seems to be vague enough on how questions of value are decided in Walden Two, he is at least candid in admitting that science plays no part in the decisions. "The philosopher in search of a rational basis for deciding what is good has always reminded me of the centipede trying to decide how to walk. Simply go ahead and walk! We all know what's good, until we stop to think about it" (page 159). If Skinner means by this that universal agreement can be obtained on what is and what is not good, his statement is obviously false—suffering, promiscuous sexual behavior, etc., are things concerning the goodness of which a Christian and a hedonist might well disagree. But even assuming that we could cleanly separate good from bad things, this would in no way solve the problem of the behavioral engineer. Since he is charged with arranging the value systems of the members of society, and since very often a choice must be made among good things (at the very least because they can't all be realized at the same time), he must have a good idea of the order in which goods are to be ranked among themselves — which are the more important ones, and which the less. This problem scarcely permits of a ready answer.

also for determining which ones we *should* condition. Now, it is not so easy to know what we are supposing here. With respect to musical ability, for example, are we supposing ourselves to be conditioning general ability in this area, ability at baroque music, ability at Bach, Vivaldi, or what? The same question arises for musical tastes. Do we condition people to like baroque music or do we condition a fondness for music in general? This is by no means an academic question for the behavioral engineer. We shall see that his failure to solve this problem will result in the emergence of new values in society, which the behaviorist psychologist cannot have taken into consideration in his scheme of conditioning, and for the control of which he will have to resort to methods which have nothing of the respectable air of science about them.

We can distinguish various levels of what we might call value generality, and the behavioral engineer must decide, assuming him to have the suitable techniques, on which level to operate. For purposes of the discussion, we might call music in general the first, or highest, level of generality; the various periods —baroque, classical, romantic, etc.—the second level of generality; particular composers, the third level; and so on. Let us call an ability or a liking on the first level an $Ability_1$ or a $Value_1$, and so on.

Now the question is: at what value or ability level are our conditioning procedures supposed to operate? Presumably the behaviorist is not going to condition each miniscule preference or ability in each member of society. I mean he is not going to decide that so and so many people should be devotees of the late Beethoven quartets, and that so and so many people are going to be admirers of Bach piano sonatas played without the pedal. Let us assume, then, that conditioning procedures are going to be applied at the first level: we are going to produce so and so many musicians, so and so many artists, etc. We are not going to produce as a matter of deliberate policy a given number of baroque pianists, a given number of impressionists, and so on. Thus, $Value_2$ choices are not,

as the $Value_1$ choices are, the direct result of policies and practices instituted by the planners.

This is the situation we are envisaging. What could we reasonably expect from such a situation; what would be the natural result of this absence of $Value_2$ conditioning? Well, one thing we could reasonably expect would be that, in an important sense, $Value_2$ would not be anything like as stable as $Value_1$. While the number of people who have musical interests and abilities is something that we can expect to be constant (because we are fixing it) the number of people who like any *kind* of music and the number who are skilled in the production of any *kind* of music is something that is likely to vary.

So, to restrict ourselves to this specific case, we can expect there to be periods in which one sort of music is in the ascendancy and periods when this sort of music is replaced by another in the favor of the inhabitants of the society. More interesting is the fact that we can expect *new* values to be created on this level. Since, to the extent to which values on this level are unconditioned there is an area for what we might call a free interplay of competing values, there is reason to expect that there will be some sort of building on what is already in existence. Gifted musicians will see the possibility of innovating, of building upon the stock of values and knowledge which they already possess, in the same way that this was done in the old society, in the way, for example, in which Mahler is said to have built on Wagner, and Schoenberg on Mahler. And we can also expect that some of these innovations will receive acceptance on the part of some of the music lovers of the society. Remember that we are supposing their $Value_2$ choices to be unconditioned.

Thus new and unplanned values have come into existence in the society. What interest, if any, should the planners take in this fact? Presumably they are going to be very interested indeed. After all, this new sort of music, when it is performed, is going to be one of the causal factors influencing the behavior of the inhabitants of the society. And there will be all sorts of factors, on this level, which will be determinants of the behavior of the inhabitants of the society—new art forms, new ways of painting, new ways of writing and performing plays; innovations in technology; new ways of building homes, new alloys for use in such building. The possibility of a literally endless number of changes in the established order opens up. These new elements are going to be competing with each other for the attention and approval of society at large. Were the planners to step back disinterestedly from this development the very element of arbitrariness and randomness which Skinner was concerned to eliminate would reappear.

So the planners must act. If it could be shown that some new Value₂—some new style of painting, for instance—was likely to have what in the judgment of the planners would be an adverse influence on the populace, it must be stopped. The whole point of the society is that such adverse influences are to be eliminated. Thus, control is introduced at this lower level of value generality.

OR IS IT? When we speak of "control" at this level are we speaking about the same sort of thing with which we began? The answer is no. In our initial attempt at describing the behaviorist utopia, how did we suppose control to be introduced? What counted as control? Clearly, it was the conditioning of certain likes and dislikes, certain abilities and character traits. This is what Skinner seems to mean throughout *Walden Two*. This, for Skinner, is an innocuous sort of control. The planners of the society are not acting against the wishes of the members—they are shaping those wishes. People do what they want to do, although what they want to do is determined by what some others want them to want. It is in this sense, for Skinner, that Walden Two is a controlled society in which all the inhabitants are free. But the control of which we are now speaking is nothing like this at all. It consists simply in the proscription, by the authorities, of certain kinds of activities. If the planners decide that

a certain type of music is likely to have an injurious effect, they will forbid it. This is political control pure and simple.

Interestingly enough, Skinner admits that control of the kind takes place in Walden Two (page 164). If someone in the society comes up with something new, he does *not* try to bring it about that the society at large accept his innovation. He goes to the relevant planning board. It is there that the decision about the acceptability of what he has done is made. If the planners decide against his idea they will prohibit its circulation. Thus is met the threat of "arbitrariness."

It is of absolute importance to recognize the difference between control in this latter sense and behavioral conditioning. *Walden Two* seems to present us with a picture of a society in which the ordinary, "nasty" elements of political control are absent. I suppose that many readers of the book have found this to be one of its most attractive features. But, as we have shown above, this is an illusion. As long as the planners of the behaviorist utopia do not condition values and abilities down to the last thinkable atom, it will be absolutely necessary to control the society (in the ordinary sense) in order to insure that the chosen values maintain their supremacy. Whatever merits Walden Two may have, the absence of rigid political control is not one of them.

This last point obviously raises the question of freedom, now in the political sense, and not in the sense of freedom of the will. Skinner argues that the former question is one that finds an easy solution in Walden Two. If people do what they want to do (whether or not their wants have been selected by someone else) then they are free. Suppose we accepted this account. Would it then follow that the inhabitants of the behaviorist utopia are free? Surely not. Consider a citizen of the society going to the planning board convinced that his new idea will result in enormous progress in sundry fields. He wants (if the word is not too weak) to have the idea introduced. But after many hours of pleading with the planners (whom he comes to look on, at least in part, as thick-headed), he is turned down. He asks, as a last desperate move, to be permitted to give a public address on the merits of his new scheme. This too is turned down. The planners, we may suppose, feel that any propagation of the ideas they have just heard will have a markedly deleterious effect on the rest of society. This sort of situation is clearly possible in the behaviorist utopia. Skinner admits as much when he says that new ideas will have to be cleared through the relevant planning boards. But the situation we have described *is* a situation in which someone is not allowed to do what he wants to do. Thus we can grant Skinner all he asks for (in the way of a definition of freedom) and still the society he envisages is an unfree one. Not only are wants and desires (on some level) conditioned by the behavioral engineers, but any deviation from the established pattern is suppressed by those behavioral engineers when it does not accord with their own views. Walden Two may now begin to look, not like an excitingly new departure in the theory of social organization, but like an old-fashioned totalitarian society of a kind with which we are already familiar.

Thus we have seen that at every important stage in the argument for the behaviorist utopia, the position adopted by Skinner is one that cannot be maintained. But let us suppose now that none of this was shown. Let us suppose, that is, that Skinner's argument, up to this point, has been a good one. Would even that show that his recommendations are worthy of acceptance? Is a controlled society (assuming that it can do most of what Skinner says) a desirable thing? Again, I submit, the answer is no. But, given our assumption, it is not possible to show this by pointing up internal contradictions in the theory behind Walden Two. We are assuming, in some vague sense, that Walden Two can "work."

Is a working Walden Two a more desirable social organization than a free society? The answer to this question obviously depends, in part, on the sort of criteria one employs in assessing the merits of a particular form of social

organization. Given certain ends, Walden Two *is* more desirable. Frazier indicates, in the course of his advocacy of Walden Two, that an important feature of the society is that it provides the opportunity to make controlled social experiments. Obviously, Walden Two would provide a more effective medium in which to conduct controlled social experiments (of a certain kind) than would a free society. But this is, after all, a rather restricted goal. And the fact that it is so restricted renders it untenable as a justifying goal for a form of social organization. One doesn't construct a society for the purpose of experimenting with its members. Skinner recognizes this, and what he regards as justifying the society is something else. Walden Two is supposed to represent an extremely progressive society, and one remarkably well adapted to achieve the goals set for it. It is in these terms that the issue between Walden Two and a free society must be discussed.[10]

ONE OF THE MOST important criteria by which we judge societies, of course, is a great degree of satisfaction of material wants—that is, the society must be an economically successful one. And the economic question is especially important in regard to Walden Two: much of the glamor of the life there proceeds from the fact that the inhabitants, having to work no more than four hours a day, have a great deal of leisure for the pursuit of culture and general self-improvement. Unfortunately, I am afraid that there is not much use in discussing this aspect of Skinner's ideas. He states, in his book, that the economics of a society are "child's play," and, indeed, he proceeds to deal with economic problems much as a child would. His ideas here are simply naive socialism, of the silliest sort. One example: once in a while, the children in

---

10 Of course, a free society does not have goals set for it in the same sense that Skinner's controlled society would, for there is no one in a position to set goals for everyone else. All we mean here by the goals of a free society are the ends which, in considering it, we would like it to achieve.

Walden Two are sent out into the world and given a

sort of detective assignment. The game is to establish a connection in the shortest possible time between any given bit of luxury and some piece of poverty or depravity. The children may start with a fine residence, for example. By going in the service drive they may be able to speak to a colored laundress hanging out clothes. They induce her to let them drive her home. That's enough [page 206].

Enough for what? To prove that all wealth in a free enterprise system is gotten unfairly? To prove that wealth in a society is like a pie, and that if some have more others must necessarily have less? Does Skinner know what an economic cost is, and that there are fortunes to be made by entrepreneurs who can discover ways of cutting costs which their competitors have not yet realized? Does Skinner know that there exists a question of the practicability of rational allocation of resources in the absence of a market for capital goods—in such a situation as obtains in Walden Two, for instance? Offhand, one would have considered an economics primer required reading for a society-builder. But in any case, the economic problems of a utopian socialist community are much beyond the scope of our discussion here. Let us, therefore, pass on to the more general question of social control vs. the decentralization characteristic of a free society.

I have mentioned that Skinner admits the necessity for political control over new ideas. This concession occurs in his discussion of the "Walden Code," a system of maxims regulating the conduct of the members of the community in an incredibly detailed way: the Code even governs how introductions between people are to be made, establishes what is to count as rudeness in a conversation and prohibits (for the sake of psychological health) the deliberate expression of gratitude between members of the society. Now, in regard to this Code, Skinner states:

As to disagreement, anyone may examine the evidence upon which a

rule was introduced into the Code. He may argue against its inclusion and may present his own evidence. If the Managers refuse to change the rule, he may appeal to the Planners. But in no case must he argue about the Code with the members at large. There's a rule against that.[11]

What this involves, then, is that every innovation in social life will have to gain the approval of the behavioral engineers. Thus, the distinction between Walden Two and the open society becomes as clear-cut as possible, and we are in a position to introduce what is probably the chief argument for freedom.

Let us attempt to state this argument in the form of an analogy—the analogy between society as a whole considered as an organization for the acquisition and communication of knowledge, and any given semi-organized field within society serving the same functon. If advances in social knowledge (in the best ways of meeting the problems that arise in human life) are best promoted by a system of rigid controls such as Skinner's why not apply this system to science and the arts? If we established a commission of the best physicists, say, who would decide what lines of thought subordinate physicists would be allowed to follow up, is it likely that breakthroughs in this science would be as frequent as in these past centuries of "anarchy," when each physicist has done as he wished? In other fields, to cite illustrations is virtually to close the case as far as these disciplines are concerned: who would wish that Bradley and Bosanquet — the outstanding British phi-

---

[11] It ought to be pointed out, incidentally, that the "scientific" nature of Walden Two is always stated rather than shown. That is, Frazier's defense of a particular practice in his community takes the form not of the presentation of any pointer readings, but simply of suggestive inferences about human beings, much as might occur in a conversation between two educated persons with an interest in "what makes people tick." (Sometimes, indeed, it descends somewhat beneath this level—see for instance his argumentation concerning the irrelevancy of history, with his vague but impassioned championsh'p of "the *Now*" [page 239].) But, presumably, Skinner is not calling for the acceptance of any of the particular practices he describes (for which he gives no "laboratory evidence" at all); it is rather the *method* which he wants us to accept.

496

losophers of their day — had been commissars of philosophy, empowered to decide whether Russell and Moore would be allowed to present their ideas to the public? Who would wish to have set Haydn in a similar way as arbiter over the young Beethoven?

These examples illustrate the principle that the progress of ideas is not served by casting over any given field — and *a fortiori,* over society as a whole — the mental limitations of one mind or one group of minds, no matter how superior a position they occupy in regard to other individual minds.

Now, it may be objected that the analogy is a false one; that the behaviorist psychologists would occupy, in relation to their wards, an extremely superior position, not at all comparable to that of Haydn to Beethoven. That is, the behaviorist might argue: "Of course, we would not wish a young innovating genius to have his hands tied by the established and conservative leaders in his field. But this would not be the case with human behavior. It is not the ideas of a young Beethoven that will be 'suppressed' by our behavioral engineers; it is simply the 'ideas' of the masses of uninspired, generally mediocre men and women, and they will assuredly gain in our system."

But such a rebuttal fails to see the full implications of the problem of innovation. Very often, innovation depends not only on qualities internal to the innovator (which conceivably could be predicted by a system of testing), but on a unique combination of circumstances in which the innovator finds himself. As Hayek describes the situation:

. . . we have no way of predicting who will at each step first make the appropriate move or what particular combinations of knowledge and skills will suggest to some man the suitable answer, or by what channels his example will be transmitted to others who will follow the lead. It is difficult to conceive all the combinations of knowledge and skills which thus come into action and from which arises the discovery of appropriate practices or devices that, once found, can be accepted generally. But from the countless number of humble steps taken by anonymous persons in the course of doing familiar things

in changed circumstances spring the examples that prevail. They are as important as the major intellectual innovations which are explicitly recognized and communicated as such.[12]

TO PUT ANYONE in charge of a field of human activity — or of human activity in general — is necessarily to place him in a position of arbiter over every potential innovator. The original question remains: "Why doesn't Skinner propose establishing commissions in each science and art, to pass judgment on the efforts of all its practitioners?"

It seems clear, then, that innovation will not be promoted by a controlled society. But perhaps a controlled society is in the best position to make use of the knowledge already available (we are speaking now of "social knowledge"— the sort of thing with which the "Walden Code" deals). Actually, it is difficult to know what to say here, because Skinner appears to be maintaining a position little short of incredible. When he says, for instance, that the expression of gratitude is not to be allowed between members of society — does he mean this literally? Will it, under all possible circumstances, represent an infraction of the Code to express gratitude? What if a man saves my life at the risk of his own? Or, to put it more strongly, what if he submits to torture, in order to conceal my place of hiding from my would-be murderers? Does Skinner mean to say that I will have to clear it with a board of behavioral engineers before I express my gratitude? Perhaps the rule concerning gratitude, when it emerges from the laboratories, will contain a clause permitting its expression in certain cases. But then, how many clauses will it contain? In general, how will it be possible for a group of men — endowed, as we may assume them to be, with a great deal of scientific psychological knowledge — to foresee all the possible combinations of circumstances which occur in social life, circumstances which often include the pitting of one generally-accepted rule against another?

---

[12] F. A. Hayek, *The Constitution of Liberty* (Chicago: University of Chicago Press, 1960), p. 28.

497

Since it is clearly impossible, perhaps Skinner could allow a certain leeway in the interpretation of his gratitude rule. But it requires little insight to see that this would be a fatal breach in his system. Once people are permitted a degree of personal discretion in the application of a behaviorist "truth," it becomes possible for them to modify the rule itself, in the way that judges have made deadletters of various laws by their interpretations of them. Control over behavior would once more pass from the hands of the psychologists to those of society at large, the very situation Walden Two was created to eliminate. Thus, we must assume that no leeway will be allowed in the interpretation of the various behaviorist maxims. Now, what does this imply? It implies that the only place where society's accumulated knowledge can be refined and fitted for application to an infinitely great variety of circumstances is in the laboratories of the behavioral psychologists. If someone thinks that a received rule ought to be modified in its application to the particular situation in which he finds himself, he is not allowed to do so. He must obey the rule as it has been handed down to him, and await the judgment of the behavioral engineers as to the permissibility of his suggested modification. Isn't it obvious that this would bring about virtually the *least* flexible and *least* adaptable society imaginable? To arbitrarily exclude by far the larger segment of society from the work of adapting received rules and maxims to various situations is to eliminate all these minds as centers for acquiring, refining and passing on knowledge. Such a procedure would make sense if there were good reason to believe that the minds put in control were omniscient — but our previous discussion of free will and selective conditioning does not support that claim, at least as far as one important behaviorist is concerned, and it is unlikely that the case would be different with his fellows.

The argument for freedom is — quite unfortunately, from the viewpoint of the prospects for a free society — an enormously complicated and abstract one, and we have only touched the surface here.[13] But, I hope that enough has been said to suggest that Walden Two is hardly a rival to a free society with respect to its ability both to changing conditions and to promote progress.

A word is perhaps in order for those who have read *Walden Two* and are made enthusiastic by its promise of a better existence for all, with less frustration and fewer misdirected lives than we see around us today. The important thing to realize is that the choice before us is not between whatever improvements behavioral psychology offers us in the problems of arranging our lives, and the benefits a free society offers us in the way of innovation and progress. Skinner's utopia indeed precludes the advantages accruing from the free play of ideas and the clash of values of the open society, but the reverse is not the case. In an uncontrolled social setting, people are free to adapt their lives in the light of behavioral psychology, and, if a substantial part of what Skinner claims for his ideas is true, then the same society which gave birth to them will be free to apply them to advantage.

The real value of the book, I think, is that it performs one of the functions credited by John Stuart Mill to even the most erroneous doctrines: by energetically presenting the case for a centrally-directed social order, it leads us to reconsider fundamentals, and forces us to re-examine and refine the arguments for the open society. Thus, while we may thank Skinner for promoting this end — which was indeed no part of his intention — those of us who are reasonable must decline the offering.

---

[13] Much the most profound discussion of these problems which I have come across is contained in Hayek's *Constitution of Liberty.* An interesting discussion of Skinner's social ideas from a psychological point of view is provided by Carl R. Rogers, "The Place of the Individual in the New World of the Behaviorial Sciences," in *On Becoming a Person* (Boston: Houghton Mifflin, 1961), pp. 384-402.

Benjamin Constant

RALPH RAICO

499

"HE LOVED LIBERTY as other men love power," was the judgment passed on Benjamin Constant by a contemporary. His life-long concern, both as a writer and politician, was the attainment in France and in other nations of a free society, and at the time when classical liberalism was the spectre haunting Europe—in the second and third decades of the last century—he shared with Jeremy Bentham the honor of being the chief intellectual protagonist for the new ideology. But it is not only for his elevated and disinterested love of freedom, nor for his historical importance that Constant merits being remembered: there is something to be gained in the study of his works by individualists aiming at the development of a political philosophy that will avoid the errors both of certain 18th century liberals and of 19th century conservatism.

Although in his day he was the most famous liberal spokesman on the Continent, Constant was never as well-known in the English-speaking world; especially today, when he shares the neglect into which his party has fallen, something will have to be said of his career.[1]

He was born near Lausanne, Switzerland, in 1767, a descendant of Huguenots who had fled France following the revocation of the Edict of Nantes. Little need be noted of his generally erratic upbringing, except that he enjoyed a cosmopolitan education, studying at the universities of Erlangen and Edinburgh; the latter was at the time a center of Whig ideas, and boasted a faculty which included Adam Smith and Adam Ferguson. Constant was early attracted to Parisian life, and entered the world of the salons shortly before the beginning of the Revolution. He was absent in Germany until the fall of the Jacobins, returning in 1795, when he quickly became closely associated with Madame de Stael, and began a life of political pamphleteering. A brief period as a member of the Tribunate under Napoleon was ended after a too ardently expressed demand that the legislative assembly be allowed a voice in the making of laws—Constant and his friends were purged, Napoleon complaining of the "metaphysicians" in the assembly who were forever seeking to tie his hands. There followed a period of intense opposition to Bonaparte. At this time, Constant composed his *On the Spirit of Conquest and Usurpation*,[2] a demonstration of to what extent the aims and methods of Napoleon were out of keep-

[1] The most complete biography of Constant in English is that of Elizabeth Schermerhorn, *Benjamin Constant: His Private Life and His Contribution to the Cause of Liberal Government in France* (New York: Houghton Mifflin, 1924).

[2] Published in Hannover, in 1813. It is reprinted in Edouard Laboulaye, ed.; *Cours de Politique Constitutionnelle* (Paris: Guillaumin, 1872), vol. ii, pp. 129-282. There have been several English translations of *On the Spirit of Conquest*, and the reader may consult this book for a good example of Constant's political and social thought.

Ralph Raico is an Editor-in-Chief of NEW INDIVIDUALIST REVIEW.

ing with the spirit of the new *bourgeois* world. He joined other liberals in enlisting under Napoleon's banner, however, during the Hundred Days, on the supposition that the great general would now be compelled to rule as a constitutional monarch. At this time, Constant drafted the constitution under which Napoleon was to have governed. With Waterloo and the restoration of the Bourbons, Constant joined the liberal opposition, serving in the Chamber of Deputies and acting as a brilliant and forceful critic of every governmental policy which he viewed as inconsistent with the rights of man. This was the period of his greatest influence, when he enjoyed a vast European reputation and inspired groups of young disciples as far away as Warsaw. He died in 1830, shortly after the establishment of the July Monarchy.

With two important facts regarding Constant, we will not be concerned here, although they merit mentioning. First, that he occupies an honorable place in the history of French literature, principally through his short novel, *Adolphe*; and, second, that, like the hero of this work, his was a painfully introspective intellect, and his a personality that found it impossible ever to be less than studied and analytical. His psychological problems and the complex emotional life to which they led have provided most of the content for the studies of Constant which have appeared up until the present. While it is likely that these aspects of his personality had a certain bearing on his political and social thought, it did so in too complex a way to warrant closer examination here.

FRANCE HAS, together with England and Scotland, contributed more than any other nation to the theory, if not to the practice, of liberty. In the line of great French liberals, which begins about the second quarter of the 18th century with Montesquieu, Constant was the first of the generation following the Revolution. This circumstance was of the greatest significance for the development of his political ideas, and to it may be traced the fact that he tended to regard political

problems from a somewhat different viewpoint from that of most of the earlier liberals. This is most evident in his attitude toward the power of the central government.

Turgot and the Physiocrats, for example, had championed the extension of state power in the interests of "reform." These liberals saw the economic life of France hamstrung by the guilds and by an incredibly circumstantial mercantilist regulation; its social life irrationally structured on the basis of nobility of birth; its intellectual life, though intense, yet furtive and often even subterranean, because a large number of persons and bodies—from the Sorbonne to some influential duchess at Versailles — had the *de facto* power of ordering any book they wished committed to the flames; and they blamed the casual heaping up of tradition for such an intolerable state of affairs. They thought that what was needed was the action of an enlightened, ordering mind, endowed with sufficient power to sweep aside the machinations of all those who had a vested interest in the traditional encumbrances on freedom. For this reason, the *philosophes* (both those among them who were essentially liberals, and those who cannot fairly be classed as such) were enthusiasts of the "enlightened despotism" fashionable among certain rulers of the time. This is also the reason that led virtually the whole philosophical party wholeheartedly to support Louis XV in his suppression of the *parlements*; since these law courts had been the only legal check on the power of the king, the favor shown by the *philosophes* for this arbitrary action would otherwise be difficult to understand.[3]

With the upheaval of the Revolution, however, most of the institutions of the Old Regime which had (with government sanction, to be sure) acted as centers of privilege, were swept away. Industrial

[3] The inability of many of the French liberals to fully appreciate the operations of a spontaneous, undirected social order has been emphasized by F. A. Hayek; cf. his stimulating essay, "True and False Individualism," in *Individualism and Economic Order* (Chicago: University of Chicago Press, 1948).

freedom was granted to all, Protestants and freethinkers no longer had to fear imprisonment for manifesting their beliefs, there was one law for commoner and noble. The focus of all threats to individual freedom became the government itself. The Church, nobility, guilds and other corporations which, endowed with coercive privilege, had vexed the free functioning of men, left the stage, and across the gap created by their disappearance the individual and the state, for the first time, stood alone facing each other. And now the liberals' attitude toward the state underwent a change.

Where previous French liberals had seen a potential instrument for the establishment of liberty, and one that might at times even safely be used for the realization of certain "philosophical" values, writers like Constant started to see a collection of standing threats to individual freedom: government is "the natural enemy of liberty;" ministers, of whatever party, are, by nature, "the eternal adversaries of freedom of the press;" governments will always look on war as "a

means of increasing their authority." Thus, with Constant, the chief articulator of his generation's liberal ideals, we see the beginnings of classical liberalism's "state-hatred," which, after the 18th century's ambiguous attitude, marks its theory to the present day.[4]

Another feature distinguishing Constant from earlier liberals was what he conceived to be the ethical ends of social organization. In this respect, the *philosophes* had anticipated the central idea of Bentham, Constant's fellow liberal and almost exact contemporary. While the liberalism of writers like Mercier de la Rivière and Du Pont de Nemours, like Bentham's, was based exclusively on a utilitarian ethic, Constant's had a vaguer, but, it will appear to many, a more elevated foundation. This ought to be emphasized, since many writers on the history of liberalism — both conservatives and modern left-liberals—often write as if utilitarianism were historically the sole philosophical basis of liberalism. This was not the case with many of the most prominent liberals, including Constant, who emphatically rejected utilitarianism:

> . . . is it so true that happiness—of whatever sort it might be—is the unique end of man? In that case, our road would be quite narrow, and our destination not a very lofty one. There is not one of us, who, if he wished to descend, to restrict his moral faculties, to degrade his desires, to abjure activity, glory and all generous and profound emotions, could not make himself a brute, and a happy one . . . it is not for happiness alone, it is for self-perfectioning that destiny calls us. . . .[5]

Thus, Constant found the ethical ends which he wished to realize through a system of liberty not in the greatest-happiness principle, but in the development and enrichment of personality. This view was in keeping with the humanism then prevalent in Germany, and was possibly, in the case of Constant, traceable to his study of Kantian philosophy, and to the influence of cer-

501

---

[4] Cf. Henri Michel, *L'Idee de l'Etat.*
[5] *Cours de Politique Constitutionnelle,* vol. ii, p. 559.

tain of his many German friends, including Schiller and especially Wilhelm von Humboldt.

THE AIM OF ALLOWING the widest possible sphere for individual development meant, in Constant's thinking, the restriction of government action within the narrowest possible limits, namely, defense against external and internal aggression:

> Whenever there is no absolute necessity, whenever legislation may fail to intervene without society being overthrown, whenever, finally, it is a question merely of some hypothetical improvement, the law must abstain, leave things alone, and keep quiet.[6]

The same conclusion is arrived at by another line of reasoning. To demand that individual activity be interfered with is to demand that individual judgment give way to the judgment of the government. Now, no matter how tenaciously the partisans of state action attempt to cling to abstract terms, in the last analysis their program calls for substituting the opinion of certain government officials for individual judgment, and this aspect of the problem may be stated in this way: is there good reason to suppose the government officials will as a rule make more intelligent decisions regarding whatever it is they wish to legislate about than the individuals concerned? Constant believed the answer to be definitely negative, and offered an interesting analysis of the drawbacks of government decision-making.[7] In the first place, the government officials will presumably be chosen, directly or indirectly, by the very people whom they are supposed to manage, and it is therefore unlikely that their outlook will be appreciably in advance of that of society as a whole. In fact, the officials will probably share the prejudices and restricted views of the relatively unenlightened majority, rather than the values and thinking of the progressive and innovating minority.

---

[6] *Commentaire sur l'ouvrage de Filangieri* (Paris: Dufard, 1824), p. 70.
[7] *Ibid.*, pp. 55-70.

Page Forty-eight

In addition, Constant held, decisions arrived at by political officials exhibit certain other undesirable but necessary features: (1) errors in legislation spread their effects throughout society, while individuals' errors are limited in their consequences to a much smaller circle; (2) the effects of such erroneous laws will fall more on others than on the legislator, who thus has less of an interest in correcting them (at least, less of an interest in proportion to their bad effects) than a private citizen has in modifying his own errors, the burden of which falls on himself; (3) the fact that the legislator is further removed from the effects of his action brings it about that a greater period of time is required for modifying it, if it should prove wrong, than is the case with private individuals; (4) since legislators are continually under the eyes of hostile observers, modification of errors involves loss of prestige, and is also difficult for this reason; (5) finally, legislation has the defect of all collective decisions: it is a "forced give-and-take between prejudice and truth, betwen interests and principles," while decisions taken by individuals have the chance of being, in this sense, purer. Thus, Constant concludes, although in a regime of *laissez faire* we will have to renounce many grand and glittering undertakings on the part of the state, the chances and costs of errors in legislation are so great that, on net, the sacrifice will be well worth it.

The sphere in which individuals would be free to pursue their activities in accordance with their own values and judgment was to be delimited by a system of rights, which included the customary demands of the classical liberals: personal liberty (including the abolition of Negro slavery and all other forms of involuntary servitude), freedom of religion, freedom of the press, economic liberty, and so on.

Constant did not occupy himself particularly with economic questions. In this field he was first and last a disciple of the economists, especially of Adam Smith and J. B. Say, but asserting the principle of economic non-intervention in even more absolute terms than was customary with the professional economists, and going so far as to criticize the latter for not adhering firmly enough to their motto of *laissez faire, laissez passer*.[8] But the more interesting aspect of Constant's thought is his political philosophy, and it is to this that we now turn.

IN A SENSE, Constant's political theory may be considered a rebuttal to that of Jean-Jacques Rousseau, whose ideas in this field had gained increasing influence toward the end of the 18th century, coming to constitute something like the official ideology of the Jacobin, or democratic, party. Like Locke, Rousseau had posited an original social contract, but where the English philosopher had attempted to employ this notion as a foundation for civil rights, in Rousseau's conception the contract involved the total surrender by the individual of his life, liberty and possessions into the hands of the community. It is perhaps not too much of an over-simplification to say that Rousseau's idea amounted to a Hobbesian system, in which the despot is replaced by society as the great Leviathan, but for one important qualification: Rousseau recognized the dangers involved in his scheme, and believed they could be met by stipulating that, in return for the loss of rights as against society, the individual would be assured of an equal share with all other individuals in the sovereignty, in the determination and exercise of the "General Will." Accepting the idea that social life necessarily brings with it the total alienation of one's rights, Rousseau was thus the modern originator of the notion that freedom in a social context is identifiable with a condition of equal submission to the interests of the community and equal participation in the exercise of political power.

Constant believed that the championship of unlimited popular sovereignty by Rousseau and others represented much less of a break with the historical political pattern than might at first appear to be the case. What had happened was that these thinkers

saw in history a small number of men, or even a single man, in possession of an immense power, which did much harm, but their wrath was directed against the possessors of power, and not against the power itself. Instead of destroying it, they only dreamt of displacing it. It was a scourge, and they regarded it as a conquest.[9]

Constant admitted the sovereignty of the people, in the sense that no government whose authority is not delegated to it by the people, is a legitimate one. But from this sense of sovereignty

it does not follow that the universality of the citizens or those who are invested by them with sovereignty, can dispose as supreme master of the existence of individuals. There is, on the contrary, a part of human existence which necessarily remains individual and independent, and which is of right outside of all social competence.[10]

In analyzing Rousseau's conception of freedom, Constant had occasion to enter into an interesting historical explanation of the Rousseauian idea. He distinguished two senses of freedom: the liberty of the ancients, and that of the moderns, and asserted that Rousseau, as well as the Jacobins during the Revolution, had been attempting to re-introduce the sort of liberty which had been prevalent in the republics of classical antiquity, but which was, for various historical reasons, now outmoded. How this analysis was relevant to the state of opinion at the time may require some explanation.

DURING THE 18th CENTURY, the veneration of the classical reached such proportions that it has been referred to by one historian as a "cult." If few went to the lengths of the admittedly oversensitive Madame Roland, who as a girl wept for not having been born a Roman or a Spartan, the commonly-accepted picture of the typical citizen of the ancient republics as austerely virtuous and natural led many to consider whether the institutions which had pro-

503

---

[8] *Ibid.*, p. 14.

[9] *Cours,* vol. i, p. 9.
[10] *Ibid.*

duced this presumably ideal human being could not be reproduced in France with similarly beneficent effects. This cult achieved its peak during the Revolution, and especially with the triumph of the Jacobins. Now thousands were sent to their deaths, cities were razed and wars declared, all accompanied by the invocation of what amounted to a schoolboy's vague but over-heated notion of "ancient liberty." This acceptance of the worst forms of tyranny—from arbitrary arrest and trial without jury to conscription, the "blood tax"—to the doubtlessly sincere cry of "liberty" resulted in much confusion. Conservatives were often even led to the conclusion that the tyrannical excesses were somehow connected with an "excess" of liberty, and resolved that in the future Jacobin tyranny would be avoided by a ruthless suppression of all liberal demands. But, Constant held, the truth of the matter was that what was involved were two different senses of "liberty": one, the sort of "liberty" generally characteristic of the ancient world—consisting in equal powerlessness before the state and equal participation in public affairs—was perfectly compatible with all the specific measures which were destructive of the second sort of liberty, the liberty characteristic of modern times. This was a liberty having to do above all with the sphere of private life, and one in which political activity plays a very subordinate role:

> Inquire, first of all, gentlemen, what, in our day, an Englishman, a Frenchman, an inhabitant of the United States of America, understands by the word, "liberty." It means for everyone to be under the dominion of nothing but the laws, not to be arrested, detained, or put to death, nor maltreated in any way as a consequence of the arbitrary will of one or more individuals. It is for everyone to have the right to express his opinion, to choose and exercise his occupation; to dispose of his property and even to abuse it; to go and come without having to obtain permission, and without having to give an accounting of his motives or actions. It is, for each man, the right to join with other individuals, either to confer on their interests, or simply to fill his hours and days in a manner more conformable to his inclinations

and his fantasies. Finally, it is the right for each to influence the administration of the government, either by the nomination of all or of certain functionaries, or by representations, petitions and demands, which authority is more or less obligated to take into consideration.[11]

Constant makes some suggestive observations as to why political liberty can no longer be considered a significant enough good to outweigh the sacrifice of private liberties:

> The most obscure citizen of Rome and of Sparta was a power. This is no longer the case with the simple citizen of Great Britain or of the United States. His personal influence is an imperceptible element in the social will which impresses on the government its direction.[12]

Even leaving aside the question of the desirability of this way of life, man could, in the present day, simply not be a political animal in the sense proposed by the partisans of antiquity. Thus, the preservation of liberty in the modern sense becomes our chief task.

Rousseau had argued that, given popular sovereignty, there was no longer any need for guarantees against state power: if the sovereign was identifiable with the totality of the citizens, it was foolish to think that it would act in such a way as to harm the citizens. The speciousness of this reasoning, obvious enough in itself, was made explicit by Constant:

> . . . as soon as the sovereign is to make use of the force which it possesses, that is, as soon as it is necessary to proceed to a practical organization of authority, since the sovereign itself cannot exercise the authority, it delegates it. . . . The action done in the name of all necessarily being willingly or unwillingly at the disposition of an individual or of a few individuals, it comes about that in giving oneself to no one, one gives oneself, on the contrary, to those who act in the name of all.[13]

At the beginning of the age of democratic government, Constant insisted on a truth which doctrinaire democrats of

---

[11] *Ibid.*, vol. ii, p. 541.
[12] *Ibid.*, p. 545.
[13] *Ibid.*, vol. i, pp. 10-11.

504

the Rousseauian sort have tended to overlook: "The people which can do anything it wishes is just as dangerous, is more dangerous, than any tyrant, or, rather, it is certain that tyranny will seize hold of this right granted to the people."[14] The worst outrages of the Terror could be regarded as logical deductions from Rousseau's principles, and "the *Social Contract,* so often invoked in favor of liberty, is the most terrible auxiliary of every form of despotism."

Having established the necessity of limits to state power, Constant had to seek for a system of effective guarantees to maintain such limits.

AFTER THE REVOLUTION and the Napoleonic period, it had become a fact too obvious for anyone to deny that the mere proclamation of a list of rights was in no way a sufficient guarantee of freedom:

> All the constitutions which have been given to France have equally accorded individual liberty, and under the empire of these constitutions, individual liberty has been ceaselessly violated. The point is that a simple declaration does not suffice. What is required are positive safeguards; what is required are bodies powerful enough to employ in favor of the oppressed the means of defense sanctioned by the law.[15]

That is to say, if individual rights are not to be a dead-letter, certain institutional arrangements must be developed and encouraged which can be counted on to work toward the maintenance of constitutional guarantees. In one sense, everything with which Constant concerned himself — from bicameralism, through freedom of the press and private property, to religion—may be viewed as an addition to the edifice of guarantees. In general, these positive guarantees may be divided into two sorts: there are those which are positively established by state action, and have to do with the form of the government itself, and there are those which consist in extra-governmental forces which there is good reason

to believe can also be relied upon to serve the function of limiting government action to its proper sphere.

As regards the first category, Constant's thinking represents no major innovation. Rather, his merit in this regard is that of having been the systematizer of the structure of the liberal state, to the point where an eminent French historian of thought could say of him that he "invented liberalism."[16]

The method of limiting state power which, since the time of Montesquieu, had been thought of as most effective by the liberals was that of turning the state in against itself, through a system of division of powers. The author of *The Spirit of the Laws* had observed that "it is an eternal experience that anyone who possesses power tends to abuse it. . . . In order that power should not be abused, it is necessary so to arrange matters that power should be checked by power." If every increase in the power of some arm of the state could be counted on to meet the resistance of other arms of the state, then, because, while it extended the sphere of the former functionaries, it narrowed that of the latter, there would result another case of a great social good being achieved by tapping the vices of men. In this way, the will to power of state officials would be directed not so much against the rights of the people as against the power of other officials. The system of checks and balances and the division of powers were not, therefore, what one social democratic writer has recently called them: "contrivances, so dear to the [classical] liberals, for guarding against the possibility that governments might govern";[17] they were instead reasonable institutionalized protections against the virtual certainty that governments would try to govern too much.

---

14 *Ibid.,* p. 280.
15 *Ibid.,* p. 146.

16 Emile Faguet, *Politiques et Moralistes du Dix-neuvième Siècle* (Paris: Société Française d'Imprimerie, 1891), p. 255.

17 Harry K. Girvetz, *The Evolution of Liberalism* (New York: Collier, 1963), p. 105. In this passage, Prof. Girvetz goes so far as to include even "bills of rights" within the sweep of his Voltairian irony. Since he prefers to consider himself a "liberal," his book turns out to be a good illustration of its own sad theme.

The system of checks and balances was, in Constant's thought, to operate at many different points in the structure of government, and the general outlines of his scheme will be familiar enough to anyone acquainted with the American Constitution. There was to be a bicameral legislature, including a House of Peers to be selected independently of democratic opinion. This was an institution which had been demanded by the Anglophile, or moderate liberal, party as early as the first year of the Revolution, and a number of historians, including Acton, have seen in the rejection of this proposal the first ominous signs of the thoughtless Rousseauian spirit that was to lead to the Convention. Constant further divided power between the legislature and the ministry, and between these two branches and the judiciary, which was to consist of judges whose immovability from office was guaranteed. A further limit on the power of the central government was implied in a system of departmental and municipal rights, an idea which had never found much acceptance in France, accustomed for centuries to the centralizing efforts of the monarchy.[18]

Besides the division of powers, another political guarantee of rights was to be found in a certain degree of popular representation in the government. But Constant insisted on restricting the franchise to property-holders. The extent to which democracy was necessary for the maintenance of liberty could, he thought, be served by such a limited franchise, and he was skeptical of the benefits of a more democratic system. He had seen Napoleon made Consul for life, and later Emperor, on the basis of universal manhood suffrage; he saw that in the situation in which France found itself during the Restoration, it was primarily the more prosperous and educated classes which were the bearers of the new liberal ideas. The masses of workers and, especially, peasants, cared less for the introduction of a liberal state than for the preservation of the old ways, to

which they were accustomed—indeed, this was the reason why the only significant group which was interested in a mass-based suffrage at this time was a certain wing of the reactionary party.[19]

A major reason for Constant's disinclination to extend the franchise was the question of property:

> If, to the liberty of the faculties and of industry, which you owe them [the lower classes], you join political rights, which you do not owe them, then these rights, in the hands of the greatest number will inevitably serve to invade property. They will march toward it by this irregular route, instead of following the natural route, labor. . . .[20]

Although in historical retrospect the attempt to limit the franchise appears to have been unrealistic, Constant at least has the merit — as this passage shows—of having foreseen one of the principal features of modern democracy.

In addition to the guarantees of individual rights which were built into the system of government itself, Constant looked to certain social institutions to provide further guarantees. One of the most important of these was the press, and freedom of the press in this way took on a double character: it was itself a precious right, and it acted as one of

---

18 Constant's constitutional ideas are elaborated on in his *Principes de Politique* and *Reflexions sur les Constitutions et les Garanties*, both reprinted in the *Cours*, vol. i, pp. 1-381.

19 Georges Weill, *La France sous la Monarchie constitutionnelle* (Paris: Alcan, 1912), p. 5. As a rule, conservatives rejected democracy in the 19th century because of its connection with the French Revolution, and because they viewed it as part-and-parcel of the new-fangled liberal system. But the rivulet of conservative thinking which looked on democracy as a good tactic for depriving the liberal middle classes of predominance in the legislatures was sufficiently important to merit more attention than it has been given. Its chief practical consequence was the establishment of universal manhood suffrage in the Constitution of the North German Confederation, in 1867, by the Junker Bismarck, who was explicitly guided by the consideration just cited (cf. Gustav Mayer, *Bismarck und Lassalle* [Berlin: Dietz, 1928], pp. 33-39). The obvious fact that if the masses are anti-liberal democracy will be as much a peril to liberty as any other system is now forcing itself on the attention of even its more unreserved panegyrists, as they reflect on the civil liberties controversy in the United States; concern with this problem is sometimes put in the form of the question: "If put to a plebiscite, could the Bill of Rights gain a majority in America today?"

20 *Cours*, vol. i, p. 55.

506

the most powerful non-political guarantees of all other rights as well. The function of the press as a tribune for those whose rights were violated was incessantly emphasized by Constant:

> Everyone now knows that freedom of the press is nothing else than the guarantee that the acts of the government will be made known to the public, that it is the sole means of such publication, that without such publication the authorities are free to do what they will, and that to trammel freedom of the press is to place the life, property and person of every Frenchman in the hands of a few ministers.[21]

He looked, as we have mentioned, on the ministers, of whatever political complexion they happened to be at the moment, as the "eternal adversaries of freedom of the press." During his career as deputy in the French legislature, at the period of the Bourbon Restoration, Constant tirelessly fought all the various expedients which an ingenious and anxious government devised to interfere with this freedom. He was considered the parliamentary expert on the subject, and, in view of the place that debates in the French legislature occupied in the affairs of the whole continent, the great European defender of this liberty.

AN IDEA WHICH SEEMS to have originated with Constant is that a further guarantee against despotism is to be found in certain extra-governmental institutions capable of tying the loyalties of men against the day when the state might once again, as in the time of Robespierre, attempt to become the be-all and the end-all of social life. It was for this reason that he severely criticized the reckless spirit of uniformity and the senseless passion for pseudo-mathematical "symmetry" which inspired many of the Revolutionary measures; which, for instance, hatched Sieyes' suggestion that the departments, having replaced the traditional provinces, should be designated by number rather than by name, and which led, at the Jacobin Club of

Strasbourg, to the interesting question being raised of whether it might not, after all, be better to guillotine Alsatians who were "divisive" enough to cling to German as their chief language. "It is remarkable," observes Constant, "that absolute unity of action, without any limits, has never found greater favor than in a revolution made in the name of the rights of man." Every institution with a claim to the loyalty of men was another potential enemy for a state aiming at total control; this was particularly true of such powerful social elements as regionalism:

> The interests and memories which are born of local customs contain a germ of resistance which authority suffers only with regret, and which it hastens to eradicate. With individuals it has its way more easily; it rolls its enormous weight over them effortlessly, as over sand.[22]

It is in this light that we should also view Constant's attitude toward religion, to the study of which he devoted many years. His works on this subject are no longer read, but they contributed to the post-18th century attitude, which no longer considered religion to have originated as a priestly invention ("when the first knave met the first fool"), but as a response to a deeply-rooted need. The writers of the Enlightenment had also, with few exceptions, been bitterly hostile to organized religion in general, and particularly to the Catholic Church. Faced with an often savage religious intolerance, thinkers like Voltaire and Diderot explicitly championed control of the Church by the State,[23] believing the only alternative to be the reverse order of control. Constant, however, held that, given religious toleration as an established right, guaranteed as other rights were, religion could, from a strictly political point of view, serve the same sort of valuable function as regionalism. He welcomed it as a similar "divisive" element in social life, and warned against the proposal of the *philosophes* of com-

507

[21] *Ibid.,* p. lxi.

[22] *Ibid.,* vol. ii, pp. 170-171.

[23] Kingsley Martin, *French Liberal Thought in the Eighteenth Century* (London: Turnstile, 1954), pp. 136-37.

bining the spiritual and political powers in the same hands:

> What does it matter if spiritual pretensions have given way to political authority, if this authority makes of religion an instrument, and thus acts against liberty with a double force?[24]

CONSTANT'S BREAK with the Enlightenment and the Revolution by no means meant that he was sympathetic to the ideas then being advanced by conservative writers like de Maistre and Bonald, who attempted to erect the Christian notion of Original Sin into the theoretical underpinning for a system of oppression, arguing for a state strong enough to keep a firm check on natural man. Constant could not imagine how politicians could be thought not to have participated in the Fall, and saw no merit in this

> bizarre notion according to which it is claimed that because men are corrupt, it is necessary to give certain of them all that much more power . . . on the contrary, they must be given less power, that is, one must skillfully combine institutions and place within them certain counterweights against the vices and weaknesses of men.[25]

Furthermore, his respect for traditions as encumbrances on government action did not mean that he was prepared, as were the conservative writers of his day, to enshrine simply any tradition. The touchstone for him was the employment of force in connection with the traditional arrangement. He rejected both the program of some of the Revolutionaries, who had been eager enough to use force to destroy traditions which did not fulfill their personal, "philosoph-

ical" values, and the program of the conservatives, who typically recommended the use of state power for opposite ends. Constant was content to leave changes in traditional institutions to the workings of forces outside of the state:

> If I reject violent and forced improvements, I equally condemn the maintenance, by force, of what the progress of ideas tends to improve and reform insensibly.[26]

In the last analysis, Constant was as much an opponent of conservatism as of the Jacobin system, and on much the same grounds: both involved violent interference with the rightful sphere of the individual's private judgment and action, the seed-bed from which emerge the things that make social life worthwhile. It is interesting to note, in this connection, that when faced with the beginnings of the socialist movement, in the form of the Saint-Simonians, Constant thought it appropriate to associate them with the representatives of the closed societies of the past; they wished, he asserted, simply to be popes over the economic organization of society, and "priests of Memphis and Thebes" over its intellectual life.[27]

BENJAMIN CONSTANT MAY serve as a good rebuttal to the stereotype of the classical liberal as anti-religious, utilitarian and fanatically democratic, a stereotype which is often employed by contemporary conservatives who insist on confusing classical liberalism with Philosophical Radicalism. And for everyone sincerely interested in discovering a liberalism which will avoid some of the errors of certain liberal thinkers of the past, Constant may be looked on as a good starting point.

---

[24] *Filangieri*, p. 27.
[25] Cited in Georges de Lauris, *Benjamin Constant et les Idées Libérales* (Paris: Plon, 1904), p. 6.

[26] *Cours*, vol. ii, p. .172n.
[27] Sébastien Charléty, *Histoire du Saint-Simonisme* (Paris: Hachette, 1896), p. 54.

NEW BOOKS AND ARTICLES

THE FOLLOWING IS A SELECT LIST OF BOOKS AND ARTICLES WHICH, IN THE OPINION OF THE EDITORS, MAY BE OF INTEREST TO OUR READERS.

Alfred Avins, ed., *Open Occupancy vs. Forced Housing Under the Fourteenth Amendment* (New York: Bookmailer, 1963). This symposium includes contributions from a large number of legal scholars and judges, evaluating the basis for legislation outlawing discrimination in housing by builders and landlords. It is particularly timely at present.

Israel M. Kirzner, *Market Theory and the Price System* (Princeton, N. J.: Van Nostrand, 1963). A textbook in intermediate price theory designed for undergraduates, by a contributor to *New Individualist Review*. Although Prof. Kirzner presumes that his readers have already had a course in elementary economics, some students without such training may find it useful, since, in the author's words, "determined efforts have been made to subordinate geometry to economic reasoning."

Leonard W. Levy, *Jefferson and Civil Liberties: The Darker Side* (Cambridge, Mass.: Harvard University Press, 1963). A fairly conclusive demonstration that the revered saint of civil liberties was not all that he was cracked up to be outside of the area of religious dissent. One surprise is Jefferson's stand on the Alien and Sedition Acts. In opposition to Madison's view that seditious libel should not be an offense, he argued merely that the question should be left to the states.

Oskar Morgenstern, *On the Accuracy of Economic Observations* (Princeton, N.J.: Princeton University Press, 1963, new edition). An influential economist questions the value of most modern statistical economics. His ideas on this subject are presented in a more popular form in an article, "Qui Numerare Incipit Errare Incipit," *Fortune*, October, 1963.

Karl Popper, *The Open Society and Its Enemies* (Princeton, N.J.: Princeton University Press, 1963), paper. A reprint of the classic defense of the free society against the totalitarianism of Plato and Hegel. A new collection of Prof. Popper's essays has also been published recently: *Conjectures and Refutations* (New York: Basic Books, 1963). While most of the essays concern the philosophy of science and the history of philosophy, there are several interesting discussions of political and social topics, such as "Towards a Rational Theory of Tradition," and "Utopia and Violence."

Murray N. Rothbard, *America's Great Depression* (Princeton, N.J.: Van Nostrand, 1963). Dr. Rothbard, whose name will be familiar to our readers, presents an analysis of the Crash of '29 and the subsequent depression, based on the Austrian theory of the business cycle. His conclusion is that, far from being an unanswerable instance of the failure of the market economy, the Crash is attributable to a government-sponsored policy of credit-expansion, while the Great Depression itself was aggravated and prolonged by the measures taken by the government to alleviate it.

Robert H. Bork, "Civil Rights—A Challenge," *New Republic*, August 31, 1963. Prof. Bork presents a clear case against the proposed civil rights bill now before Congress. In a reply, the editors of the *New Republic* accuse Bork of advocating a principle (neo-liberalism) which "would today require the repeal of the industrial revolution." See also Bork's reply in the September 21, 1963, issue, where Bork continues his assault on the dominant social-democratic position on civil rights and the Negro revolution.

Richard J. Whalen, "Here Come the Conservatives," *Fortune*, December, 1963. Mr. Whalen provides a brief history of the revival of conservatism in America in the post-war period. He is careful to distinguish the many, often conflicting, strains of thought at work in this revival, but concludes that conservatives "have thrust themselves forward as a force that Liberalism can never again ignore." An excellent introduction to an important contemporary American phenomenon.

509

Page Fifty-five

NEWE BOKES & ARTICULLES

YE FOLLOWING IS A SELECTE LISTE OF BOKES AND ARTICULLES WHICH, IN YE OPINIONE OFF YE EDITORS, MAYE BEE OFF INTEREST TO OVRE READERS.

John Selden, *Of the Dominion, or, Ownership of the Sea, Two Books. In the first is shew'd, that the sea, by the law of nature, or nations, is not common to all men, but capable of private dominion or proprietie, as well as the land. In the second is proved, that the dominion of the British sea, or that which incompasseth the isle of Great Britain is, and ever hath been, a part or appendant of the empire of that island. Written at first in Latin, and entituled, Mare clausum seu, De domino maris, by John Selden. Translated into English, and set forth with som additional evidences and discourses, by Marchamont Nedham.* (London: Published by special Command, Printed by William Du-Gard, by appointment of the Council of State: and are to be sold at the Sign of the Ship at the New Exchange, 1652). A noteworthy study in the tradition of private roads, private police forces, and private ownership of courts.

Orders Appointed to bee executed in the Citie of London, for setting Roges and idle persons to work and for relefe of the poore. (London: John Daye, dwelling over Aldersgate, 1580). [Title page bears text of Proverbs 16 and Psalm 61.] A captivating study of social security legislation in England and its effects upon the level of unemployment.

Sir John Fortescue, *A learned commendation of the politique lawes of England; wherein by most pitthy reasons and euident demonstrations they are plainely proued farre to escell as well the Ciuile lawes of the Empiere, as also all other lawes of the worlde, wyth a large discourse of the difference betwene the ii gouernements of kindomes; whereof the one is onely regall, and the other consisteth of regall and politique administration conjoyned. Written in Latine aboue an hundred yeares past, by the learned and right honorable maister Fortescue knyght, lorde Chauncellour of England in the time of King Henry the vi, And newly translated into Englishe by Robert Mulcaster.* (London: R. Totell, 1573). A learned commendation of pitthy reasons and euident demonstrations which has been plainely proued farre escelled by its advertising agency.

Newe Indiuidualist Reuiewe, A pitthy journall of euident articulles thoughtfully and thought-provokingly written on indiuidualist ideas and proposals by some of the leading conservative and libertarian writers of today and tomorrow—articulles like those in the issue you have just read.

510

Society lives and acts only in individuals
. . . Everyone carries a part of society on
his shoulders; no one is relieved of his share
of responsibility by others. And no one can
find a safe way for himself if society is
sweeping toward destruction. Therefore
everyone, in his own interests, must thrust
himself vigorously into the intellectual battle. None can stand aside with unconcern;
the interests of everyone hang on the result. Whether he chooses or not, every man
is drawn into the great historical struggle,
the decisive battle (between freedom and
slavery) into which our epoch has plunged
us.

—Ludwig Von Mises

*The Intercollegiate Society of Individualists, a non-partisan, non-profit
educational organization, deals with ideas. ISI places primary emphasis on
the distribution of literature encompassing such academic disciplines as
economics, sociology, history, moral philosophy, and political science. If
you are a student or teacher, you are invited to add your name to the ISI
mailing list. There is no charge, and you may remove your name at any
time. For additional information, or to add your name to the list, write the
nearest ISI office.*

To Educate for Liberty

INTERCOLLEGIATE SOCIETY OF INDIVIDUALISTS

629 PUBLIC LEDGER BUILDING · PHILADELPHIA 6, PENN. · WAlnut 5-5632
Midwestern Office: 505 LEMCKE BUILDING · INDIANAPOLIS 4, INDIANA · MElrose 9-5551
Western Office: 1436 EL CAMINO REAL · MENLO PARK, CALIFORNIA · 323-0047

VOLUME 3
NUMBER 3
AUTUMN 1964

New
INDIVIDUALIST
Review

THE CONSERVATISM OF
RICHARD M. WEAVER

1. THE SOUTHERN TRADITION

2. THE HUMANITIES IN A CENTURY
OF THE COMMON MAN

REFLECTIONS ON THE LOSS OF LIBERTY

GEORGE J. STIGLER

CLASSICAL LIBERALISM AND TRADITION

RALPH RAICO

Vol. 3, No. 3   35 cents

NEW INDIVIDUALIST REVIEW

Volume 3 — Number 3

NEW INDIVIDUALIST REVIEW is published quarterly by *New Individualist Review, Inc.,* at Ida Noyes Hall, University of Chicago, Chicago 37, Illinois.

Opinions expressed in signed articles do not necessarily represent the views of the editors. Editorial, advertising, and subscription correspondence and manuscripts should be sent to NEW INDIVIDUALIST REVIEW, Ida Noyes Hall, University of Chicago, Chicago 37, Illinois. All manuscripts become the property of NEW INDIVIDUALIST REVIEW.

Subscription rates: $2.00 per year (students $1.00).

The Conservatism

of Richard M. Weaver

With the death of Richard M. Weaver last year, American traditionalism lost one of its most respected and sensitive representatives. Besides being a professor of English at the University of Chicago for many years, he was the author of two books which gained him wide regard as a conservative critic of modern society and culture: Ideas Have Consequences *and* The Ethics of Rhetoric. *His works display the distinctive character of his thinking and his concern for values shared by few of his fellow intellectuals.. They have contributed a great deal to the intellectual renaissance of American conservatism in the widest sense. We are pleased, therefore, to be able to present two of his unpublished articles, with the kind permission of his brother-in-law, Mr. Kendall Beaton, and Mr. Louis Dehmlow, the executor of his literary estate.*

The Foundations of Weaver's Traditionalism

LIKE OTHER AMERICAN traditionalists, the late Prof. Richard Weaver expressed an "affection for the proliferating variety and mystery of traditional life, as distinguished from the narrowing conformity and equalitarianism of most radical systems."[1] He envisioned human existence as possessed of an element of mystery, and from that he derived his moral beliefs and his regard for tradition; however, in many respects his ideas were different from those of other conservatives. First, he was oriented not toward the Christian religion, although he certainly respected particulars of its doctrine, but rather toward Platonism. Secondly, he was influenced by the Southern agrarian tradition much more than by the British conservative tradition as expressed by Burke. On some policy questions Weaver agreed with non-conservatives, but his agreement was coincidental, and it followed from his particular ideas, not from actual similarities with other doctrines.

To elaborate, Weaver adhered to the concept of universals which are valid without respect to time or place. He referred to universals as "objective truth" and included standards of human

---

James Powell is a third-year student at the University of Chicago, majoring in economics and the history of ideas, and an editorial assistant of NEW INDIVIDUALIST REVIEW.

[1] Russell Kirk, *The Conservative Mind* (Chicago: Regnery, 1953), p. 8

conduct and transcendental goals of human action prescribed by Providence. He believed that universals provided the only true knowledge —"the reality which is perceived by the intellect," not "that which is perceived by the senses."[2] As a consequence of these initial postulates, he envisioned the ideal of humanistically developed man: development of all creative human faculties in an orderly fashion. He opposed human development and expression which did not respect order, and thus he valued forms highly. Man, he thought, is a chaotic organism by nature and does not achieve meaning and worth until discipline is imposed upon him and his actions are rendered intelligible; meaningful human action presupposes conformity to some forms. To Weaver forms were qualitative; they provide the measure for human achievement. Universals provide just such forms, or conventions, that alone elevate human existence to a civilized level.

Weaver asserted in his book *Ideas Have Consequences* that the concept of universals has been progressively abandoned by Western man, who adopted in its stead what he termed "modernism." He traced the origin of Western decline to the acceptance of nominalism in the Middle Ages. Nominalism denied that there were universals, and it superceded the logical realism of the scholastics — which was a development of Platonic thought. "For four centuries," Weaver lamented, "every man has not only been his own priest but also his own professor of ethics, and the consequence is an anarchy which threatens even that minimum consensus of value necessary to the political state."[3] From the rejection of universals he traced a growing cultural disorder; man has devalued achievement as he has ignored forms, and the West—inevitably—has waned. He argued that education no longer tends to develop recognition of moral values or to induce intellectual faculties to conform to standards; in many cases man has abandoned such standards and

has adopted "pragmatic," "materialistic" ones. He pointed to the same sort of trend away from forms in art and in literature, particularly in the romantic phases of each: "That man is the product of discipline and of forging, that he really owes thanks for the pulling and tugging that enables him to grow — this concept left the manuals of education with the advent of Romanticism."[4] Weaver concluded that intellectually nominalism has produced chaos.

He pointed to indications of decay in human relations. As one, the posture of mass media — sensationalizing the obscene and violating privacy—defies "every definition of humanity." Further, since people value privacy and peaceful reflection less, they are much less intrigued, involved and stimulated by personalities and regard other human beings as mere associates. How to win friends and influence people is one publicized concern; yet: "to one brought up in a society spiritually fused — what I shall call the metaphysical community — the idea of a campaign to win friends and influence people must be incomprehensible. . . . And the art of manipulating personalities obviously presumes a disrespect for personality."[5] A disrespect by man of man has followed only too naturally from a disrespect of universals.

HE INSISTED THAT in political and economic affairs were the most telling evidences of Western decline. The democratising influences of the past century have promoted a primary concern among masses of people for quantity rather than quality. The democratic preoccupation with the wants of majorities entails, he argued, severe restriction of the aristocratic concern for manners, taste, oratorical distinction and political competence. Democratic politicians have typically catered to the crude tastes of majorities and have offered them whatever they have wanted, even at the sacrifice of prudence; aristocratic men of affairs, such as Randolph of Roanoke,

---

[2] Richard M. Weaver, *Ideas Have Consequences* (Chicago: University of Chicago Press, 1948), page 3
[3] *Ibid,* p. 3

---

[4] *Ibid,* p. 114
[5] *Ibid.* p. 31

have, by contrast, tended to act according to canons of reason and restraint. Randolph, in fact, represented to Weaver the ideal representative of American individualism.[6] But democratic writers have mercilessly assailed aristocratic ideas and have eroded their former respectability and influence.

Weaver scorned the consumer democracy of the free market and its necessary concomitant — commercialism. His first objection was that continually fluctuating market values readily convince those who deal with economic affairs that there are no absolutes. On the market some things prevail at one time and others at another time; similarly in the market of ideas, there is no guarantee of permanent dominance for the concept of universals — or for any other one. Second, in the place of concern for universals, a flourishing commercialism offers people material goods; in effect, in Weaver's view, it encourages materialism. Third, the free market allows multitudes of consumers to judge which things will prevail and which will not. That Western man has been "his own priest" and "his own professor of ethics" explains the decline of the West, and so the first premise of the market — the sanction to free choice — is itself a cause of the difficulties of modern man.

Paradoxically, though, Weaver vigorously defended an institution that provides the foundation for the free market; the inviolable right to private property, to him "the last metaphysical right." He so called it because it does not depend upon social usefulness for its acceptance. His valuation of property derives from his view of a natural connection between honor, responsibility and a personal relationship to property. He referred to the "honor of work" and seemed to have in mind the notion that work, honorable in itself, accumulates property, and hence property is merely an extension of one's labor — and of oneself. And people would tend to be more responsible if they have a material stake — real property — in the course of human affairs. Thus, private property enables that sanc-

tuary of privacy which Weaver felt was so essential for worthwhile human development.

THE SECOND POINT in favor of property is that in an age when defenders of universals are few, the institution of private property makes resistance to the ideas and pressures of a majority physically possible; property thus affords minorities the liberty to think and to act as they so choose. As there is danger that the modern and efficient state can achieve close surveillance over the affairs of citizens, and that human development will be smothered, there is crucial need for a means of frustrating such invasion of privacy; Weaver felt that private property was the last bulwark against intrusion, and that as such it acquires particular value. It provides the most hopeful method of salvaging the pluralistic social development which results only from unhampered privacy.

However, Weaver's defense of private property *per se* is not to be construed as a defense of finance capitalism; for by "private" he meant "personal," and corporate property certainly is not owned by individual persons. "Such property is, on the contrary, a violation of the very notion of *proprietas*. For the abstract property of stocks and bonds, the legal ownership of enterprises never seen, actually destroys the connection between man and his substance without which the metaphysical right becomes meaningless. . . . Property in this sense becomes a fiction useful for exploitation and makes impossible the sanctification of work. The property which we defend as an anchorage keeps its identity with the individual."[7] Not only was he apprehensive of encroachments upon privacy by corporations, but he also thought that aggregations of corporate power — property — would entail further enlargement of government and diminuition of liberty. He opposed the institution of corporate property because he thought it stripped property of privacy. Hence, Weaver opposed industrialization which produced urbanization, the extension of

---

[6] Weaver, "Two Types of American Individualism," in *Modern Age*, vol. 7, Spring, 1963, pp. 119-134

[7] *Ideas Have Consequences*, p. 133

521

the market and economic concentration. Weaver's solution to the problem of governmental and corporate power was to have "distributive ownership of small properties: these take the form of independent farms, of local businesses, of homes owned by the occupants, where individual responsibility gives significance to prerogative over property."[8]

FROM THE IDEAS which we have discussed followed directly the kind of tradition which Weaver revered: the agrarianism of the Old South. It was infused with aristocratic qualities — education, refinement, honor, provincialism. Each person owned property, ideally, and he mingled his own labor with the soil. His environment was peaceful and reflective, and his spiritual concerns were uninterrupted by the strains of an urban, commercial and materialistic civilization. Schools provided true education — not mass instruction — that enabled a person to develop restraint, taste and refinement. Such a way of life was honorable, but it was, again, possible only in a society in which each person owned some property.

Weaver aimed "to draw a line between respect for tradition because it is tradition and respect for it because it expresses a spreading mystery too great for our knowledge to compass."[9] "There is something in its [the South's] sultry languor," he continued, "and in the stubborn humanism of its people, now battling against the encroachments of industrialism — and with so little knowledge of how to battle — which tells me that for better or for worse this is my native land."[10]

IN SPITE OF the atypical nature of some of his basic ideas, Weaver was,

522

after all, a part of the traditionalist movement. His thought, therefore, is to be distinguished from that of writers oriented in a libertarian direction, who are the heirs of the classical liberal tradition. He was in the first instance concerned with societal wholes rather than with individuals. He valued highly a "sense of community": loyalty by a people to a set of traditional ideas and beliefs. And it was from his concern with wholes that his regard for liberty followed.

But he valued "rational liberty," not liberty *qua* liberty such as J. S. Mill once did.[11] Weaver opposed the notion of progress which aroused enthusiasm in such writers as Macaulay and Spencer. While agreeing with certain liberals on some matters — such as with Acton's anti-democratic attitudes — his traditionalist point of view was radically different from a liberal one.

His major contribution, it appears to me, was that of being an effective spokesman for a point of view too little articulated today, and thus a contributor to the vigorous libertarian-traditionalist dialogue.

JAMES POWELL

———

[8] *Ibid*, p. 133
[9] Weaver, "Up from Liberalism," in *Modern Age*, vol. 3, Winter, 1958-59, p. 28
[10] *Ibid*, p. 28

———

[11] In another contribution to *Modern Age* he asserted that cultural freedom is defensible because man by nature must develop a culture, and culture cannot develop in a repressed environment. Hence, culture has rights, e.g.,: "For the freedom of cultures as wholes, two rights must be respected: the right of cultural pluralism where different cultures have developed, and the right of cultural autonomy in the development of a single culture. In a word, cultural freedom on this plane starts with the acknowledgement of the right of a culture to be itself," from "The Importance of Cultural Freedom" in *Modern Age*, vol. 6, Winter, 1961-62. We should note that this line of argument is radically different from that of any one of a number of liberals who talk in terms of individual rights and development. The issue of cultural freedom would seem to be another instance of *coincidental* agreement between a conservative and a liberal view.

I. THE SOUTHERN TRADITION

MANY YEARS AGO the historian Francis Parkman wrote a passage in one of his narratives which impresses me as full of wisdom and prophecy. After a brilliant characterization of the colonies as they existed on the eve of the Revolution, he said, "The essential antagonism of Virginia and New England was afterwards to become, and to remain, an element of the first influence in American history. Each might have learned much from the other, but neither did so til, at last, the strife of their contending principles shook the continent." If we take Virginia as representing the South and New England as representing the North, as I think we may fairly do, we can say that this situation continues in some degree down to the present. Each section had much to learn from the other: neither was willing to learn anything and that failure produced 100 years ago the greatest tragedy in American history. Today it appears in political friction, social resentment, and misunderstanding of motives despite encouraging signs of growing amity.

This amity will clearly depend upon an appreciation, which Parkman found so sadly lacking, of what each has to offer. You certainly never get anywhere in mutual understanding among peoples or nations by assuming in advance that the other fellow has nothing whatever to offer. We would never think of assuming that in the case of the English or the French or the Chinese, or even the American Indians. But I only report what I have observed if I say that there appears a tendency on the part of a good many Americans to assume that the American South has nothing to offer—

nothing worth anybody's considering. That is a proposition in itself, and it needs to be examined in the light of evidence.

My principal theme, therefore, will be those things the South believes it has contributed to this great, rich, and diversified nation and which it feels have some right to survive and to exert their proportionate influence upon our life.

Before I can do this, however, I shall have to say something about what the South is—what makes it a determinate thing, a political, cultural, and social entity, which by the settlement of 1865 is going to be part of the union indefinitely.

IT IS VIRTUALLY A TRUISM in American political thinking that the South has been a kind of nation within a nation. You have no doubt learned that "nation" is a hard thing to define in any ultimate sense. But taking the term in the practical, working sense usually employed, we can say that there are a number of evidences of Southern nationalism. The political unity of the section often referred to by the phrase "the solid South" is a fact of considerable notoriety. Its ideological unity, or its community of belief about certain ideas, certain institutions, and certain figures of history is only a little behind the political unity. And the unity of its culture, expressed in its way of life, it speech, its cookery, and its manners, has maintained itself surprisingly in the face of a variety of conditions on the inside and considerable pressure from the outside. I am

523

inclined to think that Southern culture shows a degree of centripetalism, or orientation toward a center, which is characteristic of all high cultures.

In dealing with the factors which have produced this unity of thought and feeling in the South, it seems best to take them in the order of their historical emergence.

The first step toward understanding the peculiarities of the Southern mind and temper is to recognize that the South, as compared with the North, has a European culture—not European in the mature or highly developed sense, but more European than that which grew up north of the Potomac and Ohio rivers, in several respects, even more European than that of New England.

The South never showed the same interest in seceding from European *culture* that the North and West showed. It played an important and valiant part in the Revolution, but this was a political separation. After the Revolution it settled down quite comfortably with its institutions, modelled on eighteenth century England. A few stirrings of change, I believe, there were in Virginia, but not enough to alter the patterns of a landowning aristocracy. While Emerson in New England was declaiming, "We have listened too long to the courtly muses of Europe," the South was contentedly reading Sir Walter Scott, not, as Russell Kirk has shrewdly pointed out in his *The Conservative Mind*, just because it liked romance but because in Sir Walter Scott it found the social ideals of Edmund Burke. And Burke is one of the great prophets of conservative society. The European complexion of Southern culture showed itself also in other ways. It showed itself in the preservation of a class society—one might more truly say in the creation of a class society—for very few who settled in the South had any real distinction of family. It appeared in the form of considerable ceremonial in dress and manners. It was manifested in the *code duello*, with all its melancholy consequences. It appeared in the tendency of Southern families who could afford it to send their sons to Europe for their education—even Edgar Allen Poe received some of his schooling in England. And it appeared in a consequential way in their habit of getting their silver, their china, their fine furniture and the other things that ornamented Southern mansions from Europe in exchange for their tobacco, cotton and indigo.

Whether the South was right or wrong in preserving so much of the European pattern is obviously a question of vast implications which we cannot go into here. But I think it can be set down as one fact in the growing breach between South and North. The South retained an outlook which was characteristically European while the North was developing in a direction away from this—was becoming more American, you might say.

There are evidences of this surviving into the present. A few decades ago when Southern Rhodes scholars first began going to England, some of them were heard to remark that the society they found over there was much like the society they had left behind. England hardly seemed to them a foreign country. This led to attempts by some of them to reassert the close identity of Southern and Western European culture, to which I expect to refer again later.

THE SECOND GREAT FACTOR in the molding of Southern unity and self-consciousness was the Civil War. Southerners are sometimes accused of knowing too much about the Civil War, of talking too much about it, of being unwilling to forget it. But there are several reasons why this rent looms very large in the Southerner's memory, and why he has little reluctance in referring to this war, although it was a contest in which he was defeated.

To begin with, Southerners, or the great majority of them, always have believed that their part in this war was an honorable one. Far from regarding themselves as rebels, they felt that they were loyal to the original government, that is to say, they believed that they were fighting to defend the government as it was laid down at Philadelphia in 1787 and as recognized by various state ordinances of ratification. This was a

524

government of restricted power, commissioned to do certain things which the states could not do for themselves, but strictly defined as to its authority. The theory of states' rights was a kind of political distributism which opposed the idea of a powerful centralized government. The Southern theory then as now favored the maximum amount of self-determination by the states and it included, as a kind of final guarantee that states' rights would be respected, the principle of state sovereignty, with its implied right of secession.

In the Southern view, it was the North that was rebelling against this idea which had been accepted by the members of the Constitutional Convention in 1787. Or to put it in another way, the North was staging a revolution, the purpose of which was to do away with this older concept of the American government. The South refused to go along with the revolution, invoked the legal safeguards which it believed to exist, and then prepared to defend itself by force. You may recall that the late historian Charles A. Beard found enough substance in this to call the Civil War "the Second American Revolution" in his *Rise of American Civilization*. Thus in this second American Revolution the Northerners were in the role of patriots, the Southerners in the role of English, if we keep our analogy with the Revolutionary War.

In all great crises of history where you have a legal principle challenged by a moral right, you find people flocking to both standards. The one side says it believes in the duty of upholding the law. The other side says it believes in the imperative necessity of change, even at the expense of revolution. Though the Civil War may not look quite so simple to us now, this is the way many people saw it. A number of years ago, Gerald Johnson wrote an ingenious little book on Southern secession, in which he referred to it as the struggle between the law and the prophets. The South had the law and the North had the prophets, in the form of the abolitionists and also of the advocators, both heard and unheard, of a strong central government, unimpeded by theories of states' rights.

The legal aspects of an issue which has been so long decided can now have only academic interest. But if any of you wish to see a statement of the South's legal position on state sovereignty and secession, the best source is a little book by a man named Bledsoe—A. T. Bledsoe —*Is Davis A Traitor?* Bledsoe was a Kentuckian, and he brought to the task of writing this defense an interesting set of qualifications. He was a lawyer, a professor of mathematics, and for ten years he had been a colleague of Lincoln at the bar of Springfield. Also—and probably this is pertinent to mention, since we are talking here about a metaphysical debate—he had written a book-length refutation of Jonathan Edwards' *Freedom of the Will*. I do not know whether this is true or not, but it has been said that the appearance of *Is Davis A Traitor?* in 1866, was one of the things that made the North decide not to bring Davis to trial. At any rate, the failure to bring Davis to trial was naturally taken by the South as a sign that the North's legal case was too weak to be risked in court.

These are the chief things causing Southerners to feel that, whatever the claims of moral right and wrong, they had the law on their side.

Now we come to the fact of the Civil War itself. It was impossible that a struggle as long and bitter as this should not leave deep scars. Americans, particularly those of the present generation, are prone to forget the magnitude of this civil conflict. The United States lost more men from battle wounds and disease in the Civil War than in any other war of its history, including the Second World War. The battle front stretched from Pennsylvania to New Mexico, and included also the seven seas. A good many of the wars of history have been decided by two or three major battles. In our Civil War at least eighteen battles must be accounted major by reason of the number and resources involved. The minor battles run into scores, and the total number of engagements—somebody once counted them up—is as I recall, something more than 2200. Of this eighteen major battles you might call five or six "critical" in a sense that, with a more decisive result, they might have ended the war right there or have turned it in

525

favor of the side which eventually lost. I would include in my list of critical battles Shiloh, the Seven Days, Sharpsburg, Gettysburg, and Chickamauga. So you can see it was really a knock-down drag-out fight.

THERE IS A FURTHER FACT to be noticed in discussing the effect of this war. Nearly the whole of it was fought on Southern soil. With the exception of the Gettysburg campaign, and John Hunt Morgan's raids into Indiana and Ohio, and the small but famous St. Albans raid in Vermont—a group of Confederates in disguise came down from Canada, shot up the little town of St. Albans in Vermont, took the bank deposits and got back across the border —the North was physically untouched. There is a great difference between reading about a war your boys are fighting 500 miles away, and having the war in your midst, with homes being burned, farms being stripped, and your institutions being pulled to pieces. I'll bet any Japanese or German today will testify to this. The war was much more a reality to the people of the South than to those of the North, and it has remained such down to the present.

A natural question to come up at this point is, why should anybody care to remember or write histories about a war which left his country a hollow shell? In order to explain this, I shall have to tell you something else from the Southern credo, something that goes along with this faith in the legal case. It has been a prime factor in preserving Southern morale and in maintaining that united front of the South which I am afraid has been such a vexation to the rest of the country. And the only way I can really tell this is by an anecdote, even though I have to explain the anecdote.

The story goes that a ragged Confederate soldier was trudging his way home from Appomattox. As he was passing through some town, somebody called out to him by way of taunting. "What'll you do if the Yankees get after you?" And his answer was, "They aren't going to bother me. If they do, I'll just whip 'em again." The point of the anecdote, which may need to be explained, is that the answer was at least half serious. It was a settled article of belief with the Southern soldiers—echoed in numberless Confederate reunions — that although they had lost the war, they had won the fighting — that individually they had proved themselves the equal, if not the superior of their adversary and that the contest had finally been decided by numbers. There is no point in going into the merits of the argument here. But it is easy to see how, right or wrong, it had a great effect in preserving Southern pride, and even in maintaining a spirit of defiance which to this day characterizes a good bit of Southern policy.

It also helps to explain why the South has written so voluminously about the war, and why in libraries today, for example, you can find a biography of practically every Confederate General of any eminence whatever, and sometimes three or four. A quick check of the card files in Harper library reveals ten full-length biographies of William Tecumseh Sherman, but fourteen of Stonewall Jackson, plus biographies of Stoneman, Pleasanton, Grierson, Bedford, Forrest, Stuart, and a definitive biography of Lee by D. S. Freeman; but no definitive biography of Grant. The remark has been made that in the Civil War the North reaped the victory and the South the glory. If you consult the literature of the subject very extensively you find a certain amount of truth in that.

Evidently there was enough substance in the legend to nourish the martial tradition of the South, and to support institutions like VMI, the Citadel and the A & M College of Texas, which do not have counterparts in other sections of the country.

This brings the story down to Reconstruction; which somebody has described as "a chamber of horrors into which no good American would care to look." If that is an exaggeration, it still seems fair to say that this was the most dismal period of our history—a bitter, thirty-year sectional feud in which one side was trying to impose its will on the other, and the other was resisting that imposition with every device of policy, stratagem and chicanery that could be found. We must realize that no people willingly accepts the idea of being reconstructed in the image of another. That is, in fact, the ultimate in humiliation, the suggestion that you must give up your mind, your inherited beliefs and you way of life in favor of that of your invaders. There was a critical period when, if things had been managed a little worse, the South might have turned into a Poland or an Ireland, which is to say a hopelessly alienated and embittered province, willing to carry on a struggle for decades or even centuries to achieve a final self-determination. That was largely forestalled by the wisdom of a few Northern leaders. The work of Lincoln toward reconciliation is well known but that of Grant, at Appomattox and also later, I think has never been sufficiently appreciated. And the act of Lee in calling for reunion once the verdict of battle has been given was of course of very great influence.

IT WAS AN immeasurable calamity that Lincoln was not allowed to live and carry out his words in the lofty and magnanimous spirit which his speeches reflect. He was himself a product of the two sections, a Kentuckian by birth, an Illinoisian by adoption. He understood what had gone into the making of both. As it was, things were done which produced only rancor, and made it difficult for either side to believe in the good faith of the other. It is unfortunate but it is true that the Negro was forced to pay a large part of the bill for the follies of Reconstruction.

By all civilized standards the period was dreadful enough. George Fordt Milton has called his history covering those years *The Age of Hate*. Claude Bowers has called this *The Tragic Era*. If you desire a detailed account of what the South experienced in these years probably the best source to go to is *Why the Solid South, Reconstruction and Its Results*, (ed. Hilary Herbert) by a group of Southern leaders, including a number of governors of states. This is of course, a Southern view, but it tells you from the

inside something about the financial, political, and social chaos that prevailed in those years.

Unquestionably Reconstruction did something to deepen the self-consciousness of the Southern people, to make them feel less American rather than more so. They became the first Americans ever to be subject to invasion, conquest, and military dictation. In estimating the Southern mind it is most important to realize that no other section of America has been through this kind of experience. In fact it is not supposed to be part of the American story. The American presents himself to the world as ever progressing, ever victorious, and irresistible. The American of the South cannot do this. He has tasted what no good American is supposed ever to have tasted, namely the cup of defeat. Of course, that experience is known to practically all the peoples of Europe and of Asia. This circumstance has the effect of making the mentality of the Southerner again a foreign mentality—or a mentality which he shares in respect to this experience with most of the peoples of the world but does not share with the victorious American of the North and West. He is an outsider in his own country. I have often felt that the cynicism and Old-World pessimism which the rest of the country sometimes complains of in the South stems chiefly from this cause. The Southerner is like a person who has lost his innocence in the midst of persons who have not. William A. Percy, going from a plantation on the Mississippi Delta to the Harvard Law School found that Northern boys were "mentally more disciplined" but "morally more innocent" than Southern boys. His presence is somehow anomalous; he didn't belong.

It is sometimes said, with reference to these facts, that the South is the only section of the nation which knows the meaning of tragedy. I am inclined to accept that observation as true and to feel that important things can be deduced from it. Perhaps there is nothing in the world as truly educative as tragedy. Tragedy is a kind of ultimate. When you have known it, you've known the worst, and probably also you have had a glimpse of the mystery of things. And if this is

527

so, we may infer that there is nothing which educates or matures a man or a people in the way that the experience of tragedy does. Its lessons, though usually indescribable, are poignant and long remembered. A year or so ago I had the temerity to suggest in an article that although the South might not be the best educated section in the United States, it is the most educated—meaning that it has an education in tragedy with which other educations are not to be compared, if you are talking about realities. In this sense, a one-gallon farmer from Georgia, sitting on a rail fence with a straw in his mouth and commenting shrewdly on the ways of God and man— a figure I adopt from John Crowe Ransom—is more educated than say a salesman in Detroit, who has never seen any reason to believe that progress is not self-moving, necessary and eternal. It would seem the very perverseness of human nature for one to be proud of this kind of education. But I do believe it is a factor in the peculiar pride of the Southerner. He has been through it; he knows; the others are still living in their fool's paradise of thinking they can never be defeated. All in all, it has proved difficult to sell the South on the idea that it is ignorant.

In a speech made around the turn of the century, Charles Aycock of North Carolina met the charge of ignorance in a way that is characteristic in its defiance. Speaking on "The Genius of North Carolina Interpreted," he said,

> Illiterate we have been, but ignorant never. Books we have not known, but men we have learned, and God we have sought to find out.
> [North Carolina has] nowhere within her borders a man known out of his township ignorant enough to join with the fool in saying "There is not God."

You will note here the distinction made between literacy and knowledge—a distinction which seems to be coming back into vogue. You will observe also the preference of knowledge of men over knowledge of books—this is where our Southern politicians get their wiliness. And you will note finally the strong emphasis upon religiosity.

(It has also been claimed that this tragic awareness perhaps together with the religiosity is responsible for the great literary productiveness of the South today. That is a most interesting thesis to examine, but it is a subject for a different lecture.)

For a preliminary, this has been rather long, but I have felt it essential to present the South as a concrete historical reality. One of the things that has prevented a better understanding between North and South, in my firm belief, is that to the North the South has never seemed quite real. It has seemed like something out of fiction, or out of that department of fiction called romance. So many of its features are violent, picturesque, extravagant. With its survivals of the medieval synthesis, its manners that recall bygone eras, its stark social cleavages, its lost cause, its duels, its mountain flask, its romantic and sentimental songs, it appears more like a realm of fable than a geographical quarter of these United States. Expressed in the refrain of a popular song, "Is It True What They Say About Dixie," the thought seems to be that the South is a kind of never never land from which the nation draws most of its romance and sentiment, but to which, for this very reason, you do not assign the same weight in the equation as you do to the other sections. Well the sentiment and the romance are there, in considerable measure, but there is a substratum of reality too. People are born and die in the same way as elsewhere: if you prick them, they bleed. The vast majority of them have to work for a living and in a hot climate too. The South also votes in national elections. For this reason, especially, it is important that the nation should see it as a reality and not a fiction, understand it better, both with respect to its likenesses and its differences. (And I certainly would assent to the proposition that the South ought to understand the nation better.) In the foregoing I have tried to present to you something of the peculiar history and formation of the South. In the time remaining I shall try to explain some of the peculiar—in the sense of being fairly distinct in this country— attributes of mind and outlook. It is

528

scarcely necessary to add that these have many connections with that history.

I shall begin by saying something about the attitude toward nature. This is a matter so basic to one's outlook or philosophy of life that we often tend to overlook it. Yet if we do overlook it, we find there are many things coming later which we cannot straighten out.

Here the attitudes of Southerners and Northerners, taken in their most representative form, differ in an important respect. The Southerner tends to look upon nature as something which is given and something which is finally inscrutable. This is equivalent to saying that he looks upon it as the creation of a Creator. There follows from this attitude an important deduction, which is that man has a duty of veneration toward nature and the natural. Nature is not something to be fought, conquered and changed according to any human whims. To some extent, of course, it has to be used. But what man should seek in regard to nature is not a complete dominion but a *modus vivendi*—that is, a manner of living together, a coming to terms with something that was here before our time and will be here after it. The important corollary of this doctrine, it seems to me, is that man is not the lord of creation, with an omnipotent will, but a part of creation, with limitations, who ought to observe a decent humility in the face of the inscrutable.

THE NORTHERN ATTITUDE, if I interpret it correctly, goes much further toward making man the center of significance and the master of nature. Nature is frequently spoken of as something to be overcome. And man's well-being is often equated with how extensively he is able to change nature. Nature is sometimes thought of as an impediment to be got out of the way. This attitude has increasingly characterized the thinking of the Western world since the Enlightenment, and here again, some people will say that the South is behind the times, or even that it here is an element of the superstitious in this regard for nature in its originally given form. But however you account for the attitude, you will have to agree that it can have an important bearing upon one's theory of life and conduct. And nowhere is its influence more decisive than in the corollary attitude one takes toward "Progress."

One of the most widely received generalizations in this country is that the South is the "unprogressive section." If it is understood in the terms in which it is made, the charge is true. What is not generally understood, however, is that this failure to keep up with the march of progress is not wholly a matter of comparative poverty, comparative illiteracy, and a hot climate which discourages activity. Some of it is due to a philosophical opposition to Progress as it has been spelled out by industrial civilization. It is an opposition which stems from a different conception of man's proper role in life.

This is the kind of thing one would expect to find in those out-of-the-way countries in Europe called "unspoiled," but it is not the kind of thing one would expect to find in America. Therefore I feel I should tell you a little more about it. Back about 1930, at a time when this nation was passing through an extraordinary sequence of boom, bust, and fizzle there appeared a collection of essays bearing the title *I'll Take My Stand*.[1] The nature of this title, together with certain things contained, caused many people to view this as a reappearance of the old rebel yell. There were, however, certain differences. For one thing, the yell was this time issuing from academic halls, most of the contributors being affiliated in one way or another with Vanderbilt University. For another, the book did not concentrate upon past grievances, as I am afraid most Southern polemic has done, but rather upon present concerns. Its chief question was, where is industrialism going anyhow, and what are its gifts, once you look them in the mouth? This book has since become famous as "The Agrarian Manifesto." As far as content goes, I think it can fairly be

529

―――
[1] P. Smith, *I'll Take My Stand; the South and the Agrarian Tradition*, by 12 Southerners (New York: Harper Brothers, 1930).

Page Thirteen

styled a critique of progress, as that word is used in the vocabulary of modern publicity and boosting.

Although the indictment was made with many historical and social applications, the center of it was philosophical; and the chief criticism was that progress propels man into an infinite development. Because it can never define its end, it is activity for the sake of activity, and it is making things so that you will be able to make more things. And regardless of how much of it you have, you are never any nearer your goal because there is no goal. It never sits down to contemplate, and ask, what is the good life? but rather assumes that material acquisition answers all questions. Language something like this was employed by John Crowe Ransom, one of the most eloquent of the spokesmen, in his chapter, "Reconstructed but Unregenerate."

"Progress never defines its ultimate objective but thrusts its victims at once into an infinite series," Mr. Ransom said. And he continued, "Our vast industrial machine, with its laboratory center of experimentation, and its far-flung organs of mass production, is like a Prussianized state which is organized strictly for war and can never consent to peace."[2] "Industrialism," he declared, "is rightfully a menial, of almost miraculous cunning, but no intelligence; it needs to be strongly governed, or it will destroy the economy of the household. Only a community of tough conservative habit can master it."[3] The South, Mr. Ransom felt, was such a community, and he went on to praise it for its stability, its love of established things, its veneration of the past—for all of those qualities which are generally thought to make up Southern backwardness. Mr. Stark Young, the well-known novelist and theatrical critic, defended the ideal of aristocratic indulgence and aristocratic leadership. "We can put one thing in our pipes and smoke it," he wrote, "there will never again be distinction in the South until—somewhat contrary to the doctrine of popular and profitable democracy—it is generally clear that no man worth anything is possessed by the people, or sees the world under a smear of the people's wills and beliefs."[4] There are many other pungent passages which might be quoted, but these should be enough to show that it was a militant book. As you can see, its bias was anti-industrial, anti-scientific, anti-popular. It defended the values of a culture rooted in the soil. Just what the effect was, however, is hard to estimate. But no one conversant with Southern history and culture will deny that it expressed some feelings which survive pretty strongly into the present and which may be found any where from the mansions of the *nouveau riche* in Atlanta to the mountain cabins of East Tennessee and Kentucky.

ANOTHER CARDINAL POINT, touched on here and there in the volume, is the Southerner's attachment to locality. The Southerner is a *local* person—to a degree unknown in other sections of the United States. You might say that he has lived by the principle that it is good for a man to have a local habitation and a name; it is still better when the two are coupled together. In olden days a good many Southerners tried to identify their names and their homes: thus we read in history of John Taylor of Caroline, of Charles Carroll of Carrollton; of Robert Carter of Nomini Hall; of the Careys of Careysbroke; of the Lees of Westmoreland County. With the near liquidation of the old land-owning aristocracy this kind of thing became too feudal and fancy to keep up. Nevertheless, something of it remains in a widespread way still; the Southerner always thinks of himself as being from somewhere, as belonging to some spot of earth. If he is of the lucky few, it may be to an estate or a plantation; if not that, to a county; and if not to a county at least to a state. He is a Virginian, or he is a Georgian in a sense that I have never encountered in the Middle West—though the Indiana Hoosiers may offer a fair approximation. Very often the mention of a name in an introduction will elicit the remark, "That is a Virginia

530

[2] *Ibid.,* p. 8.
[3] *Ibid.,* pp. 15-16.

[4] *Ibid.,* p. 338.

name" or "That's a South Carolina name," whereupon there will occur an extensive genealogical discussion. Often this attachment to a locale will be accompanied by a minute geographical and historical knowledge of the region, a loving awareness of details, of the peculiar physiognomy of the place. Andrew Nelson Lytle once complained in an article that in the world since 1914, nobody has known who he was or where he was from. The South has certainly felt the pressure toward rootlessness and anonymity—which are sometimes named as among the chief causes of modern psychic disorders—but I believe it has resisted the pressure better than most parts of the United States and Europe. It still looks among a man's credentials for where he is from, and not all places, even in the South, are equal. Before a Virginian, a North Carolinian is supposed to stand cap in hand. And faced with the hauteur of an old family of Charleston, South Carolina, even a Virginian may shuffle his feet and look uneasy.

THE PRIDE OF local attachment is a fact which has two sides; it is a vice and a virtue. It may lead to conceit, complacency, and ignorance of the world outside. It frequently does lead to an exaggerated estimate of the qualities and potentialities of the particular region or province. The nation as a whole is acquainted with it in the case of Texans, who have developed this Southern attribute in an extreme degree. I was teaching out in Texas about the time we were ending the Second World War. A jocular remark that was passed around with relish was: "I know we are going to win the war now. Texas is on our side." It was a fair gibe at Texan conceit.

But on the other side, provincialism is a positive force, which we ought to think about a long while before we sacrifice too much to political abstractionism. In the last analysis, provincialism is your belief in yourself, in your neighborhood, in your reality. It is patriotism without belligerence. Convincing cases have been made to show that all great art is pro-

vincial in the sense of reflecting a place, a time, and a *Zeitgeist*. Quite a number of spokesmen have pleaded with the South *not* to give up her provincialism. Henry Watterson, a long-time editor of the Louisville *Courier Journal,* told an audience of Kentuckians, "The provincial spirit, which is dismissed from polite society in a half-sneering, half-condemnatory way is really one of the forces of human achievement. As a man loses his provincialism he loses, in part, his originality and, in this way, so much of his power as proceeds from his originality." He spoke caustically of "a miserable cosmopolitan frivolity stealing over the strong simple realism of by-gone times." He summed up by asking, "What is life to me if I gain the whole world and lose my province?"

Thirty years later Stark Young, writing in the agrarian manifesto to which I referred earlier, pursued the same theme. "Provincialism that is a mere ramification of some insistent egotism is only less nauseous than the same egotism in its purity . . . without any province to harp on. But provincialism proper is a fine trait. It is akin to a man's interest in his own center, which is the most deeply rooted consideration that he has, the source of his direction, health and soul. . . . People who give up their own land too readily need careful weighing, exactly as do those who are so with their convictions."[5] What often looks like the Southerners' unreasoning loyalty to the South as a place has in this way been given some reasoned defense. Even Solomon said that the eyes of a fool are in the ends of the earth. One gives up the part for the whole only to discover that without parts there is no whole. But I have said enough about the cultural ideal of regionalism. If you would be interested in a book which brings these thoughts together in a systematic treatment, see Donald Davidson's *The Attack on Leviathan.*

Despite what I have said about this love for the particular, which is another name for love of the concrete, the Southern mind is not by habit analytical. In fact the Southern mind has little capacity

531

5 *Ibid.,* pp. 343-345.

for analysis and I think one could almost say that it is opposed on principle to analysis. There seems to exist a feeling that you do not get at the truth of a thing—or that you do not get at a truth worth having—by breaking the thing in pieces. This explains undoubtedly why the South has always done so poorly in business and technology, which demand analytical methods. The Southern mind is, on the other hand, synthetic and mythopoeic—it seeks out wholes, representations, symbols. Especially is it mythopoeic, or given to the creation of myths and stories. The American tall tale was a creation of the Southern frontier. And one cannot go into a mountain community in Eastern Kentucky or to a plantation in say, Alabama, and open his ears to the talk of the people without having borne in upon him an amazing wealth and variety of stories—dramatic, intense, sometimes grotesque. As a mine of material for the creative writer there is nothing to compare with it anywhere else in America. I have heard people ask where William Faulkner gets that stuff that goes into his novels—whether he dreams it in nightmares, and so on. No one who had spent any time in Mississippi with his ears open would have to ask that question. He would know to what extent incidents and stories of this kind enter into the imaginative life of Mississippians. This mythopoeic or poetic —in the Aristotelian sense — faculty is surely behind the present flowering of the Southern novel and short story. It has already given us an interesting body of fiction, and it may one day give us a great literature. The South is not so much sleeping as dreaming, and dreams sometimes beget creations!

FINALLY SOMETHING MUST be said about the South's famous conservatism — famous or infamous, depending upon your point of view. It is certainly a significant fact, but it has not gone wholly uncriticized at home. Walter Hines Page, growing up as a young man in North Carolina, spoke bitterly of what he called "an unyielding stability of opinion." Having

failed in his effort to do anything with it, he declared that "the only successful rebellion was an immediate departure." He then fled North, to become editor of *The Atlantic Monthly* and eventually our ambassador to Britain during the Wilson Administration. Ellen Glasgow satirized it in her urbane novels of Virginia life. Thomas Wolfe took a few hefty swings at it in his description of old Catawba. And there have been others who have complained of a stifling uniformity of thought on many subjects.

With some of these specific protests I would gladly agree, yet there is perhaps another light in which we can see this "unyielding stability of opinion." Stability has its uses, as every considerate man knows, and it is not too far-fetched to think of the South as the fly-wheel of the American nation. A fly-wheel is defined by the science of mechanics as a large wheel, revolving at a uniform rate, the function of which is to stabilize the speed of the machine, slowing it down if it begins to go too fast and speeding it up if it begins to go too slow. This function it performs through the physical force of inertia. There are certain ways in which the South has acted as a fly-wheel in our society. It has slowed down social change when that started moving rapidly. And, though this will surprise many people, it has speeded up some changes when change was going slowly. Without judging the political wisdom of these matters, I merely point out that without Southern order, the New Deal probably would have foundered. Without Southern votes, the Conscription act would not have been renewed in 1941. Generally speaking the South has always been the free trade section. It is not very romantic or very flattering to be given credit only for inertia. But conservatism is not always a matter of just being behind. Sometimes conservatives are in the lead. I could give you more examples of that if I had time. It requires little gathering up of thread to show that a mind produced by this heritage is diametrically opposed to communism. With its individualism, its belief in personality, its dislike of centralized government, and its religiosity, the South sees in the communist philosophy a combination of all it detests. If that issue comes to a showdown, which I hope does not happen, there will never be any doubt as to where the South stands.

I suspect that a good many of you entertain thoughts of changing the South, of making it just like the rest of the country, of seeing it "wake up." It seems to me that the South has been just on the verge of "waking up" ever since I have been reading things about it. My advice is to be modest in your hopes. The South is one of those entities to which one can apply the French saying, "the more it changes the more it remains the same." Even where you think you are making some headway, you may be only heading into quicksand. It waits until you are far enough in and then sucks you under. It is well to remember that the South is very proud of its past, hard as it has been; it does not want to be made over in anybody else's image, and it has had a century of experience in fighting changes urged on it from the outside. I agree with W. J. Cash that the Southern mind is one of the most intransigent on earth; that is, one of the hardest minds to change. Ridiculing its beliefs has no more effect, as far as I have been able to observe, than ridiculing

a person's religious beliefs — and the Southerner's beliefs have been a kind of secular religion with him: that only serves to convince him further that he is right and that you are damned.

INTRANSIGENCE IN ITSELF, however, is not good, of course. No mind ought to be impervious to suggestions and the influence of outside example. Intercommunication and cross fertilization are necessary. I covet a chance to talk someday to a Southern audience on what they need to learn from the North. But these express two-way relationships. It is a peculiar blindness to assume that the factors which have produced you are real, whereas the factors that have produced the other fellow are unreal. Those succeed best who go forward in the spirit of inquiry, seeking to understand the lines of force, and above all, realizing that there is something to be learned wherever complete lives are lived. With this kind of attitude it is possible for Virginia to learn from New England and New England from Virginia with a happy result that Parkman visualized but did not live to see.

2. THE HUMANITIES IN A CENTURY
OF THE COMMON MAN

THE CURRENT DEFENSE of humanities does not take into account the depth of the tide running against them, probably because it is politically unsettling to do so. But if we wish to acquaint ourselves with prospects we shall soon be grappling with as pressing realities, we shall have to look more candidly at what is undermining this historic body of study. If certain forces continue unabated, humanistic training as we have known it is not likely to survive another generation.

The first point to take into account is the paradoxical fact that the humanities are a discipline. I say paradoxical because there is a certain anomoly in asking the human being to undergo a regimen in order to become more human, or more *humane*, if we may give a focused meaning to the latter word. For the humanities are not the spontaneous, loose, and thoughtless expression of the human race, but on the contrary a highly difficult, concentrated, and directed expression which aims at a center — man at his best, not man transmuted into an angel, which is the proper study of divinity, but man incarnate, which is today, man in this world, making the best of his estate as he responds to its colors and configurations. That is why we can today admire the humanism of Greece and Rome, with indifference to the other tendencies of this civilization. Like every humanism, theirs was an achievement in sensibility and expression, and their brilliance was such that the modern world has up until now been glad to emulate. But it has always been accepted as a starting point that this emulation required education and effort, so that he who engaged in it sought to make himself over in accordance with an ideal superior to his untutored self. That would seem to be the premise of all humanistic study: the best which has been thought and said in the world was not uttered in a babble, but came slowly and often at the cost of self-torture, or at least of the mortification of passing desire. Education in the humanities has always meant a study of the classics, and a classic is a sort of cultural leader, to whom we submit ourselves out of our faith in edification.

Those who have been brought up on a humanistic education assume that there is something in the monuments of humanism which compels a respect. I fear that they are only taking a constant of their own lives to be a universal constant, which does not exist. Once before a long night descended upon these monuments. They were there to plead their case, but you cannot plead to those who will not hear. I should like to echo Whitman here, and say that if to have great poets, there must be great audiences, to have a victorious humanism, there must be a humanized audience. Enough has been said elsewhere of the dehumanizing pressures under which we labor; and acute observers have long detected in modern men, and not solely among those who are low-placed, an impulse to reach for the metaphorical pistol when the word culture is mentioned. There seems to be growing up an attitude of truculence, and nothing is more fatal to an appreciation of

past accomplishment. There are plenty of signs that the traditional respect for artistic and intellectual distinction is being displaced by reverence for political power and institutions. The first of these requires a belief in personality, and the second tends to require a disbelief in it. That may prove the fundamental difference between them.

It is a commonplace of recent history that about 1930 our age turned sharply political. The impulse has been so strong in the 30's and 40's as to carry along with it, like some engrossing wave, a large part of all artistic expression. Artistic work came to be judged by whether or not it contributed to a conception of progress, and the term progress implies, of course, a direction. If we had to give a name to that direction, we would not have to seek beyond "social democracy." This is a quite elastic term which covers, on the one extreme, the palest social amelioration, and on the other the strictest type of state-managed economy, requiring total regimentation. But whatever the form, social democracy exhibits two tendencies which are serious for the future of the humanities. One of these is a change in the structure of society, and the other a disposition of society's income.

The first tendency works to break down the categories which have hitherto existed in favor of an undifferentiated mass. Without raising the question of whether these classes which have been privileged in the past have deserved their fortune, it can be asked whether society is not thereby sacrificing its strength. It seems to be incontrovertible that all progress in the higher meaning of that term — the progress which is the carrying out of an enlightened moral ambition — has not come from society fused as a mass, but from society held in a kind of counterpoise. Aristotle has illustrated this truth through an analogy with music. A state ceases to be a state when what is harmony is allowed to pass into unison. Now the mass seems to be this state of unison, which is without the principle of counterpoise. In the other type of society, which has proved creative, we have numberless arrangements in which men are functionally placed against men, since this is in very fact its integrating principle. There is a substratum of unity, of course, for without that even our definition would collapse. The principle of counterpoise works in such a way that one element plays its part and gets its living by being poised against another element. The one is commissioned to get as much as it can out of the other, more than would ever be granted without the pressure of its demand. The requirement is always made in the name of some higher order, or liberty, or degree of enlightenment. For example, in this functional counterpoise we have teachers against students, policemen against citizens, buyers against sellers, managers against employees. It is the pluralistic kind of arrangement, in which one group stands for and enforces an ideal of performance like a competitor in a contest, *viz.,* especially teachers and policemen, and the rest of us profit by their necessary though at times irksome office. The effect of this arrangement is to make society vertebrate, if we may vary the figure. I do not see what social democracy is going to substitute for this structure. What has been suggested or exhibited thus far is a more simple and more rigid pattern, which is without the flexibility of the healthy organic body. Now the humanities have in the past exerted their authority from a kind of limited autonomy; they have been one of the weights holding us in a counterpoise. In the new state, what is going to "enforce" the humanities? It is becoming clear that if the state does not do it, it will not be done; and yet if the state does it, it will likely be done in a way that will prove fatal.

This brings us to the second tendency, which is the economic transformation accompanying the process we have just sketched.

Everyday observation brings home to us that as the modern state expands its power, it becomes more jealous of the rights of individuals. It grows more rigorous in the exercise of the authority it owns; and secretly, one fears, it determines to extend its reach. It is inevitable that in this development it should become more curious about what individuals do with their incomes. Its level of understanding here is pretty low; expenditures for food, clothing, and shelter it can grasp, but as it seeks to placate the greatest number, things beyond these will be sold to it with increasing difficulty.

Let us consider for a moment the way in which it has brought the individual's economic life under surveillance. First, the state somewhat timidly lays an income tax, applied at the outset to the wealthy, who are few and conspicuous. Next, on a plea of emergency, or extended social welfare, it increases the rates sharply, making them virtually confiscatory on the upper levels. This fact is not presented in defense of an unregenerate capitalism; its relevance to the argument appears when one recalls what has happened in this country to private donations to universities. As someone has remarked, you cannot eat up your millionaires with taxes and have them too.

The state finally adopts the withholding tax, which has the practical effect of putting everyone on the government payroll, since the government first looks at the salary, decides what fraction of it the individual shall have, and then passes on the remainder. Thus the private company becomes in effect a kind of disbursing agent for the government. This circumstance, which seems to have gone largely unnoticed, is symbolic in the highest degree of the trend even in "free" countries toward state collectivism. The bearing upon the case of culture is just this: what is going to happen to the supernumerary, non-utilitarian part of our activity when every individual is virtually on a government expense account? The inescapable conclusion is that the sum which goes for "brave, translunary things" is going to be politically determined—and inspired.

The modern world is creating an ideology whose hero is the satisfied consumer. He is the common denominator, and the offices of the state are to serve him, and not some imponderable ideal. This state serves, moreover, with an ever-increased efficiency. Today, everything is under control; nothing slips through; there is less chance than ever

535

before that the state will fail of its announced aim. Populations have been numbered, incomes have been listed; techniques have become machine-like. We must therefore consider the chance of the humanities in a social democracy whose policies will be efficient, as far as its light goes, but whose ideals encounter an insistent pull downward.

At this certain point objections arise. "Culture," which in common parlance stands for the humanities, is still a word with a great deal of prestige; it yet has associations of value which would induce politicians to sponsor it even if they felt no attachment to it. It is frequently seen that social democratic parties are more liberal than others in recognizing the claims of culture. They pledge large outlays for education and a better deal for the artists and intellectuals under their regime. The promise is fair, but it has to be distinguished from the performance for the plain reason that it is uttered as part of the ideal, and does not reflect the forces which will mold the actual. It is one thing to promise in the name of the people reverence for great art and intellectual distinction, but this is a situation in which the will, or it might be more accurately described, the impulse, of the people is going to determine. After all, one of the chief aims of social democracy is the removal of those barriers which in traditional or formalized societies stand between the people and an immediate fulfillment of their wishes.

What is likely to happen is this: in the primitive or heroic days of social democracy we would very likely get commissars or administrators who believe genuinely in the humanities and who would put up a battle for them. One is compelled to suppose that they would be battling as individuals, against indifference from above and poorly educated taste from below. For a time they might do much, but it would be foolish to mistake in this case accident for essence. For these men would be individualists, and sooner or later they would be supplanted by others closer to popular sympathy. It is likely that their very success would be held against them, so refined are the arts of political detrac-

tion. They would be described as aloof from the people, or as thwarters of the popular will; for, in fact, they would be representing an "undemocratic" force. Their successors would be the political type, who know all too well how to commit a murder while concealed under the cloak of popular sentiment. They will give the public what it wants and provide the rationalization. This is the fate in store for all state-controlled culture.

Anyone who thinks this is a fanciful alarm should reflect upon what has been done to public education in the United States. The boast of the innovating "progressive" schools is that they prepare the youth for a changing world. *Would it not be incomparably more sensible to prepare the youth to understand why the world is changing?* This is what the humanities do. There is little appeal here to the exponents of progressive education because they have no desire to rise above the confusion. If they did, they would soon be at odds with the weight and mass of general opinion. Consequently, in our present educational system, popular pressure and specious doctrines have almost extinguished the idea of discipline. Yet I am inclined to think that this system has been better protected than one could expect the humanities to be in a pure social democracy.[1]

There are further reasons for saying that we have reached a point at which these dangers are not purely speculative. We are able to examine three years of socialist rule in Britain, which indicates that we have not been expressing undue alarm. I shall cite two passages from a "Letter from England," by D. S. Savage, appearing in the Spring, 1946, issue of the *Hudson Review.* "A Labour government is in power and, so far from fostering the arts and subsidizing artists as some of its more gullible adherents

---

[1] Let us look at a special example which should serve to define the issue. Will anyone reasonably contend that the money which has been expended by the Rockefeller Foundation on education and research would have accomplished as much if it had passed through the hands of publicly elected officials? The fact that it was a privately managed corporation able to define what it wanted and above all, able to wait for long-term results, has made possible its great contribution.

among the intelligentsia had hoped, it is proving on the whole inimical to cultural values; an implicit doctrine of 'bread alone'—that is, bread and guns — prevails." Mr. Savage ventures a prediction of his own. "It seems possible that as the social order hardens into shape we shall witness the emergence of two cultures — an official and an unofficial, the one well-paid, flashy, and sterile, drawing upon the talent of debauched artists and intellectuals, and the other surviving only through extreme enthusiasm and devotion."

It is an historic truth which holds good for the past several centuries of our life that culture has developed from the liberty of the superior individual to love superior things. Whether these individuals established foundations, or whether they merely sustained a market for works of distinction out of their earned or unearned surpluses, the result was as we have seen. The essential condition was that the individual had a power of decree. We have observed that the new social regime does not permit the individual much power of decree, and it is very jealous of these surpluses. Its present humor is to describe them as theft and to appropriate them on one pretext and another. We arrive then at a state in which the single, sensitive, imaginative person cannot project his will in this fashion. As Paul Valery has suggested, liberty in the modern "free" state is simply a liberty to be like the masses because political control is vested in them. They feel "free" because what they will is made law. The more one resembles the mass man, the freer he is because his impulses run the same channel as theirs. And if he is antipathetic to the idols of the mass, he may be very unfree, because mass law and mass ethos are enforced with peculiar rigor, and there is no court of appeal. Traditional forms of government now in disfavor provided a better haven for the individualist because they felt some distrust of their own power and often relaxed it in administration. It is the special mark of the mass that it has not such feeling about its power, and is exhilirated to see it brutally exercised. For its attitude toward the non-conven-

tional, see our daily tabloids.

In summary, we face a future in which the mass is going to determine with increasing power what is done with the total productivity of the nation. There is little chance that it will devote a substantial part of that productivity to the development of pure science (unless science can be hitched to some wagon like preparation for defense in war), or to the creation of works of art which baffle or offend it.

It is now time to look at one or two aesthetic difficulties which will prove handicaps in an age dominated by this new mentality. I shall consider the first of these as the aesthetic plebeianism. There is an aesthetic of common life and an aesthetic of noble life, and the two are far from meeting. To find a principle that distinguishes them it is only necessary to point out that they correlate closely with optimism and pessimism. The noble view of life, which is the view that has conditioned art in the past, tends always to be pessimistic for the plain reason that life "does not measure up." It is not satisfactory when compared with that clear pattern which the believer in excellence has in his soul. This is clearly proved by the fact that the arts of tragedy and satire have flourished in ages which were predominantly aristocratic, that is to say, ages which accepted as a reality the distinction between good and bad men, or actions. It could not be otherwise, for satire is the reproof of man, and the very plot of tragedy depends upon the "good" man struggling in a net of evil. Whoever thinks he knows how the world ought to be feels a certain melancholy that it is not so. In all great art therefore there is a certain pessimistic overcast. Art is a kind of protest, a transfiguration. It has been remarked that if one looks below the surface of two of the most dazzling periods of creativeness in history, the Greek and the Elizabethan, he finds a well of melancholy. Shakespeare's plays deepened in gravity as the man matured.

But what occurs when life is made not the subject of a critique, but an occasion for relaxed joyousness and animal abandon? There have been signs

537

for years that we are passing out of one climate of belief into another. A significant witness is that tragedy has all but disappeared. And if this is but a beginning, it may be no exaggeration to say that the new climate is to be anti-artistic and anti-cultural. We may be faced with a time when the root-idea of standards, which is the anchor of all humanistic discipline, is to be eradicated. Indeed, our expression here may be too cautious, for the extent to which knowledge has been displaced by opinion makes this almost now an actuality.

The aristocratic view of life is waning because the mass everlastingly insists that the world be represented as *pleasant*. One quality which the crowd is never able to acquire is a hardheadedness sufficient to accept the realism of the world. For this reason it falsifies whatever it touches, and there is no hope for true art where the principle at work is falsification. To foretell the kind of art expression which the mass is going to demand, and demand effectively by reason of its economic power, one has only to look at today's media of mass circulation. The preferred themes are romantic love (this seems to be a modern version of the Aphrodite Pandemos, which is distinct from the Aphrodite Ouranios of the ancients, and from the courtly love of the mediaevals), success stories, fantasies, comedy with elements of violence and sadism. I suspect that the truest index to this mentality is the comic strip, whose offenses against taste and astheic theory it would be impossible to number. But present in all of them is the unrelenting demand that the world be subjectivized to accord with our humor. The herd man never grows reconciled to the fact that life is a defeat, and that this defeat is its real story. He wants instead a pleasing fiction by which his hopes are ingeniously flattered. It is not pressing the matter too far to say that what he wants is *deception*.

What we are actually contending with in these aesthetic plebeianisms is the mass' deep-seated and enduring hostility to the idea of discipline. It does finally require some discipline of mind to accept the fact that life is not a triumphal progress, but a sadly mixed affair with many a disenchantment. When Arnold talked of seeing things steadily and seeing them whole, he must have had reference to just this evasiveness and flabbiness of mind which it is the function of culture to remove—where it can. It will never do that where the ideal is the thing made easy.

The psychological springs of this hostility are not far to seek. The mass can never grant that there is something superior to its *habitus* and its way of conduct. For as soon as it grants the existence of such, it is under a theoretic discipline. The mass is a jealous sovereign. Those who challenge it from a superior level it seeks to destroy with the *ad hominem* attack. It is daily verifiable that in a culture so maintained, the best rewarded of those who work in the arts are soothers and entertainers.

A secondary problem posed by the aesthetic plebeianism is the impossibility of maintaining a meaningful criticism. Obviously this aesthetic can never circumvent the criterion of popularity. It finds itself always in the tautologous position of saying that because a thing is popular, it is good; and because it is good, it is popular.

Art criticism is here in the same dilemma as political democracy when the latter sets up the voice of the people as the voice of God. Either it must accept its own proposition and say that the people is infallible, and can never for one minute, or in one action, go wrong; or else it must yield its whole position. If one admits that the people can even for a minute be deluded; that is to say, that one man or one minority can be right for a minute and the people wrong, then he admits the existence of a right that is not determined by the people. I feel this to be so important that I shall try to put it in another way. The moment one grants that the people can sometimes err, even temporarily, even when bamboozled by demagogues or the press, he has scuttled the thesis of the popular determination of truth. For he has already admitted that the people may be one thing and the truth another, and this could never be if popular opinion were the sole determinant of what is true.

Now when we apply this finding to the humanities in a mass society, the same interesting thing is revealed. Either popular impression is infallible, and the people are the only judge of what they should have, or else one must admit the existence of an independently grounded aesthetic. As soon as the latter is admitted, however, the beautiful and the non-beautiful become constants, and there is something superior to the popular taste, which may be applied to it. But I fear the mass is too intractable an animal to grant these existences after it has sensed the way they are tending.

Put into language, its denial seems to take this form: it does not matter if we disdain the moral earnestness of Christianity; it does not matter if we refuse to think with the clarity of the Greeks; it does not matter that we cannot dramatize with the success of the Elizabethans; it does not matter if we fall below the eighteenth century in elegance of manner. It does not matter? I suppose one can argue here only by begging the question and saying that it is blasphemy not to prefer the good and obey its commandments. And possibly it is as much as we can do about the condition of modern man to say that he is blasphemous. In the past he has blasphemed idols that were set up for him; and now he blasphemes those which he set up for himself when he repudiates the humanities.

The second difficulty may be, at some deeper level, the source of the first. As a teacher of humanities, I have grown disturbed over an attitude which is appearing in students, including those with some endowment of sensibility. I could describe it briefly by calling it a distrust of all rhetoric. The great passages of the past, the flights of Milton, of Burke, of Arnold, are lost upon them; and they show an active distrust of contemporary matter which is rhetorically presented. The power of language to stir, or to direct the feelings of man, seems only to provoke them to an antagonism. This has gone so far that the once-familiar rhetoric of pulpit and platform is beginning to seem an anachronism. Two different interpretations can be put upon this development.

The first is that the new generation has become scientific-minded and is insisting upon pure notation in all discourse. That is to say, it has accepted the advice of the semanticists and has resolved to have no traffic with words whose objective reference is dubious. They are impatient of anything which lacks the objective correlative, and so when language passes from a sort of literal correspondence with what is signified, to metaphor, as all rhetoric must, they simply cease to accept. Since they cultivate the scientist's detached outlook upon the world, emotion is for them mere disturbance in what ought to be clear communication. Pure notation will give them knowledge in the same way that mathematics does, or nearly so. And as for making up their minds about how to feel about a thing, well, that can wait—perhaps upon the development of yet another science.

The second interpretation, which I believe to be the true one, is that our generation is losing faith in the value of value. It will appear on a moment's reflection that this is the same as losing faith itself. Ours is not so much a generation of vipers as a faithless generation. Since the whole of humanistic study is based upon the acceptance of value, here is where the decay has its source. People have suffered much in the past decades, and they have not often been told the truth by their political leaders. It may be that there has set in as a defense a kind of psychic numbness. Since all feeling brings imposition in its train, there is a will not to feel. (I have noted among more than one student a kind of shrinking from propaganda as though it were a dreaded plague loose in the world—which in a way it may be.) Now we approach the ultimate in disenchantment.

Here would be cause for rejoicing if it were possible for man to live in a devalued world, but man is simply not that kind of animal. He has got to show his inclinations. And with the death of value there is every possibility that he will do it in grotesque, unintelligible ways, in fetishism and explosions of hard feel-

539

ing, in demonism and vandalism. There is not the slightest possibility that he is less a creature of feeling than before. But the old gods have gone and the new gods have not arrived. It may be that in the interim he will turn into an idol smasher. The humanities seem high on the list of the things he will rudely reject, or allow to drift into obscurity. I fear that this is the meaning of the hatred of the old spacious rhetoric, with its tendency to elevate all that is described.

Most surveys of the plight of the humanities I have seen fall into wishful conclusions.

One supposition is that the colleges will be able to save them by a reform of curriculum. In response to this we see the inauguration of courses in general education. But this seems to be in essence only a streamlining. The courses are recast, made more compact and better integrated. The new conception, however, is hardly a discipline in the humanities such as used to season the graduates of our universities. It may easily degenerate into another requirement like the ubiquitous English com-

position. The intention is good, of course, but the hope is not great. There was a time when a cultural education was income-producing for the legions that take it, and that means inevitably a different kind of education. Statistics on what the returned veterans have studied in our universities will prove the point.

Or it is supposed that larger grants to this and that will restore the balance. These will be gratefully received, and they will help, but it is sanguine to suppose that they will restore the balance in a displacement so huge as the one taking place before our eyes. I have already shown that public sources of such grants have a very limited independence and could not long survive political attack. A grant to the humanities today is like a contribution to a church whose doctrines we have no thought of honoring with practice. I doubt that anything large and vigorous can be sustained on this.

Teachers of the humanities are going the way of teachers of Latin and Greek and elocution unless we have something like a Second Coming of faith in the values.

New Individualistic Review welcomes contributions for publication from its readers. Essays should not exceed 5,000 words, and should be type-written. All manuscripts will receive careful consideration.

Reflections on the
Loss of Liberty

GEORGE J. STIGLER

THE CONSERVATIVES have been in high alarm at the encroachments on liberty by the state for at least 30 years. It would be possible to amass a volume of ominous predictions on the disappearance of individual freedom and responsibility, and not by silly people.

Yet if we canvass the population we shall find few people who feel that their range of actions is seriously curtailed by the state. This is no proof that the liberties of the individual are unimpaired. The most exploited of individuals probably does not feel the least bit exploited. The Negro lawyer who is refused admission to a select club feels outraged, whereas his grandfather was probably a complaisant slave. But neither is complacency a proof of growing tyranny.

So let us look at what liberties, if any, the typical American has lost in the recent decades of growing political control over our lives. Let us face this American as he completes his education and enters the labor force. Of what has he been deprived?

Some additional barriers have been put in the way of entrance into various occupations. Some barriers consist of the direct prescription of types of training; for example, to teach in a public school one must take certain pedagogical courses. More often, the state imposes tests — as for doctors and lawyers and barbers and taxi drivers — which in turn require certain types of training in order to be passed.

George J. Stigler, an Editorial Advisor to NEW INDIVIDUALIST REVIEW, is Walgreen Professor of American Institutions at the University of Chicago, and President of the American Economic Association.

But few people consider such restrictions on occupations to be invasions of personal liberty. The restrictions may be unwise — those for school teachers are generally so viewed by the university world — but since the motive is the protection of users of the service, and since the requirements are directed to competence even when they are inefficient or inappropriate, no question of liberty seems involved. No one, we will be told, has a right to practice barbering or medicine without obtaining the proper training. The freedom of men to choose among occupations is a freedom contingent on the willingness and ability to acquire the necessary competence. The mentally and physically untalented man has no inherent right to pilot a commercial plane, or any other type.

For consider: we surely do not say that a man born with weak or clumsy legs has been denied the portion of his liberty consisting of athletic occupations. At most a man is entitled to try to enter those callings which he can discharge at a level of skill which the community establishes.

"Which the community establishes." The obverse of the choice of occupations is the choice of consumers. It can be said that the denial of my right to patronize lawyers or doctors with less preparation than the majority of my fellow citizens deem appropriate is the complementary invasion of my liberty. Why should the community establish the lowest levels of skill and training with which I satisfy my needs?

The answer is, of course, that on average, or at least in an appreciable fraction of cases, I am deemed incompetent to perform this task of setting standards

541

of competence. I am, it is said, incapable of distinguishing a good surgeon from a butcher, a good lawyer from a fraud, a competent plumber from a bumbler, and so on.

Now one could quarrel with both sides of this position: neither has my own incompetence been well demonstrated (especially when account is taken of my ability to buy gurantees of competence) nor has anyone established the ability of other judges to avoid mistakes or at least crudity of judgment. But these are questions of efficiency much more than of justice, so I put them aside not as unimportant but as temporarily irrelevant.

The real point is that the community at large does not think a man should have the right to make large mistakes as a consumer. The man who cannot buy drugs without a prescription does not really rebel at this undubitably expensive requirement. The man who is denied the services of a cheaper and less well trained doctor or teacher does not feel that he has been seriously imposed upon.

THE CALL TO the ramparts of freedom is an unmeaning slogan in this area. If we were to press our typical American of age 22, he would tell us that some infringements on his liberties would be intolerable, but they would be political and social rather than economic: free speech should not be threatened — at least by McCarthy — and Negroes should not be discriminated against. No economic regulation of consumers would elicit serious objection, and this younger person would often be prepared to go even farther in regulating consumers in areas such as health and education. We would have to propose policies remote from current discussion, such as compulsory location of families to hasten racial integration, before we should encounter serious resistance to public controls in principle.

Governmental expenditures have replaced private expenditures to a substantial degree, and this shift poses a related problem to liberty. The problem seems less pressing because private expenditures have increased in absolute amount even though public spending has risen in this century from perhaps 5 to 25 per cent of income. Yet the shift has been real: we can no longer determine, as individuals, the research activities or dormitory construction of universities, the housing of cities, the operation of employment exchanges, the amount of wheat or tobacco grown, or a hundred other economic activities. But again the typical American finds each of these activities worth while — meaning that he thinks that the activity will not be supported on an adequate scale by private persons.

ON A CLOSER VIEW OF THINGS, some restrictions on individuals as workers will strike most Americans as unfair, especially if they are presented as indictments. Complaints will be aroused by a demonstration that political favorites have been enriched by governmental decisions which excluded honest competitors — and of course this can be demonstrated from time to time, or perhaps more often. The complaint, however, will involve equity much more than liberty.

This conclusion, that Americans do not think that the state presently or in the near future will impair the liberties that a man has a right to posses is, of course, inevitable. It is merely another way of saying that our franchise is broad, our representatives will not pass laws to which most of us are opposed, or refuse to pass laws which most of us want. We have the political system we want.

The conservative, or traditional liberal, or libertarian, or whatever we may call him, will surely concede this proposition in the large. He will say that this is precisely the problem of our times: to educate the typical American to the dangers of gradual loss of liberty. One would think that if liberty is so important that a statue is erected to her, the demonstration that a moderate decline of personal freedom leads with high probability to tyranny would be available in paperback at every drugstore. It is not so easy to find. In fact, it may not exist.

That there have been many tyrannies no one will dispute, and indeed it is at least as easy to find them in the twentieth century as in any other. Moreover, the loss of vital liberties does not take place in a single step, so one can truly say that a tyranny is entered by degrees. But one can easily reverse this truism and assert that some decrease in liberties will always lead to more, until basic liberties are lost. Alcoholics presumably increase their drinking gradually, but it is not true that everyone who drinks becomes an alcoholic.

THE NEAREST APPROACH to a demonstration that the tendency of state controls to increase beyond the limits consistent with liberty is found in Hayek's *Road to Serfdom*. But Hayek makes no attempt to prove that such a tendency exists, although there are allegations to this effect.[1] This profound study has two very different purposes:

(1) A demonstration that *comprehensive* political control of economic life will reduce personal liberty (political and intellectual as well as economic) to a pathetic minimum.

---
1 For example:
 "Although competition can bear some admixture of regulation, it cannot be combined with planning to any extent we like without ceasing to operate as an effective guide to production. Nor is 'planning' a medicine which, taken in small doses, can produce the effects for which one might hope from its thoroughgoing application. Both competition and central direction become poor and inefficient tools if they are incomplete; they are alternative principles used to solve the same problem, and a mixture of the two means that neither will really work and that the result will be worse than if either system had been consistently relied upon. Or, to express it differently, planning and competition can be combined only by planning for competition but not by planning against competition." (p. 42)
And again:
 "Yet agreement that planning is necessary, together with the inability of democratic assemblies to produce a plan, will evoke strong demands that the government or some single individual should be given powers to act on their own responsibility. The belief is becoming more and more widespread that, if things are to get done, the responsible authorities must be freed from the fetters of democratic procedure." (p. 67)
Such passages are, however, warnings of the consequences of comprehensive socialization rather than arguments that it is inevitable.

I may observe, in passing, that this argument seems to me irresistible and I know of no serious attempt to refute it. It will be accepted by almost everyone who realizes the import of *comprehensive controls*.[2]

(2) If the expansion of control of economic life which has been underway in Britain, the United States, and other democratic western countries should continue long enough and far enough, the totalitarian system of Nazi Germany and Fascist Italy will eventually be reached.

This second theme is not an historical proposition — and no historical evidence was given: it is the analytical proposition that totalitarian systems are an extreme form of, not a different type from, the democratic "welfare" states to whom the book was addressed. Hayek was telling gentlemen drinkers, and especially some Englishmen — who were becoming heavy drinkers, not to become alcoholics.

The twenty-five years that have passed since the outbreak of World War II have seen further expansions of political control over economic life in the United States, and in most western European nations except Germany. Yet no serious diminution of liberties deemed important by the mass of educated (or uneducated) opinion has taken place. Another hundred years of governmental expansion at the pace of these recent decades would surely destroy our basic liberties, but what evidence is there that such an expansion will continue? Quite clearly, no such evidence has been assembled.

IT IS ONE THING to deny that evidence exists for the persistence of present trends to where they will endanger our liberties, and quite another to deny that such a momentum exists. Or, differently put, where is the evidence that we *won't* carry these political controls over economic life to a liberty-destroying stage?

---
2 For a recent restatement of this view by a person not identified with "conservative" views, see the essay by K. E. Boulding, "The Dimensions of Economic Freedom," in E. O. Edwards ed., *The Nation's Economic Objectives* (Chicago: University of Chicago Press, 1964) esp. pp. 119-20

543

This may be an impeccable debating point, but it will carry much less conviction than an empirical demonstration of the difficulty of stopping a trend. When men have projected the tendency of a society to a distant terminus, they have invariably committed two errors. The tendency develops in a larger number of directions than the prophet has discerned: no tendency is as single-minded as its observer believes. And the tendency encounters other and contradictory forces in the society, which eventually give the course of events a wholly different turn. We have no reason to believe that the current prophets are any wiser.

SO I CONCLUDE: we should either fish or cut bait. On the subject of liberty the conservative should either become silent, or find something useful to say. I think there is something useful to say, and here is what it is.

The proof that there are dangers to the liberty and dignity of the individual in the present institutions must be that such liberties have already been impaired. If it can be shown that in important areas of economic life substantial and unnecessary invasions of personal freedom are already operative, the case for caution and restraint in invoking new political controls will acquire content and conviction. We cannot scare modern man with incantations, but we can frighten him with evidence.

The evidence, I think, will take a variety of forms:

1. A full study of the barriers of men to entry in occupations, and of the extent to which the barriers can be defended on social grounds, will demonstrate, I believe, that the area of occupational freedom has been seriously restricted simply for reasons of ignorance, or special interest. If this is correct — if the present practices will not bear close review — the danger of further extensions of such barriers will be substantially reduced.

2. The widespread belief in the incompetence of the individual and the efficacy of economic censorship of tastes is the second large area of potential invasion of personal freedom. This development has surely not benefited from close study: it has happened that errors of judgment or deficiencies of knowledge of a tiny fraction of consumers have led to restraints being imposed on all consumers, without even checking what gains are achieved by the censorship. My own study of the S.E.C., indeed, reveals a clear instance of where the gains are not worth the cost. If consumers are wiser than the public believes, and if political intervention is not infallible and economical, we shall be better able to stop future invasions of the consumer's freedom.

I do not know whether justice is more or less important than liberty, or whether they are even fully separable. The standards of justice under political direction of economic life, I conjecture, are deplorably low:

3. The state is now the giver of many valuable rights. The favorites get TV channels, or oil import quotas, or F.D.I.C. charters, or leases on federal grazing lands, or N. Y. state liquor store licenses, or waivers from the local zoining board. Who has studied the bases on which these favors are allotted? I suspect that a careful study would display vast caprice, much venality, and a considerable number of calluses on applicants' knees and navels. The harshness of competition may mellow somewhat in public repute when alternative systems of distributive justice are studied.

Studies of the types here proposed will, I am reasonably confident, give vitality and content and direction to fears for liberty in our society. But whether the studies confirm the need for reform and vigilance in preserving freedom, or suggest that such fears are premature, they are essential to remove this subject from the category of cliché. It is no service to liberty, or to conservatism, to continue to preach the imminent or eventual disappearance of freedom; let's learn what we're talking about.

544

The Fusionists on

Liberalism and Tradition

RALPH RAICO

THE PUBLICATION OF a symposium on the question, "What is conservatism?"[1] provides us with an opportunity to explore once again a complex of issues frequently raised in these pages — that having to do with the differences between libertarianism and conservatism. In this article, I shall not attempt to deal with all of the areas covered by these differences, nor with the essays of all twelve contributors to Meyer's symposium. Instead, I shall deal merely with certain aspects of the attempted reconciliation of the two philosophies that goes by the name of "fusionism."

Frank S. Meyer and M. Stanton Evans are the two most notable exponents of the fusionist position, and they present their case in two essays in the present volume.[2] The problem they are trying to solve may be stated in this way: the term "conservative" when applied to various writers in America today (especially when applied by social democratic writers, who usually have little familiarity with the literature) appears, on closer examination, to be equivocal. The authors of the following two statements, for example, although they are both sometimes considered "conservatives," clearly have widely divergent approaches to so basic a question as the nature of government:

> In mankind's experience, government has always figured as an institution publicly representing shared insights into the meaning of life, God, man, nature, time.[3]

> Society cannot exist if the majority is not ready to hinder, by the application or threat of violent action, minorities from destroying the social order. This power is vested in the state or government. . . . Government is in the last resort the employment of armed men, of policemen, gendarmes, soldiers, prison guards, and hangmen. The essential feature of government is the enforcement of its decrees by beating, killing, and imprisonment.[4]

There are, in fact, as Meyer and Evans point out, two distinct groups of writers which the term "conservative" in its current sense encompasses: those whose intellectual forebears are to be found chiefly in the ranks of the classical liberals of the 18th and 19th centuries (this group would include Hayek, Friedman,

545

Ralph Raico is the Editor-in-Chief of NEW INDIVIDUALIST REVIEW.

[1] Frank S. Meyer, ed., *What is Conservatism?* (New York: Holt, Rinehart and Winston, 1964). 242 pp. $4.95.

[2] Meyer, "Freedom, Tradition, Conservatism"; Evans, "A Conservative Case for Freedom."

[3] Gerhard Niemeyer, "Risk or Betrayal? The Crossroads of Western Policy," *Modern Age*, Spring, 1960, p. 124. The context makes it clear that Prof. Niemeyer regrets the passing of this conception of government.

[4] Ludwig von Mises, *Human Action* (New Haven: Yale University, 1949), pp. 149, 715.

von Mises, etc.), and those who trace their ideas back primarily to Burke and the 19th century conservatives (Kirk is the best-known representative of this group, which also includes others associated with *National Review* and *Modern Age*). The first group is called by Meyer the "libertarians," and the second the "traditionalists." Often libertarians and traditionalists attack one another vigorously, and some in each camp have even maintained that the two view-points are fundamentally at absolute odds. It is true that members of the two factions very often have had similar opinions on questions of immediate political importance (which is one of the chief reasons why they are looked on as factions of one movement), but anyone who has read the works of the two groups is aware that there exist significant differences on a more basic level. These have

546

to do with such matters as the weight given to tradition, the arguments used for freedom, the priority allowed freedom as against other values (order, virtue, and so on), as well as with (as the quotations from Niemeyer and von Mises show) what I am afraid we may have to call the "philosophical presuppositions" of the two view-points. The imposing task the fusionists have undertaken, then, is to resolve the differences between libertarians and traditionalists— and this by showing that both have something of fundamental value to contribute to a common "conservatism" (for that is to be the name of the amalgamated movement), and that both are likewise at fault in certain respects.

WHAT THE LIBERTARIAN (or classical liberal) has to offer, the fusionists maintain, is a good understanding of the meaning of freedom, of the dangers facing it, and especially of the connection between economic and other forms of freedom. He is mistaken, however, in disregarding "value" and the moral law, and in having no understanding of the goal and *raison d'être* of freedom, which is "virtue." The traditionalist, on the other hand, is the complimentary figure to the libertarian, and brings to the syn-

thesis a—as the phrase goes—deep commitment to moral value, to virtue and so on. Moreover, he understands the part that tradition must play in the life of society, while the libertarian typically "rejects tradition." Thus, the stage is set for the synthesis, which will consist in a political philosophy developed on the basis of "reason operating within tradition," and upholding freedom as the highest secular end of man and virtue as the highest end of man *tout court*.

It will be seen that anything approaching an exhaustive critique of this thesis would be impossible here.[5] What I shall attempt to do, therefore, is simply to clear some ground by examining certain points in the fusionist thesis, with the aim of helping to provide the basis for a more analytical and less rhetorical discussion of these issues than has sometimes been the case in the past.

Before one can determine to what extent, if any, classical liberalism[6] must be modified, it is absolutely crucial, of course, for one to have a correct conception of what classical liberalism means. It appears to me, however, that in this regard, conservative and fusionist writers, while quite dogmatic, are also quite mistaken. As a rule, they are in the habit of treating liberalism in a casual, off-handed way, scarcely ever bringing forward any actual evidence to substantiate their rather free-swinging claims. At the risk of seeming unfair to M. Stanton Evans — which is certainly not my intention — I shall submit *his* conception of classical liberalism, which appears to me fairly typical of this view, to an extended analysis.

Evans states:

The libertarian, or classical liberal, characteristically denies the existence of a God-centered moral order,[7]

[5] For a broader discussion of the fusionist position, see the forthcoming article by Ronald Hamowy in *Modern Age*: "Classical Liberalism and Neo-Conservatism: Is a Synthesis Possible?"

[6] In what follows, I shall be using the terms "classical liberalism," "liberalism," and "libertarianism" interchangeably.

[7] In a footnote to his essay (p. 232), Evans asserts that he is using "libertarian" to mean "the chemically pure form of classical liberalism," including the "acceptance of [an] anti-religious philosophy." Presumably he has abandoned this

to which man should subordinate his will and reason. Alleging human freedom as the single moral imperative, he otherwise is a thoroughgoing relativist, pragmatist, and materialist. [p. 69]

In this amazing statement, Evans asserts the following concerning the "typical" classical liberal or libertarian:

(1) he denies the existence of a God-centered moral order;[8]
(2) he alleges human freedom to be the single moral imperative;
(3) aside from (2), he is a complete relativist, pragmatist, and materialist.

Let us deal with these allegations in detail.

(1) This is false, of course, in regard to the many liberals who were Christians (*e.g.*, Ricardo, Cobden, Bright, Bastiat, Madame de Stael, Acton, Macaulay, etc.).[9] Indeed, many classical liberals (in-

---

terminology in the passage quoted here. For if he has not, then the assertion of the anti-religiousness of the libertarian would be merely an uninteresting tautology, entailed by Evans' personal terminology, and, moreover, the passage would then have to read: "The libertarian, or classical liberal, *necessarily* denies . . ."

[8] It is difficult to see why Evans modifies the term "God-centered moral order" with the clause, "to which man should subordinate his will and reason." Presumably, the assertion of the existence of *any* moral order entails that one should subordinate one's will to it. As for the subordination of reason to this order, I take this to imply that God's moral order is not knowable by reason alone. Why such a view, even supposing that the typical libertarian maintained it, should be thought to be associated with freethinking and atheism, it is impossible to say. For it appears to be precisely the position of the Catholic Church: "Whilst therefore *the Catholic believes that the moral law is knowable to man by sheer reason and experience*, being the law of man's very nature, he believes that the fulfilment or non-fulfilment of it has more than natural implications." Thomas Corbishley, S. J., *Roman Catholicism* (London: Hutchin's University Library, 1950), p. 57 (ital. added). Since I cannot see that this clause could lead to anything but a confusion of the issue, I feel justified in ignoring it.

[9] While it is logically possible for one to be a Christian and at the same time to have some other "center" than God for one's moral system, still the rule has been that those professing Christianity have attributed to God the central role in their ethical systems. I am therefore taking the Christian faith of a classical liberal as *prima facie* disproof of Evans' assertion.

cluding present-day ones) have felt that the connection between their political and their religious and ethical views has been a very intimate one. Frédéric Bastiat, for instance, who, because of his "superficiality" and "glib optimism" is sometimes taken to be the very paradigm example of a classical liberal, expressed himself as follows towards the end of one of his more important works:

There is a leading idea which runs through the whole of this work, which pervades and animates every page and every line of it; and that idea is embodied in the opening words of the Christian Creed — I BELIEVE IN GOD.[10]

John Bright was the man who, with Cobden, and for twenty years after Cobden's death, was the leader of the Manchester School in British politics and political and economic thought — surely a typical liberal, if there is such a thing. Yet the following characterization of Bright, by his most authoritative biographer, hardly seems compatible with Evan's description:

Religious feeling, in its simplest form, was the very basis of his life. He was always a Friend [*i.e.*, Quaker] before everything else; and a servant of God; a man of deep, though ever more silent devotion.[11]

Although Christians were probably, and theists certainly, in the majority, it is true that a certain number of liberals *were* atheists or (much more frequently) agnostics: J. S. Mill, Herbert Spencer, John Morley, etc. Nevertheless, the following points ought to be made: (a) the denial of a "God-centered moral order" has been no more characteristic of classical liberalism than its affirmation; (b) even if a majority of liberals had been atheists and agnostics, the connection is so far accidental and historically-conditioned, and not logical; (c) supposing the majority of liberals to have been tainted with unbelief in one form or another, Evans still presents no reasons

---

[10] *Harmonies of Political Economy* (Edinburgh: Oliver and Boyd, 1870), Part II, p. 150. Emphasis in text.

[11] G. M. Trevelyan, *The Life of John Bright* (Boston: Houghton Mifflin, 1914), p. 104.

547

548

for dismissing the liberalism of Christian writers like Bastiat.

(2) The second charge — that the classical liberal or libertarian alleges "human freedom as the single moral imperative"— can hardly be seriously meant. Does Evans mean to say that liberals characteristically do not believe benevolence, or even lack of malice, to be morally enjoined on men? This cannot have been true of the many Christian liberals, and neither was it the case with the non-Christians, *least of all the Benthamite utilitarians* among them. Evans mentions only two names in connection with his general description: J. S. Mill and Herbert Spencer. Spencer explicitly states that, in addition to justice (respect for the rights of others), the moral code enjoins both "negative" and "positive" beneficence, the latter being the capacity to receive happiness from the happiness of others.[12] This may not be an especially elevated view of our moral obligations, but it is nonetheless sufficient to contradict Evans' statement, at least in regard to one of the only two writers he mentions by name. But the statement is even more erroneous in regard to the utilitarian liberals. J. S. Mill makes their position clear in his well-known essay, "Utilitarianism":

> I must again repeat what the assailants of utilitarianism seldom have the justice to acknowledge, that the happiness which forms the utilitarian standard of what is right in conduct, is not the agent's own happiness, but that of all concerned. As between his own happiness and that of others, utilitarianism requires him to be as strictly impartial as a disinterested and benevolent spectator. In the golden rule of Jesus of Nazareth, we read the complete spirit of the ethics of utility. To do as you would be done by, and to love your neighbor as yourself, constitute the ideal perfection of utilitarian morality.[13]

Far from being "characteristic" of classical liberalism, (2) is an attribute for which I doubt that a *single* example could be found in the whole history of liberalism.

(3) EVANS GIVES US virtually no idea of what he might mean by these three highly-charged terms, "materialist," "relativist," and "pragmatist," so we will have to deal with them as best we may.

"Materialist" may have a precise philosophical, or a loose vulgar, meaning. Taken in the first sense, the assertion would be absurd: if *any* metaphysic were characteristic of liberalism, it would probably be idealism in one form or another, not materialism. Taken in the vulgar sense of addiction to, or espousal of, "material" (usually sensual) pleasures, the assertion is also invalid. It is, indeed, hardly worth rebutting, since to support this allegation, Evans only adduces a statement by — Ernest Renan. We might as well point out, however, that, even ignoring the fact that "materialist" is scarcely a fair description of Bentham's form of hedonism, and certainly not of J. S. Mill's, the German liberals of the Classical period— *e.g.,* von Humboldt and Kant — and the French liberals of the Restoration—*e.g.,* Constant and Madame de Stael—assuredly had ideas on ethics and the destiny of man independent of any form of the pleasure philosophy.

In Evans' view, the liberals were also typically "pragmatists." Whether this is supposed to mean that they were followers of Peirce and William James, or, in some looser sense, that they believed that the truth was "what works," is unclear. It would be tedious to attempt to salvage this claim by lending it some semi-reasonable meaning, and then showing that even then it had no foundation in fact. The rebuttal of the assertion, therefore, will wait upon its being given some sense.

Evans also claims under (3) that the liberals, aside from their adherence to freedom, have been complete "moral relativists."[14] This brings up an issue

---

[12] *Social Statics* (New York: Appleton, 1880), pp. 83-84.

[13] *Utilitarianism, On Liberty and Representative Government* (New York: Dutton, 1950), p. 16.

[14] At times Evans implies that, not only are libertarians moral relativists, but that, in consequence of this, *they do not even hold that any-*

which is frequently raised by conservatives: often, the essence of the "moral crisis of our age" is seen in the decline of faith in "absolute values." It should be clear that the question of moral relativism *vs.* moral absolutism cannot even be intelligently approached until we know what is to be understood by these terms, but conservatives, in discussing the subject, generally fail to indicate their meaning. In general philosophical discussion, the most important senses of the term "moral relativism" appear to be: (a) the idea that moral rules are defeasible, *i.e.,* are not unconditionally valid; and, more frequently, (b) the idea that "it is logically possible for two persons to accept verbally conflicting ethical statements without at least one of them being mistaken.[15]

(a) The idea that moral rules must be absolute in the sense that they are binding under all empirically possible conditions appears to be a sense in which conservatives often use the term. And yet it seems to me hardly a defensible position. Is it, after all, possible to cite a single moral injunction with content (not, *e.g.,* "It is good to do the Will of God") and with application to social questions (not, *e.g.,* "It is good to love God") which is unconditionally valid? Would it, for instance, be impermissable under *all* possible conditions to take the life of a man whom one knows to be innocent? It seems to me that circumstances could well be imagined in which this would be the reasonable — possibly even the moral — thing to do. Whether or not supported by classical liberals, moral absolutism in this sense appears to me to be an untenable position, the rejection of which cannot rightfully be made the grounds for censuring anyone.

(b) The more common sense of "moral relativism" is the position that it is possible for what appear to be contradictory ethical statements to be true at the same time. A relativist in this sense might hold, for instance, that ethical statements are simply reports of the speaker's subjective feelings, and, therefore, the statement, "Murder is evil," may be true or false, depending on the actual feelings of the person who uttered it. Another form of this second sense would be that of a relativist who might hold that it is impossible to make ethical judgments transcending the bounds of different societies, and that an ethical statement may be "true" in one society and "false" in another. In this sense of relativism, however, the utilitarians (to take the group Evans probably has chiefly in mind) were almost paradigm *absolutists.* The reason for this is obvious. For any given situation in which an ethical judgment is to be made, the facts are what they are: one decision will maximize happiness, while a different one will not maximize it.[16] Thus, although we may be mistaken in our decision, still, in principle, there is only one true judgment in each ethical situation.

Thus, of the two most important senses of "moral absolutism," one is a sense in which, whatever the liberals may have thought, it cannot reasonably be defended; the other is a sense for which many adherents of moral absolutism can be found among the classical liberals.

549

I HAVE SPENT a good deal of time — and probably the reader's patience as well—in discussing these two sentences. But my justification lies primarily in the circumstance that these statements well summarize the inaccurate conception — "impression" would perhaps be a better word — of classical liberalism which many conservatives hold and propagate. It may well be that classical liberalism is superficial, unrealistic and obsolete; apparently modern-day conservatives are eager to join most of the rest of the 20th century in announcing so. But before we can accept this evaluation — and

---

thing is immoral! E.g., (addressing the libertarians): "If there were no objective standards of right and wrong, why object to tyranny? If murder and theft are *not* immoral, why object to them either singly or in the mass?" (p. 72; ital. in text). We will, however, deal only with the first claim.

15 Richard B. Brandt, *Ethical Theory* (Englewood Cliffs, N. J.: Prentice Hall, 1959), pp. 271, 154.

16 I am ignoring those very few cases in which the net utility of two different courses of action will be exactly the same.

with it the idea that liberalism must at least be substantially modified—we must be satisfied, as so far we cannot be, that it is really classical liberalism which has been demolished, and not a strawman.

NOW I WANT TO turn my attention to one of the chief problems which Meyer's and Evans' fusionism must attempt to solve: that of *tradition*. The role of tradition is often seen as the crux of the division between the two wings of what is allegedly basically one movement; the traditionalists, not unnaturally, emphasize tradition, while the libertarians are said to reject it. But just what is at issue here would be much clearer if, instead of scornful references to the French Revolution and the "apotheosis of reason," conservative and fusionist writers had outlined, in a more or less systematic way, what they have in mind when they speak of "tradition," and what they claim for it and why. Nowhere is lack of precision in this whole area more regrettable than in the repeated assertion that the classical liberals "reject tradition." The rejection of tradition can mean many different sorts of things, and depending on what is meant, it may be a good or a bad thing.

If it means, for example, that the traditionality of an idea is not to be taken by the political philosopher as an argument for its truth, then the rejection of tradition, as far as I can see, is totally unobjectionable. For to defend the truth of an assertion on the basis that it has been the traditional belief of our society, presupposes that any belief that has been traditionally accepted by our society is very likely to be a true one. But contrary examples are available in too great an abundance to permit of any confidence in such a premise. Thus, recourse to tradition in abstract, speculative argument is invalid.

On the other hand, when we say that a person accepts tradition, we might mean that he believes that tradition ought to play a large part, not in the *evaluation of putative truths*, but in *the functioning of society*, which is obviously a different thing. Here a person might

argue along these lines: science is one thing, and life another. A systematic Cartesian doubt may be useful in the scientific enterprise, but, applied to social life, it would make mankind like "the flies of summer." It is necessary for the continuance of society, it could be argued, that a good deal of our moral code, for instance, be taken simply on faith, at least by the great majority of people, and probably by everyone. It would be intolerable to have the existence of organized society depend on each individual arriving at the indispensible moral rules through his own reasoning. Thus, there must be some means of attaching people to these rules. One of the most powerful of these means, the argument might continue, is tradition. People who could not follow the abstract arguments for the moral code nevertheless obey it, because of the affection and regard surrounding *mores* which have been adhered to for a very long time. Now, this is a plausible argument, and may well be substantially correct. The important thing to realize, however, is that it involves something completely different from maintaining the truth of a given assertion on the basis of its traditionality.

Now, the second category may be further subdivided: there are traditions that are maintained in the *social* sector (typically the sector of free interaction among individuals) and there are traditions pertaining to the *government* sector (typically the sector of force or the threat of force). An example of traditionality in the social sector would be the continuance of Christianity in its received forms as the result of the private decisions, habits, etc., of people; an example in the realm of governmental activity is (or was, 200 years ago) the continuance of the persecution of Protestant "heretics" in France, Spain, etc.— that is, a tradition involving violent interference with the peaceful actions of individuals. Now a classical liberal may be an atheist, or he may be a Christian, or he may hold some other position on this question. If he is an atheist, it is likely that he will personally disapprove of the continuance of Christianity as the freely-accepted religion of individuals; his private opinion is likely to be that people would be more happier, more rational, or whatever, if they abandoned Christianity. If the classical liberal is a Christian, then presumably he will be pleased to see the continuance of the tradition of Christian belief. Thus, on this question concerning a tradition in the *social* sector, liberals may have various personal views of their own, but liberalism itself has no policy recommendations to make whatsoever; does not, in fact, concern itself with the matter. How does it stand with the second sort of traditional arrangement, that pertaining to the government sector?

Here, before we can answer this question, we are compelled to make yet another distinction (and, as regards the libertarian-conservative controversy, possibly the most important one to be made): there are some traditional governmental arrangements which involve interference with the basic rights of the individual — the persecution of Protestants in France under the Old Régime, for example. Others, however, pertain to the structure of the government itself, and may not, in the first instance, have anything to do with individual rights at all, as, for example, a traditional adherence to bicameralism. In the case of the first sort of traditional governmental arrangement, the classical liberal characteristically and by the logic of his principles recommends the abolition of the tradition, *i.e.*, recommends that the government cease doing certain things. With regard to *this* category, then, the liberal may be said to "reject tradition"— that is, he holds that the traditionality of the arrangement can be no argument in its favor. It must be tested against certain standards, and, if it is found wanting, steps must be taken towards its elimination.

The case is different with the second sort of traditional governmental arrangement: that pertaining to the structure of government itself, as, for example, the extent and conditions of the franchise, and the form of the government (constitutional monarchy, republic, etc.). Such issues do not involve basic individual rights, in the sense that religious freedom and freedom from involuntary serv-

itude are basic. Their function, from the liberal point of view, is to aid the preservation of the basic rights, and they may therefore vary to a great extent, depending on time and place. As Edouard Laboulaye, probably the outstanding French liberal of the later 19th century, put it:

> Whatever may be the epoch or the country, whatever the form of government or the degree of civilization, every man has the need to exercise his physical and spiritual faculties, to think and to act. Russian or Englishman, Frenchman or Turk, every man is born to dispose of his person, his actions and his goods. . . . With political liberties it is not the same; they change according to the time and country. One does not always have need of the same guarantees [of liberty]; as the form of attack varies, so does that of the defense.[17]

551

TO SUMMARIZE OUR rather rough classification of the senses of tradition (which is offered, with some trepidation, as a tentative basis for discussion):

I. tradition in scientific and philosophical discourse: the traditional acceptance of a truth claim may be adduced as evidence in support of the claim;

II. tradition in the functioning of society: the traditionality of a societal arrangement may be adduced as good reason for continuing the arrangement. This may apply either to:

A. the social (non-governmental) sector, *i.e.*, to traditions not involving government action, or to

B. the governmental sector. Under B we have

  I. political traditions violating basic individual rights, and,
  II. political traditions (primarily those having to do with the structure of government itself) which do not violate basic individual rights.

[17] Edouard Laboulaye, *Le Parti Libéral: son Programme et son Avenir* (Paris, 1871), pp. 121-22.

In considering the differences between libertarianism and fusionism (as well as conservation), I would locate the significant and challenging disagreement regarding tradition primarily under II A. That is, while classical liberalism as a rule restricts itself to attempting to secure individual rights by operating on the government sector (and in this endeavor may well make use of traditional political elements), fusionist and conservative writers claim that certain traditions within the social sector must often be regarded as necessary conditions for the preservation of liberty and ought to be actively cultivated and promoted by all supporters of a free society. This is especially true, in their view, of religion. The idea is suggested at times by Meyer and Evans, and is put succinctly by Stephen Tonsor, in his interesting essay, "The Conservative Search for Identity," in the present volume:

> Religion is important to the democratic state not only because it preserves the fabric of society but also because it acts as the most important power to check the aggressive, centralizing, and totalitarian tendencies of the modern s t a t e. without a strong religion, which remains outside and independent of the power of the state, civil liberty is unthinkable. The power of the state is, in part, balanced and neutralized by the power of the church. The freedom of the individual is most certain in that realm which neither church nor state can successfully occupy and dominate. [p. 150]

This represents, of course, a historical and sociological hypothesis concerning an alleged casual connection between religion and freedom. If true, it could indicate that certain policy recommendations might be in order which libertarianism would tend to frown on (Tonsor himself maintains that tax money ought to be used to support church schools). In any case, it is a thesis which ought, I think, to be elaborated and critically and dispassionately examined, for it appears to me to be the most interesting and the most plasible of the fusionist claims.

This is only one of a number of important issues raised by fusionism which it is impossible to go into here. The claim that libertarians believe in the "innate goodness of man," and err in ignoring the reality of "original sin" (whatever might be meant by these two notions) is also one that should sometime be submitted to critical examination, if only because it is so often advanced. More important would probably be a discussion of the principle aim of fusionism: in place of our support of a free society for all our various ends (or simply for itself), to substitute support of it because it is a means to one particular end, namely "virtue," in whatever sense Meyer and Evans attach to the term.

Finally, it should be evident that none of what has been said here is to be taken as indicating hostility or rancor towards the authors whose writings have been discussed. In contrast to a number of conservatives, Meyer's and Evans' real concern for freedom is obvious. And that their intentions are good ones is evidenced by the statement of Meyer:

> . . . the development of a common conservative doctrine, comprehending both emphases [traditionalist and libertarian]—cannot be achieved in a surface manner by *blinking differences or blurring intellectual distinctions with grandiose phraseology.* [p. 18, ital. added]

Certainly a true and important judgment. It is unfortunate that, in the heat of battle it is too often forgotten.

H. L. Mencken and

The American Hydra

WILLIAM H. NOLTE

H. L. MENCKEN'S major complaint with the nation at large may be reduced to one often repeated lament: America is without an intellectual aristocracy that would give it direction and order. This absence of an intellectual class free to inquire and interpret, to act on its own prerogatives, to function autonomously without regard for the opinions of the mass also explains, in large part anyway, Mencken's disapproval of democracy. Like many another artist—Melville comes at once to mind — Mencken was unable to reconcile democracy with order. And it was order that prevented man from running amuck in chaos. Moreover, it was order, or form, that gave universality to art. The modern democratic state resembles nothing more than the drunken beggar on horseback, riding off in all directions. Though it is impossible, and not even wholly desirable, to prevent that beggar from doing as he jolly well wishes, Mencken did attempt rather successfully to slow him down and make him sit up in the saddle as if he were sober. This service was performed by attacking one of the most virulent outgrowths of democracy: Puritanism. (I should explain that I use the

William H. Nolte, Assistant Professor of English at the University of Oregon, has contributed articles to the *Southwest Review* and *Texas Quarterly*, and has a forthcoming study of H. L. Mencken.

word *democracy* — which by now is perhaps without any specific meaning — as the antonym of *aristocracy*.)

Mencken performed, broadly speaking, two major services for the national letters: he led the attack on Puritanism, which had crippled the artist in America for generations; and he gave great aid to a large number of the best writers America has produced.

Down to the 1920's in America, the "master" of the arts had things pretty much his way. He was powerful, he was confident, he was popular. He was the proud descendant of Puritanism in its narrowest sense. He still violently objected to anything that smacked of heresy; especially did he object to the modern-day Maypole dancers. He represented the "moral viewpoint," the "closed vision," the "narrow outlook"— call it what you will. This ogre haunting the dreams of honest writers had over the years taken many shapes in the daylight world of actuality. In the first two decades of this century, the Puritanical restrictions were upheld in art by a class of men — the academicians; and by a philosophy — the so-called New Humanism. Moreover, the stronghold of Puritanism in the social realm had moved from New England to the South. Mencken's criticism of the professor, of the New Humanist, and of the South is of one cloth.

THE FOUNDING FATHERS of New England came to America to establish one particular type of freedom—the freedom to enforce their own narrow beliefs without any deviations.[1] Indeed, one of the first things the college student learns in a course on early American literature or history is that the concept of the Pilgrims which he acquired from high school must be radically revised. It is really an example of *un*learning, which is the most powerful of all antidotes to the conditioned mental reflex, to superstition, and to prejudice. In Europe the Puritans had been persecuted largely because they were public nuisances, malcontents unable or unwilling to live and let live, similar in many ways to the God-crazy Anabaptists who were wont to run through the streets naked and howling to the invisible powers and principalities of the air. Only in a land uninhabited by civilized man could the Puritan hope to set up his peculiar kingdom of God. In America he had to contend only with the Indian, who was an easy prey for the sharp-trading, vindictive Puritan. In his book article for December, 1921, of the *Smart Set*, Mencken took to task those historians who credited the Puritans with the invention of most of the liberal institutions and ideas, such as they were, in America. (Mencken, incidentally, was in the forefront of those who, in the 1920's, called for new and realistic appraisals of the American past.) "There is not a single right," Mencken wrote, "of the citizen of today, from free speech to equal suffrage and from religious freedom to trial by jury, that [the Puritans] did not oppose with all their ferocious might." Actually, as Mencken pointed out then, and as we now know for certain, it was the non-Puritan immigrants to New England who were responsible for overthrowing the Puritan and setting up free institutions in the country.

To [the anti-Puritans] we owe everything of worth that has ever come out of New England. They converted the sour gathering of hell-crazy deacons into the town-meeting; they converted the old pens for torturing little children into public-schools; they set up free speech, free assemblage, a free press, trial by jury, equality before the law, religious freedom, and manhood suffrage; they separated church and state; they broke down the old theology and substituted the rationalism that was to come to flower in New England's Golden Age. The Puritans were absolutely against all of these things. They no more gave them to the Republic than they gave it Franklin or Emerson. What they gave it was something quite different: the shivering dread of the free individual that is still the curse of American civilization. They gave it canned patriotism, comstockery, intolerance of political heresy, Prohibition. They gave it Wilsonism, Burlesonism, and the Ku Klux Klan.[2]

THE MAIN IDEAS of Mencken on Puritanism may be found in "Puritanism as a Literary Force," one of the major documents of American criticism. Aside from its value as a penetrating analysis of the debilitating effects of Puritanism on art, "Puritanism as a Literary Force" served as a spark to ignite the most bitterly waged critical war of the century. At the time of its publication (in *A Book of Prefaces*, 1917; the other three essays in the volume are on Conrad, Dreiser and Huneker) Mencken was at the height of his powers as a literary critic. He was 37 years old and not yet disenchanted with the profession of book criticism (it should always be remembered that Mencken's best literary criticism was done *before* the twenties, the decade over which he reigned as America's leading man-of-letters. Moreover, *A Book of Prefaces* was his first important volume of criticism (not counting the book on Nietzsche, which was primarily exposition). And it stands today, along with various essays in the *Prejudices* volumes as the best writing he was ever to do in that particular area. Indeed, within ten years after it appeared, Mencken had given up criticism of *belles lettres* except for occasional pieces and comments that continued to see print until his death in 1956.

---

[1] See the excellent preface to *The Puritans* (New York: Harper & Sons, 1938), edited by Perry Miller and Thomas H. Johnson.

---

[2] H. L. M., "Variations upon a Familiar Theme," *The Smart Set*, Dec., 1921, p. 139.

Inevitably, the reigning America-First critics fell on *A Book of Prefaces* like angels on the Antichrist. Never before in America had a writer directed such a blast against an American sacred cow. And to publish such an un-American essay just when the nation was making the world safe for democracy was more than any right-thinking man could stand. The reception of *Prefaces*—which had a small sale in 1917, but enjoyed a wide audience when reissued in 1924—is a good gauge of Mencken's popularity. Only a few rebels could stomach him during the war (Sgt. Edmund Wilson, for example, read and re-read the book, which convinced him more than any other single work that literary criticism was a worth-while profession); after the return of the conquering armies, a whole generation accepted the Menckenian theses as gospel.

In the opening pages of "Puritanism as a Literary Force," Mencken made it clear that Puritanism as a theological doctrine was pretty much exploded: "That primitive demonology still survives in the barbaric doctrines of the Methodists and Baptists, particularly in the South; but it has been ameliorated, even there, by a growing sense of the divine grace, and so the old God of Plymouth Rock, as practically conceived, is now scarcely worse than the average jail warden or Italian padrone."[3] But as an ethical concept, Puritanism lived on in all its fury. To Mencken, the American still described all value judgments, even those of aesthetics, in terms of right and wrong. It was only natural that such "moral obsession" should strongly color our literature. In the histories of all other nations there have been periods of what Mencken called "moral innocence — periods in which a naif *joie de vivre* has broken through all concepts of duty and responsibility, and the wonder and glory of the universe have been hymned with unashamed zest." But in America no such breathing spells have lightened the almost intolerable burdens of man. For proof of this continued moralism, one need only to glance at the critical articles in the newspapers and literary weeklies—that is, at those of the period before and during World War I. "A novel or a play is judged among us, not by its dignity or conception, its artistic honesty, its perfection of workmanship, but almost entirely by its orthodoxy of doctrine, its platitudinousness, its usefulness as a moral tract. A digest of the reviews of a book of Ibsen's *Hedda Gabler* would make astounding reading for a Continental European."[4] Had not most of the critics of Dreiser's *The Titan* indignantly denounced the morals of Frank Cowperwood, the novel's central character?

That [Cowperwood] was superbly imagined and magnificently depicted, that he stood out from the book in all the flashing vigour of life, that his creation was an artistic achievement of a very high and difficult order—these facts seem to have made no impression upon the reviewers whatever. They were Puritans writing for Puritans, and all they could see in Cowperwood was an anti-Puritan, and in his creator another. It will remain for Europeans, I daresay, to discover the true stature of *The Titan*, as it remained for Europeans to discover the true stature of *Sister Carrie*.[5]

When one encounters an American humorist of high rank, Mencken said, he finds further evidence of the Puritan mind. Aside from Ambrose Bierce, actually a "wit" and not at all well known, there had been few scurvy fellows of the Fielding-Sterne-Smollett variety. Mencken believed that our great humorists "have had to take protective colouration, whether willingly or unwillingly, from the prevailing ethical foliage, and so one finds them levelling their darts, not at the stupidities of the Puritan majority, but at the evidences of lessening stupidity in the anti-Puritan minority." Rather than do battle against, they have done battle for, Philistinism— and Philistinism is just another name for Puritanism. Mencken might easily have found an exception to his generalization here in the person of George Ade, whose "fables" could hardly be said to support Philistinism. But then Ade was

555

---

[3] H. L. M., *A Book of Prefaces* (New York: Alfred Knopf, 1917), pp. 197-198.

[4] *Ibid.*, p. 200.

[5] *Ibid.*, p. 201.

a singular case; besides, he did not offer much as a witness for the prosecution—and Mencken was intent on prosecuting. Mencken saw his favorite American artist, Mark Twain, as a perfect example of the American whose nationality hung about his neck like a millstone.

> One ploughs through *The Innocents Abroad* and through parts of *A Tramp Abroad* with incredulous amazement. Is such coarse and ignorant clowning to be accepted as humour, as great humour, as the best humour that the most humourous of peoples has produced? Is it really the mark of a smart fellow to lift a peasant's cackle over *Lohengrin?* Is Titian's chromo of Moses in the bullrushes seriously to be regarded as the noblest picture in Europe? Is there nothing in Latin Christianity, after all, save petty grafting, monastic scandals and the worship of the knuckles and shin-bones of dubious saints? May not a civilized man, disbelieving in it, still find himself profoundly moved by its dazzling history, the lingering remnants of its old magnificence, the charm of its gorgeous and melancholy loveliness? In the presence of all beauty of man's creation—in brief, of what we roughly call art, whatever its form—the voice of Mark Twain was the voice of the Philistine.[6]

In tracing the development of Puritanism in America, Mencken found two main streams of influence. First, there was the force from without, that is, the influence of the original Puritans, who brought to the New World a philosophy of the utmost clarity, positiveness and inclusiveness. Actually, Mencken had no great objections to the original Puritans' philosophy, or at least so he says in a letter to Gamaliel Bradford, dated October 24, 1924; what he objected to was that philosophy's "perversion, by Methodists, Rotarians and other such vermin."[7] Although the original Puritan often possessed a good education (he was not infrequently a Cambridge or Oxford graduate) and even "a certain austere culture," he was almost sure to be hostile to beauty in all its forms. Nature, it must be remembered, fell with Adam, and like Adam is at the mercy of wan-

ton demons. To copy nature is to copy corruption. There is little, if any, of the dionysian spirit, the *Ja-sager* philosophy, in the preachments of Puritan divines.

The eighteenth century saw the passing of the Puritans as a powerful body of law makers. Deism undermined the old theology; epistemological studies replaced metaphysics. The proper study of mankind was thought to be man. Skepticism was all but universal among the learned of Europe, and Americans still imported their ideas wholesale from the mother countries. Both political and theological ideas were imported from France, where Voltaire, Diderot, D'Alembert and the other Encyclopedists were giving an entirely new direction to world philosophy. Mencken noted that even in New England, the last stronghold of the old Puritanism, this European influence was felt: "there was a gradual letting down of Calvinism to the softness of Unitarianism, and that change was presently to flower in the vague temporizing of Transcendentalism." This decline of Puritanism proper was not, however, an unalloyed blessing. For as Puritanism "declined in virulence and took deceptive new forms, there was a compensating growth of its brother, Philistinism, and by the first quarter of the nineteenth century, the distrust of beauty, and of the joy that is its object, was as firmly established throughout the land as it had ever been in New England." With the passing of the Adamses and the Jeffersons, Mencken remarked, the nation was quickly turned over to the tradesmen and the peasants. There was, he maintained, but one major difference between American peasants and those of other nations: the American peasant was listened to; he possessed power. (There is, of course no such thing as a peasant in America today—only social unfortunates.) With the election of Andrew Jackson, a man with whom Mencken violently disagreed and yet admired as a strong individual, Philistinism became the national philosophy. Jackson did what had not been done before: "he carried the mob's distrust of good taste even into the field of conduct; he was the first to put the rewards of conformity above the dictates of common decency; he founded

---

[6] *Ibid.,* pp. 203-204.
[7] Guy J. Forgue, ed., *Letters of H. L. Mencken* (New York: Alfred Knopf, 1961), p. 271.

a whole hierarchy of Philistine messiahs, the roaring of which still belabours the ear." The chief concern of Americans ever since the official triumph of mobocracy has been politics; what's more, politics tended to absorb the rancorous certainty of the fading religious ideas; the game of politics had turned itself into a holy war.

The custom of connecting purely political doctrines with pietistic concepts of an inflammable nature, then firmly set up by skillful persuaders of the mob, has never quite died out in the United States. There has not been a presidential contest since Jackson's day without its Armageddons, its marching of Christian soldiers, its crosses of gold, its crowns of thorns. The most successful American politicians, beginning with anti-slavery agitators, have been those most adept at twisting the ancient gauds and shibboleths of Puritanism to partisan uses. Every campaign that we have seen for eighty years has been, on each side, a pursuit of bugaboos, a denunciation of heresies, a snouting up of immoralities.[8]

THE PERVASIVENESS of Puritan ethics (not, remember, theology) in America placed all purely aesthetic concerns in limbo. Mencken stated that with the exception of Whitman there was hardly a major writer who used the materials of his own age for subject matter. He used Algernon Tassin's *The Magazine in America* (1916) to support his thesis that the literature of the ante-bellum period was almost completely divorced from life as men were then living it. Only in such "crude politico-puritan tracts" as *Uncle Tom's Cabin* was there

[8] *A Book of Prefaces*, pp. 212-213. It should be unnecessary to remind the reader that today many high government officials are waging, by their own frequent admissions, a "moral" war against the infidelity of Communism. Of course, the Communists are themselves fully aware of the effectiveness of moral judgments against the enemy. In his long introduction to *Patriotic Gore*, Edmund Wilson composed a devastating indictment of all those who employ morality as a justification of or cloak for acts which are clearly motivated by self-interest. Although he does not exempt other nations from this disease, Wilson concentrated on the American's extraordinary ability in this particular form of causistry.

any attempt made to interpret, or even to represent, the culture of the time. (The fact that Mrs. Stowe was chastised in her own day for her "realistic" novels only supports Mencken's contention.) Later, the culture found historians, and in at least one work—*Huckleberry Finn*—it was depicted with the highest art, but Twain's *magnum opus* was a rare exception. The nineteenth-century novelists did not even sentimentalize the here and now in the manner of Mencken's contemporaries. The best minds of that period were engaged either in business or politics. The few competent men of the period who were artists almost without exception forsook the present for the non-political, non-social realms of Arcadia or El Dorado. It is evident that much of the material in "Puritanism as a Literary Force" was condensed in the later essay on "The National Letters" (in *Prejudices: Second Series*, 1920). For example:

Fenimore Cooper filled his romances, not with the people about him, but with the Indians beyond the sky-line, and made them half-fabulous to boot. Irving told fairy tales about the forgotten Knickerbockers; Hawthorne turned backward to the Puritans of Plymouth Rock; Longfellow to the Acadians and the pre-historic Indians; Emerson took flight from earth altogether; even Poe sought refuge in a land of fantasy. It was only the frank second-raters—*e.g.*, Whittier and Lowell—who ventured to turn to the life around them, and the banality of the result is a sufficient indication of the crudeness of the current taste, and the mean position assigned to the art of letters. This was pre-eminently the era of the moral tale, the Sunday-school book.[9]

IN THE SEVENTIES and eighties, with the appearance of such men as Henry James, Howells, and Twain (Mencken also listed Bret Harte even though he never considered him a good second-rate artist), a better day seemed to be dawning. These writers gave promise of turning away from the past to the teeming and colorful life that lay about

[9] *A Book of Prefaces*, pp. 214-215.

them. The promise, however, was not fulfilled.

Mark Twain, after *The Gilded Age,* slipped back into romanticism tempered by Philistinism, and was presently in the era before the Civil War, and finally in the Middle Ages, and even beyond. Harte, a brilliant technician, had displayed his whole stock when he had displayed his technique: his stories were not even superficially true to the life they presumed to depict; one searched them in vain for an interpretation of it; they were simply idle tales. As for Howells and James, both quickly showed timorousness and reticence which are the distinguishing marks of the Puritan even in his most intellectual incarnations. The American scene that they depicted with such meticulous care was chiefly peopled with marionettes.[10]

To return to "Puritanism as a Literary Force." The force from within was, in essence, a force of "conditioning." The American tended to view all the workings of God, fate, man and nature as exemplifications of a moral order or structure or pattern, just as his forebears had done. The rebel, that is, the writer who made an earnest attempt to depict his surroundings realistically rather than romantically or sentimentally, had had little influence on the main stream of American literature. Such writers as Hamlin Garland began as realists but soon saw a rosy light and devoted themselves to safer enterprises; Garland ended his days by composing books on spiritualism, or, as Mencken put it, by "chasing spooks." (Garland, as well as Howells, refused to sign the Dreiser Protest, a petition objecting to the ban placed on *The "Genius."* In the early days of the twentieth century, there had been a few realists—for example, Ambrose Bierce, Frank Norris, Stephen Crane, David Graham Phillips, Henry Fuller, Upton Sinclair—but their rebellion was apparently ineffectual.

The normal, the typical American book of today is as fully a remouthing of old husks as the normal book of Griswold's day. The whole atmosphere of our literature, in William James' phrase, is "mawkish and dishwatery." Books are still judged among us, not by their form and organization as works of art, their accuracy and vividness as representations of life, their validity and perspicacity as interpretations of it, but by their conformity to the national prejudices, their accordance with set standards of niceness and propriety. The thing irrevocably demanded is a "sane" book; the ideal is a "clean," an "inspiring," a "glad" book.[11]

In addition to the impulse from within, or the internal resistance, there was a pervasive Puritan influence from without. No examination of the history and present condition of American letters, Mencken believed, could have any value at all unless it took into account the influence and operation of this external Puritan force. Supported by the almost incredibly large body of American laws, this power resided in the inherited traits of Puritanism, which were evident in the "conviction of the pervasiveness of sin, of the supreme importance of moral correctness, of the need of savage and inquisitorial laws." The history of the nation, Mencken wrote, might be outlined by the awakenings and re-awakenings of moral earnestness. The spiritual eagerness that was the basis for the original Puritan's moral obsession had not always retained its white heat, but the fires of moral endeavor had never gone out in America. Mencken remarked that the theocracy of the New England colonies had scarcely been replaced by the libertarianism of a godless Crown when there came the Great Awakening of 1734, "with its orgies of homiletics and its restoration of talmudism to the first place among polite sciences." The book-bumping of Jonathan Edwards' "Sinners in the Hands of an Angry God" stands as a testament to that holy resurrection of Almighty Sin.

During the Revolution, politics superceded theology as the national pastime, and there was a brief period of relative quiet. But no sooner had the Republic emerged from the throes of adolescence than "a missionary army took to the field again, and before long the Asbury revival was paling that of Whitefield,

---

[10] *Ibid.,* pp. 217-218.

[11] *A Book of Prefaces,* pp. 224-225.

Wesley and Jonathan Edwards, not only in its hortatory violence but also in the length of its lists of slain." From Bishop Asbury down to the present day, that is, to World War I, the country was rocked periodically by furious attacks on the devil. On the one hand, the holy *Putsch*

took a purely theological form with a hundred new and fantastic creeds as its fruits; on the other hand, it crystallized into the hysterical temperance movement of the 30's and 40's, which penetrated to the very floor of Congress and put "dry" laws upon the statute-books of ten States; and on the third hand, as it were, it established a prudery in speech and thought from which we are yet but half delivered. Such ancient and innocent words as "bitch" and "bastard" disappeared from the American language; Bartlett tells us, indeed, in his "Dictionary of Americanisms," that even "bull" was softened to "male cow." This was the Golden Age of euphemism, as it was of euphuism; the worst inventions of the English mid-Victorians were adopted and improved. The word "woman" became a term of opprobrium, verging close upon downright libel; legs became the inimitable "limbs"; the stomach began to run from the "bosom" to the pelvic arch; pantaloons faded into "unmentionables"; the newspapers spun their parts of speech into such gossamer webs as "a statutory offense," "a house of questionable repute" and "an interesting condition." And meanwhile the Good Templars and Sons of Temperance swarmed in the land like a plague of celestial locusts. There was not a hamlet without its uniformed phalanx, its affecting exhibit of reformed drunkards.[12]

Mencken argued that the Civil War itself was primarily a result of the agitations of anti-slavery preachers. He admitted that to many historians the anti-slavery feeling had economic origins, but he insisted, probably correctly, that the war was largely the result of ecstatically moral pleas. In "The Calamity at Appomattox" (in the *American Mercury* for September, 1930), Mencken attributed the Negro's bondage in the South today to the fact that the war was won by the North. Before the surrender

12 *Ibid,* pp. 227-229.

at Appomattox, there was little hatred of the Negro in the South. More importantly, the Negro would most certainly have been made a freedman before the end of the nineteenth century anyway, and without the resulting hostility between the races. The Union victory, as Mencken stated, simply deprived the best southerners of any say in national and regional affairs, and placed the lower orders—the scalawags, carpet-baggers, freed slaves, and poor white trash—in the saddle. The Negro, of course, was soon disfranchised again, but the power remained in the hands of incompetent whites.

The Puritan of the days between the Revolution and the Civil War was, according to Mencken, different from the *Un*-Puritan and neo-Puritan of the postbellum period. The distinguishing mark of the Puritanism of this middle period, at least after it had attained to the stature of a national philosophy, was its appeal to the individual conscience, its exclusive concern with the elect, its strong flavor of self-accusing. Certainly the Abolitionists were less concerned with punishing slave-owners than they were with ridding themselves of "their sneaking sense of responsibility, the fear that they themselves were flouting the fire by letting slavery go on." The Abolitionist was willing, in most cases, to compensate the slave-owner for his property. The difference between the new Puritanism with its astoundingly ferocious and uncompromising vice crusading and the Puritanism of the 1840's was of great degree, if not of kind: "In brief, a difference between *r*enunciation and *d*enunciation, asceticism and Mohammedanism, the hair shirt and the flaming sword." After going through a number of stages and fads, neo-Puritanism found its apex in comstockery. And in comstockery there was a frank harking back to the primitive spirit.

The original Puritan of the bleak New England coast was not content to flay his own wayward carcass: full satisfaction did not sit upon him until he had jailed a Quaker. That is to say, the sinner who excited his highest zeal and passion was not so much himself as his neighbor; to borrow a term from psychopatholo-

559

gy, he was less the masochist than the sadist. And it is that very peculiarity which sets off his descendant of today from the ameliorated Puritan of the era between the Revolution and the Civil War. The new Puritanism is not ascetic, but militant. Its aim is not to lift up saints but to knock down sinners. Its supreme manifestation is the vice crusade, an armed pursuit of helpless outcasts by the whole military and naval forces of the Republic. Its supreme hero is Comstock Himself, with his pious boast that the sinners he jailed during his astounding career, if gathered into one penitential party, would have filled a train of sixty-one coaches, allowing sixty to the coach.[13]

In accounting for the wholesale ethical transvaluation that came after the Civil War, Mencken pointed to the Golden Calf; in short, Puritanism became bellicose and tyrannical when it became rich. History shows that a wealthy people are never prone to soul-searching. The solvent citizen is less likely to find fault with himself than with those about him; what's more, he has more time and energy to devote to the enterprise of examining the happy rascal across the street. The Puritan of America was, generally speaking, spiritually humble down to the Civil War because he was poor; he subscribed to a *Sklavenmoral*. But after the Civil War prosperity replaced poverty; and from prosperity came a new morality, to wit, the *Herrenmoral*. Great fortunes were made during the conflict, and even greater wealth followed during the years of the robber barons. Nor was this new prosperity limited to a few capitalists only; the common laborer and the farmer were better off than ever before.

The first effect of prosperity was, as always, a universal cockiness, a delight in all things American, the giddy feeling that success has no limits. "The American became a sort of braggart playboy of the western world, enormously sure of himself and ludicrously contemptuous of all other men." Mencken observed that religion, which is always dependent upon its popularity for survival, naturally began to lose its inward direction

and take on the qualities of a business enterprise. The revivals of the 1870's were similar to those of a half century before except that the converts at the later date were more interested in serving than in repenting. The American Puritan was less interested in saving his own soul than in passing salvation on to others, especially to those reluctant individuals who hung back and resisted the power of divine grace. It became apparent to the more forward-looking ecclesiastics that the rescue of the unsaved could be converted into a big business. All that was needed was organization. Out of this unabashed industrialization of religion came a new force, one that still exerts great influence on American society. "Piety was cunningly disguised as basketball, billiards and squash; the sinner was lured to grace with Turkish baths, lectures on foreign travel, and free instructions in stenography, rhetoric and double-entry bookkeeping." Religion lost its old contemplative nature and became an enterprise for the public relations man, the bookkeeper and the extrovert. In short, religion was "modernized." What was true at the time Mencken wrote this essay is, as a pragmatist would say, even more true in the 1960's.

After giving the necessary background material, Mencken then devoted a lengthy section of his essay to the workings and accomplishments of Anthony Comstock and his associates. The various laws, state and national, which Comstock got passed offer the contemporary reader a sorry spectacle of the vice crusader's power. As a public figure, Old Anthony was as well known as P. T. Barnum or John L. Sullivan. He had disciples in every large city who were just as eager for blood as he was. Since there were few American writers brash enough to challenge the inquisitors, Comstock and company were forced to turn to foreign works. Rabelais and the *Decameron* were naturally banned (they are still being banned in various American cities today); Zola, Balzac and Daudet were driven under the counters; Hardy's *Jude the Obscure* and Harold Frederic's *The Damnation of Theron Ware* were also among the victims.

---

[13] *Ibid,* pp. 231-232.

560

These are but leading examples of the purge. In fact, Comstock got 2,682 convictions out of 3,646 prosecutions and is credited by his official biographer with having destroyed 50 tons of books, 28,682 pounds of stereotype plates, 16,900 photographic negatives, and 3,984,063 photographs. That such a Herod's record could have been compiled was largely a result of the postal laws, which, of course, Comstock was responsible for in the first place. The very vagueness of the law was of great convenience to the prosecutors. That a novel like George du Maurier's *Trilby*, which I read in search of damning evidence, could have been widely condemned as "lewd," "obscene," and "lascivious" is next to incredible. It merely provides further proof that Swift's *Gulliver's Travels* is a good deal closer to reality than it is to fantasy.

It is held in the leading cases that anything is obscene which may excite "impure thoughts" in "the minds . . . of persons that are susceptible to impure thoughts,"[14] or which "tends to deprave the minds" of any who, because they are "young and inexperienced," are "open to such influences"[15] — in brief, that anything is obscene that is not fit to be handed to a child just learning to read, or that may imaginably stimulate to lubricity of the most foulminded. It is held further that words that are perfectly innocent in themselves — "words, abstractly considered, [that] may be free from vulgarism"—may yet be assumed, by a friendly jury, to be likely to "arouse a libidinous passion . . . in the mind of a modest woman." (I quote exactly! The court failed to define "modest woman.")[16] Yet further, it is held that any book is obscene "which is unbecoming, immodest. . . ."[17] Obviously, this last decision throws open the door to endless imbecilities, for its definition merely begs the question, and so makes a reasonable solution ten times harder. It is in such mazes that the Comstocks safely lurk. Almost any printed allusion to sex may be argued against as unbecoming in a moral republic, and once it is unbecoming it is also obscene.[18]

Mencken then cited numerous cases to show that the defendant was helpless in proving his innocence against any of a whole host of charges of immorality. Besides, Dr. Johnson was obviously right when he stated that no man would want to go on trial, even if possessed of absolute proof of his innocence. Obviously, neither author nor publisher ever knew what might pass the watchful eyes of the self-appointed smut-hounds and defenders of decency. Competent work invariably was banned while the frankly prurient and vulgar went unmolested. Mencken was never in favor of denying anything or anyone the freedom of speech, but he was indignantly amazed that the serious work of an Auguste Forel or a Havelock Ellis should be barred from the mails while the countless volumes of "sex hygiene" by filthy-minded clergymen and "smutty old maids" were circulated by the million and without challenge.

Frank Harris is deprived of a publisher for his *Oscar Wilde: His Life and Confession*" by threats of immediate prosecution; the newspapers meanwhile dedicate thousands of columns to the filthy amusements of Harry Thaw. George Moore's *Memoirs of My Dead Life* are bowdlerized, James Lane Allen's *A Summer in Arcady* is barred from the libraries, and a book by D. H. Lawrence is forbidden publication altogether; at the same time half a dozen cheap magazines devoted to sensational sex stories attain to hundreds of thousands of circulation. A serious book by David Graham Phillips, published serially in a popular monthly, is raided the moment it appears between covers; a trashy piece of nastiness by Elinor Glyn goes unmolested. Worse, books are sold for months and even years without protest, and then suddenly attacked: Dreiser's *The "Genius,"* Kreymborg's *Edna* and Forel's *The Sexual Question* are examples. Still worse, what is held to be unobjectionable in one state is forbidden in another as *contra bonos mores*.[19] Altogether,

---

[14] U.S. *vs.* Bennett, 16 Blatchford, 368-9 (1877).

[15] *Idem*, 362; People *vs.* Muller, 96 N. Y., 411; U.S. *vs.* Clark, 38 Fed. Rep. 734.

[16] U.S. *vs.* Moore, 129 Fed., 160-1 (1904).

[17] U.S. *vs.* Heywood, judges charge, Boston, 1877. Quoted in U.S. *vs.* Bennett, 16 Blatchford.

[18] *A Book of Prefaces*, pp. 263-265.

[19] The chief sufferers from this conflict are the authors of moving pictures. What they face at the hands of imbecile State boards of censorship is

there is madness, and no method in it. The livelihoods and good names of hard-striving and decent men are at the mercy of the whims of a horde of fanatics and mountebanks, and they have no way of securing themselves against attack, and no redress for their loss when it comes.[20]

It was no wonder, Mencken wrote, that American literature down to World War I was primarily remarkable for its artificiality. He compared our fiction to eighteenth-century poetry; it was just as conventional and artificial, just as far removed from reality. In America, and probably only here, could an obvious piece of reporting like Upton Sinclair's *The Jungle* create a sensation, or Dreiser's *Jennie Gerhardt* evoke such astonishment and rage. As an editor of the *Smart Set* Mencken was fully aware of the dangers lying in the path of any publisher who attempted to give his readers quality writing. Since his magazine was frankly addressed to a sophisticated minority, sold for a relatively high price, and contained no pictures or other baits for the childish, Mencken assumed that "its readers are not sex-curious and itching adolescents, just as my colleague of the *Atlantic Monthly* may assume reasonably that his readers are not Italian immigrants." Nevertheless, he was constantly forced to keep the comstocks in mind while reading a manuscript sent him by an author. He warned his contributors, though he never admitted this publicly, to be sure to keep clothes on their female characters at all times. Mencken was a man marked by the Puritan elements in the country, and he knew it. But he certainly possessed nothing resembling a martyr complex. As he wrote Dreiser in 1921, the joy of living in America "does not lie in playing chopping-block for the sanctified, but in outraging them and getting away with it. To this enterprise

described at length by Channing Pollock in an article entitled, "Swinging the Censor," in the *Bulletin of the Author's League of America* for March, 1917.

[20] *A Book of Prefaces*, pp. 273-274.

I address myself. Some day they may fetch me, but it will be a hard sweat."

ALTHOUGH OUR LITERATURE was policed and picketed by a small band of comstocks, the fact remains that the American people offered little resistance; they were perfectly willing to be led by their noses like so many cattle. The American was "school-mastered out of gusto, out of joy, out of innocence." He could in no way understand William Blake's belief that "the lust of the goat is also to the glory of God." When the comstocks examined *The "Genius"* to determine its harmful effect on immature female readers, they tacitly admitted, Mencken wrote, that "to be curious is to be lewd; to know is to yield to fornication." The medieval doctrine that woman is depraved was, and, for that matter, still is widely accepted in our own century. The right-thinking man must do all he can to save her from her innate depravity. "The 'locks of chastity' rust in the Cluny Museum: in place of them we have comstockery. . . ." Though censorship is nothing like so powerful today as it was forty years ago, and we must credit Mencken with having done much to deprive the censors of their power, there are still numerous evidences of the puritanical perversion. The most cursory look at television, for example, will provide the spectator with enough sadism to last a lifetime, but it is still impossible to portray a normal sex relationship in any way even resembling a realistic manner. It is also ironic that Roman Catholic censors, particularly the Legion of Decency, have taken up where the more nearly pure descendants of New England Puritanism left off. Once the object of Puritan prejudice, the Catholic Church now wields the whip in many areas of the country. Boston, now a Catholic stronghold, remains the laughing-stock of the nation. What hungry young novelist doesn't nightly pray that his latest book will receive the free advertising that goes with being banned in Boston?

NEW BOOKS AND ARTICLES

THE FOLLOWING IS A SELECT LIST OF BOOKS AND ARTICLES WHICH, IN THE OPINION OF THE EDITORS, MAY BE OF INTEREST TO OUR READERS.

Milton Friedman and Anna J. Schwartz, *A Monetary History of the United States,* 1867-1960. Princeton, Princeton University Press, 1963. $15.00. A mammoth study of the history of United States monetary policies and the money supply since the Civil War.

H. L. A. Hart, *Law, Liberty, and Morality.* Stanford, Stanford University Press, 1963. $3.00. A largely successful attack on the Conservative position espoused by Sir Patrick Devlin (and in the nineteenth century by James Fitzjames Stephen) that "society" has the right to enforce "its" moral code against dissenters, even in the absence of direct injury to innocent parties.

Two books of note have appeared recently by W. H. Hutt, distinguished economist of the University of Capetown, South Africa, and a consistent opponent of the policies of apartheid: *The Economics of the Colour Bar.* London, Andre Deutsch, 1964. 5 shillings, paper. His theme is that "the restrictionist policies arising from the racialist doctrines of the Nationalist Government and the efforts of the higher-paid workers to protect privileged positions in the labour market would not have been possible had the economy been run on competitive lines. But this has not happened because investors and managements have been intimidated by politicians wielding the planning powers of the state." Available from the publisher at 105 Great Russell St., London, W.C.1, England. And: *Keynesianism—Retrospect and Prospect.* Chicago, Regnery, 1963. $7.50. A major contribution to the body of anti-Keynesian literature. Professor Hutt supplies an impressive amount of factual and theoretical economic evidence for his arguments.

563

George J. Stigler, *The Intellectual and the Market Place and Other Essays.* New York, The Free Press of Glencoe, 1963. $2.50. A collection of highly readable essays on economic and political topics. The title essay should be familiar to NIR readers.

Ernest van den Haag, *Passion and Social Constraint.* New York, Stein and Day, 1963. $6.95. A new work by one of the foremost contemporary conservative sociologists, discussing the problems raised by the fact of limitation from the viewpoint of the fields of anthropology, sociology, and psychoanalysis.

Alfred Avins, "Freedom of Choice in Personal Service Occupations: 13th Amendment Limitations on Antidiscrimination Legislation," *Cornell Law Quarterly,* Winter 1964, pp. 228-256. An historical survey of antidiscrimination legislation and its human limitations, tending slightly to the polemical; but well reasoned and well documented.

William Letwin, "What's Wrong with Planning: The Case of India," *Fortune,* June 1963, pp. 118 ff. An illustrative discussion of the problems India now faces because of central planning and public ownership.

Jesse W. Markham, "Anti-Trust Trends and New Constraints," *Harvard Business Review,* May-June 1963, pp. 84-92. A detached survey of recent antitrust developments which look less like attempts to foster competition and more and more like protectionism.

AS A MAGAZINE . . .

reaches maturity in the publication field it is often blessed with the growth of a loyal and dedicated following. This hard core of zealots will stick with a magazine through thick and thin, hard times and good. NIR is fortunate in having a larger percentage of these "hard core" readers than the average periodical. We would like to present here a sampling of the encouraging praise and constructive criticism we have received over the past few months:

"Your recent issue on the Federal Regulatory Bureaus was well written and very informative. I just wanted to let you know that we have passed a resolution abolishing the ICC in our neighborhood."

"The publishing policies of your periodical have brought a new meaning to the word 'quarterly' in American magazine circles."

564

"As one of the more responsible extremist publications, NIR is, I feel, a valuable contributor to the Great Conversation and to the world's store of Great Ideas. Mankind needs NIR; mankind needs the vigor which NIR lends to dialogues between peoples. The fact that sometimes you do go just a bit far out sometimes—like selling the lighthouses, really!—does not in any way diminish your service or, as Sir Servapali Chutney was fond of putting it, your 'contribution,' to humanity."

"Leafing through back issues of NIR, I came across Mr. Hurt's 'Sin and the Criminal Law.' It is good to see a member of the responsible right who believes that moderation in pursuit of vice is no virtue."

NEW INDIVIDUALIST REVIEW   II

IDA NOYES HALL
University of Chicago, Chicago 37, Illinois

Please enter my subscription for one year at $2.00 ☐   Students, $1.00 ☐

(Two years at $3.75, students, $1.75)

I also enclose a contribution of $...................................

NAME ....

ADDRESS ....

IF STUDENT: SCHOOL.............................. YEAR OF GRAD.................

Society lives and acts only in individuals
. . . Everyone carries a part of society on
his shoulders; no one is relieved of his share
of responsibility by others. And no one can
find a safe way for himself if society is
sweeping toward destruction. Therefore
everyone, in his own interests, must thrust
himself vigorously into the intellectual battle. None can stand aside with unconcern;
the interests of everyone hang on the result. Whether he chooses or not, every man
is drawn into the great historical struggle,
the decisive battle (between freedom and
slavery) into which our epoch has plunged
us.

—Ludwig Von Mises

The Intercollegiate Society of Individualists, a non-partisan, non-profit educational organization, deals with ideas. ISI places primary emphasis on the distribution of literature encompassing such academic disciplines as economics, sociology, history, moral philosophy, and political science. If you are a student or teacher, you are invited to add your name to the ISI mailing list. There is no charge, and you may remove your name at any time. For additional information, or to add your name to the list, write the nearest ISI office.

VOLUME 3
NUMBER 4
SPRING 1965

New
INDIVIDUALIST
Review

A JOURNAL OF CLASSICAL LIBERAL THOUGHT

| Spring 1965 | 50 cents | Vol. 3, No. 4 |

NEW

INDIVIDUALIST

REVIEW

NEW INDIVIDUALIST REVIEW

SPRING 1965 **Volume 3 — Number 4**

571

NEW INDIVIDUALIST REVIEW is published quarterly by *New Individualist Review, Inc.*, at Ida Noyes Hall, University of Chicago, Chicago, Illinois 60637.

Opinions expressed in signed articles do not necessarily represent the views of the editors. Editorial, advertising, and subscription correspondence and manuscripts should be sent to NEW INDIVIDUALIST REVIEW, Ida Noyes Hall, University of Chicago, Chicago, Illinois 60637. All manuscripts become the property of NEW INDIVIDUALIST REVIEW.

Subscription rates: $2.00 per year (students $1.00). Two years at $3.75 (students $1.75).

IN MEMORIAM

Robert M. Hurt

The editors and staff of *New Individualist Review* join with his family and his friends in mourning the tragic death of Robert M. Hurt. His contributions to this magazine covered the entire scope of its operations and reflected the wide range of his own abilities. The signed articles which he wrote demonstrated both his capacity for research and analysis, and his deep concern with the extension of freedom; his sense of humor was manifested in some of our advertisements; and more than any other person he is responsible for placing *New Individualist Review* on a firm financial base.

When he left the University of Chicago to join the faculty of Princeton University, we believed that he was launched on a career that promised high achievements; he had so much ability.

He was a friend to each of us, and a stimulating companion whose zest for his own special fields of the law and economics did not dampen his interest in matters as diverse as the philosophy of logical positivism and the domestic political situation in the new nations of Africa, and whose good temper and good humor kept animosity out of even the most heated discussion. He was a keen thinker, a thorough scholar and a dear friend; we will remember him with esteem, affection, and sorrow as we grieve for his untimely death.

The Revival
of Traditional Liberalism

A druggist's assistant who, after listening to the description of pains which he mistakes for those of colic, but which are really caused by inflammation of the caecum, prescribes a sharp purgative and kills the patient, is found guilty of man-slaughter. He is not allowed to excuse himself on the ground that he did not intend harm but hoped for good . . . .

We measure the responsibilities of legislators for mischiefs they may do, in a much more lenient fashion. In most cases, so far from thinking of them as deserving punishment for causing disasters by laws ignorantly enacted, we scarcely think of them as deserving reprobation. It is held that common experience should have taught the druggist's assistant, untrained as he is, not to interfere; but it is not held that common experience should have taught the legislator not to interfere till he has trained himself. Though multitudinous facts are before him in the recorded legislation of our own country and of other countries, which should impress on him the immense evils caused by wrong treatment, he is not condemned for disregarding these warnings against rash meddling . . . .

—Herbert Spencer[1]

573

A DISCUSSION OF the revival of liberalism should begin with a description of what it is—particularly since our latter-day reactionaries have stolen the name. They have stolen the label for a good reason: it stands for the opposite of what they propose. These reactionaries are attempting to disguise their desire to apply the interventionist policies of seventeenth-century mercantilism to twentieth-century society.

Literally, liberalism meant to liberalize or liberate—to make free—to permit men

to do or say whatever they wished. Of course, there was a constraint implied in this. No man could do anything which affected the liberty of others. To permit some men to intervene in the lives of others would be the opposite of making men free. This would make some men unfree—subject some men to tyranny by others. The classical liberal was and is opposed to all forms of tyranny.

This constraint on the individual, to preclude what has been called license, implies equality in the right to be free. Opposition to all tyranny is equalitarian. Unfortunately, some economists imbued

Yale Brozen is Professor of Business Economics at the University of Chicago and an Editorial Advisor to *New Individualist Review*. He has contributed numerous articles to professional journals.

[1] Herbert Spencer, *The Man Versus the State* (New York: Appleton, 1897), pp. 338-39.

with the equalitarianism in liberty implied by opposition to tyranny came to confuse liberalism with another position —equalitarianism in the distribution of income. They began to scrutinize every public policy for its effects on the distribution of income.

"A growing number of economists, indeed, implicitly argue that no other injustice equals in enormity that of large differences in income."[2] From this position began the rationalization of intervention to make those lower on the income scale better off by methods other than removing the barriers to self-improvement or to charitable actions by private persons. At first it was argued that the state should be used to transfer income from those higher on the income scale. From this it was an easy step to forcing people low on the income scale (and others) to do what the interventionist felt would be good for them, even though these people did not wish to do these things. The new tyranny was born —or rather the old tyranny was re-born.

Historically, the rise of liberalism was in opposition to tyranny from two sources. One source was the tyranny of private persons or associations such as monopolies and guilds (usually through a grant of power from the sovereign). Monopolies and guilds could and did prevent men from consuming things which otherwise would have been available. They could and did prevent men from seeking and obtaining jobs otherwise available to them. While tyranny in this form may seem to be a small thing, it was odious not only because some men had the power to dictate economic conditions to others, but also because such dictation could be used to bend men to accept the political dictates of those possessing the power.

The second source of tyranny was the state—those who manned the political apparatus. The possessors of political power could grant or withhold favors and could thus bend men to their will. Not only could they withold favors, but they also could take punitive action, even going so far as to take the lives of those who would not obey them. As one writer has said, "Government is in the last resort the employment of armed men, of policemen, gendarmes, soldiers, prison guards, and hangmen. The essential feature of government is the enforcement of its decrees by beating, killing and imprisonment."[3] The spectacle of some men forcing others to crawl, or possessing such power, was shocking to those bred in traditions of liberty.

NEVERTHELESS, DESPITE a long tradition in the United States of constant battle to reduce the amount of power by some private agents — such as businesses — we have permitted much coercion by other private agents, notably trade unions; at the same time we have allowed enlarged powers to be assumed by the state, opening up new possibilities for unwanted coercion. Trade unions in the city of Chicago, for e x a m p l e, prevent anyone from becoming a plumber or a plastering contractor unless his father or his uncle was a member of the plumbers' union or the Plasterers' Institute. Political dissenters find building inspectors invading their homes and hauling them into court for presumed violations of the building code. Those in the restaurant and grocery business who disagree with the men in power find their establishments do not measure up to the standards of health inspectors. Property assessments have a suspiciously uniform tendency to rise for those property owners who do not go along, while they tend to decrease for those who "play ball." The Federal administration's Bureau of Internal Revenue has harassed newspapermen and steel executives who do not a g r e e with the Administration's views.

The power of the government has grown as it has, in part, because native Americans have had little experience with tyrannical governments. There has been a naive trust in the good will, the

---

[2] G. J. Stigler, *Five Lectures on Economic Problems* (London: Longmans, 1948), p. 1.

[3] L. von Mises, *Human Action* (New Haven: Yale University Press, 1949), p. 715.

beneficence, and even the omnipotence of government. Many Americans have felt that whenever the government does something, it must be in their interest and that their government will not take advantage of them.[4] The modern "liberal," the reactionary in disguise, suspects every businessman of an intent to bilk him. On the other hand, he trusts every bureaucrat and trade union officer to look out for his interest. I, on the contrary, suspect everybody of looking out for his own interests, be he businessman, bureaucrat, union officer, c o n s u m e r, Congressman, workman, or the ordinary citizen. I am somewhat willing to trust a businessman to serve me well since any attempt to bilk his customers will mean that he will lose business to competitors. This, at least, means that it is to his self-interest to serve me well.

The average politician I trust a great deal less since he is quite willing to serve my interest badly if the support he gains at my expense is crucial to his election. Besides, he can confuse the issue by offering a few items in his platform which have some appeal to offset the other things which are distasteful. In every election, I have had to choose either the grab bag of proposals offered by one party, 95 per cent of which are distasteful, or the grab bag offered by the other party, 97 per cent of which are distasteful. That is hardly a choice. At least, when I buy a General Motors automobile, I do not have to buy GM gasoline, GM schools for my children, GM garbage collection service, GM old age annuities, or GM anything else. In a free market, I can separate my decisions on what automobile I buy from my choice of what gasoline I consume, which service station I patronize, which mechanic I go to for repairs, or which company insures my car or administers the funds I save for my retirement income.

In a political market, choosing the party which offers the best school program means I may also have to take a poor street repair program, inferior garbage collection services, and indifferent operation of the water works. For that reason, I prefer that the government do less rather than more. I can make more of each of my decisions separately from other decisions. Thomas Jefferson expressed this very pointedly when he said, "That government is best which governs least."

I think another reason that Americans have allowed their government to take on an uncontrollably large number of functions is because we have improved so many things and solved so many problems (by private action, in most instances) that we think all problems can be solved—and we are an impatient people who believe it is better to take care of our problems today instead of next year.

575

As one of my colleagues has put the matter:

> Our faith in the power of the state is a matter of desire rather than demonstration. When the state undertakes to achieve a goal, and fails, we cannot bring ourselves to abandon the goal, nor do we seek alternative means of achieving it, for who is more powerful than a sovereign state? We demand, then, increased efforts of the state, tacitly assuming that where there is a will, there is a governmental way.
>
> Yet we know very well that the sovereign state is not omnipotent. The inability of the state to perform certain economic tasks could be documented from some notorious failures. Our cotton program, for example, was intended to enrich poor cotton farmers, increase the efficiency of production, foster foreign markets, and stabilize domestic consumption. It is an open question whether twenty-eight years of our farm program have done as much for poor cotton farmers as the trucking industry and mail-order houses.[5]

---

[4] A letter received by the author is typical: "The only theoretical treatments of the minimum wage laws I have seen suggest that they are unfavorable to the economy as a whole. But somehow I find it hard to believe that the law could be passed and extended and the level raised several times if it is supported by nothing more than wishful thinking." October 26, 1964.

---

[5] G. J. Stigler, "The Government of the Economy," G. J. Stigler and P. A. Samuelson, *A Dialogue on the Proper Economic Role of the State* (Chicago: University of Chicago Graduate School of Business, Selected Papers no. 7, 1963), pp. 3-4.

Page Five

Now that we have lived so long with government intervention in our economy, a few professional economists have begun to examine the results of that intervention. Some findings from these examinations are beginning to appear and affect, at least, the attitudes of an increasing number of scholars. If any resurgence of liberalism is occurring, this is the primary place where it is apparent to me. However, I am extremely poorly informed on the attitudes of undertakers, bricklayers, Republicans and Democrats.

Four years ago, an opinion study showed that 73 per cent of the college economists of this country were definitely in favor of additional government intervention in the economy. Sixteen per cent were opposed. The rest expressed no leaning either way.[6] An opinion study done last year showed that the group opposed to additional government intervention had grown to 35 per cent and the group still in favor of more intervention had shrunk to about 50 per cent.[7]

WHAT ARE THE studies leading to this change in attitude? First, I should mention a group of studies examining the effects of regulation of the transportation industries by the Interstate Commerce Commission, Civil Aeronautics Board, and the Federal Maritime Commission. One study done a few years ago points to several features of transportation regulation which produce undesirable results.[8] Let me cite one instance of the way in which railroad-trucking regulation has worked. The railroads petitioned the ICC for permission to reduce freight rates on cigarettes in the early 1950's. They had lost most of the cigarette transportation business

to trucks since the rail rate on cigarettes was higher than the truck rate. The railroads examined their cost of transporting cigarettes and found they could make money at much lower rates than they had been charging. After extended hearings, during which the reduction was not allowed to go into effect, the ICC finally decided that the railroads had an inherent advantage over trucks in moving cigarettes and, therefore, should have the business. In their wisdom, the ICC commissioners decided to divert business to the railroads, not by acceding to the railroad request for permission to reduce rates, but by raising truck rates.[9]

If this were an isolated and exceptional act of the Commission, it would produce little reaction. However, a recent study of the behavior of the Commission in its founding days, 1888-1890, indicates that raising rates is an old Commission tradition.[10] Before the ICC was formed by the Interstate Commerce Act of 1887, railroads between Chicago and New York entered into agreements with each other to maintain prices at specified levels on Chicago-New York shipments of corn and grain. These agreements were seldom successful. Railroads secretly sold transportation services at less than the agreed-upon price, and frequently at much less. In practice, the cartel of railroads rarely found it possible to maintain the agreed-upon price.

After 1887, the ICC was empowered to prevent the setting of long distance rates below the level of short haul rates. Since cutting the long haul rate between Chicago and New York made it necessary to also cut short haul rates, the net result was that railroads stopped competing for long haul business by cutting rates. After 1888, Chicago-New York rates were not kept low by competition between railroads. Rates tended to stay at

[6] National Opinion Research Center, *A Personal Interview Survey of College Economics Teachers* (mimeographed).

[7] Chase Manhattan Bank, "321 Economists Comment on Key Public Issues," *Business in Brief,* Nov.-Dec., 1963.

[8] J. R. Meyer, M. J. Peck, J. Stenason and C. Zwick, *The Economics of Competition in the Transportation Industries* (Cambridge: Harvard University Press, 1959).

[9] James C. Nelson, *Railroad Transportation and Public Policy* (Washington: The Brookings Institution, 1959).

[10] P. W. MacAvoy, *Trunk Line Railroad Cartels and the Interstate Commerce Commission 1870-1900: A Case Study of the Effects of Regulation on Price* (multilithed).

the levels railroads had attempted to set by agreement before they had the ICC to run their cartel for them.

We also suffered the usual consequences of cartel operation. High prices induced over-investment in the railroad industry, draining capital from other uses where we needed tools and equipment, creating over-capacity (from which the railroads are still suffering) and causing under-utilization of the available plant because the business available was restricted by high prices. Incidentally, the ICC is now asking for additional legislation from Congress to strengthen its power to operate as a cartel authority.

Still another study in the transportation industry, this time the effect of regulation of the price of transportation of processed foods, has produced shocking findings. This category of transportation was formerly exempt from regulation under the general exemption of agricultural commodities. The exemption was narrowed by the 1958 Transportation Act to exclude processed agricultural commodities. After this phase of transportation came under regulation by the ICC, transportation charges promptly jumped by 20 per cent.[11]

IT IS NOT ONLY the ICC which behaves this way in the transportation industry. The CAB withdrew certification from North American Airlines and drove them out of business after they pioneered air coach transportation. North American carried passengers for 30 per cent lower fares than other airlines, despite the subsidies received by these other airlines, with never an accident during the time they carried 6,000,000 passengers.[12] An intra-state airline (which is exempt from CAB regulation because it flies intra-state) flying today in California from Los Angeles to San Francisco, carries passengers at lower fares than those which prevail on any regulated airline segment of comparable length and traffic density (and makes just as much money on its investment).[13]

The Federal Maritime Board forces all subsidized ship lines to join the ocean conferences which cartelize ocean transportation. Conference-set rates are higher than those charged by ship owners and operators who are not members of the conference. Not only does the Board force higher rates on American shippers, but also follows policies in its construction and operating subsidy program which result in the inefficient design and operation of American ships. American ships carry bigger crews and are more expensive to operate than foreign ships. Since American seamen's wage rates are higher than those of foreign seamen, you would expect labor-saving features to be built into American ships that would not be found on foreign ships. Instead, the reverse is true. Because the operating subsidy provided by the federal government is based on the excess of the American crew costs over foreign crew costs, no subsidized ship operator finds it to any advantage to pay the extra cost of labor-saving equipment.[14]

So much for some of the material developed in a few of the recent studies of the transportation industry. These data are not the sort to make economists feel that the heavy hand of government is beneficent or produces results preferable to those that will occur in a free market.

RECENT STUDIES of public utility regulation do not make this bit of intervention any more appealing, although this is the one area that more economists have agreed upon as being a proper sphere for government intervention than any other. A study of the Federal Power

577

[11] Reported by Dr. George Hilton at the Conference on Regulated Utilities, June 15, 1963, at the Center for Continuing Education, University of Chicago.

[12] For a concise discussion of the CAB see S. Peltzman, "CAB: Freedom from Competition," New Individualist Review, Spring 1963, pp. 16-23.

[13] M. R. Colberg, D. R. Forbush, and G. R. Whitaker, Business Economics (Homewood, Ill.: Irwin, 1964), pp. 130-31.

[14] A. R. Ferguson, E. M. Lerner, J. S. McGee, W. O. Oi, L. A. Rapping, and S. P. Sabotka, The Economic Value of the United States Merchant Marine (Evanston: Northwestern University Press, 1961).

Commission regulation of the natural gas industry has shown that regulated field prices of natural gas sold to interstate pipe line companies are about seven per cent higher than they would be in the absence of regulation of field prices.[15]

A study of the regulation of prices for electric energy reaches the conclusion "that it is very doubtful whether consumers have been saved as much by public regulation of the electrical utilities as they have had to pay, directly and indirectly, for regulation."[16] Another study shows the prices for electricity and gas are *higher* in those states where commissions severely restrict the rate of return on investment (to less than 6½ per cent) than in those which do not. In those jurisdictions where electric companies are allowed to earn more than 6½ per cent return, the average price for 500 KWH to a residential consumer was $9.82. In those jurisdictions where the rate of return was restricted to less than 6½ per cent, the average cost to a residential consumer for 500 KWH per month was $10.14.

A study of gas utilities reached a similar finding. The companies allowed to earn more than 6½ per cent charged $8.62 for 100 therms of residential gas service. Those restricted to less than 6½ per cent charged $10.58 (about 20 per cent more).

Here is a paradox that non-economists find hard to believe, much less understand. How can a company make more by charging less? The answer lies in the fact that those companies allowed to earn more than 6½ per cent can attract the capital which can be used to install cost-saving equipment; allowing them to earn more thus benefits the consumer. Profits in the American economy are, by and large, not made at the expense of the consumer. They are made by doing a better job in production or design of product — by benefitting consumers.

Some sacred cows of those economists who believed most profits are made by monopolizing were slaughtered by this study. Even more, it casts grave doubts on the usefulness of government intervention in the one area which most economists have agreed required regulation to prevent monopolistic exploitation of consumers.

CONCERNING AGRICULTURE, farmers themselves seem to be reaching the conclusion that they are worse off *with* government intervention than without it—or at least wheat farmers seem to have reached this conclusion, judging by the latest wheat referendum. Farmers have found they received higher prices for wheat with government intervention, but they also endure higher costs as a consequence of acreage restrictions on their operations. The Agricultural Program conveys little benefit to most farmers at great expense to every taxpayer. Since farmers have begun to discover this, economists, too, are gradually becoming aware of it.

Some recent studies by agricultural economists have demonstrated that many of the programs supposedly designed to benefit the farmers have been hurting them. It seems obvious that subsidizing the use of fertilizer and machinery would help farmers by reducing their costs of production. What has seemed to be so obviously true turns out to be completely false. The increased output with subsidies has driven prices down with the result that farmers are not any better off. Those who are tenants and obtain their return from their labor are worse off because labor values are decreased by the substitution of fertilizer and equipment.[17] Those who are owner-operators are worse off not only because the return earned by their labor is reduced, but also because that earned by their land is decreased. Fertilizer and equipment are substitutes for land and sub-

[15] R. W. Gerwig, "Natural Gas Production: A Study of the Costs of Regulation," *Journal of Law and Economics*, V (1962), 69-92.

[16] G. J. Stigler, "The Government of the Economy," in Stigler and Samuelson, *op. cit.*, p. 6. See also: G. J. Stigler and C. Friedland, "What Can Regulators Regulate? The Case of Electricity," *The Journal of Law and Economics*, V (Oct. 1962), 1-16.

[17] D. G. Johnson, "Labor Mobility and Agricultural Adjustment," in E. O. Heady, H. G. Diesslin, H. R. Jensen, and G. L. Johnson ed., *Agricultural Adjustment Problems* (Ames, Iowa: Iowa State College Press, 1958), pp. 163-72.

sidizing their use reduces the return to land compared to what it otherwise would be.[18]

The farm p r o g r a m s of the federal government have not only failed to benefit the farmer, but they have also been mutually off-setting with their only net result being a higher tax burden and a waste of resources. The spectacle of multi-billion dollar reclamation programs putting more land under cultivation occurring side-by-side with a soil bank program taking land out of cultivation does not appear to be a more rational management of the economy than that resulting from the operation of free markets. Yet, the main argument of interventionists has been that the government can plan rationally. They have argued that the free market is at best non-rational but usually irrational. In the face of this evidence, it appears that government planning is far more irrational than even the severest critics of free markets could ever impute to the operation of the market.

ANOTHER GREAT disillusionment being suffered by the interventionists is the result of the examination of the programs presumably designed to benefit the poor and the disadvantaged. Urban renewal programs were launched with a great fanfare of propaganda concerning what they would do to improve the housing of the poor. The net result of our urban renewal programs has been increased cost of housing for the poor and the destruction of the livelihoods of hundreds of small businessmen. A typical urban renewal project is one in Chicago which had these results: 4,632 dwellings used by the lowest income groups in Chicago were destroyed. These were replaced by 2,040 apartments now used by middle income families.

In effect, 4,600 low income families were forced out of their homes and told to go find other housing. With the reduced supply of low-rent units, they typically had to pay higher rents in bidding for the remaining supply. A Chicago Housing Authority study of relocation in 1952-1954 showed that the average rent paid by the dispossessed before destruction of their homes was $37 per month. The average rent this group paid after being dispossessed went to $67 per month.[19] It hardly helps the poor to take their homes away and force them to rent more costly residences.

ANOTHER MEASURE which interventionists thought would help the poor was the passage of minimum wage legislation. They believed Sidney and Beatrice Webb, who argued that "higgling in the market" would reduce all wages to bare subsistence (or below). They believed that employers have the power to exploit their employees. All that had to be done to improve the lot of the poor was to pass a law which would stop the exploitation of labor by employers.

As it turned out, it has become evident that employers were paying people what they were worth. As the minimum wage rate has been raised, more and more people have been laid off who were not worth the higher wage rate[20] or have failed to find jobs which would otherwise have been available.[21] They were not being exploited. They were receiving low wage rates because they were not worth any more. The people laid off have been forced to take jobs not covered by the minimum wage law where they received even lower

[18] D. G. Johnson, "Output and Income Effects of Reducing the Farm Labor Force," *Journal of Farm Economics* XLII (Nov. 1960), 779-96.

[19] Cited by Professor Joel Segall in a paper presented at Rockford College, December 2, 1962, from Chicago Housing Authority sources. A published study by The Chicago Housing Authority (*Rehousing Residents Displaced from Public Housing Clearance Sites in Chicago, 1957-58*) showed that the median rent paid by 161 families occupying housing destroyed by the Authority in 1957 was $51/month in the destroyed housing. After relocation, these families paid a median rent of $77 — an increase of 51 per cent.

[20] J. M. Peterson, "Employment Effects of Minimum Wages, 1938-50," *Journal of Political Economy*, LXV (Oct. 1957), 412-30.

[21] D. E. Kaun, *Economics of the Minimum Wage: The Effects of the Fair Labor Standards Act*, (Ph.D. Dissertation, Stanford University, 1964).

579

wage rates than in the jobs they lost[22] or they have remained unemployed. Unemployment among teenagers, for example, has gone from 595,000 in 1949, when the minimum wage rate was $0.40 per hour (and large unemployment might have been expected because this was a depression year), to 979,000 in 1963, a prosperous year, a year in which the minimum wage rate was raised to $1.25 per hour. To the extent that teenagers are inexperienced, unskilled workers, they are the ones who have been priced out of the market by the rise in the minimum wage. Even my interventionist friends are beginning to believe that all teenagers should be exempted from the application of minimum wage laws. Perhaps they will soon learn that we should simply repeal all minimum wage laws.

One more point should, I think, be made in connection with teen-age unemployment. A leading interventionist, Willard Wirtz, Secretary of Labor, believes that the solution to this problem lies in extending compulsory education by another two years. It is typical of the interventionists that they suggest simple answers based on the treatment of all people as if they were identical, homogeneous units. It is typical that they will force people to do what they regard as being good for these people, whether or not those whose freedom is being infringed regard this as desirable. As a matter of fact, the proportion of fourteen to seventeen-year olds in school has increased from 83.3 per cent fifteen years ago to 90.3 per cent today.[23] This is in response to the fact that wage incomes of those with more years of schooling have gone up more than the wage incomes of those less educated.

Of those who are not in school, I would venture the guess that most of them were not finding the schooling available to them useful or rewarding. Forcing them to remain in school would be more likely to reduce the efficiency of the educational process than to improve the skills and make employable these unwilling drinkers at the fountain of knowledge.

FINALLY, LET ME turn to the most telling charge which has been made against free markets. The primary weapon of the socialists in their attack on free enterprise is the business cycle and the suffering caused by cyclical unemployment. If classical liberalism and the *laissez faire* for which it stands is vulnerable to attack, cyclical unemployment is the Achilles heel.

On this score, recent studies of the causes of the business cycle have disclosed that the primary cause is a change in the rate of growth of the stock of money.[24] A turn in the rate of increase in the stock of money is followed by a turn in business and employment. A downturn in the rate of increase in the stock of money is followed by a downturn in employment about six months later, on the average.

Let me describe a few instances: Sharp rises in Federal Reserve rediscount rates and imposition of penalty rates on borrowers occurred in late 1919 and in the first half of 1920. This caused a decline in the stock of money. The reduction in the stock of money was followed by an increase in unemployment from 1.5 million in 1920 to over 5 million persons in 1921.[25]

[22] Y. Brozen, "Minimum Wage Rates and Household Workers," *Journal of Law and Economics*, V (Oct. 1962), 103-9.

[23] U. S. Bureau of the Census, *Statistical Abstract of the United States: 1964* (Washington: U. S. Government Printing Office, 1964), p. 109. For information on the relation of education to income, see *Ibid.*, p. 115.

[24] M. Friedman, "The Demand for Money: Some Theoretical and Empirical Results," *Journal of Political Economy*, LXVII (Aug. 1959), 327-351; M. Friedman and D. Meiselman, "The Relative Stability of Monetary Velocity and the Investment Multiplier in the United States, 1897-1959," in Commission on Money and Credit, *Stabilization Policies* (Englewood Cliffs, N. J.: Prentice-Hall, 1963), pp. 165-268. M. Friedman, "The Monetary Studies of the National Bureau," *The National Bureau Enters Its Forty-Fifth Year* (New York: National Bureau of Economic Research, 1964), pp. 7-25. Annual Report. M. Friedman and A. J. Schwartz, *A Monetary History of the United States* (Princeton: Princeton University Press, 1963).

[25] R. F. Wallace, "The Use of the Progressive Discount Rate by the Federal Reserve System," *Journal of Political Economy*, LXIV (Feb. 1956), 59-68.

580

The contraction of Federal Reserve credit in late 1928 and early 1929 caused a decrease in the stock of money which started unemployment rising.[26] It jumped from 1.6 million in 1929 to over 5 million in 1930. The decline in money stock was intensified after September 1931 by deflationary actions on the part of the Federal Reserve when it panicked over the loss of gold. The result was a horrifying rise in unemployment to over 12 million persons in 1932.

The increases in required reserve ratio by the Federal Reserve Board in August 1936, and again in March 1937, and once again in May 1937, turned the stock of money down and sent unemployment soaring.[27] From approximately 6 million in mid-1937, unemployment rose to over 11 million in 1938.

Turning to the post-war period, fluctuations in unemployment were considerably milder. Nevertheless, we find the same relationship holding between governmental manipulation of the stock of money and unemployment. The rise in the required reserve ratio in February, June and September of 1948, along with other Federal Reserve actions in the government bond market, began a decrease in the stock of money which sent unemployment in 1949 to almost 4 million from the 2 million level of 1948.[28]

Again, in 1952, the Federal Reserve Board reduced the rate of increase in the stock of money.[29] At mid-1953, unemployment started to climb, doubling to about 3.5 million in 1954.

Still again, the Federal Reserve Board reduced the rate of increase in the money supply in 1956.[30] Recession began in mid-1957 and the unemployment level rose to over 5 million in 1958.

In 1959, the Board began limiting the reserves available to banks and started a downturn in the stock of money.[31] Recession began in early 1960 with unemployment again rising to over 5 million in 1961.

I have gone into some detail to show that the primary cause of cyclical unemployment does not lie in the unregulated behavior of free men in free markets. Those who have argued for greater governmental intervention on the grounds that a free enterprise system is unstable have chosen the wrong target for their criticism and the wrong means to cure the problem which worries them. The source of instability has been the government. The cure for instability is less government — not more. We would have less instability if the Federal Reserve Board stopped toying with the supply of money.

The study of the causes of cyclical unemployment has had a great unsettling effect on those economists who have thought we needed more government activity in the economy.[32] Most have not yet accepted the conclusions of the study. They are resisting the recognition that they have been wrong and they have attempted to refute the study. The attempts to date have failed; the data are too overwhelming. Opinion in the profession is starting to swing, even though old ideas do not die easily, especially since repetition seems to be regarded as a more cogent proof of a proposition than any evidence a scholar can offer.[33]

581

---

[26] L. Currie, "The Failure of Monetary Policy to Prevent the Depression of 1929-32," *Journal of Political Economy*, XLII (April 1934), 145-77.

[27] M. Friedman and A. J .Schwartz, *A Monetary History of the United States, 1867-1960* (Princeton: Princeton University Press, 1963), pp. 543-45.

[28] *Ibid.*, pp. 604-610.

[29] "Bank Reserves, Bank Credit and the Money Supply: 1951-1963," *Federal Reserve Bank of St. Louis Review*, XLV (Oct. 1963).

[30] *Ibid.*, pp. 4-5.

[31] *Federal Reserve Bank of of St. Louis Review, Loc. Cit.*

[32] George J. Staller, "Fluctuations in Economic Activity: Planned and Free Market Economies, 1950-1960," *American Economic Review*, LIV (June 1964), 385-95, shows that the eight planned economies of the European Communist Bloc were more unstable than the free market countries composing the Organization for Economic Co-operation and Development in the period of the fifies.

[33] For example, J. A. Schumpeter, *History of Economic Analysis* (New York: Oxford University Press, 1954), has referred to the reluctance of economists to recognize that bank loans create deposits. He remarks, "This is a most interesting illustration of the inhibitions with which analytical advance has to contend and in particular of the fact that people may be perfectly familiar with a phenomenon for ages and even discuss it frequently without realizing its true significance and without admitting it into their general scheme of thought."

I WOULD LIKE to close by quoting an observation of a nineteenth-century German immigrant to America:

Here in America you can see how slightly a people needs to be governed.... Here are governments, but no rulers — governors, but they are clerks. All the great educational establishments, the churches, the great means of transportation, etc., that are being organized here—almost all of these things owe their existence not to official authority, but to the spontaneous cooperation of private individuals. It is only here that you realize how superfluous governments are in many affairs in which, in Europe, they are considered entirely indispensable, and how the opportunity of doing something inspires a desire to do it.[34]

The most telling and effective recent evidence casting doubt on the beneficence of government and the presumed inability of free markets to serve the common good, and such social goals as improving the lot of the average man, is provided by the "miracle" of West Germany[35] and Japan, and the failure of the socialized governments in the Iron Curtain countries. We might put this in the words of a recent cartoon showing two Russian officials chatting with each other. One is saying, "When all the world is Communist, where will we get wheat?"

---

[34] Carl Schurz, in one of his writings.

[35] See E. Sohmen, "Competition and Growth: The Lesson of West Germany," *American Economic Review*, XLIX (Dec. 1959), 936-1003. J. Hennessy, V. Lutz, and G. Scimone, *Economic "Miracles"* (London: Andre Deutsch, 1964).

Reprints of this article are available from *New Individualist Review*. Single copy, 15 cents. Ten or more copies, 10 cents each.

Constitutional Mythology

GORDON TULLOCK

MYTHS, AS A PART of literature, can be entertaining and even illuminating, but if they are believed and acted upon they can be dangerous. There is such a dangerous myth which is widely believed at the present time by Americans. This myth, that "the Constitution is what the Supreme Court says it is," has the logical corollary that no action taken by the Supreme Court can be unconstitutional, and hence that decisions by the court are binding upon the executive and legislative branches. If the myth were true, then it would mean that the system of checks and balances set up in our constitution is incomplete. The powers of the legislative and executive branches are subject to checks, but those of the judicial branch are uncontrolled. Given the care which the drafters of that historic document obviously took to give no person or organization absolute power, this would be most surprising. The founders of our nation did not feel that the form of government they established could safely be trusted to the good will or self-restraint of any individual or body of men. Instead they built into the structure of government a system in which possible abuse of power by any branch could be checked by the others. If the popular myth of supreme court supremacy were true, then we would have to conclude that the found-

ing fathers distrusted the elected legislature and the elected president, but somehow felt no suspicion of the appointed supreme court. Surely this is absurd.

The power of the Supreme Court to declare acts of Congress unconstitutional was first established in the famous case of *Marbury v. Madison* by Chief Justice John Marshall. It is interesting that this case concerned a "plain violation" of the rights of five individuals. The Court refused to take action to redress the wrong to these individuals because it held that the act which gave them the right to sue before its bar was unconstitutional. In other words, it put enforcement of the Constitution above human rights. The reasoning upon which it did so is still the foundation of the doctrine of unconstitutionality.

Marshall's argument, adhered to by all commentators from his day to the present, may be summed up by one paragraph from his decision:

> Certainly all those who have framed w r i t t e n constitutions contemplate them as forming the fundamental and paramount law of the nation, and consequently, the theory of every such government must be, that an act of the legislature, repugnant to the constitution, is void.[1]

Clearly this paragraph would make as much sense if the words "executive" or "judiciary" were substituted for "legislature." The view that the executive or

---

Gordon Tullock is Associate Professor of Economics at the University of Virginia. His latest book is *The Politics of Bureaucracy;* he is co-author of *The Calculus of Consent.*

---

[1] *Marbury v. Madison,* 5 U. S. (1 Cranch) 137, 177 (1803).

Page Thirteen

the judiciary is not bound by the Constitution would as much subvert the document as the view that the legislature is not so bound. It is true, of course, that we must not expect to find the court announcing that its own acts are unconstitutional, any more than we should expect to find the legislature passing laws which it explicitly states are unconstitutional. In each case the constitutional check is imposed from the outside, not by a given branch of the government judging its own acts.

The same principle will be found to fit the remainder of *Marbury v. Madison*. Marshall was a judicial officer engaged in deciding whether he would obey a law duly passed by the legislature and signed by the President. As such he confined his language to this particular problem and did not discuss the complementary problems which would arise if the court made an unconstitutional determination. Nevertheless, his language is still convincing if it is applied to the converse problem. As an illustration let us make the necessary changes for two and a half paragraphs:

> If, then, the [executive] is to regard the constitution, and the constitution is superior to any [judicial decision], the constitution and not such [decision], must govern the case to which they both apply.
> Those, then, who controvert the principle that the constitution is to be considered, [by the executive], as a paramount law, are reduced to the necessity of maintaining that the [President] must close [his] eyes on the constitution and see only the [decision].
> This doctrine would subvert the very foundation of all written constitutions. It would declare that . . . [a decision] which, according to the principles and theory of our government, is entirely void, is yet, in practice, completely obligatory. . . .[2]

THE CONTRARY VIEW, that decisions of the Supreme Court are superior to the Constitution because "the Constitution is what the Supreme Court says it is" has never been claimed by the

Court, although a Chief Justice once said this in a speech. The Court in its decisions always claims that it is bound by the Constitution. It does not purport to have the power to change the Constitution, only to interpret and to apply it. It is, of course, true that the Constitution is a rather short document and almost 175 years old for the most part. Interpretation under these circumstances may frequently involve interstitial law making; in fact this is the main function of the Supreme Court. There is, however, a great difference between deciding what the Constitution should mean in an area where it is unclear, and deliberately going against the plain words of the document. A decision, for example, that the Senate must be elected according to population would clearly and obviously be unconstitutional.

Marshall, however, had one more problem after he had demonstrated that the Constitution was superior to the acts of a branch of the government; he had to show that the Court was charged with a duty of enforcing the Constitution. His method was simple: he pointed out that the Constitution "direct[s] the judges to take an oath to support it."

> This oath certainly applies in an especial manner, to their conduct in their official character. How immoral to impose it on them, if they were to be used as the instruments, and the knowing instruments, for violating what they swear to support![3]

Continuing this line of reasoning, the final full paragraph of his decision reads:

> Thus, the particular phraseology of the constitution of the United States confirms and strengthens the principle, supposed to be essential to all written constitutions, that a law repugnant to the constitution is void; and that *courts,* as well as other departments, are bound by that instrument.[4]

The argument, again, makes as much sense if the name of another department is substituted for that of the judiciary, as Marshall explicitly recognizes in the

---

584

[2] 5 U. S. (1 Cranch) at 178.

[3] 5 U. S. (1 Cranch) at 180.
[4] 5 U. S. (1 Cranch) at 180. (Italics in original.)

last full line of the above quotation. The same sentence of the Constitution which requires judges to support the Constitution also requires legislators, and other officials of the government, to swear to support it. Surely the oath is not more binding on one class of officials than on another. Let us repeat our experiment and substitute the executive for the judiciary in two more paragraphs of this fundamental decision:

> Why does . . . [the President] swear to discharge his duties agreeably to the constitution of the United States, if that constitution forms no rule for his government? if it is closed upon him, and cannot be inspected by him?
> If such be the real state of things, this is worse than solemn mockery. To prescribe, or to take this oath, becomes equally a crime.[5]

It is hard to see why this is less reasonable as a matter of constitutional law than the original version. If Chief Justice Marshall's reasoning was correct for the judiciary, clearly it is also correct for the executive and the legislature.

My argument that the Congress and the Executive also have responsibilities for preserving and protecting the Constitution, although it would have been acceptable to such liberals as Justices Black and Douglas in the late thirties, will be vigorously contested today. The argument which may be offered against it is that there must be a single ultimate authority to decide constitutional problems, and that the Supreme Court is that authority. This can be divided into two parts, an argument that a single authority is logically necessary, and that the Constitution established such an authority in the Supreme Court. The first, or logical, argument, although superficially plausible, is fairly easily answered. It would, of course, be impossible to have two or three bodies each issuing authoritative interpretations of the Constitution if these interpretations were equally binding upon the citizen and likely to conflict. We are not, however, faced with a dilemma of choosing between two equally unattrac-tive alternatives, the one involving multiple and possibly conflicting authorities with power to interpret the Constitution and the other involving a single arbitrary authority. If the founding fathers had seen the problem in this light they would surely not have set up an appointed body as the ultimate sovereign. They had just fought a war to free themselves from the control of appointive royal governors, and there is no reason to believe that they would have wished to place themselves and their descendants under the complete control of a body of men who were not removable no matter how bad their decisions.

THAT THE DRAFTERS of the Constitution did not even think in terms of giving ultimate power to the Court can be readily seen from the provision of the Constitution that "the Supreme Court shall have appellate Jurisdiction, both as to Law and Fact, with such Exceptions, and under such Regulations as the Congress shall make." (Article III, Section 2.) The right of Congress to make exceptions in the jurisdiction of the Supreme Court, upheld by that Court in *Ex Parte McCardle*,[6] a case involving civil rights, is clearly inconsistent with the view that the Court is the ultimate authority on constitutional questions.

If we return to *Marbury v. Madison* we see that Marshall did not claim any sort of ultimate authority for the Court. He simply said that where he thought the Constitution and a law conflicted he would carry out his oath of office and refuse to enforce the law. Until very recently this purely negative concept of the duty of the courts in constitutional questions was the dominant theory. The whole subject was traditionally described under the rubric of "judicial review," and that review amounted to "little more than the negative power to disregard an unconstitutional enactment."[7] This negative view of the problem of protecting the Constitution raises none of the logical problems of conflict-

585

---

5 5 U. S. (1 Cranch) at 180.

[6] 74 U. S. (7 Wall.) 506 (1868).
[7] Massachusetts v. Mellon, 262 U. S. 447, 488 (1923).

ing determinations of constitutionality while at the same time avoiding the grant of ultimate power to one body. Normally any act of the government will require the co-operation of two or three of the main branches of government. If the act initiated by one branch is constitutional, the other branches are required to co-operate. If the initial act, on the other hand, is unconstitutional then the other branches are required by the oaths that their officers have taken to uphold the Constitution, to refuse to play any part in destroying the constitutional guarantees. This is the famous system of "checks and balances" which the drafters of the Constitution thought more desirable than dependence upon the good will and self-restraint of a small body of men.

In practice, of course, the bodies initiating action in our system have normally been the legislature and the executive. The courts, until very recently, seldom took the initiative. This meant that most cases in point have been resolved through refusal by the courts to carry out unconstitutional acts of the legislature rather than through refusal by the legislature or executive to enforce unconstitutional decisions of the courts. The only major effort at judicial legislation prior to the last two decades was the Dred Scott case, which was, quite rightly, not enforced by many state governments and reversed "on the slight, bare slopes of Gettysburg." However, the recent outburst of judicial activism, which contrasts so strongly with the restraint characterizing previous courts even in the exercise of their negative power of judicial review, has raised an essentially new problem. Although the court still talks the language of simply applying the Constitution, it now acts as though it were a sort of superior legislature, not only imposing new laws, but also actually changing the Constitution by its decisions. No longer are constitutional decisions largely limited to refusals to enforce laws; they now frequently take the form of positive orders to other branches of the government and general rules for the control of citizens. Most of the civil rights cases and the reapportionment decisions are of this nature.

Under these circumstances the right of the other branches to "check" the Supreme Court by refusing to apply its decisions when they violate the Constitution, a right long held in abeyance, becomes a matter of first importance.

Even if a supreme authority is not logically necessary in a system where each branch checks the others, it might still be true that the Constitution did establish such an ultimate arbiter in the form of the Supreme Court. This is, however, not the case, for there is nothing in the language of Article III of the Constitution which directly assigns to the Supreme Court any special duties with respect to the Constitution. If the Constitution conferred such special powers on the Court it did so implicitly, not explicitly; and it is hard to see where supreme power is implied for the Supreme Court. The judiciary is given "the judicial power of the United States." If they had been written in 1964, these words might be construed as implying arbitrary power of the Court to interpret the Constitution in any way it sees fit. But this mythological view of judicial power was not held in 1789. Nor did Marshall claim such power. He made only the following claim:

> So if a law be in opposition to the constitution; if both the law and the constitution apply to a particular case, so that the court must either decide that case conformably to the law, disregarding the constitution; or conformably to the constitution, disregarding the law; the court must determine which of these conflicting rules governs the case. This is of the very essence of judicial duty.[8]

The statement of the role of the Court is acceptable; but it is also a duty of the executive to decide which of two conflicting laws is to be enforced, especially if one of these laws is the Constitution itself.

THE PRESIDENT HOLDS a unique status in that the Constitution itself specifies the content of the oath he must take on assuming office. This oath concludes with the words "[I] will, to the

---

[8] 5 U. S. (1 Cranch) at 178.

best of my Ability, preserve, protect, and defend the Constitution of the United States." The obligation devolving on the President is clearly more weighty than the mere duty "to support" the Constitution, the requirement specified for oaths to be subscribed to by all other officials including judges. In carrying out his duty to execute the laws, the President must, of course, make constitutional decisions. If he feels that a given law enacted by Congress is unconstitutional, he may veto it; and this is one of the reasons given by presidents for their vetoes. If an unconstitutional law is passed, he must follow his oath and refuse to enforce it. This, although it may appear novel, is simply a description of what the President has always done. The Attorney General frequently considers the constitutionality of various laws, and his rulings on such points are normally accepted by the executive arm.

A particularly interesting case has arisen in recent years with respect to defense appropriations. Congress quite frequently feels that some certain arm or weapon is more important than the executive believes. Congress has, therefore, tried to get the executive to spend more money than the Department of Defense requests for such arms, and it may put a specific provision in the appropriation act requiring that the money be spent. The intent of such provisions is to give the President the choice of vetoing the entire defense appropriation or spending the money. Since Truman, however, the executive branch has uniformly held that such provisions are unconstitutional and hence has refused to carry them out. No court was involved in this highly important decision on a constitutional issue, and clearly it does not involve any usurpation of judicial power by the executive.

The members of Congress are not only sworn to support the Constitution; they also tend to run heavily to lawyers, and hence are apt to be interested in constitutional questions. The question of whether a given measure is constitutional is frequently discussed on the floor of the two houses, and a consensus seems to prevail to the effect that unconstitutional acts should not be passed.

If the President requests legislation which appears to the members of Congress to be unconstitutional, they should refuse to pass it. It is always a little hard to determine exactly why Congress has taken any given action since there will normally be many different arguments offered by different members; but it is reasonably clear that there have been occasions when legislation has been rejected or modified for constitutional reasons. Again this involves no usurpation of judicial prerogatives. Congress is unique in that the Constitution specifically limits its power to making "Laws which shall be necessary and proper for carrying into Execution the foregoing Powers, and all other Powers vested by this Constitution in the Government of the United States. . . ." Surely Congressmen asked to appropriate money for a purpose they believe unconstitutional may refuse. The view that Congress shall refrain from considering constitutional questions is not only absurd but also directly contrary to the established practice of our government.

Thus it is not only the Constitution, but long established practice, which gives to each of the three branches of the government the right to check the others if their acts are unconstitutional. The Supreme Court has seldom experienced such checks, but this simply reflects the fact that it has seldom taken positive action which required checking. Surely the restraint of previous judges does not give the present Court positive powers to do anything it wishes.

The well thought out plan of checks and balances is completely negated by the myth of judicial supremacy. Only if we feel assured that the Justices are not like other men, that they neither make mistakes nor try to extend their authority, will we favor a system giving them ultimate power. Our officials are sworn to uphold the Constitution, not the Supreme Court. Where judicial decisions conflict with the Constitution they should keep their oath and uphold the Constitution. The statesmen who drew up our Constitution did not leave the protection of our liberties solely to nine fallible men.

587

Page Seventeen

Prospects for South Africa

DENIS V. COWEN

THIS PAPER IS concerned with the political future of South Africa; that is to say, the future of some 16 million people occupying a territory approximately one-third the size of the United States, in one of the most richly endowed, beautiful and temperate zones of the earth's surface. These 16 million people, my fellow South African citizens, are quite normal, friendly human beings, with ordinary human virtues and vices; but they are troubled and perplexed — and in varying degrees, humbled — by the tremendous challenge in human relations which faces them.

Most readers are aware of the broad outlines of the South African government's racial policy — a policy which has excited so much attention and criticism in the international community that I need do little more than mention its essential features.

The South African government of the day — which has been in power for some sixteen years — does not believe that there is any future for any political system whereunder the various racial and cultural groups in South Africa would live together on terms of equality in one undivided country. Some 10.5 million blacks of the full blood, belonging to several tribes, speaking several Bantu

languages, and at varying stages of development, cannot, they say, form a stable political structure on terms of equality with 3.5 million whites who wish to preserve their own cultural heritage. In addition, there are a half-million Asians and 1.5 million people of mixed blood, who live mainly in Cape Province. Whites, for their part, belong to two groups having much in common, but yet they each have their distinctive character; 60 per cent (nearly 2 million) are Afrikaans-speaking (i.e., their home language is Afrikaans, though most of them speak English as well), and Calvinist in religion. The remaining 40 per cent are primarily English-speaking and either more tolerantly Protestant (Episcopalian, Presbyterian, Congregationalist), or Roman Catholic in religion. About 5 per cent of the whites are Jewish. In short, not only is South Africa multi-racial; it is multi-cultural.

Given such a population structure, any attempt to share political power between whites and non-whites in a single political system is seen by most whites as involving self-immolation. "One man, one vote" in an undivided society, or anything which may lead to it, it is said, would involve cultural suicide and the eventual abandonment of a way of life. The blacks, it is argued, would "swamp" the whites; and what is more, as they are on the whole the "have-nots," the character of the economy would soon be changed out of all recognition.

Denis V. Cowen is currently Professor of Law at the University of Chicago Law School. He was formerly Dean of the Law Faculty at the University of Cape Town.

PLACING NO FAITH in constitutional guarantees and devices for minority protection — which have tended in many parts of Africa, and indeed in South Africa itself, to be mere scraps of paper — the overwhelming majority of South African whites accordingly feel that there is no health in any deliberate attempt to bring about a common political society between blacks and whites. In this predicament, the better hope, they argue, lies in the opposite direction — it should be, in short, in the direction of "separate development" of the main racial groups in their own homelands, leading to eventual independence or partition. At the same time, it is recognized that the various population groups — black and white — are now, and are likely to remain, very largely economically interdependent, whatever their political future may be. European nations, it is argued, are a similar case; and the Common Market is taking care of the resulting organizational problem. Accordingly, Dr. Verwoerd would like to see political separation, coupled at the same time with increasing economic integration, not only between the population groups of South Africa, but also between the various South African groups, on the one hand, and the African states north of the Limpopo, on the other.

That, in basic outline, is Dr. Verwoerd's plan for separate development; stated, I hope, as fairly — though not as eloquently — as he would state it in equally short compass. Nothing would be easier than to show the defects in this policy. Indeed, even its ardent supporters recognize that, given the most favorable circumstances, the achievement of Dr. Verwoerd's goals would take many years; would involve great sacrifices on the part of the whites, if the eventual partition is to be fair; and that in the intervening years there would be many injustices and anomalies.

Meanwhile, under the guidance of a very efficient administration (as efficient as any in South Africa's history) the country continues to prosper — even to boom — economically. Industrially and economically speaking, South Africa is the continent's giant, so far in advance of

all the rest that economists do not even group South Africa along with other African territories. Much the same is true of education and the organization of the learned professions.

But beneath the fair surface there is tension; and the cost of implementing the government's racial policy is very high in terms of human suffering. Having written several detailed indictments of the policy myself,[1] it is not my intention to repeat the performance now. I have not changed my convictions about the basic immorality of racialism. Nor have I changed my opinion about the economic and political arrangements in South Africa. I still hope and believe that one day racial tension will no longer exist in a fully integrated South Africa. At this stage, however, I think that it is more profitable to call attention to certain facts which tend to be overlooked in discussions about South Africa; to say why I believe that my country has a very good chance of pulling through to the achievement of a satisfactory future; and to give some idea of what may, I think, be done to help.

One will appreciate that I speak without any brief from either the exponents or the critics of the South African government's policies. The only brief I hold is *for* my country, and *all* its people.

Perhaps the best way to present my subject is to deal with it under three headings.

First, I would like to review briefly why it is that South Africa matters; why her political future deserves the very serious attention and encouragement of people beyond her borders.

Second, I would invite the reader to look at the South African scene from the point of view of what, in the past, has actually happened, and what, in the future, is likely to happen—as distinct from what some of us would have liked to have seen, or may yet wish to see take place. In other words, I suggest that it

589

——
[1] See, e.g. "Call for a Dialogue in South Africa," *New York Times*, May 17, 1964, Sec. 6, p. 19 *et seq. The Foundations of Freedom* (Oxford: Oxford University Press, 1961). *Liberty, Equality, Fraternity Today* (Johannesburg: South Africa Institute of Race Relations, 1961).

may be useful to focus attention on the actual facts, and try to predict probable events as distinct from speculating as to what *ought* to have happened and what *ought* yet to be. Under this heading, it is my intention to place before you — somewhat bluntly and flat-footedly — a series of axioms about South Africa.

Third, while concentrating on the "is," and the "likely to be," rather than the "ought to be," it may be useful for me to suggest a few maxims concerning what may be done to help the situation in South Africa; and, in particular, what sort of action should be avoided, as being calculated to aggravate the present distemper rather than cure it, for I would not like it to be thought that we should have no interest in the sphere of the "ought-to-be."

I have been induced to adopt this method of treatment (that is to say, the formulation of axioms and maxims), because a similar procedure was recently used in an article by Mr. Philip Mason, in the October 1964 issue of *Foreign Affairs*.[2] With some of Mr. Mason's conclusions I am in complete agreement. From others, however, I would differ sharply. Nevertheless, I would commend his article to you, suggesting my own remarks as required supplementary — dare I say, corrective — reading!

AT THE LEVEL of international power politics, South Africa's significance is considerable, although she is not yet a member of the nuclear club. At summit conferences, and notably in the lobbies of the United Nations, a determined effort is being made by the Afro-Asian bloc to bring the South African government to its knees, as the saying goes. More particularly, Britain and the United States, South Africa's two largest trading partners, are being told that continued trade with South Africa bolsters up and encourages a regime which the Afro-Asian nations regard as

an affront to their dignity and self respect. Accordingly, they are asking for a full scale trade boycott, backed by a blockade. They say, quite bluntly, that Britain and the United States must choose between them and South Africa.

The threat must be taken seriously. Not only would it be difficult to overestimate the determination of the Afro-Asian bloc to bring about a change in the political structure of South Africa, but a suitable occasion for involving the older and greater powers may actually present itself in the near future. Thus, it is quite possible (some say it is very probable) that next year the International Court at the Hague may feel itself compelled to give judgment against South Africa in regard to her administration of the South West African Mandate, and to call u p o n Dr. Verwoerd's government to abandon their racial policies in that territory. It is by no means clear that the judgment will, in fact, go against South Africa; but if it does, and if South Africa refuses to comply with the court's order (which, again, is not a foregone conclusion), the United States and Britain — being pledged to uphold the rule of law — might find it difficult to resist a call for immediate sanctions; and this could be the flash point for a major international confrontation.

In any event, whichever way the South West African judgment goes, the Afro-Asian bloc — aided and abetted by Russia and China, who seek, I believe quite cynically, merely to make political capital out of their "support" in terms of the overall "cold war" — will continue to press for international intervention in South Africa. In a world bemused with argument and agitation about skin color, South Africa has become a convenient pawn in a power struggle towards ends which have nothing to do with color.

Already there have been several resolutions in the General Assembly which make it abundantly clear that the South West African issue is only *one* string in the bow of the Afro-Asian block. To change the metaphor, it is no more than a convenient *casus belli*. Whatever happens in the World Court on that issue,

———
[2] P. Mason, "South Africa and the World, Some Maxims and Axioms," *Foreign Affairs*, Oct. 1964, p. 150.

they insist that there are bigger issues at stake. South Africa, they assert, presents a unique case in the modern world of a denial of human rights on the score of color. It is said that the denial of rights is so flagrant and unique that the issue cannot possibly be regarded as a domestic one; that it is, accordingly, the legitimate business of the world community; and, more particularly, the duty of the world community to put an end to the outrage.

It may be observed that quite apart from this very high-tensioned legal and moral question, South Africa also matters at the international level because it is the world's greatest producer of gold, uranium, and diamonds; one of the world's greatest producers of wool, and possesses vast deposits of coal and iron ore and other minerals. In addition, its industrial growth in recent decades has been phenomenal. None of the larger powers can be indifferent to the question of who controls this wealth and for what purpose. Indeed, only a few months ago, Dr. Nkrumah of Ghana let one of his cats out of one of his bags when he declared that South Africa's mineral wealth rightly belongs to black Africans, to be shared north of the Limpopo.[3]

At a very much deeper level, South Africa matters, too, because it presents the world's race and color problems in microcosm. If these problems can be satisfactorily resolved in South Africa — and when I say "satisfactorily," I mean at depth, with roots in sincere conviction, and not merely on the surface, or in unwilling token compliance with law — if these problems can be solved in South Africa, something enduring will have been wrought for the benefit of the world as a whole. In this regard, one will recall that the ratio between whites and non-whites in South Africa is approximately the same as the overall world ratio. Moreover, pressures and tensions are felt at the same points — that is to say, in regard to opportunities for education, jobs, housing, social and marriage relations, and in the churches.

THUS FAR I HAVE emphasized South Africa's significance from the point of view of shared international concern. At the same time, it should be borne in mind that South African affairs may also — all too easily and all too unfortunately — become part of the domestic political power struggle in the U.S. and Great Britain. One may recall how Israel's affairs long bedeviled local American politics. It should not be overlooked that today American Negroes not only hold something very like a balance of domestic political power, but they are tending increasingly to identify their own "freedom fight" with the "freedom fight" of their "black brothers in Africa." (I am quoting Dr. Martin Luther King.) Indeed, on this whole aspect, Dr. King's recent acceptance speech, when receiving the Nobel Peace Prize, is full of significance.[4]

And now having tried to put my subject into broad perspective, it is time for me to get down to the facts. I turn, therefore, to the enumeration of a few suggested axioms — or brief statements — concerning the essential and often overlooked facts of South African life.

First Axiom: My first axiom relates to the importance of cleaving to *facts*, as distinct from myths, illusions, and falsehoods about South Africa. Moreover, it is essential not only to cleave to facts, but to have regard to *all* the relevant facts, and not merely a selected group of facts; and, further, it is no less essential to weigh the facts *dispassionately*, and in full perspective. All this is emphatically not easy, because — and here is my first axiom — the South African situation, or racial predicament, is highly *complex*, shot through with deep emotion, conditioned by historical events, and, in the result, one may be sure that the surface appearance is almost invariably misleading.

Too many of the alleged friends of liberalism in the modern world approach the facts of the South African racial situation (and indeed other racial situations) with *fixed inflexible ideas*—sometimes based on sheer expediency; often

591

---

[3] *New York Times*, July 10, 1964, p. 2.

[4] *New York Times*, Dec. 11, 1964, p. 33.

with no rationally based or other deep-seated convictions; yet they cling to and brandish their ideas with a bigotry, self-righteousness, rancor, and prejudice, which is the very negation of true liberalism.

Beware of the professional "do gooders"; also beware of both the professional apologists for, and the professional critics of, South Africa. Both are likely to be wide of the mark.

To hear some of the white-washers of South Africa talk, one would imagine that the country has no problems *at all.* They fool nobody but themselves. On the other hand, to hear some of its traducers hold forth, one would imagine that the whites spend all their time killing and torturing the blacks.

Second Axiom: South Africa presents a situation to live with and improve, not a "problem" capable of instant solution.

Most of South Africa's critics, well meaning though they may be, tend to overlook the magnitude and frightful difficulty of the human situation with which we are concerned. We speak of a "color problem" as if one could "solve" (that is to say, "remove") it by an effort of the will and the intelligence. This is almost pathetically naive! There is no room here for easy generalizations in terms of "good guys and bad guys." Nor is there any one magic formula which will dissolve the dark clouds. Certainly "one man—one vote" is not the answer—potent as that slogan may have been in some parts of Africa as a weapon in the early stages of the struggle for political power or emancipation, as distinct from the achievement of prosperity or true freedom. Dr. Nkrumah's "Seek ye first the political Kingdom and all else will be added unto you" is not only sacriligious, but also over-simplistic.

We should be constantly on guard against over-simplifying the South African scene in terms of one issue. The black man's effort to better himself in the modern world is often regarded as being simply and solely a color struggle —an effort to erase color-prejudice. This is an over-simplification. It is probably

nearer the mark to suggest that what is taking place the world over is a vast revolution in which social, economic, and educational opportunities are being redistributed. The non-whites are, on the whole, the "have-nots" and color tends to be the external and visible sign of a pressure point in a social and economic process. The process itself, however, is not exclusively, and maybe not even basically, concerned with color.

Let me hasten to add that when I say that South Africa's predicament may have to be "lived with" rather than "solved," I am not being an apologist for much that is deplorable in present government policies. I say this because in the semi-lunacy which pervades some so-called "liberal" circles, if one does not support violent and bloody revolution in South Africa, one tends to be sworn at as being a "white supremacist."

Nor am I a complacent believer in a policy of drift, against which Mr. Mason rightly inveighs. I do not believe that the mere passage of time necessarily brings about an improvement in human affairs. On the contrary, it is obvious that human situations may be lived with more or less successfully. And South Africa is not being all that successful!

Again, I do not advocate inaction. But on the other hand, I most emphatically repudiate the proposition that *any* action is better than no action. What we need is *wise* action — effective action— about which I shall have a little to say under the heading of Maxims. Wisdom is often the product of old fashioned and (among the shallow) discredited virtues, such as honesty and humility.

Third Axiom: Bad as apartheid, or separate development, are — and, let me repeat, I would not even try to defend any of the acts of stupidity and cruelty which have been perpetrated in its name —no one has yet come up with an alternative, *which would be acceptable to both whites and non-whites.* In fact, apartheid, like democracy, may be the worst form of government; but at the moment, *as a matter of practical politics,* there is nothing better in sight. Indeed, those who are serious-minded and sincere enough to get beyond vague generalities (such as, *something* must be done!), differ hopelessly as to what *specific* form of government should replace the p r e s e n t dispensation.[5] The Afro-Asian bloc gets no further than the proposition: Leave the basic political structure to the decision of all the people of South Africa on a one man—one vote basis at a national convention. And this the whites will not soon or willingly accept. Any proposed change in South Africa must be acceptable to the whites as well as to the blacks if peace and inter-racial harmony are to result.

Fourth Axiom: No alternative blueprint for South Africa's future has any chance of *sticking* unless the whites, as well as the non-whites, want it and willingly accept it.

In elaboration of this axiom, I would remind you that in no sense of the term are the 3.5 million whites in South Africa colonists. Many of them have been in the country as long as the white man has been in America. They have no other home. What is more, they have as good a title to some of the country as the Bantu-speaking settlers, who arrived at about the same time from the north. The whites are grimly determined to stay on in South Africa, and I have no doubt that they will do so. For one thing, the dominant Afrikaans-speaking group have their own language, their own church, and their own mores, for the preservation of which they fought grimly over a period of many generations. They will fight to the death for them now. In this they would, I believe, be joined by the English-speaking whites.

Indeed, the population as a whole — white as well as non-white — are bent on *working out their own destiny*. What is more, despite talk to the contrary, I believe that many South African non-whites would resent outside interference

as bitterly as the whites.

Fifth Axiom: There is no likelihood of a local black revolution ever developing or succeeding in South Africa, unless it is aided and abetted by the great powers abroad. Certainly there will be no Congo, no Algeria, no Zanzibar in South Africa unless the great powers, and in particular the United States and Great Britain, deliberately cripple South Africa's economy and her government.

My reasons for this conclusion are:

(a) The South African whites are strong and determined. Rightly or wrongly, they believe that for them all is at stake. Above all, they believe in themselves. However perplexed they may be by their problems, they are tough and effective.

(b) The vital immediate decisions concerning South Africa are being taken and will, during the foreseeable future, continue to be taken *in South Africa*. In other words, the kind of withdrawal action which an external metropolitan power took in respect of, say, the Congo, Algeria, or Zanzibar, is simply "not on" in South Africa. Mr. Wilson, the present Prime Minister of England, may, perhaps, call the vital shots in Southern Rhodesia. I cannot see his doing so in South Africa.

(c) The more aggressive local opposition to apartheid has either been silenced or induced to acquiesce in the emerging patterns now being devised very largely by the whites. At the same time, I am bound to confess that I regard this silencing of black leadership as a seriously unhealthy factor. I am worried by the fact that so many of the articulate black political leaders are in jail, both because (quite apart from the humanities) I believe it necessary to encourage the fullest dialogue at all levels, and because a suppressed political view-point tends to become a political cancer. But at present I am concerned to state facts, not evaluate them.

(d) The spread of wealth in South Africa (uneven as it is between black and white) and, especially, the geography of South Africa are unfavorable to revolution. To begin with, economically,

593

---

[5] My own formula for a non-racial, fully democratic federal form of government, with a court-enforced bill of rights—elaborated at length in my book *Foundations of Freedom*—is one of several proposed "alternatives" to the present dispensation, which as yet has made no serious impact.

the whites and the non-whites are too heavily interdependent. Secondly, the overall economic conditions are not nearly bad enough for revolution. Compared with black states in the North, and with many other states in the world, South Africa's non-whites are indeed, on the whole, economically fairly well off. Thirdly, the South African terrain is open and free from jungle; and, finally, the bland, sunny weather is just too good to encourage and sustain a violent revolution.

The point I am making is that South African affairs *need not* necessarily come to a crisis point, unless this is deliberately engineered by the great powers.

Sixth Axiom: If the great powers were to heed the Afro-Asian call to bring the South African government to its knees, the consequence would be extremely grave. Assuming that economic sanctions (and they would have to be universal and total), coupled with a naval blockade, *could* bring South Africa to her knees (and that is a very big assumption), how thereafter, I ask, in the ensuing chaos, would the country be governed? An immediate consequence, I believe, would be the need for indefinite international police action. White resistance would be stiffened and great and lasting bitterness would ensue. Not only would it be difficult for foreign powers to maintain peace in the presence of an embittered white minority, with the black majority clamoring for change, but the problem of restoring South Africa as a peaceful, productive, and independent country would, to say the least, be most formidable.

Seventh Axiom: One of the greatest threats to a sane outcome in South Africa — as, indeed, to sanity and health anywhere in Africa — is the ugly growth of anti-whiteism in the modern world. The whites, no doubt, have done much to bring this upon themselves, but it is often despicably nourished by white "freedom fighters" (for a variety of their own reasons). White racism is infernally evil; black racism, let me add, is no less evil — a point which I was delighted to hear Mr. Adlai Stevenson

Page Twenty-four

make (at long last) in the United Nations recently.[6]

Eighth Axiom: My eighth and last axiom is perhaps the most important. Most people in South Africa — including, let me emphasize, a great many Afrikaners — recognize that changes in South Africa's political structure must come about. The white man knows and concedes that he cannot survive as a dominating and privileged minority. But, while the outside world clamors for change, *it is all too often overlooked that changes are, in fact, taking place.*

Barely three years ago, in my book *The Foundations of Freedom,* I criticized the Bantustan experiment in the Transkei on the score that it was retrograde and undemocratic, more particularly because the idea of popular voting was entirely excluded as being alien to the Bantu mentality.

The government's policy has since changed radically; under the revised Transkeian constitution voting is now allowed to take place on a substantial scale — a definite step, in my view, in the right direction; and so this particular piece of criticism largely falls away.

EVIDENCE OF CHANGE for the better is manifest to anyone who is honest enough to keep his eyes open, and humble enough not to expect the immediate advent of the millenium.

This is especially true in South Africa's industrial life; African minimum wages are rising steadily; last February the Minister of Labour stated in the Senate that there would be no ceiling to the skills Africans would be allowed to acquire in the border areas (a change in policy which has enormous possibilities); and, in the big cities, the wastefulness and inequity of "job reservation" is beginning to break down in the face of economic realities.

Again, a few years ago, it would have been unthinkable for Nationalist newspapers to refer to Africans as "Mr." and "Mrs." This is now being done. This may be a trivial point to those who have

6 *New York Times,* Dec. 15, 1964, p. 16.

no experience of, or sympathy with, South Africa; but for anyone familiar with the history of this country, it is by no means an insignificant change, and — to many — most encouraging.

In short, the situation still holds within it elements of fluidity. While some doors are shutting, others are opening.

I have said that in my view the South African situation has within it elements of fluidity. It is of cardinal importance to keep the situation fluid, and to avoid inducing an overall rigidity through malicious action, or short-sighted action. What, then, can be done to help; and what in the first place, should be avoided? These questions bring me to the enumeration of a few maxims.

First Maxim: There is no health in attempting to fight evil with evil. More particularly, attempts to engineer internal violence, sabotage, and bloodshed can have no beneficial effect. Those who have engineered or condoned murder and violence — often from the safety of sniping points abroad—have achieved little more than trouble and imprisonment for young men and women, deceived by their charm and rhetoric, but left behind to face the music. What is more, they have provided an excuse for increasingly drastic laws. Indeed, there is much truth in the old French proverb that "without the gift of grace, men tend to become like the evil they oppose."

Second Maxim: Attempts to pull South Africa and her government to their knees by isolation, boycotting, etc., are, in my view, mischevious and irresponsible — unless accompanied by a practical and acceptable alternative form of government. As to such an alternative, the boycotters are notoriously silent.

Third Maxim: Just as black racism is not the antidote for white racism, so too "appeasement" is not the antidote for black racism. You may be sure that no black racist would admire or like the United States or Britain any more for succumbing to the blackmail implicit in the now current Afro-Asian threat: "Choose between our friendship (no matter what the merits of the particular issue may be) or South Africa's friend-

ship." The United States and Britain must be prepared to tell black men that they are often as wrong as white men — precisely because they *are* men; that each specific issue should be decided on its specific merits, and not by reference to an allegedly universal but crude yardstick: "If you are not against South Africa's government you are against us."

I am aware that there are some black racists who argue that there is no room for the whites anywhere in Africa. And it is possible that this may yet prove to be the real and horrible issue. "Africa for black Africans!" Happily, this is not the view of most non-whites in South Africa. What South African non-whites understandably desire in their country is a more equitable sharing of power and opportunities, which is not the same thing as a rejection of the whites.

Fourth Maxim: Mere negative shibboleths like "abandon apartheid" are not going to get anyone anywhere. Even the more positive call for a national convention to work out a new deal for South Africa is not really helpful, unless one has workable ideas about what is to happen if the government of the day, of what is after all still a sovereign state, refuses to summon it; and even more to the point, what is to happen if the delegates to such a convention do not agree on a new dispensation. On these specific but crucial points, one will again find the busybodies conspicuously silent or unhelpful.

Fifth Maxim: If international intervention can be justified at all in South Africa, it ought to be justified by reference to an issue of real principle — as distinct from mere expediency — and, what is more, in the application of any genuine principle, there can be no room for "double standards."

In this regard, I was disappointed by Mr. Mason's article. Mr. Mason argues that South Africa's race relations, unlike race relations anywhere else in the world, should not be regarded as a matter of domestic jurisdiction, but are the world's legitimate business because, he says, South Africa is *uniquely* guilty of a denial of human rights. South Africa alone uses the legal process to accord different treatment to men by reason *only* of their color — over which they have no control.

There are several things very wrong with Mr. Mason's argument.

In the first place, color discrimination, bad as it is, is not the only kind of denial of human rights which should excite Mr. Mason's indignation. Hungary and Ghana have, it would seem, been guilty of some fairly massive denials of human rights in recent years. Why single South Africa out as a scapegoat?

Secondly, it is by no means the case that South Africa alone is guilty of racial discrimination, *backed by law*. The Indian Tamils, not so long ago, were ruthlessly disenfranchised by law in Ceylon; and even Denmark draws certain important distinctions between Danes and Greenlanders. Moreover, and this is even more to the point, the absence of racially discriminatory laws from the statute book does not afford an exoneration from vicious racialism in men's hearts and in actual practice. Indeed, when one looks at the facts — as distinct from mere theory and black-letter law — the body of sinners swells mightily, as you will discover if you talk to Asians in Zanzibar and throughout East Africa; Tamils in Ceylon; Malays and Chinese in Malaya; and many dark-skinned people even in the United States and Britain.

I do not mention these facts because I believe that by saying "you too," one thereby finds an excuse for South Africa's sins. Why single South Africa out as a scapegoat, I ask again?

Thirdly, it must be remembered that the South African government quite seriously rejects the contention that it is guilty of a denial of human rights, when it regards racial origin as a legitimate criterion for distinguishing between human beings. Arguing that racial origins are relevant to legitimate governmental objectives in the particular circumstances of South Africa, it places reliance on something like the "separate but equal" doctrine which once obtained in the United States. If today South Africa

is admittedly a unique exception in putting forward such an argument, her government would reply that unique problems call for unique remedies. Nowhere else, they contend, within the confines of one country, does one find a comparable racial pattern to that obtaining in South Africa — where the whites are outnumbered by three to one.

I DO NOT PERSONALLY subscribe to the South African argument. On the contrary, I oppose it for reasons which I have set out at length in another place. My point here is simply that it calls for a serious answer, in the course of which the issue of *bona fides* — that of South Africa as well as that of her critics — may have to be faced.

Fourthly, the attempt to find something unique about South Africa's case is to miss a golden opportunity to internationalize the problem of race-relations and human rights — whenever and wherever that problem is to be found; and to internationalize it in a mature and effective way.

For some years it has been recognized among international lawyers that the whole argument about the right of a sovereign state to do what it will with its own subjects within its own boundaries is becoming more and more out of date. What is needed is the encouragement and growth of this point of view; and the rededication and strengthening of the United Nations as a more clear-sighted, impartial, and rational enforcement-agency against the infringement of human rights, *wherever and whenever such infringements occur*. These goals, I believe, are not helped forward by the over-simplified and often hypocritical performance of singling out South Africa as the world's scapegoat. International law and organization are as yet a very tender plant. There is danger that its growth may be blighted by anger where coolness is needed, and by hate where there is need for compassion, charity, and above all honesty.

At the same time, there is much solid and worthwhile work that can be accomplished quietly day by day. As an example of such work, I value none more highly than keeping the channels of communication open between South Africa and what is good and more humane in the world beyond her borders. In such an enterprise, international trade and commerce have, I believe, a vital role to play.

There is an honored place for "industrial statesmanship" in South Africa. The standard of living of the African can and should be raised; African wages can and should be substantially increased on the basis of merit alone (bringing them nearer to white wages) without making enterprises uneconomic; tactful pressures can be brought to bear to relax still further the immoral and economically wasteful "job reservation" laws; new skills and know-how can be imparted to Africans; in short, the vast productive talent and purchasing power of nonwhite South Africans are ready for full and fair development; and here I would place the emphasis on the role of fairness.

Only a person with a rigid a priori view would regard such suggestions as these as an indefensible bolstering up of Dr. Verwoerd's government. I prefer to regard it as what it more properly is — an opening up of new and wider horizons; an opportunity to demonstrate that efficiency and economic laws are color blind; an opportunity, in the constructive climate of commerce and industry, *and in day to day contact,* to treat men and women of all races as they should be treated, for let us never forget that there are no laws against charity — no laws capable of determining the look in a man's eye and the tone of his voice; and finally, such an enterprise may be an instrument helping to consolidate and cement the interdependence of all men everywhere.

The blacks and the whites not only need each other but are too strong to destroy each other. Indeed, South Africa may demonstrate that economic realities are more potent than political dogmas. Earlier I indicated that I was an integrationist. I am; and I would suggest that, paradoxical as it may seem, the quickest and best route to stable and lasting integration may be the seemingly longest and the least dramatic way. Economic integration, which Dr. Verwoerd favors, may, despite his apparent views to the contrary, not only make eventual political and social integration inevitable, but it may also produce the only safe foundation for its enduring stability.

597

New Individualist Review welcomes contributions for publication from its readers. Essays should not exceed 5,000 words, and should be type-written. All manuscripts will receive careful consideration.

Note on the Election

BENJAMIN A. ROGGE

This communication was written in October before the close of the campaign.

THE ELECTION WILL probably be over by the time this reaches print, and conservatism as a potent political force will be dead. A fine man will have suffered a humiliating defeat and the modern-liberals in his party will be planning a ruthless purge of all those who were closely associated with his candidacy. The stage will have been set for the spectre of the "Goldwater debacle" to haunt the candidacy of every conservative for years to come.

In the meantime, his most passionate supporters will be using their special journals of opinion to vent their disappointment and bitterness in angry explanations of why it happened. Some will say that the campaign was badly conducted (which it was); some, that Goldwater was sabotaged by the modern-liberals of the press, radio and television (which he was); some, that he was defeated by one of the most effective, ruthless and corrupt politicians of the modern era (which may or may not true). The Minutemen will be laying in more rifles and the head of the John Birch Society will be proving to his own satisfaction that Goldwater's defeat was engineered by members of his own party, acting as conscious agents of the Communist conspiracy.

The truth, I suspect, lies quite elsewhere, and it is this possibility that I wish to explore. My own interpretation of the election can be simply stated: In a democratic society, under normal circumstances, no radical reorientation of social policy can be achieved by simple political organization and political action. Or to put it another way: As a general rule, for groups concerned with ultimate principles, elections just don't matter!

Let me put it still another way: Given the absence of any feeling of crisis in the American society and given the general acceptance of modern-liberalism by most Americans who count, Goldwater was foredoomed to crushing defeat. All of this was perfectly evident long before Goldwater was nominated. The great mistake was made, not during the campaign, but precisely when those conservatives who pride themselves on being activists and on "knowing how to get things done," decided that conservatism could be brought to America by what would amount to a political *coup.* Goldwater's own clear, good sense in thinking that the time was not ripe and that he could serve the cause better by continuing as Senator from Arizona was overpowered by the passion of the leaders of the Draft-Goldwater group and by their assurance that they had the know-how to get the job done.[1]

This assurance was bolstered by the ease with which the organization swept through the San Francisco Convention. But of course, it is no great task for a well-organized minority to take over a committee (and that is what a political convention most resembles); in fact, it is done every day.

Benjamin A. Rogge is Professor of Economics at Wabash College and an Editorial Advisor to *New Individualist Review.* He is co-author of the college textbook *Introduction to Economics.*

[1] See William A. Rusher, "Suite 3505: The Inside Story of How, When and Where the Goldwater Candidacy Was Conceived and Launched," *National Review,* Aug. 11, 1964, pp. 683-86.

598

Goldwater might have won, had the country been plunged in a deep crisis of some kind at the time of the campaign. The victories of the Erhard "social market economy" in Germany in the late forties and more recently of the conservatives in Brazil were both made possible by the wide-spread sense of impending disaster in the societies involved. As John Maynard Keynes wrote with such excellent foresight in 1936: "At the present moment people are unusually expectant of a more fundamental diagnosis; more particularly ready to receive it; eager to try it out, if it should be even plausible."[2] Certainly the philosophical and political success of the ideas he presented in the book in which these words appear would attest to the significance of timing in attempts at radical change.

IN ANY CASE, it was precisely those who pride themselves on their practical wisdom who launched this most impractical and tragic of all modern political actions. *The country was simply not yet prepared to accept the conservative position. Goldwater's campaign could not build on any solid foundation of widely accepted ideas on society, economics, and the state.*

This became apparent the moment Goldwater made the slightest threatening gesture in the direction of any specific element of the welfare state, e.g., social security. The response was so immediate and frightening that his campaign strategy made an obvious switch, to concentrate on corruption in the Johnson administration and to promise a rather mystical rebirth of honesty and integrity in government and of "morality" in society.

As Hayek pointed out to us long ago, honesty and integrity in government are not functions of which party is in power, but of the power over economic decisions possessed by those in government.[3]

[2] J. M. Keynes, *The General Theory of Employment, Interest and Money* (New York: Harcourt, Brace, 1936), p. 383.

[3] F. A. Hayek, *The Road to Serfdom* (Chicago: University of Chicago Press, 1944), particularly the chapter on "Why the Worst Rise to the Top."

But the people were not ready to reduce the power of government, and Goldwater and his advisors had no place else to go.

Nor could much be made out of foreign policy issues. Goldwater's interventionist posture in foreign affairs was just like Johnson's, only more so. The Goldwater principles of non-intervention and limited government on the domestic scene seemed to mix poorly with his promise of aggressive, interventionist action on the foreign scene. Whether he was more or less right than Johnson on foreign policy is not at issue. The question is whether there was any fundamental difference between the two in principle, and no such difference could be made to stick (not even the charge that Johnson was "soft on Communism").

Let me repeat: Goldwater lost because those who count in America weren't prepared to accept his ideas. The lesson would seem to be that *the real function of conservatism in America is not to try to win elections but to try to win converts.* The real battle is, as always, a battle of ideas. It matters less what name I drop into the ballot box on election day than what ideas I drop into the common pool during my lifetime.

Not a single one of the principles of limited government and individual freedom has been proved wrong by the Goldwater defeat (just as not a single one would have been proved right by a Goldwater victory). Nor has a single principle of the interventionist, welfare state been proved right by the Johnson victory.

Ideas are still evaluated by a different and more fundamental process, and perhaps it is time that we got back to work on that process. Let us forget for a while all attempts to be clever at political organization. Let us return to our problems of understanding, analysis, and clarity of exposition of the ideas of freedom. If we do our work well, we may some day be rewarded by the only lasting kind of political victory — a situation in which the ideas of freedom are so generally accepted in *both* parties that it will make little or no difference which one wins.

Economic Liberalism

in Post-War Germany

WILLIAM   S.   STOKES

600

. . . I do not believe that the idea of a "German mircle" should be allowed to establish itself. What has taken place in Germany during the past nine years is anything but a miracle. It is the result of the honest efforts of a whole people who, in keeping with the principles of liberty, were given the opportunity of using personal initiative and human energy. If this German example has any value beyond the frontiers of the country it can only be that of proving to the world at large the blessings of both personal and economic freedom.

—Ludwig Erhard[1]

DR. THEODOR HEUSS, the distinguished first president of the West German Federal Republic, once addressed himself to the question as to why the German has worked hard in recent times. He concluded: "he has had to; there has been no other way for him to earn his living in a country so restricted in area."[2] On the other hand, Professor Louis L. Snyder advances the thesis that German history and social, economic, and political institutions have conditioned the German to an acceptance of authoritarianism. When the elite members of society order the German to work hard, he responds instantly by working hard.[3]

The German people are indeed hard-

working in the West German Federal Republic. They are also imaginative, inventive, efficient, affluent, and humane. In a major policy address delivered by Dr. Gerhard Schröder, Federal Minister of Foreign Affairs, on April 3, 1964, certain facts were revealed which demonstrate clearly that economic progress is continuing in West Germany. Dr. Schröder said, among other things:

With a gross national produce of some 380,000 million Deutschmarks we are at the head of all Common Market countries. Our share in the overall GNP of the EEC comes to

William S. Stokes is Senior Professor of Comparative Political Institutions at Claremont Men's College. He is a leading authority on international relations and a leading specialist in Latin American affairs.

[1] L. Erhard, *Prosperity Through Competition* (New York: Praeger, 1958), p. 116.
[2] T. Heuss, "German Character and History," *Perspective of Germany, Atlantic Monthly,* March 1957, p. 103.
[3] L. Snyder, *German Nationalism: The Tragedy of a People* (Harrisburg, Pa.: Stackpole, 1952), pp. 521, *passim.*

almost 40 per cent. Our industrial production has increased by more than 180 per cent between 1950 and 1963, which means that, together with Japan and Italy, we top the list of all industrialized countries of the free world. As regards automobile production we are second only to the United States. The volume of our external trade amounts to 111,000 million Deutschmarks, which makes us today the world's second trading nation. In recent years, Germany alone has provided roughly twice as much development aid as all the Communist countries taken together.[4]

Although the explanations for German effectiveness in producing and distributing goods and services provided by Dr. Heuss and Professor Snyder are interesting and perhaps useful, they do not quite cover the situation. One can stand on the border between East and West Germany and, bereft of all of the quantification devices of behavioralists, o b s e r v e the obvious differences in productivity in the two systems.[5] East Germany has the better agricultural land, yet weeds compete with the corn for nutrients in the soil. Even the very young and the very old willingly contribute to agricultural production in West Germany. Workers in the urban centers of East Germany are apathetic and careless, whereas standards of individual performance are high in West Germany. Although repeated so frequently that the whole world must know, it is nevertheless worth saying once more that the contrast between East and West Berlin proves strikingly the superiority of capitalism over socialism. The people in East Germany, of course, are just as German as those in the Federal Republic. If Dr. Heuss' thesis were valid, they should buzz with economic activity. On the other hand, if Professor Snyder's thesis were valid, they should respond with great zeal to the admonitions of their Communist leaders: They certainly live under one of the most authoritarian systems the world has ever known. But the fact is that the People's Democracy in East Germany lags far behind the West German Federal Republic in economic development.

This paper will attempt to show that economic reforms in the direction of a private enterprise, market-oriented economy were primarily responsible for the rapid economic development which has taken place in West Germany in recent years. Special attention must be given to Ludwig Erhard and to Wilhelm Röpke, since Erhard provided the leadership and the policies and Röpke many of the principles of classical liberalism which were embraced by the government of West Germany. Other men in public life in Western Europe have shared the views of Erhard and Röpke. Where they have been able to persuade their governments to move from the planned state (*dirigisme*) to economic liberalism, the results in terms of economic development have been similar. Such men include Reinhard Kamitz in Austria, Luigi Einaudi in Italy, Jacques Rueff of France, Walter Eucken, and Per Jacobsson.[6] It is not merely that economic liberalism has produced a dynamic and creative economic system, important as this fact is, but that the value implications of classical liberalism have extended to social and political life as well.

THE SPIRIT OF the White-Morgenthau Plan permeated the military occupation of Germany in its early years. It was planned that by 1949 Germany's overall industrial capacity would be reduced to about 50 to 55 per cent of the prewar 1938 level (excluding the construction and building materials industries). The "planned reduction in Germany's resources" would result in "a 30 per cent cut in the standard of living" as compared with the average standard of living before the war (1930-38).[7] About

601

---

[4] G. Schröder, "Germany's Position and Germany's Future," *The Bulletin* (Bonn: Press and Information Office of the German Federal Government), April 7, 1964.

[5] My statements here are based on personal observations in East and West Germany, East and West Berlin, summer, 1960.

[6] W. H. Chamberlin, "The Twilight of the Planners," *The Freeman*, May, 1964, pp. 23-24.

[7] Military Government of Germany, *Monthly Report of the Military Governor U. S. Zone: Reparations and Restitutions*, No. 9 (April 20, 1946), p. 1.

6.6 million Germans were killed during the war, 3.5 million were disabled, and more than 15 million lost their homes.[8] Many parts of Germany were literally flattened. Although the initial policy was to disable rather than rebuild, the United States never intended to starve Germans to death. Between July 1, 1945, and March 31, 1950, total United States aid to West Germany was $3,801 million. As of July 31, 1952, the figure was somewhat greater. The United States claimed officially that the economic aid was used for purposes of achieving recovery in Germany. "In one form or another some 4 billions of dollars of United States aid have been applied to the economic recovery of West Germany in accordance with a policy of assistance to a defeated foe unduplicated in history and in violent contrast to the treatment accorded the areas of Germany under Soviet domination."[9] In a very broad sense, this statement may be accurate. However, the economic aid was not used to construct new industries or activate agriculture. "Nearly all of this aid represents the cost of procuring and shipping food, industrial raw materials and like commodities to Germany."[10] An official report of the Military Government describes United States policy as of 1946: "No attempt has been made to do extensive rebuilding while new construction has been absolutely prohibited."[11]

Although the United States government spent billions of dollars in Germany, policies of rationing, price control, centralized direction, restriction, and restraint — coupled with a failure to stabilize the monetary situation and manage the inflation — resulted in a virtually stagnated economy: "by the end of 1945 industrial output was no more than 25 per cent of 1936 and perhaps as little as

15 per cent of the highest wartime level."[12] The plants operating by the end of 1945 represented about 15 per cent of the total industrial establishments in the United States zone. However, such plants were operating at no more than 5 per cent of capacity.[13] About 20 per cent of the German population in the United States zone was receiving public assistance in some form or other.[14] Little improvement could be claimed in 1946. The official report for the period stated: "Industrial production is estimated at only 10-12 per cent of current capacity in the United States Zone."[15] As of late 1949, the economic situation in Berlin could only be described as deplorable. About 25 per cent of the residents were unemployed. The Soviets looted to a point of reducing industrial capacity about 80 per cent. By the end of 1949, 800,000 of the 2.1 million total population or 38 per cent were being subsidized by some form of public aid.[16]

Despite the heavy expenditures of United States dollars, few Germans ate well. In the first 21 months of the occupation, rations were as low as 1,180 calories per person per day; and in only 8 out of the 21 months did the rations reach 1,550 calories per day in the American zone.[17] Average weight continued to decline from sub-standard figures in June 1946, resulting in a nutritional status so low "as to entail excessive morbidity and

---

[8] *Die Welt* (Hamburg), Aug. 24, 1959.

[9] Office of the U. S. High Commissioner for Germany, *Report on Germany, Sept. 21, 1949-July 31, 1952* (Washington, D. C.: U. S. Government Printing Office, 1952), p. v.

[10] *Ibid.*, p. 49.

[11] Military Government of Germany, *Monthly Report of the Military Governor, U. S. Zone: Manpower, Trade Unions and Working Conditions*, No. 8 (March 20, 1946), p. 8.

[12] Office of Military Government for Germany (U. S.), *Economic Developments Since Currency Reform,* Special Report of the Military Governor, November, 1948, p. 2.

[13] Military Government of Germany, *Monthly Report of the Military Governor, U. S. Zone: Report of the Military Governor,* No. 2 (Sept. 20, 1945), p. 10.

[14] Military Government of Germany, *Monthtly Report of the Military Governor, U. S. Zone: Public Welfare,* No. 2 (Sept. 20, 1945), p. 3.

[15] Military Government of Germany, *Monthly Report of the Military Governor, U. S. Zone: Report of the Military Governor,* No. 6, (Jan. 20, 1946), p. 5.

[16] Office of the U. S. High Commissioner for Germany, *1st Quarterly Report on Germany, Sept. 21-Dec. 31, 1949* (Washington, D. C.: U. S. Government Printing Office, 1950), p. 34.

[17] Military Government of Germany, *Monthly Report of the Military Governor, U. S. Zone: Food and Agriculture,* No. 20 (March 1, 1946-Feb. 28, 1947), p. 1.

mortality from infectious diseases in general and respiratory diseases in particular." The increased incidence of tuberculosis is explained by weight deficiency and overcrowding.[18]

In a speech delivered at Antwerp, Ludwig Erhard described the character of the German economy just prior to the currency reform:

> It was a time when most people did not want to believe that this experiment in currency and economic reform could succeed. It was a time when it was calculated that for every German there would be one plate every five years; a pair of shoes every twelve years; a suit every fifty years; that only every fifth infant would lie in its own napkins; and that only every third German would have a chance of being buried in his own coffin. That seemed to be the only life before us. This demonstrated the boundless delusion of planners that, on the basis of raw material stocks and other statistical data, the fate of a people could be determined for a long period in advance. These mechanists and *dirigstes* had absolutely no conception that, if a people were allowed once more to become aware of the value and worth of freedom, dynamic forces would be released.[19]

LUDWIG ERHARD, who was elected director of economic administration of the bi-zonal economic area on March 2, 1948, before becoming Minister of Economic Affairs in the new government and Chancellor in 1964, made clear in party circles and in the Military Government that he sought the destruction of planning and the institution of a market oriented economy. He found some opposition within his own party (the Christian Democratic Union or CDU-CSU). The Social Democratic Party (SPD), Marxist influenced and socialist in a formal, official fashion, naturally despised everything Erhard stood for in the field of economics. In addition, there was apparently a preponderance of economic planners, mostly United States university professors, acting as advisers in the Military Government. Although Erhard is a friend and supporter of the United States, various statements in one of his books suggest that he had a difficult time with the economists in the Military Government. For example, he says: "It was strictly laid down by the British and American control authorities that permission had to be obtained before any definite price changes could be made. The Allies never seemed to have thought it possible that someone could have the idea, not to alter price controls, but simply to remove them."[20]

Again, when Erhard put currency stability in the forefront of his objectives, the Allies "in a heated 'war of memoranda,' preferred full employment . . . [to] the stability of our currency . . . . nearly all forces joined for a general attack on the market economy, forgetting that only through greater productivity and free competition, on the basis of the stability of our money, could we secure our position in the world markets."[21] When Erhard wanted to lower certain taxes and to remit others in order to step up consumption and lighten the burden on the economy, the Allies "at first refused permission for this tax reform."[22] Other words and phrases in his book further indicate the reluctance of the American authorities to accept economic reform: "interventions from the Americans"; the Income Tax Law of April 23, 1950 "was finally sanctioned by the Allies"; etc.[23] The head of the E.C.A. mission in Germany expressed his distaste for what Erhard was doing by describing the German tax system as the most "anti-social in the world." Erhard says that "there was constant pressure from the U.S.A. to introduce controls . . . ."[24]

The first great reform which Erhard achieved was the Tripartite Currency Reform, officially promulgated June 18, 1948 (Military Government Law No. 61), effective June 20. The reform retired the

603

---

[18] Military Government of Germany, *Monthly Report of the Military Governor, U. S. Zone: Report of the Military Governor,* No. 13 (Aug. 20, 1946), p. 16.

[19] Erhard, *op. cit.,* p. 10.

[20] *Ibid.,* p. 14.
[21] *Ibid.,* pp. 32-33.
[22] *Ibid.,* p. 35.
[23] *Ibid.,* pp. 39, 41.
[24] *Ibid.,* p. 39.

Reichsmark and established the Deutsche Mark. There would be DM 10 billion in the western zones (DM 11 billion on agreement of at least three-fourths of the Boards of Directors of the Bank Deutscher Länder of at least six of the Länder).[25]

From 1935 to 1945, the currency in circulation had increased from about RM 5 billion to over RM 50 billion. Bank deposits grew from about RM 30 billion to over RM 150 billion. Reich debt increased from RM 15 billion to RM 400 billion, "excluding war damage and other war-connected claims of RM 300 to 400 billion . . . . By 1946 the national income had been reduced from RM 60 billion to about RM 25 billion to 30 billion in 1936 prices." It was estimated that the black market controlled 50 to 60 per cent of production, with prices often fifty to several hundred times the official prices.[26]

Erhard quotes Jacques Rueff and Andre Piettre as to the immediate effect of the currency reform in West Germany, and the paragraph is worth quoting here:

The black market suddenly disappeared. Shop windows were full of goods; factory chimneys were smoking; and the streets swarmed with lorries. Everywhere the noise of new buildings going up replaced the deathly silence of the ruins. If the state recovery was a surprise, its swiftness was even more so. In all sectors of economic life it began as the clocks struck on the day of currency reform. Only an eye-witness can give an account of the sudden effect currency reform had on the size of stocks and the wealth of goods on display. Shops filled up with goods from one day to the next; the factories began to work. On the eve of currency reform the Germans were aimlessly wandering about their towns in search of a few additional items of food. A day later they thought of nothing but producing them. One day apathy was mirrored on their faces while on the next a whole nation looked hopefully into the future.[27]

The bi-zonal index of industrial production increased from about 47 per cent of 1936 in May 1948 to 75 per cent in November[28] and to 140 per cent by mid-1952.[29] Lutz, Sohmen, Wright, and Röpke agree that currency reform was the beginning of the general policy of freedom of economic opportunity (*Gewerbefreiheit*) which, year after year, has continued to produce highly satisfactory results.[30]

Wilhelm Röpke has provided the best description of the nature of the economic reforms:

The essence of the German economic reform corresponds to the sickness which it was intended to cure. If the sickness was that combination of collectivism and inflation which we have designated as repressed inflation, the therapy for it had to consist, on the one hand, in the elimination of inflationary pressure and, on the other hand, in the elimination of the apparatus of repression (maximum prices, rationing, controls, and other interferences with free prices) and the restoration of market freedom, free prices, competition, and entrepreneurial incentives. Freedom in the realm of goods, discipline in the realm of money — those were the two principles upon which rested the German economic revival from 1948 onwards, and they have remained the foundation of German prosperity in spite of all the many concessions made to interventionism and the welfare state.

The reform of 1948 was constituted, then, of two parts: the overcoming of inflation and the dismantling of the apparatus of repression. The first was accomplished by the monetary reform, the second by the economic reform represented in the res-

---

[25] Office of Military Government for Germany (U. S.), *Economic Developments since Currency Reform*, pp. 3-4.

[26] Office of Military Government for Germany (U. S.), *Monthly Report of the Military Governor: Report of the Military Governor*, No. 36 (June, 1948), p. 6.

[27] Erhard, op. cit., p. 13.

[28] Office of Military Government for Germany (U. S.), *Economic Developments since Currency Reform*, p. 3.

[29] Office of the U. S. High Commissioner for Germany, *Report on Germany, Sept. 21, 1949-July 31, 1952*, p. 233.

[30] F. A. Lutz, "The German Currency Reform and the Revival of the German Economy," *Economica*, XVI (May, 1949), 122-42; E. Sohmen, "Competition and Growth: West Germany," *American Economic Review*, XLIX (December, 1959), 986-1003; D. M. Wright, *Post-War West German and United Kingdom Recovery* (Washington, D. C.: American Enterprise Association, 1957); W. Röpke, *Economics of the Free Society* (Chicago: Henry Regnery Co., 1963), esp. pp. 246-50.

toration of the market economy. Thus were the twin pillars of genuine economic order reconstructed from the chaos and the paralysis of the inflationary planned economy: the steering and motive power of free prices and the stability of the value of money.[31]

It is hard not to agree with Röpke when he says that "here is to be found the most convincing case in all history against collectivism and inflationism and for market economy and monetary discipline."[32]

In my opinion, the most important result of currency reform was that human beings became important again. Individual dignity and self-respect were restored. It was the economic success of the early reforms, however, which provided the government with the means to behave in a humane manner. In order to assist some 13,090,000 expellees and refugees to find new homes and jobs and become a part of the West German community, more than $14.3 billion had been spent by January 1961. About 12.5 per cent of the total national product is devoted to social welfare functions (although Erhard makes crystal-clear his opposition to the concept of the paternalistic state). Restitution payments to the victims of the Nazi tyranny have been recognized to the extent of $7.8 billion, half of which has already been paid. The Federal Government has met its defense obligations through expenditures of $19,223 million ($21,823 million if aid to Berlin is included) in the period 1950-1960.[33]

No one knows or can measure the creative potentialities of human beings. The best way to discover who is capable of achievement is to permit all to try, each in accordance with his own inclinations and ideals. In Germany since 1949, talent has burst to the surface where none was ever suspected of existing. The tremendous increase in vertical mobility has already changed attitudes and perhaps values as well in the direction of representational government. With free-dom, individuals have experimented with many kinds of social and economic activities. Inevitably, the like-minded have formed voluntary organizations to discuss and, more recently, scrutinize government to see that no one in authority jeopardizes the new-found liberty.

The achievements of the "social market economy" and republican government under federalism should not be exaggerated, however. West Germany is not rich in natural resources, except for coal. No matter how inventive, ingenious, and hard-working Germans may be, relatively full employment and a high level of prosperity depend to an important degree upon an international climate that permits free, fair access to raw materials and markets. The CDU-CSU Government has succeeded in bringing about agreements liberalizing trade in the European area, but a reversal of this trend would have a negative effect. Although about 5.5 million homes were built in the period 1950-1960, construction techniques are less advanced than in the United States. Retail merchandising, especially in food, must be improved if people are to obtain high quality products at low cost.

One reform which Erhard hoped to accomplish early in his administration was the modernization of agriculture and the elimination of subsidies. When the Bonn government assumed power in 1949, the many small farms were divided into about 25 million tiny scattered strips, resulting in "an enormous waste of time, labor and land resources and seriously handicapping mechanization."[34] The "Green Plan," which is the term used to designate the program of government subsidies, distorts the market and delays the fundamental solution to the problem of producing inexpensive fruits, vegetables, meat, and dairy products. The elimination of subsidies, tariff reform, and consolidation (by voluntary means, not by government coercion) of the small plots represent goals which Erhard has not yet been able to realize.

605

---

[31] Röpke, op. cit., p. 248.

[32] Ibid.

[33] The Bulletin (Bonn), Jan. 17, 1961, pp. 1-2.

[34] Office of the U. S. High Commissioner for Germany, 7th Quarterly Report on Germany, April 1-June 30, 1951 (Washington, D. C.: U. S. Government Printing Office, 1951), p. 80.

ERHARD AND THE FOUNDING Fathers of the Bonn system believed that a private enterprise, market-organized economic order was essential for political liberty and freedom. When the White-Morgenthau policy was abandoned and West Germany was permitted to attempt national regeneration in the political realm, the Germans advanced their views to the military authorities.[35] After much deliberation, the three Military Governors submitted an Aide-Memoire to the Parliamentary Council meeting at Bonn on November 22, 1948, outlining the constitutional principles which the occupation authorities believed should be incorporated into the new "basic law" (*Grundgesetz* rather than *Verfassung* because the Founding Fathers at Bonn wanted to reserve the term "constitution" for the organic statute of a reunited Germany). The Aide-Memoire is a remarkable document, because its recommendations are the result of searching analysis of why the representative system failed in the Weimar Republic, culminating in the Nazi tyranny. As the Aide-Memoire does not seem to be well-known, or, at least, is not often mentioned in scholarly studies of Germany, it is perhaps worthwhile to insert the provisions here:

"They [the Military Governors] believe that the Basic Law should, to the maximum extent possible, provide:

"a. For a bicameral legislative system in which one of the houses must represent the individual states and must have sufficient power to safeguard the interests of the states;

"b. that the executive must only have those powers which are definitely prescribed by the constitution and that emergency powers, if any, of the executive must be so limited as to require prompt legislative or judicial review;

"c. that the powers of the federal government shall be limited to those expressly enumerated in the constitution, and, in any case, shall not include education, culture, health (except, in this last case, to secure such coordination as essential to safeguard the health of the people in the several states); and that its powers in the field of public welfare be limited to those necessary for the coordination of social security measures; and that its powers in the police field be limited to those especially approved by the Military Governors during the occupation period;

"d. that the powers of the federal government in the field of public finance shall be limited to the disposal of monies, including the raising of revenue for purposes for which it is responsible; that the federal government may set rates and legislate on the general principles of assessment with regard to other taxes for which uniformity is essential, the collection and utilization of such taxes being left to the individual states; and that it may appropriate funds only for the purpose for which it is responsible under the constitution;

"e. that the constitution should provide for an independent judiciary to review federal legislation, to review the exercise of federal executive power, and to adjudicate conflicts between federal and *Land* authorities as well as between *Land* authorities, and to protect the civil rights and freedom of the individual;

"f. that the powers of the federal government to establish federal agencies for the execution and administration of its responsibilities should be clearly defined and should be limited to those fields in which it is clear that state implementation is impracticable;

"g. that each citizen have access to public office, with appointment and promotion being based solely on his fitness to discharge the responsibility of the position, and that Civil Service should be non-political in character; and

"h. that a public servant, if elected to the federal legislature, shall resign his office with the agency where he is employed before he accepts election."[36]

---

[35] For an account of the drafting of the Bonn *Grundgesetz* from the German point of view, see P. H. Merkl, *The Origin of the West German Republic* (New York: Oxford University Press, 1963), p. 269.

[36] Office of Military Government for Germany (U. S.), *Monthly Report of the Military Governor: Report of the Military Governor*, No. 41 (November, 1948), pp. 87-88.

606

How unnerving and even galling the provisions of the Aide-Memoire and, indeed, the Bonn Basic Law must be to the modern-day "liberal." Both sources prove that one can "turn the clock back" to the principles of classical liberalism, such as individualism, voluntarism, genuine division of powers, states' rights, and most important of all, limited government.

BUT WHAT ABOUT the Social Democrats? What has been the impact of the return to classical liberalism insofar as their ideological and policy posture is concerned? Are they sincere in rejecting socialism in favor of the "social market economy" now in force?

Although the SPD until very recently opposed every major foreign and domestic policy of the Bonn Government, it is possible to argue that the party has now shifted fundamentally in the direction of strong, if not militant anti-Communism, and that it now supports the private enterprise economic system. It is difficult to conceive how a party could so radically change its position in so short a period of time, but there is evidence that this is what has happened.

The left-right conflict in the SPD over socialism and capitalism was resolved in a draft program published in the SPD paper *Vorwärts* on September 10, 1959. The program eliminated the term "class struggle" and included only one reference to the "privileges of the ruling class." It moved away from socialism and endorsed private enterprise in such phrases as "prosperity for all"; "freedom of choice for consumer goods"; and "free initiative for entrepreneurs." However, other phrases in the program indicated that the Party intended to remain at least partly leftist: "democratic socialism"; "just socialist order"; and "competition as far as possible and planning as far as necessary."

The program called for nationalization of coal and power, control of the management of large industries, cartel regulation, investment supervision, and competition by public enterprises. It preferred respect for religious institutions and endorsed their protection by law and accepted the principle of national defense. The convention of the SPD held at Bad Godesberg approved the major provisions of the draft program on November 16, 1959. Thus, the Bad Godesberg program replaced the Heidelberg program of 1925 and committed the SPD to new policies of private property, a free economy, and national defense. The Bad Godesberg program clearly rejects Marxism and denies that socialism can be made a substitute for religion. The orthodox Marxists at the convention remained almost completely silent, and only 16 out of 340 delegates voted against the program. The public press made clear that the wing of the party which supported the anti-Communist and moderate economic views of Willy Brandt had triumphed over the leftists who had dominated the party in recent years.[37]

IT IS THE ATTITUDES and values which individuals hold and cherish which determine the character of a state, regardless of the forms, structures, laws, or constitutions which may be in force at any given time. It is true that political and governmental institutions contribute to the value pattern of a society, but the family, Church, education, social classes, and the economic system also play important roles. If one seeks a society of free men organized in an independent state, it is logical to assume that the possibilities for success are maximized by creating as complete a climate of freedom as possible. If I interpret the evidence correctly, this has been the position of the leaders of the new German state since the inception of the Federal Republic in 1949 and even before, since the currency reform was in 1948. By honoring the concept of the worth and dignity of the individual Erhard and his supporters have unleashed talent and ability which almost overnight produce a dynamic economic system which in turn made values of vol-

607

---

[37] See W. Brandt, *The Ordeal of Co-existence* (Cambridge, Mass.: Harvard University Press, 1963), p. 112, *passim*.

untarism, fluidity and mobility in the class system meaningful. Since freedom is indivisible, it is only logical to insist on the establishment of a government limited to a range of functions compatible with personal liberty.

Since man is fallible and his institutions necessarily imperfect, one should not overestimate the achievement of the renewed application of principles of classical liberalism in a single country. In West Germany over three-fourths of the adult population had only eight years or less of schooling in 1949. Educational opportunities have increased since that time, of course. However, children are still separated at about age ten into the small group preparing for university or professional education and the large majority who face early terminal education and employment. Good as the system is in many respects, it may deny the country the skills and leadership which a longer and more flexible education might produce. The present system probably reduces mobility, makes the class structure more rigid, and aggravates individual and group conflict. The retention of the old division (almost a caste system) of the *Beamten,* civil service officials with a formal certificate of appointment, and the *Angestellte,* or employees, has a similar effect in the public service.

In the political and governmental field, the partial use of proportional representation permits fragmented, "functionary" parties, although West Germany is practically a two-party country in national elections. Single member constituencies and majority voting may replace proportional representation completely in time, thus compelling party leadership to behave more considerately and responsibly toward party members. Although the right-wing movements have declined in influence since about 1951-1952 and the major parties are committed to the principle of representation, there does not seem to exist any large degree of popular enthusiasm for the mechanical aspects of the Bonn system. Many Germans do not regard it wholly as their own creation. I was told many times: "It's all right, but when we achieve reunification, we will put our heads to the task and come up with something better." Perhaps so, but in the meantime it is possible to conclude that the German experience proves once more that some ideas are better than others, and that sometimes those which have prevailed in the past serve the needs and idealistic aspirations of man better than those which happen to be popular at present.

It has seemed to me that the achievements of Bonn have contributed to the defeat of socialism in the Western European countries. In a trip to the major countries of the Far East in 1963, a research experience which permitted me to talk to heads of state, men in public life, scholars, and businessmen, I found that there was widespread awareness of the German case study. I seemed to detect an awareness of the fact that those countries in the Far East which have taken steps to free their economy (Japan, Taiwan, and the Philippines for example) were regarded as having achieved a more impressive economic and political experience than those which have moved in the direction of state interventionism and planning (such as Indonesia, Ceylon, Burma, or India). As a Latin Americanist, I have many times called attention to the strong penchant for left or right-wing collectivism among both large and small countries in the Western Hemisphere. In the last ten years, however, and especially in the past several years, much evidence has appeared to suggest that people with power and influence in the community are re-examining the principles of classical liberalism, particularly in the economic realm. The case study of Germany in particular, Western Europe in general, and most recently, Spain, which is in the process of dismantling state controls, appears in the literature and in the discourse of knowledgeable people. Even in the United States itself it might be said that some change of direction can be discerned.

Property Law
and Racial Discrimination

ROBERT M. SCHUCHMAN

RECENT CIVIL RIGHTS legislation, both state and federal, has incorporated the premise that the right to use and dispose of private property is limited by the concept that all persons are deserving of an equality of treatment, regardless of race, creed, or nationality. It is not our purpose to review "public accommodations" legislation. Instead, we shall examine the judicially-inspired thesis that the doctrine of racial equality serves as a constitutional limitation on the use and disposition of property, regardless of the presence or absence of statute.

The first pertinent problem considered by the federal courts in this century was the obverse of the principal question here. The issue presented in *Buchanan v. Warley*, 245 U.S. 60 (1917), was whether the government could, through legislation, impose a racial preference on the use and disposition of property. An ordinance of the city of Louisville prevented the residential occupancy of a lot by "a person of color" in a block where the greater number of residences were occupied by white persons. A sale of private property to a Negro in such a block was declared to be void.

The law was defended on the ground that it was a proper exercise of the police power of the state. It was claimed that the ordinance "tends to promote the public peace by preventing racial conflicts;

that it tends to maintain racial purity; that it prevents the deterioration of property owned and occupied by white people . . . ." 245 U.S. at 73-74.

A white person sold a residential lot to a Negro in a "white block." When the buyer refused to fulfill the contract, relying upon the racial occupancy ordinance, the seller sued for specific performance, claiming that the Louisville act violated the Fourteenth Amendment to the Constitution.

In its decision, the United States Supreme Court upheld the right to freely dispose of one's property regardless of the local law. The Court said that:

> The effect of the ordinance under consideration was not merely to regulate a business or the like, but was to destroy the right of the individual to acquire, enjoy, and dispose of his property. Being of this character, it was void as being opposed to the due-process clause of the Constitution.
> 245 U.S. at 79-80.

It further said that:

> The Fourteenth Amendment protects life, liberty, and property from invasion by the States without due process of law. Property is more than the mere thing which a person owns. It is elementary that it includes the right to acquire, use, and dispose of it. The Constitution protects these essential attributes of property.
> 245 U.S. at 74.

It must be stressed that *Buchanan v. Warley* does not speak in terms of the equal protection clause of the Fourteenth Amendment. The decision emphasizes

Robert M. Schuchman received his LLB from Yale Law School, where he was an Earhart fellow in economics. He is currently with the law firm of Casey, Lane, and Mittendorf in New York City.

609

the "essential attributes" of the rights of property, attributes which, it is said, are protected by the ancient concept of due process of the law.

RACIAL RESTRICTIONS on the alienation of property, when imposed by the government, were struck down in subsequent decisions even when couched in the guise of a zoning regulation. Thus, in *City of Richmond v. Deans,* 37 F.2d 712 (4th Cir.), *aff'd,* 281 U.S. 704 (1930), the court held as violative of the Fourteenth Amendment a zoning ordinance which prohibited the sale of a residence on a block "where the majority of residences on such street are occupied by those with whom said person is forbidden to intermarry . . . ." Because that question was not before the court, it did not rule on the constitutionality of the law prohibiting intermarriage.

The rule that the alienation of property was entirely free from restrictions based on the racial preferences of the state was again upheld in a 1932 case in Missouri. However, the decision in this case left the door open for future regulation if such regulation was found to be for the public welfare.

> Private property cannot, under the guise of police power, be subjected to unreasonable annoyance and arbitrary restriction of its use where public welfare can in no way receive benefit by such restriction.
> *Women's Kansas City St. Andrews Soc. v. Kansas City,* 58 F.2d 593, 598 (8th Cir. 1932).

Now it was no longer a question of the "essential attributes of property." The basic issue was said to be whether "public welfare" could in any way "receive benefit." Since the racial ordinance did not benefit the public welfare, it was stricken.

The constitutional power of the states to attach a racial preference to the exercise of the rights of property seemed a settled issue after *Buchanan v. Warley* and the subsequent line of cases. A governmental body could not, constitutionally, command a property owner to restrict the sale and use of his property

to members of a specified race or color.

These early cases dealt with statutes; they were concerned with the limits of the law as exercised through the police power, not with the purely private arrangements of men. If the state could not impose racial preference by law, then the next and obvious question was: Could the state impose racial non-preference on private property and private arrangements by the use of law?

As we have noted, *Buchanan v. Warley* held that a racially restrictive ordinance was void not because it interfered with the federal government's notions of equality, but because it infringed upon the essential rights of property held by the individual. However, when state laws imposing non-discrimination on private arrangements were challenged in the courts, a completely new rationale was used to uphold the laws.

The New York Civil Rights Act provided, *inter alia,* that no labor organization could deny a person membership or equal treatment because of race, color, or creed. In *Railway Mail Ass'n v. Corsi,* 326 U.S. 88 (1945), the union challenged the Act on the ground that, in line with *Buchanan v. Warley,* it was an unconstitutional "interference with its right to selection of membership and abridgment of its property rights and liberty of contract." It was argued that the right of property to be free from one brand of government racial preference implied freedom from any other preference.

The Supreme Court disagreed and held that property was only free from legislation imposing racial discrimination, not from that imposing racial equality:

> A judicial determination that such legislation violated the Fourteenth Amendment would be a distortion of the policy manifested in that amendment, which was adopted to prevent state legislation designed to perpetuate discrimination on the basis of race or color.
> 326 U.S. at 93-94.

THUS THE PROTECTION of the right of property by the Fourteenth Amendment, in the racial context, became a simple expression of the racial policy preferences of the state. No longer was the right to use property free from the racial preference of law a part of the "essential attributes of property," as far as freedom from positive law restriction was concerned.

The development of the law from a general protection of property rights to a judicially approved mirror of public policy is echoed in the area of purely private arrangements. Contemporaneous with the line of cases concerning laws which express racial preference in property relations is a trend of decisions affecting private agreements and decisions on the use and disposition of property.

The first of these cases concerned the so-called "restrictive covenant" in real property. A racial restrictive covenant is typically an agreement among property owners, binding on the land for a specified number of years, which declares that no property in the area covered by the contract may be sold, leased, or used by members of the Negro race.

Historically, racially restrictive covenants on land were considered to be valid and enforceable contracts. They were agreed upon voluntarily by the contracting landowners, were secured by a valuable consideration, and any new buyer took possession subject to and with notice of the restriction. Except for an isolated case in 1892, such covenants were consistently upheld, except where they violated the common law policy against unreasonable restraints on alienation, or where enforcement was deemed inequitable because of the changed character of the neighborhood. But, after *Buchanan v. Warley,* challenge after challenge was made to these covenants on the ground that they denied the excluded race due process of the laws.

The courts generally rejected this argument without much comment. The *Buchanan* rule was held to apply solely to state action. When purely private parties agreed to a restriction, there was no constitutional violation and no rights were denied by enforcement of the covenant. A clear statement of the early judicial reaction to the racial covenant challenge may be found in the lower court opinion in *Corrigan v. Buckley,* 299 Fed. 899 (D.C. Cir. 1924), which upheld the covenant, stating:

> The constitutional right of a Negro to acquire, own, and occupy property does not carry with it the constitutional power to compel sale and conveyance to him of any particular private property. The individual citizen, whether he be black or white, may refuse to sell or lease his property to any particular individual or class of individuals .... Such a covenant is enforceable, not only against a member of the excluded race, but between the parties to the agreement.
> 299 Fed. at 901.

This was a restatement of the "essential attributes of property" argument embodied in *Buchanan v. Warley.* Just as a property owner was free to sell to a Negro despite laws attempting to negate this right, he could agree to refuse to sell to a Negro without state interference. The denial of due process occurred when the state dictated a racial preference in property, not when individual property owners expressed this preference.

On appeal, the Supreme Court affirmed the lower court holding in *Corrigan v. Buckley,* 271 U.S. 323 (1926). The Court emphasized that the due process clause of the Fifth and Fourteenth Amendments was a "limitation only upon the powers of the General Government, and is not directed against the action of individuals." 271 U.S. at 330. Hence, there was no substantial federal question involved in the enforcement of private restrictive covenants. The Court dismissed, without much comment, the novel contention that the Court decree enforcing the covenant was itself state action, and such enforcement therefore denied due process of law to the petitioner.

Such was the state of the law when, in 1948, the landmark case of *Shelley v. Kraemer,* 334 U.S. 1, reached the Supreme Court. On February 16, 1911, thirty out of a total of thirty-nine owners of property in a certain lot in St. Louis, Missouri, signed an agreement, subsequently recorded, which provided in part:

611

. . . the said property is hereby restricted to the use and occupancy for the term of Fifty (50) years from this date, so that it shall be a condition all the time and whether recited and referred to as [sic] not in subsequent conveyances and shall attach to the land as a condition precedent to the sale of the same, that hereafter no part of said property or any portion thereof shall be, for said term of Fifty-years, occupied by any person not of the Caucasian race, it being intended hereby to restrict the use of said property for said period of time against the occupancy as owners or tenants of any portion of said property for resident or other purposes by people of the Negro or Mongolian **Race.**

On August 11, 1945, Shelley, a Negro, purchased a parcel of land in the lot concerned. On October 9, 1945, the white landowners in the lot brought suit to enforce the terms of the restrictive covenant. The Supreme Court of Missouri granted the relief, holding the agreement effective and concluding that enforcement of its provisions violated no rights guaranteed by the Federal Constitution. *Kraemer v. Shelley*, 355 Mo. 814, 198 S.W. 2d 679 (1946).

Shelley took his appeal to the United States Supreme Court. Chief Justice Vinson, in his decision, noted initially that the racial restrictions of this private agreement "could not be squared with the requirements of the Fourteenth Amendment if imposed by state statute or local ordinance," 334 U.S. at 11. But this was a voluntary, private restriction, and a different rule of law applied:

. . . the action inhibited by the first section of the Fourteenth Amendment is only such action as may fairly be said to be that of the States. That Amendment erects no shield against merely private conduct, however discriminatory or wrongful.
We conclude, therefore, that the restrictive agreements s t a n d i n g alone cannot be regarded as **viola**tive of any rights guaranteed to petitioners by the Fourteenth Amendment. So long as the purposes of those agreements are effectuated by voluntary adherence to their terms, it would appear clear that there has been no action by the State and the provisions of the Amendment have not been violated.
334 U.S. at 13.

SO FAR, this is just a restatement of the old law. But Shelley argued, and the Court agreed, that the mere enforcement of these admittedly lawful covenants constituted state action in violation of the Fourteenth Amendment. The reasoning of the Court in this regard is so vital for an understanding of later applications of the "state action" doctrine that I take the liberty of quoting from the decision at some length:

It is clear that but for the active intervention of the state courts, supported by the full panoply of state power, petitioners would have been free to occupy the properties in question without restraint.
These are not cases . . . in which the States have merely abstained from action, leaving private individuals free to impose such discriminations as they see fit. Rather, these are cases in which the States have made available to such individuals the full coercive power of government to deny to petitioners, on the grounds of race or color, the enjoyment of property rights in premises which petitioners are willing and financially able to acquire and which the grantors are willing to sell. . . . Nor is the Amendment ineffective simply because the particular pattern of discrimination, which the State has enforced, was defined initially by the terms of a private agreement. State action, as that phrase is understood for the purposes of the Fourteenth Amendment, refers to exertions of state power in all forms. And when the effect of that action is to deny rights subject to the protection of the Fourteenth Amendment, it is the obligation of this Court to enforce the constitutional commands.
334 U.S. at 19-20.

The decision in *Shelley v. Kraemer* was shattering in its impact. It held, in effect, that although private racial preference contracts were perfectly valid and legal, their enforcement was unlawful. The Court treated the equitable enforcement of a restrictive covenant as a positive discriminatory act of the state, bringing it within the limitations of the Fourteenth Amendment.

This analysis, it would seem, entirely misconstrues the historical role of courts of equity. Moreover, it ignores the distinction between the judicial function of enforcing positive law and that of settling private disputes and construing private agreements. In the *Buchanan v. Warley* situation, the courts were called upon to enforce a legislative enactment expressing racial preference. It was because the underlying act, an expression of the positive law, was contrary to the Fourteenth Amendment, that the enforcement of the law was also barred.

The private agreement in *Shelley v. Kraemer* presents an entirely different situation. There, the underlying act was a voluntary private covenant, admittedly in violation of no law. The role of the court was not one of enforcing a coercively based government measure. Rather, the court was to act as a neutral arbiter of private disputes by carrying out the solemn agreements of a contractual society. In its enforcement of private contracts, the courts should not judge the substance of such contracts. Private agreements, to this observer, need not reflect the prevailing government policies. Otherwise, liberty of contract is a sham.

IT HAD BEEN accepted doctrine in the Anglo-American community that courts were not to write the contracts of men: they were to construe and then enforce them, regardless of which party had the better bargain, so long as the bargain was not illegal. Those who dislike a contract need not agree to it. When a person received notice of a restrictive covenant on a property he wished to buy, he was free to accept it with the covenant or not make the purchase. The novel doctrine of *Shelley v. Kraemer* places the courts in the position of rewriting the bargain to conform to current majority sentiment. To say the least, this is not an expression of freedom of contract.

Numerous cases since *Shelley v. Kraemer* have extended the "state action" thesis even further. In the companion case to *Shelley*, *Hurd v. Hodge*, 334 U.S. 24 (1948), the Supreme Court considered the enforcement of a restrictive covenant in the District of Columbia. Inasmuch as the Fourteenth Amendment applies only to the states, and not to the District, a different rationale than that relied upon in *Shelley* was required.

One contention of the petitioners in *Hurd v. Hodge* was that "judicial enforcement of the covenants is contrary to . . . treaty obligations of the United States contained in the United Nations charter." 334 U.S. at 28, n.4. To this and other arguments the Court stated that enforcement was

> . . . judicial action contrary to the public policy of the United States, and as such should be corrected by this Court in the exercise of its supervisory powers over the Courts of the District of Columbia. The power of the federal courts to enforce the terms of private agreements is at all times exercised subject to the restrictions and limitations of the public policy of the United States as manifested in the Constitution, treaties, federal statutes, and applicable legal precedents. Where the enforcement of private agreements would be violative of that policy, it is the obligation of courts to refrain from such exertions of judicial power.
> 334 U.S. at 35.

Here, as in *Shelley*, we see the notion that property must be used in accordance with the majority sentiment of the day dignified into a governing juridical principle. The final statement of this doctrine, as applied to restrictive covenants in real estate, appeared in the case of *Barrows v. Jackson*, 346 U.S. 249 (1953). A sale of restricted real estate was made to a Negro purchaser and, under the authority of *Shelley v. Kraemer*, he was permitted to occupy the lot without challenge. However, the owners of the adjoining properties, who were parties to the restrictive covenant, sued the white vendor of the lot in question for money damages for breach of contract.

Here it could hardly be argued that "state action" was being used to exclude Negroes and deny rights guaranteed by the Fourteenth Amendment. Unlike *Shelley*, the court was not asked to enforce the contract and expel the Negro purchaser. Rather, the covenanting parties sought to hold the violating party liable for his breach. The Supreme Court disagreed however, and, in a terse decision, disallowed the recovery of dam-

613

ages under the authority of *Shelley v. Kraemer.*

The new departure of the Court in *Barrows v. Jackson* was emphasized by Chief Justice Vinson in a vigorously worded dissenting opinion. It will be recalled that Vinson actually wrote the opinion in *Shelley v. Kraemer.* Yet, in *Barrows,* he said:

> The majority seems to recognize, albeit ignores, a proposition which I thought was made plain in the *Shelley* case. That proposition is this: these racial restrictive covenants, whatever we may think of them, are not legal nullities so far as any doctrine of federal law is concerned; it is not unlawful to make them; it is not unlawful to enforce them unless the method by which they are enforced in some way contravenes the Federal Constitution or a federal statute.
>
> * * * * * * *
>
> The majority identifies no non-Caucasian who has been injured or could be injured if damages are assessed against respondent for breaching the promise which she willingly and voluntarily made to petitioners, a promise which neither the federal law nor the Constitution proscribes. Indeed, the non-Caucasian occupants of the property involved in this case will continue their occupancy undisturbed regardless of the outcome of the suit.
> 346 U.S. at 261, 262.

As Chief Justice Vinson pointed out, the *Shelley* doctrine goes much further, as applied, than a mere ban on enforcement of private agreements expressing racial preference. Despite all the verbiage about the lawfulness of these agreements in themselves, the Court actually struck down the underlying voluntary agreements. Since *Shelley v. Kraemer,* the Supreme Court has extended the "state action" rule to prohibit more and more p r i v a t e uses of property. In a society where broken agreements can only be enforced through the judicial system, it has declared that, in effect, all contracts partake of state action. As the Supreme Court put it: "Once courts enforce the agreement the Sanction of government is, of course, put behind them [sic]." *Railway Employe's Dep't. v. Hanson,* 351 U.S. 225, 232 n.4 (1956). No longer is the Court the neu-

tral enforcer of private contracts; instead, it becomes a participant in the contract.

The *Shelley* rule was extended to labor union contracts in *Brotherhood of R.R. Trainmen v. Howard,* 343 U.S. 768 (1952), where it was held that, under the Railway Labor Act, a union could not make a contract where race was a determinent of employment. One of the reasons therefore was that since Congress authorized the system of collective bargaining through union representatives such representatives would act in violation of the Constitution if they deprived a worker of benefits because of his race. 343 U.S. at 773.

ANOTHER FACET of the *Shelley* doctrine is whether a member of the excluded race has a right to use another person's private property when the exclusion is based solely upon race. The recent trend of decisions concern not judicial enforcement of racial restrictive contracts, but judicial compulsion directed against those voluntarily agreeing to abide by such contracts.

An early case dealing with the question was *Rice v. Sioux City Memorial Park Cemetery,* 349 U.S. 70 (1955). The contract of sale of a burial lot in the cemetery provided that "burial privileges accrue only to members of the Caucasian race." The Cemetery, acceding to its own contract, refused to bury a certain Winnebago Indian. The decedent's widow sued the Cemetery to compensate her for its action. She argued that judicial recognition of the validity of the racial clause in the burial contract would violate the Fourteenth Amendment and, in addition, the provisions of the United Nations Charter.

The Supreme Court of Iowa denied relief to the widow. It held that, under *Shelley v. Kraemer,* it could not compel the Cemetery to obey its contract by excluding non-Caucasians. However, where the Cemetery was only relying upon the racial clause as a defense to an action, the court could not reform the contract by enforcing it without regard to the racial clause. Moreover, the court said,

614

the provisions of the United Nations Charter "have no bearing on the case."

The widow appealed the decision to the United States Supreme Court, which granted certiorari. The Court split down the middle, four Justices for affirmance, four for reversal. Under the traditional rules of the Court, an evenly-divided court is treated as an affirmance of the lower court, but no opinion is filed. Hence, the reasoning of the Justices in this case is unknown, although four jurists apparently believed that the racial restriction in the burial contract could not be privately enforced by the Cemetery. The Iowa Legislature then passed a statute prohibiting denial of burial solely on account of race. This law, governing future burial contracts, made the *Rice* situation a moot question.

But more recent cases have probed more deeply into the issue of a private right to express racial preference on one's own property. In Wilmington, Delaware, a Negro was refused service in a privately owned and operated restaurant which was, however, in quarters leased from the municipal parking agency which owned the building. The Negro sued to compel the restaurant to serve him, on the ground that the restaurant had sufficient proximity to state action for denial of service to constitute a violation of the Fourteenth Amendment. From an adverse decision in the Supreme Court of Delaware, he appealed to the United States Supreme Court.

In, *Burton v. Wilmington Parking Authority*, 365 U.S. 715 (1961), the Court reversed the d e c i s i o n, holding that state action was involved in the restaurant, and the Negro could not be denied service because of his race. It was found that the Parking Authority and the city of Wilmington owned the land and the building in which the restaurant was located; the building, a municipal garage, was dedicated to a "public use"; the costs of acquisition, construction, and maintenance of the building were publicly defrayed; and the restaurant gained the benefits of proximity to the parking facility. 365 U.S. at 723, 724. The Court concluded that:

Addition of all these activities, obligations and responsibilities of the Authority, the benefits mutually conferred, together with the obvious fact that the restaurant is operated as an integral part of a public building devoted to a public parking service, indicates that degree of state participation and involvement in discriminatory action which it was the design of the Fourteenth Amendment to condemn.
365 U.S. at 724.

The *Burton* case, as can be seen, goes further than *Shelley v. Kraemer*. The issue is no longer limited to judicial enforcement of private contracts. In *Burton* the question is whether private uses of property, in terms of racial preference, can be restricted by the courts on the ground that there is "state participation and involvement" in the private property. The overwhelming involvement of the state in all aspects of private property today leads to the conclusion that the *Burton* doctrine can be used to eliminate virtually all expressions of racial preference by private owners on private property, as a matter of constitutional law. Moreover, the doctrine can be used to restrict other voluntary uses of property which do not conform to prevailing majority sentiment.

615

A FEW EXAMPLES of the broadness of the concept of "state involvement" demonstrates how easily private property can be limited merely by redefining it as government-involved p r o p e r t y. *Smith v. Holiday Inns of America, Inc.*, 220 F. Supp. 1 (M.D. Tenn. 1963) was a class action to enjoin the defendant motel from continuing its policy of refusing to accept Negroes as guests. The land for the motel had been acquired by the city of Nashville as part of an urban redevelopment project. The Holiday Inns purchased the land from the city, paying full market value, without tax rebates; the Inns erected the motel with its own funds and at no cost to the public; the operating motel paid all relevant taxes; and, it was found, the state had no interest in the property and no voice in the management, operation and control of the motel.

This did not satisfy the court, however. Since the deed to the property contained several reservations and covenants placed there by the state and federal governments, to insure future uses of the land in harmony with the redevelopment project, the court held that the state was "involved in private conduct to a significant extent," and the private motel was compelled to drop its policy regarding Negro guests.[1] 220 F. Supp. at 8.

Another recent case, *Simkins v. Moses H. Cone Memorial Hospital*, 323 F.2d 959 (4th Cir. 1963), demonstrates how participation of any sort by a government entity in private property takes that property out of the voluntary sector and places it in the coercive sector of the economy. *Simkins* was an action by Negro physicians, dentists, and patients to compel private hospitals to end racial discrimination. The hospitals, which were entirely private, had accepted federal aid under the Hill-Burton Act (Hospital Survey and Construction Act), 42 U.S.C.A. §291. The court held that acceptance of federal monies placed the hospitals under the rule of the *Burton* case, and Negroes could not be excluded as either doctors or patients:

> Weighing the circumstances we are of the opinion that this case is controlled by Burton . . . . Here the most

---

[1] *Smith v. Holiday Inns of America, Inc.,* has been affirmed by the Court of Appeals for the Sixth Circuit. 336 F.2d 630 (6th Cir. 1964). The Court noted that the Civil Rights Act of 1964 would plainly render the motel's policy of racial exclusion illegal, but, since neither party raised mootness as a defense, they considered the case on its merits.

The motel operator attempted to bring the case outside the rule of the "sit-in" cases by contending, on appeal, that the excluded Negro failed to prove that the motel's actions were "under color of any state law, statute, ordinance, regulation, custom or usage." The Court rejected this argument, stressing that this motel was part and parcel of a large, significant, and continuing public enterprise, *i. e.,* the urban redevelopment project. Thus, state action exists and the exclusion of Negroes in this context violates the Fourteenth Amendment.

Despite this holding, the Court emphasized that "We do not hold that the mere fact that a State agency once held title to a piece of property affects private title forever after with some public quality." It will be interesting to see if the Supreme Court adheres to this admonition.

significant contacts compel the conclusion that the necessary "degree of state [in the broad sense, including federal] participation and involvement" is present as a result of the participation by the defendants in the Hill-Burton program. The massive use of public funds and extensive state-federal sharing in the common plan are all relevant factors, ... But we emphasize that this is not merely a controversy of a sum of money . . . . As the case affects the defendants it raises the question of whether they may escape constitutional responsibilities for the equal treatment of citizens, arising from participation in a joint federal and state program allocating aid to hospital facilities throughout the state. 323 F. 2d at 967.

TO SUMMARIZE these cases, it has been held that "state action" or "state involvement" exists in private property when that property is: (a) leased from the government, and is physically part of a government project; (b) purchased from the government, with the government attaching some covenants restricting use to the deed of sale; and (c) the beneficiary of federal financial assistance. In each situation, the private property owner has been held subject to the same restrictions as a government body.

The most recent Supreme Court extensions of the "state involvement" doctrine have been in the celebrated "sit-in" cases in the South. In each of these cases, civil rights demonstrators entered the "white only" section of segregated lunch counters or restaurants; they demanded service and refused to leave until served. The store manager, following the restaurant's policy, refused to serve them and asked them to leave; when they refused, he called the police, who arrested the demonstrators for criminal trespass. The defendants were convicted, the lower courts finding a clear case of trespass on property wherein the owner did not want their continued presence.

In reversing these cases, the Supreme Court found "state involvement" present in every instance. *Peterson v. Greenville,* 373 U.S. 244 (1963), for example, involved a city where the local ordinance required separation of the races in restaurants (clearly an unconstitutional ordinance). Said the Court:

> It cannot be denied that here the City of Greenville, an agency of the State, has provided by its ordinance that the decision as to whether a restaurant facility is to be operated on a desegregated basis is to be reserved to it. When the State has commanded a particular result, it has saved to itself the power to determine that result and thereby "to a significant extent" has "become involved" in it, and, in fact, has removed that decision from the sphere of private choice.
> 373 U.S. at 247-48.

But, it was argued, the store manager removed the demonstrators because he wanted to run a segregated restaurant, independent of any ordinance. Thus, it was a private decision, without state involvement. Chief Justice Warren disagreed:

> These convictions c a n n o t stand, even assuming, as respondent contends, that the manager would have acted as he did independently of the existence of the ordinance. . . . When a state agency passes a law compelling persons to discriminate against other persons because of race, and the State's criminal processes are employed in a way which enforces the discrimination mandated by that law, such a palpable violation of the Fourteenth Amendment cannot be saved by attempting to separate the mental urges of the discriminators.
> 373 U.S. at 248.

After reading *Peterson v. Greenville,* one would think that the touchstone of state involvement was the local segregation ordinance. In other words, absent the ordinance, the store manager could segregate Negroes to his heart's content; it was only because the city government decreed segregation that the private decision to segregate was unlawful. But in the companion case of *Lombard v. Louisiana,* 373 U.S. 267 (1963), also written by the Chief Justice, there was no ordinance or statute compelling racial segregation in restaurants. The store manager called upon the demonstrators to leave his premises without any local command of law to guide his decision. The Supreme Court found state involvement present anyway. In lieu of an ordinance, the Court found that during the civil rights crisis in the city of New Orleans, the Mayor and the Superintendent of Police had issued statements condemning violence, opposing the "sit-in" movement, and calling for an end to the demonstrations. Although these statements were not made with the force of a law behind them, the Court held that they constituted sufficient "state involvement" to nullify the private decision of the store manager:

> A State, or a city, may act as authoritatively through its executive as through its legislative body. As we interpret the New Orleans city officials' statements, they were determined that the city would not permit Negroes to seek desegregated service in restaurants. Consequently, the city must be treated exactly as if it had an ordinance prohibiting such conduct . . . . These convictions, commanded as they were by the voice of the State directing segregated service at the restaurant, cannot stand.
> 373 U.S. at 273-74.

The development of the law on private racial preference from *Buchanan v. Warley* to the "sit-in" cases has been most extraordinary. From the position that individuals were free to express a racial preference in the use of their property, regardless of ordinance or statute, we have come to the point where private racial preference is invalid if the Mayor expresses the same preference.

The notion that private property is to be treated as if it were an agency of the government whenever the state is "involved" in that property is a most comprehensive doctrine. In a country where every business must be licensed by the state; every profession must be authorized by the state; every piece of real estate must conform to zoning laws, building codes, fire regulations, housing ordinances, etc.; every labor union must be certified by the state; and almost everybody receives money from the state; in such a regimen one is hard pressed to find any substantial voluntary action which does not have "state involvement" to some degree.

If this be true, then the sphere of private contract and use of property is

617

severely restricted. None can deny that discrimination solely on the basis of race is morally indefensible. But the right to discriminate, the right to express a preference in the use of one's property which is at variance with the prevailing majority sentiment is of the very essence of liberty. It is possible that if the state involvement doctrine were alive a century ago, in the days of Dred Scott, the Court would have ruled that a property owner was obligated to treat Negroes as chattels, that manumission was illegal. Today the pendulum is on the other side, in favor of racial equality. But the principle remains: If state involvement means state determination of the uses of property, then private property is a nullity.

For those who may think this analysis far-fetched, and who may disbelieve that this is the trend of judicial decision, I close with the analysis of one of our most advanced jurists, Mr. Justice Douglas. Believing that the majority view in *Lombard v. Louisiana* did not go far enough, Justice Douglas wrote a concurring opinion in which he expressed the view that there was "state action . . . wholly apart from the activity of the Mayor and police." 373 U.S. at 278. This is the basic substance of his commentary:

> Places of public accommodation such as retail stores, restaurants, and the like render a "service which has become of public interest" in the manner of the innkeepers and common carriers of old. . . . In our time the interdependence of people has greatly increased; the days of *laissez faire* have largely disappeared; men are more and more dependent on their neighbors for services as well as for housing and the other necessities of life. By enforcing this criminal mischief statute, invoked in the manner now before us, the Louisiana courts are denying some people access to the mainstream of our highly interdependent life solely because of their race.
>
> When the doors of a business are open to the public, they must be open to all regardless of race if *apartheid* is not to be engrained in our public places. It cannot by reason of the Equal Protection Clause become so engrained with the aid of state courts, state legislatures, or state police.

There is even greater reason to bar a State through its judiciary from throwing its weight on the side of racial discrimination in the present case, because we deal here with a place of public accommodation under license from the State.

State licensing and surveillance of a business serving the public also brings its service into the public domain. This restaurant needs a permit from Louisiana to operate; and during the existence of the license the State has broad powers of visitation and control. This restaurant is thus an instrumentality of the State since the State charges it with duties to the public and supervises its performance. The State's interest in and activity with regard to its restaurants extends far beyond any mere income-producing licensing requirement.

There is no constitutional way, as I see it, in which a State can license and supervise a business serving the public and endow it with the authority to manage that business on the basis of *apartheid,* which is foreign to our Constitution.
373 U.S. at 279, 281, 282-83.

See also the concurring opinion of Mr. Justice Douglas in *Bell v. Maryland.* 378 U.S. 226, 242 (1964).

THE CONCLUSIONS expressed by Mr. Justice Douglas have been incorporated into the Public Accommodations section of the Civil Rights Act of 1964. However, the statute finds the authority of Congress to interfere with the racial policies of private owners in the plenary power granted the federal government by the Commerce clause of the Constitution.

The view of Justice Douglas goes much further. He enunciates a trend of juridical thinking which holds that all private properly used for business purposes is, as he phrased it, "an instrumentality of the State." If this be true, then private business establishments must indeed conform to the current judicial interpretation of the Constitution, even absent all civil rights laws. The pattern of decision reviewed by this paper demonstrates that in the conflicts between the imposition of normative values by the state and the liberty of private property, it is property which is being sacrificed.

NEW BOOKS AND ARTICLES

THE FOLLOWING IS A SELECT LIST OF BOOKS AND ARTICLES WHICH, IN THE OPINION OF THE EDITORS, MAY BE OF INTEREST TO OUR READERS.

Armen A. Alchian and William R. Allen, *University Economics*. Belmont, Calif., Wadsworth Publishing Co., 1964. $11.35 (text edition $8.50). An excellent new introductory economics text by two well-known UCLA Professors — both of the "Chicago School" — designed to relegate Samuelson's text to the role of an inferior good.

Martin Anderson, *The Federal Bulldozer*: *A Critical Analysis of Urban Renewal*, 1949-1962. Cambridge, Mass., The MIT Press, 1964. $5.95. The first major analysis of the federal urban renewal program since its inception. In the opinion of Edward C. Banfield of Harvard University, "There may be some fine points to quibble about, but *The Federal Bulldozer* makes rubble of the urban renewal program."

George J. Stigler, "Public Regulation of the Securities Markets," *The Journal of Business*, April 1964. Prof. Stigler presents fundamental criticisms of the recently published *Special Study of the Securities Markets* on grounds of both methodology and validity of its conclusions, saying "Once we ask for the evidence for its policy proposals, the immense enterprise becomes a promiscuous collection of conventional beliefs and personal prejudices." The article is mainly devoted to setting forth a few statistical models by which the efficiency of the securities market might be judged both before and after the establishment of SEC regulation. In the October 1964 issue of *The Journal of Business* two articles appear in reply, and sharply criticize several points which Stigler makes in the earlier article; but they fail on the whole to refute the thrust of his argument. In his rebuttal, also appearing in the October 1964 issue, Prof. Stigler comments: "The issue is precisely that of the use of 'scientific method' versus 'common sense.' Either we present explicit hypotheses and test them by the developing techniques of the social sciences, or we rely upon the a priori case for protecting investors plus the scandals revealed by a Pecora, or the a priori case for letting men conduct their own affairs plus the counter-scandals revealed by some new counter-Pecora."

Ronald Hamowy, "Liberalism and Neo-Conservatism: Is a Synthesis Possible," *Modern Age*, Fall 1964. A noteworthy attack upon the position that classical liberalism and modern conservatism can be synthesized into a single right-wing philosophy. Hamowy argues that both classical liberalism and modern conservatism arise from distinct and separate traditions of thought, and that their basic premises are fundamentally in conflict.

The fifth volume of the *Journal of Law and Economics* (dated October 1962) has been issued, and includes articles by George J. Stigler, Ronald Coase, Yale Brozen, and others. Of all American scholarly journals, this annual publication is undoubtedly the one most solidly in the classical liberal tradition. A complete set (five issues) may be obtained for $12.50 (students $5.00) by writing: Prof. Aaron Director, *The Journal of Law and Economics*, University of Chicago Law School, Chicago, Illinois 60637.

Philip B. Kurland, "The Supreme Court 1963 Term, Foreword," *Harvard Law Review*, November 1964. A lengthy evaluation of the decisions handed down by the Supreme Court during 1963 which is generally critical of the path the court is taking. Prof. Kurland notes four movements which have gained strength

619

during the last decade: "the emerging primacy of equality as a guide to constitutional decision . . . the effective subordination, if not destruction, of the federal system . . . the enhancement of judicial dominion at the expense of the power of other branches of government, national as well as state . . . [and] the absence of workmanlike product, the absence of right quality [in the decisions of the court]." In regard to the first of these movements, he notes the more and more frequent tendency of the court to appeal to the equal protection clause rather than to the due process clause of the Fourteenth Amendment. "There are two primary problems that arise under the equal protection clause. The first is the ambiguity inherent in the relevant term, whether it be 'equality' or 'equal protection of the laws.' The second major difficulty results from the possible conflict of the notion of equality with that of liberty or some other fundamental constitutional value."

Regenery has published two new books on or by Albert Jay Nock: his autobiography, *Memoirs of a Superfluous Man* (Chicago, 1964. $5.95), is reprinted from the 1943 edition which is no longer available; and Robert J. Crunden, *The Mind and Art of Albert Jay Nock*. Chicago, 1964. $4.95. The latter is an excellent intellectual biography, and contains an appendix listing his uncollected articles.

Richard M. Weaver, *Visions of Order: The Cultural Crisis of Our Time*. Baton Rouge, La., Louisiana State University Press, 1964. $4.50. A posthumous collection of Prof. Weaver's essays concerned with an elaboration of the uses of order and tradition in society, and a critique of modern-liberalism and sentimental democracy.

Hanson W. Baldwin, "Should We End the Draft?," *New York Times Magazine*, Sept. 27, 1964. The military expert of the *New York Times* summarizes the major arguments for and against ending conscription, while lending the weight of his authority to the opinion that "there is not much doubt that long-term professional services — active and reserve — are better suited to the military requirements of the atomic age than large, semi-trained, rapid-turnover forces drafted or induced to serve by the prospect of the draft."

Prof. Ernest van den Haag of the New School discusses the question of Negro intelligence in an interesting interview published in *National Review* ("Intelligence or Prejudice?," December 1, 1964). His conclusions are essentially: (1) There is no scientific evidence supporting the currently popular theory that no innate intelligence differences exist between ethnic groups; (2) There is some, although not conclusive, evidence that the contrary is true; and (3) that even if (2) were proven to be the case, genetically determined intellectual inferiority of the members of a particular race in no way implies their moral inferiority. See also the criticisms and reply in the Feb. 9, 1965, issue of *National Review*. On the same theme there is an excellent review of Weyl and Possony's *Geography of Intellect* in the *University of Chicago Law Review*, Spring 1964, by Warren Lehman. Rather than dealing with the shoddy and unscientific approach of the authors, Lehman concentrates on the possible legal implications of their conclusion that interracial intelligence comparisons indicate sharp distinctions exist. Lehman attacks the thesis — interestingly enough shared by many violent anti-racists — that scientific evidence on the intellectual inferiority, superiority, or equality of one race over another is relevant to their legal (and particularly constitutional) status.

The latest (we think) issue of *Focus Midwest* (Vol. III, Number 6) is devoted to a "roster of the right wing" which runs the gamut from the American Farm Bureau to the Soldiers of the Cross and the American Nazi Party. If one is inured to the incredibly unsophisticated approach manifested by the leftist counterparts of The Christian Crusade, he will find much information of interest and value in this publication.

Lyndon Johnson Got 130% of The Votes Needed to Lose!

The great victory of Conservatism at the polls in November must not cause the Forces of Freedom to be lulled into complacency. Even though 26 million right-thinking Americans spoke out against moral decay, we must remember that 40 million misguided people—besotted by pornography and drugged by fluoridated water—confusedly endorsed the status quo!

We must use our strength to press onward! No resting on our laurels! In the next election the triumph will be even greater! We will boost our strength to 40% of the electorate. Conservatism has come, seen, and conquered!

We at NEW INDIVIDUALIST REVIEW stand solidly in the mainstream of this great march, urging onward the flood of victory. The Editors of NIR, however, would remind our compatriots only that

> (1) The enemy is stronger than ever, although recent political events may make us unduly optimistic.
>
> (2) To stay alert, we must stay well informed and pure.
>
> (3) NIR doesn't cost very much.

REMEMBER . . . When roving Communist bands come through your community, they must not find an economically illiterate populace . . . Subscribe to NEW INDIVIDUALIST REVIEW!

NEW INDIVIDUALIST REVIEW   12

IDA NOYES HALL
University of Chicago, Chicago, Illinois 60637

Please enter my subscription for one year at $2.00 ☐   Students, $1.00 ☐
(Two Years at $3.75, Students, $1.75)

I also enclose a contribution of $. . . . .

NAME . . . .

ADDRESS . . . .

IF STUDENT: SCHOOL . . . . YEAR OF GRAD . . . .

622

ESSAYS IN THE HISTORY OF ECONOMICS

By GEORGE J. STIGLER

Professor Stigler is one of the most distinguished proponents of the Chicago school of economics, a group of economists past and present who have stressed the value of the free, competitive market. This volume is a collection of some of his articles on the history of economic theory. Professor Stigler himself chose the essays which include his reflections on originality in scientific progress; the politics of political economists; the development of utility theory; Ricardian value and distribution; perfect competition; Fabian socialism; marginal productivity theory; and the Giffen paradox.

400 *pages* $6.95

THE CREATIVE ORGANIZATION

Edited by GARY A. STEINER

These various papers are the result of a recent seminar at the Graduate School of Business of the University of Chicago. Among the participants were Bernard Berelson, Jerome S. Bruner, and Paul Meehl representing social scientists, Ralph W. Tyler and W. Allen Wallis speaking for the educators, and B. E. Besinger, Peter Peterson, and David Ogilvie, for the executives. Conclusions drawn at this seminar point to no easy solution for the establishment of a creative organization. The central problem may well be, in Mr. Steiner's words, "to learn the difference between creating productivity and producing creativity."

June, 288 *pages* $5.00

CAPITALISM AND FREEDOM

By MILTON FRIEDMAN

These provocative and controversial essays discuss the proper role of competitive capitalism in a free society. " . . . this book is a brilliant defense of libertarianism by a cogent, intellectual spokesman." — EDWIN McDOWELL, *Christian Economics.* " . . . an eloquent, spirited, and provocative book to show how the ideal of personal freedom may be realized in— and only in—a system of competitive capitalism." —EDWARD C. BANFIELD, *National Review.* " . . . anyone with faith in the power of government to improve our lot will find it difficult and hazardous exercise to match wits with Milton Friedman." —HENRY C. WALLICH, *Challenge.*

Cloth $3.95
Paper $1.50

THE UNIVERSITY OF CHICAGO PRESS

Chicago and
London

VOLUME 4
NUMBER 1
SUMMER 1965

New
INDIVIDUALIST
Review

FINANCING HIGHER EDUCATION

BENJAMIN A. ROGGE

TRENDS IN THE
U. S. SUPREME COURT

PHILIP B. KURLAND

HOW SOVIET PLANNING WORKS

G. WARREN NUTTER

• • •

LEWY'S "THE CATHOLIC
CHURCH AND NAZI GERMANY"

STEPHEN J. TONSOR

A JOURNAL OF CLASSICAL LIBERAL THOUGHT

Summer 1965   50 cents   Vol. 4, No. 1

NEW INDIVIDUALIST REVIEW

SUMMER 1965   **Volume 4 — Number 1**

629

NEW INDIVIDUALIST REVIEW is published quarterly by *New Individualist Review, Inc.,* at Ida Noyes Hall, University of Chicago, Chicago, Illinois 60637.

Opinions expressed in signed articles do not necessarily represent the views of the editors. Editorial, advertising, and subscription correspondence and manuscripts should be sent to NEW INDIVIDUALIST REVIEW, Ida Noyes Hall, University of Chicago, Chicago, Ill. 60637. All manuscripts become the property of NEW INDIVIDUALIST REVIEW.

Subscription rates: $2.00 per year (students $1.00). Two years at $3.75 (students $1.75).

NEW

INDIVIDUALIST

REVIEW

A JOURNAL OF
CLASSICAL LIBERAL THOUGHT

EDITORIAL STAFF

Editor-in-Chief • Ralph Raico

Associate Editors • J. Michael Cobb • James M. S. Powell
Robert Schuettinger

Editorial Assistants • Douglas Adie • Burton Gray
Edwin Harwood • Edward Kimak • James A. Rock
Ernest L. Marraccini

EDITORIAL ADVISORS

Yale Brozen • Milton Friedman • George J. Stigler
University of Chicago

F. A. Hayek   Benjamin Rogge
University of Freiburg   Wabash College

630

Complaints of the loss of individuality and the lessening of respect for the person and his rights have become a commonplace of our time; they nonetheless point to a cause for genuine concern. NEW INDIVIDUALIST REVIEW, an independent journal associated with no organization or political party, believes that in the realm of politics and economics the most valuable system guaranteeing proper respect for individuality is that which, historically, has gone by the name of classical liberalism; the elements of this system are private property, civil liberties, the rule of law, and, in general, the strictest limits placed on the power of government. It is the purpose of the Review to stimulate and encourage explorations of important problems from a viewpoint characterized by thoughtful concern with individual liberty.

Financing Higher Education

in the United States

BENJAMIN A. ROGGE

THE PURPOSE OF THIS study is to explore certain current and expected problems in the financing of higher education in the United States. In particular, it will be directed to an evaluation of one method of solving these problems: the method of full-cost pricing of the services of higher education.[1]

The central thesis of the study is that full-cost pricing has much to recommend it, both as a solution to the pressing financial problems of higher education and as a solution to other serious problems flowing from below-cost pricing. It is argued that the traditional reasons advanced to support the need for subsidy to higher education, even if accepted, do not demand below-cost pricing as the method of subsidy. A secondary thesis is that the case for subsidy has itself been both exaggerated and distorted and requires careful reexamination.

No time need be spent here establishing the fact that the colleges and universities of this country, both public and private, do indeed face a serious financial problem. This is one of the best publicized facts in the United States today. In sum, the story is that of an industry which confronts a financial crisis because of a fast-rising demand for its services.

Benjamin A. Rogge, a faculty advisor to *New Individualist Review*, is professor of political economy at Wabash College, and is currently at work on a book on the economics of discrimination.

This statement of the problem is used deliberately to throw in sharp relief the unique character of the industry. It is one in which the service is sold for much less than its cost of production.[2] It is this and this only which makes an increase in demand a matter of deep concern rather than a reason for optimism. An increase in the size of a student body usually means a larger deficit —a deficit that must be financed through public and/or private subsidy.

To most students of the problem, including most college and university presidents, the problem is simply one of raising more money to meet the larger deficits. To only a few does it seem to be reason for a careful and thorough reexamination of the nature and purposes of higher education and of the financial arrangements most likely to promote those purposes. It is the thesis

631

---

[1] The findings may or may not be relevant to elementary and secondary education. At the very least, this relevance would have to be established by a study specifically directed to those two stages in the education process. In this regard, the reader's attention is called to an article in the *New Individualist Review*, Vol. III, Number 1, Summer 1963, by Robert L. Cunningham, "Education: Free and Public," in which he discusses a system of publicly financed but privately managed elementary and secondary educational institutions.

[2] A study of various collections of data reveals that the revenues from tuition charges cover from 15 per cent to 25 per cent of the costs at publicly-controlled institutions and from 45 per cent to 55 per cent of the costs at privately-controlled institutions.

of this study that such a reexamination is badly needed. In particular, to view the problem as simply a desperate need for expanded subsidy to higher education is to ignore the many problems that are associated with below-cost pricing — problems that will not be solved even if the expanded subsidy is secured.

This study is designed to concentrate attention on how educational services are *priced,* not on how the buyers of those services secure the funds to pay the prices asked. That is, full-cost pricing does not rule out private and/or public subsidies to individual students. There are really two questions here: One is how the service should be priced, and the other is who should ultimately bear the cost of the service. Both will be examined, but the first will receive the more careful study.

TO SUBJECT HIGHER education to economic analysis may seem to be laying profane hands on a sacred symbol Such is the mystique of this "industry" that it must not be appraised with the vulgar calculus of the market place.

Yet, "the vulgar calculus of the market place" still remains as the most humane method man has yet devised to solve those problems of allocation and division which are ubiquitous and permanent in human society. This we have accepted as a people by our continued commitment to the free market form of economic organization. We profess our faith in this form of economic organization for the economy at large, but deny that it is suited to the purposes of higher education. Free market pricing is deemed appropriate for most goods and services, but is rejected in pricing the services of higher education. The reasons advanced to support this position will be examined, but attention will be directed first to certain effects of this policy on the educational system itself. The question to be examined can be phrased in this way: How does below-cost pricing affect the college and university system of this country?

The impact of below-cost pricing on higher education will be examined in four parts: problems of finance, problems of rationing, problems of motivation, and problems of educational efficiency.

To most observers the *only* problem presented by below-cost pricing is the financial problem—the deficits that must be underwritten by the taxpayer or the private donor. Admittedly the financial problem is a serious one. This fact is clearly evidenced in the increasing tendency for college and university presidents (even of tax-supported institutions) to be fund-raisers first and educational leaders and scholars second.

The college or university president must of necessity be a professional begger and the pressure of performing in this role is undoubtedly one of the factors leading to the rapid turnover of presidents in American colleges and universities.

The financial problem presented by below-cost pricing *is* a serious one and is rapidly becoming a problem of fantastic proportions. Given the fact of below-cost pricing, there seems to be no solution to this problem that does not involve a significant increase in the burden of the taxpayer. Nor does it seem likely that it will be solved without increasing reliance on funds supplied by the Federal government.

THE FINANCIAL PROBLEM, however, is not the only problem presented by below-cost pricing, nor is it even necessarily the most serious. At least as serious is the rationing problem which comes from selling educational services at well below the price which would clear the market.

The price of a good or service in a free market is not only a source of funds to cover the costs of the good or service. It is also the instrument which answers the question of to whom the available supply is to go. That is, the price *rations* the total number of units available among those who wish to buy the product. It does this on the principle that the product is to go to those who are willing to give up the most *i.e.,* pay the highest price) to obtain it.

The acceptability of this principle need not be debated here. It is important only to note that it is a device for rationing.

Moreover, it is a device that clears the market and that operates without any need for the seller to choose among buyers on some personal basis.

To set a price below the market price is to create an excess of quantity demanded over quantity supplied, whether the product be sirloin steak, rental housing, or education. This, in turn, requires of the seller that he find some way to determine whose requests for the product are to be granted and whose denied.

The problem of rationing the available educational services is fast becoming one of the major problems of higher education. This has brought into sharp relief the issue of the rationing principle to be used. The generally accepted principle is that educational opportunities are to go to those possessed of the greatest potential for intellectual activity; but closer examination reveals that this principle can be questioned on both practical and theoretical grounds.

If the principle is accepted, the first task is to *measure* potential for success in college. No one who has served on the admissions committee of a college or university would argue that this is a simple task. On the contrary, it is one of the most difficult tasks of college administration. Techniques for measuring potential are being improved each year, but mistakes are still made and will continue to be made under the best of measurement programs.

Somewhat less difficult, but no less trying, is the task of determining which students are to be permitted to continue in school, once admitted, and which are to be denied further access to the services of higher education.

The rationing technique under discussion here—whether applied in the selection of students for admission or in the selection of those to continue—operates in such a way that it often appears to the rejected student as a personally discriminatory technique. The rationing system of the free market at least has the advantage of operating as does the system of justice represented by the blindfolded goddess holding the scales. It does not ask "Who are you?" or "What kind of a person are you?" or "Did your mother or father attend this college?"

but only "Are you willing to pay the price?" Cruel as this may sometimes seem in practice, it would appear on balance to be less cruel and less humiliating than the personalized techniques of non-market rationing.

YET EVEN IF POTENTIAL for intellectual growth and general success in college could be measured with complete accuracy and in such a way as to leave no room for personally discriminatory decisions, there would still exist serious questions of the appropriateness of this principle. It seems to rest on the assumption that large jars should be filled with the purest wine, while smaller jars should receive nothing but such rainwater as they can catch from the skies. If education is opportunity for personal growth, are we to deny it in some arbitrary way to those unfortunate enough to start from a lower level or to possess less absolute capacity for growth? Is 30 per cent growth for the bright student more to be preferred than 30 per cent growth for the less able student?

Is it not possible that the brighter student is more capable of educating himself than the weaker student; that in fact it might *not* be nonsense to say to the quick-minded student, "Go educate yourself," and to the less-gifted student, "Come, we will try to help you"? As a matter of fact, current practice on United States campuses is moving toward independent study programs for the gifted students — a back-handed recognition of the fact that to such students the traditional apparatus of the college may not be important. This is not to argue that admission should be limited to the *bad* student, but only to indicate that the principle that admission should be limited to the *good* student can be questioned.

Suppose this same principle of making educational opportunities available only to those with high potential to benefit from these opportunities were applied to other goods and services. The sale of opera tickets would then be restricted to those who could establish ability to enjoy opera, wine would be sold only to the recognized connoisseur, and most

633

wives would be denied the privilege of attending baseball games with their husbands.

For almost all other goods and services we assume that the individual is the best judge of whether or not he is receiving his money's worth. Only in education do we give to the seller the power to make this decision for the buyer.

It might be answered that this is made necessary by the fact that college students are too immature to make this decision for themselves. This answer ignores the fact that the family of the college student participates in this decision and that we permit this same family to make most other decisions for the children in the family. Why is the family less able to make decisions about education than about medical care or clothing or housing for the m e m b e r s of the family?

In sum, the rationing principle in current use in higher education in the United States today is questionable in both philosophy and in practice.[3] Yet below-cost pricing makes some such arbitrary and capricious method of rationing a necessity.

UNDER THE PRICE SYSTEM, a unit of any given product goes to the one who is willing to give up the most to get it. This is a rationing principle which tends in part to be a measure of strength of motivation. It tends to weed out those who have no great interest in the product. The effect of far-below-cost pricing in higher education is to admit many who have no strong desire to be educated — thus the curious situation in which professors and deans must be constantly belaboring students to take that which they are supposed to desire. We are in the position of a grocer who must keep close watch on his customers to see that they do not pay for the mer-

chandise and then try to get out of the store without it.

Moreover, the effect on the motivation of teachers is equally significant. To the extent that their incomes derive from sources other than student fees, they are freed from some part of the necessity of really attending to the interests and wishes of their students. It is curious how irritated teachers become at any suggestion that their product be evaluated by their customers. They seem to really desire that each teacher be judge in his own cause or, at worst, that he be judged by his colleagues (who, of course, should not be so vulgar as to consult s t u d e n t opinion on his work as a teacher).

A number of the points under discussion here are well made in Adam Smith's *The Wealth of Nations*. Smith comments at length on the effect of divorcing teachers' income from student fees as follows:

In other universities, the teacher is prohibited from receiving any honorary or fee from his pupils, and his salary constitutes the whole of the revenue which he derives from his office. His interest is, in this case, set as directly in opposition to his duty as it is possible to set it. It is the interest of every man to live as much at his ease as he can; and if his emoluments are to be precisely the same, whether he does or does not perform some very laborious duty, it is certainly his interest, at least as interest is vulgarly understood, either to neglect it altogether, or, if he is subject to some authority which will not suffer him to do this, to perform it in as careless and slovenly a manner as that authority will permit. If he is naturally active and a lover of labour, it is his interest to employ that activity in any way from which he can derive some advantage, rather than in the performance of his duty, from which he can derive none.

If the authority to which he is subject resides in the body corporate, the college, or university, of which he himself is a member, and in which the greater part of the other members are, like himself, persons who either are, or ought to be teachers, they are likely to make a common cause, to be all very indulgent to one another, and every man to consent that his neighbour may neglect his duty, provided he himself

___

[3] College faculties usually give enthusiastic endorsement to this rationing principle. Could this be because they find it easier and more pleasant to interest the already interested, to seem to produce growth in those destined to grow anyway? This in an understandable feeling, but it seems something less than sufficient as a justification for the principle.

is allowed to neglect his own. In the university of Oxford, the greater part of the public professors have, for these many years, given up altogether even the pretence of teaching.[4]

He then comments on the effect of loss of student control in the choice of teachers:

If in each college, the tutor or teacher, who was to instruct each student in all arts and sciences, should not be voluntarily chosen by the student, but appointed by the head of the college; and if, in case of neglect, inability, or bad usage, the student should not be allowed to change him for another, without leave first asked and obtained; such a regulation would not only tend very much to extinguish all emulation among the different tutors of the same college, but to diminish very much, in all of them, the necessity of diligence and of attention to their respective pupils. Such teachers, though very well paid by their students, might be as much disposed to neglect them, as those who are not paid by them at all or who have no other recompense but their salary.

If the teacher happens to be a man of sense, it must be an unpleasant thing to him to be conscious, while he is lecturing to his students, that he is either speaking or reading nonsense, or what is very little better than nonsense. It must, too, be unpleasant to him to observe, that the greater part of his students desert his lectures; or perhaps, attend upon them with plain enough marks of neglect, contempt, and derision. If he is obliged, therefore, to give a certain number of lectures, those motives alone, without any other interest, might dispose him to take some pains to give tolerably good ones. Several different expedients, however, may be fallen upon, which will effectually blunt the edge of all those incitements to diligence. The teacher, instead of explaining to his pupils himself the science in which he proposes to instruct them, may read some book upon it; and if this book is written in a foreign and dead language, by interpreting it to them into their own, or, what would give him still less trouble, by making them interpret it to him, and by now and then making an occasional remark upon it, he may flatter himself

that he is giving a lecture. The slightest degree of knowledge and application will enable him to do this, without exposing himself to contempt or derision, by saying any thing that is really foolish, absurd, or ridiculous. The discipline of the college, at the same time, may enable him to force all his pupils to the most regular attendance upon his sham lecture, and to maintain the most decent and respectful behavior during the whole time of the performance.

The discipline of colleges and universities is in general contrived, not for the benefit of the students, but for the interest, or, more properly speaking, for the ease of the masters. Its object is, in all cases, to maintain the authority of the master, and whether he neglects or performs his duty, to oblige the students in all cases to behave to him as if he performed it with the greatest diligence and ability. It seems to presume perfect wisdom and virtue in the one order, and the greatest weakness and folly in the other. Where the masters, however, really perform their duty, there are no examples, I believe, that the greater part of the students ever neglect theirs. No discipline is ever requisite to force attendance upon lectures which are really worth the attending, as is well known wherever any such lectures are given.[5]

In sum, then, while the student may find it pleasant to have his education subsidized, the price he pays for this is loss of control over his education. He who pays the piper will call the tune, and if the student is not the one who pays the piper, he cannot call the tune. Moreover, the divorce of teacher income from student fees has a tendency to encourage inefficient and ineffective teaching and to encourage teachers to treat their teaching duties as a necessary evil to be disposed of as quickly as possible to permit them time for more important activities. An exaggeration? Perhaps, but who can say that he has never seen such tendencies at work?

The small, private colleges have the reputation of providing the best quality of teaching in higher education. Why is this? It is difficult to believe that it has no connection at all with the fact that such institutions derive 50 per cent

635

[4] Adam Smith, *The Wealth of Nations* (Modern Library Edition), pp. 717-18.

[5] *Ibid.*, pp. 719-20.

or more of their revenues from student fees. Thus, the quality of the teaching has an important effect on the revenues of the college and the administration is forced to encourage and demand of its faculty a high quality of teaching service.

The effect, then, of below-cost pricing is to make of our colleges a collection of students, many of whom have no real desire to make use of the opportunity, and a collection of teachers who are under no real necessity to provide a high quality of teaching services.

THE PROBLEMS OF educational efficiency are usually discussed under the heading Problems of Academic Freedom; but "academic freedom" is really a misnomer. It should not be confused with freedom in the sense of those rights which are guaranteed to Americans in the Bill of Rights. It is altogether fitting and proper that a person should be free to worship as he pleases (or not to worship at all), to think as he pleases, to speak and write as he pleases *without fear of reprisal by government*. In fact, these rights are the very cornerstone of any free society and they are literally worth dying for; but to say that Paul Robeson should be free to sing the Internationale is a far different thing from saying that we must pay him for singing it. We may believe that Gus Hall should be free to publish books advocating communism, but we are not violating his freedom when we refuse to buy them. Now perhaps we are missing a chance to become better educated by refusing to buy them and that brings us to the point here. So-called academic freedom is really a question of educational efficiency, of the improved understanding which comes from being exposed to a variety of points of view.

No teacher has an inherent right to present a point of view and to be paid for presenting it. If his customers wish not to pay to hear his point of view, this may be unwise on their part; but it is not a violation of any inherent freedom. In fact, to force them, say, through the taxing power of the government to pay a teacher to present a point of view which they do not wish presented is a violation of an important freedom—the freedom of each man to spend his money as he pleases. Consider, for example, the injustice that would be done if the trustees of a college which demands acceptance of the Apostle's Creed as a condition of employment were to be forced to hire or to continue to employ an acknowledged atheist in the interest of academic freedom, or if a Quaker college were forced to hire General Mark Clark as its president.

Insisting that what is called academic freedom does not really involve freedom, however, it not to minimize its importance. On the contrary, even though it is really a question of educational efficiency, it is a very important question. It *is* important that students be given an opportunity to hear and read a variety of points of view, particularly on questions of social policy. In the words of John Stuart Mill, "There is always hope when people are forced to listen to both sides; it is when they attend only to one side that errors harden into prejudices."

THIS BRINGS US BACK finally to the matter of below-cost pricing. The necessity for finding funds to fill the gap between students fees and total costs is always potentially dangerous to the integrity of an institution, to its continued ability to offer a program which embraces a wide range of social philosophies and which is otherwise educationally efficient.

The reasoning runs as follows: While the piper must inevitably be subject to pressure from those who pay him, his opportunity to play a varied and personally satisfying concert is the greater the more numerous the sources of his support and the less dependent he is upon the support of one payer or one group of payers. In other words, his best protection lies in a wide diffusion of the economic power which he confronts. For example, if an institution becomes dependent on a government for support, the government will be strongly tempted to call the tunes. This control can and has been used to dictate not only the "proper" social philosophies for teachers but the "proper" content of the curriculum as well. Even the assumption

636

that the government is controlled by majority vote of the citizenry is cold consolation to a professor or an institution that prefers the point of view of the minority.

In the same way, for a private college to become dependent on a few men of wealth, or on a relatively homogeneous alumni body or on corporation giving, is to create a potential for control and dictation. Of course, a mixing of all of these with student fees does provide considerable diffusion of power, and this is the real strength of the private college as compared to the public; but even this mixing may leave a few men or a few corporations in a position to wield extraordinary influence on the policies of the college. It must be insisted that there is no violation of inherent right if these men or corporations insist on exerting the influence they possess. They have helped to pay the piper and they have a right to call some of the tunes, but this is a situation in which the educational efficiency of the institution may not be maximized. Now sometimes these money-givers from among the philistines have a better idea of what the college should be doing than does the faculty and administration, but there is no reason to believe that their influence will always be benign.

Below-cost pricing combined with public and/or private subsidy creates a situation in which the integrity of the educational institution is not protected by that diffusion of economic power ranged against it which is the real protection of all units—households and firms alike —in a competitive market economy. The private colleges and universities—both because they depend more heavily on student fees and because they draw subsidies from a greater variety of sources— do seem more capable of maintaining an educationally efficient program than do the large, state-supported institutions. The argument is not that the public donor is more given to intervening or is less tolerant than the private donor. The argument is that the public donor agency may have control of as much as 80 per cent of the revenue sources of the institutions with which it is involved, whereas the private donor rarely has control over more than a small fraction of the revenue sources of the institutions with which he is involved.

BUT WOULD NOT FREEING the colleges from subsidy-oriented control and placing them under customer control be a move from the frying-pan into the fire? Is the college student really equipped to evaluate the service he is buying?[6]

This is a difficult question to answer. If I may be permitted to draw from my own experiences as a college teacher and college dean, I would say that the student is a much better judge of the quality of the educational services he is receiving than he is commonly held to be. In the main, students *are* able to distinguish between those faculty members who provide excellent learning opportunities and those who provide mediocre or worse. The testimony on which the student has been convicted as a poor judge is the testimony of those who are themselves the object of the judging and who have traditionally resented the very practice of student appraisal.

And here again it must be remembered that the student's family often participates in the decision-making, adding the maturity of adult critical faculties to the immediate impressions of the student.

However, the greatest benefit to be derived from customer control is that the judgment of no one customer is critical to the operation of the institution. No small group of legislators, no small groups of corporations or individuals, must be placated for the institution to survive and prosper. Nor need all institutions serve the same type of customer. The critical customer can be told to go elsewhere, because no one customer is

637

---

[6] Thus, Howard Mumford Jones of Harvard University writes, "It is a misleading function when the concept of learning is, as is too often the case, sacrificed to the concept of teaching; when, for example, adolescents are solemnly asked to rate mature scholars in terms of their entertainment value in the classroom, and an administration in turn seriously accepts these callow judgments as a factor in the keeping and promoting of scholars." H. M. Jones, "The Service of the University," *ACLS Newsletter,* Winter, 1956-57, p. 12.

of great significance. To repeat, it is not the "quality" of the power wielders but the diffusion of power under customer control that protects the integrity of the institution.

In sum, below-cost pricing inevitably creates a threat to what has been called "academic freedom," or "educational efficiency." To expect those who provide the subsidies to refrain from interfering with the operation of the school is to make a demonstrably weak assumption. On the other hand, to do as many seem to feel appropriate, to somehow "force" the donors (perhaps through the operation of an organization like the American Association of University Professors) to keep their hands off the institutions they have subsidized is to deny another important freedom—the freedom of each man to choose the purposes to which his money resources are to be put. This is particularly true when the donor is the taxpayer who does not have the immediate option of stopping his contributions. He is ordered to pay and then is told that he must not question the purposes to which his money resources are to be put. Under the system of below-cost pricing there is no way of guaranteeing so-called "academic freedom" that does not involve a denial of other freedoms — or that does not demand of the donor a superhuman restraint from directing the uses to which his funds are to be allocated.

TWO PRIMARY ARGUMENTS are advanced in support of below-cost pricing. One is based upon the assumption that the benefits of higher education flow not only to the students who are the direct customers of the schools, but also to society at large—that every member of society profits from being surrounded by and led by an educated citizenry. The other is the pure egalitarian argument that the principle of equality of opportunity demands that each young man and each young woman be given the opportunity of attending college, regardless of ability to pay for the services rendered. These arguments will be examined in turn.

The traditional thesis is that the student "captures" only a part of the gain that flows from his college education. Some part of the gain flows to society at large. Thus, in the Northwest Ordinance of 1787 we find the following statement: "Religion, morality and knowledge being necessary to good government and the happiness of mankind, schools and the means of education shall forever be encouraged."

The student tends to push his purchases of education only to the point where the *private* gain from another unit would be equal to the cost of another unit. However, it is in society's interest that he push his purchases beyond this to the point where the *social* gain from another unit would be equal to the cost of that unit. This requires that the student receive a subsidy sufficient to induce him to purchase the additional units of education.

But even if this principle be accepted, below-cost pricing does not inevitably follow. The subsidy could be provided directly to the student to permit him to pay the market price to whatever institution he chooses to attend. We have implemented our desire to provide bread to those who do not have the means to buy it, not by asking bakeries to sell all bread at below-market prices and then subsidizing the bakeries, but rather by providing a direct subsidy to the families involved. In particular, we have not insisted on the government actually operating bakeries to take care of this problem. The thesis under study does *not* establish a need for government-operated educational institutions, and in fact, on other grounds, there is good reason to prefer privately operated to publicly operated colleges and universities.

Nor does this thesis establish any case for below-cost pricing of (or even for subsidy to) *all* the services now provided by higher education. It seems to establish a case only for those programs of education which contribute to the citizenship qualities of the individual. Surely those courses which are primarily vocational in nature make only an insignificant contribution to the development of the citizen.

Professor George Stigler of the University of Chicago has commented on this issue as follows:

The basic defense for public and private subsidy of higher education is of course that it confers large social benefits, quite aside from any benefits accruing to the individual. This defense is largely wrong, simply as a matter of fact. The majority of college students concentrate their efforts on vocational studies whose general social value is measured, comprehensibly and with tolerable accuracy, by the earnings of the graduates. In 1954, of 187,500 bachelor's and first professional degrees received by men in the United States, 63.1 per cent were vocational degrees. For women the corresponding percentage was 54.8. The largest fields were:

Business Administration	35,255
Engineering	22,264
Education	16,885
Medicine	16,458
Law	8,687
Agriculture	7,687

The general scientific and cultural values of these disciplines scarcely call for something like a 50 per cent subsidy of the costs of institutions of higher learning.[7]

The principle of social benefit at best calls for subsidy only to the traditional liberal arts programs of colleges and universities and even there does not require below-cost pricing as the technique of implementation. Direct subsidy to the individual student would serve equally as well.

Finally, it might be argued that the social benefits deriving from formal higher education have been much exaggerated. These benefits probably come primarily at the lower levels of education, particularly in the instruction each child receives in the basic skills of communication. Once a young person has acquired these skills, a whole world of knowledge is opened to him, a world in which formal classroom education is only one of many alternatives. It would be difficult to prove that the college graduates in this country have been "better" citizens (if even a yardstick could be found) than the high school graduates. Far from under-emphasizing the importance of formal higher education, we may have grossly exaggerated its im-

_____
[7] G. J. Stigler, "The Economic Theory of Education," an unpublished manuscript.

portance to the maintenance of our free society.

THE SECOND ARGUMENT advanced in support of below-cost pricing is that equality of opportunity must be assured and that this demands equal educational opportunity for all.

In the first place, it should be pointed out that this too would justify only subsidy *in some form*, and provides no specific support for below-cost pricing of the services of higher education. On the contrary, below-cost pricing is a technique that subsidizes the sons and daughters of the wealthy as well as the sons and daughters of the poor. If the goal is to make education available to those who cannot afford it, below-cost pricing is a very blunt and wasteful instrument. Thus, even if the egalitarian view is accepted, far from justifying below-cost pricing, it condemns it as an inefficient means of achieving the desired end.

But the thesis that equal access to higher education, regardless of financial ability to pay for it, is a *sine qua non* of equality of opportunity is not of unquestionable validity either. Support for this thesis usually involves pointing to the demonstrably higher lifetime earnings of college graduates *vis-à-vis* non-college graduates. The inference is drawn that the college education is itself the *cause* of the higher earnings.

One of the most important principles of statistics is that correlation is not the equivalent of causation. In this case, the high correlation between years of education and lifetime earnings may derive in part from the fact that those who attend college possess a generally higher potential to achieve than those who do not. These same people would probably attain to higher income positions even if they were not to go to college. In the same way, those who attend college tend to come from higher-income families than those who do not, and they have such advantages as may come from a firmer financial base as a platform for the launching of a career. Finally, there is good evidence in the current and recent economic history of this country that a young man or woman without a college education is capable of making

639

Page Eleven

rapid economic progress.[8]

Moreover, those who wish to be educated do not face just the one alternative of formal, classroom education. Each person in our modern society is surrounded by opportunities for acquiring the knowledge, skills, and understandings that are the end-product of higher education. One increasingly important set of such opportunities is to be found in the education programs sponsored by business firms for their employees. In addition, there is evidence that the young adult, with some work experience behind him, makes much better use of educational opportunities than does the young person of 18 to 22.

In other words, there is no clear evidence that income earning possibilities are a direct function of education; and even if this could be established, it would still be difficult to prove that formal college education is the only kind of educational opportunity which promotes this end.

Admittedly, there are certain professions (*e.g.*, law, medicine, and engineering) which are open only to those with a certain minimum of formal education; but in most of those cases, the lifetime earnings of those who received the training would easily permit them to pay for their education on a deferred-payment basis. All that is needed here is a capital market that will permit the treating of professional education as an investment in personal capital.

Confirmation of this thesis is found in one unexpected place: in a book whose central thesis is that higher education must be even more subsidized than at present, including a substantial increase in Federal aid to higher education. The book is *A New Basis of Support for Higher Education,* by Thad L. Hungate, Controller and Professor of Education, Teachers College, Columbia University.

In one paragraph he says, "While students and parents may continue to finance student living costs, neither fees nor living expenses should bar a student who has met defined state standards and has been admitted to and accredited for attendance. State aid should supplement family means as needed for this purpose." [9] Yet in the very next paragraph he adds, "It is considered likely that each beneficiary of a college education so lifts his lifetime earnings that the increased taxes he pays will more than repay to society the initial capital it has invested in him."[10] If his increased earnings will permit him to repay the taxpayer, they will also permit him to repay a lending agency on the private capital market! Far from establishing a case for public subsidy, this statement weakens the case for public subsidy and strengthens the case for letting each student finance his own education from some combination of current and anticipated resources.

In sum, the argument that higher education must receive public subsidy to assure equality of income-earning possibilities is questionable in both theory and practice. There is no clear evidence that a formal, college education is itself a cause of higher lifetime earnings; but if it could be established, it would establish not a need for public subsidy, but rather a need for an improved capital market to permit students to pay for their schooling out of the higher earnings produced by that schooling.

IT MIGHT BE ARGUED that the primary inequality associated with less than universal higher education is a *social* inequality, that the non-college person is denied entry to the social circles of the college graduates. This may or may not be true. Certainly there is some evidence that many Americans

---

[8] An interesting reason for one advantage of the college graduate over the non-college person is to be found in the comment of an executive of one of the large steel companies. He says that his company hires so many college graduates each year in its executive development program, not because they have found college graduates to be clearly superior to non-graduates, but because the union rules on seniority prevent them from advancing the really good men from the work force into positions of responsibility. The same rules do not govern the young college graduates hired directly into the management group, and from this follows the company's search for college graduates!

[9] T. L. Hungate, *A New Basis of Support for Higher Education* (New York: Bureau of Publications, Teachers College, Columbia University, 1957), p. 7.
[10] *Ibid.*

look upon the college degree as little more than a card of admission to "polite" society. This case is usually stated less boldly by the philosophers of American higher education. Their stress is upon the "democratizing" influence of our educational system. Thus, Howard Mumford Jones writes,

> . . . the American university operates, and operates successfully, because it is staffed by Americans reared on that simplest of all formulas for getting men to work together, the democratic formula . . . . The great virtue of this remarkable invention is that it rests upon a particular theory of education, including higher education, as a form of public service. The great reproach brought against the ivy colleges in the old days was, indeed, that they did not recognize this doctrine, but were on the contrary expressive of snobbery. The eventual response of the ivy colleges to this reproach is, I think, illuminating. They did not defend the necessity, perhaps even the duty, of creating an intellectual elite; . . . on the contrary, they demonstrated that they are just as public and popular as anybody else. With us, in truth, the popular theory has triumphed over the concept that the nation needs an intellectual elite, and the notion of the university as a service institution prevails in the United States to a degree that astonishes the foreign scholar.[11]

It may well be that making the college degree available to all has a levelling effect on the social system. The colleges and universities may be primarily institutions dedicated to the task of giving young people membership cards in an eventually universal club of college graduates. If so, it is serving a futile purpose. Nothing is surer than that man will develop forms of social differentiation and if one form is eliminated, another will take its place. To pander to envy is hardly a useful and noble role for higher education.

Nor is it likely that the quality and nature of its services will remain unaffected by this goal. Already there is good evidence of the impact of the demand of education for all on the qualitative characteristics of higher education. It would be interesting to speculate on

[11] H. M. Jones, op cit., pp. 9-10.

what would happen to the quality of a "prestige" car like the Cadillac if we were to endeavor to make one available to each family so that no family would have to feel inferior to another. It is quite legitimate to argue that education must be made available to all because otherwise education becomes an element in an unwanted social differentiation, but to so argue is to attempt to satiate man's unlimited capacity to envy his fellow man. Also, it must carry with it certain modifications in the character of higher education which not all would find desirable.

IN SUMMARY, THE following conclusions can be drawn: The present system of below-cost pricing of higher education creates a number of serious problems. These include the problem of deciding which young people are to be admitted to college and then which are to be permitted to continue; the problem of low motivation of many students; the problem of motivation of faculty members created by the fact that they are not paid by their students; and the problem of educational efficiency created by the need to find resources to cover the annual deficits of colleges and universities. The arguments presented to establish the desirability of public and/or private subsidy to higher education, even if accepted, do not demand below-cost pricing. They call only for subsidy in some form, and the problems associated with below-cost pricing suggest that the subsidy should be provided in other ways, perhaps through grants to individual students.

The arguments for subsidy to higher education are not of unquestionable validity. The "social benefit" argument seems to have been exaggerated and at best would apply only to the non-vocational types of higher education. The "equality of opportunity" in the opportunity-to-income sense, cannot be verified by a study of the recent and current economic history of this country. If it could be verified, it would establish not a case for subsidizing higher education, but rather a case for an improved capital market to permit students to borrow against future earnings to meet current educational expenses. The "equality of opportunity" in the sense of opportunity to acquire the social status of a college-trained person may be valid, but this would make of higher education a technique for satisfying a futile and none-too-noble purpose.

IF THE ARGUMENTS developed in this article were to be accepted as valid, what policy changes would seem to be required? Would these changes not call for an unrealistic assumption of the willingness on the part of the American people to modify the traditional arrangements in higher education? Certainly it is true that traditional arrangements cannot be changed quickly or with ease —and this is not an unmixed evil. A certain caution in making changes is usually wise.

It is particularly difficult to secure any reduction of subsidies to special groups, and in particular to secure reduction of subsidies coming from public funds. Those who lose the subsidy lose a considerable sum per capita; those who are relieved of paying for the subsidy gain only a small sum per capita. Thus, the subsidized tend to be much more vocal and aggressive than the subsidizers. However, there is a growing awareness of the frightening financial load of higher education to be expected in the next 10 or 15 years. Some state legislators are already demanding that the state-supported schools increase tuition charges to students.

Clearly any changes would have to begin with the charges at state-supported schools. The private colleges and universities cannot hope to move much closer to full-cost tuition charges until the tuition charges at state-supported schools are increased substantially. The differential in tuition costs already operates to place the private schools at a serious competitive disadvantage.

The first step would seem to be for state-supported institutions to set up a pattern of tuition increases designed to increase the percentage of costs covered by tuition payments. This pattern could call for a final position in which the revenues from tuition fees would be approximately equal to total costs. This could probably be done, of course, only if the state were to also provide an increasing supply of straight grants or loans to students. It would seem to be desirable to move as quickly as possible to the use of only loans to students pursuing strictly vocational courses, and to increase the ratio of loan money to grant money for all students. These state loans and grants could also go to students attending privately operated colleges and universities. This would certainly be consistent with the general principle, but the private colleges would probably be able to bring students in touch with private sources of loan or scholarship money and might probably prefer to do so. In fact, there would be good reason for the state governments to vacate the lending position as rapidly as the private money market could service the needs of students.

This article is basically neutral on the question of whether government aid should come from local and state units or from the Federal government. However, the principle of diffusion of power would seem to establish a preference for local and state units. Also, the general reduction in the financial responsibilities of government for higher education under this plan would largely dissipate the case now being made for Federal aid to higher education.

IT IS PROBABLY unrealistic to expect that higher education in this country could be recast in the ultimate pattern implied in this study; but it is not unrealistic to suppose that p r o g r e s s could be made in bringing all tuition charges closer to the level of full-cost, in greater use of loan techniques in the financing of all education and in the financing of vocational education in particular, and in making greater use of the private capital market in the financing of investments in education. T h e s e changes would also tend to place an increasing emphasis on private as compared to public sponsorship of institutions of higher education. If the arguments advanced in this article are valid, all of these changes would work to the benefit of higher education and of the American society.

Page Fourteen

Trends in the

U. S. Supreme Court

PHILIP   B.   KURLAND

I INTEND TO CONFINE my observations to the constitutional aspects of the Supreme Court's work. It is here that the Court performs its unique role as ultimate arbiter of the meaning of our fundamental law; law beyond the power of the other branches of the government to revise and, for the most part, beyond the control of the people themselves.

Looking over the past decade of the Court's work — roughly the period between the school desegregation cases[1] in 1954 and the reapportionment cases[2] of 1964, one quickly discovers that the Justices have wrought more fundamental changes in the political and legal structure of the United States than during any period in our history since Mr. Chief Justice Marshall first wrote meaning into the abstractions of the Constitution's language. To make my essential point at the outset, the problem is not primarily whether in one's personal opinion these changes are good or bad; but whether the Supreme Court, constituted as it is by nine lawyers with life tenure and politically irresponsible, is the proper organ of government to accomplish the goals it may decide to set for this country.

Philip B. Kurland is the editor of The Supreme Court Review, and a professor of law at the University of Chicago. He is a frequent contributor to law reviews.

THREE DOMINANT MOVEMENTS are evident in the Court's recent work. First and foremost has been the emerging primacy of equality as a guide to constitutional decision. Perhaps an offshoot of the Negro Revolution that the Court helped to sponsor in *Brown v. Board of Education*,[3] the egalitarian revolution in judicial doctrine has made dominant the principles to be read into the Equal Protection clause of the Fourteenth Amendment rather than the Due Process clause, heretofore the polestar of Supreme Court action. Just as the Court read its own notions of appropriate governmental policy into its creation of substantive due process in the period that culminated in the 1930's, so we now have a similar construction by the Court of what the Swiss have most appropriately called "substantive equal

---

[1] *E.g.*, Brown v. Board of Educ., 347 U.S. 483 (1954).

[2] *E.g.*, Reynolds v. Sims, 377 U.S. 533 (1964); Lucas v. Colorado General Assembly, 377 U.S. 713 (1964).

[3] 347 U.S. 483 (1954). In retrospect, the importance of *Brown* inheres as much in the fact that it shook the equal protection clause completely loose from its moorings in history as in its substantive ruling. This is not to suggest that theretofore history had been a controlling factor in the application of the equal protection clause, but only that it had not been, as it would now seem to be, totally irrelevant except in its more fictionized versions.

protection." The decisions in the school segregation cases, the sit-in cases, and the reapportionment cases are merely the most prominent of a very large number of decisions pushing this egalitarian theme. Quite clearly the movement is at its inception; certainly it is nowhere near its conclusion.

Two fundamental difficulties face the Court in this effort, or would face the Court were it more conscious of its obligation to justify and explain its judgments. The first is the question whether the Equal Protection clause empowers the Court to eliminate not only the inequalities imposed by law, but the inequalities that derive from non-governmental action or inaction, the social and economic inequalities as well as the political inequalities. Until now the Court has successfully avoided confrontation of the problem either by finding governmental action where few others can discover it, as in the sit-in cases that preceded the Civil Rights Act,[4] or by sweeping the problem under the rug, as in the sit-in cases decided by the Court since the Civil Rights Act.[5]

The second major problem presented by the new egalitarian movement is the task of adequately reconciling the competing claims of equality on the one hand with liberty and other fundamental guaranties on the other.[6] Again the confrontation has not been publicly made, although the conflict was revealed in the 1963 Term in the Court's split over its own power to command that private business concerns make their premises, goods, and services equally available to all.[7] The split in the Court was all the more interesting because it separated Mr. Justice Black, heretofore the acknowledged intellectual leader of the "liberal" wing of the Court, from Justices Goldberg and Douglas, who have now assumed the role of leading the levellers. Mr. Justice Goldberg, for example, expressed himself — extracurricularly—as believing that equality and liberty were one and the same.[8]

This short article is not the place to document further my proposition of the Court's new egalitarian pose. Those who are hardy may find some of the details set out in a recent article of mine in the Harvard Law Review.[9] Those of you who are foolhardy can look forward to seeing them expressed at greater length in a book I hope to publish soon.

LET ME TURN THEN to the second prominent theme of current Supreme Court adjudication. This one, however important, is hardly novel. I am referring to the effective subordination, if not destruction, of the federal system. This movement is not entirely disparate from the egalitarian push, for each is a drive toward uniformity and away from diversity. Equality demands uniformity of rules. Uniformity cannot exist if there are multiple rulemakers. It follows that the objective of equality cannot be achieved except by the elimination of authorities not subordinate to the central power. It, too, is an important part of our political and social and economic movement away from diversity towards conformity.

Because of its lack of novelty there is no need to dwell on the Court's behavior on this front. Perhaps the most amazing fact about the Court's recent infringements on state authority is that, having taken so much power away from the states, it continues to find more to take away. But one point should perhaps be made clear. Governor Rockefeller in his 1962 Godkin lectures at Harvard said:

[4] *E.g.*, Peterson v. Greenville, 373 U.S. 244 (1963).

[5] *E.g.*, Hamm v. City of Rock Hill, 379 U.S. 306 (1964).

[6] On the question of the meaning to be assigned the term "equality" see Wollheim, "Equality," in *Proceedings of the Aristotelian Society, 1955-56*, London, LVI, p. 281; I. Berlin, "Equality," *ibid.*, p. 301. On the question of the appropriate resolution of conflict between "liberty and equality," compare R. H. Tawney, *Equality* (4th ed.; New York: Capricorn Books, 1952), with F. A. Hayek, *The Constitution of Liberty* (Chicago: Univ. of Chicago Press, 1960). The comparison is not intended to suggest that "liberty" is the watchword of conservatism and "equality" the battle cry of revolution.

[7] Bell v. Maryland, 378 U.S. 226 (1964).

[8] Arthur J. Goldberg, "Equality and Governmental Action," 39 N.Y.U. L. Rev. 205, 207 (1964).

[9] "The Supreme Court, 1963 Term, Foreword," 78 Harv. L. Rev. 143 (1964).

"The reports of the death of federalism, so authoritatively asserted in the nineteen-thirties, were, as we have seen, highly exaggerated."[10] But the Governor obviously had a different concept of federalism in mind than I do here. Certainly, as the Governor pointed out, state governments are bigger than ever, both in the amount of money they secure and disperse and in the number of tasks they perform; but this reflects not the continuance of federalsm but merely the growth of the role of government in modern society.

As Rector K. C. Wheare of Exeter College, Oxford, in his book on federalism, has pointed out: "What is necessary for the federal principle is not merely that the general government, like the regional governments, should operate directly upon the people, but, further, that each government should be limited to its own sphere and, within that sphere, should be independent of the other."[11] As you all know, there are today few, if any, governmental functions performed by the states that are not subject either to the direct control of the national government or to the possibility of preemption by the national government. The concept of separate sovereignties within this country is now largely a matter of history. Vestigial remains are perhaps still to be found in the fields of education and health and the administration of criminal justice, but even here state power is clearly on the wane. It is especially in the area of control of police and prosecution that the Court has, in recent years, drawn the reins tighter and tighter.

It would not be correct to leave the impression that this fundamental revision of governmental structure was brought about solely by the Court. Advances in transportation, communication, and science, which reduced the size of the world, were the primary causes. The rise of the United States as a world power was certainly a most important factor. And the essential default of the states in failing to assume the responsibilities that were theirs cannot be ignored. But the Court, too, has made and is making its contribution. It may be that federalism is no longer desirable or feasible. The question remains, who should make that judgment. Ought it, or must it, be the Court?

THIS BRINGS ME TO the third of the major trends discernible from a study of the Court's efforts over the past ten years. I have in mind the enhancement of the judicial dominion at the expense of the power of other branches of government, national as well as state. Again it is not a novel theme. In the past, the Court's powers have risen and declined like the business cycle; but like the recent economic prosperity, the Court's recent dominance has been unusually long-lived and shows no signs of recession. (Automation creates no problems here.) There was, at one time, a fairly substantial area of governmental action that the Court had wisely declared off-limits for itself. The reapportionment cases seem to have dealt a fatal blow to the idea that there are certain functions of government beyond the competence of the Court to perform. There was, at one time, a notion that the Supreme Court was a court like other courts, called upon to resolve specific controversies between specified parties and not to lay down general blueprints for the reorganization of society. For Mr. Justice Brandeis, for example, if not for his successor: "If the Court were to exercise its grave function of reviewing the validity of co-ordinate branches of government, the Court must be careful to keep within its appointed bounds as a condition of judging whether others had kept within theirs."

This calls to mind the fact that the Court in recent years has struck down so much Federal legislation as unconstitutional that it is reminiscent only of the activities of the nine old men in their frustrated attempt to dam the tide of the New Deal. Certainly it is true that the Court has engaged in this pastime of judicial review since it was invented by Mr. Chief Justice Mashall in *Marbury v.*

645

---

[10] N. A. Rockefeller, *The Future of Federalism* (Cambridge, Mass.: Harvard Univ. Press, 1962), p. 29.

[11] K. C. Wheare, *Federal Government* (4th ed.; New York: Oxford University Press, 1964), p. 14.

646

Madison. Even so, striking down two statutes in a single Term is a little better than par for the course; and that is what the Court accomplished at the 1963-64 Term. In an opinion by Mr. Justice Douglas, it held that it was so unreasonable as to be unconstitutional for Congress to say that the benefits of citizenship conferred on a foreign-born person are dissipated when the citizen returns to his homeland for an indefinite period of time, perhaps never to return to this country.[12] In an opinion by Mr. Justice Goldberg, *Aptheker v. Secretary of State,* it held that no legitimate governmental purpose could be served by denying passports to all members of the Communist Party and therefore no legitimate governmental purpose could be served by denying passports to the chairman of the Communist Party and its chief theoretician.[13]

IT IS ONLY FAIR TO note, however, that the Court treats its own precedents with no less disdain than it accords Congressional legislation. Indeed, a Court that considers its pronouncements to be "the law of the land" might be expected to pay more respect to its own opinions. The fact of the matter is that the number of its own cases overruled by the Court in the past decade, either openly or covertly, have accelerated at such a rate as almost to remove the hyperbole from Mr. Justice Roberts' charge that the Court's judgments were coming to be like railroad excursion tickets, good for this day only.

I shall not burden the reader with the details of my complaint about the technical deficiencies of the Court's performance except to quote from an article written over seven years ago by two members of the Yale Law School faculty, in which they said:

> The Court's product has shown an increasing incidence of the sweeping dogmatic statement, of the formulation of results accompanied by little or no effort to support them in reason, in sum, of opinions that do not

opine and of per curiam orders that quite frankly fail to build the bridge between the authorities they cite and the results they decree.[14]

I would report here only that the difficulties suggested have become exacerbated rather than resolved in the more immediate past.

The Court has not, however, acted entirely without excuse for its behavior, although there are some who think the excuse is not adequate. The essential justification is that the Court has acted, perhaps overacted, as the conscience of a nation when no other branch of our government was capable of demonstrating adequately decent behavior. Certainly there is merit in the argument when one considers the conduct of our other governmental departments in the face of the abuses that the community has rained on the Negro; the evils of McCarthyism, and the continued restrictions on freedom of thought committed by the executive and legislative branches of our national and state governments; the refusal of the states and the nation to make it possible for the voices of the disenfranchised to be heard; the continued use of police tactics that violate the most treasured rights of the human personality. The list may be substantially extended, but to no good purpose here. There can be little doubt that the other branches of government have failed in meeting some of their most fundamental obligations to provide constitutional government.

This justification may be inadequate, however, because the Court's conduct has gone far beyond the necessity suggested by the action or inaction of the elected officials of our government. Or it may be inadequate because, as Learned Hand once told us, "a society which evades its responsibility by thrusting [it] upon the courts . . . in the end will perish."[15]

THE SOLUTION OF THE problem of excessive judicial power, of what Leon-

---

[12] Schneider v. Rusk, 377 U.S. 163 (1964).

[13] Aptheker v. Secretary of State, 378 U.S. 500 (1964).

[14] A. M. Bickel and H. Wellington, "Legislative Purpose and the Judicial Process: The Lincoln Mills Case," 71 Harv. L. Rev. 1, 3 (1957).

[15] *The Spirit of Liberty* (2nd ed.; New York: Alfred A. Knopf, 1953), p. 164.

ard Boudin called, in the 1930's, "Government by the Judiciary," of what Morris Ernst damned at the same time as "The Ultimate Power," is not to be found in the various gimmicks that have been suggested for limiting the Court's jurisdiction or subordinating it to so silly an institution as "The Court of the Union," any more than it was to be found in 1937 in Roosevelt's "court-packing plan." The answer must be found in making the judicial branch of the government politically more responsible without impinging on its independence. It should be remembered, as Sir Winston Churchill was fond of pointing out, that the success of Anglo-American democracies has depended in no small part on the independence of the judiciary.

Such an answer, if it is to be found anywhere, may possibly be found in the responsible utilization of the amending power. I would emphasize the qualification that the utilization of the amending power must be responsible. Recent efforts to push amendments through state legislatures without the knowledge of the people of the states is not what I have in mind, for there are, of course, serious dangers in an expanded use of power of constitutional amendment. The people of California have only recently provided us with some examples of silly, if not tragic, behavior in this regard. Professor Paul Freund has told us that the essential difficulties are threefold.[16]

The first, and I think the most important, is that "proliferating amendments would impair the sense of attachment to the old and familiar, the spirit of loyal devotion to a deeply rooted institution." The second is that amendment may precede second thoughts that would demonstrate the undesirability of the amendment. The third is that an amendment may create more difficulties than it would solve.

In no small measure, the Founding Fathers anticipated two of these difficulties in providing for the means of con-

stitutional amendment. The method is sufficiently cumbersome to assure that no large number of amendments could be successfully promulgated. The same lack of ease of amendment would provide more than adequate time for second thoughts to prevent unduly hasty action. The problem of the "risk of substituting new dissatisfactions for old, new uncertainties for old perplexities," can be avoided only by dealing with proposed amendments with the care received, for example, by the proposed School Prayer Amendments in the House Judiciary Committee.

There is, however, a prerequisite to the utilization of the amending process, a prerequisite that will both justify the process and, in many instances, make it superfluous. That prerequisite is a real comprehension on the part of the electorate of the role and performance of the Supreme Court. The obligation of this understanding falls particularly on the leaders of the community, for, I think I can say without fear of being proved wrong, that the press has failed in its obligation to educate the public about the decisions of the Court. It is also unfortunately true that the bar has failed in this regard; too few lawyers are themselves concerned with the efforts of the highest judicial tribunal in the land. Only an educated public can understand whether judicial decisions appropriately call for constitutional amendment. At the same time, an educated and aroused public may make the Court politically more responsible than it has been. It may, at times, even convince the Court itself to reconsider constitutional judgments that it has promulgated. History shows that the Court understands that, to use Professor Thomas Reed Powell's phrase, "a switch in time saves nine."

In conclusion, like another unsuccessful campaigner, I would remind you that the people get the kind of government they deserve. He was speaking of the elected branches of government, but I think it is also true of the Supreme Court. If the country thinks it deserves better, it should do something about it.

16 P. A. Freund, "To Amend—or Not to Amend —the Constitution," New York Times Magazine, December 13, 1964, pp. 33ff.

647

How Soviet Planning Works

G. WARREN NUTTER

IN AN AGE OF romantic pragmatism, such as we now endure, keeping faith with logic, principles, or the facts is likely to be considered a curious eccentricity, perhaps deserving tolerance on occasion but seldom worthy of emulation. Nothing succeeds, in such an age, quite like success. Surely, nothing fails like failure. Never mind if you are wrong as long as you succeed. Right or wrong, beware only of failure.

Rationalization waxes as reason wanes, and here enters the role of the intellectual; for he is set off from other mortals as much by his impressive powers of rationalization as by anything else. To him, failure is no more difficult to "explain" after the fact than is success, even when the one historically follows the other and the two "explanations" are mutually inconsistent. Hence we grow accustomed to the spectacle of intellectuals scurrying to get off one bandwagon that has stalled and onto another that is gathering speed.

As a case in point, when it was popular only a short time ago to believe that the Soviet economy was sweeping all before it, the main body of Western intellectuals spoke almost of one voice in praising the Soviet brand of central planning as the reason for success. In urging their own countries to heed this unmis-

takable lesson of history. Learned articles were even being written on "why Stalin was necessary." Now the mob has swung around in the opposite direction; now they accuse this same system of bringing about inevitable economic failure and applaud Soviet officials for talking about reform. Why this change in attitude, one might ask? Can it be simply because it is no longer popular to view Soviet economic performance as an unprecedented and unmarred string of successes? The failures that were always there to be seen by the discerning eye have become too apparent to be hidden from anybody by propaganda. In many ways there is little difference in the realm of intellectual discussion between what goes on inside and outside the Soviet world. The basic difference, perhaps, is the intensity of argument. Formerly Soviet literature contained the most uncritical adulation of centralized planning. Now it contains the most severe criticism.

BUT THIS IS ALL BY way of introduction, because I want to discuss another, though related, kind of romanticizing that has helped make scholars blind to what was really happening in the Soviet economy. I have in mind the propensity to idealize, to elevate form above substance, to impute purpose to chance—in brief, to see order in disorder or even in chaos. The point is that West-

G. Warren Nutter, professor of economics at the University of Virginia, is an authority on economic planning in the Soviet Union, and the author of *Growth of Industrial Production in the Soviet Union*.

ern scholars have not, as a rule, seen the Soviet system for what it really is: a set of institutions that has arisen out of an historical process of trial and error, and survived the various tests along the way. Their vision of the system has instead been almost idyllic, imposing a logic of design, a purity of function, and a simplicity of structure that have little or nothing to do with reality. Thus, the typical textbook on the Soviet economy has an early chapter on central planning that usually begins with a discussion of what one would want to do if one ran an economy; continues with an analysis of how one could efficiently do this by somehow solving an impressive array of simultaneous equations; and concludes with a description of how Soviet planning performs these functions. In other words, the actual system is made to conform with a preconceived ideal whether it does or not.

Perhaps a better way to understand central planning would be to start with the definition given by Mark Spade in his charming little book *Business for Pleasure,* the sequel to *How to Run a Bassoon Factory.*[1] Spade says: "The difference between an unplanned business and a planned one is this: (1) In an unplanned business things just happen, i.e. they crop up . . . . On the other hand: (2) In a *planned* business things still happen and crop up and so on, *but you know exactly what would have been the state of affairs if they hadn't.*" There is, of course, more to the matter than this, but not as far as planning itself is concerned. We all know about the "best laid plans of mice and men," and yet we persist in applying the term "planning" to quite different social processes. We forget that this word was put into currency for its propaganda value, not its descriptive accuracy.

Instead of talking about planning, central or otherwise, we should be talking about ways of organizing social activity. At base, social organization must be achieved through custom, contract, or authority. No society has ever existed—

---

[1] N. Balchin (pseud. M. Spade), *How to Run a Bassoon Factory; or, Business Explained and Business for Pleasure* (London: H. Hamilton, 1956).

or could exist—that relied on one principle to the full exclusion of the others, and hence the only sensible way to distinguish societies is in terms of the different roles played by each.

There is, however, a point to visualizing pure forms of social organization, if only to get our thinking straight. Let us start with an imaginary society ruled solely by authority. This would be best described as a corporate or hierarchical order. Everything that is done is done in response to an order passed down from a superior to a subordinate. Everybody has a boss—everybody, that is, except the supreme boss. The prototype is a military force, and a society exclusively run by a corporate order would simply be an army.

BY CONTRAST, ORGANIZATION by contract means a social order based on mutual interaction or voluntary association, whichever way one wishes to think of it. The purest form is the ideal market place, where individuals freely exchange their wares for mutual benefit.

No one but a diehard and deluded anarchist can conceive of a society based solely on contract. No one but a demented and doomed dictator can conceive of one based solely on authority. In any event, there are no historical examples of either, and there will never be any. All this is painfully obvious, not to mention trite. The family itself is an authoritarian body, though it may not always be clear who is the boss. A private enterprise—the organizing entity in a market economy—is also a corporate form; and no authoritarian system of any size can survive without some markets and other realms of mutual interaction within it.

But to get down to cases. The Soviet system may be described as basically a corporate order with a large area of contractual and customary behavior — some authorized, some merely tolerated, and some strictly illicit. The functioning of the economy is necessarily conditioned by this mixture of elements, and it is misleading to neglect any of them. As in the case of all economic systems, organization of the Soviet economy has three aspects. First of all, there must be

649

planning or thinking ahead. Second, there must be basic decisions on what the economy is to try to do. Third, there must be administrative d i r e c t i o n of activity.

Planning, in the narrow sense used here, is essentially a staff function. Somebody sits down and reviews the record of past performance, imagines how things have or could be changed to alter that performance, and maps out a program or programs designed to achieve goals supplied by somebody else. No society can keep going unless somebody, somewhere is looking ahead in some degree, but this is just another way of saying that man differs from other animals in at least this respect. It is equally clear that no society can run on planning alone.

Obviously somebody has to have the power to decide which program is to be followed. In the Soviet Union, this power is focused in a small self-perpetuating elite, and ultimately in the hands of one man or, at most, a small committee of men. Yet this group cannot decide everything. Like the great generals of history, it must leave small decisions to lieutenants if it is to make the big ones. The cardinal decision, as far as the economic sphere is concerned, is how the fruits of social activity are to be divided, first, between the state and the populace, and, second, between the present and future in each case. The overriding objective is reasonably clear and simple: enhancement of Soviet power, and thereby the power of the elite; but there remains the more important question of how this goal can be realized. In particular, there is the annoying problem of how to get the right mixture of power now and power in the future.

Let us put the problem in its crudest form. Military force is surely a key element in Soviet power, yet a smaller force now makes possible a larger one in the future. Similarly, the volume of goods available both now and in the future is not independent of what is given to the populace. The basic question boils down to this: When, in point of time, should the power of the state be maximized? The subsidiary problem is then how to arrange affairs to get the desired result.

These are the kinds of decisions the Soviet planners must make, and they make them on the basis of the configuration they perceive in the giant chess game they are playing with the world. Just as to plan is not to decide, so to decide is not to do. Somebody has to get things done—to organize and manage activities with at least the intent of fulfilling basic decisions. This, in fact, is what most people seem to have in mind when they speak of "central planning"; and so I want to center the remainder of my remarks on how the Soviet economy runs.

FIRST, LET ME REPEAT my opinion that one gains little in understanding from abstract theorizing about central planning. Perhaps there will be a time when it will be relevant to talk about how Kosygin, or somebody else, optimized this or that through material balances or electronic computers or input-output techniques or linear programming or some as yet undiscovered but revolutionary device of social engineering; but that time is not now, and it was less so every year one goes back in Soviet history. Let me further state—as a simple act of faith, if you will—my conviction that it is beyond the ingenuity of man, no matter how far the science of social engineering may progress, to devise ways of running a society as large as the Soviet Union without significant recourse to contract or custom. Unless, that is, one is willing to abandon altogether the notions of efficiency and rationality, and to quit raising the question of how end results are related to original intentions.

Whatever may be the ultimate limits of a corporate order, the fact is that the Soviet economy is run only in part by command and obedience. It is also run by adjustment and even by inertia. There is no more sense in attributing all good or ill in the Soviet economy to centralized direction, without regard to the role played by markets and related institutions, than there is in saying that a man stays alive by breathing in, regardless of what he does about breathing out.

Markets pervade the Soviet economy, and their role has steadily grown since the early thirties. Some, like the so-called collective farm market, are open and legitimate. Others pass through the various shades of gray. Who has not heard of the "fixers" and "pushers"—the *tolkachi?* Of institutionalized influence peddling — the system of *blat?* Of the elaborate markets for exchanging apartments? Of "speculators" and other entrepreneurs, who sometimes achieve momentary fame on their day of execution? And so on and on. It is literally inconceivable that centralized direction could have functioned as well as it has without these pervasive, built-in shock absorbers and flexible linkages. I recall the words of a disillusioned young Russian engineer who, while vacationing in Yalta some eight years ago, struck up a brief acquaintance with me. "You know what communism means?" he a s k e d me. "Communism means," he said without waiting for an answer, "that if you have enough money, you can buy whatever you want." And there was the collective farm manager whom I asked about planning in agriculture. "Of course, there are agricultural plans," he replied. "But," he added, "they depend on the weather."

LET US TURN TO another widespread misconception about Soviet planning. Textbooks often describe Soviet economic programs, as if they were a series of boxes within boxes. According to this view the first box to be built is the grandest one of all: the long-range plan, formerly for five years and now for seven. Even this box is said to have its general contours determined by a fifteen or twenty-year plan. Once the long-range plan is constructed, the only problem remaining, we are told, is to fit the smaller boxes inside it, one for each successively smaller time period. The actual schedules of day-to-day activity—the quarterly and monthly plans—are viewed as miniatures of the grander scheme.

This all sounds fine, and it would make sense except for one troublesome detail: the system just does not happen to work this way. Western scholars in general have merely repeated in their writings what they have read in Soviet textbooks. Until very recently, they have not studied in depth, using the most primary sources available, how the system actually works.[2]

THE LONG-RANGE PLAN is a hazy vision of things it would be nice to have. It sets forth, for a limited number of key items, targets to keep one's eye on. In other words, it gives something to shoot at and shout about — something concrete that the populace and economic agencies can be exhorted to attain. In no other important sense can it be considered a blueprint of the economic program for the intervening years. It does not attempt, for instance, to set a time schedule of achievements.

Now, consider two additional things: first, goals for the future grow out of experience of the past; and, second, it takes time to prepare reports on accomplishments and prospects. The result is that a goodly portion of the period being planned for is eaten away by preparation of plans. It is not unusual for a long-range plan to be published as late as a year after the period has started.

What, then, keeps things going in the meantime? The technical answer is current plans, on an annual, quarterly, and monthly basis. But these plans obviously have to be drawn up before there is a long-range plan of which they are supposed to be a carefully fitted part. And this is not the end: current plans also take time to draw up. The first quarter may be over before the annual plan is ready, the first month before the quarterly plan is ready, and so on. By that time, what has actually taken place is

651

[2] In fact, to my knowledge the only scholar to devote himself in earnest to this task is Eugene Zaleski of the National Center of Scientific Research in France. To anyone who wants to know the true mechanics of the Soviet planning process, I strongly commend Zaleski's treatise *Planification de la croissance et fluctuations économiques en U.R.S.S.*, a work to appear in three volumes. The first volume was published in French in 1962, and an English translation is now in press. I will try here merely to sketch, in boldest outline, the basic characteristics of the process— at least, as I understand it.

likely to be rather different from what has emerged as the plan. So the plan has to be revised to correspond with actual performance, and the process repeats itself. Through this constant readjustment of current plans to achievements, plans and performance converge in the course of the year. No wonder *Pravda* can publish such high percentages of plan fulfillment at the end of each year. The plan referred to is, of course, the final revised version.

Similiarly, in the course of either a short or a long period, plans can be attained—if this should remain an overriding objective—by the rather simple expedient of letting things slide in those large areas where no precise goals are set, or where the goals have a relatively low priority. There are plenty of built-in shock absorbers—or residual claimants, if you will—to dampen the blows of miscalculation. If this does not work, there always remains the expedient of throwing the whole plan away and starting over, as was done, for example, in 1957 and 1958. The question to ask, of course, is: Which is chicken and which is egg? Does performance derive from plan or plan from performance? The answer is that the relation goes both ways, though it is much stronger, in my opinion, from performance to plan than from plan to performance.

THE CRITICAL ELEMENT of muddling through can be shown in another way. Let us ask the question: What are the agencies that draw up plans, make basic economic decisions, and run things? As far as planning is concerned, the name Gosplan—State Planning Agency—immediately pops to mind: but one grows dizzy tracing out the shifting assignments and personnel of this agency in the postwar period alone. The terms of reference for this agency were changed no fewer than eight times between 1945 and 1964, almost once every two years.

Let me illustrate. In 1945 Gosplan had four major tasks: (1) planning of supplies, (2) planning on a current basis, (3) planning on a longe-range basis, and (4) compiling and processing statistics.

The planning of supplies was withdrawn in 1946, processing of statistics in 1947. In 1953, planning of supplies was reassigned to Gosplan, only to be withdrawn two years later along with current planning. At this low point in 1955 and 1956, Gosplan was responsible for long-range planning alone, but in 1957, both planning of supplies and current planning were returned to its province. Three years later, it was relieved of its duties in long-range planning and restricted to planning of supplies and current planning. After another two years, its role was precisely reversed: It was made responsible solely for long-range planning. Finally, in 1964 its duties were expanded to encompass part but not all of current planning. There has, of course, been rather more stability in the decision-making nexus, essentially the Presidium of the Communist Party and of the Council of Ministries. Here important shake-ups have occurred only four times. At the level of actual administration, however, there has been vacillation back and forth between territorial and functional principles of organization since 1957, and no equilibrium arrangement is in sight. This is to say nothing of the frequent reorganizations of ministries, state committees, and the like, and the c o n s t a n t reshuffling of personnel.

Let me try to disarm my critics in advance by admitting that I have exaggerated elements of disorder in the Soviet system to make a point. Make due allowance, if you will, for this exaggeration. Is it even so possible to visualize Soviet planning as a process with dominant order, purposes, and continuity? I think not. Let us describe it for what it is: a set of institutions that has arisen out of an historical process of trial and error and survived the various tests along the way. These institutions make the economy go, sometimes reasonably well and sometimes quite poorly. Beneath everything there is the elemental force of momentum, which carries the economy forward from one day to the next whether plans have been properly attended to or not. Then, also, there are the many loose and flexible links that allow bending without breaking.

652

THIS IS FAR FROM THE picture conjured up by loose talk about theories of central planning. There is no command headquarters in the Soviet economy where brilliant scholar-leaders are solving a horde of simultaneous equations, pausing intermittently to issue the orders that mathematical solutions say will optimize something or other. Nor is there a simple mechanism whereby these orders are transmitted or carried out. If I may now conclude where I began, I would stress again the mischief of romanticizing. If they had faced the facts in the first place, would the intellectuals of our society have fallen down so badly in their job of guiding public understanding of the Soviet economy? Perhaps so. But at least they would have an honorable excuse.

Collectivism in Social Theory

EDWIN HARWOOD

There is no scientific sense whatever in creating for oneself some metaphysical entity to be called "The Common Good" and a not less metaphysical "State" that, sailing high on the clouds and exempt from and above human struggles and group interests, worships at the shrine of that Common Good.
—*Joseph A. Schumpeter* [1]

THE BELIEF THAT THE natural law framework of society is essentially corporative, that society requires a hierarchy of enlightened leadership with its most important social institutions receiving their legitimacy from a common ideological core and their operating directives from a central political directorate, has tended to unite social democrats, fascists, and even, it would seem, some religiously i n s p i r e d neo-traditionalist thinkers. In the view of these, a government equipped with sufficient powers over human and material resources should be able to achieve a maximum of rationality and morality in society; and market-capitalism, which produces a division of political and economic powers, leads to the deterioration of a moral society.

It is too often forgotten that many liberal bourgeois social thinkers who were not socialists themselves have contributed to this critique of capitalism, partly as a result of their acceptance of that genre of social metaphysics alluded to above. In the case of the French sociological school, an essentially moral critique of capitalist industrial society was abetted by social scientific research and reinterpretation. Aiming to correct basic theoretical flaws in the atomistic-utilitarian conception of human action and motivation, these outwardly liberal thinkers emphasized the coercive and regulatory functions of all social organization. They argued that it was necessary to recognize the importance of moral and cultural constraints in human action. As a member of society, man regulates his action in accordance with social values and tempers his hedonism with moral and religious considerations; in any case, his felicific calculus is as much the product of cultural tradition as it is of a basic schedule of biologically fixed needs.

This attack on atomistic utilitarianism (the psychological-methodological basis of English political economy and of its radical off-shoot, Marxism), received its major impetus from the French school of sociology, from men like Saint-Simon and Comte at an earlier period, and later from Durkheim and Mauss.[2]

---

[1] J. A. Schumpeter, "The Communist Manifesto in Sociology and Economics," *The Journal of Political Economy*, LVII (June 1949), 208.

[2] A good critique of the wholistic presuppositions of the French school of sociology can be found in F. A. Hayek, *The Counter-Revolution of Science* (New York: The Free Press of Glencoe, 1964).

Edwin Harwood did his undergraduate studies at Stanford University, is currently a graduate student in the department of sociology at the University of Chicago, and has published several articles in scholarly journals.

It should be noted that while the French sociologists were hostile to capitalism and suspected that it was the chief cause of industrial civilization's presumed moral anarchy, the French critique of utilitarian theory did not derive from their ideological principles, but rather it rested on the accepted canons of scientific investigation alone. On the other hand, it is clear that if a good case could be made for theories which stressed the *social* determinants of human action and which asserted that man's nature is nothing if not social, then societies which appear consistent with the utilitarian analysis would be more likely to appear unnatural; that is, historical aberrations to be corrected by a generous corporative impulse. Hence, there is indeed an ideological bias in the early French sociological theorizing.[3] In the writings of Comte, Mauss, and Durkheim one finds many concrete recommendations for a corporative social order, and they attempted to support these recommendations with their scientific studies.[4]

AMERICAN SOCIOLOGY of the 1930's manifests a strong imprint of French concepts and the anti-capitalist bias discussed above. This may have been understandable in view of the solid empirical contributions of Durkheim and his students; but the task of carrying forward their program of research on the industrial order and its disabilities extended to more than just scientific considerations. It included, in addition, adapting the French assault against "chaotic capitalism" to the American social terrain of the 1930's—admittedly a time which was not exactly propitious to theories favorable to capitalism, especially among social scientists not trained in

economics. The separation of the moral and political order of society on the one hand from the operations of the market on the other, a separation which is never complete even in advanced capitalist societies, was one of the "natural aberrations" which the French fulminated against. This theme was soon taken up by a group of American sociologists and social-anthropologists, some of them men of indisputably great stature, like Elton Mayo and W. Lloyd Warner. In their work one finds the same admixture of political critiques with scientific explanation. Both of these writers write eloquently about the need for society to re-integrate itself in the interest of all contending factions. Their recommendations for a more rigid and unified hierarchy, and for a greater coordination of economic interest groups by political institutions is consonant with the corporative conception outlined above;[5] but if social peace and quiet are such vital needs, why not recommend the proscription of those political freedoms and that type of parliamentary squabbling and naughtiness which—at least in the view of right- and left-wing authoritarians — only serve to magnify and exacerbate rather than resolve existing tensions and social antagonisms! Why not leave off with the terminological trepidation. Call it what it properly is: a fascist solution.

What had been with the French and certain of these American social scientists a critique of existing capitalist society and an argument for a corporative social order, one in which the economic sector of society would again be put to a moral harness, became transformed into a highly general theory of social organization.

INSTRUMENTAL IN THIS development was the work of Talcott Parsons. In a brilliant early work, *The Structure of Social Action,* Parsons continued the dialogue with utilitarian individualist thought which the French had spearheaded. Ten year later, in

655

[3] A. Gerschenkron has given an interesting economic explanation of the attraction which corporative and mildly socialistic ideological currents had in France, even among the entrepreneurial and financial bourgeoise. "Economic Backwardness in Historical Perspective," in B. Hoselitz, ed., *The Progress of Underdeveloped Areas* (Chicago: University of Chicago Press, 1952).

[4] Cf. Emile Durkheim, "Preface to the 2nd edition," *The Division of Labor in Society* (New York: The Free Press of Glencoe, 1964).

[5] E. Mayo, *The Human Problems of an Industrial Civilization* (New York: The Macmillan Co., 1933), Chs. 6-8; W. L. Warner and J. O. Low, *The Social System of the Modern Factory* (New Haven: Yale University Press, 1951), pp. 181-196.

The Social System, he developed a distinctive theory of his own. Emphasis in this theory, which was not meant to be a theory of any one type of social system but of all social systems, was given to the postulate of shared values, of norms held in common by the inhabitants of a political community. Basic social antagonisms based on class and political divisions were secondary phenomena which had to be explained but were not of central relevance. What is the difference here between Parsons' extrapolation of French sociological thought and what the French themselves believed? Parsons' theory does not allow for distinctions between types of social systems, distinctions which are essential to a proper understanding of different societies at different stages of historical development. There was, for example, no attempt to distinguish between actual ongoing corporate states on the one hand — socialist and feudalist societies are similar in terms of the heavy-handed political centralization and statist natural law premises they advance—and capitalist society with its institutionalized independence of economy from polity. The French recognition of the fact that capitalist society differed from what they conceived of as a more natural social order was lost sight of in the emerging general theory developed by Parsons.

Parsons wanted to talk about society in general. This led him to the kind of pitfalls which I intend to discuss now. We shall consider one application of his general theory, his explanation of social stratification: the way in which men come to differ in terms of income and prestige. This theory of stratification is erroneous because it derives from a wholistic conception of social life and such a conception, I argue, is not at all adequate to the task of describing capitalist societies.

Parsons assumes that the reward and prestige which a given occupation garners depend upon "society's" evaluation of the contribution of that occupation to the survival needs of the society. Occupations felt to be vital to the continuation of society will receive much more prestige and income than occupations which are not so vital. Sufficient consensus exists, in Parsons' view, to insure that the income of a position will not be discrepant with its social value. A moral order being common to all men within the social system, such consensus about the relative ranking of services and occupations would never be problematic; but if a discrepancy should occur, if occupations of great importance were to receive less income than would be warranted by their importance, serious strains would be engendered. Some agency would have to intervene to insure that the important occupations received their due share of the economic distribution.[6]

That is the theory in a nutshell. It assumes that social systems have stable ideological cores from which unambiguous rankings of different occupations can be derived. It assumes that men come to a uniform evaluation of the survival needs of their societies—indeed, that societal survival is foremost in their minds when it comes to ranking jobs and allocating material rewards. It assumes, further, that situations in which a discrepancy exists, as for example in the case of jobs or trades which have high income but are morally reprehensible, can be considered abnormal and productive of social strain. Then, of course, they must be "corrected." Is it not possible, however, in contrast to Professor Parsons' view, to think of a market which does not follow the moral guidelines of some social elite, but allocates income to those who best provide for the wants of the mass of consumers?

These individuals may not measure up to the standards of the cultural elitists. They may actually provide services and goods felt to be petty and trivial; but the financial power of the consuming public is a basically democratic power, and it lies at the very roots of those discrepancies between the presumed moral attributes of an occupation and that occupation's income which are more the rule than the exception in healthy capitalist states. It is often only

_____

[6] T. Parsons, "A Revised Analytical Approach to the Theory of Social Stratification," in R. Bendix and S. M. Lipset, eds., *Class, Status and Power* (New York: The Free Press of Glencoe, 1963), pp. 92-129.

the elitist intellectuals who must perceive a harmony of social functions where harmony does not in fact exist; and it is usually the intellectuals and the unsuccessful who feel that things moral and material must be brought back "into line."

IN COLLECTIVIST societies a general consensus regarding the relative worth of different social functions, if it does not actually exist among the populace at large, can indeed be enforced by the intellectual, military, or feudal elites. Only this type of society, approximated by contemporary socialist states and feudalist regimes, can attempt to coerce the flow of income into channels which maintain consistency between the income and the presumed moral worth of a given occupation or social position. It is well known that a market freely organized can be frustrated in its effective allocation on the basis of demand, and thus the central administrative apparatus of the state can assign wages and salaries on the basis of criteria irrelevant to economic efficiency. In feudal and socialist regimes, merchants, entrepreneurs, tradesmen, and kindred social types of the third estate usually do not receive the material rewards that they would otherwise receive for their services in a democratic capitalist society.

Since a free market would have provided these social types with income felt to be inappropriate to the economic worth of their social functions, kings and comrades must have recourse to measures which will bring income into line with social prestige or what *they* feel to be society's needs. Heavy taxation continually enforced, as in Bourbon France, or capriciously, as in the England of Charles I, sumptuary legislation—now, with changing fashions, referred to as "rationing"—and downright expropriation are among the measures which a social elite can employ to make certain that income will be allocated on the basis of political or "moral" criteria. I must confess that the socialist elites have carried out their task in this matter with much greater efficiency than the former Western monarchs and feu-

dal princes; but I think that in terms of the ideal-typical distinctions I am trying to draw in this paper, it is safe to contrast feudal and socialist social systems on the one hand with capitalist societies on the other.

Professor Parsons and those sociologists who have followed him in this theory of social stratification never made these crucial distinctions between capitalist societies on the one hand, and socialist and feudal regimes on the other. They are not advocating a return of control over economic operations to a social and political elite—in short, a transformation of capitalist society into a socialist order—because they believe that there are no crucial distinctions. I am not saying that they are not personally aware of important differences. I am arguing that their explanation of social stratification does not take these differences into account.

657

I CANNOT DEAL WITH all of the underlying assumptions in this theory, in particular, with the assumption that society has a set of survival needs which are clear to most men in society, and which, when clearly understood, give rise to a uniform set of occupational evaluations. I leave this assumption for more versatile metaphysicians than myself to grapple with. The belief, however, that widespread social consensus exists with respect to the value of different economic services and social roles, that men not only agree upon the relative ranking of different social functions but in addition, experience strain and distress when they perceive how occupations and other social functions of high prestige receive modest incomes, strikes me as being contrary not only to common sense but also to historical experience. Consider the social and political upheaval in seventeenth century England. The enclosure movement which developed in the wake of the Tudor Reformation, as a response to the sale of monastery lands to enterprising nobles and burghers, created concern among the highest ruling elements of the society, Church and Crown.

The greater efficiency of the monas-

658

tery lands, after having been sold to enterprising private individuals, increased the pressure on other landholders to raise rents and rationalize agricultural practices. There were other factors at work here, among them the decline in the purchasing power of the coinage, while rents in many cases had remained unchanged since feudal times. Nobles and gentry responded by jacking up rents, and by turning a large part of their lands into pasture for the production of wool. The lower ranks of the peasantry, the copyholders in particular, had a difficult time defending their rights to their private plots as well as to the commons in manor courts run by the very nobles and gentry they were up against. The Crown was disturbed by the growing social dislocations in the countryside. The rationalization of social relations between peasant and manor brought about by the commercialization of land was felt to undermine the power of the Crown—although Henry's sale of Church lands and the campaign against the private feudal armies of the nobility were themselves factors in the decline of manorial paternalism.[7]

In the end, of course, the anti-capitalist measures of Laud, the High Commission, and Charles' Privy Council were put to the block as squarely as was the Archbishop's head. The combined triumph of agricultural capitalism in alliance with urban mercantile capitalism meant far more than just the end of a corporate feudal society. It meant, in addition, the end of a coerced consensus on the relative moral worth and prestige of different social functions. It meant that low-born bourgeois would obtain the full value of their economic contributions. They would also have more wealth than many of the high-born, and in time, more power too. Parliament, in denying the Crown's right to impose arbitrary taxes, in particular, to sell and grant exclusive franchises which interferred with the efficiency of the market system, abolished in the process the use

of political power for the control of economic life, for the diverting of the flow of goods and income away from the strata to which they would normally be destined under free market conditions. The sundering of the polity from the market meant—and this is most important for understanding the inadequacy of sociological theories of stratification like Parsons'—that the prestige which some elite judges to be merited by a social function will not necessarily correspond to the income received by that function in a capitalist society. There is also an absence of consensus about the relative importance of different social functions in capitalist society. Leftist intellectuals do not think as highly of businessmen as the latter do of themselves; ward-heelers are thought very highly of by lower-class, ghettoized immigrants, but that doesn't assure them entry into clubs and upper-class salons.

In seventeenth century England, on the other hand, the nobility and court had sufficient social and political resilience to continue to determine what style of life and family background constituted high social worth, but they lost the ability to insure that the stream of goods and material comforts would correspond to this other dimension of social class. Capitalism's triumph was not postponed because it had a falling out with some presumed "common-value" system which had assured consensus on the relative worth of different social functions. It triumphed because certain strata, fortunately aided by an aristocratic element with strong commercial interests, the Tory Radicals of their age, took the political initiative in seeing that the market system worked without Stuart political and religious fetters. England attained this goal much earlier because its bourgeoisie was much more advanced. It was favored over France and the other continental countries for a number of other reasons which John U. Nef has dealt with at length in his *Industry and Government in France and England: 1540-1640*. That work is among the best I know for gaining an understanding of why parliamentary democracy and capitalism triumphed so early in England.

---

[7] See R. H. Tawney, *The Agrarian Problem in the 16th Century* (New York: Longmans, Green and Company, 1918); C. Hill, *The Century of Revolution: 1603-1714* (Edinburgh: Thomas Nelson and Sons, Ltd., 1962).

WE HAVE DEALT AT some length with the myth of a "common-value" system, at least as applied to capitalist social systems, and I think that in the process we have learned why collectivist sociological theories apply to collectivist societies and not to the more pluralistic democratic capitalist system. If one considers, for example, R. H. Tawney's political tracts, *Equality* and *The Acquisitive Society,* or Karl Polanyi's *The Great Transformation,* one finds a quite stubborn awareness of the fact that capitalist civilization is neither a moral unity with a common ideological core nor a system that assures that income and prestige will follow what these anti-capitalist intellectuals consider to be their proper channels. These men are *advocating* a unified, morally integrated society, one in which a centralized political directorate would have the power to determine the moral value and "functional contribution" of various occupations and services. Although I heartily disagree with the ideas of these two thinkers, I must confess that they have a more acute understanding of the nature of social class and stratification in capitalist society than non-socialist social scientists such as Parsons and his followers. That the general theory of social stratification advances conceptions unsuited to the contours of capitalism is most clearly revealed in the statement made by two of Parsons' followers regarding the dilemma of private property and inherited wealth:

> . . . as social differentiation becomes highly advanced and yet the institution of inheritance persists, the phenomenon of p u r e ownership emerges. [By this I assume they mean ownership without unsubtly obvious functions.] In such a case it is difficult to prove that the position is functionally important or that the scarcity involved is anything other than extrinsic or accidental. It is for this reason, doubtless, that the institution of private property in productive goods becomes more subject to criticism as social development proceeds towards industrialization.[8]

[8] K. Davis and W. E. Moore, "Some Principles of Stratification," *American Sociological Review,* X (April 1945), 242-49. W. L. Warner's *Social Class in America* develops a similar theory of

This seems to be a striking admission. Having noted the obdurate legal fact of inherited wealth, Davis and Moore are arguing that with time people will come to reject the right of private ownership of productive firms and will insist that such material reserves be re-allocated on the basis of some more valid criterion of social contribution. This may or may not be an accurate description of current historical tendencies. It is clearly an admission of the inadequacy of their theory to account for the dynamics of class and stratification in capitalist states. What they are saying really is that with time, social reality will "catch up" with the propositions of their theory, the day when some Ministry of the Moral Order will insure that large blocs of wealth do not go into the hands of rentiers—Captains of Non-industry, if I may pervert somewhat a phrase coined by David Riesman; but will go to those who make the most important contributions to that somewhat mysterious and elusive end, societal survival.

These men pretend not to advocate but only to describe what is. The advocates of a collectivist society, however, are not only honest advocates but clearly cognizant of the important differences between the dynamics of class and stratification under capitalism on the one hand, and the mechanisms which operate in collectivist states on the other. I do not care for the collectivist goals of the French sociologists or the Marxian mecca of orthodox socialism; but I am concerned to see that the distinction between corporative and capitalist societies be fully understood for what it is, rather than being submerged by a general theory which admits of no important differences.

For this reason, I tend to feel that the older political polemics which recognize these differences have more scientific relevance and analytic clarity than altogether inapplicable abstractions about society in general. The latter have attained the orthodox scientific goal of universality with the result that we understand not more but less about the functioning of modern western societies.

stratification. (New York: Stratford Press, Inc., 1949), p. 8.

Justice, "Needs," and Charity

ROBERT L. CUNNINGHAM

And for **bonnie** Annie Laurie
I'd lay **me** down and dee
(William Douglas, *Annie Laurie*)

660

Each heart recalled a different name
But all sang "Annie Laurie"
(Bayard Taylor)

DEFINITIONS ARE generally regarded as the best and most effective means of ensuring that our use of words is exact and clear. The advantages of following the recommendation: Define your terms! are seldom questioned; but to define a term like "justice," a word that combines a strong eulogistic flavor with a wide ambiguity of meaning, is to engage in a dangerous occupation, for one is implicitly engaged in recommending an ideal, and thus any definition given is inevitably persuasive. There may be no agreement on the application of "justice," no agreement on the criteria which ought to determine its use, there may be an inconsistency of application which reflects confusion of thought, but there will be unquestioning adherence to the proposition that *justice* is a good thing. When it proves possible to shift the application of a term like "justice" (or "democracy" or "liberty" or "socialism") one may very well have won an important battle, for, implicitly, interests are

Robert L. Cunningham, professor of philosophy at the University of San Francisco, is a contributor to philosophical journals, and currently engaged on a major work on social justice.

thus redirected, values legislated in or out of existence, and the range of relevant "explanatory" information changed.

That such a shift in the application of "justice" has occurred is not really in doubt. "Justice" now usually refers not so much to a moral habit some individuals have and others, more or less, lack, but to a sort of institutional arrangement which it is the goal of political programs to achieve. Part of the load of favorable connotations formerly carried by "charity" (now redefined and carrying s o m e w h a t dyslogistic overtones), "love," and "mercy" have been shifted to "justice." Commutative justice is "out"; distributive or social justice is "in." "Social justice" and "universal prosperity" or "happiness" are often used coextensively.

I shall attempt to show that if this shift has occurred, it has considerable importance for men of intelligence and good will: for it is an analytical proposition that men of good will and intelligence will strive for *justice*. A few centuries ago, a somewhat analogous shift occurred—a shift in the meaning of "selfish" which led men to accept as true the proposition: "All action is really self-ish"—with the result that many were seduced from attending to their duties; fortunately a Bishop Butler was then available to make the appropriate distinctions and to show that the proposition was true only when "selfish" is used in a trivial and uninteresting sense.

JUSTICE HAS traditionally been considered to be a necessary modality of government action. If one says, "that's unjust," one has implicitly said, "government has no business doing that"; and if one can justifiably say, "doing that will promote or foster justice," one has given a good (though not necessarily a sufficient) reason for saying, "government ought to do that." Now, one way of broadening the legitimate range of government activity is to broaden the scope of "justice," and it does appear true that certain sorts of activity hitherto attached to "charity" (love, sympathy, affability, kindliness, spontaneous likings, friendliness, friendship) are now attributed to "justice"—usually *social* justice (the very *best* things these days are characterized as "social"). There are certain advantages to this broadening of "justice." "Justice" connotes rationality, austerity, rigor, and admits of being pressed into fixed formulae and codes. The virtue of justice counteracts the crude egoism of the individual, but only in a minimal way, for it demands that all men be treated equally—and there are only a limited number of ways in which men *are* equal. "Charity," and "mercy" even more so, connotes sentiment, softness, the glorification of instincts and whims, non-rationality. There is this difference too between charity and justice: Justice calls for treating *A* and *B* equally, whether *A* is a friend and *B* an enemy, or *A* one's mother and *B* one's mother-in-law. "A judge who respects the person is unjust." Justice calls for the methodological exclusion of charity; but charity does not call for treating *A* and *B* equally. We love what is like ourselves and since some are more like us than others are, we love them more than we love the others. There are gradations of love or charity, but not of justice: We

can love one more than we love another, but cannot treat one more justly than we treat another. As Joseph Pieper has written, "If love says: 'Whatever belongs to me should belong to the one I love, too,' justice proclaims: 'To each his own.' "[1]

When strict (commutative) justice is called for by the situation, it must *never* be overruled or replaced by charity. If I borrow fifty cents from a friend, promising to repay fifty cents the next day, it would be unjust of me not to repay what I owe when it is due: to refuse to do so (when able) is a paradigm of injustice. It would also be morally unreasonable to strike an attitude of generosity and, when the money is due, say: "Here, take the fifty cents: you need it more than I do"; or out of "charity" to say: "I won't keep the fifty cents, nor will I give it to you; I'll give it to some poor person who needs it more than either of us." Nor is it true that the claim to justice and to mercy are of equal weight. "There is," James Martineau says, "a vast interval between the obligation which I have openly incurred in the face of my neighbor's conscience and that which is only privately revealed to my own."[2] But if charity be brought under the aegis of social justice, then it may well be that some will argue that social justice ought to overrule commutative justice. The exquisite charity of the saint scarcely permits his justice—hardly different from that of the honest tradesman —to appear; and similarly, scarcely will social justice allow commutative justice to appear.

Notice also another limitation on the rectification of "justice" to designate what was traditionally designated by "charity." Ordinary language is a few paces behind the verbal redistricting that has gone on. "He needs it more than I" justifies giving another charity, but hardly justice; and it makes sense to say, "I owe you $50 for the suit I got from you," but hardly any sense to say, "I (we) *owe* you $50 because you are unemployed."

---

[1] *Justice* (New York: Pantheon Books, 1955), p. 58.
[2] *Types of Ethical Theory* (New York: Macmillan, 1886), II, p. 122.

Page Thirty-three

WHY NOT, HOWEVER, broaden the designation of "just" to include much of what was hitherto included under "charitable"? If government will now promote charity, mercy, love—why not? For a very simple reason, indeed: because government has no goods of its own to distribute in charity and mercy. What goods it has it obtained from others who were (implicitly) threatened with violence if they did not pay what they "owe." There is all the difference in the world between helping the poor by a free gift, and being ready to take away from the rich what he would otherwise unjustly—by the criteria of social justice—retain and then giving this to the poor. "Christ's bidding to the rich is most imperative. It is necessary to stress that while He urged the rich young man to 'distribute unto the poor,' He did not tell the poor to take upon themselves to redistribute by taxation the rich young man's wealth. While the moral value of the first process is evident, that of the second is not."[3] Though the (individual) moral duty of charity logically presupposes that of strict justice—since even when exercising charity to the highest degree, one can give only what is one's own—if government is acting as a charitable agent, its charity can now be seen as demanded by social justice.

One tends to be struck, over and over again, with the unreal, not-in-this-world atmosphere in which many philosophers tend to discuss justice. The problems that seem important to solve have to do with *distribution*—there is no discussion of *costs*. The underlying model seems to be one in which there exists a mountain of goods to which individuals come with claims of various sorts, and government's job, with the advice and consent of the philosopher, is to judge which and how many of these goods are to be distributed to *A*, to *B*, to *C*. In such a world the only problem is that of *a just distribution* — how this mountain of goods got there is irrelevant, or at least uninteresting; for this model does not even permit the raising of the issue of whether or not these goods already belong to someone, whether it is private property that is being (re-) distributed. W. K. Frankena, for example, asks us to consider the notion of comparative allotment as central to distributive justice. Suppose, he says, "society" is "alloting" goods to people. Then society may be justified in "giving *C* a banjo, *D* a guitar, and *E* a skin-diving outfit."[4] Note well the paternalistic model: Surely these are the gifts a father would give his children, say at Christmas; and note that the question of how it is that the father raises the money to pay for these goods does not arise. Nor does the question of how it is that one knows just what is good for each child arise; but is it appropriate to use the actions of a wealthy and wise father as a model for government action?

MERCY IS AN EVEN more unseemly sort of virtue than charity in our modern world. The man who practices it places himself above his neighbor, who is put in the position of receiving alms, in the position of dependence on an overlord. Can anything less democratic be imagined? Nor is mercy a *radical* virtue: the merciful man tends to deal with symptoms rather than root-causes, and is guilty, as Aurel Kolnai puts it, of "wishing to relieve the pain of the incurably sick instead of eliminating sickness from the world." One can see that if the "mercy of the rich and powerful" can be eliminated from the world—by being made unnecessary as a result of the substitution of systematic social justice—the world will have gained in objectivity, rationality, and human dignity.

Notice also another advantage of broadening the extension of "justice": those who receive what they "need" are no longer put in the position of one who receives charity or mercy, but of one who receives *his just due*. "Means tests" are out, for they were appropriate only when a man could not have been said to "deserve" help. It was argued traditionally that the fact that each person is not due the fulfillment of his

---

[3] Bertrand de Jouvenal, *The Ethics of Redistribution* (Cambridge: Cambridge University Press, 1951), p. 14.

[4] "The Concept of Social Justice," in R. B. Brandt, ed., *Social Justice* (Engelwood Cliffs, N.J.: Prentice-Hall, 1962), p. 7.

662

"needs" follows directly from the proposition that "neither can it be affirmed *a priori* that there exists in the external world a sufficiency of goods for the needs of all, nor can it be affirmed *a priori* that one's needs constitute a sufficient title to claim from others what belongs to them."[5] Now the "logic" of the word "need" is interesting. If I say "I need X," there is, by contrast with my saying "I want Y," a connotation of constancy, absoluteness, definiteness, a suggestion that what I say I need is almost physiologically demanded, and a suggestion that costs are irrelevant; the things I "need" are things that surely benefit me, but what I "want" may not do so. I can compare, for instance, my wife's telling me, *"I want a new rug"* with her saying, *"We need a new rug."* The connection between *"X needs Y"* and *"X (morally) ought to have Y,"* though not an entailment, is not purely contingent; but it makes sense to say *"X wants Y, but maybe he (morally) ought not to have it."* In English we speak not of urgent, critical, crying, vital, or essential *wants* —but of urgent, critical, crying, vital, or essential *needs* (and this is so even though the noun "want" connotes the stability of "need"—a connotation not at all p r e s e n t in the use of the verb "want"). To speak then of an economy as potentially capable of satisfying all our "needs" is to imply that there is a constant and unchanging set of goods and services called "our needs" and also that a finite amount of wealth will enable us to satisfy these needs. But as economists point out over and over again, the notion of "need" is not an analytically useful one.

We are inclined to *say* that we *need* too many sorts of things, from more protein in our diet or a longer vacation, to a new car, more highways, more and better teachers, more missiles, more water in California. This is to say that "need," like "want," is a vague word, *connoting* constancy and definiteness but *denoting*, in many of its uses, nothing more definite than "want." "I need" is used persuasively to say "I want." When some-

one says: "I (or more usual, *we*) need X," one should, I think, follow the suggestion made by Alchian and Allen and respond: "You say you *need X, but in order to achieve what? At what cost of other goods or 'needs'? And at whose cost?"[6]* These questions are obviously relevant when someone says *"I want X";* they are no less relevant when someone says *"We need X."* The only practical way, of course, of distinguishing "wants" and "needs" is to give some authority the power to define what are to be counted as "needs" and what are to be counted only as "wants"—but this course of action would have some rather o b v i o u s l y undesirable consequences which need not be discussed here.

D. D. RAPHAEL ARGUES that unequal treatment *can* be justicized on the basis of different needs: "We think it right to make special provision for those affected by special needs, through disability, such as mental or physical weakness, or through the slings and arrows of outrageous fortune. . . . Here, it would seem, we go *against* nature, and think ourselves justified in doing so."[7] Nonetheless, would we not find it strange to *say:* "He's a *just* man because he gave more attention to the poorer students than to the average students"; or to say: "He's a *just* man because he helped the child the bigger boys knocked down." It may be *right* to give greater attention to poorer students, or to help the injured child—but is it *just* (that is do we now *say* that it is "just")? It may be *right* "to meet these special needs . . . [by] an attempt to bring such people up to the normal level of satisfactions, or as near to it as we can"—but is it *just* to spend more on some than on others? Mortimer Adler once argued that if it takes two or even three times as much money to educate the less intelligent to an acceptable norm, the money should be spent. Per-

663

---

[5] Gustavo del Vecchio, *Justice* (New York: Aldine, 1952), p. 142.

[6] *University Economics* (Belmont, Calif.: Wadsworth, 1964), p. 72.

[7] "Justice and Liberty," *Proceedings of the Aristotelian Society, 1950-51,* London, LI, reprinted in M. Minitz, ed., *Modern Introduction to Ethics* (Urbana, Ill.: University of Illinois Press, 1958), p. 468.

haps; for maybe there are good (possibly utilitarian) reasons for doing so — but are they justicizing reasons? It may be right for a father to spend a great deal of money to send a crippled child to special schools, but if the other children question the justice (or "fairness") of this procedure, can the father give good justicizing reasons? T h o u g h charity never overrules justice, one may—and perhaps the crippled boy's siblings morally ought to—give up that to which one is justly entitled; but ought government to use the threat of coercion to achieve the same goal?

If a man asks for a dollar for a bed for the night, few would say I ought to give it *in justice;* but if that man votes himself a dollar from me, do I *now* owe it to him in justice? It is hard to see that the fact that he now has the government at his back to enforce his "claim" makes all the difference between a request for mercy and a demand for justice.

There may be a sense in which college professors "deserve" higher pay (everyone might be better off if abler men were attracted to teaching, etc.); it might be right to "work for" higher pay; but is it *unjust* that people have not chosen to spend a greater amount of their wealth on education?

One may well be able to defend the proposition that "private property has a social function"; but is this appropriately interpreted to mean that if you have more property than I, you ought *in justice* to give me some? This is egalitarianism with a vengeance and, as Kolnai says, "the trouble with the true egalitarian is precisely that he is unable to see a fat person beside a lean one without being tempted to assume that the former must have fattened on the flesh and blood of the latter."[8]

It is conceivable that robbing Peter to pay Paul (the model of the welfare state?) may sometimes, in marginal situations, be justified; but never justicized. It is a considerable step from "the pursuit of happiness" to a claim to happiness *rationed* out by a government which guarantees social justice—aside from the fact that here as in all other cases where scarce goods are rationed, the goods tend to disappear.

Is it not odd that people will "fight" to raise social security benefits with all the solemnity proper to the performance of a religious duty? One is reminded of the Marxist prophecy which "required from its disciples no other belief than that in the force of bodily appetites and yet at the same time satisfied their most extravagant hopes."[9] What used to be called "selfishness" is made out to be not only permissible but a moral duty, the motive power behind the achieving of world social justice. "The 'divine discontent' that makes me crave for three rooms instead of two and two radios instead of one is a revolutionary force which deserves not only to be acknowledged but venerated."[10] If striving after limited equality is justice, then striving after total equality is striving for the consummation of justice.

IT IS NOT, I THINK, irrelevant to note parenthetically that there is good reason to believe that when legislators respond to popular demand for "public services" solely on the basis of "needs" criteria, overinvestment tends to result. This is also the case when government provides "private" goods to individuals without the use of pricing. It is doubtless true, as Kolnai writes, that we may be ready to dispense with "the fine connoisseurship of delicious dukes if in compensation we are relieved from the presence in our midst of illiterates, uncared-for consumptives, and persons ignorant of the use of soap."[11] But the means we choose, whether "just" or not, often fail to achieve their goal. Milton Friedman has argued, successfully I think (*pace* Galbraith: "Public services have . . . a strong redistributional effect. And this effect is strongly in favor of those with lower incomes."[12]), that with the excep-

8 "The Common Man," *Thomist,* XII (1949), 285.

9 Michael Polanyi, *The Logic of Liberty* (Chicago: University of Chicago Press, 1951), p. 105.
10 Kolnai, *op. cit.,* p. 303.
11 *Ibid.,* p. 295.
12 "Let Us Begin: An Invitation to Action on Poverty," *Harpers,* March, 1964, p. 24.

664

tion of direct transfer payments to the poor, all types of social welfare measures have the effect of taxing the poor to help the rich.[13] This is to say that there is a net transfer from the poor to the rich when measures such as those making education "free" to the poor are passed (mainly at the higher, but even at lower, educational levels); freeways (not tollways) are built; "public housing" is provided (more housing than is built is first destroyed, and so the average cost of the housing available is raised); areas are "redeveloped"; "medicare" legislation is passed (the very poor are already well taken care of); "social security" is passed (benefits are, partly, paid for by a regressive tax); and legislation is passed to help farmers, only some of whom are poor (but raising the price of food for everyone else); or to help "senior citizens," only some of whom are poor; etc.

The way the poor are dealt with is reminiscent of the way wolf packs are dealt with by the Eskimos. They plant razor-sharp knives clasp down in the ice and rub the blades with a little seal blood. The wolves, attracted by the blood, lick the knives, cutting their tongues. They are greedily delighted by the seemingly unending supply of nourishing blood they can lick off the knives. They stand there licking until they drop in their tracks from the loss of their own blood, then freeze to death in the snow.

Gregory Vlastos argues that "since humanity has lived most of its life under conditions of general indigence, we can understand why it has been so slow to connect provision for special need with the notion of justice, and has so often made it a matter of charity; and why 'to each according to his need' did not become popularized as a precept of justice until the first giant increase in the productive resources. . . ."[14] But is this not a rather odd position? In the past, when we could not satisfy needs adequately, it was the function of *charity* (sympathy, pity, generosity) to provide help to the needy; today, when most people are not needy, charity is no longer called for, but we must *in justice* bring the few needy who remain up to par. When there are a great many needy people, pity them; when there are only a few who are not really so needy — in advanced countries, for in most of the world many people are still (biologically) needy — give them justice. Few would want to deny that with the passage of time sensitivity to the demands of justice can increase (or decrease), or that sensitive, pitying awareness of human misery can increase (or decrease). Yet is it not simply obfuscation (though persuasive) to confuse the two verbally, to say what was called for by "charity" on one day is called for by "justice" on another; and that the extent of remediable misery is sufficient to call for the verbal transmutation of "charity" into "justice." We must give *justice* to our poor fellow-Americans, but need give only charity to the rest of the world's poor.

Ceteris paribus, all of us would prefer a state of affairs where social rewards, privileges, wealth, power, and prestige were proportional to the individual's use of his talents. We would like to see reward proportioned to "merit," not only in heaven, but here and now on earth. What holds people back is the recognition that they lack divine knowledge and power (recalling the old saw of what would heaven be like if God sometimes put people in the wrong mansions?) Most political theorists also feared that some man or group of men might acquire the power to decide what another's status ought to be, and that therefore freedom would be diminished.

ALTHOUGH IN UTOPIA reward should correspond to merit, and not necessarily to performance (which may depend on luck), *we* cannot very well judge *merit*. We may, however, feel that there are ways to get an idea of *motivation;* and for anyone influenced by Kant, motivation may be thought to be the near-equivalent of merit. From this viewpoint, it appears that businessmen are inspired mainly by the profit-motive, when we should prefer them to be motivated by a desire to promote the "com-

665

13 Cf. *New York Times Magazine*, October 11, 1964; *Capitalism and Freedom* (Chicago: University of Chicago Press, 1962), Chs. 11, 12.

14 "Justice and Equality," in R. B. Brandt, ed., *op. cit.*, p. 42.

mon good"; but since there is no logically necessary connection between performance and income, we can, by interfering with the market system, attempt to establish some sort of correlation between preferred motivation and high income.

This sort of thinking is, however, moralistic, and leads only to confusion between the end of the activity and the end of the actor. Yet certainly *what* is done should count for more than *why* something is done: a Torquemada does no less harm for being nobly motivated. Should we no longer interest ourselves in the finality of an activity but only in the finality of the agent, we shall find highly motivated activity driving out highly beneficial activity. "Let us stop talking about people's motives. I don't care what people's motives are. I want to know what they are doing and what the effects are, and which ones are good and which ones are bad. I don't care why you hold this office or why you run this business. It will always be true, I should think, that people will go into business to make money. What is wrong with that?"[15]

Is it not better to strive for less than "(re-) distributive justice"—namely, for visible and evident commutative justice which does not directly count the personal effort of a man's work but only the result—realizing that moral value, while the highest, is not the sole value, and is the least measurable by empirical methods. It is better to give up a dream for the perfectly just society—which, as a matter of fact, the unsuccessful would find more unbearable than now, when chance and fortune so clearly have enormous roles to play and they can blame luck rather than lack of merit for their condition. Given the climate of opinion about the very wealthy—whether based on envy or not—a man is unlikely to choose commerce and industry unless the material rewards are relatively great. The only way a "philistine" has of knowing whether his efforts have *any* merit is by his profit-and-loss account. If this standard of successful service is scorned, the function of the market in allocating

resources to successful producers is destroyed. Running a department store well is not the noblest of all humanly befitting activities, a *bonum honestum*, and the best people know it. (The Greeks called such activity *banausic*—"the man at the stove."

The lower the possible "profits," the less the interest in putting one's economic life on the line. The losses are as great as ever, and speculative economic investment of the sort that, when successful, means great service to the consumer and so great wealth to the entrepreneur, is stillborn. How far we have departed from the attitudes reflected in Samuel Johnson's remark that "there are few ways in which a man can be more innocently employed than in getting money"! As long as it appears desirable to raise the general standard of living, if not for oneself then at least for one's fellows in one's own country and the rest of the world, one had better make sure that those who engage in productive pursuits are not deprived of sufficient material rewards to encourage them to continue their useful other-serving activity, even though whole-hearted moral approval cannot be given them. The envious man who for "moral" reasons refuses to pay the price asked for the services he demands ("How can *any* man be worth a million dollars a year?") will shortly find these services are unavailable. One must not forget, as Hayek reminds us, that in a sense all of us are striving to achieve the status of the "idle rich," those whose activities are not governed by desires for material gain.

What is true of the wealthy with respect to the poor is true also to wealthy nations *vis-à-vis* poorer nations: One may, by redistribution, kill the proverbial goose. Further, if it is "just" to *re*-distribute the "profits" of the wealthy to the poor in one's own country, is it not quite as "just" for people of poorer countries to claim that the goods of the wealthy nations ought to be redistributed among them? Is not "social justice" being violated in a world in which an American auto worker belongs to that two per cent of the earth's population whose income is highest?

15 John Courtney Murray, *The Corporation and the Economy* (Santa Barbara, Calif.: 1959), p. 43.

Page Thirty-eight

The 1964 Election

Rusher on Goldwater:

IT MAY BE USEFUL if I describe some of the considerations that motivated those who sought to draft Senator Goldwater, and who in the process seem to have annoyed Professor Rogge so vastly. ("Note on the Election" by Benjamin A. Rogge, *New Individualist Review*, vol. III, no. 4, Spring 1965).

First let me say that I agree with a large part of Professor Rogge's underlying thesis. It is perfectly true that America, in 1964, "was simply not yet prepared to accept the conservative position." Furthermore, I will cheerfully go the extra mile and concede that the probable outcome of the struggle was plainly foreseeable from the outset. One mild caveat here: No election is ever totally predictable, and it was always possible, even if only slightly so, that our expectations were unduly pessimistic, or that external events—the "deep crisis" mentioned by Professor Rogge—might arise to confound them. My own not terribly libertarian view was quoted in the November 1962 issue of *Foundation:* "there will inevitably come a time when the American people determine that world Communism must be destroyed. If that time comes before November of 1964, Goldwater will be elected. If it comes after 1964, he will be defeated."

Yet Professor Rogge seems to think he has the argument won if he can only manage to establish that Senator Goldwater was doomed to lose. He throws in a few unkind remarks about the excessive zeal of the Draft-Goldwater forces, and concludes with a ringing appeal to conservatives "not to try to win elections but to try to win converts."

This is sound enough as far as it goes, but I think it omits some important considerations. There is, first of all, the question of what obligation (if any) we owe to the democratic process. Granted that conservatives are a minority in this country, does it inexorably follow that they should not "fight the good fight, run the good race," in Bryan's hackneyed phrase? How, if conservatism is too delicate a bloom to be buffeted by the rough winds of the electoral process, are the American people even going to learn what it is, let alone be converted to it?

Beyond such considerations, and at a lower but by no means unimportant level, I urge Professor Rogge to consider the striking increase in the size, and the even more striking increase in the general articulation, of the conservative movement as a result of the Goldwater campaign. It will not, I think, be seriously denied that ten years ago there were far fewer conscious, committed conservatives in this country than there are today. Even two years ago, when the National Draft-Goldwater Committee was publicly proclaimed, conservatives were comparatively unaware of each other's existence, and hence of their united strength. Today, despite the disappointment naturally engendered by Senator

667

Goldwater's defeat, conservatives are vastly better organized and infinitely more experienced in the ways of practical politics than they have ever been before.

A final observation. After the defeat of Richard Nixon in 1960, it was universally assumed that the inevitable course of the Republican Party was leftward—to Rockefeller, and perhaps even beyond him; but what is the comparable expectation today, nine or ten months after the "debacle" of the Goldwater drive? It is, of course, widely asserted in Republican Party circles that a "conservative can't win"; but is one not struck by the paucity of voices arguing that its destiny lies with Rockefeller (or Kuchel,

_____

[1] William A. Rusher is publisher of *National Review* and one of the organizers of the Draft Goldwater committee in 1964.

or Lindsay, or some other authentic modern-liberal) in 1968? The general assumption seems to be that we are in for Mr. Nixon or somebody more or less like him—perhaps Romney; and I have no hesitation in saying that this passion for the middle of the road is generated, and indeed dictated, by the show of force put on by the conservative Republicans under Senator Goldwater last year. No Republican convention in the near future will be able to ignore their wishes altogether — thanks to Senator Goldwater's effort in 1964.

For all of the above reservations, I repeat that I agree with much of Professor Rogge's central thesis. The real battle is, and will always be, the battle of ideas. Conservatives must labor to build that better mousetrap; only then will the world beat a path to our door.

—**WILLIAM A. RUSHER** [1]

668

Reply to Mr. Rusher:

IT MAY BE symptomatic of the general concern of conservatives with consistent principles that Mr. Rusher and I continue to dispute various points on the periphery of a central core of agreement. Were we modern-liberals, we could bed down together in the spacious accommodations of complete pragmatism, perhaps even co-authoring a book on the danger to society of "true believers."

I agree with Mr. Rusher that the key to my thesis is the almost-fact that Senator Goldwater was doomed to lose, right from the start. He was running as a candidate of one of the two major political parties in the country, and the function of a political party at election time is to win the election—not to educate the electorate. A party can win only by offering a candidate and by taking a position near the center of the normal distribution curve of public philosophy; only

by offering what, if not an echo, is at least only a semi-choice. If this be true, then the only way a real change can be made in the policies of the country is by moving this "locus of possible choice" to the left or to the right. What the modern-liberals have succeeded in doing is to move this locus significantly to the left. What we must do is move it back to the right.

Is there no role for political action then? Yes, but it is not the central role, which belongs to education in its broadest sense. Political action in local areas (including whole states) where the locus of possible choice is already to the right can be successful—witness the number of conservative voices in the houses of Congress in recent decades. In fact, one of the tragedies of the Goldwater candidacy was that his crushing defeat carried many of these men into at least temporary oblivion as well. As Congressmen or Senators they *were* in a position to educate the electorate; now the task is more difficult.

If a political party happens by chance to select a candidate not from the center, it will be forced to remake his image so that he appears to be so—and with this remaking goes most of the chance for the candidacy of a Goldwater to be educational. While the last campaign may have trained some conservatives in political action, it did *not* educate the public to conservatism, nor even sharpen the issues between conservatism and modern, social democratic liberalism. In fact, these issues were hardly debated. For Goldwater to have really taken his stand on these issues would have been immediate political suicide. Thus he was forced to make concessions that will not help conservatives in their long-run battle for men's minds. For example, when I now criticize social security, I am told that "even Barry Goldwater wasn't *that* reactionary."

I come out right where I did before: The candidacy of Barry Goldwater was not helpful to the chances in the long-run of moving America in the direction of individualism and limited government.

—**BENJAMIN A. ROGGE**[2]

[2] Benjamin A. Rogge is an advisor to *New Individualist Review*.

669

The View from

London Bridge

STEPHEN J. TONSOR

The Catholic Church and Nazi Germany by Guenter Lewy. New York, McGraw-Hill, 1964. 464 p. $7.50.

IN OCTOBER 1840, Thomas Babington Macaulay, Whig-Protestant and the most widely-read and influential English historian of the nineteenth century, reviewed Leopold von Ranke's *The Ecclesiastical and Political History of the Popes of Rome, during the Sixteenth and Seventeenth Centuries*. In Macaulay's time Roman Catholicism, after two centuries of decline which culminated in exile and imprisonment for Pius VII by Napoleon, was demonstrating a vitality and dynamism which enabled it to threaten both Protestantism and liberalism. Macaulay and Ranke explored and expanded upon the sins of Rome, but both recognized and were puzzled by her permanence. In a famous passage from Macaulay's review of 1840 he observed:

> Nor do we see any sign that the term of her long dominion is approaching. She saw the commencement of all the governments and all the ecclesiastical establishments that

now exist in the world; and we feel no assurance that she is not destined to see the end of them all. She was great and respected before the Saxon had set foot on Britain, before the Frank had passed the Rhine, when Grecian eloquence still flourished at Antioch, when idols were still worshipped in the temple of Mecca. And she may still exist in undiminished vigour when some traveller from New Zealand shall, in the midst of a vast solitude, take his stand on a broken arch of London Bridge to sketch the ruins of St. Paul's.[1]

Now, a century later, Guenter Lewy in his recent book has rediscovered the Scarlet Lady and, while most of the secular and religious press of the United States is filled with the spirit of ecumenism and the excitement of Vatican II, has indicted her once more on the grounds of immorality and institutional opportunism. His study is fascinating and complex both because of the problems which it raises and the motives which lie behind its charges. Its tone of ill-concealed hostility and its unnerving assumption of moral superiority are matched only by the thoroughness of its documentation and the clarity of its analysis. Mr. Lewy clearly possesses what Justice Holmes described as an "instinct for the jugular."

Stephen J. Tonsor is professor of history at the University of Michigan. He is a specialist in the history of ideas, and a contributor to professional journals.

[1] T. B. Macaulay, "Von Ranke," in *Works* (London: Longmans, Green, 1897), VI, p. 455.

There is a certain naive charm in those historians who discover, with an intensity of moral indignation which nearly lifts them above the moral insensitivity and the common fallibility of mankind, that Popes sin, that prelates mistake institutional advantage for the will of God, that even good men, indeed saints, are not much better than the average run of their fellow men. They somehow forget that moral grandeur is not the hallmark of fallen man; that Moses doubted, that David murdered and fornicated, that Solomon as all his people before and after him, turned away from Jehovah to whore after false Gods and to live in injustice and iniquity; that Peter, reckoned by Catholics as the first pope, denied Jesus three times when Jesus' hour of passion had come; that Judas among the chosen twelve betrayed; that mistaken Paul assisted at the martyrdom of Stephen. Those who stand at some distance from Holy Scripture and the common experience of mankind are always surprised at the history of Christianity; forgetting somehow that we are formed of the dust of the earth. Perhaps the error lies in a generous overestimation of the moral resources of human nature rather than a deeper commitment to morality. This emphasis upon perfectability and innate goodness is a common characteristic of recent Protestantism, of Whig politics, and of liberal humanism. The view, however, from London Bridge leaves few illusions and holds few surprises. The Old and New Testaments should be required reading for graduate students in history, not because they are good history, nor because they expound the basic religious attitudes and values out of which our society has developed, but because they give us such a long, uninterrupted, and candid view of the nature and possibilities of this creature, man.

AT THE WAR'S END IN 1945 a myth seemed in the process of crystalizing. As with other myths the myth of the opposition of the Catholic Church to National Socialism had its roots in reality. From the outset there had been tension and open hostility between Catholicism and National Socialism; but the myth and the world ignored those wide areas of agreement and open cooperation between National Socialism and German Catholicism, and chose to overlook the curious ambivalence and friendly neutrality so often exhibited between the Holy See and the Nazi State. Only history was capable of pointing the finger of guilt and disestablishing a myth which comforted both the Roman Church and the new Germany.

The truth, when it is finally established, will be far more interesting than the myth and far more consistent with past history and with our experience of human behavior. Yet the truth is not easily come by and there is reason to suspect that the truth in all its ramifications is still and will long be incompletely known. There is a great deal more evidence in the Vatican archives which the Church owes the world. Its effects upon world opinion cannot be more damaging than the silence which has cloaked this important aspect of contemporary history; but when the evidence is all in, there is reason to suspect that an important aspect of the truth will be a sympathetic analysis and understanding of motive. It is precisely this understanding of motive which is absent in both Rolf Hochhuth's play, *The Deputy*, and Guenter Lewy's *The Catholic Church and Nazi Germany*. Lewy gives us, in his study, with great care, detail, and accuracy, the facts. But in history, aside from the know-nothing histories of the positivists, the facts are always less than the truth.

As we also might suspect, the facts are far more damning than the truth. There is the fact that German Catholicism was hostile to the Weimar Republic; that it marshalled its great power against the ideological and social pluralism, the liberalism, the democracy, the secular tone of Weimar Germany. The Church's vision was dominated by the ideal of an authoritarian state whose object was the promotion of virtue and true religion. The libertarian secularism of the Weimar Republic could only be considered by the Church as social disease, the work of Jews, liberals, Freemasons, and Bolsheviks.

671

There was, moreover, the fact to reckon with that German Catholics were enthusiastic nationalists who, since the days of the *Kulturkampf,* had been stung by the charge that Catholicism was incompatible with German patriotism. In an effort to prove themselves both good Catholics and good Germans they displayed an understandable but excessive devotion to "national rebirth," militarization, and the revision of the Versailles treaty. Since this "national rebirth" was obviously being achieved under the leadership of the National Socialists, Catholics in large numbers joined the party and enthusiastically supported the Nazi program. As Guenter Lewy points out, such actions were not limited to the secularized laity. Numerous priests and bishops supported National Socialism out of patriotic motivation.

672

THE CONCLUSION IS plain. Traditional German and Catholic anti-semitism p l a y e d an important role in strengthening the accommodation between National Socialism and Catholicism. It is too easy to see anti-semitism as George Mosse does in his recent study, *The Crisis of German Ideology,*[2] as the product of volkish ideas and a social response to the crisis of the emergence of German society into modernity. Anti-semitism is much more complicated than the partial explanation which Mosse proposes. It is clear that its roots were to a substantial degree cultural and religious and reach back into German and Christian history to a point well before the beginning of the nineteenth century. It was easy for German Catholics, consequently, to be at best insensitive to the fate of the Jews under National Socialism, though most of them did not support the morally monstrous "final solution."

There was, too, the very human effort on the part of the Church to derive some advantage from an accommodation with the dynamic National Socialist movement. When Rome was captured by the Allies in World War II, a cynic remarked of the behavior of the Roman citizenry

---

[2] (New York: Grosset and Dunlap, 1964).

Page Forty-four

in welcoming the Allied armies, "Everybody loves a winner, but the Romans love them just a little more." There is a strong (if we are to judge from the historical record) parallel between Rome's citizens and the clergy of the Roman Church. It is all too easy to see the hand of Providence supporting the successful conqueror and the triumphant tyrant. A belief in Providential history leads almost inevitably to the assumption that "whatever is, is right."

Additionally there is a confidence in the Church, born of the divine promise and two thousand years of experience, that the Church can outlive its enemies, profit from their concessions, and eventually assist in their undoing. But in accommodating to National Socialism through the Concordat of July 1933, the Church put its stamp of approval upon a criminal regime and opened the way for a recognition of that regime within Germany and abroad. The cooperation of the Church went well beyond the Concordat. The Church played an important role in the Saar referendum, in the remilitarization of the Rhineland, in the Austrian Anschluss, in the German war effort, 1939-1945, and in the "crusade against Soviet Bolshevism." The Catholic press in Germany was frequently little more than an extension of Goebbels' propaganda ministry and German bishops and priests often spoke the party Chinese of the Nazis.

Ultimately the worst sins of the German Catholic Church and of the Papacy were those of omission; the failure to speak out against racism, persecution, the violation of the peace, murder on a scale hitherto unknown in human history, in morally unambigious terms. To be sure, there were infrequent statements from the German bishops and the Papacy, but they were couched in the muted and esoteric language of encyclical-Latin. If Jesus Christ had spoken this language he might have been appointed to the Sanhedrin.

THESE ARE THE "FACTS." There are explanations possible which are more sympathetic than those adduced by Guenter Lewy. George O. Kent's article, "Pope

Pius XII and Germany: Some Aspects of German-Vatican Relations, 1933-1943,"[3] is, at certain points, both more exact and more charitable than Lewy's account. Klaus Epstein's discussion of the problem, entitled "The Pope, the Church and the Nazis,"[4] is the sanest, deftest, and most knowledgable review of the whole matter. Still, if the worst possible construction is put on the "facts," Pius XII and his fellow bishops emerge as figures of singular moral grandeur when compared with their fellow bishops of earlier date. Given the moral condition of the world in the thirties and forties, that any objective moral standards were maintained (as indeed they were) was a signal victory. That these standards were not forcefully voiced or adequately implemented is only another in the long series of moral failures which serve to remind Catholics of the human dimension of their Church. Nor is this simply an easy way of shunting moral responsibility. "Woe to the world because of scandals! For it must needs be that scandals come, but woe to the man through whom scandal does come." (Matt. 18: 7)

If a more charitable construction is placed on the events of 1933-1945, it is frequently understandable that the protests were necessarily weak and ineffectual. Pius XII was frequently forced to weigh saving Catholic souls as against saving Catholic and Jewish lives. His choice was wholly in accord with that which he thought the more important obligation. One is tempted to reply to Lewy's condemnation of the German Church for having failed to foster an active resistance to Hitlerism by asking where, during the period of 1933-1945, the Jewish resistance was? Is it not possible that those who suffer indignity and persecution without resisting also do God's work? One may question the reasonableness of such inaction; it is difficult to question the motive.

WHATEVER MAY BE the "ultimate truth," Catholicism need not fear a tem-

porarily "bad press." Religion is rooted in responses which are not, fortunately, contingent upon the moral probity of its communicants or its leaders. The more interesting and fundamental questions, however, concern the attitude of the Catholic Church which made the initial enthusiasm of German Catholics for National Socialism possible and, secondly, the danger which this set of ideas still poses for the Catholic Church. In terms of these ultimate questions Guenter Lewy's final chapter "Catholic Political Ideology: The Unity of Theory and Practice" is perhaps the most interesting and important part of his book.

Since St. Paul, the political theory of Catholicism has been unsatisfactory. It has been unsatisfactory largely because the Church at first saw itself and mankind as pilgrims and strangers on earth. The time between Christ's ascension and his second coming was thought to be short, and life in the interim was provisional. Political institutions were not important to the Christian who had his treasure elsewhere. As eschatological expectation waned and the institutional Church solidified its forms and achieved victory in the struggle with paganism, some accommodation between the supernatural order which the Church represented and the secular state was necessary. Eusebius viewed the Empire of Constantine the Great as the embodiment of God's kingdom on earth, and Constantine was elevated, at his death, to sainthood. (Catholic churchmen have been making the same error as Eusebius from that day to this.) As the centuries passed Church and State were ever more completely identified. In the Christian East the identification was complete and the State emerged as the dominant partner in this strange and uncertain relationship. In the Christian West the Church with difficulty maintained its independence from the State, and the struggle of the medieval papacy to establish a theocracy left a permanent impress upon Catholic political theory.

In its growing recognition of permanence and its accommodation to temporal society, the Church identified itself ever more closely with the authoritarian culture of the medieval era. It grew pro-

673

[3] American Historical Review, LXX (Oct. 1964), 59-78.
[4] Modern Age, IX (Winter 1964-65), 33-94.

gressively more difficult to distinguish the boundaries of the realms of nature and of grace as the so-called "medieval synthesis" developed. So close, indeed, was this identification between the Church and its cultural context that when, as was inevitably the case, medieval society began its long process of transition and dissolution, the Church failed to adjust its institutional structure or its political theory to the new culture which was emerging. It continued down to the last decade to maintain the necessity for a close and intimate association between Church and State and an authoritarian social order. Its views were, and in many instances remain, anti-democratic, anti-pluralistic, anti-liberal, anti-capitalistic. It is for this reason that the Church opposed liberal democratic political and social forces in the reactionary first half of the nineteenth century, when the restoration Church dreamed of a medieval revival and an alliance between throne and altar.

It is for this reason that neo-romantic Papal social theory at the turn of the century created the grotesque intellectual charade of "corporatism," grounded, as it was, upon an imperfect understanding of medieval s o c i e t y. It is true, as Lewy points out, that Pope Leo XIII revolutionized Catholic political theory by divorcing it from emphatically teaching the necessity of monarchy as a state form for the welfare of the Church. Yet while other state forms were recognized as *licit,* the presumption of correctness was clearly in favor of authoritarianism. This is the basic reason that the Church welcomed the dissolution of liberal democratic governments in Italy, Germany, and Spain in the 1920's and 1930's. Nor need we point to Europe in quest of evidence. One need only recall the rasping voice of Father Charles Coughlin, leaf through an old file of *Social Justice,* or study the iconography of the Shrine of the Little Flower in Royal Oak to understand the full implications of the so-called "social teachings" of the Church in the 1930's. In this atmosphere the fact that Father Coughlin circulated the anti-semitic *Protocols of the Elders of Zion* was no accident. It should be remembered that the Church resisted the anti-Christian aspects of National Socialism. Its guilt lay in the fact that it espoused a political phantasm which bore no relationship to the economic, cultural, or religious reality of modernity. Finally, there is no assurance at the present time that Catholic political theory has broken with the traditions of a thousand years.

Implicit in the difficulty is the fact that Catholic theologians have confused the temporal with the divine order, have confused man's culture, which is man's creation, with God's revelation. When man's culture, which always is imperfect, erring, and inextricably bound up with man's creaturely imperfection and sinfulness, is elevated to a position of absolute validity (as it is in so much of contemporary Catholic social thought), the Church invites disaster. The institutions of man are neither eternally valid nor unambiguously moral. Even the most perfect of institutions, the Church, bears eloquent testimony to the imperfections inherent in man's condition. It is for this reason that the Church dare not attach itself to a particular social or political order. The attachment to the older authoritarian order of Western society was the source of the failure of the Church to meet squarely the challenge of totalitarianism.

674

REVIEW:

Passion and Social Constraint by Ernest van den Haag. New York, Stein and Day, 1963. 368 p. $6.95.

AMONG CONTEMPORARY American sociologists, Ernest van den Haag is perhaps the most creative and the most independent; the unique character of his work is doubtless owing, at least in part, to a most catholic upbringing. Born in Holland of Dutch parents, van den Haag was reared in Germany and later studied in France, Italy, and America. He remained for ten years in Italy, spending part of this time at the University of Bologna. After later receiving a doctorate in economics from New York University, he embarked on a career in psychoanalysis, and although he is a practicing analyst, van den Haag is best known today for his contributions to sociology.

This broad and varied background is reflected in a distinctive contribution to American social science. Whereas the overwhelming majority of his colleagues are modern-liberal in viewpoint, van den Haag is an avowed conservative. Whereas modern psychoanalytic theory has gradually blended orthodox Freudianism into the ego-oriented psychology of the neo-Freudians and their related cohorts, van den Haag holds firmly to Freud. In an age when form and order are held by many to be no longer applicable to art, literature, or even to society, when a slovenly relativism is the favored approach to life and art, van den Haag advocates an old-fashioned reliance on moral and aesthetic "truths." He calls a spade a spade, and vulgarity, vulgarity. Popular Western culture is vulgar, he says, and for him that vulgarity is not redeemed by the material it offers for his acerb humor.

Both van den Haag's background and his philosophical position are reflected in *Passion and Social Constraint.* Opinion and fact are carefully delineated and distinguished, however; a precision not often shown by van den Haag's modern-liberal colleagues.

The opening section of the book deals with personality, which is handled from an orthodox Freudian point of view. Van den Haag presents the Freudian developmental position clearly, carefully limiting the number of "technical" terms he uses, concisely defining those he does employ, and thus managing to be easy to read without diluting what he has to talk about. In presenting evidence for and against his interpretations, he does not engage in the currently all-too-common serpentine manipulations of logic whereby a particularly embarrassing set of facts is somehow made to lead to a conclusion directly opposed to that obviously called for. In those very few instances when the facts do not seem to justify van den Haag's interpretation, he quite candidly resorts to a salvation-is-by-faith-and-faith-alone appeal, and invokes Freud to settle the dispute—this touch of dogmatism at least provides a consistent framework for the analysis and interpretation of the existing evidence.

The most controversial aspects of the book derive from van den Haag's insistence on the inherent "limitations of man's nature and on the tragic nature of human destiny." The essence of this strictly Freudian position is that biology sets limits on man's development; culture determines only to what extent his biological potential may be fulfilled. Social change cannot eradicate basic differences between men. Hence social change will never accomplish all that its egalitarian advocates hope for.

675

THE SECOND SECTION of the book, that dealing with society, blends the predominantly psychoanalytic approach of the personality section with van den Haag's conservative approach to sociology. He treats such standard sociological topics as group membership, tensions and rivalry, power and authority, cultural constraints, class and caste, but in a refreshingly original manner. Of particular interest here is the material dealing with prejudice and the Supreme Court's desegregation decisions. Van den Haag argues that it is impossible to prove "that prejudice is clinically injurious." If prejudice cannot be shown to be clinically injurious, then no damage has been wrought of which a court may properly take judicial notice. Van den Haag discusses the famous study of Dr. Kenneth Clark, which was cited as evidence before the Court and which declared that Negro children in a segregated school suffered psychological injury. Van den Haag points out that the same tests administered to Northern Negro children in integrated schools showed even greater manifestation of the behavior interpreted by Clark as the outcome of injurious, that is, prejudiced treatment. On the basis of Clark's logic these findings should lead to the conclusion that desegregation is psychologically more injurious; and therefore that segregation should prevail as a means of protecting Negro children from psychological harm.

Van den Haag's distaste for what he considers a distorted egalitarianism becomes most apparent in Part III of this book. Interestingly, he, like his modern-liberal counterparts, is vitriolic in denouncing the popular culture of today, but where they blame this deterioration on the corrupting influence of advertising and other mass media, he feels that advertising does not *create* taste, but merely *reflects* the abysmally low level of public taste. Advertising has pandered to the populace, but advertising has not created its vulgarity. The responsibility for that lies with the same leveling influences which have lowered the purchasing power of those cultivated persons who have "individual taste" while raising the purchasing power of the masses so fast that they have not been able to acquire, via education and acculturation, a respectable level of personal taste. The free market has operated to translate tastes into economic demand under these circumstances, and that demand has evoked the corresponding supply.

Whatever one's opinions on the individual and social issues discussed in this highly readable book, one cannot fail to be impressed by the clarity of van den Haag's exposition. Contemporary sociological jargon is little in evidence here. Van den Haag also manages to make seemingly dull topics fascinating by introducing historical examples (Frederick II's experiment to determine the natural speech of children—their nurses were instructed not to talk to them; but instead of speaking any language, all the children died). This interesting synthesis of psychoanalysis and sociology presents a truly novel discussion of contemporary mass society in a book which the educated layman can enjoy, and which the social scientist should respect.

—RICHARD McCONCHIE [1]

[1] Richard McConchie is currently pursuing graduate studies in psychology at Columbia University.

NEW BOOKS AND ARTICLES

THE FOLLOWING IS A SELECT LIST OF BOOKS AND ARTICLES WHICH, IN THE OPINION OF THE EDITORS, MAY BE OF INTEREST TO OUR READERS.

Milton Friedman and Anna J. Schwartz, *The Great Contraction*. Princeton, N. J., Princeton University Press, 1965. $1.95. A paperback reprint of those chapters in their monumental *Monetary History of the United States, 1867-1960* (Princeton: Princeton Univ. Press, 1963) pertaining directly to the years of the Great Depression. Prof. Friedman remarks in the preface that the idea of a smaller reprint was given him by a student, with the idea in mind of bringing the work within reach of undergraduates and others unable to avail themselves of the complete work.

Vera Lutz, *French Planning*. Washington, D. C., American Enterprise Institute, 1965. An analysis and criticism of the "soft" economic planning pursued by France in recent years. This, and other worthwhile and scholarly publications, are available from the American Enterprise Institute at little cost. Address: 1200 Seventeenth Street N.W., Washington, D.C. 20036.

James J. Martin, *American Liberalism and World Politics, 1931-1941*. New York, Devin-Adair, 1963. 2 vols. $22.50. An extremely detailed exposition, largely from the pages of the *Nation* and *The New Republic*, of the shift in American left-wing circles from a position generally pacifistic and critical of the Versailles settlement, to one demanding a crusade against the Axis Powers. *The New Republic* and *Nation's* profuse apologiae for Stalin's forceful measures of internal policing in Russia during this period provide some amusement.

Richard Perlman, *Wage Determination*: *Market or Power Forces*. Boston, D.C. Heath and Co., 1965. $1.50. A timely paperback collection directed to the controversy of "countervailing power" or supply and demand in the labor market. Contributor Fritz Machlup proposes that the entrepreneur does equate marginal productivity with marginal costs in hiring simply through his feel of the situation.

Prof. P. T. Bauer of the London School of Economics, a specialist in the field of underdeveloped countries, criticizes in the June 29, 1965, issue of *National Review* ("Capitalism and African Economic Development") the ideas on this subject of the in-vogue Swedish economist, Gunner Myrdal. Myrdal, Bauer finds, like so many other writers in this field, "takes the case for comprehensive [government] planning for granted without argument." Yet, "it is by no means obvious why an economy should progress more rapidly, if what is produced is determined largely by the government, rather than by individual consumers and producers." Prof. Bauer is, along with B. S. Yamey, author of *The Economics of Underdeveloped Countries*, an excellent introduction to the field.

Robert L. Cunningham, Professor of Philosophy at the University of San Francisco and well known to *NIR* readers, dissects the basic claims of the Triple Revolution group on automation in the current (Summer 1965) issue of *Modern Age*. Far from ranking with the works of Copernicus and Galileo, the ideas of this highly-publicized organization, Cunningham demonstrates, consist largely of a few shopworn economic fallacies, with an admixture of odd linguistic usage.

Edwin L. Dale, Jr., "The Big Gun on Poverty," *The New Republic*, August 7, 1965. A writer on economic affairs for *The New York Times* points out the far greater efficacy in combatting poverty of greater economic growth over particular governmental programs. "Jobs have increased rapidly in the very

677

places where the great bogey, automation, was supposed to cause trouble. . . . By the test of income, 450,000 families moved out of the poverty class last year, almost none of them touched by the poverty program. . . . The main conclusion is that an increase of one percentage point in the national rate of economic growth solves far more problems of human misery, insofar as they stem from unemployment or low income, than all the retraining programs, union resistance to automation, poverty programs, distressed-areas programs and the rest put together."

Theodore Draper, "The Roots of the Dominican Crisis," *The New Leader,* May 24, 1965. An interesting, objective analysis of the situation in the Dominican Republic following the ouster of Trujillo. Draper criticizes especially the incredibly incompetent handling of Latin American relations by the United States in general, and the Johnson Administration in particular. "In effect, the decision against Bosch was a decision against democracy and decency as the bulwarks against Communism."

Harry Kalvin, Jr., *"The New York Times* Case," *1964 Supreme Court Review.* Chicago, University of Chicago Press, 1964. Prof. Kalvin of the University of Chicago Law School discusses the content and the larger significance of the Supreme Court's actions in striking down the libel ruling of a lower court: "In brief compass, my thesis is that the Court, compelled by the political realities of the case to decide it in favor of the *Times,* yet equally compelled to seek high ground in justifying its result, wrote an opinion which may prove to be the best and most important it has ever produced in the realm of freedom of speech. . . . analysis of free speech issues should hereafter begin with the significant issue of seditious libel and defamation of government by its critics rather than with the sterile example of a man falsely yelling fire in a crowded theater." The implications of the *Times* case extend far beyond the usual notions of "democratic open discussion": "If [a society] makes seditious libel an offense, it is not a free society no matter what its other characteristics."

Spencer MacCallum, "Social Nature of Ownership," *Modern Age,* Winter 1964-65. Mr. MacCallum discusses the sociological role of property in human society and traces its functions logically prior to the State from the point of view of anthropology, and presents it as a workable alternative to state action. His discussion represents a serious and valuable contribution to classical liberal thinking in areas where the point is usually granted to the authoritarian position *a priori.*

An interesting article appeared in the July 24, 1965, issue of *The New Republic*: "Concern About LBJ," by John Osborne. Among the sources of concern cited is the curious tone struck by Presidential Aide Jack Valenti, who recently stated, in a speech in Boston: "The Presidency is a mystical body, constructed by the Constitution, but whose architecture was conceived in the inner crannies of a people's soul." Valenti also referred, according to Osborne, to President Johnson as "a father to lead us," and claimed that the President was fortified by a "Godly osmosis" [*sic*].

An excellent new journal is called to the attention of the libertarian reader: *Left and Right,* among whose editors appear Dr. Murray N. Rothbard and Leonard Liggio, both *NIR* contributors. *Left and Right* emphasizes an anti-Cold War position, from a libertarian point of view. Subscriptions to this journal, published three times yearly, are available from: *Left and Right,* Box 395, Cathedral Station, New York, N.Y. 10025, for $2.50 per year. Another interesting publication recently brought to our attention is *Innovator,* a monthly in the newsletter format, featuring "applications, experiments and advanced developments of liberty." Subscriptions are $2.00 per year. Write: *Innovator,* P.O. Box 34718, Los Angeles, Calif.

678

Coming This Fall From Regnery

LIFE WITHOUT PREJUDICE
and other Essays

by Richard Weaver

> Selections of his most important and mature essays.

$3.50

NEW GATEWAY EDITIONS

THE INVISIBLE HAND

by Adrian Klaasen, editor

> Essays in classical economics by such leading economists as George Stigler, Ludwig von Mises, Friedrich Hayek, Allen Wallis and Milton Friedman.

$2.45

SELF CONDEMNED

679

by Wyndham Lewis

> This is a novel of great style and force about an Englishman who exiled himself to Canada during World War II. Considered by T. S. Eliot to be Lewis' most significant work.

$1.95

FADS AND FOIBLES IN MODERN SOCIOLOGY

by Pitirim A. Sorokin

> One of the leading contemporary sociologists exposes the non-scientific and half-scientific elements in modern sociology and the related disciplines. Dr. Sorokin searingly debunks the use of obtuse jargon and sham-scientific slang, testomania — the overuse of intelligence, projection, ink-blot and thematic apperception tests — the "Grand Cult of 'social physics' and 'mental mechanics' " and the obsolescent philosophy too widely adhered to by social science.

$2.45

CREATION AND DISCOVERY

by Eliseo Vivas

> Essays in criticism and aesthetics. This book includes analyses and critiques of Dostoyevsky, Kafka, Dreiser, Henry and William James, discussions of the major aesthetic theories and problems of aesthetics.

$2.45

Henry **Regnery** Company PUBLISHERS

114 West Illinois Street, Chicago, Illinois 60610

In August 1963 We Promised:

"NEW INDIVIDUALIST REVIEW will NOT publish articles by James Baldwin, Ralph McGill, Walter Lippmann, J. William Fulbright, Arthur Schlesinger, Jr., Gore Vidal, Jean-Paul Sartre, or Howard N'Bongo-Bongo, Prime Minister of Anthropophagia;

"NIR will not tell you how affluent you are, or urge you to write your Congressman to triple your income-tax, so that the country can eliminate squalor in the public sector;

"NIR will not attempt to distinguish between in-itself and for-itself in the Theater of the Absurd, or compare Bertholt Brecht favorably with Shakespeare;

"NIR will not claim that Portuguese rule in Angola is the single greatest threat to world peace today;

680

"NIR will not assert that American businessmen are morally inferior to the Mau Mau."

WE KEPT THIS PROMISE. This alone would be worth the price of a subscription, even if we sent you 60 pages of blank paper every three months. But we do more—we send you a magazine full of thoughtful and thought-provoking discussions of individualist ideas and proposals, by some of the leading classical liberal writers of today and tomorrow — articles like those in the issue you've just read.

HOW CAN YOU POSSIBLY LIVE WITHOUT NIR? SUBSCRIBE TODAY!

ESSAYS IN THE HISTORY OF ECONOMICS

By GEORGE J. STIGLER

One of the most distinguished proponents of the "Chicago School" of economics, Professor Stigler has selected from his published writings the essays to be included in this volume. He ranges over such diverse topics as originality in scientific progress, the politics of political economists, the development of utility theory, Ricardian value and distribution, Fabian socialism, perfect competition, marginal productivity theory, and the Giffen paradox. "Professor Stigler writes with a wit that is even more to be cherished than his erudition. Economics would never have been called the dismal science if there had been a nineteenth-century Stigler."—*The Economist.*

400 *pages* $6.95

THE CREATIVE ORGANIZATION

Edited by GARY A. STEINER

"The creative organization in fact prizes and rewards creativity. A management philosophy that stresses creativity as an organizational goal, that encourages and expects it at all levels, will increase the chances of its occurrence. But it is one thing to call for creativity, another to mean it, and still another to reward it adequately and consistently when it occurs."

The coexistence of the creative organization and the creative temperament was the topic of a recent seminar sponsored by the Graduate School of Business of the University of Chicago. Here are papers presented by social scientists Bernard Berelson, Jerome S. Bruner, and Paul Meehl; educators Ralph W. Tyler and W. Allen Wallis; and executives B. E. Besinger, Peter Peterson, and David Ogilvy, together with lively exchanges of opinion and an "Overview" by Mr. Steiner.

288 *pages* $5.00

UNIVERSITY OF CHICAGO PRESS
Chicago/London

VOLUME 4
NUMBER 2
WINTER 1966

New
INDIVIDUALIST
Review

A JOURNAL OF CLASSICAL LIBERAL THOUGHT

Winter 1966   75 cents   Vol. 4, No. 2

NEW INDIVIDUALIST REVIEW

WINTER 1966 Volume 4 — Number 2

687

Due to unavoidable technical difficulties, we have been forced to omit the Autumn 1965 issue of *New Individualist Review*. The present Winter 1966 issue follows the Summer 1965 issue as Volume IV, Number 2. Subscriptions will not be affected by this omission; each subscriber will receive four issues for a one-year subscription.

NEW INDIVIDUALIST REVIEW is published quarterly by *New Individualist Review, Inc.*, at Ida Noyes Hall, University of Chicago, Chicago, Illinois 60637. Telephone 312/363-8778.

Opinions expressed in signed articles do not necessarily represent the views of the editors. Editorial, advertising, and subscription correspondence and manuscripts should be sent to NEW INDIVIDUALIST REVIEW, Ida Noyes Hall, University of Chicago, Chicago, Illinois 60637. All manuscripts become the property of NEW INDIVDUALIST REVIEW.

Subscription rates: $3.00 per year (students $1.50). Two years at $5.75 (students $2.75).

NEW

INDIVIDUALIST

REVIEW

**A JOURNAL OF
CLASSICAL LIBERAL THOUGHT**

EDITORIAL STAFF

Editor-in-Chief ● Ralph Raico

Associate Editors ● J. Michael Cobb ● James M. S. Powell
Robert Schuettinger

Editorial Assistants ● Douglas Adie ● David D. Friedman
Burton Gray ● Edwin Harwood ● Thomas C. Heagy
James A. Rock ● Ernest L. Marraccini ● John C. Moorhouse

EDITORIAL ADVISORS

Yale Brozen ● Milton Friedman ● George J. Stigler
University of Chicago

F. A. Hayek   Benjamin Rogge
University of Freiburg   *Wabash College*

688

Complaints of the loss of individuality and the lessening of respect for the person and his rights have become a commonplace of our time; they nonetheless point to a cause for genuine concern. NEW INDIVIDUALIST REVIEW, an independent journal associated with no organization or political party, believes that in the realm of politics and economics the system most effectively guaranteeing proper respect for individuality is that which, historically, has gone by the name of classical liberalism; the elements of this system are private property, civil liberties, the rule of law, and, in general, the strictest limits placed on the power of government. It is the purpose of the Review to stimulate and encourage explorations of important problems from a viewpoint characterized by thoughtful concern with individual liberty.

Herbert Clark Hoover:

A Reconsideration

THE AMERICAN PEOPLE have been subjected to a battery of political and historical myths; of these one of the most virulent has been the Hoover Myth. During the Great Depression, the Democrats held Herbert Hoover aloft as the wretched symbol of poverty and iniquity; but with the passing of the Depression, new times and new issues evaporated the old Democratic antagonism. The field was thereby cleared for the Hoover hagiographers, who have rushed in, unopposed (to paraphrase Mencken's immortal comment on the Woodrow Wilson idolators), to nominate Herbert Clark Hoover for the first vacancy in the Trinity. We have been regaled ad infinitum with the wisdom, the individualism, the sagacity, the lovability, and the glory of Herbert Hoover; and we have countless times been instructed on the horrors of the smear campaign waged against him by Charlie Michelson and the Democratic National Committee during his Administration. Throughout the Right-wing, numberless pilgrimages were made to Hoover's suite in the Waldorf Towers, and countless Right-wingers have been honored to refer to him as "The Chief." It is high time to redress the balance.

The hand-wringing over the Michelson smear campaign may be disposed of at

Murray N. Rothbard is the author of *America's Great Depression, Man, Economy, and State,* and other books and articles. He is currently editor of the journal *Left and Right,* and working on a history of the United States.

the start. Any public official, any politician, must expect to be subject to vigorous attacks, some justified, some not. Every president since Washington has been subjected to such attacks, and thus the public has been kept alert and vigilant to possible error and wrongdoing. Why should Hoover enjoy a special exemption from criticism? It is curious to see the same people who distributed with zeal and relish *A Texan Looks at Lyndon* bewail the tragedy of Hoover's ordeal. Despite the repeated harangues of his idolators that Hoover was not a "politician" and should therefore not have been treated as such, Hoover *was* a politician and cannot be allowed to escape the responsibility for his chosen profession.

THE MYSTERY OF Herbert Hoover begins, not in 1928 or 1932, but in 1919, when he was boomed for the *Democratic* nomination for the Presidency by such left-wing Democrats as Louis Brandeis, Herbert Croly, Ray Stannard Baker, Colonel Edward Mandell House, and Franklin D. Roosevelt. Yet, less than two years later, the Left-wing of the Republican Party was able to force Hoover on a reluctant Harding as a Secretary of Commerce whose powers had been vastly enlarged. What manner of man was this to be so beloved by *both* parties? It might be said that Hoover's greatness or goodness was so evident as to lead to his being courted by both parties; but to the wiser and more skeptical this story is suspiciously familiar. If a hard-core member of the Establishment may be defined as someone who somehow manages to land in a high government post whichever party is in power, Herbert Hoover may be considered to be the first *ur*-Establishment man of modern American politics.

It must be noted at the outset that any definitive study of Hoover at this point in time is almost impossible, but the blame for this situation must lie largely with Hoover himself. Hoover never released his papers for study by the scholarly public; hence the only information about his career has come from Hoover's own *Memoirs*—almost unbearably self-righteous and free from acknowledgment of error, *even* for political memoirs — and from Hoover's friends and supporters. As a result, critics have been discouraged from writing about Hoover, and we are left with a flood of worshippers, none of whom acknowledges a single error or flaw in their hero. Franklin D. Roosevelt, at least, had his John T. Flynn; where is Hoover's?

One significant example will give much of the flavor of the Hoover reminiscences. Hoover's recent book on Woodrow Wilson in the war and post-war years of World War I is almost as worshipful of Wilson as recent biographies have been of Hoover; or, rather, the book is a series of paeans to Wilson by Hoover, interspersed with paeans to Hoover by Wilson. Virtually the only act of Wilson's disapproved by Hoover was his famous call for a Democratic Congress in 1918, a call that angered the American public in its repudiation of the Wilsonian Republicans (such as Hoover) who had joined ardently in the war policy. Naturally, Hoover was shocked at this brusque slap at Republicans who had subordinated themselves to Mr. Wilson's war. How did Hoover react? In his book, he registers his sharp disapproval of the Wilson appeal; and yet, at the time, Hoover not only did *not* attack the Wilson plea; instead, he publicly rallied to the President's support, understandably angering Republicans in the process. Hoover states:

> Deeply as I believed that this appeal was a mistake and a wholly unwarranted reflection on many good men, . . . I addressed a letter to . . . a Republican friend, in which I supported the President's appeal for a Congress favorable to him. I did so because I believed that the President's hand in the Treaty negotiations would be greatly weakened if the election went against him. The publication of this letter created a storm around my head. The Chairman of the Republican National Committee denounced me violently.[1]

There is no hint of apology, no hint of remorse for Hoover's act; instead, there is, characteristicaly, only the proud reference to Woodrow Wilson's praise of Hoover's deed:

> My dear Hoover:
>
> Your letter . . . has touched me very deeply, and I want you to know not only how proud I am to have your endorsement and your backing given in such generous fashion, but also what serious importance I attach to it, for I have learned to value your judgment and have the greatest trust in all your moral reactions. . . .[2]

And that is *all* of Hoover's reference to the matter; for Herbert Clark Hoover, at least, wrapped securely in the mantle of morality and the enthusiasm of Woodrow Wilson, the case is closed.

THE HERBERT HOOVER story begins in 1899, when Hoover, a very young mining engineer and manager, was sent to China by his employers, the London mine consulting firm of Bewick, Moreing and Co. It is fitting that Herbert Hoover launched his career in enterprise, not on the free market, but in the midst of a mercantilistic struggle among claimants for mixed governmental and private property. Moreing had joined forces with a wily operator and recipient of special privilege in China, one Chang Yen Mao, who conveniently held the simultaneous posts of head of the Chinese Bureau of Mines in two provinces, *and* head of the "private" Chinese Engineering and Min-

---

[1] H. Hoover, *The Ordeal of Woodrow Wilson* (New York: McGraw-Hill, 1958), p. 17.
[2] *Ibid.*

ing Company. Hoover became Yang's deputy in managing the mines in *both* of Yang's capacities, public and private. Herbert Hoover emerged from years of competition among numerous foreign powers for the Chinese prize with the first leg up on his mining fortune.

The next years of Hoover's life, during which he built a multi-million dollar mining fortune, have not been generally detailed, and they are badly in need of scholarly work. Suffice it to say that Hoover's high qualities as a mining manager were undoubtedly primarily responsible for the amassing of the fortune, and enabled him to strike out on his own as an international mining consultant in 1908.

HOOVER SOON BEGAN TO display the ignorance of economics and predilection for statism that was to mark his public career. In 1904, at the age of thirty, he informed the Transvaal Chamber of Commerce that he had achieved lower mining costs in Australia *because* labor had been paid higher wages; thus, Hoover had already adopted the egregious fallacy that wage rates are determined by the good or ill will of the employer rather than by the competitive market, *and* that high wage rates lead to greater efficiency and lower costs rather than the other way round. Four years later, Hoover reiterated these views, and, in his *Principles of Mining*, went further to embrace the institution of labor unions. Unions, he declaimed, "are normal and proper antidotes for unlimited capitalistic organization. . . . The time when the employer could ride roughshod over his labor is disappearing with the doctrine of *'laissez faire'* on which it is founded. The sooner the fact is recognized, the better for the employer."[3] He went on to challenge, in a neo-Marxist manner, the orthodox laissez faire view that labor is a "commodity" and that wages are to be governed by laws of supply and demand. It is not surprising that, in 1912, Herbert Hoover enthusiastically supported and voted for Theodore Roose-

velt's Progressive Party, for Hoover had become the very model of an "enlightened" left-wing Republican, a man of the Establishment. Superficially, his views might be called "socialistic"; but it would be more precise to term them "mercantilist" or "state capitalist" or "monopoly capitalist," for Hoover, like his fellow Establishment liberals then and since, was not about to abandon state power to a dictatorship of the proletariat or even to Fabian social workers.[4] In the house of statism there are many mansions.

By 1914, Herbert Hoover, having made a substantial fortune in mining, was eager to try his hand at "public service." The First World War brought him his chance, and it was Hoover's luck that the opportunities that came his way were such as to lend him that mantle of saintliness and advanced morality which he was always able to wrap around his political activities more snugly than most of his fellows.

When Belgium was occupied in the fall of 1914, a group of American businessmen resident in London and Brussels formed a Commission for the Relief of Belgium, and Hoover agreed to serve as its head. The massive relief effort to Belgium, continuing throughout the war, gained Hoover immense publicity, and "The Chief" and "The Great Engineer" had now become "The Great Humanitarian." Actually, while it was no doubt admirable that Hoover and the group of wealthy American businessmen serving as his top aides accepted no compensation for their efforts, the operation was in no sense true charity. Neither was it really humanitarian and apolitical, as Hoover and its eulogists maintained.

In the first place, to be truly charity, aid must be voluntary and not compulsory; and yet the overwhelming bulk of contributions to Belgian relief came not

691

---

[3] *Principles of Mining* (New York: McGraw-Hill, 1909), pp. 167-68.

[4] This, of course, has nothing to do with the attempt of such "libertarian Trotskyites" as Tony Cliff and Raya Dunayevskaya to dub the Soviet Union "state capitalist," which is true only in the jejune sense that under socialism the state is the owner of the country's capital. On the contrary, the term is most aptly used to describe the mercantilist, interventionist policies of modern capitalist countries, and to distinguish them from socialism.

from private citizens but from Western governments. Secondly, from the beginning the C.R.B. was tied in with governmental policy, particularly of the supposedly neutral American, and the definitely warring Belgian, governments. On the American side, Hugh Gibson, secretary of the American Legation at Brussels, was one of the main originators of this unusual Commission. Belgian officials were vital leaders of the whole operation, and the notoriously Anglophiliac Walter Hines Page, the American Ambassador to London, was strongly committed to the whole idea.

The curious point about the C.R.B., and one that highlights the spuriousness of its neutrality and divorce from politics, is the question, why Belgium? Why a massive relief program to Belgium (and Northern France), and none anywhere else in war-torn Europe? The evident answer is that the C.R.B. was conceived as an extremely clever device to focus the continuous attention of the American people on the supposedly unique sufferings of Belgium, and *thereby* to lead people to keep focussing on the allegedly heinous crime of Germany in warring against "poor little Belgium." The "poor little Belgium" line was the main focal point of the mendacious propaganda of Great Britain, especially in sentimental and poorly-informed America, and it was undoubtedly instrumental in sucking America into perhaps the most senseless and ill-conceived war in which it has ever engaged. Certainly, it was a war with unprecedently bad consequences, for America and for Europe. As Walter Millis has put it:

> When the appeals for aid for the starving Belgians began to come in, offering a sudden practical outlet for the overwrought American emotions, the response was immediate — and the Allies found themselves in possession of still another incomparable propaganda weapon. That the relief of suffering could in any way compromise our neutrality hardly occurred to the Americans who poured out their contributions; but the Allied leaders understood very well that every request for funds in that cause was a conceded demonstration of German brutality and every answering . . . penny doing its part to

cement the emotional alliance with the Entente Powers.[5]

Of course, few Americans stopped to realize that the major cause of starvation in Belgium — and in the rest of Europe — was the brutal British blockade, which cut off even such non-contraband items as food from the people of the Continent.

THE IMAGE OF Herbert Hoover as an "isolationist" is as distorted as that of Hoover as an individualist. While apparently originally opposed to American entry into the war, by the Spring of 1917 Hoover had gone over to the pro-war camp, and sent Wilson a warm telegram of congratulations for his war message. Hoover promptly returned to the United States to take a leading part in the "war socialism" which marked America and the leading European participants in World War I.

It is almost impossible to exaggerate the fateful consequences, for America and the world, of the collectivism and central planning engaged in by the leading countries in the First World War. Here was the watershed of our time; and here was the model of collectivism, in a great many of its features: for fascism and naziism; for the central planning of the early New Deal years and during World War II; and for the "military-industrial complex" of the present day. The totalitarian changes of our age began in the impact of World War I, and Herbert Hoover played a large part in their inception.

Being "The Great Humanitarian," Hoover was appointed Food Administrator (also known as "Food Czar" or "Food Dictator") by President Wilson. In accepting, Hoover insisted that he alone have full authority, unhampered by boards or commissions. So eager indeed was Hoover to get started that he set up the Food Administration illegally, several months before it was authorized by Congress. Hoover urged Wilson to set up single Czars in every field, and was

---

[5] W. Millis, *Road to War* (Boston: Houghton Mifflin, 1935), pp. 73-74. Also see H. C. Peterson, *Propaganda for War* (Norman, Okla.: Oklahoma University Press, 1939), p. 66.

692

also responsible for Wilson's creation of the War Council, which served as the overall organ for the central planning of the economy.

Hoover's food-control act imposed the strictest control of any area of war planning. As the historian of government price control in World War I put it, the act "was the most important measure for controlling prices which the United States took during the war or had ever taken."[6] The measure set the pattern for twentieth century American collectivism: Behind a facade of demagogy about the necessity for keeping prices down and regulating business, the Federal government organized a gigantic cartellizing program to keep prices *up* and "stabilize" business under the guidance of government. Thus, the masses would come to think of the Federal government as their proconsul in control of business, while in reality it was the servant of those business interests who wanted monopoly privilege and a quieter life against the rigors of a competitive market.

TWO OUTSTANDING examples were the Hoover wheat and sugar control programs during World War I. Wheat price control was organized as a result of propaganda that the government must step in to see that wicked "speculators" did not push the price too high; but somehow, the government never got around to fixing maximum prices; instead the prices it fixed were *minima,* and these minima w e r e systematically pushed higher in order to maintain the bloated wartime wheat prices after the end of the war. The method of such control was through a gigantic licensing system, under which every food manufacturer and dealer had to be licensed — and to keep its license — from the Federal government. Profits were guaranteed at "reasonable" amounts by fixing cost-plus margins, and any overly greedy competitor who dared to raise his profits above pre-war levels by cutting his prices were severely cracked down on. Hoover organized a Grain Corporation, "headed

___
6 P. W. Garrett, *Government Control Over Prices* (Washington, D. C.: Government Printing Office, 1920), p. 42.

by practical grain men," which purchased most of the wheat in the country and sold it to the flour mills, all the while undertaking to guarantee millers against loss, and to maintain the relative position of all the mills in the industry. Wilson and Hoover also kept the industry happy by requiring all bakers to mix inferior products with wheat flour at a fixed ratio, something which the bakers were of course happy to do since they were assured that all their competitors were being forced to do likewise. All this was initiated in the name of "conserving" wheat for the war effort.

The fiercely-conducted drive to keep down sugar prices, in contrast, was far more sincere — sincere because the raw sugar came largely from Cuba, and the sugar *refiners* were in the United States and other allied countries. The fact that increased sugar demand *should* have raised sugar prices by the workings of the free market made no impression on the sugar refining interests or on the Allied governments. Hoover and the governments of the Allies therefore organized an International Sugar Committee, which undertook to buy all of the sugar demanded in those nations at an artificially low price, and then to allocate the sugar, in the manner of a giant cartel, to the various refiners. On the other hand, of course, the price of sugar could not be forced *too* low, since then the marginal American cane and beet sugar producers would not be getting their divinely-appointed "fair return." Therefore, the Federal government set up the Sugar Equalization Board to keep the price of sugar low to the Cuban producers while keeping it high enough to the American sugar refiners; the Board would buy the Cuban sugar at the low price and then resell at the agreed-upon higher price. Since an excessively low price of sugar would have caused high public consumption, production was directly ordered to be cut, and consumption by the public was severely rationed.

The food industry, as well as other industries in the Wilson-Baruch program of war collectivism, were delighted with the cartellizing and "stabilizing" (part of which was accomplished by enforcing compulsory standardization of parts and tools, a standardization which eliminated many small specialty businesses in machine tool and other industries, and forced production into a smaller number or bigger firms). Thus, Hoover

> . . . maintained, as a cardinal policy from the beginning, a very close and intimate contact with the trade. The men, whom he chose to head his various commodity sections and responsible positions, were in a large measure tradesmen. . . . The determination of policies of control within each branch of the food industry was made in conference with the tradesmen of that branch, meeting at intervals in Washington. It might be said . . . that the framework of food control, as of raw material control, was built upon agreements with the trade. The enforcement of the agreements once made, moreover, was intrusted in part to the cooperation of constituted trade organizations. The industry itself was made to feel responsible for the enforcement of all rules and regulations.[7]

694

DURING HIS LONG REIGN as Secretary of Commerce in the 1920's, Herbert Hoover carried forth the principles of advancing governmental cartellization of business; production was restricted and cartellized as much as possible by appeals to "elimination of waste," trade associations of business were promoted, export industries were encouraged and promoted abroad, "standardization" was furthered. It was this encouragement of industrial self-regulation, with the governmental mailed fist kept in the background to crack down on the maverick competitor, that launched the characteristic Hoover emphasis on "voluntary" action, and that enabled him to establish specious distinctions later between his own "voluntary" program and the compulsory measures of FDR. Also typical of Hoover's "voluntarism" was heavy emphasis on propagandizing the public. Thus, in his program as Food Czar in the First World War:

> The basis of all efforts toward control exercised by the Food Administration was the educational work which preceded and accompanied its

measures of conservation and regulation. Mr. Hoover was committed thoroughly to the idea that the most effective method to control foods was to set every man, woman, and child in the country at the business of saving food. . . . The country was literally strewn with millions of pamphlets and leaflets designed to educate the people to the food situation. No war board at Washington was advertised as widely as the United States Food Administration. There were Food Administration insignia for the coat lapel, store window, the restaurant, the train, and the home. A real stigma was placed upon the person who was not loyal to Food Administration edicts through pressure by schools, churches, women's clubs, public libraries, merchants' associations, fraternal organizations, and other social groups.[8]

Perhaps Herbert Hoover's outstanding "accomplishment" as Secretary of Commerce was to impose socialism on the radio industry. Even though the courts were working out a satisfactory system, based on private property rights in radio frequencies—under which one frequency owner could not interfere in the radio signals of another[9]—Hoover by sheer administrative fiat and the drumming up of "voluntary cooperation" was able to control and dictate to the radio industry and keep the airwaves nationalized until he could secure pasage of the Radio Act of 1927. The act established the government as inalienable owner of the airwaves, the uses of which were then granted to designated licensed favorites, the favorites being kept in line by the Federal Radio Commission's unchallenged control of the licensing power. If private "squatters' rights" had been permitted in radio (and subsequently in television) frequencies, we would have had a genuinely free press in the airwaves. As it is, we have had an air medium totally regulated and integrated into the Federal Establishment. More than anyone else we have Herbert Hoover to thank for government ownership and regulation of radio and television.

[7] *Ibid.,* pp. 55-56.

[8] *Ibid.*

[9] See R. H. Coase, "The Federal Communications Commission," *The Journal of Law and Economics,* II (Oct. 1959), 30-31.

Hoover was also the first great proponent of Federal dams, and was the initiator of the Grand Coulee, Hoover Dam, and Muscle Shoals projects. Improvement of navigation or reclamation was to be at the expense of the taxpayer and of the flooded private property owners, for the benefit of the recipients of cheap water and cheap power. Hoover was insistent, however, that the Federal government should not *itself* go into the p o w e r business; instead, it should thoughtfully build the plants and then *lease* them to private enterprise. Here is another example of state monopoly capitalism: the active use of the Federal government to promote monopoly and subsidize privilege.

UNDOUBTEDLY THE SINGLE most collectivist and despotic governmental action during the ascendancy of Herbert Hoover was Prohibition. It is characteristic of Herbert Hoover that he was one of Prohibition's most ardent supporters. Prohibition, of course, should be quite congenial to modern conservatism. All the arguments for prohibition of narcotics and gambling apply here too: Statistics show that people under the influence of liquor commit more crimes; let a workingman spend his money on liquor and he will become attached to it and waste his money there rather than spend it on nourishing and wholesome food for his children, etc.

Hoover acted in all this like a typical conservative, i. e., glorifying the State and its sacrosanct Laws over the liberty of the individual. His definitive statement on Prohibition as a whole: "Our country has deliberately undertaken a great social and economic experiment, noble in motive and far-reaching in purpose. It must be worked out constructively."[10] Whereas the only way to break down Prohibition was to destroy its enforcement, Hoover maintained that violation of one law destroys respect for all laws, and greatly expanded the nefarious institution of the Federal Prohibition Agent, attempting to make him incorruptible.

---

[10] *Memoirs* (New York: Macmillan, 1952), Vol. II, p. 201.

To the very last, Hoover stood fast for the "noble experiment."

As befitting one of the major leaders in the twentieth century drive for replacing quasi-laissez faire by a tightly controlled and cartellized system, Herbert Hoover favored trade unionism, and the dragooning of the worker into large, "responsible" unions that could be integrated into the New Order. Thus, during 1919/20, Hoover directed for President Wilson a Federal conference on labor-management relations. Under Hoover's aegis, the conference, which included "forward looking" industrialists such as Julius Rosenwald, Oscar Straus, and Owen D. Young, as well as labor leaders and economists, adopted Hoover's recommendations: wider collective bargaining, attacks on company unions, abolition of child labor, national old-age insurance, and government arbitration boards for labor disputes. In 1920, Hoover arranged a meeting of leading industrialists of "advanced views" to try to persuade them to tie in more closely with the American Federation of Labor; Hoover, incidentally, was always close to the A.F.L. leadership.

Hoover committed two striking acts of pro-union interventionism during the 1920's. One was his movements against the steel industry: Steel was operating on a twelve hour day, and groups of Social Gospel ministers suddenly found Biblical sanction for the alleged immorality of any working day over eight hours. Hoover assumed the mantle of evangelical *cum* secular power to force steel to grant an eight hour day. Conducting a skilful propaganda campaign, Hoover induced President Harding to launch several bitter attacks on the steel industry. Finally, in June 1923, Hoover wrote a letter for President Harding to send to Judge Gary of U.S. Steel, sternly chastising the steel companies. This Presidential pressure turned the tide and forced the steel companies to capitulate.

Hoover also played a large role in helping to bring about the compulsory unionization of the railroad industry, and did so long before the Wagner Act. The railroad unions had waxed fat as a result of Federal government favoritism during World War I, when the government had temporarily nationalized the railroads (the government operated the roads, and the old owners reaped the profits which the government turned over to them). During the severe (though short-lived) depression of 1921, the railroads asked for wage cuts, and the unions angrily hit back by calling a nation-wide strike. When Attorney General Daugherty acted to preserve person and property by obtaining an injunction against union violence, Herbert Hoover, winning Secretary of State Hughes to his side, persuaded the weak-willed Harding to withdraw the injunction.

Despite Hoover's actions, the unions lost the strike, and so they decided to use the power of Federal coercion to establish themselves in the industry. They finally achieved this goal in the Railway Labor Act of 1926, which guaranteed compulsory unionism (collective bargaining for all) to the railway unions, and imposed compulsory arbitration. Most of the railroads went along with the plan because railroad strikes were now outlawed; but the bill was drafted by union lawyers Donald Richberg and David E. Lilienthal, *and* by Herbert Hoover.

HOOVER WAS ALSO THE victim of a terribly inadequate grasp of economics, leading him to accept the popular "new economics" of the 1920's.[11] The "new economics" stood economics on its head; whereas economics saw that high wage rates in prosperous countries came about as a *result* of capital investment and high productivity, the "new" thinkers concluded that American prosperity had come about *because* employers paid high wage rates. In reality, the market determines wages, and not the goodheartedness or the wisdom of the employer. The employer in modern India who decided, out of the goodness of his heart and/or from reading economic nonsense peddled by Hoover or old Henry Ford, to triple his wage payments would quickly find himself bankrupt. Hoover deduced from

this the union slogan that during depressions the worst thing that could happen was lower wage rates. It was this lowering that helped wipe out unemployment and end previous depressions relatively quickly; and it was Hoover's personal use of the mailed fist in the velvet glove to *prevent* such lowering that kept wage rates increasingly and disastrously above market wages during the years 1929-33. This intervention insured that the Depression could not be relieved by natural market forces, or unemployment be lowered from disastrous Depression-born levels.

It was indeed as a depression-fighter that the nation came to know Herbert Hoover best. In all previous depressions, the Federal government had pursued a laissez faire attitude, keeping hands off and letting market forces bring about recovery quickly; and the recovery always came, no matter how steep the depression at the start.[12] But Hoover had long determined that *he* was not going to pursue such a "reactionary, Neanderthal" course. He would rush in, to plan, to inflate, to push up wages and prices and insure purchasing power. He had determinde that he would *plan,* that he would use the full resources of government, all the modern tools of the new economics, to push the economy out of the Depression. And he did just that, except that the results were not quite what the Great Engineer had anticipated.

In pushing through his program, Herbert Hoover created virtually all the lineaments of the New Deal; the New Deal was in fact Herbert Hoover's creation, and historians, now removed from the partisan squabbles of the New Deal period, are increasingly coming to recognize this fact. Massive public works programs, government relief, inflation and cheap money on a grand scale, government deficits, higher taxes, government loans to shaky businesses, farm price supports, propping up of wage rates, monopolizing the oil industry and restricting produc-

---

[11] This movement is not to be confused with the Keynesian "new economics" of the 1930's.

[12] The government's key role in producing depressions in the past is a question which cannot be gone into here. For a discussion of this aspect of the problem, see M. N. Rothbard, *America's Great Depression* (Princeton, N. J.: Van Nostrand, 1963), Part I.

696

tion, war against the stock market and stock speculation—all these crucial facets of the New Deal program were launched *con brio* by President Hoover.[13]

Hoover's method of forcing wage rates to remain high was typical of his pseudo-"voluntarism." He lost no time; as soon as the stock market crash broke, Hoover, in November 1929, called all the major industrialists to the White House and told them that they must pledge to keep wage rates up; that, whatever happened, the brunt of the Depression must fall on profits, not wages. This is precisely what did happen; wages were bravely kept up, especially in the larger firms, profits collapsed, and losses, bankruptcies, and mass unemployment ensued and remained unresolved. Since prices continued to fall, fixed wage rates meant that *real* wages (in terms of purchasing power) rose, aggravating the unemployment problem still further. Only in the small firms, hidden from public view, could quiet and secret wage cuts be agreed upon, and the workers continue to be employed. This was indeed the first severe depression in history in which real wage rates *rose* rather than fell: with the result that the Depression was intensified and rendered quasi-permanent. Even when wage cuts finally came, hesitantly, after several years of steep depression, they were so designed as to have little effect. For "humanitarian" reasons, they were largely put through in the higher income brackets and among executives: this, of course, could have little effect in stimulating employment where it was needed: among the lower-income, rank-and-file workers.

Addressing the White House conference, Hoover described his wage-floor agreements as an

> . . . advance in the whole conception of the relationship of businesses to public welfare. You represent the business of the United States, undertaking through your own voluntary action to contribute something very definite to the advancement of stability and progress in our economic life. This is a far cry from the arbi-

trary and dog-eat-dog atttiude of the business world of some thirty or forty years ago.[14]

The American Federation of Labor was ecstatic over this new era in combatting depressions: "The President's conference has given industrial leaders a new sense of their responsibilities. . . . Never before have they been called upon to act together. . . ." The United States, it proclaimed, would "go down in history as the creator of [an] . . . epoch in the march of civilization—high wages."[15]

One of the most irritating facets of Herbert Hoover was his unshakable conviction that he had never committed a serious mistake. He had entered the White House at the peak of economic prosperity; he had left it, after a new departure in economic planning, in the midst of the most intense and long-lasting depression the United States had ever known. Yet not once, either then or later, did Herbert Hoover falter in his absolute conviction that his every act was precisely what should have been done. In his acceptance speech for renomination, Hoover proclaimed:

> We might have done nothing. That would have been utter ruin. Instead, we met the situation with proposals to private business and to Congress of the most gigantic program of economic defense and counterattack ever evolved in the history of the Republic. We put it into action.[16]

Indeed he did, and "utter ruin" was precisely the result. Yet never once did Hoover falter in his attacks against all criticism, from left or right. Neither was this simply campaign oratory, for never once in his later years, when he was considered by friend and foe alike as a living symbol of laissez faire, did Herbert Hoover fail to look back upon every one of his disastrous deeds, from fighting the Depression to bolstering Prohibition. without finding them right and good. Every four years, Hoover could be depended upon to issue a campaign mani-

[13] For a more extensive discussion and analysis of the Hoover New Deal, see *ibid.*, Part III.

[14] W. S. Myers and W. H. Newton, *The Hoover Administration* (New York: Scribners, 1936), p. 34.

[15] *The American Federationist* (March 1930), p. 344.

[16] E. Lyons, *Herbert Hoover, A Biography* (New York: Doubleday, 1964), p. 300.

697

festo proving proudly and conclusively that the Republican Administrations, far from being exemplars of laissez faire, pioneered in the burgeoning statism of the twentieth century.

THERE SEEM TO BE several important lessons embedded in the story of the Hoover myth. One, of course, is the great dimensions of the myth, of the total misinterpretation, on all sides, of the Hoover record. Far from being a libertarian, Hoover was a statist par excellence, in economics and in morals; and his only difference from FDR was one of degree, not of kind: FDR only built upon the foundations laid by Hoover. Secondly, the very pervasiveness of the myth poses some sharp questions about the Right-wing that has so earnestly fostered it. There can be only two explanations of this phenomenon: Either the Right-wing shows itself monumental in stupidity, by mistaking statism for laissez faire; and/or, more significantly, the Right-wing's professed devotion to free enterprise and the free market is only rhetorical, and it will cheerfully welcome a statism slanted in typically conservative directions. A third lesson is that anyone genuinely devoted to freedom and the free market must, once and for all, discard the whole putrescent world-view of the unique diabolism of Franklin Roosevelt and his New Deal. The plain fact is that the New Deal was rooted far back in the past, in the Hoover Administration, and further back into the Progressive period and beyond. Genuine believers in freedom and a free market must cease to regard the American system as having been a grand and splendid one until an unaccountable break came in the 1930's. They have to realize that they must be far more "radical" than they have ever remotely conceived.

698

With the current issue, Winter 1966, the single copy price of *New Individualist Review* has been raised from 50 cents to 75 cents. Our subscription rate has been increased proportionately to $3.00 and $5.75 for one- and two-year non-student subscriptions, and to $1.50 and $2.75 for one- and two-year student subscriptions. This increase has been made necessary by the expansion of the magazine to its present size.

Readers who have entered their subscriptions prior to February 1, 1966, will continue to receive *New Individualist Review* under the previous subscription rates. No change has been made in the duration of existing subscriptions.

Twelve Thoughts

on Inflation

W. H. HUTT

THE PRESENT WRITER'S interest in the phenomenon of inflation goes back at least forty-five years. He was then an undergraduate at the London School of Economics. The famous Edwin Cannan, at whose feet he was studying, had taken the delightful gesture of suing the British Government under the Profiteering Act for selling pound notes at above their gold value. Cannan wanted to bring home to the public the extent to which inflation had debased the pound sterling.

As a teacher of business administration during the last thirty-eight years, the writer's attention has been repeatedly forced back to this question of the spasmodic, yet persistent, depreciation of money. How can businessmen co-ordinate the private sector of the economy effectively when the most important measuring-rod of all—the *monetary* unit—has been left with no reliable, defined value? Units of length, volume, and weight have been universally defined with meticulous care; but dollars, lire, francs, and pounds have been allowed to change in every significant attribute over time. Hence, the aim in this article is to record briefly the twelve most important practical conclusions to which the thought of an academic lifetime on this issue has led the author.

W. H. Hutt is Professor of Commerce and Dean of the Faculty of Commerce at the University of Capetown, South Africa. Among his published works are Keynesianism—Retrospect and Prospect, The Theory of Collective Bargaining, and The Theory of Idle Resources.

(1) Nearly all inflations have been intentional, calculated actions of governments, however reluctant they may have been. No monetary depreciation in history has ever occurred in which governments have not purposely taken the steps needed to bring it about or, alternatively, have not deliberately refrained from action which could rectify any inadvertently caused inflationary tendencies. If monetary systems had rested solely on private contracts to redeem credit instruments (according to some stipulated standard) inflation could never have occurred.

(2) From time immemorial *princes* debased currencies. To such an extent did this happen that almost invariably the emergence of representative government in different parts of the world was followed by legislation to remove the right of monarchs to reduce the metallic content of moneys. But curiously, with the transfer of the kingly power to parliaments, no similar constitutional limitations were imposed upon elected governments. There *have* been suggestions in the United States, since the Second World War, that the continued decline in the purchasing power of the dollar should be brought to an end by incorporating the objective of a stable price index, by amendment, into the Employment Act of 1946; but the leadership which could have forced governments to take so difficult a step has thus far been lacking.

699

Page Thirteen

(3) When governments plan the programs which force up the cost of living they are usually reluctant. If they (or their advisers) could conceive of some means other than inflation for keeping their supporters happy they would make use of them; but provided the public generally does not predict the speed with which it is to occur, or its duration, inflation accords governments an easy access to income—unauthorized by democratic process—with which to purchase popularity, as well as an easy means — although a clumsy and unjust means — of temporarily alleviating the most common causes of disco-ordination in an economic system.

(4) Inflation can serve as a sort of palliative or anaesthetic which deadens the pain of a serious economic disease, namely, disco-ordination due to different categories of prices coming to be wrongly related to one another. Various types of restraint on competition permit wage rates and prices to be fixed too high to permit the full flow of output to be purchased from uninflated income, or too high in relation to price expectations. When one kind of labor or its product is priced too high, the sources of demand for non-competing labor and products are reduced; and if prices generally are rigid downwards, a cumulative decline in activity is set in motion. In the absence of inflation, therefore, the symptoms of the disco-ordination so caused are unemployment and depression.

AN ORGANIZED depreciation of the monetary unit, however, *may* bring about some sort of reco-ordination of the price system, in spite of its injustice. *Under favorable conditions*, it can cause the prices realized for products to rise more rapidly than the costs of making them. This may render profitable the employment of some presently unutilized or under-utilized productive capacity. For instance, if costs such as wage rates have been fixed higher than the public can afford to pay for the full supply of labor, a slowing down of output, with unemployment, is threatened. Inflation can then raise prices in relation to costs

and so keep the economy going. Similarly, if producer-dominated marketing commissions have forced up the prices of primary products (raw materials or food) so that the public begins to be unable to afford to buy all that is being produced, again inflation can, in a crude sort of way, rectify the position by validating the higher prices. *But all this depends, of course, upon the public as a whole not expecting it.*

Eventually the recipients of wages *as a whole* and the farmers *as a whole* receive no more for their services. Their persistent striving to squeeze more for themselves out of the common pool is self-frustrating because the prices of the things which *they* have to buy are equally forced up by the process; but elected labor union officials can often retain their jobs only if they can show that they have raised wage rates year by year; and organized farmers habitually think it right that they should be paid a little more each year for their products. Hence in this inflationary age, wage rates and primary product prices tend to be raised, again and again, above what the public could afford in the absence of concurrent inflation; and so it seems as if the whole fatuous process has to be kept going.

(5) When the prosperity achieved by inflationary means happens to be accompanied by thrift, economic growth will occur, although in a less productive form than non-inflationary growth; and the easily won and largely illusory development tempo then gives rise to a confusion of growth with rising prices, a confusion which politicians (not surprisingly) encourage. But growth is purely a matter of thrift. Rising prices are *not* a condition for growth. On the contrary, there are good reasons for regarding inflation as, on balance, a discouragement of growth. In countless ways, rising prices tend to induce consumption. In particular, the "money illusion" all too easily causes insufficient provision to be made for depreciation and the maintenance of "real capital" intact.

(6) The result of trying continuously to co-ordinate by inflation is that the

basic causes of the disorder so crudely rectified are never tackled. For this reason, inflation is a more insidious and virulent manifestation of the disease of disco-ordination than unemployment and recession; for the latter, being more painful, create incentives for fundamental reform.

(7) The origin of the most serious disco-ordinations of the modern economic system lies ultimately in the corrupting influence of a tradition whereby governments have come to be regarded as beneficent distributors of favors to the people, the people in turn rewarding governments by keeping them in power. This tradition creates a situation in which governments can intimidate minorities (unless the minorities happen to be able to disturb the balance of political power). Business managements become disheartened and obsequious; and because inflation seems to offer the only way out, they acquire the habit of acquiescence in it. At the same time politically powerful groups or institutions are given virtual carte blanche to pursue purely sectionalist objectives. That is why the private use of coercive power — the most obvious cause of disco-ordination in the pricing mechanism—has come to be tolerated.

(8) The crucial task, yet the most difficult task, of a truly planned regime is to secure co-ordination without inflation; and that means, in the first place, protection of the community from such sectionalist actions—particularly on the part of trade unions—as are calculated to reduce the flow of wages and other forms of income and render its distribution less equitable. A reduced flow of uninflated wages is always the consequence of any forcing up of wage rates (and hence product prices) in certain sectors otherwise than through free market pressures. If governments were aiming at (i) the maximization of the wage-flow, and (ii) equality of opportunity as a determinant of the distribution of wages, they would be *ipso facto* achieving effective co-ordination, for both rising prices *and* unemployment would then be simultaneously eliminated. But to achieve this result they would be forced to take the initially unpopular step of enshrining the right of all, and particularly of the poorer classes or races, to keep the price of their labor at a minimum. For instance, if equality of opportunity, distributive justice, and economic efficiency had been primary objectives in the United States, the minimum wage laws, which have slowed down the industrial progress of Negroes in the underdeveloped South, would never have been passed.

For identical reasons, governments would have to prevent other forms of contrived scarcity. A good example is the price supports which have become common where governments have been directly active in agricultural marketing. When the prices of primary products and food are raised, people have less uninflated income to spend on other things; and if the prices of these other things are rigid, that must mean the unemployment of some of the productive factors which manufacture them also. Dynamic forces cause cumulative contraction.

701

(9) THE TECHNIQUE OF inflation demands that governments and their agencies shall continuously deceive the public about the fact, the speed, and the duration of inflation intended. Ministers of Finance have here no option but to employ what has been called the "necessary untruth." Unless they do employ this technique, inflation will lead to costs rising as rapidly as prices, or in advance of prices, thereby destroying the whole purpose of inflation. Moreover, yields on fixed interest bonds will be forced up and yields on equities forced down. As Professor Ludwig von Mises has insisted:

> These enthusiasts [for inflation] do not see that the working of inflation is conditioned by the ignorance of the public and that inflation ceases to work as soon as the many become aware of its effects upon the monetary unit's purchasing power....This ignorance of the public is the indispensable basis of inflationary policy. . . . The main problem of an inflationary policy is how to stop it before the masses have seen through their rulers' artifices.[1]

[1] L. von Mises, *The Theory of Money and Credit* (New Haven, Conn.: Yale University Press, 1953), pp. 418-19.

Page Fifteen

The phrase "necessary untruth" was used in 1949 by the *Manchester Guardian*[2] in justifying the conduct of the British Chancellor of the Exchequer, Sir Stafford Cripps, who, just before the British devaluation of that year, and after it had been finally planned, had categorically denied on no fewer than nine occasions that it was intended. The British Government had secretly discussed the proposed step for some time, almost inevitably setting into circulation rumors of what was contemplated. They had finally decided to devalue, it seems, at least three weeks before they were ready to put their decision into effect. They had to discuss it first with the United States, Canada, and the International Monetary Fund. In the meantime it became imperative to mislead the trustful for the benefit of the mistrustful.

It had for some time been governmental technique to pretend, in order to dissuade rational reactions, that "suspensions" of convertibility were merely temporary breaches of obligation. Thus, in 1931 there occured one of the most disturbing examples of the necessity to mislead in order successfully to reduce the value of a nation's currency: Dr. Vissering, head of the Netherlands Bank, telephoned Mr. Montagu Norman, Governor of the Bank of England. He inquired whether his bank would be justified in retaining the sterling it was holding. Dr. Vissering received from Norman an unqualified assurance that Britain would remain on the gold standard. He believed what he was told. In consequence, his bank lost the whole of its capital; for the very next day Britain abandoned gold. Through the same act, the Bank of France lost seven times its capital.[3]

Two years later, using the argument that he wanted "to control inflation," President Roosevelt persuaded Congress to give him extraordinary discretionary powers in the monetary field. Then, in April of that year, he decided to call in all privately owned gold "as a temporary measure." There was no suggestion that the real purpose was a forced depreciation of the dollar in terms of gold, the issue of an enormous number of notes, with open market operations by the Treasury and Federal Reserve System to acquire government securities and hence perpetuate the depreciation.

The fact that the Bank of France had been called upon to falsify its balance-sheet in 1925, in order to maintain confidence, had been regarded as a shocking incident by those who understood what had happened.[4] But exactly the same *kind* of deception is inevitable if inflation is ever to be continuously successful. A delightful euphemism is "creating a favorable climate of opinion"!

Because a policy of creeping inflation must rely upon persistent deception, its survival in the modern world is obvious evidence of the corruption of government and of the disintegration of trustworthy relations between governments.

In 1922, in negotiating a settlement with the American Debt Funding Commission, Britain had confined herself, on the whole, merely to asking that the rate of interest should be 3½% in accordance with her credit standing. Professor B. M. Anderson, at that time economist to the Chase Bank, commented: "The British were superb in this. They were proud, magnificently proud. They asked little consideration."[5] Perhaps Britain was then the loser, in material terms; but can we be indifferent to the moral deterioration which has subsequently become evident, recorded in an era which demands "necessary untruth"?

(10) The disintegration of *faith in money* (ultimately, of *faith in government*) has involved the peoples of the world in formidable material costs. In the pre-1914 era, simply because no one ever doubted that "banks of issue" would honor convertibility obligations, there were no balance of payments difficulties, no hot money flights, no devaluation scares, no complaints of world liquidity shortages, no restraints on international

702

[2] September 21, 1949.

[3] B. M. Anderson, *Economics and the Public Welfare* (New York: Van Nostrand, 1949), p. 246; also, W. A. Morton, *British Finance, 1930-1940* (Madison, Wis.: University of Wisconsin Press, 1943), p. 46.

[4] B. M. Anderson, *op. cit.*, pp. 154-56. Anderson refers to the *Commercial and Financial Chronicle* (New York), April 11, 1925.

[5] B. M. Anderson, *op. cit.*, p. 293.

settlements, no blocking of foreign balances, and no quantitative trade restrictions for balance of payments purposes. In that co-ordinated era, even such *concepts* (which the present disco-ordinated age treats as everyday notions) would have been incomprehensible.

The enormous administrative costs of today's "controls" are obvious enough; but the losses due to the economic distortions they cause—domestically and internationally—are incomparably heavier. World disco-ordination is a product of the continuous misdirection of expectations which the inflationary technique necessitates.

(11) THE ONLY WAY IN which the general public can discourage inflation is to make it unprofitable. They can do this when they are in a position to insist upon fixed income contracts being revised *ahead of* instead of following the price increases at which official policy is aiming (perhaps via "escalator clauses"), and refusing to accept the dishonest assurance that their insistence can be a cause of inflation. A similar discouragement is effected when investors learn to avoid fixed interest bonds, except at very high yields to compensate for monetary depreciation.

(12) When more and more people begin to understand what is happening, a government which wishes to persevere with inflation is forced to take authoritarian action. It has to discourage or prevent *those who understand* from using market institutions to escape the destruction of the real value of their savings. In other words, when enlightenment spreads, for a government to engineer rising prices successfully demands eventual resort to price controls, rent controls, import controls, exchange controls, controls of capital issues, "income policies," and so forth. In the absence of inflation, all controls of this kind (or extra-legal "persuasions" with the same object, backed by arbitrary state power) have no purpose.

TO WHAT GENERAL conclusion are we led after consideration of these twelve

points? Is it not that the gradual drift of the so-called "free world" towards a totalitarian concentration of power has had its origin in the creeping inflation which, dating from the 1930's, seems to have been mainly inspired by Keynesian teachings? Through public acquiescence in perpetually rising prices, we are threatened with an emergence of the sort of social order which, less than three decades ago, the blood of countless patriots was spilled to prevent.

In recording these thoughts, is the writer the victim of a futile nostalgia—a naive longing for the nineteenth century era? Has not inflation perhaps been an inevitable step towards a slow, inexorable transfer of consumer freedom (and the entrepreneurial freedom which is its consequence) to the state? Certainly there are those who, with a dogmatism of Marxian stubborness, will argue that, once the institutions of representative government had been conceded, politicians were bound, sooner or later, to discover the potentialities of twentieth century techniques of persuasion and propaganda; whilst that discovery could not fail to mean the ultimate passing of authority to those most skilled, or most uninhibited, in controlling the minds and purchasing the support of political majorities. If they are right, the stereotype of the state as the donor of benefits was predestined to emerge; recourse to inflation had necessarily to follow; and as the community began to be more difficult to deceive, and started to use the remnants of the free market economy to evade the burden of inflation, the urge to totalitarian government became irresistible.

To those who are inclined, for such reasons, to acquiesce in, or make terms with, the totalitarian trend, the "classical" type of analysis, like that presented above, seems to have become irrelevant. What the rulers of modern society *now* need, they feel, are formulae which assist officialdom in maintaining a nice balance between plausibility or electoral acceptability on the one hand and mitigation of the more obvious causes of unrest on the other. It comes to be regarded as more important, therefore, for economists to be experts in semantics than ex-

703

perts in explaining dispassionately to students and the public the nature of the economic process. Indeed, governments have no alternative but to choose economic advisors from those who understand their basic problems, all of which center on the need for the retention or winning of office. Accordingly it becomes the duty of the universities to provide the required training. Useful economics, they will insist, is "operational." That is, it is a kind of economics which takes politically decided objectives for granted, concentrates on the problems which arise in seeking those objectives, and isolates the kinds of data (and types of statistical analysis) which are of service in satisfying the politically powerful and placating the politically weak.

Would inflationary policy (with its eventual totalitarian outcome) have been inevitable, however, if the public had been taught the above twelve truths (if they are truths) about inflation? Suppose economists in the leading universities had maintained their political independence and reiterated with unanimity the simple points we have stressed. Would not the authority attaching to their teachings, together with the almost self evi‑dent irrefutability of the propositions themselves (to men of affairs), have forced the abandonment of inflation? And in renouncing the inflationary remedy for disco‑ordination, would not the state have been forced to re‑assume its traditional task of protecting the co‑ordinative mechanism of the price system from sabotage by sectionalist action? Would not suppression of the private use of coercive power have permitted the social discipline of the free market to bring different categories of prices into harmonious relationship with one another, without inflationary validation?

But this was not to be. From the middle thirties — for reasons which cannot be discussed here — Keynesian economists slowly got the upper hand, not only in the counsels of governments but in most of the universities. "Classical economics," the product of more than a century of disinterested, scientific thinking, was pushed aside as fundamentally wrong. It was replaced by the more plausible doctrines of Keynes' *General Theory* — doctrines built on a number of obscurely enunciated propositions which, because obscurity all too easily suggests profundity, greatly impressed the layman—an influence which was magnified through the subsequent elaboration of the propositions by mathematicians.

The fact that, since the war, every unique Keynesian theory which clashes with classical economics seems to have been tacitly abandoned, in the sense that it can no longer be rigorously defended,[6] has hardly discouraged the continued indoctrination of students of economics in the new orthodoxy. Indeed, so strongly is a powerful Keynesian establishment now entrenched within the universities, and so influential are the vested interests it has built up, that even non‑Keynesian economists have mostly felt themselves forced to attempt to persevere with its concepts. The most widely used textbooks remain Keynesian, and the young student of economics is seldom made aware that ideas like those explained in this article can be seriously entertained except by cranks. Yet the present writer is convinced that, if free and fair competition between the Keynesian and "classical" notions had been permitted, only the latter could have survived.

AS THINGS ARE, THE Keynesian thesis which — as one apologist put it — "removed inhibitions against inflation," still dominates policy in Britain, in the United States, and, indeed, in most parts of the world. Governments, relying on the fruits of a technological progress which current policy has hampered but not prevented, will not easily renounce the myth that they can foster the spending of a country into prosperity and growth whilst they simultaneously "fight inflation."

---

[6] For the evidence supporting this assertion the reader's attention is directed to the present author's *Keynesianism — Retrospect and Prospect* (Chicago: Regnery, 1963), chap. xix, "The Retreat"; and his recent article, "Keynesian Revisions," *South African Journal of Economics,* XXXIII (June 1965), 101‑13, reprinted in the *Rampart Journal,* I (Winter 1965), 1‑18.

Raico on Liberalism

and Religion

M. STANTON EVANS

IN A RECENT issue,[1] *New Individualist Review* carried an article by Ralph Raico which was among other things an extended attack upon a contribution of mine to *What Is Conservatism?*[2] I had intended a reply before this, but the pressure of journalistic duties, followed by a rather hectic session of the Indiana legislature, has intervened. I trust, however, that the nature of the subject will make this belated continuation of it of some interest to *New Individualist Review*'s readers.

The article which ignited Raico's displeasure argues that the imperatives of freedom and religious authority were not, as sometimes asserted, incompatible, but complementary. In so alleging, I briefly sketched the outlines of what I call "classical liberal" philosophy and traditional conservatism, trying to show that the alleged contradictions were more a matter of mortal confusion than of philosophical necessity. In rebuttal, Raico contended my discussion of classical liberalism was mistaken, both in the round and in its several particulars; that I had along with other conservatives and divers spokesmen for modernity, erred in calling this school of thought "superficial, unrealistic, and obsolete."

My first observation on this charge is that my views on "classical liberalism," however broadly or narrowly the term

may be defined, do not coincide with the usual modernist critique of it. I am in general agreement with the economic views of the classical liberals. I happen to think that, in discussing the secular modulations of freedom and the secular conditions most agreeable to its continuance, Herbert Spencer is hard to surpass. It is precisely in this respect, of course, that the views of the classical liberals are nowadays most disparaged.

Where I depart from classical liberalism's most famous spokesmen is the point at which modern collectivists tend to agree with them—in their mechanical, materialist, and relativist view of human nature and ethical principles. As I tried to argue in my previous article, the classical liberals all too clearly foreshadowed modern-liberalism in this respect, and helped lay the ethical foundation for the rise of the total state they wanted to avoid.

In lumping together the critics of classical liberalism, therefore, Raico is liable to give the reader a wrong impression of my differences with nineteenth century spokesmen for laissez faire. My position is not one of blanket condemnation, but rather one of arguing that, while the secular views of the classical liberals are by and large correct, their ethical views in the long run undermine the freedoms they thought they were protecting.

M. Stanton Evans is the editor of the *Indianapolis News* and author of *Revolt on the Campus, The Liberal Establishment,* and co-author of *The Fringe on Top.*

[1] Vol. III, No. 3, Autumn 1964.
[2] (New York: Holt, Rinehart, and Winston, 1964.)

My argument is so insistent on this point that Raico, despite his tendencies toward amalgam, perforce devotes most of his comment to battling against it. Once more, however, he neglects to keep the categories of the discourse in order. My purpose in *What Is Conservatism?* was, in part, to examine the philosophical strain in Western society which, as most characteristically put forward in England and America during the past century, I identify with the terms "libertarian" and "classical liberal." I explicitly note that *some* people who put themselves in this category do not fit my definition, since they do profess religious sentiments. "To the extent they do," I say in an explanatory note which appears with the article and which in fact appeared with it in its original incarnation as far back as 1960, "I trust my terminology will not obscure the fact that the argument of this essay is not an attack on such 'libertarians,' but a vindication of them."

Raico chooses to ignore the meaning of this statement, feigning to believe my critique includes everyone in the nineteenth century, religious or otherwise, who embraced the principles of freedom. He then cites certain examples of religious devotees of liberty as disproof of my argument. The deficiencies of this tactic are so grave as to be, in themselves, fatal to his position. He in effect ignores the definition I explicitly set forward, as the central condition and point of my article; bootlegs another definition of his own without making it explicit; glosses over the transposition in terms by suggesting I have employed his categories despite my direct statement to the contrary; and then taxes me for violation of his unstated taste in noun substantives. If I had used the categories he appears to favor, there would have been no point to the article in the first place. The purpose of my essay was to examine that class of people who *do* believe irreligion and liberty to go hand in hand, and to argue that they are mistaken. *Of course* there have been libertarian spokesmen who also believed in a profoundly religious view of the universe; I acknowledge the existence of such people in my article. More, I cite them as examples of the *correct* view of things, *in opposition* to those who believe irreligion the handmaiden of freedom. Burke, Smith, Acton, and Tocqueville are some I mention explicitly. To bring these people up as a rebuttal to my assertions about irreligious classical liberals is comparable to citing Barry Goldwater as proof that Lyndon Johnson is not a Democrat.

Thus launched into obscurity, Raico proceeds to divide his argument unevenly among a number of points. In some places, he seems to object to the argument that there *are* people who believe liberty can be protected by tearing down religious authority. Secondly, and in this modulation he consumes most of the space in his criticism, he argues that, whatever the general case with people of this description, classical liberalism is not the correct label for them. Like Pascal, I am not much inclined to argue about names so long as I know what is meant by them. If Raico wants to call such people by another name, well and good; let us have the name; we can then go on, using Raico's terminology, to explore the real issues involved. While he quarrels with my use of the term, Raico ignores the specific content I give it and neglects to say what terminology he would himself apply to the irreligious-libertarian point of view so that it might in some way be discussed. His approach suggests he either does not grasp the import of my article, or else does not want to talk about it. In either event, he has not answered it.

Finally, and this may be the reason Raico neither acknowledges the real nature of my argument nor reformulates it in his own terms, he goes on to suggest that, although there *are* irreligious classical liberals, their views are a matter of indifference, since the maintenance of freedom is a purely secular business. On this score, he begs the question to which my article is addressed. My view is exactly that the maintenance of freedom is not, and cannot be, purely secular, and that the profession of irreligious, relativist ethics is in the long run harmful to liberty. At no point does Raico close with my views on this score, as he would have to do if he paraphrased them correctly rather than presenting them in caricature.

To sustain his criticism while omitting substantive argument, Raico undertakes a laborious analysis of my statement that the classical liberal "characteristically denies the existence of a God-centered moral order, to which man should subordinate his will and reason," alleges human freedom, "as the single moral imperative," and otherwise is a "thoroughgoing relativist, pragmatist, and materialist." His comment is that the classical liberal is not in fact like this, and that the characterizations are in several instances meaningless anyway.

As to the irreligious nature of "classical liberals," I have already noted Raico's principal tactic. At different points in his article, he directly or indirectly accuses me of ignoring or "dismissing" certain religious classical liberals. In point of fact, I "dismiss" no religious classical liberals; they are the very type of correct reasoning suggested by my article, men who combine *both* ethical affirmation and concern for human freedom. They are the heroes of the piece. This is the most frivolous of his arguments, and I have no doubt belabored it sufficiently already.

MORE TO THE POINT is a second version of Raico's position — that although irreligious classical liberals do exist, they are no more numerous than the religious sort, and that their irreligion has no necessary connection with their libertarian views. This argument from statistical insignificance is patently incorrect. Whatever the numerical incidence of such people, the issues raised by them are still there, and still distressing. It is their position, not that of an Acton or Tocqueville, which has given rise to philosophical contention within the ranks of conservatives; it is their position which clashes directly with what is understood to be conservative ethical theory; it is their position which is emphasized nowadays in public discourse, in part by critics of conservatism, but also by sectarians within the conservative camp. The whole purpose of the article was to discuss these deep-going

differences—to take the "libertarian" and "authoritarian" positions in their most antinomian terms, in order to explore the philosophical tensions between them. To reconcile Acton with Burke, while no doubt a problem to test the mettle of political philosophers, would be nothing to the purpose, since both occupy, comparatively speaking, middle ground. But to explore the possibility of uniting Spencer's economics with de Maistre's ethical theory, although clearly too ambitious a project for my talents, is very much to the purpose indeed. The latter effort speaks to the philosophical stress within the conservative camp today, and which was recognized by de Tocqueville more than a century ago. Raico faults me with not taking the solution to the problem as the statement of it.

As to whether the agnostic strain in libertarian philosophy is important enough to merit this kind of treatment, and to justify using "classical liberalism" as an eponym for such belief, the names of Mill and Spencer should be sufficient answer. Raico passes over these giants of classical liberal thought as though they were but random faces in the crowd, preferring the example of John Bright. But to adduce the atypical Quakerism of Bright as proof of the religious character of classical liberalism is no more convincing than to cite the formal devoirs of the National Council of Churches as proof of the religious character of modern-liberalism. The Bright example fails on at least three counts. First, while Bright was sincerely theistic, the emphasis of his public advocacy (and private contention within the Society of Friends) was on the secular aspects of reform, and it was in this secular business that the entire impact of his public career was made. Ficino and Erasmus were, in their way, equally pious; yet it was the pagan secularism they mixed with Christianity which left its mark on Renaissance scholarship, and it was in its thrust toward secularism that the Renaissance helped shape the modern consciousness. Second, Bright occupies little or no place in the theoretical development of classical liberalism, any more than a LaFollette or Borah occupies a place in the theoretical development of modern-lib-

707

eralism. Bright was all free trade and extend-the-franchise, and while a consistent libertarian and a man of probity, he was a politician and not a philosopher. Third, precisely because Bright was not a philosopher, he was not called upon to square his private theism with the implications of classical liberal chiliasm and environmentalist notions about man. When such a confrontation of thought *was* made by nineteenth century liberals, it is noteworthy that they either repudiated liberal assumptions (as did Acton), or else repudiated Christian ethics (as did Spencer).

If we would understand the philosophical tendencies of classical liberalism, we must turn to its explicit theorists, as represented in the clear line of development from Hume to Sumner. In this history, Mill and Spencer have a pre-eminent claim upon our attention. It is from them that classical liberal philosophy received its most powerful impulses and most characteristic form. It is from them that the notion of irreligion united with secular liberalism continues to draw sustenance. Mill is still considered the great aboriginal spokesman for civil liberties. Spencer, above all other men, put the impress of his thought on the rationalization of the free enterprise system, ably assisted in America by the complementary efforts of Sumner. To suggest classical liberal thought *was* religious, *with the exception of Mill and Spencer,* is very much like suggesting late Victorian culture, *with the exception of Darwin and Huxley,* affirmed special creation. To argue that we should hold the immense force of the ideas generated and formalized by these two powerful intellects—ideas which long dominated English and American thought and which in their ethical tendencies are all too unhappily attuned to modern disintegration—at parity with the opinions of Madame de Stael is equivalent to saying we cannot identify Communism with Marx and Engels because Proudhon also has his claims in the matter. Mill and Spencer alone would, I think, justify appropriating "classical liberalism" to describe anti-clerical libertarianism, and for making it the object of considerable examination. But they do not, of course,

stand alone. To their names might be joined those of Diderot, Condorcet, Faguet, Hume, Godwin, Paine, Bentham, Sumner, Nock, Mencken, and Miss Ayn Rand, to mention only a few.

If any of these deserves to be mentioned along with Mill and Spencer, it is Sumner, whose formulation of classical liberalism looms enormously in any conspectus of American thought. It was Sumner who preached to Americans the evolutionary ethics of which Spencer was the acknowledged master, and taught that all values are relative to the needs of time and place; whose views became embodied in American thought and practice and translated into law through the labors of Mr. Justice Field and others on the Supreme Court; who preached the radical disjunction of liberal sentiment from religious profession, and whose inconsistencies foretold the unhappy results of that separation. Himself a Puritan by temperament and upbringing, Sumner believed the Protestant Ethic could stand on its own secular merits even after society, like himself, had put its religious beliefs in the drawer never to retrieve them. He believed it possible to construct a purely materialist and relativist system while maintaining the strict moral outlook indicated by his Puritan ancestry. The experiment has not worked. Once the religious underpinning was removed, the subtle comprehension of material forces desired by Sumner could not be counted on to sustain human motives toward liberty and self-reliance, as our own era has all too conclusively demonstrated. Sumner helped demolish the moral foundations which alone can support a regime of freedom.

So much for classical liberals' not believing in a "God-centered moral order." On the secondary point that classical liberals do not believe man should subordinate his will and reason to this order, Raico generously refrains from annihilating me because he considers it of small importance. He then goes on, in a footnote, to say even Christians do not necessarily believe man *should* subordinate his will and reason to the divine order, citing a commentary in paraphrase of St. Thomas. His construction of this point is in error. St. Thomas believed a portion of the divine order, revealed in the Natural Law, apprehensible by reason; he did not, however, believe it was validated by reason. The ultimate *sanction* for all truth, natural and divine, is in the Christian view of the will of God. Raico has got Christian orthodoxy hopelessly turned around, as he will readily discover if he opens the *Summa* to Question XCI, Articles 2, 3, and 4.

On the issue of a *causal* connection between irreligion and libertarian attachment, enough has been said, I think, to show that Raico has twisted my position inside-out. "Even if a majority of liberals had been atheists and agnostics," he says in supposed rebuttal to my position, "the connection is so far accidental and historically-conditioned, and not logical." The burden of my argument, of course, is precisely that there *is* no logical relationship between the anti-religious views of Mill, Spencer, et al., and the establishment of the free society they desired. On the contrary, I argue that lack of religious grounding leads to slippage from freedom. Mill's intellectual career is a perfect example of this.

The connection between libertarian views and anti-religious tendencies is, therefore, not causal, but adventitious. That the dominant spokesmen for classical liberalism gravitated to anti-religious thought is a matter not of integral connection but of historical fact. The relation, to use Hume's terminology, was not causal, but conditional—apparently founded in the assumption which has vitiated modern thought from the Renaissance forward, that supernatural authority is the enemy of freedom. This assumption, far from being my own, is the chief target of my article.

RAICO NEXT objects to my statement that classical liberals elevated human freedom as "the single moral imperative." Other values, he says, were also cherished by them. The reader of Spencer's *Principles of Ethics* and *Social Statics* will be constrained to disagree with Raico's interpretation of this author. The necessity of a regime of freedom is Spen-

cer's "first principle"; all other principles he deduces from the irrefragable rightness of liberty. Raico incorrectly alludes to Spencer in his effort to prove otherwise. Spencer's *summum bonum* is the existence of mutually sacrosanct zones of freedom for all men—the ability of each to do as he pleases so long as he respects the equal ability of everybody else. He states and restates this as the first law of moral philosophy, recommended by science, logic, and the intuition of fitness which is the final authority for every value system. "Positive" and "negative" beneficence are not moral values, but utilitarian functions of the human mind which enable it to comprehend and enjoy the balance of freedoms that is the end and justification of all other principles. Negative beneficence consists in refraining from encroachment upon other men's satisfaction; positive beneficence is the ability to derive part of one's own satisfaction from the fact that the general system of freedom has displaced the reign of license in which one man's desires are satisfied at the expense of another's. In the second category, Spencer's disquisition greatly resembles Hume's treatment of "sympathy" in the *Treatise,* in which benevolent tendencies are ultimately derived from the self-regarding faculties. Spencer's view is even more mechanical than Hume's (subsequently modified in the *Inquiry Concerning The Principles of Morals*), because it clearly views this tendency as a means toward achievement of universal freedom. "Positive" and "negative" beneficence, in Spencer's system, are props to his first principle of mutual liberty, and derive their sanction from it. Freedom is, for Spencer, quite obviously the "single moral imperative." Spencer's inconsistency in bringing "intuition" into play at this juncture is characteristic of the classical liberal position as a whole, even when the matter is not made as explicit as Spencer makes it. My point is that, given the relativist-utilitarian ethics of the Mill-Spencer school, there is no logical reason to exempt human freedom from the potencies of the system. If morality is the function of secular arithmetic or the adjustment of secular means to secular

709

ends, or a coefficient of the evolutionary struggle, then it is altogether possible that, somewhere along the line, freedom must give way to the calculus, the adjustment, or the evolution. This was a conclusion Mill and Spencer were loath to draw, in effect excepting liberty from their mechanical systems. This is, to be sure, an inconsistency; but again, it is not my position, but the position of the classical liberal spokesmen whom I am criticizing.

Finally, Raico questions my use of the terms "materialist," "pragmatist," and "relativist," alternately claiming them to be untrue or professing himself baffled by my meaning. Each of them refers to the classical liberal tendency of deriving value from the conjunction of secular phenomena and subjective apprehension. Spencer is an aboriginal "materialist" in the philosophical sense; value for him arises from the evolutionary progress of history toward its "higher" forms; good and bad are the terms we give to the adjustment of means to ends in the battle for biological and cultural survival. As for "pragmatism," both Mill and Spencer were pragmatists a half-century before James and Dewey; both test values by their practical consequences. Spencer's language in *Social Statics* is pragmatic at every turn. If the reader will peruse Mill and James consecutively on the subject of religion, he will find the first values it because it provides rules for moral life, suggesting a secular substitute would do as well or better, and the second favors it because it evokes a release of vital energies. It should be obvious to the rudest intelligence that both men take a "pragmatic" view of religion—judging it solely by its "practical" effects in the secular world.

Both Mill and Spencer, finally, are clearly relativists in the sense that they deduce value criteria from secular and largely subjective phenomena. Both begin with the pleasure-pain calculus, making right and wrong a function of human comfort; Spencer superadds the asserted "laws" of evolutionary development. To assert this utilitarian view is a form of "absolutism," as does Raico, taxes credibility even in an Orwellian generation.

Presumably, all criteria of value are "absolute" in a sense if one is prepared to act upon them; to a dope addict, securing the next fix is the most compelling of absolutes; but we would be justified in launching further inquiry before anointing him as a moral absolutist. According to received notions of intelligible discourse, "absolutism" holds values to exist independent of subjective apprehension. Mill-Spencer utilitarianism makes values consist exclusively in such apprehension. "The facts are what they are," Raico says of the pleasure-pain calculus; but "happiness," as Spencer himself noted, is not a fact, it is a state of mind; the greatest good for the greatest number" is not a fact, it is a matter of opinion. To make these things the measure of value is to throw all fixed and objective values out the window, to make right and wrong a function of secular stress and contention; it is relativism par excellence.

ALMOST ALL of the foregoing, however, is oblique from the main point, and I have gone into it only because failure to respond to Raico's charges might give some readers the impression that I conceded their correctness. The fact of the matter, however, is that even if I could settle all of these differences to Raico's satisfaction, or he to mine, the outstanding issues of freedom and authority would be no closer to resolution than before. While clarity in the use of terms is desirable, it is chiefly important as it helps us to advance in substantive understanding. I am therefore reluctant to leave the present discussion with a *pro forma* defense of my previous article, which I fear would create an unhappy emphasis on lesser issues at the expense of greater ones. Let me, then, repeat what I consider to be the chief topic before us, namely: *Can a regime of political freedom long exist without the underpinning of religion and moral sentiment derived from Judaeo-Christion revelation?* There is a considerable history of modern Western thought, ranging from Diderot to Mencken, which says it can, and which has worked great influence in contemporary America and

710

elsewhere. The important point about this school is not whether we call it or some subdivision of it "classical liberalism," but whether its major premises are true or false. A certain number of "libertarians" today appear to think they are true. I for one think they are dangerously false. That is the issue, and the terminology of the thing — while I happen to believe my own usage is justified —is of little or no importance compared to the substance of it.

Reply to Mr. Evans:

BEFORE I DEFEND my critique against Mr. Evans' rebuttal, I should like to explain briefly why I took time to attack Evans' article in the first place.

In their attempt to carve for themselves a position of relevance in discussions of contemporary social problems, conservative writers sometimes present a sketchy philosophical outline of the historical development of classical liberalism, attempting to show deeper reasons for its decline than those readily admitted by classical liberals themselves. The attempt has been supported by writers such as Russell Kirk, Frank S. Meyer, and Eric Voegelin. Dr. Kirk, for instance, sees the original flaw in the liberals' excessive commitment to individualism, especially in the form of economic liberty:

> . . . central direction endeavors to compensate for the follies of reckless moral and economic atomism. . . . [The liberals'] sentimental liberalism soon became shocked at its own practical consequences; the economic competition and spiritual isolation which resulted from the triumph of their ideas provoked among them a reaction in favor of powerful benevolent governments exercising compulsions.[1]

Mr. Meyer, an advocate of economic liberty, identifies the seed of corruption in liberalism rather as its supposed utilitarian ethic:

> This transformation [from individualistic to collectivistic liberalism] was the result of a fatal flaw in the philosophical underpinnings of 19th-century liberalism. It stood for individual freedom, but its utilitarian philosophical attitude denied the validity of moral ends firmly based on the constitution of being.[2]

Eric Voegelin imagines he can see a close connection between classical liberalism and Bolshevism: both, he thinks, imply the "permanent revolution," in that they attempt the impossible—changing the nature of man.[3] And so on, with other conservative authors.

It appeared to me that for once someone ought to call a conservative to account for his flamboyant and unsubstantiated claims regarding classical liberalism; for once, the canons of precise definition and relevant evidence, which

Ralph Raico, Editor-in-Chief of *New Individualist Review*, is an instructor of history at Wabash College and a member of the Mt. Pelerin Society.

[1] *The Conservative Mind* (Chicago: Regnery, 1953), pp. 89-90.

[2] *In Defense of Freedom* (Chicago: Regnery, 1962), pp. 1-2.

[3] "Der Liberalismus und seine Geschichte," in *Christentum und Liberalismus* (Munich: K. Zink, 1960), pp. 23-25.

serious scholars in all disciplines apply, ought to be applied here, too. It seemed to me, furthermore, that Evans had presented us in his article with a startling example of these conservative defects, and that the article could profitably be examined from this point of view.

NOW TO DEAL WITH Evans' rebuttal. Is it true that I have confusedly interpreted his claims, besides being wrong on a number of factual points?

First comes the terminological question, less interesting than the others, but unavoidable, since here is where I am supposed to have decisively confused the issues.

What does Evans mean by "classical liberalism"? Does he mean what everyone else does—that is, in one description, the social philosophy whose best representatives were Tocqueville and Acton?[4] Does he mean that great intellectual and political movement of the eighteenth and nineteenth centuries, so vast and various that no particular philosophical pre-suppositions bind all of its adherents, but only their commitment to individual liberty—to private property, civil liberties, and parliamentary and constitutional government? If the reader considers classical treatments of the subject, say Ruggiero's *History of European Liberalism* or (on a more analytical level) Von Mises' *The Free and Prosperous Commonwealth*, he will see what is meant by classical liberalism when the world at large discusses the history of ideas.

Evans claims, on the contrary, however, that he was clearly and consistently using "classical liberalism" in an odd sense: he was using it to designate only the atheistic and agnostic classical liberals (what he wants to call the theistic classical liberals is not made clear—possibly he wants to refer to Bastiat and Adam Smith as "conservatives"). It seemed to me otherwise. In my article, I point out that Evans has a footnote to the effect that in his usage "libertarianism . . . signifies the chemically pure

form of classical liberalism, with all of its metaphysical implications." Now, in the first place, it ought to be clear that this passage implies that libertarianism is one subspecies of classical liberalism (its "chemically pure form"), other subspecies of which, less chemically pure, do not share libertarianism's anti-religious position. This indicated to me that Evans, at least at this point, was using "classical liberal" in more or less its received meaning, and simply wanted to define "libertarian" in an unconventional way.

Then, in the text, Evans equates libertarian and classical liberal, stating: "The libertarian, or classical liberal, characteristically denies the existence of a God-centered moral order. . . ." Now this certainly *sounds* like a *description;* that is, it sounds as if Evans is accepting the usual definition of classical liberal, and saying that, while there may have been a few liberals who were religious, characteristically and as a rule they were not religious. If he were keeping to the definition in the footnote, the passage wouldn't make sense: it would then have to read, "libertarians *necessarily* and by *definition* deny the existence . . . ," etc.

If the reader still thinks it was unreasonable of me to suppose that Evans was using classical liberalism in its usual sense (or, at least, that its usual sense was one of those in which Evans was using the term), let him consider the following, from Evans' original article:

> While labelling someone a classical liberal is not necessarily an insult, it must be pointed out that today's conservatives, although opponents of statism, are generally not Manchesterians.

Doesn't this imply that Evans was taking the Manchesterians to be one school (the only school?) of classical liberalism? But how could this be, if he was exclusively using classical liberal to mean agnostic or atheistic classical liberals? Both leaders of the Manchester School, Cobden and Bright, were Christians.

Evans tries to trivialize this terminological point by speaking of varying "tastes" in noun substantives. But there is very good reason for preserving a

<hr />

[4] H. J. Laski, as quoted in F. A. Hayek, *The Constitution of Liberty* (Chicago: University of Chicago Press, 1960), p. 530.

modicum of consensus on the way terms are to be used. Imagine what trouble would be caused if each time anyone wrote on the history of ideas, he used terms like "liberal," "conservative," "socialist," "utopian," etc., in odd and unconventional ways. For one thing, intellectual history as an on-going enterprise would become impossible. It is at least equally important to keep to the same definitions of key terms in one and the same article.

LET US ASSUME, though, that Evans had made it clear in his article that in levelling his series of charges he had in mind only the non-religious classical liberals of the past and present: men like John Stuart Mill and Herbert Spencer, and, in our own day, most of the free enterprise economists whose names would come most readily to mind. Is it true that these men "allege human freedom as the single moral imperative"? Evans really does hold that they do, evidentally: An irritating premise of his, which comes out also in his rebuttal, is that a person who is not religious can have no ethical beliefs or concerns. Thus he refers to the religious classical liberals, "men who combine *both* ethical affirmation and concern for human freedom," as if an agnostic liberal never affirmed any ethical principles. Evans' position is that non-religious liberals did not and do not believe that anyone has a moral obligation to tell the truth, or to avoid malice, or to save another person's life even at no risk to oneself. Can this really be the case?

Well, I quoted in my critique a well-known passage from J. S. Mill's essay, *Utilitarianism,* part of which tells us that:

> In the golden rule of Jesus of Nazareth we read the complete spirit of the ethics of utility. To do as you would be done by, and to love your neighbor as yourself, constitute the ideal perfection of utilitarian morality.[5]

---

[5] *Utilitarianism, On Liberty and Representative Government* (New York: Dutton, 1950), p. 16.

Evans prefers in his rebuttal not to take cognizance of this point. Instead, declining to withdraw his claim, he attempts to show that it is true of Herbert Spencer. Even if this were true, it would prove nothing, since innumerable agnostic and atheistic liberals could be cited who do, indeed, believe that there are ethical imperatives beyond simple respect for the liberty of others. Yet far from being "quite obvious" that freedom for Spencer is the single moral imperative, it is quite obviously false. This is not the place to go into a detailed examination of Spencer's ethical system (I find Evans' exposition confusing); but this is what Spencer says:

> [There are] many actions which from hour to hour are gone through, now with an accompaniment of some pain to the actor and now bringing results that are partially painful to others, but which nevertheless are imperative. . . . Though the pains which the care of many children entail on a mother form a considerable set-off from the pleasures secured by them to her children and herself, yet the miseries immediate and remote which neglect would entail, so far exceed them that submission to such pains up to the limit of ability to bear them becomes morally imperative as being the least wrong.[6]

The point about natural law and Roman Catholicism is trivial and quickly disposed of. One of the things wrong with classical liberals, in Evans' view, is that they deny that there is any divine "moral order to which man should subordinate his will and reason." Of course, the existence of *any* moral law means that one should subordinate one's will to it: this isn't in question. What is at issue is just what Evans meant by the liberals' denial that reason ought to be subordinated to the moral law. If, as seemed likely, this meant that they denied that the moral law was unknowable

---

[6] H. Spencer, *The Data of Ethics* (New York: Burt, n. d.), p. 311. Spencer elsewhere in the same work (p. 28) states: "Lastly, we inferred that establishment of an associated state, both makes possible and requires a form of conduct such that life may be completed in each and in his offspring, *not only without preventing completion of it in others, but with furtherance of it in others.* . . ." Italics supplied.

713

by reason and had to be accepted purely on faith, then I don't see why this should be considered especially atheistic; for the denial of the arbitrariness and irrationality of the moral law is precisely the position of the Catholic Church. Again, I don't understand Evans' exposition in his rebuttal on this point: neither his distinction between (in St. Thomas' view) the moral law being apprehensible by reason, but not validated by it, nor how Evans is using "sanction." The important point is that if one believes with St. Thomas and the Catholic Church[7] that the moral law can be discovered by reason, then there is nothing sinister or atheistic about the liberals' position. Furthermore, it is then possible for an agnostic to come to an appreciation of morality, without any personal religious faith. On this problem of the connection between morality and reason, Evans blinks the distinction among Christian churches, and seems to want to have Calvin legislating for Christendom.

I do not find that Evans' rebuttal illuminates to any great extent what he might have had in mind when he charged classical liberals with being "materialists," "pragmatists," and "relativists." We are given no definition of materialism, no evidence that classical liberals were and are "characteristically" materialists. Spencer doesn't appear to have been a materialist, *pace* Evans,[8] but what if he had been? Mill was a phenomenalist; that is, he thought that matter was nothing but the possibility of certain mental states[9] — rather the opposite of a materialist. What do these two examples prove about the characteristic position of classical liberalism?

Evans doesn't really meet my objection to his use of "pragmatism," either. He states that Bentham, the Mills, etc., were pragmatists long before Charles Peirce and William James (the founders of the school), because they believed in an instrumentalist theory of value. But the essence of pragmatism lies in its theories of meaning and truth, and the one sentence definition Evans is seeking is *not* that pragmatism holds *value* to be determined by "what works," but that it holds *truth* to be so determined,[10] i.e., the difference between: "this action is good," and "this statement about the properties of copper is true."

FINALLY, WE COME TO the modern-day conservative bugaboo, "relativism." Here, too, Evans, like other conservatives who write on the subject, still owes us a definition. I don't think the one he gives in his rebuttal — deducing "value criteria from secular and largely subjective phenomena" — is really adequate. For one thing, it is uncertain, on the basis of this, whether someone who holds a *fiat justicia, pereat mundus* natural law position, but with no supernatural elements, would fall into the category of "relativist"; if he would, it would be a fairly unserviceable definition. For another thing, the definition doesn't make "relativism" the opposite of Evans' "absolutism," which "holds values to exist independent of subjective apprehension." J. S. Mill's utilitarianism, for instance, would be both relativist and absolutist in Evans' definitions: relativist, because its criterion of good is whatever promotes human happiness, and thus it may be said to deduce its criterion from a secular phenomenon — human happiness; it would be absolutist, though, because it insists, for example, that although all the people of a country might *think* it good to undertake aggressive war, this would not make it a good thing: its goodness is "independent of the subjective apprehension" of the actors, and is to be tested by whether the action actually

[7] "For Aquinas . . . the human being does not receive the moral law simply as an imposition from above: he recognizes or can recognize its inherent rationality and binding force, and he promulgates it to himself." F. C. Copleston, *Aquinas* (Baltimore: Penguin, 1963), p. 214. On the position of the Catholic Church, see T. Corbishley, S. J., *Roman Catholicism* (London: Hutchin's University Library, 1950), p. 57.

[8] F. A. Lange, *The History of Materialism* (London: Routeledge and Kegan Paul, 1957), Vol. III, p. 190.

[9] L. Wood, "Recent Epistemological Schools," in V. Ferm, ed., *A History of Philosophical Systems* (New York: Philosophical Library, 1950), p. 531.

[10] B. Russell, *A History of Western Philosophy* (New York: Simon and Schuster, 1945), pp. 815-18.

does promote human happiness and welfare.

There is nothing "Orwellian" in my suggestion that utilitarianism can be considered an "absolutist" ethic; by one definition commonly accepted among philosophers, it is so considered.[11] If Evans wants to deny that utilitarianism may be judged to be absolutist, if he wants to continue to maintain that liberals and libertarians were and are characteristically "relativists," let him provide acceptable definitions and then cite some evidence.

Incidentally, it seems interesting that conservatives typically don't spend just a bit more time explaining in a clear manner what they have in mind by terms such as "relativism" and "absolute values," considering that these make up such a large part of their stock-in-trade.

I think I have given good reason to believe that I was justified in my original critique of Evans' article. The question remains, however, why didn't I deal with the substantive issues, with Evans' thesis — why did I limit myself to discussing just his attack on classical liberalism?

FIRST OF ALL, WE MUST ask: Exactly what is Evans' thesis? Exactly what is the thing in the absence of which a free society cannot be maintained? Is it belief in the "Judeo-Christion" revelation, or a belief in a particular variety of Protestantism? In his rebuttal, Evans traces many of our troubles to the decline of the Protestant Ethic — this decline is supposed to make self-reliance less popular and the welfare state more tempting, and the liberals were, he alleges, foolish to suppose they could undermine the Protestant Ethic and not expect people to gravitate towards dependence on the state. But Max Weber's point was precisely that the Protestant Ethic was *not* characteristic of Roman Catholicism, or even of Lutheranism, but primarily of Calvinism

and related sects.[12] Here the role of the doctrine of predestination was crucial, in Weber's statement. If it is the Protestant Ethic which is a necessary condition for the preservation of a free society, are we then committed to saying that a free society cannot be preserved without a general belief in predestination?

Let us assume that Evans' thesis is the one he explicitly states: "A regime of political freedom cannot long exist without the underpinning of religious and moral sentiment derived from Judaeo-Christian revelation." Why didn't I go on to discuss this? The answer is that, although I consider this an interesting and important question, Evans purely and simply presents not the slightest evidence for "his thesis."[13] We cannot consider vague references to the moral crisis of our time, plus the example of John Stuart Mill — overworked as these both are — to be evidence in any scientific sense. If someone wanted seriously to maintain that a free society cannot be preserved in the absence of a commitment on the part of the great majority of the people to Christian revelation, a number of questions would immediately arise. Here are a few:

(1) What were the real causes of the decline of liberalism, beginning around 1870? To what extent did Christianity itself contribute to this, in the form of the numerous Christian Socialist and Christian Social movements in Europe and America? To what extent was the decline of liberalism due to the decline of the authority of the science of economics, and to what degree was this, in turn, caused by the view, often supported by Christian moral sentiment, that economics was "inhuman" and "selfish" in its view of human nature?

(2) Assuming that a free society is only possible if people believe that it is called for by the Christian holy scriptures, how

715

[11] R. B. Brandt, *Ethical Theory* (Englewood Cliffs, N. J.: Prentice-Hall, 1959), p. 154.

[12] M. Weber, *The Protestant Ethic and the Spirit of Capitalism* (New York: Scribner's, 1958), pp. 73-74, 84-85, 110-17.

[13] Just as he presents no evidence — nor any reference to evidence elsewhere — for the statement in his rebuttal that the classical liberals "helped lay the ethical foundation for the rise of the total state they wanted to avoid."

can such a belief be long sustained if, in fact, these writings *do not* call for a free society? Assume that at any given time everyone believes in capitalism because he thinks that it is entailed by revealed Christian doctrine; unless it really *is* so entailed, then this supposed iron-clad support for capitalism must be expected to crumble as people realize that the entailment does not exist. Now, why does Evans, and why do so many conservatives, suppose that free enterprise and limited government *are* called for by Christian doctrine? Most of the Christians who have lived, and most Christians today, would disagree with this interpretation. Examples are really superfluous: The whole history of intolerance and persecution, the opposition of most Christian churches to capitalism down to, in our own day, John XXIII's *Mater et Magistra* — all this indicates that most Christians have found their faith perfectly compatible with all kinds of infringements on liberty. If Evans could demonstrate that Christian doctrine calls for capitalism, it would represent a real landmark in the history of thought.

(3) Another difficulty that arises for anyone who wants to maintain that Christian revelation provides a much firmer basis for ethics (and thus for a free society) than any secular philosophy is able to propose, is the fact that very few people would be prepared to accept certain clear Biblical statements in this field. Who now agrees with Exodus 18:22 —"Thou shalt not suffer a witch to live." How many friends of freedom are completely comfortable with Romans 13:1-2— "The powers that be are ordained of God. Whosoever therefore resisteth the power, resisteth the ordinance of God: and they that resist shall receive to themselves damnation." How many people find that, on reflection, there is a great deal of practical good sense in: "Take no thought for your life, what ye shall eat, or what ye shall drink. . . . Take therefore no thought for the morrow: for the morrow shall take thought for the things of itself." (Matthew 6:25, 34) On what basis do we choose among the various ethical imperatives contained in the Bible, which we will take seriously

and which not; which we shall interpret literally and which we shall reinterpret in some more convenient manner?

(4) Evans states, in his rebuttal: "If morality is the function of secular arithmetic or the adjustment of secular means to secular ends . . . then it is altogether possible that, somewhere along the line, freedom must give way to the calculus. . . ." Here we have another hidden assumption — that unlike non-supernatural ethical systems, Christianity presents us with an air-tight body of moral rules: it consists of the orders given by God to man, which are clearly expounded in various revelations and backed up by the very powerful sanctions available to the Divinity. This is, however, a very naive view, I think, and anyone holding it is obliged to acknowledge the existence of the following argument and attempt to answer it: Exactly what is it that God tells us in an unambiguous way concerning our ethical obligations? Are there any rules which we are commanded to follow, telling us what to do under given conditions in a manner much more precise than some ethic such as utilitarianism? If we turn to the Bible, we find a number of such rules given, such as: Thou shalt not kill, thou shalt not steal (sometimes taken as a divine rule governing the proper social attitude towards private property), etc. Now, if the religionist conservative claimed that "Thou shalt not kill" is an unconditional rule (at least in reference to human beings), I think I could understand in what sense Christian ethics is more absolutist than, say, utilitarianism; in what sense Christianity presents what Evans calls "fixed and objective values" which utilitarianism does not present. Utilitarianism, as far as I can see, proposes no such unconditional, absolute rules. Yet surely there are no conservative religionists who favor an *absolute, unconditional* acceptance of this rule, for that would make impermissable both American military action in Viet Nam and capital punishment. So in just what sense is the Biblical injunction against killing more absolutist than the utilitarian one?

I am not aware that any religionist conservative has really dealt with any of these questions, and certainly Evans has not. It is much easier to flog non-supernatural ethical systems for being vague and indeterminate, and consequently responsible for all kinds of catastrophes, always with the implication that one has himself a really solid ethic in reserve.

FINALLY, I SHOULD like to make the chief point implied in my attack on Evans' original article somewhat more explicit: the fact is that much too much passes muster in conservative writings that is nothing more than uninformed rhetoric. That almost all conservative publicists are guilty of this, at least sometimes, is scarcely the best kept secret on the Right. I for one am finally getting bored with the sophomoric misuse of technical philosophical terms; with sketchy outlines of the "course"

of modern history; with constant attacks on the French Enlightenment, on human reason, and on the *hubris* of modern man; and with worldly-wise references to Original Sin and the absurdity of progress. Let conservative writers follow the example of present-day classical liberal economists, who adhere to the accepted rules of scholarly discussion in their confrontation with their leftist counterparts. The typical approach of the conservative cultural critics, on the other hand, since it is rhetorical and unanalytical, does not allow for progress being made towards the solution of the issues under discussion. If conservative publicists find the scholarly approach too tedious, they ought to recall that no one is *compelled* to write on intellectual history or philosophy.

—RALPH RAICO

717

Anglican and Gallican Liberty

FRANCIS LIEBER

718

Francis Lieber, scholar and political writer, was born in Prussia in 1800, emigrated to America in 1827, and soon thereafter became an American citizen. His career was divided between teaching at the University of South Carolina and Columbia College, and such public services as the composition of legal rules to protect non-combatants and their property in time of war (his suggestions were adopted by Lincoln for the Union Army and subsequently embodied in the Hague Conventions of 1899 and 1907). His main energies, however, were devoted to a comprehensive statement of liberalism, the social philosophy which was his lifelong concern. The following selection, from his Miscellaneous Writings,[1] *is a characteristic example both of Lieber's liberal political thinking and his admiration for his adopted country.*

IN THE SPHERE of political freedom there arise, as in all spheres of unfettered action, different schools, to borrow a term from the province of philosophy and that of the arts. It is thus that we have in the province of political freedom an Anglican and Gallican school. The term Anglican has been adopted here for want of a better one. We stand in need of a term which designates characteristics peculiar to the Anglican race in Europe, here, and in other parts of the world. If they are not all peculiar to this race, they are at least characteristics which form very prominent marks of its politics.

Page Thirty-two

It is by no means the object here to show the gradual development of modern liberty and of the Anglican characteristics, their causes, and the circumstances under which they developed themselves, but rather to point out in what at this moment consist the striking features of these two political schools. With this view, it may be stated at once, that Anglican liberty distinguishes itself above all by a decided tendency to fortify individual independence, and by a feeling of self-reliance. The higher the being stands in the scale of nature, the more d i s t i n c t is its individuality until it reaches in man its highest degree, and among men again we find the same principle prevailing. The higher, the more intellectual, and the more ethical the being is, the more prominent is also his own peculiar individuality. The same progress is observed in the scale of civil liberty. Individuality is almost annihilated in absolutism—whether this be of a monarchical or a democratic cast — while the highest degree of freedom (in the Anglican view of the subject) brings out the individuality of every one and the individual activity of each, as best it seems to him, in its freest play. Independence in the highest degree, compatible with safety and broad national guarantees of liberty, is the great aim of Anglican liberty, and self-reliance is the

---

[1] This text is taken from *Miscellaneous Writings of Francis Lieber,* Vol. II, *Contributions to Political Science* (Philadelphia: J. B. Lippincott, 1881). pp. 377-88. This essay appeared originally in a newspaper published at Columbia, South Carolina, June 7, 1849.

chief source from which it draws its strength. At no period has the deplorable absorbing concentration of power which characterizes the political systems of the continent of Europe during the seventeenth and eighteenth centuries obtained a footing among the Anglican peoples, although it was several times strenuously attempted. All the maxims of the common law most dear to the people, and most frequently quoted with pride as distinguishing it favorably from the civil law, embody this manly feeling of individual independence.

Everywhere is liberty considered by the Anglican nation to consist, in a very high degree, in a proper limitation of public power. Anglican liberty may be said to consist, essentially, in a proper restriction of government, on the one hand, and a proper amount of power on the other, sufficient to prevent mutual interference with the personal independence among the people themselves, so that order and a law-abiding spirit becomes another of its distinctive features. No people of the past or present have ever made use of the right of association, even where it fully existed, equal to the vast and at times gigantic application of this right to great practical purposes of a social, as well as political, character among the English and Americans. Public interference is odious to them. Government, to them, is not considered the educator, leader, or organizer of society. On the contrary, in reading the many constitutions which this race has produced, and the object of which is to define the spheres of the various public powers and to fix the rights of the individual, we almost fancy to read over all of them the motto, "Hands off."

This tendency of seeking liberty, above all, in untrammelled action has produced among others the following great effects.

The untrammelled action or absence of public interference (which of course must in its nature be almost always of an executive character) has not been restricted to individuals, but as a matter of course the spirit has extended to institutions and whole branches of power, so that time was allowed to them to grow, to develop themselves, and to acquire their own independent being; consequently, we find the word *law* possesses a meaning very different from that which the corresponding words have even in their most comprehensive sense with other nations; we find a common law rooted deeper in the people than any enacted law or constitution; we find a parliamentary law (no *"reglement"*); we find the indispensable principle of the precedent of greater p o w e r than minister or crown, even though it be worn by a Stuart, or a Henry the Eighth.

Secondly, a consequence of the principle of self-reliance is that liberty is conceived far more essentially to consist in a great amount of important rights than in a direct share in the government. The latter is sought after as a security and guarantee for the former.

Thirdly, Anglican liberty consists in or produces the utmost variety, as all untrammelled life and unfettered individual actions necessarily do. Equality (if sought in aught else than in equality of freedom from interference, and if believed to consist in uniformity alone) is monotony, and becomes the opposite to life and action.

Fourthly, the Anglican race has mixed up subjects purely social with politics far less than any other race, and, it may be safely averred, has allowed itself to be less misled by phantoms, and adhered more to positive realities in the sphere of public life, than any other division of mankind.

EVERY GREAT PRINCIPLE or movement of mankind has its own characteristic fanaticism, caricature, or mischievous extravagance. This applies to all movements, religious, social, or political, and Anglican individualism leads, if carried beyond its proper line, to selfish isolation and heartless egotism. The fanaticism of Anglican individualism is Utilitarianism as it has been taught by some. But it must not be forgotten that we speak here of civil liberty alone. No American or Englishman has ever maintained that we can do without patriotism, without devotion to the public, and it is a striking fact, admitted by all, that nowhere is shown so much public spirit, during successive periods, as by the

719

Anglican people, although it might have been supposed that their individualism would have led to the opposite. The reason is that Anglican liberty makes the people rely upon themselves, and not upon public power; they feel, therefore, that they ought to help each other and to depend upon their own united action, and not call for the aid of government at every step.

From a point of view, therefore, which belongs to Anglican liberty, the French device — Liberty, Equality, Fraternity, will appear in this light: Liberty is aspired to by all; it is the breath of conscious man. If equality means absence of privilege, unfounded upon political equivalents, it is comprehended within the term of liberty; if it mean, however, social uniformity, it is rather the characteristic of absolutism, and not of liberty. For if liberty means unrestrainedness, it implies variety. Bating the monarch, there exists nowhere in Europe or America a degree of equality equal to that in all Eastern despotisms, or that which existed in the worst period of Athens, where democratic absolutism was consistently carried out; where ultimately the principle of equality required the razing even of talent, fitness, and virtue, and the *lot* decided upon appointments. After the principle of equality had been established in such a manner, Aristotle described democratic liberty (or what we, according to modern terminology, would call democratic absolutism) as consisting in this: that every citizen is, in regular turn, ruling and ruled. Diversity is the law of all organic life, and despotism and freedom find their parallels in nature, in inorganic matter, and organic bodies. As to fraternity, it is the broad principle proclaimed by Christ; it is the divine principle of all social existence; it is one of the wells from which we shall draw, to irrigate our otherwise sterile life; it is like charity, like honesty, like forbearance, and to be true, ought to be infused into all our actions and measures, but it is no *right*, it is not *liberty;* nor does it necessarily indicate freedom. There is in some respects more political fraternity among Mohammedans than, unfortunately, among Christian people. Not that we put any slight value upon

720

fraternity; Christians ought to have far more; but we merely mean to show that it is not necessarily connected with liberty. Fraternity exists often in the highest degree among the rudest tribes. That this device was adopted during the first French revolution was natural. It had a meaning in contradistinction to the utterly selfish and immoral state of things which had existed and which it was a settled purpose to destroy; but its resumption in the present third French revolution leads to misconceptions or rests on a confusion of ideas, which seems as great as if in America a political banner were raised with the motto, Liberty, Love of our Enemy, and Salvation; or Liberty, Production, and Daring. All these are excellent or sacred things, but used as distinctive political characteristics would either have no meaning or might easily be made to mean mischievous things.

QUITE DIFFERENT from Anglican is Gallican liberty. The history of England distinguishes itself from that of all the other nations of Europe by nothing more than by the fact that, in that country alone, the nobility assimilated itself at a very remote period with the people. As early as in the year 1215 the noblemen did not wholly forget the people. The plodding husbandman was included in the Magna Charta; and repeatedly afterwards we find the knights siding with the citizens. The nobility of all other countries, however, were and remained selfish, oppressive and rebellious barons. Louis XI and Richelieu greatly broke their power in France, and Louis XIV completed the work. No citizen-liberty h a v i n g existed in that country, Louis found himself perfectly unlimited so soon as he had changed the baron into the servile courtier; and now a system of such absorbing centralization began that, when he died, he left France without institutions (if we take the term in the Anglican sense, meaning institutions with an independent and individual existence), as he left her without money and without morality in the leading classes. The absorbing centralization of power went on in all successive periods, and whatever changes of government have taken place, the process of centralization was only speeded on by it. The ball was ever rolling in that direction. The first French revolution, whatever benefit it otherwise produced, accelerated and perfected it much; Napoleon carried it still further, and a minister of the present provisional government, M. Ledru Rollin, lately declared, in one of his proclamations, that France should imitate the example of Paris, which he called the center and representative of French virtue, intelligence, action, and patriotism. How strange a similar declaration of an English minister, with reference to London, would sound in the ear of an Englishman, or of our President with reference to New York, or any state of ours![2]

Concentration of the most stringent kind existing, and it being neither disrelished nor suspected by the people, it is obvious that, coupled with the idea of liberty, in contradistinction to despotism, it can produce no other idea than equality—an equal change of "ruled and being ruler"; and since equality, with this political meaning, is a practical impossibility with a nation so vast as the French, we have the further consequence that, practically speaking, equality means in France always the exclusive sway of a certain class. He that seeks now to sway is the *Ouvrier,* and *Bourgeoisie* has actually become a name of shame or hatred, as the term *noblesse* had become in the first revolution.

Gallican liberty, then, is sought in the *government,* and, according to an Anglican point of view, it is looked for in a wrong place, where it cannot be found. Necessary consequences of the Gallican view are that the French look for the highest degree of political civilization in *organization,* that is, in the highest degree of interference by public power. The question whether this interference be despotism or liberty is decided solely by the fact *who* interferes, and for the benefit of which class the interference takes place, while according to Anglican views this interference would always be either absolutism or aristocracy, and the present dictatorship of the *ouvriers* would appear to us an uncompromising aristocracy of the *ouvriers.*

The universal acknowledgment of organization makes the Frenchmen look for every improvement at once to government. Self-reliance does not exist in detail. While the British race seeks for one of the great applications of liberty in free trade, the French call for organization of labor, and M. Louis Blanc has proposed a plan, accordingly, w h i c h would appear to us as insufferable tyranny, and annihilation of individuality. While we have seen, in the Anti-Corn-Law League, a mighty private association coping with the most powerful interest that ever existed in a legislature, the British land-owner, and ultimately forcing government to fall into its own ranks, we do not find a solitary club in Paris pursuing one detailed practical measure, but all discuss the best *organization,* and to the Minister of Justice, and of Worship, and to others whom previous "organization" had already created, a Minister of Labor, and even one of Progress has been added, if the papers have informed us correctly. In Anglican liberty the movement not only begins with the people, but also the practical carrying out. In France, liberty is expected to begin practically with government organization and to descend to the people.

721

---

[2] The most remarkable fact in history, so far as centralization is concerned, is probably the last French revolution (of 1848). A minority — but allow even a majority—of a single city changes a monarchy into a republic; the republic is telegraphed into the provinces and France is a republic, without any attempt at resistance, any show of adhesion to the former government, any struggle. If all France had been so thoroughly prepared for the republic (which we now know was not the case) that nothing more than the breathing of the name was necessary, the former government must long before have collapsed. If this was not the case, the so-called republic would not have been received so easily, were not the French accustomed to receive everything from Paris, fashions, pronunciations, and orders, and even now telegraphic despatches telling the prefect Monsieur so and so, that *Il n'y a plus de roi,* or some such thing. Is not the people in a very abject state where such things can occur? Is this not Russian? Does it not remind of the worst times of Rome? The French often, nay, almost universally, confound this submission to Paris with laudable patriotism. But this only shows the more the absorbing centralization which exits in France.

This is so true, that a large number of the French (we believe it to be a minority, but it is the active and loud minority) seem to have wholly discarded the idea that liberty is the main object to be striven for, and call for a *social* reorganization. A very busy and widespread club at Paris has actually hoisted a banner on which the word Liberty is omitted, bearing the following device: Equality, Solidarity, Fraternity. Here, then, we have the caricature of French liberty, as we have in ultra-utilitarianism that of Anglican freedom. Equality and solidarity are necessary elements of all politics. Without solidarity no nation could be a nation, no state a state. Every one is obliged to bear with laws which he considers bad, or the consequences of a war which he condemns. It is the price we pay for living in a civil society; but if solidarity be elevated into a distinctive mark of a specific political or social system it is the death-blow to individualism, and a Spartan republic, destroying even the family, must be the consequence. Here, too, is to be found the reason of the striking phenomenon that at all periods the fanatics who have attempted the abolition of private property always made war against exclusive or individual marriage at the same time. Many communists have preached it, and many religious fanatics in the Middle Ages have attempted it.

The fact that Gallican liberty expects everything from *organization,* while Anglican liberty inclines to *development,* explains why we see in France so little improvement and expansion of institutions; but when improvement is attempted, a total abolition of the preceding state of things—a beginning *ab ovo* —a re-discussion of the first elementary principles.

ANGLICAN LIBERTY produces variety, as was stated before, and demands absence of unnecessary restraint; Gallican liberty demands uniformity and even uniforms, so odious to Americans. A proclamation of the provisional government, dated April 30, 1849, actually begins with the words: "Considering that the principal of equality implies uniformity of costume for the citizens called to the same functions," etc., prescribing a costume—coat, waistcoat, and pantaloons, to the members of the national assembly— that assembly which, according to the expression of the provisional government itself, is the highest representative of national sovereignty that has ever assembled, and into whose hands that same provisional government will lay down its power. Nothing can show more distinctly the difference between Anglican and Gallican liberty than that this order was possible.

In England and America, the principle of liberty dictates that all that can be done by private enterprise ought to be left to it, and that the people ought to enjoy the fruits of competition in the highest possible degree. In France, on the other hand, the provisional government made arrangements to buy up all the railways so soon as the king had been expelled.

All political changes, according to Anglican liberty, are intended more efficiently to protect the changes which society has worked for itself; according to Gallican liberty, the great changes are intended to be, not political, but social, organized by government: that is, according to Anglican liberty, forced upon society by the successful party, which, nevertheless, may be a very small minority owing to the peculiar power which, in the great system of concentration, Paris exercises over France, and which all movable masses exercise over populous cities—an influence considered salutary according to Gallican views of liberty, and disastrous according to Anglican.

THE OBJECT OF this paper has been to show the difference of the two schools, and it would be foreign to the subject to dwell upon the generous enthusiasm which pervades at this moment large parts of the French people, and, coupled as it is with the fearful reminiscences of former days, has produced some very remarkable effects; but enthusiasm cannot last, and, if it could, it cannot become a substitute for individualism, an indispensable element of our ethical nature. Enthusiasm is a necessary element of all great actions of individuals as well as masses, but he who founds upon it plans of a permanent state of things, whether in worship or politics, deprives his system of durability. Nothing can insure principles against an early withering but institutions. No ruler, however popular or brilliant, no period, however glorious, and no enthusiasm, however generous, can produce lasting good if they do not lead first of all to the foundation of expansive institutions. Nations must neither depend upon popular rulers, nor trust their own enthusiasm. If they do, everything is frail and evanescent, and the continuity of the state, without which there is no law, order, strength, or greatness, is rendered impossible.

This remark leads us to the last observation we mean to make upon the difference of Anglican and Gallican liberty. The Anglican race is a decidedly institution-loving and institution-building race, as the Romans were, who built up the civil law. They are conservative as well as progressive, and believe that conservatism is as necessary an element as progression. The fanaticism of conservatism is a Chinese idolatry of the past and the old. The French, on the other hand, as they appear, at least in modern times, are philosophizing, often brilliant, organizers, and resemble in this more the Greeks, who built up no law but whose philosophers proposed invented governments. The fanaticism of this disposition is a restless re-beginning at every step and denial of the necessity of continuous progress.

It must have appeared to the reader that the writer of this paper is an advocate and lover of the principles of Anglican liberty; that he believes the French are mistaking democratic absolutism for democratic liberty; that the whole Continent will have to pass through long periods of ardent struggle before it can rid itself of the consequences of the unhallowed centralization which a b s o l u t e princes in their blindness mistook for power and fastened upon the people; that he is a devoted friend to independence and the liberty of the individual, which, in his opinion, need be as little connected with selfishness as Christianity is, although this religion, above all others, throws man upon his individual responsibility, thus raising him immeasurably; that, however dazzling the effects of democratic absolutism occasionally may be, it is still not freedom, which, like dew, nourishes every blade in its own individuality, and thus produces the great combined phenomenon of living nature; and that he would infinitely prefer a life in one of our loneliest log-houses to a barrack-residence of absolute equality, stifling his own individuality and that of every one of his fellow-citizens, however brilliant that barrack might be furnished.[3] But whether these are the views of the writer or not, is of little importance. The truth remains the same, that the difference pointed out by him exists between the two modes of liberty, that they differ widely, and that it behooves every sincere friend of liberty to reflect maturely on the subject and to come to clear results; especially on the European continent, where liberty is in a nascent state, and is of course exposed to be seriously injured in the tender age of her infancy; while a closer geographical connection with France often leads to the adoption of measures and views peculiar to that country, when no intrinsic reason for doing so exists. The European continental countries have had their periods of absorbing and life-destroying centralization. The principles of our liberty, therefore, are peculiarly necessary to the people of the European continent. Many of them seem to fall into the same unfortunate delusion of expecting everything from *organization* by public power.

---

[3] The writer is no admirer of the feudal ages. He has repeatedly given views of that period, the essential principles of which with its graduated allegiance are wholly unfit for our nobler freedom. Whenever he has spoken of individual freedom in this paper, he has meant individual independence within *nationalized* societies, under the protection of broad, wide, organic, pervading civil liberty—the very opposite to mediaeval spitefulness, arrogation, lawlessness, unnational and unsocial liberty.

The Uneasy Case

for State Education

E. G. WEST

724

This article has been adapted by the author from his recent book Education and the State, *published in London by the Institute of Economic Affairs.*

THE CASE FOR substantial government intervention in primary education is normally examined by political economists in the context of two principles: "state protection" and "neighborhood effects." According to the first, if it is generally agreed that the state exists basically to give protection to its members, it must have special obligations to children since they are least able to protect themselves on their own. According to the second principle, the way I choose to act often has serious spillover effects upon my neighbors; and similarly the actions of my neighbors, taken individually, can substantially affect me. The choice of any one individual to educate, or not to educate, his children is shown to be a particular case in point. Even if all individuals choose voluntarily to purchase education they may still "underinvest" from the point of view of society as a whole. This being so there is again said to be a strong presumption in favor of government intervention.

E. G. West has been lecturing at the University of Newcastle-on-Tyne, and will take up a Readership in Economics at the University of Kent at Canterbury, England, in 1966. He is currently engaged in a research fellowship at the University of Chicago.

Page Thirty-eight

The first part of this article attempts to examine the "protection principle" in more than usual detail. The second part will raise questions which are not normally raised about the empirical foundation for common assumptions about the "neighborhood effects" of education.

WHATEVER THE MEANING of laissez faire, the most ardent of its nineteenth century English supporters rarely argued that it should operate outside the boundaries of a proper legal framework. Within this framework they were prepared to make many exceptions to their general principle of freedom of contract and their special reservation for children was a prominent example of this attitude. However much they disliked over-interfering governments, they believed that some element of governing was necessary. But what was the true duty of government? The answer of one of the classical economists, Nassau Senior, disciple of Bentham and friend of John Stuart Mill, was quite clear:

I detest paternal despotisms which try to supply their subjects with the self-regarding virtues, to make men by law sober, or frugal, or orthodox. I hold that the main, almost sole, duty of Government is to give protection. Protection to all, to children as well as to adults, to those who cannot protect themselves as well as those who can.[1]

[1] *Suggestions on Popular Education* (London: J. Murray, 1861), p. 6.

Senior went on to remind his readers that children were more defenseless than others. In view of this the state had extra protective obligations towards them and in particular there was a strong presumption in favor of state intervention in education. This view, which seems to have been readily accepted by liberal economists ever since,[2] will now be examined in more detail in order to gather its precise implications.

A MOMENT'S REFLECTION will show that it is much easier to state the "protection of minors" principle than to draw practical policy conclusions from it. If it is agreed that the state should be responsible for seeing that children are protected, the question arises: whom should it appoint to carry out this duty in practice? The first obvious point to clear up before deciding this issue is for the state to ascertain from its members how important a role they want the family to play. If they aim at giving the family a central place, then the question of protecting infants cannot be settled in isolation of this policy, for it establishes a presumption in favor of delegating the duty of child protection first and foremost to the parents and only withdrawing this arrangement when special circumstances require it. For these reasons the following remarks of John Stuart Mill, which seem to have had widespread influence on this subject, were too evasive and too legalistic:

> In this case [education] the foundation of the *laissez-faire* principle breaks down entirely. The person most interested is not the best judge of the matter, nor a competent judge at all. Insane persons are everywhere regarded as proper objects of the care of the state. In the case of children and young persons, it is common to say, that though they cannot judge for themselves, they have their parents or other relatives to judge for them. But this removes the question into a different category; making it no longer a question whether the government should interfere with individuals in the direction of their own conduct and interests, but whether it should leave absolutely in their power the conduct and interests of somebody else.[3]

Few would disagree with Mill's general sentiments. If we do not tolerate cruelty to animals still less should we allow the possibility of continued cruelty to children by granting *absolute* power over them to any single person. But Mill was mistaken in assuming that the common argument, that parents and relatives could judge for their children, was a claim for *absolute* power. What most people envisage is something in the nature of a *fiduciary* power, to be removed in cases where abuse can be shown.

Whatever the true interpretation of his statement, Mill's anxiety to put this question into a different category did not make it any less important or less urgently in need of an answer: for the state is not a disembodied entity; it has to work through individuals to whom it prescribes certain powers. Now the function of supervising a child is such a personal and delicate matter that it is most important to visualize it in the form of a competition for influence between one individual, the parent, who by nature is closer to the child and therefore has better opportunity for gaining knowledge of its best interests, and another individual, appointed by the state, who has the advantage of some presumed expertise in protecting children. When the problem is expressed in this way the question of *absolute* power is beside the point. Certainly the difficulty is not one which can be solved easily by any universal or dogmatic ruling. Accordingly, the following analysis is not intended to stake an unconditional claim for any of the parties concerned, but is merely an attempt to examine the issues objectively. Insofar as I am critical of the ability of the "protection" argument to justify universal state schooling, it must be emphasized that my criticism is not to the prejudice of the "neighborhood effects" argument for this system.

---

[2] See, for instance, Milton Friedman, *Capitalism and Freedom* (Chicago: University of Chicago Press, 1962), p. 86.

[3] *Principles of Political Economy* (London: Longmans, 1915), p. 957.

BEFORE WE CAN CHOOSE those individuals deemed to be best able to protect a child, we have to solve the even more difficult task of defining the danger against which we are trying to protect it. Even state action against physical cruelty is not always simple to administer since the criterion is rarely a matter of unanimous agreement. But at least where physical injury has resulted in permanent damage to an individual, then the evidence is usually so obvious that the case for state protection against further assault is clear enough. In education, on the other hand, the argument is for protection not against physical injury but against ignorance. Here it is often more difficult to see in what respect any faculties can be said to be permanently injured, either in effect or in intention. When, for instance, the head of a temporarily distressed family sees his five- and six-year-old children remaining ignorant of reading and writing, we cannot say that their faculties are injured in the same sense as in the case of physical brutality. In this instance, the faculties of learning need not in any way be permanently damaged; it is quite possible for them to remain intact to be used later. If the state does decide to intervene in such cases, therefore, it cannot be on the grounds of the same sort of protection as that directed against physical aggression of any kind; rather is it likely to be based on the widely accepted principle of government relief of poverty. This initial clarification seems necessary if we wish to avoid using the term "protection" with its more usual connotation.

But there is a much more stubborn difficulty. When we now speak of protection against ignorance, we have to ask: ignorance of what? A person may be most ignorant of one thing but quite expert at another. Too hasty attempts to prescribe learning priorities can lead to results which not only endanger spontaneity and individuality but which can involve fundamental contradictions in any society which professes to encourage and support the ideal of liberty. Confusion on this subject often arises from a dogmatic insistence that the relevant ignorance is necessarily ignorance of

what is taught in schools between statutorily prescribed ages. Schooling is only one instrument in the removal of ignorance; if other means are being used, the need for protection may well be superfluous. There are additional sources of learning in real life: the parent, the family, its friends, the church, books, television, radio, newspapers, correspondence courses, etc., "on the job training," and personal experience. J. S. Mill himself can be quoted in this respect:

> Even if the government could comprehend within itself, in each department, all the most eminent intellectual capacity and active talent of the nation, it would not be the less desirable that the conduct of a large portion of the affairs of the society should be left in the hands of the persons immediately interested in them. The business of life is an essential part of the practical education of a people; without which, book and school instruction, thought most necessary and salutary, does not suffice to qualify them for conduct, and for the adaptation of means to ends. Instruction is only one of the desiderata of mental improvement; another, almost as indispensable, is a vigorous exercise of the active energies; labor, contrivance, judgment, self-control: and the natural stimulus to these is the difficulties of life.[4]

The best means by which individuals are likely to "protect" themselves or their children from "ignorance" should therefore be open to constant comparative appraisal. That a parent, for instance, wishes to take his child away from school at an early age does not necessarily signify that he is negligent. Insofar as the school has become less efficient than other means of education, the parent himself may be acting from motives of protection and be making the same kind of shrewd comparative assessment that he makes before transferring his buying from one source of his child's food or clothing supply to another. Again, to assume that the education given in a school is always and under all circumstances to be preferred to alternative types of education is probably to assume also that all schools and home environments are homogeneous. This is by no

[4] *Ibid.*, p. 948.

means self-evident—especially in a changing society. It is interesting a recall that J. S. Mill himself was deliberately kept at home throughout his childhood by a father who was strenuously motivated by protective impulses. His father, James Mill, indeed kept his son away from school, "lest the habit of work should be broken and a taste for idleness acquired."[5] It is quite true that James Mill has been the subject of severe criticism from subsequent state educationists on the ground that he was too forceful a task-master. The question is, however, whether a state school could have produced a "better" John Stuart Mill. Such questions, of course, give rise to all sorts of speculations, but no apology is offered for asking them, since, as I hope to show, they lie at the root of the problem I am discussing.

THE "PROTECTION OF minors" argument has in the past been used to support pressure not merely to educate a *minority* of neglected children but also to establish *universal* schooling whereby *every* child is provided for by state schools. There are two major difficulties in the way of our accepting such reasoning, the first political and the second economic. On the political difficulty, it must first be observed that in order to justify a vast and comprehensive system comprising thousands of new state schools one must establish that such provision is needed to fill an obviously widespread deficiency and that the *majority* of parents and relatives are either negligent or ignorant. Now if this is the contention, it must imply either widespread schizophrenia or self-abnegation, for it envisages an electorate which virtually condemns most parents and relatives for being ignorant or negligent about their children when that same electorate consists to a large extent of the parents and relatives themselves. Otherwise, the question immediately arises of why, if such ignorance and negligence is so serious, should we presume that it will not equally express itself at the

ballot box and with equally "unfortunate" results when the parents and relatives choose their representatives?

The extent of this presumed schizophrenia could best be checked by a survey among parents to ask their intentions if given hypothetical refunds of indirect and direct taxes in the form either of money vouchers spendable only on education in lieu of "free" state education or of income tax allowances. The only statistical survey that has attempted to elicit answers to this question suggests that negligence would be far from typical.[6] Alternatively we can make an historical investigation to discover parental behavior before the inception of state education, bearing in mind that such state intervention had to be supported by increased tax revenues which might otherwise have been spent voluntarily on education. I think it can be shown from historical evidence that nineteenth century parental behavior was much more responsible than is commonly supposed.[7]

The second major difficulty in the way of accepting the "protection" argument to justify a universal state school system is an economic one. Nowhere does it seem to have been shown why other forms of state intervention could not achieve the intended result of state protection more effectively and with less cost than the present system of state schools (which amounts virtually to a system of *nationalized* schools). Much as John Stuart Mill wanted the protection of children, even he did not in the end prescribe compulsory state schools, nor even compulsory private schooling, but only compulsory *education*. Accordingly he held that the state should be interested not merely in the number of years of schooling but in checking the results of education whatever its sources, and he contended that an examination system was all that was necessary. If a young

727

5 J. S. Mill, *Autobiography* (New York: Holt, 1873), p. 36.

6 See *Choice in Welfare, First Report* (London: Institute of Economic Affairs, 1963), Part III.

7 See E. G. West, *Education and the State* (London: Institute of Economic Affairs, 1965), chaps. ix, x, and xi. The English government did not make education compulsory in the nineteenth century until most parents were already sending their children to school voluntarily. The same can be said of the State governments in the United States.

person failed to achieve a certain standard, then extra education would be prescribed at the parents' expense. Another sanction which Mill also entertained was to make the right to vote conditional on some minimum degree of education.

Under Mill's scheme, if it were operating today, it is conceivable that some children would attempt to attain the necessary standards by much more dependence on parental instruction,[8] correspondence courses, evening classes, local libraries, etc. These in turn would be measured against particular services offered by the private schools whose relative efficiency would be measured by parents and their children in terms of the size of their classes, for instance, or the qualifications of their staff and the personal attention they gave the children.[9] There are examples of this kind of minimum state intervention in other spheres. Thus although the state insists on the acquisition of a minimum competence in driving before allowing persons to take their vehicles on the roads, it has so far found it unnecessary to prescribe the particular way in which persons should acquire the knowledge and the skill, or to nationalize the driving schools and supply training "free" by raising taxes on all. Again, protection against the supply of adulterated food to children (or to anybody else) is effected simply by a system of inspection,

----

[8] In England and Wales there are 100,000 qualified women teachers at home compared with 160,000 teaching in schools. It is obvious that there are thousands of parents who are qualified, even in this formal sense, to teach in their own homes. Under Mill's system it is doubtful whether all this educational capital would be as underused as it is today. Since under his scheme the state would not have involved itself in the heavy taxation now needed to finance "free" schools, average incomes after taxes would be much higher. These added incomes would, for instance, enable many married teachers quietly to buy the help of auxiliaries in the form of domestic help and/or labor-saving devices to allow them time to teach their own five- or six-year-olds at home. Today it is just conceivable that the government could allow tax rebates for this purpose, but the administrative and political obstacles are formidable.

[9] Bearing in mind that everybody would be more able to afford tuition-charging schools to the extent that they would be asked to pay less indirect taxation (which nobody now escapes) than a state "free" school system makes necessary.

reinforced by regulations, breaches of which are punishable by the law.

THE CASE OF FOOD IS interesting. Protection of a child against starvation or malnutrition is in the same category of importance as protection against ignorance. It is difficult to envisage, however, that any government, in its anxiety to see that children have minimum standards of food and clothing, would pass laws for compulsory and universal eating, or that it should entertain measures which lead to increased taxes in order to provide children's food "free" at local government kitchens or stores. It is still more difficult to imagine that most people would unquestioningly accept this system, especially where it had developed to the stage that for "administrative reasons" parents were allocated those stores which happened to be nearest their homes; or that any complaint or special desire to change their pre-selected stores should be dealt with by special and quasi-judicial inquiry after a formal appointment with the local "Child Food Officer" or, failing this, by pressure upon their respective representatives on the local "Child Food Board" or upon their Congressman. Yet strange as such hypothetical measures may appear when applied to the provision of food and clothing, they are nevertheless typical of English and American state education as it has evolved by historical accident or administrative expediency.

Presumably it is recognized that the ability in a free market to change one's food market when it threatens to become, or has become, inefficient is an effective instrument whereby parents can protect their children from inferior service in a prompt and effective manner. If this is so, then one should expect that the same arguments of protection would in this respect point in the direction not of a state school system where it is normally difficult to change one's "supplier" but in the direction of a free market where it is not. In this sense one must question John Stuart Mill's assertion that in the case of education the principal of laissez faire breaks down entirely; for if by laissez faire he meant (as he seems to have meant) a free market system, then our reasoning suggests on the contrary that this is a technique which with some qualifications is admirably suited to protection of all kinds and not least the "protection of minors."

So much for the analysis of the basic issues in the "protection" thesis. The conclusion is that if there is a logical case for a *universal state school system*, as distinct from marginal intervention to meet special cases, we must look elsewhere than the protection principle.

THE ABSENCE OF A justification for state intervention on the grounds of the "protection principle," brings us to the second line of reasoning, which is widely believed to give still stronger support for such intervention. As previously indicated, this belongs to what is known as the "neighborhood effects" argument; a brief general account of its present place in economics may be helpful prior to the particular application of it to education.[10]

Roughly speaking, the "neighborhood effects" argument stems from the common observation that "no man is an island." Many of his actions intentionally or unintentionally affect other people. Where these spillover effects are very pronounced, and do not show any signs of ever being organized or brought under control by the market, one's normal reaction is to explore the possibility of government intervention. The most obvious instance of the resort to government is seen in the establishment of a state system of law and order to curb and to make socially accountable individual acts of aggression. Here, indeed,

we have the basic *raison d'être* of the state in the first place. Beyond personally aggressive private actions, however, there are other particular "neighborhood effects" which are also identified and often listed in a descending order of seriousness or scope. Several of these are also commonly claimed to warrant state intervention. The most frequently quoted example in economics is the firm whose factory chimneys offend the neighborhood with smoke and thereby cause people outside the factory to spend extra amounts on laundries, bronchitis cures, etc. Another alleged instance is the injury to "local amenities" caused by the "unfortunate" construction of a new house by a private speculative builder. Again there is the individual motorist who parks his car to the detriment of other road users. Campaigns to make socially accountable those responsible for road traffic and aircraft noises or exhaust fumes also belong in the same category of "neighborhood effects." All of them are cited as cases where the costs taken into account by the individual in the market are unlikely to include any element of what are called *social* costs.

One must observe already that although most people react to such situations by readily calling upon government to put these things right, they do not immediately see how complicated is their request. For one thing, if they examine more carefully the above examples of social costs they will see that they are not exclusively a consequence of private action. The noise from publicly-operated airways, buses, and trains, for instance, has its ultimate sanction not in private action but in public legislation, that is, in government itself. Nationalized chimneys give off smoke no less than private ones. Public gasworks can spoil amenities while offensive smells can come from publicly operated sewage works.

A further complication is that social costs can be negative as well as positive; that is, some spillover effects may be unintentionally *beneficial* to the neighborhood. Thus a farmer who drains his own land may improve that of the neighboring farm, even though he cannot charge for benefits rendered. Still more complex are the many instances where

729

---

[10] For the application of the neighborhood effects argument to education in England, see the *Report of the Committee on Higher Education* (London: HMSO, 1963), I, chap. i, and Appendix IV, Part III. See also *15 to 18 Report of the Central Advisory Council for Education* [Crowther Report] (London: HMSO, 1963), chap. vi. For further modern critical treatment of the general argument, see J. M. Buchanan, "Politics, Policy and the Pigovian Margins," *Economica*, XXIX (Feb. 1962), 28; R. H. Coase, "The Problem of Social Cost," *Journal of Law and Economics*, III (Oct. 1960), 1-44; and R. Turvey, "On Divergence between Social Cost and Private Cost," *Economica*, XXX (Aug. 1963), 309-13.

both positive and negative social costs are produced by the same agent. An example of this is where a new industrial plant gives off smoke (detrimentally) but also reduces unemployment in the same neighborhood (beneficially). Again the owner of the plant could be the central or local government as well as a private company.

It seems to have been widely believed at one time that the moment that one had pointed out a privately originating "neighborhood effect," such as that of the smoke-laden atmosphere, actual intervention by the state was adequately justified. This, however, is not so. The identification of a "neighborhood effect" is only a *necessary* but not a *sufficient* condition for intervention. There are many serious offsetting considerations, the most important being that the task of measuring the chain reaction of costs and benefits is often insuperable. The administrative costs of intervention alone may be so high as to exceed the net benefits which such action sought to secure, even if they could be measured.[11] Furthermore, it is likely that a particular mode of state intervention to meet a privately originating "neighborhood effect" may itself incur a second (publicly originating) "neighborhood effect" which has still more serious consequences than the first. For instance, suppose that the government responds to the smoke pollution of a factory by placing a special local tax upon the offending firm. The resulting increase in relative costs of production may so discourage the expansion of the same firm as to encourage it to invest its surplus funds elsewhere. The result may be that the firm's decision is now the cause of another "neighborhood effect," not smoke pollution this time but the more serious problem of unemployment.[12]

How then does the "neighborhood effects" analysis apply to education? Political economists usually have two particular instances in mind. The first is expressed in their contention that the *social* benefits of education are not confined to the "educatee" but spread to society as a whole, most noticeably in the form of reduced crime and more "social cohesion." This can be expressed negatively: The private actions of an uneducated person may have unfortunate consequences for others in society. The idea seems to be, for instance, that just as the government can do something about "anti-social" smoke (e.g., by taxation) it can do something about "anti-social" conduct (e.g., by education). The second general example is the idea that education is an investment whose benefits also spill over to the *economic* advantage of society as a whole. There is nothing in this argument so far to justify government provision of schools. If the government were satisfied that neighborhood effects were substantial, it could increase the quantity of education by a mixture of subsidies, vouchers, and compulsory legislation. But what is the evidence for neighborhood effects? Are economists' assumptions always well grounded?

CONSIDER FIRST THE familiar proposition that state provision of education will successfully meet the "neighborhood effect" of crime. It will be helpful first to give a few quotations to illustrate the widespread influence of the idea both in the nineteenth century and today.

In 1847 T. B. Macaulay proclaimed in Parliament:

> I say that all are agreed that it is the sacred duty of every government to take effectual measures for securing the persons and property of the community; and that the government which neglects that duty is unfit for

---

[11] Expressed more formally: the persistence of such "externalities" as smoking chimneys may be quite consistent with optimal allocation of resources since the costs of using the market and/or government agencies to correct them may be larger than the potential gain.

[12] Another aspect requiring deeper analysis: the larger the influx of new residents to the area, the more harmful the effects of the smoke and the higher the tax necessary. But this increasing tax is itself *an increasing harm to the firm*, thus encouraging it to move or expand elsewhere.

Since each new resident is not aware of the harm he is imposing on the firm and its employees, he is causing an adverse neighborhood effect; and one which is not counteracted by government intervention, but indeed has its origins in such intervention. This is the argument of R. H. Coase, *loc. cit.*

730

its situation. This being once admitted, I ask, can it be denied that the education of the common people is the most effectual means of protecting persons and property?[13]

In the previous year W. T. Thornton had typically expressed the prescription of the Utilitarians:

No one now denies that proper schools for the lower orders of people ought to be founded and maintained at the cost of the state. The expense no doubt would be considerable, but it would scarcely be so great as that already incurred for prisons, hulks, and convict ships; and it is certainly better economy to spend money in training up people to conduct themselves properly, than in punishing them for their misdeeds.[14]

Such Utilitarian calculation of the crime-reducing potentialities of formal education is still in evidence among responsible authorities today. Thus, referring to the "neighborhood effects" of education, the Robbins Report on Higher Education (1963) said:

There are, of course, also important social and political benefits of education which accrue to the populace as a whole—a better informed electorate, more culturally alive neighborhoods, a healthier and *less crime-prone population,* and so on. What is not always recognized is that these social and political consequences may in turn have significant economic effects — the efficiency with which goods are exchanged is obviously enhanced by general literacy, *to the extent that education reduces crime* (even if only by keeping children off the streets during the day) the country can shift resources that would have had to be used for the police function to other ends, and so on.[15]

The Robbins Report makes this statement before freely admitting that the evidence is still not sufficient to make it anything more than an inspired hunch. The Crowther Report of 1959 and the Newsom Report of 1963, referring to the

education of persons between fifteen and eighteen years (which include the most crime-prone ages), although much more hesitant on the matter, nevertheless, as I shall show in more detail below, favored still more education in the current twentieth century campaign against delinquency and crime.

IN THE LIGHT OF THE "neighborhood effects" argument examined in the preceding paragraphs, what can be made of its application to education? It is important to remember the complications; not only must the "neighborhood effect" be first identified in a meaningful way, but also the possible side-effects of the proposed government intervention itself should all be examined before such intervention is fully justified. How far then, first of all, has the particular "neighborhood effect" relationship between education and crime been reasonably established in practice? In other words, what evidence have we to show that the belief in state education as a general insurance against crime is anything more than dogma?

In answering such questions the early economists were inclined to rely upon crude statistics. Because the latter were presented as showing an inverse relationship between crime and education (usually measured by the degrees of schooling) the general inference was that ignorance (or the deprival of schooling) was a major cause of crime. To the extent that poverty was connected with ignorance and undesirable habits, it too was thought to be an important contributory factor. In view of this kind of reasoning it would be intriguing to know the reaction of these early commentators to present-day statistical evidence, for this shows that crime has increased at the same time as state education has been growing. Certainly this does not deny that crime could have grown equally or even more in the absence of state education; but scientific objectivity demands that all things should be suspect, especially where there is a positive correlation. One can at least speculate, judging by their weakness for such crude statistical inferences on this sub-

---

13 House of Commons, *Hansard,* April 19, 1847.

14 W. T. Thornton, *Over Population and Its Remedy* (London: Longman, 1846), p. 379.

15 *Report of the Committee on Higher Education* (London: HMSO, 1963), Cmnd. 2154, Appendix IV, Part III, Para. 54. Italics supplied.

ject, that the early economists would be tempted to point to the possibility that our *state* education, as distinct from their nineteenth century *parochial* education, was a predisposing cause of crime!

Today indeed there is at least a growing scepticism about the potentialities of state education as a crime reducer. Thus *The Times Educational Supplement* in 1963 declared:

> It is strange that as education spreads and poverty decreases, juvenile crime should steadily rise.[16]

Similarly, the idea that poverty is a major cause of crime is not so confidently held. Indeed some social scientists conclude from the evidence that the idea has no firm basis. Lady Wootton writes:

> . . . it is a conclusion which would, I think, have surprised our grandfathers. The converse was implicit — and sometimes explicit — in the thought of not so many generations ago; as it is implicit also in the thought of those who express disappointment that the coming of a "welfare state," which they believe (though mistakenly) to have banished poverty, has not also greatly reduced the criminal statistics.[17]

The most energetic nineteenth century advocates of state education would no doubt have been also perplexed by the fact that the same welfare state which has failed to reduce crime is one which also includes an extensive education system financed by public funds of unprecedented magnitude.

Today, of course, we would claim to be much more aware of the complexity of crime and its causes. Certainly much more sophisticated reasoning surrounds the subject and it has been established in particular that a proportion of convicted persons is suffering from mental disorders which, it is claimed, need psychiatric treatment. Many other possibly conducive factors are still being investigated and these include divorce, broken homes, the persistence of crime in some families, poor church attendance, mothers' employment outside the home, health, and type of employment. Meanwhile an ordinary person may be forgiven the thought that highly organized crimes today call for such a degree of skill and intelligence that education can only serve to be a complementary rather than a competitive factor. The cleverer the criminal the more effective the crime. But it is interesting to observe that so far English social scientists have not even yet reported any very clear correlation between education and crime. Thus in 1958 Lord Pakenham published the results of research into the causes of crime (financed by the Nuffield Foundation), which included the following observation:

> I do not think, however, that the distinguished experts, including the representatives of the National Union of Teachers who gave evidence before us, would claim that, up to the present, much progress has been made in connecting education and crime.[18]

Insofar as people today still press for more education to reduce crime they usually mean a lengthening of the school life, i.e., a rise in the school-leaving age. In this connection we touch upon a piece of evidence which English educationists have found particularly perplexing. The Crowther Committee (1959) discovered the fact that the last year of compulsory education was also the heaviest year for juvenile delinquency and that the tendency to crime during school years was reversed when a boy went to work. Not only was this a long-standing phenomenon but also when in 1947 the school-leaving age was raised from fourteen to fifteen the most troublesome age group moved up from the thirteen-year-olds to the fourteen-year-olds.[19]

HOW SHOULD AN economist treat such information within the general framework of the "neighborhood effect"

732

[16] September 1963. Mr. William Singer, President of the Ulster Teachers' Union, told his annual conference on April 21, 1965: "There is a growing body of opinion which believes that our educational system must bear its share of responsibility for many of the problems of behavior, which show themselves in juvenile delinquency and vandalism."

[17] Barbara Wootton, *Social Science and Social Pathology* (London: Allen and Unwin, 1959), p. 80.

[18] *Causes of Crime* (London: Weidenfeld and Nicholson, 1958).

[19] Crowther Report, *op. cit.*, Para. 63.

analysis? It seems reasonable at least for him to conclude that the popular belief, as quoted for instance from the Robbins Report that state education makes the public less crime prone, is unsupported by the available evidence. Beyond this he could argue, but with less certainty, that the evidence showed a *prima facie* relationship in the opposite direction, i.e., that state education involved *adverse* external effects and aggravated or even helped to cause the prevailing trend towards increased criminal behavior. Certainly one could not object to the tentative conclusion that if any further official action were to take place it should first concentrate on a proper investigation of this question and that in the meantime there was to be a presumption against any further increases in the duration of compulsory schooling on this account.

It therefore comes as a surprise to find the Crowther Report concluding that there was nothing in the current state of affairs

> . . . to make any thoughtful person doubt the value of being at school; indeed, the delinquency may arise, not because boys are at school, but because they are not at school enough.[20]

As is well known in Great Britain, the Report argued for the raising of the compulsory school-leaving age. In doing so it referred to the *beneficial* external effects on society of presumed increased economic growth,[21] but at the same time it apparently refused to consider the possibility of any *adverse* external effects. Yet the Crowther policy of first raising the school-leaving age despite the evidence about delinquency and then trying to justify the measure after the event by offering hopes of future improvements in schooling seems to start at the wrong end. Indeed, such proposals seem to substitute dogma for reason and to betray the attitude that come what may the schools should not yield. In this attitude they probably reflect the limitations of state-sponsored committees which inevitably comprise many members and witnesses such as local education officers, state school headmasters, and the heads of teacher-training establishments who have a direct interest and belief in the expansion of state education itself. Such committees seem to welcome the rationality implicit in the "neighborhood effect" argument when it suits them, but are too ready to discard it the moment it becomes inconvenient.

The Crowther Committee contended that delinquency among older pupils probably arose because a boy had more time on his hands to get into mischief when at school compared with when he was at work. The Newsom Report[22] (on the education between the ages of thirteen and sixteen of pupils of average or below average ability) pointed out the difficulty of getting enough staff and resources to keep the boys occupied sufficiently. Accordingly this Report recommended that: "The school programme in the final year ought to be deliberately outgoing—an initiation into the adult world of work and leisure."[23] Again, undaunted by the evidence, the Report also recommended the raising of the school-leaving age. Once more the innocent observer must be allowed to question why, if the rate of delinquency declines when boys go out to work, should the commencement of this work be delayed still further *in favor of schemes for simulating work in school?* Why do we accept indiscriminately arguments about the need to protect young people from the "uncertain pressures of adult life" as long as possible and neglect the possibility that the pressures of school life may be in some cases the crucial ones? Such thoughts are not so revolutionary when it is remembered that, in these days, going out to work does not necessarily mean the end of formal education, since technical colleges and day-release schemes are now typically provided for the young worker's continued instruction. Those who show an overweening concern about the welfare of school-

733

---

[20] *Ibid.*

[21] This proposition is examined in West, *op. cit.,* chap. vii.

[22] *Half Our Future* (London: HMSO for the Ministry of Education, 1963).

[23] *Ibid.,* p. 79.

leavers do not seem to have shown why their proposals for extra protection could not be implemented, for instance, by schemes for appointing special supervisors, which would have the additional merit of being far less expensive than schooling. This is not of course to argue that all expenditure on further schooling is wrong. Where it is appropriate, and this may apply to most people, it is to be welcomed; but to apply a measure to all on the grounds that it is suitable to some is to sacrifice prudence to mere legislative expediency.

The reduction of crime is only one of many kinds of social benefit which society is supposed to expect from education; but it has been selected here for first attention because of its prominence in traditional reasoning and because it is a good illustration of the facility with which unchallenged and unverified theories can become assimilated in the folklore of educational debate. In addition to the errors of fact which are involved in it, such thinking also suffers through a lack of conceptual clarity. What do we mean when we say that *education* reduces crime? Are we thinking of education in the wide sense or do we mean only formal schooling? If the former, what *kind* of education have we in mind? If the latter, do we mean only *state* schooling or do we include non-state schooling?

The "reduction of crime" is only one of the propositions which economists normally associate with "neighborhood effects." Space does not allow a review of all of them, so the remainder of this article will confine itself to one more example of unsupported assumptions in this field: the assumption that widespread literacy could not have been achieved or maintained today without the predominant role of government.[24]

MANY ECONOMISTS ARE anxious to remind us that without widespread literacy it would be difficult to maintain a market economy as well as a political democracy. What, then, is to be feared? Was the populace *not* making itself literate before the government stepped in?

To what extent does nineteenth century history indicate that the English people, for instance, were in need of governmental help on this account? The evidence shows indeed that the majority of people in the first half of the nineteenth century did become literate (in the technical sense) largely by their own efforts.[25] Moreover, if the government played any role at all in this sphere it was one of saboteur!

As long ago as the first few years of the nineteenth century it was a subject for government *complaint* that the ordinary people *had become literate;* for the government feared that too many people were developing the "wrong" uses of literacy by belonging to secret "corresponding societies" and by reading seditious pamphlets. In 1803, for example, Thomas Malthus echoed the government's fears by asserting the probability that: "The circulation of Paine's *Rights of Man* . . . has done great mischief among the lower and middle classes of this country."[26] Far from subsidizing literacy, the early nineteenth century English government placed severe taxes on paper in order to discourage the exercise of the public's reading and writing abilities. Yet despite this obstacle, by the time government came around to subsidizing on a tiny scale in the 1830's, between two-thirds and three-quarters of the people (according to one modern specialist[27]) were already literate. Even then the subsidies were financed from a taxation system which burdened the poor more than the rich.[28]

---

[25] See West, *op. cit.*, chap. ix.

[26] T. R. Malthus, *Essay on Population* (London: Dutton Everyman, 1958), p. 190.

[27] R. K. Webb, "The Victorian Reading Public," in *From Dickens to Hardy* (London: Pelican Books, 1963).

[28] Moreover, the effects of the subsidies to schools were probably more than offset, in the early years at least, by the continuation of the "taxes on knowledge," i.e., the enormous taxes on paper, newspapers, and pamphlets which were not removed until the 1850's and 1860's. Here we have a good instance of the way in which government action itself (this time the way

---

[24] Further detailed investigation of assumptions concerning other allegedly favorable spillover effects from education, for instance, upon economic growth, equality of opportunity, and social cohesion, will be found in West, *op. cit.*

Those who argue that the system, not of government subsidy, but of government provision in the form of nationalized schools, was the key to the expansion of literacy have an even more difficult task. Using one of the generally accepted indexes of nineteenth century literacy, the figures showing the number of persons signing the marriage register with marks, it is argued that in 1870 when nationalized schools (called board schools) were introduced, 20 per cent of the men and 27 per cent of the women were signing their names with a mark. Much of the subsequent improvement in literacy, so the argument continues, must therefore be attributed to the 1870 legislation. One must observe, however, first that even if such figures are accepted they indicate that most people were already literate without the help of the nationalized schools. In other words, this evidence does not demonstrate the need for *universal* provision of these schools. Second, that judging by the growth rate in literacy prior to 1870 it is not clear that at least as good an improvement would not have occurred without the 1870 Act. Third, the men signing the marriage register in 1870, having an average age of 28 years, had on the average

---

in which taxation was levied) can result in socially adverse spillovers or "neighborhood effects" (i.e., social costs). If it were seeking the *positive* neighborhood effects of education, it would have been more practical for the government first to have attended to the *negative* neighborhood effects for which *it* was responsible; that is, it should have abolished the "taxes on knowledge" before considering subsidizing the pursuit of it. To subsidize and tax the same activity is illogical and costly.

left school seventeen years before. If most people learn to read and write at school, an assumption which seems to be implied in this sort of reasoning, the 1870 marriage registers in England reflect the schooling of the early 1850's. A more appropriate figure to test the literacy rate of school leavers around 1870 is that of the 1891 Census. This shows that only 6.4 per cent of the men and 7.3 per cent of the women were signing the registers with a mark. These men must have left school on an average around 1874. They could therefore have barely benefitted from the new state schools since the building program had scarcely got underway at this time. Finally, there is no evidence that the state school system, which had become universal by the time of the Second World War, has been a complete success. Even by 1948 there were still in England and Wales 5 per cent of fourteen-year-old school-leavers officially classified as nearly or completely illiterate.

Here then we have the paradox of a public managing to educate itself into literary competence from personal motives and private resources, despite the obstacle of an institution called government which eventually begins to claim most of the credit for the educational success. The notion held by many people that had it not been for the state they or at least most of their neighbors would never have become educated is a striking monument to the belief of the Victorian legal theorist Dicey, that people's opinions and convictions eventually become conditioned by the legislated institutions they make themselves.

735

South Africa Reconsidered

THOMAS MOLNAR

In our Vol. III, No. 4 issue, New Individualist Review *carried an article by Professor Denis Cowen, of the Law School of the University of Capetown, "Prospects for South Africa." Professor Cowen is a confirmed and outspoken opponent of the Nationalist Administration's policy of* apartheid. *A reply to Professor Molnar's communication will appear in a forthcoming issue of* New Individualist Review.

THE TONE OF WRITERS against South African apartheid policies is generally so vituperative that one must welcome Prof. Cowen's article in the Spring 1965 issue of *New Individualist Review* (Vol. III, No. 4) for its relative moderation. As one example of the usual "approach" to South African affairs in our press, I wish to mention only the document, published in March 1965 by the Carnegie Endowment for International Peace.

Under the title, *Apartheid and the UN: Collective Measures,* the Carnegie Endowment, supposedly devoted to peace on earth, recommends the most drastic aggression against South Africa, including naval blockade, combat operations by small naval, air, and land forces, and

---

Thomas Molnar is Professor of Romance Languages at Brooklyn College. He is the author of a number of books, among them *The Decline of the Intellectual, The Future of Education, The Two Faces of American Foreign Policy,* and *Africa, A Political Travelogue.*

military occupation. The authors of the document go so far in their warlike enthusiasm as to set down in advance the probable casualty figures, dead, wounded, and prisoners: close to forty thousand, although they thoughtfully add that "a percentage of these personnel would be returned to duty." That they expect a war of no small scale and violence is indicated in their closing sentence: "The statistics are based on experience gained from World War II and Korea. These estimates will vary based upon intensity of combat, enemy capabilities, training of troops, etc. Consequently they should be used with caution."

I mention this monstrous instance of warmongering by an organization nominally devoted to peace in order to suggest the difficulty Prof. Cowen, mindful of world opinion, must have faced in writing his article—in a climate of clamoring demagoguery in which common sense is practically suppressed, or at least suspected. Yet Prof. Cowen himself seems to me to yield to ideological pressure a n d consequent unrealistic thinking in too many passages of his text. In what follows I wish to point out these passages.

Cowen shares his premises with the ideological liberals when he assumes that all South Africa must do is to comply with the demands of "world opinion" and the United Nations for peace to descend on that beautiful country and its population. His arguments are surprisingly naive, although he himself warns the reader against the views of liberals and do-gooders. Everything would turn out all right, he says, and the world would turn its attention elsewhere if a non-racial democracy were established in South Africa in the framework of a federal form of government in which the courts would enforce a bill of rights protecting the minority races.

This is, of course, not a new formula; indeed Mr. Cowen, under the disguise of impartiality, has taken out a leaf from the Progressive Party's program, backed in South Africa exclusively by starry-eyed liberals and misguided intellectuals. I would point out to Mr. Cowen, as I did to Mrs. Helen Suzman, sole parliamentary spokesman of the Progressive Party, that almost the totality of the South African electorate is violently opposed to this program, hence that it is simply not enforceable except by military action such as that outlined in the above-quoted document.

Furthermore, it should also be stated (and Mrs. Suzman, in private conversation, found no counter-argument) that in recent history very few bills of rights, or other legal guarantees, proved more than fragile paper barriers when the (racial, national, religious, etc.) majority wanted to have its own way. After all, what good did the Bill of Rights do for the American Negro in the last one hundred years, since Abraham Lincoln emancipated him and restored him to full citizenship? There is every reason to believe that if full parliamentary democracy is introduced in South Africa, with universal suffrage for all races, the majority. which is black, will in no time submerge the entire country. To everybody who tries to view the South African situation with some clarity of judgment it is evident that the white, Indian, Chinese, Griqua, and Coloured minorities would be swept away by a triumphant black majority and by the one-party State.

BEHIND PROF. COWEN'S faith in the "federal" or "democratic" solution (incidentally: democracy has not survived even the first years of independence anywhere in Africa), there is his equally unrealistic belief that the UN is, now or potentially, an impartial enforcement agency of human rights wherever they are threatened. It would be tedious to list the examples of UN failure to act (Budapest and Tibet come easily to mind), except when the two great powers which dominate it, the United States and the Soviet Union, decide to push it in the direction they occasionally favor together. But it is nothing less than scandalous to suggest that Africa, which has witnessed horrible UN atrocities in Katanga, amply documented by the International Red Cross, should again be the scene of "peace enforcement" by that organization. I know that among liberals in South Africa there is the same ideology-spawned faith in the moral superiority of the UN as among members of the Western intelligentsia; but the dream of a few utopian minds ought not to become the platform of a country's policies.

The fact is that the UN, and a number of other agencies and countries whom Mr. Cowen implicity trusts and quotes, are irrevocably hostile to South Africa because it is a bulwark of anti-Communism, hence of Western defenses in the South Atlantic and the Indian Ocean. (Taiwan cannot be accused of "racial discrimination," yet the same circles are hostile to it.) Displaying a strange naiveté, Mr. Cowen admits the fact of this hostility, even though he and I would disagree on its motives. He admits, namely, that even if South Africa were to comply with the UN claim, now debated before the World Court at The Hague, on South West Africa (which Pretoria has administered since 1920 under a League of Nations mandate), other issues would be found to attack it. He also quotes Kwame Nkrumah who lays claim, in the name of "Africa," to the South African mineral wealth. He also argues that since the American Negroes hold now "the balance of political power" in the United States (!), Pretoria had better change its racial policies before Washington, pressured by Negro groups at home, intervenes with pressures of its own.

Like an irresponsible Santa Claus, Mr. Cowen chooses to hold out some rewards for the South Africans in case they become good children and obey the UN's solicitous advice. If South Africa solves its race problem, Mr. Cowen writes, it will provide the world with a beautiful example of racial peace. More than that: Since the ratio of races (white to non-white) in the world is roughly the same as in South Africa, the example would become truly convincing! This is not exactly a scholarly argument, nor does it mention that racial strife exists between all races (in Africa: between blacks and Arabs, Indians and blacks), that it is not an invention of those devilish whites.

In this rather long, yet incomplete, comment on Mr. Cowen's text I did not wish to introduce a counter-analysis of apartheid and other related matters, domestic and foreign, in the light of which they must be viewed for the sake of intelligibility. I merely wanted to point out that behind Prof. Cowen's apparently objective and sweetly benevolent arguments one finds the same assumptions, b a s e d on the quicksand of illusions, which have so far created tragedy and bloodshed for African whites and blacks alike.

738

REVIEW:

Alchian and Allen's
"University Economics"

STANLEY G. LONG

University Economics by Armen A. Alchian and William R. Allen. Belmont, California: Wadsworth Publishing Co., 1964. 924 p. $8.95.

ABOUT A YEAR AGO while riding in a railroad club car I got into a conversation with several publisher's representatives, who were with one of the well known textbook firms. While talking about texts for the economics principles course, one of them was quite knowledgeable about frequently cited strengths and weaknesses of his company's products and also those of his competitors. (It is one of the duties of publishers' representatives, when calling at universities and colleges, to make lists of "strong points" and "weak points.")

Commenting one one of his firm's books, I said that it seemed sound, that I was contemplating adopting it, and that I supposed that that particular book was my second choice in the field (although I couldn't then decide what my *first* choice was).

"That's why it's the number two seller in the field; it's everyone's second choice," returned my friend triumphantly.

Our exchange suggests something about the textbook industry, or at least the section of that industry devoted to producing new principles-of-economics books. Location theory suggests that it is often in the interest of a second mobile hot dog seller just invading a beach to

Stanley G. Long, an instructor in economics at Knox College, has an M.A. in economics from Northwestern University, and is currently a Ph.D. candidate there. He has also pursued economic studies at Cambridge, Uppsala, and Vienna.

locate near an already existing one. Studies of product differentiation in, say, consumer-durable-producing oligopolies lead us to expect many quite similar brands each trying to capitalize on the success of competitors and being just different enough to give the advertising department some extra push buttons, or what-have-you, to write about. Similarly with our number-two textbook: Everything is there, and its (justifiable) claim for serious consideration rests on being able to persuade some potential customers that it covers each (or most) of the "essential areas" just a little better than any of its slightly differentiated substitutes. See for example any or all of the good texts by Samuelson, Bach, McConnell, Reynolds, Fels, Harris, Ferguson, and Kreps, to name most of the leading contenders in the field. Each has certain distinctions, such as being the first to incorporate the "Keynesian Cross" into an elementary text, being unusually encyclopedic with respect to topics covered, being unusually well written, etc. Yet the nature of the textbook market is such that each book tries to appeal to the largest possible audience, and in so doing often seems to imitate the others. The fact that the book selection process is often one of committee decision accentuates the tendency to include all possible topics.

UNIVERSITY ECONOMICS cannot be considered as simply another entrant into a crowded field trying simultaneously to be discreetly and marginally new and yet enough like "the others" so that potential customers (who are of course, from the standpoint of decision making, the professors, not the students) may continue to use last year's lecture notes and not be threatened by any really new approach or organization. *University Economics,* rather, offers a real alternative choice, and in the opinion of this reviewer, a good one indeed. The student who sustains his interest through this book in an introductory economics course will understand a great deal more about resource allocation than he could have obtained from the price theory sections of perhaps any other introductory text with which I am familiar. The probability of continuing interest is increased both by Alchian and Allen's prose style and by the use of some "gimmicks," especially a series of provocative questions at the end of each chapter. Unfortunately, our student who has sustained his interest through the book, while having acquired a firm grasp of pricing and allocation theory and of the process of economic reasoning, will not have learned much about macro-economic analysis, that is, the national-income-determination process from what seems to be an overly short and mechanical section on the simple income determination model. The presentation of a simple model to show equilibrium national income and a discussion of monetary and fiscal policy using such a model is more satisfactory elsewhere.[1] So, the strength of the text and its emphasis lie in its superior treatment of exchange, production, and distribution. To many of us the strength here will outweigh the cost of having to supplement the macro-economic sections, and I have no quarrel with the authors' decision to forego a separate section (presumably of equal "weight") on every possible policy "area." Let me make it clear that I do not consider the national income sections unusable; it is only the relative strength to which I refer. The implications for a second edition are evident, however.

A STRONG CASE CAN BE made for placing a rather greater emphasis on resource allocation than has been the

[1] E.g., P. A. Samuelson, *Economics* (New York: McGraw Hill, 1964).

Page Fifty-four

vogue for at least the last decade. It has been convenient to separate national income determination from price analysis as if these two parts of economic reasoning had nothing to do with one another, and as if the principles of resource allocation were inapplicable in periods of less than full employment. However convenient, this is simply wrong. The reason for this simplifying assumption in the organization of our texts was, of course, that the macro-economic or national income analysis was something rather new, developing from the discussion started by Keynes' *General Theory* and finding its way into textbooks only after World War II. The experience of this intellectual revolution and the overwhelming impact of the Great Depression caused a generation of economists to direct most of their energies to this one single problem. Perhaps it was necessary to attack the then "conventional wisdom" in order to pave the way for a more orderly analysis of the goal of economic stability; but it needn't have been done at the cost of converting the analysis of prices (in many of the texts) to a bag of tricks. (Some of the writers on my list are more guilty of this than others.) Today, moreover, the idea that *particular policy proposals* are automatically contained in a particular theory, Keynes' or anyone else's, seems silly. Theories must be accepted or rejected on their own merits, according to established rules of evidence; and the policy proposals one advocates depend also on what *normative* goals one has chosen to support.

Once the ideological brush has been cleared, then, income analysis becomes an important tool for analyzing monetary and fiscal policies (or the lack of them); and the saving-equals-investment equilibrium is a simpler notion to understand than the supply-and-demand equilibrium (although it has fewer important uses than the latter). Thus, once we no longer have to knock down Classical straw men or be forced to defend any particular policy along *with* a body of analyses, I would claim that the essentials of macro-economics are needed to understand public discussion of policies about price stability, growth, full employment, etc.; but that having understood the essentials, most important economic issues involve discussions of resource *allocation,* or broadly, price theory. George Stigler has claimed that for every time a citizen is called upon to hold a responsible opinion about economic policy when macro-economic theory can be used, he can use price theory ninety-nine times.

> Questions devoted primarily to maintaining employment are posed so infrequently, and are even then (as in the appropriation acts) so completely dominated by allocative questions that for practical purposes they are an infrequent and minor problem for the citizen. . . . Would intense concentration on the basic logic of price theory, applied to . . . real problems, give a vastly better and more lasting training than the current encyclopedic texts? Surely the answer is yes.[2]

I might be inclined to make the ratio 49 to 1, but I qualitatively agree. To put my position rather differently, I would claim that the problem of aggregate demand is a very important one (too much leads to inflation, not enough to depression, etc.), and that it is vital that the supply of money, tax schedules, and government expenditures be in a proper relationship to business and consumer expenditures so that we avoid disaster; but we *have* the knowledge to take care of this. (Here is not the place to demonstrate that Keynes was a conservative.) Given that we have this knowledge, beginning economics students should learn about it; but not to the exclusion of learning about the analysis of problems of resource allocation which have so much wider applicability.[3] It is in this presentation of the problems of exchange, production, and distribution that *University Economics* excels.

ALCHIAN AND ALLEN take greater care than usual to emphasize that economic analysis and value judgments

should be identified and separated. That there should be occasional lapses from this ideal is perhaps inevitable. Even as one who considers himself a classical liberal, I was occasionally disturbed by implicit value judgments in the text, often in the form of omitted qualifications. Although they are mentioned later in the book in short sections, I would like to see more frequent and explicit reference to (i) the existence of externalities; (ii) the fact that the distribution of income depends on acceptance of a set of institutional arrangements about which a value consensus, or even one person's value judgment, is of a different order than a value consensus about, say, "economic efficiency." Aside from what I would call purely technical problems, e.g., economic stabilization and the provision of "pure public goods," those areas about which a classical liberal might question the ability of "open markets" to provide a "satisfactory" answer usually concern situations involving externalities or situations of "unsatisfactory" distribution of income.

An understanding of the working of markets, however, is perhaps our best safeguard against misguided idealists and special interest pleaders being able to alter the economic solution by trying (or claiming to try) to obtain one result (with respect to externalities or income distribution) but achieving another.

At this point, however, I am grinding one of my own axes about which I happen to feel rather strongly. I am often upset by the neglect of these two issues, externalities and income distribution, when policy proposals are being advanced which are designed to further classical liberal goals. However, Alchian and Allen's analysis must be judged as just that, analysis, regardless of their implicit policy position, which it would seem *is* classical liberal. As analysis it comes very well indeed. Here is a new introductory economics text that rescues price theory from the status of a mechanical puzzle which some treatments have given it, and while I have dealt with it primarily as an undergraduate text, the first thirty chapters could well be recommended as introductory or review reading for the interested layman.

741

---

[2] "Elementary Economic Education," in *The Intellectual and the Market Place* (New York: The Free Press of Glencoe, 1963), pp. 82-84.

[3] See P. A. Samuelson, *op. cit.,* 4th and later editions, on the "Neoclassical Synthesis": Once problems of aggregate demand are attended to, allocation becomes more important.

NEW BOOKS AND ARTICLES

THE FOLLOWING IS A SELECT LIST OF BOOKS AND ARTICLES WHICH, IN THE OPINION OF THE EDITORS, MAY BE OF INTEREST TO OUR READERS.

Two books have appeared recently compiling some of the essays and letters of Randolph Bourne: *The World of Randolph Bourne,* edited with an introduction by Lillian Schlissel. New York: Dutton, 1965. $2.25, paper. And: *War and the Intellectuals,* edited with an introduction by Carl Resek. New York: Harper Torchbooks, 1964. $1.95, paper. Bourne is of interest as one of the very few radical American intellectuals of the early 1900's who was not swept along in the euphoria of "Mr. Wilson's War." In many often brilliant passages Bourne is able to capture and express the same anarchistic sentiments felt by many of today's "conservatives."

Frank S. Meyer, ed., *The African Nettle.* New York: John Day, 1965. $5.00. A symposium on the current situation and the prospects for Africa, including articles by P. T. Bauer on African economic policy; W. H. Hutt on the collectivistic policies used to keep living standards for the blacks depressed in South Africa; Sir Roy Welensky; Elspeth Huxley; and others.

742

The essays of Mihajlo Mihajlov, the young Yugoslavian intellectual, which recently led to his being sentenced to a nine-month prison term (later commuted to five months on probation and suspended sentence) have been issued by Farrar, Strauss and Giroux. *Moscow Summer* (New York: 1965, $3.50) were held to violate the Yugoslavian law against "damaging the reputation of a foreign state" (the Soviet Union). Specifically in question was Mihajlov's discussion of the Russian concentration camps, e.g.: "The first 'death camps' were not really established by the Germans, since they were founded by the Soviets. In 1921 [under Lenin and Trotsky], in the vicinity of Archangel, the first death camp, known as Homogor, was formed with the sole purpose of physically exterminating the prisoners. . . ." Another indication of Mihajlov's transgression of the acceptable limits of debate in Yugoslavia as set by the Tito regime is a letter from Mihajlov, quoted in an interesting article in the June 1965 issue of *Encounter* ("Letter from Belgrade," by Anatole Shub), in which he maintains that in the U.S.S.R. "serfdom still obtains, because the agricultural workers are administratively bound to the *kolkhoz.*"

E. G. West, *Education and the State.* London: Institute of Economic Affairs, 1965. 40 shillings. From the review in *The Times Educational Supplement* (London), November 12, 1965: "Dr. E. G. West, an economics lecturer in Newcastle University, has produced a remarkably able and lively critique of the system and principles under which education is provided by the state. He denies that the majority of working-class parents are not to be trusted. By going back to the days before the 1870 Act, when education was neither free nor compulsory, he attempts to show that the great majority of working-class parents were prepared to spend money on it. . . . If working-class parents were prepared to back the choice they then possessed with money, why should they be presumed unfit to choose today when they are so much richer?" In another review, Giles St. Aubyn writes: "If myths were as self-evident as truths are supposed to be, they would collapse of their own accord; but endowed opinions tenaciously resist destruction regardless of the errors they contain. Dr. West's book none the less is calculated to reduce even the strongest fortifications to rubble. *Education and the State* is perhaps the most important work written on the subject this century." [*The Sunday Times* (London), November 21, 1965.] Copies may be ordered directly from the IEA, Eaton House, 66A Eaton Square, London S.W.1, England.

Martin Anderson, "Urban Renewal: The Claims and the Facts," *Harvard Business Review*, XLIII (Jan.-Feb. 1965), 6-20ff. Prof. Anderson of Columbia University is the author of *The Federal Bulldozer* (Cambridge, Mass.: MIT Press, 1964), a large-scale study of the urban renewal program. Anderson's scientific investigations have led him to the conclusion that the arguments in favor of governmental urban renewal programs are largely mythical, and that the interest of the public at large — as distinguished from that of certain special interest groups — would be better promoted by abolishing the programs. His findings are summarized in this article, which is available from the American Conservative Union in pamphlet form without charge. Write: ACU, Suite 1101, 1010 Vermont Ave., N.W., Washington, D.C. 20005.

Prof. Colin D. Campbell of Dartmouth College and his wife have written an article entitled "You'll Never Get Back All Those Old-Age 'Contributions' " in the *Washington Post,* November 7, 1965, Section E. Campbell points out on the basis of calculations made in the article from typical Social Security payments, benefits, and life expectancy, that the average worker would be much better off if the system did not exist: "Even from a private insurance company, the cost of a $3024 annuity at age 65 is about $45,000, $9000 less than the accumulated amount of a worker's tax payments." He further points out that at 4 per cent interest, the typical worker could provide out of savings as much as the Social Security program provides, and still have an accumulated $38,000 to pass on to his heirs. Campbell discusses in brief the inequities in the present system as regards women, bachelors, the poor, and those workers over sixty-five who choose to continue to work. "The Social Security system started out as a program to help wage earners provide themselves with a minimum income in their old age. It has evolved into a combined insurance, welfare, and giveaway program with inequities that are difficult to justify."

743

John Gregory Dunne, who writes an occasional column on TV and radio for *The New Republic,* had a provocative article in the November 6, 1965, issue of that magazine ("Whose Dissent Do You Hear?"). His main thesis: "I think it can be argued that the three major networks are indirectly responsible for the proliferation of paranoid [Right-wing] broadcasters. The reason is that there is nothing on the air today remotely passing for responsible dissent. The news departments of all three networks are in the hands of an Establishment consensus, bounded on one side by Eric Sevareid, on the other by Howard K. Smith." The frequency with which William Buckley graces the airwaves does not invalidate this description because, "As Proust was the pet Jew of the anti-Semites, so Buckley is the pet Conservative of the Establishment." Dunne argues for more conservatives on radio and television, which would have the effect of inducing Americans to consider "whether opposition to Medicare can be dismissed simply as hostility to old people, or support of the bracero program only as an excuse to exploit Mexican wetback labor."

Michael E. Levine, "Is Regulation Necessary? California Air Transportation and National Regulatory Policy," *The Yale Law Journal,* LXXIV (July 1965), 1416-47. In this detailed study of the operation of free market forces in Los Angeles-San Francisco air transportation, Mr. Levine concludes: "The CAB should draw a lesson for national regulation from the Los Angeles-San Francisco market and amend the present regulatory scheme so that all markets are freed from restrictive economic regulation. . . . [The] air space is public property, restrictions on the use of which were initially imposed in response to fears of economic evils. Since examination of the Los Angeles-San Francisco market shows that these fears are unjustified, there is no reason why we need continue to deny the opportunity to serve the public to those prepared to risk capital to do so. It is neither wise political nor economic policy to mark out an area of activity as the preserve of a few corporations who have the good fortune to have been operating on May 14, 1938."

Wesley McCune, director of Group Research, Inc., was for some reason or other asked to address the meeting of the Intellectual Freedom Committee of the American Library Association in Washington early this past year (his speech is reprinted in the June 1965 issue of the *American Library Association Bulletin*). His talk naturally concerned the threat from the Radical Right, and served to "alert" librarians to the "flood" of Radical Right propaganda they may expect to receive soon (what librarians *do* with such materials is primly left to their own civilized consciences). Typical of McCune's technique, and indicative of why he so annoys conservatives and classical liberals, is the following: After discussing the activities of the old stand-bys — like Gerald L. K. Smith and Billy James Hargis — McCune warns librarians of one of the newer threats: ". . . a group . . . headquartered at Wabash College and called the Principles of Freedom. . . . The key man in this planned operation is Dean Benjamin Rogge, . . ." whom McCune further identifies through Rogge's curious and suggestive connections with the Foundation for Economic Education and the Intercollegiate Society of Individualists. *New Individualist Review* recommends the speech especially to (a) modern-liberals who wish to avoid having to rebut the arguments for consistent capitalism; and (b) conservatives who would like to see a McCarthy-*redivivus* in action.

Herbert Spencer, "The New Liberalism," *The Freeman*, November 1965. This reprinting of excerpts from Spencer's "The New Toryism" and "From Freedom to Bondage" represents a welcome effort to bring to the general public today some of the classic arguments for liberty as set down by one of the best minds of the last century. These essays were directed to those of Spencer's contemporaries who, he thought, were forgetting the basic principle of liberalism: "to diminish the range of governmental authority and to increase the area within which each citizen may act unchecked." This article is a good introduction to Spencer's political thought, and is available on request from: The Foundation for Economic Education, Irvington-on-Hudson, New York 10533.

Kenneth Vinson, "Prohibition's Last Stand," *The New Republic*, October 16, 1965. A professor of law at the University of Mississippi reports on that state's curious official attitude on hard liquor: while it is prohibited by law throughout the state, there also exists a state excise tax on it. The situation lends itself easily to the arbitrary use of the police power, which has been employed, according to Prof. Vinson, particularly against civil rights workers and others out of step with the officially sanctioned *mores* regulating race relations in that state.

Sampling of Distinguished Paperbacks

745

Few Readers Realize . . .

. . . the impact a controversial young magazine such as NEW INDIVIDUALIST REVIEW can have upon the mass movements of our age. But who can ignore the lesson of recent events in Andorra? Taking to the barricades with submachineguns in one hand and (thanks to our energetic representative at the University of Andorra Business School) copies of NIR in the other, the Andorran Freedom Fighters held off government troops for three days while, behind closed doors, high level theoreticians in the Andorran Liberal Party debated the questions raised in the last, provocative issue of NEW INDIVIDUALIST REVIEW.

The moderate majority deftly sidestepped the issue of contracting the army and police force out to a private company (amidst shouts of "shame!" and "Yalta!" from one faction) and finally succeeded in getting the Party to broadcast the following statement on the rebel station, Radio Free Andorra:

746

(1) NIR is not typically conservative;

(2) NIR is not typically left-wing;

(3) NIR is refreshingly different; and

(4) NIR doesn't cost very much!

When the Revolution sweeps your neighborhood, be prepared! Take to the barricades with a copy of NIR. Subscribe today!

NEW INDIVIDUALIST REVIEW   14
IDA NOYES HALL
University of Chicago, Chicago, Illinois 60637

Please enter my subscription for one year ☐ $3.00; Two years ☐ $5.75

(Students, one year ☐ $1.50; Two years ☐ $2.75)

I also enclose a contribution of $..

NAME ....

ADDRESS ....

CITY .... STATE .... ZIP CODE ....

IF STUDENT: SCHOOL .... YEAR OF GRAD. ....

APOSTLES OF THE SELF-MADE MAN
Changing Concepts of Success in America
By JOHN G. CAWELTI

Thirty per-cent of the businessmen in the United States will either "make it" or be broken this year. Those who "make it" are termed "successful"—those who don't are failures. But how does one define success? What does our society say about success and failure? The definitions change with the times, from "Protestant Virtue" to the "Rat Race" and back again. Mr. Cawelti draws from many sources, both literary and otherwise, to trace the evolution of that enigmatic goal everyone strives for—success! "... lightened by a pawky humor ... an extremely entertaining volume to read."—GERALD W. JOHNSON, *The New Republic*. 279 *pages*, $6.95

THE POLITICS OF MODERNIZATION
By DAVID E. APTER

In modernizing societies the mood fluctuates between an exciting sense of new freedom and hope and fear, cynicism and opportunism. In this, the first major study of the processes of modernization, the struggle that has given meaning to our generation, Dr. Apter brilliantly analyzes the basis for both extremes. His main theme is the consolidation of authority during periods of modernization and the exceptional opportunities for creative choice which arise in times of upheaval. His far-reaching, profound analysis is based on the contention that in political life, the significant can only be understood in moral terms. 481 *pages*, $7.50

A PERIL AND A HOPE
The Scientists' Movement in America, 1945-1947
By ALICE KIMBALL SMITH

How did the scientists who developed the atomic bomb react to its first explosion during World War II? Mrs. Smith and her scientist-husband, Cyril Stanley Smith, lived at Los Alamos, while he worked on the Manhattan Project. Her intimate association with these men and her reporter's eye for detail combine to present a living document of the scientists' efforts to wrest control of the bomb from the military and turn it over to the civilians. "... fully and critically documented, compassionately written, painstakingly detailed. It is both lively and exact."—PHILLIP MORRISON, *The Scientific American*. 591 *pages*, $10.00

UNIVERSITY OF CHICAGO PRESS
Chicago/London

VOLUME 4
NUMBER 3
SPRING 1966

New
INDIVIDUALIST
Review

THE TRIPLE REVOLUTION:
  A NEW METAPHYSICS

A JOURNAL OF CLASSICAL LIBERAL THOUGHT

Spring 1966   75 cents   Vol. 4, No. 3

NEW INDIVIDUALIST REVIEW

A JOURNAL OF CLASSICAL LIBERAL THOUGHT

Spring 1966   Volume 4 -- Number 3

753

NEW INDIVIDUALIST REVIEW is published quarterly by *New Individualist Review, Inc.,* at Ida Noyes Hall, University of Chicago, Chicago, Illinois 60637. Telephone 312/363-8778.

Opinions expressed in signed articles do not necessarily represent the views of the editors. Editorial, advertising, and subscription correspondence and manuscripts should be sent to NEW INDIVIDUALIST REVIEW, Ida Noyes Hall, University of Chicago, Chicago, Illinois 60637. All manuscripts become the property of NEW INDIVDUALIST REVIEW.

Subscription rates: $3.00 per year (students $1.50). Two years at $5.75 (students $2.75).

NEW

INDIVIDUALIST

REVIEW

A JOURNAL OF
CLASSICAL LIBERAL THOUGHT

EDITORIAL STAFF

Editor-in-Chief • Ralph Raico

Associate Editors • J. Michael Cobb

James M. S. Powell • Robert Schuetinger

Editorial Assistants • David D. Friedman

Burton Gray • Thomas C. Heagy

Ernest L. Marraccini • John C. Moorhouse

EDITORIAL ADVISORS

Yale Brozen • Milton Friedman • George J. Stigler

University of Chicago

F. A. Hayek   Benjamin Rogge

University of Frieburg   *Wabash College*

754

Complaints of the loss of individuality and the lessening of respect for the person and his rights have become a commonplace of our time; they nonetheless point to a cause for genuine concern. NEW INDIVIDUALIST REVIEW, an independent journal associated with no organization or political party, believes that in the realm of politics and economics the most valuable system guaranteeing proper respect for individuality is that which, historically, has gone by the name of classical liberalism; the elements of this system are private property, civil liberties, the rule of law, and, in general, the strictest limits placed on the power of government. It is the purpose of the Review to stimulate and encourage explorations of important problems from a viewpoint characterized by thoughtful concern with individual liberty.

The Triple Revolution:
A New Metaphysics

KARL BRUNNER

MAN'S CONCERN WITH salvation is ancient indeed. For millenia he has relentlessly poured out his intellectual resources in this pursuit. The pressures and frustrations of reality have demanded consoling orientations toward the universe and the social environment, and man has proved almost more than equal to this challenge of "existential anxiety." A profusion of products has been created to satisfy this demand; and over the centuries a rich pattern has evolved, from the biomorphic interpretations of the cosmos as in primitive societies, up to the metaphysical systems of modern philosophy and theology.[1]

A concern for salvation in this world and this life through the manipulation of institutional arrangements is not entirely new. This secular eschatology shares with other types of *Erlösungslehren* an essentially noncognitive, emotive-pictorial use of language and the commitment to a global strategy. It holds that redemption from evil cannot be assured by a piecemeal procedure of trial and error. The social order must be totally reshaped in order to achieve salvation. Deliverance comes through a force or a process which invariably destroys the inherited social organization, and thus opens the path to the New Jerusalem.

The theme is old and has been played in many variations; but the clash of ideologies permitted by an open society inevitably generates new conceptions. Among the products recently cast up we note in particular the *Manifesto of the Triple Revolution,* prepared by an Ad Hoc Committee for the Triple Revolution, and issued in March 1964 with an admirable sense for publicity. A variety of programs on radio and television have since been devoted to the diffusion of the Word. Articles in magazines and newspapers have similarly elaborated the message. In this article I intend to analyze the claims and proposals of the "Triple Revolution" group from the standpoint of economic theory, and then indicate some of the wider philosophical implications of this phenomenon.

The *Manifesto* opens with a declaration that "mankind is at a historic conjuncture which demands a fundamental

755

Karl Brunner is the Everett D. Reese Professor of Economics and Banking at Ohio State University. He studied at the State University of Zurich, Switzerland, and the London School of Economics.

[1] An excellent analysis of the structure of metaphysical conceptions can be found in Ernst Topitsch, *Vom Ursprung und Ende der Metaphysik* (Vienna: Springer Verlag, 1958). This analysis has a general bearing on the nature of non-cognitive belief-systems pervading our society.

re-examination of existing values and institutions." The historic conjuncture results from "three separate and mutually reinforcing revolutions": cybernation, weaponry, and human rights. The *Manifesto*, however, barely mentions the last two, and concentrates on the cybernation revolution. It is claimed that the advent of complex computers, data-processing and self-regulating machines, creates an historical break in the evolution of social life. "A new era of production has begun. Its principles of organization are as different from those of the industrial era as those of the industrial era were different from the agricultural." The new machines, it is claimed, introduce a regime of unlimited productive capacity.[2] With cybernation, abundance has become a "fact"; scarcity is the result of obsolete institutions and inappropriate values. With abundance abounding, rationing and allocation mechanisms become redundant.

In the Marxist eschatology, the state was expected to wither away. Not so according to some prophets of the Triple Revolution. The economic organization is expected to vanish, but the state will absorb society.[3] While paradise could (almost?) immediately be achieved, inherited institutions and values prevent its realization. An economic organization based on private property and guided by market price signals converts the impact of cyber-

nation into rising poverty, expanding unemployment, and corrosive "alienation of man." The new machines displace people in droves, first from manufacturing industries and agriculture, and subsequently from the service industries. Man cannot compete with these machines. Poverty, therefore, expands and men become totally alienated from a hostile society. In the new era dominated by cybernation and automation, it has become impossible to achieve full employment in the context of a market economy. Fiscal policy may, admittedly, provide some transitory remedies; but they are of dubious value in alleviating the unavoidably growing unemployment.[4]

THE NATURE OF THE ultimate society remains strangely obscure, however. We seem assured that it will be a Good Society which will have exorcised the curse of alienation brought on by a market system of economic organization. There is, however, no discussion of the institutional arrangements of the new society of abundance which will have vanquished

2 This assertion is frequently repeated in elaborations of the theme. Gerard Piel states, for instance, that $200 billion of Gross National Product "is going unconsumed." This remarkable assertion is obtained from the statement that there are 20 million families "whose level of life is something like three or four thousand dollars short of what our society has come to regard as a minimum scale"; see *A Conversation: Jobs, Machines, and People* (Santa Barbara, Calif.: Center for the Study of Democratic Institutions, 1964), p. 4.

3 The reader may find the following references illuminating: "If all of us are going to be provided with enough to go around, rationing isn't necessary any longer." (Statement by Robert Theobald, *ibid.*, p. 21. Michael Harrington discusses in another publication the existing prospects of Utopia. The vanishing of all economic problems in

Utopia is characterized in a manner which creates the definite impression that this event is feasible and worth exploring as an achievable goal. The discussion appears in *Cacatophia and Utopia* (Santa Barbara, Calif.: Center for the Study of Democratic Institutions, 1965). The point is particularly clear when we read (on p. 24) about "intellectuals...willing to sacrifice and struggle to create Utopia or a decent society." On p. 10 of the same *Conversations*, W. H. Ferry asserts that "we have entered a society of abundance, and economy of plenty, as against our former economy of scarcity."

4 The consequences for unemployment have been elaborated fulsomely. A sample may be noted here: Theobald states that until the new era, "more and more people were rising out of the poverty level....But today we are moving into a situation where people are being thrown out of the abundant society." *Jobs, Machines, and People*, pp. 4-5. Piel, never to be left behind in the supply of impressive assertions, formulated a law of worker displacement as follows: "...the displacement of workers in both white-collar and blue-collar functions is proceeding at an exponential rate, that is, proceeding at the square of time." Mr. Piel concedes that the operation of his law is somewhat offset by a growing popula-

the Satan of Scarcity. One point only emerges with clarity: The vanishing amount of labor required to assure abundance suggests that any connection of income with productive effort is totally obsolete, and in a "deeper sense" immoral. Incomes must be disbursed independent of productive contribution.

Instead of a description of institutional arrangements and of their manner of operation in the new society, we are offered tortuous debates on the New Morality required for a society which radically dissociates income from productive effort. The agonizing discussions about the inappropriateness of inherited moralities yield no enlightenment concerning the mode of operation of the new society. It is not clear whether *any* income whatsoever may be claimed by the individual eager to share abundantly in the abundance, or whether a limited income is assigned to every member of society "according to his needs." The vague references which may be culled from pamphlets suggest the second inter-

pretation. Should this be correct, one wonders about the justification for such limited allocations in the midst of "unlimited" plenty.

We are, however, provided with somewhat more information concerning the transition from the old to the new order. Massive government programs and a massive expansion of the government sector and government activities are necessary to alleviate "the physical and psychological miseries" created by cybernation in a market system. The key word is definitely "massive," whether it pertains to public education, public works, low cost housing, rapid transit systems, or public power systems. Among the etcetera may be noted income redistribution through taxation (on a massive scale, of course); and extensive use of licensing, and minimum wage laws are also proposed. In summary, the *Manifesto,* supplemented by individual elaborations and comments offered by its propounders, casts a "cacotopian" gloom over contemporary society and its economic organization, and reveals the promise of a Happy and Good Society achievable through radical social engineering and an appropriate reshaping of moral values. It also traces suggestive outlines of a program to alleviate the pains of transition.

Many people no doubt find the arguments used to support the *Manifesto's* approach appealingly plausible. The impact of new machines on the workers directly affected appears quite simple and obvious. Such impressions, however, possess a most ambiguous significance. For many centuries they confirmed that nobody could live on the other side of the earth, and it seemed just as obvious to most men that the sun revolves around the earth. The history of many sciences clearly shows that impressions must be carefully distinguished from observation reports. Impressions transcend a mere recording of observations in that they contain interpretative conjectures

757

---

tion, which mysteriously raises aggregate demand for output. This increase thus absorbes a portion of the displacement. He continues, however, to emphasize that "the problem is the enlarging gap between the employed labor force and the more rapidly increasing size of the labor force as a whole." Employment may still rise for a few years, but "within a decade employment is going to level off and begin to fall." (*ibid.*, p. 10) Other statements supplied by the group suggest that unemployment has already begun to rise: "I accept the fact that full employment at this junction in time is a misleading goal if by full employment is meant the traditional kind of jobs in the private market — a market that has filed in the last five years to produce the kind and number of jobs necessary." (Holstein in *ibid.*, p. 15). And lastly, we may consider the central "facts" adduced by the *Manifesto,* p. 7: "(a) the rate of productivity increase has risen with the onset of cybernation; (b) an industrial economic system postulated on scarcity has become unable to distribute the abundant goods and services produced by a cybernated system or potential in it; (c) surplus capacity and unemployment have thus coexisted at excessive levels over the last six years; (d) the underlying cause of excessive unemployment is the fact that the capability of machines is rising more rapidly than the capability of human beings to keep pace; and (e) a permanent impoverished and jobless class is established in the midst of potential abundance."

bearing on the observations noted. Consequently, they provide no evidence for the underlying and hidden theoretical notions. Moreover, the psychological sense of conviction accompanying such implicit interpretations cannot possibly establish their truth. The history of man's knowledge supplies many examples demonstrating the inadequacy of the most convincing, most obvious, and most plausible impressions of our environment. A critical examination of the ideas which the *Manifesto* advances with an overpowering sense of urgency for immediate radical action thus acquires considerable importance. That such an examination can only be conducted by means of technical economic theory is due to the nature of the subject matter. I shall proceed in this manner with some reluctance, since I feel certain that my treatment is destined to receive much less attention in the popular press than did the *Manifesto of the Triple Revolution.* Yet in the last analysis, after all, it is through economics and not prophecy that we can come to the truth in this matter.

THE EXISTENCE OF "idle" resources has often been observed in both market and non-market economies. On this point, the two types of economic organizations do not differ. They do differ, however, in the manner of occurance and the appropriate interpretation of the phenomenon.

The market process releases signals in the form of price movements which reallocate resources and output. If information about evolving market structures and the reallocation of resources were available without cost, resources would move instantly in the directions determined by the changes in demand and supply. In the context of a "full-information world" with no adjustment costs, economic resources would never be "idle," and markets would always be cleared. But this is not our world. Information must be produced, or gathered, at a positive social and private opportunity cost. Resources with alternative uses must be invested to collect, evaluate, and comprehend information about market positions. The more information one requires, and the more rapidly one wishes to collect a given amount of it, the greater will be its cost. Similarly, the readjustment of inherited resource-utilization patterns also necessitates a specific allocation of resources with alternative uses. Readjustment involves costs, which rise with both its magnitude and its speed.

Once we recognize the crucial role of the costs of information and adjustment, we can arrive at a more intelligent understanding of the nature of the market process. Idle resources will then appear as a rational attempt to minimize the costs of information and adjustment in the face of shifting demand and supply patterns. Consider, for instance, the position of a landlord having lost some tenants and being left with a number of vacant apartments. There is always a sufficiently large reduction in the rent which would lure new tenants immediately. Nevertheless, landlords rarely choose this option. The likelihood of his taking this action would be substantially greater if the landlord could immediately terminate the tenure of provisional low-rent tenants. But this action is precluded by the tenants' behavior. They insist, as a rule, on some minimal period of assured tenancy. This behavior is a consequence of the readjustment costs noted above. If readjustments imposed by others proceeded without inconvenience, i.e. without cost, tenants would be indifferent between two apartments differentiated only by the existance or absence of an advance notice before having their lease cancelled. The existence of readjustment costs thus induces tenants to prefer contracts requiring advance notice and preferably longer advance notice. This latter condition is due to the greater costs of readjustment when it must be done at greater speed. Under these circumstances the landlord will reject the option of immediately luring a tenant by lowering the rent. The market has informed him so far that he can rent the apartments at the accustomed prices. He has at the moment no information which would rationally justify a lowering of his rents.

Keeping an apartment vacant, coupled with a continuous sampling of the market and calling information to the attention of potential buyers, thus forms an alternative to immediate and large rent reductions. Both alternatives involve costs: the direct purchase of other resources (advertising, real estate agents, etc.) or the allocation of one's own resources (showing customers around, etc.). The latter includes most particularly the cost of the immediately available lower revenue foregone by holding the apartment vacant. The resampling of the market yields, on the other hand, information on the maximum price obtainable. The more a supplier samples the market, the greater is the probability that he will find somone willing to pay a higher price; and the higher this price, the greater the return for the landlord. The returns diminish, though, as the period of resampling and information distribution lengthens. On the other side, the marginal cost of information persists or may even increase; and so the landlord will reach a point where he will maximize his profits. A bargain is struck at the best price sampled at the moment. Under this wealth-maximizing action, however, emerges an unused, an "idle" resource, viz. vacant apartments. Yet simply to call these apartments "idle resources" is dangerously misleading. It conveys an impression of functionless, useless, and inefficient waste; and this is not necessarily the case. Vacancy emerges from a rational use of resources in the face of incomplete information and substantial adjustment costs. Holding apartments vacant implies, under the circumstances indicated, a more economical usage of resources, in response to the relevant operation of informational and adjustment costs.

THE SAME FORMAL analysis applies to any asset, as, for example, labor. The workers' search for jobs and the employers' search for employees, the collection of information about jobs and employee characteristics, do not proceed without substantial costs. Moreover, the adjustment of the supply of labor services to the range of new job opportunities is not costless; neither is the hiring and firing of employees. A discharged worker could always find a job, quite immediately, at a sufficiently low wage. Yet if the market indicated up to the time he was discharged that he could reasonably expect to find jobs at accustomed conditions and the inherited wage, he would reject the option of an immediate job at lower wages and prefer to sample the market through appropriate search activities. The search would involve costs of various types, foremost of course the potential wage forfeited by remaining unemployed and searching for a job of the same type and wage as the old. The nature of the prevailing relief and unemployment benefit systems modifies this cost, and thus affects the outcome substantially. This sampling of the population of potential buyers of labor services supplies the unemployed worker with an expanding volume of information. If the market situation for his general skills is fundamentally unchanged, the repeated resampling yields a rising maximal wage offer. The rate of increase diminishes, however, with repeated sampling; and the worker will accept employment when marginal adjustment and inform-

759

ation costs (modified by benefits) threaten to exceed the expected increment in the maximal wage offered.

The market situation may, however, change fundamentally during a worker's search for one of two reasons: either because a change in the general supply conditions has permanently lowered the relative demand for his special skills, or because the aggregate demand for output is falling. In the first case, the information collected through persistent resampling of the market will always disappoint the worker. The low wage offers experienced will induce him eventually to readjust his anticipations and, consequently, his labor supply decision. This readjustment presents him with a choice between two courses of action: either to accept employment at substantially lower wages on the basis of unspecialized skills, or to invest some resources (and thus incur additional costs) in order to acquire new skills. In either case, he will eventually find employment — after possibly a substantial revision of anticipations and matching reservation prices.

In the second case, a different situation emerges. The initial anticipation level and reservation price of the discharged worker correspond to the information previously available through his employment. The unemployed worker thus samples the market with the anticipation of finding a similar job at the accustomed wage. But while he slowly acquires information, aggregate demand declines and thereby changes the phenomena sampled.

The maximal wage offers fail to rise in the manner expected and may even fall. Anticipation-level and reservation price will gradually be adjusted downwards, in the absence of legal or institutional constraints. Nevertheless, they will lag behind the decline in aggregate demand. An indefinite period of unemployment will eventually be absorbed as soon as the aggregate demand stablizes, even without a subsequent increase, though such an increase would be a necessary condition for absorption of unemployment in the case where institutional constraints prevent a downward adjustment of wages. Otherwise, this increase in business activity *accelerates* absorption.

THIS OUTLINE OF AN economic analysis of unemployment may be summarized in the following manner: Unemployment is broadly determined by: (a) the nature of the costs govering information gathering and adjustments in the types and directions of the labor supply (relief and benefit systems and opportunities for choice between employment and non-employment activities may play a crucial role at this point); (b) the magnitude and frequency of relative shifts in demand for products; (c) the magnitude and frequency of shifts in the supply conditions of product markets, particularly in the underlying technology shaping production; and (d) the comparative variability of aggregate demand for output. It is the variability relative to the prevailing speed of information diffusion and the associated adjustment speed of anticipations and reservation prices which actually matter in this context.

It follows from these considerations that larger marginal adjustment costs, smaller marginal information costs, and large and frequent demand shifts compounded by an accelerating technological impact on production tend to raise the average level of unemployment generated by the market process. Furthermore, the larger the relative variability of aggregate demand for output, the larger are the fluctuations of unemployment around its average

760

as determined by the above set of factors. [5]

The analysis outlined above, based on general economic theory, provides an interpretation of unemployment. It also determines a balance of social costs, the social cost of unemployment juxtaposed with the social cost of lowering average unemployment or holding its level below some ceiling. One may also use this analysis to investigate the nature of institutional arrangements which contribute to reduce both types of costs and, most particularly, assure a continuous close balance of the types of costs. [6] Moreover, we can extract some general information from this analysis about the impact of cybernation on the level of unemployment. The effect of cybernation essentially coincides with the broad pattern of consequences emanating from new technologies observed over a long period in the past. *It will effect the level of unemployment only in the cases where cybernation involves an accelerated rate of technological innovation. In addition, it would require a continuous acceleration in order to raise the average level of unemployment persistently.* So far the balance of evidence assembled by investigators of technological innovation yields little support for the assertion that innovation has been accelerated and definitely no support for the expectation of a *continuous* acceleration. This finding does not deny the existence of substantial social readjustment costs associated with the impact of cybernation; and one might legitimately raise the issue of the proper distribution of these costs. One could reasonably expect that cybernation would sharpen the wage differential between skilled and unskilled, and within the skilled group itself shift the balance of wages and employment conditions in favor of the professionally better educated. The readjustment costs and the differential impact on labor types will occur, however, independently of the level of unemployment due to the rate of acceleration of the cybernation process. Our analysis cannot be understood therefore to imply a smug indifference. It emphasizes, on the contrary, the importance of appropriate institutional arrangements designed to minimize the social adjustment costs associated with the continuous introduction of new technologies. Economic analysis can even be usefully applied to clarify the consequences of various arrangements for distributing these costs among different groups of our society. No rational choice among these arrangements can be made without careful application of this underlying analysis. [7]

761

5 The above analysis implies that the economic process continuously operates to absorb into employment the labor force supplied. Two major implications follow: (a) over the long-run, employment and employment potential move closely together; and (b) the length and magnitude of an expansion is correlated with the length and depth of the previous contraction. The first point has been emphasized by A.C. Pigou and the second particularly by Milton Friedman. The reader may be usefully reffered to the textbook by A.A. Alchian and W.R. Allen, *University Economics* (Belmont, Calif.: Wadsworth Pub. Co., 1964), chap. xxxi, p. 546. This chapter presents an excellent analysis of unemployed resources. My account has been strongly influenced by my discussions with Armen A. Alchian.

6 This formulation covers an attention devoted to monetary and fiscal policy designed to remove the pronounced accelerations or decelerations in aggregate demand (relative to the speed with which information is circulated) which has generated all major fluctuations in unemployment.

THIS ANALYSIS, BASED on validated economic theory, yields no "paradox of poverty amidst abundance" nor

7 My survey of "A Highly Miscellaneous and Imperfect Bibliography of the Triple Revolution," prepared by W. H. Ferry, yielded no indications or references to an analysis comparable to the analysis supplied by contemporary economic theory. Oral discussions with various signers of the *Manifesto* supplied no references to any analysis or evidence about the "change of the world." One signer admitted upon repeated questioning by Allen Metlzer that he had not analyzed the problem; but then, he simply *knew* that the world had changed.

any general erosion of employment opportunities. The *Manifesto of the Triple Revolution* is quite correct in its assertion that economic analysis denies such "paradoxes" and gloomy predictions. One might have reasonably expected, therefore, that the *Manifesto* would present (or refer to) an alternative analysis of economic processes, combined with a careful assessment of the relevant evidence which would enable us to appraise the comparative validity of the conflicting theories. At this point, however, an astonishing fact emerges. The prophets of the Triple Revolution have simply failed to provide any such alternative theory. Analysis appears to be replaced by the assertion that the structure of the world has fundamentally changed. As a result of this unspecified historical break, expanding poverty and rising unemployment are the necessary consequences of the patterns of innovation presently at work. Nevertheless, "observations" are adduced apparently as evidence in support of the non-existent analysis. The following are statements culled from the *Manifesto*: [8]

(1) It is noted that productivity per man-hour rose at an average pace above 3.5 per cent since 1961. This acceleration of productivity is attributed to the impact of new machinery.

(2) Prices of machines replacing labor are low compared to the annual wage of the replaced worker.

(3) It is increasingly more difficult to create the increment in aggregate demand necessary to absorb the growing labor force into employment.

(4) Unemployment rates averaged 5.7 per cent in the earlier 1960's. Teenage unemployment has risen steadily, and minorities exhibit a comparatively high unemployment rate.

(5) Nearly 4 per cent of the labor force sought full-time work in 1962 but could find only part-time jobs.

(6) Many men and women stopped looking for employment and withdrew from the labor force. It is reasonable to estimate that over 8 million people are not working who would like to have jobs today as compared with the 4 million shown in the official statistics.

(7) The number voluntarily withdrawn from the labor force is continuously increasing.

(8) Labor force participation rates are declining.

(9) The stablization of the unemployment rate at 5.5 per cent does not reflect the market's absorption of labor into employment but rather withdrawal of discouraged would-be workers from the labor force.

(10) During the period 1957 to 1962 more than half of the new jobs were created in the public sector. The private sector almost ceased to create new jobs, with the exception of the service industries.

THE STATEMENTS listed above contain a weird mixture of interpretative assertions, vague conjectures, and observations. Some of the statements have simply no bearing as evidence for the *Manifesto's* thesis, but instead contribute to an appropriate psychological receptivity on the part of unwary readers (including the signers of the *Manifesto*?). This applies particularly to points (1), (2), (4), (8), and (10). All these points are quite consistent with an explanation based on the previously developed analysis of no discriminating evidence and thus no support for the *Manifesto's* central thesis. It should be noted, in particular, that the unemployment patterns alluded to under point (4) are quite closely associated with the repeated extensions of minimum wage laws and the rise in minimum wages. Economic analysis implies that both the extension and increase in minimum wages will raise the unemployment rate of teenagers and of the least skilled workers. It is especially Negroes, therefore, who are unfavorably affected by the legisla-

---

[8] I found almost no useful material bearing on this aspect in supplementary writings.

tors' desire "to help the poor."[9] Similarly, the observed variations in the growth rate of labor productivity can be explained within the framework of economic analysis. Neither recent growth rates nor observed accelerations assume levels significantly different from past cyclical experiences. Moreover, the growth rate declined somewhat in the past year and the current year compared to the levels reached in the earlier expansion phases. These observations yield little support, indeed, for the *Manifesto's* thesis of a revolutionary breakthrough.

Point (2) deserves some further attention. The statement, while emotively suggestive, is almost meaningless. Information about the machine price relative to the annual wage is not sufficient to yield implications bearing on our issue. And point (3), of course, is not an observation: It remains a sheer unsupported conjecture suggested by the retardation of the economic process over the period 1957 to 1961 compared to the movements before 1957. The sluggish retardation of the 1950's has been replaced meanwhile by a surging and maintained expansion. Both retardation and subsequent acceleration, nevertheless, require an explanation.

The upswing, beginning in 1949 and ending in the summer of 1953, was supported by a substantial monetary expansion. As a matter of fact, the growth rate of the monetary base (i.e., the volume of high-powered money is-

sued by the Federal Reserve authorities) accelerated until 1952 and moved to levels not reached since 1945. The resulting surge in aggregate demand continued to lower unemployment rates even beneath the typical sharp decline accompanying the first phase of an upswing. A different pattern emerged with the upswing beginning in the late summer of 1954. The initial acceleration in the monetary base was suddenly broken in 1955 and its subsequent growth rate was held to a comparatively low level and even declined gradually during 1957. Some indications suggest that money demand contracted over the middle 1950's. This fall contributed to maintain the initially acquired momentum for some time in spite of the retardation in the base.[10] Still, the pronounced deceleration of the monetary base probably weakened somewhat the movement of aggregate demand. Unemployment declined sharply for some months but resisted further erosion after that. The next cyclic period, beginning in early 1958 and terminating around the middle of 1960, was characterized by a pronounced acceleration of the monetary base followed by a remarkable deceleration. The early acceleration contributed to prolong the rapid decline of unemployment rates from their peak until the turn of the year 1958/59. But the sudden deceleration obstructed absorption of unemployment beyond this level. Unemployment thus rose at the beginning of the downswing from a higher low point than before. Furthermore, the sharply restrictive monetary policies were not attenuated by changing demand factors which contributed to raise the velocity of spending. The period from 1957 to 1961 may very well be characterized as a time of comparative monetary restriction. This

763

---

9 Many well-meaning people are deeply offended when informed of this effect of minimum wages. The offense is frequently so great that analysis and evidence are simply disregarded. Emotive commitments easily dominate cognitive commitments. This behavior is, however, closely associated with a pervasive misconception, viz., that moral judgments are a sufficient condition for policy actions. The role of analysis, of a necessary knowledge about the structure of social processes, seems to escape the professional moralizers. One could reasonably argue that proper cognition also deserves a moral obligation. If one accepts this obligation one will wonder about the singular immorality of the professional moralizers who implicitly deny this particular moral obligation. Is it because it is too dangerous and inconvenient?

---

10 The reader may usefully consult the chapters on postwar velocity in the superb book by M. Friedman and A. J. Schwartz, *A Monetary History of the United States, 1867-1960* (Princeton: National Bureau of Economic Research, 1963).

monetary restriction differentiates this period from both the early postwar adjustment phase (1945 to 1949) and the first post-adjustment phase (1949 to 1957). The monetary restriction resulted in higher unemployment, a serious retardation of employment in the private sector, and sluggish movement of production and Gross National Product. Monetary policy was however decisively reversed in 1961. There emerged the longest acceleration in the monetary base ever observed and attributable to Federal Reserve action since the Federal Reserve started operations in 1914. Moreover, this acceleration pushed the growth rate of the monetary base to levels not observed since the war. This remarkable monetary expansion gradually and persistently lowering unemployment rates, contrary to the "cacotopian gloom" of the Triple Revolution, was also accompanied by a rapid expansion of production. Gross National Product, and even employment in the private sector.

The comparative stagnation of employment in the private sector from 1957 to 1961/62 was thus a consequence of a severe monetary restriction. If this stagnation had been the first symptom of the cybernation revolution, as suggested by the *Manifesto* and its supplementary elaborations, then the subsequent movements of private employment and unemployment could not have occured. Yet they did occur and they were the natural outcome of a historic monetary expansion most admirably engineered by the Federal Reserve authorities. [11]

UNDER THE STIMULUS of an appropriate monetary and fiscal policy, the market process created ample opportunities for employment. The relevant development may be usefully sketched with the aid of the comparative movements of *employment* and *employment potential*. The latter describes the "portion of the total population which is of approximate working age." [12] Such a comparison is particularly pertinent for the appraisal of points (6) and (7) mentioned above. These assertions made by the *Manifesto* would merit attention if the population's employment potential grew substantially more than actual employment. Morover, the *Manifesto's* case rests chiefly on an accelerated divergence of employment and employment potential since the turn of the decade. From 1948 to 1964 total population at working age (twenty to sixty-four) rose at an average rate of 0.9 per cent, whereas employment rose at an average rate of 1.07 per cent. "Since April 1961, while total employment has increased at a 1.7 per cent annual rate, population aged twenty to sixty-four is estimated to have increased at a rate of about 1.1 per cent per annum, and population aged eighteen to sixty-four increased at a 1.3 per cent rate. [13] Thus, it follows that, contrary to the assertions trumpeted in the *Manifesto,* jobs and employment have been growing more rapidly than the population of working age. The assertions made by the Triple Revolution group simply have no basis.

---

[11] The observations noticed expose the falshood of point (9). First, the unemployment rate was not stablized at 5.5 per cent, but fell gradually. Secondly, if unemployment rates had been kept from rising by the withdrawal of "discouraged and defeated" workers from the labor force, one would expect employment — particularly private employment — and the labor force to be stationary. All three magnitudes rose persistently, however; and the statement under point (9) is quite untenable.

[12] This quote and the material summarized is from the *Federal Reserve Bank of St. Louis Review*, XLVI (Oct. 1964), 1-4.

[13] The assertion under point (6) that 8 million people would like to work in addition to the 4 million officially reported to be unemployed is almost fantastic. There is not even a hint of a suggestion how this figure is "reasonably estimated." Neither is there even a clue to an analysis which determines such "reasonable" estimation. Furthermore, my survey of the literature yielded no material elucidating this assertion.

Observations on the relative parti cipation of various population groups in the labor force yield additional information bearing on the relevance of the *Manifesto's* ideas. The participation rate of males in the labor force declined from 84.5 per cent in 1947 to 78.6 per cent in 1964. The participation rate of females rose on the other hand from 31 per cent to 37.4 per cent over the same period. The observation makes little sense if one believes that machines remove workers from the labor force and that service industries are increasingly exposed to the calamity of cybernation.

Still there remains the decline in the participation rate of males. How is this to be explained? It is important to recognize that this decline results from the falling participation rates of two specific age groups. Males between fourteen and nineteen years lowered their participation rate from 54.3 per cent in 1947 to 43.6 per cent in 1964, and males sixty-five and over lowered their rates from 47.8 per cent to 28 per cent over the same period. A slight decline can also be found for the age group fifty-five to sixty-four. The other age groups show either no significant change or even a slight increase. Moreover, there is no indication of any break in the participation of the middle group in the labor force. The assertions listed under points (5) and (7) simply do not hold for the central core of our working age population.

But what about teenagers and the oldest group? Do they not confirm the claims of the *Manifesto*? The answer is, No. Cybernation cannot be used to explain the peculiar pattern of evolving participation rates. The wholesale destruction of jobs under the Cybernation Revolution would create a random pattern of discouragement and defeat involving also the broad range from twenty years to fifty-five years. It would also affect the females over twenty years, whose participation rates have all been rising. What actually occurred

is that considerable extension of the Social Security system, of pension plans and associated devices, expanded income outside of employment for older age groups. This gradual change in opportunities modified the comparative advantages and disadvantages of retirement and induced a growing number of older people to prefer a retirement status. It should be noted however that this process operated only on the male worker and is only reflected in the male participation rates. Our argument does not apply to the females, and we do observe that their participation rate in the age group fifty-five to sixty-four rose by 66 per cent from 1947 to 1964 and even increased slightly for those sixty-five and older. Once more, this movement yields no support for the thesis of wholesale and widely ramified job destruction through cybernation.[14] The decline of teenage participation also can be understood as a response to peculiar institutional changes and expanding wealth. Expanded schooling has created opportunities for additional education, and increasing income has enabled families to exploit these opportunities. Repeated extentions of the minimum wage laws may also have contributed to the withdrawal of teenagers from the labor force and induced them to stay longer in school.[15] Moreover, the decline in the teenagers'

14 A survey article prepared by Jacob Mincer adduces some noteworthy observations which bear on the interpretation of the decline in the participation rates of older men. "In 1951, 22 per cent of retired claimed layoffs as a cause of retirement; only 9 per cent claimed it in 1963." Moreover, "compulsory retirement age was quoted by 22 per cent recently, compared to 11 per cent in 1951; poor health by 35 per cent, compared to 41 per cent earlier; and preferences for leisure by 17 per cent, compared to 3 per cent in 1951." *Labor Force Participation and Unemployment: A Review of Recent Events,* unpublished manuscript.

15 The reader may find the following passages from Jacob Mincer's manuscript illuminating. The age group fourteen to seventeen "had particularly severe declines during three cyclical troughs, as well as from fifty to fifty-one, fifty-five through fifty-seven, and sixty to sixty-one. The latter...and two former declines coincide

participation rate is a long-run phenomenon and exhibits no acceleration in the last five to ten years. This observation again is difficult to reconcile with the claims advanced by the *Manifesto*.

THE PECULIAR assertions listed under points (5) and (7) possibly refer to the existence of "disguised unemployment." This phenomenon is associated with the cyclical sensitivity of the labor force, i.e., the partial dependence of the labor force on aggregate demand. It follows therefore that reported unemployment understates the actual loss in employment occurring during a downswing. The disguised loss of employment has been estimated in several ways. Moreover, it has been suggested on occasion that reported and "disguised" unemployment are both components of some complete measure of employment loss. A more careful examination, based on economic analysis, renders this conception very dubious. The additivity of the two groups appears in the context of an argument which postulates that absorption of labor into employment from either group occurs at approximately equal net levels of marginal productivity; and most particularly, the marginal productivity of the unemployed in either group is supposed to be zero. This assumption is very doubtful, indeed. A growing number of people possess a meaningful choice between employment and non-employment activities, and in the marginal productivity (or marginal utility) of these non-employment activities may be quite substantially above zero. The

relevant attraction of such non-employment activities is mirrored in the large turnover of participants in the labor force. An average participation ratio of 50 per cent does not mean that 50 per cent of the population is always in the labor force and 50 per cent is never in the labor force. There prevails a frequency distribution of participation time. Some people participate more continuously, others much less, and the resulting average over a given period yields 50 per cent. But this very behavior reveals the existence of attractive alternatives to employment activities. The positive marginal productivity of non-employment activities existing for a number of groups implies that the opportunity costs of job-searching and job-assessment (i.e. the costs of information) are quite sizeable. It follows therefore that "the net gain from moving into the labor force and the net loss from leaving it...can be quite small" for this group of people. The existence of non-employment activities with positive marginal productivity determines a pronounced supply elasticity with respect to market conditions — changing market conditions induce substitutions between employment and non-employment activities. Under these conditions, merely adding together reported and "disguised" unemployment misconceives the nature of productive labor. Additivity also misconstrues and badly exaggerates the loss in welfare terms. The opportunities for non-employment activities are particularly relevant for the so-called secondary labor groups, which include a good portion of the females, and the older and single males. The behavior of this secondary group confirms our supposition: The labor force participation of this group is remarkably responsive to employment conditions. The substitution elasticity between employment and non-employment conditions of this group induces a sensitive shift in time allocation between employment and non-employment activities. This analysis of "disguised unemployment"

---

with Federal increases in minimum wages and the extension of coverage. Since 1956 this group had a drastic increases in unemployment with little change afterward. ...Supporting evidence for the probable role of minimum wages in the labor market experience of this group is provided in a regression analysis of teenage unemployment by Arnold Katz...."

eliminates the *Manifesto's* assertions listed under points (5) and (7) from further consideration until some analysis worthy of attention is supplied.

Unemployment data mean very little by themselves; they require careful interpretation, and only analysis supported by relevant evidence yields a reliable interpretation. The movements of unemployment figures must be considered within the context of shifting patterns created by a changing and expanding economic system. This applies especially to the interpretation of the apparent growth of unemployment since the early fifties. No doubt, unemployment rates during the 1958 recession exceeded the unemployment rates during the 1954 recession. Similarly, unemployment rates during the upswing initiated in 1958 exceeded the unemployment rates during the expansion of 1954 to 1957. During the recession of 1961, however, unemployment rates were lower than at the previous low point and were also lower than during the recession of 1949. In addition, unemployment rates in the autumn of 1965 were close to unemployment rates in late 1948. This evolution in employment rates yields little support for the apocalyptic assertion of a total discontinuity in the nature of the economic process occurring around the turn of the decade. On the other hand, there exists some evidence suggesting that average unemployment rates will gradually rise with increasing affluence given our values and institutional arrangements. Increasing

16 The passage in the text is also based on the manuscript by Jacob Mincer previously mentioned. We may again usefully quote from this manuscript: "Given some scope for timing of their activities, work in the labor market will be preferred at times when search costs are low and job conditions attractive....The optimization of timing of labor force activities creates the illusion of disguised unemployment. The more economical the timing, the larger the number of disguised unemployed.... The paradox simply reflects the myopic preoccupation with GNP, when broader considerations motivate behavior."

wealth raises the demand for schooling and also the demand for leisure. More extensive enrollment in schools induces a lower labor force participation of younger people, while Social Security arrangements and pensions exert a similar effect on the older age groups. The decreasing labor force participation of these groups reveals itself predominantly through an increasing proportion of intermittent work, increased labor turnover, and an increased proportion of inexperienced workers among both employed and unemployed. These trends are reinforced by the growing participation of women. The range of relevant tradeoffs between employment and nonemployment activities will continue to grow. This change in the structure of employment is a natural response to expanding opportunities and not a symptom of impending catastrophe. Slowly rising unemployment rates are therefore not a harbinger of growing and entrenced poverty but the epiphenomenon of deepening affluence and a broader range of relevant choices. Should this argument be supported by subsequent analysis and evidence we would conclude that *unemployment rates of the primary group consisting of males between twenty-five and fifty-four years of age provide a much better index of the unemployment situation.* This central core group probably reflects the movements of "involuntary unemployment" much more reliably. Interestingly enough, these data substantially refute the dismal projections of the *Manifesto of the Triple Revolution.*

767

ECONOMIC ANALYSIS yields no case for the Triple Revolution. Of course, the Masters of the *Manifesto* were aware that "conventional analysis" denies their assertions, so they have dismissed economic analysis.[17] It is quite clear, however, that they fail completely to understand the nature of this analysis, why it rejects their assertions, and on precisely what grounds. They provide no critical examination of any empirical theories supported by economics nor any reference to such examinations; nor do we find a comparison of the merits of received economic theories, which have successfully explained observable phenomena, with a carefully and explicitly constructed alternative theory justifying their contentions. Similarly, any careful analysis of the institutional arrangements which are suggestively proposed in order to ease the pain of transition is completely absent. The behavior patterns and the consequences which may be expected to arise from these proposed arrangements pose a serious problem both for the general welfare and for the survival of an open society. Even less is heard about the ultimate society of happy, just, and de-alienated abundance. They tell us nothing of the nature of such a society, of its institutional arrangements and its general mode of behavior. Are we supposed to infer the emergence of a millenium, a paradise maintained for "humanized man" with "creatively adjusted highest values"?

The fundamentally metaphysical character of the whole Triple Revolution venture comes into focus in many details. Analysis and evidence are dismissed in favor of emotive phillipics — a play on words replaces analysis, moral agonizing and impressionistic references substitute for evidence. The play on the words "scarcity" and "abundance," for instance, provides an excellent example of the irresponsible misuse of language, of the surreptitiously emotive use of a pretended cognitive category. The economist applies the term "scarcity" to describe the relative limitation of an inherited resource situation in the context of a given technology. This limitation exists relative to the values pursued by individual members of a society. Scarcity is reflected in the curcumstances that every allocation of resources to particular tasks involves a sacrifice of some other valuable tasks; and this fact continues to exist even with cybernation. No society of our empirical world will ever be able to extract from its resources a total satiation of the wants of every member of that society. The principle of scarcity continues to prevail even in very affluent societies. The prophets of the Triple Revolutionary paradise carelessly shift the meaning of their words from "abundance" as denial of the economist's "scarcity" to "abundance" as an emotive-effective description of a large and rising real income per capita. From such a confusion of concepts, only confusion can result.

A similarly effective usage dominates the term "facts." Direct observations, interpretive guesses, and wild conjectures are equally referred to as "facts." No doubt, facts may be hard to recognize; but not *that* hard, provided the difference between metaphysical speculation and empirical-rational procedures is maintained. The impresssionistic misuse of language, in particular, is such as to constitute a scandal. Innumerable examples of this could be adduced. Here is a brief sampler:

...people are increasingly outside ...our social structure. ... [18]

17 This dismissal is not complete. It certainly applies to price theory, the explanation of market and allocation processes. However, the Masters appear to accept a somewhat naive version of Keynesian theory. On p. 6 of the *Manifesto*, military expenditures are presented as a "strong prop" of the economy. It appears that reductions in government expenditures would exert serious deflationary consequences independent of other policies, e.g., monetary policies. There is at present no evidence in support of such a position. The recently published Grand Debate in the *American Economic Review* LV (1965), 753-92, agrees at least on one point: the simple textbook versions of Keynesian-type theories, which apparently influenced the *Manifesto's* statement, may be safely shelved.

18 Helstein, *Jobs, Machines, and People*, p. 2.

768

Vague allusions to scientists working for the joy of achievement appear sufficient to justify a totally new society which does not have to rely on wealth incentives.[19] And look at this hoary fallacy:

In the society of scarcity, one man's well-being could be increased only at the expense of other men's well-being.... [20]

Michael Harrington pronounces that "the question of collectivism has been settled."[21] A survey of his writings shows, however, no analysis nor even a remote hint of relevant evidence supporting this claim. Or, catch this one:

...Technology is in charge and men are not in charge.[22]

And an absolutely delicious example:

...at precisely the moment all economic problems disappear... we would have a finished society in which men would die not from floods or plagues or famines, not from their own idiocies about the economy. They would die from death, and at that point the historical shell around the fact of death would be broken. For the first time society would face up to death itself.[23]

A favorite procedure of the group involves references to single examples to support far-reaching generalizations. This applies particularly to the relation between cybernation-automation and unemployment.

The dislocation and disemployment that occur simply add the people to the twenty million families some of whom by now have had several generations living in this state.[24]

Or, we may read:

But these sectors, which have been soaking up the disemployed from productive and extractive functions, are beginning to fail to soak them up. New jobs are *not* being created in these fields. [25]

Both statements are, of course, palpably false. The first implies that unemployment should increase at a rate equal to gross dismissals from work. This assertion is immediately rejected by observation. Piel's contention cannot survive exposure to observations on the movement of employment in non-manufacturing activities outside the government sector.

THE IMPRESSIONISTIC misuse of language is particularly reflected in a persistent confusion of value statements and cognitive statements. The proper separation of the two types of statements has been painfully slow in man's history, and the distinction is often felt to endanger most of man's elaborate constructions for orienting himself in a manner satisfying to his psychological needs. The logical clarification of these statements has therefore encountered deep-seated hostility. The careful separation of value assertions and theoretical statements forms, however, an absolutely crucial precondition for any progress of knowledge. This does not preclude their interaction in the analysis of rational action; but the explicit recognition of the mutual spheres of value assertions and cognitive statements exhibits the logical impossibility of deriving factual statements or even policy statements from value assertions only.

A major consequence of the tangled confusion involving valuations and theoretical statements deserves particular attention. As human beings, we do not respond at random to the various types of statements. Reactions to value judgements are much more pronounced than those to cognitive statements.

769

---

19 *Ibid.*, pp. 21-22
20 *Ibid.*, p. 23.
21 *Cacatophia or Utopia*, p. 8.
22 *Ibid.*, p. 12.
23 *Ibid.*, p. 21.
24 Hellstein, *Jobs, Machines, and People*, p. 5.

25 Piel, *Ibid.*, p. 6.

This response pattern creates a surreptitious domination of value judgements over intellectual processes. A pervasive effect of the very language we use strengthens this pattern. The apparently autonomous existence of language induces a belief that since value judgements are articulated in sentences which exhibit the same grammatical form as cognitive statements, the two types of statements are of the same logical form. Cognition thus becomes irrelevant and even appears obstructive to the reformation of the world in the light of one's valuation. At the very base of the Triple Revolution is rejection of critical analysis; we can thus recognize a radical rejection of man's noblest achievement: his struggle, always endangered by entrenched ideologies, to respond intelligently to the challenge of his environment through a systematization of an ancient trial and error procedure.

An act of faith thus replaces the empirical assessment of human institutions; and the patiently piecemeal but reliable improvement of our lot is sacrificed to a dream.

Agnosticism and Morality

HENRY HAZLITT

I THINK I SHOULD begin with a confession of faith — or lack of faith. I am an agnostic. Having made this confession, I think I should go on to say just what an agnostic is, and is not, and just what kind of agnostic I consider myself to be.

An agnostic is, first of all, a man who confesses his own ignorance — specifically, his own ignorance of the ultimate nature of the universe, of the ultimate destiny of man, of whether the universe has or has not a "purpose," and finally, of whether there is or is not a God or Supreme Being governing the universe.

It is possible to define an agnostic by two negatives: Although, on the one hand, he is not convinced of the existence of God, he is not certain of His non-existence either. A man who declares himself to be an atheist declares that there is no God. The agnostic replies that such a statement is mere dogmatism, and assumes knowledge and evidence that do not exist. Yet, there is a wide range of possible differences, intellectual and emotional, among agnostics; and I think I should explain just where I stand in that spectrum. An agnostic may merely be one who confesses his

Henry Hazlitt is a Contributing Editor of *Newsweek*, and author of a number of books, among them *Economics in One Lesson, The Foundations of Morality,* and *The Failure of the New Economics.*

personal ignorance of whether or not there is a God. He may be willing to admit that perhaps others know, or *can* know, or at least that mankind may *someday* know. I should not blankly deny this last possibility, but I regard it as enormously improbable.

771

The human intellect is wonderful, judged by animal standards; it has recently shown itself capable of accomplishments that a highly intelligent man before the birth of Aristotle would have thought impossible, and, in fact, of accomplishments that would have amazed even Leibnitz or Newton or Darwin. Yet the human intellect is primarily an instrument for dealing with practical problems. While it is capable of amazingly abstract concepts, it can carry back the chain of cause and effect only for a finite and limited distance. This little animal brain, weighing three or four pounds, and these limited animal senses, were not evolved to comprehend infinite time or space, or the complexity of an infinite number of facts; or a First Cause.

The human brain has, of course, achieved wonderful results by inventing and manipulating symbols, as in mathematics; but these results, I think, lead us to deceive ourselves as to the true extent of our knowledge. Any man can *say* "a million," or "a billion," or a "hundred billion," and write down the symbols or perform various operations with them in a matter of seconds or minutes; but how many men can have a true conception of even a million —a million dollars or a million miles or a million anything else: As an economic journalist I have been stuck, in recent years, with how little impression it makes on people to tell them that we have a five billion dollar budget deficit, or that we have given away more than one hundred billion dollars in foreign aid.

The more a man knows, the more he realizes the extent of his ignorance, and the greater that ignorance seems to him. One of the most striking examples of this is Sir Isaac Newton, the greatest intellect of his age, and possibly the greatest that has ever lived: "I do not know what I may appear to the world," he wrote, "but to myself I seem to have been only a boy playing on the seashore, and diverting myself in now and then finding a smoother pebble or a prettier shell than ordinary, whilst the great ocean of truth lay all un-discovered before me."

I became an agnostic, as I remember, at the age of seventeen or eighteen; and I gave up my belief in God and human immortality painfully and reluctantly. Today my agnosticism is more thor-oughgoing than it was then. I remember being for some time attracted by Herbert Spencer's concept of the Unknowable; but I later decided that Spencer knew too much about the Unknowable. He knew that it *was* un-knowable; he seemed also to know just where the Unknowable began, and the exact dividing line between it and the Knowable. I decided that none of these things were known and probably could not be known.

Today I am not sure that I know even the meaning of the ultimate religious or philosophical *questions*, let alone the positive or negative answers. What is the meaning of the question: "Is there a God?" or "Is there a Supreme Being?" What is the meaning of the answer: "There *is* a God" or "There is no God"? How would we establish whether either answer is true? What sort of evidence would we look for to establish the truth or the probable truth of our answer? What necessary consequences would follow from the truth or falsity of either answer? What necessary difference, for example, would the truth or falsity of either answer make in our own earthly goals or our own conduct?

What sort of concept lies behind the words either of the theist or the atheist, "Do you believe in a personal God?" What is meant by "personal" in this connection? That God looks like a human being—like the God painted by Michelangelo on the ceiling of the Sistine Chapel, for example? That he is the size of a human being? Or twice the size? Or how many times the size? That he has a definite location in space—"in h e a v e n," for example? That he is "within us"? Like a microbe? Exactly what does this spacial metaphor mean, and is it consistent with belief in a "personal" God? Or does a "personal" God simply think or feel like a human being? Think with our limitations, or without them? Feel the way a person feels? But in what respect? Surely not in physical appetites, or in sexual drive, or in energy or fatigue, or in ambition or frustration, or in seeing the same things as beautiful, indifferent, or ugly—or in showing the same tastes and responses that make up at least nine-tenths of all human feelings and actions.

LET US ABANDON THESE insoluble problems and come to a problem that seems at first glance more soluble. Let us ask: How do, or how should, our intellectual answers—whether theism, atheism, or agnosticism —affect our *attitude* toward the universe—our trusts and hopes and f e a r s, for our-selves or for mankind, our goals, our morality, our attitude towards each other? A large number of modern philos-ophers have concluded, in despair of knowing what to *believe,* that the essence or religion *is* simply such an attitude. I have myself been attracted by the statement of Gerald Heard, for example, that the essence of religion is a belief that the universe is friendly;

772

but this attitude of trust in the universe, as regards its intentions towards mankind, rests on a belief. What is the ground or justification for this belief? To be sure, the universe has been friendly enough toward man *in the past* to make it possible for him to evolve, to multiply, to live longer, and to increase his material satisfactions enormously. What reason, though, do we have for assuming that this will go on indefinitely, that the earth will not grow cold—or collide with a comet or some other body? Hurricanes, tornadoes, floods, droughts, and earthquakes are, after all, a matter of annual occurrence, and seem to be entirely indifferent to our human hopes or prayers.

I have given time to confessing and explaining my reasons for doubt. I am not triumphant about my doubts. I am not eager to infect anybody else with them. I am not eager to undermine anyone else's religious faith. In brief, I am not eager to *argue* for my doubts; I am merely trying to explain them.

What I do wish to state, however, is my conviction that *one's belief or lack of belief on religious matters neither logically should, nor in fact does, affect one's actions, goals, and moral conduct to anything like the extent that is commonly imagined*. This conviction rests on both empirical and on deductive grounds. Those who are acquainted with the history of moral philosophy know that there is no sharp and consistent difference between the moral injunctions preached by the pagan philosophers and by the early Christian philosophers. There is no sharp and consistent difference between the "justice" of Socrates and Plato, between the "golden mean," the "temperance" and the "high-mindedness" of Aristotle, between the virtues preached by the Stoic philosophers, by Epictetus with his counsels to "endure" and "refrain," by Marcus Aurelius and his precept to "reverence the gods and help men" — and the virtues recommended by, say, Thomas Acquinas. In fact, as Henry Sidgwick reminds us: "The moral philosophy of Thomas Aquinas is, in the main, Aristotelianism with a Neo-Platonic tinge." And when Aquinas lists the moral virtues by which others receive their due, his list of such virtues, to the number of ten, "is taken *en bloc* from the *Nicomachean Ethics*."[1]

It is not merely in moral philosophy, however, but in prevailing commonsense ethics, that we find, in spite of peripheral differences, a great central core of agreement in the moral codes of different nations and peoples and even of historical eras, notwithstanding fundamental differences in religion. Practically all widely-shared moral codes have been *against* domestic murder and violence, law-breaking, looting, banditry, theft, ingratitude, treachery, lying, promise-breaking, etc. Practically all such codes have been *for* law and order, domestic peaceableness, promise-keeping, truth-telling, loyalty, mutual aid, good manners, etc.; and all this for the simple reason that justice and morality are absolutely indispensable for the very preservation of society.

For the same reason, whatever different names they may have given to it, or whatever aspect they may have emphasized, all moral codes have implicitly recognized that the very function and goal of a moral code is, on the negative side, to prevent or minimize violence, conflict and strife; and on the positive side, to promote human well-being and happiness. The minimum goal of our moral rules is to avoid conflict and collision, to learn how to keep out of each other's way. In a wider setting moral rules are necessary so that we can all reasonably count on each other's statements, promises, and

---

1 *Outlines of the History of Ethics* (1886), pp. 141-42.

773

actions, so that we not only may avoid acting at cross-purposes but can co-operate with each other to promote our mutual welfare.

TOO MUCH TIME HAS been wasted in moral philosophy in comparing or contrasting the relative necessity and merits of "egoism" and "altruism." There is no basic conflict, but co-incidence and harmony, between the rules of action that would do most to promote the welfare of the individual and those that would do most to promote the welfare of society. One could hardly promote one without promoting the other, or harm one without harming the other. It is in the interest of every individual to live in an orderly, peaceful, secure, co-operative—i.e., a moral—society. Social co-operation is the heart of morality, and the means by which each of us can most effectively supply his own wants and maximize his own satisfactions.

Whether or not a man believes in God, he has exactly the same reasons for following the rules of prudential ethics. If he is an idler, a spendthrift, or a gambler, a glutton, a drunkard, or a drug addict, he will pay the same penalties for his sins in the one case as in the other. Whether or not a man believes in God, he has exactly the same reasons for obeying the traffic laws: they exist for his own protection as well as the protection of others, and if he violates them he takes the same risks with his own life as well as the same risks with the law. Finally, whether or not a man believes in God, he is likely to have the same sympathy with his fellow men, the same respect for their opinion, the same desire for their good will, and the same impulse to act decently towards them. "It is a curious assumption of religious moralists," once wrote Santayana, "that their precepts would never be adopted unless people were persuaded by external evidence that God had positively established them. Were it not for divine injunction and threats,

everyone would like nothing better than to kill and to steal and to bear false witness."[2] The religious moralists who hold this view assume that those who do not believe in God are moral only because they are afraid of being caught. Yet their own argument also assumes that religious people are moral chiefly because they believe that God will reward them if they are, and punish them if they are not.

Those who are truly moral, in fact, whether theists, agnostics, or atheists, are so because they believe that virtue is its own reward, and sin its own punishment. They believe that good actions promote human well-being, including their own, and that evil actions injure others as well as themselves. In brief, whether we are Catholics, Protestants, Jews, agnostics, or atheists, we can agree on essentially the same moral code. If most of us, even if we are professed Christians, cannot always bring ourselves to love each other, most of us, religious or non-religious, can be brought to see the advantages of being decent and polite and even kind to each other.

Morality, in other words, is autonomous; it is not dependent on one's religion. As Stephen Toulmin has put it, writing from the standpoint of a religious man:

Where there is a good moral reason for choosing one course of action rather than another, morality is not to be contradicted by religion. Ethics provides the *reason* for choosing the "right" course: religion helps us to put our *hearts* into it.[3]

Finally, as William James wrote: "Whether a God exist, or whether no God exist, in yon blue heaven above us bent, we form at any rate an ethical republic here below."[4] This, I think, is the best if not the only basis on which

2 *Dominations and Powers* (New York: Scribners, 1951), p. 156.
3 *An Examination of the Place of Reason in Ethics* (Cambridge: Cambridge University Press, 1950), p. 219.
4 "The Moral Philosopher and the Moral Life," (1891), in *Pragmatism and other Essays* (New York: Washington Square Press, 1963), p. 223.

774

it is possible for the religious and the non-religious to co-operate intellectually in moral, legal, and political philosophy.

This does not mean that any of us need abandon religious or ontological speculations. On the contrary, we should all strive to keep alive the sense of wonder and awe before the inscrutable mystery of the universe, before the tremendous mystery of existence—not merely of the existence of mankind, but of the existence of anything, the existence of a grain of sand, or of the planets, the sun, the solar system, the stars, the Milky Way, the constellations and galaxies without end. The difference between a philosopher and a philistine, between a thinking man and a Babbitt, is that the thinking man has not lost his sense of wonder. In his *Voyage of the Beagle*, Darwin tells us how, at one place where the ship anchored, the native savages were enormously curious about the rowboats in which the British came ashore; but they showed no interest in the ship itself. It was so far beyond their understanding that they simply took it for granted. It is a very limited and shallow mind that takes the existence and nature of the universe for granted.

LET US BY ALL MEANS keep alive our interest in ultimate questions; but let us recognize that they *are* ultimate questions, *final* questions. Our own conclusions on these matters, if we arrive at any, should not be made the necessary *premises* for agreement on practical actions or policy.

All of my readers are, I take it, devoted to a greater or lesser degree to liberty; and among the liberties that all of us hold most precious is liberty of opinion—for ourselves and for others. If we respect this, we will not insist that others must accept our own particular religious, epistemological, or ontological premises before we will even condescend to argue with them on moral, legal, or political questions.

775

Wage Rates, Minimum Wage Laws, and Unemployment

YALE BROZEN

ALONG WITH THE weather, sex, health, and taxes, one of the most widely discussed topics in America is wage rates. We have had an abundance of guide posts offered for determining the changes which should be made in wage rates. Union strategists have insisted in times past that wage rates should rise when the cost of living goes up, whatever "cost of living" may mean. They do not accept the converse proposition that wage rates should go down when the cost of living goes down, however. In the latter case, they argue that a decline in cost of living means a depression is coming or has arrived and, therefore, wage rates should be raised to increase purchasing power and prevent the depression.

Another guide post offered in times past (and last year by Mr. Reuther) concerns the relationship between wage rates and profits. Still another relates wage rates to an acceptable level of living. Most recently, wage rates and changes in them have been linked to changes in average output per man-hour. The General Motors contract of a decade ago provided for

changes in wage rates linked to the change in the consumer price index of middle income urban families, plus an annual improvement factor which happened to be approximately the same as the increase in output per man-hour in the American economy in the preceding several decades.

Four years ago last January, the Council of Economic Advisors entered the discussion of guide posts for wage rate increases. They were moved to do this because, as they said at the time, "...wage decisions affect the progress of the whole economy" and, therefore, "...there is legitimate reason for public interest in their content and consequences."[1] They repeated their suggested guide posts in 1964 because, as they said, "If cost...pressures should arise through the exercise of market power...we would be forced once more into the dreary calculus of the appropirate trade off between 'acceptable' additional unemployment and 'acceptable' inflation."

The Economic Advisers have advised that, "The general guide for wages is that the percentage increase in total employee compensation per man-hour

Yale Brozen is Professor of Business Economics at the University of Chicago and an Editorial Advisor to *New Individualist Review*. He has contributed a number of articles to professional journals.

1 "Annual Report of the Council of Economic Advisors," *Economic Report of the President* (Washington: Government Printing Office, 1962), p. 185.

be equal to the national trend rate of increase in output per man-hour."[2] The Council has provided a measure of recent trends (1952-64) in the annual rates of growth of output per man-hour in the private economy. They suggest that the latest five-year trend in productivity, amounting to 3.2 per cent, should be *the* guide for wage rate increases. They seem to believe that if wage rates plus fringe benefits in each industry rise by 3.2 per cent, then the average cost of labor will rise by 3.2 per cent.

If hourly labor costs increase by 3.2 per cent on the average *in each industry,* however, average compensation per man-hour would rise by 4 per cent. Many wage earners obtain wage increases by leaving low paying jobs (such as those in agriculture) for higher paying jobs — without any change in the rates paid for specific positions. The average wage does rise, then, without any change in wage rates, about 0.6 to 0.8 per cent per year. Subtracting this out of the 3.2 per cent rise in output per man-hour for the total private economy would imply that the Council's suggested guide rate would be achieved with an average annual rate of change of 2.5 per cent per year in money wage rates (including fringe benefits as part of the wage, or employee compensation) in each industry.

The Council does not believe that every wage rate should be increased exactly by the rate of overall productivity increase. Their report says that "specific modifications must be made to adapt (the guide posts) to the circumstances of the particular industry."[3] For instance, they say "Wage rate increases would fall short of the general guide rate in an industry *which could not provide jobs for its entire labor force.*"[4] Also, they would fall short where "wage rates are exceptionally high because the bargaining position of workers has been especially strong."[5]

THE COUNCIL OF Economic Advisors should be complimented for its recognition of the fact that wage rates in some industries are too high to permit all those who would like jobs in those industries to obtain them. They should also be complimented for recognizing that money wage rate increases must be smaller in the future if we are to have more rapid economic growth and decreased unemployment without inflation. The Council recognizes that the upward movement of some wage rates and prices is the result of agreements between strong unions and employers, and that "the post-Korean war years were marked by the coincidence of relatively large wage increases with declines in industry employment."[6] The fact that unduly high wage rates decrease the number of jobs available and the number of people working in an industry is obviously understood by the Council and is clearly implied in its report.

Several things are left unsaid, however, which should receive explicit recognition. The Council dwells on the inflation which may be caused by large wage rate increases. They fail to recognize that large wage rate increases for some workers come not only at the expense of causing some to become unemployed, absent inflation, but also at the expense of workers in other sectors of the economy.

I would estimate that 10 per cent of the labor force of the United States receives wage rates about 15 per cent

777

2 "Annual Report of the Council of Economic Advisors," *Economic Report of the President* (Washington: Government Printing Office, 1965), p. 108. This same advice appeared first in the 1962 report where the Advisors said, "The general guide for non-inflationary wage behavior is that the rate of increase in wage rates (including fringe benefits) in each industry be equal to the trend rate of over-all productivity increase." (p. 189)
3 "Annual Report of the Council of Economic Advisors," *Economic Report of the President* (Washington: Government Printing office, 1962), p. 189.

4 *Ibid.*
5 *Ibid.*
6 *Ibid.,* p. 175.

higher than they would in the absence of wage laws and governmental support of trade unions.[7] The result is that 90 per cent of the U.S. labor force receives wage rates about 5 per cent lower than they would otherwise obtain. The *net* result is greater inequality in the division of income and about 3 per cent less total wage income for U.S. wage earners, or about 10 billion dollars less than they would otherwise earn as a group (including those whose wage rate is excessive).

To illustrate this in terms of the experience of one state, let us consider some occurrences in Michigan. Wage rates in transportation equipment manufacturing in Michigan not only rose more than in other manufacturing industries in the state, but also rose, between 1950 and 1957, by 10 per cent more than in the *same* industry in the other four East North Central states (Wisconsin, Ohio, Indiana, and Illinois).[8] Overall employment in the auto industry declined in part as a result of overly large employment cost increases. In Michigan, where the greatest increase in wage rates occurred, the decline in employment was greater than for the industry as a whole. Between 1954 and 1958, there were 85,000 more jobs lost in Michigan than in the other four East North Central states. In 1954, Michigan employed 41,000 *more* workers in transportation equipment manufacturing than the other four states. In 1958 it employed 44,000 *fewer* workers in the industry than the other states. Michigan became a depressed area, in employment terms, largely because employment costs increased so drastically in its major industry.

7 For the data on which this estimate is based, see H.G. Lewis, *Unionism and Relative Wages in the United States* (Chicago: University of Chicago Press, 1963), pp. 8-9, 286-95.

8 S.P. Sobotka, "Michigan's Employment Problem: The Substitution Against Labor," *Journal of Business,* XXXIV (1961), 124. For a fuller treatment of the subject see S.P. Sobotka, *Profile of Michigan* (New York: Free Press of Glencoe, 1963).

Not only did employment in Michigan suffer; in addition, workers in other industries in Michigan suffered. Those becoming unemployed in the transportation equipment industry sought jobs in other fields. Many found jobs in other manufacturing industries. The consequence was, however, lower compensation for those in the other industries. More jobs were made available only by restricting the rise in wages which otherwise would have occurred. Hourly earnings in these "other" industries rose 6 per cent less than the rise in these same industries in the other four East North Central states. Although employment in these industries in Michigan increased more than in other states, this represents a less productive use of the labor than its employment in transportation equipment. If wage rates and other employment costs in transportation equipment had not been raised so much in Michigan, hourly earnings would have gone up more in the other manufacturing industries. High hourly earnings for auto workers came at the expense of workers in other industries.

THIS BRINGS US TO the second point which the Council failed to make explicit in its concern over the inflationary impact of unduly large wage rate increases. The power of unions is focused on certain sectors of the economy, such as transportation, auto manufacturing, and coal mining. Their use of power and the consent of employers to agreements which incorporate unduly high costs of employment decreases the number of jobs available in these sectors of the economy. Since these are industries in which output per man-hour is high, declining employment in these industries forces men to take jobs in low productivity sectors of the economy. The net result is a lower average output per man-hour for the economy than otherwise

778

would be attained. Excessive wage hikes in some parts of the economy cause our productivity to rise less rapidly (and average wage income to rise more slowly) than it otherwise would.

The experience of coal miners illustrates this point. Coal mining hourly earnings rose by $1.95 or 163 per cent from 1945 to 1960; bituminous coal mining employment dropped from 385,000 to 168,000. By way of comparison, in the same period, manufacturing production worker hourly earnings rose $1.24 or 122 per cent, and manufacturing employment rose from 15,524,000 to 16,762,000. The differential in hourly earnings in favor of coal miners increased from 18 to 39 per cent. Many of the coal miners who lost their jobs (and men who would have found employment in coal mines) took manufacturing jobs. In these jobs, their productivity and their wage income is lower than in coal mining. If we had more coal miners mining coal and fewer coal miners in other industries today, average output per man-hour in the private sector of the economy would be higher (and the record of the annual rate of increase in output per man-hour would be better), average wage income would be higher, and inequality would be less.

Excessive wage hikes in some industries slow the increase in output per man-hour in the economy as a whole for another reason besides forcing people out of high productivity into low productivity occupations. To make men worth employing in coal mining or auto manufacturing at high wage rates, the amounts of capital per man employed must be increased enough to raise the productivity of the men remaining in the industry to the point where employment costs can be covered. This is the process known as automation. Concentration of large amounts of the available capital on a few men in these industries reduces the capital available per man in the rest of the economy. With less capital per man, output per man-hour in other industries is lower than it otherwise would be. The distortion in the allocation of capital caused by distortions in the wage structure prevents average output per man-hour from reaching otherwise attainable levels. The result is a poorer record of increase in output per man-hour, a poorer record of growth, and lower incomes on the average for all.

The most important point that the Council has overlooked is that their proposed guides will have no influence on the determination of wage rates anyway. They worry about some wage rates being too high, about the unemployment caused in some areas of the economy by the overpricing of labor, about the slowing in the growth rate caused by increasing unemployment; but they suggest no effective means for preventing these unhappy events from occurring. They suggest that "an informed public...can help create an atmosphere in which the parties to (wage decisions) will exercise their powers responsibly."[9] This is much like expecting the flood waters rolling toward a threatened town to stop because an informed public recognizes the tremendous damage that will be done.

If an "informed public" does recognize that it and the country are being damaged by excessive wage increases, and that these excessive wage increases are the result of union power and legislative enactments, what should it do? The Council proposed no action! It seemes to be sufficient for the Council that the public recognize that the wage increases are excessive and damaging. The President has added that it is his intention to "draw public attention to major actions by either business or labor that flout the public interest in non-inflationary price and wage standards."

9 "Annual Report of the Council of Economic Advisors," *Economic Report of the President* (Washington: Government Printing Office, 1962), p. 185.

779

IT IS UP TO THE public, evidently, to figure out what it should do. The Council is not about to tackle this thorny problem. One thing the public might do is to tell the Council to tell the Secretary of Labor to stop raising the minimum wage rates he sets under the powers vested in him by the Walsh-Healy and Davis-Bacon Acts. In 1964, he raised a great many rates. Most of these he raised by much more than 2.5 per cent — usually by 5 per cent or more. Most of these rates were excessive before he raised them. According to the Council's guide posts, they should not have been raised at all. He raised rates in one case to $6.10 an hour, surely a clear instance in which the advice of the Economic Advisors would have been not to raise such a high minimum wage rate.

Since the Secretary of Labor has surely read the Council's report, however, I would advise the public to forget about asking the Council to speak to the Secretary of Labor. Instead, the public should speak to its Congressmen about repealing the Walsh-Healy and the Davis-Bacon Acts. These are pernicious Acts which, on the one hand, increase costs to the government and increase our taxes, and, on the other hand, prevent people from getting jobs who would like to have them.

Additional steps I would suggest to make the Council's advice effective is to reduce the power of labor unions. The public should insist on enforcment of laws during strikes. Assaulting and threatening people on their way to work is against the law in any jurisdiction about which I know.

Still another step I would suggest is the repeal of the increases which have occurred in the minimum wage rate set by the Fair Labor Standards Act. On September 3, 1965, there was an increase in the minimum wage from $1.15 to $1.25 an hour for a large group of employees, in addition to the group whose minimum wage was raised to $1.25 in September 1963. This will be and was an increase of 8.7 per cent in the wage rate of the very groups now suffering the greatest incidence of unemployment. It comes on top of a 15 per cent increase made two years ago. Not only is this a much greater increase than the 3.2 per cent rate of rise suggested by the Council — it is an increase for a group of people *who cannot now find jobs*. The Council has said "wage rate increases [should] fall short of the general guide rate (in occupations) which cannot provide jobs for their [entire] labor force."[10] The greatest unemployment we have is among the less educated, less skilled, low productivity, low wage groups. Teen-age unemployment amounts to 13 per cent, and Negro unemployment is 9 per cent. The Council's advice points strongly to the inadvisability of any wage rise in this group, much less an 8.7 per cent increase.

Certainly, this is not a time to enact still higher minimum wage rates. Yet, a bill is now before Congress which would increase rates from $1.25 to $1.60 and extend coverage to seven million additional jobs. When this passes we will doubtless find the number of applicants for the Job Corps skyrocketing.

We have seen the damage done by previous increases in the minimum wage rates. Newspapers a few months ago reported 1,800 women discharged in crab meat packing plants in North Carolina because of the increase in the minimum from $1.15 to $1.25 which went into effect last September. When the rate was increased from 75 cents to $1.00 in 1956, unemployment among workers under nineteen and females over forty-five rose, despite an increase in total employment by 1.8 million in 1956 over the levels prevailing in 1955, and a decline in unemployment in all other groups. Normally, increasing employment decreases unemployment

---

10 *Ibid.*, p. 189.

in all groups.[11] It failed to do so in 1956 because of the overpricing of less skilled workers.

I remember vividly a dramatic example of the effect of the increase in the 1956 minimum wage. I visited friends in Nashville late in 1956 and remarked on the fact that they had acquired a maid since my previous visit in 1955. They told me that they had hired a Negro girl because the wage rate of maids had dropped, and they had to pay only 50 cents an hour. I expressed my astonishment and asked what had happened. They told me that local textile mills had been hiring girls at 80 cents an hour in 1955. When the minimum wage rate went up to $1.00 an hour in 1956, many of the mills reduced their work force and were no longer hiring Negro girls.[12]

Similar results occurred in 1950 when the minimum wage rate was raised from 40 cents to 75 cents an hour. Professor John Peterson of the University of Arkansas found, from surveys of large southern pine saw mills before and after the imposition of the 75 cent minimum wage in January 1950, that 17 per cent of the workers in mills whose average wage had been below the minimum lost their jobs.[13] Again, when the Fair Labor Standards Act came into operation in October 1938, workers in the seamless hosiery industry in Western Pennsylvania suffered unemployment. The imposition of a minimum wage rate of 25 cents an hour at that time caused layoffs and a drop in employment in Western Pennsylvania at the very time when employment in the United States was rising.

IN ADDITION TO THE actual unemployment caused by increased min-

imum wage rates, there is also a decrease in the opportunities for youngsters to obtain training which prepares them for productive employment. To put this in terms of a specific example, an automobile parts jobber testified: "We had always had a training program for new employees which in itself is expensive, and when the minimum wage was increased, we had to discontinue this training program and hire only people as we needed them on a productivity basis. In other words, the average number of employees that we now have is about 5 per cent lower than before the minimum wage was increased."

I could go on giving illustrations of the unemployment caused by minimum wage laws and their effects on freedom of choice among occupations, but this should be sufficient to convey the point. Instead, let me turn to another kind of minimum wage imposition and its effect.

We are very concerned in Chicago about the large number of adolescents who drop out of high school and are unable to find jobs. The problem manifests itself in part in high juvenile delinquency rates. These boys would like to engage in some kind of activity, preferably filling a job. Many of them used to be employed as elevator operators at $1.00 to $1.25 an hour. The elevator operators, union has succeeded in imposing a minimum wage of $2.50 an hour for operators in downtown Chicago buildings. The result is that owners of buildings have found it economical to spend $30,000 per elevator to automate their lifts and make them self-operating. Since the tax, insurance, depreciation, and interest costs of automating an elevator amount to $8,000 per year, it did not pay to automate when two shifts of operators cost only $5,000 per year. The union has succeeded in driving the two-shift cost of operation to over $10,000 per year. The result is elevator automation, no jobs for elevator operators, and a policing problem of unskilled

781

11 Ibid., p. 232.
12 Y. Brozen, "Minimum Wage Rates and Household Workers," Journal of Law and Economics, V (1962), 103-9.
13 J.M. Peterson, "Employment Effects of Minimum Wages, 1938-50," Journal of Political Economy, LXV (1957), 419.

teen-agers which is getting out of hand. I think this example speaks for itself. Thirteen per cent of the teen-agers who would like to have jobs cannot find them because of the minimum wage rates set by the unions, by the Secretary of Labor, and by law.

Perhaps I should quote the words of a U.S. Senate report at this point, "The conditions of insecurity and hopelessness that characterize the lives of many unemployed young people threaten their acceptance of traditional American ideals. What they need and cannot find is jobs. Given jobs, many of them will make a successful transition into the adult world and a useful contribution to the nation's strength. Without jobs, continuing moral degeneration is inevitable."

782
The power of unions to prevent people from taking jobs they would like to have is a major factor in causing some people to suffer the circumstances described in this Senate report. Perhaps it is an anticlimax to add that the power concentration in union hands is also a major factor in causing some wage rates to rise much more rapidly than the Council of Economic Advisors' guide lines would allow. Yet the Council has made no suggestion for limiting concentrations of power. It simply offers some meaningless rhetoric about the necessity for having an informed public opinion as a way of enforcing its suggestions.

There is quite a list of actions the Council could have suggested which would make its words meaningful. The fact that its words are not is demonstrated by a series of wage rate increases which have occurred since their guide posts were suggested — wage rate increases exceeding 3.2 or even 4 per cent. The New York electricians' increase is a notorious instance. Typographers on New York newspapers struck for a 26 per cent increase in compensation, surely an amount far in excess of 3.2 per cent. Longshoremen were granted an 8 per cent increase

as a result of the pressures exerted by the Federal government during a strike. The Teamsters negotiated a contract providing a 5 per cent annual increase just a year ago. In the first six months of this year, the average wage increase in new settlements amounted to 4 per cent, exclusive of increases in fringe benefits. One-third of the workers covered by new settlements received increases of 5 per cent or more. The agreement negotiated last fall between the Communication Workers and the Michigan Bell Telephone Company provided a 5 per cent increase in wage rates and fringe benefits. The U.A.W. won a 4.9 per cent annual increase for each of three years in 1964. This is 50 per cent higher than the guide line.

THE COUNCIL'S GUIDE lines for wage setting are meaningless in terms of informing the public, providing a guide for employer-union bargaining, or for guiding employers who have no union with which to contend. Certainly, no one has paid much attention to the Council's guide posts, except where unions have used them as an argument for getting a bigger wage increase than they might otherwise be able to justify. However, they are meaningless for very good reasons other than the fact that no one uses them.

First, the increase in average output per man-hour is highly variable year to year. The overall trend of several past years has no necessary relationship to the change in any one year. If one examines productivity changes from year to year, it is clear that average output per man-hour decreased between 1920 and 1921, increased between 1923 and 1924, decreased between 1926 and 1928, decreased again between 1929 and 1933, etc. This is highly variable behavior. Any constant rate of increase even in real wage rates, much less money wage rates, would result in unemployment in some years, shortages of labor in other years, and allocation of much labor to the wrong places every year.

Aside from the fact that past output-per-hour trends do not provide a guide for *real*-wage rate changes in a specific year, they are of no help at all in judging proper changes in *money* wage rates. Money rates fell from 56 cents an hour in 1920 to 52 cents an hour in 1921 — a 7 per cent decrease — yet real wage rates went up 4 per cent because of an even greater decline in consumer prices. If money wage rates had been increased 3 per cent between 1920 and 1921, we would have had a 14 per cent rise in real wage rates and 10 million unemployed instead of 5 million in 1921.

The Council pays little attention to the possibility that real wage rates may increase through a declining level of product prices as well as by a rising level of money wage rates. In view of our balance of payments problems at this time, this should be the preferred method of raising real wage rates.

If we are going to engage in the sport of setting guide posts for wage increases, I would like to enter a candidate. I would like to suggest my guide post in the form of an answer to the question, "How can employers recognize the circumstances which dictate a change in the wage level or wage structure?" Of course, any time a company's profits fall or it incurs a loss, it would like to decrease its wage costs. In some cases, this may be the proper action to take; but, in other cases, a decrease in wage rates may increase costs or may cause the company to lose even more.

On the other hand, when profits increase, as they did for General Motors last year, for example, should wage rates be raised? Again this may or may not be the proper action. It depends upon the circumstances. How can we tell what to do, then, if the proper

action is not directly related to profitability?

THE BEST SINGLE guide to the proper action is the relationship of the quit rate of currently employed persons to the rate of receipt of qualified applications for jobs. If the quit rate in a given company exceeds the qualified-applicant rate, the wage rate may be too low. People do not ordinarily quit jobs in appreciable numbers unless alternative jobs are available which are more attractive than those they are leaving. If the quit rate is high, we would probably find that better paying jobs, or jobs more attractive for some other reason, are available. A low qualified-applicant rate also indicates this sort of situation. Retaining a work force, then, may require an increase in the level of wage rates.

Now, one may notice that my suggested guide line is in the form of advice to employers. I am not interested in getting the public into the act, nor in getting government into the act. The only people in the act should be those who are employing men, and the men who would like to have the jobs. This is true for the determination of overtime rates as well as straight time wage rates. We should not impose penalty rates by law on employers for employing men over forty hours a week. If men desire additional income, wish to work more than forty hours per week, and are willing to do so for rates less than those required by the Fair Labor Standards Act, that should be their privilege as free men.

Further, one may notice that my advice to management is hardly necessary. It simply says, pay as much as you must to obtain the labor force you require; but do not pay any more than you must. Any company not trying to do this is not a business — it is a philanthropic operation. How long it

783

can survive depends only on how long it can go on giving money away, or rather, how long the stockholders are willing to hold stock in a company giving away their money. Also, any company paying higher wage rates than it *must* to attract the work force it wants, and keep turnover rates as low as is profitable, is not serving the public well. It is providing fewer jobs than men would like to have and less product than its customers would like to have. If employers will follow their own interests by raising wage rates only when their quit rates go up (or threaten to do so), they will be serving the economy in general as well as their own interests.

In advising that quit rates should be the primary indicator in determining the appropriateness of a wage change, all I have really said is that wage rates should be set at the levels at which free marekts would set wage rates. Perhaps this might be better said by using a quotation from Henry Simons. He pointed out that

The proper wage in any area or occupational category is....the wage that will permit the maximum transfer of workers from less attractive, less remunerative, less productive employments....We imply that any wage is excessive if more qualified workers are obtainable at that wage than are employed — provided only that the industry is reasonably competitive as among firms. Reduction of rates (in these circumstances) would permit workers to enter who otherwise would be compelled to accept employment less attractive to them and less productive for the community or to accept involuntary unemployment....

The basic principle here is the freedom of entry — freedom of migration, between localities, between industries, between occupational categories. If such freedom is to exist....wages must fall to accommodate new workers in any area to which many qualified persons wish to move. Freedom of migration implies freedom of qualified workers, not merely to seek jobs but to get them; free entry implies full employment for all qualified persons who wish to enter. Whether the wage permits an adequate family scale of living, according to social service workers, is simply irrelevant ....what really matters is the judgment of workers who would be excluded by an excessive wage as to the *relative* merits of the employment in question and of employment in less attractive alternatives actually open to them. Other things equal, the wage is too high if higher than the wage in actually alternative employments. Ethically, one cannot go beyond the opinion of qualified workers seeking to transfer. If in large numbers they prefer employment here to the alternatives and cannot get it, the wage is excessive. [14]

I should add that the Council of Economic Advisors itself believes this, although it tries to avoid saying so. The Council does not think much of its own guide posts and prefers the one suggested here, as I will demonstrate shortly.

WHAT IS FRIGHTENING about the Council's discussion of guide lines for the economy is the implication that they know how to make wage decisions and price decisions which are in the public interest. Some idiot is likely to take this seriously and set up a regulatory agency to set wage rates and prices. It is not a long step from setting guide lines for the economy to guiding the economy. Down that road lies tyranny.

That the possibility is real is evidenced by the appointment two years ago of a member of the Council who believes the government should set up an Industry Economics Agency which

14 H.C. Simons, "Some Reflections on Syndicalism," Economic Policy for a Free Society (Chicago: University of Chicago Press, 1948), pp. 140-41.

would set specific prices and wage rates — not just generalized national guide lines — and which would hold corporations over a certain size and unions to "new standards of public accountability." The Council has not yet gone this far, but there is talk about a so-called early warning group to watch for price and wage changes which do not conform to the guide lines.

The Council of four years ago did not even take its own rule for wage setting in terms of change in output per man-hour seriously. After offering its general rule it said, "wage rate increases would exceed the general guide rate in an industry which would otherwise be unable to attract sufficient labor." [15] This, of course, is what any employer does when he finds he cannot obtain as many employees as he wishes. He bids a higher wage to attract more people, frequently bidding substantial premiums above even

union-set wage rates when he cannot find enough men. Also, the Council said, "wage rate increases would fall short of the general guide rate in an industry which could not provide jobs for its entire labor force." [16] This, of course, usually occurs in markets where there are large numbers of unemployed men — and no legal minima, or union power to prevent this. What the Council has said in these statements is that supply and demand in free markets should determine wage rates.

I am heartily in favor of those measures and those laws which maximize wage income and minimize inequality. If the labor legislation which I have discussed, and the guide lines proposed for determining changes in wage rates were good for labor as a whole, that would be the end of the matter for me. I question the virtue of these measures because they decrease labor income, limit the opportunity to obtain jobs and to engage in meaningful activity, and increase inequality.

785

15"Annual Report of the Council of Economic Advisors,' *Economic Report of the President* (Washington: Government Printing Office, 1962), p. 189.

16*Ibid.*

Economic Development and Free Markets

REED J. IRVINE

THE IDEA THAT THE wealth of nations can be expanded most rapidly by governmental direction of their economies is not a traditional socialist concept. In the broad sweep of economic thinking Adam Smith pioneered the view that governmental intervention was a hindrance, not an aid to economic development. He examined what was going on around him in England and some parts of Europe, and he came to the conclusion that if men were given a high degree of freedom to produce, trade, and consume, productivity would rise and consumers would be better satisfied.

The socialists, including Karl Marx, did not dispute the contention that economic freedom led to great productivity. They could not, for they had all about them the overwhelming evidence of the Industrial Revolution which showed that this was true. Note this description of the process of economic development under capitalism by Friedrich Engels:

...the bourgeoisie shattered the

_____

Reed J. Irvine holds the position of Advisor in the Division of International Finance of the Board of Governors of the Federal Reserve System, and is currently chief of the Asia, Africa, and Latin America Section.
The views expressed in this article are those of the author and do not necessarily reflect the views of the Board of Governors of the Federal Reserve System.

feudal system, and on its ruins established the bourgeois social order, the realm of free competition, freedom of movement, equal rights for commodity owners, and all the other bourgeois glories. The capitalist mode of production could now develop freely. From the time when steam and the new tool-making machinery had begun to transform the former manufacture into large-scale industry, the productive forces evolved under bourgeois direction developed at a pace that was previously unknown and to an unprecedented degree.

What bothered the nineteenth century socialists was not the inability of the capitalistic free market to bring about rapid economic development. On the contrary, many of them were appalled by the extent and pace of the economic change caused by the Industrial Revolution in England. They were all highly critical of what seemed to them to be an unjust distribution of the fruits of production. Marx and Engels shared these views, but they also advanced the idea that this tremendously dynamic productive system would eventually break down because of defects that were inherent in it. They perceived what they thought was a fatal flaw in the constant drive for greater productivity and what they

_____

[1] F. Engels, "Socialism: Utopian and Scientific," _The Selected Works of Karl Marx_, (New York: International Publishers, 1962) Vol. I, pp. 165-66.

thought was a tendency to minimize the use of labor and the payment of labor. They maintained that this would eventually bring the whole system crashing down and open the way to socialism.

The fact that economic history has failed to bear out the dire predictions of their prophets ought to be a source of profound embarrassment to Marxist theorists. The capitalist states have had their crises, but none of them ever proved fatal, and these economies have not only recovered but have gone on to create and distribute to the workers, as well as to the capitalists and rentiers, wealth on a scale undreamed of in the nineteenth century.

The dogma has had to be adjusted to this stubborn refusal of the facts of history to bear out the Marxian hypothesis. We hear less and less about the increasing misery of the exploited workers in the capitalist economies. Even rarer are the predictions of the eventual collapse of the developed economies of the West.

In lieu of this we have a new dogma —one which Marx would never recognize. One might say that just as Marx turned Hegel upside down, so have the modern Marxists turned Marx upside down. Socialism is no longer the synthesis that is supposed to emerge from the inevitable collapse of the most developed capitalist states. Rather, socialism is now presented as the engine of economic development itself. Capitalism, with its bourgeois emphasis upon free trade and free competition, is now portrayed as a system that is useless if not harmful for any underdeveloped country that hopes to see its wealth increase. While Marx and Engels saw in capitalism an irrepressible drive to expand production and productivity which would inevitably bring about its collapse, the modern socialist sees capitalism as completely lacking in dynamism with a fatal tendency toward total stagnation. Socialism is said to be the energizing medicine which the states stagnating under free market systems need to propel themsleves into the industrial age. This view has been accepted even by some modern-liberals, one of whom has put this new dogma in these words:

> Only in Russia and China do they, the submerged masses, find a model of how in backward countries great masses of people can raise themselves quickly by their own bootstraps.

> The Communists are expanding in Asia because they are demonstrating a way, at present the only obviously effective way, of raising quickly the power and the standard of living of a backward people.[2]

THE EMPIRICAL EVIDENCE no more supports this new hypothesis than it does the original theory of Marx. While the world has been awed by Soviet space feats, the people of Eastern Europe have grown increasingly critical of the failure of the communist economic system to provide housing, food, clothing, and other consumer goods in the desired quantities and qualities. While these countries boast of impressive rates of economic growth, their statistics have concealed serious economic failures. This is true not only in agriculture, where the disastrous effects of the communist policies are notorious, but also in industry.

This is why the revolutionary proposal that profit incentives be introduced into the Soviet economic system have made such headway throughout Eastern Europe. The proposal was first made by Professor Y.G. Liberman of the Economic-Engineering Institute of Kharkov in September 1962. Although the Liberman proposals were opposed by communist "conservatives" as being capitalistic, they were introduced in the Soviet Union on an experimental basis in July 1964. More recently, fol-

787

---

2 Walter Lippmann, *Washington Post*, November 13 and December 12, 1958.

lowing Khrushchev's overthrow, the Soviet government announced that it was pleased with the results of the experiment and indicated that it would be extended to other plants. This triggered an announcement by Czechoslovakia that it was completely revamping its economic system to reduce centralized planning and control, and placing greater reliance on profit incentives and the law of supply and demand. A report from Prague summed up the trouble with the old system in these words:

> Through centralized planning and control, resources were squandered on almost every imaginable industrial product — from airplanes to xylophones. This over-extension produced intolerably high costs of production, manpower shortages and, above all, a loss of quality in comparison with the products of more-specialized competitors. Prague was forced to sell cheaply abroad and the cost of living here soared. There was no way to reverse the trend because central planning of production could control only quantity, not quality. It could not enforce technological improvement, innovation and refinement, which depend upon the producer's interest in his goods. [3]

Hungary has introduced "capitalistic" reforms, and Poland is clearly moving in the same direction.

An economic system which has been exposed as suffering from such serious inherent defects in the countries which have tried the hardest to make it work can hardly be recommended as a model to other countries. Where it has been tried in countries even more dependent upon agriculture than those of Eastern Europe, the results have been even more disastrous. Cuba, once one of the most prosperous countries of Latin America, was impoverished by communism in less than five years. China, within a decade of the communist take-over, was shaken to her foundations by the disastrous consequences of the economic follies of the communists. Economic debacles have struck or are threatened in such countries as Indonesia, Burma, Ceylon, Guinea, Mali, and Algeria as a result of their adoption of the "socialist" approach to economic growth. Retrogression, not progress, has been the hallmark of communist experimentation in the less developed countries.

What of the charge that capitalism is too lacking in dynamism to be useful to developing countries in the modern age? This too is refuted by the evidence.

The striking contrast between the economic restoration of West Germany under free-market capitalism and the painfully halting recovery of East Germany under socialism tells a great deal about the relative dynamism of the two systems. Of course, the socialists did not anticipate this result. Paul Hagen, a German socialist, in his book *Germany After Hitler,* which was published during the war, said that unless Germany adopted a system of "democratic planning, as against a restoration of profit capitalism" the economic outlook for Germany and Eruope would be a dark one. He thought that restoring the old system would amount to sentencing millions of Germans to death and would endanger European reconstruction. [4] Fortunately for Germany, Ludwig Erhard did not share these dogmatic doubts.

Japan, like West Germany, has displayed tremendous economic dynamism in the postwar period, while remaining wedded to free enterprise. In 1945, Japan's physical destruction was so complete and the demoralization of her people so thorough, that some observers thought it might take a century for her to recover economically from the war. It actually took

3 *New York Times,* November 6, 1964.

4 P. Hagen, *Germany After Hitler,* (New York: Farrar and Rinehart, 1944), pp. 138-48.

less than a decade. Manufacturing output exceeded the prewar level in 1953. Six years later it had doubled, and by mid-1964 it had doubled again. Japan is now the third largest producer of steel in the world, ranking behind the U.S. and the U.S.S.R. Japanese consumer goods are not only abundant at home, but they are being sold in great quantities all over the world. Japanese exports, despite discrimination in some markets, more than quadrupled between 1953 and 1963.

It should be noted that this achievement represents a great deal more than merely the recovery from the destruction wreaked by the war. The development of synthetic fibers during the war meant that Japan could not place such heavy reliance on earnings from raw silk exports as she had prewar. Cotton textiles, another prewar pillar of Japan's foreign trade, also offered diminished prospects as other countries developed their own mills and restricted imports.

The Japanese knew that they would have to trade to survive, but ten years ago no planner could possibly have predicted the course their trade would take. The Honda motorcycle which has since taken a good part of the world by storm was still little more than a gleam in the eye of a struggling young mechanic. Transistor radios were still unheard of, the world was just beginning to hear that the Japanese could make optical goods that rivalled German goods in quality, and the idea that the Japanese might give the Swiss competition in watches would have been considered a joke.

Fortunately, under the free-market system, it was not necessary for any planner to predict or even understand the possibility of these developments. They came about because of the dynamism of the free-market system — that same drive for greater efficiency, greater production and greater sales which had so forcefully impressed Karl Marx. The export of these and thousands of other items in tremendous quantities has earned for Japan the means to pay for the huge amounts of food, fuel, raw materials, machinery, equipment, and consumer goods that she needs to keep her great industrial machine operating and keep her people well-fed and contented. Although Japan has 96 million people crowded into four mountainous islands whose total land area is less than that of Paraguay, they have been able to achieve a reasonably high standard of living. This has been steadily improving in recent years as productivity has gone up. Unemployment is negligible and wage rates are now said to be comparable to those in Southern European countries. The rise in real wages has averaged about 4.5 per cent a year since 1951.

It may be argued that Japan and Germany are exceptional cases, since both had already attained a high degree of industrial development before the Second World War. Recovery and further rapid growth may be easier than starting from scratch — even if it did not so appear to observers at the end of the War.

What about other countries? Are there any which were not already industrialized which have shown signs of development in recent years?

THERE HAS BEEN a striking rise in industrial activity throughout the world in the postwar period, and many of the countries of Asia, Africa, and Latin America have participated in this. One of the most interesting examples is that of Hong Kong — both because its growth has been so rapid and because its economic policies have been in such striking contrast to those prescribed by the communists. Hong Kong is perhaps the closest approximation to nineteenth century laissez faire capitalism that exists in the world today. In the words of a recent publi-

789

cation of the U.S. Department of Commerce:

Hong Kong is unique among the world's markets in that it presents virtually no artificial barriers to trade. As a free port, the colony has no protective duties or quantitative restrictions on imports; no difficulties are encountered in obtaining import licenses or foreign exchange; no cumbersome procedures or delays hinder the clearing of merchandise through customs; the Hong Kong dollar is stable and freely convertible....Indeed, the concept of free trade and private enterprise is heartily supported and practiced by all segments of the business and official community and has probably been the single most important factor accounting for the phenomenal development of the colony's commerce and industry over the past decade. [5]

Before the War Hong Kong had been little more than a bustling entrepot for China. She resumed this role after the war for a few years, but the communist takeover on the mainland forced a dramatic change in her status. Hong Kong could no longer depend on the entrepot trade for survival. Moreover, her population was being heavily swollen by refugees from the mainland. No planner decreed that Hong Kong should emphasize industry, but it soon became apparent to a large number of people that it might be profitable to start manufacturing enterprises there. Labor was abundant and cheap, taxes were low, red tape was virtually non-existent, raw materials and machinery could be imported freely, and Hong Kong had the whole world for her market.

A start was made in cotton textiles, and by 1957, little Hong Kong was becoming a competitor to be reckoned with in the world's textile markets. The entrepot trade continued, but as early as 1957, about a third of her

5 U.S. Department of Commerce, *Hong Kong, A Market for U.S. Products*, (Washington: Government Printing Office, 1964), p.viii.

exports consisted of goods produced in Hong Kong. This ratio grew to three-fourths by 1961.

Hong Kong does not publish an index of industrial production, but some idea of the rate of increase of manufacturing output can be obtained from the statistics on registered factories and employment. In 1950, there were 1,752 such factories employing 92 thousand workers. By the end of 1963, there were 8,348 thousand factories employing 354 thousand workers. Thus the number of factories had nearly quintupled while factory employment had nearly quadrupled. However, these figures considerably understate industrial employment. According to the 1961 census, 39 per cent of the population was employed, and just over half, or 610 thousand was employed in industry.

Hong Kong's industrial development has had to overcome the handicaps of a shortage of land and fresh water. Virtually all raw materials have to be imported, including fuels. This means that industry has not had the advantage of cheap electric power.

Nevertheless a most impressive array of manufactured products is now being produced. Cotton textiles are still the most important single product. At the end of 1963, 632 thousand spindles and 19.3 thousand looms were in operation. Over 540 million square yards of cotton cloth were produced, and most of this was exported. Other important industries include plastic products, shipbuilding and shipbreaking, machinery manufacture, cement, aluminum products, clocks and watches, enamelware, electrical equipment and appliances, foodstuffs and beverages, footwear, leather goods, electronic goods, hardware, optical goods, and clothing.

A decade ago Hong Kong was hardly anything more than an insignificant spot on the map as far as most people were concerned. Today, she is one of the major trading countries in Asia —

790

and indeed, in the world. In 1963, only four Latin American countries, Argentina, Brazil, Venezuela, and Mexico, surpassed Hong Kong in the value of exports. This is a remarkable achievement for 3.6 million people crowded into an area of only 391 square miles which is almost completely devoid of natural resources.

As in the case of Japan, this dynamic economic expansion resulted in higher incomes and improved living standards for the working people of Hong Kong. In spite of the influx of refugees from the "workers' state" on mainland China, which in 1960 and 1961 helped boost the population of Hong Kong by an incredible 7 per cent a year, labor shortages have developed. Wages, while still low by Western standards, have risen sharply in recent years. Since the increase in the cost of living has been one of the lowest in the world, there has been a substantial increase in real wages.[6]

One indication of the improvement in living standards is the sharp drop in the death rate and the infant mortality rate in the last decade. The crude death rate has fallen to 5.5 per thousand, one of the lowest in the world. The infant mortality rate has been cut by 64 per cent since 1948 to the level of 32.9 per 1000 live births in 1963.[7] This is considerably lower than the rate for non-whites in the United States, and it compares with rates in Central America and Mexico which range from 80.2 for Mexico to 91.3 for Guatemala (1962 data).[8]

HONG KONG'S POSTWAR growth is a striking demonstration of just how dynamic a developing free economy can be. It does not prove that every free economy will necessarily be eq-

6 *Hong Kong Report for the Year 1963,* (Hong Kong: Government Press, 1964), pp.50-51.
7 *Ibid.,* p.453.
8 *U.N. Statistical Yearbook,* 1963.

ually dynamic. The colony has had some advantages and some disadvantages not found in other developing countries. Not every country can duplicate Hong Kong's accomplishments even if it pursues identical economic policies. Some countries suffer from even more serious economic handicaps than Hong Kong. Some are so isolated geographically that they are at a serious disadvantage in international trade. Many have a large number of inhabitants who do not easily adapt to new and more efficient modes of production. Others are beset by political instability and strife which discourage saving and investment.

When a country which suffers from serious disadvantages such as these does not make rapid economic progress, the communists invariably place the blame on whatever degree of economic freedom the government may permit.

It would be wrong to pretend that there are always easy, quick solutions to many problems such as these. Economic freedom cannot overcome all such handicaps. Some curtailment of freedom is indispensable to the attainment of a reasonable degree of order and security in society, as Thomas Hobbes long ago convincingly argued in the *Leviathan.*

It would be equally wrong to argue that all of these problems can be solved by abolishing all individual economic freedom, as the communists propose. This is not merely because freedom is itself something which men prize highly, frequently more highly than material progress. It is because freedom, when properly used, can accelerate material progress enormously. To use an analogy, an excess of lubricating oil may cause a motor to malfunction. This does not mean that you try to operate the equipment without any oil at all. The amount of freedom in an economy, like the lubricating oil in a motor, has to be adjusted to the varying conditions that exist.

791

Page Thirty-nine

The communists, by dogmatically propagandizing against this valuable economic "lubricant," have succeeded in influencing policy in many countries toward minimizing the degree of economic freedom that is permitted. They have systematically labored to magnify the obstacles to economic development in free economies. They have worked to intensify political instability and insecurity, they have done their best to discourage the induction of needed savings from abroad, they have tried to frustrate efforts to increase labor productivity and needed rationalization in the allocation of economic resources. All this has been done to prove that freedom has to be eliminated. The result has been that many economies are functioning at far less than the highest possible level of efficiency either because they have permitted too much liberty to those whose main objective has been to keep the economy from performing satisfactorily, or because they have given in to unreasonable pressure to restrict freedom which might improve the functioning of the economic machine.

The experience of Japan and Hong Kong, where these machinations have had no success, deserves careful study and emulation by the countries of the world which wish to develop economically.

792

New Individualist Review welcomes contributions for publication from its readers. Essays should not exceed 5,000 words, and should be type-written. All manuscripts will receive careful consideration.

The Sources of Monopoly

SUDHA R. SHENOY

793

IN THIS ARTICLE I wish to examine, very briefly, the tacit assumption universally made, even by free-market writers, that monopoly is a natural market phenomenon, arising out of normal market processes. I hope to show that, on the contrary, the conditions of monopoly cannot arise except in connection with government intervention.

The characteristics of monopoly are usually given as follows: (a) exclusive control over the whole—or a very high proportion—of the output of a commodity lacking close substitutes (or control over a group of commodities that are close substitutes to each other); arising out of, and maintained by, (b) barriers to entry that are tacitly assumed to be spontaneously thrown up by normal market forces; or (c) the two together (exclusive control over supply and barriers to entry), enabling the monopolist to restrict output below, and thus raise prices above, the competitive level.

For our purposes the most important assumption to consider is the second, barriers to entry. [1] Before going on to examine some of these, I should first like to suggest that exclusive control over the supply of a (physically distinct) commodity does not mean that the "monopolist" is isolated from, or insulated against, the effects of competition—using the term to indicate a dynamic market process. The range of substitution open to the consumer is not something which is fixed once and

for all, and which can be ascertained by simple "observation." We seem to have here a confusion between the economic and the technological notions of substitution. Whether commodities are to be regarded as complementary or as substitutes depends not on their technological characteristics, nor on the opinion of the economist, who is only an observer, but on the real actions of individuals taken in their aspect as consumers. Products may be treated differently by different consumers at different times: a housewife may today treat cornflakes and shredded wheat as perfect (economic) substitutes, while tomorrow she may differentiate sharply between them if in the meantime her family has acquired a taste or a dislike for either. Again, wash-and-wear shirts may be seen as providing substitutes for laundry services; and home canning may similarly provide competition for the large firms producing canned goods. In short, there may be all sorts of unexpected sources of competition on the market.

To return to the notion of bars to entry: It has been argued that costs may form a barrier, in the sense that the optimal size of the plant in a particular field may be "large" compared to the size elsewhere. The necessity of having to raise large amounts of capital,

Miss Shenoy is pursuing studies toward the B.Sc. (Econ.) degree at the London School of Economics.

---

1 See, for instance, the long and comprehensive list compiled by J.S. Bain, "Conditions of Entry and the Emergence of Monopoly," in E. H. Chamberlin, ed., *Monopoly and Competition and Their Regulation* (New York: Macmillan, 1954). Also see the discussion by E.A.G. Robinson, *Monopoly* (London: Nisbet and Co., 1941), chaps. i and ii.

however, cannot be said to prevent entry, since if sufficient profits were anticipated the capital would be forthcoming, either from savings or by withdrawing it from other uses; and if sufficient returns were not anticipated, this would indicate that the existing firm was efficient enough in meeting the demand so that the setting up of another firm would be unprofitable, or at least less profitable than using the resources elsewhere.

Nor can it be said that cut-throat competition can establish a monopoly by driving all firms except one out of business: since whenever the "monopolizing" firm attempted to raise its prices again, it would be inviting other firms to enter the field. [2]

794

WHAT ABOUT MONOPOLY arising out of exclusive control over some essential factor of production—e.g., a natural resource or a trade secret? Now here again, a rise in relative prices would render profitable the search for substitutes,[3] or the use of techniques or factors that would not otherwise be profitable. Moreover, the possession of a "trade secret" by a firm must be counted as part of the skills forming its owner's property.

Goodwill, advertising, and product differentiation are said to create monopolistic positions and barriers to entry by, so to speak, "attaching" consumers to a particular supplier, so they do not readily turn to alternative sources of supply. Here, too, the economist cannot decide for the consumer his

2 See W. A. Leeman, "The Limitations of Local Price-cutting as a Barrier to Entry," *Journal of Political Economy,* LXIV (1956), 329-34; for the classic Standard Oil story, see J. S. McGee, "Predatory Price Cutting: The Standard Oil (N.J.) Case," *Journal of Law and Economics,* I (1958), 137-69; J. Chamberlain, *The Enterprising Americans: A Business History of the U.S.* (New York: Harper and Row, 1963), pp. 146-56.

3. An excellent example is Indian jute: The Indian Government believed that since India had exclusive control of jute production, it was safe to charge heavy export duties and thus raise prices. The outcome of this was not the reaping of monopoly revenues, but a great expansion of production of substitutes for jute, such as kraft paper.

range of substitution, since this would depend on the latter's own preferences (including his laziness or other costs involved in acquiring information about possible substitutes). It would always be open to competing firms to try and persuade consumers of the superiority of their own products and services, since presumably the "attachment" of the consumer to a particular firm bears some relation to its performance, or to his beliefs about its performance. Moreover, to speak of such things as advertising and good will as creating monoplistic positions would seem to imply that consumers react like puppets. The function of these two is probably better described as conveying information to consumers. The concept of product differentiation is subject to the same ambiguities as that of the range of substitution: is the product "different" from the viewpoint of the technologist, the engineer, the economist-observer, or the consumer; and whose viewpoint is most relevant?

For these considerations, I will suggest that the sources of monopoly cannot be found in market processes, as their working has usually been interpreted; and I will propose that the chief sources are governmental acts of intervention, for here we have a clearly identifiable and unambiguous class of barriers to entry. We can clearly and unambiguously identify a restriction of market supply below the competitive level, and the corollary of raising prices above the level they might otherwise have attained.

In the case of such interventions as exclusive patents, grants, charters, concessions, permits, licenses, tariffs, and quotas, this restrictive effect is quite plain. All of these reduce the number of sources of market supply— the number of firms that would otherwise be present in the market. Yet we may also perceive this restrictive effect arising out of such interventions as progressive taxation, labor legislation, and the special privileges granted to labor unions. Progressive taxation prevents the accumulation of additional capital, to the comparatively greater detriment of those firms and individuals seeking to establish themselves, and to the advantage of established firms and the already-wealthy. Firms cannot expand except as they save out of their rising incomes or borrow out of the rising incomes of others. Insofar as these incomes are taxed away at progressive rates, new firms and individuals seeking to rise are placed at a comparative disadvantage to those who may fall back on previously accumulated capital. If "large" firms and "wealthy" individuals are prevented from growing larger or wealthier, the comparatively smaller firm and poorer individual are prevented from rising at all. [4]

The effect of labor legislation is to raise total costs above the level they would have otherwise attained. This in turn implies that fewer firms will be able to continue in, or newly enter, the fields where such legislation is applied. In other words, we have here a formidable cost barrier to entry. [5] Labor unions have been granted the special privilege of using private coercion; they may use this power to cartelize an industry, or give de facto monopoly to a single firm, by preventing the entry of firms who would seek to cut costs, or by driving certain firms out of the field. That unions in the United States have used their special privileges to cartelize numerous areas of economic activity seems to be one of the major conclusions emerging from such investigations as those of Senator McClellan and his Committee. [6]

SO-CALLED "FAIR TRADE" laws, which set minimum prices or purport to set minimum standards, also operate to reduce competition and thereby create semi-monopolistic positions. [7] And then there are, of course, the cartels and monopolies, especially in the agricultural sectors of developed economies, that have been deliberately organized by governments. [8] For these reasons, we find that, historically, government intervention has almost invariably been connected with the emergence of monopolies. We may examine some specific examples of this:

In the United States, the presence of tariffs on manufactured goods almost certainly facilitated the emergence of monopoly-like situations in the manufacturing sector of the economy in the latter half of the last century by limiting the effectiveness of international competition. The remedy, however, was sought in further intervention, in the form of antitrust legislation. This at least prevented further monopolization, by making cartelizing contracts unenforceable at law, thus permitting domestic competitive forces to operate; [9] but legal opinion in the country does not seem certain whether uniform pricing by independent firms should be taken as evidence of competition or collusion, while every attempt at price cutting seems to be taken as evidence of a desire to monopolize. [10]

In Germany, contracts in restraint of trade were declared enforceable at law by the Supreme Court, thus eliminating the emergence of competition via the activities of "chiselers"; later,

795

---

4 For a discussion of the various results of progressive taxation, see especially F. A. Hayek, *The Constitution of Liberty* (Chicago: University of Chicago Press, 1960), chap. xx and the references given there.

5 See the brief remarks by P. T. Bauer, "Regulated Wages in Under-developed Countries," in P. Bradley, ed., *The Public Stake in Union Power* (Charlottesville: University of Virginia Press, 1962), pp. 348, 353; see also the discussion in W. H. Hutt, *The Theory of Collective Bargaining* (Glencoe, Ill.: The Free Press of Glencoe, 1954), and in H. C. Simons, "Some Reflections on Syndicalism," *Economic Policy for a Free Society* (Chicago: University of Chicago Press, 1948), pp. 121-59.

6 See Simons, *ibid.*, and also S. Petro, *Power Unlimited: The Corruption of Union Leadership* (New York: Ronald Press, 1959).

7 See especially Simons. *loc. cit.*

8 See L. C. Robbins, "The Inevitability of Monopoly," *The Economic Basis of Class Conflict* (London: Macmillan, 1939), and the remark by Hayek, *op. cit.*, p. 265, and also chap. xxiii.

9 See W. Roepke, *The Social Crisis of Our Time* (London: Wm. Hodge and Co., 1950), p. 251n; J. Chamberlain, "The Morality of Free Enterprise," in F. S. Meyer, ed., *What is Conservatism?* (New York: Holt, Rinehart and Winston, 1964). But also see S. Petro, "The Menace of Antitrust," *Fortune*, November 1962, pp. 128-31.

10 See the brief remarks by F. A. Hayek, "Unions, Inflation and Profits," in Bradley, *op. cit.*, pp. 54-56, and *The Constitution of Liberty*, p. 265.

the government actively engaged in the formation of cartels, even making cartelization compulsory. [11]

In South Africa, diamond mining was gradually becoming a more competitive industry when the government, alarmed at the prospective loss of revenue from its share of the profits of one of the companies, decreed that thenceforward mining was to be by license only. [12]

In Great Britain, monopoly was never a serious problem during the free trade period of the nineteenth century; it became a problem only with the abandonment of free trade in the early twentieth century, and with the acceptance by the courts at about the same time of the enforceability of restrictive contracts, if the restrictions were "reasonable." [13] In Britain, also,

796

the government has engaged actively in the cartelization of the trucking and coal mining industries, as well as of agriculture. [14]

In India, comprehensive exchange and import controls, together with comprehensive and detailed regulation of every aspect of business life, insure that competition is never allowed to emerge. [15]

The conclusion to which all these considerations would seem to lead is that monopoly is not, as so many have supposed, a natural, market phenomenon at all; but that, on the contrary, it does not arise except in conjunction with government intervention.

---

11 See especially F. Boehm, "Monopoly and Competition in Western Germany," in Chamberlin, *loc. cit.*

12 See the account given by E.A.G. Robinson, *op. cit.*, pp. 49-53.

13 See the account given by Robinson, *op. cit.*, pp. 49-53.

14 See J. B. Heath, *STILL Not Enough Competition?* (Hobart Paper No. 11; London: Institute of Economic Affairs, 1963), p. 22.

15 See B. R. Shenoy, *Indian Planning and Economic Development* (Bombay: Asia, 1962); and by the same author, "A Report on Ten Years of Economic Planning in India," *New Individualist Review*, Winter 1964, pp. 13-20, also see P. T. Bauer, *Indian Economic Policy and Development* (London: Allen and Unwin, 1960) for a more general discussion.

What's Wrong With Right-to-Work Laws

HIRSCHEL KASPER

ALTHOUGH THERE IS NO necessary reason why public policy proposals should be consistent with one's political philosophy, it can be embarrasing for classical liberals to say one thing and lobby for another. The recent debate on the issue of whether to maintain Federal legislation to enable states to pass Right-to-work laws presents just such a striking anomaly. A correct reading of classical liberal philosophy requires disapproval of legislation, Federal or state, which forbids private parties to engage in a mutually beneficial exchange, unless that private contract eliminates liberty or is an element of increased coercion. Given our existing economy. Right-to-work laws should be seen as antithetical to those who prefer more liberty and less governmental coercion.

Since this line of reasoning may not be clear, a brief discussion of the background of Right-to-work legislation may be useful. When there is a federal system of government, legislation on the same matter may arise from both the central Congress and the state

Hirschel Kasper is Assistant Professor of Economics at Oberlin College. He received his Ph.D. from the University of Minnesota in 1963, and has published several articles on labor in scholarly journals.

legislatures. The Supreme Court has decided that national legislation preempts state legislation in labor-management relations, as well as in many other areas. In this light, Congress wrote into the 1947 Taft-Hartley Act a provision, Section 14(b), which said specifically that the Act should not

> ...be construed as authorizing the execution or application of agreements requiring membership in a labor organization as a condition of employment in any State or Territory in which such execution or application is *prohibited by State or Territorial law.*

The effect of such Congressional legislation is to allow states to prohibit union-management contracts which require union membership as a condition of employment. About two-fifths of the states, mostly in the South and West, have taken advantage of Section 14(b) of the Taft-Hartly Act and passed restrictive legislation to outlaw "union shop" agreements. The state laws, referred to as Right-to-work laws, thus derive from the Congressional legislation; and if Congress had repealed Section 14(b), there is no doubt that the state legislation would have been invalidated.

It is not immediately apparent why a classical liberal should favor legislation which forbids unions and firms from signing a contract which requires union membership as a condition of employment. Certainly, there would be opposition to legislation which prohibited contracts from including provisions on hours, grievance procedures, and working conditions. Union security provisions requiring workers to join unions and to pay union dues are as much a legitimate condition of employment as requirements that workers arrive at work on time and perform their jobs satisfactorily. All of these conditions of employment are coercive of the employees who would prefer to work under other arrangements; but there is no especial diminution of liberty, certainly not in modern-day America. The right to work for a particular firm under an employee's own conditions has not been recognized, and is likely to remain secondary to the right of a firm and a union to establish mutually satisfactory rules for employment.

TO A CLASSICAL LIBERAL, the denial of a union shop, where it is desired both by labor and by management, is a needless and arbitrary reduction in liberty. All workers in each of the nineteen states with Right-to-work laws are denied by statute the opportunity of working in a union shop. Just as an open, competitive society will give birth to firms which can take advantage of the propensity of women to prefer to work from 10:00 A.M. to 3:00 P.M., so it will give birth to firms which hire workers who prefer not to join unions, for whatever reason. This is more than an academic point, since total union membership in the United States is less than one-fourth of the total labor force, and less than one-half of the number of "potential" or "eligible" union members. The open society is far more protective of the liberty of

workers to work under conditions which they prefer than a society which prohibits certain working conditions.

In addition, it is not obvious that union shop provisions should be prohibited in order to improve labor-management relations. On the contrary, there is a strong presumption for allowing the parties to the bargain the widest latitude in working out for themselves those conditions of employment which improve the labor-management relations climate. Bargaining practice suggests that union security provisions are obtained by the union only at the cost of foregoing some other demand. Reportedly, management often "sells" a union shop provision for a five-cent per hour wage increase. Since there is so little known about the impact of union security provisions on labor-management relations, there is every reason to suppose that the regulation of union security ought to be left to the parties involved.

Although all unions might prefer stronger union security provisions, companies are of mixed opinion. Some firms believe that the climate of labor-management relations is improved when unions are assured of members without continuing incidents of bickering; others believe just the opposite. In one case, the labor agreement of a large farm implement manufacturer includes the text of a union security provision which it would want but cannot have because such is not "legally possible under Iowa and Federal laws" (according to the agreement). Thus, the existence of a Right-to-work law interferes with the right of private parties to sign agreements and to commit private property in accordance with their preferences. The effect is to coerce the parties to the bargain and, in our society, to increase the liberty of none.

Let me emphasize that the argument here is not one of whether union security provisions are good or bad; the argument is whether there should be legislation which prohibits them.

IT IS DIFFICULT TO shake the suspicion that many people favor Right-to-work laws because of the presumption that such legislation will weaken the political and economic power of unions. Regardless of whether this presumption is correct, and most of the evidence is in the other direction, this kind of legislation is a most obtuse way of accomplishing the goal. If the opposition to unions is to be based on liberal tenets, it should be focused on the nature of unions and collective bargaining per se, and not on those kinds of government interference which on any other grounds would be inherently indefensible.

Although Right-to-work laws interfere with the right of private contract and must be coercive, if they are effective, it does not follow that repeal of such legislation is neutral with respect to private property. The concern here is that some workers, currently employed in Right-to-work states, who would prefer jobs where union member-ship is not a condition of employment, would suffer a loss of property if their unions obtained union shop contracts. These workers have accumulated rights in the form of pensions, insurance, and, most important, seniority, which they would lose should they have to take another job to avoid union membership. One compromise which would increase freedom, preserve property rights, and minimize coercion might be the repeal of all Right-to-work laws — i.e., repeal of Section 14(b) — but with the provision that all currently employed workers who are not now members of a labor union would not be compelled to join a union as a condition of employment. All new employees in firms which have union shops would be required to join the union as a condition of employment. Such a compromise would ease the transition for workers and unions in states with Right-to-work laws, since job opportunities in those states are increasing at a faster rate than in the economy as a whole.

799

"Fragile" Constitutions

W. H. HUTT

PROF. THOMAS MOLNAR'S courteous criticism of Dr. Denis Cowen's interesting article on "Prospects for South Africa" [1] reminds me of an occasion some years ago when I was addressing a meeting of the South African Institute of Race Relations (from the floor). The question of constitutional protection of minorities had arisen. I put forward the proposition that "the essence of an effective constitution is that it is built on mistrust, not on faith." I can remember the murmer of disapproval — even seething indignation — which swept over the gathering. Most of the kindly, well-meaning people present — many of them clergy — could simply not contemplate so cynical a view.

Several years before that, at another meeting of the same Institute, I had argued that the prospect of an African majority, through the ultimate extension of the franchise on the basis of "one man, one vote," created wholly justifiable fears on the part of the Whites. I suggested that, if the sharing of political power with the Africans was ever to be peacefully achieved, it would have to be based on constitutional entrenchment of the rights of the three

minorities — the Whites, the Coloureds (i.e., the half-castes), and the Indians. I suggested further that, for the presently-enfranchised Whites to be persuaded to share their virtual monopoly of political power, it would be absolutely essential to renounce the principle of universal suffrage on a common roll and accept some form of weighted franchise.

I was told that the Africans would never agree to any such arrangement; that the very suggestion implied a slight on the majority race and a wish to maintain them in a permanent condition of inferiority and subordinacy; and, much to my regret, my proposal evoked an angry attack in the press from Alan Paton, for whom I have a profound admiration as a genuine humanitarian and one of the greatest novelists of this generation.

Professor Molnar's position appears to be exactly the opposite to that of the sentimentalists whose opposition I have recorded. He seems to argue categorically that no effective constitutional protection for minorities, such as the Whites in South Africa, is possible, unless the constitution denies *all* political representation to the majority group. Those who believe, as the Progressive Party in South Africa does,

---

W. H. Hutt has been Professor of Commerce and Dean of the Faculty of Commerce at the University of Cape Town, South Africa. He is currently Visiting Professor of Economics at the University of Virginia.

[1] The two articles mentioned appeared, respectively, in the Winter 1966 and Spring 1965 issues of *New Individualist Review.*

that the solution lies in the direction of limitations on voting rights, he describes as "starry-eyed liberals and misguided intellectuals." Actually, that Party happens to be the only political party of which I myself have ever been a member, and I hardly deserve to be called "liberal" in the current American sense of the word.

The sole reason why I felt compelled to join the Progressives a few years ago was that they are the only party in my country which has any glimmering of insight into the imperative need to restrain majority power. However wrong they may be on some issues, they do perceive that, if we are to find any democratic solution to the incipient racial conflict which history has bequeathed us, it is the state which we must somehow control.

Yet we are reminded by Prof. Molnar that very few bills of rights and constitutions have "proved more than very fragile paper barriers." This is undoubtedly true; but his point is, we should notice, not that constitutional entrenchments cannot be effective when they are enforced, but that constitutions will be torn up when they are unpalatable to majorities.

The tearing up of the 1910 constitution of South Africa through the subterfuge of packing the Senate, and the absence of Constitutional restraint to prevent political appointments to the Supreme Court of the United States (which appointments have led to the Court's functioning on vital issues — as I once heard it put — "like a constitutional convention in permanent session"), ought properly to shake the faith of those who, like myself, believe that minorities *can* be effectively protected by entrenched constitutional provisions with a rigid separation of powers.

But if a constitution is framed by those who have studied dispassionately the manner in which time-serving politicians have in the past trampled on bills of rights, and who recognize therefore that their task must be carried out in an atmosphere of the utmost distrust of politicians and parliaments, and even of judges, must they necessarily fail? Obviously, a more effective means of ensuring judicial independence and preventing judicial tyranny than has yet been achieved in the United States is needed. Moreover, the question of control of the police and the armed forces is also a vital issue.

I DO NOT THINK THE leaders of the Progressive Party in South Africa have gone nearly far enough in their studies of these and other aspects of the working of constitutions. The complex racial difficulties with which they are faced demand more imagination and inventiveness than they have yet given to their task; but they are pioneers among realistic political thinkers about race relations in South Africa. They deserve every encouragement and the frankest criticism from their friends.

May not the attitude of Prof. Molnar on this issue have been influenced by a belief that a more humane form of apartheid is possible? Does he believe that the "separate development" of Africans in Bantustans like the Transkei, in which they will be permitted local government rights and ultimately perhaps (although this is very unlikely) some measure of political independence, can provide a statesmanlike solution?

The truth is that, in spite of all the efforts to bring about segregation of *one* of the races in South Africa — the Africans — they seem to be in the process of integration into the White economy at an accelerating pace. As a very wise resolution submitted to a meeting of the Institute of Race Relations recently put it, "Segregation is an ideal....It does not exist in any general or fundamental form in South Africa. The fact of integration and the ideal of segregation are on different planes and do not admit of a middle

801

course between them...." And the resolution suggests that one proper field of activity is, therefore, "demonstration of the fact of integration and exploration of ways to live with it. ..."

In spite of strenuous, indeed ruthless, governmental attempts to turn back the tide, economic integration is growing. Is it really conceivable, then, that a minority race will be able permanently to deny equality of opportunity to the other races, who constitute an overwhelming majority of the population, and to withhold from Africans the effective right to vote in the areas in which most of them must work? If Prof. Molnar thinks that this is possible, does he not invite the application

to himself of his own epithet, "starry-eyed"?

When the minorities in my country fear eventual domination by the Africans — possibly imbued with the spirit of African nationalism and thirsting for revenge — these minorities are, of course, fearing what nationalists can achieve through the machinery of the state. The Progressive Party and Dr. Cowen are thinking in terms of preventing the abuse of state power. If Prof. Molnar maintains that they have not yet satisfactorily solved the problem of how to do so, I agree with him. But surely he cannot contend that they are groping for a solution *in the wrong direction.*

802

Origins of Apartheid:

In the following excerpts from his book, Economics of the Colour Bar, *Prof. Hutt discusses the origins of* apartheid. *In the opinion of the Editors, an awareness of the history of* apartheid *is important in light of the preceding discussion.*

WE DO NOT . . . find in colour prejudice as such the main origin--nor, perhaps, even the most important cause--of most economic colour bars. The chief source of colour discrimination is, I suggest, to be found in the natural determination to defend economic privilege (the preservation of "customary economic relationships between the races"), non-Whites simply happening to be the essentially underprivileged groups in South Africa. Certainly colour custom and colour prejudice have been persistently exploited in efforts to win electoral support for

measures which seek to curb the tendency of the profit system to admit the poorer races to better opportunities; but such casuistic exploitation of custom and prejudice does not make it the prime motive for the exclusion of competition from the despised or feared Coloureds, Asiatics or Africans.... [1]

Because of the shortage of skilled personnel in South Africa at the beginning of the century, artisan immigrants, reared in the traditions of the emergent restrictionist ideologies and British trade unionism, were brought to fill artisan and foreman posts. It is hardly surprising that, after the Boer war (and together with their Afrikaner comrades after 1907), they should have endeavored to enforce a sort of closed shop which denied all opportunities for advancement to their non-White comrades. The political background of the period had produced stereotypes which actively encouraged the formation of labour unions, and the strike power so

[1] W. H. Hutt, *The Economics of the Colour Bar* (London: Institute of Economic Affairs, 1964), p. 27.

created seems to have enabled the Whites to perpetuate the ratio of White to non-White wage-rates which had been established by the 1880's. In this way, the unions managed not only to preserve the remuneration of their members against the competition of their fellow Whites, but later to forbid the training of Africans for employment in responsible, supervisory and skilled occupations.

What was probably at that time the most blatant colour bar of history (although by no means the most burdensome) received the force of law in 1911. The motive was industrial peace; but it was sought *via* an appeasement of the militant White labour organization, which appeared then to be growing in strike power and political support.

The beginnings of militant unionism date from the 1880's and 1890's when branches of British labour unions were opened in South Africa. The leadership was in the hands of typical union officials of the British type—hard, ruthless but scarcely Marxist. Quite early in South African labour history, however, the influence of the extreme Left seems to have been discernable, and resort to violence in support of strike action was not uncommon. This tendency was probably due to infiltration of the class-war idea from foreign countries rather than from the relatively respectable British trade unionism of the day.... [2]

During the First World War, the White miners' union had succeeded in enforcing wage-rate increases many times larger than those obtained by the unorganized Africans. But the position of the latter had in some respects improved because, through the emergency, they had been permitted to undertake semi-skilled work especially as drill-sharpeners. This opportunity for a small proportion of Africans mitigated the increased costs of mining gold, the price of which rose to a premium after the war for a short period only. When it was obvious that the sterling price

2 *Ibid.*, pp.58-59.

of gold would return to its standard level, the mine-owners naturally attempted to retain Africans in semi-skilled tasks and tried further to obtain some relaxation of other wasteful provisions enforced through regulations under the 1911 Colour Bar Act. They asked for a ratio of 10.5 Africans to 1 White; but the labour union demanded 3.5 to 1. A disastrous strike followed in 1922. The miners were supported by a general strike on the Rand, which developed into virtually an armed uprising. Those who revolted were mainly Afrikaners, but as always the extremists of the Left were experts in the art of fishing in troubled waters. W. H. Andrews, who was shortly to become Secretary of the Communist Party in South Africa, played a leading role in this fight for White privilege. The revolt was crushed but powerful publicity had been given to the notion that the Whites were fighting against capitalist exploiters for the preservation of their traditional and rightful economic supremacy. In that sense, the strike, which has been called the "colour bar strike," was a victory for Andrews and those who called themselves socialists.

At the time of the strike, the overwhelming majority of the white miners (foremen or artisans, as distinct from executives) were Afrikaners from the Transvaal and the Orange Free State, and their anti-colour indoctrination had been fruitfully exploited from the first by the Marxist-indoctrinated inspirers and leaders of the insurrection, such as Andrews. The result was a great boost to the South African Labour Party, which was modelled more or less on its British counterpart and was on the best terms with the British trade-union movement. In 1924, largely through the impact upon White opinion of the 1922 strike, it obtained the chance of sharing in government through a coalition formed with the Nationalist Party, a socialistically-oriented party representing Afrikaners who accepted the principle of White supremacy and non-White subjection. Without this active

803

Page Fifty-one

co-operation of a typically British sort of Socialist party to form a Labour-Nationalist "Pact," the era which introduced the most serious forms of colour injustice might never have emerged....[3]

THE "RATE FOR THE JOB" was the vital principle in the most powerful yet most subtle colour bar that has ever operated. Equal pay for equal work (i.e., for identical outputs of a given quality) is a result of the neutrality of the free non-discriminatory market. It is no method of achieving such a market. When the standard wage-rate is forced above the free market level (whether through legal enactment or the strike threat), thereby reducing the output which can be produced profitably, it must have the effect of preventing the entry of subordinate races or classes into the protected field or of actually excluding them from it. This has been by far the most effective method of preserving White privileges, largely because it can be represented as non-discriminatory. Whereas some of the policies of the Labour-Nationalist Pact amounted to blatant discrimination (such as the deliberate dismissal of non-Whites in order to employ Whites in government service), the effects of the "civilized labour" restraints have been far more important. They have rendered much more formidable the restraints imposed by custom and prejudice that have debarred non-Whites from avenues of economic advancement. They have, indeed, had a more unjust impact than "influx control" and "job reservation" under apartheid....[4]

The initial disadvantages of the non-Whites due to home background and lack of resources for investment in their own education have in themselves been a minor hindrance to their progress. It will generally pay private enterprise to see that education, both general and technical, is made available where openings for the employment of the attributes and skills acquired are not likely to be suppressed. But powerful custom or prejudice, collusive action and legal enactment, by closing potential avenues of employment may destroy the motive for investment in human capital. Indeed, it will be wasteful for the state, for business concerns or for individuals to devote their energies and limited incomes to such purposes. But there would have been an irresistibly strong demand for developing the industrial usefulness of the Coloureds if it had not been for fears that any such move would have encountered other legislative steps to render unusable the skills so developed. The profit motive is powerful; but when it is likely to be overruled by legislation or regulation its power to serve the community is hamstrung....[5]

I have tried to show that in South Africa it has been to the advantage of investors as a whole that all colour bars should be broken down; and that the managements of commercial and industrial firms (when they have not been intimidated by politicians wielding the planning powers of the state) have striven to find methods of providing more productive and better remunerated opportunities for the non-Whites....[6]

The virtues of the free market do not depend upon the virtues of the men at the political top but on the dispersed powers of substitution exercised by men in their role as consumers. In that role, a truly competitive market enables them to exert the energy which enforces the neutrality of business decision-making in respect of race, colour, creed, sex, class, accent, school, or income group. The reader will have noticed that at no time have I claimed that the free market which released the "liberating force" has been motivated by altruistic sentiment....[7]

3 *Ibid.*, pp.68-69.
4 *Ibid.*, pp.72-73.

5 *Ibid.*, p.79.
6 *Ibid.*, p.173.
7 *Ibid.*, pp.174-75.

Kefauver and
Populist Economics

SAM PELTZMAN

In a Few Hands: Monopoly Power in America by Estes Kefauver, Baltimore: Penguin Books, 1965. 246p. $1.25, paper.

THE LATE SENATOR Estes Kefauver first came into prominence in the early 1950's as chairman of the Senate crime investigating committee. After he had made two unsuccessful bids for the Democratic Presidential nomination, his name reappeared in the headlines in 1958 when the Senate Subcommittee on Antitrust and Monopoly conducted hearings under his chairmanship on industrial pricing practices. *In a Few Hands* summarizes some of the more lurid findings which made those hearings newsworthy and serves as a vehicle for the Senator's random thoughts on the problem of monopoly in American industry.

Since the book is about monopoly, it was to be expected that Senator Kefauver would define the beast. The etymologically correct definition — a market served by one seller — applies to none of the industries discussed in the book (drugs, steel, baking, automobiles). Most of the time Senator Kefauver seems to apply the term to an industry dominated by a few firms, but he never does precisely define it. Sometimes it

Sam Peltzman is Assistant Professor of Economics at U.C.L.A., and a Contributing Editor to *New Individualist Review*. He received his Ph.D. from the University of Chicago in 1965.

appears that the word "monopoly" is just longhand for "bad" — since a monopoly, whatever it is, is bad, many, if not all bad things derive from monopolies. This utter failure to make necessary intellectual distinctions is well illustrated by the Senator's discussion of the drug industry.

Here we have an industry in which Kefauver is able to cite numerous examples (pp. 11-23) of small competitors substantially undercutting their larger rivals in order to win orders, and he suggests that the availability of cut-price drugs is fairly widespread (p. 24). To be sure, price competition doesn't characterize all drugs; but the Senator makes it quite clear that the most notable exceptions are to be found among patented drugs.[1] Now, of course, price competition is absent here because of a *legally enforced* monopoly and has nothing to do with the particular market structure of the drug industry. Whatever else it may be, it is not the purpose of the patent laws to promote price competition in drugs or any other patented product but to prevent precisely that. If price competition in drugs now protected by patent is deemed desirable, then it is the patent law and not the structure of the drug industry which has to be changed.

If the drug industry, where it is unprotected by law, doesn't exhibit the

805

[1] *Op. cit.*, pp. 23-25, 36.

Page Fifty-three

evil pricing policies of monopolistic industries, what other evil doings can it be saddled with? In answering this question Senator Kefauver makes much of some of the defective drugs that have been introduced onto the market in recent years, e.g., thalidomide, chloromycetin, MER/29. The tragic consequences of the introduction of these drugs is well-known, and the Senator recounts them for his reader. Yet, again, the connection of all this with the market structure of the drug industry is never made clear. Do such mistakes occur more frequently because the drug industry is dominated by a few large firms, or would such events occur about as frequently if there were ten thousand equal sized drug producers? Surely it would seem that the losses incurred by way of law suits, damaged trade reputation, etc., would weigh as heavily against relatively large as against relatively small firms. Implicitly Senator Kefauver must have believed that these losses were somehow not as great for the relatively large firms, or that such firms derived some special gains from selling bad drugs; if he didn't believe this, why the association of the practice with "monopoly" and not, say, with stupidity? The reason for this belief is never spelled out, however, and it will remain a mystery to those who do not share the Senator's animus against the drug industry.

Since Senator Kefauver's discussion of other industries is no more precise and no less confused than that of the drug industry, it is easy to wonder if he was trying to make any point at all. He was; but it surfaces amidst contradiction, and it turns out to have nothing to do with monopoly at all.

SENATOR KEFAUVER'S central point becomes obvious when one compares his discussions of the steel and baking industries. The steel industry is chided for various monopolistic pricing practices — rigid prices, implicit collusion whereby all firms adopt the prices set by one of them, etc. If this or any industry is to serve the public interest, according to Senator Kefauver, the firms in it really ought to compete against each other in the most vigorous manner:

> It is this free spirit of individualistic behavior which gives to the public the benefits of competitive enterprise, namely lower prices and better quality. It is this same spirit which earns the enmity of the monopoly for its unsettling and disturbing impact upon established ways of doing things, not to speak of the disruptive consequences on [sic] monopolistic pricing and profits. [2]

Now, sometime after World War II some baking companies prospered by acting as the Senator believed steel companies should. They penetrated many markets by offering lower prices than existing bakers. Predictably, this forced some established bakers out of business. Yet this particular disturbance of established ways of doing business is *not* welcomed by Senator Kefauver. It is, instead, cause for complaint that "small producers, unable to stand up under the pressure directed against them by the giants of the industry, are disappearing from the American scene." [3] All of a sudden the laudable "competitive enterprise" recommended to the steel industry becomes, when practiced by baking companies, evil "competitive warfare." [4] The desideratum is no longer the "free spirit of individualistic behavior" but rather "free and *reasonable* competition." [5] Why this palpable contradiction, this switch from the ethics of competition to the ethics of the cartel? The answer has already been suggested: The aggressive bak-

---

2 *Ibid.,* p. 138.
3 *Ibid.,* p. 143.
4 *Ibid.,* p. 139.
5 *Ibid.,* p. 144. Emphasis added.

ers, because of their success, have become *large;* they are replacing *small* bakers. This really is the crux of the matter. Both the aggressive baker and the somnolent steelmaker are bad mainly because they are big. It would do little good to point out that large absolute size has nothing per se to do with monopoly; that, in fact, many of the small bakers replaced by large, nationwide bakers were local monopolies; and that a few large companies competing in several local markets make for a more competitive industry than several local monopolies. Senator Kefauver simply seems to have had a tropistic reaction against big corporations (the TVA excepted) which he embellished with the nostalgia for rural and small town America that comes from his Populist political heritage.[6] He tends to identify this advocacy of an economic system composed of many, physically small firms with advocacy of the competitive system and opposition to monopoly. The normal functioning of a competitive system will, of course, comprehend cases where large firms win out over small firms. At no point in his book, however, does the Senator point to any such event as an example of the healthy functioning of a competitive economy. Where such events are alluded to, as with the baking industry, the context is the triumph of evil bigness over the victimized innocence of the small.

Once Senator Kefauver's basic premise becomes clear, many of the other points he makes become explainable, if not particularly understandable. Take, for example, his discussion of the relationship between monopoly and the development of a community — "monopoly" for these purposes being identified with the dominant importance of large absentee-owned industries in a community's economic life. To monopoly, or rather to this grotesque *A is*

bad, B is bad, therefore A is B* definition of monopoly, Senator Kefauver attempts to attribute, in whole or part, each of the following community ills or presumed ills: shoddily built houses, slums, high bankruptcy rates among small retail stores, high infant mortality rates, lack of popular interest in literature and education, low church membership, a diminution of the spirit of neighborliness and good fellowship, and excessive time spent by youths in pool halls.[7] This incredible list could be expanded. Some may be tempted to find in all this a reflection of the type of mentality that moved men to burn witches in former times. To Senator Kefauver, however, it must have appeared the simple truth that where the desirable attributes of the small Tennessee town have vanished, big companies captained from the far-off metropolis are the cause of it all. Anyhow, talking against monopoly is these days more socially respectable than witch burning.

IT IS PERHAPS fortunate that all Senator Kefauver, the co-author of an important antitrust statute, did in his book was to talk against monopoly. He made no important policy recommendation for remedying what he conceived to be the monopoly problem. In fact, he is at his most perceptive where he discusses and rejects certain remedies advanced by others. He rejects general government price regulation, for example, because of a clear recognition that where it already exists — e.g., airlines, railroads, natural gas — such regulation has become little more than a shield for cartelization.[8]

807

---

6 *Ibid.,* pp. 160-61.

7 *Ibid.,* pp. 170-71, 177-78, 183
8 Cf. C. D. Stone, "ICC: Some Reminiscences on the Future of American Transportation," *New Individualist Review,* Spring 1963, pp. 3-15; S. Peltzman, "CAB: Freedom from Competition." *ibid.,* pp. 16-23; R. W. Gerwig, "Natural Gas Production: A Study of Costs of Regulation," *Journal of Law and Economics,* V (1962), 69-92.

BOOKS:

Freedom Under Lincoln by Dean Sprague, Boston: Houghton Mifflin Co., 1965. 345 p. $5.95.

808

THE COMPLETION, a year ago, of the centennial celebration affords an opportunity for a more sober re-evaluation of the Civil War's continuing influence upon American life and thought. *Freedom Under Lincoln* is a useful contribution to Civil War history which also offers timely instruction for our own day. In a dramatic and interesting way, it tells the story of the suppression of civil liberties in the United States as the Lincoln Administration struggled to preserve the Union. In the unprecedented experience of trying to cope with the problems of secession and civil war, the North lived in a state of public hysteria. Fearful for the safety of the capital at Washington and of the border slave states of Maryland, Kentucky, and Missouri, the President, without consulting Congress, suspended the writ of habeas corpus and permitted Secretary of State Seward to order the arbitrary martial arrest and imprisonment of hundreds of American citizens.

More than in any other crisis in the nation's history, the Civil War raised the question of the extent of the individual's loyalties and responsibilities in relation to his government. Though there was justifiable concern in the North over the presence there of thousands of Southern sympathizers, it was nevertheless tragic that the Lincoln Administration felt forced to abandon traditional American rights and freedoms. In addition to the sudden arrest of citizens whose loyalty was suspect — often on the flimsiest sort of hearsay evidence — newspapers were coerced or suspended, state legislatures dissolved, and free elections corrupted. Soldiers home on leave heightened the intolerant militarist atmosphere in the North while, again and again, as Sprague's book demonstrates, the doctrine of military necessity was used improperly to justify harsh measures. More often than not, the appeal to national security, in areas far removed from the battlefield, was simply an excuse to cloak the expansion of Federal power over the states and individual citizens. In the author's words, "the policy of repression did have a tremendous impact on the nation. It fundamentally altered the balance of power between the Federal and state governments, laying the groundwork for such actions as the national draft and the Federal income tax."

Fortunately, most of those imprisoned were held only for short periods of time — as the protests against the arbitrary arrests grew in volume and intensity. Some of those taken away, such as James Wall of New Jersey who later became a United States Senator, actually derived a certain political benefit from their imprisonment and never stopped talking against the War. After 1861, when the immediate military safety of the North was largely assured, the suppression of dissent was directed mainly against those who advocated the prompt negotiation of a peace settlement with the South; and later, in 1863, when Clement L. Vallandigham was arrested for stating his peace views, the famous midnight knock on the door by agents of Secretary Seward or Stanton had become a rare event. As the brave but scattered voices of dissent were silenced, the growth of national power over the individual become more and more a component part of the preservation of the Union.

ALTHOUGH THE BROAD outlines of the American democratic process were preserved, and although Lincoln himself exercised a mild and humane influence within his Administration, it is clear nevertheless that the Civil War did great violence to the Constitution it sought to safeguard. In the very process of extending freedom to the Negro slaves, countless Americans were temporarily deprived of their civil liberties and personal freedom. That the ultimate legacy of the Civil War was, however, one of hope rather than despair is indicated in the author's concluding quotation from the Supreme Court's classic postwar defense of individual rights in the celebrated Milligan case of 1866. In language which has echoed to our own time, the Court held that "the Constitution of the United States is a law for rulers and people, equally in war and in peace, and covers with the shield of its protection all classes of men, at all times, and under all circumstances."

—*ARTHUR A. EKIRCH. JR.*[1]

1 Arthur A. Ekirch, Jr. is Professor of History at the State University of New York at Albany. He is the author of *The Decline of American Liberalism* and *The Civilian and the Military*.

809

Page Fifty-eight

NEW BOOKS AND ARTICLES

THE FOLLOWING IS A SELECT LIST OF BOOKS AND ARTICLES WHICH, IN THE OPINION OF THE EDITORS, MAY BE OF INTEREST TO OUR READERS.

Robert M. Hurt and Robert M. Schuchman, "The Economic Rationale of Copyright," *American Economic Review,* LVI (May 1966), 421-32. The authors, who were both closely associated with *New Individualist Review,* argue that copyright is not the most suitable way either to protect property rights in publication or to promote publication. "If we believe in the theory that an author is entitled to certain moral rights as an extension of his personality, then traditional tort law protection could satisfy our objectives short of a copyright monopoly grant. If we are attracted by the analysis of the Register of Copyrights, that society has an obligation to support the creators of literary products, our goal could be achieved by other methods of reward than copyright, such as tax exemptions for royalties or payment of cash bounties for literary creation....We can say that the traditional assumption that copyrights enhance the general welfare is at least subject to attack on theoretical grounds; the subject certainly deserves more investigation and less self-rightious defense."

811

One of the most interesting and lively publications on the market today is *Innovator,* devoted to "applications, experiments, and advanced developments of liberty." In its June issue, several authors provide the reader with information about the origins of the government postal monopoly, and the *non-governmental* origins of most of the technological advances which the industry has made. An earlier issue (January 1966) carried articles concerned with the question of privately owned roads and highways, as opposed to the present system of government-maintained roads.   Published in newsletter format, a year's subscription is $2.00. Write: *Innovator,* Box 34718, Los Angeles, Calif. 90034.

Grant McConnell, "P.R. in the Forests," *Sierra Club Bulletin,* April 1966. Prof. McConnell, of the Department of Political Science at the University of Chicago, cites evidence in this article to add the United States Forest Service to the list of regulatory agencies taken over and made to serve the interests of those supposedly regulated: "As with other reforming and formally independent agencies, time and exposure took their toll. In order to survive and also maintain its bureaucratic autonomy, the Forest Service had to accomodate itself to the interest groups whose activities it was supposed to regulate. Over time, the service, like such other independent regulatory agencies as the ICC, the CAB and the SEC, acquired as its own constituency a particular industry, in this case lumber. Thus, in symbiotic relationship, there lies behind the Forest Service a strongly organized and determined lumbering industry." Write: Sierra Club, 220 Bush Street, San Francisco, Calif. 94104. This article is an adaptation of one by the same title which appeared in the *Nation,* December 27, 1965, and additional material is in Prof. McConnell's recent book, *Private Power and American Democracy* (New York: Alfred A. Knopf, 1966), $4.95.

Jora R. Minasian, "Television Pricing and the Theory of Public Goods," *Journal of Law and Economics,* VII (October 1964), 71-80. This article, in the form of an analysis of the theory of public goods advanced by Prof. Paul A. Samuelson, is a fine addition to the literature on pay television. Prof. Minasian is chiefly concerned with the additional choices in programming which would be yielded by subscription TV, since, of the two, subscription pricing would be more responsive to minority consumer wants. This article should be read in conjunction with R.H. Coase's article, "The Federal Communications Commission," in the second volume of the *Journal* (1959). For subscriptions or single copies, write: *The Journal of Law and Economics,* University of Chicago Law School, Chicago, Illinois 60637. Single copies, $2.50; students, $1.00. The *Journal* is issued annually; subscription prices are multiples of single copy prices.

Two articles in major publications have recently noted a striking comparison between the United States today and the first years of the Roman Empire: Thomas Molnar, "Imperial America: A Look into the Future," *National Review,* May 3, 1966, and Hans J. Morgenthau, "The Colossus of Johnson City," *New York Review of Books,* March 31, 1966. Although the two authors differ markedly in their political views, both writers recognize that Empire may work unintended effects upon American federal institutions. These articles, and many others offering a more thorough treatment

812

of the subject, ought to be of interest (i) to conservatives who advocate a vigorous foreign policy but limited government at home, and (ii) to social democrats who oppose such a foreign policy but favor a vigorous government at home. Specifically to be recommended is a pamphlet by Garet Garrett, first published in 1952 and reprinted in his book *The People's Pottage* (Caldwell, Idaho: Caxton Printers, 1953), entitled "The Rise of Empire." This short piece is an excellent, perceptive analysis of the degeneration of a republic into an empire through the actions of a strong central executive and an aggressive foreign policy. A condensed reprint of this article appeared in the Winter 1966 issue of *Left and Right* (Box 395, Cathedral Station, New York NY 10025; 85 cents).

An informative discussion of the recent Supreme Court ruling in the Ginzberg and other pornography cases is provided in the April 11, 1966, issue of *The New Leader,* by Richard Morgan of Columbia University ("The Court and Obscenity"). Morgan emphasizes the lack of logic and arbitrariness of the Brennan decision against Ginzberg, underwritten by Warren, Fortas, and two other Justices. The issue is dealt with also in an editorial in the April 19, 1966, issue of *National Review* ("Ginzberg and Pornography"), a contribution to the discussion notable not so much for the light it casts on the problem as for the insight it provides into the thinking of contemporary American conservatives. *National Review's* editorial comment exhausts itself in irrelevent sallies against "the hypocrite Ginzberg...a pornographer-for-profit," the foolishness of some of his supporters, etc. The focus is on personalities, and missing entirely is any discussion of the one important question: *Should the government be permitted to censor any publication simply on the grounds of obscenity; and if so, Why?*

"The Draft is Unfair," by Jack Raymond. *The New York Times Magazine,* January 2, 1966. A brief summation of the reasons underlying the frequent charge of unfairness leveled against conscription as it operates in the United States. We will hopefully be excused for considering the most significant part

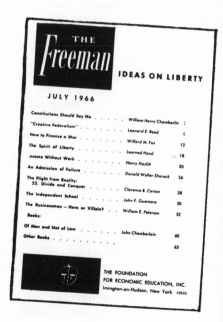

of the article to be the extended comments by Prof. Milton Friedman, who favors an all-volunteer military force except in cases of wars on the scale of World War II (but his position on volunteer forces holds for cases such as Viet Nam). States Friedman: "Conscription is a tax in kind — that is, forced labor imposed on the young men who are drafted or who volunteer to serve because of the threat of the draft. One of the great advances in human freedom was the conversion of taxes in kind to money taxes. A similar advance would be attained now by repealing conscription and using volunteer enlistments to staff our armed forces. In order to do so, we would, of course, have to make military service sufficiently attractive in terms not only of pay but of career opportunities and conditions of service to get the number of men we need. But this is an advantage, not a disadvantage. It would be not only more equitable but also more efficient." Friedman considers that the estimated increased cost of the volunteer system ($4-6 billion) is somewhat exaggerated, and thinks that the taxpayers would be ready to accept the increased costs in order to abolish a bad institution.

In the second issue of *Left and Right,* published last Autumn, Murray N. Rothbard has an article of major interest on "Liberty and the New Left." The author persuasively maintains that the New Left — in contradistinction to the old Left — places a good deal of emphasis on values which the libertarian also shares: decentralization of power, personal autonomy, distrust of government, its bureaucracy and police. Moreover, certain writers closely associated with the New Left, e.g., Paul Goodman, are proving interestingly attracted to the voluntarism of laissez faire capitalism.

Ronald Hamowy, "Left and Right Meet," *The New Republic*, March 12, 1966. Ronald Hamowy of Stanford University, discusses the transposition which has taken place between Right and Left: whereas the New Left seems to be libertarian, the Right-wing has become more statist in the last decade. This article appears also in a book *Thoughts of the Young Radicals*, published by *The New Republic*, and available from them for 75 cents.

In its April 21 and April 28, 1966, issues, *The Village Voice* featured a report on Synanon, the radically different and relatively extremely successful method of treating narcotics addicts ("The Synanon Way," by Ross Wetzteon). "In an area where statistics are more inconclusive than usual, the most conservative estimate is that Synanon has nine times the 'cure-rate' of any other method. Other estimates are bolder — no other method works at all." Especially interesting from the viewpoint of libertarians is the fact that Synanon has been developed and the centers were started for its application completely independent of any governmental agency. New York City recently offered the organization a grant of $328,000, but this was turned down. Marvin Tobman, one of the leaders of the school, explained that if money comes from the government, "no matter how much it is, it's no good. All the money would mean is that we'd become dependent. Pretty soon they'd be sure to get their hooks into us and before you know it they'd be saying you have to put this bed over there and move that chest of drawers over there. We'd end up just another run-of-the-mill flophouse. This way it's all ours." Funds for the organization come from private donations (averaging $25-30), private organizations such as Yale University, and from the proceeds of Synanon Industries, Inc., "the largest distributor of pens on the West Coast."

Know Your Enemy!!

The editors of NEW INDIVIDUALIST REVIEW have recently, through their highly placed contacts in the Communist Empire, come into possession of a fantastic and hitherto secret Communist blue-print for world domination. Entitled BLUE-PRINT FOR WORLD DOMINATION, it was composed in the depths of the Kremlin in 1920, by a noted Bolshevik writer, and has been ratified and re-ratified by numerous Communist Congresses and countless Communist deeds. Every patriotic American must familiarize himslef with this shocking and sobering document! Here are the Conclusions, as set forth by its author, the well-known Bolshevik leader, V. I. LENIN.

816

"In order to conquer the world for our Godless Creed we must employ infinite craftiness and patience. The most difficult nation to vanquish will be the United States, for there the people are basically prosperous, moral, and un-revolutionary, because of the inspiring achievements of free enterprise. After the United States has been initially softened up by the abolition of the gold standard and the introduction of welfare legislation, we will begin this Three-Point Program for victory over America:

"(1) First we will trick them into banning prayer in the public schools. Just as fluoridation of water destroys the body, so the elimination of public-school prayer destroys the spirit.

"(2) Then, in keeping with our almost Oriental immoralism, we will begin the steady introduction of pornographic materials—both those which are rankly so, and those which we will camouflage as "avant-gardism"—into American society. Pornography will be the chief weapon in our campaign to rot out the moral fibre of America, but abstract art and 12-tone music are not to be neglected in this connection.

"(3) Our final take-over will be preceded by an unparalleled crusade to destroy the magazine, NEW INDIVUDUALIST REVIEW. This quarterly journal, because it is so highly informative, entertaining, and intellectual, is perhaps our single most serious problem in the United States, rivalled only by the Strategic Air Command. To destroy NEW INDIVIDUALIST REVIEW is to make America a plum ripe for the picking!"

Block Communist
Plans for World
Domination
Today! Subscribe
to NEW INDI—
VIDUALIST
REVIEW!

The Journal of

LAW & ECONOMICS

VOLUME VII	OCTOBER 1964	PRICE $2.50

Aaron Director . . . . . . .The Parity of the Economic Market Place

Harold Demsetz . . . . . . The Exchange and Enforcement of Property Rights

The Rt. Hon. Sir
  Kenneth Diplock . . . . Antitrust and the Judicial Process

Kenneth W. Dam . . . . . .Trademarks, Price Discrimination and the Bureau of Customs

Abba P. Lerner . . . . . . .Conflicting Principles of Public Utility Price Regulation

Jora R. Minasian . . . . . .Television Pricing and the Theory of Public Goods

Paul A. Samuelson . . . . .Public Goods and Subscription TV: Correction of the Record

A. W. Coats . . . . .The Role of Authority in the Development of British Economics

Roger W. Weiss . . . . . . .The Case for Federal Meat Inspection Examined

John S. McGee . . . . Government Intervention in the Spanish Sugar Industry

THE UNIVERSITY OF CHICAGO LAW SCHOOL

The Journal of Law and Economics is published annually in October by the University of Chicago Law School. It specializes in the discussion of public policy. The editor of Volumes I to VI was Aaron Director. Subsequent volumes have appeared under the editorship of R. H. Coase.

All volumes of *The Journal of Law and Economics* may be obtained for the price of $2.50 per volume. However, the Journal is also available at a *special student rate* of $1.00 per volume. Those students wishing to obtain all volumes of *The Journal of Law and Economics* issued to date (through Volume VII) should remit $8.00, or, if they wish also to include Volume IX (October 1966), $9.00. Please make all remittances payable to the University of Chicago Law School. Send orders and remittances (and if wishing to pay at student rates, particulars of student status) to:

Publications Secretary
The Journal of Law and Economics
University of Chicago Law School
1111 East 60th Street
Chicago, Illinois 60637

THE NATION'S ECONOMIC OBJECTIVES
Edited by EDGAR O. EDWARDS

Contributors: Kenneth E. Boulding, Arthur F. Burns, Lester V. Chandler, Seymour E. Harris, Simon Kuznets, Fritz Machlup, Edward S. Mason, *and* Jacob Viner. "This book will be a source of pride and pleasure to economists. We can be proud of the demonstration that some economists have something important to say to the public and can say it in an understandable and interesting way." —*HERBERT STEIN, American Economic Review.* 167 *pages Paper, $1.75 Cloth, $4.95*

STRATEGIC POWER AND SOVIET FOREIGN POLICY
By ARNOLD L. HORELICK and MYRON RUSH

"...a first-rate piece of work — original in presentation and conclusions, sound and often brilliant in its analysis, and extremely well written." — *HANS J. MORGENTHAU.*

The authors brilliantly analyze the crucial relationship between strategic military power and Soviet foreign policy, showing how the Soviet leaders have been both attracted by the political potentialities of nuclear weapons and sobered by their dangers. They detail the inner workings of the massive Soviet effort to deceive the West about the USSR's ICBM superiority and the way in which the Soviet leaders attempted to manipulate Western beliefs about the strategic balance to their advantage in Berlin. The Cuban missile crisis, which resulted from Soviet failure in Berlin and the collapse of the "missile gap" myth, is analyzed as it may have been viewed from Moscow. The book concludes with an examination of future alternative Soviet military-foreign policies likely to be considered by the present Soviet leaders in the light of past failures. A RAND Corporation Research Study. *224 pages, $5.95*

THE GARDEN AND THE WILDERNESS
Religion and Government in American Constitutional History
By MARK DE WOLFE HOWE

"...a totally absorbing series of lectures on the tradition of church and state relations in the United States....Mr. Howe does not quarrel with the Supreme Court's conclusions in a notable series of decisions...but he wishes the justices were better historians....an instructive book and a timely one" - *MERRILL D. PETERSON, Virginia Quarterly Review.*

208 pages, $4.50

UNIVERSITY OF CHICAGO PRESS
Chicago/London

In Canada, University of Toronto Press

VOLUME 4
NUMBER 4
SPRING 1967

New
INDIVIDUALIST
Review

A JOURNAL OF CLASSICAL LIBERAL THOUGHT

Spring 1967 $1.00   Vol. 4, No. 4

BOUND VOLUMES OF
NEW INDIVIDUALIST REVIEW

The Editors of **New Individualist Review** are pleased to announce in conjunction with publication of the first number in our fifth volume the issue of a small number of complete, bound sets of the journal which will be available for distribution in December of 1968. These rare and valuable sets will include the three out-of-print issues of **New Individualist Review** which are not available to the general public, and unavailable in most libraries; issues, we might add, containing articles by F.A. Hayek, Milton Friedman, Murray N. Rothbard, as well as all of the original editors of the journal.

This announcement is being made in the endeavor to supplement our subscription revenues with contributions from readers and supporters who may have been unaware of our need and dependence upon supplemental contributions for continued publication. The number of bound sets of **New Individualist Review** which will be available is strictly limited by the availability of the out-of-print numbers; it may be impossible to repeat this offer. If you would like to obtain one of these sets and assist **N.I.R.** in its publication, please send your check in the amount of $100.00 or more to **New Individualist Review**, Ida Noyes Hall, University of Chicago, Illinois 60637.

NIR Back Issues

Certain back issues of NEW INDIVIDUALIST REVIEW can be purchased for a limited time at the special rate of $1.00 per copy. Among the issues presently available are those containing:

"Sin and the Criminal Law," by Robert M. Hurt (II/1)

"National Review: Criticism and Reply," by Ronald Hamowy and William F. Buckley, Jr. (I/3)

"The Fusionists on Liberalism and Tradition," by Ralph Raico (III/3)

"Civil Liberties in the Welfare State," by Robert M. Schuchman (II/3)

"The Uneasy Case for State Education," by E.G. West (IV/2)

"Why Not A Volunteer Army?" by Milton Friedman (IV/4)

A complete set of the available back copies (fourteen issues) may be ordered for $13.00, postpaid. The three out-of-print numbers can be provided by xerographic reproduction at a cost of $4.00 each. Address inquiries to:

NEW INDIVIDUALIST REVIEW
Ida Noyes Hall, University of Chicago
Chicago, Illinois 60637

NEW INDIVIDUALIST REVIEW

A JOURNAL OF CLASSICAL LIBERAL THOUGHT

SPRING 1967   VOLUME 4, NUMBER 4

823

NEW INDIVIDUALIST REVIEW is published quarterly by *New Individualist Review, Inc.*, at Ida Noyes Hall, University of Chicago, Chicago, Illinois 60637. Telephone 312/363-8778.

Opinions expressed in signed articles do not necessarily represent the views of the editors. Editorial, advertising, and subscription correspondence and manuscripts should be sent to NEW INDIVIDUALIST REVIEW, Ida Noyes Hall, University of Chicago, Chicago, Illinois 60637. All manuscripts become the property of NEW INDIVIDUALIST REVIEW.

Subscription rates: $3.00 per year. Two years at $5.75.

Second printing revised. Copyright 1968 by *New Individualist Review, Inc.*, Chicago, Illinois. All rights reserved. Republication of less than 200 words may be made without specific permission of the publisher, provided NEW INDIVIDUALIST REVIEW is duly credited and two copies of the publication in which such material appears are forwarded to NEW INDIVIDUALIST REVIEW.

NEW

INDIVIDUALIST

REVIEW

EDITORIAL STAFF

Editor-in-Chief • J. M. Cobb
Associate Editors • David Levy
James M. S. Powell
Editorial Assistant • J. Huston McCulloch
Contributing Editors • Robert L. Cunningham
Bruce Goldberg • Sam Peltzman
Ralph Raico • Robert Schuettinger

EDITORIAL ADVISORS

Yale Brozen • Milton Friedman • George J. Stigler
University of Chicago
F. A. Hayek   Benjamin A. Rogge
University of Freiburg   Wabash College

824

Complaints of the loss of individuality and the lessening of respect for the person and his rights have become a commonplace of our time; they nonetheless point to a cause for genuine concern. NEW INDIVIDUALIST REVIEW, an independent journal associated with no organization or political party, believes that in the realm of politics and economics the system most effectively guaranteeing proper respect for individuality is that which, historically, has gone by the name of classical liberalism; the elements of this system are private property, civil liberties, the rule of law, and, in general, the strictest limits placed on the power of government. It is the purpose of the Review to stimulate and encourage explorations of important problems from a viewpoint characterized by thoughtful concern with individual liberty.

Why Not a Volunteer Army?

OUR MILITARY FORCES currently require the services of only a minority of young men. At most, something like one-third will have seen military service by the time they reach twenty-six. This percentage is scheduled to decline still further as the youngsters born in the postwar baby boom come of age. Some method of "selective service" is inevitable. The present method is inequitable, wasteful, and inconsistent with a free society.

On this point there is wide agreement. Even most supporters of a draft like the present one regard it as at best a necessary evil; and representatives of all parts of the political spectrum have urged that conscription be abolished — including John Kenneth Galbraith and Barry Goldwater; the New Left and the Republican Ripon Society.

The disadvantages of our present system of compulsion and the advantages of a volunteer army are so widely recognized that we can deal with them very briefly. The more puzzling question is why we have continued to use compulsion. The answer is partly inertia — a carryover from a total war situation, when the case for a volunteer army is far weaker. But even more, the answer is the tyranny of the status quo. The

Milton Friedman is Paul Snowden Russell Distinguished Service Professor of Economics at the University of Chicago, and past President of the American Economics Association. This article is an amplified text of his paper presented to the Conference on the Draft held at the University of Chicago in December 1966.

natural tendency of an administrator of a large, complex, and ongoing activity is to regard the present method of administering it as the only feasible way to do so and to object strenuously that any proposed alternative is visionary and unfeasible — even though the same man, once the change is made and it becomes the existing method, will argue just as strenuously that *it* is the only feasible method.

This bureaucratic stand-pattism has been reinforced by a confusion between the apparent and the real cost of manning the armed forces by compulsion. The confusion has made it appear that a volunteer army would be much more expensive to the country and hence might not be feasible for fiscal reasons. In fact, the cost of a volunteer army, properly calculated, would almost surely be less than of a conscripted army. It is entirely feasible to maintain present levels of military power on a strictly volunteer basis.

The other disadvantages that have been attributed to a volunteer army are that it might be racially unbalanced, would not provide sufficient flexibility in size of forces, and would enhance the political danger of undue military influence. While the problems referred to are real, the first and third are in no way connected with the use of voluntary or compulsory means to recruit enlisted men and do not constitute valid arguments against abolishing the draft. The second has more merit but devices exist

Page Three

to provide moderate flexibility under a voluntary as under a compulsory system.

There is no reason why we cannot move to volunteer forces gradually — by making conditions of service more and more attractive until the whip of compulsion fades away. This, in my opinion, is the direction in which we should move, and the sooner the better.

A volunteer army would be manned by people who had chosen a military career rather than, at least partly, by reluctant conscripts anxious only to serve out their term. Aside from the effect on fighting spirit, this would produce a lower turnover in the armed services, saving precious man-hours that are now wasted in training or being trained. Also it would permit intensive training and a higher average level of skill for the men in service; and it would encourage the use of more and better equipment. A smaller, but more highly skilled, technically competent, and better armed force could provide the same or greater military strength.

A volunteer army would preserve the freedom of individuals to serve or not to serve. Or, put the other way, it would avoid the arbitrary power that now resides in draft boards to decide how a young man shall spend several of the most important years of his life — let alone whether his life shall be risked in warfare. An incidental advantage would be to raise the level and tone of political discussion.

A volunteer army would enhance also the freedom of those who now do not serve. Being conscripted has been used as a weapon — or thought by young men to be so used — to discourage freedom of speech, assembly, and protest. The freedom of young men to emigrate or to travel abroad has been limited by the need to get the permission of a draft board if the young man is not to put himself in the position of inadvertantly becoming a law-breaker.

ONE GOOD EXAMPLE of the effect on freedom of a volunteer army is that it would completely eliminate the tormenting and insoluble problem now posed by the conscientious objector — real or pretended.

A by-product of freedom to serve would be avoidance of the present arbitrary discrimination among different groups. A large faction of the poor are rejected on physical or mental grounds. The relatively well-to-do used to be in an especially good position to take advantage of the possibilities of deferment offered by continuing their schooling. Hence the draft bears disproportionately on the upper lower classes and the lower middle classes. The fraction of high-school graduates who serve is vastly higher than of either those who have gone to college or those who dropped out before finishing high school.

A volunteer army would permit young men, both those who serve and those who do not, to plan their schooling, their careers, their marriages, and their families in accordance with their own long-run interests. As it is, the uncertainty about the draft affects every decision they make and often leads them to behave differently than they otherwise would in the correct or mistaken belief that they will thereby reduce the chance of being drafted.

Substitution of a volunteer army (or of a lottery) for the present draft would permit colleges and universities to pursue their proper educational function, freed alike from the incubus of young men — probably numbering in the hundreds of thousands — who would prefer to be at work rather than in school but who now continue their schooling in the hope of avoiding the draft, and from controversy about issues strictly irrelevant to their educational function. We certainly need controversy in the universities — but about intellectual and educational issues, not whether to rank or not to rank students for their draft boards.

Similarly, the community at large would benefit from the reduction of unwise early marriages contracted at least partly under the whip of the draft and from the probably associated reduction in the birth rate. Industry and government would benefit from being able to hire young men on their merits, not their deferments.

So long as compulsion is retained, inequity, waste, and interference with freedom are inevitable. A lottery would only make the arbitrary element in the present system overt. Universal national service would only compound the evil — regimenting all young men, and perhaps women, to camouflage the regimentation of some.

If a very large fraction of the young men of the relevant age groups are required — or will be used whether required or not — in the military services, the advantages of a volunteer army become very small. It would still be technically possible to have a volunteer army, and there would still be some advantages, since it is doubtful that literally 100 per cent of the potential candidates will in fact be drawn into the army; but if nearly everyone who is physically capable will serve anyway, there is little room for free choice, the avoidance of uncertainty, and so on. To rely on volunteers under such conditions would then require very high pay in the armed services, and very high burdens on those who do not serve, in order to attract a sufficient number into the armed forces. This would involve serious political and administrative problems. To put it differently, and in terms that will become fully clear to non-economists only later, it might turn out under these special circumstances that the implicit tax of forced service is less bad than the alternative taxes that would have to be used to finance a volunteer army.

Hence, for a major war, a strong case can be made for compulsory service. And indeed, compulsory service has been introduced in the United States only under such conditions — in the Civil War, World War I, and World War II. It is hardly conceivable that it could have been introduced afresh in, say, 1950, if a system of compulsory service had not so recently been in full swing. As it was, the easiest thing to do when military needs for manpower rose was to reactivate the recent wartime technique.

Under conditions found at present, the number of persons who volunteer for armed service is inadequate to man the armed forces, and even so, many who volunteer do it only because they anticipate being drafted. The number of "true" volunteers is clearly much too small to man armed forces of our present size. This undoubted fact is repeatedly cited as evidence that a volunteer army is unfeasible.

It is evidence of no such thing. It is evidence rather that we are now grossly underpaying our armed forces. The starting pay for young men who enter the armed forces is now about $45 a week — including not only cash pay and allotments but also the value of clothing, food, housing, and other items furnished in kind. When the bulk of young men can command at least twice this sum in civilian jobs, it is little wonder that volunteers are so few. Indeed, it is somewhat surprising that there are as many as there are.

TO MAN THE ARMY with volunteers would require making conditions of service more attractive — not only higher pay but also better housing facilities and improved amenities in other respects. It will be replied that money is not the only factor young men consider in choosing their careers. This is certainly true — and equally certainly irrelevant. Adequate pay alone may not attract, but inadequate pay can certainly deter. Military service has many non-monetary attractions to young men—the chance to serve one's country, adventure, travel, opportunities for training, and so on. Not the least of the advantages of a volunteer army is that the military would have to improve their personnel policies and pay more attention to meeting the needs of the enlisted men. They now need pay little attention to them, since they can fill their ranks with conscripts serving under compulsion. Indeed, it is a tribute to their humanitarianism — and the effectiveness of indirect pressure via political process — that service in the armed forces is not made even less attractive than it now is.

The personnel policies of the military have been repeatedly criticized, and, with no spur, repeatedly left unreformed. Imaginative policies designed to

827

Page Five

make the armed forces attractive to the kind of men the armed services would like to have (plus the elimination of compulsion which now makes military service synonomous with enforced incarceration) could change drastically the whole image that the armed services present to young men. The Air Force, because it has relied so heavily on real volunteers, perhaps comes closest to demonstrating what could be done.

The question how much more we would have to pay to attract sufficient volunteers has been analyzed intensively in the Department of Defense study of military recruitment. Based on a variety of evidence collected in that study, Walter Oi estimates in his paper[1] that a starting pay (again including pay in kind as well as in cash) of something like $4,000 to $5,500 a year — about $80 to $100 a week — would suffice. This is surely not an unreasonable sum. Oi estimates that the total payroll cost (after allowing for the savings in turnover and men employed in training) would be around $3 billion to $4 billion a year for armed forces equivalent to 2.7 million men under present methods of recruitment, and not more than $8 billion a year for armed forces equivalent to the present higher number of men (around 3.1 or 3.2 million men). Based on the same evidence, the Defense Department has come up with estimates as high as $17.5 billion. Even the highest of these estimates is not in any way unfeasible in the context of total Federal government expenditures of more than $175 billion a year.

Whatever may be the exact figure, it is a highly misleading indication of the cost incurred in shifting from compulsion to a volunteer army. There are net advantages, not disadvantages, in offering volunteers conditions sufficiently attractive to recruit the number of young men required.

This is clearly true on the level of individual equity: the soldier no less than the rest of us is worth his hire. How can we justify paying him less than the amount for which he is willing to serve?

How can we justify, that is, involuntary servitude except in times of the greatest national emergency? One of the great gains in the progress of civilization was the elimination of the power of the noble or the sovereign to exact compulsory servitude.

ON THE DIRECT budgetry level, the argument that a volunteer army would cost more simply involves a confusion of apparent with real cost. By this argument, the construction of the Great Pyramid with slave labor was a cheap project. The real cost of conscripting a soldier who would not voluntarily serve on present terms is not his pay and the cost of his keep: it is the amount for which he would be willing to serve. *He* is paying the difference. This is the extra cost to him and must be added to the cost borne by the rest of us. Compare, for example, the cost to a star professional football player and to an unemployed worker. Both might have the same attitudes toward the army and like — or dislike — a military career equally; but because the one has such better alternatives than the other, it would take a much higher sum to attract him. When he is forced to serve, we are in effect imposing on him a tax in kind equal in value to the difference between what it would take to attract him and the military pay he actually receives. This implicit tax in kind should be added to the explicit taxes imposed on the rest of us to get the real cost of our armed forces.

If this is done, it will be seen at once that abandoning the draft would almost surely reduce the real cost — because the armed forces would then be manned by men for whom soldiering was the best available career, and who would hence require the lowest sums of money to induce them to serve. Abandoning the draft might raise the apparent money cost to the government, but only because it would substitute taxes on the general population in money for taxes on certain "selected" young men in kind.

There are also some important offsets even to the increase in apparent money

---

[1] See his article, pp. 13-16, this issue.

cost. In addition to the lower turnover, already taken into account in the estimates cited, the higher average level of skill would permit further reductions in the size of the army, saving monetary cost to the government. Because manpower is cheap to the military, they now tend to waste it, using enlisted men for tasks that could be performed by civilians or machines, or eliminated entirely. Moreover, better pay at the time to volunteers might lessen the political appeal of veteran's benefits that we now grant after the event. These now cost us over $6 billion a year, or one-third as much as current annual payroll costs for the active armed forces — and they will doubtless continue to rise under present conditions.

There are still other offsets. Colleges and universities would be saved the cost of housing, seating, and entertaining hundreds of thousands of young men. Total output of the community would be higher both because these men would be at work and because the young men who now go to work could be offered and could accept jobs requiring considerable training instead of having to take stop-gap jobs while awaiting a possible call to the service. Perhaps there are some effects in the opposite direction, but I have not been able to find any.

Whatever happens to the apparent monetary cost, the real cost of a volunteer army would almost surely be less than of the present system and it is not even clear that the apparent monetary cost would be higher — if it is correctly measured for the community as a whole. In any event, there can be little doubt that wholly volunteer forces of roughly the present size are entirely feasible on economic and fiscal grounds.

It has been argued that a military career would be so much more attractive to the poor than to the well-to-do that volunteer armed services would be staffed disproportionately by the poor. Since Negroes constitute a high proportion of the poor, it is further argued that volunteer armed forces would be largely black.

There is first a question of fact. This tendency is present today in exaggerated form — the present levels of pay are *comparatively* more attractive to blacks than the higher levels of pay in voluntary armed forces would be. Yet the fraction of persons in the armed forces who are black is roughly the same as in the population at large. It has been estimated that even if every qualified Negro who does not now serve were to serve, whites would still constitute a substantial majority of the armed forces. The military services require a wide variety of skills and offer varied opportunities. They have always appealed to people of varied classes and backgrounds and they will continue to do so. Particularly if pay and amenities were made more attractive, there is every reason to expect that they would draw from all segments of the community.

In part, this argument involves an invalid extrapolation from the present conscripted army to a volunteer army. Because we conscript, we pay salaries that are attractive only to the disadvantaged among us.

829

BEYOND THIS QUESTION of fact, there is the more basic question of principle. Clearly, it is a good thing to offer better alternatives to the currently disadvantaged. The argument to the contrary rests on a political judgment: that a high ratio of Negroes in the armed services would exacerbate racial tensions at home and provide, in the form of ex-soldiers, a militarily trained group to foment violence. Perhaps there is something to this. My own inclination is to regard it as the reddest of red herrings. Our government should discriminate neither in the civil nor in the military services. We must handle our domestic problems as best we can and not use them as an excuse for denying blacks opportunities in the military service.

One of the advantages cited for conscription is that it permits great flexibility in the size of the armed services. Let military needs suddenly increase, and draft calls can be rapidly stepped up, and conversely. This is a real advantage, but can easily be overvalued. Emergencies must be met with forces in being, however they are recruited. Many months now elapse between an increase in draft calls and the availability of additional trained men.

The key question is how much flexibility is required. Recruitment by voluntary means could provide considerable flexibility — at a cost. The way to do so would be to make pay and conditions of service more attractive than is required to recruit the number of men that it is anticipated will be needed. There would then be an excess of volunteers — queues would form. If the number of men required increased, the queues could be shortened, and conversely.

The change in scale involved in a shift from conditions like the present to a total war is a very different matter. If the military judgment is that, in such a contingency, there would be time and reason to expand the armed forces many-fold, either universal military training, to provide a trained reserve force, or stand-by provisions for conscription could be justified. Both are very different from the use of conscription to man the standing army in time of peace or brush-fire wars, or wars like that in Viet Nam which require only a minority of young men.

The flexibility provided by conscription has another side. It means that, at least for a time, the Administration and the military services can proceed fairly arbitrarily in committing U. S. forces. The voluntary method provides a continuing referendum of the public at large. The popularity or unpopularity of the activities for which the armed forces are used will clearly affect the ease of recruiting men. This is a consideration that will be regarded by some as an advantage of conscription, by others as a disadvantage.

THERE IS NO DOUBT that large armed forces plus the industrial complex required to support them constitute an ever-present threat to political freedom. Our free institutions would certainly be safer if the conditions of the world permitted us to maintain smaller armed forces.

This valid fear has been converted into an invalid argument against voluntary armed forces. They would constitute a professional army, it is said, that would lack contact with the populace and become an independent political force, whereas a conscripted army remains basically a citizen army. The fallacy in this argument is that such dangers come primarily from the senior officers, who are now and always have been a professional corps of volunteers. A few examples from history will show that the danger to political stability is largely unrelated to the method of recruiting enlisted men. Napoleon and Franco both rose to power at the head of conscripts. The recent military takeover in Argentina was by armed forces recruiting enlisted men by conscription. Britain and the U. S. have maintained freedom while relying primarily on volunteers, Switzerland and Sweden while using conscription. It is hard to find any relation historically between the method of recruiting enlisted men and the political threat from the armed forces.

However we recruit enlisted men, it is essential that we adopt practices that will guard against the political danger of creating a military corps with loyalties of its own and out of contact with the broader body politic. Fortunately, we have so far largely avoided this danger. The broad basis of recruitment to the military academies, by geography as well as social and economic factors, the ROTC programs in the colleges, the recruitment of officers from enlisted men, and similar measures, have all contributed to this result.

For the future, we need to follow policies that will foster recruitment into the officer corps from civilian activities — rather than primarily promotion from within. The military services no less than the civil service need and will benefit from in-and-outers. For the political gain, we should be willing to bear the higher financial costs involved in fairly high turnover and rather short average terms of service for officers. We should follow personnel policies that will continue to make at least a period of military service as an officer attractive to young men from many walks of life.

There is no way of avoiding the political danger altogether, but it can be minimized as readily with a volunteer as with a conscripted army.

Given the will, there is no reason why the transition to volunteer armed forces cannot begin at once and proceed gradually by a process of trial and error. We do not need precise and accurate knowledge of pay and amenities that will be required. We need take no irreversible step.

OUT OF SIMPLE justice, we should raise the pay and improve the living conditions of enlisted men. If it were proposed explicity that a special income tax of 50 per cent be imposed on enlisted men in the armed services, there would be cries of outrage. Yet that is what our present pay scales plus conscription amount to. If we started rectifying this injustice, the number of "real" volunteers would increase, even while conscription continued. Experience would show how responsive the number of volunteers is to the terms offered and how much these terms would have to be improved to attract enough men. As the number of volunteers increased, the lash of compulsion could fade away.

This picture is overdrawn in one important respect. Unless it is clear that conscription is definitely to be abolished in a reasonably short time, the armed services will not have sufficient incentive to improve their recruitment and personnel policies. They will be tempted to procrastinate, relying on the crutch of conscription. The real survival strength of conscription is that it eases the life of the military high command. Hence, it would be highly desirable to have a definite termination date set for conscription.

The case for abolishing conscription and recruiting our armed forces by voluntary methods seems to me overwhelming. One of the greatest advances in human freedom was the commutation of taxes in kind to taxes in money. We have reverted to a barbarous custom. It is past time that we regain our heritage.

831

Conscription in a

Democratic Society

RICHARD   FLACKS

832

I DO NOT SEE HOW it can be denied that the institution of conscription is by definition alien to a genuinely free society. Therefore, I want to stress at the outset my view that the abolition of this institution ought to be a very high priority for Americans. This goal is, however, utopian so long as the United States continues to follow a policy based on the assumption that the status quo in every part of the world must be maintained by American military power. Thus, the only really worthwhile question to ask about conscription — how we can get rid of it — cannot be answered without debating the whole scope of American foreign policy.

It is, however, not entirely fruitless to raise some questions about the way in which conscription is used by our society, given the assumption that some form of Selective Service is going to be with us for the indefinite future. This may be particularly necessary for those of us who oppose the draft altogether, since much of the present discussion con-

cerns how best to *extend* the scope of military training institutions, and how better to *integrate* them into the fabric of American life. My concern here, then, will be not with the many inequities of the present draft system, but with discussing ways of limiting the impact of this alien system and of preventing or diluting some of its more pernicious effects.

In my view, a fundamental flaw in the current draft system is that it reinforces and exacerbates a serious constitutional weakness in American political life, namely, the enormous delegation to the President of power in international commitments, to wage war and mobilize national resources and public consent, which is not substantially checked or limited by private power. The institution of permanent, compulsory military service facilitates the freedom of the President in this regard and enables him to deploy military forces on a very large scale without achieving prior popular consent. Such built-in Presidential irresponsibility is intrinsically repugnant; from a pragmatic point of view, its consequences can be read in Viet Nam.

It is my hope that serious study will be given to ways in which Presidents can be made responsible for their international policies, and to mechanisms by which the Presidential ability to mobil-

Richard Flacks is Assistant Professor of Sociology at the University of Chicago. He is author of a number of articles, and has actively supported the Students for a Democratic Society and other New Left organizations. This article is adapted from the paper presented to the Conference on the Draft held at the University of Chicago in December 1966.

Page Ten

ize for war can be balanced and checked. Many of the most important considerations in this regard lie outside the scope of this paper; but, it seems to me, there are ways in which the contribution of the Selective Service System to Presidential irresponsibility can be reduced or reversed.

First, it seems to me inadmissible that those most likely to be compelled to kill and die for often highly questionable policies do not even have the right to vote. If we are going to draft eighteen, nineteen, and twenty-year-old men, then we ought to allow them access to the ballot box. This, I think, would not be merely a formalistic reform, permitting young men to ratify their own induction, although it might turn out to be only that. Rather, it seems plausible that the introduction of large numbers of young people into the political arena would create a substantial new constituency for policies of restraint and internationalism — a constituency which might provide some check on the patriotic hawking of elderly politicians.

Second, it seems to me that we ought to adopt the notion, which prevails in some other countries such as Canada, that conscripts ought not to be used indiscriminately in foreign wars. The only legitimate use for draftees ought to be for the defense of the nation's most vital interests. Senator Gruening's proposal to prevent the President from using conscripts involuntarily in combat without specific Congressional mandate seems to me to be a reasonable, if minimal, way to insure some Congressional check on Presidential power. A stronger, and in my view more legitimate, proposal would be to prevent the use of draftees in combat (who do not subsequently volunteer for such duty) without a specific declaration of war. In any case, some mechanism of this sort would be a desirable way of bringing the power of the President to escalate conflicts under some degree of democratic control, while establishing conscription as an institution for national defense rather than an instrument for imperial adventure.

Third, it seems to me necessary to increase the freedom of citizens to resist being mobilized for wars of questionable justification. One way to do this is to broaden the grounds for conscientious objection. Conscientious objection can be founded on philosophical and political grounds as well as religious ones. Moreover, if there is any sense to the distinction between just and unjust wars, then it is improper to deny the possibility of conscientious objection to particular wars. There is, as far as I can tell, no practical difficulty in establishing whether a young man is a sincere objector on non-religious grounds, which is not present under the present definition of conscientious objection. It seems to me inconsistent with our best traditions to compel a young man to fight a war against his conscience, even if his basic values have been shaped by philosophical or political rather than religious influences; and it would seem to me desirable from the point of view of limiting Presidential power, if each inductee had the freedom to test whether his conscience would be violated by serving or fighting in behalf of current policy.

FINALLY, I WOULD argue that the traditional view of the draft as an alien institution must be preserved, and all attempts to make conscription a permanent, integral feature of American society must be firmly resisted. The common goal of liberals and democrats in the coming period ought to be to reduce rather than enhance areas of compulsion in American life. On this view, there is serious danger in some of the proposals now being offered to reduce the inequities of Selective Service. I refer here not only to attempts to revive universal military training, but to well-intentioned suggestions of universal conscription for "national service." The idea of national service for youth is an exciting one, but the notion that it should be compulsory or tied to conscription is literally totalitarian. Similarly, the proposals to expand the scope of induction to include unqualified youth, so that they may receive the educational benefits of the armed services, is highly reminiscent of the procedures of a garrison state. It is

833

834

not a matter for pride that the best opportunities of self-improvement for underprivileged youth are offered by the military, or that the only fully integrated educational institution in our society is the army. This situation is a measure of the default of the larger society; the war on poverty is not going to be won by giving the military even more control over the lives of young men.

The only really worthwhile goal of an affluent society as regards its youth is to promote the maximum possible freedom and opportunity for self-development. At present upper status youth have enormous opportunity for years of higher education, and many avenues open for cultural enrichment and personal fulfillment. These opportunities are widely buttressed by public subsidies in the form of free tuition, scholarships, fellowships, loans, etc. In the long run, the only way to reduce the inequities of the draft and to offset present trends toward a quasi-caste system among youth, is to extend these privileges, opportunities, and subsidies (where necessary) to all youth. What appears to be needed is a massive opening-up of the range of choices for youth so that each has a chance to select experiences of service, of education and training, of cultural enhancement and self-realization.

I want to conclude by indicating an important problem posed by these suggestions for limiting the uses of conscription. The present system has the apparent virtue of permitting a partial mobilization for wars as large as Viet Nam, without substantially increasing the militancy of the population, without developing major war fever, and without very widespread suppression of dissent. It may well be that mechanisms such as those proposed here which would limit the Executive's freedom of action in this regard will "back-fire," and produce more systematic efforts to engineer full popular support for war efforts. This situation would be dangerous domestically; it could also lead to more rapid escalation of conflicts. Such considerations should be given due weight; but on the other hand, we need to ask whether the costs added by these constraints might not make Presidents more cautious and rational when they make decisions about the deployment of military forces.

At any rate, these proposals to limit the uses of conscription and to resist its integration into American society seem to run counter to the drift of present policy. The likelihood of their adoption by Congress in the near future seems very small. In this situation, it is heartening that a significant number of inductees have decided to risk jail by undertaking legal tests of the current definition of conscientious objection, by refusing induction during a war which they perceive as unjust and illegal, by emigrating to Canada, and by publicly refusing to report for combat duty in such a war. These men may well be speaking for a sizeable portion of their generation in questioning the legitimacy of conscription. They deserve the highest degree of support from those concerned to preserve and extend democratic values.

The Real Costs of a

Volunteer Military

ONE OF SEVERAL proposed alternatives to the current draft is the establishment of an all-volunteer force. To say that a particular alternative such as an all-volunteer force is preferable to the current draft implies that the cost of this alternative is, in some sense, lower than the cost of procuring military personnel with the current draft system. Yet in his statement before the House Armed Services Subcommittee, T. D. Morris, Assistant Secretary of Defense, indicated that an all-volunteer force of 2.65 million men would increase military payroll budgets by $4 to $17 billion per year.

The budgetry payroll of the Department of Defense is *not*, however, the economic cost of labor resources allocated to the uniformed services. The presence of a draft has surely affected both the level and structure of military pay; moreover, the men who actually entered active military service were recruited or conscripted through manpower procurement programs which rely in differing degrees on the coercive influence of a draft liability. A change

Walter Y. Oi is Associate Professor of Economics at the University of Rochester. He was for several years Manpower Consultant for the Departure of Defense, and participated in the University of Chicago Conference on the Draft, December 1966.

to a purely voluntary force would have to be accompanied by increases in military compensation, and substantial changes in the procurement channels through which men are recruited into the armed forces. The composition and structure of an all-volunteer force would thus differ significantly from that of the present force, which contains many men who were enlisted under the pressure of a draft liability. A third alternative, such as the lottery, would yet produce a different composition of the armed forces; but this article will deal with cost comparisons for only two military manpower procurement arrangements— a purely voluntary one, and the one which has evolved under the current draft law.

There are at least three senses in which the maintenance of a defense establishment entails a financial cost: (1) budgetry cost, (2) cost to the economy, and (3) cost to the individual military service participants. According to the defense budget for fiscal year 1965, the cost for active-duty military personnel was $12.7 billion, while retirement benefits accounted for another $1.4 billion. If the higher levels of military pay which are required to attract sufficient volunteers were applied to the probable age structure of a voluntary force, this writer obtains an estimate of the budgetary cost that is $4 billion greater than that of a mixed conscript and volunteer force.[1]

The financial cost of military personnel provides a measure for the value of the civilian outputs that could have been produced by the labor which was allocated instead to the armed forces; but this concept of cost completely ignores the welfare loss due to the occupational preferences of the individuals themselves for military versus civilian employments. In a sense, it is just a measure of technical efficiency, indicating the alternative cost in terms of foregone civilian output that was required to achieve given goals of military preparedness. The concept of full economic cost, on the other hand, acknowledges the occupational preferences of prospective recruits. If an individual has an aversion for service life, he could, in principle, be compensated enough to induce him to volunteer. Presently, individuals who would require such compensation are involuntarily inducted, while others reluctantly volunteer before they are drafted. These imputed compensations to overcome aversions for military service would be included in any computation of the full economic cost of acquiring military personnel; but our task here is merely to arrive at an estimate of financial costs. Finally, it must be remembered that the mechanics of the current draft law impose costs in the form of uncertainties on youths in the draftable ages. The incidence of inductions (who will be drafted) and the time of induction are not known in advance.

TO EVALUATE THE comparative costs of an all-volunteer force and of the force which has evolved under current law, this writer first examined the implications of a continued draft which produced a mixed force of conscripts, true volunteers, and draft-motivated, reluctant volunteers. It was assumed for this paper that active duty force strengths in the years ahead (1970-75) would return to their pre-Viet Nam levels of 2.65 million men, in order to utilize available Department of Defense data.

The manpower procurement channels which have evolved under the current draft are reflected in the patterns of active military service which were observed in the six years prior to Viet Nam, 1960-65. An anaylsis of these patterns indicates the probable characteristics of a mixed force under a continued draft. In order to maintain a force strength of 2.65 million men, annual accessions of 507,700 men must be recruited or conscripted from civilian life. With a smaller male population in the period prior to Viet Nam, roughly 59 per cent of males who were physically and mentally qualified for military service entered the active duty forces. By 1970-75 it is projected that only 38.5 per cent of qualified males of military age will be demanded by the armed services.

To estimate the cost of an entirely voluntary force, it is necessary first to consider the case assuming that the draft would be abolished with no accompanying changes in pay or other recruitment incentives. Under this assumption, the services would obviously lose the draftees who had accounted for 21 per cent of the accessions to enlisted ranks in 1960-65. In addition, a significant fraction of regular enlistees could properly be called reluctant volunteers who enlisted in preference to being drafted. The incidence of reluctant volunteers was inferred from a survey of responses to the question:

If there had been no draft, and you had no military obligation, do you think you would have volunteered for active military service?

If the draft were eliminated, reluctant volunteers would also likely be lost from the armed forces. Voluntary enlistments in all services could be expected to fall by 38.1 percent, and to the regular army alone by 43.2 per cent. Moreover, these surveys indicate that 41.3 per cent of

---

[1] The reader is directed to the author's "The Costs and Implications of an All-Volunteer Force," in Sol Tax, ed., *The Draft* (Chicago: University of Chicago Press, 1967), chap. xxii, pp. 221-51.

newly commissioned officers were motivated to enter military service because of the threat of being drafted.

The fall in initial accessions due to the loss of conscripts and reluctant volunteers would result in a decline in the sustainable force strength. Since a voluntary force, however, would enjoy a greater rate of re-enlistment, the decline in strength would be smaller than the fall in accessions. The annual turnover rate of Army enlisted men is around 25 per cent when over half of accessions are draftees and reluctant volunteers. If all enlistments were true volunteers, it is estimated that the turnover rate could be lowered to 17 per cent.

The improved retention patterns which can be expected to apply to an all-volunteer force were then used to estimate the gross flow demand for accessions to achieve the assumed strength objective of 2.65 million men. The deficit between requirements (gross flow demand for assumed strengths) and voluntary enlistments could be eliminated by attracting more volunteers with higher military pay. To eliminate a deficit of 1.6 (the ratio of requirements to voluntary enlistments) in the Army, it was estimated that first term military pay would have to be increased by 68 per cent, from $2,500 to $4,200 per year. As a result, the pay of career men in the Army would have to increase by 17 per cent also. In addition to higher levels of military pay, the move to a voluntary force would imply a change in the composition of the armed services — the age structure would move to a larger fraction of older men in the career force. It would also be anticipated that a smaller fraction of officers would be college graduates.

IN BOTH THE MIXED and voluntary type of miltary force, 2.65 million men, it is assumed, would be required to maintain the defense of the nation, and thereby would be kept out of the civilian labor force. The financial cost to the economy can thus be defined as the opportunity cost equal to the value of goods and services that could have been produced by these servicemen. If servicemen were paid the same incomes as civilians of comparable ages and educational attainments, the men in the mixed force would earn $13 billion per year. The corresponding figure for the voluntary force would be $14.2 billion, or some 9.1 per cent higher than the mixed force, reflecting a preservation within the armed forces of the acquired military skills and experience of the older men, while in the mixed force many of the men do not remain in the services beyond their initial term — thus losing this experience. Although the voluntary force has a lower average educational attainment, it also contains older men who usually earn higher salaries than younger men, and on balance the age effect outweighs the smaller average education. To the extent that military service is not a perfect substitute for civilian job experience, the financial cost to the economy of the present type of mixed force contains a downward bias: civilian employment experience provides a man with skills he can take directly to a new job, while military experience is only partially useful in later employment.

The financial cost to individual military service participants is restricted to their monetary losses, suffered by those men who were coerced into active military service by the draft liability. By 1970-75, it is projected that only 55,300 men would need to be involuntarily drafted; but another 153,700 men per year would be expected to volunteer for enlisted ranks because of their draft liabilities. By using data for 1963-64, this writer was able to arrive at estimates of annual civilian and first-term military incomes for these reluctant service participants. The differentials between alternative civilian and military incomes represents an implicit tax that is placed on those who were forced to serve. If each draftee serves 1.9 years, and each reluctant volunteer for 3.5 years, the aggregate implicit tax which is borne by members in this age group is estimated to be $691 million. To the extent that some officers (notably doctors and dentists) serve an initial tour of active duty because of the draft, the

837

size of this invisible tax is even larger. If reluctant participants were compensated for their aversion to military service life, it is estimated that the military pay budget would have to be increased by $826 million a year. This is the amount of the implicit tax, or cost, that is imposed on men who are coerced into military service by the draft. If the true volunteers were awarded the same pay as the reluctant service participants, the economic cost of the draft then easily exceeds the budgetary cost of moving to an all-volunteer force. It should be noted that these financial costs altogether disregard the welfare loss through the occupational preferences of individuals for military versus civilian jobs.

To sum up, a force strength of 2.65 million men could be achieved on a purely voluntary basis by 1970-75 if the military pay budget were increased by approximately $4 billion. Because of its higher retention rates, only 27.5 per cent of qualified males in each age class would be needed to sustain this voluntary force. On the other hand, if the draft is continued, the higher personnel turnover in a mixed force would mean that 38.5 per cent of all qualified males will have to enter military service each year. Some men will be involuntarily inducted, while others reluctantly volunteer because they might be drafted.

838

The Politics of Conscription

BRUCE K. CHAPMAN

THE BELIEF THAT political arrangements afford an efficient means to resolve problems, and the abstraction from potential special-interest pleadings, inspires much of the reliance upon government action and the distrust of the voluntary sector apparent in public policy today. The examination of the interrelationship between incompetence and the automatic political stabilizers which preclude any radical elimination of this incompetence is a most underworked field. The operations of the Selective Service System in the United States provide a sterling example of gross bungling by a political agency generating a continued demand for reliance upon that agency.

Illustrative of one aspect of bungling by Selective Service is its handling of the I-A pool of men available for service. At any point in time, the Selective Service System does not know how many men are available to be inducted, how many will be available the following month, how many are needed by the Army, or even where the men are located geographically. This is a serious indictment, and it can be supported by

Bruce K. Chapman, former publisher of *Advance* and editorial writer for the late *New York Herald Tribune*, is co-author of *The Party That Lost Its Head* and author of *The Wrong Man in Uniform*, from which this article is an excerpt.

examining the evidence provided by the Selective Service System itself.

In February 1966, General Hershey appeared before the Subcommittee on Education of the House Committee on Education and Labor to explain just how the draft was working and why it was necessary for students to be threatened with induction. General Hershey sent the Subcommittee a projected estimate of the draft's situation during the first half of 1966, containing arithmetic errors which left 100,000 men unaccounted for. It was returned. In the second version, the Selective Service claimed that given the I-A pool at the end of January, the number of new nineteen-year-olds being classified I-A, draft calls of 40,000 men per month, and enlistments of 50,000 per month, the I-A pool of "available" men would be exhausted and actually deficient of 5207 men on June 30, 1966. This alarming prediction convinced many that a draft of students was justified.

But it was not accurate. Monthly draft calls did not reach 40,000 during the whole spring, nor, for that matter, until October. February's call was 29,400; March, 22,400; April, 21,700; May, 34,600; June, 18,500. Selective Service overestimated its needs by more than a third during the period; indeed, February, March, and April quotas were already known to Hershey when the projections were made. The estimate of enlistments may have been more accurate, but Hershey's assertion that they represented a drain on the I-A pool was not. According to the Department of Defense, nearly half of the new enlistments (45 per cent in 1965) come from men under nineteen, men who are not yet in the I-A pool, and who, because of their enlistment, never will be. Another part of the 5,000 (for instance, deferred students) is also drawn from outside the I-A pool at the time of their enlistment. Finally, the Selective Service's estimates neglected to take into account the new manpower acquired by its own reclassification of some I-Y's (those with temporary mental and physical deferments) or those gained by the Army's lowering of its mental standards.

Consequently, perhaps much to the surprise of draft officials, there was no manpower crisis at the end of June. No one knows how many young men on the draft's borderline were reclassified during that period and called up by local boards anxiously anticipating an imminent shortage. How can the draft make such mistakes?

Early in 1966, the author attempted to find out, following up a public remark by General Hershey which described a clogged "pipeline" of paperwork in the draft bureaucracy. Some men's reclassification and induction papers were—and are—handled more efficiently than others. The ones whose papers were delayed or stalled are said to be in the "pipeline," and while it is likely that some inefficiency must arise in any system, in January 1966 General Hershey said some 500,000 men out of less than 650,000 in the whole I-A pool were in the pipeline. According to a source at the Labor Department's Office of Manpower, Automation and Training, the problem has been growing since 1957, when only about 20,000 men were in the pipeline. By 1966 General Hershey could declare, "I've never been in a time where the situation was more confusing than it is

now, in terms of having numbers of registrants I could really count."[1]

WHEN A MAN TURNS eighteen he must register for the draft. If by age nineteen he does not obtain a deferment, he is classified I-A and is subject to induction. There presently are some 500,000 men turning nineteen each month, of whom about 30,000 will be classified I-A, while the others are either temporarily or permanently deferred. Other men come into the I-A pool, for example, when they lose their II-S student deferment upon graduation. Within the I-A pool, however, there are priorities for drafting. All single men aged nineteen to twenty-six, oldest first, are supposed to be called before married men, who also are called oldest first. Therefore, when a man is called up, supposedly all the other men of greater priority have already been drafted. But if in the process of being inducted, some men higher up had their papers delayed, they are "not available" to meet a particular month's call, and someone further down on the lists—maybe a married man or a student who has to be reclassified for the purpose—is called instead. In January 1966, 522,472 out of 641,958 men in the I-A pool were "not available" to meet monthly quotas.

With local draft boards directed by the Selective Service System, and with the "entrance and examination" (i.e., "induction") centers directed by the Department of Defense, it is not easy to trace the vagaries of the "pipeline." The Selective Service System tends to blame the jam-up on the Pentagon, and a spokesman for the Army (which has charge of the induction centers) refers to it as "an internal problem of the Selective Service." There is reason to think it is the fault of both.

The efficiency of the induction centers in processing the men is a fit subject for debate. When a man takes his mental and physical tests, the Army is required to return the results, in two sets, to the registrant's local draft board within five days. An Army survey late in 1965

1 "Draft Now Hits Men Long Thought Safe," *New York Herald Tribune*, January 23, 1966, p. 16.

showed the five-day processing going smoothly, with a national backlog of only 6,000 men's papers at any one time. Yet the Selective Service figures at the beginning of the new year showed 114,062 men whose *first* set of test results had not been returned to local boards, and another 63,510 whose *second* set had not been returned. Both sets must be in the draft board's hands before a man can be ordered to report for induction.

Some men, as a result of the delays, are never drafted at all. A young man of the author's acquaintance in New York who was graduated from law school one June at age twenty-five was reclassified then, but was not notified to report for an examination until December—on Christmas Eve, in fact. The examination was conducted on New Year's Eve. The young man passed his twenty-sixth birthday on the 14th of February and, telephoning his draft board, found they were still awaiting receipt of his second set of test results. This is where the pipeline problem begins to develop, according to the Selective Service officials, criticizing the Army. Since the Army runs the induction centers, the Selective Service System feels there is little it can do to speed things up.

At the end of June 1966, the Department of Defense finally owned up, though indirectly, to the induction center delays, now claiming that the previously unacknowledged backlog of incomplete cases had been reduced by 32 per cent; but even on the day the Pentagon statement was released, a Boston registrant the author later interviewed was personally prodding an Army induction center to locate and deliver to the Selective Service the results of a physical examination given in December 1965, more than six months before.

The pipeline jam is even more severe outside the induction centers than within them. Among 522,000 men "not available" in the January 1966 statistics were 225,452 who were ordered for mental and physical examinations but whose papers informing them just where and when to report were delayed, "shuffling back and forth between draft boards and induction centers," as one draft spokesman put it. There are also pipeline lags for other reasons. Some 82,937 men in January 1966 were ordered for induction, but had to wait for room to open for them in an Army training camp. There must be a twenty-one day wait, by law, so that draftees can straighten out personal affairs. Since the Army can only take about 35,000 men per month, the pipeline bulge is still remarkably large. There are always a few men awaiting hearings or decisions on appeals, and some "delinquents" — including young men ignorant of the requirements to register at eighteen and a few genuine draft-dodgers—who make up the balance in the pipeline.

ONE INTERESTED AND close observer of the draft process is the Labor Department's Office of Manpower, Automation and Training, which likes to keep track of large movements of people to gauge their effect upon the labor market. An official there told the author in early 1966 that he found the draft's manpower dilemma hard to understand. "So far as we can judge," he said, "there should be no problem meeting needs even with increased calls." He then succinctly summed up much of the pipeline problem—and the inequities it causes—by ascribing it to the inefficiency of the draft's national operations. "Their bookkeeping is not that exact. They don't feel secure unless they can see where the next million men are coming from."[2]

The Viet Nam war has necessitated the draft's reaching deeper into its I-A pool and lowering the induction standards. Thus more people than at any time since the Korean War are being directly affected by the Selective Service System's operations. Draftees stand a better chance of being sent to Viet Nam than regulars, since only 12 per cent of the Armed Forces are draftees, while 33 per cent of the men in Viet Nam are draftees. Consequently, parents and other adults who have tended to shrug off the draft

841

---

[2] *The Wrong Man in Uniform* (New York: Trident Press, 1967), p. 47.

as a necessary annoyance are now becoming alarmed that some men are being taken from civilian life and involuntarily assigned to combat by an inherently inequitable system. The war, which is only tangentially relevant to the draft imbroglio, has made possible the development of the draft as a public issue.

Ironically, the war may also be the most effective instrument for suppressing or at least stalling consideration of draft reform. The argument is made that to debate the draft now will falsely encourage the Communists in Viet Nam and falsely raise the hopes of young men now faced with the draft here at home. Yet the use of the Viet Nam war to inhibit debate on the draft was fortuitously deterred by Secretary McNamara himself, at a speech in Montreal, when he scored the lack of universality in the draft as inequitable and suggested a program of national service; and again by the President in July 1966, when he appointed a commission to study draft operations and in August described the draft's rules as a "crazy quilt."

Lacking a spontaneous market process for eliminating mistakes, the viability of political solutions to various problems depends on official willingness to change, to realize and correct mistakes. Indicative of official attitudes within the Selective Service System, General Hershey commented in 1955:

> There are many things that we would like to change in our present law. There are many things we would like to change in its operation. The question is whether, if you start changing them, you may not open up many other problems, and if we are going to have a democracy everybody must have their chance for a change. What the thing is going to look like when we get through many times impels us to go ahead with the evils that we face, so we live in some sort of accommodation with them rather than to jump into those we cannot foretell because, smart as we think we are, we haven't been able to forecast the fu-

ture so that we could be 100 per cent accurate. . . .[3]

One would think that such a reactionary attitude would have sent Congress into spasms of indignation. Imagine the Secretary of State or the Secretary of Labor admitting in public that changes in our foreign policy or labor laws might be needed but should be ignored, lest one reform lead to another.

Perhaps because the draft was such a rolling political issue in 1940, it is now a sacrosanct one. General Hershey and a number of other politicians are all eager to keep the quadrennial question of draft extension falling on an odd-numbered year, believing it makes less difference how long the draft is extended than when it expires. He said of the 1966 bill, "Let us hope, pray, or what not that the thing expires on a year that is not divisible by two. There are several reasons that I need not explain to you why this is so."[4] The years "divisible by two" are election years, of course, and Hershey feared the influence of an aroused public. Whenever the draft extension has come up for review since 1951 there have been demands from a handful of Congressmen that it be extended for only one or two years, and a complete examination be made during that time of the whole draft situation. The *Congressional Record* shows that each time, some of the critics have been persuaded and others simply overwhelmed by spokesmen for the House and Senate Armed Services Committees, who argue that four years is needed to give Congress the time it needs to really investigate the problems of the draft and to devise new legislation. In 1963, Rep. Robert Kastenmeier of Wisconsin pointed out this pattern during House debate, but was himself apparently persuaded, for he joined reluctantly in voting the extension. The House vote that year was 373 to 3; in the Senate the bill passed unanimously after ten minutes of debate.

---

[3] American Council on Education, *Proceedings of the Conference on Military Manpower*, ed. by R. F. Howe (Washington, D.C., 1955), p. 19.

[4] *Ibid.*

Later, when criticism arises, Senate and House Armed Services Committees have typically referred newsmen to the Selective Service System, where General Hershey modestly declares that he only administers the laws; if Congress wants to change them, that's their business. Critics are soon then told that the draft will come up for extension again in another year or two, and the whole matter can be looked into then. A variation of the draft lobby's runaround technique is shown in the behavior of the House Armed Services Committee and its chairman, L. Mendel Rivers of South Carolina. When criticism of the pipeline and other aspects of the draft mounted in late 1965 and early 1966, Rivers told inquirers that his committe would begin hearings on the draft within a month. Public statements of such a pledge were made in early January 1966 and repeatedly thereafter; brief hearings were held in late June. Yet, then they were limited to testimony from General Hershey, a Defense Department spokesman, and several interested Congressmen. Chairman Rivers set the tone at the outset by declaring that while conscription might be "inimicable [*sic*] to our basic concept of individual freedom, we as a nation recognize that the alternatives can only result in jeopardizing our national security and then in turn, our precious heritage of freedom."[5] Having thereby opened and closed in the same breath the most important question of the hearings, Rivers, not surprisingly, was as markedly uninterested in exploring the efficiency of the draft as a manpower procurement system, as he is markedly uninterested in permitting other committes of Congress — such as Labor and Education — to hold hearings on the subject. Rivers in the past has been a supporter of higher military pay, but not primarily as a way of reducing the need for a draft, for he clearly isn't persuaded of any connection; and regrettably his committe, like its Senate counterpart, does not want a wide-ranging investigation.

---

[5] Statement of Rep. L. Mendel Rivers, June 22, 1966.

A somewhat different version of the stall against major draft reform can be seen in the attitude of the White House from 1964 to 1966. President Johnson has said as little as possible on the subject, and whatever his motivations, his actions have seemed more to anticipate and quiet the draft's critics than to spur reform.

ADLAI STEVENSON was the first major politician after the war to call for abolition of the draft, a 1956 Presidential campaign stand that was roundly attacked as irresponsible. Eight years later, in early 1964, the same proposal — unhappily also presented without the body of supporting research and analysis — was almost unnoticed when made by Senator Barry Goldwater. The Senator and his opponents in both parties apparently thought there were better issues to debate, and the draft question quickly dropped out of sight. It bobbed up again briefly in April 1964, when a group of sixteen Republican Congressmen of various ideological shades let it be known that they had prepared a long series of attacks on the draft and intended to take the House floor to demand a Congressional investigation.

Three days before the Republican floor presentation, President Johnson called a hasty press conference to announce that he had just that day directed the Department of Defense to conduct a full-scale analysis of the draft, to be completed at the cost of one million dollars by June 1965. What the President did not say was that a study ordered by the late President Kennedy was then seven months underway in the Defense Department, and that a concurrent investigation of the matter, underway in the Department of Labor, was being shelved under Pentagon pressure. When the Republican group, led by Congressman Thomas B. Curtis, took the floor three days later, they found that the Johnson statement had stolen their thunder and their press coverage. The Republican draft critics realized they

843

844

had been outmaneuvered; some were particularly angry and suspicious of the Department of Defense's assignment to investigate its own operations. Rep. Curtis, one of the earliest and most determined draft critics in the country, told the House,

My experience in Washington leads me to fear that any policy submitted by the Department of Defense, regardless of how much consultation occurs with other affected agencies, will be a policy in which every dispute has been settled in favor of the Department of Defense. This means that the very important considerations bearing on the draft that normally fall within the purview of the Departments of Labor and of Health, Education and Welfare, just to name two, will be downgraded to the Defense Department's interests. . . . [I also] fear that the Department of Defense will either ignore completely or will refuse to communicate to Congress and the public information that would not redound to the benefit of the Defense Department and its creature, the Selective Service System.

Every man who has ever served in the peacetime army is well aware of the staggering amount of featherbedding and goldbricking that goes on. It is practically a maxim that if a job can reasonably be done by two men in four hours, it will require six men for eight hours.[6]

Could the Pentagon be counted upon to expose the military's own waste of manpower, thereby embarrassing itself and the President? Could the Pentagon be counted upon to hunt down training functions which could better be performed by civilians? Curtis predicted that each branch of the service would resist the proposal of such reforms in a Pentagon study for fear of losing its own relative power and prestige in the notorious inter-service rivalry.

Would the Pentagon expose any abuses of law and regulation by its own staff? Curtis charged that "it has been candidly admitted by Army recruiting sergeants, in private conversation, that beyond a certain point they are quietly advised 'from above' . . . not to recruit any more young men . . . because if Army recruiting figures showed how easy it is for the Army to meet its force levels through voluntary enlistments, Congress would review the necessity of the draft."[7] What was needed, Curtis asserted, was to call a number of recruiting sergeants to testify under oath about this alleged practice, and *that* the Department of Defense was unlikely to do. Nor was it likely to examine the implications of the "evasion mentality" caused by the draft or the socio-economic effects of "channeling" men into jobs and other situations approved by the draft authorities. In short, Curtis expected a whitewash.

Congress as a whole felt that it was best to let the President have his way. In 1959, under a Republican President, Senator Mike Mansfield (D-Montana) argued vehemently against a Presidential commission on the draft, saying, "It is about time that we got away from attempting to meet every problem by the appointment of a commission." Senator Richard B. Russell (D-Georgia), Chairman of the Senate Armed Services Committee, caustically observed that "Usually we end by getting the same recommendations from the commissions that we have had from the Department of Defense on the same subject. It is really a new way of asking for the views of the Department of Defense." Senator Lyndon B. Johnson of Texas apparently agreed, and helped defeat the commission proposal in the Senate. By 1964, President Johnson felt differently about Presidential commissions, as did Senators Mansfield and Russell.

A number of Congressmen, however, principally Republicans, were skeptical of the much-touted Defense Department study. Curtis read into the *Congressional Record* a newspaper column by John McLaughry describing the Johnson device as a "phantom committee" which "in practice . . . does little or

---

[6] *Congressional Record*, June 25, 1964, pp. 15056-57.

[7] *Ibid.*, p. 15057.

nothing. Its main purpose is to quiet the demands of Congress by assuring the public that something is being done."

IN THE SPRING OF 1965, when the study was due to appear, the only evidence of it was a calculated leak to the press t h a t abandoning conscription would be too costly to consider. Inquirers in June 1965 were told that the study was on the desk of Secretary McNamara, awaiting transmittal to the President. Summer passed, and autumn, and winter. By June 1966, a year after the completion date, the study had yet to be released, and its contents were still a secret even to General Hershey.

When Rep. Rivers held his hearing in the summer of 1966, a statement by Thomas D. Morris, Assistant Secretary of Defense for Manpower, was billed as an unveiling of the Pentagon report. Yet, though the Rivers committee seemed adequately satisfied with it, the statement was nothing more than a report on a report, touching on only a few of the charges leveled against the system, and giving no evidence that the Departmen of Defense had attempted a definitive study.

The twenty-three page, wide-margined, double-spaced Pentagon paper gave away its bias early by describing the growing supply of new manpower in America as "A principal problem affecting the operation of the draft system," as if abundance were a "problem" and not an opportunity. It noted that the percentage of men age twenty-six (the effective final date of draft vulnerability) with military service had dropped from 70 per cent in 1958 to 46 per cent in 1966 and would drop to 42 per cent in 1974 if the present size of the military were maintained, and to only 34 per cent if it were restored to the levels that preceded the Viet Nam build up.

Nonetheless, the Pentagon said it had concluded that the draft was an essential influence toward supplying the military manpower. "To document this in-

fluence," said Mr. Morris, "a questionnaire survey was made of a representative sample [of military personnel] to determine the extent to which the draft influenced their decision to enter military service." That "survey" concluded, on the basis of one simple question, "Would you have entered service if there had been no draft?," that only 41 per cent of regular officers and 38 per cent of enlistees would join without the pressure of the draft. Apparently no deeper probing of motivation was attempted! The Pentagon paper did not explain, for example, why its survey made no distinction between men who said they would have enlisted if there had been alternative influences and those who would not have enlisted under any circumstances. The Army, which has the hardest time getting enlistees, issued a report two years before the Pentagon study based on a more detailed survey which produced quite different results. The Army study is clearly more thorough and convincing than that released by the Pentagon; but the Pentagon apparently ignored it and came to the pessimistic conclusion that without the draft the military could not maintain its force levels.

As if pretending to test the hypothesis that increasing the levels of military pay would provide the necessary additional recruits for an all-volunteer military, the Pentagon reported on a survey that asked boys sixteen to nineteen whether pay alone would induce them to join the military if there were no draft. The findings were ("surprisingly") that "equal pay with civilian life was considered the most important inducement by less than 4 per cent." But pay alone is not the "most important inducement" in almost any career, especially in the minds of sixteen- to nineteen-year-olds; and if it were, many would not admit it. Nonetheless, good wages certainly *are* one important — an essentially important — inducement to almost anyone. The higher re-enlistment rate of blacks, who tend to come from poorer circumstances than whites, shows the importance of pecuniary rewards in the mili-

845

tary. Here again, the Pentagon study's probing of motivation was simplistic, if not simpleminded.

The final estimates of how much pay scales and total outlays would have to be increased to provide an all-volunteer military not only differed by billions of dollars from the estimate leaked to the press the previous year, and with those of Secretary McNamara himself, but were so widely divergent — "pay increases of 110 per cent to 280 per cent" and the total increase in funds "from $6 billion to $17 billion" — as if to indicate that if implemented it would mean a $6300 *average raise* for every person in the military. Presumably it does not take into account any of the substantial savings from drastically reduced manpower turnover. If the figures did take such savings into account, they are even more outrageous, since the average pay raise implied in them would be higher still. It is useful for perspective to note that the median personal income for employed males in the United States is $5431 (1963 Census sample), much less than the average pay *raise* implied in the Pentagon scale figures.

The fears of a whitewash expressed by Rep. Curtis and other critics were fully realized in the Pentagon's statement. Extensive surveys and reams of "raw statistics" were alluded to, but not presented; one could not tell whether they really existed or not; and the all-important matter of just what prejudices and assumptions were programmed into the Pentagon's computers on this study along with those statistics was anything but clear. What was clear was that the Pentagon was going to placate only the most tepid draft critics. Yet, no sooner had it been unveiled than once again President Johnson attempted to head off the attackers by announcing a blue-ribbon Presidential "National Advisory Commission on Selective Service," another *deus ex machina,* or if you will, another *machina ex deo,* this time operated by Burke Marshall, former Assistant Attorney General.

WHILE THIS COMMISSION was given a supposed full mandate, true friends of draft reform must be forgiven for their skepticism. For one thing, the commission operated for only five months (until January 1, 1967), and Presidential commissions have a way of meeting only occasionally anyway, calling important and busy people to Washington for brief deliberations on the work that the commission staff has undertaken. While outside authorities were consulted, their opinions were weighed entirely in private, and the public has no way of knowing what was or was not going on. What's more, since most members of such commissions on complex issues — however well intentioned — are handicapped by their relative lack of familiarity with the operations of the governmental departments affected by their study, they tend to be overly deferential to the spokesmen for those departments. There is little likelihood, for example, that the Presidential commission on the draft seriously challenged the validity of the Department of Defense's manpower statistics, for most potential doubters would founder on their own lack of expertise, the commission's relative lack of resources, and the critically debilitating lack of time.

But perhaps the draft critics, at last, have caught on. When the commission was announced after the Johnson Pentagon study, Rep. Curtis was only the most vehement on his denunciation of the conveniently timed action. Said the *New York Times* editorially, "If Mr. Johnson thinks it desirable to call for a fresh study after finding the Pentagon's work disappointing, Congress appears justified in a study of its own. After all, it has no assurance that the next Presidential study will be any better than the last."[8] Democrats such as Senator Nelson of Wisconsin and Representatives Kastenmeier and Reuss, also of Wisconsin, and Republicans such as Wednesday Group members Morse of Massachusetts, Bell of California, and Reid of New York, as well as Rumsfeld

_____
[8] *The New York Times,* July 5, 1966, p. 36.

of Illinois, are demanding a disinterested investigation of the draft and its possible alternatives. Most believe a joint special committee of Congress, made up of members of Armed Services, Education and Labor, Appropriations, and other affected committees, should conduct the investigation in full view of the public and with ample resources and time to do the job properly.

It may be futile to expect anyone to live up to their mistakes, unless they are placed in a position where they cannot do otherwise, but the realization of this weakness should encourage the construction of institutions to avoid the temptation. The need is as close as your local draft board.

847

NIR NEEDS YOUR HELP

A Small theoretical-political journal such as **New Individualist Review** is not able to avail itself of the techniques of mass advertising and distribution which enable larger publications to reach their full potential audience. We need your help. If every reader would do one or more of the following things to increase the circulation of **NIR,** the continued existence and success of this journal would be assured:

(1) If you are not now a subscriber, you can enter a subscription for yourself; **and**

(2) You can introduce **NIR** to your friends and urge them to subscribe. Quantity discounts are available for this purpose.

(3) You can urge your local or school library to subscribe. A library subscription makes an excellent donation, since it may introduce the journal to dozens of people.

(4) Our subscription prices cannot cover the full cost involved for optimal management and promotion of a journal such as this; these prices only cover production costs purposely to encourage as wide a readership as possible among undergraduates. Our capital deficit is made up by voluntary contributions from individuals, which are tax deductable. Any donation which you might be able to afford at this time would be gratefully received.

If you agree that this is a useful journal which ought to be read by more people, we sincerely urge you to help us in the above ways to further the growth of classical liberal ideas.

Emigration as an

Alternative to the Draft

JOE MICHAEL COBB

848

An iron despotism can impose no harder servitude upon the citizen, than to force him from his home and occupation, to wage offensive wars, undertaken to gratify the pride or passions of his master.
—The Hartford Convention, 1815 [1]

THE PROBLEM OF LOYALTY and patriotism in modern society is one so surrounded with emotional tension that only two approaches to the subject are usually observed. In polite circles it may be unfashionable to discuss the subject at all: the assumption that everyone is adequately patriotic and loyal is almost universal, and insofar as one may rarely consider the question of his own ultimate loyalties, so one will not in general doubt his neighbor's feelings. The second approach to the problem of loyalty and patriotism may be regarded as gauche, but it is not unknown: whenever it is discovered that a person is openly unpatriotic or suspected of disloyalty, the feelings of fear and animosity dominate one's reactions. Since the rise of nationalism and the appearance in this century of the phenomenon of total war, there seems to be no middle

ground for discussion of this question. The task of this article is to raise the question of loyalty in the context of emigration, and to discuss some of the factors surrounding a decision to reject the government of one's homeland and seek freedom abroad.

It may be an overstatement to characterize a decision to emigrate with the word oppression, especially in reference to a Western nation such as the United States, but oppression is not a quantifiable, aggregative concept, such as per capita income; nor is it a quality easily isolated and tested by sociologists and political scientists, such as the absence of habeas corpus or the secret ballot. Oppression is necessarily an individual assessment of social well-being. The increasing degree to which the subject of leaving the United States to avoid the draft is considered by young men, and the number of recent magazine and newspaper articles about those who

---

J. M. Cobb is Editor-in-Chief of *New Individualist Review*. He received his A.B. in Economics from the University of Chicago in 1966, and is currently doing graduate work there.

[1] *The Proceedings of a Convention of Delegates* (Hartford, Conn., 1815), p. 11.

have done so, tend to indicate that impressment is no more acceptable in the service of a democratic government than it was under the repressive, feudal regimes of Europe during the last century.

Of all the demands made upon their subjects by European governments that of compulsory military service has been among the strongest influences causing emigration. . . . This enforced service in the army and navy has been among the causes giving to the United States immigrants from Russia, Germany, Denmark, Austria, and Italy.

Conscription has been more of a factor in Germany, from which country thousands of young Germans have emigrated annually in order to avoid compulsory military service. Evidence of this is found in the official announcements of the penalty and punishment to which they have been sentenced. This has been particularly true since 1866, the right of emigration, which had been regarded as a fundamental one, being limited in that year by the restriction that it could not be permitted by emigration to avoid this duty. It was this compulsory service in the army and navy that caused many young men to whom passports were refused to emigrate across the frontiers. In Austria the law rendering every able-bodied man liable to military duty prompted not a few young men to leave the country before they reached the age of twenty.[2]

It is evident from discussions of the subject with that one per cent of Americans who are currently serving involuntarily, or who face induction within the next few years, that compulsory military service is regarded widely as a bitter imposition on their lives.[3]

It is not germane here to analyze whether we, in some detached overview, consider military service a burden or a privilege. It is clearly not a sought-after employment; if it were, there would be no need for conscription. Yet it may be

unpleasant without being oppressive, if the draftee is resigned to it and regards it as his duty. The majority of adult, male Americans who have served — especially those who fought the three wars — regard a term of military service as *the expected thing* for any young man to do, as it was indeed for them. It does not seem possible for resisters to organize any effective movement against conscription in the face of this monolithic attitude towards the military; those who try are scorned, those who are inducted soon learn that any attitude other than docile cooperation can be perilous. The concern in this article is with the obstacles placed in the path of that minority who would rather emigrate than perform military service, by a government determined to shore up an anti-liberal institution with illiberal restrictions on a basic freedom.

The rationale for military impressment is cogently stated in the words of Mr. Chief Justice White, in the decision upholding the constitutionality of the World War I draft:

> It may not be doubted that the very conception of a just government and its duty to the citizen includes the reciprocal obligation of the citizen to render military service in case of need and the right to compel it.[4]

The argument is that of the social contract — those who desire the benefits of a free society must bear the costs of those benefits: everyone pays taxes, everyone refrains from violence, everyone serves two years in the army. Oddly, it is *not* the case that the *contrapositive* argument is accepted by the government. On the basis of the social contract rationale, a citizen who is willing to forego the privileges of living in the United States should be allowed to emi-

849

[2] F. J. Varne, *The Immigrant Invasion* (New York: Dodd, Meade and Co., 1913), pp. 43-44.

[3] Cf. "Evading the Draft: Who, How and Why," *Life Magazine*, Dec. 9, 1966, pp. 40-43.

[4] Selective Draft Law Cases, 245 U.S. 366, 378 (1917). The Court cites Vattel, *Law of Nations*, Book III, chaps. i and ii. In addition the Government argued: "Compulsory military service is not contrary to the spirit of democratic institutions, for the Constitution implies equitable distribution of the burdens no less than the privileges of citizenship." 245 U.S. 366, 368.

850

grate without any further obligations to the United States. That person would have entered into a new social contract, with his chosen country, to pay its taxes, obey its laws, and serve in its army instead. The government of the United States, however, does not permit the nullification of military obligations by emigration.

Although the United States maintains no general barriers to emigration, it is significant that the Selective Service System has in the past operated to deny the right of emigration, and currently maintains regulations which cast doubt upon the legal status of draft-liable emigrants. Only extreme tyrannies impose repressive general laws. The modern state — "absolute, minute, regular, provident, and mild" — imposes piecemeal restrictions, upon only small minorities at one time: a practice guaranteed to maintain a general opinion of support and loyalty. Yet if oppression is piecemeal, one must examine in each case whether a restriction on emigration exists, because a general freedom of exit is fraudulent if those groups who might seek to claim it are expressly kept in.

IT IS NOT COMMONLY realized that the United States imposes any restrictions upon exit. The actual statutes passed by Congress do not explicitly forbid emigration by men of draft age, and it is usually only Acts of Congress which we consider relevant. Under Title I, Subsection 10(b)(1), of the Universal Military Training and Service Act, however, "The President is authorized to prescribe the necessary rules and regulations to carry out the provisions of this title."[5] The regulations so promulgated stitch together a binding network of law with which, entirely on its own initiative it seems, the Executive branch of government has denied young men of draft age a significant human right.[6] A detailed examination of the regula-

tions is necessary to make this denial clear. In an attempt to make the avoidance of military service as difficult as possible, the Selective Service regulations provide:

> When it becomes the duty of a registrant or other person to perform an act or furnish information to a local board or other office or agency of the Selective Service System, the duty or obligation shall be a continuing duty or obligation from day to day and the failure to properly perform the act or the supplying of incorrect or false information shall in no way operate as a waiver of that continuing duty.[7]

It is by virtue of this declaration by the Executive of a perpetual duty, without any provision of machinery or conditions under which it may be cancelled, that all citizens and resident aliens of the United States between ages eighteen and twenty-six are legally obligated to perform military service — expatriation or emigration notwithstanding. The details and severity of this regulation will be made clear in the course of this article.

One further regulation of the Selective Service System bears upon the question of emigration in a direct way. It is important to note the wording of the single condition imposed upon the issuing agencies:

> The Director of Selective Service, the State Director of Selective Service, or the local board may issue to a registrant a permit to depart from the continental United States, the State of Alaska, the State of Hawaii, Puerto Rico, the Virgin Islands,

---

[5] 62 Stat. 619.

[6] Cf. *Universal Declaration of Human Rights* (New York: United Nations, 1948), Articles 13 and 15.

[7] *Code of Federal Regulations*, Title 32, chap. xvi, sec. 1642.2. In Fogel v. United States, 162 F.2d 54 (1947), the court upheld a conviction over appellant's argument that the statute of limitations applied. Mr. Justice Sibley, dissenting, wrote: "The theory of the conviction is that by doing nothing he renewed his crime every day to the date of the trial; which amounts to saying there is no statute of limitations for this offense. This seems to me not to be in accord with authority, when the thing which is made a crime is the failure to perform a continuing duty, when nothing at all happens after the crime became complete." *Ibid.*, p. 56. See note 21 below.

Guam, or the Canal Zone to any place which is not within any of those areas *whenever the registrant's absence is not likely to interfere with the performance of his obligations* under the Universal Military Training and Service Act, as amended. Such permit shall be issued by completion of a Permit for Registrant to Depart from the United States (SSS Form No. 300).[8]

One might argue that emigration cancels all such obligations, and therefore the issuance of the permit would not "interfere" with their performance; but it is clear on the basis of its past actions that the Selective Service System does not hold such a position. At the present time, a permit is not actually required for exit, but the Selective Service System has indicated that this permit is the only insurance one would have against being declared delinquent and prosecuted. That the Selective Service authorities regard this discretionary power over travel with satisfaction, and are willing to use it, can be inferred from a close reading of the following quotation from the eighteen volume official history of Selective Service during World War II, discussing emigrant aliens (who could presumably use foreign passports to leave the United States with greater ease than citizens):

> Finally, alien registrants who had departed from the United States and were no longer residing here were classified IV-C. Such classification was authorized as a practical solution to an awkward situation. There was some doubt and difference of opinion as to the extent of the liability under the Selective Service law for an alien who had departed from the United States.
>
> As a practical matter, however, the System had no means of enforcing the orders of a local board upon an alien outside of the country. On the other hand, the board had to continue processing and reprocessing such cases, to report them to the United States attorney as delinquents and to make other futile motions of this nature. Consequently, a procedure was adopted whereby

such registrants were placed in a class not available for service. Under the revised regulations if an alien so classified returned to the United States, he was subject to prosecution for any penalties he had incurred before departing and any subsequent obligations which had occurred for him under the act.

> On the whole, this solution was in the best interests of Selective Service. Aliens liable for training and service could not leave the country without the consent of their local boards. The Immigration and Naturalization Service of the Department of Justice cooperated wholeheartedly in this regard. Thus, the control of the System over the departure of aliens and its inability to enforce orders, after the alien had departed, appeared to justify the adoption of the IV-C classification procedure.[9]

Here is an excellent example of bureaucratic thoroughness. In spite of "some doubt and difference of opinion as to the extent of the liability . . . for an alien who had departed from the United States," rather than remove such emigrant alien from the rolls as no longer liable for military service to the United States, the Selective Service authorities decided to keep his dossier for possible use against him if he should ever return, perhaps to visit friends or on vacation. On the other hand, if the person should attempt to obtain permission from the government before departing, the police powers of the Department of Justice would be there to intervene.

ALTHOUGH INVOLVING other factors as well, the treatment of Japanese Americans during the Second World War provides an interesting study of one group of people obviously subject to oppression who were denied the chance to emigrate by Selective Service, and subsequently ordered to report for induction. Again from the official history,

851

---

[8] *Code of Federal Regulations,* Title 32, chap. xvi, sec. 1621.16. Emphasis supplied.

[9] U. S. Selective System, *Problems of Selective Service; Special Monograph No. 16* (Washington: Government Printing Office, 1952), Vol I, *Text,* pp. 117, 120.

852

the Selective Service authorities ob-
liquely admit this denial of the right
of emigration:

The alien problem was one of the
first to demonstrate the effectiveness of coordination between local
boards and their State Headquarters.
On the west coast large numbers of
Japanese registrants began asking
permission from their local boards
to leave the United States. This was
a new and troublesome situation and
the boards turned to State Headquarters for advice. The pattern was uniform enough from board to board
that the State Directors of this part
of the country felt the problem must
be met directly and promptly. They
therefore held meetings with the
Japanese leaders of the Pacific Coast
States who indicated their disapproval of such action by Japanese
registrants. The State Headquarters
concerned then recommended that
the boards disapprove the requests.[10]

The decision of the individual concerning his loyalties and attitudes toward various duties was never considered relevant; a group policy was formulated w i t h Procrustean disdain.
"Thus, it was that the initial contact
of Selective Service with many Japanese
American and Negro registrants was
not with men who lacked patriotism, but
with those who to a considerable extent
were just not 'sold' on the war."[11]

Prior to Pearl Harbor, Japanese Americans were drafted like other ordinary
citizens, but from February 1942 they
were considered by the War Department
as generally unacceptable for service.[12]
In January 1944, the Selective Service
System altered its policies, however, pursuant to a War Department decision of
the preceding November. The new approach was to screen every eligible registrant, and to induct those found acceptable.[13]

The reintroduction of Selective
Service for Japanese Americans in
January 1944 came without advance
notice and apparently as a rather
complete surprise to many residents
of War Relocation Authority Centers. Almost immediately, the number of requests for repatriation or
expatriation showed a marked increase. . . . This was done not only
by men disloyal to the United States,
but also by those whose interest was
solely draft dodging. Some of the latter could not even speak the Japanese language and had no relatives,
property or other apparent interest
in Japan.

In a War Department memorandum, dated March 30, 1944, it was
stated that requests for repatriation
or expatriation to Japan made by
Japanese American citizens who
were liable for military service
would be considered an effort to
evade such duty if filed after January 21, 1944, or when the registrant's
induction was imminent.[14]

It is clear that the government maintained an exceedingly hostile attitude
toward those who sought to emigrate as
a means of cancelling military obligations.

In general, Japanese Americans who
made strong enough statements of disloyalty during their individual screen-
ings by Selective Service after January
1944 would have been found unacceptable to the military authorities, thereby
avoiding the draft without actually being expatriated. By its own admission,
however, the Selective Service System
was so inefficient and uncoordinated
with the War Department that many
clearly disloyal registrants were still
classified as acceptable even months after a change in their status or opinions.[15]
When these registrants were occasionally ordered to report for induction,
which they refused to do, the courts consistently upheld the authority of the government to deny the right of emigration,
to detain the individual, and to order
him into the Army if he should be classified as acceptable. In the case of Hideichi
Takeguma et al., defendants were con-

[10] *Ibid.*, pp. 222-23.

[11] U. S. Selective Service System, *Special Groups; Special Monograph No. 10* (Washington: Government Printing Office, 1953), Vol. I, *Text,* p. 67.

[12] *Ibid.*, p. 117.

[13] *Ibid.*, pp. 123-24.

[14] *Ibid.*, pp. 128-29.

[15] *Ibid.*, pp. 127, 136.

victed of failing to report for induction even though the government had granted their requests for expatriation, while detaining them in fact for the duration of the war. The court held:

> It remains to be considered whether or not the granted expatriation request by the other two appellants, together with the order of exclusion and segregation, are so inconsistent with the order to report for induction as to void the latter order. . . . If, as these two appellants claim, this completed act of expatriation transformed them f r o m United States citizens into subjects of Japan, hence alien enemies, appellants have not gained their goal for the reason that alien enemies who are acceptable to the military authorities (and these appellants were) still may serve in the land and naval forces of the United States.[16]

The injustice of this practice was remarked by one District Court Judge, who acquitted other defendants on different grounds:[17]

> It is shocking to the conscience that an American citizen be confined on the ground of disloyalty, and then, while so under duress and restraint, be compelled to serve in the armed forces, or be prosecuted for not yielding to such compulsion.[18]

This case, *Kuwabara v. United States,* is mentioned here only because it stands in such contrast to the general attitude of the courts, and the Selective Service System, towards the role of citizens in respect to the state. The right of emigration and the social contract rationale for duties to the state both imply a liberal, individualistic orientation: an individual may not transgress the laws of society, but the decision to obey or to emigrate is his own; his loyalty is some-

thing he extends to the state, not something the state can demand by reason of an accident of birth.

DURING THE PAST DECADE the Supreme Court has acted to restore to American citizens many rights of foreign travel which formerly had been infringed by the Passport Division of the Department of State, and by Congress.[19] Mr. Justice Douglas, delivering the opinion of the Court in *Kent v. Dulles,* wrote:

> The right to travel is a part of the "liberty" of which the citizen cannot be deprived without due process of law under the Fifth Amendment. So much is conceded by the Solicitor General. In Anglo-Saxon law that right was emerging at least as early as the Magna Charta. . . . Freedom of movement across frontiers in either direction, and inside frontiers as well, was a part of our heritage. . . . Freedom of movement is basic in our scheme of values.[20]

With language this strong, one might speculate that the Supreme Court would guarantee a draft-liable individual the right to emigrate, but the Supreme Court has not yet addressed itself specifically to these questions.[21] Given the

853

---

[16] Hideichi Takeguma v. United States, 156 F.2d 437, 440 (1945).

[17] Defendents were in fact incarcerated by the internment center authorities and denied the opportunity either to obey or disobey the order to report for pre-induction physical examinations.

[18] Kuwabara v. United States, 56 F. Supp. 716, 719 (1944).

[19] E.g., Kent v. Dulles, 357 U.S. 116 (1957); Aptheker v. Secretary of State, 378 U.S. 500 (1963); and United States v. Laub, 385 U.S. 475 (1967).

[20] 357 U.S. 116, 125-26.

[21] There is no decided Supreme Court case concerning the application of the statute of limitations vs. the continuing duty concept. The lower courts in general follow Fogel v. United States, 162 F.2d 54 (1947), but two recent cases, Graves v. United States, 252 F.2d 878 (1958), and Venus v. United States, 266 F.2d 836 (1959), both in the Ninth Circuit, show a marked hesitancy to follow the continuing duty theory of Fogel. If the precedent of Fogel is overturned by the Supreme Court when an emigration case is finally decided—as authority would suggest; cf. United States v. Irvine, 98 U.S. 450 (1879), Prendergast v. United States, 317 U.S. 412 (1943), and Fiswick v. United States, 329 U.S. 211 (1946) —emigration as a practical method of nullifying Selective Service obligations after five years would be established, provided the statute of limitations applied to the particular case. The *right* of emigration as a cancellation of Selective Service obligations, however, will not be

emotional atmosphere surrounding the issue of compulsory military service — and resistance to it — and considering that the courts have never been very receptive to the pleas of citizens against the Selective Service laws,[22] the question is moot. This writer was unable to locate any decisions relating directly to the question of emigration per se, and by the nature of the crime, there are no decisions involving those who fled and have not been brought to court by reason of their permanent residence abroad. Apparently extradition for draft evasion has not been widely used, although several recent indictments may yet alter that; we may soon see more vigorous prosecution of dissenters. Unfortunately for our purposes here, the willingness of the Selective Service System to allow delinquents to avoid criminal prosecution by reporting for immediate induction has probably very much reduced the chances of these points of law being considered by the courts.

The ease with which a person may leave the United States, especially the ease with which Americans can enter Canada or Mexico, is well known. The point of this discussion has not been to assert that a person would be physically prevented from departing if he were liable for conscription. Enforcement is not adequate to check all tourists passing into Canada and Mexico in order to apprehend draft evaders. Our concern, however, is with the absence of any lawful means of cancelling the military obligation through emigration, and the continuing liability and threat

of apprehension and prosecution to a draft-liable individual who chooses to emigrate rather than serve. To a classical liberal, the accident of being born in Detroit rather than Windsor, or Seattle rather than Vancouver, for example, ought to have no bearing upon the freedom of that person to renounce loyalty to the United States and seek Canadian citizenship, and to enjoy all privileges thereof — *including the treaty rights of traveling and carrying on business in the United States*. Under present law, the accident of birth is all-important: the government does not regard citizenship as an accident.

The anti-liberal attitude of the United States government may be merely a reflection of the prevailing majority opinion — that if a man will not loyally serve the country of his birth, he ought to be permanently exiled or imprisoned; but this is hardly an attitude conducive to or compatible with other widely held beliefs in the United States, such as freedom of opinion and speech, the right to travel, etc. It is not the case that a person who emigrates from the United States forfeits all liberty and rights enjoyed by American citizens, for Britons, Canadians, Australians, and many other nations share the liberal heritage with citizens of this country. Americans would be very disturbed if France, for example, were accustomed to detain and conscript United States citizens of French ancestry vacationing in Paris, even if only first-generation immigrants were so liable. The United States government, on the other hand, actively engages in the harassment of expatriates who emigrated in order to avoid military service. The administrative regulations of the Department of State, for example, provide:

Aliens ineligible to citizenship or who departed to avoid service in the Armed Forces. An alien shall be re-refused a nonimmigrant visa under the provisions of section 212(a)(22) of the [Immigration and Nationality Act, as amended] if, having other than nonimmigrant status, he departed from or remained outside of the United States on or after Sep-

---

established merely by overturning Fogel, because the concept of social contract cancellation through emigration implies an immediate termination of duties, not just an acquisition of immunity from prosecution after five years. There is further the problem that the Government might successfully argue to the Supreme Court that the statute of limitations *is suspended* during the period of the emigrant's residence abroad, under the provisions against "fugitives from justice." 18 U.S.C.A. 317.

[22] Cf. United States v. Cornell, 36 F. Supp. 81 (1940); United States v. Garst, 39 F. Supp. 367 (1941); United States v. Herling, 120 F.2d 236 (1941), affirming United States v. Rappaport et al., 36 F. Supp. 915 (1940).

tember 8, 1939 to avoid or evade training or service in the United States Armed Forces.[23]

The purpose of a regulation such as the above can only be to place as large a penalty as possible upon foreign nationals, unfortunate enough to have been born in the United States or to have lived here, who did not make the decision to emigrate until after age eighteen, when it was too late to escape the military obligation lawfully (since the requirement to register and serve commences on that date). In terms of practical enforcement, though, it would seem that Canadians would be less likely to be affected by this hostile attitude because of a loophole arising from cordial United States-Canadian relations:

> The provisions of section 212(a) (26) of the [Immigration and Nationality Act, as amended] relating to the requirements of valid passports and visas for nonimmigrants are waived by the Secretary of State and the Attorney General, acting jointly, in pursuance of the authority contained in section 212(d)(4) of the Act under the conditions specified for the following classes:
>
> (a) *Canadian nationals, and aliens having a common nationality with nationals of Canada or with British subjects in Bermuda.* A visa shall not in any case be required of a Canadian national, and a passport shall not be required of such a national except after a visit outside of the Western Hemisphere. . . . [24]

Although the probabilities of arrest are smaller for those draft evaders who might become Canadian citizens, the permanent danger of imprisonment still represents a serious threat to all former Americans, especially if the Attorney General were to become more concerned with emigre draft dodgers and were to have such persons placed under sur-

veillance. It is already the case that some draft-liable emigrants to Canada have been arrested at the border upon returning to the United States to visit friends or conduct business.

ALTHOUGH THE PRESENT Selective Service regulations made pursuant to the Universal Military Training and Service Act deny the social contract premise which defends the Act, there are marginal circumstances by which many people desiring to emigrate would be able to avoid the trap which closes on one's eighteenth birthday. Once a person (whether citizen or alien) has registered with the Selective Service System, his only recourse if he wishes to emigrate is either to violate the law and risk imprisonment, or to fulfill the required term of service beforehand. Even aliens who wish to return to their own countries are no less subject to this unfortunate dilemma than citizens victim of an "accident of birth." Aliens do, however, have more flexibility with regards the registration requirement, if they know the construction of the regulations.

Certain categories of aliens who can claim a permanent foreign residence can qualify for the status of "non-residents," and not be required to register. The most likely persons to avoid the military dilemma in this way are students, who as non-residents would not have to register for Selective Service and not be faced with the age-extending problem of the II-S classification. These persons would be expected to leave the United States upon completion of their studies, but would not be barred from returning to or later seeking citizenship in the United States. For a person with dual citizenship — discussed below — it would be necessary to emigrate to his other homeland prior to the age of eighteen, and then apply for a non-resident student visa for college in the United States.

Aliens not qualifying for a non-resident student visa would be required to register with the Selective Service Sys-

855

---

[23] *Code of Federal Regulations*, Title 22, chap. i, sec. 41.91 (a) (22). Italics in the original. The restriction is broadened by the Act itself to include immigrant visas also. 66 Stat. 184.

[24] *Code of Federal Regulations*, Title 22, chap. i, sec. 41.6 Italics in the original.

tem at age eighteen or within ninety days after entering the United States. The regulations give aliens the option of declaring themselves resident or non-resident, the former being subject to conscription immediately and the latter being allowed one year to finish their business and depart or be registered as resident aliens. Because of the diplomatic problems involved in drafting aliens, however, the government has provided SSS Form No. 130, which allows resident aliens to declare that they do not wish to perform military service, and that they accordingly foreswear the opportunity ever to obtain American citizenship. The execution of this form is irreversible — even if the person decided later to serve in the military, he could never obtain American citizenship; and if he subsequently departed from the United States, he might be denied re-entry under the State Department regulations quoted above, unless he could utilize the Canadian loophole. The existence of the possibility of obtaining such an exempt alien classification, Class IV-C, merely by renouncing future United States citizenship would suggest interesting possibilities for dual citizens and pre-eighteen emigrants; but the liberal ideal is far from being realized when ordinary citizens cannot escape impressment similarly.[25]

The most interesting category of aliens involves those born with both United States citizenship and some other citizenship. Such persons are typically those born abroad of United States parentage, or born in the United States of foreign

parents. Such dual citizens usually must choose between their two "homelands" before age twenty-five, at which time the choice is deemed to have been made for them by virtue of residence. For purposes of qualifying under Selective Service in some non-liable category, the choice for non-United States citizenship would have to be made prior to the eighteenth birthday; but since the person would still be a minor, this would have the beneficial effect of not damaging the possibility of a change of heart later — whereupon the person could regain full, natural-born American citizenship. To avoid as much as possible the appearance of one's name on government lists, the correct procedure of choosing non-United States citizenship involves obtaining documents from the foreign government, passport, health certificate, drivers license, etc., establishing that citizenship, rather than executing any renunciation of United States citizenship because the latter is automatically terminated when foreign citizenship is obtained. To escape Selective Service, it is only necessary to successfully terminate United States citizenship prior to age eighteen, and, if returning to the United States, then to execute SSS Form No. 130 and obtain a IV-C exempt alien classification.

Because of the many anti-liberal aspects involved in being a citizen of some particular country — passport restrictions, draft liabilities, taxation, and property penalties — it would seem desirable from the standpoint of a classical liberal to allow the individual himself to make the choice of citizenship (natural-born if possible, because naturalized citizens are restricted in many countries in minor ways, as in holding public office or residing abroad for long periods) rather than leaving this highly significant choice up to an accident of birth. For these reasons, it would not be surprising if in the future a large number of Americans were to spend a summer or a year in Canada, coinciding with the birth of a child (the timing of birth could be accurately controlled within a month's vacation period by birth control measures), especially if conscrip-

---

[25] The person who might obtain a IV-C classification by executing SSS Form No. 130 must be distinguished from those emigrants fortunate enough to have obtained a IV-C classification from their local boards under C.F.R., Title 32, chap. xvi, sec. 1622.42(c), which provides: "In Class IV-C shall be placed any registrant who is an alien and who has departed from the United States. Such alien shall be placed in Class IV-C even though he is a delinquent but this classification shall in no way relieve him from liability for prosecution for violation of the selective service law. If any registrant so classified under the paragraph returns to the United States, his classification shall be reopened and he shall be classified anew." See also the quotation cited in note 9 above.

tion is not soon abolished in the United States. Such children could be reared and attend school in the United States, and by qualifying for a non-resident visa even obtain a college degree in this country. Once such children had passed military age (twenty-sixth birthday) they would still be free to return permanently and, if they desired, take out United States citizenship.

THE ONLY LAWFUL WAY in which a United States citizen can avoid military service through emigration is to depart from the country before age eighteen and renounce his citizenship once abroad. Legally, it would be absolutely necessary to renounce United States citizenship, since all citizens, whether at home or abroad, must register at age eighteen — and the goal is not to register. Such a person would become in effect a stateless person for the period of time required for naturalization in his new homeland, and would not qualify for a passport during this period (though limited foreign travel would be possible with documents of identification obtainable from most governments). Persons planning to maximize their freedom and violate the law if necessary in the short run, provided likelihood of arrest is minimal, would probably be able to cut the period of time as a stateless person to two years (under current United States passport regulations) simply by acquiring a new passport immediately before departing and not renouncing citizenship at all, but waiting for it to become forfeit when they acquire their new citizenship after five years (Canada or United Kingdom). This same tactic could be used without violating the law by emigrating prior to age fifteen.

In all of the above examples, the co-operation of the individual's parents would be absolutely necessary, inasmuch as the person must be a minor to emigrate and avoid military service thereby. In the extreme case, the parents would accompany the child to his adopted country. It might not be unreasonable to expect a family of Quaker or pacifist

convictions to take this step with the fate of their minor children in mind, although most parents would consider the suggestion absurd. A more likely case might be the sending of children abroad for school or college with the knowledge that they would initiate foreign naturalization proceedings as soon as possible. Except for Canadian schools, this would mean not seeing one's children for some time unless the parents themselves went abroad on vacation. If the realization of the full impact of conscription did not occur to the individual until the age of seventeen, even then it would not be too late to decide upon a Canadian or British university, and parents might be much more receptive to that suggestion than to any other. The prestige of study abroad might outweigh any objections they would have to the suggestions of emigration and renunciation of citizenship. The laws of citizenship and nationality are intricate, and it is unlikely that a teenage boy would have the knowledge or sophistication to research the problems adequately. For this reason, the above cases are purely hypothetical; but for purposes of this article, it is useful to set forth the full picture of Selective Service and emigration law, loopholes included. If the fact that United States military obligations commence at age eighteen — and not at birth — were more widely known, it seems likely that fewer draft resisters would attempt conscientious objection status, which requires two years of menial alternative service as objectionable on libertarian grounds as military service, or fall afoul of the law when finally fleeing the United States to avoid impressment. It seems intellectually more honest to confront one's attitudes toward military service and loyalty to a government which compels it, and to reject the government outright through emigration, rather than to attempt to evade the law — in effect taking the benefits of a country without paying the costs. Most individuals, however, are caught in the Selective Service trap simply because they innocently register at age eighteen without realizing that they could have taken other options.

857

The decision to renounce United States citizenship is one that few Americans would ever make. Certain metaphysical characteristics attach to the citizenship of one's native land that tip the scales heavily against giving it up, although one might live abroad for many years. Even in this cosmopolitan age, we see Britons and expatriate Americans living in every major city of the world, with no diminution of loyalty and attachment to their homes. Our purpose in this article has been to discuss the surprising denial of freedom to an oppressed minority who might want to escape through emigration; a minority which does not share the loyalty of most. In the nineteenth century, America welcomed with open arms the Germans and Eastern Europeans who fled military service and burdensome taxation in their homelands. Now that America itself has shouldered the double burden of world empire and domestic *dirigisme* we ought to be less hostile and intolerant towards those among us who still remember the old American dream and want to follow it to whatever land it has now gone.

858

Anti-Militarism and Laissez Faire

JAMES POWELL

IN THE NAME OF a pragmatic national defense, the United States since World War II has reversed its traditional presumptions against conscription. In part, of course, this reversal, and the popular acceptance of conscription as a regular feature of American life, has been a product of the major wars with which this country has been involved; peacetime conscription has been heralded from 1945 on as a way of preventing another war. That there is much support, however, for conscription as an instrument of social reform — national service — indicates that conscription is not strictly a military phenomenon, but is a consequence of the general presumptions for state-oriented over citizen-centered policy, which have guided social reform for many decades.

The state-oriented presumption in the case of conscription has been the doctrine of "service obligation." According to this doctrine, the government defines certain occupations as fulfilling the "national interest," and is empowered to compel people to follow such occupations. Finally, the government claims that the whole process is an uplifting experience. Thus, Lt. General William Knudsen testified before the House Committee on Military Affairs: "So I can tell you from my own experience that a period of one year in the service of the State or of the Government will have a tendency to make men more democratic. They will all be together. They will learn each other's ways and learn to look upon the Nation as a whole. They will be more patriotic when they get through with their service, and they will never forget the time that they had working for their country."[1] General Eisenhower has stated his ideals of military service many times, as in this case:

> If UMT accomplished nothing more than to produce cleanliness and decent grooming, it might be worth the price tag — and I am not altogether jesting when I say this. To me a sloppy appearance has always indicated sloppy habits of mind.
>
> But above and beyond these advantages of UMT is the matter of attitude toward country. If a UMT system were to become a fixture of our national life, I think that resentment against military obligation would die away, that virtually every young man would take pride and satisfaction in giving a year of his life to the United States of America. After all, the good instincts lie near the surface of the young. Patriotism, a sense of duty, a feeling of obligation to country are still there. They

James Powell is Associate Editor of *New Individualist Review.* He received his A.B. in History from the University of Chicago in 1966, and is currently doing graduate work there.

[1] Statement of Lt. Gen. William S. Knudsen, House Committee on Military Affairs, Nov. 27, 1945.

are the noblest and the most necessary qualities of any democratic system, and I am convinced that UMT would help call them to the surface once more.[2]

Or consider General Hershey's assessment of the creative potential of the threat of military service: "You are trying to use the deferment on the one hand as the carrot and the induction as the whip if you want to call it that, to keep the person channeled into scientific schools, into engineering schools, into medical schools. . . . The practice is going to be that the rare bird, if you want to call him that, is so useful that we keep the threat of service over him in order to keep him useful."[3] The idealization of compulsion which is implicit in conscription marks it as a paradigm of state-oriented policy.

However sincerely people might believe in the idea of service obligation, it is opposed to the values of a citizen-centered social order which relies upon voluntary social cooperation. That the idea of service obligation masks a policy which, however widely accepted today, is nonetheless just another kind of state-worship, is illustrated well by the following:

> The Army trained men for unconditional responsibility at a time when this quality had grown rare and evasion of it was becoming more and more the order of the day. . . . it trained men in personal courage in an age when cowardice threatened to become a raging disease. . . .
> The Army trained men in resolution while elsewhere in life indecision and doubt were beginning to determine the actions of men.
> The Army trained men in idealism and devotion to the fatherland and its greatness while everywhere else greed and materialism had spread abroad.
> The young man who practiced obedience during this time could

then learn to command. By his very step you could recognize the soldier who had done his service.[4]

The similarity between Hitler's statement and much Congressional testimony, for instance, should appear as no accident, but as an indication of how far state-oriented ideas have been implanted in American thought. In some situations the requirements for national defense might include conscription, but recognition that such unusual situations might occur is not at all equivalent to the general belief that conscription is a good thing.

THERE ARE PROBABLY three elements of the general belief in conscription, or the doctrine of service obligation. First, conscription sanctions Executive prerogative. National defense requires professional expertise of the sort possessed by administrators, not legislators; and the presumption is that whatever aspect of defense policy receives the endorsement of the Executive agencies should be enacted substantially as proposed, particularly in a time of crisis. Each time the draft law has expired, since 1951, there have been perfunctory hearings, and the Congressional committees have reported, and Congress has voted, to extend the draft virtually unmodified. Congress has functioned more to enact than to deliberate upon the recommendations of the Executive. Or, as Garet Garrett described the government of an empire: "The word *executive* came to have its new connotation. For all the years before when you spoke of the executive power of government you meant only the power to execute and administer the laws. Henceforth it would mean the *power to govern.*"[5] Conscription has illustrated the chief aspect of Executive government — the tendency of the Executive both to gather administrative knowledge and to formulate policy.

860

[2] D. D. Eisenhower, "This Country Needs Universal Military Training," *Reader's Digest*, Sept. 1966, p. 55.

[3] Statement of Lt. Gen. Lewis B. Hershey, Director, Selective Service, Senate Committee on Armed Services, March 5, 1959.

[4] A. Hitler, *Mein Kampf* (Boston: Houghton Mifflin, 1943), pp. 280-81.

[5] G. Garrett, *The People's Pottage* (Caldwell, Idaho: Caxton, 1965), p. 130.

Second, arguments for conscription have invariably involved the assumption that voluntary incentives would never attract sufficient military manpower. The Marshall Commission, for instance, innocently reported that "a draft law has been necessary precisely because there have not been enough volunteers to meet military manpower needs."[6] Similarly, General Mark Clark, Chairman of the Civilian Advisory Panel, testified before the Senate Armed Services Committee that "a draft law will be required for national security purposes for the indefinite future."[7] There is no suggestion in the Marshall Commission Report, or in any other testimony on the draft, that incentives affect the number of people who enlist. Nor is there any suggestion that in certain circumstances the draft could — and *should* — end altogether; a regular feature of testimony on the draft is the supposition that we must rely, indefinitely, on compulsion to sustain our national defense.

Third, conscription has survived at least in part because of the belief that military service exacted through compulsion is more noble and patriotic than those careers people voluntarily pursue. By and large this has been the moral position which the American Legion has always represented to Congress, as in 1963: "Our nation should never be without an obligation for every youth to serve his country in a military capacity and a system for their selection so to serve."[8] Conscription is moral because it is service to the *state*. This idea, of course, is the first principle of any authoritarian regime, and justifies the ultimate subversion of all civil liberties.

Fortified by the idea of service obligation, lobbyists for conscription seldom have argued that their conclusions are

the results of empirical investigation. Certainly no one has testified before Congress to indicate what sorts of evidence would certify those claims as humbug. Does Selective Service intend merely to acquire temporary possession of a specified quantity of people? Is the goal to encourage career enlistments? Or to allocate manpower most effectively? Or to follow those policies most consistent with personal freedom? One consequence of *not* stating the claims of Selective Service in such a way that the empirical implications are clear, has been to avoid the implication that in certain circumstances Selective Service should end altogether.

Many people have argued that conscription is most objectionable as an aspect of militarism, but the state-oriented ideas which justify conscription apply to non-military policies as well. Last May, Secretary of Defense McNamara offered his well-publicized proposal for universal two-year "service to country."[9] Shortly after McNamara's speech, Senator Javits joined the crusade: "Secretary McNamara's proposal was aimed at 'voluntary' service by both men and women. It is my feeling that it would be almost impossible to make such a concept work as a practical matter. I propose that universal national service be made compulsory for young men, giving them the option of selecting what form it should take within permissable categories established by the government."[10] President Johnson evidently lent his implicit support to the universal "voluntary" service idea: "The call for public service therefore cannot be met by professionals alone. We must revive the ancient ideal of citizen soldiers who answer their nation's call in time of peril. We need them on battlefronts where no guns are heard but freedom is no less tested."[11] Again: "We must move toward a standard that

861

---

[6] National Advisory Commission on Selective Service, *Report*, 1967, p. 12.

[7] Statement of Gen. Mark W. Clark, Chairman of the Civilian Advisory Panel on Military Manpower Procurement, Senate Committee on Armed Services, April 12, 1967.

[8] Statement of William C. Doyle, Chairman, National Security Commission, American Legion, Senate Committee on Armed Services, March 12, 1963.

[9] R. S. McNamara, "Address before American Society of Newspaper Editors, Montreal, Canada," Office of Assistant Secretary of Defense (Public Affairs), May 18, 1966.

[10] J. K. Javits, "Administration Should Support National Service Concept," Office of Jacob K. Javits, May 22, 1966.

[11] *The New York Times*, May 12, 1966, p. 14.

no man has truly lived who only served himself. . . . To move in this direction, I am asking every member of my Administration to explore new ways by which our young people can serve their fellow men."[12] Secretary of Labor Wirtz expressed his belief in universal service, last November,[13] and more recently Sargent Shriver indicated that universal service should begin at the age of sixteen.[14] The popularity of the universal service idea shows how slender is the protection to civil liberties offered by civilian supremacy over the military; both civilian and military regimes have acted in blatant disregard of civil liberties, and universal service merely extends to civilian experience some of the features of state-oriented, military life.

862

INDEED, THE GROWTH, if it should occur, of non-military, but authoritarian, labor conscription would be the result of the confluence of socialist and pacifist ideas. These ideas have worked not to mitigate the assaults upon civil liberties which conscription entails, but to deflect the assaults from military to non-military pursuits; socialism has preserved the state-oriented—compulsory— aspect of service to a civilian rather than a military state. One of the most influential statements in the history of American pacifism, William James' "Moral Equivalent of War," illustrates this kind of socialist-pacifism clearly:

> If now — and this is my idea — there were, instead of military conscription a conscription of the whole youthful population to form for a certain number of years a part of the army enlisted against *Nature,* the injustice would tend to be evened out, and numerous other goods to the commonwealth would follow. The military ideals of hardi-

hood and discipline would be wrought into the growing fibre of the people; no one would remain blind as the luxurious classes now are blind, to man's real relations to the globe he lives on, and to the permanently sour and hard foundations of his higher life. To coal and iron mines, to freight trains, to fishing fleets in December, to dishwashing, clothes-washing, and window-washing, to road-building and tunnel-making, to foundries and stoke-holes, and to the frames of skyscrapers, would our gilded youths be drafted off, according to their choice, to get the childishness knocked out of them, and to come back into society with healthier sympathies and soberer ideas. They would have paid their blood-tax, done their part in the immemorial human warfare against nature, they would tread the earth more proudly, the women would value them more highly, they would be better fathers and teachers of the following generation.[15]

Many pacifists have accepted James' idea of national service, and have indicated thereby that however extensively war has figured in the suppression of civil liberties, pacifism as such does not provide a basis for defending civil liberties. In fact, those pacifists who favor compulsory national service as a way of avoiding wartime service promote both the suppression of civil liberties and war against individuals. The suppression of civil liberties is clear enough; war against individuals occurs through the attempts to enforce compliance with national service regulations. When human relations are voluntary, non-compliance with a contract eventually results in termination of the contract; the most effective way to enforce mutual exchange is simply to deny a non-compliant party the benefits of mutual exchange. When, however, a contract is compulsory, enforcement by termination of contract obviously cannot occur; instead, government must administer punishments to enforce compliance. Moreover, such punishments conceivably could occur indefinitely, for non-compli-

---

[12] "Remarks of the President at Montgomery County Fair, Dayton, Ohio," Office of the White House Press Secretary, Sept. 5, 1966, pp. 4-5.

[13] W. Wirtz, "Policy for Youth," *Vital Speeches of the Day,* Jan. 1, 1967, p. 162.

[14] Statement of Sargent Shriver, Senate Subcommittee of Employment, Manpower, and Poverty, March 23, 1967.

[15] S. Lynd, ed., *Nonviolence in America: A Documentary History* (Indianapolis, Ind.: Bobbs-Merrill, 1966), p. 147.

ance could occur indefinitely. To enforce national service on everyone, government must extend to civilian experience the discipline of military-type law.

The implication of national service is that the loss of civil liberties and the war against recalcitrant individuals is worthwhile because compulsion is the most effective way of developing and allocating human resources, and thereby of resolving social problems. Of course, nowhere in the national service literature is there a demonstration that this contention is true, and certainly there is never any indication of what sorts of evidence would confirm or invalidate the contentions. By not weighing the claims of national service scientifically, people have opted to bear the costs — or rather shuffle the costs upon others — without securing comparable benefits. The losses, as with military conscription,[16] would occur as (1) budgetary costs, (2) welfare costs to the nation as a whole, and (3) the implicit forced labor tax borne by the service-conscripts. As in the case of military conscription, one result of not stating the claims for national service scientifically is avoidance of the implication that in certain circumstances national service should be abolished—if it ever should be established in the first place. Certainly the shoddy, unscientific way in which national service is usually advanced does not separate moral and empirical arguments; and it is never clear whether people favor national service empirically as a method of resolving problems, or whether they favor national service as a matter of principle.[17] If the former is true, then the arguments should be regarded as sheer hokum until they are presented scientifically so they can be evaluated. If the latter case is true, then the conflict between libertarian, citizen-centered ideas, and state oriented ones, is abundantly clear; and it is clear that only from libertarian, and not from pacifistic grounds, can one develop principled opposition to oppression.

AS A WAY OF fostering exploration of libertarian ideas, we reprint in this issue three articles by men who have illustrated two aspects of the libertarian tradition. One is that the presumption for voluntarism requires exhaustion of voluntary incentives before adopting conscription. Taft, for instance, conceded that on certain rare occasions the requirements of national defense might include conscription, but he added:

I did oppose the Selective Service Act of 1940, and am still opposed to the compulsory draft of men in time of peace *until every voluntary method has been tried* to obtain the men necessary for the force required for defense.[18]

Great Britain followed this presumption and did not resort to compulsion in World War I until mid-way through the hostilities, in 1916. The other point is that for each of these people anti-conscription was but one element of their libertarian points of view; compulsion in the case of conscription was more overt but not much more serious than compulsion in other areas of life. Hopefully, reprinting these articles will illustrate by example that there is indeed a coherent tradition to which people can refer for a principled opposition to conscription.

THE LIBERTARIAN tradition thrived not as antimilitarism, although that was one element of libertarian thought, but as a general presumption for personal rights, civil guaranties, private property, and constitutional, republican government. Militarism and conscription have thrived not so much because these particular ideas are popular, but because state-oriented ideas generally are popular. The most peaceful, non-militaristic century in modern history—the nineteenth—was also the century in which free trade flourished more than it ever had before, or since; in which the rule of law was extended, at

863

---

[16] See the article by Walter Y. Oi in this issue.

[17] E.g., D. J. Eberly, ed., *A Profile of National Service* (New York: Overseas Educational Service, 1966), *passim.*

[18] *A Foreign Policy for Americans* (Garden City, New York: Doubleday, 1951), p. 124. Emphasis supplied.

least in part, to many European countries and in which libertarian ideas governed the major features of state policy. The British Empire, at the zenith of its influence during the nineteenth century, never employed conscription. And the growth of imperialism toward the end of the nineteenth century was but one part of the movement of ideas that embraced higher trade barriers, the growth of state monopolies, of special labor laws, of compulsory health insurance, and other policies which marked a more vigorous role for government.

Decisive to the continuation of conscription is the general presumption that government is morally and technically qualified to administer the lives of citizens; only by overthrowing this presumption, and reviving libertarian ideas, can conscription be ended. Merely opposing compulsion in the case of conscription promises only a futile, rear-guard harassment of government. Non-libertarians who are anti-conscription have reason empirically to doubt the possibilities of ending conscription without wholly reversing the presumption for state-oriented over citizen centered policy.[19]

863

864

---

[19] For a fine introduction to antimilitarism in America, see A. A. Ekirch, *The Civilian and the Military* (New York: Oxford University Press, 1956). A useful general survey is A. Vagts, *A History of Militarism* (New York: Norton, 1937), and since reprinted. There are many articles of one sort or another dealing with conscription, and one of particular interest, on the efforts exerted by the military to reverse traditional American presumptions against conscription, is H. Baldwin, "The Military Move In," *Harpers*, Dec. 1947, pp. 481-89. The *Nation* is probably the only publication which has preserved a long tradition of opposition to conscription; see in particular the issues during and shortly after World War I—when its editors were both anti-conscription and libertarian.

THE ANTI-MILITARIST TRADITION:

Robert A. Taft, 1940

Until his death in 1953, Robert A. Taft was an enlightened spokesman for liberal ideas in financial affairs, in foreign policy, and in military policies. He was elected to the United States Senate in 1938, 1944, and 1950, and was the ideal Republican candidate for President in 1952. His speech in opposition to the Burke-Wadsworth bill, which proposed peacetime conscription in America for the first time in history, is a classic and we reprint it here with only a few changes.[1]

WE FACE TODAY NOT one emergency but two. The first is from abroad; the second is from ourselves. While I do not agree with those who think that Hitler is about to attack the United States, nevertheless we must all recognize that for the next ten years we face a new kind of world. The development of the totalitarian nations, their effective war machines, and their complete lack of regard for international morals have created this new condition. We cannot rely on the sanctity of any treaty or any promise which may be made by the German Government and perhaps by the other governments. I believe that the same condition will exist whether the German attack on England succeeds or fails. England can hardly hope to overwhelm Germany for years to come. There will always be the possibility of the breaking up of the British Empire. We must provide for that possibility. I have voted for all the various appropriations increasing the size of the Navy and of the air forces. We are agreed that we must have a navy able to defend both the Atlantic and Pacific coasts. But surely it is the duty of Congress to consider as respects each measure brought before it the character and extent of the emergency. . . .

For we face another kind of emergency at home. We have steadily drifted toward centralized government. We have given it power to regulate everything and everybody. There is a bill pending in Congress to give the President power to take property of any kind; to fix all prices, to assign every man to a designated position. There is a bill pending providing for a capital levy, taking a large proportion of every man's property in exchange for one per cent government bonds. In short, proposals made by responsible men, if added together, would create exactly the kind of government in this country which exists today in Germany. There are many who urge with the proponents of the Burke-Wadsworth bill that the emergency requires a complete recasting of American life, a dedication of our entire energies to defense alone, and subordination of every principle on which the American Republic is based.

[1] This text is taken from the *Congressional Record*, Appendix, September 6, 1940, pp. 5490-92. The article was originally presented as a radio address by Senator Taft on September 5, 1940.

865

It is said that in time of war we have not hesitated to establish a dictatorship. I am afraid we would do so again, whether it is necessary or not. But that is a very different thing from establishing a dictatorship in time of peace on the ground that an emergency exists. In wartime it is frankly done for war purposes, and when the war is over the people know it is time to resume their powers. While the power is exercised, most of those exercising it are intensely inspired by patriotic motives, and politics is largely adjourned. But no one knows when a peace emergency is over. We have been enjoying a continuous emergency for the last seven years. The present emergency may well last for ten years without war reaching our shores. Arbitrary powers granted today may never be resumed.

It is just as dangerous to exaggerate the emergency as it is to underestimate the emergency. When an emergency exists it is all the more important that we retain our respect for the principles of constitutional American government, and that we go no further in modifying them than is absolutely essential.

. . . It is not necessary that we set aside the right of free debate, and a free press, and free speech. It is not necessary, to avoid regimentation by Hitler, that we forget all the Bill of Rights and the protection of minorities and authorize some Executive to conscript men and conscript property.

I am convinced that it can be worked out, retaining the principles of individual liberty for which it was founded, if we try. I am convinced that to meet the threat of a totalitarian nation we need not make ourselves totalitarian. I shudder when I hear the words "total defense." I do not know what "total defense" means, unless it means the subjugation of every other principle of our life to the one subject—military defense. If the words mean anything, they mean that the energies of every individual shall be devoted to defense, and that we shall wipe out from our minds every other goal. That is not true today; I hope it may never be true. At a time like this it is peculiarly necessary that with every measure we take we see that the principles of American freedom are guarded well. Never has the American way of life been in such danger—danger as much from within as from without.

IT IS SAID THAT A compulsory draft is a democratic system. I deny that it has anything to do with democracy. It is far more typical of totalitarian nations than of democratic nations. It is absolutely opposed to the principles of individual liberty, which have always been considered a part of American democracy. Many people came to this country for the single purpose of avoiding the requirements of military service in Europe. This country has always been opposed to a large standing army, and it has been opposed to the use of the draft in time of peace. I shrink from the very setting up of thousands of draft boards, with clerks and employees and endless paper work and red tape; from the registration of 12,000,000 men and the prying into every feature of their lives, their physical condition, their religious convictions, their financial status, and even their hobbies.

The draft is said to be democratic because it hits the rich as well as the poor. Since the rich are about 2 per cent of the total, it is still true that 98 per cent of those drafted are going to be the boys without means. It doesn't make much difference to the poor boy whether the other 2 per cent go or not. To be snatched out of his life work may be a tragedy for a poor boy, but the rich boy will have no trouble finding another job if he is any good at all. As a matter of fact under the volunteer system you would probably get a greater percentage of wealthy boys than under the draft. This is because the wealthier boys all go to college, and the percentage of enlistment from the colleges has always been higher. The need for the defense of this country against nations thousands of miles distant is brought home to those in the colleges more forcibly than it is to the boy who is employed locally, to whom international affairs are a long distance off. Under a volunteer system the poor boys who already had good jobs would not have to go.

It is said that under the draft the slacker will stay at home and leave the burden on the patriots. But in the first place, the number of real slackers is negligible in the whole picture, and under the bill any real slacker has an easy "out." All he has to do is marry a lady who has no other means of support. The number of marriages in recent weeks has increased by thousands.

THE PRINCIPLE OF A compulsory draft is basically wrong. If we must use compulsion to get an army, why not use compulsion to get men for other essential tasks? We must have men to manufacture munitions, implements of war, and war vessels. Why not draft labor for those occupations at wages lower than the standard? There are many other industries absolutely essential to defense, like the utilities, the railroads, the coal-mining industry. Why not draft men for those industries, also at $21 a month? If we draft soldiers, why not draft policemen and firemen for city and state service? The logical advocates of the draft admit this necessary conclusion. Senator Pepper, of Florida, has said that he believes the President should have power to draft men for munitions plants. Mr. Walter Lippmann says that if the conscription bill is to serve its real purpose it must not be regarded as a mere device for putting one man out of twenty-five into uniform but must be regarded as a method of mobilizing the men of the country for the much larger and more complicated task of industrial preparedness. In short, the logic behind the bill requires a complete regimentation of most labor and the assignment of jobs to every man able to work. This is actually done today in the Communist and Fascist states, which we are now apparently seeking to emulate.

There has been, very properly, a great outcry against the action of the Senate in authorizing the Secretaries of War and Navy to seize any industrial plant needed for the manufacture of munitions. I voted against that amendment because I do not see the necessity for that any more than for the drafting of men and because it gives uncontrolled discretion to the Secretary of War and the Secretary of the Navy. But at least the owners of such plants are to be fully compensated for their property, while men who are drafted may be forced to give up jobs paying $50 a week to receive a soldier's pay, at most equivalent to $15 a week. Their time is conscripted without compensation.

The argument in favor of conscription proves too much. If the emergency is as great as alleged, then we should adopt a completely socialized state and place ourselves and our property at the disposal of the government. That is fascism. It could only be justified if it were the only possible alternative to the subjugation of the United States by fascism from without.

Is it really necessary to take this long step toward a system in which the state is everything and the individual is nothing? What kind of an army do we want? The developments of the present war have shown that great numbers of men in the trenches are no longer the prime requisite for success. France had universal conscription, but it did them no good against a highly organized, modern, mechanized army. According to all the best military advice, what we need today is an army of experts. We have all kinds of estimates of the number needed in the United States, but the best opinion is that an expert army of not more than 750,000 men would serve every purpose of defense. In January the President only requested funds for an army of 227,000 men. Even on May 31, after the Germans had broken through in France and France was collapsing, the President was satisfied with an army of 280,000 men, and General Marshall himself estimated on June 4 that an army of 400,000 would avoid the necessity of mobilizing the National Guard and give a reasonable liberty of action up to January. Now the "ante has been boosted" to 1,200,000 men. This bill has put the cart before the horse. It is trying to provide a method of raising men before

867

anyone has decided how many men should be raised. Up to this time the Army has had no authority to recruit men, in excess of 375,000 plus the National Guard of 225,000; has had no authority to invite boys into training camps for military training.

As far as the Regular Army is concerned, conscription is the poorest possible method of getting it. Men are chosen at random from all kinds of occupations, mostly unrelated to the Army. After one year they naturally return to the jobs which they were forced to give up. Someone else equally unwilling and equally inexperienced has to be given a year of partial training. There is only one way to get the kind of Army we need today—that is to make the Army an occupation sufficiently attractive so that men will go to it as a matter of choice. Why should we expect men to accept pay equivalent to approximately $15 a week? Privates in the Army get board, lodging, and clothes, equivalent perhaps to $40 a month, plus $21 in cash, a total of $61 a month. They should certainly get the equivalent of $100 a month. The Army does not want a lot of men who leave at the end of one year or even of three years; they want men who are sufficiently satisfied to stay indefinitely.

It is said that the voluntary-enlistment plan has broken down. Of course that is utterly untrue. In spite of inadequate pay and in spite of three-year enlistments, from which a man cannot escape if a better job is offered, it has been accomplishing everything which had been asked of it. Men are enlisting today at a rapid rate — 40,000 enlisted in the month of August. Yet there has been no really serious effort to enlist men, and no call by the President for volunteers. In fact, he has publicly discouraged college boys from enlisting.

Men are looking for jobs with reasonable pay. In New York City this year it was necessary to fill a position as sanitation man at $1,800 a year, which, considering the cost of living in New York City, is not very much more than Army pay plus support. There were 84,000 applications from New York City alone.

Of course the men who enlist in the Army, like the men who get jobs in any industry, are those who at the time are out of work. There are more than 5,000,000 men out of work today, looking for jobs. There are over 1,700,000 on W.P.A. and over 200,000 in the C.C.C. camps. The government is paying these men in a way which makes W.P.A. and C.C.C. more attractive than the Army. We have not the right to require these men, as a condition of government aid, to accept employment in the Army; but surely, if we make the Army only reasonably attractive, many of them will prefer the Army to W.P.A. or C.C.C.

How utterly ridiculous it is to make 700,000 men give up good jobs at a time of life when they are first making real progress, while many millions of men out of work, and 1,200,000 boys coming of age every year, are looking for jobs. The idea that the Army is the most unpleasant occupation in the world, into which men must be forced against their will, is archaic and fallacious. In time of war Army service is dangerous, but if we prepare adequately, we should not be at war, and the Army for the most part is a peacetime, highly specialized occupation with only a chance of danger. Experience shows that men do not avoid an occupation because there is a chance of danger. There are dangerous civilian occupations — work with high-tension wires, work in tunnel construction, work in coal mines; and there is never any difficulty in finding men interested in those occupations.

The Air Corps is the most dangerous part of the Army, but more men want to enlist than can be accepted. The Army has many advantages, a clean and regular life without great responsibility, an attraction in the very discipline and order which appeals to some men and offends others very greatly. The Navy always has a waiting list because they pay their men more adequately to try to make their service attractive. The Army should be just as attractive today. We already have 650,000 men available under existing law. We will have no difficulty in getting 750,000 or 950,000 or 1,200,000 under the volunteer system, if the Army is made as attractive to the average man as many other jobs furnished by industry.

As for the Reserve, we have never tried getting men for military training camps. No such camps are in existence except for Reserve officers. Of the 1,200,000 boys who graduate from high school or college every year, a large proportion could be persuaded to take a year in the military training camps at the government's expense before starting on their life work. Within a very few years we would build up all the Reserve we could possibly need. An attempt to raise whatever Army is necessary by a volunteer appeal will unquestionably meet with success if that attempt has the wholehearted cooperation of the Administration and of the Army; that it will furnish 400,000 men if that many are needed, before the complicated draft is working.

There are some who have felt that the emergency is so immediate that only the draft will meet it. Obviously that is not today the official view. The President has just transferred fifty destroyers to England in exchange for bases which will not be ready for a year. If Hitler were about to overwhelm England and attack the United States, the President obviously could not weaken our Navy by depriving it of fifty destroyers now in active service. The alleged need immediately for a huge Army is based on the theory that our Navy is inadequate. The President has just determined that the Navy is completely adequate and can even afford to surrender fifty of its fighting craft. What has happened to the emergency supposed to justify this drafting of men, so complete a departure from American tradition and so long a step toward dictatorship? No; we obviously have a reasonable time before Mr. Hitler can possibly organize an attack on the United States. It is no easy task to transport an army across 3,000 miles of water while our Navy is in existence. We have time to do our job in the right way. We have time to get the kind of voluntary expert mechanized Army we really need. We have time to do the job without upsetting and perhaps wrecking hundreds of thousands of lives. We can do it without excitement and hysteria, without breaking down the fundamental principles of the American Republic. We can do it without over-estimating the emergency, and sinking all the principles we love in the slough of total defense.

Free men, free enterprise, free speech are the cornerstones of the American Republic. If the Burke-Wadsworth bill should become law, we will have to accept that limitation of freedom. But we should be all the more vigilant to oppose the further limitations on freedom. The more we yield to the demand for arbitrary power, the more power will be demanded, until freedom will be as nonexistent in America as it is in Germany today. In fact we may even be turning over these destroyers to Germany to be used against us, for the British may have to surrender their fleet, according to the William Allen White Committee. Of course, in case of British defeat any pledge of the present British Government would be worthless, for the Government would not be there. Obviously the President must consider our fleet more than adequate for defense.

869

Oswald Garrison Villard, 1916

870

Oswald Garrison Villard was a genuine liberal and pacifist throughout most of his life. He was the grandson of William Lloyd Garrison, the great abolitionist and founder of the Liberator. *Villard inherited the New York* Evening Post *from his father, Henry Villard, and edited that until he sold it in 1918. He was editor of the* Nation *for many years until its sale in 1932, serving thereafter as a contributor until 1940—when the* Nation *opted both for an interventionist foreign policy and domestic statism (after 1929, even Villard did not escape these latter influences). In 1940 he severed all connections with the journal. We reprint here his editorial from the* Nation[1] *as a brisk rebuttal to the widespread notions that conscription and universal military training are democratic and beneficial to society. It is worth noting that this and other of his best statements on conscription appeared during a period in his life when he was most laissez faire in his opinions and furtherest away from socialism.*

IN THE YEARS to come none of the many amazing phenomena of 1916 will, we are sure, cause greater wonderment than our recent discovery that univer-

[1] This text is taken from the *Nation,* CII (May 11, 1916), 510-11. Although published as an unsigned editorial, authorship has been verified with copies of the *Nation* in the possession of the publishers bearing Villard's notes.

sal military service is the cure-all for every one of our American ills. Do we wish to defend our country? We have but to adopt the system of training every boy to be a soldier, and the problem is solved. Do we wish to become industrially efficient? Then let us forget all about vocational training, but give every American a year under arms, and presto! we shall outdo Germany in scientific efficiency and management. Is our youth lawless and undisciplined? Universal compulsory service will end that once and for all. Is our democracy halting? It is the tonic of a democratic army that we need, in which all men shall pay for the privileges of citizenship by a year of preparation for poisonous gas and of learning how to shoot. Our melting-pot is a failure? Then let us pour into it the iron metal of militarism, and it will fuse every element at once. Finally, if we need an American soul—and the war has suddenly taught us that this glorious country lacks a soul—it is the remedy of universal military service that is to supply our spiritual needs and give us the ability to feel as one, to think as one, to steer towards our destiny as of one mind.

It is all so alluring and so entrancingly easy, the wonder is that we have never thought of it before. We saw it going on in France and Germany and Russia, but it seemed altogether repulsive in its forms. Americans to be conscripted? Heaven forbid. There rose before us the unutterable cruelties of non-commissioned officers and some of the officers — visions of the men who have come to our shores with hands mutilated to avoid the barracks, with their open immoralities, their bitter hardships, the loss of three years of so many working lives. The "Red Rosa," Rosa Luxembourg, with her 10,000 authenticated instances of cruelties to German soldiers, inflicted by their own countrymen behind the screen of official authority, explained to us why so many young Germans emigrated before coming of military age. We saw in universal Russian service a complete reason for the failure of the Russian revolution [1905], for the survival of the corrupt bureaucratic government. We knew of men of noble spirit in every land crushed by the whole system. We saw in the development of the Prussian military clique not merely the fine flower of militarism, but the true fruits of universal service. We recalled, too, James Madison's belief that "large armies and heavy taxes are the best-known instruments for bringing the many under the domination of the few."

But it now seems that we were mistaken in all this; that our failure to progress financially, economically, and spiritually as rapidly as we should have done has been due solely to our failure to grasp at the panacea that lay so easily within our reach. Take the education of our boys. The other day at a joint meeting of two schoolmasters' associations there were divided views on some issues, but none apparently as to the utter lawlessness of our American youth and the complete failure of our private schools to reduce them to subordination by means of mental and moral discipline. And so there were many who grasped with joy at the idea of the universal-military-drill to retrieve for them the ground lost by their own failure to do the fundamental thing they pledged themselves to accomplish. Of course, they knew little or nothing about universal service; perhaps it was the unexplored mystery of it that appealed. Many Americans are quite sure that the latest untried remedy, be it some law, or the initiative and referendum, or the recall of judicial decisions, or some other panacea, is, by reason of its very newness, just the medicine for a given ill they have been looking for. So with these school-teachers. Ignoring the fact that our private military schools have been anything but popular, and only in exceptional cases of high standing, they turn to military drill as to a last straw. One can admire their courage while marvelling at their judgment. Fortunately, those particular teachers heard the European system of a nation in arms denounced by one of their number, who had served in Austria both as private and as officer.

WHAT THEY DO not see any more than the Stanwood Menkens who, never having borne arms, yet know that universal service is what we need to make patriots by the million, is that the spirit of compulsory service makes directly against the American ideal, for it inculcates blind obedience to the will of others, subordination to those who are masters not necessarily because of superior wisdom or fitness, but largely because of accident. It often means cringing before men who abuse their powers, particularly over men of finer instincts and antecedents — just as the late Karl Bitter was driven to desert from the Austrian service by intolerable persecutions. It is not without significance that there is a suicide a day among the private soldiers in Germany in time of peace — no record being kept of unsuccessful attempts at self-destruction. Again, as Major-Gen. O'Ryan, of the New York National Guard, has put it, the primary thing that military service teaches is that the soldier shall *stop thinking* and become an automaton — to do only what his officers tell him. And usually there is a steadily widening cleft between him and those officers.

Once we valued American self-assertiveness, independence of thought and action, mental alertness, yes, even the happy-go-lucky Yankee initiative and individuality, as some of our best characteristics. Now we are to prefer men cast in one mold, drilled in one way of thinking, and into obedience to their

871

rulers. Formerly, we deemed it most worth while that all men should have their own opinions, express them freely, and differ with their rulers as they saw fit — since their rulers were but their servants. As for making patriots, universal military service makes Socialists and deserters. There is nothing whatsoever democratic about it, save that it applies to all men alike. Where universal service is most efficient, there is every kind of distinction as to regiments and individuals. The peasant serves three years, the "gentleman" one. The favors shown to the Guard regiments in Germany have led to more than one bitter debate in the Reichstag. What can there be democratic about an army? Its whole fundamental principle is that of a hierarchy in which everybody responds automatically and blindly to the will of a commander-in-chief. What system could be more directly opposed to the democratic theory?

872

THE ANTI-MILITARIST TRADITION:

Daniel Webster, 1814

This famous speech, which Webster delivered in the House of Representatives in December 1814, is reprinted here in its entirety.[1] It is an example of Webster in his prime, when he opposed conscription and favored free trade. It was in large measure Webster's work which defeated Mr. Madison's conscription proposal in 1814, and we hope his words may have some influence on today's Status Quo, which has lined up behind Mr. Johnson's conscription. It is both amusingly enlightening and sadly regrettable that so many of the concepts of the Federal Republic which Webster defended and relied upon in his lifetime have completely passed away in this century.

MR. CHAIRMAN: AFTER the best reflection which I have been able to bestow on the subject of the bill before you, I am of the opinion that its principles are not warranted by any provision of the Constitution. It appears to me to partake of the nature of those other propositions for military measures

[1] This text is taken from D. Webster, *Writings and Speeches* (Boston: Little, Brown, 1903), pp. 55-69. The article was originally delivered as a speech on the floor of the House of Representatives, December 9, 1814, in opposition to President Madison's proposal for compulsory military service; the speech was transcribed afterwards by Webster himself.

which this session, so fertile in inventions, has produced. It is of the same class with the plan of the Secretary of War; with the bill reported to this House by its own Committee for filling the ranks of the regular army, by classifying the free male population of the United States; and with the resolution recently introduced by an honorable gentleman from Pennsylvania (Mr. Ingersoll), and which now lies on your table, carrying the principle of compulsory service in the regular army to its utmost extent.

This bill indeed is less undisguised in its object, and less direct in its means, than some of the measures proposed. It is an attempt to exercise the power of forcing the free men of this country into the ranks of an army, for the general purposes of war, under color of a miltary service. To this end it commences with a classification which is no way connected with the general organization of the militia, nor, to my apprehension, included within any of the powers which Congress possesses over them. All the authority which this government has over the militia, until actually called into the ranks of an army, for the general purposes of war, under color of a mili-power it has exercised. It now possesses the further power of calling into its service any portion of the militia of the States, in the particular exigencies for which the Constitution provides, and of governing them during the continuance of such service. Here its authority ceases. The classification of the whole body of the militia, according to the provisions of this bill, is not a measure which respects either their general organization or their discipline. It is a distinct system, introduced for new purposes, and not connected with any power which the Constitution has conferred on Congress.

But, sir, there is another consideration. The services of the men to be raised under this act are not limited to those cases in which alone this government is entitled to the aid of the militia of the States. These cases are particularly stated in the Constitution, "to repel invasion, suppress insurrection, or execute the laws." But this bill has no limitation in this respect. The usual mode of legislating on the subject is abandoned. The only section which would have confined the service of the militia, proposed to be raised, within the United States has been stricken out; and if the President should not march them into the Provinces of England at the north, or of Spain at the south, it will not be because he is prohibited by any provision in this act.

This, sir, is a bill for calling out the militia, not according to its existing organization, but by draft from new created classes; — not merely for the purpose of "repelling invasion, suppressing insurrection, or executing the laws," but for the general objects of war — for defending ourselves, or invading others, as may be thought expedient; — not for a sudden emergency, or for a short time, but for long stated periods; for two years, if the proposition of the Senate should finally prevail; for one year, if the amendment of the House should be adopted. What is this, sir, but raising a standing army out of militia by draft, and to be recruited by draft, in like manner, as often as occasion may require?

This bill, then, is not different in principle from the other bills, plans, and resolutions which I have mentioned. The present discussion is properly and necessarily common to them all. It is a discussion, sir, of the last importance. That measures of this nature should be

debated at all, in the councils of a free government, is cause of dismay. The question is nothing less than whether the most essential rights of personal liberty shall be surrendered, and depotism embraced in its worst form.

I HAVE RISEN, ON this occasion, with anxious and painful emotions, to add my admonition to what has been said by others. Admonition and remonstrance, I am aware, are not acceptable strains. They are duties of unpleasant performance. But they are, in my judgment, the duties which the condition of a falling state imposes. They are duties which sink deep in his conscience, who believes it probable that they may be the last services which he may be able to render to the government of his country. On the issue of this discussion, I believe the fate of the government may rest. Its duration is incompatible, in my opinion, with the existence of the measures in contemplation. A crisis has at last arrived, to which the course of things has long tended, and which may be decisive upon the happiness of present and of future generations. If there be anything important in the concerns of men, the considerations which fill the present hour are important, I am anxious, above all things, to stand acquitted before God and my own conscience, and in the public judgment, of all participations in the counsels which have brought us to our present condition and which now threaten the dissolution of the government. When the present generation of men shall be swept away, and that this government ever existed shall be matter of history only, I desire that it may be known that you have not proceeded in your course unadmonished and unforewarned. Let it then be known, that there were those who would have stopped you, in the career of your measures, and held you back, as by the skirts of your garments, from the precipice over which you are plunging and drawing after you the government of your country.

I had hoped, sir, at an early period of the session, to find gentlemen in an-

874

other temper. I trusted that the existing state of things would have impressed on the minds of those who decide national measures, the necessity of some reform in the administration of affairs. If it was not to have been expected that gentlemen would be convinced by argument, it was still not unreasonable to hope that they would listen to the solemn preaching of events. If no previous reasoning could satisfy them, that the favorite plans of government would fail, they might yet be expected to regard the fact, when it happened, and to yield to the lesson which it taught. Although they had, last year, given no credit to those who predicted the failure of the campaign against Canada, yet they had seen that failure. Although they then treated as idle all doubts of the success of the loan, they had seen the failure of that loan. Although they then held in derision all fears for the public credit, and the national faith, they had yet seen the public credit destroyed, and the national faith violated and disgraced. They had seen much more than was predicted; for no man had foretold that our means of defense would be so far exhausted in foreign invasion, as to leave the place of our own deliberations insecure, and that we should this day be legislating in view of the crumbling monuments of our national disgrace. No one had anticipated that this city would have fallen before a handful of troops, and that British generals and British admirals would have taken their airings along the Pennsylvania Avenue, while the government was in full flight, just awaked perhaps from one of its profound meditations on the plan of a conscription for the conquest of Canada. These events, sir, with the present state of things, and the threatening aspect of what is future, should have brought us to a pause. They might have reasonably been expected to induce Congress to review its own measures, and to exercise its great duty of inquiry relative to the conduct of others. If this was too high a pitch of virtue for the multitude of party men, it was at least to have been expected from gentlemen of influence and character, who ought to be supposed to value

something higher than mere party attachment, and to act from motives somewhat nobler than a mere regard to party consistency. All that we have yet suffered will be found light and trifling in comparison with what is before us, if the government shall learn nothing from experience but to despise it, and shall grow more and more desperate in its measures, as it grows more and more desperate in its affairs.

IT IS TIME FOR Congress to examine and decide for itself. It has taken things on trust long enough. It has followed executive recommendation, 'til there remains no hope of finding safety in that path. What is there, sir, that makes it the duty of this people now to grant new confidence to the Administration, and to surrender their most important rights to its discretion? On what merits of its own does it rest this extraordinary claim? When it calls thus loudly for the treasure and the lives of the people, what pledge does it offer that it will not waste all in the same preposterous pursuits which have hitherto engaged it? In the failure of all past promises, do we see any assurance of future performance? Are we to measure out our confidence in proportion to our disgrace and now at last to grant away everything, because all that we have heretofore granted has been wasted or misapplied? What is there in our condition that bespeaks a wise or an able government? What is the evidence that the protection of the country is the object principally regarded? In every quarter that protection has been more or less abandoned to the States. That every town on the coast is not now in possession of the enemy, or in ashes, is owing to the vigilance and exertions of the States themselves, and to no protection granted to them by those on whom the whole duty of their protection rested.

Or shall we look to the acquisition of the professed objects of the war, and there find grounds for approbation and confidence. The professed objects of the war are abandoned in all due form. The contest for sailors' rights is turned into

875

a negotiation about boundaries and military roads, and the highest hope entertained by any man of the issue, is that we may be able to get out of the war without a cession of territory.

Look, sir, to the finances of the country. What a picture do they exhibit of the wisdom and prudence and foresight of government. "The revenue of a state," says a profound writer, "is the state." If we are to judge of the condition of the country by the condition of its revenues, what is the result? A wise government sinks deep the fountain of its revenues — not only 'til it can touch the first springs, and slake the present thirst of the treasury, but 'til lasting sources are opened, too abundant to be exhausted by demands, too deep to be affected by heats and droughts. What, sir, is our present supply, and what our provision for the future resource? I forebear to speak of the present condition of the treasury; and as to public credit, the last reliance of government, I use the language of government itself only, when I say it does not exist. This is a state of things calling for the soberest counsels, and yet it seems to meet only the wildest speculations. Nothing is talked of but banks, and a circulating paper medium, and exchequer notes, and the thousand other contrivances which ingenuity, vexed and goaded by the direst necessity, can devise, with the vain hope of giving value to mere paper. All these things are not revenue, nor do they produce it. They are the effect of a productive commerce, and a well ordered system of finance, and in their operation may be favorable to both, but are not the cause of either. In other times these facilities existed. Bank paper and government paper circulated because both rested on substantial capital or solid credit. Without these they will not circulate, nor is there a device more shallow or more mischievous, than to pour forth new floods of paper without credit as a remedy for the evils which paper without credit has already created. As was intimated the other day by my honorable friend from North Carolina (Mr. Gaston) this is an attempt to act over again the farce of the As-

signats of France. Indeed, sir, our politicians appear to have but one school. They learn everything of modern France; with this variety only, that for examples of revenue they go to the Revolution, when her revenue was in the worst state possible, while their model for military force is sought after in her imperial era, when her military was organized on principles the most arbitrary and abominable.

LET US EXAMINE the nature and extent of the power which is assumed by the various military measures before us. In the present want of men and money, the Secretary of War has proposed to Congress a military conscription. For the conquest of Canada, the people will not enlist; and if they would, the treasury is exhausted, and they could not be paid. Conscription is chosen as the most promising instrument, both of overcoming reluctance to the service, and of subduing the difficulties which arise from the deficiencies of the exchequer. The Administration asserts the right to fill the ranks of the regular army by compulsion. It contends that it may now take one out of every twenty-five men, and any part, or the whole of the rest, whenever its occasions require. Persons thus taken by force, and put into an army, may be compelled to serve there during the war, or for life. They may be put on any service, at home or abroad, for defense or for invasion, accordingly to the will and pleasure of the government. This power does not grow out of any invasion of the country, or even out of a state of war. It belongs to government at all times, in peace as well as in war, and it is to be exercised under all circumstances, according to its mere discretion. This sir, is the amount of the principle contended for by the Secretary of War.

Is this, sir, consistent with the character of a free government? Is this civil liberty? Is this the real character of our Constitution? No sir, indeed it is not. The Constitution is libelled, foully libelled. The people of this country have

876

not established for themselves such a fabric of despotism. They have not purchased at a vast expense of their own treasure and their own blood a Magna Charta to be slaves. Where is it written in the Constitution, in what article or section is it contained, that you may take children from their parents, and parents from their children, and compel them to fight the battles of any war in which the folly or the wickedness of government may engage it? Under what concealment has this power lain hidden which now for the first time comes forth, with a tremendous and baleful aspect, to trample down and destroy the dearest rights of personal liberty? Who will show me any Constitutional injunction which makes it the duty of the American people to surrender everything valuable in life, and even life itself, not when the safety of their country and its liberties may demand the sacrifice, but whenever the purposes of an ambitious and mischievous government may require it? Sir, I almost disdain to go to quotations and references to prove that such an abominable doctrine has no foundation in the Constitution of the country. It is enough to know that that instrument was intended as the basis of a free government, and that the power contended for is incompatible with any notion of personal liberty. An attempt to maintain this doctrine upon the provisions of the Constitution is an exercise of perverse ingenuity to extract slavery from the substance of a free government. It is an attempt to show, by proof and argument, that we ourselves are subjects of despotism, and that we have a right to chains and bondage, firmly secured to us and our children by the provisions of our government. It has been the labor of other men, at other times, to mitigate and reform the powers of government by construction; to support the rights of personal security by every species of favorable and benign interpretation, and thus to infuse a free spirit into governments not friendly in their general structure and formation to public liberty.

The supporters of the measures before us act on the opposite principle. It is their task to raise arbitrary powers, by construction, out of a plain written charter of National Liberty. It is their pleasing duty to free us of the delusion, which we have fondly cherished, that we are the subjects of a mild, free, and limited government, and to demonstrate, by a regular chain of premises and conclusions, that government possesses over us a power more tyrannical, more arbitrary, more dangerous, more allied to blood and murder, more full of every form of mischief, more productive of every sort and degree of misery than has been exercised by any civilized government, with a single exception, in modern times.

The Secretary of War has favored us with an argument on the constitutionality of this power. Those who lament that such doctrines should be supported by the opinions of a high officer of government, may a little abate their regret, when they remember that the same officer, in his last letter of instructions to our ministers abroad, maintained the contrary. In that letter he declares, that even the impressment of seamen, for which many more plausible reasons may be given than for the impressment of soldiers, is repugnant to our Constitution. It might therefore be a sufficient answer to his argument, in the present case, to quote against it the sentiments of its own author, and to place the two opinions before the House, in a state of irreconcilable conflict. Further comment on either might then by properly foreborne, until he should be pleased to inform us which he retracted, and to which he adhered. But the importance of the subject may justify a further consideration of the arguments.

CONGRESS HAVING, BY the Constitution, a power to raise armies, the Secretary contends that no restraint is to be imposed on the exercise of this power, except such as is expressly stated in the written letter of the instrument. In other words, that Congress may execute its powers, by any means it chooses, unless such means are particularly prohibited. But the general nature and object of the Constitution impose as rigid a restriction on the means of exercising power as could be done by the most explicit injunctions. It is the first principle applicable to such a case, that no construction shall be admitted which impairs the general nature and character of the instrument. A free constitution of government is to be construed upon free principles, and every branch of its provisions is to receive such an interpretation as is full of its general spirit. No means are to be taken by implication which would strike us absurdly if expressed. And what would have been more absurd than for this Constitution to have said that to secure the great blessings of liberty it gave to government an uncontrolled power of military conscription? Yet such is the absurdity which it is made to exhibit, under the commentary of the Secretary of War.

But it is said that it might happen that an army could not be raised by voluntary enlistment, in which case the power to raise armies would be granted in vain, unless they might be raised by compulsion. If this reasoning could prove anything, it would equally show, that whenever the legitimate power of the Constitution should be so badly administered as to cease to answer the great ends intended by them, such new powers may be assumed or usurped, as any existing Administration may deem expedient. This is the result of his own reasoning, to which the Secretary does not profess to go. But it is a true result. For if it is to be assumed, that all powers were granted, which might by possibility become necessary, and that government itself is the judge of this possible necessity, then the powers of government are precisely what it chooses they should be. Apply the same reasoning to any other power granted to Congress, and test its accuracy by the result. Congress has power to borrow money. How is it to exercise this power? Is it confined to voluntary loans? There is no express limitation to that effect, and, in the language of the secretary, it might happen, indeed it has happened, that persons could not be found willing to lend. Money might be borrowed then in any other mode. In other words. Congress might resort to a *forced* loan. It might take the money of any man by force, and give him in exchange exchequer notes or certificates of stock. Would this be quite constitutional, sir? It is entirely within the reasoning of the Secretary, and it is a result of his argument, outraging the rights of individuals in a far less degree than the practical consequences which he himself draws from it. A compulsory loan is not to be compared, in point of enormity, with a compulsory military service.

If the Secretary of War has proved the right of Congress to enact a law enforcing a draft of men out of the militia into the regular army, he will at any time be able to prove, quite as clearly, that Congress has power to create a Dictator. The arguments which have helped him in one case, will equally aid him in the other, the same reason of a supposed or possible state necessity, which is urged now, may be repeated then, with equal pertinency and effect.

Sir, in granting Congress the power to raise armies, the people have granted all the means which are ordinary and usual, and which are consistent with the liberties and security of the people themselves, and they have granted no others. To talk about the unlimited power of the government over the means to execute its authority, is to hold a language which is true only in regard to despotism. The tyranny of arbitrary governments consists as much in its means as in its ends; and it would be a ridiculous and absurd constitution which should be less cautious to guard against abuses in the one case than in the other. All the means and instruments which a free government exercises, as well as the ends and objects which it pursues, are to partake of its own essential character, and to be conformed to its genuine spirit. A free government with arbitrary means to administer it is a contradiction; a free government without adequate provisions for personal security is an absurdity; a free government, with an uncontrolled power of military conscription, is a solecism, at once the most ridiculous and

878

abominable that ever entered into the head of man.

SIR, I INVITE THE supporters of the measures before you to look to their actual operation. Let the men who have so often pledged their own fortunes and their own lives to the support of this war, look to the wanton sacrifice which they are about to make of their lives and fortunes. They may talk as they will about substitutes, and compensations, and exemptions. It must come to the draft at last. If the government cannot hire men voluntarily to fight its battles, neither can individuals. If the war should continue, there will be no escape, and every man's fate and every man's life will come to depend on the issue of the military draft. Who shall describe to you the horror which your orders of conscription shall create in the once happy villages of this country? Who shall describe the distress and anguish which they will spread over those hills and valleys, where men have heretofore been accustomed to labor, and to rest in security and happiness. Anticipate the scene, sir, when the class shall assemble to stand its draft, and to throw the dice for blood. What a group of wives and mothers and sisters, of helpless age and helpless infancy, shall gather round the theatre of this horrible lottery, as if the stroke of death were to fall from heaven before their eyes on a father, a brother, a son, or a husband. And in a majority of cases, sir, it will be the stroke of death. Under present prospects of the continuance of the war, not one half of them on whom your conscription shall fall will ever return to tell the tale of their sufferings. They will perish of disease and pestilence, or they will leave their bones to whiten in fields beyond the frontier. Does the lot fall on the father of a family? His children, already orphans, shall see his face no more. When they behold him for the last time, they shall see him lashed and fettered, and dragged away from his own threshold, like a felon and an outlaw. Does it fall on a son, the hope and the staff of aged parents? That hope shall fail them. On that staff they shall lean no longer. They shall not enjoy the happiness of dying before their children. They shall totter to their grave, bereft of their offspring and unwept by any who inherit their blood. Does it fall on a husband? The eyes which watch his parting steps may swim in tears forever. She is a wife no longer. There is no relation so tender or so sacred that by these accursed measures you do not propose to violate it. There is no happiness so perfect that you do not propose to destroy it. Into the paradise of domestic life you enter, not indeed by temptations and sorceries, but by open force and violence.

But this father, or this son, or this husband goes to the camp. With whom do you associate him? With those only who are sober and virtuous and respectable like himself? No, sir. But you propose to find him companions in the worst men of the worst sort. Another bill lies on your table offering a bounty to deserters from your enemy. Whatever is most infamous in his ranks you propose to make your own. You address yourselves to those who will hear you and advise them to perjury and treason. All who are ready to set heaven and earth at defiance at the same time, to violate their oaths and run the hazard of capital punishment, and none others, will yield to your solicitations. And these are they whom you are allowing to join ranks, by holding out to them inducements and bounties with one hand, while with the other you are driving thither the honest and worthy members of your own community, under the lash and scourge of conscription. In the line of your army, with the true levelling of despotism, you propose a promiscuous mixture of the worthy and the worthless, the virtuous and the profligate; the husbandman, the merchant, the mechanic of your own country, with the beings whom war selects from the excess of European population, who possess neither interest, feeling, nor character in common with your own people, and who have no other recommendation to your notice than their propensity to crimes.

879

Page Fifty-seven

Nor is it, sir, for the defense of his own house and home, that he who is the subject of military draft is to perform the task allotted to him. You will put him upon a service equally foreign to his interests and abhorrent to his feelings. With his aid you are to push your purposes of conquest. The battles which he is to fight are the battles of invasion —battles which he detests perhaps, and abhors, less from the danger and the death that gather over them, and the blood with which they drench the plain, than from the principles in which they have their origin. Fresh from the peaceful pursuits of life, and yet a soldier but in name, he is to be opposed to veteran troops, hardened under every scene, inured to every privation, and disciplined in every service. If, sir, in this strife he fall — if, while ready to obey every rightful command of government, he is forced from his home against right, not to contend for the defense of his country, but to prosecute a miserable and detestable project of invasion, and in that strife he fall 'tis murder. It may stalk above the cognizance of human law, but in the sight of Heaven it is murder; and though millions of years may roll away, while his ashes and yours lie mingled together in the earth, the day will yet come when his spirit and the spirits of his children must be met at the bar of omnipotent justice. May God, in his compassion, shield me from any participation in the enormity of this guilt.

880

I WOULD ASK, SIR, whether the supporters of these measures have well weighed the difficulties of their undertaking. Have they considered whether it will be found easy to execute laws which bear such marks of despotism on their front, and which will be so productive of every sort and degree of misery in their execution? For one, sir, I hesitate not to say that they cannot be executed. No law professedly passed for the purpost of compelling a service in the regular army, nor any law which, under color of military draft, shall compel men to serve in the army, not for the emer-

gencies mentioned in the Constitution, but for long periods, and for the general objects of war, can be carried into effect. In my opinion it ought not to be carried into effect. The operation of measures thus unconstitutional and illegal ought to be prevented by a resort to other measures which are both constitutional and legal. It will be the solemn duty of the State governments to protect their own authority over their own militia, and to interpose between their citizens and arbitrary power. These are among the objects for which the State governments exist; and their highest obligations bind them to the preservation of their own rights and the liberties of their people. I express these sentiments here, sir, because I shall express them to my constituents. Both they and myself live under a constitution which teaches us that "the doctrine of nonresistance against arbitrary power and oppression is absurd, slavish, and destructive of the good and happiness of mankind." [New Hampshire Bill of Rights] With the same earnestness with which I now exhort you to forebear from these measures, I shall exhort them to exercise their unquestionable right of providing for the security of their own liberties.

In my opinion, sir, the sentiments of the free population of this country are greatly mistaken here. The nation is not yet in a temper to submit to conscription. The people have too fresh and strong a feeling of the blessings of civil liberty to be willing thus to surrender it. You may talk to them as much as you please, of the victory and glory to be obtained in the enemy's provinces; they will hold those objects in light estimation if the means be a forced military service. You may sing to them the song of Canada Conquest in all its variety, but they will not be charmed out of the remembrance of their substantial interests and true happiness. Similar pretences, they know, are the grave in which the liberties of other nations have been buried, and they will take warning.

Laws, sir, of this nature can create nothing but opposition. If you scatter them abroad, like the fabled serpents' teeth, they will spring up into armed men. A military force cannot be raised in this manner, but by the means of a military force. If the Administration has found that it cannot form an army without conscription, it will find, if it ventures on these experiments, that it cannot enforce conscription without an army. The government was not constituted for such purposes. Framed in the spirit of liberty, and in the love of peace, it has no powers which render it able to enforce such laws. The attempt, if we rashly make it, will fail; and having already thrown away our peace, we may thereby throw away our government.

Allusions have been made, sir, to the state of things in New England, and, as usual, she has been charged with an intention to dissolve the Union. The charge is unfounded. She is much too wise to entertain such purposes. She has had too much experience, and has too strong a recollection of the blessings which the Union is capable of producing under a just administration of government. It is her greatest fear, that the course at present pursued will destroy it, by destroying every principle, every interest, every sentiment, and every feeling which have hitherto contributed to uphold it. Those who cry out that the Union is in danger are themselves the authors of that danger. They put its existence to hazard by measures of violence, which it is not capable of enduring. They talk of dangerous designs against government, when they are overthrowing the fabric from its foundations. They alone, sir, are friends to the union of the States, who endeavor to maintain the principles of civil liberty in the country, and to preserve the spirit in which the Union was framed.

881

NEW BOOKS AND ARTICLES

THE FOLLOWING ARE A SELECTION OF ITEMS AND NOTES WHICH, IN THE OPINION OF THE EDITORS, MAY BE OF INTEREST TO OUR READERS.

Two fine anthologies have appeared in paperback: Arthur A. Ekirch, *Voices in Dissent*, New York, Citadel, 1966. $2.45. And: Staughton Lynd, *Non-Violence in America: A Documentary History*, Indianapolis, Bobbs-Merrill, 1966. $3.45. Both anthologies, in particular the one by Ekirch, could use a generous dose of bibliographic citation to indicate where the fervent reader could find more information. The currents of liberty and peace run through both books, and they illustrate well the surviving ideas of natural law: that social organization should be citizen-centered rather than state-oriented and that laws are to be judged by the citizenry, as individuals; laws must be judged according to criteria independent of the state.

Richard Flacks, Florence Howe, and Paul Lauter, "On the Draft," *The New York Review of Books*, April 6, 1967. Another example of an interesting article dealing with the draft and American empire, illustrating once again the features of thought shared by the "New Left" and many on the "Old Right." Consider this comment on national service: "One of the main hand-wringers, Margaret Mead, describes national service at work: 'Every individual, including the physically handicapped, the mentally defective, the emotionally disturbed, the totally illiterate, would be registered, and every one of these, according to their needs or potentialities, would be assigned to types of rehabilitation, education, and different kinds of service with different sorts of risks, benefits, and requirements.' Oddly, despite this description, national service advocates persist in calling the system 'voluntary.' To deal with at least two million new men annually (to say nothing of women), the system would require an enormous Federal bureaucracy, fantastic expenditures for training and maintenance, and expansion of service opportunities beyond anything now imaginable. Besides, service is probably best rendered by those who freely give it.

"Above all, national service — perhaps servitude is a more appropriate term — would mean an enormous jump in the degree of control by a central authority over the lives of Americans. Assignments to the military, to service, or to rehabilitation would finally be made not according to individual ability or interest, but by a centralized manpower planning commission, according to established definitions on national priorities. In this light, national service can be seen as the present draft writ large: 'channeling' no longer applied 'indirectly' — the 'American way' — but by compulsion. The system becomes a machine, in which men are considered as a 'national resource,' to be developed, channeled, enriched, molded, utilized, exploited, and above all, nationalized — in the public interest, to be sure."

John M. Swomley, Jr., who has long opposed conscription, recently smoked out national service in "The National Service Proposal," *Christian Century*, January 11, 1967. Swomley has some silly (favorable) ideas about a guaranteed annual income, minimum wage laws, and "free" health services, but he does point out that the decisive inequities of conscription do *not* occur simply because not all people are conscripted: "The real inequity of military conscription lies at this point of pay, not simply in the fact that some young men are drafted and others are not. The real inequity is that we are drafting men when there is no need to do so except to keep down the taxes of the rich whose financial interests are being preserved around the world by the low-paid soldiers. . . . It is one thing to provide voluntary service opportunities; it is quite another to institute a national service program whose pivotal concepts are peace time conscription and service to humanity via the nation." Donald J. Eberly replied in "National Service: Purpose and Potential," *Christian Century*, April 5, 1967. Eberley's main argument appears to be that life is full of coercion, anyway. Indeed! Barry Goldwater added a final touch to the assault on national service: "These so-called liberals, who want to fasten a domestic fascism on our young people, are simply following the line originally set by Robert McNamara who, months ago, suggested turning the draft system into a social service system in which every young American would be compelled to serve the state." (Los Angeles Times Syndicate, April 17, 1967) Is Goldwater a party to the New Left?

The February 1967 issue of *Moderator*, "the national magazine for leading college men," contains an article on conscription entitled, appropriately enough, "The Problem of Being Patriotic," written by *Moderator's* editor Philip R. Werdell and publisher Sherman B. Chickering. The thrust of the article is in a very non-radical, conservative direction: service to society is good, and the existence of military impressment is alienating an entire generation from all traditional forms of loyalty. The authors have familiarized themselves with the arguments in favor of a volunteer military, and present them cogently in arguing against a national lottery or compulsory service of any kind. The disturbing aspect about the author's thesis concerns the notion of *service to society* — they argue for a massive transformation of American motivational incentives to counteract and reverse the trend toward alienation among today's youth. Their program, although strictly within the framework of liberal principles, choice, voluntarism, etc., includes an appeal to colleges and universities, corporations, and government to give "those who have served" a special, higher status position or preferences in employment. A person of libertarian opinions cannot help but be cautious when approached by such allies, because the conscious erection of social pressures to induce a certain mode of behavior is no more acceptable than the imposition of legal sanctions — in fact social pressures can be more insidious because no libertarian would think of allowing *intolerance* to become a tort liability (as most modern-liberals would, for example.) There is much to be said in defense of social alienation, but clearly an Establishment publication such as *Moderator* would not think of this. It is difficult to conceive, for example, the revival of classical liberal opinions toward government without the breeding ground of alienated hostility toward "those in power." Classical liberalism was born in an era of alienation and hostility toward kings; what choked and almost killed it at the end of the century was an optimistic trust in The People and popular government. This trust in government — "we *are* the government" — is the foundation of social democratism and the welfare state ideal, and if the Right (or Left, maybe) is ever going to succeed in dismantling the deadening hand of the state it might well be better to encourage social alienation.

883

We had been hoping that voluntarism would be the irresistible wave of the future, but there are a number of people conspiring against that prospect. Last May, Secretary of Defense McNamara proposed that we adopt some form of compulsory national social service: "It seems to me that we could move toward remedying that inequity [not everyone is drafted] by asking every young person in the United States to give two years of service to his country—whether in one of the military services, in the Peace Corps, or in some voluntary developmental work at home or abroad." ("Address of Robert S. McNamara before American Society of Newspaper Editors, Montreal, Canada, May 18, 1966," Office of Assistant Secretary of Defense [Public Affairs], p. 14.)

Last fall, President Johnson suggested the national social service idea: "We must move toward a standard that no man has truly lived who only served himself. . . . To move in this direction, I am asking every member of my Administration to explore new ways by which our young people can serve their fellow men." ("Remarks of the President at Montgomery County Fair, Dayton, Ohio, September 5, 1966," Office of the White House Press Secretary, pp. 4-5.)

In November, Secretary of Labor Wirtz called for a stampede to NSS: *"First, that it be required that every boy and girl 'register in' with the local community when he or she reaches age eighteen. Second, that it be recognized as the community's obligation to provide every youth with the opportunity to receive at that point two years of further education, occupational training, a chance to participate in a service program, or a job. Third, that it be recognized as the youth's obligation, in return, to use this opportunity."* After pausing to say that his scheme, ideally, would be voluntary, Wirtz added: "There are strong reasons, at the same time for beginning to think through the possibilities of a firmer, tougher course." ("Policy for Youth," *Vital Speeches,* January 1, 1967, pp. 163, 165.)

884 More recently still, Poverty Commissar Shriver recommended that compulsory national social service be opened to people at age sixteen: "I favor the registration and testing of all young Americans at age sixteen — females as well as males. The Peace Corps and VISTA and the Job Corps have all proven — once again — that women are just as courageous and patriotic and hard working as men. Thousands, perhaps millions, of young women would like a chance to help their country by performing recognized national service and such service should *not* be restricted to combatant military service. It's an archaic sentimentalism which excludes young women from selective service in the generic sense of those words." ("Statement by Sargent Shriver before the Senate Subcommittee on Employment, Manpower, and Poverty, March 23, 1967," p. 1.)

Collecting all of these luminous ideas together is Donald J. Eberly, Executive Director of the National Service Secretariat, a recently-formed lobby; Eberly asserts: "In the free market economy the law of supply and demand operates to fill the most essential jobs. But the needs that are met are primarily private or personal — the provision of electric can openers or automatic dishwashers. Some of the more fundamental needs in the area of human and natural resources — concerns very much in the public domain — are left to the agencies of the community, state and Federal governments." To satisfy basic, human, social, crying needs, Eberly would "establish universal volunteer service as a national goal, and rename the Selective Service System the National Service System and the Selective Service Boards the National Service Boards." Happily, "a program of national service provides youths not only with an opportunity to serve their country, extend their education and broaden their experience but also offers them increased individual freedom." *A Plan for National Service,* Washington, National Service Secretariat, November 1966, pp. 11, 29, 51.

Whether all of these proposals were sparked by the approaching expiration of the current draft law is not clear; but what is clear is the brand of Left-fascism that the proposals represent.

One book, excellent for its polemical approach, which has received little attention is Jean Carper, *Bitter Greetings; the Scandal of the Military Draft,* New York, Grossman Publishers, 1967. $5.00. The following quotation from the book's introductory chapter may serve to whet one's appetite: "Ironically, officials of the Selective Service in some of their press releases pat themselves on the back for never having suffered a scandal. . . . Nevertheless, it would be a joke of the blackest kind for the American people to join in Selective Service's celebration of itself. For the truth is that the draft enjoys no *small* scandal. Its very existence, its operation, its Orwellian schemes and powers for controlling the nation's youth constitute a scandal of monstrous proportions. Contending there is no scandal in the draft is like saying there are no blackheads on that portrait of corruption rotting away in Dorian Gray's attic. For the draft, like the degenerate Dorian, suffers no small blemishes; it is corrupt of spirit all the way through."

The December 1967 issue of *Ramparts* reprinted selections from an official Selective Service document entitled "Channeling" which illustrates the totalitarian philosophy of such a system and its functionaries. "The psychology of granting wide choice under pressure to take action is the American or indirect way of achieving what is done by direction in foreign countries where choice is not permitted. . . . From the individual's viewpoint, he is standing in a room which has been made uncomfortably warm. Several doors are open, but they all lead to various forms of recognized, patriotic service to the Nation. Some accept the alternatives gladly — some with reluctance. The consequence is approximately the same." All that is denied is the freedom to choose an "unapproved" course of action which more nearly fulfills the individual's notion of what his life should be.

885

Probably the two best books to have appeared on this subject are James C. Miller III, ed., *Why the Draft?* Baltimore, Penguin Books, 1968. $1.25. And: *The Draft?* prepared for the Peace Education Division of the American Friends Service Committee. (New York, Hill and Wang, 1968. $1.25.) Both books argue strongly against conscription and in favor of voluntarism, and both are impressive for their scholarship and the careful, scientific treatment of this highly emotional subject. The A.F.S.C. book, *The Draft?*, takes a completely pacifist point of view, arguing against all military service; and does an excellent job of destroying the case for conscription, as well as the more difficult job of building a case against all militarism. The Miller book, *Why the Draft?* argues positively for a volunteer army on the grounds of feasibility and optimality, and against conscription because it is simply not the best way of doing the job and has bad side effects as well. Both books were prepared by high-powered research teams, and this division of labor produced two superior books.

The source of most of the technical arguments against procuring military manpower through compulsion which are used by almost every other work on the subject is the economic research of men such as Prof. Walter Y. Oi, who presents his findings in the *American Economic Review*, LVII (May 1967), 39-62; and also in Sol Tax, ed., *The Draft* (Chicago: University of Chicago Press, 1967), pp. 221-51. Other technical articles of note are Stuart H. Altman and Alan E. Fechter, "The Supply of Military Personnel in the Absence of a Draft," *American Economic Review*, LVII (May 1967), 19-31; and W. Lee Hansen and Burton A. Weisbrod, "Economics of the Military Draft," *Quarterly Journal of Economics*, LXXXI (August 1967), 395-421. Additional articles in the Sol Tax book, which is a symposium covering all points of view and not merely the case for a volunteer army, include one by Kenneth Boulding, President of the American Economics Association, questioning the legitimacy of the national state; and several others which appear in revised form in this issue of N.I.R.

LIBERALS OF THE WORLD:
UNITE!

Our Hour of Need is upon us. The time is fraught with peril for the most promising development in the non-Western freedom movement—the Arabic Edition of *New Individualist Review*. Our latest foreign language edition is in grave danger, threatened with extinction by the International Postal Monopoly, the United Nations, and the fine hand of the COMINTERN itself.

To crush the rising tide of revolution which everywhere has followed upon the first publication of our SYMPOSIUM ON CONSCRIPTION, the government of Egypt has launched a drive to deny *New Individualist Review's* Arabic edition the free use of international postal services. In the United Nations debate devoted to the issue, the Egyptian Ambassador demanded:

> . . . that the United Nations declare the Arabic edition of *New Individualist Review* to be the greatest threat to peace in the Middle East—stirring discontent among the harmonious Egyptian people and spreading sedition by its challenge of ancient truths. All nations must rise to fight the anarchists, who preach such treason as "Taxes In Money, Not Forced Labor" and "Emigration Before Conscription" and the like. No government is safe; no military force is secure. In Sinai alone, thousands of soldiers left the battlefield with cries of "Freedom Now; Down With Military Servitude!" on the very eve of Israeli attacks. . . .

The United States Ambassador demonstrated the cunning solidarity of all government agents when threatened by the stirrings of liberation. His reply:

> We wish to assure the State of Egypt that the Arabic edition of this odious publication—judging by the contents of the English edition—will trouble the peace no longer. The United States government has a great tradition of respect for freedom of speech; as President Johnson once said, "Freedom of Speech is a First Class Freedom." Of course, this *New Individualist Review* is mailed third class . .

FRIENDS OF

FREEDOM,

You must not fail us!

Subscribe Today!

Vote with your dollars.

The Journal of

LAW & ECONOMICS

VOLUME XI	APRIL 1968	PRICE $2.50

THE UNIVERSITY OF CHICAGO LAW SCHOOL

The Journal of Law and Economics is published by the University of Chicago Law School twice annually, in April and October.

All issues of **The Journal of Law and Economics** may be obtained for the price of $2.50 per issue. However, the **Journal** is also available at a special student rate of $1.00 per issue.

The subscription rate for the **Journal** will be $5.00 for two issues each year ($2.00 to students), with the following discounted rates for extended subscriptions: two years, $9.50 (students, $4.00); three years, $13.50 (or $6.00); four years, $17.00 (or $8.00); and five years, $20.00 (or $10.00 to students). Those students wishing to obtain all volumes of the **Journal of Law and Economics** issued to date (through Volume X) should remit $10.00. Please send orders and remittances (and particulars of student status if you are applying for the student rate) to:

Publications Assistant
The Journal of Law and Economics
University of Chicago Law School
1111 East 60th Street
Chicago, Illinois 60637

VOLUME 5
NUMBER 1
WINTER 1968

New
INDIVIDUALIST
Review

A JOURNAL OF CLASSICAL LIBERAL THOUGHT

Winter 1968 $1.00   Vol. 5, No. 1

BOUND VOLUMES OF
NEW INDIVIDUALIST REVIEW

The Editors of **New Individualist Review** are pleased to announce in conjunction with publication of the first number in our fifth volume the issue of a small number of compete, bound sets of the journal which will be available for distribution in June of this year. These rare and valuable sets will include the three out-of-print issues of **New Individualist Review** which are not available to the general public, and unavailable in most libraries; issues, we might add, containing articles by F.A. Hayek, Milton Friedman, Murray N. Rothbard, as well as all of the original editors of the journal.

This announcement is being made in the endeavor to supplement our subscription revenues with contributions from readers and suporters who may have been unaware of our need and dependence upon supplemental contributions for continued publication. The number of bound sets of **New Individualist Review** which will be available is strictly limited by the availability of the out-of-print numbers; it may be impossible to repeat this offer. If you would like to obtain one of these sets and assist **N.I.R.** in its publication, please send your check in the amount of $75.00 or more to **New Individualist Review**, Ida Noyes Hall, University of Chicago, Illinois 60637.

NIR Back Issues

Certain back issues of NEW INDIVIDUALIST REVIEW can be purchased for a limited time at the special rate of $1.00 per copy. Among the issues presently available are those containing:

"Sin and the Criminal Law," by Robert M. Hurt (II/1)

"National Review: Criticism and Reply," by Ronald Hamowy and William F. Buckley, Jr. (I/3)

"The Fusionists on Liberalism and Tradition," by Ralph Raico (III/3)

"Civil Liberties in the Welfare State," by Robert M. Schuchman (II/3)

"The Uneasy Case for State Education," by E.G. West (IV/2)

"Why Not A Volunteer Army?" by Milton Friedman (IV/4)

A complete set of the available back copies (thirteen issues) may be ordered for $12.00, postpaid. The three out-of-print numbers can be provided by xerographic reproduction at a cost of $4.00 each. Address inquiries to:

NEW INDIVIDUALIST REVIEW
Ida Noyes Hall, University of Chicago
Chicago, Illinois 60637

NEW INDIVIDUALIST REVIEW

A JOURNAL OF CLASSICAL LIBERAL THOUGHT

WINTER 1968   VOLUME 5, NUMBER 1

NEW INDIVIDUALIST REVIEW is published quarterly by *New Individualist Review, Inc.*, at Ida Noyes Hall, University of Chicago, Chicago, Illinois 60637. Telephone 312/363-8778.

Opinions expressed in signed articles do not necessarily represent the views of the editors. Editorial, advertising, and subscription correspondence and manuscripts should be sent to NEW INDIVIDUALIST REVIEW, Ida Noyes Hall, University of Chicago, Chicago, Illinois 60637. All manuscripts become the property of NEW INDIVDUALIST REVIEW.

Subscription rates: $3.00 per year (students $1.50). Two years at $5.75 (students $2.75).

NEW

INDIVIDUALIST

REVIEW

EDITORIAL STAFF

Editor-in-Chief • J. M. Cobb
Editor • James M. S. Powell
Associate Editors • David Levy
Ernest L. Marraccini • Robert Schuettinger
Editorial Assistant • J. Huston McCulloch
Contributing Editors • Robert L. Cunningham
Bruce Goldberg • Ronald Hamowy
Sam Peltzman • Ralph Raico

EDITORIAL ADVISORS

Yale Brozen • Milton Friedman • George J. Stigler
University of Chicago
F. A. Hayek   Benjamin A. Rogge
University of Freiburg   *Wabash College*

894

Complaints of the loss of individuality and the lessening of respect for the person and his rights have become a commonplace of our time; They nonetheless point to a cause for genuine concern. NEW INDIVIDUALIST REVIEW, an independent journal associated with no organization or political party, believes that in the realm of politics and economics the system most effectively guaranteeing proper respect for individuality is that which, historically, has gone by the name of classical liberalism; the elements of this system are private property, civil liberties, the rule of law, and, in general, the strictest limits placed on the power of government. It is the purpose of the Review to stimulate and encourage explorations of important problems from a viewpoint characterized by thoughtful concern with individual liberty.

The Rhodesian Calumny

W. H. HUTT

I HAVE LIVED FOR thirty-seven years in race-troubled South Africa and during that time I have been observing, thinking about, and occasionally writing about, the superficially intractable problems of color prejudices and racial domination. I have seldom felt that the politicians were leading wisely on the always delicate and sometimes explosive issues of race antagonisms, either in my own country or in adjacent countries. Yet during the 1950's and early 1960's, there was one area in which there were hopeful signs of emerging enlightenment. I refer to the now disintegrated Federation of Rhodesia and Nyasaland.

With rare statesmanship, commendable realism, and courage, the Welensky regime had brought about in the Federation an all too brief era of peaceful and prosperous development under the rule of law, independent courts, integrity of administration, and as rapid an orderly modernization as the world had ever witnessed. Nowhere else had Blacks and Whites got on with one another better under the stresses of radical sociological change and economic progress. Order was maintained by a tiny *unarmed* police force, more than half of which was African. Time-rooted color prejudices were being slowly dissolved whilst, for Southern Rhodesia, the 1961 Constitu-

tion had not only laid down a non-racial voting qalification, but, through a Declaration of Rights, provided for the unconstitutionality of legislative discriminations on the grounds of race or color.

Unfortunately the British government, placing the ambitions of a handful of power-hungry African politicians above the interests of the inarticulate African masses, decided to break up this great experiment. Nevertheless, in the present Rhodesia, the 1961 constitution (with minor amendments) has survived: and under it, *the most promising deliberate attempt the world has ever seen at creating a wholly democratic, multi-racial society has continued.*

But persistent pressures from the new totalitarian and nationalistic African governments, which were understandably hostile to a genuine democracy in their continent, have demanded that it be crushed; and the belief of the White Rhodesians that Britain and the United States were siding with the totalitarians drove Ian Smith's Government (legally elected under the 1961 Constitution) into a Declaration of Independence in 1965.

The present position is that Britain, the United States, and the United Nations reject the system under which the right to the franchise in Rhodesia is independent of race or color and based on very modest educational and/or property qualifications. They want a system which confers the right to vote unconditionally upon four million tribal Africans. That is what the quarrel is about. Yet Rhodesia was offering, in the middle of Africa, a continuous object lesson in

895

W. H. Hutt has been Professor of Commerce and Dean of the Faculty of Commerce at the University of Cape Town, South Africa; currently Visiting Professor of Economics at Wabash College. His book, *Economics of the Colour Bar*, remains one of the principal works on the origins and impact of racial legislation in South Africa.

growing racial and color harmony, under *classical democracy*.[1]

Ian Smith's regime, whilst solemnly pledged to "unimpeded progress to majority rule"; and prepared to entrench this objective by any bona fide technical means the world might demand ("by solemn treaty if necessary"); and prepared further to lighten materially the franchise requirements (under adequate safeguards), is nevertheless doggedly resolved to preserve the Western heritage for all races to share, and not to permit its destruction (which nearly all White Rhodesians believe would be the outcome under "one man, one vote"). The only limitations on the franchise are, in fact, of the kind that J. S. Mill advocated in his classic *Representative Government* (1861).

896

I allege that Americans have been grievously misled about the facts. The frankness of Ian Smith and his colleagues in expressing their fears of the *unconditional* enfranchisement of Africans, has been subtly used, by unscrupulous reporters, to create an impression that the Rhodesian government is keeping the Africans in political subjection. That is false.

ADMITTEDLY, THERE *are* White supremacists in Rhodesia. They support the present Government *faute de mieux*, because it is at least staving off African uni-racial totalitarian rule. Today they are taking advantage of the backlash caused by anger at the injustice of sanctions and pressing for an *apartheid* policy. If the supremacists gain power and put back the clock, will it not be the fault of Britain and the United States?

The present situation may easily confuse the superficial observer. Originally the threat, and later the actuality of sanctions, together with unprecedented internal efforts (mainly by non-Rhodesians) at subversion, have forced the Rhodesian government into defensive action. It is easy to represent emergency steps as normal policy. The white leaders of Rhodesia are not Nazis. Some have a proud war record.

The extent to which, through press, radio, television, and pulpit, the American public has been misinformed on this issue is fantastic. I can illustrate by a few out of *hundreds* of examples. In September 1966, the influential *Newsweek* (relying upon a reference by Ian Smith to Dr. Verwoerd's personal kindliness: words of sympathy following the latter's assassination) remarked that "the Rhodesian leader made it plain that his support for white supremacy was unshaken." Rep. D. M. Fraser told Congress shortly before that the Rhodesian government "favors rule by a racial minority through policies aimed at excluding virtually all Africans." Various politicians (mostly ill-informed, but still irresponsible) have referred to "racial and political injustice" in Rhodesia (these are President Johnson's words), or expressed similar blanket condemnations. Ambassador Goldberg told the world through the United Nations that Rhodesia involved "the seizure of power by a minority bent on subjugating a vast majority on racial grounds." And a host of other seemingly well-informed and trustworthy authorities have succeeded in slandering the rulers of Rhodesia by deepening the impression that Africans are being denied democratic or human rights by a White minority.

Actually, Rhodesia offers free political institutions, the rule of law, a judiciary with an independence of politics which most Americans would find difficult to believe, a free enterprise economy, and few surviving *state-imposed* (I stress this qualification) barriers to equality of economic opportunity. It *was* also a happy and internally peaceful area until recently, order having been maintained since the beginning of the century by a tiny force of *unarmed* police. That was, of course, before the return of saboteurs trained in China, Algeria, and Tanzania. Otherwise, since World War II, persons of all races had obviously been learning to live with one another under increasing amity.

---

[1] It is as essential to distinguish between "classical democracy" (i.e., the form of representative government advocated by the "classical liberals") and what is commonly called "democracy" today, as it is to distinguish between "classical liberalism" itself and what is today commonly called "liberalism."

The greater proportion of the 220,000 Whites (which includes many whose enterprise and industry had created the civilization established in Rhodesia) had undergone an agonizing readjustment of deep-rooted racial attitudes. They had come to accept not only the inevitability of equality of political opportunity, but also the wisdom of a policy aimed at deliberately hastening progress toward the day when the majority of the qualified electorate would be Africans. Moreover, prior to the imposition of sanctions, Rhodesia had been prosperous. Its GNP had almost doubled during one decade, providing more than proportional benefits to the African section of the population and attracting an enormous number of foreign Africans to share in temporary employment opportunities.

The main source of discord was a small group of African leaders, imbued with a faith in their ability to serve their people, but often spurred on chiefly by personal ambition; and sometimes understandably bitter in the light of humiliations and indignities which they may have had to endure. Among this group, the politicians' ubiquitous hunger for power was whetted by the apparent prospect of *early* African supremacy. They had just witnessed a succession of capitulations which had conferred sudden status, privilege, and wealth on similarly placed African leaders to the north. They were aware of the dominating population of mainly tribal Rhodesians whose votes could obviously be won by appeals to perfectly natural envy as well as to color resentments, nationalist emotions, and class antagonisms. All this seemed to suggest that, with determination and the right stategy, office and honor were within their grasp. They found they were *thwarted by the entrenchment of a non-racial political equality, a reasonably achievable franchise available on equal terms for every literate and responsible Rhodesian, whatever his color.*

WHY SHOULD GOVERNMENTS which claim, at least, to be striving for the eradication of color prejudices and racial injustices wish to crush this genuinely democratic society? One reason is, I believe, that American and British politicians tend to think in terms of the aspirations of African *politicians*. They are not directly concerned with the welfare of the African masses, who, unlike their leaders, are not possible future voters at the United Nations; and sometimes the Western politicians seem to think that it is expedient to retain the friendship of "moderate" leaders in African territories; whilst even the moderate leaders find it desirable, for popularity reasons, to appease the racial emotions and resentments of the black peoples. If they did not, they could not survive, it is felt, against more extreme rivals.

A more difficult question is, why should so many who obviously do sincerely wish to eliminate surviving inequalities of opportunity and respect between Black and White in the world, also wish to destroy the most propitious experiment in non-discriminatory representative government that mankind has known? I can conceive of only one answer: because of culpable news-slanting by reporters, newspaper correspondents, editors, and radio and television staff.

What I cannot explain satisfactorily to myself is why those in control of propaganda resources should have a *vested interest* in misinforming the world on so vital an issue. Yet the blatant fact remains that the number of people outside Rhodesia who know the facts about that country is almost infinitesimal, and the occasional attempts of these few to correct misrepresentations have had little success. For instance, during the year 1966, I can recall seeing only two really unslanted references in New York newspapers to the policy of the Smith Government. One was in a very well informed letter from John Davenport (of *Fortune*), and the other a brilliant letter, quoted from the English press, of Elspeth Huxley's.

Now there are some aspects of the racial situation in Rhodesia which critics abroad might deplore, whilst giving full recognition to the democratic, non-racial objectives of the Smith Government. I shall shortly refer to policy aspects

897

which I myself regard as wrong or ill-conceived; but it has been a tactic of those who are hostile to Rhodesia's aim of preserving Western civilization for gradual sharing with the Africans, to refer to these aspects and, through references to her friendship with the Republic of South Africa, to imply that Rhodesia is following an *apartheid* policy.

It is true, of course, that South Africa has tactfully assisted Rhodesia's resistance to sanctions, yet this is not because there is any basic similarity in objectives. It is due to fear that the overthrow of Smith's regime would lead to the early establishment of a hostile black nationalist dictatorship on the northern boundary of South Africa. The Rhodesians are genuinely grateful for this support in their hour of need, and official references to the Republic are understandably amicable; but the proclaimed racial policies of the two countries, whatever their merits or demerits, are at present diametrically *different*.

Let us consider the allegations of racial discrimination in parliamentary representation, with general political bondage for the Africans. In truth, every Rhodesian at the age of twenty-one upwards has the right to qualify for the vote (or to stand for election) on the same terms, irrespective of his race, color, or ancestry. Moreover, the franchise qualifications are surprisingly moderate when one considers the need, in so complex a racial situation, for insuring that voters shall be able to understand something about the issues on which they will be expected to exercise ballot-expressed judgments.

The qualification is based on education or property, or a combination thereof. Thus, on the so-called "A" roll (providing for 50 of the 65 seats in the legislature) completion of primary education *plus* either an annual income of £528 (say $1300) *or* property of £1100 is one of the conditions which qualifies a voter.[2] But *no* property or income standard is applied if four years of secondary education have been completed (a provision intended, I understand, to bring as many moderately qualified young Africans, as rapidly as possible, onto the "A" roll). And there are other, alternative conditions for qualification. For the "B" roll (providing for 15 seats only) the requirements are much more lenient. For persons over thirty years of age, income of only £132 *plus* completion of primary education will qualify, as will completion of two years of secondary education with no age, property, or income requirement. Again, there are other means of qualifying. The "B" roll qualifications were intended to insure immediate representation by African members in Parliament.[3]

FOLLOWING THE *TIGER* talks, the Smith regime had been willing to accept even easier franchise qualifications. The Rhodesian government was, indeed, prepared to lean over backward in its efforts to refute the slander that its object was to perpetuate the subordinacy and inferiority of the Africans. Now I submit that, unless by some stratagem Africans are prevented from exercising their rights, even under the present provisions, there is nothing to justify the sanctions through which Britain and the United States have been trying to bring the regime to an end. Let it be clearly understood that there is no parallel in Rhodesia to the subterfuges which have, in the past, denied *constitutional* rights to Negroes in some parts of the United States. Moreover, there are no grounds whatsoever for the suggestion that educational opportunities are being deliberately withheld from Africans, or not reasonably available. (I shall return to this point.) Nor can the Whites be shown to be using the dominating parliamentary majority power which the franchise conditions at present accord them in order to legislate against equality of opportunity in the economic sphere. Even if they did, the Declaration of Rights, with the Consti-

---

[2] It should be noticed that *this* qualifying income is less than one quarter of the family income regarded by the U. S. Bureau of Labor Statistics as the poverty or "deprivation" level.

[3] There are 13 African representatives in Parliament.

tutional Council's power to declare such measures unconstitutional, would stand in their path.

If Rhodesia's critics had merely demanded even more ironclad constitutional entrenchment to insure that African rights should not be subsequently revoked, there is not the slightest doubt that the Smith Government would have agreed to this, although not in a form which would have given a veto right to the "B" roll voters. The intransigence of the White Rhodesians rests in their determination not to let the future of their land—a progressive country which their courage, industry, and integrity have built up—be determined by a "one man, one vote" referendum in which almost wholly tribal and illiterate Africans were allowed to vote.

The political protection of these presently voteless Africans is secured through the "Declaration of Rights," which provides for what are termed "fundamental rights and freedoms." Equality of treatment in all legislation is guaranteed to every Rhodesian ". . . whatever his race, tribe, place of origin, political opinions, color or creed, subject to respect for the rights and freedoms of others." To pronounce on the constitutionality of proposed legislation (in the light of this "Declaration") there is a Constitutional Council, of *predominantly non-white membership*. Its members are nominated and chosen by an electoral college consisting of the existing and any former chairman of the Council, members and former members of the Council, judges and retired judges, and the President of the Council of Chiefs.

THROUGH THE CHANCE of history and tradition, few of the four million Africans were able to play more than a passive role in the development of their country. Hardly any were capable of being more than unskilled collaborators with the hard-earned savings, enterprise, energy, and skill of the White settlers. This was due, as every *intelligent* Rhodesian knows, not to any innate inferiority of the Black people, but to history and the absence of earlier

opportunity. Insofar as there remains any *deliberate* perpetuation of practices or procedures which deny opportunities to Africans, there is something which any "classical liberal" like myself would never hesitate to censure; and any *unintended* perpetuation of racial economic inequalities can equally be subjected to exposure and criticism. Yet White property owners, including landowners, have never been responsible for racial discrimination — at least *not in that role*.

But are the political rights conferred under the sort of franchise conditions I have briefly indicated a mere sham, as is often alleged? Let us consider the educational facilities available for Africans as a path to enfranchisement. Rep. Donald M. Fraser told Congress last year that "the Smith regime refuses to provide education above the primary school level for a meaningful number of Africans," and Mr. Joseph Palmer, Assistant Secretary of State for African Affairs, recently told the California Institute of Technology that "relatively few Rhodesian Africans are permitted the facilities to complete the highest secondary grade or go to college." These assertions are false.

What are the facts? To get the matter into perspective we must remember that, although the Whites make up only one-twentieth of the population, they provide 98 per cent of the *direct* taxes collected. In spite of the fact that 220,000 Whites alone must for some time finance educational development for 4,000,000 Africans, *the most impressive achievement of the regime and the most impressive planned achievement is precisely in respect to secondary education*. A top priority in the reforms introduced by the Field Government in 1962 was a rapid speeding up in the provision of secondary schools. In the period since then, 45 new secondary schools have been established. The present program aims at offering secondary school education to 50 per cent of those Africans who complete primary school; and for the rest a system of correspondence courses is to be provided.

If the opportunities available in Rhodesia are seized, progress toward the

899

time when responsible Africans will hold the balance of power should not be protracted. A team of three Americans, headed by Rep. John Ashbrook, has recently reported, after a study of the situation at first hand, that there have been "spectacular advances" in educacation and that "the demand for . . . places in secondary schools has yet to equal the supply." Far from being *excluded* from opportunities, Africans are not yet voluntarily taking advantage of the facilities available. In vocational training the same apathy on their part is slowing down the progress hoped for.

Over a decade, enrollment of Africans in *primary* schools has doubled, enrollment in *secondary* schools has increased six-fold, and enrollment as a whole has tripled. Ashbrook's team points out, quite pertinently, that in Britain "only 34 per cent continue to go to school after age 15." In Rhodesia the *target* for Africans alone is 50 per cent. Unless sanctions succeed in sabotaging the most rapid advance in educational facilities which any African area has ever experienced, in three years time all Rhodesian children of all races will have an opportunity of achieving a complete primary education. Expenditure on education, which is the biggest item in Rhodesia's budget, has trebled over the last seven years and has been accelerating. Moreover, as far as university education is concerned, a deliberate policy of discrimination in favor of Africans in respect to scholarships and loans has been followed. In the words of the Ashbrook Committee, the Rhodesians have "struggled valiantly to pull the African into the twentieth century."

These facts, which can easily be verified, ought to have been known to Rep. Fraser and to Mr. Palmer. If they did not trouble to check their facts but based their allegations upon reports of newspaper correspondents, articles in popular periodicals, and the like, their speeches were recklessly irresponsible. But should the facts as I have stated them be doubted, let one of the large foundations finance a visit to Rhodesia by a small body of disinterested members of the academic profession—*chosen for their known independence from affil-*

iation or association with any political party—and let them report, from first hand contact, on what is happening. The overall aim of the program, planned in 1962, may well be over-ambitious, almost naive in its optimism and idealism; but what chance has it when the world tries to destroy the regime which boldly conceived of it?

AT TIMES, I GET the feeling that it is hopeless to try to expose the repeated misrepresentations and false stereotypes that have been created, particularly in the minds of American Negroes. I can illustrate by a typical distortion. On one occasion a reporter told the world that Ian Smith had declared "There will be no black rule in my time." This alleged assertion made headlines everywhere and it is constantly repeated; but the repeated denials seldom get printed, let alone make headlines. What Smith had actually said, in a CBS telecast, and I quote from Anthony Harrigan's *One Against The Mob,* was: "If we had a black nationalist government — a black extremist government in my lifetime, then I believe we would have failed in our policy . . . [which] has always been no discrimination between black or white."

A report published in the American press on September 18, 1967 said that Prime Minister Wilson was sending aides to Rhodesia to seek "acceptance of eventual African majority rule." How tendentious and subtly mendacious it all is! There *is* majority rule under non-discriminatory franchise qualifications, and the whole plan, guaranteed since 1961, contemplates an eventual African majority of votes on both the A and B rolls as soon as the Africans have used the rapidly growing facilities to achieve education or to qualify under the other responsibility tests. Moreover, the hackneyed insistence that "all sections of Rhodesian opinion, black and white, should be consulted" is equally tendentious; for already, under the present constitution, all sections who can be reasonably assumed to be capable of envisaging the issues have equal rights under the franchise provisions. But if "all sec-

900

tions" is a euphemism for Nkomo and the PCC, and Sithole and ZANU, anything short of immediate black supremacy seems certain to be rejected.

How much wiser and commendable is Ian Smith's attitude towards the whole franchise problem! He has said: "We hope the time will come when we shall have Black and White in Parliament and nobody will start counting heads to decide whether there are more Blacks than Whites."

Do those Americans or British who applaud the "tough" line taken against Rhodesia *know* that this is the spirit with which the government of that country has faced its appallingly difficult task? How many who feel indignation at the supposed "oppression" of the Africans in Rhodesia know that, in advising his countrymen about how to act in face of brutal attacks, perfidious misrepresentations, and vindicative sanctions, he urged them all to exercise "courtesy, kindness and understanding towards all peoples, especially those of other racial groups . . . to maintain the highest standards in everything that you do: in your work, in your play, in your thoughts, especially when thinking of other people; in your general demeanour. . . ." Are these the words of a Rhodesian Hitler determined to treat the Africans as the Nazi regime treated the Jews? Yet that *is* the image which has been created of Ian Smith.

Yet is there political freedom in Rhodesia? Is there not suppression of effective opposition? Again, I have found that most Americans and Britons who have been interested in the subject believe that the expression of anti-government *views* is somehow restrained. The truth is, I think, that the restrictions imposed have been aimed not at *opinion* but firstly at incitement to mob violence, terrorism, and intimidation, and secondly at more subtle attempts to destroy morale.

It is possible that, through an element of war hysteria created by world hostility and organized misrepresentation of their aims, the Rhodesian government has gone beyond what has been needed to prevent instigation to disorder; but confronted with sustained cold war aggression, together with the burden of sanctions, it was vital that they should maintain legitimate hopes of success in their struggle to preserve non-racial democracy. Although the newspapers of Salisbury and Buluwayo (which are under a single British ownership) have a justified reputation for responsibility, they have pursued a policy of supporting Britain right or wrong. Their news presentation and comments were obviously felt to be destructive of good racial feelings, and even worse, destructive of *faith* in the power of Rhodesia to survive the world's aggression (through sanctions and otherwise).

The Rhodesian government had no journals of their own of similar influence; short of nationalizing the press, they were led to drastic censorship; and the power to censor remains. The Ashbrook Committee reports that it is the Administration's "earnest hope that the worst rigors of censorship are past. . . . If the editors would only be a little more co-operative, the whole unpleasant business could be brought to an end."

901

THE SORT OF PROBLEM which has to be resolved can be illustrated by difficulties encountered at the University College of Rhodesia recently. As in virtually every college or university of the free word, a few Communist *sympathizers* among staff and students (of course, "they are not Communists," we are always assured) appear to work for the "other side" in the cold war. They work as unobtrusively as they can, but their task is to spread dissention and inspire "demonstrations." Now it was the hope of the Smith Government that the College could train a growing number of Africans to take their part among Rhodesia's future rulers, and that within its walls the old prejudices, antagonisms, and misunderstandings could be eradicated. A minority among the staff, however, (mostly British) seemingly indoctrinated with the notion that the fomentation of race hatred, and the quiet implementation of class and race war are legitimate in the struggle against "capitalist imperialism," were causing serious friction. They seemed to be inculcating

Page Nine

resentments and the spirit of revenge among the African students. The deportation of certain lecturers who were believed to be guilty of this abuse of academic freedom has naturally been represented as, in itself, a denial of that freedom.

A typical misrepresentation can be mentioned. Last year the College entertained the Principal of the University of Cape Town, Dr. J. P. Duminy. At the ceremony, a deplorable demonstration was organized among some of the students on the grounds that the principal of "a segregated university" was being honored. The American journal, *Christianity and Crisis,* subsequently published an article which sought to justify this insult to an eminent academician, by describing the invitation to Dr. Duminy as "provocative to the African students." Yet the University of Cape Town is (and will always remain, I hope) open to students of all races. Segregation is imposed by the government of South Africa upon students wishing to attend, not by the University's own decision or regulations. Moreover, every year after he was appointed, Dr. Duminy, together with the Chancellor of the University, played his role in an annual ceremony and procession of protest at which the "torch of academic freedom" is carried—a torch which was ceremonially and solemnly extinguished when academic *apartheid* was enacted. The writer must have known these facts. Why did he suppress them?

If, in these circumstances, the Rhodesian government has resorted to press censorship and suspension of the rule of law (and of *habeas corpus*) in dealing with suspected troublemakers, the criticisms of those far from the scene ought, at any rate, to be guarded. There are no racial riots and no *obvious* signs of smouldering discontent among the great mass of Rhodesian Africans. From that angle, whatever the demerits of the regime, it has its concomitant virtues. Ashbrook's Committee reported of the Rhodesian capital: "The only troops in evidence are a handful of smiling Africans. . . . On the streets white and black mingle with one another with every appearance of courtesy and good humor.

. . . During the whole of our visit, we never heard a siren; . . . we never noticed so much as a sidearm. . . . The perceptive American knows that racial tensions can be sensed; but he senses none of these tensions here." We must remember that, due to the infiltration of saboteurs trained abroad, Africans who wished to co-operate in the democratic order, by enrolling as voters or by actually voting, were for some time in danger of being murdered, tortured or having their houses and crops destroyed and their cattle maimed. After Rhodesia's independence, the Zambia Broadcasting Corporation, with the collaboration of the BBC, explicity exhorted participation in sabotage and murder. This seemed incredible to me when I first heard of it; but it is true. Tape recordings exist and the text has been published. Both the PCC[4] (formerly ZAPU) under Nkomo, and ZANU[5] under Sithole, are supported by the two great Communist powers. Captured bombs, grenades, and machine-guns together with sabotage instruction manuals from various places beyond the Iron Curtain have been produced in the courts.

The first big campaign for lawlessness and disorder was rapidly suppressed by the loyal and efficient Defence and Police Forces.[6] Internal peace then ruled for some time; and a second large-scale effort launched from Zambia recently appears also to have been effectively suppressed. Those who forecast wide-spread bloodshed following the Declaration of Independence have been proved wrong, although many Africans lost their lives and their property at first.

IN DEFENDING THE Rhodesian regime from contemporary misrepresentations, I must not leave the impression that, in my judgment, the Africans have no legitimate grievances. There *are* surviving discriminations. How rapidly the causes of the discrimination can be removed will depend upon the wisdom of

---

[4] People's Caretaker Council.

[5] Zimbabwe African National Union.

[6] It is perhaps significant that, at the rank and file level, Africans constitute the majority in the Defence and Police Forces.

those elected as the weight of the African vote gradually increases. Moreover, as I have already insisted, there *are* supremacists in Smith's Rhodesian Party. But the Prime Minister himself vehemently and indignantly denies that his policy is moving towards *apartheid*. He maintains—and with patent sincerity, I believe — that his government stands for non-discrimination and the right of all to progress on merit.

U.S. Representative J. D. Waggoner claimed recently that "Segregation is unknown in Rhodesia. It is forbidden by law. Public facilities, hotels, bars, buses and the like are open to one race as well as another." That *is* broadly the position; but a cultured African is, I understand, still subject to indignities and affronts, mainly from Whites of a lower social class; and exclusions by subterfuge occur here in other spheres,[7] fortunately not in the University College, or in public transport, or in public buildings. In housing, de facto segregation persists fairly widely, but only in the sense in which this assertion is still equally true of the United States, and it is basically an income segregation. (The most stupid follies of *apartheid* are not found in Rhodesia).

The remaining major discrimination *imposed by law* against Africans is, in my opinion, that due to segregation maintained under the *Land Apportionment Act*. There is, I believe, almost universal agreement that this Act must eventually be drastically amended; but the case against precipitate action is strong. What *were* the objects of the *Land Apportionment Act?* The British Parliament passed it with two aims in mind:

The first aim was to attract settlers with enterprise and know-how capable of developing the flow of real income for the benefit of all races (which aim has been realized). The Act was in the na-

_____
[7] Segregation in schools has not discrimination as its purpose, but maintenance of standards. This is not just hypocrisy. No one believes, I think, that it will survive African progress in the cultural and educational fields. The Ashbrook Committee reported, after interviewing three African members of the Rhodesian Parliament, "They do not urge even the integration of elementary and secondary classrooms."

ture of a contract with the settlers who responded. If there was any element of privilege conferred by the contract, it resembles the monopoly promised to prospectors everywhere—to induce them to risk capital in searching for the earth's hidden wealth.

The second aim was to protect land allocated to African ownership from purchase by Whites. There is, I understand, no *legal* restraint on the sale of agricultural land in White ownership to Africans: the chief protection the Act provides is for Blacks, not Whites.

Mr. Palmer told his audience that "the acreage reserved for the white minority consists of the best land." That is not true. In a reply to Mr. Palmer, the Rhodesian Ministry of Information has pointed out that "there was a slightly higher percentage of higher fertility soils in the African area than in the white area, nearly twice the percentage of medium fertility soils and, while only 37 per cent of Rhodesia has a rainfall above 20 inches, half the African areas fall within this zone."

Now it is complained also that the area of land *per head* possessed by Whites is incomparably greater than that possessed by Africans *per head*. Of course, but should that be a grievance? The Whites equally remain in possession of a proportionally greater capital *per head* in other forms; but it was the capital which their enterprise, stubborness, expertness, and energy could alone have created. What is now their land was hardly capital when they took it over. It was virtually valueless—almost wholly unproductive scrub. Many of the critics of Rhodesia *seem* to be arguing that the Whites should be dispossessed of that property simply *because* they are Whites. But the principle of non-discrimination condemns privilege, not property. Privilege may become property—e.g., import licenses may become assets—but property is not privilege. It cannot be held that the Whites *exploited* the Africans they employed.

THE CHIEF OBSTACLE to a more rapid achievement of equality of economic opportunity on the part of Rho-

903

desian Africans is to be found, however, in the labor market. This is an aspect of the problem, however, which Rhodesia's critics all pass over. Just as in the Republic of South Africa, the most powerful color bars in Rhodesia do not arise from quite honest exclusions in "job reservation" form, or from the indirect but still obvious exclusions via "group areas" and "labor allocation" forms. It is the simple insistence on "the rate for the job" which creates the really vicious color injustices. The principle of "equal pay for equal work" prevents the African from discounting his initial inferior training for many types of work required in modern society, the extra costs of employing him (including the unrest which labor union leaders can initiate by playing on the color prejudices of the Whites). It confines him on the whole, therefore, to occupations of relatively low productivity and value, and it destroys the business incentive to invest in the inculcation of industrial skills. Where the Rhodesian Africans are progressing economically is in the spheres where the standard rate cannot be enforced and labor union power cannot be exerted—in the white collar occupations, journalism, and the civil service. In the professions and in business, the qualified Africans encounter merely the kind of obstacles (not imposed by law) which similarly qualified Negroes encounter in the United States. But it is through restraints in the labor market, of a kind which are defended by practically all Rhodesia's critics, that the key injustices can be discerned.[8] Whether African leaders wise enough to perceive this reality are likely to emerge in the near future is very doubtful. But as the

political progress of Africans under the present constitution will be to some extent dependent upon economic progress, their leaders will have every incentive to rescue their people from the tyranny of "the standard wage-rate."

Of course the constitution withholds present majority power from the Africans, but the purpose is to insure their eventual sharing in the heritage of the West by preventing their destruction of it; and the planned gradualness is surely to be welcomed. Blacks as well as Whites are stupidly emotional on the skin color issue in all areas of contact all over the world. The problem is aggravated when color prejudice is merged, as it usually is, with class prejudice. With gradualness and steadfast policy, these prejudices can be dissolved; but demagogues demanding haste can sabotage the process.

Those who, like myself, regard color prejudice as the worst social evil of the contemporary era must strive for the removal of the sanctions which were imposed against Rhodesia after she was condemned, *unheard and unrepresented,* by the United Nations. If we want the most hopeful planned attempt the world has ever experienced to achieve a free multi-racial society to be allowed to demonstrate its potentialities—for the benefit of all—we must, indeed, go even further. Rhodesia deserves generous compensation for the harm already caused, mainly to innocent Africans, from past efforts to compel her to capitulate to the prospect of black totalitarian racism; and in the United States, if the Negroes were rationally and disinterestedly led, we should find them fighting for the right of the Rhodesian Africans to qualify for a democratic and prosperous future; and that means their protection from the "one man, one vote" tyranny which capitulation to the PCC and ZANU would surely impose upon them.

---

[8] Since NRA, in the United States the *relative* progress of *male* Negroes appears to have been confined solely to the white collar field (clerks, salesmen, teachers, or professional men), and to the entrepreneurial field, or to professional sport.

Community, Leadership

and Progress

LET US BEGIN OUR discussion with a few observations of basic characteristics in every human community. First, the members of a community are unequal with respect to both the distribution of their abilities as well as the hierarchy of their wants and aspirations. Secondly, we can distinguish between two forms of social life in every community: the communitarian forms of life and the contractual forms of life. The former we define as the accepted principles of behavior, such as justice, truthfulness, and love, which each member of the community is expected to observe. The latter serves the purpose of harmonizing, or equilibrating, different interests of the community members through exchange. Thirdly, the relationship between the two forms of life is one of mutual interdependence. The communitarian forms of life determine the quality and content of contractual agreements; that is, the quality of contractual agreements is constrained in a specific way by the prevailing communitarian forms of life. At the same time, any deviation of contractual agreements from the principles of behavior would, if that deviation is accepted by the community, force the communitarian forms of life to adjust in order to embrace the novelty. Consider for example the his-

tory of the institution of marriage in a number of European communities. For some time the communitarian forms of life had prescribed that a mature girl must show an unquestionable obedience to her father including, of course, the acceptance of the man whom he selected to be her husband. When in the course of time young people had begun to choose their own partners, the quality of contractual agreement with respect to the institution of marriage changed and its acceptance — notwithstanding the resistance of the prevailing communitarian forms of life — brought about changes in the accepted principles of behavior. It became possible for a girl to reject her father's choice of mate without fear that it could result in her eventual alienation from the community.

Finally, the interaction between the communitarian and contractual forms of life in a community leads to the emergence of a number of social institutions. Some of those institutions are impartial, that is, they serve the purpose of reducing social conflict created by the confrontation of all the different interests and aspirations of the community members (e.g., open-market competition, democratic elections), while some others are founded with the explicit purpose of promoting the self-interest of specific groups in the community (e.g., trade unions, government-sheltered monopolies).

Svetozar Pejovich is Associate Professor of Economics at Texas A&M University.

Consider a community as it moves along through time. If there were no changes in the quality of contractual agreements the community life would flow through time undisturbed. The role of its rulers would be limited to the supervision of contractual agreements and to keeping them in agreement with the prevailing principles of behavior. A number of communities in Africa and Asia, where life has not changed for centuries, offer a good example of this type of communitarian life.

It is true, of course, that the years of accumulated experience must contribute to some improvements in the execution of contractual agreements. Those improvements, however, would only introduce changes in the data of the system but not add new phenomena. In other words, only some *quantitative* changes could be expected to take place within the firmly established framework of a "routine" life community. The meaning of time in a "routine" life community, as it emerges from our discussion, is an *objective* one: the sequence of events is independent of the action of the actor; man's activity can be predicted, i.e., it is given to him objectively from without. Life in a community of this type is unimaginative and uninspiring.

IT WAS SAID THAT the contractual forms of life serve the purpose of satisfying human wants through exchange. We must now make a clear-cut distinction between the "existing" or "known" wants and "newly created" wants. The former are wants which have been accepted by the community for some time and whose satisfaction can be attained through the prevailing contractual forms of life. The latter are wants — let us call them potential wants — which someone would like the community to become aware of, try them out, accept, and thus include in the sphere of "existing" wants. For example, the concept of equality before the law had not belonged to the sphere of "existing" wants in medieval Europe, but its later acceptance by the majority of European communities indicates that it was a definite potential want.

The introduction of potential wants calls for a *change* in the quality of contractual agreements; but the *acceptance* of a change in the contractual forms of life must lead, as we have seen, to a re-adjustment in the communitarian forms of life. It follows that the actualization of potential wants, i.e., the injection of a novelty into the community's life is an act of social-reorganization. This kind of social change we shall call progress, because the community's voluntary acceptance of new wants and, consequently, of new forms of life indicates that it considers them superior to the old ones. We conclude that progress involves a double variation: the quantitative changes, i.e., more of the same, and the qualitative changes, i.e., successful actualization of potential wants.

It appears that human progress is triggered by a group of men whose vision is not constrained by the prevailing forms of life, and who are capable of overcoming the inevitable resistance of the prevailing social institutions. The fact that the action of these men — let us call them *free agents* — means an injection of something new into the community's life implies that the outcome of their action can only be anticipated, not predicted. The free agent, therefore, must knowingly and willingly accept the risk of seeing his ideas and, consequently, himself rejected by the community.

> While wear and tear of time and the passivity of matter naturally dissipate the things of this world and the energy of history, the creative forces which are characteristic of the spirit and freedom and are also their witness and which normally find their point of application in the effort of the few — thereby destined to sacrifice — constantly revitalize the quality of this energy. Thus, the life of human societies advances and progresses at the price of many losses.[1]

Thus, in a "progressive" community a new meaning for time emerges: the sequence of events becomes dependent on the action of the free agent. In Western

---

[1] J. Maritain, *The Rights of Man and Natural Law* (New York: Charles Scribners' Sons, 1943), p. 30.

Europe free agents emerged from the ranks of small traders, bankers, artisans, and craftsmen, i.e., from the ranks of the rising middle class. The middle class wanted to distinguish itself from the lower classes of wage and farm labor, while at the same time it was envious of all the honors, privileges, and status enjoyed by the nobility. The members of this class turned their attention to commercial activity and the accumulation of wealth, and in doing so they re-organized the social structure of the West.

SO FAR WE HAVE discussed two types of communities: the "routine" life community and the "progressive" community. The former is leaderless, that is, there exists no man in that community capable of disrupting the circular flow of life by offering something new to its members, something which they have not known or tried before. A "routine" life community has its own elite and rulers, to be sure, but those people are not its leaders; their job is to preserve peace and order within the existing social framework. The "progressive" community has its true leader: the free agent. He is the man who injects into the community's life, usually at a great risk to himself, something essentially new, something which is not an outgrowth of the past. He provides his community with an energy capable of disrupting its routine life and with a *choice* between new and old forms of life.

If our concept of progress — social changes voluntarily accepted by the community — is a sound one, then we can conclude that human progress depends on the rate at which free agents are able and willing to *suggest* changes; and the number of *suggestions* must, obviously, depend on the number of the people who are given freedom to make them. It follows that the central problem of human progress is to find the social organization, or environment, most conducive for carrying out innovating actions. I submit that the environment in which each and every man is allowed to be his own exclusive agent, in which each and every man enjoys freedom from organized groups, and in which no social institu-

tions serving some specific group interests are sheltered by the community rulers, will make each and every man a potential leader (free agent).

The presence of the class of free agents in a community is likely to mean the difference between degeneration and creation, mechanical life and inspiring life. In a "routine" life community the leaderless man adjusts himself to the world. In a "progressive" community, thanks to the presence of free agents, man constantly improves the world.

In addition to the two types of communities discussed above there exists a third type which we may call the "changing" community. Consider for example what is happening today in a number of emerging countries in Africa and Asia. The idea of progress had hit the elite rulers of those communities from without long before the class of free agents emerged, thus forcing the respective elite governments to assume the role of sole innovator and to "legislate" progress by compelling the people to accept new forms and ways of life.

The trouble is, of course, that in the absence of impartial social institutions such as open-market competition and democratic elections it becomes quite difficult if not impossible to ascertain whether social changes imposed by the government have been voluntarily accepted and, thus, considered superior to the old forms of life by the community at large. Since the acceptance of social changes instituted by the government is coercive rather than voluntary it may well be that the government sponsored changes do not mean the actualization of people's potential wants and, hence, progress. While it is often argued that an important advantage of the "changing" community is that it helps its members to break away from the old forms of life, the fact remains that this type of community is promoting change rather than *progress*. Consequently, there is no reason to believe that social changes which people are *compelled* to accept represent the pattern of social development preferred by them.

The conclusion of this paper, of course, is that progress cannot be legislated from without, or suppressed altogether from

907

Page Fifteen

within, although it can be impeded. It depends on the presence of free agents, a group of people not constrained in a specific way by prevailing forms of life and who are willing to accept the risks of carrying out their vision; it accelerates when the right of each to act as his own exclusive agent is protected; it grows in the absence of social institutions promoting some specific interests; and because it depends on the community's freedom to accept or reject proposed social changes, it depends on the existence of impartial social institutions. Only those social changes which the community voluntarily accepts can be properly called progressive, and social restrictions on the non-conforming lifestyle of free agents represents as mistaken an approach to society's optimal welfare as forced adoption of changes from outside.

908

SELL NIR TO YOUR FRIENDS

The Political Thought

of Michael Oakeshott

JAY   A.   SIGLER

PROF. MICHAEL OAKESHOTT, of the London School of Economics, is widely regarded as the most articulate and influential conservative political theorist in England today. A successor to the chair of Harold J. Laski, eminent Marxist theorist, Prof. Oakeshott has dealt extensively with refining a conception of conservatism within the tradition of Edmund Burke and St. Thomas Aquinas. While resisting the creation of an orthodox conservative ideology to counteract the dominant liberal ideology, Oakeshott has sought to provide a philosophical basis for criticism of liberalism. As founder of the *Cambridge Journal,* Oakeshott sought to provide an outlet for English conservative thought. Since Prof. Oakeshott is a philosopher, historian, and critic of some note we find in his writings possibly the epitome of the best in conservative thought.

The importance of the conservatism of Prof. Oakeshott is due to his philosophical rigor and consistency. The philosophical basis for Oakeshott's conservatism is to be found in his first book, *Experience and its Modes,* written in 1933, when Oakeshott was thirty-two years old. In an effort to identify the basis of all knowledge as the totality of empirical experience taken as a coherent whole, Oakeshott insisted that only in

the coherence of experience could truth be found.[1] From this standpoint, a slice of experience, which Oakeshott calls "a mode of experience," may be considered an abstraction from reality, not reality itself.[2] The tendency to confuse the abstraction of ideology with the concrete world of experience was a fundamental error which Oakeshott sought constantly to avoid, as his later work indicates. This awareness generates his philosophic suspicion of all ideological generalizations.

Even history can provide no sure guide to political activities:

> Both the active politician and the writer on politics, both the reformer and the conservator invoke the oracle of history and interpret its answer according to their predisposition, giving out their conclusions as the lessons of history. But history itself has neither the ideas nor the language wherewith to teach practical conclusions.[3]

History itself is experience, just like the experience of the contemporary environment.[4] Abstractions drawn from it, since they describe only a portion of reality, cannot be wholly "true." Patriotism, a love of the past, is often based on a fan-

Jay A. Sigler is Assistant Professor of Political Science at Rutgers University.

---

[1] *Experience and Its Modes* (Cambridge: The University Press, 1933), p. 323.
[2] *Ibid.,* p. 327.
[3] *Ibid.,* p. 316.
[4] *Ibid.,* p. 99.

cied past, or a remembered past, rather than the historical past. It is this part, which is known as *our* past, which forms each nation's private view of history.[5] It is in that "political past" rather than the actual, historical past that Oakeshott finds the source of a nation's traditions and customs. It may not be "truth" but it may provide the best guide to future action.

Many political beliefs which appear to be coherent doctrines turn out on examination to be less than that. It may be that "the social and political beliefs of representative democracy are more in the nature of a tradition and a tendency than a well-knit doctrine."[6] Most competing contemporary ideologies are superficial and non-philosophical, enjoying in this respect no superiority over contemporary democracy. Among contemporary social theories "the Catholic social and political doctrine stands far above any of the others, for it at least has the help of a profound thinker, St. Thomas Aquinas, and is not dependent for its philosophy on some vague leaning towards a half understood and wholly confused pragmatism."[7] Oakeshott finds many of the principles of conservatism in Catholic philosophy.[8] Certainly, he feels we have much to learn from the coherence and consistency of that system.

In traditional political philosophy the search for an entire and coherent understanding of political life as an aspect of total civilization engaged the greatest thinkers. In high political philosophy mere reflection on political life is replaced by "the intellectual restoration of a unity damaged and impaired by the normal negligence of human partiality."[9] Such classical political philosophies are not now being written. Political ideology is a pale shadow of a political philosophy, an abstraction of an abstraction. In any event, the great political philosophies did not believe, as do contemporary ideologists, that political activity is a good in itself, but believed, instead, that politics "is contributory to an end which it cannot itself bring about."[10] With the disappearance of the belief in high moral ends, the scope of activity of the political thinker is diminished. Oakeshott himself plays the role of critic of ideology rather than builder of a massive system of political philosophy.

IN OUR LIFETIME the attempts to construct metaphysical systems of thought have been replaced by the construction of scientific theories. Oakeshott, although respectful of the achievements of modern science, is suspicious of attempts to transfer the methods of science to the arena of politics.[11] Yet the belief "that politics, at their best, are the science of the arrangement and improvement of human societies in accordance with certain abstract ideals" has been the main "inspiration of political activity in Western Europe for the last two hundred years."[12] Fascism, rather than being a reaction to the rational ideas of contemporary liberalism, is seen by Oakeshott as a rejection instead of far older traditional ideas of representative government, ideas which liberalism, with its project of a science of politics, also rejects.[13] This is what makes scientific politics a dangerous conception. The academic study called "political science" is also condemned by Oakeshott as unsuitable even for university undergraduates, because no such scientific understanding as yet exists.[14]

This is an age in which Oakeshott sees an almost universal speculative interest in morals and politics; but Oakeshott feels that undue interest in morals and politics is a sign of an unhealthy society. It is an age when the coherence of a universal philosophical scheme is impos-

[5] *Ibid.*, p. 103
[6] *The Social and Political Doctrines of Contemporary Europe* (Cambridge: The University Press, 1939), p. xvi.
[7] *Ibid.*
[8] *Ibid.*, pp. xix-xx.
[9] Introduction to *Leviathan*, by Thomas Hobbes (New York: Macmillan, 1947), p. x.

[10] *Ibid.*, p. lxix.
[11] "Science and Society," *Cambridge Journal*, I (July 1948), 696-97.
[12] "Scientific Politics," *Cambridge Journal*, I (March 1948), 349-50.
[13] *Ibid.*, p. 351.
[14] "The Study of Politics in a University," in *Rationalism in Politics* (New York: Basic Books, 1962), p. 329n.

sible.[15] The alleged stability of earlier ages is largely exaggerated. It may be true that other ages "possessed more reliable habits of behaviour, but a clear view of the ends of human existence has never been enjoyed except by a few rare individuals."[16]

In a scientific age such as our own, Oakeshott reminds us that the methods of science depend upon the faithfulness of the scientist "to the traditions of scientific inquiry."[17] Politics itself is a "second-rate form of human activity, neither an art nor a science."[18] The study of politics "should be an oecological study of a tradition of behaviour,"[19] not a pursuit for false hopes of human engineering or a rashly optimistic science of politics. We must be humble in the face of human variety and the fallibility of human "rationality." No political theory or ideology can grasp the whole of experience. There is no chart of politically rational theory.

In political activity, then, men set sail on a boundless and bottomless sea; there is neither harbour for shelter nor floor for anchorage, neither starting-place nor appointed destination.[20]

The concept of tradition is central to Oakeshott's approach. A "tradition of behaviour" is "a principle of continuity" which is derived from the past and extends into the future. It is not learned as an abstract idea, but is a "concrete, coherent manner of living in all its intricateness."[21] The coherence of human activity, what gives life its pattern, is inherent in the activity of living. The elements of the pattern are called "customs, traditions, laws."[22] Oakeshott goes so far as to say that "in general, constitutional tradition is a good substitute for philosophy."[23] In simpler terms, a "tradition of behaviour" is a better guide to political conduct than any theory or ideology because it is based upon the whole of life, rather than upon some abstraction derived from life. Experience is a more trustworthy guide than any book, but "even in the most favourable circumstances," it may take "two or three generations to acquire" the political traditions of a society.[24]

AN IDEOLOGY, FOR Oakeshott, is an abridgement of a tradition. The conversion of a "habit of behaviour" into a comparatively rigid system of abstract ideas creates a "politics of destruction and creation" as a substitute for "the politics of repair."[25] It is of the essential character of an ideology that it presents itself as knowledge. However, ideology "by itself is always an insufficient guide" because political fact, actual experience, must always precede political activity.[26] Ideology, then, is always false knowledge because it is an abstraction of reality, even at its best. Oakeshott finds himself opposed to ideology in any form, including conservative ideology. It is the distinguishing feature of Oakeshott's variety of conservatism that he sees the opposition of conservatism and liberalism as one of contrary claims to knowledge. This peculiar feature of Oakeshott's conservatism is that it attempts to make the lack of a specific program or doctrine a merit rather than a shortcoming. The conservative is one who is sceptical "about the possibility of . . . perfection," one who is determined "not to allow human life to be perverted by the tyranny of a person or fixed by the tyranny of an idea."[27]

Oakeshott identifies the source of ideological infection as the development of what he calls "modern Rationalism." The rationalist stands for independence

911

[15] "The Universities," *Cambridge Journal*, II (May 1949), 530.
[16] *Ibid.*, p. 520.
[17] "Rational Conduct," in *Rationalism in Politics*, p. 103.
[18] Introduction to *Leviathan*, by Thomas Hobbes, p. **lxiv.**
[19] "Political Education," in Peter Laslett, ed., *Philosophy, Politics and Society* (New York: Macmillan, 1956), p. 19.
[20] *Ibid.*, p. 15.
[21] *Ibid.*, p. 17.
[22] "Rational Conduct," *op. cit.*, p. 105.

[23] "Contemporary British Politics," *Cambridge Journal*, I (May 1948), 475-76.
[24] "Rationalism in Politics," in *Rationalism in Politics*, p. 30.
[25] *Ibid.*, p. 21.
[26] "Political Education," *op. cit.*, p. 9.
[27] "Scientific Politics," *op. cit.*, p. 357.

912

of mind on all subjects at all times, irrespective of tradition or authority. Confident of his capacity for "reason" the rationalist "has no sense of the cumulation of experience"[28] and optimistically pursues the "politics of perfection" heedless of the limits of unaided reason and regardless of the disturbances and injuries he may cause. The philosophy of John Locke, of Bentham, and Godwin encouraged this faith which has resulted in the mixed blessings represented by the ideas of "open diplomacy, the planned society, federalism, nationalism, votes for women, the world state and the destruction of the Austro-Hungarian Empire."[29] The flaw in the rationalist theory is the assumption of the existence of a mistake-proof apparatus called a "mind" which is an independent instrument made capable of dealing with experience by means of externally imposed educational training.[30] Brushing aside accumulated customs and habits, the rationalist romantically assumes that each generation begins with a fresh political and social slate. The existence of a mentally discoverable "natural law" is a typical rationalist error, and is rejected by Oakeshott."[31]

Against the charge that the rejection of rationalism creates an irrational position, Oakeshott replies that rationalism itself is not a "rational" doctrine and that the definition of "rational" behavior includes more than the rationalists admit. Oakeshott defines "rational" conduct as "faithfulness to the knowledge we have of how to conduct the specific activity we are engaged in," and "acting in such a way that the coherence of the idiom of activity to which the conduct belongs is preserved and possibly enhanced."[32]

Scientific activity is "rational" to the extent to which it follows its own traditions of procedure. Political activity is "rational" to the extent that the politician proceeds in accordance with the customs and traditions of the nation.

Nations are "hereditary, co-operative groups, many of them of ancient lineage" which enjoy a past, a present and a future.[33] Democracy and other ideologies are not subject to export because they are not formal belief systems but are contained within the tradition of a nation. Politics, then, becomes a "pursuit of intimations,"[34] a present conversation with the past on behalf of the future.

THE BUSINESS OF THE politician is to prevent the concentration of power in a society and to break up all concentrations of power which have the appearance of becoming dangerous.[35] Thus Oakeshott is strongly in favor of antimonopoly legislation, although also a friend of the institution of private property. He defends private property as the surest bulwark for personal liberty; but the maximum diffusion of the power which springs from ownership is the proven source of liberty. Massive corporate businesses or massive labor organizations both threaten liberty by imposing limitations upon the prerogatives of individual behavior. The possession of private property permits a man to choose among groups and to move freely within society; and a freely competing economic system is the essence of personal freedom.[36]

Collectivism is the enemy of freedom, but it may be found in many guises. Collectivism and freedom are the real alternatives. The collectivist rejects the idea

---

[28] "Rationalism in Politics," op. cit., p. 2
[29] Ibid., p. 6.
[30] "Rational Conduct," op. cit., pp. 85-87.
[31] "Science and Society," op. cit., p. 696. He also rejects the concept of natural rights in "Rationalism in Politics," op. cit., p. 27n.
[32] "Rational Conduct," op. cit., pp. 101-2. As Oakeshott states: ". . . it is important that a writer who wishes to contest the excessive claims of 'Rationalism' should observe the difference [between rational inquiry and 'rationalism'] because if he fails to do so he will not only be liable to self-contradiction . . . but also he will make himself appear the advocate of irration-

ality, which is going further than he either needs or intends to go." "Scientific Politics," op. cit., p. 349.
[33] "Political Education," op. cit., p. 2.
[34] Ibid., p. 13.
[35] "Contemporary British Politics," op. cit., p. 486.
[36] "The Political Economy of Freedom," in Rationalism in Politics, pp. 46-48. In certain cases Oakeshott entertains the idea that government monopoly might be preferable to American-style private radio and television. "The B.B.C.," Cambridge Journal, IV (June 1951), 553-54.

of the diffusion of power and insists upon the necessity of central direction. The creation of great unified power is necessary to this end and ultimately a collectivist government must enforce its imposed order at the price of liberty.[37] The collectivist fails to understand the "poetic character of all human activity" and the ultimate result of such a society is that "everybody (with the partial exception of the planners themselves) is deprived of so much freedom that the regime would at once be recognized as a tyranny" if we were not deluded into thinking that we had exchanged a new freedom for our lost freedom.[38]

The word "conservative" itself is really a description of an emotional disposition more than a creed or doctrine. It signifies a preference for the familiar to the unknown, experience to the experimental, an acceptance of the need of change within the framework of accepted rules and practices. The conservative, who is a reluctant innovator, believes that the role of government is limited to keeping the peace, rather than including the power to impose choices. He believes this because he is suspicious of any claims to political expertise, and aware of the essentially selfish pursuit of happiness. Yet a man could be radical in all other respects while being conservative in his politics. The conservative accepts the world and people as they are, with all their flaws and imperfections.[39] Ultimately, Oakeshott is in agreement with Hobbes, whom he greatly admires, in that:

> Here in civil society is neither fulfillment nor wisdom to discern fulfillment, but peace . . . the only thing in human life, on Hobbes's theory, that can be permanently established.[40]

SOME HAVE SAID OF Oakeshott that his ideas are unoriginal, but it may be, as Bernard Crick suggests, that Oakeshott has written "two or three of the subtlest political essays of the century."[41] Another critic claims that Oakeshott has assumed the posture of anti-politics, of one who is bored with politics and politicians.[42] Regardless of the final appraisal, it still seems true, as Russell Kirk insists, that Oakeshott's essays reveal the low estate of American conservatism.[43] It is this author's contention that a thorough reading of Oakeshott's writings reveals a consistent philosophical approach to modern conservatism, a consistency lacking in American conservatism, as it is in most contemporary political thought.

If Oakeshott is extremely historical, this is not inappropriate for a conservative.[44] If Oakeshott is deeply concerned with the dangers of planning, this too, is consistent with the mainstream of modern conservatism.[45] It is true, as Peter Viereck insists, that American conservatism lacks a long tradition rooted in feudalism;[46] but that does not necessarily disprove Oakeshott's contention that all societies have traditions which are guides to present action. Neither is it a fair criticism to suggest that a conservative position need be doctrinaire, or contain particular programs or actions.[47]

913

---

[37] "The Political Economy of Freedom," op. cit., p. 51.

[38] "Contemporary British Politics," op. cit., p. 484. War is considered by Oakeshott to be the enemy of freedom because it encourages that artificial unity which is the aim of the collectivist planner. "The Universities," op. cit., p. 525.

[39] "On Being Conservative," in Rationalism in Politics, pp. 168-96.

[40] Introduction to Leviathan, by Thomas Hobbes, p. lxvi.

[41] "The World of Michael Oakeshott," Review of Rationalism in Politics, Encounter, XX, No. 6 (June 1963), 65.

[42] David Marquand, "Floating," Review of Rationalism in Politics, New Statesman, LXIV (October 26, 1962), 574.

[43] Review of Rationalism in Politics, American Academy of Political and Social Science, Annals, CCCXLVII (May 1963), 181.

[44] "In the demonstration of the validity of ideas history had been, in truth, one of the great weapons of the conservative. From history one may derive a behaviorial criticism of both revolution and reform." F. G. Wilson, "The Anatomy of Conservatives," Ethics, LXX (July 1960), 276.

[45] "But the conservative concern, always the same, has been consistently with the 'planners,' the thinkers of abstract schemes, the know-better innovations of the politically unresponsive intellectuals." Gerhart Niemayer, Review of Conservatism in America, by Clinton Rossiter, Journal of Public Law, IV (Fall 1955), 443.

[46] Peter Viereck, Conservatism Revisited (Rev. ed.; New York: The Free Press, 1962), p. 143.

[47] See Willmoore Kendall, The Conservative Affirmation (Chicago: Henry Regnery Co., 1963).

The achievement of Prof. Oakeshott has been to provide a contemporary restatement of the essence of conservatism, based on a consistently maintained philosophical position. In doing so, Oakeshott borrows from many preceding conservative thinkers, composing an amalgam of his own. Although rejecting, with Burke, Hobbes's attempt to create a scientific politics,[48] Prof. Oakeshott is close to accepting Hobbes's view of human nature. Although discarding the idea of natural rights, Oakeshott retains a deep admiration for Aquinas, from whom Oakeshott draws some of his own views regarding the proper role of government.[49]

Oakeshott admittedly builds on the work of Henry Simons in his essay on private property,[50] but he goes beyond Simons to provide a logical defense of private property as a necessary part of individual freedom. Oakeshott is not merely echoing Burke's famous statement: "The individual is foolish . . . but the species is wise,"[51] when he rests his case against rationalism by citing the "tradition of behavior." He is trying, instead, to counteract the abstractions of rationalist innovators with the concrete facts of everyday and historical experience. It is Oakeshott's aim to indicate the method of political knowledge and by his success in achieving that goal he must be judged.

---

[48] Edmund Burke, *Burke's Politics,* ed. by R.J.S. Hoffman and P. Levack (New York: Alfred A. Knopf, 1949), p. 228.

[49] St. Thomas maintains that it is the function of the political ruler merely to maintain peace and order by seeing to it that all the services of public administration and defense are performed, thus removing all impediments to the good life. See G. H. Sabine, *A History of Political Theory* (New York: Henry Holt, 1950), p. 250.

[50] *Economic Policy for a Free Society* (Chicago: University of Chicago Press, 1948).

[51] Burke, *op. cit.,* p. 227.

Two Decades of Economic Planning in Yugoslavia

LJUBO   SIRC

DURING THE SECOND World War, the Yugoslav Communists were so certain of being in possession of the absolute truth that they did not hesitate to jockey for power from the very beginning of the struggle against the occupying German and Italian armies. Thus in Slovenia, they issued a decree, at the end of 1941, to the effect that anybody fighting the enemy outside the Communist dominated Liberation Front would be considered a traitor and liquidated. Many a non-Communist resistant was driven into collaboration by the resulting pressure.

Simultaneously the Communists, whose number was twelve thousand at the beginning of hostilities, persistently denied any intention of introducing "social changes" after the war and kept promising free elections and everything that goes with them. Yugoslavia being a country of small landowners, the main field for recruitment of the partisan detachments was the peasantry, which made it expedient for the Communists to underline the advantages individual peasants would obtain should the Communist rule be established. They promised the peasants more land, although nobody knew where more land was to

Ljubo Sirc is Reader in Economics at the University of Glasgow, and a native of Yugoslavia. He is author of a study in economic planning for the Institute of Economic Affairs, London.

come from, as the entire arable area was under cultivation and the share of big estates was negligible. The Communist flirtation with the peasants led some foreign observers into believing that they were agrarian revolutionaries.

In order to obtain Allied recognition, Tito, who had emerged as the leader of the National Liberation movement, concluded an agreement with the exiled Yugoslav government in London after repeated interventions by the leading Allied personalities on both sides. This agreement guaranteed all sorts of democratic liberties for the population, politicians, and the democratic parties. Yet when the war was over, Yugoslavia found itself firmly under the control of the Liberation Army, officered mainly by Communists, and of the political police, an exclusively Communist domain. The letter of the agreement with the London Government may have been sometimes abided by, but the spirit certainly never was.

During 1945 and 1946 hardly any reforms were introduced; the time was spent on tracking down "collaborators" and bringing them to justice, but the definition of "collaboration" was so wide that practically anybody, patriot or no patriot, whom the Communists did not like could be fitted in. If somebody could not, there was always the possibility of trumped up charges.

915

Page Twenty-three

In addition, many people were killed without any trial at all. Although the Nazi rule in Yugoslavia was extremely ruthless, the Germans are quite right in pointing out that a large part of the over 1.5 million Yugoslav war victims were due to internal strife; and a substantial number of these were liquidated by the Communists, sometimes for good reason, sometimes only in preparation for the final take-over. The massacre continued after the war when some 300,000 people were done away with; the prisons overflowed and many people, mainly members of the German minority in Yugoslavia, were driven over the border to Austria. There was sufficient horror around to terrorize the population into silent submission.

A person must be utterly convinced of the correctness of his cause to take upon himself this destruction of human life and this infliction of suffering to establish himself firmly in the saddle. Even if one accepts the possibility of such firm conviction—and many Communists must have been convinced that they were up to something remarkable—there is still something pathological about it.

In the eyes of the Yugoslav Communists, Stalin was the depository of all wisdom and knowledge of how to abolish all evils and human failings. They had some difficulties with him, but this was because the Yugoslavs were too zealous to tolerate Stalin's cautiousness. His aim was to make the Western Allies believe that he had turned into a Russian nationalist, and then to take them by surprise when they least expected it. Stalin was afraid that the Yugoslavs would spoil his game by their zeal and even advised them to pose as monarchists.

The obvious thing for the Yugoslav admirers of Stalin to do was to take a leaf out of the Soviet book, which they did. In the spring of 1947, they produced a Five Year Plan which was closely modeled on the Soviet plan, although the two countries could hardly be more different than they are. The Soviet Union possesses a vast territory and has a population at least ten times larger than Yugoslavia. The traditional economic freedom of peasants in Yugoslavia goes partly back to the Austrian Emperor

Joseph II in the second half of the eighteenth century, and in other parts to the liberation from the Turks, while in Russia the feudal relations lingered almost into the twentieth century. The individual character of Yugoslav agriculture was further strengthened by a land reform after the first World War.

In spite of these substantial differences between the two countries, the Yugoslav Communists applied the Soviet methods of economic development, possibly pushing them to the extreme, so that the French Professor Marczewski went on record as remarking on the planned rate of growth of the Yugoslav national income:

> In fact, in the long term the average rate of growth proposed for the national income seems impossible to achieve. Until now the highest rates of growth in the economic history of the world have never surpassed 8 per cent. . . . It is impossible to explain these figures except by the complete lack of experience of the Yugoslav planners who appear to have copied Soviet rates without understanding what they really meant.[1]

THE SYSTEM TAKEN over from the Soviets tended to rigidity and uniformity because it did not know any of the economic and accounting calculations which help the enterpreneur at least approximately adjust to circumstances and thus contribute to the maximization of welfare. Yugoslav planning was based on a few very simple tenets.

The central principle was, naturally, the abolition of private property, from which according to Marx every evil stems. His reason for this is the theory of surplus value, the part of the product allotted to capital owners. Following the labor theory of value, all charges for the use of producer goods were disregarded except for a purely nominal interest rate on short-term bank credits.

The only criterion used for the allocation of capital and other resources was the teaching of Marxist dialectical ma-

---

[1] J. Marczewski, *Planification et Croissance economique des democraties populaires* (Paris: Presses Universitaires, 1956), p. 134.

terialism that the means of production determine productive relations, which means the social system. Their conclusion was that the most modern equipment should be used, because this would help the introduction of "socialism" as a stage on the way to full "communism." The choice of technique was not adapted to circumstances, and, as in the Soviet Union, it was thought and planned that manufacturing had to prevail over other branches of the economy, particularly agriculture; within manufacturing industry by far the greatest stress had to be on the production of producer goods and power; and within this framework the leading link was machine building. Even the disparaged market indicators were harnessed in the interest of this policy. The fixed prices of raw materials and capital goods were kept very low, and the prices of consumer goods very high. Yet since no distortion of prices could make possible a shift in the direction of the economy exactly as desired by the Communists, the market forces were considered as "anarchy" fed by "spontaneity," and soon completely disregarded and replaced by planning — the "conscious direction of extended reproduction." At the same time, the fact that people value present things more than future things, that food today is more important than a television set ten years hence, was neglected, which led to the adoption of a practically unlimited planning horizon, to the idea that even the most important present needs can be sacrificed to the "luminous future."

The collective satisfaction of needs was considered much preferable to individual consumption, so that most "distribution" tended to be organized by the state. Distribution, however, was considered "non-productive" anyway and neglected, so that often even available goods did not reach the public.

Before this system copied from the Soviet Union could get underway, Stalin found that Tito had become too big for his shoes and decided to cut him down to size. In a way, the Yugoslav Communists were more Stalinist than Stalin and several times tried to jump the gun, act in advance of the time table carefully worked out by Stalin to take the West by surprise and gain full control of Eastern Europe. Stalin thought that this would not do and was in addition jealous of Tito, who succeeded in making a name for himself in Yugoslavia and in the world, so he did not entirely depend on Stalin's reflected glory. Soon there was a complete rift with which ideology had very little if anything to do.

One of the proofs for this explanation is that the first reaction of the Yugoslavs was an attempt to prove that they were good Communists. They clamped down on their bourgeoisie and dragged more people to prison and administrative forced labor camps. A fully fledged collectivization campaign was started and agriculture utterly disrupted. When it proved that it was impossible to fulfill the Five Year Plan of 1947, the priorities provided for in this Plan were brought into play, carrying further the initial lopsidedness. Inessential investment, i.e., investment in consumer goods production was dropped, and the concentration on heavy industry stepped up. To make things worse, even depreciation was not used for the replacement of worn-out equipment, but was channelled into new industries, so that many branches, especially agriculture, textiles, and housing, suffered from disinvestment. In other words, the branches most essential for supplying the population with necessities were run down in order to provide means for the completion of the Giants of the Five Year Plan. Table I shows the intended and the actual structure of "productive" investment.

Thus many more resources were concentrated on manufacturing industry in the period 1950-56 than originally planned, although the first Five Year Plan was underfulfilled in all other respects. In fact, it had to be extended for another year, to 1952, and from then economic activity was carried on until the end of 1956 on the basis of provisional one-year plans — due to the fact that the entire basis of planning began to be questioned. Nevertheless, the belief that the concentration on "key projects" would solve all problems persisted in spite of all the other changes described below. From 1947 until 1956, the investment in "basic" industries (iron and non-

917

ferrous metallurgy, machine tools, ship-building, electrical appliances, and construction materials) amounted to 51.2 per cent of industrial investment and reached its peak in 1952 with 57.3 per cent. To this 31 per cent invested in power production has to be added.

A change came about only in 1957, when the second Five Year Plan was introduced with the aim of "eliminating the disproportions [shortages and bottle-necks] arising from the policy of industrialization and forced expansion of

cal targets, laid down in detail by the centralized plan, led to a much worse confusion and anarchy than had ever been seen under the working of spontaneous market forces. The search started for simplified indicators which would make the functioning of the factories coherent and would also give some scope for the workers' administration. Marxism, however, proved a tremendous stumbling block in this respect. The wish was to introduce some kind of "automatism," or invisible hand, by which well

918

TABLE 1

ALLOCATION OF TOTAL INVESTMENT

Period	Industry	Agriculture	Forrestry	Construction	Transport	Trade
1947/49	50.3	8.4	3.2	3.7	28.9	4.9
1950/52	64.3	5.6	1.2	3.7	22.4	2.4
1953/56	58.7	6.4	1.7	3.3	23.7	4.9
1957/59	43.3	17.3	1.7	3.6	26.1	8.5
1960/62	50.9	14.3	1.8	3.3	21.2	8.7
1963/65	54.4	12.6	1.9	3.5	17.6	9.0
Plan for 1947/51	51.8	8.6	1.6	1.6	31.0	3.5

heavy industry."[2] In this period the concentration of investment in industry was reduced to just over 40 per cent, of which only 31 per cent went into "basic" branches.

WHEN THE YUGOSLAV Communists finally admitted in 1950 that Stalin was directly involved here, and not some obscure Soviet officials who misinformed Stalin about the real state of affairs in Yugoslavia, they also embarked on the first deviation from the Soviet orthodoxy. They abandoned—at least in theory — the principle of *"odinanachalie,"* of the absolute control by the government appointed factory manager, and introduced workers' councils.

Yet they also began to realize that the running of factories according to physi-

managed factories would be rewarded and badly managed works punished. It became obvious that it did matter how much capital was used by an enterprise and that therefore there had to be some kind of charge on the use of capital; but this could not be the interest rate, because it was deemed to be un-Marxist.

Ten years later, the same problem arose in the Soviet Union, when Liberman's proposals to introduce a profit rate were aired. From many quarters they were assailed and it was claimed[3] that in a Marxist country there could be no serious consideration of using a percentage charge on capital—profit rate —but that a percentage charge on wages fund—a "surplus" rate—was the only possible solution. Such a surplus rate was introduced in Yugoslavia in 1952 under the name of "the rate of accumulation."

---

2 Savka Dabcevic-Kucar, "Decentralized Socialist Planning: Yugoslavia," in Hagen, ed., *Planning Economic Development* (Homewood, Ill.: Irwin, 1965).

3 E.g., A. Bachurin and A. Pervukhin, "K voprosu o pribyli pri socialisme," ["On the Question of Profits in Socialism"], *Voprosy ekonomiki,* September 1963.

This rate not surprisingly proved to be unworkable and was replaced after a year of confusion, in 1954, by the interest rate. Thus the first of the basic Marxist principles which should have brought Yugoslavia unprecedented prosperity went overboard, under the impact of the requirements of economic efficiency. Of course, the interest rate did not and still does not work properly in Yugoslavia, but the need for a scarcity charge on capital was at least recognized.

The introduction of the "automatism" also called for commodity prices based on supply and demand, but those in charge still believed that manipulated prices could influence actual economic relations in desired directions, and therefore decided to keep the prices of raw materials and agricultural goods down. In fact the agricultural prices were so low that they depressed the real earnings of peasants from sales of their produce in 1952 on average to 42 per cent of their pre-war earnings. On top of this, there came very high direct taxes.

The passive resistance of the peasants, however, forced the Communists to stop their campaign for agricultural collectivization by direct and indirect pressure, initiated in 1948, and to allow them to pull out of government-sponsored cooperatives, which they almost all did. For a few years the peasants were left alone, which led to a considerable improvement in agricultural production as compared with the disastrous year 1952, when agricultural production was lower by about one-third than in the late 1930's.

After the introduction of interest rates, the intention was to allocate the capital to those offering the highest return at capital auctions, but this soon proved unacceptable. The expected return on capital invested in heavy industries was so low that investment into these branches would remain well under that desired by the government. Therefore, auctions between industries were abandoned and limited to auctions within the same branch, while the allocation between branches was according to the provisional yearly plans, and later to the Five Year 1957-61 Plan which however provided, as mentioned, for a much more sensible distribution between consumer goods and producer goods and thus led to a considerable increase in consumption from the very low level of 1952, when consumption, total and per capita, might have been down by as much as one-third of the pre-war consumption. In fact, during this relaxation in 1957-58, total consumption probably caught up with what it was before the war.

But while consumption improved, the key projects worked at low capacities, which made the Communists think that there must be something wrong even with the very halfhearted application of market indicators. Since they could no longer make up their minds to scrap the market altogether, they found the ingenious solution that the market was all right for day to day decisions, but "the fundamental economic development could not be spontaneous, but had to be based on the conscious social process of reproduction by planned direction." And the third Five Year Plan of 1961-65 was designed for "further accelerated economic expansion on the basis of a more balanced growth."

As a result fixed investment in basic industries, which was reduced to 13 per cent of "productive investment" in 1958 from 37 per cent in 1952, went up again to 29 per cent in 1961-62. Total fixed industrial investment jumped from 42 in 1959 to 52 in 1961 at the expense of agricultural investment, down from 21 per cent in 1959 to 15 per cent in 1961, and investment in transport, down from 24 per cent in 1959 (28 in 1957) to 16 per cent in 1962 (17 in 1963).

THIS REVERSAL TO Marxist-Leninist investment policy resulted in the economic crises of 1962 and 1965, marked by stepped up production of unsaleable goods, increase in foreign debt, and inflation. One is entitled to wonder how it was possible to revert to the old pattern of investment in spite of the fact that market forces had made themselves increasingly felt since 1952. The answer is that investment allocation remained concentrated in the hands of various federal and other investment funds (in 1964, 68 per cent of total fixed investment) which obeyed Plans and political

919

criteria instead of economic indicators, and that the rest was mainly re-investment. In addition, old habits were at work — anything metallic was still considered to bring prestige—and the interest rates were still pegged too low, particularly in view of the inflation, to force investors to be selective and choose the most efficient projects.

The result of these attempts in the 1960's for achieving accelerated growth by renewed concentration on equipment production led to more increases in inventories (see Table 2) and to the establishment of more capacities never to be used.

Such wasteful factories would have to go out of business if their inventory keeping were not financed by a constant flow of bank credit. This credit cannot be repaid, of course, because the inventories are never sold, which all leads to inflation (taking the form of considerable increases in money supply if not always of rising prices, since these are largely controlled and were completely frozen in the spring of 1965). From 1956 to 1964, the volume of production (including waste) rose 2.2 times and the money supply 4.7 times, from 553 billion to 2,577 billion dinars, to which another 1344 billion dinars have to be added, al-

TABLE 2

INVENTORY INCREASES AND RATES OF GROWTH

Year	Inventory Increases (percentage of national income)	Annual rates of growth	
		Industrial Production	Capital Goods Production
1958	9.0	11.0	13.0
1959	11.1	13.0	17.0
1960	11.0	15.0	20.0
1961	8.8	7.0	4.0
1962	6.3	7.0	1.0
1963	8.9	16.0	15.0
1964	13.0	16.0	19.0
1965	14.6	8.0	N.A.

The figures on inventory increases in Table 2 are from the OECD report on Yugoslavia in 1965, with the exception of the figures for 1964 and 1965 which come from official Yugoslav abstracts which in 1964 admitted, for the first time, a substantial "difference" defined as "a result of opposite fluctuations [including changes in prices, customs duties, inventories, period delimitations, statistical coverage, etc.]." Clearly, "inventories" tucked away amongst other items account for the predominant part of this "difference." There are no corresponding figures for new capacities established but never used, but it is allowable to estimate that in the years of higher growth of industrial production about one-third of this production will never satisfy any human needs at all. (In 1965 "increases in stocks" was finally introduced as a separate item in the national income accounts.)

though the enterprises, public bodies, and individuals holding them are restricted in their use. As a consequence, the purchasing power of the dinar in terms of living costs was reduced to 3.8 per cent of its pre-war purchasing power, although the normal pre-war circulation of banknotes (6 billion dinars) was restored in 1945.

The OECD report of 1965 advocated an incomes policy for Yugoslavia because the OECD experts believed they had traced the origin of Yugoslav inflation primarily to incomes and not to the financing of increasing stocks of unusable products. Yet, in spite of more freedom for profit distribution, if any is made, within the enterprise it is hard to believe that the Communist League had so lost its grip over the workers administration that they could not stop any unwarranted increase in incomes. On the other hand, there would often be no money to distribute, were the banks not prepared to finance increasing stocks of inventories. The OECD also stressed that there was no deficit budgeting on current account; but deficit budgeting on capital account is no better, especially in Yugoslavia where investment frequently produces no fruit at all.

As a result of this strange kind of economic development, Yugoslavia kept sucking in large quantities of foreign resources, which had to tide her over bottlenecks in the heavy industries, production of primary goods, and food production. From 1952 to 1962 it had been receiving American aid to the tune of about $100 million a year. Besides, it contracted foreign debts amounting to $800 to $1000 million by 1962 and to $1400 million by 1965. For obvious reasons this could not continue forever. For this reason, the dinar was devalued from 50 to 300 dinars to the dollar in 1952, to 750 in 1962, and to 1250 in 1965. Because of various duties and subsidies and of tying imports to exports, these moves in the exchange rate do not influence foreign trade directly; but they are a reflection of the dinar's loss of purchasing power.

Another lapse back from the more liberal policies of the mid-1950's was an attempt to win the fight against private peasants by starving them of any investment, which began to be concentrated on the 15 per cent of the agricultural area owned by "social estates." The only result here was that the law of diminishing returns set in, and the products of the "estates" cost twice as much as the products of private peasants. Furthermore, the "estates" worked at losses in spite of various bonuses paid to them.

THE CRISIS INTO which the Yugoslav economy ran in 1962 and again in 1965 posed once more the classic question of the proper economic role of planning and the market. The crisis of 1962 was so clearly engineered by the Plan providing for high investment in "basic" industries that President Tito called for "better planning." There was even talk about scrapping the Plan altogether, which did not happen, but the confidence in the Plan fell so much that it was no longer considered a particularly useful guide for anybody.

Waterston described the equivocal situation in 1962:

> . . . the federal plan no longer lays down production quotas for enterprises. This does not mean, however, contend the planners that the federal plan has become only a hypothesis of the future development of the economy, for the overall targets of the economy as shown in the federal plan, are still legally binding. Nevertheless, the practical significance of this position is hard to understand, since no person or enterprise is held legally accountable for fulfilling any target of the federal plans.[4]

The reforms as envisaged after the 1962 crisis were not carried through because the Communists shrank back from laying large portions of industry idle and relaxing more controls. The result was another crisis in 1965, which shook the planning even further.

The European Economic Commission Report on Planning published in 1965 says—obviously on the basis of a Yugoslav official submission—that, in Yugoslavia, the enterprises enjoy:

> complete independence of a c t i o n [and that they] use plans as indications of expected changes in demand . . . in so far as they prove to be correct forecasts of the market situation—though they can follow their own market research if they consider that to be more accurate."[5]

This is apparently the end of all claims that plans possess extraordinary virtues. It is intended now to drop annual plans altogether and to decentralize investment in the hands of enterprises. A new midterm plan is being worked out, but there are already voices which warn against "planning burdened with high growth rates."[6] In 1962 an official spokesman thought that it was better "doing less but doing it better."

921

---

[4] A Waterson, *Planning in Yugoslavia* (Baltimore: The Economic Development Institute, IBRD, 1962), p. 39.

[5] United Nations, Economic Commission for Europe, *Economic Survey of Europe in 1962* (Geneva, 1962), part 2, *Economic Planning in Europe*.

[6] *Ekonomski politika*, March 5, 1966.

One of the goals the Communists set out to accomplish was the equalization of the economic development of various Yugoslav regions, which were and continue to be very differently developed. Slovenia has almost three times the national income per capita of Macedonia, Bosnia, or Montenegro (see Table 3).

TABLE 3

NATIONAL INCOME BY REGION

Region	Nat'l Income per capita	Average Wages
Serbia.	90	93
Croatia.	120	104
Slovenia	195	130
Bosnia-Herz. . .	71	94
Macedonia. . . .	69	86
Montenegro . . .	73	91

(Average wage-level nationwide = 100)

The equalization should have been brought about by considerable transfers of accumulated capital from some regions to others. Table 4 is an indication of what was happening.

The table shows that in spite of the substantial shifts of capital from more developed regions to less developed, there was hardly any change in the shares of various regions in the social product. This is understandable, since production does not depend only — or even foremostly — on the availability of capital. Substantial parts of the national income of Slovenia and of the more developed parts of Croatia and Serbia were withdrawn and allotted to less developed Southeastern regions. There was hardly any proportionate economic progress in the subsidized regions, however, which increased the resentment in the parts of the country which had to supply the subsidies. There is talk now of reducing the transfers to only 2 or 3 per cent of the national income.[7]

Such large-scale transfers of resources are possible only under a regime which controls — through various budgets and funds—about one half of the national income. Under normal circumstances there would be transfers from region to region —although much smaller—in the form of private investment which would remain the property of people from the transfering region and would be more properly managed.

The yearly rate of growth of the total Yugoslav national income from 1947 to 1962 was 6.6 per cent, and of the national income per capita 5.4 per cent. This is less than in the cases of Greece, Italy, and Western Germany, but the picture becomes worse if it is taken into account that in these countries personal consumption rose in step with the national income, while in Yugoslavia it was badly lagging behind. Before the war, in Yugoslavia at least 75 per cent of the national income was consumed; after the war the personal consumption (including social insurance benefits) fell to 50 per cent of the national income: from 1947 to 1962 total output increased by 132 per cent over the pre-war level, but consumption by only about 66 per cent. This gives a compound annual rate of the growth in total consumption of 3.4 per cent and of the consumption per capita of 2.2 per cent.

This is particularly bad in view of the enormous efforts: Investment regularly amounted to about 30 per cent of the national income. However, the capital-output ratio was very bad for a country at the Yugoslav stage of development, amounting to 6.5/1 for the period 1948-1964. In 1948-1952 it was 10/1, then it fell to 3/1 in the comparatively relaxed period from 1956-1960, but again climbed to 8/1 in the subsequent period up to 1964, when a new Marxist-Leninist investment drive was started. The Communists themselves admit this to be very bad and discuss the possibility of a capital-output ratio of 2.5/1 in the future.

The welfare of the Yugoslav population was sacrificed to investment and to government expenditure which very often did not contribute to welfare at all, but was used for public ostentation. The investment was in branches of industry for which the Yugoslav market is too small, for which there are not enough raw materials and other cooperating factors, and which produce at cost

---

[7] *The Times* (London), June 14, 1966.

far above the world market price.[8] Thus many of the new industries work at low capacities (e.g., machine tools at below 60 per cent) although they turn out unsaleable goods (according to the Vice-Chairman of the central government, Gligorov, the value of inventories in 1967 was about 80 per cent of the national income, while 20 to 30 per cent is more consistent with experience in market economies. It cannot even be hoped that these new branches will contribute to the welfare of the population later on. They are obsolete and badly organized.

WHAT WAS WRONG? The Communist economic ideology, as explained at the beginning of this article, led the Yugoslav government to embark on

missed. About 10 per cent of the industrial labor force was unemployed, and about as many had to leave to work abroad. This latter development was particularly grave for Communists who had always represented migration as a consequence of capitalist incompetence.

The most advanced and capital-intensive techniques were used, while there was a shortage of capital and highly skilled labor and unskilled labor was available in abundance. Thus the equipment produced is even today so expensive that it is often cheaper to do things by hand, not to speak of the cheapness of imported equipment.

There is such a discrepancy between supply and demand, particularly of producer goods, that the economy can only run at tolerable utilization of capacity if large-scale investment continues to be

923

TABLE 4

REGIONAL PRODUCTION AND CAPITAL TRANSFERS

Region	Percentage of Fixed Capital		Percentage of Nat'l Income	
	1947	1960	1947	1960
Serbia.	31.5	36.3	42.8	38.0
Croatia.	(58.2)	(41.7)	26.0	26.0
Slovenia			14.2	15.7
Bosnia-Herz.	6.1	15.8	11.5	13.4
Macedonia.	3.4	4.1	5.0	5.0
Montenegro	0.8	2.1	1.2	1.4

large-scale investment in branches of industry for which there was not sufficient management talent or technical skill. The Yugoslav technicians managed to produce complicated machinery, but not at a cost comparable with costs in other countries.

The production of some kinds of machines was pushed at full speed, while other machines needed in conjunction with them or raw materials and intermediate products were disregarded because they were technically less glamorous. Large numbers of unskilled workers were available, but the investment was not adapted to them. When streamlining began, numerous workers had to be dis-

carried through, to the obvious danger of more capacity being created which it will be difficult to utilize. This circular investment has been indulged in until now; but at present the futility of this practice seems to be fully realized, because it has become clear that the capital structure of productive capacity is completely divorced from both the derived demand for producer goods and the final demand for consumer goods. Very large quantities of resources are used, but this results in very little welfare.

In many ways it is much easier to start from scratch than to put right a structure completely distorted by investment which bears no relation to actual demand. To make matters worse, the system has for such a long time favored passive obedience that it is now

[8] See Karlo Buhman, "Industry in the New Economic Conditions," *Review of International Affairs* (Belgrade), October 5, 1965.

very difficult to change the attitudes of the population and prod people into being resourceful and prepared to take responsibility. The will of the Yugoslav population to work and to show initiative was also shattered by the fact that personal incomes and personal consumption were exceedingly low when compared with the efforts which were demanded from them, particularly when the resulting public and investment funds seemed clearly to be largely wasted.

The Communist government has come to realize this and now says that increased personal incomes and personal consumption are a sine qua non for further increases in production; but this is very difficult to achieve when the economy is as distorted as all Communist economies are. When Malenkov tried to step up consumer goods production in the Soviet Union in 1954, this proved impossible because of the lack of raw materials and appropriate machinery.[9] There, as in Yugoslavia, the development of heavy industry proved to bear no relation to the actual needs of the country and to be largely *l'art pour l'art.*"

THE YUGOSLAV REFORM in 1965 should have remedied this situation by substantially cutting down on investment and by sharply reducing government expenditure. This was easier said than done, because it meant a further reduction in the already low utilization of heavy industry capacities, the laying idle of many prestige works, and the dismissal of large numbers of workers. These workers should in fact have been made available for the production of badly needed consumer goods, but who was to organize their production and where were the equipment and raw materials to come from? The planners had not kept in mind in the previous decades that machine tool manufacture has ultimately to provide specific machines for specific purposes and not just large numbers of machines. When the Yugoslav government decreed that henceforward investment would have to be

"profitable" and not "political" it meant precisely that it had to result in equipment needed for the production of consumer goods which are in demand and should not merely swell production by whatever it happened to turn out.

Even if the Yugoslav heavy industry today produces the right type of equipment, it is still often not at the right price or of the right quality. This could be corrected by opening the borders and exposing Yugoslav producers to the competition of foreign products; but since the Yugoslav productivity in the prestige industries preferred by the Communist planners is so low that they had no hope of competing at the previous exchange rate, this was changed by 66 per cent to protect domestic producers from the same competition Yugoslavia invited. Since there was also a shortage of raw materials, it was decided to increase their prices to make their production more attractive and force enterprises to use them with greater care and economy. The agrarian prices were raised by 32 per cent, coal prices by 36 per cent, etc. This has led to major price adjustments: the cost of living rose by 30 to 50 per cent, according to region, and even by 70 per cent in some cities. All this has led to a new inflationary round, by which, it is considered, the devaluation of 1965 has been rendered useless.

This is not the main problem at the moment, however. While cuts in investment, reductions in government expenditure, opening of the borders, and readjustment of prices were certainly moves in the right direction, the question remains: Who is going to run the Yugoslav economy, who is going to be the moving spirit behind it? Up until now the Communists have relied on the central planners, but now it turns out that they are unable to coordinate and control the economy. The present answer seems to be decentralization of investment and current decision-making in the hands of workers' councils. Is this going to work? For at least a decade, Yugoslav authors have been stressing that economic responsibility has to be reintroduced if the economy is to start working properly again. Lack of responsibility was one of the main criticisms against central plan-

---

[9] S. P. Pervushin, *Production, Accumulation, Consumption* (Moscow, 1965), p. 33. Quoted in the *Neue Zürcher Zeitung,* March 13, 1966.

ning. What is the likelihood that this criticism will be met by the new decentralized system?

It would seem that the link between a worker and his enterprise is insufficient to expect any responsibility. The worst that can happen to an irresponsible worker is that the factory might close down and the worker have to find a new post, where he would obtain the same guaranteed income as before. On the other hand, if the enterprise worked particularly well, workers would be paid higher wages out of profits. However, substantial disparities between wages of equally skilled workers were normally felt to be an injustice, so that in Yugoslavia constant attempts had to be made at "equalizing the business conditions," that is eliminating the influences of market changes and technological choices on profit. What then becomes of entrepreneurial functions? Further, workers feel that they cannot be responsible for the original decision of founding an enterprise (which cannot be made by the workers' council) that does not possess any potential for profitability, or for the current decisions which they cannot understand. There must be many of such latter decisions, because of those employed in the economy 7.1 per cent have no education at all and about 50 per cent have only four or fewer years of school.

In view of this still troubled situation, there are voices that it would be better to revert to "enlightened state-appointed management" than to rely entirely on workers' councils. It is unlikely that this would take the country very far, because the men who are presently called managers are appointed on the basis of political instead of economic criteria, and their education is bad—25 per cent have only a primary school education.

It is hard to imagine how any progress can be achieved in the market economy without falling back on private initiative —enterprises directed by those who can make them work at a profit—at least in agriculture and small-scale industrial and artisan establishments. Something on these lines seems to be happening in Yugoslavia, although very slowly and tentatively. The larger enterprises can

hardly be saved without large-scale technical, commercial, and financial cooperation from abroad.

In 1967, investment in fixed capital has been reduced and national income and industrial production have been stagnating. Stocks of finished goods keep increasing, but, because of a credit squeeze, they have to be financed from capital accumulations intended for new fixed investment. The impression is that, without solving the question of economic responsibility and initiative, necessary structural changes will not take place.

After twenty years, it has become abundantly clear that the economic principles introduced by the Yugoslav Communists in the late 1940's did not lead to unprecedented growth but to utter confusion and waste. One is told that the advantages of "private ownership of the means of production" are being widely discussed in the Yugoslav Communist circles. This amazing development amounts to a complete reversal of the original Marxist teaching, in the name of which the Communists felt entitled to impose suffering on the population and suppress all liberties.

After a full circle has been thus concluded, disillusionment and disgust prevail in Yugoslavia among the youth, as exemplified in a letter addressed "To you, our fathers" and published in the students' weekly of Ljubljana:

I believed in what we then called "our glorious past." I believed in what we called "searching" or "the present" and what we called "our future." Today, I no longer believe in all this. I do not believe in the society which by force we want to call socialist. I do not demand answers to my questions, but I do demand the right to find them myself and to be allowed to stick to them. This is all.[10]

It turned out that freedom of thought and freedom of speech are not an impediment to economic progress, but rather a necessity if economic policy reminiscent more of black magic than of a rational approach is to be prevented.

10 *Studentska Tribuna* (Ljubljana), March 9, 1966.

Page Thirty-three

925

Marxism and Alienation

DAVID LEVY

NOT TOO MANY YEARS ago there was no Marxist challenge to the rationale for a market system which deserved to be taken seriously; Mises and friends did their work so well that advanced Western socialists adopted the market as their own, and even communists learned the glories of directing resource allocation by an Invisible Hand. Much has changed; a streamlined form of Marxism has returned to present the market with a most formidable challenge. The thesis, which we shall call the alienation argument, that the market's operation systematically forces workers to participate in a psychologically damaging method of production, is widely pressed by a number of well known social thinkers,[1] a surprisingly large number to judge their influence from the almost nonexistent counter attacks. The major deterrent to hostile examination of this challenge must be the patent absurdity to which the conclusions can be pushed. That the subject matter of the challenges seems to fall within disciplines which are not overly concerned with a study of the workings of the market system has also not helped stimulate debate.

Interest in alienation arose with the discovery and gradual translation of an earlier and previously unknown body of Marx's writings which can justify the creation of a greatly different Marxism:

both more liberal and not chargeable for unfulfilled predictions and internal contradictions. The tale of this growing discussion and the application of his ideas has been told many times in readily available form.[2]

The proponents of the alienation argument contend that a market system with an advanced form of the division of labor wreaks psychological havoc on workers. Although the philosophy of alienation can be linked with the theory that man is alienated whenever he works for income rather than for the sake of the work itself,[3] we shall only deal with a more relevant version which contends that the division of labor by its infinite specialization imposes *costs* on the workers. Or, as Marx writes in *Capital*:

> manufacture . . . seizes labour-power by its very roots. It converts the labourer into a crippled monstrosity, by forcing his detail dexterity at the

David Levy is an Associate Editor of New Individualist Review. He received his B.A. in Economics from the University of California at Berkeley in 1966, and is currently doing graduate work at the University of Chicago.

---

[1] Eric Fromm, *Marx's Concept of Man* (New York: Frederick Unger, 1961), pp. 43-58; Robert Tucker, *Philosophy and Myth in Karl Marx* (Cambridge: Cambridge University Press, 1961), pp. 234-43; Daniel Bell, *End of Ideology* (New York: Free Press, 1960), pp. 335-68.

[2] Fromm, op. cit., pp. 1-3, 69-74; Dirk J. Struik, "Introduction" to Karl Marx, *Economic and Philosophical Manuscripts* (New York: International Publishers, 1964), pp. 47-56. Attention cannot be too often directed to Lukacs' stupendous feat; the prediction of the content of the early Marxian manuscripts prior to their discovery, and to the service of scholarship performed when the masters of the Soviet Union convinced him of the error of his ways and brought him back to the light. Bell, op. cit., pp. 343-44.

[3] Marx, op. cit., pp. 110-11.

expense of a world of productive capabilities and instincts. . . .[4]

Or, from a non-Marxist vantage, Daniel Bell argues:

> The most characteristic fact about the American factory worker today —and probably the worker in factories in other countries as well—is his lack of interest in work. Few individuals think of "the job" as a place to seek any fulfilment. There is quite often the camaraderie of the shop, the joking, gossip, and politicking of group life. But *work* itself, the daily tasks which the individual is called upon to perform, lacks any real challenge, and is seen only as an irksome chore to be shirked, or to be finished as fast as possible.[5]

Our analysis will proceed by a roundabout historical method: we will examine the alienation argument as it was developed in *Capital* to clear up some muddled interpretations of Marx's ideas and then we will give some examples of a related discussion in classical economic literature. By reformulating the alienation argument to meet one of the few detailed criticisms, we can easily see a failure which is so fundamental that no reformulation can make it stand as a viable non-ascetic criticism of a functioning market system. Those interested neither in an examination of the later Marxian system nor a glance at a bit of economic intellectual history are invited or warned to skip the next two sections.

WE WILL NOT GO INTO a detailed examination of the early body of Marx's thought, for there are no conflicting interpretations in which we will be interested. There are, however, two dominant interpretations of Marx's thoughts on alienation in *Capital*. Eric Fromm and others[6] argue against the older "exploitation" reading, according to which Marx's denunciation of capitalism depends on his theory that the worker is paid less than his value; they stress that alienation is the dominant idea in Marx's published economic writings as well as in the earlier unpublished ones. Bell and others[7] defend the classical view and argue that in *Capital* problems of alienation are forgotten, or as Bell says, relegated to literary references and treated only as a problem of technology to be solved by automation.

The critical point to remember while reading Marx is the importance of technology in his system. It is changing technology which brings about changes in the social order, the division of labor, and through its influence on the division of labor, to alienation in capitalism.

The first conception of the division of labor which Marx considers is co-operation, where work differs from a purely atomistic variety largely in that workers are side by side. Although this form of organization requires a mass of capital, the lack of highly developed tools or machines implies that individuals do not specialize in production:

> Simple co-operation is always the prevailing form, in those branches of production in which capital operates on a large scale, and division of labour and machinery play but a subordinate part.[8]

Co-operation does not present psychological problems of alienation:

> mere social contact begets in most industries an emulation and a stimulation of the animal spirits that heighten the efficiency of each individual workman.[9]

> When the labourer co-operates systematically with others, he strips off the fetters of his individuality, and develops the capabilities of his species.[10]

The next form of the division of labor, manufacturing, arises

927

---

[4] Karl Marx, *Capital* (Moscow: Foreign Languages Publishing House, n.d.), Vol. I, p. 360.

[5] Bell, *op. cit.*, p. 367.

[6] Fromm, *op. cit.*, pp. 69-80; Tucker, *op. cit.*, pp. 165-76 (with reservations); Struik, *op. cit.*, pp. 49-56, 234-35 (with different reservations).

[7] Bell, *op. cit.*, pp. 335-67; Lewis Feuer, "What is Alienation? The Career of a Concept," in *Sociology on Trial*, eds. Maurice Stein and Arthur Vidich (Englewood Cliffs, N. J.: Prentice-Hall, 1963), pp. 136-37. Fromm, *op. cit.*, p. 73, cites others.

[8] Marx, *Capital*, p. 335.

[9] *Ibid.*, p. 326.

[10] *Ibid.*, p. 329.

from the union of various independent handicrafts, which become stripped of their independence and specialised to such an extent as to be reduced to mere supplementary partial processes in the production of one particular commodity.[11]

Or, alternatively

from the co-operation of artificers of one handicraft; it splits up the particular handicraft into its various detail operations, isolating, and making these operations independent of one another up to the point where each becomes the exclusive function of a particular labourer.[12]

Here the influence of technology is clearly emphasized.

928

Manufacture is characterised by the differentiation of the instruments of labour — a differentiation whereby implements of a given sort acquire fixed shapes, adapted to each particular application. . . . The manufacturing period simplifies, improves, and multiplies the implements of labour, by adapting them to the exclusively special functions of each detail labourer. It thus creates at the same time one of the material conditions for the existence of machinery . . . [13]

The result is a "productive mechanism whose parts are human beings."[14]

Here the adverse effects of the division of labor make their unwelcome appearance: "The one-sidedness and the deficiencies of the detail labourer become perfections when he is a part of the collective labourer."[15] Yet this leads to the further development of a class of the unskilled which

develops a one-sided speciality into a perfection, at the expense of the whole of a man's working capacity, it also begins to make a speciality of the absence of all development.[16]

Marx compares the difference between co-operation and manufacture in a passage which we have partially quoted before:

While simple co-operation leaves the mode of working by the individual for the most part unchanged, manufacture thoroughly revolutionises it, and seizes labour-power by its very roots. It converts the labourer into a crippled monstrosity, by forcing his detail dexterity at the expense of a world of productive capabilities and instincts. . . .[17]

There is yet a final stage in the development of the division of labor, however, as modern industry destroys the technical foundations of the older division of labor:

Modern Industry never looks upon and treats the existing form of a process as final. The technical basis of that industry is therefore revolutionary, while all earlier modes of production were essentially conservative. . . . it is continually causing changes not only in the technical basis of production, but also in the functions of the labourer, and in the social combinations of the labour-process.[18]

With the need for mobility caused by modern industry's creation of an industrial reserve army (in conjunction with the falling rate of profit and the class polarization), the bondage of man to detail work is swept away. Modern industry should

replace [the] detail-worker of to-day, crippled by life-long repetition of one and the same trivial operation, and thus reduced to the mere fragment of a man, by the fully developed individual, fit for a variety of labours, ready to face any change of production.[19]

We see therefore that alienation cannot be *Capital's* chief criticism of capitalism, because in fully developed capitalism, alienation is no longer a problem.

---

11 *Ibid.,* p. 338.
12 *Ibid.*
13 *Ibid.,* pp. 341-42.
14 *Ibid.,* p. 338.
15 *Ibid.,* p. 349.
16 *Ibid.,* p. 350.

---

17 *Ibid.,* p. 360.
18 *Ibid.,* pp. 486-87.
19 *Ibid.,* p. 488. Georges Friedmann, *Anatomy of Work* (New York: Free Press, 1962) mistakes this as a picture of the ideal socialist society and fails to see that this is Marx's picture of the last stage of capitalism.

Fromm's reading of Marx is singularly unfortunate; he has ignored the crucial changes in technology. Further, if it were true that Marx is seriously concerned with alienation in *Capital* we would expect the same picture of the ideal state which we find in his earlier writings to emerge. Instead of the utopian version in *German Ideology*:

> In communist society, where nobody has one exclusive sphere of activity but each can become accomplished in any branch he wishes, society regulates the general production and thus makes it possible for me to do one thing today and another tomorrow, to hunt in the morning, fish in the afternoon, rear cattle in the evening, criticize after dinner, just as I have a mind, without ever becoming hunter, fisherman, shepherd or critic.[20]

we find in *Capital*:

> when the working-class comes into power, as inevitably it must, technical instruction, both theoretical and practical, will take its proper place in the working-class schools.[21]

Bell's reading of Marx is closer but he fails to see Marx's detailed treatment of the progress of the division of labor and alienation. Further, alienation does not disappear with automation, but with the creation of interindustry mobility brought about by the industrial reserve army.

A REFINED VERSION of the alienation argument goes back to Adam Smith:[22]

> In the progress of the division of labour, the employment of the far greater part of those who live by labour, that is, of the great body of the people, comes to be confined to a few very simple operations, fre-

quently to one or two. But the understandings of the greater part of men are necessarily formed by their ordinary employments. The man whose whole life is spent in performing a few simple operations, of which the effects too are, perhaps, always the same, or very nearly the same, has no occasion to exert his understanding, or to exercise his invention in finding out expedients for removing difficulties which never occur. He naturally loses, therefore, the habit of such exertion, and generally becomes as stupid and ignorant as it is possible for a human creature to become. The torpor of his mind renders him, not only incapable of relishing or bearing a part in any rational conversation, but of conceiving any generous, noble, or tender sentiment, and consequently of forming any just judgment concerning many even of the ordinary duties of private life. Of the great and extensive interests of his country he is altogether incapable of judging; and unless very particular pains have been taken to render him otherwise, he is equally incapable of defending his country in war. The uniformity of his stationary life naturally corrupts the courage of his mind, and makes him regard with abhorrence the irregular, uncertain, and adventurous life of a soldier. It corrupts even the activity of his body, ... His dexterity at his own particular trade seems, in this manner, to be acquired at the expence of his intellectual, social, and martial virtues. But in every improved and civilized society this is the state into which the labouring poor, that is, the great body of the people, must necessarily fall, unless government takes some pains to prevent it.[23]

929

This is not an isolated point in the *Wealth of Nations* for Smith argues at length that barbaric societies and agricultural occupations are intellectually stimulating and in a similar vein "people of some rank and fortune" don't have the problem of the laboring poor.[24]

---

[20] Cited in Fromm, *op. cit.,* p. 42.

[21] Marx, *Capital*, p. 488.

[22] Adam Smith, *Lectures on Justice, Police, Revenue and Arms,* ed. Edwin Cannan (New York: Augustus Kelley, 1964), pp. 255-58. If I had known E. G. West's note, "Adam Smith's Two Views of the Division of Labor," *Economica,* XXXI (1964), 23-32, before writing this section, much time would have been spared.

[23] Adam Smith, *Wealth of Nations* (New York: Modern Library, 1937), p. 734. Bell, *op. cit.,* p. 227, refers to this argument with Smith, but does not tie it in with his treatment of alienation. In the sociological literature Hegel is universally credited with inspiring Marx, which indicates I suppose that Stigler's General Incompetence Theorem applies outside of economics also.

[24] Smith, *Wealth of Nations,* pp. 127, 735-37.

This argument clearly differs from Marx's in important respects; Smith ignores any implications for the welfare of the workers and worries only about the effect of the division of labor on the worker's ability to be a good citizen. Nonetheless Smith and Marx agree on the central thesis that productive activity is the dominant force shaping the worker's mental state; although Smith is optimistic enough to think that education can remedy the problem.[25]

Smith's argument is reproduced by J. B. Say:

A man, whose whole life is devoted to the execution of a single operation, will most assuredly acquire the faculty of executing it better and quicker than others; but he will, at the same time, be rendered less fit for every other occupation, corporeal or intellectual; his other faculties will be gradually blunted or extinguished; and the man, as an individual will degenerate in consequence.[26]

Say's American editor disagrees, and cites Dugald Stewart's argument:

The extensive propagation of light and refinement arising from the influence of the press, aided by the spirit of commerce, seems to be the remedy to be provided by nature against the fatal effects which would otherwise be produced, by the subdivision of labour accompanying the progress of the mechanical arts: nor is any thing wanting to make the remedy effectual, but wise institutions to facilitate general instruction, and to adapt the education of individuals to the stations they are to occupy.[27]

An interesting critical literature arose in the notes of various editions of the *Wealth of Nations*. McCulloch strongly dissents from Smith's argument in his edition.

As well as asserting that the evidence contradicts the proposition that manufacturing laborers make bad soldiers,[28] he argues:

The weaver, and other mechanics of Glasgow, Manchester, Birmingham, etc. possess far more general and useful information than is possessed by the agricultural labourers of any part of the empire. And this is really what a more unprejudiced inquiry into the subject would lead to anticipate. The various occupations in which the husbandman successively engages, their constant liability to be affected by so variable a power as the weather, and the perpetual change in the appearance of the objects which daily meet his eyes, and with which he is conversant, occupy his attention, and render him a stranger to that ennui and desire for adventitious excitement which must ever be felt by those who are constantly engaged in burnishing the point of a pin, or in performing the same endless routine of precisely similar operations. This want of excitement cannot, however, be so cheaply or effectually gratified in any way as it may be by *stimulating*, that is, by cultivating the mental powers. Most workmen have no time for dissipation; and though they had, the wages of labour in old settled and densely peopled countries are too low, and the propensity to save and accumulate too powerful, to permit their generally seeking to divert themselves by indulging in riot and excess. They are thus driven to seek for recreation in mental excitement; and the circumstances under which they are placed afford them every possible facility for gratifying themselves in this manner. By working together in considerable numbers they have what the agriculturists generally want, constant opportunities of discussing every topic of interest or importance; they are thus gradually trained to habits of thinking and reflection; their intellects are sharpened by the collision of conflicting opinions; and a small contribution from each individual enables them to obtain supplies of newspapers and of the cheaper class of periodical publications.[29]

Thus the worker's job influences his intelligence but in exactly the opposite manner that Smith argues. Further and more importantly, intelligence is stimu-

---

[25] *Ibid.*, pp. 734-35.
[26] J. B. Say, *A Treatise on Political Economy* (New York: Augustus Kelley, 1963), p. 98.
[27] *Ibid.*, p. 99.
[28] Adam Smith, *Wealth of Nations*, ed. John R. McCulloch (Edinburgh: Blac, 1863), pp. 350-51.

[29] *Ibid.*, p. 58. We know that Ricardo agreed with McCulloch on this point. *Works and Correspondence of David Ricardo*, ed. Piero Sraffa (Cambridge: Cambridge University Press 1962), Vol. IX, pp. 192-93.

lated by social contact and discussion, a point Smith did not make.

Rogers, while not necessarily contradicting Smith's analysis, argues that the evils which Smith denounces are no longer relevant:

> The experience of modern society affords a corrective to this sweeping charge. The manufacturing populations of many large towns, among whom the division of labour is carried to the farthest limit conceivable, are honourably distinguished by the energy with which they have furthered the means of local education through the maintenance of mechanics' institutes, libraries, and schools. This machinery of adult education has been generally adopted in many towns, especially in Lancashire and Yorkshire, and there are no persons more alive to the benefits of education than the factory hands of the north-west counties of England. There were other reasons which made such people indifferent to public questions in Smith's days, and in particular the exclusion of the mass of artisans from all political power.[30]

The Garnier edition defends Smith from McCulloch:

> This passage on the moral superiority of the agricultural population relative to the urban working class is one which best illustrates the sincerity and genius of the founder of political economy. . . . McCulloch asserts, in a note, if the agricultural population had ever been intellectually and morally superior to the industrial population, it is not today; he maintains that today the English industrial workers are more intelligent than the farming peasantry. . . . McCulloch is completely refuted by the recent inquiries into the condition of the handloom weavers. The commissioners state that the weavers were formerly an intelligent and moral class, but from poverty they have become brutalized and morally degraded, falling into the condition of the lowest class of the English nation. . . . Therefore Adam Smith is still right today; agricultural work is more favorable to morality, human understanding, and health than mod-

ern industrial work, especially as it is found in England today.[31]

Marshall devotes a considerable discussion to the related problem of industrial boredom: he is interested in the worker's quality of life, and if a more tedious but less tiring work allows pursuit of intellectually stimulating interests outside the job, then there is no social problem, only cause for rejoicing.[32] Thus the type of work in which a man is engaged forms only a slight influence in the stimulation of intelligence. Marshall also observes that any truly tedious job will be the easiest to mechanize and hence will most likely disappear.[33]

Undoubtedly there is a much greater literature on the subject than I have indicated, both in the studies of the conditions of the poor and perhaps in the theoretical literature of the eighteenth and nineteenth centuries.[34] However, one bit of information exists which should settle any interest in priorities. In the introduction to the new edition of Rae's *Life of Adam Smith*, Jacob Viner writes:

931

---

[30] Adam Smith, *Wealth of Nations*, ed. James E. Thorold Rogers (2nd ed.: Oxford, 1880), Vol. II, p. 365.

[31] Adam Smith, *Richesses des Nations*, trans. Germain Garnier (Paris: Chez Guillaumin, 1843), pp. 167-68.

[32] Alfred Marshall, *Principles of Economics* (Variorum ed.; London: Macmillan, 1961), pp. 261-64.

[33] *Ibid.*

[34] See for example Allen Clarke, *The Effects of the Factory System* (London: Grant Richards, 1899), pp. 72-78. I particularly like Clarke's observation, "It may happen, if the factory system continues, that the operatives' heads will, in course of time, shrink to a rudimentary fraction of empty skull, just as man today has at the base of his spinal column the bit of bone which proves that he once sported a simian tail." (p. 73) On the other hand, Whately Cooke Taylor, *Modern Factory System* (London: Kegan Paul, Trench, Trubner & Co., 1891), p. 435, argues: "As a matter of fact, the progress of the factory system has directly resulted in a very wide diffusion of education; nor should its indirect offices be overlooked. The inestimable importance of order and regularity in daily life has been more than once commented on. The influence on intelligence of constant association with others in a common object could not be easily overstated." Taylor was a factory inspector and had no great love for many of the results of the factory system. John A. Hobson, *The Evolution of Modern Capitalism* (London: Walter Scott, 1894), p. 380, argues: "Industry which is purely monotonous, burdensome, uninteresting, uneducative, which contains within itself no elements of enjoyment, cannot be fully compensated by alternate periods of consumption or relaxation."

There is one issue on which Smith and Ferguson cover common ground, as also John Millar, Robert Wallace, and later, after the publication of *The Wealth of Nations,* a host of writers including notably Karl Marx, and that is the proposition that division of labor tends to degrade labor, the *"Entfremdung"* or *"alienation"* issue. Here Adam Smith has clear claims to priority as far as British writers are concerned, although according to Marx, who was not acquainted with Smith's contributions to the *Edinburgh Review* in 1755, it was Smith who was taught by Ferguson, rather than the other way around. But all of these, except perhaps Marx, were started on this line of thought by a "French author," or at least an author writing in French, Jean Jacques Rousseau, and none of them made a secret of his indebtedness. . . .[35]

932

IN THE ONE elaborate attack on the alienation argument I know, Nathaniel Branden makes two objections to the theory of alienation which are relevant for our purposes: (i) the division of labor and specialization produces material well-being on which our lives and happiness depend, and (ii) the wages paid to a man are objectively determined by market forces, "the only rational and just principles of exchange." [36]

These criticisms, however, do not seem to come to grips with at least some of the proponents of the alienation argument. Consider Bell's point:

> For the unions to challenge the work process [to help rid the economy of alienation] would require a radical challenge to society as a whole: . . . it is to question the logic of a consumption economy whose prime consideration is lower costs and increasing output. Moreover, how could any single enterprise, in a competitive situation, increase its

costs by reorganizing the flow of work, without falling behind its competitors? But this is not only a failing of "capitalist" society. In the socialist societies, sadly, there have been almost no imaginative attempts to think through the meaning of the work process. . . .

> For underdeveloped countries, where living standards are pitifully low, it is difficult to talk of sacrificing production in order to make work more meaningful to the worker. Yet these are not, nor should they be, put in either/or terms. Engineers have learned that if efficiency considerations are pushed too far— if work is broken down into the most minute parts and made completely monotonous — they become self-defeating. The question is always one of "how much." But the question must be stated and placed in the forefront of considerations.[37]

This argument surely does not involve a denial of the need for a division of labor or indeed of a market process.

To meet Branden's criticisms formally we can reformulate the alienation argument as follows: workers have preferences for material wage income, income in the form of leisure, and in addition, income in the form of the type of productive activity in which they are engaged. Hence, they are willing to exchange a certain amount of wage goods for an amount of leisure or employment in a more desirable productive activity. Yet, the argument goes, the capitalistic system is rigid and run by those interested in producing material goods, the worker has no choice; he is denied the ability to choose between the forms of income, he is forced to take material goods and forego employment in desirable productive processes. Thus because wages and productive activities are joint operations it is impossible for a worker to obtain an optimal allocation of income. In a word, he is alienated. The solution presumably is some form of economic system in which a more optimal form of the division of labor can emerge.

This formulation meets Branden's objections: the question is not whether income is desirable (his first point) or whether a functioning competitive labor

---

[35] Jacob Viner, "Guide to John Rae's *Life of Adam Smith,"* in John Rae, *Life of Adam Smith* (New York: Augustus Kelley, 1965), pp. 35-36. Viner is borne out in his thesis that Marx was not started independently of the British discussion—there is no reference to Rousseau in the index to the text of the *Economic and Philosopical Manuscripts,* although there is a citation to Say on alienation, p. 161.

[36] Nathaniel Branden, "Alienation," in Ayn Rand, *Capitalism: The Unknown Ideal* (New York: New American Library, 1966), pp. 269-71.

---

[37] Bell, op cit., pp. 367-68.

market produces an optimum in terms of material income (his second) but whether the market correctly allocates intrapersonal distribution of income, broadly defined.

Once the problem is so stated the solution is trivial. Take the case: How does the market allocate income between material income and leisure? If there are workers who would like to exchange wage goods for more leisure, then there exists a wage such that it will be to the advantage of the employer to adjust the terms of employment to the workers' desires. This is not to say the employer is necessarily indifferent between employees working any hours at a given wage rate; but that it is possible to adjust production to different hours desired, if workers are willing to pay for more leisure by accepting lower wages. This argument is valid under the condition that production functions are uniform throughout the economy. On a more reasonable assumption of different production processes, workers can allocate themselves among employers with different desires for hours to be worked and hence receive a more constant wage rate. (Significantly Marx could not see how the market would operate in this case—in his system, hours of employment are determined by political power). [38]

The problem of the exchange of wage goods for employment in different production processes is completely analog-

ous: the employer would be willing to make the trade if it meant that he could produce with less cost. This would be the case if his laborers accept a real wage sufficiently low to compensate for the employer's loss in adopting a different process of production. Again the argument is correct even in the case where all industry production functions are the same, and of course the effect becomes stronger when we recognize the existence of a myriad of production processes.

The implication of this argument is that alienation in a functioning market economy is simply an aspect of scarcity. Income in any form is rarely a free good and we should expect workers to be dissatisfied about their productive activity, in the sense that they would be rather doing something else, *if* their material income were not changed, just as we should expect that they do not have enough material goods to satisfy all of their needs. Industrial alienation is thus no viable criticism of the market any more than scarcity would be.

If the concept of alienation or worker dissatisfaction is to have any use, another major problem must be cleared up: how is on the job income shared among the family? Income and leisure can be shared, but it is not at all obvious that income from employment in a more desirable production process can be similarly distributed. A serious study of worker "dissatisfaction" would have to investigate this relationship.

---

[38] Marx, *Capital*, p. 299.

933

The Economic and Social Impact of Free Tuition

ARMEN A. ALCHIAN

RARELY DO educational issues provoke as much passion as the proposal to raise tuition fees in California colleges. Unfortunately, the passion has not been matched by reason — it is hard to find a clear statement of the consequences of or reasons for a zero tuition or a high tuition fee. It is hard to determine from the public comments whether the antagonists differ about what the consequences of alternative tuition arrangements would be or have different preferences with respect to well perceived consequences. Some defenders of zero tuition have asserted that zero tuition is necessary for aid to poorer students, for the maintenance of our great system of higher education, for the preservation of free and prosperous society, for achievement of great social benefits, for educational opportunity for all, is a hallowed century-old tradition, and that tuition is a tax on education. Some proponents of tuition fees have argued, for example, that the university and colleges are harboring delinquents who

Armen A. Alchian is Professor of Economics at the University of California, Los Angeles. He is co-author of the textbook *University Economics* and author of a number of important articles on costs and property rights. Acknowledgement is made to the Lilly Endowment, Inc. for a research grant to U.C.L.A. during which the present article was written. The opinions expressed here in no way reflect any conditions of that research grant.

would not be there with full tuition, the poor are aiding the rich, students should pay tuition in order to appreciate their education, taxes are excessive, and low tuition requires exploitation of an underpaid faculty, to cite a few. Most of these arguments are so patently fallacious or nonsensical or irrelevant that they do disservice to the more intelligent arguments. But there are some propositions that merit closer examination. To evaluate them it is first necessary to identify at some length the issues that are involved in analyzing and thereby choosing among the alternatives — and in the process make clear my own preferences. If I overlook significant objectives or consequences, perhaps others will be stimulated to fill the gaps.

The issues represent a classic topic for applied economics — the effects of different means of allocating scarce resources among competing claimants. A rational analysis of the consequences of tuition systems requires separation of two questions: (1) Who should bear the costs of education? (2) If someone other than the student should pay for his education, in what form should the aid be given?

Unless the distinction between these two issues is grasped, confusion is inevitable. The case for zero tuition is *not* established by demonstrating that aid to students is desirable. Full tuition may still be desirable, with the desired aid taking the form of explicit grants-in-aid or scholarships from which the student pays the tuition fee of his chosen school.

The issue of the most desirable form of aid should be separated from still another closely related question: What is the desired method of financing and controlling *colleges* — as distinct from financing *students?* For example, aid to students in the form of zero tuition means also that the state finances the colleges' activities directly by legislative appropriations with the students and their parents having less influence on financing and controlling the activities of colleges. Where student aid is in the form of grants-in-aid or scholarships, students and parents paying full tuition to their chosen colleges have a greater role in determining which colleges shall be financed and rewarded for superior performances. Recognition of these differences in effect explains why some people have asserted the administrators and members of state universities and colleges, which are currently financed by direct legislative appropriation, have sought from self-interest, rather than educational interest, to maintain the impression that zero tuition is the only feasible or sensible means of aid to students — in order to repress student influence and control over the colleges while retaining the influence of politicians.

ADVOCATES OF subsidization of college students (regardless of the method) assume that if each student bore the full cost there would be too little college education as well as a decrease of educational opportunity. What makes it desirable to have more education than if students pay full costs? Several arguments are advanced. Let us discuss these in ascending order of sophistication.

(1) "Although the costs of education are less than the gains to the students themselves, some are unable to finance their education now. A subsidy would provide educational opportunity to the poor." (2) "Cultural education, though not profitable in market earnings, and hence not capable of being paid for out of enhanced earnings, is nevertheless desirable." (3) "Even if every student acquires as much education as is worthwhile to him, he would take too little, because the individual ignores the beneficial social gains indirectly conferred on other members of society — giving what some people call 'external social effects.' Therefore, society at large should induce students to take more education than indicated by their private interests."

The argument that the poor can not afford to pay for a profitable college education is deceptive. What is meant by a "poor" person. Is he a college calibre student? All college calibre students are rich in both a monetary and non-monetary sense. Their inherited superior mental talent — human capital — *is* great wealth. For example, the college calibre student is worth on the average about $200,000, and on the average, approximately $20,000-$50,000 of that has been estimated as the enhanced value derived from college training, depending upon his major field and profession.

Failure to perceive this inherent wealth of college calibre students reflects ignorance of two economic facts. One is the enormous human wealth in our society. Every good educator recognizes that inanimate capital goods are not the only forms of wealth. The second fact is the difference between current earnings and wealth. For example, a man with a million dollars worth of growing trees, or untapped oil is a rich man — though he is not *now* marketing any of his wealth or services. So it is with the college calibre student. Though his *current* market earnings are small, his wealth — the present wealth value of his future earnings — is larger than for the average person. This is true no matter what the current earnings or wealth of his parents. It is *wealth,* not current earnings nor parent's wealth, that is the measure of a student's richness. College calibre students with low current earnings are not poor. Subsidized higher education, whether by zero tuition, scholarships, or zero interest loans, grants the college student a second windfall — a subsidy to exploit his initial windfall inheritance of talent.

935

This is equivalent to subsidizing drilling costs for owners of oil-bearing lands in Texas.

There remains an even more seriously deceptive ambiguity — that between the subsidization of college education and provision of educational *opportunity*. Educational *opportunity* is provided if any person who can benefit from attending college is enabled to do so despite smallness of *current* earnings. Nothing in the provision of full educational *opportunity* implies that students who are financed during college should not later repay out of their enhanced earnings those who financed that education. Not to ask for repayment is to grant students a gift of wealth at the expense of those who do not attend college or who attend tuition colleges and pay for themselves. This is true because, for one reason, our tax bills do not distinguish between those directly benefitted by having obtained a zero tuition educational subsidy and those not so benefitted. Alumni with higher incomes pay more taxes, but they do not pay more than people with equal incomes who financed their own education or never went to college.

MANY DISCUSSIONS about educational opportunity refer to proportions of students from poorer and richer families at tuition free colleges. However strong the emotional appeal, the proportion of rich and poor family students is relevant only to the separate issue of wealth redistribution, per se, consequent to state operated zero tuition education. It has nothing to do with the extent of educational opportunity. Though data for California colleges and taxes suggest that lower income groups provide a smaller proportion of students than of taxes to support education, such comparisons are irrelevant, so far as provision of educational *opportunity* is concerned. These data tell how much wealth redistribution there is among the less educated, the poor, the educated, and the rich. That wealth redistribution is good or bad depending upon whether one believes the educational system should be used as a device to redistribute wealth as well as to enhance wealth, knowledge, and educational opportunity. No matter how zero tuition in tax supported schools may redistribute wealth, the provision of full educational opportunity does *not* require redistributions of wealth. Yet, it seems to me, many people confuse these two entirely separate issues or think the latter is necessary for the former. To think that college calibre students should be given zero tuition is to think that smart people should be given wealth at the expense of the less smart.

When some zero tuition university alumni say that without zero tuition they could not have attended college, they should have a modest concern for the implications of that statement. One poor, "uneducated" resident of Watts, upon hearing Ralph Bunche say that he could not have had a college education unless tuition were free, opined, "Perhaps it's time he repay out of his higher income for that privilege granted him by taxes on us Negroes who never went to college." That reply spots the difference between educational opportunity and a redistribution of wealth.

Full educational *opportunity* would be provided if college calibre students could borrow against their future enhanced earnings. Students could repay out of their enhanced future earnings. Although, currently, loans are available from private lenders and also from publicly supported loans, a subsidy could provide a state guarantee of repayment of educational loans exactly as housing loans are guaranteed for veterans. Students could select among optional repayment methods. Some could contract to repay in full with interest; others could opt for a sort of insurance system, whereby the amount repaid was related to their income, with upper and lower limits to amounts repaid being specified. A host of possibilities are available. In fact today with income taxes, the college alumni are repaying part of the educational costs via taxes (but so are others who did not attend college).

Some people are impressed by the size of the debt that a college graduate would have to repay, but they should be impressed with the fact that the debt is *less* than the enhanced earnings he has thereby obtained and is an indication of the wealth bonanza given the student who is subsidized by society.

There remains one more facet of the educational opportunity argument. Even if a college education may be a very profitable investment for some person, he may, because of inexperience or lack of confidence, not appreciate his situation or be willing to borrow at available rates of interest. This presumably is an argument for subsidizing those students who lack confidence or understanding of their possibilities, and it may be a meaningful argument on its own ground, but it is not an argument for subsidizing "poor" students.

Pleas are made for subsidizing *cultural* education which, though it may add nothing to the student's future market earnings, will enhance his general welfare. But a person's welfare is increased if he gets more food, housing, recreation, beer drinking, and fancier cars. It would seem therefore that the relevant argument for helping students is one of helping them regardless of whether they wish their welfare increased via cultural education or better food. A grant of money to be spent as the recipient deems appropriate is an efficient form of aid — as judged by the recipient. Subsidized cultural education rather than money gifts could be justified if the giver knows better than the recipient what is good for the recipient. I cannot make that leap of faith for the collegiate student, although other people do it easily and confidently.

A case can be made for subsidizing the poor *and* the rich to take more education — more than a person would take when motivated by his own interests alone. It is often said there are privately unheeded, net social benefits, so each person will under-invest in education from the social point of view, regardless of whether he is rich or poor; but we must separate the illusory from the real external available gains.

EDUCATION MAKES A person more productive, as a doctor, lawyer, merchant, or engineer. Other people benefit from his greater productivity, because more engineers enable lower costs of engineering services for the rest of society. Engineers, looking only to their private gain would, it is said, undervalue the total benefit of having more engineers; too few people would seek sufficient engineering education. If this sounds persuasive, economics can teach you something. The increased supply of engineers reduces the prices of engineering services — even if by only a trivial amount — and thereby reduces the income of *other* engineers. Their income loss is the gain to the rest of society. This is a *transfer* of income from existing engineers to non-engineers; it is *not* a net social gain. The benefitted parties gain at the expense of existing members of the engineering profession, who lose some of their scarcity value as more educated people are created. This is a transfer from the more educated to the less educated. A striking awareness of this effect is evident in the advocacy by labor groups of immigration restriction. Restricting the inflow of laborers of particular skills prevents reductions in wages of incumbent workers with similar skills and prevents a transfer of wealth from them to the rest of American society. An immigrant or a more educated person would have provided an increased product and he would have obtained that value by the sale of his services, but the lower wages to that *type* of services would have transferred some of the incomes of similar workers to the rest of society. This external *transfer* effect is not a net contribution to social output. It is not a reason for subsidizing education.

For external effects to serve as a valid basis for more education two conditions must be satisfied: (1) There must be a net social *gain* (not transfer) unheeded by the student. The ability to read reduces dangers and inconvenience to other people; ability to be sanitary enhances health of other people, or economic education may—but probably will not — prevent passage of socially detrimental, special interest legislation. These are examples of education with external social gains, which we shall assume are

937

not heeded by the student in his private actions because they do not affect the marketable value of his services. Professional education of doctors, engineers, lawyers, economists, mathematicians, etc., has not been shown to fit in that category. Perhaps education at the undergraduate collegiate level in the elements of law, psychology, political science, mathematics, economics may make f o r better *non-market* decisions or actions.

I confess to a strong suspicion that such education is most significant at the grade school level, diminishes at higher levels, and disappears for professional or cultural, artistic, personal satisfaction courses, and is possibly *reversed* at graduate levels (by overtraining and insistence on excessively high standards of training for granting of licenses to practice in some professions — though this is a point the validity of which is not crucial to the main issue here).

(2) The second condition is that there must be *further* external gains unheeded by students at the college level. The fact of having *achieved* net external gains is not sufficient to warrant subsidization. The crucial condition is the failure to achieve still further available *incremental* net social gain from *further* education. Before concluding that they exist because of a tendency for people to ignore them, we should note that people attend college for reasons other than financial marketable gain. College attendance for personal reasons includes cultural, artistic education, and attendance to find mates. All these tend to extend education beyond maximizing one's market wealth and possibly even beyond that yielding unheeded social gains. But the facts are not conclusive in *either* direction.

Incidentally, an especially common but erroneous contention, presumably relying on the external effect, is that the growth, prosperity, and unusual position of California depend upon the free tuition, higher education system. What does this mean? If this means that free tuition has contributed to higher wealth for the educated then this is no argument for either free tuition or more education. If it means the prosperity and growth of aircraft, electronics, motion picture, or agricultural industries in California are dependent upon free tuition, the contention remains unsupported by any analytic or factual evidence, and in fact can be falsified by comparisons with other states. Even if it could be demonstrated that *subsidized* higher education was responsible, the issue of *free* tuition would still not be touched. If this means that free tuition did attract some people to seek their education in California, they proceeded to reap the gain in their own higher income. If they provided a real net social benefit, it should have exceeded the extent of their subsidization to be justifiable. The same proposition holds for residents of California. If this argument is accepted, it is difficult to justify charging newcomers a full tuition while permitting existing residents a "free tuition." Yet, we have seen no proponent of zero tuition advocate zero tuition for all newcomers from all other states. If this means that the higher incomes for more people increase tax receipts, then the relevance of that completely escapes me. If this means California has a larger population, then this means higher land prices. But in so far as benefits to "California" have any relevance, I believe they should be viewed as benefits to people in California rather than as benefits to owners of a geographically identified piece of land, unless by "California" one means "land owners or politicians," who indeed do prefer larger populations as a source of political power and higher land values.

To induce students to take more education than is privately worth their while — in order to obtain the otherwise unheeded external gains — does call for payments to students. If a student were paid for doing what he would have done anyway, or if his education were subsidized to increase *his* wealth, he would be receiving a gift. But a payment (whether as zero tuition or a money payment) to the student to *extend* his education, for the sake of achieving *real*, external benefits that he otherwise would have not produced, is a payment for services, much as if he were to build houses, for the benefit of the rest of society. Such payments may well be independent of the income or future income of the student as well as of his parents. Though there is nothing that says the rich would provide less real external effects from more education, my conjecture is that the rich would in any event take more education than the poor for cultural reasons and would therefore require a smaller inducement to take the "optimal" extra amount of education for external social benefits. This can form a basis for advocating more educational inducements to the poor than to the rich, but not necessarily by a zero tuition inducement to rich and poor alike.

It should be noted however that there is already subsidization of higher education by private philanthropy on a scale that staggers the imagination. The endowment funds of colleges and philanthropic foundations aiding education runs into the scores of billions. Even if only half that were used to subsidize education (and the rest for research), the amount can not be regarded as minor, on any standard.

NO MATTER WHAT your beliefs about the validity or relevance of the preceding consideration, let us accept them, for the sake of analysis of alternative *means* of providing aid, for full educational opportunity, cultural aid, or extra inducements to education. (Of course, those who think the preceding arguments are too weak to warrant taxpayers' giving aid to college students can ignore all that follows, for to them there is no case for any state action, nor of zero tuition). The rest will want to ask, "What is the best form of aid or inducement?"

We can enable or induce students to take more education with the following offer: "On the condition that you take certain kinds of education, we shall bear enough of the costs to induce you to do so." The costs he would have borne are the income foresaken and the tuition costs. (Food and living costs can be ig-

nored for he would be incurring them no matter what he did). Which of the following is the preferred way of extending that aid to potential students? (1) We pay directly the costs of extra education by operating the school to provide the extra education; this is the zero tuition system. (2) We pay him an equal amount on the condition he take the additional, specified type of education, but he decides which school to attend and he pays the tuition to the school. This is an educational voucher or G.I. type educational bill-of-rights (used after World War II for veterans).

The first requires *also* that the state directly finance and operate the school providing the education; the second permits the student to choose from competing schools and direct payment to the school he chooses. These two alternatives are sufficient to illustrate the major implications of zero versus high tuition modes of subsidy. The wealth effect for the student is superficially the same in either case, and the financial cost to the subscriber can be the same in each case, once it is decided how much education to subsidize for whom. The costs to the subscriber may be the same, but the results are not.

In the California state system of higher education, the tuition fee is zero for *all* state schools and for -*all* kinds of training, regardless of whether it contributes to a net social gain or not, and regardless of how rich the student is.

Zero tuition implies that the appropriate aid or subsidy for every student of a state school is exactly equal to the tuition cost no matter what subject he takes. No basis for zero tuitions as being the proper amount has ever been presented; maybe the aid should be even larger, to compensate for foresaken earnings.

Because low or zero-tuition schools are believed to have a larger proportion of less wealthy students than high tuition colleges, zero tuition schools are believed to do a better job of providing educational opportunity for less wealthy students. But this entails the earlier confusion between provision of *opportunity* and provision of a wealth *bonanza;* zero

939

tuition schools give bigger wealth gifts to the mentally able students than do the high tuition schools.

Of course, higher tuition will, *other things left unchanged,* reduce the number of financially insecure students attending tuition colleges. The case for raising tuition is not that aid should be denied but instead that "zero tuition" is a less desirable means of providing aid to students; it entails undersirable controls and political interference with education and lowers the quality of education. Yet there is another method of providing full educational opportunity *and* at the same time improving the quality and quantity of education and reducing political controls. That alternative is a system of full tuition supplemented by grants-in-aid to those who qualify as financially insecure and deserving students.

It is important to note that the financing of *colleges* to provide education is different from subsidizing *students.* The zero tuition is a subsidy to the *college* as well as to the student. Subsidies to *students* alone can be provided with a full tuition system; in fact they are now being so provided by many private schools that do charge full tuition.

The alternative to the zero tuition method of providing educational opportunity or giving aid is tuition, *with* loans or with grants of money. The critical difference, in my opinion, between no tuition and tuition, under these circumstances, is that the former lets the state politician and college administrator and faculty directly exert more control over education whereas the latter enables the student to exercise more power by his choice of college.

Subsidies to whatever extent desired could be provided by a system of grants-in-aid via scholarships. That would appear to be more expensive *administratively* (but only administratively) than zero tuition, precisely because an effort is made to eliminate the haphazard bonanzas in the zero tuition system. The presumption is that the cost of selecting the students to be subsidized is less than the savings from the avoidance of subsidies to all students.

Tuition with grants-in-aid to students is not visionary. It is proven, practical, economical and currently used. New York State already has a large system of Regents scholarships. California has a smaller scale system with about 2,000 scholarships. After World War II, the Federal government granted millions of veterans educational vouchers for tuition, books, and incidental expenses under an enormously successful act known as the G.I. Bill. All these granted aid regardless of the student's current financial status. In California the university and state colleges now receive about $500 million annually directly from the legislature. That would finance 250,000 scholarships of $2000 each. The university's budget would finance 125,000 students, more than the number now attending.

At present many arrangements exist whereby private colleges take into account the financial status of students in deciding how much tuition to charge each student. Even more efficient would be a system of loans with interest to be repaid after graduation out of the student's enhanced earnings. Under a loan system, the problem of filtering rich students from the financially distressed would be reduced to trivial dimensions, since the rich would have little, if anything, to gain by borrowing. This would provide full educational opportunity with little need for a means test.

Full tuition does not in any way restrict the achievability of full education opportunity. That can be achieved explicitly and openly by the scope of grants and subsidized loans. Just as social security and welfare payments are made in money with the recipient choosing his purchases from competing producers, so a full tuition system with grants-in-aid or loans would enable separation of the issue of the amount, if any, of the subsidy from that of the best means of providing and controlling education.

Under a system of full tuition fees, with whatever loans and scholarship voucher grants are deemed desirable, students could choose their education from the whole world. Any accredited college or educational institution

940

whether it be for barbers, television technicians, beauty operators, mechanics, butchers, doctors, lawyers, or historians could serve. Ours would then really be the best educational system in the world; no longer would Californians be confined to California state operated schools. Whatever one's beliefs about the desirable degree of subsidy for more education, and whatever his beliefs about who should get it, the full tuition voucher coupled with scholarships and loans would magically open a new, larger world of choice.

An alternative form of aid to students is a tax-credit allowance whereby parents, or students, could later receive a tax offset to their payments for tuition. This would put private college students on a more equal basis with low tuition public colleges. In my opinion, this would be equality at the wrong level of equality. Rather than give tax credits as a means of maintaining zero tuition. I would prefer placing a tax *liability* on students attending public colleges with low or zero tuition. Whereas the tax credit provides subsidies and aid to all students at the expense of non-students, the tax-liability assessment places the costs of providing the education more squarely on those who benefit from the education. A tax credit gives *equal* treatment to private and public college students — at the expense of non-students. A tax-liability gives equality to private and public college students and to college and non-college people, with each bearing only the costs of service provided for their benefit. If tax-liability assessments are out of the question politically, the tax credit would be the next best; but it would not achieve one of the major purposes of a full tuition system.

WITH FULL COST tuition, competition among California colleges, and even among academic departments would change. Instead of competition for funds being negotiated among university committees, deans, regents, state college boards, a n d legislators, competition would rely more on classroom behavior of instructors who would be more de-pendent on student attendance *vis-a-vis* other departments and other colleges. This would enormously enhance the power of the student in the former zero tuition colleges. Giving students more attention and influence in the university would indeed occur, exactly as the customer exercises more power at the grocery — by his purchases and choice among competing products and stores, but not by leaping over the counter and insisting on power to run the store, as occurs with current protest. Currently at the grade school level many parents are turning to private schools precisely because the parents can choose more fully the kind of education given their children — via the power of the purse. The poorer people do not have that option — but they would with a tuition-grant system.

Since the producer usually knows more about what he is producing than does the consumer, the producer illogically tends to conclude that he is a better judge about the appropriate quality and quantity for the consumer. This tendency is especially rewarding if the producer can thereby obtain a sheltered competitive position in the production of the good. He would tend to produce a quality and quantity in a style related more to that which enhances his welfare and less to what students and parents prefer.

It is easy to see that with zero tuition the university faculty benefits from research and graduate activity that builds an impressive publication record and research status, with the currently less rewarding teaching of undergraduates being relegated to the less "distinguished," lower-ranking faculty or graduate students. The "publish or perish" rule would be less powerful under full tuition, because teaching would become a more important source of student directed funds. Survival of the better teachers who are weak in publication would be enhanced. It is interesting and amusing to note, incidentally, that students at the University of California are now attempting to protect some members of the faculty from being dropped because of inadequate research and pub-

941

lication. The protection comes by the students "donating" funds to hire the man to give classes; this *is* a voluntary, spontaneous full tuition system. If allowed to expand, students would determine who was on the staff and who got the bigger incomes, just as they now decide which restaurants shall survive and prosper.

This is a simple application of the old, powerful, fundamental principle of behavior. The lower the price at which goods are distributed, relative to the market value, the greater the degree of discrimination and arbitrary criteria that the "seller" will display. Its corollary is that the lower the seller's right to the monetary proceeds, the greater his gain from underpricing the goods. The gains to the university administration and faculty from low tuition are classic examples, first expounded in Adam Smith's *The Wealth of Nations*. The greater the portion of a college's funds coming from tuition fees, the greater the power of the students and the greater the role teaching will play in the survival and prosperity of the members of the faculty. The less will the faculty choose which students shall attend, how they shall behave, etc. The lower is the ratio of tuition payments, the greater the power of the faculty over the students because the students are less able to exert significant effects on the financing of schools or departments as a reward for "good" performance — as they can with restaurants. The faculty says "education is different" and students are poor judges of good education; students are swayed by popular, theatrical teachers and do not appreciate the more valuable scholarly teachers. One wonders how students happen to go to the better and possibly tougher schools in the first place. The faculty of any college prefers lower tuition — until the budget expenditures can not be met from non-tuition sources. And even then there is conflict of interest within the college between those who are threatened by the budget cut and those with tenure who are not. If the cut, or loss of income, would mean merely fewer undergraduates and fewer *new* teachers, clearly the least difficult

resolution from the current faculty's interest is the reduction in new students, rather than an increase in tuition.

WITH ZERO TUITION the state schools have expanded relative to higher tuition private colleges, and the state university with its higher salaried teachers and more expensive education is more attractive to students than the state colleges and junior colleges. The ex-president and the administrators of zero tuition institutions correctly insist that *zero* tuition is the great principle underlying the *growth* of the university; but it is not a source of better education for California students. We should not confuse the *amount* of money with the *way* the money is obtained. More and better education, as judged by students, could be obtained at the same, or less, cost with the full tuition control of colleges coupled to loans and whatever grants-in-aid are desirable.

With full cost tuition, the less expensive junior colleges would attract students and income from the university and colleges. Predictably, the few administrative voices heard in favor of higher tuition seem, from my observation, to come from junior college administrators — who believe they would out-perform the university if put on a quality-cost basis of competition for students.

A counter argument to the preceding propositions is that junior college education is "inferior" to university education. Although the quality of the university as a research institution is high, not as much can be established for its quality as a teaching institution to educate college students. The move to junior colleges with full tuition would occur if the more expensive university education were not matched by the higher quality as judged by students and parents. The university would have to improve its teaching to hold students at its higher costs. If it could not, the results would constitute evidence that the high cost and high quality combination was not a superior combination of quality, cost, and quantity. A Rolls-Royce gives higher quality transportation than a Ford, but it does not follow that more Rolls should be produced than Fords. *Education* must be judged by the quality, quantity, and costs, rather than in terms of only those who are educated at the highest, most expensive levels.

Yet, despite this patent fact of life, when faced with a budget cut the administrators of the state university plump four square for "quality at all costs" — for maintenance of quality education for a selected few regardless of how many must be turned away and given instead an "inferior" education. On what criterion is it established that it is better to maintain the level of quality of education for fewer students at the cost of sacrificing education for others? Would one argue that in the event of a social security reduction, we should reduce the *number* of recipients in order to maintain the quality of those lucky enough to keep getting social security payments? But analogies aside, the elite, authoritarian arguments by university administrators and faculty for a given level of quality, regardless of the sacrifices imposed on excluded students or on tax payers is sobering evidence of the seductiveness of self-interest pleading.

THE FACULTY AND administration of higher education in California has evolved in the zero tuition environment, with appropriately adapted behavioral traits. They have learned to use that political structure; they have learned how to appeal to the political processes and to legislators and governors for more financing. They have been almost exclusively reliant on the political process. They praise politicians for statesmanlike, responsible b e h a v i o r when the university budget is increased; but if it is decreased, they cry of political interference. Having accepted almost exclusive dependence on financing directly from the political and legislative processes, they should not complain of "political interference" when that same political process examines more intently the budget and the operations of the university. Are they really surprised that the venerable law "He who pays, controls" still is effective?

Legislators generally tend to favor direct state legislative financing of education coupled with no tuition, rather than full tuition with grants-in-aid. The closer the tuition approaches full cost, the less the power of the legislators over the educational institutions. It is not entirely accidental that Congress used a grant-in-aid system for veterans; there was no Federal college system.

We must constantly remember the difference between paternalism and independence. Independence from the competition of political processes and politicians' interests can be enhanced by full tuition, but it will bring greater dependence on competition among educators in satisfying students' whims and interest. Either the students pay and control, or the political processes and politicians do. Yet some of the faculty seem to think they can avoid both. For educators there is no free lunch nor "free" tuition.

The situation reminds one of the Russian plight. Dissatisfaction with the quality of goods produced by Russian firms is sparking attempts to restore market prices as reflections of consumers' interests. While the Russian economists and consumers advocate more control via the market, producers and politicians show far less interest in weakening their power by moving away from Socialism.

There remains a subtle, but effective means whereby full tuition would lead to *more* education than if directly provided by government at zero tuition. As matters stand now, an education at a tuition school may be worth $2000, or say, $500 *more* than the education at zero tuition state schools. For that superior education worth $500 *more*, the student would have to pay the full tuition cost of $2000. He gets no relief for not using state schools. If education were on a full tuition basis, this obstacle to more and higher quality education would be removed. We should not assume that spending more by government for *direct* provision of education necessarily yields more education. This phenomenon, I conjecture, is powerful at all levels of education.

943

A PREFERENCE FOR full tuition implies nothing whatsoever about the desirable extent of aid or subsidy to students. Unfortunately much of the debate has erroneously assumed that zero tuition is a necessary or a preferred method of aid while full tuition is a device to avoid aid to students. No matter how much aid, if any, should be given to students, the case for full tuition does not rest on a denial of aid. It rests on the premise that, whether or not aid is given to students, the financing of schools should be controlled more directly by students and their parents because the kind of education thereby made available is deemed to be better — by those who advocate full tuition.

Full tuition, plus grants-in-aid to whatever extent one believes is justified, directs educational activities more to the interest of students and less to that of the university staff. And after all, is it not the students whose interests are fundamental rather than the university's, as an institution? Is it the students' interests as reckoned by students and parents rather than the convenience to the educators that is a better guide? My choice of answers is obvious. I suspect that these are the crucial issues on which advocates of zero tuition will differ with me.

My opposition to zero tuition arises because I do not like the way it redistributes wealth, nor do I like the totality of the effects of the kinds of competition it induces relative to that which would prevail under full tuition, supplemented by grants and loans. The latter yields more variety of educational opportunities and just as much educational opportunity and presumptively, greater detectability and survival of superior education. It reduces the producers' control over the products that the customers can have. The influence of selecting their colleges and controlling payments is a trait with high survival in the world outside of academia and which should be cultivated. The decreased role of the state and political activity in administering education is also a consequence I find congenial. Higher tuition would improve the quality of education rather than reduce it. The quantity would be affected not by either a zero or high tuition, but by how much is spent for education. Zero tuition does not mean more is spent for education, nor that more poor people can attend. To believe it does is to think zero tuition is the only or best way to subsidize or aid students — and that contention begs the fundamental question of what is the best way.

All these consequences seem to work against my interests as a member of a zero tuition college. If I thought this one exposition of economic analysis and one man's preferences really were capable of converting our system of educational subsidies from the zero tuition to a full tuition system with scholarships, loans, and vouchers, I might be less willing to expose it, for the price may be high enough to make me join with those who, whatever may be their reason, prefer the Holy Zero, (excuse me, the *free*) tuition system.

Books

Friedrich Engels: His Contributions to Political Theory, by Fritz Nova. New York, Philosophical Library, 1967. 115p. $4.50.

The German Revolutions; The Peasant War, and Revolution and Counter Revolution, by Friedrich Engels. Edited and with an Introduction by Leonard Krieger. Chicago, University of Chicago Press, 1967. 246p. $2.45.

ENGELS HAS NEVER emerged from Marx's shadow. He was generally self-effacing and, as the man who systematized dialectical materialism, is generally shunned by those who study Marx as a philosopher of alienation and emphasize the humanist aspects of Marxism. Neither of the recent biographies is much good. Yelena Stepanova paints Engels as a revolutionary saint, and her solid research has been translated into muddled English; Grace Carlton shows him as a good-natured man somehow led astray by Marx, without whose maleficent influence Engels would have lived happily and dully ever after; the Carlton book is interrupted by tirades against Marx and Engels for their failure to appreciate the perfection of English institutions and empiricism, and it ends up even more dogmatic than the Stepanova work, which at least has some reading behind it.

Both biographies are essentially personal in emphasis, presenting Engels as hero or victim, and Gustav Mayer's impressive work, which assessed Engels and his ideas, is out of print both in the original and in the one-volume English abridgment. Therefore, Fritz Nova's book, which purports to discuss some of Engels' ideas, ought to be a good thing.

Unfortunately, it turns out to be not so much written as simply sorted into chapters, presenting quotations and paraphrases without any comment. The first chapter, "Social Theory: To Condemn or Condone?" is characteristic. The gist of the assembled statements (which Nova does not sum up) is that Engels thought political theory was well enough so long as it did not insulate the theorist from all contact with the real world, and so long as the theory was not wrong.

The ten-page chapter on Reformism and Revolution provides no hint of what Engels meant by revolution; there is no differentiation between statements made in 1844 and those made thirty-odd years later, as if Engels' opinions necessarily formed an unchanging whole; and there is no mention, much less analysis, of those references to the possibility of a peaceful transfer of power that give Marxist revisionism some claim to canonical authority. Not only is there no analysis, but the selection of quotations is erratic.

Nova's conclusion is that he has "not found any justification for reducing Engels to not much more than an accessory of Marx," but he makes no effort to prove that Engels *was* significant in himself. Engels was surely no appendage of Marx, but neither did he work in a vacuum. Nor should he be written about in a vacuum. Anyone who sets out to discuss Engels' ideas, even if he restricts himself to one of those fields such as natural or military science on which Marx rarely trespassed, ought to make some attempt to define the relation of his topic to Marxism in general. To list Engels' statements on politics or any other subject, without putting them into any context, can prove nothing more than what Nova has proven: that Engels wrote some things himself. And this could be ascertained by glancing at the index to the Marx-Engels *Werke*. Why is Engels important? Nova invokes Karl Kautsky, who is "generally regarded the most important successor to Marx and Engels," who said that Engels was an influence on him.

Certainly more than this can be said about Engels. In 1844 when Marx was still largely immersed in the study of Hegel, Engels had decided that the advance of industrialism in England was the most important thing going on in the world and that the accompanying ideology of classical liberalism was cor-

945

respondingly important; and he had begun the Marxist critique of liberalism as fundamentally a species of hypocrisy. After that he watched, advised, and criticized the world revolutionary movement for fifty years. In the course of this involvement, he wrote a great many books and articles, most of which are significant in one context or another, and which must be analyzed, discussed, and thought about.

Engels is not likely to be ignored altogether. International Publishers keeps some of his works available in paperback (including the "Outline of a Critique of Political Economy," in Marx's *Economic and Philosophical Manuscripts of 1844*), the University of Manchester Press has a recent translation of *The Condition of the English Working Class in 1844*, and now we have a new edition of *Revolution and Counter-Revolution*. The *Peasant War* was already available but fits in well here, and *Revolution and Counter-Revolution*, a series of articles that Engels wrote for the New York Tribune in 1851-52, shows him as an effective English stylist. He has plenty of opportunity to be scathing as he discusses the ineptitude and half-heartedness of the German middle-class revolutionaries of 1848-49. The book is a useful treatment of that particular revolution, and considered as a Marxist document it, like the *Peasant War,* illuminates some fundamental propositions of the Marxist attitude toward revolution: that bourgeois progressives are exceedingly unreliable allies, and that revolutions are matters of classes and epochs, not of conspiratorial or military expertise.

Leonard Krieger's introduction discusses sensibly the relationship between Marx and Engels (though "Engels' addiction to Germany in contrast to Marx's propensity for France" greatly overstates this point of difference) and analyzes the importance of Engels' two histories both in relation to their subjects and in relation to Marxism. They are made to illuminate major problems of Marxist thought, such as the relationship of history and philosophy and the relationship of free-will and determinism, and they gain in intelligibility and interest by being put in context. The analysis is on a very high level, but it is perhaps even more important that — in contrast to Nova — Krieger recognizes the necessity to ask questions.

—**MARTIN BERGER**[1]

James Mill: Selected Economic Writings, edited by Donald Winch. Chicago, University of Chicago Press, 1966. 452p. $12.50.

IT SHOULD COME AS no surprise to libertarians accustomed to meeting their ideas presented by others in surrealistic form that an inordinate number of efforts in the field of economic intellectual history are grotesquely inadequate. Prof. G. J. Stigler has gone to great lengths to show the casualness of scholarship in even such simple tasks as quoting accurately and naming theorems in such a way that they bear some non-random relation to the names of the theorems' initial propounders.[1] Still no amount of secondary cynicism can quite cushion the shock of, say, reading Max Lerner's "Introduction" to the *Wealth of Nations*.

Perhaps naively, we can hope that more readily available works can help reduce some of the heinous crimes committed in the name of intellectual history — if their presence will not necessarily inspire more careful scholarship, at least reviewers will have to search less for the material to point out inadequacies. The great new editions of Ricardo, Bentham (economic writings), J. S. Mill (about one third has been published) and the forthcoming volumes of the bicentennial edition of Adam Smith may generate a more precise reading. Thus we should welcome the University of Chicago's present and promised publication of the Scottish Economic Society's *Scottish Economic Classics*. Concentrating on those whose theories are

---

[1] Martin Berger is currently doing graduate work in history at the University of Pittsburgh.

[1] George J. Stigler, *Intellectual and the Market Place* (New York: Free Press of Glencoe, 1963), pp. 57-62.

comparatively unknown even inside academic economic circles: McCulloch, Steuart, Lauderdale, and Anderson, these new and forthcoming editions should make economic intellectual history less a game for antiquarians and entice more research in primary sources.

In the first volume of *Scottish Economic Classics,* Dr. Winch has compiled three of James Mill's most important economic pieces: *An Essay on the Impolicy of a Bounty on the Exportation of Grain* (which is so rare that J. A. Schumpter did not know it),[2] *Commerce Defended,* and *Elements of Political Economy,* along with "Smith on Money and Exchange," "Whether Political Economy is Useful," selections from *History of British India,* and "Extracts from Oral Evidence on the affairs of the East India Company." In addition Winch provides a biographical sketch, commentary on Mill's early economics, and an informal bibliography, not to mention an index.

I will not commend the editor for all his obvious hard work: virtue and book sales, after all, are their own reward; but I would examine one rather interesting point Dr. Winch raises which enters into serious interpretative problems with implications outside economics.

Winch asserts that Mill draws from Ricardo's economics the thesis that rent, being a residual, is the optimal subject for taxation because there are no effects on resource allocation:

> Mill went a good deal further than either Ricardo or McCulloch were willing to go. . . . Mill attempted to implement the radical conclusions which he drew from Ricardo's interpretation of the rent doctrine. Though this is seldom realised, Mill's influence on the Indian land revenue system represents perhaps the single most important application of Ricardian economics in practice.[3]

Ricardo himself did not support such a program:

It would be difficult to separate pure rent from profit on capital invested by the land-owner, and therefore a tax on contractual rents might inhibit the improving landlord. But, as always, Ricardo was willing to face the logical consequences of his doctrines, and does not seem to have been afraid of considering the possibility of complete land nationalisation.[4]

But Mill's conclusions are readily deducible from Ricardo's theories:

> In upholding the principle of taxing rent Mill was merely taking to its logical political conclusion, Ricardo's argument that there was an inherent conflict between the interests of land-owners and rest of the community.[5]

This is a profoundly misleading reading of Ricardo. Winch correctly describes the allocation aspects of Ricardo's theory but ignores the political constraint of equal treatment under law which Ricardo always imposed on his policy proposals.

It is true that Ricardo believed that neutrality in taxation is an important goal:

> The duty which I have here proposed, is the only legitimate countervailing duty, which neither offers inducements to capital to quit a trade, in which for us it is the most beneficially employed, nor holds out any temptations to employ an undue proportion of capital in a trade to which it would not otherwise have been destined. The course of trade would be left precisely on the same footing as if we were wholly an untaxed country, and every person was at liberty to employ his capital and skill in the way he should think most beneficial to himself. . . . we should offer no temptations to capitalists, to employ their funds and their skill in any other way than they would have employed them, if we had had the good fortune to be untaxed, and had been permitted to give the greatest development to our talents and industry.[6]

947

[2] Joseph A. Schumpter, *History of Economic Analysis* (New York: Oxford University Press, 1954), p. 476.

[3] Donald Winch, "James Mill and David Ricardo," in the book reviewed, p. 197.

[4] *Ibid.,* p. 198.

[5] *Ibid.*

[6] *Works and Correspondence of David Ricardo,* ed. Piero Sraffa (Cambridge: Cambridge University Press, 1962), Vol. IV, p. 244. All further references will be by volume and page.

Further there is no doubt taxes on rent would be neutral,[7] but Ricardo refuses to recommend such taxation, on grounds of isonomy:

> It must be admitted that the effects of these taxes would be such as Adam Smith has described [neutral]; but it would surely be very unjust, to tax exclusively the revenue of any particular class. . . .[8]

This concern with equal treatment is not an isolated instance in Ricardo. He opposes inflation, in spite of the fact that it might benefit the more productive classes, because it implies unequal treatment by government action;[9] he opposes repudiation of the national debt in spite of distributional advantages on the same ground;[10] he even supports tariffs to equalize the tax burden between landowners and the rest of society.[11]

THUS RICARDO'S opposition to taxes on rent and Mill's support are indications of a rather deep split in political philosophy, not as Winch implies, a difference on the feasibility of measuring rent. The harmony/disharmony of interest interpretation of Ricardo and classical economics has blighted the profession since at least Halevy's monumental *Growth of Philosophical Radicalism* but is useless as a rationalization for Ricardo's policy proposals.[12] As a student of Jacob Viner, Winch of course does not subscribe to the silly harmony theory: but it is a shame he still finds the disharmony part of Halevy's theory at all useful to explain Ricardo's policy. Ricardo did not favor class legislation against anyone, regardless of whether their interests were harmonious with the rest of society; and indeed as mentioned above is willing to put tariffs on corn to reduce the *inequality* of the tax burden on landlords. Nor does a harmony reading help understand any other part of Ricardo's theory of policy: what is at question is whether a competitive price system produces some sort of an optimum, which Ricardo usually argues that it does, and importantly how do we go about getting out of the messes the government got us into. Ricardo develops and widely applies a theory of compensation to solve the problem that even the best reforms will hurt someone. This cannot be explained by a harmony/disharmony approach.

But enough carping. This new edition of James Mill gives complete (or nearly so) versions of important economic works and selections of minor pieces, in addition to interesting commentary. It is most valuable, but, unfortunately if quotations must be critical, one must compare them to the original. This writer found seven minor errors in the first eighteen pages (including table of contents and introduction) of the *Elements*.

—DAVID LEVY

---

[7] I, 204.
[8] *Ibid.*
[9] VI, 233.
[10] I, 245-46.
[11] IV, 264.
[12] Elie Halevy's harmony/disharmony interpretation is that Ricardo's static theory is a harmony view of the world. The labor theory of value states that all are paid according to their labor, hence the competitive price system produces a constrained version of the best of all possible worlds. His dynamic theory implies an inherent conflict between landlords and the rest of society: population increases by Malthusian principles forcing up the price of corn, increasing money wages, decreasing profits, and increasing rent. The decrease in the rate of profit will slow down economic progress, thus the landlord benefits at the expense of society. Elie Halevy, *The Growth of Philosophical Radicalism*, trans. Mary Morris (Boston: Beacon, 1966), p. 319ff.

NEW BOOKS AND ARTICLES

THE FOLLOWING ARE A SELECTION OF ITEMS AND NOTES WHICH, IN THE OPINION OF THE EDITORS, MAY BE OF INTEREST TO OUR READERS.

John Kenneth Galbraith, whose recent book *The New Industrial State* (Boston: Houghton Mifflin, 1967) should escape public notice, has just written an important tract on the Viet Nam war; important because of Galbraith's prominent position among the anti-war faction of the Establishment. *How To Get Out of Vietnam* (New York: Signet Books, 1967. 47p. 35 cents.) sets down in cogent form the most important assumptions usually made by opponents of the Viet Nam involvement, and after thoroughly illustrating if not documenting those assumptions, draws the necessary conclusions: ". . . it is now a war that we cannot win, should not wish to win, are not winning, and which our people do not support. . . ." (p. 32) Galbraith's thoughts raise an important issue in the minds of certain observers of the pro- and anti-Viet Nam debates, the fact that both positions make unproven, and at worst undemonstrated, assumptions about the nature of "the enemy." Galbraith rather carefully demolishes, for example, the usual anti-Communist approach to foreign involvement (he concludes: "The enemy coalition—the empire—against which our operation was launched turned out not to exist. This cannot have happened very often in history. . . ." [p. 15]); but to do so he relies in turn upon his own assumptions as to the nature of the Communist governments, assumptions which those who disagree with him cannot accept because he dismisses any "world-wide coordination" aspect of Communism and styles it all as Titoist nationalism. It would seem that any useful discussion of American foreign policy must grapple with the empirical documentation of assumptions such as these; but such documentation would seem to be either unobtainable in a scientifically acceptable form, or, if available, much too dispersed and unorganized to be usefully marshaled. A third possibility is also plausible, given the political Left-Right polarization of foreign policy discussions: the factual evidence which may be in the possession of known anti-Communists is suspect by men such as Galbraith because a mutual trust in the others' integrity is lacking—those in possession of facts damaging to the position of their opponents are considered capable of fraud to defend their own position. Likewise, those who fear the less than pleasant prospect of a global American Empire policing the free world at enormous cost in lives, money, and domestic liberty are seen as dangerously blind and naive, and dismissed with vague references to Munich and America First. It becomes, on the one hand an act of faith that "international Communism" is a terrible menace to free men everywhere, and on the other that "Cold War paranoia" is regimenting free men at home and extinguishing rational foreign policy abroad.

949

The editors of *New Individualist Review* have been divided for some time as to what editorial position to adopt on this question, and have sidestepped the issue in favor of omitting articles devoted to foreign policy. In the future, we would like to consider for publication well written and thoroughly documented articles on these general questions. We invite our readers to assist us in this endeavor.

Dan Cordtz, "Social Security: Drifting Off Course," *Fortune*, December 1967, pp. 104-7ff. The Social Security System, which for three decades has been the holiest of sacred cows in the American political barn, has come under increasing investigation in the past three years, possibly as a result of the surprising reaction Sen. Goldwater's campaign encountered in 1964—surprising to the campaigners, although not to their opponents. It is a tribute to the extent that conventional wisdom can be subverted by scholarly investigation and exposure that the number of articles critical of Social Security has expanded, and that a few books have appeared reopening the question. Diligent effort by Right-wing scholars has forced even non-political studies to examine Social Security with critical questions in mind. It can be hoped that election campaigns in 1968 or 1972 may see the Social Security System dismantled entirely.

Prof. Harry Kalven, Jr., of the University of Chicago Law School, examines the applicability of the Constitutional guarantees of freedom of the press to the radio and TV broadcasting industries in the October 1967 issue of *The Journal of Law and Economics* ("Broadcasting, Public Policy and the First Amendment"). He argues that the United States wrongly has two traditions in freedom of expression, one relating to the press and the other to broadcasting. He then goes on to show that precedents exist in other fields for application of the First Amendment (for example, motion pictures and second class mailing rights) which could easily be extended to radio and TV in the event of a legal show-down before the Supreme Court. The entire Volume X (207 pp.) is available for $2.50 ($1.00 for students) from the *Journal;* see their ad in this issue. Additional articles of interest in that volume include Milton Friedman on "The Monetary Theory and Policy of Henry Simons," and articles by James Buchanan, Paul Samuelson, and Jora Minasian on the question of public goods, which was initiated in the *Journal of Law and Economics,* Volume VII (1964). Libertarian theorists ought to pay greater attention to the theory of public goods, inasmuch as these discussions of the marginal cases for private property bring into greater clarity and even question some of the fundamental arguments for laissez faire.

An old controversy on the Right has reappeared, which our readers may be interested in following more closely as it develops. In the January 1968 issue of *The New Guard,* official magazine of Young Americans for Freedom, is reprinted Frank S. Meyer's famous article "The Twisted Tree of Liberty," which was originally composed in reflection on the debate between *New Individualist Review* editor Ronald Hamowy and William F. Buckley, Jr. in the November 1961 issue of N.I.R. It is pure speculation to comment upon what might have encouraged *The New Guard* to pick up the article for reprinting from *National Review* (Jan. 16, 1962), but the recent review of Meyer's *Moulding of Communists* in Murray N. Rothbard's journal of libertarian thought, *Left and Right,* might have had something to do with it. Taking Meyer (and by implication, Burnham and the rest of the Right-wing ex-Communists) to task for singlemindedly directing American conservatism toward hard-nosed foreign policy objectives, Rothbard analyzes Meyer's description of the typical Communist trainee (and later cadre) and points out, interestingly enough, that exactly the same moral condemnations can be made against any secretive organization man—including most especially FBI and CIA agents, who exhibit most of the traits Meyer identifies with Communism. The reader may be interested in examining Rothbard's discussion of Meyer, inasmuch as Meyer *is* widely read on the Right, and Rothbard has a number of interesting things to say, but not the audience. The review appears in the Spring-Summer 1967 (Vol. 3, No. 2) issue of *Left and Right,* and would be available for 85 cents from them at Box 395, Cathedral Station, New York, N. Y. 10025.

An attack on Establishment "liberalism" from a radical point of view is presented in *The Great Society Reader: The Failure of American Liberalism,* by Marvin E. Gettleman and David Mermelstein (Vintage Books; $2.45, paper), a reader containing speeches, essays, etc., by Lyndon B. Johnson, Sargent Shriver, and Arthur Schlesinger, as well as Paul Goodman, Tom Hayden, Hans Morgenthau, and other critics of the current spirit of the times as manifested in Wash-

951

ington. Most interesting to N.I.R. readers would probably be the contribution of Murray N. Rothbard, libertarian economist and editor of *Left and Right*. In an essay entitled "The Great Society: A Libertarian Critique," Prof. Rothbard stresses the congruence of the Johnsonian program with the corporate state trend of American politics during most of the twentieth century. Of particular interest is his assertion that: "The cruelest myth fostered by the liberals is that the Great Society functions as a great boon and benefit to the poor; in reality, when we cut through the frothy appearances to the cold reality underneath, the poor are the major victims of the welfare state"; and Rothbard goes on to cite more than a dozen major elements of the welfare state—from minimum wages and urban renewal to inflation and the farm subsidy program—which penalize the relatively poor to the advantage of the relatively rich.

Harry G. Johnson, *Economic Policies Toward Less Developed Countries*. Washington, Brookings Institution, 1967. $6.95. In the discussion of economic assistance and trade between the industrialized nations and the underdeveloped world, much attention has been given to governmental structuring and planning, which involves almost necessarily restrictions on free market activity. Johnson's survey brings out with great clarity and insight the essential features and interrelations among the leading proposals for improving international economic relations. The book is particularly noteworthy for its exposure of the economic fallacies in arguments for various forms of interference. Protectionist approaches by both rich and poor countries are contrasted unfavorably with an optimal system which would combine free trade, realistic exchange rates, and the provision of aid on the basis of net resource requirements.

A number of other Conservative publications are beginning to notice a controversy which N.I.R. joined in its November 1961 issue: Ayn Rand and her philosophy of Objectivism have been the object of a recent article by M. Stanton Evans in *National Review* (October 3, 1967), and the Objectivist leaders (i.e., official spokesmen of the Nathaniel Branden Institute) have come under sharp attack by a disenchanted "student of Objectivism," Jarret B. Wollstein, in the *New Guard* (October 1967). Evans addresses himself to what he sees as the twin failure of Miss Rand logically to construct an ethical system which can support the kinds of behavior she favors, and her neglect of the need for a spiritual, particularly Christian, underpinning for society. The points directed by Evans to the first issue seem well taken, although he pauses to puzzle that N.I.R. saw fit to criticize Rand in spite of the seeming agreement in practical matters; the puzzle is solved by reading Prof. Goldberg's article in the November 1961 issue more closely. His second point is weaker; consider the assertion: "The ancients could conceive of no authority higher than the *polis;* they believed the state had a total lien on man's energies and affections." Socrates' argument in the *Apology* seems to invalidate such a generalization.

On a more personal level, Wollstein gives a detailed account of the troubles he encountered when he attempted to propagate the virtues of Objectivism. His report contains a truly amazing chain of events, with the Objectivist establishment performing some rather non-voluntaristic acts—including at one point the threat of force. What makes this report particularly interesting is the direct manner in which it supports Whittaker Chambers' savage attack on the Randians in *National Review* (December 1957). Chambers accused Miss Rand of being a fascist. In spite of some rather ill-mannered letters from Objectivists, this charge has often seemed curious. How, after all, can one detect authoritarianism in any form in Ayn Rand's highly voluntaristic philosophy? Indeed, Evans takes Chambers to task for the self-evident contradiction in the charge.

One line of analysis which has not been followed by any of those interested in the subject is the relation, long stressed by many inside of the classical liberal tradition, between toleration of opposing views and the fundamental rationalist recognition that it is possible to be in error. Prof. Karl Popper has warned that the great danger of irrationalist philosophy comes from its ability to dismiss any and all criticisms without considering the validity of the criticism. Hence, it is possible for some Marxists to reject logical arguments on the basis of the class interests of potential propounders. An indirect test for the tolerance of a philosophy may consist of an examination of the type of arguments which if accepted would prove the philosophy fundamentally in error. In the case of Objectivism, this examination ought to be facilitated because it goes to great lengths to stress the axiomatic and definitional bases of its arguments. In Miss Rand's recent *Introduction to Objectivist Epistemology* (New York: The Objectivist, Inc., 1967. 77 pp. $1.95.) she develops her theories of axioms and definitions and defends them as being of the greatest importance: "Do you want to assess the rationality of a person, a theory or a philosophical system? Do not inquire about his or its stand on the validity of reason. Look for the stand on axiomatic concepts. It will tell the whole story." (p. 56). "The truth or falsehood of all of man's conclusions, inferences, thought and knowledge rests on the truth or falsehood of his definitions." (p. 47). Axioms in her system are self-evident, their denial will lead to contradictions; an axiomatic concept "is implicit in all facts and in all knowledge. It is fundamentally given and directly perceived or experienced, which requires no proof or explanation, but on which all proofs and explanations rest." (p. 52). Definitions represent the identification of the nature of the things defined. Although it is obvious that Miss Rand has not followed the mathematical discussions of axiomatic systems, she does profess a high regard for higher mathematics. The fundamental theorem of Gödel of course proves that for very general systems it is not possible to prove a set of axioms are both consistent and complete; but knowledge of an even older body of mathematical thought would be sufficient to demonstrate the misleading nature of her concept of axioms—it is well established that geometries denying the classical parallel axiom can be constructed as consistently as Euclidean geometry.

953

The well established fact that it is not always possible to resolve axiomatic questions by examining only the consistency of the deductions from those axioms destroys the possibility of discussion with Miss Rand over differences in axioms. The relevant tests differ from those which Miss Rand establishes as a check on the validity of her axioms—consistency will not suffice. Similarly, her discussion of what must happen when people disagree over definitions is singularly unhelpful; appeals to objective reality (her phrase) are useful only if one knows how to appeal. Perhaps an illustration of her procedure will show the great difficulties one would encounter if he wished to discuss fundamentals. Miss Rand defines man as a rational animal in the sense that man is capable of being rational, unlike other animals. If definitions are as important to her system as she alleges, we should certainly want to ascertain the correctness of this particular definition. Yet surely this definition is every bit as true as a definition of man as a religious and altruistic animal in that unlike other animals he is capable of being both. Now one must ask, how would Miss Rand propose to bring objective reality in to test the definitions? She does consider, and reject, divergent definitions of man, but without really indicating why. Unfortunately, the revelations of objective reality are not for the uninitiated.

Such is Miss Rand's fundamental irrationality: Many of the interesting problems she discusses are solved with appeals to definitions pulled out of hats; axioms which can't be tautological if used logically, but which nevertheless look like tautologies; and a very large dose of faith. Prof. Goldberg argued in his article for N.I.R. in 1961 that Objectivism is an approach which goes nowhere; perhaps it is time to consider Whittaker Chambers' charge that Objectivism leads to somewhere far worse.

954

The Journal of

LAW & ECONOMICS

VOLUME X   OCTOBER 1967   PRICE $2.50

THE UNIVERSITY OF CHICAGO LAW SCHOOL

The Journal of Law and Economics has been published annually by the University of Chicago Law School since 1958. The growing interest in the law-economics area has suggested that it would be desirable to undertake more frequent publication. It has therefore been decided to increase the issues published each year to two, one to appear in April and the second to appear in October. The new arrangement will start with Volume XI, with the first number of the Volume appearing in April 1968, and the second in October 1968.

All issues of **The Journal of Law and Economics** may be obtained for the price of $2.50 per issue. However, the **Journal** is also available at a special student rate of $1.00 per issue. Those students wishing to obtain all volumes of **The Journal of Law and Economics** issued to date (through Volume X) should remit $10.00.

The subscription rate for the **Journal** will be $5.00 for two issues each year ($2.00 to students), with the following discounted rates for extended subscriptions: two years, $9.50 (students, $4.00); three years, $13.50 (or $6.00; four years, $17.00 (or $8.00); and five years, $20.00 (or $10.00 to students). Please send orders and remittances (and particulars of student status if you are applying for the student rate) to:

Publications Assistant
The Journal of Law and Economics
University of Chicago Law School
1111 East 60th Street
Chicago, Illinois 60637

Studies in Philosophy, Politics, and Economics

Friedrich A. Hayek

These eloquent, vigorous studies voice Hayek's endeavor to make "the philosophical foundations of a free society once more a living intellectual issue, and its implementation a task which challenges the ingenuity and imagination of our liveliest minds." His concerns range from the nature of economic theory to the philosophy of David Hume; from the ethical basis of free enterprise to the appeal that socialism has for intellectuals; from the way *The Road to Serfdom* was received to a critique of *The Affluent Society*.
1967   LC:18436   356 *pages*, $6.50

The Economic Life of the Ancient World

Jean-Philippe Lévy

Translated by John G. Biram

Here is a concise, comprehensive, and readable overview of the economic life of the ancient Mediterranean world, tracing the evolution of man's economic activity from the Greco-Oriental cultures before Alexander to the Fall of Rome. Professor Lévy describes the premonetary states, the advent of money, the growth of commerce, and the social consequences of commercial activity for each of the periods covered. No comparable survey has ever appeared before in English. The material presented is arranged for easy reference.
1967   LC:67-20575   147 *pages*, $5.00

Public and Private Enterprise

John Jewkes

Here is a fresh approach to the vital subject of the proper roles for private enterprise and government in national economic life. Jewkes argues that economists have failed to perform adequately their function of pointing out the real elements of economic decision that enter into public policy-making. He warns of the dangers of public monopoly and presents the case for the free market. "... a witty and penetrating attack on the contemporary mania for socialism, planning, redistribution of income, and other forms of governmental economic controls." —Henry Hazlitt, *National Review*.
1967   LC:66-12709   94 *pages*, $2.25

The Economics of Trade Unions

Albert Rees

Here is a critical look at the impact of unions on wages, prices, employment, productivity, and the distribution of income. An "... analysis of trade unions in forthright, lucid, and cogent manner without the usual overlarding of descriptive institutional material or the qualifications besetting most texts." —Solomon Barkin, *Industrial and Labor Relations Review*. "... a small gem ... lucid and economical treatment of a large and complex subject." —*American Economic Review*. Formerly in the "Cambridge Economic Handbook" series, this book now appears as a *Phoenix* paperback.
1962 LC:62-9741 208 *pages Cloth* $3.50, *paper* $1.50

University of Chicago Press, Chicago 60637

CUMULATIVE
INDEX

962

963

969

973

975

976

979

991

992

993

Book Design by JMH Corporation, Indianapolis, Indiana
Typography by Typoservice Corporation, Indianapolis, Indiana
Printed and bound by Edwards Brothers, Inc., Ann Arbor, Michigan